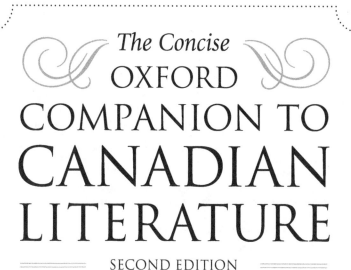

The Concise
OXFORD
COMPANION TO
CANADIAN
LITERATURE

SECOND EDITION

EDITED BY WILLIAM TOYE

OXFORD
UNIVERSITY PRESS

OXFORD
UNIVERSITY PRESS

Oxford University Press is a department of the University of Oxford.
It furthers the University's objective of excellence in research, scholarship, and education by publishing worldwide.
Oxford is a registered trade mark of Oxford University Press in the UK and in certain other countries.

Published in Canada by
Oxford University Press
8 Sampson Mews, Suite 204,
Don Mills, Ontario M3C 0H5 Canada

www.oupcanada.com

Copyright © Oxford University Press Canada 2012

The moral rights of the author have been asserted
Database right Oxford University Press (maker)

First Published in 2001.
Second Edition Published in 2010.

Library and Archives Canada Cataloguing in Publication

The concise Oxford companion to Canadian literature / edited by William Toye. – 2nd ed.

An abridged ed. of: The Oxford companion to Canadian literature.
ISBN 978-0-19-542885-8 (bound).–ISBN 978-0-19-544529-9 (pbk.)

1. Canadian literature--Dictionaries. 2. Canadian
literature–Bio-bibliography. I. Toye, William, 1926–
II. Title: Oxford companion to Canadian literature.

PS8015.C65 2010   C810.9'0003   C2010-904818-0

PAGE 204: From 'body of my death', Patrick Friesen, *Earth's Crude Gravities*, 2007, Harbour Publishing. PAGE 227: excerpt from
'Your phone number' from *Evenings at loose ends* by Gerald Godin. Translation by Judith Cowan. Signal Editions, Véhicule Press.
PAGE 243: excerpted from *Creation* by Katherine Govier. Copyright © 2002 Katherine Govier. Reprinted by permission of Random
House Canada. PAGE 301: excerpt from 'The perils of geography' from *The perils of geography* (Brick Books, 1995). Permission
granted by author and publisher. PAGE 328: from *Beyond this dark house* by Guy Gavriel Kay. Copyright © Guy Gavriel Kay, 2003.
Reprinted by permission of Penguin Group (Canada), a Division of Person Canada Inc. PAGE 361–62: from *Crow Lake* by Mary
Lawson, published by Chatto & Windus. Reprinted by permission of The Random House Group Ltd. Copyright © 2002 Mary
Lawson. Reprinted by permission of Knopf Canada. PAGE 627: excerpted from *A complicated kindness* by Miriam Toews.
Copyright © 2004 Miriam Toews. Reprinted by permission of Knopf Canada. PAGE 644: excerpted from *The assassin's song* by
M.G. Vassanji. Copyright © 2007 M.G. Vassanji. Reprinted by permission of Doubleday Canada.

Oxford University Press is committed to our environment. This book is printed on Forest Stewardship
Council certified paper, harvested from a responsibly managed forest.

Printed and bound in Canada.

MIX
Paper from
responsible sources
FSC
www.fsc.org   FSC® C004071

1 2 3 4 — 15 14 13 12

IN MEMORY OF

P.K. Page

Mordecai Richler

Robert Weaver

Preface

This is an updated edition of *The Concise Oxford Companion to Canadian Literature*, published in 2001. The *Concise* appellation alludes to the inclusion only of books by francophone writers that are in translation and to the omission of some long survey entries that appeared in *The Oxford Companion to Canadian Literature* (1983) and its second edition (1997), which I co-edited with Eugene BENSON. For the present volume the end of the year 2007 is the cut-off date for books published in 2001 and after. These are usually described in some detail. Titles published in 2008 and 2009 (and some in 2010), however, are referred to, but only briefly.

In my Preface to the previous edition I said that 'the new authors in these pages amount to an interim coverage.' Needless to say, in the period 2001–10 there was an explosion of publications by 'new' Canadian writers of fiction and poetry as well as by authors who already had entries in the *Companion*. The editor (who is 84) cannot help but think of the early years of his career, in the 1950s, when Canadian publishing was in a precarious state and only a very few publications in fiction, poetry, and non-fiction, from year to year, gave any promise of the richness of today's publications.

I have dropped one entry, *The MOUNTAIN AND THE VALLEY* (the entry on Ernest BUCKLER accounts for this), but I have added forty-two new entries (not all of them are on writers), written over two-and-a-half years. Inevitably I'll be criticized for the authors I have neglected. (There are just so many books one person can read within a certain period.) I'll be upfront, however, and aid my critics by listing the new entries. They are BABSTOCK, *BEAUTIFUL LOSERS*, BERGEN, BIBLIOASIS, BLUNT, BÖK, BOYDEN, BUSH, *CNQ: CANADIAN NOTES & QUERIES*, COMPTON, CORMORANT BOOKS, CRUMMEY, 'DAVID', *DIVISADERO*, DJWA, FISCHMAN, GIBB, GILMOUR, GRAY (Charlotte), HARVEY (Kenneth J.), HUMPHREYS, ITANI, JARMAN, LACEY, LAWSON, MacDONALD (D.R.), MacMILLAN, MARSH, MARTEL, MOORE (Lisa), MULHALLEN, NEW, ORMSBY, PYPER, REDHILL, SAKAMOTO, *SECOND SCROLL*, SPALDING (Esta), TOEWS, WACHTEL, WILSON (Budge), and WINTER. I regret that my reading time could not encompass other writers who might seem to deserve entries. I hope, nevertheless, that readers of this *Concise Companion*, as I have conceived it, will find much in it to interest and inform them.

June 2010   WILLIAM TOYE

Contributors

Maroussia Ahmed

Geraldine Anthony

Ivor Arnold

Stan Atherton

John Ayre

Janet Baker

Douglas Barbour

Francesca Benedict

Eugene Benson

Katherine Berg

Raymond Bertin

Diane Bessai

Joseph Bonenfant

Nicole Bourbonnais

Colin Boyd

Russell Brown

Diana Brydon

Roberta Buchanan

Peter Buitenhuis

William Butt

Marie J. Carrière

Robert Cockburn

Fred Cogswell

Andrew Cohen

Joan Coldwell

Don Coles

John Robert Colombo

Rebecca Conolly

Nathalie Cooke

Dennis Cooley

Terrence Craig

Terry Crowley

Burke Culen

Tara L. Curtis

Steven J. Daniel

Frank Davey

Marie C. Davis

Bernard Delpêche

Lovat Dickson

Madeleine Dirschauer

Sandra Djwa

Kathleen Donohue

Max Dorsinville

Dennis Duffy

François Dumont

Leon Edel

Renate Eigenbrod

Sarah Ellis

Susan Elmslie

Howard Engel

John English	Christopher Innes
Margery Fee	Patricia Irwin
George Fetherling	David Jackel
David Flint	Kim Jernigan
Janet Friskney	Karl Jirgens
Robert Fulford	Chris Johnson
George Galt	J. Kieran Kealy
Keith Garebian	L.W. Keffer
Gary Geddes	Reinhold Kramer
Carole Gerson	Joy Kuroptawa
Robert Gibbs	Eva Kushner
Barbara Godard	M. Travis Lane
Noreen Golfman	David Latham
Judith Skelton Grant	David Leahy
Michael Greenstein	Barbara Leckie
Stefan Haag	Alexander Legatt
Kathryn Hamer	Pierre H. Lemieux
Geoff Hancock	Rota Herzberg Lister
Annika Hannan	Douglas Lochhead
Dick Harrison	Grant Loewen
David M. Hayne	Robert Lovejoy
Jeffrey Heath	Mary Lu MacDonald
Allan Hepburn	Barbara McEwen
Paul Hjartarson	S.R. MacGillivray
Anthony Hopkins	Robin Gedalof McGrath
Shawn Huffman	Louis K. MacKendrick
Renée Hulan	Ken MacKinnon
Michael Hurley	Carrie MacMillan

Lorraine McMullen

Jay Macpherson

Laurent Mailhot

John Margeson

Joyce Marshall

Keavy Martin

Kerry Mason

Hugo A. Meynell

Jacques Michon

Marianne Micros

Orm Mitchell

Ian Montagnes

Christopher Moore

Lianne Moyes

Laura J. Murray

Elaine Nardocchio

Elaine Kalman Naves

Graeme Nicholson

Gerald Noonan

Stephanie Nutting

Ed Nyman

Shane O'Dea

Jean O'Grady

David O'Rourke

F. Hilton Page

Ruth Panofsky

George L. Parker

Michel Parmentier

Donna Palmateer Pennee

Michael Peterman

Penny Petrone

James Polk

Zailig Pollock

Lisbie Rae

Magdalene Redekop

Keith Richardson

Lucie Robert

Katherine Roberts

Ian Ross Robertson

Linda Rogers

Constance Rooke

Marilyn Rose

Catherine Ross

Malcolm Ross

Jennie Rubio

Mary Henley Rubio

Lori Saint-Martin

Judith Saltman

Heather Sanderson

Peter Sanger

Robert J. Sawyer

Stephen Scobie

Howard Scott

Wendy Scott

Andrew Seaman

Antanas Seleika

Ben-Z. Shek

Sherry Simon

Antoine Sirois

David Skene-Melvin

Patricia Smart

Donald Smith

Paul Socken

Alexander Sokalski

Sam Solecki

D.O. Spettigue

David Staines

Charles R. Steele

Peter Stevens

Rosemary Sullivan

Fraser Sutherland

Wendy K. Sutton

Michael Tait

Thomas E. Tausky

M. Brook Taylor

Richard Teleky

Jules Tessier

Donald F. Theall

Sharon Thesen

Gillian Thomas

Deborah Torkko

William Toye

Rhea Tregebov

Elizabeth Trott

Claude Trottier

James H. Tully

Marino Tuzi

Pierre-Louis Vaillancourt

Frederick Vaughan

Maïr Verthuy

Miriam Waddington

Anton Wagner

Robert S. Wallace

Germaine Warkentin

Jack Warwick

Elizabeth Waterston

Robert Weaver

Justine Whitehead

Patricia Whitney

George Wicken

Ann Wilson

George Woodcock

Lorraine York

Alan R. Young

Sally Zerker

Francis Zichy

Cynthia Zimmerman

A

Aboriginal legends and tales. Legends and tales are part of the oral traditions inherited by Canadian Natives from their forefathers and preserved through countless recitations. Because they are not a homogeneous people, because they speak a number of languages, practise many diverse customs, and hold many distinctive beliefs, their mythology is varied and vast.

From the beginning of the seventeenth century, when early missionaries first recorded a number of Huron and Algonquin tales in their *JESUIT RELATIONS*, Native stories have been gathered piecemeal by such interested laymen as traders, explorers, travellers, clergymen, and Native agents. Towards the end of the nineteenth century the 'doomed-culture theory'—the belief that the Natives would soon be extinct—prompted a more systematic effort to preserve their oral heritage. Expeditions of anthropologists, ethnologists, folklorists—and, much later, sociologists—went to live and work in specific regions among particular tribes. These trained specialists recorded the tales verbatim, transcribing them into literal translations, in simple English, with little or no attempt at literary style, in order to preserve their integrity. In many instances their publications offered the narratives in the original, with an interlinear literal English translation, thus adhering as closely as possible to the forms in which the tales were told. Interpreting and evaluating their materials from the point of view of their academic disciplines, these specialists produced numerous valuable scholarly studies. And, in an effort to systematize Aboriginal lore, they applied a European system of categories and classifications. To prove their pet hypotheses they exaggerated similarities to Scandinavian, Greek, and Hindu mythologies and found Jewish and Christian analogies; they also studied resemblances among the tales themselves. Though many modern scholars have deemed such comparative studies futile speculation, recurrent patterns and motifs do exist in Aboriginal legends and tales and they transcend geographical and linguistic barriers: otherworld journeys; heroic encounters with supernatural powers; animal wives and husbands; animal divinities; powerful magicians; guardian spirit quests; the ritual observance of animal corpses; and belief in the significance of dreams, in the indwelling spirit of every created thing (inanimate and animate), in the coupling of all animate and inanimate things or beings (even colours and words), and in the magical power of numbers (4—Ojibwa; 5—Athabascans). Metamorphosis and anthropomorphism are essential and significant features. And plots may offer ancient tribal rituals (those of the shaking tent, sweat lodge, bearwalk, Sun, rain and ghost dances, potlatch), and purification and expiation ceremonies, as well as initiation, puberty, and mortuary rites. The vision quest—requiring fasting, prayer, deprivation, and ceremonial purity—holds a prominent place in Native legends and tales.

The culture hero or trickster-transformer figure, who brings about the origins of life as a series of transformations, is the central character in the majority of Canadian Native myths. Human or animal, he is known to the different tribes under various names. Raven, of the Pacific coast tribes, accounts for the existence of all things—the sun, moon, stars, fire, water, even the alternation of tides; for the Cree and Saulteaux, Wisakedjak (there are many phonetically similar versions of his name) is responsible for shaping the existing world; the Mi'kmaq Glooscap and the Ojibwa's Hare made the world ready for man; Nanabozho, son of the West Wind and greatgrandson of the Moon, gave the Ojibwa the necessities of life; and for the Plains Native peoples, Coyote or 'old man', who existed on earth before mankind, when humans and animals were not really distinct, is credited with putting the world in order.

At times the hero-trickster is presented in antithetical roles: as an actual creator or as a helper who might either co-operate with or thwart the creator; as a beneficent culture hero and helper of mankind or a malevolent being; as an all-wise, powerful shaman or a credulous fool; as a crafty trickster able to change himself into animal and human shapes or the butt of ridicule; as a joker or a scapegoat who often falls victim to his own and others' wiles. His adventures, whether mischievous or not, always lie in well-known localities within the territory of the band that tells these stories. The trickster performs his altruistic services first to satisfy his own ends and only incidentally for men. A variety of animals—wolverine, badger, raccoon, mink, crow, fisher—might also be selected as trickster-transformer.

I

Aboriginal legends and tales

For non-Native readers preoccupied with exact chronology and factual details, Native chronicles based on oral traditions are disappointing. The constant evocation of a confusing assemblage of mythological figures, and the frequent introduction of supernatural causes and interventions, have created a hodgepodge of details concerning historical origins. Countless variations of a single tale, even within the same tribe or band, are confusing: the treatment of a story may be altered by the taste, gender, or life circumstances of the narrator, as well as by the place and time of the telling, and even the particular audience. West Coast families have handed down their own versions of stories that often contradict the traditions of their neighbours; there is no interest in reconciling such differences. Although the Iroquois form of government inspired the praise and emulation of the American founding fathers, and their traditions are among the most systematic and coherent, their chronicles lack historical data. For example, details concerning Deganahwidah—the chief who carried out such an important constitutional change as the formation of the League of the Iroquois—are often obscure and casual. The famous Ojibwa interpreter and author, Peter JONES, stated that the Natives' 'notions as to their origins are little better than a mass of confusion'. Many traditions, he claimed, were founded on dreams, 'which will account for the numerous absurd stories current amongst them'.

Because of their many wanderings and because the history of European-Native relations has obscured many original Native values and attitudes, much legendary lore has been debased and distorted by later generations, or has entirely disappeared and been forgotten by the living. Elements of European thought and missionary teaching (Bible stories had a strange fascination for Natives) have been so assimilated into an acculturated tradition that it is difficult to separate the European accretions from authentic Native lore. The *Jesuit Relations* state that the notion of the Great Manitou in its personal sense was introduced by the Jesuits themselves; that the concepts of one incorporeal god, the devil as prince of darkness, the distinction between good and evil gods and the pitting of one against the other, and the belief in future punishment or in an abode of evil spirits, were all foreign to the Algonquin tribes. In modern times some tribes (with only a handful of elderly Natives remembering) tend to emphasize what is most recent in their collective memory, relating stories of events that took place since the advent of whites.

Native folklore, as it is commonly recorded by scholars, presents other difficulties. Language manipulation is a problem in the translation process. Since collectors have depended chiefly on the broken English of (mostly aging) Native informants or of Métis interpreters, both of whom were unable or unwilling to translate or explain the full implications of the words or episodes, mistranslations and misconceptions have undoubtedly arisen. And the more literary the English texts, the more apt they are to misinterpret the originals. The Euro-Canadian mind—with its different conceptions of time, the supernatural, material possessions, the phenomena of nature, and humour—finds it difficult to comprehend and appreciate Native mythology. Foreign to Western sensibilities are totemism, metamorphosis, and animism; a moral code that, while it prescribes right conduct, glorifies the ingenious rogue whose cleverness seems to deserve success (fools deserve to be duped); and the realistic and imaginative depictions of erotic love, procreation, and excretory processes.

For the non-Native, transcriptions of oral myths lack dramatic emphasis and highlights, subtlety, characterization, and plot motivation. Anecdotal and episodic, they tend to be a potpourri of unrelated and incomplete fragments, often very brief and almost incoherent; some are merely summaries of reports or events. To people schooled in the English literary tradition (including many Natives who understand little of the language of their ancestors), the rambling conversational manner and exaggerated action of Native myths can be tedious, their arcane subject matter and hermetic meanings frustrating.

According to Natives themselves, much of the dramatic power and fun of their mythology and folklore emerge only when their stories are told in performance in the Native language. Many tales (some of which were sung) comprise the dramatic portions of ritual, festival, and ceremony—elements considered more important than plot and characterization. In print—particularly in English—they lose their dramatic force; but the Native linguistic context brings to life their pungent wit and rich vein of comic pleasantry, metaphorical skill, imagination, and psychological insight. Their humour—sometimes considered obscene by non-Natives—provides comic relief in a violent world; the variations and incongruities, which detractors find chaotic, mirror the rich diversity the Natives saw in nature. Indeed, there are scholars today whose knowledge of Native languages and traditions has led them to recognize an appropriateness and coherence in Aboriginal myths and folklore—in the context of the Native way of life—that had not previously been understood.

Countless Native tales have been retold and interpreted by non-Natives. Partly because of the demands of the marketplace, much reshaping and editing has been effected: references to sex, procreation, and excretory matters expunged or minimized; difficult allegories and allusions either ignored or simplified; repetitions, digressions, asides, and obscurities omitted; missing links provided; loose structure tightened; a 'childishness' concealed; and poor syntax and faulty grammar corrected. To be fair, these editorial revisions have often been carried out with every attempt to recreate the spirit of the Native originals, but the well-intentioned desire to extract English storytelling elements from them has sometimes led to total misrepresentations. Generally speaking, non-Native storytellers, unable to fathom the Native mind, have failed to master Native material.

Native writers have begun to object strongly to the corrupt and intrusive writing process that non-Natives have applied to their stories, and particularly to the appropriation of their stories by non-Natives. Basil H. JOHNSTON, for example, decries the misconceptions and misrepresentations surrounding Nanabush: 'To look upon stories concerning him as no more than fairy tales intended solely for the amusement of children serves only to inhibit further inquiry into, and an appreciation of, Algonquian oral traditions. It is only within the context of Ojibway perception of the world and of the individual, and of tribal customs as commemorated in oral traditions and in ritual, that Nanabush may be more fully understood.' Lenore KEESHIG-TOBIAS states emphatically that 'stories are power'; their appropriation is 'culture theft, the theft of voice'. Some—like Beth Brant, Marie Annharte Baker, and Emma LaRocque—regard the oral as *Native*, in conflict with the *written*, which they identify with the colonizer's medium, English, the language of 'the enemy'. As a result, Native writers have begun to reclaim and recover their stories, retelling the old and creating new ones as traditions and events unfold into the future. A few, like Keeshig-Tobias, have taken up storytelling seriously as a profession and an important art form. Some, however, are finding it difficult to include features from oral narratives in their written works. In Maria CAMPBELL's words: 'It was hard, we had to change from telling a story to a group of people to being alone and telling the story to the paper'.

Bibliography. There is a staggering collection of Native folklore, more from some tribes than from others. Much of it lies buried in journals of learned societies (collected more for scientific than literary reasons) like the American Folklore Society, the Royal Society of Canada, the Canadian Institute, and the British Association Committee, and in reports and bulletins of government agencies, such as the Geological Survey of Canada and the National Museum of Canada. The first professional collector to record the myths of Canada's Native peoples in English was the American ethnologist Henry Rowe Schoolcraft (1793–1864), who worked among the Ojibwa of the Great Lakes and was probably most responsible for popularizing the Natives' oral literature. His *Algic researches* ... (2 vols, New York, 1839) provided the earliest source material for compilers and editors. In 1956 Mentor L. Williams brought together Schoolcraft's *Indian legends from Algic researches, The myth of Hiawatha, Oneóta, The red race in America, and Historical and statistical information respecting ... the Indian tribes of the United States.* Dr Franz Boas (1858–1942), considered to be the first professional anthropologist to do field work in Canada, and other anthropologists associated with him, collecting and analyzing masses of texts and tales, made significant scholarly contributions, many of which were published by American agencies such as the Smithsonian Institution, Bureau of American Ethnology: these included *Tsimshian texts* (Bulletin 27, 1902) and *Tsimshian mythology based on texts recorded by Henry W. Tate* (1916, rpr. 1970). Another notable collector was Marius BARBEAU, whose *Huron and Wyandot mythology with an appendix containing earlier published records* (Geological Survey of Canada, Memoir 80, no. 11, 1915), treats such subjects as literary style, themes, and diffusion in the Introduction. Much that has been recorded here shows the influence of European tales, riddles, and fables; English translations are given. Barbeau's *Indian days on the western Prairies* (National Museum, Bulletin no. 163, Anthropological Series no. 46, 1960) contains narratives from the Stoney Indians of the Morley Reserve in Alberta. Barbeau himself wrote *Haida myths; illustrated in argillite carvings* (Bulletin 127, Anthropological Series no. 32, 1953). Diamond Jenness (1886–1969), chief anthropologist of the National Museum of

Aboriginal legends and tales: bibliography

Canada (1926–48), was the author of a number of valuable scientific reports on the tribes of Canada, notably *The corn goddess and other tales from Indian Canada* (Bulletin no. 141, no. 39, 1956), for which he selected 'such tales as appear to possess literary merit'. Pioneer collectors of Northeast Woodland lore were Silas T. Rand (1810–89), missionary and philologist, and Charles Leland. They produced the earliest and the two most frequently cited authentic sources: *Legends of the Micmacs* (New York and London, 1894), in which Rand offers stories of Glooscap, the central figure of northeastern Algonquin mythology, and *The Algonquin legends of New England; or myths and folklore of the Micmac, Passamaquoddy, and Penobscot tribes* (Boston, 1884), in which Leland makes detailed comparisons with the Norse eddas and sagas.

Since the late nineteenth century there have been countless collections of 'Indian' legends by non-Natives. Legends recounted by Natives began to appear in the 1970s, published in Native and non-Native newspapers and collected in numerous books, including: *The life and traditions of the red man* (Bangor, Maine, 1893; rpr. 1979) by Joseph Nicolar; *Legends of Vancouver* (1911, new edn 1961) by the famous Mohawk poet Emily Pauline JOHNSON, who adapted the legends of the Squamish tribe told to her by Chief Joseph Capilano; *Abenaki Indian legends; grammar and place names* (1932) by Henry Lorne Masta; *Tales of the Kitimat* (1956) by William Gordon Robinson; *Men of Medeek* (2nd edn 1962), as told in 1935–6 to Will Robinson by Walter Wright, a Tsimshian chief of the Kitselas Band of the Middle Skeena River—this material concerns the legendary city of Tum-L-Hanna and the migration westward to Kitselas Canyon in British Columbia; *Legends of my people: the great Ojibway* (1965) by the prominent Ojibwa artist, Norval Morrisseau; *Son of Raven, son of Deer* (1967), a collection of twelve tales of the Tse-Shaht people by George CLUTESI, who also wrote an apologia for his people's potlatch ceremony in *Potlatch* (1969). *Tales of Nokomis* (1970) by Patronella Johnston presents Ojibwa legend and custom within the narrative framework of children visiting their grandmother. In *Voice of the Plains Cree* (1973) Ruth M. Buck edited legends collected by the Rev. Edward AHENA-KEW (1885–1961). *Squamish legends* (1966) was edited by Oliver N. Wells from tape-recorded interviews with Chief August Jack Khahtsahlano and Domanic Charlie. *Visitors who never left: the origins of the people of Damelahamid* (1974)—translated by Chief Kenneth B.

Harris, a Tsimshian chief, in collaboration with Francis M.D. Robinson—is a collection of eight myths dealing with the origin and history of the Native peoples from the regions of the Skeena and Nass Rivers in northern British Columbia. In *Wild drums* (1972) Alex Grisdale relates tales and legends of the Plains Natives to Nan Shipley. See also *Tales of the Mohawks* (1975) by Alma Greene (Forbidden Voice); *Ojibway heritage* (1976), which offers ceremonies, rituals, songs, dances, prayers, and legends of the Ojibwa by Basil H. Johnston, who also published *Tales the Elders told: Ojibway legends* (1981); *The adventures of Nanabush: Ojibway Indian stories* (1979) told by Sam Snake, Chief Elijah Yellowhead, Alder York, David Simcoe, Annie King, compiled by Emerson Coatsworth and David Coatsworth; *Kwakiutl legends* (1981) as told to Pamela Whitaker by Chief James Wallas; *Tagish Tlaagu Tagish stories* (1982), told in English by Angela Sidney; *Where the chill came from: Windigo tales and journeys* (1982) translated from the Swampy Cree by Howard Norman; and *Ojibway ceremonies* (1983) by Basil Johnston.

Other publications are: *Micmac legends of Prince Edward Island* (1988) by John Joe Stark, *Glous'gap stories of the Micmac Indians* (2000) retold by Michael B. Running Wolf and Patricia Clark Smith, and *Earth elder stories: the Penayzitt path* (1988) by Alexander Wolfe. *Write it on your heart: the epic world of an Okanagan storyteller* (1989) contains the stories of Harry Robinson (1900–90) transcribed by Wendy Wickwire, who tried to retain their original flavour and sound, setting them typographically in lines structured to evoke the speech rhythms without attempting to polish the English. In his review of the book, Thomas KING wrote: 'In reading Robinson one is forced to read the story out loud, thereby closing the circle, the oral becoming the written becoming the oral.' See also Basil Johnston's *Tales of the Anishinaubaek* (1993) and *The Manitous, the spiritual world of the Ojibway* (1995).

Aboriginal literature:

Native and Métis literature. I. HISTORICAL BACKGROUND. The literature of the Native peoples of Canada had its origins in an oral tradition that was rooted in, and transmitted through, the social contexts of storytelling and ceremony. Storytelling included all types of myths, legends, tales, and folklore, while compositional elements of ceremony offered a wide range of songs, ritual chants, drama, poems, prayers, and orations. This spoken

4

literature was first printed when scattered specimens were translated into French and recorded in the *JESUIT RELATIONS*. The missionaries expressed amazement at the Native people's literary faculties, Father Paul Le Jeune observing that 'metaphor is largely in use among these Peoples' (1636). Because Native peoples associate an idea with an object, with visual memory, they invariably make use of metaphors and analogies, and because they pay more attention to the implications or suggested meanings of their words—the connotative as opposed to the specific or denotative meaning—their metaphors embody an emotional force. It is this power of arousing emotion by making apt comparisons that constitutes one of the great strengths of their oratory. Oratorical skill was held in the highest esteem. Le Jeune stated that a Native leader was obeyed in proportion to his use of eloquence because his followers had no other law than his word. In his *Relation* of 1633 Le Jeune commended a Montagnais chief for a 'keenness and delicacy of rhetoric that might have come out of the schools of Aristotle or Cicero'. In his *Relation* of 1645 Father Jérôme Lalemant quotes a speech given by an Iroquois spokesman to Governor Montmagny at Québec that illustrates the orator's style: 'Onontio, thou hast dispersed the clouds; the air is serene; the Sky shows clearly, the Sun is bright. I see no more trouble. Peace has made everything calm: my heart is at rest. I go away very happy.' Sentences are short and straightforward. Language is clear and simple. A nature image dramatizes the speaker's feelings. A poetic quality and a certain grace permeate the entire speech, while courtesy as well as a sense of dignity and a laconic reserve dominate. If the occasion warranted a long speech, however, the Native had appropriate metaphors and vocabulary, a syntax that allowed him to formulate complex relationships between ideas, as well as employing a vivid imagination and literary inventiveness.

In time numerous samples of Native eloquence in translation, from different tribal cultures across Canada, appeared in the writings of white explorers, traders, travellers, adopted captives, missionaries, and settlers. Admired chiefly for their literary value rather than for their content, they were recorded to illustrate certain stylistic qualities: 'pathos', 'caustic wit', or 'genial pleasantry'.

The Native predilection for figurative and symbolic language, for allegorical meanings and allusions, contributed greatly to the problems of exact translation into French and English. The eighteenth-century English fur trader Alexander Henry recognized this dilemma when he explained that 'The Indian manner of speech is so extravagantly figurative, that it is only for a very perfect master to follow and comprehend it entirely.' The speeches of two outstanding eighteenth-century warrior-orators—the Ottawa war chief Pontiac (1720–69) and the Iroquois Thayendanegea, better known as Joseph Brant (1742–1807)—exemplify Native eloquence at its best. Pontiac could not write, but his recorded speeches in council outlining his vision of a separate, independent Native confederacy allied to the French inspired the revolt in 1763–4 of nearly all the tribes around Lake Superior, and as far south as the lower Mississippi. His dictated letters to British and French officials are also impressive, demonstrating the cunning of an astute warrior, a brilliant diplomat, or a wily politician as the need arose. The great orator Joseph Brant was a spokesman for the Mohawk Loyalists who moved to the Grand River (Ontario) in 1784. Besides his speeches, his extant writings consist mainly of letters to British and American military and civil authorities, and to royalty, many of them expressing his idealistic vision of an independent Native confederacy that would be a sovereign ally of the British. Written in lucid, direct, highly persuasive English, and notable for their patrician tone, they can be read in W.L. Stone's *Life of Joseph Brant* (2 vols, New York, 1838) and Charles M. Johnston's *The valley of the Six Nations* (1964). The celebrated Shawnee Chief Tecumseh (1768–1813), renowned for his military genius, also used his remarkable oratorical talents not only in his attempts to unite the Native peoples into a western confederacy but also in support of the British cause in the War of 1812. Tecumseh's famous speeches in council reveal his adroit reasoning powers as well as his keen political sense, at times combining dry sarcasm with rich metaphor.

The many treaties that emerged out of the complexities of Native-white relations over the span of three centuries also represent recorded Native literature. During treaty-making sessions, which resembled ancient councils in their drama and ceremonial formality, orators delivered highly rhetorical speeches using the ancient formulaic metaphors of chain, fire, sun, tree, road, hatchet, and pipe, and made traditional analogies to the natural world while they poured forth their embittered eloquence in defence of home and hunting ground. Western orators of the late nineteenth century—like Crowfoot,

Aboriginal literature: Native and Métis

Poundmaker, Big Bear, Sweet Grass, and Misto-wa-sis—kept alive the tradition of their forefathers to persuade and lead by means of the oratory of exhortation, which contained inherited images and a strong element of didacticism and aphoristic, dignified language; their speeches can be read in A. Morris's *The treaties of Canada with the Indians* ... (1880, rpr. 1976).

2. THE NINETEENTH CENTURY. The first signs of literary creativity in English among the Native peoples appeared as a result of organized missionary efforts to convert them. Christianized Natives, some of whom became missionaries (mostly Methodist), were encouraged to write for an international audience in order to create interest in, and possibly raise money for, the Native peoples. Since they wrote for an international audience of Christian philanthropists, they had a deliberate aim: to encourage compassion and support for the 'poor Indian', who required patience and understanding in the process of being assimilated into the blessings and benefits of European civilization. Their mainly autobiographical works present a wealth of proudly recounted historical information about tribal beliefs, ceremonies, customs, and folklore; ironically, for the modern reader, they are pervaded by deep Christian piety and biblical cadences, the Bible being the predominant literary influence in these peoples' lives. Their books comprise the first body of Canadian Native literature in English; they also offer the first written evidence of the ideas, responses, and feelings of individual Natives, as opposed to the collective expressions contained in myths and legends. The first Canadian Native to publish a book in English was George COPWAY, who wrote *The life, history, and travels of Kah-ge-ga-gah-bowh (George Copway), a young Indian chief of the Ojibwa nation, a convert to the Christian faith, and a missionary to his people for twelve years* ... (Albany, N.Y., 1847). An instant success, it was reprinted six times by the end of the year and republished in London under the title *Recollections of a forest life* ... (1850). Copway's most famous work, described by himself as 'the first volume of Indian history written by an Indian', is *The traditional history and characteristic sketches of the Ojibwa nation* (London, 1850). One contemporary newspaper praised his 'biting satire', 'pungent anecdote', 'strokes of wit and humour', 'touches of pathos', and 'most poetical descriptions of nature'. His success as a writer brought him international recognition and he toured Europe as a celebrity, writing of his experiences in *Running sketches of men and places in England, France, Germany, Belgium and Scotland* (New York, 1851). Another remarkable Native author was the Rev. Peter JONES. Interpreter, translator, author, Native-rights leader, preacher, and the first Native Methodist minister in Canada, he was a prolific and indefatigable writer who played a vigorous role in the religious and secular life of his time. His autobiography, *Life and journals of Kah-Ke-Wa-Quo-Na-By (Rev. Peter Jones) Wesleyan minister* (Toronto, 1860), was published posthumously, as was his *History of the Ojibway Indians; with especial reference to their conversion to Christianity* (London, 1861; rpr. 1970). His English prose is highly personal and literate, and occasionally amusing and anecdotal. The writings of two other Native ministers reveal the lucid, correct style that many of these men attained. *Journal of the Reverend Peter Jacobs* ... (Toronto, 1854) is a straightforward factual record of the three-month journey from Toronto to York Factory of Peter JACOBS, who was a keen observer; his diary entries are written with precision and clarity. *The diary of the Reverend Henry Budd 1870–1875* (1974), edited by Katherine Pettipas for the Manitoba Record Society Publications, offers the personal record of a former Hudson's Bay Company clerk who was a farmer, teacher, and for thirty-five years a missionary in the remote diocese of Rupert's Land. He was the first ordained Native Anglican minister in North America (1858). A number of other educated Natives also wrote and published. George HENRY was the author of two pamphlets: *Remarks concerning the Ojibway Indians, by one of themselves, called Maungwudaus, who has been travelling in England, France, Belgium, Ireland, and Scotland* (Leeds, 1847); and *An account of the Chippewa Indians, who have been travelling among the whites in the United States, England, Ireland, Scotland, France and Belgium* (Boston, 1848)—which, along with Peter Jones' reactions, offers the earliest-known detailed impressions of Europeans from the Native perspective.

The best-known Native writer before and after the turn of the century was a poet, Emily Pauline JOHNSON, author of *The white wampum* (London, 1895), *Canadian born* (1903), and *Flint and feather* (1912; rev. 1914; rpr. 1997). Her collections of short fiction included *Legends of Vancouver* (1911) and *The moccasin maker* (1913), which was published posthumously. John Brant-Sero (Ojijatekha, 1867–?), of Hamilton, Ontario, saw himself as the historian of the Six Nations Indians, dedicated to make known his 'hitherto untold lore', and gave public concerts and lectures in Great Britain and North

America. He translated 'God Save the King' into Mohawk and wrote six articles.

3. THE 1960S AND 1970S. In the 1960s more and more Native newspapers and periodicals sprang up across Canada to provide a forum for politically conscious Native organizations, and for speeches, essays, and reports, as Native activists began to attack and criticize the dominant society. Whether in speech or essay, they reacted politically to their problems in a frank and often angry and bitter manner, and in language that is sometimes flamboyant but always direct and forceful. Concerned with the wrongs inflicted on their people, they were more interested in content than in literary style. Native-authored books—frequently written with the aid of a collaborator or amanuensis—revealed five trends: (1) a pan-Native approach that played down tribal affiliation and focused on a common Native identity, while sometimes shifting from emphasis on the shared experiences of the group to the single experiences of the individual; (2) a greater diversification of literary genres; (3) inspirational writing intended to provide a sense of historical continuity and making use of ancient beliefs and values; and (4 and 5) two militant approaches: one that advocated separation from the dominant society, and another that sought an as-yet-undefined revisionist presence in society. *The statement of the Government of Canada on Indian policy* (1969), the controversial 'White Paper' that recommended the abolition of special rights for Native peoples, sparked a burst of literary activity. An immediate and angry reaction to the government proposals came from the Alberta Cree Harold Cardinal in *The unjust society: the tragedy of Canada's Indians* (1971). He argued shrilly for the retention of special rights within the strengthened contexts of treaty and the Indian Act, and his book, which gained national prominence, became a classic on the Native situation in Canada. Arguing a minority point of view, William Wuttunee, a Calgary Cree lawyer originally from Saskatchewan, opposed special status as a barrier to progress, and in his controversial *Ruffled feathers: Indians in Canadian society* (1971) advocated instead integration, individual development, and a radical change in the Native psyche itself.

The growing self-consciousness of Native peoples in the 1970s produced more protest literature, some of it written by militant patriots and couched in strident, sloganistic language. Examples of such books are *Prison of grass: Canada from the Native point of view* (1975) by Howard Adams; Harold Cardinal's *The rebirth of Canada's Indians* (1977); *Half-breed*

(1973) by Maria CAMPBELL; and *We are Métis* (1980) by Duke REDBIRD.

Antitheses of such angry presentations were a number of popular histories focusing on personal experience as well as family and tribal traditions. In *The feathered U.E.L.s* (1973), Enos T. Montour recreates some memorable occasions in the lives of the first Native United Empire Loyalists and their descendants. He combines fully dramatized scenes with dialogue and folksy entertaining anecdotes. *My tribe the Crees* (1979) by Joseph F. Dion, a treaty Cree descendant of Big Bear, traces the history of the Crees before the arrival of the white man and provides insights, from a Native perspective, into the Northwest Rebellion of 1885. This was edited by Hugh A. Dempsey, who also edited *My people the Bloods* (1979), drawn from a book-length manuscript entitled 'Indians of the Western Plains', completed in 1936 by Mike Mountain Horse (1888–1964). It is well written and of historical interest. *The ways of my grandmothers* (1980) by Beverly Hungry Wolf records the ancient ways of the Blood women as well as some personal and tribal history. Two historical books have a strong quality of prophecy and vision: *The fourth world: Indian reality* (1974) by George Manuel and Michael Posluns, in which the background of Manuel as a Shuswap from British Columbia is used to trace the Canadian Native's struggle for recognition, and Manuel offers his vision of a fourth world where the values of special-status people are integrated with those of all peoples; and *These mountains are our sacred places* (1977) by Chief John Snow, of the Wesley band of Stoney Indians, who records the past of his people in a moving and sometimes lyrical prose.

Biography, and its allied forms, is a favourite genre of Native writers. At their best, such books—which are sometimes the result of taped interviews, collaborations, or translation—have a good-humoured, warm, flowing narrative style. *Recollections of an Assiniboine chief* (1972) by the highly articulate Dan Kennedy (Ochankugahe, 1877–1973), a Saskatchewan Assiniboine, brought together his writings of the twenties, thirties, and forties and offered primary data about his tribe's history and culture in an engaging and informative style. *Guests never leave hungry: the autobiography of James Sewid, a Kwakiutl Indian* (1969) describes Sewid's successful adjustment to the culture change in British Columbia. Anahareo, who had lived with the famous Englishman turned Ojibwa, Grey Owl (Archibald Stansfeld BELANEY), wrote *Devil in*

Aboriginal literature: Native and Métis

deerskins: my life with Grey Owl (1940, rpr. 1980), and *Grey Owl and I: a new autobiography* (1972). *First among the Hurons* by Max Gros-Louis, in collaboration with Marcel Bellier, translated from the French by Sheila FISCHMAN, is the autobiography of a Québec chief who played a vital role in the James Bay project. *No foreign land: the biography of a North American Indian* (1976) by Wilfred Pelletier (edited by Ted Poole) tells, in a straightforward manner, of Pelletier's life in two worlds—both on and off the reserve. *Buffalo days and nights* (1976), containing the memoirs of Peter Erasmus (1833–1931), the last surviving member of the Palliser Expedition of 1857–60, as told to Henry Thompson in 1920, was published by the Glenbow-Alberta Institute. It includes an introduction by Dr Irene Spry, copious footnotes, a bibliography, and an index that make it by far the most scholarly of these memoirs. *I am an Indian* (1969), edited by the non-Native Kent Gooderham, was the first anthology of Native literature to be published in Canada, containing a wide assortment of literary forms—from legends, essays, and stories, to poems by such well-known Native writers as Duke Redbird, Chief Dan George, Howard Adams, Alma Greene, Ethel Brant Monture, and George CLUTESI.

The social-protest poetry of the angry young Duke Redbird, among others, was balanced by an output that expressed a new affirmative spirit and often featured wit and irony. In fact *Loveshine and red wine* (1981), the collected verse of Duke Redbird, reflects both these attitudes: a mellow, loving, mature Redbird, as well as the angry young man. Chief Dan George's lyrical responses to life are enjoyable, and his vision of the divine in living things is mirrored in his prose poem 'My heart soars' (1974). In 1977 the Highway Bookshop published two collections of verse: *Wisdom of Indian poetry* and *Okanagan Indian*, by the West Coast Native Ben Abel, who writes gentle lyrical verse and is most compelling when he deals with his own experiences. George Kenny, an Ontario Native, is the author of *Indians don't cry* (1977), in which the best poems are permeated with a sense of the abiding ironies of Indian life. *Poems of Rita Joe* (1978) is an autobiographical sequence by a Mi'kmaq woman, Rita JOE, detailing the experiences and values that helped her define the Native perception of life. The texts of a few of the poems offer both Mi'kmaq and English in parallel columns.

Native stage plays based chiefly on tribal ritual, legend, and ancient custom also appeared in the 1970s. The versatile Duke Redbird's *Wasawkachak* (1974) used traditional and contemporary song and dance in dramatizing the creation of humanity. *October stranger* by George Kenny was performed in Monaco at the sixth International Theatre Festival in 1977. *Ayash* by Jim Morris, a stage adaptation of an ancient Ojibwa legend, had its premiere in Sioux Lookout, Ontario, on 18 Feb. 1983.

The best Native short-story writer of the period was the gifted Basil JOHNSTON. His entertaining *Moose meat & wild rice* (1978) uses gentle irony and satire to poke fun at the pretensions and prejudices of Native and non-Native alike.

4. 1983 TO 2000. The creative output in this period surpassed the great upsurge of literary activity in the 1970s, to which must now be added the great diversity and iconoclasm of Native writing. Some writers, like Basil Johnston, Lenore KEESHIG-TOBIAS, Rita Joe, and Jeannette ARMSTRONG, are writing bilingually, using their own Native languages and English. This body of new writing is distinguished by a wide range of forms. Beatrice Culleton (Métis, b. 1949) was the first Native to tackle the novel: *In search of April Raintree*, (1983; reissued in 1984 minus a graphic rape scene; rpr. 1992). Set in Winnipeg, it is the moving account of two Métis sisters who are raised by different foster parents to develop in antithetical directions. Two years later Jeannette Armstrong published *Slash* (1985, rev. 1990). Thomas KING wrote three well-received novels: *Medicine River* (1990, rpr. 1996), which has been made into a television film, *Green grass, running water* (1993), and *Truth and bright water* (1999). Two novels by Ruby Slipperjack (b. 1942), *Honour the sun* (1987) and *Silent words* (1992), are told respectively from the point of view of a young girl and boy growing up in small isolated Native communities in Northern Ontario. The award-winning Jovette MARCHESSAULT, a major figure among contemporary Québec feminist writers, draws upon the details of her own life in her three novels translated from the French: *Like a child of the earth* (1975, rpr. 1988), which chronicles a childhood paradise on the banks of the St Lawrence; *Mother of grass* (1980, rpr. 1989), which tells of her hardships and poverty in the slums of Montreal's inner city and ends with the death of her beloved grandmother, the author's comfort and mentor; and *White pebbles in the dark forests* (1990)—which traces a reconciliation between men and women, children and parents, and includes elements of myth and visionary experiences. Joan Crate's first novel, *Breathing water* (1990)—told from

the point of view of a Métis cocktail waitress newly married to her former boss, a rich Greek hotel owner—demonstrates an astonishing mastery of technique. The three novellas by Jordan Wheeler (b. 1964) in *Brothers in arms* (1989)—'Hearse In Snow', 'Red Wave', and 'Exposure'—deal with the relationship between pairs of Native brothers trying to re-establish contact after years of separation, and to reconnect with their ancestral past. In *Keeper'n me* (1994, rpr. 1995), Richard Wagamese, a former award-winning columnist for the *Calgary Herald*, draws upon his own life as an Ojibwa to tell of foster homes, street kids, jail, and finally recovery through the redemptive powers of his Native family and tradition. This was followed by *A quality of light* (1997), about the affectionate, and then difficult, relationship between Joshua Kane, an Ojibwa, and Johnny Gerhardt, a white. *Stones and switches* (1994) is a promising first novel by Lorne Simon (Mi'kmaq), who was killed in a car accident shortly before it was published. His friend Richard Van Camp (Dogrib) is the author of *The lesser blessed* (1996). Both are effective first novels about young Natives growing up. Following the success of her story collection *Traplines* (see below), Eden Robinson (Haisla) published her first novel, *Monkey Beach* (2000). Narrated by Lisamarie Hill, who had run away to Vancouver and is back living with her family in Kitamaat Village in northern B.C., in Haisla territory, it begins with the shocking news from the Coast Guard that the seiner *Queen of the North*, with her younger brother Jimmy on board as a deckhand, is overdue. There follows a vivid reminiscence of the life of an extended family, in which Jimmy is prominent. In the easy, voluble exchanges of family and friends, and their humour, a certain sophistication rules, yet Lisa has a powerful dreamlife, and ghosts, spirits, and good and bad medicine are taken for granted by Ma-ma-oo (grandmother), keeper of the old traditions—and these seep into the narrative in lyrical passages of an accomplished family novel.

The short-story form is still the choice of many writers. *Achimoona* (1985) is an interesting collection of ten short stories written as the result of a workshop conducted by Maria CAMPBELL, who wrote the Introduction; three of the stories were written by Jordan Wheeler and one by his mother, Bernelda Wheeler (Cree/Saulteaux, b. 1937), a writer and broadcaster who has published three children's books. Thomas King uses the form with considerable skill, combining techniques from the oral tradition and mainstream literary conventions.

In his collection *One good story, that one* (1993), his acute ear for dialogue and the oral English rhythms and colloquial speech of his Native characters is striking. A volume of light short stories, *Food and spirits* (1991), by Beth Brant, a Bay of Quinte Mohawk, is uneven in quality; but it contains a gem, 'Turtle Girl'—which first appeared in CANADIAN FICTION MAGA-ZINE (no. 60, 1987)—about an aged black musician and a young Native girl. *Traplines* (1996, rpr. 1998), the astonishing debut of Eden Robinson, is made up of four stories—one of them, 'Contact sports', is a novella—in which hapless families, weird situations (in 'Dogs in winter' the young narrator's mother is in jail as a serial killer), and flashes of violent action are described without emotion but with narrative ease and lively dialogue.

Many Native writers experiment with the poetic form, preferring looser, and concrete, poetry over the conventional, and satire, humour, and irony over direct confrontation. Although they continue to write about the pain and abuse suffered from the cultural clash with church, state, and school during the years of 'colonization', they also write about joyful childhood memories, grandchildren, ancient beliefs, sexual love, and the beauty and rhythms of the natural and spiritual worlds. Daniel David MOSES showed himself to be a strong and effective poet in *Delicate bodies* (1980) and *The white line* (1991). Other poets—Duke Redbird, Rita Joe, Jeannette Armstrong, Lenore Keeshig-Tobias, Marie Annharte Baker (Salteaux, b. 1942), Beth Cuthand (Cree, b. 1949), and Joan Crate—are now familiar names. Louise Halfe, a Plains Cree, published *Bear bones* and *Feathers* in 1994. Gregory Scofield (Métis/Cree)—a self-taught poet who was helped by Patrick LANE and Lorna CROZIER—has published four books of poetry: *The gathering: stones for the medicine wheel* (1993), which won the Dorothy LIVESAY Poetry Prize; *Native Canadiana: songs from the urban rez* (1996); *Love medicine and one song* (1997); and *I knew two Métis women: Dorothy Scofield and Georgina Houle Young* (1999), inspired by his mother and his aunt.

Many Natives are still choosing the autobiographical mode. Following Maria Campbell's landmark classic *Halfbreed* (1973, rpr. 1983), there have been *I walk in two worlds* (1987) by Eleanor Brass; *Indian school days* (1988, rpr. 1991) by Basil H. Johnston; *I am Woman* (1988, rpr. 1996) by Lee MARACLE; and *Inside out: the autobiography of a Native Canadian* (1990, rpr. 1995) by James Tyman. *Occupied Canada: a young white man discovers his unsuspected past* (1991, GGA), co-written by Robert

Aboriginal literature: Native and Métis

Calihoo and Robert Hunter, is Calihoo's life story that tells of degradation and desperation. Beth Brant's *Writing as witness: essay and talk* (1994) is a warm, chatty discourse that ranges over a wide range of topics, from Pauline Johnson and Pocahontas to Brant's parents, her children, and her lesbianism. In *Back on the rez: finding the way home* (1996) Brian Maracle, a former broadcaster and journalist for the Toronto *Globe and Mail*, who grew up as a non-status urban Native, writes about his first year back on the Six Nations Grand River Territory, and gives a personal account of Mohawk culture and history, as well as a description of contemporary Native life in Canada. The poet Gregory Scofield (Métis / Cree) published *Thunder through my veins: memories of a Métis childhood* (1999, rpr. 2000). His very mixed background, being separated from his mother at the age of five, his loneliness as he grew up, his discovery in his teens that he was gay—his dealing with all these things, and his flowering as a writer, are described in an expert narrative.

Oral histories are still popular. *Enough is enough: Aboriginal women speak out* (1987) is a collection of stories about being Native and female, as told to Janet Silman by a small group of women activists from the Tobique Reserve in New Brunswick who, through their struggles and demonstration marches, contributed to the passing of Bill C-31 by Parliament in June 1985 that ended more than 100 years of legislated sexual discrimination against Native women. *Kôhkominawak otâcimowiniwâwa; or Our grandmothers' lives as told in their own words* (1992), edited and translated by Freda Ahenakew, records the stories of seven Cree women who grew up in northern Saskatchewan during the 1930s. *Crazy water: Native voices on addiction and recovery* (1993), by the award-winning print and broadcast journalist Brian Maracle, features notably honest and poignant interviews with Native drug dealers, alcoholics, hookers, and con-artists. Maracle, who specializes in Native issues, has said that his idea for the book was rooted in the fact 'that native wit and wisdom is largely unappreciated'. *I'll sing 'til the day I die: conversations with Tyendinaga Elders* (1995) by Beth Brant reconstructs the stories of fourteen Mohawks and gives 'the sense of orality'.

Because of the growing need for Aboriginal literature texts in high schools, colleges, and universities, there has been a proliferation of anthologies. The first major anthology, *First people, first voices* (1983), edited by Penny Petrone, was distributed internationally and

has had many printings. *Seventh generation: contemporary Native writing* (1989), edited and compiled by Heather Hodgson, is the first anthology of poems written by Natives. It was followed by *Our bit of truth: an anthology of Canadian Native literature* (1990), edited by Agnes Grant, and *Writing the circle: Native women of western Canada* (1990), edited by Jeanne Perreault and Sylvia Vance, presenting the writings of fifty-two young, little-known First Nations women. The first Native-edited anthology is *A gathering of spirit: a collection by North American Indian women* (1984; rev. 1988) edited by Beth Brant. Thomas King edited *All my relations: an anthology of contemporary Canadian Native writing* (1990). While many of the same authors from his previous anthology are here, King also included Ruby Slipperjack, Jordan Wheeler, Jovette Marchessault, Basil H. Johnston, and Joan Crate, among others. The Introduction to *An anthology of Canadian Native literature in English* (1992), edited by Daniel David Moses and Terry Goldie (a non-Native professor at York University, Toronto), rather than interpreting the anthology offers a dialogue between Moses and Goldie—who is ambiguous about the reasons that prompted the editorial selections. In the same year appeared *Voices: being Native in Canada*, edited by Linda Jaine (Cree) and Drew Hayden TAYLOR (Ojibwa), a collection of nineteen short stories and essays by well-known writers, including Jeannette C. Armstrong, Jordan Wheeler, Lee Maracle, Gilbert Oskaboose, and others. *Steal my rage: new Native voices* (1995), edited by Joel T. Maki, grew out of a project sponsored in 1993 by Toronto's Na-Me-Res, a Native men's residence. A collection of poetry, fiction, and non-fiction, it features 34 new Native writers from across Canada who treat a wide range of topics, including the difficulties of urban life, identity problems, difficulties with self-esteem, romantic love, spirituality, and the need for self-government. *Thunder in my soul: a Mohawk woman speaks* (1993), by Patricia Monture-Angus, is a landmark collection of essays and papers by a First Nations woman scholar who addresses Aboriginal people's experience with education, racism, feminism, and the reformation of the criminal justice system.

The most exciting literary development has taken place in drama. Tomson HIGHWAY's *The Rez Sisters* (1988), and its sequel *Dry lips oughta move to Kapuskasing* (1989), both of which won Dora Mavor Moore Awards, brought the Manitoba-born Cree writer international fame. Daniel David Moses and Drew Hayden Taylor are two other award-winning Native playwrights whose dramas have received acclaim. Among the plays of Jovette Marchessault translated into English are *Night cows* (1979); *Saga of the wet hens: a play* (1983); and *Alice and Gertrude and Natalie and René [sic] and dear Ernest* (1983), which principally concerns four lesbian literary figures, Alice B. Toklas, Gertrude Stein, Natalie Barney, and Renée Vivien—and Hemingway. Marchessault's other celebration of women writers and artists, *Le voyage magnifique d'Émily Carr* (1990, GGA), was translated by Linda Gaboriau (1992).

Native literature in Canada: from the oral tradition to the present (1990) by Penny Petrone is the first book-length critical study of the literature of Canada's First Peoples. Although the concept of criticism as it is understood in the Western literary tradition does not exist in Aboriginal culture, several Native writers have taken up the role of literary critic, objecting to the Eurocentric literary standards and approaches used by non-Native academics, who, they claim, misinterpret the Native message. As a result they have been working hard to find new and culturally appropriate modes, both in literature and criticism. Some women writers—Jeannette Armstrong, Lee Maracle, Lenore Keeshig-Tobias, Beth Brant, Beth Cuthand, and Marie Annharte Baker—are passionate critics of the Canadian literary establishment, and their critical essays have been appearing in newspapers, anthologies, and journals. *Telling it: women and language across cultures* (1990) celebrates the thoughts and words of women writers and artists from Canada's fractured margins, and challenges non-marginal assumptions about the nature of writing in Canada, with Jeannette Armstrong and Lee Maracle speaking on the problems of cross-cultural communications and the appropriation of voice. According to Maracle, 'If the culture in which we live cannot accommodate new thoughts, new feelings, new relationships, then we need a *cultural revolution.' In the feminine: women and words* (1983), edited by Ann Dybikowski, et al., offers such papers as 'Transmitting our identity as Indian writers' by Beth Cuthand, 'Coming out as Indian Lesbian writers' by Beth Brant, and 'Writing from a Native woman's perspective' by Jeannette C. Armstrong. *Give back: First Nations perspective on cultural practice* (1992) includes Lee Maracle's 'Oratory: coming to theory', Jeannette Armstrong's 'Racism: racial exclusivity and cultural supremacy', and two essays by the Cree cultural activist Joy Asham Fedorick:

'Decolonizing language: reflections on style' and 'Fencepost sitting and how I fell off to one side', about the appropriation by non-Aboriginal people of Native stories. *Looking at the words of our people: First Nations analysis of literature* (1993), edited by Jeannette Armstrong, is a ground-breaking attempt in Native criticism that includes important essays by Janice Acoose and Kateri Damm, among others.

Canada's Native writers are creating a body of new writing that has an amazing versatility, vitality, and commitment. They are questioning why they should be expected to conform to the constraints of Eurocentric critical theories; they are using the language of 'the enemy' to break from a colonized past, bending and stretching mainstream rules of genre, reinventing new ones, and redefining traditional notions of orality and literacy to enrich and extend Canada's literature. Considering the power and sacredness that traditional Aboriginal cultures attribute to the word as a force of change, the Native word—whether oral or written—will never cease contributing new perspectives and insights to the literature of Canada.   PENNY PETRONE (2000).

5. 2001 TO 2007. The writers who brought Aboriginal literature into the spotlight in the 1980s—Métis author Beatrice Culleton Mosionier, Jeannette ARMSTRONG, and Tomson HIGHWAY—continue to publish after their first successes. With her novel *In the shadow of evil* (2000) Mosionier wrote what is in some ways a sequel to her gripping story *In search of April Raintree* (1983). Through evocations of Fascism, among other themes, she explores different contexts for the existence of evil, in this case sexual abuse of Aboriginal children in foster homes. Concerned about ongoing racism in Canadian society, she addresses the issue humorously in her children's story *Unusual friendships: a little black cat and a little white rat* (2002). However, it is her first novel that continues to captivate Canadian readers, including academics. It became the text chosen by Cheryl Suzak for the first critical edition of any Aboriginal-authored text in Canada (*In search of April Raintree: critical edition*, 1999), and a 25th Anniversary Edition was celebrated in Winnipeg in 2008. Jeannette Armstrong's *Slash* was reprinted in 2007, but in 2001 she published her second novel, *Whispering in shadows*, which tells the story of a female artist and activist who fights environmental and social injustice from an Okanagan worldview. She also continued with her publication of children's books: *Dancing with the cranes* came out in 2005. Tomson

Aboriginal literature: Native and Métis

Highway added to his two 'rez' plays from the eighties a third instalment, the musical *Rose* (2003). In his play *Ernestine Shuswap gets her trout* (2005), on the other hand, he draws on an event in the colonial history of the Shuswap Nation in British Columbia, which lost its rights, lands, language, and culture without any treaties ever having been signed. Fluent in his Native language Cree, Highway also created three bilingual (Cree and English) children's books, beautifully illustrated by Brian Deines: *Caribou song / atíhko níkamon*, which presents an episode from his novel *Kiss of the fur queen*; *Dragonfly kites / píwíhakanísa* (2002); and *Fox on the ice / mískwamíhk e-cípatapít* (2003). See also Highway's Charles R. Bronfam Lecture in Canadian Studies, *Comparing mythologies* (2003).

Similar to the inclusion of Cree oral traditions and Cree language in many works by Highway, who is from northern Manitoba, Plains Cree poet Louise Halfe writes her poetry from a distinctively Cree perspective, both in her poetic historical narrative *Blue marrow* (the revised edition of 2004 was nominated for a GOVERNOR GENERAL'S AWARD) and in her re-imagining of the story of 'The Rolling Head' in *The crooked good* (2007). This story from the Cree oral tradition tells about the beheading of a woman by a husband jealous of her snake lovers, and evokes themes of violence against women, demonization of women's power and sexuality, and their separation from their children if they are deemed morally inferior—to mention only a few themes that Halfe works into her poetry as a way of undermining the binary of good and evil embraced by Catholicism. Critically acclaimed Métis poet Marilyn Dumont published the award-winning poetry collection *green girl dreams Mountains* (2001), followed by *that tongued belonging* (2007). In her poetry, language and its social significance often become themes, but she writes in English only. Métis poet Gregory Scofield, on the other hand, continues with a lyrical style that intersperses words in Cree and the rhythm of Cree chants (*Singing home the bones*, 2006). An altogether different language, yet equally rich and innovative, is used in *City treaty* (2002), a book of poems by Marvin Francis, a Cree from northern Alberta. Here the poems give voice to urban Aboriginal people in a poetic diction that is 'writing the street', as was said of the poet who lived in Winnipeg until his untimely death in 2005. (His collection of poetry, *bush camp*, was posthumously published in 2008.) Métis novelist Joseph BOYDEN, who garnered much attention and praise with his First World War novel *Three day road* (2005)—and who won the GILLER PRIZE in 2008 for *Through black spruce*—often refers to the Cree language without actually using it. After Maria CAMPBELL's *Halfbreed* (1973), Lee MARACLE's *Bobbie Lee: Indian rebel* (1975), and Gregory Scofield's *Thunder through my veins: memories of a Métis childhood* (2000), it was not until 2002, with the publication of the award-winning memoir *Lake of the Prairies: a story of belonging* by Warren Cariou, that another autobiographical work by an Aboriginal author was published. Cariou explores the question of where he is coming from by telling stories of settlers and Native people at the place where he grew up and where Cree and Métis history, including his own ancestry, was silenced. A new work of fiction by an up-and-coming young Métis writer Cherie Dimaline, *Red rooms* (2007), tells the stories of hotel guests as described by the hotel's housekeeper. It has been praised for its vitality and vividness of language and humour, and won the 'Fiction Book of the Year Award' at the 2007 Anskohk Aboriginal Literature Festival.

There are two Cherokee authors living and working in Canada who are both scholars and creative writers. One is Thomas KING, University of Guelph, who became particularly well known for his novels *Medicine River* (1990) and *Green grass, running water* (1993). In 2005 he published a collection of short stories titled after the first satirical story in the collection *A short history of Indians in Canada*, but it was his 2003 Massey Lectures, also published as a book, *The truth about stories: a Native narrative*, that again drew much attention to his work. His adage 'The truth about stories is that that's all we are' is often cited in discussions of Aboriginal texts and the meaning of narratives cross-culturally. He elaborates on the stories we choose to live by and on their potential for both empowerment and disempowerment. The second Cherokee author is Daniel Heath Justice, who teaches at the University of Toronto and wrote three fantasy novels, published by the Canadian Aboriginal press Kegedonce, with the series title *The way of thorn and thunder: books 1, 2 and 3: Kynship* (2005), *Wyrwood* (2006), and *Dreyd* (2007).

Several Anishinabe writers, who started out in the eighties and nineties, maintain a strong publishing record. Ruby Slipperjack turned to a younger audience with *Little voice* (2001) and incorporated oral traditions of her community in the novel *Weesquachak and the lost ones* (2000, revised as *Weesquachak*, 2005). Her latest book, *Dog tracks* (2008), tells the story of returning to the reserve. Both Anishinabe authors Drew Hayden TAYLOR and Richard Wagamese started to become known as writers in, or shortly after, the year of Oka (1990), a political-landmark event that, like the White Paper of 1969, generated many responses from the Aboriginal writers' community. Taylor—humorist, essayist, and playwright—added to his impressive list of plays (his later work includes *In a world created by a drunken God*, 2006; *The night wanderer*, 2007; *The Berlin blues*, 2007) two books of essays by various Aboriginal authors: *Me funny*, 2005, and *Me sexy* in 2008. Like Taylor, Wagamese is also a columnist in different Aboriginal newspapers. After his first two novels on the theme of cross-cultural adoption, his award-winning third novel, *Dream wheels* (2006), takes a different spin on that same theme by creating a family of Native cowboys who 'adopt' an Afro-Canadian family, a single mother and her teenaged son, embracing the philosophy that Native people were and are the teachers in this land for *all* newcomers. In this novel he not only undermines the 'cowboy and Indian' binary, but also the common belief that Native people are defined by their victimization. Abuse is emphasized in the story of the immigrant characters, while the Native family meets challenges with great inner strength. Wagamese's most recent novel on the theme of homelessness, *Ragged company* (2008), further elaborates on his vision of Native people as teachers and healers. Although from a different perspective, the urban environment is also used as the setting in the gang novel *Dead loyalties* (2007) by Jennifer Storm, an Anishinabe writer from the new generation.

There are several Aboriginal writers from different nations on Canada's west coast. Stó:lō author Lee Maracle created another women-centred novel, *Daughters are forever* (2002). Embedded in Salish storytelling, it takes a critical look at the damaging impact of the child-welfare system on Native people and the difficulties, particularly for women, of caring for children in a traumatized society. An interesting addition to Stó:lō literature is the second edition of Henry Penner's autobiographical work *'Call me Hank': a Stó:lō man's reflections on logging, living, and growing old* (1st edn 1972; 2nd edn 2006) edited by Keith Thor Carlson and Kristina Fagan. After Eden Robinson's successful novel *Monkey Beach* (2000), mostly set on Haisla land and influenced by Haisla culture, this Haisla / Heiltsuk author published *Blood sports* (2006), a story of violent relationships among drug addicts in East

Vancouver in which she chose not to emphasize the ethnic background of her characters. Richard van Camp from the Tlicho (Dogrib) First Nation in the Northwest Territories followed his successful first novel *The lesser blessed* (1996; the German translation, *Die Ohne Segen Sind*, won a prestigious award for youth literature) with a collection of short stories, *Angel wing splash pattern* (2002). The often-anthologized story 'Mermaids' from that collection shows his ability to reach out to youth by writing in a style they can relate to and by understanding their challenges well enough to give them hope. Robert Arthur Alexie from the Teetl'it Gwich'in First Nation further north in the Territories wrote his debut novel *Porcupines and china dolls* (2002) about the impact of residential-school abuse on survivors in their adult life (unlike the award-winning residential-school story *My name is Seepeetza*, 1992, by Shirley Sterling from the Interior Salish Nation, which focuses on school experiences). The book was published by Penguin Canada in 2002, went out of print soon after, and has been republished by Theytus Books. Alexie's second novel *The pale Indian* (2005) explores intergenerational effects of adoption practices in First Nations. It illustrates in much more graphic detail than Maria Campbell's similar story 'Jacob', in *Stories of the road allowance people*, that, as the storyteller comments:

'I tink dats dah reason why we have such a hard time us peoples our roots dey gets broken so many times.'

Several collections of stories published in the last few years draw attention to the oral tradition. These include a new edition of *Write it on your heart* (2004) edited by Harry Robinson and Windy Wickwire—a third volume in that series is *Living by stories* (2005); *Trail of the spirit* (2006) by George Blondin, a Dene; and *The stone canoe: two lost Mi'kmaq texts* (2007) edited by Elizabeth Paul, Peter Sanger, and Alan Syliboy. *Telling our stories: Omushkego legends & histories from Hudson Bay* (2005) by Louis Bird was followed by the collection, also told by Bird, *The spirit lives in the mind: Omushkego stories, lives, and dreams* (2007). A significant scholarly text is *Aboriginal oral traditions: theory, practice, ethics* (2008) edited by Renée Hulan and Renate Eigenbrod.

The field of Aboriginal literatures in Canada has become so diversified and features so many authors, styles, themes, and genres that it is impossible to do it justice in a few pages. Since the publication of Penny Petrone's entry, which precedes this one, there have been

Aboriginal literature: Native and Métis

many new creative works by Aboriginal authors and also new theoretical insights into the field, for example by Métis scholar Kristina Fagan in the anthology *Creating community: a roundtable on Canadian Aboriginal literature* (2002) edited by Renate Eigenbrod and Jo-Ann Episkenew. In her article '"What About You?" Approaching the Study of "Native Literature"', Fagan questions the homogenized notion of 'Native lit' common among many critics in the eighties and nineties and explains the need for recognizing the diversity of Aboriginal cultures in Canada. Her call for a culture- and nation-specific approach is supported by Mohawk scholar Taiaiake Alfred as well as Native American advocates for 'literary nationalism', like Daniel Heath Justice in his book *Our fire survives the storm: a Cherokee literary history* (2006).

There are more and more Aboriginal scholars interpreting and disseminating Aboriginal literature. After Jeannette Armstrong's seminal book *Looking at the words of our people* (1993), Armand Garnet Ruffo edited *(Ad) Dressing our words: Aboriginal perspectives on Aboriginal literature* (2001), which was followed by the collection of mostly Aboriginal-authored essays in *Creating community*, mentioned above. Peter Cole, from the Douglas First Nation (Southern Stl'atl'imx), based his scholarship on orality in *Coyote and Raven go canoeing* (2006). *Reasoning together* (2007), edited by the Native Critics Collective in the US, includes essays by Canadian Native scholars, thereby beginning a much-needed dialogue across the border. I wish to mention also the conference on Aboriginal literature at the University of Manitoba in 2004, *For the love of words* (selected proceedings in *Studies in Canadian literature/Études littérature canadienne* 31.1), the Brandon Aboriginal Literary Festival in 2007, and the annual Anskohk Aboriginal Literature Festival in Saskatoon. Special issues of *PRAIRIE FIRE* (2001) and *Spirit Magazine* (2006) feature Aboriginal literature, and there are numerous new anthologies. *Native poetry in Canada* (2001), edited by Jeannette Armstrong and Lally Grauer, includes poets from the older generation whose works are out of print; *Without reservations: Indigenous erotica* (2003), edited by Akiwenzie-Damm, includes indigenous writers from around the world, like her previous anthology *Skins* (2000); *Staging Coyote's dream* (2006) is an anthology of First Nations drama in English edited by Monique Mojica and Ric Knowles; and the anthology *Our story* (2004) by Tantoo Cardinal and others contains fiction and non-fiction. Aboriginal women's writing is the focus of *Sky woman: indigenous women who have shaped, moved or inspired us* (2005) edited by Sandra Laronde. *Tales from Moccasin Avenue* (2006), with an Introduction by Morgan Stafford O'Neal, is an anthology of fiction, mostly by less-established Canadian Aboriginal writers; similarly supportive of young emerging writers is *Initiations: a selection of young Native writers* (2007), edited by Marilyn Dumont; while a collection of interviews, *Story keepers* (2004) by Jennifer David, records conversations with ten well-known authors of Aboriginal descent. Daniel David MOSES and Terry Goldie published the third edition of their canon-forming *Anthology of Canadian Native literature in English* in 2005.   RENATE EIGENBROD

Inuit literature. Inuit literature is as diverse and ancient a tradition as the lands and people that produced it. In Canada, the Inuit homeland extends into Labrador (Nunatsiavut), Northern Québec (Nunavik), Nunavut, and the Inuvialuit Settlement Region in the Northwest Territories; the texts from these regions appear in English, French, and the many dialects of Inuit language (often referred to generally as Inuktitut). In the late-eighteenth and nineteenth centuries Christian missionaries used both alphabetic and syllabic writing systems to translate Western classics into Inuktitut. However, the foundations of Inuit literature are the extensive oral traditions of story and song that long predated European presence in the North. Tales of the epic hero Kiviuq, or of the sea-spirit Nuliajuk (Sedna), are—despite various southern attempts at suppression—known across much of the Arctic. They exist in a variety of forms and continue to influence Inuit writers today.

There are two major sources of traditional Inuit literature: Knud Rasmussen's contributions to the ten-volume *Report of the fifth Thule expedition—the Danish ethnographical expedition to Arctic North America, 1921–24* (1928–45, 1976), and Helen Roberts's and Diamond Jenness's *Songs of the Copper Eskimos: Report of the Canadian Arctic expedition 1913–18, Vol. XIV* (1925). Selections of this material have been reprinted in collections like Guy-Marie Rousselière's *Beyond the high hills: a book of Eskimo poems* (1961), James HOUSTON's *Songs of the dream people: chants and images from the Indians and Eskimos of North America* (1972), Charles Hoffman's *Drum dance: legends, ceremonies, dances and songs of the Eskimos* (1974), John Robert COLOMBO's *Poems of the Inuit* (1981), and Neil Philip's *Songs are thoughts: poems of the Inuit* (1995). Tom Lowenstein's *Eskimo poems from Canada and Greenland* (1973), which contains new translations of material recorded by Rasmussen, is one of the most thorough collections: the introduction provides a helpful context, the material is organized by region and genre (songs of mood, hunting songs, songs of derision, and charms), and composers like Aua, Netsit, and Orpingalik are accredited. Further information about the origins of this material can be found in *Across Arctic America: narrative of the fifth Thule expedition* (1999), which contains selections from Rasmussen's journal.

Since the time of Rasmussen and Jenness, a number of books of classic Inuit stories have been collected by both Inuit and non-Inuit editors. Many publications now appear in bilingual and trilingual editions, have a high proportion of illustration, and include both transcribed oral material and texts from original manuscripts. In 1950, Thomas Kusugaq of Repulse Bay told a series of tales to Alex Spalding, who later published the English/Inuktitut volume *Eight Inuit myths/Inuit unipkaaqtuat pingasuniarvinilit* (1979). Meanwhile, Zebedee Nungak and Eugene Arima's *Stories from Povungnituk, Québec* (1969), also printed in Inuktitut and English, contains the stories behind the carvings of several Povungnituk artists. The Rev. Maurice Métayer, an Oblate missionary to the Western Arctic, collected three volumes of stories in *Unipkat: tradition esquimaude de Coppermine, Territoires-du-Nord-ouest, Canada* (1973), but he is better known for the smaller collection of translated stories, *Tales from the igloo* (1972) and *Contes de mon iglou* (1973). Agnes Nanogak, the illustrator of *Tales from the igloo*, demonstrates her storytelling and editing talents in the sequel, *More tales from the igloo* (1986), which contains a variety of Inuit animal-spouse, cautionary, and epic stories. Other collections include *How kabloonat became and other Inuit legends* (1974), by the Inuk newspaper editor Mark Kalluak, and *Stories from Pangnirtung* (1976), illustrated by Germaine Arnaktauyok, the renowned Igloolik artist. Arnaktauyok also provided the artwork for *Inuit legends* (1977), edited by Leoni Kappi of Rankin Inlet, which contains further stories collected by Maurice Métayer.

Traditional literature has achieved a greater visibility in the south by its inclusion in a variety of anthologies, such as Howard Norman's *Northern tales: traditional stories of Eskimo and Indian peoples* (1990), Agnes Grant's *Our bit of truth: an anthology of Canadian Native literature* (1990), and Daniel David MOSES and Terry Goldie's *An anthology of Canadian Native literature in English* (2005), now in its third edition. One of the most extensive anthologies

devoted entirely to Inuit literature is Penny Petrone's *Northern voices: Inuit writing in English* (1988). This volume is divided into sections on oral traditions, early contact literature, personal narratives, letters, and transitional literature and modern writing. It includes contemporary work by writers whose names are known in the North: John Amagoalik, Ruth Qanatsiaq, Sam Metcalfe, Willie Thrasher, Leah Idlout d'Argencourt, Tumasi Quissa, Susie Tiktalik, Mark Kalluak, Mary Carpenter Lyons, Martha Flaherty, Tagak Curley, Liz Semigok, Aksaajuuq Etuangat, Nelly Cournoyea, Peter Ernerk (Irniq), and Mary Simon. Much of the writing and storytelling gathered by Petrone was originally published in the many serial publications that have circulated in the North, such as *Inuit Today, Inuit Monthly, Inuvialuit, Isumavut, Up Here, Nunavut,* and *Them Days*. Robin McGrath (Gedalof) also catalogues these publications in *An annotated bibliography of Canadian Inuit literature* (1979). She went on to examine the connections between contemporary writing and oral tradition in *Canadian Inuit literature: the development of a tradition* (1984), and also to publish the small volume *Paper stays put: a collection of Inuit writing* (1980), with illustrations by Alootook Ipellie.

Classic stories, along with the life stories of Inuit elders, can also be found in the publications resulting from oral history projects, such as Susan Cowan and Rhoda Innuksuk's *We don't live in snow houses now: reflections of Arctic Bay* (1976), Hattie Mannik's *Inuit nunamiut: inland Inuit* (1998), a collection of stories by Baker Lake elders, or John MacDonald's *The arctic sky: Inuit astronomy, star lore, and legend* (1998), which was produced by the Igloolik Oral History Project. *Saqiyuq: stories from the lives of three Inuit women* (1999), a multigenerational life history project edited by the anthropologist Nancy Wachowich, records the experiences of a family of Pond Inlet women. In 2004, John Bennett and Susan Rowley published *Uqalurait: an oral history of Nunavut,* which was the product of more than ten years of work by David Webster, Suzanne Evaloardjuk, Peter Irniq, Uriash Puqiqnak, David Serkoak, and dozens of Nunavut elders. The first half of this volume organizes Inuit traditional knowledge (*Inuit Qaujimajatuqangit*) by subject, while the second half focuses on the specific experience of four different regional groups. Nunavut Arctic College in Iqaluit, meanwhile, has made an enormous contribution to the body of Inuit oral history; since 1999, it has published five volumes in its Interviewing Inuit Elders series (1999–2001),

Aboriginal literature: Inuit

three volumes in its Memory and History in Nunavut series (2000–3), and four volumes in its Inuit Perspectives on the 20th Century series (2000–2). It is also currently publishing a series of books entitled Life Stories of Northern Leaders, which contain the recollections of prominent Inuit politicians Abraham Okpik (2005), John Amagoalik (2007), Paul Quassa (2008), James Arvaluk (2008), and Peter Itinnuar (2008). All of the Nunavut Arctic College publications are available in both English and Inuktitut.

As both Robin McGrath and the Labrador scholar Dale Blake point out, autobiography has been an important form in Inuit literature. This genre has its origins in the diaries that were kept as Christianity, along with syllabic and alphabetic writing systems, spread throughout the Arctic in the late-eighteenth and nineteenth centuries. One of the earliest surviving examples is the diary of a Labrador Inuk called Abraham, who in 1880 travelled to Europe with his family, where they were exhibited in ethnographic shows, and soon died of smallpox. *The diary of Abraham Ulrikab* (2005), an English translation edited by Hartmut Lutz, was recently published with illustrations by Alootook Ipellie. Back in Labrador, memoirs soon began to follow diaries, and in 1893, seventy-four-year-old Lydia Campbell published her *Sketches of Labrador life* (1980), which was initially serialized in the St. John's *Evening Herald* (1894–5). In 1940, a Labrador woman named Anauta (Lizzie Ford Blackmore), who was working in the United States as a performer/lecturer, published an autobiography entitled *Land of the good shadows: the life story of Anauta an Eskimo woman*, while in 1964, Lydia Campbell's great-grandniece Elizabeth Goudie began writing a memoir that was later published as *Woman of Labrador* (1973).

Further west, life in the old days was also described by storytellers like Nuligak (Bob Cockney), whose Western Arctic memoir *I, Nuligak* (1966) was translated and edited by Maurice Métayer. Peter Pitseolak's *People from our side* (1975), edited by Dorothy Eber, documents the more recent contact culture through the very personal and humorous memoirs of one of Cape Dorset's legendary leaders. Eber also edited *Pitseolak, pictures out of my life* (1971), an oral biography by the famous Cape Dorset printmaker Pitseolak Ashoona. Other books about the lives of Inuit artists include Norman Ekoomiak's *An Arctic childhood* (1980), *Qikaaluktut: images of Inuit life* (1986), a bilingual book written by Baker Lake artist Ruth Annaqtuusi Tulurialik with David F. Pelly, and *The shaman's nephew:*

a life in the Far North (1999), a non-fiction book for children, co-authored by Sheldon Oberman and the Utkuhiksalingmiut artist Simon Tookoome. Much Inuit life writing centres on the difficulties of managing the influences and interventions of southern Canada. The Inuvialuk (Western Arctic) writer Alice French describes her education in an Aklavik boarding school in her memoir *My Name is Masak* (1977), and Minnie Aodla Freeman's *Life among the Qallunaat* (1978) illustrates the challenges faced by James Bay Inuit in a time of great cultural change. Anthony Apakark Thrasher, whose father was a contemporary of Nuligak, gives a much grimmer picture of urban Inuit life in *Thrasher: skid row Eskimo* (1976). Thrasher's view of life from a series of prison cells is contrasted, however, by the lyrical and humorous *Shadows* (1975), by the Rev. Armand Tagoona of Repulse Bay. In 2007, a writer named Gideon Enutsia Etorolopiaq published *Iliarjuk: an Inuit memoir* under the pseudonym 'Dracc Dreque'. *Iliarjuk*, which means 'orphan', tells the powerful, often painful story of the author's youth in Iqaluit.

Inuit writing that might be classified as fiction, meanwhile, exists in a variety of forms. In 1969, a Kangiqsujuaq woman named Mitiarjuk Napaaluk wrote a novel entitled *Sanaaq*; initially published in Inuktitut, it was recently re-released in French translation (2002) by renowned anthropologist Bernard Saladin d'Anglure. Two other short novels, *Harpoon of the hunter* (1970) and *Wings of mercy* (1972)—originally serialized in the newsletter *Inuttituut*—were written by an Inukjuak pilot named Markoosie Patsauq. Markoosie's first novel, which is prefaced by the government administrator James H. McNeill, plays upon the appetite of southern audiences for stories set in 'traditional' times. The fictional work of Michael Arvaluk Kusugak, son of Repulse Bay storyteller Thomas Kusugaq, is intended for young readers and often draws upon older traditions of storytelling. In *Hide and sneak* (1992) the heroine, Allashua, encounters an *Ijiraq*, a half-human, half-bird spirit, whom she must outwit in order to escape, while in *Northern Lights and soccer trails* (1993) another girl, Kataujaq, learns to cope with the death of her mother when she is told that those who have died are playing soccer among the Northern Lights. Kusugak also published a novel for young adults entitled *The curse of the shaman: a Marble Island story* (2006), which tells the tale of a young boy whose family's visit to the shaman Paaliaq goes disastrously wrong. The Iqaluit-born artist and writer Alootook

Ipellie, who died in 2007, also re-imagines Inuit traditions in his *Arctic dreams and nightmares* (1993), which combines a series of unique and often disturbing ink drawings with stories to match. In one tale, he retells the classic story of the sea-spirit Sedna, but resolves it with an unusual twist. More recently, the Igloolik-born journalist Rachel Attituq Qitsualik published a short story entitled 'Skraeling' in the collection *Our story: Aboriginal voices on Canada's past* (2004). In it, Qitsualik skilfully depicts an encounter in 1000 CE between the eastward-migrating Thule Inuit, the Vikings, and the Tunit, or Dorset people, whose culture would eventually give way.

In the past decade, some of the most exciting Inuit storytelling has occurred in non-print media. The work of the Montreal-based Inuk spoken-word poet Taqralik Partridge, for instance, is currently available only in online audio recordings, and was recently featured in a CBC Radio 2 concert, *Quiet is not silent* (2008). Singer-songwriter Lucie Idlout has released two CDs of edgy, decidedly untraditional songs: *E5-770 My Mother's Name* (2003) and *Swagger* (2009). Meanwhile, the Inuit film company Igloolik Isuma Productions, which produced the internationally acclaimed feature films *Atanarjuat (The fast runner)* (2000) and *The journals of Knud Rasmussen* (2006), refers to its work as part of the 'continuous stream of oral history, carried forward into the new millennium through a marriage of Inuit storytelling skills and new technology.' *Atanarjuat*, which tells the story of two brothers caught up in a family feud, is based on an Igloolik legend, while *The journals of Knud Rasmussen* depicts Igloolik life in the early 1920s and the conversion of the famous shaman Aua. Isuma, which was founded by Zacharias Kunuk, Norman Cohn, Paul Apak Angilirq and Pauloosie Qulitalik, has also produced a series of dramatized short educational films, such as *Qaggiq (Gathering place)* (1989). A sister company, Arnait Video Collective, recently released a feature film entitled *Before tomorrow* (2007), an adaptation of Danish writer Jørn Riel's novel *Før morgendagen* (1975). KEAVY MARTIN/ROBIN McGRATH.

Acorn, Milton (1923–86). Born in Charlottetown, Prince Edward Island, he served in the Second World War, suffering a serious head injury. On his return to P.E.I., he eventually became a carpenter, but gave up carpentry in 1956—after privately publishing his first collection of poems, *In love and anger*—to devote himself to poetry in Montreal, where he met Irving LAYTON, Al PURDY, and other poets. *The brain's the target* and a broadsheet, *Against a league of liars*, were both published in 1960. In 1962 he married Gwendolyn MacEWEN in Toronto, and when the marriage failed the following year he moved to Vancouver. Fifty-eight of his poems were published in *The FIDDLEHEAD* (Spring 1963), and in the same year *Jawbreakers* (1963) appeared. Throughout the sixties he became increasingly involved in political activities and many of his poems developed through public readings. At the end of the sixties he returned to Toronto. When *I've tasted my blood: poems 1956 to 1968* (1969), selected and introduced by Purdy, failed to win a Governor General's Award in 1970, a group of Toronto poets created the 'Canadian poetry award' for Acorn and named him 'The people's poet'. His next two collections were *I shout love and On shaving off his beard* (1971) and *More poems for people* (1972), illustrated by Greg Curnoe, which was dedicated to Dorothy LIVESAY, and inspired by her *Poems for people* (1947). *The island means Minago* (1975, GGA) was followed by *Jackpine sonnets* (1977), *Captain Neal MacDougal and the naked goddess* (1982), and *Dig up my heart: selected poems 1952–1983* (1983), selected by Purdy. Since Acorn's death several books of selected poems have appeared, including *The uncollected Acorn* (1987) and *To hear the faint bells* (1996) selected by James Deahl, and *The edge of home: Milton Acorn from the Island* (2002) selected by Anne COMPTON, whose Preface and long Introduction—an essay called 'The Ecological Poetics of Milton Acorn's Island Poems'—are valuable commentaries on his work.

Acorn's is a poetry of opposites, of delicacy and toughness, of 'love' and 'anger', which come together in a single dialectical vision: the delicate beauty that Acorn celebrates in humanity and nature must be defended through tough-minded, unrelenting struggle, and is the ultimate inspiration of even his most harshly aggressive works. The poems of Acorn's early maturity, collected for the most part in the first half of *I've tasted my blood*, are generally brief and straightforward, but have a subtlety of technique that gives them a surprisingly rich resonance. A sensitive ear for the nuances of North American speech rhythms and a gift for imagery, ranging from delicately precise notation to almost surrealistic evocativeness, are joined to a fine organizing intelligence. Acorn's best lyrics are miniature dramas in which conflict and resolution find expression through the subtle interplay of rhythm and imagery. It is on the basis of some of these poems, such as 'Charlottetown harbour' or 'The Island', that Acorn has come to be known as one of Canada's finest regional poets. But politics in the broadest sense is never absent from even the most lyrically descriptive of the regional poems. And many of the finest poems of the period (such as 'Poem for the astronauts' or 'Words said sitting on a rock sitting on a saint', a statement of the artist's adversary role in modern society comparable in importance to A.M. KLEIN's 'Portrait of the poet as landscape') express a kind of playfully serious wit, reminiscent of the metaphysical poets, which seems unique to Acorn and has little to do with regionalism. In the mid-sixties Acorn's poems tended to become longer and looser, the imagery less organic, speech rhythms yielding to the cruder rhythms of public exhortation and vituperation. However, in many of the poems in *Jackpine sonnets*, and in the sonnet sequence *Captain MacDougal and the naked goddess*, Acorn seems to have rediscovered the real source of his strength in the 'dialectical play of argument', which he defines as the essence of the sonnet ('Tirade by way of introduction', *Jackpine sonnets*). These sonnets and sonnet-like poems contain some of Acorn's most powerful expressions of his twin themes of love and anger. See also Ed Jewinski, *Milton Acorn and his works* (1990); Chris Gudgeon, *Out of this world: the natural history of Milton Acorn* (1996); and Richard Lemm, *Milton Acorn: in love and anger* (1999).

Adam, Graeme Mercer (1839–1912). In 1858 the Scottish-born Adam arrived in Toronto, where he eventually became head of Adam, Stevenson and Company, publishers and booksellers. He published or edited a series of important periodicals, including ROSE-BELFORD'S CANADIAN MONTHLY, of which he was editor, was a major contributor to *The* WEEK, and promoted a literary life for Canada through his choice of contributors to the periodicals he edited and his own writings. His books included works of travel and history—for example, *The Canadian North-west; its history and its troubles ...* (Toronto, 1885), in response to the Riel rebellion, and a *History of Toronto and the County of York* (Toronto, 1887)—and he contributed an 'Outline of Canadian Literature' to William Henry WITHROW's *History of Canada* (Toronto, 1876). With Agnes Ethelwyn WETHERALD he collaborated on a novel, *An Algonquin maiden; a romance of the early days of Upper Canada* (Montreal, 1887).

Adam left Canada for the United States in 1892 and died in New York.

Adams, Levi (1802–32). Probably born in the seigneury of Noyan, just east of the Richelieu River, he is mainly known as a writer for his long poem *Jean Baptiste* (1825; modern edition edited by Racy Ware, 1996), which adheres to the *ottava rima* of Byron's *Beppo* and *Don Juan*, often at the expense of logical speech patterns. Set in contemporary Montreal, it tells, in mock-heroic tones, how the bachelor politician of the title, rejected by his true love, eventually marries the willing Rosalie; it includes discursive comment on mortality, love, marriage, literature, and the law. Adams was called to the bar in 1827, when he apparently ceased writing for publication.

Adderson, Caroline (b. 1963). Born in Edmonton, Alberta, she was educated at the University of British Columbia (B.Ed., 1986) and lives in Vancouver. Her first book, *Bad imaginings* (1993), a collection of short stories, is remarkable for portraying with stylistic confidence and humour—and sharp insights, lyrical descriptions, and small surprises—a disparate assemblage of periods, places, damaged characters, and emotional landscapes. Two of the ten stories, 'Shiners' and 'And the Children Shall Rise', are about almost eerie children. 'Gold Mountain', narrated in formal nineteenth-century English by a remittance man, is about three mismatched gold seekers who have not yet reached the Cariboo. 'The Chmarnyk' is about Teo the rainmaker who, at the end of the story, stands almost naked on the hood of a car: 'Motionless, arms open, fingers spread and dripping—you were sowing rain.... Then you turned, spun round and spattered the silent crowd. Turned again, kept spinning, faster. Whirling, whirling on the slippery hood, you drenched and astounded us, became a living fountain. And then, amazing! A nimbus, seven-coloured, shimmering all around you.' 'Blood and stone' is about a widow, with a young autistic(?) son. She has an epiphany about Stephen, her 'honourable lover', when Bill, the son, asks for bread and Stephen gives him a stone: 'It shocked her more than if he had struck the boy.' In 'The Hypochondria Club', when Claire, a chambermaid, learned that her husband had been killed in the Great War, she 'buried his ring in the rose garden of the hotel. That was his funeral.... Andy had been away for twice the time she'd known him. She was more married to her yearning than to him.' But a guest, Mr Stowe, wants to romance her by giving Claire and her two friends tango lessons, then by exhibiting one of his Egyptian treasures, a mummified cat—which, when they unwrapped it, turned out to be something else. Thirteen years later Adderson published her second collection of stories, *Pleased to meet you* (2006), which for this reader was disappointing, in spite of the praise it received. The stories lack the depth, originality, and readability of those in her first collection; the characters and plots are thin and uninteresting, though they summon up everyday behaviour and verbal exchanges convincingly, sometimes amusingly. The story called 'Hauska Tutustua'—Finnish for 'Pleased to meet you'—is about the widower David, a volunteer for the Hospice Society, who visits the ailing Mr Virtanen to give him comfort. When the old man dies, it is left to David to write to his daughter, who replies in Finnish—he finds a Finnish dictionary. She then writes to him in English, saying that she is flying to Victoria and will go to Campbell River because she 'would really like to meet him.' That is the end, but one can imagine the rest. In her novel *A history of forgetting* (1999) Adderson portrays the effects of pain in the present and of horror in the past. Partly set in a hairdressing salon, it brings together unusual situations and characters: Malcolm and his lover Denis, who owned and ran a salon in Paris, move as elderly men to Malcolm's hometown, Vancouver, when Denis goes into an Alzheimer victim's decline; impressionable, uneducated Alison, an apprentice hairdresser where Malcolm works, who asks the meaning of the numbers on Mrs Soloff's arm and is ashamed and horrified when Christian explains them; the witty, ugly, kind Christian, a co-worker, who is murdered by Nazi skinhead gay-bashers. Alison becomes obsessed by a picture book about the Third Reich; she is determined to visit Auschwitz and does so with Malcolm. In a glass case filled with hair, '…she saw that the hair behind the glass was actually nothing like what she had been sweeping off the salon floor…. Hair is dead and this was the dead hair of the dead. It was the dead and the dying, becoming dust.' In *Sitting practice* (2003) love and sex are imagined in the context of impairment when the happy marriage of Ross and Iliana is transformed three weeks after their wedding by a car accident—Ross the driver, Iliana the victim. Their new life is governed by her permanent spinal damage, Ross's guilt, and (two years later) their decision to open a café in Duncan B.C. that becomes successful. Influencing this situation in various ways are

Ross's irritating, dependent, lovelorn twin sister Bonnie and her three-year-old son Bryce (to whom Ross is devoted), and Stevie, a wayward young workman who is attracted to Iliana and arouses her sexually—even though 'Sensory perception below the waist had been cut off and, to compensate, had intensified in other places. It was as if all her pleasure receptors had migrated upward.' Moving back and forth in time (repeatedly to the wedding), the novel's overload of quotidian detail, and the pointed, crucial exchanges in all-too-normal inane dialogue, do not enliven the emotional Ross (given to weeping) or Iliana, or make us care about them; the episodic narrative somehow neutralizes them. Adderson's portrayal of a loving, accidentally damaged couple is sensitive, but the potential resolution of their emotional strains is not convincing. *Very serious children* (2007) is a clever, funny book for young people about the Grants, two circus clowns who are forever performing gags, and their serious sons, Nicky—the delightful narrator, typing the text on his typewriter, who loves his parents and likes the circus characters, but is lonely—and Saggy. They eventually run away from the circus. *I, Bruno* (2007) is a story for children, perhaps written for Adderson's son Patrick.

Ahenakew, Edward (1885–1961). A Plains Cree, grandnephew of the famous Cree chief Poundmaker, he was born on the Ah-tah-ka-koops Reserve north of Prince Albert, Saskatchewan. His high school education qualified him to study at the Anglican Wycliffe College, Toronto, and then at Emmanuel College in Saskatoon; he was ordained an Anglican priest in 1912. In 1923 he collected the tales of his people from Chief Thunder Child (1849–1927), which were published posthumously in *Voices of the Plains Cree* (1973), edited by Ruth M. Buck. He also wrote *Cree trickster tales*, which appeared in *The journal of American folk-lore*, vol. 42 (Oct.–Dec. 1929), and helped to edit a 26,000-word Cree-English dictionary, which was published in 1938.

'Ahkoond of Swat, The: a threnody'. With its epigraph, '"The Ahkoond of Swat is dead."—Press dispatch', this humorous 52-line poem begins 'What, what/What's the news from Swat?' and ends 'The great Ahkoond of Swat/Is not.' The author was George T. Lanigan (1845–86). Born in St Charles (Québec) and one of the founders of the Montreal *Star*, he was working for the New York *World* when he heard the cryptic message announcing the Ahkoond's death over the wires.

Alderson, Sue Ann (b. 1940). Born in New York City, and earning an M.A. in English literature, she was made a professor of creative writing in 1992 at the University of British Columbia, and was the initiator of the university's Writing for Children Programme. Alderson has written some ten picture books, illustrated by various artists. She wrote the classic *Bonnie McSmithers, you're driving me dithers* (1974), in which a kind of psychological tug-of-war is revealed between a harassed single mother and an intelligent, obstreperous child that is resolved humorously and practically. The title, and its refrain 'and blithery blathery out of my mind', became popular incantation chants. There were two sequels: *Hurry up, Bonnie* (1977) and *Bonnie McSmithers is at it again* (1979). Alderson's subsequent books, which vary in age interest, include *The not impossible summer* (1983), *Sure as strawberries* (1992), her narrative poem *Ten Mondays for lots of boxes* (1995), and *Pond seasons* (1997), and *Wherever bears be* (1999).

Alexie, Robert Arthur. See ABORIGINAL LITERATURE: 5.

Alexis, André (b. 1957). Born in Trinidad, he grew up in Ottawa, attending French schools, and now lives in Toronto. In 2007-8 he was known for his Sunday-afternoon radio program 'Skylarking' on CBC Radio 2. *Despair and other stories about Ottawa* (1994, rpr. 1998) is a collection of strange, dark stories that feature dreamlike and surreal situations that sometimes seem disturbingly familiar. In 'The Night Piece' a teenage boy meets a young man who tells him a terrifying story of a vampire, which consumes the boy's imagination. 'Kuala Lumpur' depicts the way an adolescent boy responds to the mystifying behaviour of adults at his father's wake, creating in him a 'confusion, a welter, a tangle, a tumult'. In 'Metaphysics of Morals' a simple outing to buy a loaf of bread gives birth to a dreamlike sequence and a consideration of the source of the narrator's own good or evil impulses. Strange fetishes, bizarre lodgers, odd travelling companions, and a haunting ('As hauntings go it was dull. It was what you'd expect in Sandy Hill', an Ottawa neighbourhood)—all these and more inhabit stories that are compelling and unnerving. His novel *Childhood* (1998, rpr. 2000)—which is not only about childhood, but also about the ways of love and how people process the past—is so gracefully written, so quietly realized, that its emotional impact seems almost to seep into the reader's sensibilities. Set in a small Ontario town in the 1950s and

1960s, and then in Ottawa, the story is told by Thomas MacMillan, a man in his early fifties whose mother and maternal grandmother are both black. As he sifts through his memories, trying to understand the important people in his life, and perhaps himself, we meet his rather frightening grandmother and his mother, who abandoned him for the first ten years of his life, and the gentle and peculiar Henry Wing, the owner of a vast library who devotes himself to private scientific experiments. The novel is a moving, never sentimental, recovery of the ambiguities of memory and a longing for what has been lost. It won the Chapters / *Books in Canada* First Novel Award, and was a co-winner of the (Ontario) Trillium Award. In 2008 Alexis published *Asylum* (rpr. 2009), a long novel in which Mark, the narrator—having spent fourteen years in a Gregorian monastery in Tuscany—writes about the life and the people he knew in Ottawa in 1983 and after, during the Mulroney years. *Ingrid and the wolf* (2005) is a semi-fantasy for young people about eleven-year-old Ingrid Balasz, who lives in Toronto and is sent by her father to meet her grandmother in Hungary. There she learns her family's history and forms an important relationship with Gabor the wolf. It is a highly readable story for its age group that, unusually and expertly, combines simple though rich language with some sophisticated ideas. Alexis has also written a short play, *Lambton Kent* (1999), mostly in the form of a satiric monologue given by Ken Mtubu who, after travelling in southern Ontario, addresses the Nigerian Geographical Society, presenting 'an account of his Canadian travels in the counties of Brant, Oxford, Middlesex, Lambton, and Kent.'

Alford, Edna (b. 1947). Born and raised in the village of Turtleford, Saskatchewan, she was educated at the University of Saskatchewan, where she majored in English, and worked summers in hospitals and nursing homes for the chronically ill, experiences that inspired her early fiction. She wrote her first stories during a ten-year period living in Calgary and attending summer writing schools. In 1975 she founded the literary magazine *Dandelion*. In 1988 she won the third annual $10,000 Marian ENGEL Award for her inspired, disturbing, and original fiction. The ten stories in *A sleep full of dreams* (1981) are linked by a nurse named Arla and are set in Pine Mountain Lodge, a grim nursing home for old and terminally ill women, where the inmates struggle to survive. Her second collection, *The garden of Eloise Loon*

(1986), is made up of fourteen stories that are finely crafted, original, and sometimes upsetting. Many of them are hallucinatory and fragmented, with central themes as varied as mental breakdown and the nuclear threat suggested by cruise missiles over Alberta. One story is told from the point of view of a decomposing head; in others a plague of caterpillars invades a house, and a character tries to steal the hand of a corpse from a freezer.

Alianak, Hrant (b. 1950). Born in Khartoum, Sudan, he came to Canada in 1967 and studied economics at McGill University, Montreal, and English at York University, Toronto. He has worked as a writer, actor, and director for stage, television, and film. His plays have been seen throughout Canada, and in the United States and England. His best work is witty and theatrically inventive, sometimes dispensing with dialogue altogether: *Mathematics* (1973; prod. 1972) recounts a day in the life of a suburban couple simply in terms of properties thrown one by one onto the stage; in *Christmas* (1974; prod. 1973) an actor traces in mime the brief career and death of a Christmas tree. Both were published in his 1975 collection *The return of the big five*, and they show that even plays without dialogue can entertain a reader through the wit of the stage directions. In the same collection the characters of *Western* (1973; prod. 1972) act out sex and power games in dialogue that consists mostly of one character's calling out the title of an old Western while another responds with the name of the star. Alianak's interest in film also emerges in *The violinist and the flower girl* (1982; prod. 1972), a wordless play that imitates the pathos and melodrama of a silent film. More characteristically, he draws on *film noir* in gangster plays like *Mousetown* (1982; prod. 1974); in *The blues* (2003; prod. 1976, 2003), an atmospheric piece about four losers in a New York bar in 1951, which combines self-mocking pastiche with real sadness; and in the violent, hallucinatory *Lucky strike* (1989; prod. 1978, 1996), an experimental postmodern performance piece featuring two wounded men, a girl, two guns, a bag of money, a matchbook with one match left, a lot of movement, little dialogue, and very loud music. Alianak's sense of alienation from more recent developments in theatre is given sharp, ironic treatment in *The big hit* (1992; prod. 1992), in which a frustrated playwright (played in the first production by Alianak himself) battles with his agent and artistic director over his insistence on wordless plays with a lot of nudity in a theatre that

has become socially conscious and politically correct. Part of the joke is that in *The big hit* itself there is no nudity and dialogue carries the main weight. Though the play's central character is accused of being narrow and repetitive, and though Alianak's work can sometimes provoke the same criticism, this energetic counterblast shows his resourcefulness as a theatre artist. *The walls of Africa* (2001; prod. 2001 at Toronto's Theatre Passe Muraille) is a one-act three-character play, with twenty scenes and minimal dialogue, some of it repetitive, that relies for its effects mainly on facial expressions, body movements, silences, music and the occasional sound of waves, and lighting, which is turned on and off in four separate areas on four separate levels. (All are described in lengthy stage directions.) Mr Pym, an academic, is a shy middle-aged roomer; Mrs Shields, a slightly older divorcée, is his landlady who drinks sherry and wants tenderness; the Woman is a beautiful young fantasy woman who appears enticingly to Mr Pym in various guises but never says a word. The play takes place in London, England. Africa, apart from two references, has nothing to do with the action.

Allan, Ted (1916–95). Born Allan Herman in Montreal, he left high school early and became a dedicated Young Communist, serving in the International Brigade in the Spanish Civil War and in Dr Norman Bethune's blood-transfusion unit. His best-known book, *The scalpel, the sword: the story of Doctor Norman Bethune* (1952, with Sydney Gordon; rev. 1989), is a heroic biography (translated into nineteen languages) that is enthusiastically vivid about Bethune's personality, medical innovations, and revolutionary commitment. Acknowledging the flaws in his obsessive and mercurial temperament, Allan nevertheless occasionally sees Bethune's earlier life—including its self-indulgent phases and his sad and stormy relationship with his wife Frances—as too prophetic of his later humanitarian dedication, in Spain and China, to fundamental political and social change. A film version, *Bethune: the making of a hero*, screenplay by Allan, was released in 1990. As a playwright Allan wrote *Double image* (1957), a murder mystery whose hero impersonates his twin, which ran for five years in Paris under the title *Gog et Magog*; *My sister's keeper* (1976); and the original stage treatment of Joan Littlewood's *Oh, what a lovely war!* Allan also wrote a novel about the Spanish Civil War, *This time a better earth* (1939), short stories, collected in *Don't you know anybody else?* (1985), screenplays, and several dozen radio and television dramas.

Allen, Grant (1848–99). Although born on Wolfe Island near Kingston, Canada West (Ontario), and educated privately and in France and England, graduating from Merton College, Oxford, he spent most of his life in Surrey, England. He published at his own expense *Physiological aesthetics* (London, 1877; reissued 1977), which brought him to the attention of a few editors. But he became well known as a writer of fiction, producing more than forty novels and collections of stories. Allen presented advanced social ideas in an accessible form, such as questions of class and other social issues in *The British barbarians* (London, 1895; rpr. 1975) and feminism and women's rights in the bestseller *The woman who did* (London, 1895; rpr. 2004). The Preface is two lines long: 'But surely no woman would ever dare to do so,' said my friend. 'I knew a woman who did,' said I; 'and this is her story.' What she did was have a relationship outside marriage. Reissued in England in 1995 by the Oxford University Press in their Oxford Popular Fiction series, with a long introduction by Sarah Wintle, it has a notice in large type on the front cover: 'The bestseller that scandalized Victorian Britain.' *The typewriter girl* (1897), published under the pseudonym 'Olive Pratt Raynor', is about the position of working women at the end of the nineteenth century; its opening sentence: 'I was twenty-two and without employment.' It was reissued in 2004, edited with an introduction by Clarisse J. Suranyi. *An African millionaire: episodes in the life of the illustrious Colonel Clay* (London, 1897) introduces a character whom Frederic Dannay (half of 'Ellery Queen') described as 'the first great thief of mystery fiction', anticipating by two years E.W. Hornung's much better-known A.J. Raffles. The introduction by Norman Donaldson to a modern reprint (New York, 1980) sketches Allen's career and comments on his place in the history of detective fiction. Allen also wrote thirty works of non-fiction.

Allen, Ralph (1913–66). Born in Winnipeg, Manitoba, and educated in Ontario and Saskatchewan, he became a sports writer for the Winnipeg *Tribune* at the age of sixteen and moved to the Toronto *Globe* in 1938. After serving as a gunner in the Royal Canadian Artillery in the Second World War, he became in 1943 an award-winning correspondent for the Toronto *Globe and Mail*. In 1946 he was made managing editor of *Maclean's*, where he was renowned for his high editorial standards and influenced many subsequently important journalists, and in 1964 he was appointed managing editor of the *Toronto Star*. Despite his busy career, Allen wrote five popular novels: *Home made banners* (1946), about Canadian soldiers in the Second World War; *The chartered libertine* (1954), a satire of Canadian broadcasting; *Peace River country* (1958), about the flight of a mother and her two children from Saskatchewan to the Northwest; *Ask the name of the lion* (1962), about Congo's struggle for independence; and *The high white forest* (1964), set during the Battle of the Bulge. He also wrote *Ordeal by fire: 1915–1945* (1961), a volume in the Doubleday Canadian History Series. *The man from Oxbow: the best of Ralph Allen* (1967), edited by Christina MCCALL-NEWMAN, is a collection of his newspaper articles.

Alphabet (1960–71). First published in Sept. 1960, this adventurous little magazine from London, Ontario, was edited and distributed, and often typeset and printed, by its founder, James REANEY. It had an ever-expanding range of editorial curiosity: from myth and literature, it grew to include discussions of concrete poetry, popular music, Ojibwa art, cinema, sound poetry, and performance art. The nineteenth and final issue appeared in June 1971—seven issues short of Reaney's original hope of one issue for each letter of the alphabet.

Anansi, House of—named after an African spider god, a trickster and talespinner—began as a small Toronto publishing house that was instrumental in shaping English Canada's sense of literary identity after Expo 67. Founded by novelist Dave GODFREY and poet Dennis LEE that same year, it included among its early publications some now well-known Canadian books: by Margaret ATWOOD (*The circle game*, SURVIVAL, and, in 2008, *Payback: debt and the shadow side of wealth*), Michael ONDAATJE (*The collected works of Billy the Kid*, *Coming through slaughter*), Northrop FRYE (*The bush garden*), and George GRANT (*Technology and empire*). Among the books that followed were collections by established poets, first novels by Matt COHEN, Peter SUCH, Graeme GIBSON, Chris SCOTT, and Ray SMITH, and writing in translation from the Québec of the Quiet Revolution. In the early 1970s the original founders moved on and Jim Polk and Ann Wall stayed to continue the house's traditions—until Anansi's Canada-first stance was no longer news; many of the star writers had moved to other venues, and major Toronto publishers were beginning to realize that quality Canadian writing could sell. In August 1989 owner Ann Wall sold the house to the successful Canadian-owned trade publisher Stoddart Publishing, a business that failed. Anansi has been owned since 2002 by Scott Griffin (see the GRIFFIN POETRY PRIZE); the president and publisher is Sarah MacLachlan. In October 2007 Anansi celebrated its fortieth anniversary at Toronto's Harbourfront. It has expanded considerably—with sales of just under $5 million and a staff of twenty—becoming an influential literary publisher. Among recent novels published are *DeNiro's game* (2006) by Rawi Hage, which won the richest literary prize in the world, the Dublin IMPAC Award, and his *Cockroach* (2008); Lisa MOORE's *Open* (2002) and *Alligator* (2006), which won the Commonwealth Prize; *The law of dreams* (2006) by Peter Behrens, which won a GOVERNOR GENERAL'S AWARD; and Marie-Claire BLAIS's *Augustino and the choir of destruction*. Anansi publishes three or four poets a year, including Ken BABSTOCK, Nicole BROSSARD, Steven HEIGHTON, and Dennis LEE. Among its bestselling books are the annual Massey Lectures—including Margaret Atwood's *Payback*—and a book first published in 1968, *A manual for draft-age immigrants to Canada* by Mark Salin. Atwood's *The circle game* is still in print. Anansi also has a children's imprint, Groundwood Books. See *The Anansi reader: forty years of very good books* (2007) edited by Lynn Coady.

Anderson, Patrick (1915–79). Born in England and educated at Oxford University and Columbia University, he came in 1940 to Montreal, where he taught at Selwyn House, a private school, became a Canadian citizen in 1945, taught at McGill University (1948–50), then left Canada. As a founder and leading editor of PREVIEW he was an important catalyst in the development of Canadian poetry by disseminating contemporary techniques that influenced poets such as P.K. PAGE, A.M. KLEIN, and to a lesser extent F.R. SCOTT. His own collections of poetry—offering a striking combination of technical sophistication and an immigrant's fresh wonder at a new country in its winter—were published in this period: *A tent for April* (1945), *The white centre* (1946), and *The colour as naked* (1953)—from which poems were selected for *A visiting distance—poems: new, revised, and selected* (1976; 2nd edn 1978); and *Return to Canada: selected poems* (1977). After he left Canada, Anderson published in England three well-reviewed autobiographical works—of which the second,

Search me: the black country, Canada and Spain (1957), includes his time in Canada—and five travel books, mainly about Greece.

Anderson-Dargatz, Gail (b. 1963). Gail Anderson was born in Kamloops, British Columbia; married Floyd Dargatz, a farmer and beekeeper, in 1990; and earned a B.A. degree from the University of Victoria in 1998; they lived near Millet, Alberta. She is now married to photographer Mitch Krupp, who took the photographs that appear throughout her novel *Turtle Valley*. She teaches creative writing at the University of British Columbia and lives in the Shuswap area, the location of *Turtle Valley*.

Anderson-Dargatz's *The Miss Hereford stories* (1994), a collection of eight sharply drawn stories set in the fictional Likely, Alberta, introduced her flair for lively dialogue in a western farming family. They begin with the Miss Hereford contest (for a cow ambassador) of the Hereford Breeders' Club the day before the Likely Fall Fair, and proceed with stories about other events in the life of the narrator, Martin Winkle, from childhood to adulthood. This was followed by the striking novel *The cure for death by lightning* (1996, rpr. 1997), which is narrated by Beth Weeks, who turns sixteen in the course of the story she tells about her family in the 1940s in remote Turtle Valley, British Columbia: her farmer father, injured in the head during the Great War, who becomes tyrannical and abusive; her brother Dan; and her long-suffering mother, who keeps a cherished scrapbook of recipes, newspaper clippings, and bizarre remedies, such as the 'cure' of the title: 'Dunk the dead by lightning in a cold water bath for two hours and if still dead, add vinegar and soak for an hour or more.' The hired hands Dennis and Filthy Billy and their neighbouring Native family, and the Swede, with whom the father fights over a foot-wide length of property, are among the other people in their lives. B.C. Gothic elements—including a fatal mauling by a bear, a rape, a fire, and a suicide by hanging—are seamlessly blended with accounts of Beth's mother's delicious food (recipes given) and Beth's sensual connections with nature. A second novel, *A recipe for bees* (1998), begins and ends with the same event, the return from a long train ride of the elderly, strong-willed Augusta Olsen, who is gifted with second sight and premonitions. Times past and present are interwoven in the intervening discursive narrative to produce a portrait of Augusta's life: her marriage to Karl Olsen, a farmer whose feelings are submerged in shyness and work; the conflict between lack of money, imprisonment in a constraining household, and frustrated desire for some independence; the pleasant surprise of having a lover; the birth of a daughter; and the discovery of the joys of beekeeping and the sweetness this unexpectedly provides in Augusta's marriage late in life. Punctuating the narrative are many brief descriptions of beekeeping lore, in which the bees and their activities become understandable and even endearing in their industry and cozy cohabitation, when not endangered.

The protagonist of *A rhinestone button* (2002), which has as its epigraph two sentences from the Book of Job, is the namesake of the biblical Job. Farmer Job Sunstrum—lonely, an outsider in spite of being very good looking—also 'feared God and avoided evil', and was subjected to a series of unjust trials. The worst was when, after their father died, his brother Jacob, with his unpleasant wife Lilith and their son Ben, moved into the house on the family farm and took it over—Lilith commandeering the kitchen, where Job had enjoyed cooking. The zealous pastors of the Baptist and Pentecostal churches, and their shallow adherents—all friends and acquaintances of Job's—usually only made things worse. The author's faithful depiction of farm life and of people in a small Alberta town not far from Edmonton will strike home with anyone who has lived there; but apart from one's sympathy for the ineffectual Job, the characters are one-dimensional, cannot be imagined visually, and evoke no interest. After a tornado, the farm is sold and things look up for Job; with Liv he opens, and cooks for, a successful tea room. Romance is in the offing. *Turtle Valley* (2007) was inspired by the author's having to evacuate her parents from B.C.'s Salmon Arm fire in 1998. The narrator Kat, her husband Ezra—whom she was linked to in a rushed marriage and is disabled by a stroke—and their son Jeremy have returned to Turtle Valley, where a forest fire is approaching, to help her mother Beth (the protagonist, many years before, in *The cure for death by lightning*) and her father Gus leave their farm. This family novel begins slowly and calmly, but Kat's life soon becomes complicated and taxing. Neighbour Jude (her former lover, who still loves her) appears; Beth shows signs of early dementia; Gus is dying; Jude is constantly present; and Ezra's mood swings are intolerable. Added to this, Kat discovers in her grandmother's scrapbook and love letters a secret in her family's past, one that involves her grandfather (she sees his ghost). And the

fire encroaches. 'The day after the firestorm, when Ezra, Val [Kat's sister], Jeremy, and I drove Mom out to the farm, we found my parents' house distilled to three inches of ash in the basement.' With moments of magic realism (some ghosts) smoothly injected into the realistic family narrative, the novel testifies to the author's craft; but the emotions, the deep feelings, that presumably coloured relationships and events described, in both the present and the past, are dormant.

Angéline de Montbrun (Quebec, 1884). This novel—translated by Yves Brunelle in 1974—by Marie-Louise-Félicité ANGERS (pseud. 'Laure Conan'), Québec's first woman novelist, was published in serial form in *La Revue canadienne*, Montreal, from June 1881 to August 1882, and as a book in 1884. In the first part of the novel, composed of letters, we read that the young Angéline, who lives with her father, Charles de Montbrun, on the North Shore of the St Lawrence, is being courted by Maurice Darville. Suddenly a narrative describes M. de Montbrun's death, Angeline's disfigurement in an accident, her conviction that Maurice's ardour had cooled, and her decision to live alone. In the final part Angéline's diary entries describe her anguished solitude and her determination to devote herself to the poor of the district. The novel was praised at the time as an edifying portrait of Christian resignation, but contemporary Québec criticism has attempted to identify and unravel the psychological, autobiographical, and psychoanalytical elements in its composition.

Angers, Marie-Louise-Félicité (1845–1924). Québec's first woman novelist, who used the pseudonym 'Laure Conan', was born at La Malbaie (Murray Bay), Québec, and educated at the Ursuline Convent in Quebec City. She fell in love with a Member of Parliament, Pierre-Alexis Tremblay, and this unrequited attachment seems to have affected the rest of her life, leading to a rather solitary existence and furnishing a theme—frustrated love and the anguish attending it—that reappears in her fiction. Her novelette *Larmes d'amour*—serialized in 1878–9 and published as a book in 1899—introduces both the theme (an impossible love) and the narrative technique (a combination of epistolary and diary forms) that constitute the originality of her early fiction. A similarly frustrated love affair forms the basis of her best-known novel, *ANGÉLINE DE MONTBRUN* (Quebec, 1884), which was translated by Yves Brunelle in 1974. Her other fiction included three historical novels, two set in New France: one, *À l'oeuvre et à l'épreuve* (Quebec, 1891), was translated as *The master-motive; a tale of the days of Champlain* (1909).

Anne of Green Gables (1908, NCL; at least six other reprints are available). This enduring children's classic by L.M. MONTGOMERY—perhaps the bestselling book by a Canadian author—has never been out of print, selling millions of copies in more than fifteen languages. It has proved popular with people of all ages in several media (film, stage, television), who have responded to Montgomery's wry humour, her deflating of stuffiness, her affectionate descriptions of the Prince Edward Island countryside, and her remarkably loquacious heroine. Based partly on a Barnardo child, Ellen Macneill, who was adopted by relatives of Montgomery who were expecting a boy, the novel is about the quest of the orphan Anne Shirley for acceptance by the elderly brother and sister Matthew and Marilla, who adopt her, and by her community. Convinced that her red hair is a liability, Anne is consoled by her love of nature and her friendship with Diana Barry. Her rivalry with Gilbert Blythe ends with her winning a college scholarship, which she declines after Matthew's death in order to stay on the farm at Avonlea (Cavendish) with Marilla. Anne's transformation from ugly duckling to comely maiden leads to a compromise between the private world of her imagination and the genteel, practical world around her. Many sequels followed. The TV production of *Anne of Green Gables* (1985), written and directed by Kevin Sullivan (with Megan Follows as Anne, Colleen Dewhurst as Marilla, and Richard Farnsworth as Matthew), began a long series of televised Anne stories, released internationally. Anne's imprint on people's minds even today is indicated by three books related to the novel that were published in 2008. *Before Green Gables* by Budge WILSON is a prequel; *Imagining Anne: the island scrapbook of L.M. Montgomery* by Elizabeth Rollins Epperly reproduces more than 100 pages from scrapbooks dating from 1893 to 1910; and *Looking for Anne: how Lucy Maud Montgomery dreamed up a literary classic* (US title: *Looking for Anne of Green Gables: the story of L.M. Montgomery and her literary classic*) by Irene Gammel uncovers new connections between the novel and Montgomery's life in Cavendish and references in journal entries, both unpublished and published. There is even *The Anne of Green Gables cookbook* (1985)—by Montgomery's granddaughter, Kate Macdonald, and charmingly illustrated by Barbara

DiLella—that includes detailed recipes for Splendid Lettuce Salad, Thick and Creamy Vegetable Soup, Poetical Egg Salad Sandwiches, and Old-fashioned Lemonade.

Apprenticeship of Duddy Kravitz, The (1959, NCL; rpr. 2001, 2005). Mordecai RICHLER's fourth and best-known novel shows him as an early user of the 'black comedy' that subsequently emerged, in the 1960s, as the most prominent new feature of English-language fiction. It is a loosely episodic study of a young hustler on his way up—in the Jewish ghetto around St Urbain Street in Montreal—that is prevented from becoming either a parable of environmental determinism or an illustration of the moral bankruptcy of unrestrained ambition by its exuberance and sometimes broad comedy, as in set pieces such as the tale of the bizarre movie produced by the questionable film company Duddy created to film bar mitzvahs for the socially ambitious. Because of the way Duddy embodies so much manipulative but attractive energy, the debate on how he should be judged has been ambivalent. At the end of the novel Duddy finds victory emptier than he had anticipated, but the reader senses that he is not without achievement. Among other things he represents a new example of escape from the mythology of the ghetto and of someone who has disrupted a world that was too often static. *Duddy Kravitz* was made into a highly successful film (1974) starring Richard Dreyfus, for which Richler wrote the screenplay.

Arcadian adventures with the idle rich (1914, NCL; rpr. 2002). One of Stephen LEACOCK's most popular books, along with SUNSHINE SKETCHES OF A LITTLE TOWN, which was published two years earlier. As numerous similarities in overall structure and detail indicate, it was intended as a companion piece. It portrays the full flowering in a large American city (based on Montreal) of the seeds of corrupt materialism, already detected in small-town Mariposa. In its bitter satire of the 'conspicuous consumption' of the 'idle rich', it shows the influence of *Theory of the leisure class* by Thorstein Veblen, Leacock's teacher at the University of Chicago. Unlike *Sunshine sketches*, it shows sympathy not for those it satirizes but for their hapless victims. The inhabitants of Plutoria Street are presented primarily as hypocritical and dangerous embodiments of corrupt institutions or forces, such as the church, politics, finance, and education. As it proceeds, the book becomes progressively darker until in its final chapter, 'The Great Fight', there is a foreshadowing of the tyranny and violence that were later to grip the world in the 1920s and 1930s. A scholarly edition edited by D.M.R. Bentley was published in 2002.

Aquin, Hubert (1929–77). Born in Montreal, he was educated in philosophy at the Université de Montréal and at the Institut d'études politiques in Paris (1951–4), and then worked as a producer at Radio-Canada (1955–9) and as a scriptwriter and film director for the National Film Board (1959–63). In 1960, while working as a stockbroker for the Montreal Stock Exchange, he joined the Rassemblement pour l'Indépendance nationale (RIN). In 1964 he disappeared for a time, after stating in a press release that he was joining an underground terrorist movement; he was arrested in July 1964 while in possession of a stolen car and an automatic pistol and was transferred from Montreal Prison to the Albert Prévost Psychiatric Institute, where he spent four months awaiting trial for illegal possession of a firearm. During this period he wrote his first and most famous novel, *Prochain épisode* (1965; translated with the same title by Penny Williams, 1967); it was retranslated by Sheila Fischman and republished as *Next episode* (2001, NCL), Acquitted in Dec. 1965, Aquin had become a literary sensation. The years following were characterized by a series of dramatic incidents that indicated Aquin's inability to compromise with any established structure, professional or political. In 1968 he publicly broke with the RIN when it merged with René Lévesque's Mouvement Souveraineté-Association to form the Parti Québécois, describing the merger as suicidal for the Québec independence movement. In 1969 he became the first Québec writer to refuse a Governor General's Award (for *Trou de mémoire*) on political grounds. In 1976, after eighteen months as literary director of Éditions La Presse, he resigned publicly, accusing the editor and publisher of *La Presse*, Roger LEMELIN, of 'colonizing Québec from within'. On 15 Mar. 1977 he took a pistol left to him in his father's will and shot himself in the temple. *Prochain épisode* was hailed on publication as the great novel of Québec's revolutionary period. In fact it is about paralysis, and the impossibility of revolution, as much as it is about revolution. It recounts the attempt of an imprisoned separatist to distract himself from reality, and to rediscover his revolutionary fervour, by writing a novel. The hero of the fictional novel—a revolutionary Québec

separatist in Switzerland—after receiving instructions about the enemy he is to kill, agrees to rejoin his lover and revolutionary comrade K. (clearly a symbol of Québec) twenty-four hours later in Lausanne. But as the plot unfolds, the hero reveals himself as an artist rather than as a man of action, and in his 'infinite hesitation' becomes a 'fractured symbol of the revolution in Québec'. His enemy, H. de Heutz—in his triple identity of banker, historian, and lonely aristocrat—emerges as the double or enemy-brother of the hero, the other half of the French-Canadian psyche associated with an English Canada both hated and loved. In the perfection of its moving and complex structure, *Prochain episode* transcends the historical movement that gave it birth while remaining, as the narrator writes, clearly identified with that moment. It speaks equally powerfully of despair, and of the unceasing hope that produces metamorphosis and revolution. The three novels Aquin published after *Prochain episode*—*Trou de mémoire* (1968), *L'antiphonaire* (1969), and *Neige noir* (1974)—were attempts to make the novel into a 'total' art form. The literary influences he most often mentioned were Joyce's *Ulysses* and the work of Vladimir Nabokov, as well as the detective novels he loved, whose 'whodunit' form may have influenced the often sadistic and teasing relationship his novels establish with the reader. Alan Brown translated the first two as *Blackout* (1974) and *The antiphonary* (1973, rpr. 1983). *Neige noir*, translated by Sheila FISCHMAN as *Hamlet's twin* (1979), perhaps his greatest novel, is an 'unfinishable' film scenario and a modern reply to Hamlet; it attempts to integrate the temporal and the sacred in a philosophical meditation on time that counterpoints a violent and erotic detective-type plot. See also *Writing Quebec: selected essays by Hubert Aquin* (1988), edited by Anthony Purdy.

Archambault, Gilles (b. 1933). Born in Montreal, he received his B.A. from the Université de Montréal in 1957. The following year he went to work for Radio-Canada to present reviews of his two favourite topics, literature and jazz, and has continued to write reviews and humorous commentary on current events for radio, print media, and recently the Internet. David Lobdell has translated four of his novels—*Parlons de moi* (1970), *La fleur aux dents* (1971), *La fuite immobile* (1974), and *Les pins parasols* (1976)—as *One for the road* (1982), *The man with a flower in his mouth* (1983), *Standing flight* (1986), and *The umbrella pines* (1980). *One for the road* and *The man with a flower in his mouth* are both monologues of young middle-aged family men—at unsatisfactory turning-points in their wayward lives, steeped in dissatisfactions and feelings of failure—who are nevertheless able to describe their past and present in a swift-flowing, sympathetic narrative. While the unnamed protagonist of the first novel, whose wife has left him and who has just returned from a motor trip with his son 'on the road', ends up in despair, Georges at the end of the second novel, to his surprise, is blessed with good fortune and hope for the future. In *Standing flight* writer and journalist Julien struggles with class distinctions as he moves from a blue-collar upbringing into a professional environment, reluctant to leave his tavern friends, yet unable to curse in front of them without sounding affected. *The umbrella pines* is the portrait of the isolated members of an affluent family: Serge, soon to turn fifty, his wife Danielle, a would-be writer, their daughter Emmanuelle and her husband Yves, and the head of the family, Serge's widowed father, a rough, self-made man who has decided to remarry and move to Florida, leaving the house, Saint-Sauveur—'sitting in the shade of a row of umbrella pines'—to his son, whose life is changed by an act of violence in the family. Lobdell also translated *L'obsédante obèse et autres agressions* (1987, GGA) as *In a minor key* (1990), a collection of 136 one-paragraph mini-stories with titles.

Armstrong, Jeannette C. (b. 1948). Jeannette Christine Armstrong is a member of the Okanagan nation, was born on the Penticton Indian Reserve in British Columbia, and attended the reserve's elementary school and the Penticton Senior Secondary School. She received a Diploma in Fine Arts from Okanagan College (1975) and a B.F.A. degree from the University of Victoria. A fluent speaker of the Okanagan language, she has also studied under Okanagan elders and is co-founder and director of Penticton's En'owkin International School of Writing, the first credit-giving creative-writing school in Canada operated for and by Native people. Her poetry collection *Breath tracks* (1991)—divided into four sections: 'From the landscape of Grandmother', 'History lesson', 'Fire madness', and 'Wind woman'—is innovative in form, with free verse and concrete poems reflecting personal experiences and social and political concerns intensely and compassionately, but without sentimentality. Her novel *Slash* (1985; rev. 1990; rpr. 2007) is the story of an Okanagan Native youth's search for truth and meaning in his life as he grows into

manhood during the turbulent sixties and seventies. Non-Natives criticized Armstrong's disruptive style, the book's lack of character development and time perspective, but Native critic Lee MARACLE praised it for not being a European piece of literature: 'It is Native literature from beginning to end' (*Fuse*, July 1988). And Lenore KEESHIG-TOBIAS referred to it as 'emergence literature, a stage in the evolution of Native literature as a written art form. It is a process of learning decolonization' (*Fuse*, March/April 1988). Armstrong's second novel, *Whispering in shadows* (1999, rpr. 2000—about Penny Jackson (an Okanagan, a painter, an environmental activist, and mother of three) from youth to middle age—is not easy to follow as it jumps around in time and combines traditional narrative passages with letters, diary entries, and fragments from poems. One of these, headed 'IS THIS PART OF THE POEM OR IS IT NON-FICTION?', is a long sequence of words signifying oppressions of various kinds: 'globalization and supremacy deceit and grudging paternalism systematized racism colonial practice and government structured racialization power enforcement might makes right the colour of oppression and racism is money and blood'. The genuine emotional content of the novel, however, is unmistakable, especially when Penny is struck with cancer. Its last lines are her poem 'earth love': 'I said that I would/give my flesh back/but instead my flesh/will offer me up/and feed the earth/and she will/love me'.

The native creative process (1991) is a collaborative discourse between Armstrong and the distinguished Native architect Douglas Cardinal. Armstrong is the author of *We get our living like milk from the land: Okanagan tribal history book* (1993) and *Looking at the words of our people* (1993). She also edited (with Lally Grauer) *Native poetry in Canada: a contemporary anthology* (2001) and has written three children's books: *Enwhisteetkwa: Walk-in-water* (1982), *Neekna and Chemai* (1991), and *Dancing with the cranes* (2004), imaginatively illustrated by Aboriginal artist Ron Hall.

As for me and my house (1941, NCL). This first novel by Sinclair ROSS—recognized as a Canadian classic, and the most critically appraised of Canadian novels—portrays Philip Bentley, a clergyman, whose ministry has brought him to a small prairie town during the Depression as an ineffectual minister and a frustrated artist caught up in a vocation to which he may never have been suited. This view of Philip is tempered, however, by the reader's awareness that the story is being told through the diary entries of his wife, a woman who once dreamed of being a professional musician and chafes at her duties as a minister's wife. While Mrs Bentley can be suspected of exaggerating Philip's talent and his disaffection for the ministry, in order to justify her own desire to have him leave it (engaging in various schemes and manipulative acts towards that end), there is poignancy in her attempts to maintain and transform a difficult marriage under trying circumstances, and a degree of apparent admiration in the text for her stalwart resistance to the conformist demands of the ironically named town of Horizon. Critical approaches to the novel—from such varied perspectives as reader-response theory, feminism, semiotics, ethics, and new historicism—testify to the protean achievement this novel represents. Keath FRASER in *As for me and my body: a memoir of Sinclair Ross* (1997), however, views the novel quite differently. Late in his life Ross talked openly to Fraser (his friend) about his homosexuality and this leads to Fraser's seeing Philip Bentley as a repressed homosexual: 'By not admitting Philip's homosexuality in the novel, so it might have made a difference to the drama or effected a less stilted outcome, Ross compromised the credibility of his main heterosexual relationship. Philip is flawed ... in the sense of an artistic flaw out of which the story fails to flow but ought to.' Fraser examines the novel at length in the light of what he calls the 'false front' Ross applied to Bentley.

'At the Mermaid Inn'. This column—conducted by the poets Wilfred CAMPBELL, Archibald LAMPMAN, and Duncan Campbell SCOTT—appeared in the Toronto *Globe* every Saturday (with one exception) from 6 Feb. 1892 to 1 July 1893. The individual columns dealt with literature, painting, history, politics, and religion, and promoted Canadian literature vigorously, along with the aesthetic values that were implicit in its contributors' poetry. In response to a controversy (27 Feb. 1892) aroused by Campbell's writing that many of the stories in the Old Testament 'have been proved to belong to the class of literature called mythic' and that the 'story of the cross itself is one of the most important myths in the history of humanity', the *Globe* was obliged to publish an apology. The entire run of the column was reprinted, with an introduction by Barrie Davies, in *At the Mermaid Inn: Wilfred Campbell, Archibald Lampman, Duncan Campbell Scott in the Globe 1892–3* (1979).

Atwood, Margaret (b. 1939). Born in Ottawa, she was educated at Victoria College, University of Toronto, Radcliffe College, Cambridge, Massachusetts, and studied for three years at Harvard University. Over a career of almost fifty years she has published fourteen collections of poetry (including three *Selected poems*, first published in 1976, 1986, and 1990); ten novels; seven collections of short fiction; and five works of criticism. She is a writer of international prominence who is as well known in the USA, Europe, and Australia as she is in Canada; her work has been translated into more than thirty languages. She has received numerous awards and honours, including the GOVERNOR GENERAL'S AWARD (for *The circle game* and *The handmaid's tale*), Companion of the Order of Canada (1981), the GILLER PRIZE (for *Alias Grace*), the Medal of Honor, National Arts Club, New York (1997), the Booker Prize (for *The blind assassin*); and honorary degrees from more than ten universities, including Oxford and Cambridge. In October 2008 she received Spain's prestigious Prince of Asturias Award for Letters as 'one of the most outstanding voices of contemporary fiction'. In 2010 Atwood shared the Dan David Prize, worth $1 million, with the Indian novelist Amitav Ghosh; founded in 2002 by an Israeli businessman, it requires that each winner donate 10 per cent to graduate students studying literature.

From the time of her first publication in 1961 Atwood has demonstrated remarkable artistic control of her poetic material. Each book has a thematic unity and can be seen to elaborate a central preoccupation of her work: the role of mythology, both personal and cultural, in the individual life. Like Northrop FRYE, she is fascinated by the conventions that lie behind everyday reality, by the mythological substructures of modern culture. Atwood continually startles the reader with her imagery, which unfolds in a terse, elliptical style. The game of 'Ring-around the-rosie', alluded to in the title of her first major collection, *The circle game* (1966; rev. 1998; rpr. 2006), is one of ritual exclusion in which the known is circumscribed by a garrison of bodies that keeps out the threatening, unknown world. For Atwood the essential human impulse is to reduce an irrational and threatening environment to a closed circle of orthodoxy. Thus the writer's responsibility is to expose the conventions (psychological, linguistic, mythic) by which we invent convenient versions of ourselves. She sees modern humans as being prey to continual invasions of fear and paranoia from the subliminal mind, yet committed to an anachronistic belief in civilized order that is patently contradicted by the barbarism of the twentieth century. The rational mind must be integrated with the dark side of the psyche that has been repressed by humanistic ideas of order. To enter the wilderness of the self, then, is one of Atwood's major concerns. In *The animals in that country* (1968) another pre-occupation appears, the pioneer, 'disgusted/ with the swamp's clamourings and the out-bursts/of rocks' ('Progressive insanities of a pioneer'). In *The JOURNALS OF SUSANNA MOODIE* (1970; 24th rpr. 2007) a nineteenth-century Canadian pioneer becomes the archetypal colonial entering the unknown wilderness of the New World. Imprisoned within the outmoded conventions of the Victorian world that she carries in her head, she retreats into her own circle game projecting nostalgic Victorian preconceptions onto an alien landscape, while remaining ignorant of the challenges of her new environment. (For Atwood, as for Frye, such a garrison mentality once characterized the Canadian sensibility.) Moodie's last meditations are from under-ground. *Procedures for underground* (1970) explores the same themes in a different con-text. The title poem is indebted to West Coast Native mythology for its motifs. Entering the mirror world of the psyche, the poet becomes a shaman whose visions are threatening to her tribe. From the 'underland' she sees the world as an ambiguous landscape of violence and death—the landscape we enter in many other poems in the book. In the brief, aphoristic poems of *Power politics* (1971; rev. 1996) Atwood exposes the sadistic deceptions implicit in the myth of romantic love. Lovers are predatory, even cannibalistic; relationships are a sophisticated form of consumption: love is power politics. Each individual seeks the security of role reinforcement from the other, and remains trapped in an essential solipsism, committed only to his or her own needy appetite. *You are happy* (1974), which repre-sents an expansion of these themes, includes the brilliant sequence of 'Circe/Mud' poems in which the story of Odysseus arriving in Aiaia is retold from the perspective of Circe, whose experience represents the extortion of women, who must be entirely passive—malleable as clay to male desire. With these two books Atwood became a major voice in the feminist debate over personal relation-ships. The themes of Atwood's later poetry also include the world of modern politics and the domestic world of mother and child. The title poem of *Two-headed poems* (1978) is an elegy for a nation divided between two cul-tures: not only in the 'two-headed' national persona—represented by a 'leader' who speaks

duplicitously in two languages—but in the ensuing debate, which 'is not a debate/but a duet/with two deaf singers'. An antidote to this public cynicism appears in poems that create potent myths for the child, offering a private magic, and in a treatment of nature that reveals its benevolence in the cyclical renewal of life. In *True stories* (1981), Atwood's political concerns are transferred to an inter-national context. We live in a fragile security, cocooned from the global realities of famine, political terrorism, and war: our willed igno-rance of such evils is a form of collusion. In a peculiarly Canadian way, Atwood is a staunch moralist, essentially demanding that modern humans reinvent themselves. *Interlunar* (1984) contains the remarkable 'Snake poems', a sequence reminiscent in its eloquent lyricism of D.H. Lawrence's 'The snake', and demon-strates Atwood's total control of her voice and her material. After a poetic silence of eleven years, the poems in *Morning in the burned house* (1995) encompass many moods, from playful to sombre—in an elegiac series of meditations on the death of her father—as the poet courses back through memory, searching for the values of compassion and forgiveness. The themes and concerns and emotions that pre-vail in this collection are equalled, or exceeded, in effectiveness and resonance by those in *The door* (2007), which begins with poems about domestic matters, such as 'Resurrecting the dolls' house' and 'Year of the hen', about throwing out junk: 'the junk, in other words,/ that's blown in here, or else been saved,/or else has eddied, or been thrown/my way by unseen waves'. She writes about poetry and poets: 'The poet has come back' ends with two clever puns: 'the god of poetry has two hands:/the dextrous, the sinister'; in 'Poetry reading' she amusingly turns against the poet reading; and in the long 'Owl and Pussycat, some years later', Edward Lear's characters have become poets and the pussycat describes the idiosyncrasies of, and public indifference to, such an activity. Nature is another subject. 'The weather': 'Why were we so careless?/ we ask ourselves, as the weather billows/over the horizon';'It's Autumn': don't go 'into the faded orange wood—/it's filled with angry old men/sneaking around in camouflage gear/pretending no one can see them.' Other subjects are parents ('Butterfly', about her father's epiphany at the age of ten that led him to his career; and 'My mother dwindles') and war: 'War photo', 'War photo 2', 'Nobody cares who wins'. In the beautiful final (title) poem, in which the poet moves through life, as the door swings open and closed (death?),

Atwood

the last two lines are: 'You step in./The door swings closed.'

Atwood has explained that, for her, the novel is a 'social vehicle' that 'reflects society'. In each of her first five novels—*The edible woman* (1969, NCL), *Surfacing* (1972, NCL; rpr. 2006), *Lady Oracle* (1976, rpr. 1998), *Life before man* (1979. rpr. 1998), *Bodily harm* (1981, rpr. 1999)—the main character is a woman (a consumer research analyst, a commercial artist, a novelist, an anthropologist, a 'lifestyle' journalist) living a professional life in a modern consumer society who is forced to engage in a radical process of reassessment when the props supporting her carefully constructed version of herself are knocked out from under. Marian, the narrator of *The edible woman*, exorcises the menace of a predatory sexist society by baking an 'edible woman' cake and ritualistically offering it to her man in place of herself. In *Lady Oracle* the narrator, Joan, lives her life as if it were a trashy and melodramatic script, one of the costume Gothics she writes. When neurotic relationships and her invented personas (she has at least three identities) become too confusing, she decides to simulate her own death; but whether this escape into normalcy is successful is left ambiguous. *Life before man* is about a love triangle; but in an anaesthetized, plastic world—the puritanical world of WASP Toronto—the characters can't seem to transcend clichés of feeling. Lesje, one of the main characters, works at the Royal Ontario Museum, and prehistoric dinosaurs walk like phantoms through the pages of the novel. Atwood's implicit question is: Have we earned the right to call ourselves human? Atwood's most complex early novels are *Surfacing* and *Bodily harm*. In *Surfacing* the unnamed narrator searches the wilderness of northern Québec for her father, a botanist, who has been reported missing. Trying to re-establish contact with her past, she must re-evaluate all her cultural assumptions. In this retreat into the wilderness, which is both a literal and a psychological place, Atwood is challenging Western ways of seeing, particularly of relating to nature. The modern compulsion is to treat nature as raw material, to explain and master it in accordance with the technological myth of progress. By showing her protagonist moving through a ritual preparation that corresponds to the stages of shamanistic initiation, Atwood attempts to recover a primitive, mystical participation in nature, in which the heroine must recreate herself. In *Bodily harm* the heroine flees from a constricting consumer society and a broken relationship to another alien territory—the politically complex environment of a Caribbean island. Confronted with its stark realities, she comes to acknowledge her narcissistic entrapment in a culture where feelings are invented, packaged, and merchandised.

With *The HANDMAID'S TALE* (1985, rpr. 2007) Atwood achieved immediate international recognition for her portrait of a futuristic American society in the throes of a fundamentalist dictatorship where women, forced into servitude as handmaids, are commandeered into producing babies for the governing elite. The book shows Atwood at her most intellectually fierce, revealing how an epidemic of infertility in the Western democracies as a consequence of chemical pollution could be used by right-wing fundamentalists to impose their own repressive theocratic rule. With *Cat's eye* (1988, rpr. 1999) Atwood turned back to a more private world, chronicling the return of a middle-aged painter, Elaine Risley, to Toronto for a retrospective of her work: her re-entry into the world of her childhood allows Atwood to examine the betrayals and cruelties of adolescent females with a sympathy and humour that combine the lyrical intensity of her poetry with the social vision of her fiction. For many critics this is one of her finest novels. *The robber bride* (1993, rpr. 2007) develops this strength. Playing on the title of the sadistic Grimm's fairy tale 'The robber bridegroom', it explores the friendship among three women who are united in part by their involvement with a common nemesis, a charismatic and manipulative woman called Zenia, who, thought dead, surfaces to subvert their peace. Each woman experiences her life in retrospect, unfolding back to the encounter with Zenia, who has robbed her of the significant male in her life. The book becomes a meditation on how we concoct versions of ourselves, and elaborates Atwood's fascination with illusion, camouflage, and deception. Shrewdly understanding the narrative and dramatic potential of psychological projection, Atwood creates characters who, because wounded, have been vulnerable to another's con-artistry of the mind. *Alias Grace* (1996, rpr. 2006), a historical novel, is based on a murder case in Canada West (Ontario) in 1843. The heroine, thirty-two-year-old Grace Marks, is sixteen years into a life sentence in Kingston Penitentiary for her involvement in the murder of her employer, Thomas Kinnear, and his housekeeper/mistress, for which her supposed accomplice, fellow servant James McDermott, was hanged. Grace claims to have no memory of the murders, and, under the auspices of a group of Kingston reformers and Spiritualists, Dr Simon Jordan, a pioneer in the new science of mental illness, has been brought to Canada to determine Grace's innocence or guilt. Atwood had been fascinated by the Grace Marks story since reading Susanna MOODIE's inaccurate account of the murders in *Life in the clearings* (1853) in her high-school reader. By using the new science of psychology as backdrop to her novel, and threading it with nineteenth-century literary quotations, as well as popular ballads and newspaper clippings of the time, Atwood vividly conjures up nineteenth-century fears and fantasies about 'the female murderess'. The novel becomes a meditation on the nature of identity, memory, and the unconscious in a fascinating exploration of male-female relationships. The title of *The blind assassin* (2000, rpr. 2006)—which had simultaneous publication in five countries—is that of a popular novella, a memoir-cum-sci-fi-potboiler, published posthumously by Laura Chase; her death at the age of twenty-five in 1945 is described in the first sentence of Atwood's novel, which is narrated by Laura's older sister Iris, in her early eighties, whose infirmities do not go unmentioned. Iris recalls details of her life, and Laura's—they were the children of a prosperous button manufacturer in the fictional Port Ticonderoga in the Niagara Peninsula of southern Ontario. When their mother died they were raised by Reenie, the loyal housekeeper who was filled with tough-minded admonitions in the form of hackneyed sayings. These reminiscences are interspersed among chapters from *The blind assassin* (which turned Laura into a cult figure), describing the secret meetings of two unnamed lovers in tawdry surroundings, when the male entertains his partner with a wild and sometimes chilling pulp-fiction fantasy, having metaphorical meanings, about the planet Zycron. Iris describes her childhood, and that of strange, bright Laura, and her wayward behaviour; the appearance in their lives of a leftist young man, Alex Thomas, to whom both are attracted, who is fleeing from the law as a suspected Communist; Iris's forced marriage at eighteen, when her father's business was destroyed by the Depression, to Richard Griffen, a much older and ruthless Toronto industrialist with right-wing political ambitions—he closed the button factory after his marriage; her presence in Toronto society, coached by Richard's malevolent sister, also right-wing; and later events, including the birth of a daughter—all coloured by details of local social history and the brief intrusion of

world events, until the twists and turns of Iris's life, and Laura's, offer Gothic revelations. The sweep and intricacy of this long novel—in which three, even four, stories unfold—are given life and readability by Atwood's lucidity and her piercing, dry observations, her control of the story of two sisters and of her sometimes melodramatic material, and her skill as a storyteller as she not only conveys the disintegration over a long period of one family in southern Ontario, but arouses suspense and questions in Iris's narrative, which is not always reliable. Atwood's concerns about the future of contemporary society in the light of such things as genetic engineering, corporate greed, and the unprincipled use of new technologies gave rise to *Oryx and Crake* (2003, rpr. 2005), a dystopian fantasy, described by the author as 'speculative fiction'. Unusual for Atwood, it is written from a male point of view, that of Snowman, whom we learn about in flashbacks to his past when he was the teenaged Jimmy, and who may be the last human after a deadly virus has destroyed the population of a biotech world. Jimmy's best friend, nicknamed Crake, becomes a brilliant genetic engineer, a 'numbers person' (Jimmy is a 'words person' who memorizes countless standard words that have become obsolete). Both love Oryx, an Asian prostitute Crake has liberated. Ingeniously conceived and plotted, the novel portrays a frightening world that is eerily plausible. (See below for a later novel that is connected.) *Moral disorder* (2006, rpr. 2007) is described as a series of linked stories, but their interconnectedness and development of characters and unfolding life experiences give it the unified persuasiveness and force of a novel. Focused on the life of Nell, the narrator, it begins in her old age with husband Tig (real name Gilbert) and proceeds to 'the summer I was eleven', in a story called 'The art of cooking and serving', the title of a cookbook to which she became devoted. Drawing, surely, on some aspects of Atwood's own life, the book is enriched by authentic descriptions of social details for each period. The smooth, witty, graceful narratives cohere in a memorable personal and family history that is warm and sympathetic. In 2009 Atwood published *The year of the flood*, which looks at aspects of *Oryx and Crake* from a different perspective: we learn how Jimmy and Glenn become the Snowman and Crake, and God's Gardeners, led by Adam One, are important, along with the corporations (controlled by their security arm CorpSeCorps). The flood is apparently a plague called a Waterless Flood and all but a few humans, including Toby and Ren (their past and present are part of the narrative) are extinct. The complexities of this new speculative novel cannot be gone into here, but as a lament for the destruction of the best human qualities by the greed, stupidity, and hatefulness of humans, leavened by its masterly blending of humour, wit, and creative foresight, it is a compelling work.

Atwood has demonstrated her mastery of the short-story form, which allows for interesting technical experiments with point of view, dialogue, and epigrammatic style. In *Dancing girls* (1977, rpr. 1999), the characters—like the protagonists of her novels—are psychologically complex individuals trapped by paranoia and radical alienation. Two stories are representative: 'Polarities' is a study of madness, both inside and outside mental institutions, in which a clinically insane student proves to have a deeper understanding of the general psychosis of modern society than the so-called sane protagonist; 'The grave of the famous poet' is one of Atwood's most compassionate fictional studies of the failure of relationships. With acerbic irony she penetrates beneath the level of clichéd passion to expose love as an addictive habit. *Bluebeard's egg* (1983, rpr. 1999) contains several avowedly autobiographical stories, including 'Significant moments in the life of my mother', and 'Unearthing suite', compassionate and tender accounts of family life that demonstrate the great gap between Atwood's own childhood experience and the Gothic world that is often her fictional subject. *Wilderness tips* (1991, rpr. 2006) includes the story 'Isis in darkness', a thinly disguised tribute to her friend Gwendolyn MacEWEN. In *Murder in the dark: short fiction and prose poems* (1983, NCL), the subject is writing itself: what is the plot against the reader? The title piece describes writing as a treacherous parlour game in which the writer is the murderer, the reader her victim, and, by the rules of the game, the writer must lie. The price the writer exacts from herself justifies her sinister assumption of authority: 'If you decide to enter the page, take a knife and some matches', because the journey is horrifying: 'You can become lost in the page forever.' The last section of the book explores the varieties of darkness beneath the page where the writer enters a limbo between sanity and madness. *Good bones* (1992, NCL) is a much more playful book, parodying traditional forms such as the parable, monologue, mini-romance, mini-biography, and reconstructed fairy tale. But beneath its satiric humour, the vignettes offer serious meditations on a theme that has

long fascinated Atwood: human evolution and our hubristic arrogance in the face of the natural world. Selections from *Murder* and *Good bones* make up *Good bones and simple murders* (2001).

'Gertrude talks back' is one of the stories, in verse, in *Good bones*. ('I always thought it a mistake, calling you Hamlet.... I wanted to call you George.') In another collection of mini-fictions, *The tent* (2006, rpr. 2007), one of the longest stories (six pages), 'Horatio's version', Horatio attempts to answer Hamlet's plea 'to tell my story'. In the end he can only tell 'how things are, now, on this earth.... *So shall you hear of carnal, bloody, and unnatural acts....*' Another mini-fiction, 'Bring back Mom: an invocation', eulogizes in verse 'breadbaking Mom' of happy memory 'in her crisp gingham apron ... who made our school lunches'—and is destroyed by madness. Though sometimes playful, these mini-fictions encapsulate grievances, despair, and hopelessness ... and in the not-too-distant future an apocalypse threatens. 'Wind comes in, your candle tips over and flares up, and a loose tent flap catches fire, and through the widening black-edged gap you can see the eyes of the howlers, red and shining in the light from your burning paper shelter, but you keep on writing anyway because what else can you do?' ('The tent'). Drawings by Atwood decorate *The tent* and its striking jacket.

Contributing to Knopf's Myth Series, for which leading writers were commissioned 'to provide a contemporary take on our most enduring stories', Atwood wrote *The Penelopiad* (2005, rpr. 2006), in which the faithful wife of the absent Odysseus in Homer's *Odyssey*, beset by suitors, tells her story (and that of her twelve maids, who provide choruses, chanted or sung, and were hanged). Penelope's story is imagined by Atwood in an engaging, smooth-flowing narrative in modern English. In 2005 Atwood and Phyllida Lloyd produced a staged reading in London (Atwood as Penelope) and in July 2007 there was a production by the Royal Shakespeare Company, which opened at the National Arts Centre, Ottawa, in September.

Much informal criticism is included among Atwood's writings: the controversial SUR-VIVAL: A THEMATIC GUIDE TO CANADIAN LITERATURE (1972, rpr. 2006, with a new introduction by the author), *Second words: selected critical prose* (1982, 2nd edn 2000), and *Moving targets: writing with intent 1982–2004* (2004). *Strange things: the malevolent North in Canadian literature* (1995), in the series Clarendon Lectures in English Literature, is made up of four lectures Atwood gave at Oxford University in the spring of 1991. She also gave six Empson Lectures in 2000 at Cambridge University, *Negotiating with the dead: a writer on writing* (2002, rpr. 2003). While Atwood's Introduction to *Strange things* demonstrates her lighthearted approach to her subject, the Introduction to *Negotiating with the dead* is serious and much longer, and is followed by a Prologue. The brilliant lectures in both books display her wide-ranging knowledge of literature, which she focuses on in unexpected, illuminating ways. *Strange things*, as the subtitle indicates, is strongly Canadian in its orientation. The six lectures in *Negotiating with the dead* have the titles 'Orientation', 'Duplicity', 'Dedication', 'Temptation', 'Communion', and 'Descent: negotiating with the dead'. She received an honorary doctorate from each university. Atwood's witty and prescient CBC Massey Lectures were published in book form in October 2008—as *Payback: debt and the shadow side of wealth*—a few weeks before they were broadcast in Nov., in order, presumably, to take advantage of the general interest in the book's subject after the financial breakdown on New York's Wall Street and its world-wide consequences.

Atwood edited *The new Oxford book of Canadian verse in English* (1982, rpr. 1984), and co-edited with Robert WEAVER *The Oxford book of Canadian short stories* (1986; 2nd edn 1995; rpr. 1997).

See Rosemary SULLIVAN's *The red shoes: Margaret Atwood / starting out* (1998, rpr. 1999) and Nathalie Cooke's *Margaret Atwood: a biography* (1998). See also *Margaret Atwood: works and impact* (2000), edited by Reingard M. Nischik, professor of American literature at the University of Constance, Germany—essays by international contributors (including Atwood's close associates, Ellen Seligman, Nan Talese, Phoebe Larmore, and Sarah Cooper); *The Cambridge companion to Margaret Atwood* (2006) edited by Carol Ann Howells, a collection of essays; and *Margaret Atwood: essays on her works* (2007) edited by Branko Gorjup.

Aubert de Gaspé, Philippe-Joseph (1786–1871). Born in Quebec City, he was the scion of an old and aristocratic Québec family, and his childhood was partly spent at the ancestral manor house on the south shore of the St Lawrence River. He became a lawyer, though he retired in 1822. In his late seventies he published his historical romance *Les anciens canadiens* (1863), set at the end of the French regime and drawing on family reminiscences, relatives who served as characters, and the

family manor. It became popular with English-speaking readers in the translation by Charles G.D. ROBERTS, *CANADIANS OF OLD* (1890); a modern translation by Jane Brierley was published in 1996. For his *Mémoires* (Quebec, 1866) Aubert de Gaspé gathered hundreds of anecdotes and reminiscences that form a fascinating social history of Québec before and after the turn of the eighteenth century. They were translated by Jane Brierley as *A man of sentiment ...* (1988). Brierley has also translated stories by Aubert de Gaspé and collected them in *Yellow-Wolf and other tales of the Saint Lawrence* (1990).

Authors at Harbourfront Centre (formerly operating as the Harbourfront Reading Series). Harbourfront Centre was created in 1972 as an arts venue that presented performance art, cultural festivals, galleries, and arts workshops at its location at the foot of Toronto on the shore of Lake Ontario. Included in its first programming year (1974) was a series of literary readings. Founded by Don Cullen, the literary program was an attempt to revive the Bohemian Embassy readings, Toronto, of the 1960s. As part of Harbourfront Centre's public programming division, run by Ann Tindal, the program was managed for a period by John Robert COLOMBO, before being programmed in 1975 by Greg GATENBY. He became artistic director of the program in 1976, until that role was taken over by Geoffrey Taylor in 2003. In 1986 the program became a subsidiary company of Harbourfront Centre; its founding board was chaired by Bruce Westwood; board members have included Margaret ATWOOD, Louise Dennys, and the Right Honourable Adrienne Clarkson. Intended originally only for readings of poetry, the regular weekly gatherings expanded to include all genres of the creative written word. In 1978 George MacBeth was the first non-Canadian to read as part of the program, and was soon joined by other international authors, including John Cheever and Joyce Carol Oates. The response to these authors was overwhelming and paved the way for thousands more to come. To bring to North American audiences a type of literary festival already in existence in Europe, the reading series presented the first Harbourfront International Festival of Authors in 1980, inviting eighteen authors from around the world to read in six events over six evenings. Among the initial group was Czeslaw Milosz, who was awarded by Nobel Prize just days before the festival opened; the resulting publicity thrust the fledgling festival into the spotlight. The International Festival of Authors (IFOA)

Authors at Harbourfront Centre

remains an annual event but is now an eleven-day festival attended by more than 100 authors from as many as 20 countries who take part in readings, interviews, round tables, and a number of special events. Under Taylor's direction, Harbourfront Centre's literary programs have incorporated more genres of literature and ideas in programming than ever before, with the inclusion of a biannual event featuring travel writers, an annual event focusing on architecture and design, and an annual IFOA literary non-fiction reading featuring the winner of the Charles Taylor Prize for Literary Non-Fiction. Graphic novelists made their first appearance at IFOA in 2003, and a greater emphasis was placed on promoting literacy with the birth of several festivals for young readers: 2004 saw the addition of Step into Stories (now Young IFOA) to the IFOA program, and in 2005 the three-day ALOUD, a celebration for Young Readers, came into being. In 2007 Authors at Harbourfront Centre partnered with the Ontario Library Association to present the first Forest of Readings Festival of Trees. In 2008 this event had already grown to two days and, with around 60 authors and more than 6,500 readers from kindergarten to grade twelve in attendance, had become the largest literary event for children in Canada. Taylor also added a number of high-profile annual events to the IFOA program, including annual readings by the authors shortlisted for the Scotiabank GILLER PRIZE (in 2004), for the GOVERNOR GENERAL'S LITERARY AWARD for English-language fiction (in 2005), and for the Rogers Writers' Trust Fiction Prize (in 2008). IFOA has long supported PEN Canada by including an empty chair on stage at all events to represent an author persecuted for his work, and since 2005 IFOA has featured PEN Canada's Gala Benefit on its opening night—an event that consistently attracts superlative authors and a full house. Since its inception, Authors at Harbourfront Centre has presented more than 5,000 authors from more than 100 countries, and has ensured that Harbourfront Centre is considered the pre-eminent venue for readings in the world.

Avison, Margaret (1918–2007). Born in Galt, Ontario, the daughter of a Methodist minister, she grew up in Calgary, Alberta. She studied at Victoria College, University of Toronto, graduating with a B.A. in English in 1940 and doing graduate work for three years in the 1960s. Her first collection of poetry, *Winter sun* (1960, GGA), is intensely metaphysical, concerned with problems of belief and moral knowledge. The beautiful but desolate light of a winter sun is a metaphor for the poet's state on the edge of imminent revelation. In *The dumbfounding* (1966) the language and imagery are less inward. The title poem records the experience of a religious vision that confirmed the poet's commitment to the Christian faith, which was to direct her future work. These two collections were combined in *Winter sun/the dumbfounding: poems 1940–66* (1982). *sunblue* (1978) is the product of a profound religious conviction and explores Avison's Christian vision in poems about nature, where the natural world is used metaphorically to locate spiritual realities. *No time* (1989, GGA) is a personal book about death and the loss of friends, in particular the poet bp NICHOL and a childhood friend, Josephine Grimshaw, who is the subject of the most eloquent sequence in the book *The Jo poems*. All Avison's skill is evident: the play of rhythm and enjambment, the syntactical complexity and metaphysical imagery in the tradition of seventeenth-century poets like Donne and Herbert; and yet the poems are astonishingly direct. Few Canadian poets can match Avison in the sophistication and beauty of her linguistic and imagistic gifts, and even the reader who does not share her religious belief will find in her poetry a profound and imaginative perception of reality. This is evident also in *Not yet but still* (1997), a collection of accessible, sometimes humorous, poems that treat a wide variety of subjects and ends with the long 'Job: word and action: confrontation and resolution', containing the poet's discussions of the Book of Job, under topical headings, interspersed with those of a 'book reviewer', all of them poetic meditations that are both delightful and penetrating. *A kind of perseverance* (her 1993 Pascal Lectures at the University of Waterloo, published in 1994) is made up of two lectures that record the journey—in her words 'often unfocussed'—that led to her Christian conversion. *Margaret Avison: selected poems* (1991) includes her 'adaptations' of poems by the Hungarian writers Gyula Illyes and Ferenc Juhász. In *Concrete and wild carrot* (2002), which won the prestigious GRIFFIN POETRY PRIZE, her acquisition of many years belies the vigour and spiritual boldness of such lines as: 'Break/all our securities, and break out!/Explore only the ranges/beyond our mastering.' ('Alternative to riots ...') In 2003 an Italian-English anthology of Avison's poems appeared, *Il cuore che vede /The optic eye*, the poems translated by Brunella Antomarini, Francesca Inghilleri, and Francesca Valente. The preliminary pages contain 'Appreciations', in English and Italian, by André ALEXIS, Elizabeth HAY, Gwendolyn

MacEWEN, and Michael REDHILL; the book also contains colour reproductions of sixteen attractive paintings by Ubaldo Bartolini. *Always now: the collected poems* was handsomely published by PORCUPINE'S QUILL in three volumes (2003, 2004, 2005): One (*From Elsewhere, Winter sun, The dumbfounding, Translations*); Two (*sunblue, No time*); Three (*Not yet but still, Concrete and wild carrot, Too towards tomorrow: new poems*). MCCLELLAND & STEWART published *Momentary dark* (2006), a collection of new poems, many of which are life-enhancing and spell contentment, and *Listening: last poems* (2009), made up of most of a collection Avison left on her death, prepared for publication by Stan Dragland and Joan Eichner. See *Margaret Avison and her works* (1989) by David Kent. Avison was made an Officer of the Order of Canada in 1984.

Awful disclosures of Maria Monk (New York, 1836). This sensational book, probably a fictional memoir, describes the travails of Monk, a young Québec Protestant who converts to Roman Catholicism and becomes a nun of the Hôtel-Dieu in Montreal. There she learns, among other things, that nuns are forced to 'live in the practice of criminal intercourse with the priests' and that the offspring from these unions are killed after being baptized. Finding herself pregnant, Monk escapes to the United States and rediscovers her Protestant faith. The book sold thousands of copies in Canada, the US, and England; although many believed its revelations, others, especially both Catholics and Protestants in Montreal, denied their veracity. Doubts were raised about the book's authenticity—William Leete Stone published *Maria Monk and the nunnery of the Hotel Dieu. Being an account of a visit to the convents of Montreal and refutation of the 'Awful disclosures'* (New York, 1836)—partly because of the four 'designing men' Monk was associated with, one of them her legal guardian, though a second edition was published in the same year and a sequel in 1837. In its motifs of subterranean passages, imprisoned nuns, and secret murders the work is interesting, and its link to the Gothic novel shows how suitable this type of fiction was for anti-Catholic literature. It was reprinted in 1962 with an introduction by Allan Billington.

B

Babstock, Ken (b. 1970). Born in Newfoundland and raised in the Ottawa Valley, he lives in Toronto and is the poetry editor for the House of ANANSI, which published his three poetry collections. In *Mean* (1999), a significant debut, Babstock's tense imagery portrays aspects of his life and world—Newfoundland, adolescence, family, animals and nature, love, death (many deaths are referred to), accident, and injury—and makes them 'mean' something (gives them 'meaning'). Fishing for cod: 'Gavin slid/fingers under gills, hoisted its cold/bulk over so it thudded on the deck' ('Mainland boy in Eastport'); love: '... that rarest of gifts:/the love that survives youth's bat-blind, rigorous stretchings/to plant itself intact in the soil of maturity' ('Steady'); and its surcease: 'We have shuffled our lives/to somewhere north of wanting/each other' ('Authority'); a smashup: 'When the bike dropped it jammed/a foot-peg into asphalt. Blue/sparks spat off chrome, a dead-stop/catapult sent it clear up and//we slid right under,/holding each other.// Time stalled' ('What we didn't tell the medic'). 'Head injury card' is a series of short experimental poems with titles such as 'Unsteadiness on the feet, dizziness', 'Mental confusion', 'Persistent or increasingly severe headache'—which begins surreally: 'Further back. Feet stirruped, muzzled nurses hover/and grip. Crown of a skull slides out. Algae.' What has been called the 'free play' of Babstock's mind seems to rebuff the ordinary reader in *Days into flatspin* (2001), in such poems as 'He propositions the toilet'—'I see you still have the ring./And I still the glue of the holding/ of the fitted of the hinged/self that manages cutlery and appointments: that binged.'—which leads one to ask: What does this mean? Re this and other poems: What are they about? What is going on? *Airstream land yacht* (2006), which won the Trillium Book Award given by the City of Toronto, is divided into four sections headed, respectively, with the first two syllables and the last two words of the title. The title poem (in the 'Yacht' section) is about a trailer: 'Where in the world to go, to go?/O where in this world to go?/This big old wagon's slow, it's slow, /My beautiful wagon's/slow.' Babstock has earned generous praise from many Canadian reviewers.

Backwoods of Canada, The (London, 1836; rpr. 2000, NCL, CEECT). Catharine Parr TRAILL's first 'Canadian' book is composed of eighteen letters to family and friends in Suffolk, England, describing her departure with her husband from Scotland in July 1832, the sight of the St Lawrence River, their arrival in Montreal, and their progress through the spring of 1835, when they were comfortably settled in their own log house near present-day Lakefield, Ontario. The letters are of an optimistic and reassuring cast, drawing on Traill's fund of Christian patience and her faith in British character, as they provide a record of settlers' adventures and adjustments and dispense practical advice and information for British womenfolk contemplating 'a home amid our Canadian wilds'. Michael Peterman edited a scholarly edition (1997) published by the CENTRE FOR EDITING EARLY CANADIAN TEXTS.

Bacque, James (b. 1929). Born in Toronto and educated at Upper Canada College and the University of Toronto (B.A., 1952), he worked as an assistant editor of *Saturday Night, Canadian Packaging,* and *Canadian Homes,* and was trade editor for the MAC-MILLAN COMPANY OF CANADA (1961–8). He was a co-founder of New Press, Toronto, in 1969. He has written four modestly successful novels. *The lonely ones* (1969), reprinted in paperback as *Big Lonely* (1971), depicts a painter who becomes involved in the activities of a separatist cell in Québec in the 1960s. In *A man of talent* (1972) a bright young man, who is dean of arts at a university, becomes caught up in a conflict between student radicals and the university administration. *The Queen comes to Minnicog* (1979) portrays a fictional visit of the Queen of England to a small Georgian Bay town, employing to humorous effect stock rural types, farcical situations, and dialogue heavily dependent on malapropisms. Bacque's drive as a writer, and his knowledge of the Allied-German adversaries in the Second World War, accounts for his long, ambitious novel *Our fathers' war* (2006)—embracing the love stories of three young Germans, an Englishwoman, a French resistance fighter, and four Canadians, along with vivid war

scenes (Hitler, Churchill, Stalin, and Roosevelt also appear)—which didn't catch the attention of much of the reading public. Bacque's non-fiction is better known. *Just Raoul: adventures in the French Resistance* (1990) is a biography of Raoul Lapoterie, a Resistance hero. While working on this book Bacque found evidence of mass deaths in US-controlled camps after the Second World War, which were noted in army reports under the heading 'Other Losses'. This led him to research and write the controversial *Other losses: an investigation into the mass deaths of German prisoners at the hands of the French and Americans after World War II* (1989; 2nd rev. edn 1999). This was followed by *Crimes and mercies: the fate of German civilians under Allied occupation 1944–1950* (1997), an account of the expulsion of 15 million Germans from the eastern provinces and the Sudetenland into the Occupied Zones, and of more than 2 million deaths, after the war. *Dear enemy: Germany then and now* (2000) contains a correspondence between Bacque and Richard Mathias Mueller, a member of Hitler Youth who fought in the Second World War, in which many controversial issues are discussed.

Bailey, Alfred Goldsworthy (1905–97). Born in Quebec City, he was educated at the University of New Brunswick, the University of Toronto, and the London School of Economics. He became professor of history at UNB in 1937 and was head of the department for more than thirty years. He was made an Officer of the Order of Canada in 1978. His first two books of poetry were traditional in the style of Canadian romanticism; but meeting such writers as Robert FINCH and Earle BIRNEY in Toronto changed his approach, and he helped to establish *The FIDDLEHEAD*. His mature work appeared in *Border River* (1952), *Thanks for a drowned island* (1973), and *Miramichi lightning: the collected poems* (1981), and *the sun the wind the summer field* (1996). His central themes are the impingement of one culture on another, the aspirations of explorers and settlers, the difficulties of maintaining continuity and purpose, and nature. His style is compact and elliptical, sometimes playful, sometimes difficult. His *Culture and nationality: essays by A.G. Bailey* (1972) contains the important essay, 'Creative moments in the culture of the Maritime provinces'.

Bailey, Jacob (1731–1808). Born in Rowley, Massachusetts, he graduated from Harvard in 1755. After a brief career as a school teacher and Congregationalist minister, he converted to the Church of England. Ordained priest in 1760, and appointed to a frontier parish at Pawnalborough, Maine (then part of Massachusetts), he was resented by the largely Congregationalist community. As America slid towards open defiance of British authority, resentment of Bailey and the state-supported Church he represented sharpened. From 1774 on he was frequently harassed and assaulted. In 1779 he was permitted to depart as a Loyalist refugee for Nova Scotia, where he served as parish priest at Cornwallis (1779–82) and Annapolis Royal (1782–1808). Bailey left a voluminous amount of correspondence, journals, sermons, moral commentaries, histories, expository prose 'descriptions', fiction, and poetry. William S. Bartlet edited selections from the journals and correspondence for *The frontier missionary* (Boston, 1853), but most of his work was never published. Bailey's most sustained literary achievement lay in his poems, many of them satires. These include 'Farewell to Kennebec'(1799), a valedictory lamenting his exile from Maine; 'Character of a trimmer' (1779–80), which satirically attacks fence-sitters as well as rebels; 'America' (1780–4), an incomplete poem designed to present the Loyalist view of the cause of the Revolution; and the ambitious 'The adventures of Jack Ramble, the Methodist preacher' (c. 1785–late 1790s), incomplete in more than 9200 lines, which attacks evangelical itinerant preachers.

Baird, Irene (1901–81). Born Irene Todd in England, she came to British Columbia with her parents in 1919 and was a reporter for the *Vancouver Sun* and the *Daily Province*. She later married John Baird. In 1942 she joined the National Film Board, working in publicity and public relations, and on her retirement from the federal civil service she was chief information officer for the Department of Indian Affairs and Northern Development. Her first novel, *John* (1937), is a character study of John Dorey, a Scot who created a ten-acre haven for himself on Vancouver Island. *Waste heritage* (1939) is a classic of Canadian literature. Initially received as a stylistically imperfect but powerful and honest portrayal of the predicament and rage of the chronically unemployed in the Depression, it later came to be admired only for its accurate depiction of events based on the trek to Victoria by 1000 unemployed after the forcible expulsion of the 'sit-downers' from the Vancouver Post Office in 1938. These views neglect the thematic consistency through

which Baird created a vision of an entire society straining under tensions that could only lead to fruitless destruction. *Waste heritage* was praised when it was reissued in 2007 by the University of Ottawa Press, edited and with an introduction by Colin Hill. Baird also wrote *He rides the sky* (1941), an epistolary novel chronicling the emotions and experiences of a young man who trains as a pilot with the RAF in 1938 and is lost in battle in 1940, and *Climate of power* (1971), based on her experience of federal bureaucracy and her knowledge of the Arctic—underlying the plot are government's sincere but muddled attempts to improve Inuit culture, though in fact they destroy it.

Balconville (1980). This bilingual play by David FENNARIO was first produced in Montreal, Toronto, and Ottawa in 1979, and at London's Old Vic, to critical acclaim. The action takes place in Point Saint-Charles, Montreal, and the title refers to the name given to the working-class district where the balconies provide a dubious refuge from the stuffy, cramped apartments, and where four anglophones and four French Canadians communicate in what seems like one long quarrel: true communication is nonexistent. Prejudice, the language barrier, and the generation gap are obvious obstacles, but the real one is bitterness over the vicious circle of their lives from which there is no escape. Those who don't have work refuse to look for the kinds of menial jobs those who do have work hate. In the last lines of the play, addressed to the audience, the anglophones' question 'What are we going to do?' is echoed by the francophones' '*Qu'est-ce qu'on va faire?*' French and English are finally united in mutual despair.

Ballantyne, R. M. (1825–94). The Scottish-born writer joined the Hudson's Bay Company when he was sixteen, serving as a clerk at Fort Garry, Norway House, and York Factory until 1845, when he was transferred to posts in the Lower St Lawrence district until 1847, the year he returned home. His journals and letters provided material for his first book, *Hudson Bay; or everyday life in the wilds of North America…* (Edinburgh, 1848; rpr. 1971). With *Snowflakes and sunbeams; the young fur traders* (London, 1856)—better known as *The young fur traders*— and *Ungava* (London, 1858) he began a long and prolific career as a writer of adventure stories for boys that combined narrative skill and manly heroes in exotic settings. Ballantyne continued to exploit his experiences in the

Northwest, setting more than twenty of his 120 books in the New World. But other parts of the world provided the background for his most popular novels, which include *The coral island* (London, 1858; rpr. 1990), *Martin Rattler* (London, 1858), and *The gorilla hunters* (London, 1862).

Ballem, John (b. 1925). Born in New Glasgow, Nova Scotia, he was educated at Dalhousie University (B.A., 1946; M.A., 1948; LL.B., 1949) and Harvard Law School, where he took a post-graduate LL.M. (1950). After serving as a pilot with the Royal Navy Fleet Air Arm (1944–5) and as assistant professor of law at the University of British Columbia (1950–2), he worked in the oil industry for a decade before entering private law practice in Calgary in 1962. As a regional writer Ballem's major work is his 'Oilpatch trilogy' consisting of *Oilpatch empire* (1985), *Death spiral* (1989), and *The barons* (1991), which treat the vortex of oil, business, politics, power, and sex in Canada's oilpatch, a region Ballem knows better than any other Canadian writer. These three novels, plus *The devil's lighter* (1973), set in the Canadian Arctic, form *The oil-patch quartet* (2005). Ballem has also used his intimate knowledge of Alberta politics and the oil business in his thrillers, notably in *The dirty scenario* (1974), set in Ottawa, in which an energy crisis affecting Canada and the USA is used by the CIA to foster an annexationist plot; *The Judas conspiracy* (1976), republished as *Alberta alone* (1981), in which Alberta separates from Canada; and *The moon pool* (1978), set in the Beaufort Sea, where Inuit terrorists attempt to seize an oil rig. Ballem has also written two crime novels set in the Caribbean: *Sacrifice play* (1981) and *The Marigot run* (1984). *Manchineel* (2000), which is also set in the Caribbean, *Murder as a fine art* (2002), which takes place at the Banff Centre for the Arts, and *A murder of convenience* (2006), set in Calgary where the serial killer nicknamed TLC stalks the streets, are three 'Castle Street Mysteries'. His most important book, however, is the internationally recognized and authoritative *The oil and gas lease in Canada* (1973; 3rd edn 1999).

Barbeau, Marius (1883–1969). Born at Sainte-Marie-de-la-Beauce, Québec, the founder of modern folklore studies in Canada was educated at Université Laval (admitted to the bar in 1907) and as a Rhodes Scholar at Oxford University; he also studied in Paris at the Sorbonne and the École d'Anthropologie. In 1911 he was appointed as an anthropologist

to the National Museum of Canada, where he remained until his retirement in 1949. His major interest was folksong, and he gave the National Museum a corpus of more than 10,000 French-Canadian, Native, English, and Inuit songs. But the whole domain of the folklorist was also studied, and Barbeau was a prolific publisher of his research in countless articles and books, in English and French. His publications on Native culture included *Huron and Wyandot mythology...* (1915), *Totem poles on the Gitksan, Upper Skeena River, British Columbia* (1929), *Haida myths illustrated in argillite carvings* (1953), and *Huron-Wyandot traditional narratives in translation and Native texts* (1960). He used his knowledge of Native culture in two novels: *The downfall of Temlaham* (1928) and *Mountain Cloud* (1944). Barbeau's work on traditional French folksongs, representing the single most important corpus ever published, appeared in numerous volumes. Oxford published, and Barbeau's son-in-law Arthur Price illustrated, two collections of tales in English. The first was *The tree of dreams* (1955), which contained folk tales and legends. The twelve titles in *Les contes du gran' père sept-heures* (1950–3), written for children, led to *The golden phoenix and other French-Canadian tales* (1958, rpr. 1980), a popular children's book in which eight stories in the French series were adapted and retold by Michael Hornyansky. The recipient of many honours, Barbeau was one of the first to be named a Companion of the Order of Canada. See Laurence Nowry, *Marius Barbeau: man of mana* (1995).

Barbour, Douglas (b. 1940). Born in Winnipeg, he was educated at Acadia University (B.A., 1962), Dalhousie University (M.A., 1964), and Queen's University (Ph.D., 1976). In 1969 he joined the staff of the English department of the University of Alberta, becoming a full professor in 1982; he is now Professor Emeritus (2005–). In his first poetry collections—*A poem as long as the highway* (1971), *Land fall* (1971), and *White* (1973)—he used a free-flowing lyrical style and vibrant images to capture the nuances of western landscapes, while also introducing ideographic characters into some poems, a device carried further in *Songbook* (1973) and *He. &. She. &.* (1974). He employed sound poetry in the long narrative poem *Visions of my grandfather* (1976), but this is less evident in *Shore lines* (1979), *Stargazing* (1980), and *The harbingers* (1984), a sequence of nineteen poems that explore the archetypal significance of the three white horses of death appearing in dreams, mythology, and folklore. His poems were collected in

Visible visions: the selected poems of Douglas Barbour (1984) and *Story for a Saskatchewan night* (1990), a ten-year selection displaying the wide variety of forms Barbour has used: space is important, along with a resistance to closure. *Fragmenting body etc.* (2000), *Breath taken* (2001), and *A flame on the Spanish stairs* (2002) are more recent collections. As a literary critic Barbour is the author of *Lyric/anti-lyric: essays on contemporary poetry* (2001) and has written studies, the first three published in 1992, of four Canadian poets and their works: bp NICHOL, Daphne MARLATT, John NEWLOVE, and Michael ONDAATJE (1993).

Barfoot, Joan (b. 1946). Born and raised in Owen Sound, Ontario, she studied English at the University of Western Ontario (B.A., 1969), and from 1976 to 1994 was a reporter/editor for the *London Free Press*. She has published ten novels: *Abra* (1978, rpr. 2000), *Dancing in the dark* (1982, rpr. 1990), *Duet for three* (1985, rpr. 2003), *Family news* (1989), *Plain Jane* (1992), *Charlotte and Claudia keeping in touch* (1994), *Some things about flying* (1997), *Getting over Edgar* (1999), *Critical injuries* (2001), and *Luck* (2005). Barfoot's first novels feature women who must escape suburban domesticity in order to rediscover themselves. In *Abra* the title character abandons her comfortable lifestyle to live in isolation in a northern-Ontario cabin. *Dancing in the dark* tells the story of Edna—a housewife isolated in the suburbs, who has spent two decades keeping herself, her home, and husband in perfect condition—who is driven mad by the knowledge of her husband's affair with his secretary; this, and the desperate act it inspires, introduces the possibility of reinventing herself. *Duet for three* describes the precarious relationship of eighty-year-old Aggie and her daughter, and explores the powerful and complex bonds that unite them. *Family news* focuses on Susannah, and her reconciliations with her blood relatives and chosen family. *Plain Jane* is a dark comedy about the quiet, lonely librarian prone to elaborate fantasy whose pen-pal relationship with a wife-murdering convict creates an extended fantasy of suburban love. *Charlotte and Claude* is about two very different women who have been friends for fifty years and exchange views on love, sexuality, and aging. *Some things about flying*, a lesser novel, describes the flight across the Atlantic by two university professors who are lovers—Lila, who teaches English, and Tom, who teaches history—when one engine catches fire. The crisis, which does not end disastrously, prompts Lila's reminiscences, contacts

with other passengers, all of them uninteresting, and leads in the end to her parting from Tom. *Getting over Edgar* begins with Gwen Stone standing over the coffin of Edgar, her late husband, who had left her shortly before he was killed in a motor accident. Angry, she picks up a young bartender, David, awakens him to sexual enjoyment, and the rest of the novel is made up of the alternating stories of their subsequent lives: each has lasting meaning for the other, and the denouement, which affects them both, is both surprising and satisfying. *Critical injuries* has a more demanding and intense plot, about Isla, mother of a boy and girl by her first husband, James (who destroyed the marriage when he was arrested for molesting young women), and is very happy in her second marriage to Lyle. Once, when they want ice cream, Lyle parks in front of Goldies' Dairy Bar, Isla goes in—and is shot. Seventeen-year-old Roddy had the gun (he and friend Mike wanted to rob the store) and, alarmed when Isla suddenly appeared, let it go off; the bullet hit her spine. The novel is a detailed rendition of family relationships in the context of this and other crises, compellingly described. In the surprising final chapter, a daring conclusion, Isla (recovered down to her waist) finds herself in a state of grace. *Luck* presents ingenious variations on the theme of loss growing out of a shocking event described on the first page: Norah wakes up to find that her forty-six-year-old husband Philip Lawrence has died in his sleep. Every possible way of confronting this, and the aftermath, is explored by Norah, a painter, by Sophie, an employee (who clings to her brief affair with Phil) and less so by beautiful Beth, also part of the household: on *the first day* ('Norah screams. She leaps up.// She immediately regrets, not the leaping—who would not leap?—but the scream. It calls attention, it calls the others, she has lost the moment that was hers.'); *the second day* ('Brain cells zapped closed on the first day start popping open again, beginning the necessary, chaotic work of absorbing severe injury, adapting to fresh facts, seeking new alignments and compensating adjustments.'); *the third day*—the funeral ('Norah's eyes are locked on the plain casket, a sight that nearly knocks her to the floor. Philip is inside, right there. This is real.'). There are many recollections and incidents (Sophie takes Phil's clothes to the funeral parlour and demands that the director, Hendrik Anderson, let her see the unembalmed body privately), Norah phones Phil's first wife, Lynn (bitter though remarried with children), to tell her; Lynn turns up at the funeral with her husband and speaks (Norah responds); Sophie becomes pregnant by Hendrik and they marry happily. A year later Norah has a highly successful show of her new work; it includes three paintings of Sophie, nude (Hendrik buys them), and some of Philip. Norah's last thought is *Now what?* From the first page the novel is an authentic, clever, entertaining evolution. In 2008 Barfoot published *Exit lines*, a novel about four occupants of a retirement home—three women and a man—and their developing friendship, which is rattled when Ruth says she wants help in ending her life.

Barker's Canadian Monthly Magazine (May 1846–April 1847). Of the many pre-Confederation periodicals, this was the first whose contents were written entirely in Canada. The owner, editor, and publisher was Edward John Barker, born near London, England, in 1799. He had practised medicine before immigrating to Canada in 1832, settling in Kingston, Ontario, where he edited newspapers owned by others before beginning his own *British Whig* in 1834. *Barker's Magazine* published fiction—including the first two-thirds of J.S.Cummins' novel *Altham*—poetry, serious political articles and political satire, biographies of Canadian politicians, and reviews of books by Canadians or about Canada. Although Barker had hoped that the low price of ten shillings per annum would bring him a thousand subscribers, there were only 400, and he reluctantly ceased publication with vol. I, no. 12, at the end of the first year.

Barometer rising (1941, NCL). The protagonist of this tightly structured novel by Hugh MacLENNAN—it takes place over eight days towards the end of 1917—is Neil Macrae. He returns from the Great War in the hope of clearing himself of a false accusation of insubordination, laid by Colonel Wain, a representative of the old colonial order who happens to be his hated uncle and the father of his former sweetheart Penelope, who has another suitor, Angus Murray, though she remains faithful to Neil. The melodramatic plot unfolds against a compelling backdrop of wartime Halifax and permits frequent views of the harbour and the shipping within. When the *Imo* emerges from behind Richmond Bluff, all the characters seem to be inevitably arranged so that, after its fatal collision with the French munitions ship *Mont Blanc* and the frightful aftermath (which MacLennan witnessed as a boy), all the threads of the plot

suddenly come together in a denouement. The skilfully conveyed effects of the ships' explosions (representing the death of the old Canada), and the response as his characters survive and attempt to bring about a kind of rebirth after the cataclysm, form a parable of Canadian self-realization. With this, his first published novel, MacLennan produced a minor classic of Canadian fiction.

Barr, Robert (1850–1912). Born in Glasgow, he was taken by his family in 1854 to Canada West (Ontario) and in 1873 entered the Toronto Normal School, where he obtained a licence to teach. He was briefly a school principal before he married in 1876 and moved to Detroit, where he was a successful reporter for the *Free Press*; in 1881 he moved to London, England, to establish a weekly edition. In 1892, with Jerome K. Jerome, he founded *The Idler*, a humorous magazine for men, and went on to become a well-travelled journalist and writer who counted among his friends and acquaintances Stephen Crane, George Gissing, Henry James, Joseph Conrad, and Arthur Conan Doyle. Among his many story collections is *The triumphs of Eugene Valmont* (1906), detective stories about the delightful Valmont—seen by recent critics as a precursor to, and possibly the model for, Agatha Christie's Hercule Poirot. Barr's ear for crisp, functional dialogue, his ability to outline a situation, and his faculty for constructing, and then quickly and credibly resolving, a mystery, provide entertaining reading. See the *Selected stories of Robert Barr* (1977), edited by John Parr. Among Barr's twenty novels, *The measure of the rule* (1907, rpr. 1973) makes use of his Normal School experiences and contains some trenchant material on the education of both students and teachers, and on the social realities of Toronto boarding houses of the day. Arnold Bennett wrote in his *Journals* that Barr was 'an admirable specimen of the man of talent who makes of letters an honest trade', though he had not much, 'if any at all, feeling for literature.'

Barrington, E. See Lily Adams BECK.

Bates, Walter (1760–1842). Born in Stamford, Connecticut, he immigrated to Saint John, New Brunswick, as a Loyalist with the Spring Fleet of 1783, settling at Kingston in King's County, where he was sheriff for many years. He wrote *The mysterious stranger* (New Haven, 1817), a popular account of 'Henry Moon' (Henry More Smith), a notorious horse thief who was incarcerated in Bates' prison for a time before being pardoned and going to the United States, where he continued his criminal activities. It was also published in England under the title *Companion for Caraboo … with an introductory description of New Brunswick; and a postscript, containing some account of Caraboo, the late female imposter, at Bristol* (London, 1817)—covering the 'dreadful doings' of Smith since the appearance of the first edition. (Many other editions followed.) Bates describes, not without some admiration, the exploits of his 'hero', but explains that his book was written 'to prevent further mischiefs'. Written in a quaint, unsophisticated style, *The mysterious stranger* is an intriguing oddity in early Canadian literature and provides an insight into the rough-and-ready conditions of prisons in the early nineteenth century.

Batten, Jack (b. 1932). Born in Montreal, he graduated from the University of Toronto (B.A., 1954) and Osgoode Hall Law School (LL.B.,1957) and practised law from 1959 to 1963, when he turned his attention to writing magazine articles, and then books. He has published some forty books on sport and law, biographies (the businessman and theatre owner Ed Mirvish, the lawyer John Robinette, Tom Longboat, the Onondaga long-distance runner), and crime fiction. In the latter genre are the fast-moving novels about the Toronto criminal lawyer and jazz buff named Crang: *Crang plays the ace* (1987), *Straight no chaser* (1989), *Riviera blues* (1990), and *Blood count* (1991). Batten writes a weekly column on crime fiction for the *Toronto Star*. Among his publications since 2000 are *The Leafs* (2004), about the Toronto Maple Leafs, *The Annex: the story of a Toronto neighbourhood* (2004), and *Learned friends: a tribute to fifty remarkable Ontario advocates, 1950–2000* (2005), written for The Advocates' Society.

Bauer, Walter (1904–76). Born in Merseburg, Germany, he graduated from the teacher's college there and was a widely published author when the Nazis came to power and banned his books. Disillusioned with German attitudes, both during and after the Second World War, he immigrated in 1952 to Toronto, where he found work as a dishwasher. He attended the University of Toronto and taught in the German department from 1958 until his retirement a few months before his death. Bauer published more than seventy books in West Germany—novels, story collections, biographies, poetry, essays, and children's

books. In the last years of his life he wrote in English. Henry BEISSEL translated two collections of Bauer's lyric poetry: *The price of morning* (1968) and *A different sun* (1976). In much of his poetry Bauer explored the experience of the immigrant who, in the New World, craves the Old.

Beauchemin, Yves (b. 1941). Born in Noranda, Québec, he attended elementary school in Clova, Abitibi, before moving to Joliette, where he completed his 'cours classique' at the Séminaire. In 1965 he obtained his Licence ès lettres from the Université de Montréal. After teaching for a while and working for the Bibliothèque générale of the Université de Montréal, he worked for the book publisher Holt, Rinehart and Winston from 1967 to 1969, when he went to Radio-Québec. Among his novels translated into English, the best known is *Le matou* (1981), which has been translated into fifteen languages; the English translation, *The alley cat* (1986, rpr. 1994, NCL), is by Sheila FISCHMAN. It is a fast-paced story of fantasy and adventure. Florent Boisonneault, little thinking his action will disrupt his whole life, helps a man knocked senseless by a bronze quotation mark that has fallen from a sign. He soon receives a bizarre invitation from a witness to the accident, Egon Ratablavsky, who insists on meeting him. Later, little by little, Ratablavsky reveals a mysterious, diabolical plan. Warmly received in both Canada and France, this extraordinary novel was considered one of the best ever written in Québec and its author one of the most gifted storytellers to emerge at the time in French-language literature. *Juliette Pomerleau* (1989), translated by Fischman as *Juliette* (1995), is a long Dickensian novel about the fifty-seven-year-old landlady of a Montreal apartment building (she is also an accountant) and its eccentric tenants, including a photographer, a composer, a violinist, and a dentist, among others; there is also a search for Juliette's niece, Adèle, who has disappeared, and Juliette's relationship with Adèle's son Denis, whom she has raised. The city of Montreal and the obliteration of some of its urban landscape, music, and friendships are all important elements in this impressive novel. The hero of *Le second violon* (1996), translated by David Homel as *The second fiddle* (1998), is also middle-aged, though younger than Juliette. Nicolas Rivard is forty-five, happily married with children, but his career as a journalist has become flat and meaningless, and he wants to change his life. The death of his friend, an important Québécois writer, and Rivard's unwilling connection with a political scandal, the Robidaux Affair, bring about this change in a typically adroit and highly readable Beauchemin narrative of relationships and events. *Charles the bold: the dog years* (2006, rpr. 2007)—the excellent translation by Wayne Grady of *Charles le Téméraire: un temps de chien* (2004)—is the first volume of a trilogy, beginning with Charles Thibodeau's birth (in 1966) on the first page and taking him up to the age of twelve, when he is leaving elementary school. His 'natural gift for happiness', and exceptional intelligence and verbal fluency for a boy of his age (he is a great reader), were tested by a sequence of surprising, but plausible, hard-to-bear events, beginning with the death of his beloved mother when he was four and his father Wilfrid's descent into alcoholism and brutality (only his dog Boff gave him love, and remained with him). Chance brought him in touch with neighbours, Fernand and Lucie Fafard, who fell in love with him, nurtured him, and took him into their family (Fernand paid Wilfrid $5000), which included their son and daughter, Henri and Céline. Fending for himself much of the time, Charles is often faced with untoward episodes—for some of which he creatively found 'his means of revenge'. The climax is provided by the return of Charles's father from northern Québec—he appears on the Fafards' doorstep, as crazily demanding and threatening as ever—but all ends well. East-end Montreal in the sixties and seventies, and the political changes in Québec at the time, recur repeatedly and effectively in the background of this rich novel that smoothly narrates a multitude of events and human responses, concerning both children and their elders. Volume 2, *The years of fire* (2007, rpr. 2008), Wayne Grady's translation of the second half of *Un temps de chien*, takes Charles through high school to the age of seventeen. He excels in his studies; continues to read, particularly Balzac; contends with the fact that Fernand's hardware business is failing; with the horrible reappearance of Wilfrid, his father; with the fire that failed to destroy Fernand's store (Charles suspects Wilfrid set it); and his attempt to pay Wilfrid off by earning money making deliveries for a drug pusher. In the midst of all this he discovers sex, decides he wants to be a writer and works all night on a story, and falls in love with Céline (who has always loved him). Québec politics appears in the form of the first referendum, for which Fernand worked faithfully for the YES faction. The great René Lévesque visits his hardware store to thank him, and Charles shakes his hand—a great moment. The final words of the novel are: 'Montreal! You're going to be hearing from me! I'm going to make your ears ring!' Volume 3 of the trilogy, *A very bold leap* (2009)—Grady's translation of *Charles le téméraire: un saut dans le vide* (2009)—is an often hilarious account of Charles's first attempt to become a published writer and the jobs he takes afterwards.

Beaulieu, Michel (1941–85). Born in Montreal, he was educated at the Université de Montréal and became one of Québec's leading avant-garde poets, publishing some thirty titles. Three of his collections are available in English. The bulimia that took hold of Beaulieu in 1977 did not end until the publication in the year of his death of *Kaléidoscope: ou les aléas du corps grave* (1985), translated by Arlette Francière as *Kaleidoscope: perils of a solemn body* (1988), in which the 'you' is the poet speaking to himself. But the poetic line is so close to prose that the reader continually feels challenged by that voice, which seems so close and familiar, despite the detachment it proclaims. Other collections in English translation are *Spells of fury / Charmes de la fureur* (1984, rpr. 2003), a bilingual edition with translations by Francière, and *Countenances* (1986), a translation by Josée Michaud of *Visages* (1981, GGA).

Beaulieu, Victor-Lévy (b. 1945). Born in Saint-Jean-de-Dieu, near Rimouski, Québec, he added Victor to his given name for Victor Hugo, whose creative force and mythopoeic imagination he sought to emulate. He has constantly been in the forefront of Québec's literary development, opening a bookstore and publishing from it between 1976 and 1984 his own Éditions VLB. The quality of the books produced, his own among them, set new standards in Québec publishing. Largely self-taught, he is among the most prolific of Québec writers, producing well over forty titles to the present, among which only six are available in English. His considerable achievement is in creating convincing portraits of characters on the fringes of normality and psychological viability; he does this with an air of acceptance and even approval that makes them not unsympathetic. The influence of others who have explored through literature the shadowlands of derangement and alienation—such as Jack Kerouac, Malcolm LOWRY, and Réjean DUCHARME—is clear. The title and themes of *Don Quichotte de la démanche* (1974, GGA), which play on physical and mental deformity, sum up this aspect of this work. It was translated by Sheila FIS-CHMAN as *Don Quixote in Nighttown* (1978). (Beaulieu wrote about Kerouac in *Jack Kerouac: essai-poulet* (1972), translated by Fischman as *Jack Kerouac: chicken-essay* (1975), which explores the links between writing, criticism, appetite, and consumption.) Other novels available in English are *The grandfathers* (1975), translated by Marc Plourde, *A Québécois dream* (1979), *Jos connaissant* (1982, rpr. 1993), *Satan Belhumeur* (1984), and *Steven Le Hérault* (1987), all translated by Raymond Chamberlain.

Beausoleil, Claude (b. 1948). Born in Montreal, he was educated at Collège Sainte-Marie (Université de Montréal), the Université du Québec à Montréal, and the Université de Sherbrooke, where he received a Ph.D. in literary studies, and since 1973 has been professor of Québécois literature at Collège Édouard-Montpetit (Longueuil). Beausoleil has had an extremely prolific career as poet, critic, essayist, and translator, with more than forty publications to his credit. *Concrete city: selected poems 1972–82* (1983) is a bilingual edition containing poems translated by Ray Chamberlin from eight collections. His highly experimental work of the 1970s developed a poetics of dislocation and prized multiplicity of meaning. The big city, especially Montreal, has been painstakingly inscribed in his work from the 1980s onward, which is characterized by an intense self-questioning of his identity as a Québécois poet. He defines the central paradox of his identity as a tear through the stomach of language, for the language of America is not his own, even though America's culture informs his sense of self. Other collections available in English are *The Grand Hotel of foreigners* (1998), a bilingual edition translated by Jed English and George Morrissette, and *Life in the singular: selected poems 1993–1999* (2004), translated by Daniel Sloate.

Beautiful Joe (Philadelphia, 1894; rpr. 1994). Subtitled *An autobiography* and narrated by a dog, this very popular novel for children by Marshall SAUNDERS was designed to arouse for dogs the kind of sympathy stirred for horses by *Black Beauty* (1877; first American publication 1890). Joe's life story moves from puppy days with a brutal owner to happy times with the kind Miss Laura and the Morris family. Though unashamedly sentimental and didactic—Joe supports the views of Miss Laura and her friends on temperance, mannerliness, and worship—the novel's quick succession of exciting incidents and the sense of a likeable voice made this 'fine tale of an ugly dog' a worldwide bestseller. A 1994 reprint marked its centenary.

Beautiful losers (1966, NCL; rpr. 2004). Leonard COHEN's second novel was a publishing sensation that combined experimental novel-writing with no-holds-barred sex. Many reviewers were baffled, but it was seen, correctly, by others (those who did not damn it as being pornographic) as brilliant, an anarchic wonder very much in tune with its own decade, that of the beats, readers of Allen Ginsberg and Jack Kerouac. Academics, in some cases attempting to reduce the puzzlement, found in it an inexhaustible source of intricate explications and metaphorical meanings. The huge numbers of readers, however, were content to let the disordered text—its events, ideas, rhetorical excess, and fantasy—wash over them, to 'watch *how it happens*', caring little about overall meaning. Cohen, in a letter, described it as 'a long confessional prayer attempting to establish itself on the theme of the life of a saint'. *Beautiful losers* is without plot or coherent narrative, and the concept of time plays an insignificant part in it. But it is a rich amalgam of historical narrative, grotesque incidents, politics, religion, emotional epiphanies, and sexual fixations, punctuated with flights into prose poetry. Its topics include the Mohawks, torture, Canadian history, Québec separatism, ancient Greece, Montreal in the 1960s, sex, sainthood, and two religions—of the spirit and the flesh. The first of the novel's three books, 'The history of them all', is a long cascade of events and ideas that begins by identifying the four characters and their fates: Catherine (Kateri) Tekakwitha (1656–80), whose actual life is described in detail, is a virginal Mohawk who is baptized and becomes associated with miracles, and with sainthood (beatified in 1980, she is not yet a saint); the narrator, an anglophone anthropologist obsessed with Tekakwitha, who turns himself into a disciple and ends up a raddled old man living in a treehouse; he was the husband of Edith, an Aboriginal he married when she was sixteen (like all Cohen's women, a sex object), who is dead, having been killed seated at the bottom of an elevator shaft; F. is the narrator's francophone lover who describes himself as 'a born teacher'. The mystical universe for the 1960s that is created in *Beautiful losers* is constructed from a playful but passionate exploration of the expansion of consciousness and involves, among other things, the disintegration of character—except for that of Tekakwitha, who is on her way to sainthood.

Beck, Lily Adams (1862?–1931). The daughter of the British admiral John Moresby, she spent many years in the Orient and travelled widely before settling in Victoria, British Columbia, in 1919, the year she began her career as a writer of more than thirty books. As a popular novelist, writing under the name E. Barrington, she wrote historical romances, including *The divine lady: a romance of Nelson and Emma Hamilton* (1924), which became a silent film, and *The duel of queens: a romance of Mary, Queen of Scots* (1930), which had a great popular success. Under her own name she published collections of stories and other books rooted in Oriental philosophy and traditions.

Bedard, Michael (b. 1949). Born in Toronto, he was educated at the University of Toronto (B.A., 1971). He worked for a time in the university library, then as a pressman in a small print shop, publishing his first books, both collections of original fairy tales: *Woodsedge and other tales* (1979) and *Pipe and pearls: a gathering of tales* (1980). They were followed by *The lightning bolt* (1989), based on the Grimms' 'The fisherman and his wife', and retellings of two of Hans Christian Andersen's tales, *The tinder box* (1990) and *The nightingale* (1991). Other picture books—about famous authors and all published in 1997—are *Emily* (about Emily Dickinson), *Glass town* (about the Brontës as children), and *The divide* (about Willa Cather). *The clay ladies* (1999) features the Toronto sculptors Frances Loring and Florence Wyle, who lived in a converted church in Toronto. *The wolf of Gubbio* (2000) is based on one of the stories associated with St Francis of Assisi. The fairy tale's influence on his novels *A darker magic* (1987), *Redwork* (1990, rpr. 1996, GGA), and *Painted devil* (1994) expresses itself primarily in the clarity of Bedard's images and settings and in his mingling of fantasy and realism: he sees eternity folded in with time, dream and reality as interrelated, and the imagination as a catalyst for both good and evil. Both *A darker magic* and *Painted devil*, its sequel, combine realism, horror, and mystery in their examination of a young girl's chilling encounter with darkness as it is embodied in Professor Mephisto, a magician, whose spell is broken only by the movement of the potential victim from a state of passive observation to a state of creative action and resistance. The technically impressive *Redwork* uses Blake's visionary poetry and the second stage in alchemy—redwork—as guiding metaphors of artistic activity, involving, among other things, reconnection with one's youth as a means towards self-enlightenment. Bedard's general subject matter embraces the past and the present, lower-middle-class life, early adolescence, and the special relationship between the old and the young. His novels for young people, while challenging and intricate, are compelling. In *Stained glass* (2001) George Berkeley, who as a boy had apprenticed to the glass craftsmen at Canterbury Cathedral in England, is washing the outside of the windows of St Bartholomew's Church in Caledon (Ontario?) when the ladder's feet began to sink into the soil and the ladder crashes into one of the stained-glass windows, creating a shower of coloured glass particles. Inside the church young Charles Endicott, skipping a piano lesson, hears the crash and sees a girl lying under the window. His relationship with the mysterious, otherworldly Ambriel, and glass, particularly coloured glass, are central elements of this substantial, challenging novel.

The painted wall and other strange tales (2003) is a delightful collection of stories adapted from some of the many stories retold in the seventeenth century by Pu Sung-ling in his collection whose title translates as *Strange tales from a studio of leisure*—the most popular collection of stories in Chinese history.

Beissel, Henry (b. 1929). Born in Cologne, Germany, he studied philosophy at the universities of Cologne and London before coming to Canada in 1951. He received his M.A. in English (1960) from the University of Toronto; taught at the University of Alberta, Edmonton, where he founded the magazine *EDGE*; and is now Distinguished Emeritus Professor of English, Concordia University, Montreal, whose English faculty he joined in 1966. He is a prolific author of poetry collections, plays, and poetry translations. Beissel's strong conviction about the necessity to ground one's life in the pursuit of artistic truth is apparent in *New wings for Icarus* (1966), a long poem in four parts. His first book of shorter poems was *Face in the dark* (1970), though this volume still demonstrates an emphasis on making larger poetic statements, as it also contains parts of longer uncompleted poems. Later collections include *Cantos north* (1982), 'an epic poem about Canada in twelve cantos', *Season of blood: a suite of poems* (1985), the first book in a cycle intended to represent 'a quest for an understanding of the point humanity has reached today in its turbulent development as the dominating species on this planet.' *Across the sun's warp* (2003), the sixth volume, is one long poem and marks the first use of an atomic bomb. Other volumes are *Poems new and selected* (1987), *Dying I was born* (1992), and

Stones to harvest (1993), and *The dragon and the pearl* (2002), which grew out of a six-week lecture tour of China; it is illustrated by Arlette Francière, his wife. Beissel's plays have often focused on Canadian themes and cultures, especially in *Inook and the sun* (1973), a play for young people about the Inuit that was staged at the Stratford Festival in 1973; in 2000 it was reissued in a bilingual edition as *Inuk and the sun/Inuk et le soleil*, translated by Arlette Francière. Another play with a Native subject is *Under Coyote's eye: a play about Ishi* (1979).

Beissel was a friend of the brilliant, troubled, self-destructive Edward LACEY, a poet, and wrote an illuminating introduction to *A magic prison: letters from Edward Lacey* (1995)—the letters are to Beissel.

Belaney, Archibald Stansfeld (1888–1938) wrote under the name Grey Owl. Brought up by two aunts in Hastings, England, he dreamed and read of North America's Native peoples as a child and at eighteen, in 1906, immigrated to Canada and became a guide and packer in northern Ontario, and then joined a band of Ojibwa on Lake Temagami. In 1910 he married an Ojibwa girl and came under the influence of the band, living and hunting with them. He went through a ceremony of adoption and was given the name Grey Owl. After being wounded in the Great War, he returned to Canada as a guide and trapper in the Mississauga River country, and resumed his Grey Owl identity. His life changed in 1926 when he met Anahareo, an Iroquois girl with whom he had a passionate though stormy love affair, and who was horrified by his bloody trade as a trapper and persuaded him to save and bring into their cabin two baby beaver. Their affectionate behaviour and childlike ways made Grey Owl vow never again to take the life of another beaver. He and Anahareo went to Cabano, in northern Québec, to found a colony for the preservation of the species. The couple and their charges were discovered by the Canadian government in 1930. Grey Owl was appointed Honorary Park Warden and a home was built for him and his beaver at Lake Ajawan in Prince Albert National Park, Saskatchewan. At Cabano, Grey Owl had turned to writing to support his adopted 'family', and in 1931 published *The men of the last frontier*, about the simple life as it was lived when he first came under the tutelage of the Ojibwa and listened to their legends, and *Pilgrims of the wild* (1934), about his and Anahareo's journey to Cabano, which was published in England by Lovat

Dickson Limited and established his fame as a writer. (This resulted, in 1935–6 and 1937–8, in two highly successful lecture tours of the United States and Britain, ending with a lecture before the Royal Family at Buckingham Palace.) Two other books followed: *The adventures of Sajo and her beaver people* (1935), written for children, and *Tales of an empty cabin* (1936, rpr. 2005), an impressive collection of sketches of men and animals in a forest world, full of humour and close, affectionate observation. See Anahareo's *Devil in deerskin* (1972); Lovat DICKSON's biography, *Wilderness man* (1971); Donald B. Smith, *From the land of shadow: the making of Grey Owl* (1990); Armand Garnet Ruffo, *Grey Owl: the mystery of Archie Belaney* (1997); and Jane Billinghurst, *The many faces of Archie Belaney* (1999), an illustrated biography.

Belles-soeurs, Les (1974; rev. edn 1992). The translation by John Van Burek and Bill Glassco of a major turning point in modern Québécois theatre by Michel TREMBLAY, bears the same title (English translation: *The sisters-in-law*) in both the English and French (1968) editions. The play's first English-language production, in Toronto in 1973, was followed by productions—and revivals—in many other Canadian cities and in the USA. A poor woman, Germaine Lauzon, wins a million trading stamps and decides to give 'a stamp-pasting party' for fifteen women (only one an actual sister-in-law). They eventually steal the stamps and the play ends in an uproar. The party is a vehicle for the women to voice their social and sexual deprivations; in so doing they realize how short-lived their dreams of a better life are, how useless their rebellion. Though it frequently provokes laughter, this pessimistic drama is justly seen as a realistic depiction of the working class in Montreal, and of the conditions of women—figures of Québec's destiny simmering in revolt. A true (and perhaps necessary) metaphor for national alienation, *Les belles-soeurs* remains a landmark as a formally innovative play. The choruses and monologues that structure it express collective solitudes; and its diction (JOUAL in French)—which is used poetically, not realistically—is the language of visceral, spontaneous, and apparently disordered lamentations. Under the title *Belles-Soeurs* director René Richard Cyr and composer Daniel Bélanger presented, in April–May 2010, a well-received musical version, in which there are fifteen songs and the text has been shortened by more than half.

Benson, Eugene (b. 1928). He was born in Larne, Northern Ireland, and graduated from the National University of Ireland (B.A., 1950) and Teachers Training College, Belfast (1952). In 1954 he immigrated to Canada, where, following teaching in Saskatchewan and at the NATO Language School in London, Ontario, he did post-graduate work at the University of Western Ontario (M.A., 1958) and the University of Toronto (Ph.D., 1966, thesis supervisors were Northrop FRYE and Marshall McLUHAN). From 1965 to 1993 he taught at the University of Guelph, and was elected University Professor Emeritus in 1994. A former chair of the WRITERS' UNION OF CANADA (1983–4), he was founding co-president (with Margaret ATWOOD) in 1984 of the Canadian Centre, International PEN. He is the author of two novels. *The bulls of Ronda* (1976), about a young Canadian writer who becomes involved in the political tensions of Fascist Spain in the 1960s, is at once a political commentary, a love story, and a spy novel. *Power game* (1980) is a satire on Canadian politics and a comic examination of the power (and corruption) that surrounds the office of the prime minister of Canada. Benson has also written the libretti for four operas (composer, Charles Wilson): *Héloïse and Abelard* (Canadian Opera Company, 1973), *The Summoning of Everyman* (Stratford Festival, 1974), *Psycho Red* (Guelph Spring Festival, 1978), and *Earnest, the importance of being* (2008, composer Victor Davies). With L.W. Conolly (who co-authored with him *English-Canadian theatre*, 1987) Benson co-edited *The Oxford companion to Canadian theatre* (1989) and the *Encyclopedia of post-colonial literatures in English* (1994; 2nd edn 2005), and with William Toye *The Oxford companion to Canadian literature: second edition* (1997).

Beresford-Howe, Constance (b. 1922). Born in Montreal and educated at McGill University and Brown University, Rhode Island (Ph.D., 1950), she taught English literature and creative writing at McGill and at Ryerson Polytechnical Institute, Toronto, retiring in 1988. While living in Montreal she wrote four novels that explore the emotional lives of young women: *The unreasoning heart* (1946); *Of this day's journey* (1947); *The invisible gate* (1949); and *My Lady Greensleeves* (1955), set in sixteenth-century England and based on a documented Elizabethan lawsuit—all displaying a fluid and natural prose style suitable to Beresford-Howe's realist agenda. After settling in Toronto in 1971, she wrote the first of three critically acknowledged and popular novels that portray the day-to-day lives of contemporary women. *The book of Eve* (1973, rpr. 2001), the most successful, is about a spirited middle-class woman who suddenly, at the age of sixty-five, decides to leave her ailing and demanding husband and live as she pleases. (A successful stage adaptation, *Eve*, by Larry FINEBERG, was produced at the Stratford Festival in 1976.) In *A population of one* (1976, rpr. 2002) a sheltered thirty-year-old virgin leaves Toronto to teach in Montreal and discovers that casual love affairs are neither as easy to come by nor as desirable as she had thought. *The marriage bed* (1981, rpr. 2002) describes a few weeks in the life of a young woman with two pre-school children, and eight months pregnant, whose lawyer husband has left her, yet she continues to affirm the values and pleasures of motherhood. With wry humour these novels challenge largely uncontested ideas of their time concerning women and female identity. Irony and the courage to carry on also characterize Beresford-Howe's later fiction: *Night studies* (1985), about the lives of fourteen hapless characters at a dismal Toronto college whose concentric corridors are explicitly Dantean; *Prospero's daughter* (1988), with its English manor-house setting, about a celebrated Canadian expatriate and his manipulation of his daughter into a conventional marriage; and *A serious widow* (1991, rpr. 1993), which portrays an initially incompetent and impoverished Toronto widow who moves towards independence and self-realization.

Bergen, David (b. 1957) was born in Port Edward, British Columbia, becoming part of a large Mennonite family (he had five siblings). When he was six his school-teacher father moved his family to Manitoba, where he taught in Niverville. David Bergen himself taught high school for several years after graduating from the University of Winnipeg. Producing a large family of his own—he has four children—he balanced this responsibility not only with teaching but with writing. His first highly praised fictions led him to concentrate on writing, whose notable qualities are clarity of expression, the easy combination of natural dialogue and quotidian domesticity, and sensuous descriptions of (joyless?) erotic moments. Bergen's first book was *Sitting opposite my brother* (1993), a collection of eleven stories, four of which appeared in *The Journey prize anthology*. The title story, narrated by Thomas, is about his brother Timothy (introduced in an earlier story called 'Where you're from' as a Mennonite missionary on leave from Indonesia) and his Guyanese wife June. Thomas and his wife are visiting them for the Easter weekend at Whistler, British Columbia. He is attracted to June, though nothing is said. Towards the end of the story, when 'I was sitting opposite my brother', playing chess, Timothy suddenly says: 'June's leaving me. She told me when we were dressing for supper.'

Of Bergen's novels, *A year of Lesser* (1996) is about people who live in or near the small Manitoba town of Lesser. Johnny Fehr is a well-meaning but ineffectual man, a feed salesman who also runs a Friday- and Saturday-night drop-in centre 'for kids who had nowhere to go'; highly conscious of sin, he is baptized twice in an evangelical church. Charlene is his wife, whom he loves, and Loraine Wallace is his mistress, whom he also loves and who has a baby by him—the women accept this three-way relationship, unwillingly. Loraine's teenaged son Chris is also prominent. Suffering various losses, Johnny by the end of the novel is reduced to living in a tent. Loraine, who had asked him to leave her, finds him. '"You poor thing," she whispers. "You shouldn't have to live like this." "It's good for me," Johnny says.' On the first page of *See the child* (1999) Paul Unger learns from the town constable that his alienated teenaged son Stephen has died. 'He was lying face down in Hiebert's field.... Drowned himself in the mud.' Grief and guilt take over Paul's life and destroy his marriage—he retreats to his farm, where he keeps bees—until three years later Nicole, Stephen's girlfriend, turns up with a baby, his grandson Sky, with whom he bonds. The wayward Nicole comes and goes, attached to one man after another—including Daniel, the husband of Paul's daughter Sue—and ends up in Montana, with the unsavoury Wyatt, a lumberjack. Paul goes there, invited by Nicole, hoping to acquire Sky, but the reunion ends disastrously. The long Nicole episode is relieved occasionally by (gratuitous) passages on beekeeping and by Paul's contacts with others in his life, including his wife Lise and his daughter Sue (no longer married to Daniel), who has a boyfriend, the apparently admirable Chris, Loraine's son in *A year of Lesser*.

Teaching in Winnipeg, Bergen once pulled a teenaged girl off the railing of the Maryland Bridge, over the Assiniboine River. She was angry and struggled, but he pinned her down and saved her from suicide. This event is echoed in *The case of Lena S.* (2002, rpr. 2003). More precocious verbally, socially, and sexually than any sixteen- and seventeen-year-olds one has encountered are Mason Crowe and his beloved Lena Schellendal, 'bright and haughty and all-knowing'—and suicidal. 'Last night she wrote in her journal, "It is either him [Mason] or no one at all."' Once, conflicted after seeing his mother with her lover, Mason is led away by Lena, who says, '"You're so lovely." She pushed her tongue deep into his startled mouth and only later did he realize that that was how it would always be, she would decide what was good and fair and dirty and raw and ugly and lovely and he, he would nod and say, Yes.' Typically for Bergen, this leads to no happy ending—only to acceptance. In 1996 Bergen with his family flew to Vietnam as a Mennonite volunteer to teach English with his wife at a teachers' college in Quang Ngai. Difficulties brought an end to this and they moved to Danang, where they stayed for six months. The experience informed and enriched *The time in between* (2005, rpr. 2006). Central to this novel is eighteen-year-old Charles Boatman's time as a soldier in Vietnam when he unnecessarily shot and killed a Vietnamese boy—and his return twenty-eight years later, hoping 'to conclude an event in his life that had consumed him.' In between were his settling in British Columbia, his marriage and eventual widowhood, and his raising three children: Ada, who adores her father; Jon, whose life as a homosexual is only hinted at; and Del, who lives happily with Tomas Manik, a painter and sculptor the same age as her father. Ada and Jon, losing track of their father, fly to Vietnam to try to find him. Ada is persistent, tracking down leads, some of them false, until she is finally told about her father's end. She is given a suitcase that contains a letter from Charles to his children. 'He said that he had imagined coming back to this place and solving some mystery, that then he would understand what had happened to him. But it was not the same place. Oh, the streets were familiar and he recognized certain buildings, and the landscape, but everything else had vanished. All the inside things, the things he felt when he was an eighteen-year-old, twas gone.' A few striking Vietnamese characters, and aspects of the culture and beauty of Vietnam, are brought to life when Charles returns, and later when Ada spends time there. The novel made a strong, favourable impression and won the GILLER PRIZE. In 2008 Bergen published *The retreat*, set in 1974 at the time of the Ojibwa occupation of Anicinabe Park in Kenora, Ontario. It maintains several strands involving Raymond Seymour, an eighteen-year-old Ojibwa; Lizzy Bird, whose disturbed family joins a commune called The Retreat and falls in love with Raymond (disastrously); and the Ojibwas' protest at the Park. In 2009 Bergen won the WRITER'S TRUST Notable Author Award ($25,000).

Berger, Carl (b. 1939). Born in The Pas, Manitoba, he was educated at the University of Manitoba (B.A., 1961) and the University of Toronto (M.A., 1962; Ph.D., 1967), where he studied under Maurice CARELESS. He was appointed there in 1964 and is a professor of history. Berger's inquiries into intellectual history have deepened the understanding of the Canadian past and pointed towards new sophistication in historiography. *The sense of power: studies in the ideas of Canadian imperialism, 1867–1914* (1970) appeared at a time when Canadians were fiercely debating American influence, and argued that British imperialism had evolved in Canada as a form of Canadian nationalism. Free from previous preoccupations that had infested former inquiries when the subject was hotly contested in the political arena, Berger's work added a new dimension to historical scholarship in revealing the complicated roles that ideas play in history. Turning next to the output of his colleagues, Berger wrote the landmark work, *The writing of Canadian history: aspects of English-Canadian historical writing since 1900* (1976, GGA; 2nd edn 1986), the first in-depth analysis of how earlier historians had understood the past. Evoking the principal themes that had governed intellectual output while analyzing the country's major historians, Berger cast a mirror on an academic discipline that had been little prone to introspection. In *Science, God, and nature in Victorian Canada* (1983) he examined the intricate interplay between scientific inquiry and religion; but in *Honour and the search for influence: a history of the Royal Society of Canada* (1996) he went on to portray the difficulties that intellectuals have in fulfilling ideals.

Bersianik, Louky (b. 1930). Born Lucille Durand in Montreal, she studied French literature at the Université de Montréal, and then at the Sorbonne and the Centre d'études de radio et de télévision, Paris, where she lived for five years. She has worked as a writer and researcher for radio, television, and cinema, and taught creative writing at Concordia University, Montreal, and the Université du Québec à Montréal. Using the name Louky Bersianik, she published *L'Euguélionne* (1976)—translated by Howard Scott as *The Euguelion* (1996)—a ground-breaking feminist novel combining allegory and parable, and parody, that became an immediate bestseller. It is the story of a 'sister [Euguelion] from another planet' who has come to earth in search of the 'male of her species'. The Euguelion ('the bearer of good news', from the same Greek roots as 'evangelist', plus a feminized ending that makes the character a lioness) is a female Christ figure who discovers the bizarre state of relations between the sexes in our world, and in the process demystifies, deconstructs, satirizes, and lampoons the mythologies and conventions of human male-female relations. 'To resist is good', she proclaims, 'to transgress is better.' The Euguelion denounces sexism in language and literature and the discourses of Western philosophical tradition, and satirically demolishes Freudian and Lacanian psychology. She urges women to seize language, shape it to their needs, and write themselves into history.

Berton, Pierre (1920–2004). Pierre Francis de Marigny Berton was born in Whitehorse, Yukon, and spent the first twelve years of his life in Dawson City. (In 1995 he purchased the house where he lived, donated it to the Yukon Arts Council, and as Berton House it is a haven for writers; it is now administered by the Writers' Trust of Canada.) He was educated at the University of British Columbia (B.A., 1941), and was made city editor of the Vancouver *News-Herald* in 1942. After service in the Second World War, he joined *Maclean's*, becoming its managing editor (1952–8), and was then, until 1962, associate editor of the *Toronto Star* and a columnist who never feared to address controversial subjects. The author of fifty books, about half of which were in print in 2007, he has been credited with being the first writer to popularize Canadian history on a large scale, and with defining the Canadian identity (*Why we act like Canadians*, 1987). Berton was a well-known figure in radio and on television, particularly as a panelist on CBC's 'Front Page Challenge' for more than twenty-five years. The recipient of numerous awards and honorary degrees, he was made a Companion of the Order of Canada in 1986.

The mysterious North (1956, GGA)—reprinted as *The mysterious North: encounters with the Canadian frontier 1947–1954* (1989)—is a vivid description of the Canadian North and an appraisal of its potential, and *Klondike: the last great gold rush, 1896–1899* (1958, GGA; rev. 1972; rpr. 2001; American title *Klondike fever*) dramatically recreates the gaudy personalities who, from 1896 to 1903, were attracted to the Klondike by lust for gold. *The Klondike quest: a photographic essay 1897–1899* (1983, rpr. 2005)—visually impressive in a large format—is one of many picture books for which Berton wrote the text. He returned to the North in *The*

Arctic grail: the quest for the North West Passage and the North Pole 1818–1909 (1989, rpr. 2001). His most impressive achievement is his two-volume history of the Canadian Pacific Railway: *The national dream: the great railway 1871–1881* (1970, rpr. 2001) and *The last spike: the great railway 1881–1885* (1971, rpr. 2001, GGA)—abridged as *The great railway* (1992). His much-enjoyed gift for anecdotal history was also evident in *The invasion of Canada, 1812–13* (1980, rpr. 2001), *Flames across the border, 1813–1814* (1981, rpr. 2001), and *Vimy* (1986, rpr. 2001), which include vivid descriptions of battle and details of military history. *My country: the remarkable past* (1976, rpr. 2002) contains eighteen great Canadian stories told with Berton's usual narrative skill. Popular subjects have engaged Berton's interest: for example, *Hollywood's Canada: the Americanization of our national image* (1975); *The Dionne years: a thirties melodrama* (1977, rpr. 1992), about the Dionne quintuplets and the public phenomenon that followed their birth; and *The Great Depression 1929–1939* (1990, rpr. 2001). His extensive bibliography includes collections of his columns—such as *Worth repeating: a literary resurrection* (1998, rpr. 1999), including mostly newspaper and magazine pieces from 1948 to 1994; the texts for picture books, including *The Great Lakes* (1996), *Seacoasts* (1998), and *Pierre Berton's Canada: the land and the people* (1999); children's books, among them *The secret world of Og* (1961; rev. 1991; rpr. 2002); and memoirs: *Starting out: the days of my youth, 1920–1947* (1987, rpr. 1993) and *My times: living with history, 1947–1995* (1995, rpr. 1996).

Among Berton's last books were *Marching as to war: Canada's turbulent years, 1899–1953* (2001, rpr. 2002) about four wars—from the Boer to the Korean—in which Canada was involved, all but one described by Berton as unnecessary and wasteful of Canadian lives. *The joy of writing: a guide for writers, disguised as a literary memoir* (2003) is, as one would expect, helpful and knowledgeable—and entertainingly anecdotal—with such chapter titles as 'The Joy of Research', 'Digging Deep', and 'Storytelling'. *Prisoners of the North* (2004, rpr. 2005) is a very readable study of five people whose lives were shaped in various ways by the North: Joe Boyle, Lady Jane Franklin, Vilhjamur Stefansson, John Hornby, and Robert SERVICE.

See *Pierre Berton* (2008) by A.B. McKillop. In 1994 the Hudson's Bay Company founded Canada's National History Society to maintain its popular magazine *The Beaver*, and the Society immediately established an award to recognize excellence in popular history.

Pierre Berton was the first recipient and later in 1994 he agreed to have the award named after him. *For the love of history: celebrating the winners of the Pierre Berton Award* (2005) is an anthology of book extracts by the winners, including Berton himself and James H. GRAY, Peter C. NEWMAN, Charlotte GRAY, and J.L. GRANATSTEIN.

Bessette, Gérard (1920–2005). Born on a farm near Sainte-Anne-de-Sabrevois, Québec, he spent his early childhood in the village of Saint-Alexandre before moving to Montreal in 1930. He was educated at the Université de Montréal, obtaining a Master's degree in 1946 and a Ph.D. in 1950. From 1946 he taught at Canadian and American universities until he went to Queen's University, Kingston, where he taught from 1960 to 1979, when he began to devote his time entirely to writing. In his many novels, for which he won two Governor General's Awards, Bessette has made a major contribution to the exploration of the inner life of Québécois, showing not only the Québécois 'choirboy' in the process of becoming a Freudian, but that the ego can emerge in spite of a condition of orphanhood—the orphanhood of liberation. His first novel, *La bagarre* (1958)—translated by Mark Lebel as *The brawl* (1976)—examines three aspects of French Canada and describes the problems that confront students—three types of student, three failures: Jules Lebeuf, who hopes to become a writer and goes out with a waitress who hardly interests him, eventually opts for trade unionism; Sillery, a homosexual, chooses exile and the study of anthropology and colonialism; the American Weston plans the study of French Canadians for his thesis but abandons this in favour of journalism. *Le libraire* (1960)—translated by Glen Shortliffe as *Not for every eye* (1962, rpr. 1999)—is a witty satire on book censorship in the Duplessis era. Hervé Jodoin, after losing his job as college proctor, becomes a cynical, depressed country librarian, but once again breaks the rules and loses his job for having sold a censored book to a student. The novel attacks the hypocrisy of a situation that could be saved only by a 'quiet revolution'. *L'incubation* (1965, GGA), translated by Shortliffe as *Incubation* (1967, rpr. 1986), is important in modern Québec fiction for its exploration of the depths of the human psyche—symbolized by the labyrinthine basements of the library where the narrator Legarde works—and for its innovative, frequently imitated style: the text is an implosive and introspective first-person narration in a long, unpunctuated stream of ideas and emotions. Legarde strives to stay afloat in a world that continually threatens to drown him, and expresses despair at the degeneration of the relationships that surround him. He accompanies his dissolute friend Gordon to Montreal, where Gordon meets his former lover, Néa, after twenty years. They are both guilt-ridden for having wished the death of Néa's husband—a wish that was fulfilled. Néa longs for some 'overwhelming confrontation', a 'catastrophic event to restore her equilibrium and moral tranquility'. Because of Néa, Gordon's wife leaves him; but Néa, realizing that Gordon no longer cares for her, commits suicide. To the simple parentheses and dashes that replaced normal punctuation in this novel, Bessette added double parentheses in *Le cycle* (1971, GGA)—translated by A.D. Martin-Sperry as *The cycle* (1987)—to indicate the emergence of a character's unconsciousness; dashes frame physical observations and sensations; and single parentheses surround hallucinations of the preconscious. Three generations of the same family—seven members presented through seven interior monologues—are reunited by the death of their relative, which offers an occasion for them to consider his life and ruminate on their own problems and ruling passions.

Biblioasis. This literary press began as a used bookstore in Windsor, Ontario. After organizing a local literary festival, owner Daniel Wells began to dabble in publishing, producing a trade book and five short-story chapbooks in the fall of 2004; edited by John METCALF, they included new work by Leon ROOKE and Clark BLAISE, authors the press would later publish in trade editions. The second and third trade books published by the press were translations from the Serbo-Croatian of Goran Simic. Both were critical successes and became the foundation for the Biblioasis International Translation Series, which Stephen Henighan began to edit in 2006. In four and a half years, since 2004, Biblioasis has established itself as one of the more important literary presses in the country.

When Metcalf's editorial connections with the PORCUPINE'S QUILL ended in 2006 he joined Biblioasis as senior editor, where he has been instrumental in shaping the press's editorial vision. He and Dan Wells are the primary editors, with Eric ORMSBY contributing as poetry editor. Short-story collections are a specialty. In 2005 Wells established the in-house Metcalf-Rooke Award, which has resulted in the publication of four first collections by Patricia Young, Kathleen Winter, Rebecca Rosenblum, and Amy Jones; collections by Rooke, Patricia Robertson, and the noted American writer Bruce Jay Friedman have also been published. The press's Renditions series of reprints—the first in the country to take advantage of print-on-demand technology—has brought several important Canadian titles back into print, including Ray SMITH's *Cape Breton is the thought control centre of Canada*. Biblioasis publishes *CNQ: CANADIAN NOTES & QUERIES* thrice yearly.

Bird, Will R. (1891–1984). William Richard Bird was born in East Mapleton, Nova Scotia, and educated at Amherst Academy. After serving overseas in the Great War, he became a freelance writer and subsequently an information officer for the Nova Scotia government. The author of twenty-seven books, he was best known for his historical romances. Only four of his novels—*Private Timothy Fergus Clancy: a novel of the Great War* (1930), *Maid of the marshes* (1935), *So much to record* (1951), and *The misadventures of Rufus Burdy* (1975)—have twentieth-century settings. His eight historical novels are all set in the raw atmosphere of eighteenth-century Nova Scotia. Portraying mainly humble folk, they require little psychological analysis but are attractive for their evocation of colourful incidents, characters, and settings. Bird's best work, *Here stays good Yorkshire* (1945), introduces the rough-hewn Crabtree family, settlers in the Chignecto region in the troubled times of the American Revolution. *Tristram's salvation* (1957) and *Despite the distance* (1961) make the Crabtree saga a trilogy. Two other novels are derived from Bird's Yorkshire-settlement heritage: *Judgment Glen* (1947) and *The shy Yorkshireman* (1955). *The passionate pilgrim* (1949) is another Chignecto novel, set during the time of the Acadian expulsion. *To love and to cherish* (1953) portrays the founding of Shelburne by the Loyalists, and *An Earl must have a wife* (1969) is a lurid account of the life of a famous colonial administrator, J.F.W. DesBarres (1722–1824).

Bird's short stories were collected in *Sunrise for Peter and other stories* (1946) and *Angel Cove* (1972). Two memoirs, *And we go on* (1930) and *Ghosts have warm hands: a memoir 1916–19* (1968), describe Bird's experiences in the First World War. CEF Books, Ottawa, have reissued *Ghosts have warm hands* (1997), *The communication trench: stories and statistics from the Great War* (2000), *Thirteen years and after: the story of the old front revisited* (2001), and *Private Timothy Fergus Clancy* (2005). Bird also wrote several works of history, including *Done at Grand Pré* (1955), and three travel books.

Birdsell, Sandra (b. 1942). Born Sandra Bartlette in Hamiota and raised in Morris, Manitoba, she was educated at Red River Community College, the University of Winnipeg, and the University of Manitoba. Her life partner is Jan N. Zarzycki, she has three children, and lives in Regina, Saskatchewan. Her first collection of stories, *Night travellers* (1982, rpr. 1987), based on the fictional town of Agassiz, was followed by *Ladies of the house* (1984), which was linked to her first collection through interrelated storylines about the fictional Lafrenière family. These two collections were reissued as *Agassiz stories* (1987, rpr. 2002); the title of the American edition of these stories, *Agassiz: a novel in stories* (1991), aptly suggests that her work defies easy categorization. This was followed by *The two-headed calf* (1997), a Governor General's Award nominee. Like Alice MUNRO and Margaret LAURENCE, Birdsell writes of women's lives in rural Canada, but her work is much darker, and her refusal to disguise or underplay hopelessness has prompted some critics to liken her fiction to that of American writers Raymond Carver and Bobbie Ann Mason. Birdsell's novels—*The missing child* (1989, rpr. 1998) and *The chrome suite* (1992, rpr. 2002)—brought her further recognition. Like her short-story collections, these novels are preoccupied with generations of women whose problems go largely unresolved. Her fiction is not without humour, and while the sexual oppression of women is a dominant concern, erotic love also finds its place. When, however, Birdsell confronts what is horrific in women's lives, she does so without flinching. In *The missing child*, a complex novel that experiments with narrative structure and conventions of storytelling, the rape and murder of young girls is one of the central, devastating themes. *The chrome suite* adheres more closely to realist traditions and is also less disturbing, though it has its share of break-ups, deep disappointments, and death. Birdsell's most ambitious novel, *The Russländer* (2001, rpr. 2002), draws on her Mennonite heritage—her grandparents fled persecution in Russia and emigrated to Manitoba—and is about a Mennonite community in southern Russia. (In 1789 Catherine the Great brought Mennonites from Germany to become farmers—they were very successful.) The novel is about the families of Peter Vogt—his daughter Katya is central (she eventually emigrates to Manitoba with her husband)—and Abram Sudermann, for whom he works. On the first page is the announcement, dated Nov. 15, 1917, of a massacre at Sudermann's estate: Abram, his wife, and seven Vogts (including Peter) were murdered. Knowing this, the reader is surprised by the even tenor of the narrative that follows, describing family occurrences: beginning in the devastating year of 1917, when Sudermann's estate is set on fire, we are simply told that 'the stray dogs, tails dipped in kerosene and lit … were released to run through the ripened grain.' Telling her story as an old woman, Katya says, 'After they killed Abram they thought they had to keep on killing until no one was left. They didn't want to leave a witness.' This long, undramatic novel about a very dramatic period in Russian (and Mennonite) history—with Canadian overtones—is a remarkable re-creation of a historical period for a community of Mennonites but is not a compelling work of fiction. *Children of the day* (2005) is a longish novel (405 pages) that takes place on one day in June 1953 in Union Place, Manitoba, and is about the Vandal family. It begins with Oliver dressing in the early morning while his wife Sara—furious with him because he went to see an early sweetheart the evening before—stays in bed. Oliver is a Métis (like Birdsell's father) and Sara was born a Russian Mennonite (like Birdsell's mother)—she appears in *The Russländer*. The Vandals have ten children (Birdsell has ten siblings). The novel skilfully combines some western Canadian history—for example, Oliver finds in a tobacco can a memoir written by his grandmother, who lived through the two Riel rebellions—with memories of Oliver and Sara and, as the day passes, the activities of some of their children. They all eventually come together, and their respective problems seem to have a kind of resolution. Birdsell's *The town that floated away* (1997) is a children's book.

Birney, Earle (1904–95). Alfred Earle Birney was born in Calgary, Alberta, and was educated at the University of British Columbia, graduating in Honours English in 1926, and at the University of Toronto (M.A., 1927; Ph.D., 1938); having studied Old and Middle English at the University of London, he wrote his doctoral dissertation on 'Chaucer's irony'. Birney accepted a junior faculty position at the University of Toronto and undertook the literary editorship (1936–40) of THE CANADIAN FORUM. He began writing poetry seriously at this time, and shortly after enlisting for officer training in the Canadian army published his first collection, *David and other poems* (1942, GGA). The narrative poem 'DAVID' is said by Sam Solecki (see page 52) to form 'the cornerstone of Birney's reputation.'

Birney

After serving overseas as a personnel selection officer, in 1946 he became supervisor of the International Service of the Canadian Broadcasting Corporation. His second poetry collection, *Now is time* (1945), also won a Governor General's Award. From 1948 to 1965 he was professor of medieval literature at the University of British Columbia, where he established Canada's first Department of Creative Writing. See OUTPOSTS. He was made an Officer of the Order of Canada in 1970.

The Audenesque qualities of his first two collections, repeated in *The Strait of Anian* (1948), were followed by the ingeniously varied styles of the verse-play *Trial of a city* (1952). In his next collection, *Ice cod bell or stone* (1962), Birney unveiled a precise new free verse, a colloquial first-person viewpoint, and a strong interest in visual or 'concrete' poetry; in its poems set in Latin America he presented the first of the world-travel poetry by which he would be widely known throughout the next two decades. *Near False Creek mouth* (1964), with its innovative, contrapuntally structured title poem, also contains impressively vivid travel meditations set in South America and the Far East. Throughout the 1960s and 1970s Birney's concern to expand the technical resources of his poetry was reflected in various kinds of hand-drawn poems, typewriter-concrete poems, and chant poems that appeared in *Pnomes, jukollges & other stunzas* (1969), *Rag and bone shop* (1971), *What's so big about green* (1973), *The rugging and the moving times* (1976), *Alphbeings and other seasyours* (1976), and *Fall by fury* (1978); and in the substitution of space for conventional punctuation marks that characterizes these books and the retrospective gatherings *Selected poems* (1966), *The poems of Earle Birney* (1969), *Collected poems* (1975), and *Ghost in the wheels: selected poems* (1977). In this later work Birney repudiated the humanistic themes of his first three books to envision a vast, indifferent cosmos in whose 'mammoth corridors' human energy is little more than a glorious absurdity. *Last makings* (1991) is a volume of new and selected poems. Overall, Birney's poetry is marked by extraordinary technical virtuosity, playfulness, and openness to experimentation. Most important are his long poems 'David', 'The damnation of Vancouver', and 'November walk near False Creek mouth', which reflect both his resourcefulness as a craftsman and his profound empathy with human limitation. In his introduction to *One muddy hand: selected poems* (2007) the editor, Sam Solecki, discusses Birney's best poetry admiringly and resourcefully from a present-day viewpoint.

Birney's prose—of less interest than his poetry—includes the comic war novel *Turvey* (1949, NCL); the novel *Down the long table* (1955), which depicts the Trotskyist scene in which Birney worked in the 1930s; *Big bird in the bush* (1979), a collection of stories and sketches; and the semi-autobiographical non-fiction works *The creative writer* (1966), *The cow jumped over the moon* (1972), in which he discusses the composition of his own poems, and *Spreading time: remarks on Canadian writing and writers 1904–1949* (1980, rpr. 1989). See Elspeth CAMERON, *Earle Birney: a life* (1994).

bissett, bill (b. 1939). Although he was born in Halifax, Nova Scotia, and now lives in London, Ontario, bill bissett is mostly associated with Vancouver and the West Coast, where he was the defining figure of the Vancouver cultural scene in the 1960s. He embodied then, and to a great extent now, the vision and idealism of the so-called hippy movement. His open espousal of drug use frequently led him into legal trouble, and his books have also been the focus for charges of obscenity, in the face of which he was able to rally impressive statements of support from the cultural community. His first book of poems, *We sleep inside each other all* (1966), was followed by a steady stream of collections over a period of more than forty years, many published by his own BLEWOINTMENT PRESS, and in recent years by TALONBOOKS. Among the many titles one may mention *Awake in the red desert* (1968), *Pomes for yoshi* (1972, rpr. 1977), *Medicine my mouths on fire* (1974), *Sailor* (1978), *Seagull on Yonge Street* (1983), *Canada gees mate for life* (1985), *Animal uproar* (1987), *Hard 2 beleev* (1990), *Th last photo uv th human soul* (1993), *Th influenza uv logik* (1995), *Loving without being vulnraball* (1997), and *Scars on the seehors* (1999). There have been two volumes of selected poems: *Nobody owns th earth* (1971) and *Selected poems: beyond even faithful legends* (1980). More recent collections are *Peter among th touring boxes, text bites* (2002), *Narrativ enigma: rumours uv hurricane* (2004), *Northern wild roses: deth interrupts th dansing* (2005), and *Ths is erth thees ar peopul* (2007). bissett has been a tireless experimenter in the forms of poetry, exploring visual and sound poems, chants, collages, short lyrics and extended narratives, and poems of vision and social satire. The most obvious and obtrusive aspect of his style is his unconventional spelling and orthography: he believes that 'correct' spelling symbolizes social and political oppression. But one soon becomes accustomed to bissett's spelling, which quickly built up its own loosely phonetic conventions. The importance of the orthography is chiefly visual; bissett sees each poem as a composition on the page, with line divisions determined more by visual than by rhythmic criteria. The visual and oral elements of his work are thus separate; but the oral is important, as his readings demonstrate—especially the chants, based on Native chanting as much as on the tradition of sound poetry, and conveying a mesmeric, meditative effect that provides one of the foundations of his vision, which can be divided into the Blakean categories of 'innocence' and 'experience'. Although his evocations of an ideal state of being—attained through communion with nature, drugs, sex, and the free expression of the personality unhampered by social restraints—may seem romantic, naive, or simplistic, they are expressed with a singular intensity, and often transcend the banal images and the unsophisticated ideas. At his best, bissett writes with remarkable subtlety and quiet irony. In narrative poems such as 'Killer whale' or 'Th emergency ward', the gentle humour and ironic distance show a fine control of nuance and tone. One of his finest sequences is *Pomes for Yoshi*, in which a series of love lyrics is juxtaposed to an increasingly weird and nightmarish story of bissett's troubles in the house he lives in; yet the long closing narrative, one of his most devastating accounts of the 'straight' world, ends with the humanistic assertion that 'its/beautiful/to feel so many/ peopul around me'. bissett may be the last surviving hippy, the last poet in Canada who can still write 'far out' and get away with it. He has refused to become obsolete. As a visual artist bissett has also produced paintings, drawings, and collages. *Radiant danse uv being: a poetic portrait of bill bissett* (2006)—'Poems about bill from his friends and fellow poets'—was edited by Jeff Pew and Stephen Roxborough.

See *Bill Bissett: essays on his works* (2002) edited by Linda ROGERS.

Bissonnette, Lise (b. 1945). Born in Rouyn, Québec, she was educated at the Université de Montréal (1965–70) and pursued her doctoral studies at the Université du Strasbourg and l'École pratique des hautes études à Paris. Her journalistic career at *Le Devoir* included being a reporter, parliamentary correspondent in Quebec City and Ottawa, editor, and— from 1990 to 1998—publisher. From 1986 to 1990 she was a freelance journalist, writing a column for the Toronto *Globe and Mail* and two magazines. The recipient of several honorary degrees and other honours, including the Légion d'honneur française in Feb. 2000, she is présidente-directrice générale de la Grande Bibliothèque du Québec, Montreal.

Bissonnette's three brief novels and one collection of short stories, all translated by Sheila FISCHMAN, are modernist works of spare elegance and strong narrative drive into which understated erotica and perversities are matter-of-factly woven. *Following the summer* (1993)— *Marie suivait l'été* (1992)—takes place in a northern Québec mining community: 'The people of this land don't put down roots..... They wait, then they move on again, amidst the penury that clings to those who open the roads. That is why we know nothing about them.' We read about Marie, a schoolteacher (whose pupils 'all resemble one another..... You filter them through yourself as best you can, their affection is never sincere, no one is more duplicitous than a half-grown child'); about Marie's lover, then husband, from eastern Europe; and about Corrine, a freewheeling girl who fascinates Marie. At the end Marie, married, finds that 'It is enough to dismantle desires' and fling them away. Most of *Affairs of art* (1996)—*Choses crues* (1995)—is made up of a letter written to the woman he loves by François Dubeau, a bisexual art critic who has died of AIDS. The letter—a narrative of his life and loves in which he describes himself as an impostor (as a critic? a lover?)—is read by Marianne, his mother. One of his loves was Bruno Farinacci-Lepore, a great Italian art critic who also died of AIDS. ('He spoke of death as of a work of art, his words dry.') When Marianne finishes the letter, the novel moves towards a stunning finality. The third book in the so-called False Pretenses trilogy is *An appropriate place* (2002)—*Un lieu approprié* (2001). (The three words of the title are not only the last words of the novel but occur at least four times, referring to four different places.) We read mainly about Gabrielle Perron, who has left the PQ government as cultural minister and embarks on a new life in the Montreal suburb of Laval. We read about life in Quebec City ('It took less than six months for the area in front of 225 de la Grande Allée Est and the side entrance to the Parliament to erase Quebec City's charm.'); about a federal-provincial conference in Ottawa; the weakened sovereignty movement; Gabrielle's Ph.D. thesis and her life as a female academic; an abortion, which she describes in a letter she never sent to her lover; and her part in organizing a show to raise money for AIDS research. Bissonnette's dense, forward-moving narrative smoothly intertwines various characters, and events past and present. We meet Pierre, Gabrielle's short-term teenaged lover; her friend Marie (who raised Pierre), who leaves for Ethiopia to teach—she writes a twenty-two-page memoir in Addis; and we hear about François Dubeau (of *Affairs of art*) who, though he died of AIDS, 'was Marie's boyfriend, he slept with her', according to Pierre. 'The Viper', one of the fifteen stories in *Cruelties* (1998)—*Quittes et doubles* (1998)—is narrated by a man who had planned to kill his wife, a novelist, until she handed him her grey notebook: 'Never had I read anything so sublime from her pen. Each word found the next one amid slowly distilled rage.... Her venom is a work of genius, my grief is unending.' 'The Lovers' is narrated by a red chalk drawing of a nude woman 'in various states of arousal'—images that were 'superior for triggering an erection'. Each story has a poetic epigraph that is a quasi summary; the one for the last story, 'The Scaffold', is: 'Naked beneath her robe/she demanded the scaffold/for the handsome thief who stands there/"Her lips are honey/and my sting is innocent,"/he declared to the faltering judge/He impregnated her before the jury's eyes/The child was sentenced to life.'

Bissoondath, Neil (b. 1955). Born in Arima, Trinidad, West Indies, he came to Canada in 1973 and completed a B.A. in French (1977) at York University, Toronto, working as a teacher until 1985. He moved with his family to Quebec City, taught creative writing in French at Université Laval for several years, and then moved to London, England. Bissoondath's fiction displays the development of an assured command of narrative, and of language that can produce moments of lyrical and aphoristic brilliance. His first volume of short stories, *Digging up the mountains* (1985, NCL) was followed by a novel set in the Caribbean, *A casual brutality* (1988, rpr. 2002), and another short-story collection, *On the eve of uncertain tomorrows* (1990, rpr. 1991). His next novel, *The innocence of age* (1992, rpr. 1993), is about Pasco, who owns a greasy spoon; his son Danny, educated and smart, who finds himself confronting violence; and a wide cast of subordinate characters, all rendered convincingly and with sympathy. Although some of this fiction is set in the Caribbean, Bissoondath is not committed to exploring his West Indian background. He has cast his net wide and is as comfortable dealing with the imaginary island of Casquemada (*A casual brutality*) as he is in portraying a Japanese girl trying to make a living in Toronto (*On the eve of uncertain tomorrows*), and the lights and shadows of that city in the 1980s (*The innocence of age*). Perhaps of greatest literary significance, for its skilful recounting of a complex story of lives and relationships in different periods and places, is *The worlds within her* (1998, rpr. 1999). Moving back and forth in place and time, its settings are Canada (Toronto?), where Shakti, when her politician husband was killed, took her young daughter Yasmin, who grew up to become a popular TV news reader married to Jim Summerhayes; and an unnamed Caribbean island to which Yasmin takes her mother's ashes and where she intends to learn more about her father from his brother and sister, all of whom are of Indian ancestry. The novel is made up of a long, alternating series of brief episodes, discrete but subtly linked in their cumulative revelations. They are presented in the form of Shakti's unexpectedly sophisticated and perceptive monologues, spoken to a comatose neighbour; scenes of Yasmin's marriage and her motherhood; and reminiscences of the aunt and uncle, Penny and Cyril, who, together with Shakti, build up a detailed psychological portrait of Yasmin's father and Shakti's marriage to him. Yasmin is finally changed by what she learns. The subject of race is never far from these books. *Doing the heart good* (2002, rpr. 2003) is in the form a memoir of seventy-five-year-old Alistair Mackenzie—former professor of English, a widower, and deaf—whose duplex burned down six months before and is living with daughter Agnes, her husband Jacques (whom he calls Jack), and grandson François. His life, of which his beloved wife Mary was the mainstay, is rendered through brief stories about many acquaintances and his acute observations of them. If one considers the beautifully written text a revelation of his mind, he is appealing; but his often insensitive treatment of others makes him unappealing. The complexities and uncertainties of his life are somewhat resolved towards the end of the book. We are told—in a compelling scene—about the destruction by fire of his duplex, and why this happened. At the very end, during a Christmas dinner with his family, François smiles at him 'and it is like the dawn of a thousand suns, shining its light into a future, his and mine....' *The unyielding clamour of the night* (2005) is Bissoondath's exploration, as he has said, 'of an individual in a place ... torn by civil strife.' The place is an unnamed island nation, where the sinister insurgents are referred to as 'the Boys'. Arun, twenty-one, travels from north to south to become a schoolteacher. He meets, among others, Seth, an army captain; Mr and Mrs Jaisaram, and their sharp-tongued, entirely lifelike and appealing daughter Anjani, with whom he falls in love. The beautifully written narrative begins slowly, without energy, but as it confronts violence it rises to tense passages that arouse suspense, surprise, and shock. In 2008 Bissoondath published *The soul of all great designs,* the title referring, as an epigraph explains, to secrecy: Alec's belief that as an interior designer he must appear to be homosexual and Sue's (Sumintra's) deceiving her traditional Indian parents about the life she leads, of which Alex is at the centre.

In the controversial *Selling illusions: the cult of multiculturalism in Canada* (1994, rev. 2002), Bissoondath comments: 'One makes a life, puts down roots, and from this feeling of belonging comes the wish to be as fully part of the country as possible.' This sentence encapsulates a whole attitude to migration, a way of negotiating the binaries of centre and margin, a resistance to hyphenated identities, that informs all Bissoondath's work. It is also reminiscent of the work of his uncle, Sir V.S. Naipaul. In both writers there is no naive nostalgia, no simplistic denunciation of the West; instead there is a rigorous examination of what it means to be a migrant, of living in a world characterized by ambivalence and indeterminacy. Bissoondath's lecture *The age of confession* (2007, bilingual) was given on 26 April 2006 and inaugurated the Antonine MAILLET—Northrop FRYE Lecture sponsored by the Université de Moncton. An engaging discussion of narrative, it includes a wide range of references that include himself and his family.

Blais, Marie-Claire (b. 1939). Born in Quebec City, she left school at fifteen to work in a shoe factory. Later she took courses in French literature at Université Laval. In 1962—after the publication, when she was only twenty, of her first novel, *La belle bête,* and of *Tête blanche*—she was awarded a Guggenheim Fellowship (sponsored by Edmund Wilson). Since the appearance in 1959 of *La belle bête*—translated by Merloyd Lawrence as MAD SHADOWS (1960, NCL)—Blais has experimented in book after book with language, method, and form, using stream-of-consciousness, the crudest of street-talk, lyric symbolism, and various blends of the real and the surreal to depict her own particular world, in which evil exists as a monstrous force, relationships are doomed from the start or truncated, and children are destroyed by those around them or by the mere fact of growing up. Parents, except in some of the later works, are callous or depraved, nuns sadistic, priests venal or rascally or at least half mad. The style

is always impelling—at times stripped and subtle, at other times lyrical, incantatory, rhapsodic, or brutally forceful. Blais was appointed a Companion of the Order of Canada in 1972.

Two minor novellas of this early period— *Le jour est noir* (1962), about a group of children who see their parents' death as a betrayal, and *Les voyageurs sacrés* (1969), the story of a marital triangle in which disloyalty to a marriage is equated with disloyalty to childhood—have been translated by Derek Coltman and published in a single volume as *The day is dark and three travellers* (1967).

Une saison dans la vie d'Emmanuel (1965)— translated by Derek Coltman as *A season in the life of Emmanuel* (1966, NCL)—ranks with *La belle bête* and the three Pauline Archange novels (see below) as her most significant and characteristic works. In this powerful and tragic novel, Blais makes a statement about the rural Québec society of the time by reducing it to its bleak and brutish essence. The sixteen children of an exhausted mother and an illiterate farmer father live a life deprived of grace, beauty, and hope. All their desires and strivings for something more are in succession stifled, brutalized, or corrupted by the rigidity of their society and the indifference or viciousness of those who should look after them. Over the series of frustrations, deprivations, and mutilations that mark the first months in the life of Emmanuel broods the figure of the grandmother, the one source of warmth for the children, to the youngest of whom she appears chiefly as a sturdy pair of feet that dominate the room. It is this strong if limited embodiment of the old virtues who offers at the end a sort of summation: 'You get used to everything, you'll see'—a message less of hope than of blind animal endurance.

In Blais's three semi-autobiographical novels about a girl growing up in Québec, *Les manuscrits de Pauline Archange* (1968, GGA), *Vivre! Vivre!* (1969), and *Les apparences* (1970)—the first two of which were translated by Derek Coltman and published in a single volume as *The manuscripts of Pauline Archange* (1969) and the third translated by David Lobdell as *Dürer's angel* (1976)— a more robust central figure, the young Pauline, fights, often savagely, to maintain her integrity in a milieu in which parents, even though at times pitiable, are enemies, and friendships are curtailed by death or become distorted. There is great vitality in these books in the character of Pauline Archange herself, in her determination to live as a free individual despite the flaws in her upbringing and education, and in the sense, for the first time in Blais's work, of a layered and complex society.

Three smaller novels—*Tête blanche* (1960), translated by Charles Fullman with the same title (1961); *L'insoumise* (1966), translated by David Lobdell as *The fugitive* (1978); and *David Sterne* (1967), translated by Lobdell with the same title (1973)—deal with boys or young men who are all thwarted rebels, at odds with society and their own nature. In *Le loup* (1972)—translated by Sheila FISCHMAN as *The wolf* (1974, rpr. 2008 with an introduction by Edmund White)—the homosexual youth who is the central character, though he is drawn again and again to relationships of the most mutually destructive sort, comes to feel finally that 'love given unstintingly, even if it is given very badly, is not wasted.' *Une liaison parisienne* (1975)—translated by Fischman as *A literary affair* (1979)—is a relatively slight novel satirizing Québécois's romanticizing of the French literary scene. *Une joualonais, sa joualonie* (1973) is also satirical in intent; this time the target is those Québec writers who use JOUAL as a literary and political device. It was translated by Ralph Manheim—unfortunately with considerable misunderstanding of Québécois idiom, especially street idiom—as *St Lawrence blues* (1974). *Les nuits d'underground* (1978)—translated by Ray Ellenwood as *Nights in the underground* (1979)—is a study of the lesbian as outcast, combining vivid streettalk in both French and English with long, sinuous, looping sentences to trace the sometimes tragicomic, often tragic lives of a group that frequents a tawdry lesbian bar in Montreal. *Le sourd dans la ville* (1979, GGA)—translated by Carol Dunlop as *Deaf to the city* (1980)—returns to the underside of Montreal, this time a rundown hotel. Two condemned people—a boy with a brain tumour who longs to live and a wealthy woman devastated by the desertion of her husband—contemplate one another, unable to communicate, each hoping to read in the other's eyes some answer to their own and the world's pain. *Visions d'Anna* (1982), translated by Fischman as *Anna's world* (1984), poses the same question (why should one live?), but provides for two of the characters—two young women who have withdrawn from a world of barbarism and indifference—at least a partial answer. *Pierre, la guerre du printemps* (1984)—translated by Lobdell and Philip Stratford as *Pierre* (1991)—is the account of a disillusioned well-to-do young man who becomes involved with bikers, drugs, and vice of various sorts, but finds that there is no answer to his world-weariness there either.

L'ange de la solitude (1989)—translated as *The angel of solitude* (1993) by Laura Hodes—is a study of eight lesbians who attempt to found an ideal society. Blais's most recent accomplishment is an ambitious trilogy, which has been extravagantly praised as a masterpiece. Each novel is written in one paragraph, with the punctuation limited to a great many commas and occasionally a few periods and semicolons. Though the effect is that of an anti-novel, you are carried along once you get into it. The setting is an island in the Gulf of Mexico, and most characters appear in all three books. *These festive nights* (1997)—Sheila Fischman's translation of *Soifs* (1995, GGA)—has been described as a tropical storm, a series of long, undulating sentences that swing from past to present, from reality to fantasy, from character to character, with the occasional discourse on apparently unrelated subjects, such as music, literature, painters (the composers, writers, and painters mentioned revealing the author's knowledge). It offers a picture of the world at the turn of the last century. *Thunder and light* (2001)—Nigel Spencer's translation of *Dans la foudre et la lumière* (2001)—is a triumph of lyrical writing, like the other books, with many characters, settings, incidents, and revelations of Blais's knowledge of modern life blending into one another: 'Ari could not imagine so much horror as he contemplated the solidity of his hand and arm scored by the work he did, his body was forever, he thought, energetic, strong, and his hand would never stop sculpting, and life could not go on without the strength of this impetuous body of his. This is life's bounty, thought Jean-Mathieu as he walked, cane in hand, toward Caroline's house, almost fully hidden by a crown of palm trees...' (these are two characters introduced in *These festive nights*). Sensuous beauty (Blais uses the word 'sensuous' a lot) and danger—shootings, plane crashes, Sri Lanka etc.—punctuate the text. Difficult to follow though they are, these dense novels express with great originality 'the rhythm of life', in Blais's words. In the first eighteen pages of *Augustino and the choir of destruction* (2007)—Spencer's translation of *Augustino et le choeur de la destruction* (2005), which won a GOVERNOR GENERAL'S AWARD—we meet Petites Cendres, a transvestite; the Egyptian Lazaro—in *Thunder* Carlos had shot him in the leg over a watch and went to jail—whose desire for revenge makes him think of 'the young and angry, those destined to sensitive missions of martyrdom, thousands of them, unnamed and unnameable, candidates for suicide, flourishing in disordered ranks worldwide, staging attacks anywhere and everywhere'. We also meet Mère, 'almost eighty', and her thoughts (over several pages) on the life of Marie Curie (the Polish Maria Sklodowska), and Mère's grandson Augustino. And we read about the black Olivier, a senator, his Japanese wife Chuan, and their son Jermaine; about the hanging of five rapists in Tehran (Lazaro's thoughts); and about the music of Benjamin Britten and Olivier Messian (Mère's thoughts). The onrush of monologues and third-person descriptions conveyed in sentences punctuated mostly by commas, with no paragraphs, make it difficult to place the characters and remember their relationships. One should create a list of these as one reads (Blais does not object to making the reader work). As for Augustino of the title, a boy who wants to be a writer, he 'got up early like his father, often before dawn, and wrote, reading the words he had written from a screen placed up high where he could see the ocean, an invisible choir of destruction, I'm convinced that there are strategic missiles hidden on this island, but no one really knows, how was Augustino to face his father, Daniel, who adamantly resisted his son's desire to become a writer, what was this craziness about writing alone in his room for hours when Augustino had received a sports education...' In 2008 Blais won the GGA for *Naissance de Rebecca à l'ère des tourments*.

The exile and the sacred travellers (2000) is a collection of nine short stories and a novella translated by Nigel Spencer.

Blais's two collections of poetry were published in one volume as *Pays voilés/Existences* (1964) and republished in a bilingual edition, with translations by Michael Harris, as *Veiled countries/Lives* (1994). Blais is an effective dramatist. Two of her plays were translated by David Lobdell: *L'exécution* (1968) as *The execution* (1976), and *L'île* (1989) as *The island, a drama* (1991). Five short plays written for Radio-Canada in the late 1970s were collected in *Sommeil d'hiver* (1984) and translated by Nigel Spencer in the collection *Wintersleep* (1999); see also *The collected radio drama of Marie-Claire Blais* (2005), translated by Nigel Spencer. *American notebooks: a writer's journey* (1996) is the translation by Linda Gaboriau of articles Blais wrote for *Le Devoir* in 1963 (published in French in 1993), when she spent a year in Cambridge, Massachusetts, on her Guggenheim Fellowship.

Blaise, Clark (b. 1940). Born in Fargo, North Dakota, of a French-Canadian father and an English-Canadian mother, he spent his childhood and youth—the frequent subjects of his fiction—in various places, the American South and the Canadian Prairies among them. He was educated at Denison University (A.B., 1961) and the University of Iowa's Writer's Workshop (M.F.A., 1964), whose international writing program he directed in 1990–8. From 1966 to 1978 he was a professor at Concordia University, Montreal. After teaching for many years at the University of California at Berkeley, he divides his time between San Francisco and Southampton, Long Island.

Blaise's fiction—the short stories in *A North American education* (1973), *Tribal justice* (1974), *Resident alien* (1986), *Man and his world* (1992), and the novels *Lunar attractions* (1979) and *Lusts* (1983)—deals compassionately with the outcast and the victimized. At times appearing as connected short stories, at times as novels, his fiction generally deals with lengthy, episodic narratives replete with social and cultural detail. *I had a father: a post-modern biography* (1992) blends memoir and fictional sketch to represent the mysterious presence that is at the centre of Blaise's fiction: the magnetic, neglectful, mercurial, larger-than-life father. Often marked by bizarre violence and displacement, his narratives convey the plight of the perennial outsider—a Canadian in the American South, a backwoods boy in Canada. His heroes are always found at crossroads. The novel *If I were me* (1997) is something of a departure, with its international settings (Poland, Japan, India, Israel) and its central figure, Dr Gerald Lander, a famous psycholinguist and author of a celebrated book. His relationships with others, including his adopted African-American daughter and his son, and his reflections on his professional devotion to the subjects of language, mental deterioration, and severe dementia are woven into a short, elegant narrative that explores a brilliant man's ideas and his life to its inconclusive end in Tel Aviv.

Blaise's distinguished stories have been reissued in four volumes as *Selected stories* (with some new stories in each one): Volume One, *Southern stories* (2000), which draws on his early life in Florida; Two, *Pittsburgh stories* (2001), about years of adolescence spent in that city; Three, *Montreal stories* (2003); and Four, *World body* (2006), in which the stories have international settings and a wide range of subjects, including the Indian Diaspora and Alzheimer's disease, of which Blaise's grandfather and mother both died. He describes it and reflects on it memorably in the story 'Salad days' (the title refers to 'Alzheimer's word salad'). This is an important series of handsome books published by the PORCU-PINE'S QUILL.

Days and nights in Calcutta (1977), written in collaboration with Blaises's wife, the noted writer Bharati Mukherjee, deals with their lengthy stay in India and is comprised of separate accounts. Blaise has also written *The sorrow and the terror: the haunting legacy of the Air India tragedy* (1987, rpr. 1997), the journalistic study of a terrorist bombing. Blaise's finest non-fiction achievement, however, is *Time lord: the remarkable Canadian who missed his train and changed the world* (2000, rpr. 2001), which is both a partial biography of the great Victorian Canadian Sir Stanford Fleming—who devised and facilitated world standard time and the world-encircling sub-Pacific cable, was chief engineer of the Canadian Pacific Railway, and designed the first Canadian postage stamp (a beaver)—and a series of imaginative, beautifully written discourses on time itself and on the onset of modernism in the arts when standard time was established: 'The stirring in the arts called modernism is really the implanting of time inside all artistic constructions.' In 2010 Blaise was appointed an Officer of the Order of Canada.

Blake, William Hume (1861–1924). Born in Toronto, the grandson of the Liberal politician Edward Blake, he was educated at the University of Toronto and admitted to the bar in 1885. He published two books of essays—*Brown waters and other sketches* (1915, rpr. 1925 with a preface by Vincent Massey) and *In a fishing country* (1922)—that are similar in structure, containing essays on fishing, camping, weather, the survival of legends and witchcraft, and portraits of habitant families. In both collections Blake expresses his love of the Laurentian wilderness and admiration for its Native and French-Canadian inhabitants who lived close to nature. *A fisherman's creed* (1923) is an essay on the importance of the intellect in the elaboration of an individual religious faith. Blake's translations of Louis HÉMON's *Maria chapdelaine* (1921) and Adjutor Rivard's *Chez nous* (1924) brought to English-speaking readers two of the most traditional portraits of habitant life.

Blaser, Robin (1925–2009). Born in Denver, Colorado, he was educated at the University of California, Berkeley (B.A., 1952; M.A., 1955; M.L.S., 1956) and immigrated in 1966 to Vancouver to teach in the Department of English at Simon Fraser University, first as university lecturer, then as professor of English (1972–85), becoming Professor Emeritus. Considered a member of the so-called San Francisco Renaissance of poets and artists active in the 1950s and early 1960s, Blaser published *The moth poem* and *Les chimères* in 1964, each a series of linked poems that examine facets of an experience, image, or phenomenon. (The 'serial' poem is a form also associated with the work of other San Francisco poets such as Jack Spicer and Robert Duncan.) He was a significant influence on the West Coast poetry scene as teacher, poet, and editor. Additional collections of poetry since his arrival in Canada include *Image-nations 1–12* (1974), *Image-nations 13 & 14* (1975), *Syntax* (1983), *Pell mell* (1988), and his collected poems, *The holy forest* (1993), which includes all Blaser's previous work in addition to new work, notably an ongoing series entitled 'The great companions'; it has a Foreword by Robert Creeley. *The holy forest* was launched at an international conference held in Vancouver in June 1994 and fifty papers were presented on the conference subject, 'The recovery of the public world: a conference in honour of Robin Blaser's poetry and poetics'. The resulting Festschrift, edited by Robert Sherrin, was published in *The Capilano Review* 17–18 (Fall 1995). A revised and expanded edition of *The holy forest*—edited by Miriam Nichols, with Creeley's Foreword and a new Afterword by Charles Bernstein—was published in 2006, the year *The fire: collected essays* was published, edited with a commentary by Miriam Nichols. Blaser wrote the libretto for the English composer Harrison Birtwistle's opera *The Last Supper*, which premiered successfully in 2000 at the Berlin Staatsoper (Daniel Barenboim conducting) and at Glyndbourne, England. In the devastating libretto the horrors of the last two millennia are the dust of centuries that Christ washes off the feet of the Apostles, brought to life in the present. In 2008 Blaser—having been awarded two years earlier by the Griffin trustees their first Lifetime Achievement Award—was awarded the GRIFFIN POETRY PRIZE for *The holy forest*. He was made a Member of the Order of Canada in 2004.

Blewointment (1963–78). The first issue of this unconventionally political literary magazine, edited and published in Vancouver by poet bill BISSETT, appeared in October 1963. The magazine was characterized by its editor's personal spelling conventions, and by his view of the artist as oppressed by state and corporate 'fascism'. Five volumes, with varying numbers per volume, were published until 1968. Subsequent issues were released as unnumbered 'speshuls': notably 'Fascist Court' (1970), 'Occupation Issue' (1970), and 'End of th World Speshul Anthology' (1978). All issues were produced in crude mimeograph. Most were printed on variously sized and coloured paper and bound together with random newspaper clippings, and occasionally with one-of-a-kind drawings, so that individual copies of issues differed considerably in appearance. The content made it both a community newsletter of the arts, documenting work-in-progress by Vancouver writers and graphic artists, and a national literary magazine. As Margaret ATWOOD reported in 1969: 'It can print poetry so awful you have to be high to appreciate it and poems so good they create their own high'. Contributors constituted a cross-section of Canadian poetry, and included Atwood, bissett, Margaret AVISON, Colleen Thibaudeau, Gwendolyn MacEWEN, Earle BIRNEY, Michael ONDAATJE, George BOWERING, bp NICHOL, Al PURDY, Dennis LEE, John Robert COLOMBO, and John NEWLOVE. Blewointment Press, founded by bissett in 1967, published books in a similarly unusual mimeographed format, but confined itself mostly to writers of the 1960s Vancouver counterculture. In the mid-1980s bissett sold it to musicians David and Maureen Lee of London, Ontario, who briefly continued the press as Nightwood Editions, and then sold its backlist, in 1992, to Pulp Press of Vancouver. See *The last Blewointment anthology, volume 1, AC-LE* (1985), edited by bissett.

Bliss, Michael (b. 1941). He was born in Leamington, Ontario, and educated at a District High School and at the University of Toronto (B.A., 1962; M.A., 1966; Ph.D., 1972), where he received an appointment in the Department of History and is now University Professor Emeritus. A pivotal historian in moving historiography away from a concentration on past politics, Bliss has written numerous books of social history that are firmly rooted in his knowledge as a scholar and an academic and are also highly readable and illuminating. He first wrote a business history, *A living profit: studies in the social history of Canadian business 1833–1911* (1974). He followed this with a biography that masterfully evoked the worlds of retailing, food processing, high finance, and supply during the First World War, *A Canadian millionaire: the life and business times of Sir Joseph Flavelle, Bart* (1978). This was followed by *The discovery of insulin* (1982, rpr. 2000), a model for writing scientific

history engagingly. One of the key figures in the discovery of insulin was the subject of *Banting: a biography* (1984). *Plague: a story of smallpox in Montreal* (1991) combines Bliss's social and medical knowledge in a dramatic examination of the last major outbreak in 1886 of smallpox in the Western world. Concerned in the early 1990s about the fragmentation in Canadian historical scholarship as it sought new vistas in untold directions, Bliss turned to national political history in an account of the country's prime ministers since Confederation: *Right honourable men: the descent of Canadian politics from Macdonald to Mulroney* (1994), a lively and occasionally scathing examination of federal politics; it was revised and updated for publication in 2004, with a change in the subtitle:... *from Macdonald to Chrétien*. Bliss's medical knowledge was perhaps put to the most demanding test when he wrote *William Osler: a life in medicine* (1999), a definitive biography of the world-famous Canadian-born physician (1849–1919). His skill as a medical biographer reached a climax with the monumental *Harvey Cushing: a life in surgery* (2005), a huge biography of the famous brain surgeon. Bliss is a Member of the Order of Canada.

Blondin, George. See ABORIGINAL LITERATURE: 5.

Blunt, Giles (b. 1952). Born in Windsor, Ontario, he grew up in North Bay and then studied English literature at the University of Toronto (B.A. Hons., 1975). He lived for twenty years in New York, writing the scripts for some well-known TV crime series. He now lives in Toronto and has achieved a reputation as the author of well-conceived, well-written crime novels. Five of his novels feature the detective John Cardinal who lives in a (fictional) northern Ontario town called Algonquin Bay: *Cold eye* (1989), praised as a 'sensational literary debut'; *Forty words for sorrow* (2000, rpr. 2002), which begins when four teenagers are missing, and won the British Crime Writers' Macallan Silver Dagger Award; *The delicate storm* (2003, rpr. 2004), which won the Arthur Ellis Award for Best Crime Novel; *Blackfly season* (2005); and *By the time you read this* (2006, rpr. 2007)—the title being the first words of an apparent suicide note found near the body of a woman who had fallen from the roof of an apartment building that Cardinal was called to check up on, only to be shocked by the discovery that the body was that of his wife. But was it suicide? A departure from these novels is

No such creature (2008) in which Max, an elderly thief who only steals from rich Republicans, spends the summer touring America with his grand-nephew, eighteen-year-old Owen—they are a team, until Owen is accepted at Julliard.

Boas, Franz. See ABORIGINAL LEGENDS AND TALES: BIBLIOGRAPHY.

Boatman, The (1957). This collection by Jay MACPHERSON, one of the landmarks of modern Canadian poetry, is an intricate sequence of epigrammatic poems that is a colloquial and familiar retelling of myths. Carefully constructed from biblical and classical allusions—their strict metres recalling ballads, nursery rhymes, and hymns—the poems are organized in six parts. (A model would be William Blake's *For the sexes: the gates of paradise* or *The crystal cabinet*.) While employing simple language, charming wit, and playful humour, they are richly metaphorical, recording the struggle from a fallen vision to an anagogic vision, where the imagination is resurrected by love. The first section, 'Poor child' (reminiscent of Blake), describes the archetypal human state as fallen: man longs to return to the security of the insatiate womb. The sixth and final section is 'The fisherman: a book of riddles', and the last poem, 'The fisherman', is a portrait of man egotistically claiming the world as his idea until God intervenes and the creature realizes his 'creatureliness'. With the golden hook of love, fallen man catches the fish of wisdom. The poet seems withdrawn into a mythological world that reflects the real world as in a glass globe, as though the mythological structures represented a delicate and poignant defence against a deeply personal anguish. What intrigues the reader is the voice of the poet trying to will her own renewal. *The boatman*, which received a Governor General's Award, was reissued in 1968 with sixteen new poems, and this collection, along with Macpherson's second book, *Welcoming disaster* (1974), was republished in 1981 under the title *Poems twice told* (rpr. 2006), which includes drawings by the author, whose Acknowledgements begin: 'Twenty some-odd years ago/ Oxford took an ark in tow....'

Bodsworth, Fred (b. 1918). Born and educated in Port Burwell, Ontario, he was a reporter there and in St Thomas, Ontario, before working as reporter and editor for the Toronto *Daily Star* and *Star Weekly* (1943–6), and then *Maclean's* as assistant editor (1947–55). He lives in Toronto. As a journalist he was best known for his articles on nature: his ornithological expertise informed much of his periodical writing as well as his novels. Bodsworth's first novel, *The last of the curlews* (1954, NCL), portrays the extinction of the Inuit curlew. Following in realistic detail a lonely male's seasonal migration and doomed search for a mate, the book expresses deep sorrow and pessimism about man's interference with nature. *The strange one* (1959), published in the United States as *The mating call*, tells a similar but much more optimistic story of two geese that is complemented by a parallel plot involving people. A Hebridean-born biologist's romance with a Cree woman in the James Bay area is set against the mating of a Canada goose with a Hebridean barnacle goose that had been windswept across the Atlantic. Just as the barnacle goose resists his instincts in order to stay with his new mate, so the biologist takes a lesson from nature and remains with his lover. The plot is complicated by white racism, which drives the educated Cree woman back to her people and that the couple must combat together. In *The atonement of Ashley Morden* (1964) an RCAF bombardier's sense of his war guilt drives him to become an altruistic scientist. Afraid that his research will be redirected into germ warfare by the Canadian military establishment, he tries to destroy his work and flees to the North to live with a German girl whose father had fled the Nazis. An anti-war book that is topical in its treatment of military distortion of medical research, it too employs birds to convey a didactic parallel with nature. *The sparrow's fall* (1967) explores nature's crueller side. A missionary's preaching is seen to have had a near-fatal influence on a young Ojibwa couple whose survival in the bush depends on the killing of animals: Christian concepts imported into the North seem out of place in the elemental struggles of people so close to the land. The two Ojibwas move towards a more practical philosophy based on the obvious lessons of nature. Bodsworth's novels are sparely written and fast-paced, reflecting the care and authentic detail of an experienced journalist as well as his strong commitment to the preservation of nature, particularly in the Canadian North, and his belief that nature shows us the way to live. Bodsworth received the Matt COHEN Lifetime Achievement Award in 2003.

Bök, Christian (b. 1966). Born Christian Book, he was raised in Georgetown, Ontario, and received a B.A. in English literature from Carleton University, Ottawa, and a Ph.D. from

York University, Toronto. A virtuoso performer of sound poetry, he teaches creative writing at the University of Calgary. His first two books—published by COACH HOUSE PRESS in handsome editions—reveal a brilliant wordsmith, with a poetic imagination, who wishes to subject his writing to constraints and at the same time infuse it with references to mathematics, chemistry, and physics. His first poetry collection, *Crystallography* (1994; 2nd edn rev., 2003; 4th rpr. 2008), plays not only with images of crystals but of jewels, glass, diamonds, snowflakes, mirrors, and ice. Inspired by its etymology, the author says 'crystallography' means 'lucid writing'. He also says: '*Crystallography* is a pataphysical encyclo-paedia that misreads the language of poetics through the conceits of geology.' From the poem 'Crystals': 'A crystal is the flashpoint of a dream intense enough/to purge the eye of its infection: sight'. In the long poem 'Diamonds', set in two columns in small caps, the author's father is central. 'My father/was a sad/gemcut-ter … My father/taught me/precision … He retired, nerves/shot by the threat/of a slipped razor.' The effects of snow, ice, frost appear in the long surrealistic prose poem 'Midwinter glaciaria'. Bök is fascinated by fractals—myriad patterns, left behind by the dynamic activity at work in the world and in humans, such as the spacing of stars, a shoreline, the intricacies of veins, of snowflakes, the structure of a leaf. The poem 'Fractal geometry'—the term is an invention of Benoit Mandelbrot, who coined the word 'fractal'—begins 'Fractals are haphaz-ard maps… Don't ramble—lest you dream/about a random belt of words/brought to you by Mandelbrot.' The last words of the poem are 'a snow-/flake knows a leaf.' The design of the revised second edition of *Crystallography*, in the author's words, has a 'much cleaner, much tighter look'. The text is supplemented by a series of typographic illustrations and figures in line, rendered with extreme clarity, whose visual attractiveness makes up for their esoteric nature. The frontispiece is a collage superim-posed on the score for Mozart's K617, 'Adagio and rondo for glass harmonica' written for glass goblets, 'tuned' by water, that emit musi-cal notes when rubbed or tapped.

Bök's *Eunoia* (2001; 20th rpr. 2007; upgraded edn 2009) entered the realm of bestsellerdom—unusual for such an experi-mental work—when it won the GRIFFIN POETRY PRIZE. In an endnote Bök tells us that '"Eunoia" is the shortest word in English to contain all five vowels and the word … means "beautiful thinking".' Requiring seven years of 'daily perseverance', the book is a lipogram,

in which each 'chapter'—a succession of twelve-line paragraphs featuring one of the five vowels—uses only words with the same single vowel; and each 'chapter' must allude to a banquet, a debauch, a pastoral tableau, and a nautical voyage. The first sentence of Chapter A is 'Awkward grammar appals a craftsman.' Each chapter has a bit of a story, Chapter E being about Helen of Troy: 'Helen, the new-wed empress, weeps. Restless, she deserts her fleece bed where, detested, her wedded regent sleeps.' (Chapter O is dedicated to Yoko Ono.) Chapter U is about Ubu, the physically gro-tesque *père* Ubu of the play *Ubu Roi*, an absurdist drama by Alfred Jarry (Ubu was inspired by his ugly physics teacher) that cre-ated a sensation when it was first produced in Paris in 1896. It influenced many writers; André Gide called it 'the most extraordinary thing seen in the theatre for a long time'. For Bök 'Ubu puns puns. Ubu blurts untruth.' And he has sex: 'Ubu thrusts. Ubu bucks. Cum spurts. Ubu cums.' In the final section, called 'Oiseau' ('the shortest word in French to contain all five vowels'), the poem 'Vowels' is an anagrammatic treatment of the title, using only the letters in the title ('loveless vessels//we vow/solo love'); the next poem 'Voile', dedicated to Arthur Rimbaud, is a homophonic translation of Rimbaud's sonnet 'Voyelle' (vowel): 'Anywhere near blank rage/ you veer, oblivial', which is Bök's rendition of the original French: 'A noir, E blanc, I rouge, U vert, O bleu: voyelles,'. The book was founded on *Oulip (Ouvroir de littérature poten-tielle*—'Workshop for potential literature'), which began in Paris nearly fifty years ago and is dedicated to imposing 'severely restricted methods' on literary composition. Georges Perec's novel *La disparition* (1957) was written without using the letter E. (Bök's 'Emended Excess', dedicated to Perec, uses words whose only vowel is the letter E.) Bök is a clever user of language within the con-straints he has imposed on himself. But it is questionable whether his ingenious verbal activity—adhering to rules, rejecting the per-sonal (emotion, inspiration, intellect) and the whole idea of prosody—results in more than occasional accidental poetry; there is also much meaninglessness. The inventive out-come of the enormous task he set himself, however, deserves nothing but admiration. In late 2008 *Eunoia* was published in Britain and the first printing of 6000 copies sold out in two days; *The Times* of London included it among the top ten books of the year. The 'upgraded edition' published in 2009 contains some newly written poems.

Bök

Bök is also the author of '*Pataphysics: the poetics of imaginary science* (2006), in the series Avant-garde & Modernism Studies published by Northwestern University Press, USA. The word 'pataphysics was coined by Alfred Jarry as 'a supplement to metaphysics, accenting it, then replacing it, in order to create a philosophic alternate to rationalism'. Bök explains that 'Jarry may precede the French word '*pataphysique* with an apostrophe in order to avoid punning, but ironically, his neologism is still polysemic, since the French idiom for the English word "flair", *la patte* (the hand, or "paw", of the artist) appears in the homophonic phrase *patte à physique*—the flair of physics'. With a length of 102 pages—plus 14 pages of notes and a 9-page bibliography–'*Pataphysics* is a five-chapter essay (with many references to Steve McCAFFERY, Christopher DEWDNEY, and bp NICHOL in the Canadian chapter, 'Canadian 'Pataphysics'), whose possible brilliance can be revealed only to the favoured few who can fathom its arcane vocabulary and conceptions.

Bök is the editor of *Ground works: avant-garde for thee* (2002), an anthology of innovative Canadian writing by authors born in the thirties and forties, including many writers with entries in this *Companion* (Leonard COHEN, Audrey THOMAS, Graeme GIBSON, Ray SMITH, Michael ONDAATJE, Matt COHEN, George BOWERING, Daphne MARLATT, Dave GODFREY, Robert ZEND, Derk WYNAND, Gail SCOTT, bp Nichol, and Steve McCaffery). Bök wrote an Afterword and Margaret ATWOOD an Introduction.

Bolster, Stephanie (b. 1969). Born in Vancouver, she was educated at the University of British Columbia (B.F.A., 1991; M.F.A., 1994). She is an associate professor of creative writing at Concordia University, Montreal. Bolster's gifts as a poet were brought to public attention when her first book-length collection, *White stone: the Alice poems* (1998), won a Governor General's Award. This was followed by *Two bowls of milk* (1999), which won the Trillium Award (Ontario). Much of the poetry in these books is grounded in actuality—the two people associated with *Alice in Wonderland* in *White stone*, and individual works of art in *Two bowls*. But far from inhibiting the poetry, the considerable research that preceded the writing of the first book, and on the art works referred to in the second, simply released conversions of subject into imaginative, delicate, often captivating poems. When Charles Dodgson first met the four-year-old Alice Liddell in 1856, he wrote in his diary, 'I mark this day with a white stone'.

Some years later, when she was still a child, he photographed her, took her in a row-boat on the Thames, and told her stories. In 'Two deaths in January, 1898', when both Dodgson and Alice Liddell's father died, 'Your orphaned body rocked/as on a boat down a river one ancient, golden/afternoon, but no one to tell the stories, no one to row'. These 'biographical' poems about Alice Liddell, with their surprising and illuminating imagery, inspired by fact and fancy, have an *Alice in Wonderland* ring of truth. In *Two bowls of milk* there is a long sequence of poems on paintings by Jean-Paul Lemieux. The poem 'Virginia Woolf's mother in the blurred garden', about a photograph by Julia Margaret Cameron of her niece, begins 'Ten years before your birth, you already live/in her face, in the sharpness of her nose,/the omniscience of her eyes.' The calm, lucid, descriptive short poems of *Pavilion* (2002) allude to other of Bolster's cultural interests and draw on many books consulted (listed in the bibliographical Notes at the end). The title of the first group, 'The Stillness That Turns the House' is a quotation from a poem about Vermeer (the next poem is about a painting of a house in Delft); for other poems (among them 'Window', 'Domesticity', 'Room') Witold RYBCZYNSKI's *Home* is acknowledged. Another group is called 'The Japanese Pavilion'—that of Expo 86 in Vancouver; included are short italicized statements about Japanese manners culled from a woman's guide to the Orient. The group of untitled poems called 'Girl' (Vermeer's *Girl With a Pearl Earring*) draws on a long list of books about Vermeer that Bolster consulted: 'Before Vermeer's girl in Manhattan [*A Young Woman*]/I wanted her to let me/in. She would; she leaned//on her arm, almost in the room/already. Her pearl an affecting eye;/no tear. Her sister in The Hague [*Girl With a Pearl Earring*]//has no words. Her eyes entreat, her mouth/regrets. Or the reverse? Caught between,/the pearl turns on its axis.' Bolster has also published four chapbooks: *Three bloody words* (1996), *Inside a tent of skin* (1998), *Past the Roman arena and the cedar of Lebanon* (2006), and *Biodôme* (2006).

Bolt, Carol (1941–2000). Carol Johnson was born in Winnipeg, grew up in British Columbia, and graduated from the University of British Columbia in 1961. She and a few friends started a small theatre in Montreal; when it closed, she moved to Toronto in 1964 and married David Bolt. In the late sixties and early seventies she developed her scripts through the Collective Creation process with George Luscombe's Toronto Workshop Productions and Paul Thompson's Theatre Passe Muraille. Her early plays—*Buffalo jump* (1972), *Gabe* (1973), and *Red Emma* (1974), all developed collectively—offered a political re-interpretation of historical events. Essentially their dramatic strength lies in their colourful characters and their 'montage' of swiftly changing scenes, while idealism, heroism, and comic parody shade their historical actuality and political messages. While *Buffalo jump* explores the conflict between 'Red Evans' and Prime Minister R.B. Bennett during the 1935 unemployed workers' trek to Ottawa, and *Gabe* studies the relevance of Louis Riel and Gabriel Dumont to their modern descendants, *Red Emma* examines the nature of revolutionary commitment in the person of Emma Goldman, turn-of-the-century Russian-born American anarchist who had a colourful life before she died in Toronto in 1940. In *Shelter* (1975), a satirical rendition of the involvement of five Saskatchewan women with the contemporary political process, Bolt's earlier emphasis on myth and heroism gives way to more naturalistic presentation and rounded character development. Her most successful play, *One night stand* (1977), started from the formal challenge of creating a thriller with a small cast: a casual encounter between boy and girl moves from situation comedy to a terrifying psychological exposé. *Escape entertainment* (1981), about making and reviewing Canadian films, has exaggerated comic characters, a multi-dimensional use of film, set, and soundstage, and a pervasive conflict between romantic visions and real-life experiences. Bolt wrote widely for radio and television, to which areas she turned almost exclusively in the 1980s and 1990s.

Borson, Roo (b. 1952). Born in Berkeley, California, she was educated at Goddard College, Vermont (B.A., 1973). In 1974 she moved to Vancouver, where she worked as a library assistant at the Vancouver Public Library while studying creative writing with Robert BRINGHURST at the University of British Columbia (M.F.A., 1977). She has lived in Toronto since 1977. With Kim Maltman, her partner, and Andy Patton she is a member of the collaborative poetry group Pain Not Bread, whose first book, *Introduction to the Introduction to Wang Wei*, was published in 2000. Borson's poems are characterized by deft, delicate descriptions and sensuous images of birds, flowers, rain, and sky. Her spiritual leanings have been compared to the

'inscape' of Gerard Manley Hopkins, and to the spirituality of Denise Levertov and Margaret AVISON. The early collections *Landfall* (1977) and *Rain* (1980) contain warm and deceptively simple poems; the latter uses images of rain, water, and flowing away to suggest the loss of mortality. In *In the smoky light of the fields* (1980) time, relationships, and mortality are considered, as the narrator builds meaning out of fragments; through loss she finally comes to an acceptance of her life. *Night walk* (1981) and *A sad device* (1983) earned Borson recognition as one of the major poets to emerge in the 1980s. The latter collection, recalling her family and childhood, warns that in a mechanical world, love can be a dismantled mechanism: 'I think my heart is a sad device/like a can opener.' In *The whole night, coming home* (1984) relations between men and women are described against the 'feminine' landscapes of California vineyards and gardens. Borson's great strength was revealed in the second section, 'Folklore', a triumphant series of prose poems about decay and disintegration. *The transparence of November/snow* (1985, with Kim Maltman) is a sad book, with many cold images—moon, night, wind, snow—relating to the nature of death and defeat. *Night walk: selected poems* (1994) traces Borson's development from melancholy to moments of warmth, grace, and joy. *Water memory* (1996), celebrating moments of intense happiness, is a book of love poems, exuberant and beautiful. The poems and prose in *Short journey upriver toward Ōishida* (2004), which won both a GOVERNOR GENERAL'S AWARD and the GRIFFIN POETRY PRIZE, are a tribute to the seventeenth-century Japanese poet Bashō, who wrote a book called in English *Narrow Road to the Deep North* and *did* journey to Ōishida. (Borson writes about him in an essay at the end of the book.) Bashō's apparently precise, intense poems, and their simple, vivid nature imagery and restrained feeling, colour Borson's own poems: 'All along the summer river,/this confused heart—/wild anise and pine./*It's not a place for rest,/and not for meditation*—/It's a place of endless daydreams,/something flowing underneath reflections on the water.' ('Summer river'.) 'The mind is a horse I want to learn to ride again,/But this time, properly—/the landscape suddenly unfurling,/like a painted scroll on raw silk.' ('Seven variations on the word silk'.) In 2008 Borson published *Personal history*—a small book, little over 100 pages in length, beautifully produced by Pedlar Press, Toronto—that is a series of beautifully written prose meditations on 'things to be remembered and conveyed', including poetry (the first section is called 'Poetry as *Knowing*'), artists and art, family, and travels.

Bosco, Monique (b. 1927). Born in Vienna, she received her early education in France and came to Canada in 1948, receiving her M.A. from the Université de Montréal in 1951 and her Ph.D. in 1953. She worked for many years as a freelance journalist until she became in 1963 a professor in the French Department of the Université de Montréal and one of the pioneers of Québécois studies. She is a novelist, short-story writer, and poet, but among her many books only her novel *La femme de Loth* (1970, GGA) has been translated, by John GLASSCO, as *Lot's wife* (1975). A strong and bitter jeremiad, it is the lament of a rejected woman who has not yet broken through her fascination with a man-god. Bosco is a Member of the Order of Canada (2001).

Bouchard, Michel Marc (b. 1958). Born in the Lac Saint-Jean region of Québec, which has provided the background for several of his plays, Bouchard realized that his future lay in the theatre and he studied drama at the Université d'Ottawa. On completion of his B.A. he worked as an actor for the Atelier du Centre national des Arts, and served variously as producer, author, actor, and vice-president for several Franco-Ontarian theatre companies. Bouchard has been successful in all these capacities, but his reputation rests on his achievements as a playwright. The author of some twenty-five plays, performed internationally, he first came to critical attention in Québec with *La contre-nature de Chrysippe Tanguay, écologiste* (1984)—translated by James Magruder as *The counter nature of Chrysippe Tanguay, ecologist* (1987)—a psychodrama focusing on the experience of a homosexual couple who want their own child. There followed a psychological and symbolical drama, *La poupée de Pélopia* (1984)—translated by Gideon Schein as *Pelopia's doll* (1986)—dealing with rape and incest within the family of a famous doll maker pretending to respectability. Critics and public alike acclaimed *Les feluettes; ou La repetition d'un drame romantique* (1987—translated by Linda Gaboriau as *Lilies; or The revival of a romantic drama*, 1990, rpr. 1997)—which marked the beginning of Bouchard's national and international career. Mixing estheticism and coarseness, this baroque drama—a play within a play, in which male and female roles are taken by male prisoners—re-enacts in 1952 a series of passionate and tragic episodes occurring in 1912 that disrupted or ended the lives of those involved. Truth emerges from a tale of homosexual love, and from fantasy bordering on madness. It was filmed as *Lilies* (1996), directed by John Greyson, with Bouchard's French scenario translated/adapted by Linda Gaboriau. Of Bouchard's next plays, two have received particular recognition. *Les muses orphelines* (1989)—translated by Gaboriau as *The orphan muses* (1993, rpr. 1995)—centres on the destiny and neuroses of three sisters and a brother as these are revealed during a contrived reunion many years after they have been abandoned by their mother and have lost their father. *L'histoire de l'oie* (1991)—translated by Gaboriau as *The tale of Teeka* (1992, rpr. 1999), and into many European languages—was written initially as a play for children. Set once more in rural Québec in the 1950s, it examines the relationship between a boy, physically abused by his parents, and the goose who is his sole friend. In Bouchard's plays the emphasis on a highly theatrical structure and the use of different levels of language are trademarks. There are also recurrent patterns of homosexuality and victim/torturer relationships. Bouchard's characters are often marginalized and tormented, and self-contradictory: they struggle to distinguish between reality and fiction. And while the plots of his neoromantic dramas veer towards the melodramatic, there are no simplistic solutions. *Heat wave* (1996), the translation by Bill Glassco of *Les grandes chaleurs* (1993), is a comedy of love between two generations. The following plays were all translated by Linda Gaboriau. *The coronation voyage* (1999—*Le voyage du couronnement* (1995)—takes place in May 1953 on the *Empress of France*, filled with passengers—including an important Montreal Mafioso who expects to retire in England—planning to attend celebrations marking the coronation of Queen Elizabeth II. In *Down Dangerous Passes Road* (2000)—*Le chemin des passes-dangereuses* (1998)—three alienated brothers, on the anniversary of their father's death, visit the place where it happened. *Written on water* (2004)—*Les manuscrits du deluge* (2003)—is a poetic play about a flood that disperses the collected writings of some seniors, and their impossible struggle to recreate their pasts—which the flood has freed them from. Other of Bouchard's plays available in English are *Desire: a comedy* (1997—*Le désire*), and *Pierre and Marie ... and the devil with deep blue eyes* (1998—*Pierre et Marie ... et le démon*). The recipient of many prizes and honours, Bouchard was made an Officer of the Order of Canada in 2004.

Boucher, Denise (b. 1935). Born in Victoriaville, Québec, she obtained her teaching certificate from the École normale Marguerite-Bourgeois, Sherbrooke, in 1953, and taught at the primary and secondary level in Victoriaville from then until 1961. In Montreal she has worked as a broadcaster while also pursuing a career in journalism, contributing to newspapers and magazines. Boucher's first play, *Les fées ont soif* (1978)— translated by Alan Brown as *The fairies are thirsty*, 1982—brought her both success and controversy. Produced by the Théâtre du Nouveau Monde, Montreal, in Nov. 1978 over the opposition of the Greater Montreal Arts Council, which was accused of censorship, it is essentially a series of monologues for three voices. Three women appear on stage: the living statue of the Virgin Mary in a plaster cast; Mary, the submissive wife and mother; and Mary Magdalene, the sinner— both contemporary characters. Each is an aspect of the archetypal Holy Virgin, and together they rebel against the roles imposed upon them by the Church and patriarchal society, and express their readiness for love and dialogue. Since this *succès de scandale*, Boucher undertook other types of writing that have not been translated.

Bourinot, Arthur Stanley (1893–1969). Son of the historian Sir John Bourinot, he was born in Ottawa and educated at the University of Toronto. After serving in the First World War, the last two years as a prisoner of war, he completed his legal training at Osgoode Hall, Toronto; he was called to the bar in 1920 and practised law in Ottawa until his retirement in 1959. His *Selected poems (1915–1935)* (1935) contained the work of a deft versifier enthralled with the beauties of nature. *Under the sun* (1939, GGA) showed a new versatility in terse rhythms and free verse, and in frank poems about the Depression and the coming war. As a war poet he wrote about the Second World War in *Canada at Dieppe* (1942) and *True harvest* (1945), which were followed by numerous other collections, including *Watcher of men: selected poems (1947–66)* (1966), containing nature lyrics and contemplative and narrative poems. An active member of the Canadian literary community, Bourinot wrote critical articles, edited anthologies, and was editor of *Canadian Poetry Magazine* (1948–54 and 1966–8) and *Canadian Author and Bookman* (1953–4, associate editor 1957–60).

Bowen, Gail (b. 1942). Born Gail Bartholomew in Toronto, she was educated at the University of Toronto (B.A.), University of Waterloo (M.A.), and the University of Saskatchewan, where she almost completed a Ph.D. She was granted tenure in the English department of the University of Regina in 1986, having in 1981 become associate professor in the First Nations University of Canada (formerly University of Regina, Saskatchewan Indian Federated College), and has now retired. Bowen has received widespread acclaim for her detective series featuring Joanne Kilbourn, a fictional character who has much in common with her creator. Both are teachers at Saskatchewan universities, sometime TV panelists, and each has several children and a politically connected husband. Eleven books of the series— *Deadly appearances* (1990, rpr. 1996), *Murder at the Mendel* (1991, rpr. 1992), *The wandering soul murders* (1992, rpr. 1993), *A colder kind of death* (1994, rpr. 2001), winner of a Crime Writers of Canada Arthur Ellis Award, *A killing spring* (1996), *Verdict in blood* (1998), *Burying Ariel* (2000, rpr. 2001), *The glass coffin* (2002), *The early investigations of Joanne Kilbourn* (2004), *The last good day: a Joanne Kilbourn mystery* (2004), and *The further investigations of Joanne Kilbourn* (2006)—offer challenging puzzles and motives with a fair sprinkling of clues. But it is the added elements of the books with which her readers empathize: complex family interactions alongside everyday domestic details, prairie urban life and work, the ever-present prairie weather, and the often uneasy Native presence. In *The brutal heart* (2008) widow Joanne has married the very clever (wheelchair-bound) Zach Shreve; but she is the better sleuth when a Regina call girl is murdered.

Bowering, George (b. 1935). Born and raised in the Okanagan Valley of British Columbia, he was an RCAF aerial photographer after finishing high school. He then enrolled at the University of British Columbia (B.A., 1960; M.A., 1963). Along with fellow students Frank DAVEY and Lionel KEARNS, he became influenced by the writing and theories of the American poets Robert Duncan, Robert Creeley, and Charles Olson—who were associated with Black Mountain College in North Carolina—particularly when Duncan visited Vancouver in 1961 and Creeley became a visiting professor (and Bowering's M.A. thesis adviser) at UBC. In 1961 Bowering—with Frank Davey, Fred WAH, and others—founded the controversial little magazine TISH. He lives in Vancouver and is an Officer of the Order of Canada (2002).

Bowering

A prolific writer, Bowering has published some fifty books of many kinds since his first poetry collection, *Sticks and stones* (with a preface by Creeley), appeared in 1963 as a Tishbook (new edn 1989). Among the poetry collections that followed were *Points on the grid* (1964); *The man in yellow boots* (1965); *The silver wire* (1966); *Baseball: a poem in the magic number of 9* (1967, rpr. 2003); *Two police poems* (1968); *Rocky Mountain foot* (1968) and *The gangs of Kosmos* (1969), which together won a Governor General's Award; *Sitting in Mexico* (1970); *Touch: selected poems 1960–1970* (1971); *Selected poems: particular accidents* (1980); *George Bowering selected: poems 1961–1992* (1993), edited by Roy Miki; and *His life: a poem* (2000), actually a sequence of poems drawing on moments in his life from 1958 to 1988. Bowering has also written long, book-length poems, including *George Vancouver* (1970) and *Autobiology* (1972), which were included in *The catch* (1976), and *Allophanes* (1976); his long poems have also been collected in *West window* (1982). *Kerrisdale elegies* (1984) gained wide critical notice as a long serial poem. See also *Blonds on bikes* (1997); *Changing on the fly: the best lyric poems of George Bowering* (2004); and *Vermeer's light: poems 1996–2006* (2006), which includes a series of untitled 'imaginary poems' addressed to his late wife Angela and concludes with a twenty-six-page section, mostly in prose, called 'Rewriting my grandfather' (also published separately in 2005), in which Bowering discusses playing around with rewriting his most-anthologized poem, 'Grandfather'.

Bowering prizes spare language and minute attention to phrasing in his poetry. The hesitations at the end of his (usually) short lines register the tensions between wanting to move on, restlessly, with the speed of the moment, and wanting to observe the moment so he will not betray, by sliding past it, the exact word he is on the verge of finding. He has come more and more to think of writing as playing with the conventions of language and literature. In both his poetry and his prose fiction he observes the two chief features of postmodernism. He takes in his poetry a phenomenological position that attempts to respond to the flow of consciousness at the moment of occurrence; and in his prose fiction he assumes a semiotic position that goes out of its way to stress the artificial structures and practices of art.

Bowering's prose fiction includes short stories—collected in *Flycatcher & other stories* (1974), *Protective footwear: stories and fables* (1978), *A place to die* (1983), *The rain barrel and* other stories (1994), and a novella, *Concentric circles* (1977); the title story in *Standing on Richards* (2004) is about a former professor who decides he wants to sell his mind, as the women on Richards Street in Vancouver sell their bodies; *The boy* (2009) is a collection of new stories about the sixties in B.C. Bowering's several novels include *A mirror on the floor* (1967, GGA) and *Burning water* (1980, rpr. 2007), a metalingual narrative about George Vancouver's search for the Northwest Passage. The fiction—which also includes *Caprice* (1987, rpr. 1994), a spoof on the Western and its gendered roles—becomes increasingly parodic and metafictional. Outlaws are treated in another Western, *Shoot!* (1994, rpr. 2009), about three brothers and Alex Hare who formed the McLean Gang and were hanged in New Westminster. *Cars* (2002) is a collection of short pieces on the subject of the title. Bowering wrote them with his friend, the writer Ryan Knighton (who doesn't drive—he's blind) and he has described them as fiction, but—on his part at least—autobiographical ingredients certainly appear.

Three works of non-fiction are Bowering's 'unauthorized' take on history: *Bowering's B.C.: a swashbuckling history* (1996, rpr. 1997), *Egotists and autocrats: the prime ministers of Canada* (1999), and *Stone country: an unauthorized history of Canada* (2003). These books reject neutrality and objectivity, allowing humour, imagination, love of anecdotes, and storytelling flair (as well as research) to reveal Bowering's subjects in a fresh and personal light. He also wrote a memoir of a well-known Canadian painter, *The moustache: memories of Greg Curnoe* (1993). Bowering has said that he never wanted to write an autobiography, but there is autobiographical content in much of his non-fiction, including *The magpie life: growing a writer* (2001), which begins with an 'Alphabiography', twenty-six autobiographical accounts beginning with A for Angela, his late wife, B for birth, C for childhood, etc.; and *Baseball love* (2006), a memoir of Bowering's life with baseball.

Bowering's critical publications include *A way with words* (1982), *The mask in place: essays on fiction in North America* (1983), *Imaginary hand: essays by George Bowering* (1988), and *Left hook: a sideways look at Canadian writing* (2005), which contains a long essay on Margaret ATWOOD's famous 'hook' poem in *Power politics* and includes comments on Sheila WATSON's novel *The double hook*. His criticism is often shrewd, particularly in its discussion of poetics. *And other stories* (2001) is an anthology he edited of twenty-three stories, imaginatively chosen, by familiar/unfamiliar short-story writers. Canada's first Poet Laureate (2002–4), Bowering is an Officer of the Order of Canada.

Bowering, Marilyn (b. 1949). Born in Winnipeg, Manitoba, raised and educated in Victoria, British Columbia, where she graduated from the University of Victoria (B.A., 1971; M.A., 1973), she has made her living as a writer, editor, and teacher in the Department of Creative Writing, University of Victoria, until 1997 and since 1999 at Malaspina University College. She lives in Sooke, B.C. Her collections of poetry include *The liberation of Newfoundland* (1973), *One who became lost* (1976), *The killing room* (1977, rpr. 1991), *Sleeping with lambs* (1980), *Giving back diamonds* (1982), *The Sunday before winter: new and selected poems* (1984—nominated for a Governor General's Award), *Anyone can see I love you* (1987), *Grandfather was a soldier* (1987), *Calling all the world* (1989), *Love as it is* (1993), *Interior castle* (1994), *Autobiography* (1996), *The alchemy of happiness* (2002, rpr. 2003), and *Green* (2008). Most of these collections are represented in *Human bodies: new and collected poems (1987–1999)* (1999), with an Introduction by Dave GODFREY, who writes: 'Their initial pleasure, is the bouquet, is in precision of language and deftness of narrative, but this poetry ages well, not least because of the intelligent mind that lies behind it and the ongoing search for compassion and understanding which informs the whole body of work.' With her scholarly fascination with history and biography, Bowering is an enigmatic writer, presenting different personae, but her own voice prevails, even though (in her poetry) it is at one moment Marilyn Monroe and the next a credible dog orbiting the earth. Raised a charismatic Christian and educated in mythology, Bowering has made magic play a significant part in her poetry and fiction. Her works of fiction are *The visitors have all returned* (1979), in which prose poems combine to form an experimental and compelling novel about the relationship of two lovers; *To all appearances a lady* (1989), a novel about the Anglo-Chinese colonization of the West Coast of Canada—this is probably quintessential Bowering, describing an inscrutable femininity that dissembles as it tells; and *Visible worlds* (1997, rpr. 1999), about Albrecht Storr (much of it is related by him) and his twin brother Gerhard, a subsidiary character, and their parents, and Albrecht's friend Nathanial (Nate) Bone and his parents. Spanning the years 1934 to 1960 and set in widely dispersed places—Winnipeg, Nazi Germany,

Korea—*Visible worlds* includes occasional scenes of the laborious trek on skis from Soviet Russia to North America of a young woman called Fika that are gradually linked to the main narrative. The novel is a kind of condensed epic in which times, places, characters, and events are skilfully interwoven. *Cat's pilgrimage* (2004) begins with the unappealing fourteen-year-old Cathreen (sometimes called Cat) and other teenagers living on Vancouver Island, her mother Helena and her boyfriend Tink, a cat (Cutthroat), a dog (Breaker), a donkey, and her father Jag, who lives in Glastonbury, England—and his sister Jen, married to Colin Printer. Unhappy Cathreen flies to England to join her father, and what follows is an unusual combination of reality and magic—drawing, without achieving a seamless, persuasive narrative, on various mythological sources. *What it takes to be human* (2006)—focusing on the years 1939 to 1942—has an implausible beginning. The narrator, nineteen-year-old Sandy Grey, is sitting in a car handcuffed to a constable; on page 3 he is on a boat, his wrists handcuffed, standing in the bow. A middle-aged woman, Georgina, speaks to him, asks him what has brought him to this pass and he tells her (but not the reader; we learn later that he hit his fundamentalist preacher father over the head with a tire iron, without killing him). He asks what he should do and she replies: 'Get the hell out of here, of course!' He jumps overboard, floats, and Georgina rescues him in a rowboat. The rest of the novel follows his life in an institution for the criminally insane, where he is overseen sympathetically, except for a malevolent attendant, enjoys the work he is given with animals, is visited by Georgina, and responds well to problems and to other people (he is always human). In a contrived, melodramatic ending he is released from this imprisonment and looks forward to the future.

Boyden, Joseph (b. 1966). He grew up in Willowdale, Ontario, near Toronto, in an Irish-Catholic family—which had a mixture of Scottish, Métis, and Mi'kmaq blood in its ancestry—and studied creative writing at York University, Toronto (B.A.) and the University of New Orleans (M.F.A.), where he teaches. He has also taught in Northern College's Aboriginals program in Moosonee, Moose Factory, Fort Albany, and other places in Northern Ontario. The trace of Aboriginal blood in his background—inspiring his first publication and important elements of his second—is supplemented by military relationships: his doctor father was the highest-decorated medical officer in the Second World War and his grandfather and uncle were in the Great War—which obviously coloured his approach to his first novel. He divides his time between Louisiana and Northern Ontario and is married to the American novelist Amanda Boyden.

Boyden's first book, *Born with a tooth* (2001), introduced the work of a gifted writer whose thirteen stories reveal the life of Natives in and outside the reservation in Moose Factory—'the rez'—in well-told narratives whose apparent authenticity is all the more impressive for being written by a non-Native. The (first) title story is about seventeen-year-old Sue Born With a Tooth, the wolf that befriended her, and 'the new teacher up from Toronto': the wolf is shot, she becomes pregnant. The stories are divided into four groups named for the four points of the compass. 'South' is subtitled 'Ruin'. Painted Tongue in the story of that name is in Toronto, where it is believed nothing good can happen for a Native, and—as an alcoholic—he inevitably becomes a victim. The novel *Three day road* (2005, rpr. 2009) is an extraordinary amalgam of warfare, Native lore, and spirituality. Xavier Bird and Elijah Whiskeyjack who share a spiritual connection with nature—friends from boyhood and raised by Niska, Xavier's aunt whom he calls Auntie—enlist in what became the Great War. Niska, a Cree who lives alone in the bush, is a shaman, having access to the world of good and evil spirits. The book begins with Xavier's return to Northern Ontario. Niska meets him at a train station. '"I was told you were dead, Auntie." / "And I was told you were, too," I say.' He is a wreck, hard of hearing, addicted to morphine and with one leg. Niska takes him in her canoe on a journey of three days to where she lives. (The title refers to the dying who walk the three-day road to death.) There unfold stories Niska tells Nephew about her life, in an attempt to heal him (he may or may not hear them), and Xavier's internal monologues describing his and Elijah's war experiences. As Natives they are set apart and speak to each other in Cree. Xavier can hardly speak English, though Elijah speaks it very well, having gone briefly to a Catholic school. They soon distinguish themselves as nighttime snipers—able to move silently in their moccasins ('We have done many night hunts over the years.') and to wait patiently and silently for the right moment to shoot—in a succession of famous Canadian battles, including the Somme, Vimy Ridge, Passchendale, and Hill 70 overlooking Lens, in all of which there were enormous casualties. 'Elijah and I watch through our sniper scopes for puffs of breath on the German line that rise up from the trenches like steam and give away positions. When our artillery knocks out chunks of Fritz's line, we watch and wait for the poor soul who doesn't know any better to appear in the opening just long enough to disappear in the red spray of Elijah's bullet, or mine.' There are countless gripping descriptions of sniper attacks, many of them suspenseful. Underlying the friendship of Xavier and Elijah (who calls him X) is X's, and the reader's, discovery that Elijah likes killing for its own sake and once commits murder. In this expert, complex narrative there is perhaps an understandable anomaly: Niska and Xavier speak, respectively, no and less-than-fluent English, yet their stories are related in educated language. For *Three day road* Boyden won the Amazon.ca/*Books in Canada* first-novel prize. In 2008 he published his second novel, *Through black spruce*, which begins with a horrible dream of the former bush pilot Will Bird (the son of Xavier) about Native children in a residential school near Moosonee, Ontario. The memory of this dream, plus the decline of the traditional ways of life of the Cree who live there, resonate throughout the novel, which is also about Will's niece Annie Bird, who leaves Moose Factory for Montreal, then New York, in search of her sister Suzanne. It won the GILLER PRIZE.

Brady, John (b. 1955). Born in Dublin, Ireland, he attended Trinity College there and graduated in sociology. He came to Canada in 1975 and after a stint as an elementary-school teacher is now a full-time writer living with his family in Toronto. With Inspector Matt Minogue of the Criminal Investigation Department of the Dublin detachment of the Garda, the Irish national police force, as his 'Everyman', Brady skilfully dissects Irish society and mores in seven crime novels that rank as some of the best writing in the genre being published not just in Canada, but anywhere. His debut was *A stone of the heart* (1988, rpr. 2001), in which gunmen from the North, on the run, kill a Garda officer and Minogue is drawn into Irish-American gun-running. Winner of an Arthur Ellis Award, it transcends the formulaic pattern of the mystery as Brady explores the problems and moral ambiguities faced by the Irish at the end of a century that has seen their society riven, and holds up to the light the professional ethnicity of Irish-Americans who claim a nostalgic philosophy that rings hollow in its falseness. Brady followed this with

Unholy ground (1989, rpr. 2002) in which Minogue duels with British Intelligence in the no man's land of the 'Irish Question'. *Kaddish in Dublin* (1990, rpr. 2002) is a tour de force: the body of the son of a prominent Dublin Jewish family washed up on a beach leads Minogue into political intrigue surrounding ultra-nationalists who would resurrect the 'Troubles'. In *All souls* (1993, rpr. 2003) Minogue's investigation into the twelve-year-old murder of a young Canadian tourist in County Clare reveals the strains that tourism as an industry is bringing to a conservative and economically depressed land. *The good life* (1994) is a much more traditional thriller in which Minogue outwits Dublin's underworld, although it is not without its sociological insights. In *A Carra King* (2000) Minogue investigates the deaths of a gangster and the son of an Irish-American billionaire, which become entwined with the Irish legend of the Carra King. In *Wonderland* (2002) two Albanian men are murdered in a Dublin street in broad daylight, a drug-smuggling boss has an uneasy relationship with gangsters who put him where he is, a teenaged girl is dead from an overdose … and that's not all! At the beginning of *Islandbridge* (2005) the name of the title is described as being an area in inner-city Dublin, and in July 1983, outside a nightclub, a double murder takes place. *Poacher's Road* (2006) is probably the first novel in another series, devoted to Inspektor Felix Kimmel, an officer with the Austrian Gendarmerie. It also begins with two bodies, discovered in the woods of Austria, and an act of arson takes place the next day; secrets in Felix's own family add to the plot's complications and interest.

Brand, Dionne (b. 1953). Born in Trinidad, she immigrated to Canada in 1970, and holds a B.A. from the University of Toronto (1975) and an M.A. from the Ontario Institute for Studies in Education (1989). She lives in Toronto. A radical social activist when young, she was politicized by the Black Power movement of the 1970s, and worked as an information officer in Grenada with CUSO in 1983, when the United States invaded that country. That same year she came out as a lesbian. She said she was attempting to balance writing and political activism in her life, and the early creative work she produced attested to that determination. Her poetry collections include *'Fore day morning* (1978), *Primitive offensive* 1983); *Winter epigrams and epigrams to Ernest Cardenal in defense of Claudia* (1983); *Chronicles of the hostile sun* (1984); *No language is neutral*

(1990, rpr. 1998); *Land to light on* (1997), which won both a Governor General's Award and the (Ontario) Trillium Award; *Thirsty* (2002), winner of the Pat LOWTHER Memorial Award; and *Inventory* (2006). As a writer of fiction she has produced the short-story collection *San souci and other stories* (1988), and the novels *In another place, not here* (1996, rpr. 1997), *At the full and change of the moon* (1999, rpr. 2000), and *What we all long for* (2005).

Brand's work is centrally concerned with issues of race, gender, and cultural politics. It was fiercely polemical in tone in the seventies, eighties, and nineties, attacking colonization and the 'tyranny of mapping' that is its instrument, exposing racism in Canada as less visible but no less vitriolic than that of the United States, and lambasting the belittling and silencing of women, particularly lesbian women, by male establishments of all kinds. In celebrating struggle and encouraging resistance, Brand frequently employed what might be called 'unruly language', a counter-discourse that, guerilla-like, challenged standard English, which she associated with imperial power. Dialect, direct address, repetition, street slang, and political rhetoric were tools through which she attempted to write the disenfranchised into visibility, and hence into the discourse of power. Foremost a poet, Brand replaced the fierce rhetoric of her earlier books in the sequences of mostly prose poems in her fifth collection, *Land to light on*, by a use of felt experience and imaginings rendered in controlled, though exuberant and lyrical language. *Thirsty* is a sequence of untitled numbered poems about city life, in Toronto, and the terrible times—'the child killers in high schools, the rages on the highways, / the pushing murders in subways, killers in the street'—and focuses on Alan from the Caribbean, his mother and wife, his sudden death ('Alan fell down whispering, "… thirsty…"'), the funeral: '… before / his child the Toronto police / have to answer any one of us / time and again'. *Inventory* is one long poem, in sections, that details various sadnesses and horrors of modern life: 'I have nothing soothing to tell you, / that's not my job, / my job is to revise and revise this bristling list, / hourly'. *Ossuaries* (2010)—a pulsing evocation of modern times and human turmoil—is a collection of fifteen 'ossuaries', or long poems in three-line stanzas, each of which is a cascade of linguistically rampant images that focus on many damaging effects (the bones) of our culture, and human turmoil; there are also reflections of the observant Yasmin as her sad life is revealed.

Brand

In the thirteen eloquent essays of *Bread out of stone: recollections sex recognitions race dreaming politics* (1994, rpr. 1998)—written from the perspective that 'every public or private gathering with white people is a war zone' (followed by other war-zone gatherings—with men, with straights)—her anger is raised at 'commonsense racial ideology where white supremacy is consistent' to a new level of impassioned, aphoristic rhetoric in decrying 'the face-off between "whiteness" and all it has excluded.... We haven't been excluded, we've been repressed, and we don't need access, we need freedom from the tyranny of "whiteness" expressing itself all through our lives.' The calmer *A map to the door of no return: notes to belonging* (2001) draws on Brand's Caribbean background, travels in Canada and elsewhere, African ancestry, and other subjects. In a series of short or long paragraphs in poetic prose—*Maps* is the most frequent of the few titles—she thinks about her childhood and grandfather and uncles ('My uncle taught me to hang on to the world from the arms of books, or words at any rate.'), the black body, her arrival in Toronto ('I was in America'), the city itself, world travels, and writers—J.M. Coetzee's novel *Disgrace* ('race as a subject') and Toni Morrison ('*Paradise* is about the nature of blackness.'). There are frequent references to the metaphor of the title, the Door of No Return—'the place where our ancestors departed one world for another ... a place emptied of beginnings.' As Brand says at the very end of her book, 'After the Door of No Return, a map was only a set of impossibilities, a set of changing locations. A map, then, is only a life of conversations [for example, her book?] about a forgotten list of irretrievable selves.'

Brand's ambitious second novel, *At the full and change of the moon*, is an epic of many generations descended from the slave Marie Ursule who organizes a mass suicide on a sugar-cane plantation in Trinidad in 1824, the only survivor her two-year-old daughter Boba. We read about Boba's offspring and descendants in a narrative that is impressive in its range of characters, situations, emotions, and places (including Toronto) into the twentieth century, with frequent references to the mythic world of the earlier time. *What we all long for* is a multi-racial Toronto novel—the first chapter is a poetic description of passengers on the subway: 'People stand or sit with the thin magnetic film of their life wrapped around them.' The second chapter is headed 'Quy,' the name of a six-year-old boy who lost sight of his father's legs in the crowd

as they were leaving Vietnam. He was lifted onto a boat that sailed for eight days in the South China Sea before reaching Pulau Bidong, an island in Malaysia. His father Bo and mother Cam, sister Tuyen and brother Binh, arrive in Toronto and we read about them in 2002. Tuyen's parents. who run a restaurant, are obsessed by having lost Quy—her mother blames herself and hardly ever sleeps. Among the many friends and acquaintances of the young people there are two unreciprocated loves: Tuyen loves Carla, her neighbour, and Jackie, a black Nova Scotian who has a German boyfriend, is loved by Oku. The relationships of these and other characters—punctuated by chapters headed *Quy* describing his move to Singapore and his entry into criminal activities—are described in a narrative infused with vivid references to day-to-day life in Toronto—the city is almost another character. As one foresees from the beginning, Quy himself ends up in Toronto, having been guided there by his brother Binh. He meets Tuyen and is taken by car to meet his parents in Richmond Hill, when the melodramatic ending takes place. The lucid, often poetic language that describes all this is interrupted occasionally by a strange use of incomprehensible or inappropriate diction: '... and it surprises him out of his own declensions on fate', 'a kind of lapping shame', 'a hyperbole of pots', 'the city's heterogeneity, like some physical light'.

Earth magic (1979, 2nd edn 2006) is a book of poems for children—including skipping songs and chants—that was obviously inspired by Brand's childhood in Trinidad. The illustrations of Eugenie Fernandes in the new edition of 2006 celebrate a child's Caribbean life colourfully and joyfully.

In 2006 Brand was awarded the Harbourfront Festival Prize, and in 2009 she was named Toronto's Poet Laureate.

Brandt, Di (b. 1952). Born in Winkler, Manitoba, she grew up in Reinland, a Mennonite farming village. She was educated at the Canadian Mennonite Bible College (B.Th., 1972), the University of Manitoba (B.A., 1975), the University of Toronto (M.A., 1976), and the University of Manitoba (Ph.D., 1993). She taught English at the University of Winnipeg from 1986 to 1995, was associate professor of English and creative writing at the University of Windsor, Ontario (1997–2005), and since 2005 has occupied the Canada Research Chair in Creative Writing at Brandon University, Manitoba. A feminist writer, Brandt has published six volumes of poetry:

Questions I asked my mother (1987), *Agnes in the sky* (1990), *Mother, not mother* (1992), *Jerusalem, beloved* (1995), *Now you care* (2003), and *So this is the world & here I am in it* (2006). Place—whether it is the prairies, Jerusalem, or Windsor—is Brandt's muse, inspiring her to write lively poems about family, politics, and eroticism. One of her central themes is the relationship between mothers and daughters. Brandt is also interested in Mennonite narratives, and her work is deeply imbued with her struggle to reconcile the values of her Mennonite upbringing with her stance as a feminist. Among many other subjects *Now you care* treats pollution in 'Zone: le Détroit' ('Breathing yellow air/here, at the heart of the dream/ of the new world'; environmental depredation ('Now that it's much too late/now you care'—'Dog days in Maribor'), and a broken marriage ('Songs for a divorce'). She has also published a volume of literary criticism, *Wild mother dancing: maternal narrative in Canadian literature* (1993), based on her doctoral dissertation, and a collection of what she calls 'creative essays', *Dancing naked: narrative strategies for writing across centuries* (1996). Brandt edited with Barbara Godard *Re: Generations: Canadian women poets in conversation* (2005). See *Speaking of power: the poetry of Di Brandt* (2006) edited by Tanis MacDonald.

Brant, Beth. See ABORIGINAL LITERATURE: 4.

Brant, Joseph. See ABORIGINAL LITERATURE: 1.

Brant-Sero, John. See ABORIGINAL LITERATURE: 2.

Brault, Jacques (b. 1933). Born in Montreal, he studied philosophy there as well as in Paris and Poitiers and went on to teach in the Faculté des Lettres of the Université de Montréal. A renowned poet, as well as a writer of fiction and a critic, he is known to English-language readers through four books that have been translated. In *Within the mystery* (1986), Gertrude Sanderson's translation of *L'en dessous l'admirable* (1975), the poetry rejects formalism and sterile convention, thriving on simplicity and direct speech: it is concerned with what is seen and felt, dreamed and encountered. Brault's later poetry showed a deepening interest in what may be termed 'quotidian metaphysics'. The bilingual edition *Fragile moments 'Moments fragiles* (1985, rpr. 2000), with translations by Barry CALLAGHAN, is divided into five sections—'November murmurs', 'Posthumous affections', 'Short spells', 'Studies in solitude', and 'Almost silence'—to

evoke the frailty of existence. *On the road no more* (1994; bilingual edn rpr. 2001), David Sobelman's' translation of *Il n'y a plus de chemin* (1990), depicts, mostly in prose poems, the solitude of the vagrant for whom it is important to 'eke out a kind of life, a kind of agony'. Brault's novel *Death-watch* (1987), David Lobdell's translation of *Agonie* (1984, GGA), is partly about a student's obsession with his philosophy professor's life, discovered by reading his notebook, and partly a long commentary on a poem by the Italian poet Giuseppe Angaretti that forms the epigraph and begins: 'To die like the blighted larks/in the mirage'. *At the bottom of the garden: accompaniments* (2001)—E.D. Blogett's translation of *Au fond du jardin* (1996)—is a collection of prose *essais* that describe fifty unnamed (real and imagined) writers, pervaded by the garden of a poet's imagination.

Breakwater Books Ltd was founded in St John's, Newfoundland, in 1973. Initially its sole purpose was to publish materials that preserved the unique culture of Newfoundland and Labrador and the Maritime provinces. In recent years, however, Breakwater has been publishing cutting-edge literature in many genres, including literary and commercial fiction, non-fiction, educational books, poetry, and children's books, while at the same time continuing to support its culturally significant backlist titles. Breakwater Books, which now includes Jesperson Publishing and Breakwater Distributors, also takes great pride in fostering the careers of up-and-coming authors while continuing to support its established writers. Many of its authors maintain, and many titles reflect, strong links to Newfoundland and Labrador and the North Atlantic, while others hail from all parts of Canada as well as the United Kingdom and the United States, and write about topics of both national and international interest.

Brett, G.S. (1879–1944). George Sidney Brett was born in Wales of English parents, and educated at Christ Church, Oxford, taking a first in 'Greats' in 1902. He came in 1908 to Trinity College, Toronto, as lecturer in classics and librarian, and in 1921 was appointed professor of philosophy in the University of Toronto, becoming head of the department in 1927. He was not only a trusted administrator, but an outstanding teacher whose lectures were lightened by memorable phrases and quiet humour. A checklist of his writings contains 126 entries.

Brett

Among them are *The philosophy of Gassendi* (1908), a tribute to a long-neglected French priest, humanist scholar, scientist, philosopher, and contemporary of Descartes; *The government of man: an introduction to ethics and politics* (1919, 2nd edn 1921), which relates the historical development of moral and political ideas to the social and religious conditions that constitute their setting; and his great contribution to scholarship, the three-volume *History of psychology* (1912–21). Brett's psychology was broader in range, and more philosophical in content, than that of today; but this important work gave full scope to his vast learning. Brett has a minor presence in Canadian literature. The novelist Phyllis Brett Young—author of *Psyche* (1959) and *The Torontonians* (1960, rpr. 2007)—was his daughter. In Morley CALLAGHAN's *The Varsity story* (1948) he makes a brief appearance as 'a man with an orderly mind'. Hugh HOOD in *Reservoir ravine* (1979) relates an imaginary conversation between Brett and a newly appointed young lecturer in philosophy; while Ernest BUCKLER, in his essay 'The best place to be' (*Whirligig*, 1977), includes, from his own experience as a graduate student under Brett, a lifelike sketch that is a gracious and fitting tribute.

Brewster, Elizabeth (b. 1922). Born in Chipman, New Brunswick, she enjoyed a rural childhood in various parts of her native province. She was educated at the University of New Brunswick (B.A., 1946), Radcliffe College (A.M., 1947), the University of Toronto (B.L.S.,1953), and Indiana University (Ph.D., 1962). From 1972 until her retirement in 1990 she was on the English faculty of the University of Saskatchewan, where she is Professor Emerita. Many of Brewster's early poems interpret her rural upbringing and embody a curious tension between the intensely personal and the deliberately objective, discovering a form in memory and in the very process of writing. Old conventions are used in an original, revivifying way; and although nostalgia and reminiscence are frequently the inspiration behind her poetry, the poems themselves are remarkable for their tough honesty. Some of her early poems first appeared in small limited editions, the best of them collected in *Passage of summer* (1969). Later volumes include *Sunrise north* (1972), *In search of Eros* (1974), *Poems* (1977), *The way home* and *Digging in* (both 1982), *Selected poems 1944–1984* (2 vols, 1985), *Entertaining angels* (1988), *Spring again* (1990), *Wheel of change* (1993), *Footnotes to the Book of Job* (1995), and *Garden of sculpture* (1998). Brewster's poems are generally short, and are written for the most part in so-called free verse, but with a careful control of rhythm and cadence. Certain themes recur—an undeveloped love affair, memories of dead parents and relatives, analysis of a doubtful faith, frank reappraisals of an uneventful but satisfying life. Mainly about what she sees and feels in everyday situations, her poems universalize her own modest experience while remaining understated, impressing the reader with their sensitivity and delicate rightness, and their elegance and quiet grace. Brewster remained productive after she turned eighty. *Jacob's dream* (2002) is named for the poem 'Translating Jacob's Dream' based on Genesis 28: 11–12, when Jacob lay down, with stones for a pillow and dreamed of a ladder reaching to heaven with angels ascending and descending:'Years later, Jacob/ on his way home from exile/... acquires a new name,/Isra-El,/he who wrestles with God,/and becomes a father/to generations of God-wrestlers.' In the early 2000s Brewster converted to Judaism, referred to in the poem 'For *teshuvah*':'Blessed is the One/who guides the traveller home/from the long journey://not so much conversion,/a sharp turn in the road,/as *teshuva*, return.' *Bright centre* (2005) contains more poems inspired by the Bible ('Jacob's angels'), public horrors ('Martyrs on television'—'I watch suicide bombers/and makers of bombs/interviewed on television.'), and personal reminiscences ('Imperfect memories'—a grandnephew has 'phoned me/to ask about his grandmother,/ my eldest sister.') Her *Collected poems* appeared in two volumes (1, 2002; 2, 2004).

Brewster also published two novels. *The sisters* (1974), about a girl growing up in the Maritimes, has the feel of autobiography; *Junction* (1983) is a curiously absorbing romance about time travel in early twentieth-century Canada. Her short stories—collected in *It's easy to fall on the ice* (1977), *A house full of women* (1983), and *Visitations* (1987)—are about women who are mostly timid and lonely; their ordinariness suggests autobiography rather than fictional 'making', but intelligence and sensitivity are evident throughout. Brewster has also published two collections of stories and essays, *The invention of truth* (1991) and *Away from home* (1995). She is a Life Member of the LEAGUE OF CANADIAN POETS and a Member of the Order of Canada.

Brick: A Literary Journal. The history of *Brick* began when two small presses, Nairn Publishing

House and Applegarth Follies, were founded in 1971. Nairn struggled with a few titles, before passing along its custodianship to poet Stan Dragland, who reactivated it in 1979 as Brick/Nairn. Meanwhile, Applegarth Follies began with large ambitions that did not materialize. The first item to appear was the magazine *Applegarth's Folly* (1973), named for a pioneer settler in the London area. The publication was irregular, with issues appearing up to two-and-a-half years apart. Applegarth Press would not apply for grants, did not receive any other funding, and eventually discontinued. Dragland became associated with the enterprise when he was asked to become review editor of *Applegarth's Folly*. The second issue contained a review section that seemed too large to be contained in the magazine, so this split off in 1977 and became *Brick: A Journal of Reviews*. The thrice-annual magazine was eccentric, even quirky, with its reviews of Canadian small-press titles usually overlooked by larger review magazines, as well as reviews of books long out of print. By 1978 the publishing house had folded. Dragland and Jean McKay published twenty-four issues of *Brick* from London until 1985, including several special issues: no. 5 featured Colleen Thibaudeau; no. 8 James REANEY's play, *King Whistle*, with commentary on the Stratford railworkers' strike of 1933; no. 12 a sampler with index; no. 23 bp NICHOL; no. 24 included an index. With no. 25 Linda SPALDING became publisher, with Michael ONDAATJE and Daphne MARLATT contributing editors and a new location in Toronto. After no. 33 the magazine changed its subtitle to *A Literary Journal*. In 1993 Esta SPALDING, Linda's daughter, joined the magazine and became a contributing editor with Ondaatje; Michael REDHILL was both contributing and managing editor. The magazine expanded its publishing program to include outstanding literary and personal essays and articles by internationally known novelists and poets, with thoughts on their work and the creative work of others, alongside interviews, excerpts, unusual and unconventional writings in 'found pieces', the occasional poem, and belles lettres from some of the world's major authors. But the magazine's focus is on Canadian writing within a world context. As a journal of literary and political ideas it is considered one of the best in the English-speaking world. Many of the contributors had an association with COACH HOUSE PRESS, which produced the magazine for many years. *The Brick reader* (1991), edited by Linda Spalding and Ondaatje, contains an extraordinary number of well-known international writers, along with many Canadians; royalties from the book were donated to International PEN. On the twenty-fifth anniversary of the magazine, in 2003, Linda Spalding retired as publisher but continues to be an editor (along with Ondaatje, Esta Spalding, and Redhill, et al.). Michael Redhill is now publisher. *Brick* no. 79 (Summer 2007) is a very handsome magazine, beautifully designed with an attractive full-colour cover, a page size that is 8 ¼ x 8 ¾, more than 160 pages in length, and with black-and-white illustrations and many advertisements. The content, as usual, is full of variety and interest. See also BRICK BOOKS.

Brick Books grew out of Nairn Publishing House (see BRICK: A LITERARY JOURNAL), which ceased publishing in 1975 when Stan Dragland took it over, producing several chapbooks; he assumed the Brick/Nairn imprint in 1979 and the Brick Books imprint in 1981. Don McKAY joined as editor and co-publisher in 1977. Printed in Toronto, with the general manager, Kitty Lewis, living in London, Ontario, McKay in Victoria, Dragland in St John's (and with other far-flung editors), Brick Books has a truly national scope, publishing six new titles and three reprints a year. Among the poets on its list are Janice KULYK KEEFER, M. Travis LANE, Al MORITZ, P.K. PAGE, Robyn SARAH, and Jan ZWICKY. See the poetry anthology *New life in dark seas: Brick Books 25* (1995), edited by Dragland.

Bringhurst, Robert (b. 1946). Born in Los Angeles and raised in Utah, Montana, and Wyoming, he moved with his parents to Alberta 1952 but since the 1970s has lived in Vancouver, though he now lives in Heriot Bay, B.C. The author of many books, he has studied widely in an unusual variety of disciplines: architecture, physics, and linguistics (at the Massachusetts Institute of Technology); philosophy and oriental languages (at the University of Utah); Arabic language and Islamic history (at the Defense Language Institute, Monterey, California). Bringhurst has a B.A. in comparative literatures from Indiana University (1973) and an M.F.A. in writing from the University of British Columbia (1975). Dominated by an ambitious intention, 'no matter how preposterous and impossible it might be—to learn all the words and all the grammars of the world', he began learning Haida. A cultural historian, he is as much at ease with Aztec theology as with modern French poets. Bringhurst's own complex poems tend to fall into four main patterns. First are the dramatic monologues spoken by characters as diverse as Moses, Jacob, and Petrarch. A second group of poems is erudite and difficult, though not obscure, with elusive, often enigmatic references to pre-Socratic philosophers, Egyptian pharaohs, and primitive South American gods. A third group includes haunting poems with strong individual images, precise, often stark, diction, and controlled lines. He has published more than a dozen books of poetry since 1970s—including *Bergschrund* (1975); *Tzuhalem's mountain* (1982); *The beauty of the weapons: selected poems 1972–82* (1982); *Pieces of map, pieces of music* (1986), which includes an auto-biographical 'meditation' and an interview on his working methods; *Conversations with a toad* (1987); *The calling: selected poems 1970–1995* (1995); *The book of silences* (2001); and *New World suite no. 3* (2005)—which abundantly demonstrates Bringhurst's masterful use of images, rhythm, and sound to illuminate his erudite subjects. Some of his long poems—including *Cadaste* (1973), *Deuteronomy* (1974), *Jacob singing* (1977), and *The stonecutter's horses* (1977)—appear in limited fine editions, often in chapbooks he designed himself. The 265-page-long *Selected poems* was published in 2009. *Ursa Major: a polyphonic masque for speakers & dancers* (2003) is a play; it has an Afterword by Peter Sanger.

Bringhurst has published several books on Aboriginal cultural history, including *The raven steals the light* (1984; 2nd edn 1996), a cycle of ten illustrated Trickster stories from Haida mythology, written in collaboration with his friend, the late Haida sculptor and artist Bill Reid, and a study of Haida art and culture, *The black canoe: Bill Reid and the spirit of the Haida Gwaii* (1991, rpr. 1995). Bringhurst has long been a self-taught, though far from fluent (as he has admitted) student of the Haida language. *A story as sharp as a knife: the classical Haida mythtellers and their world* (1999, rpr. 2002) had its origins in the 5000 pages of poems and stories that the young Harvard-educated linguist John Swanton, in 1901–2, recorded (through a translator) from the lips of Skaay, the blind Ghandl, and other Haida poets and storytellers on the Haida Gwaii (Queen Charlotte Islands). The book is partly a claim for the important literary stature of the poems and stories included in the surrounding scholarly text of this readable and attractive book. On publication, however, it was attacked by the (non-Haida) scholar of the Haida language, John Enrico, author of the about-to-be published first Haida dictionary and grammar, and by a teacher of

Haida on the Haida Gwaii. They objected to the fact that material and language that had until fairly recently been entirely oral were being subjected to the scholarly work of someone who was considered to have neither the moral nor the linguistic right to transliterate a literature that is considered sacred, and without the permission of the Council of the Haida Nations. It is hard to believe, however, that in all later studies and anthologies of Haida material, by Haidas and others, Bringhurst's illuminating study will not be consulted. The essays in *The tree of meaning: thirteen talks* (2006), lectures he gave between 1994 and 2005, display his learning and imagination on such subjects as oral literatures, stories ('A story is to the sentence as a tree is to the twig ... the tree of meaning we call stories'), poetry, language, the book etc., with references to a range of cultures—those of Aboriginals, particularly the Haida, appearing over and over again. A companion book, *Everywhere being is dancing: twenty pieces of thinking* (2007), is an elegantly produced book of essays—demonstrations of the author's knowledge of languages and his grasp of many ideas and subjects that, though sometimes abstruse, still provide welcome illuminations. A few of the essays go back more than thirty years.

An authority on letter forms and book design, Bringhurst is also the author of *The elements of typographic style* (1992; 3rd edn 2004) and the editor of *The form of the book: essays on the morality of good design* (1996), a tribute to Swiss modernist typographer Jan Tschichold. In 2008 he published *The surface of meaning: books and book design in Canada*.

Broadfoot, Barry (1926–2003). Born in Winnipeg, he was educated at the University of Manitoba (B.A., 1949), lived latterly in Nanaimo, British Columbia, and pursued a multi-faceted career as a journalist. He was best known for his many carefully researched and sensitively edited oral histories—which he called 'living memories'. These include *Ten lost years 1929–1939: memories of Canadians who survived the Depression* (1973, rpr. 1997); *Six war years* (1975); *The pioneer years* (1976); *Years of sorrow, years of shame* (1977), about the treatment of Japanese-Canadians during the Second World War; *The veterans' years: coming home from the war* (1985, rpr. 1987); *The immigrant years: from Europe to Canada 1945–1967* (1986); and *Next-year country: voices of prairie people* (1988). Broadfoot was awarded the B.C. Gas Lifetime Achievement Award and was a Member of the Order of Canada.

Brooke, Frances (1724–89). The daughter of an Anglican clergyman in Claypole, England, Frances Moore was born there and grew up in rural Lincolnshire and in Peterborough. About 1748 she moved to London, where she became a distinguished woman of letters. In 1756 she married the Rev. John Brooke. Frances Brooke's first epistolary novel, *The history of Lady Julia Mandeville* (London, 1763), a sentimental work, includes a plea for Great Britain's keeping the newly conquered French colony of Canada. Shortly after it appeared, Brooke—seen off by Samuel Johnson, among others—left for 'this Canada', accompanied by her only son, to join her husband, who had been in Québec since 1760 as chaplain to the garrison. The family returned permanently to England late in 1768. Brooke is best known for her second epistolary novel, *The history of Emily Montague* (4 vols, London, 1769; rpr. 1990; CEECT 1985; NCL; Canadian Critical Editions, 2001). Comprising 228 letters, it is deservedly called the first Canadian novel, being set mostly in Canada in the 1760s. Ed Rivers, the chief male character who eventually marries Emily Montague, arrives in Québec in June 1766, during the 'interregnum of government' between the departure of Gov. James Murray and the arrival of the next governor, Guy Carleton, to whom the novel is dedicated. Besides Rivers, a retired English army officer who plans to settle in Canada, the chief correspondent is Arabella Fermor, the clever 'coquet' who is Emily's best friend. The letters, which describe many aspects of Canada, are particularly detailed on the manners and customs of the Québécois—they explore with sense and sensibility English-French relations in Canada—and the Native peoples, and on the 'sublime' scenery of places like Montmorency Falls. It was reprinted several times during the eighteenth century in both London and Dublin and translated into Dutch and three times into French. A scholarly edition, edited by Mary Jane Edwards, was issued in 1985 in the CENTRE FOR EDITING EARLY CANADIAN TEXTS series. Brooke continued to have an active writing career after her return to England. See *An odd attempt in a woman: the literary life of Frances Brooke* (1983) by Lorraine McMullen.

Brooker, Bertram (1888–1985). Born in Croydon, England, he came to Canada with his parents in 1905 and settled in Portage-la-Prairie, Manitoba, where he and his father found work with the Grand Trunk Pacific Railway. He worked at various jobs there, and in Winnipeg, before moving to Toronto in 1921, embarking on a career in advertising, and gaining recognition as a painter, illustrator, editor, columnist, novelist, poet, dramatist, and musician. In all his activities he was an innovator and a catalyst. Best known today as a pioneer of abstract painting in Canada—his best-known painting is probably the geometric *Sounds Assembling* (1928, Winnipeg Art Gallery)—he received nationwide recognition as a novelist in 1937 when *Think of the earth* (1936, rpr. 2000) won the newly established GOVERNOR GENERAL'S AWARD for fiction. A character study of a strange itinerant labourer who believes he is destined to commit an act of unmitigated evil that will ultimately lead to the salvation of humanity, this novel is perhaps best understood in the context of Brooker's conception of the spiritual and of 'consciousness', which was informed by theosophical writings, including Richard M. BUCKE's *Cosmic consciousness* (1901, rpr. 2000). Brooker wrote two other novels, both of which explore spiritual issues: *The tangled miracle: a Mortimor Hood mystery* (1936), published under the pseudonym 'Huxley Herne', a murder mystery about a missing cult leader whose disciples believe he has ascended to heaven, and *The robber: a tale of the time of the Herods* (1949), a study of Barabbas set in Palestine in the year prior to the crucifixion of Christ. Brooker's work as a poet was recognized with the publication of *Sounds assembling: the poetry of Bertram Brooker* (1980), a selection edited by Birk Sproxton, which reveals not only Brooker's fascination with the spiritual and his ability to discover it in everyday life, but his willingness to experiment with form and line. He was also active as a dramatist. Two of his plays, *Within: a drama of mind in revolt* and *The dragon: a parable of illusion and disillusion*, were produced in Herman VOADEN's Play Workshop in 1935 and 1936. Voaden described these two one-act plays as 'milestones in Canadian expressionistic theatre writing'. Both plays were published in *Canadian Drama* 11.1 (1985), with an Introduction by Sherrill Grace.

Brossard, Nicole (b. 1943). Born in Montreal and educated at the Collège Marguerite Bourgeoys and the Université de Montréal, she was active in the avant-garde Québec poetry movements of the middle sixties as founding editor (1965–75) of the literary magazine *La barre du jour*. Beginning in 1965 with *Aube à la saison in Trois*, she has published many poetry collections, two of which won Governor General's Awards (in 1974 and

1984), and novels written from a feminist-lesbian perspective. In 1991 she was awarded Toronto's Harbourfront Festival Prize and the Athanase-David Prize of the Government of Québec for the entire body of her work. She won the Molson Award in 2006. Brossard's novel *Picture theory* (1991, rpr. 2006), the translation by Barbara Godard of a book with the same title (1982), is a complex text that interweaves fiction (five women interact on a Utopian lesbian island) with a theoretical investigation (problems of representation and language are analyzed in a vast conceptual apparatus that draws on the ideas of Wittgenstein, Stein, Joyce, Djuna Barnes, and others). In a 'mathematics of the imaginary', influenced by contemporary science, Brossard offers a model of the text as a process of transformation to articulate a new (feminist-lesbian) inflection of the 'real'. A popular novel is *Le désert mauve* (1987), translated by Susanne de Lotbinière-Harwood as *Mauve desert* (1990, rpr. 1998), about a translator's work. It examines the interpretative processes one goes through in transferring a text into a different cultural milieu and considers the ethics of such a transformation. *Baroque at dawn* (1997)—a translation by Patricia Claxton of *Baroque d'aube* (1995)—returns to her *Aube à la saison* of thirty years earlier, revising its eroticism. The vertiginous, perspectival play between the character Brossard, an 'English' novelist, and the author Brossard, a Québécois, stages Brossard's continuing interest in the shifting boundary between 'art' and 'life', and in fiction as virtual reality offering manifold potentialities for transformation. COACH HOUSE PRESS has published numerous works by Brossard in translation, including the poetry collection, *Daydream mechanics* (1980), Larry Shouldice's translation of *Méchanique jongleuse* 1974), and the novels *A book* (1976), also translated by Shouldice (*Un livre*, 1970); *Turn of a pang* (1976), translated by Patricia Claxton (*Sold-out [étreint—illustration]*, 1973); and *French kiss, or, A pang's progress* (1986), translated by Patricia Claxton (*French kiss: étreinte—exploration*, 1974). These three fictions have been combined in one volume (also published by Coach House), *The blue books* (2003), in the Introduction to which Brossard refers to 'her resistance to narrative' and tells us that '*A book* put to work my fascination for the acts of writing and reading, *Turn of a pang* sought to revive the Montréal of my childhood superimposed with the cultural and political present of seventies Québec.... And *French kiss, or, A pang's progress* synthesized Montréal as a metaphor for ludic [playful,

spontaneous] writing, urban life, the French language ... The novel *Yesterday, at the Hotel Clarendon* (2005), a translation by Susanne de Lotbinière-Harwood of *Hier* (2001), may be Brossard's most brilliant book. The four main characters are Simone Lambert, an archeologist and the curator of a new museum in Quebec City; Carla Carlson from Saskatchewan, who is working on a novel there; an unnamed woman called the Narrator who also works in the museum; and Axelle Carnavale, who is revealed to be Simone's granddaughter whom she hasn't seen for fifteen years. Most of this complex fiction is made up of fragments, many of them inner monologues, those of Carla and the Narrator (and their conversations) and particularly the meditations on her past of Simone (the birth of her daughter Lorraine, who has disappeared in Mexico; her world travels with her lover Alice, a married woman with two children who dies; her interest in history). These short pieces broaden towards the end into eight beautifully written scenes (sixty-five pages), with the four characters conversing in the Hotel Clarendon, as in a play (one would like to see them performed by good actresses). They are enjoyable and engrossing, especially when Simone and Axelle uneasily come to terms with their relationship. 'NARRATOR. And what can be made from silence? SIMONE. Silence contains everything required to live happily. AXELLE. For example? SIMONE. From silence streams everything we call *art*, including the art of living. Imagining without silence or without the constraint of silence would be unthinkable...' There is a short final scene—a play within a play—rendered in Latin and translated in the Appendix. Chapter Five is by the Narrator. She refers to 'the character of Carla Carlson', so the reader's grasp of the text is pleasurably subverted one more time as the boundaries of the 'real' and the imaginary are blurred.

Other books by Brossard in translation are the collection of theoretical essays *The aerial letter* (1988)—Marlene Wildeman's translation of *La letter aeriénne* (1985)—that express 'my desire and my will to understand patriarchal reality... for its tragic consequences in the lives of women'; and the poetry collection *Lovhers* (1986), Barbara Godard's translation of *Amantes* (1980). *Intimate journal or Here's a manuscript (followed by) Works of flesh and metonymies* (2000, rpr. 2004)—also translated by Godard (*Journal intime, ou, Voilà donc un manuscrit*, 1984)—contains selections from Brossard's diary written in January-March 1983. *She would be the first sentence of my next novel* (1998), a bilingual edition with the English translation by de Lotbinière-Harwood, is a miscellany of feminist-lesbian commentaries, notes, and monologues, described by the author as 'a conference paper', written in 1992 and presented at various universities in the US and Canada. The first sentence is: 'She had been thinking about her next novel for over a year.' A very interesting non-fiction collection is *Fluid arguments: essays written in French and English* (2005), to which six translators contributed.

Erin MOURÉ and Robert Majzels have translated three poetry collection: *Installations: with and without pronouns* (2000)—*Installations: avec et sans pronoms* (1984); *Notebooks of roses and civilization* (2007)—*Cahier de roses et de civilisation* (2003), which has a stunning photographic cover showing the seats in the *Gran Teatro* in Havana; and *Museum of bone and water* (2003)—*Musée de l'os and de l'eau* (1999). *Museum* is made up of groups of very short sensuous poems. Each group has a title, such as 'Theatre: speed of water': 'for a long time in separating/the peaks of waves I touched/the water of rapture/the liquid coating of the night'; and 'The throat of Lee Miller', about a woman of renowned beauty—she was much photographed (her neck was indeed beautiful)—who, briefly in the late 1920s, lived in Paris with the artist and photographer Man Ray and was his muse, and became a photographic artist herself: 'I remember the throat of Lee Miller/one June day in Paris ... the throat of Lee Miller/no trace of a kiss'.

See *Nicole Brossard: essays on her works* (2005) edited by Louise H. Forsythe.

Brown, Audrey Alexandra (1904–98). Born and raised in Nanaimo, British Columbia, she was the last important representative of romantic poetry in Canada, deeply indebted to the English Romantic poets, especially Keats. Her five volumes of verse—*A dryad in Nanaimo* (1931; enlarged with eleven new poems, 1934), *The tree of resurrection and other poems* (1937), *Challenge to time and death* (1943), *V-E day* (1946), and *All fools' day* (1948)—reveal little artistic development. Her finest poem, 'Laodamia', which appeared in her first volume, epitomizes her poetic world: her attraction to a legendary past, her love of colourful descriptions, her musical cadences, as well as a derivative dimension. She was made an Officer of the Order of Canada in 1967.

Brown, E.K. (1905–51). Edward Killoran Brown was born in Toronto and educated at the universities of Toronto (B.A., 1926) and

Paris, from which he received in 1935 a Docteur-ès-Lettres for a major thesis on Edith Wharton and a minor one on Matthew Arnold's prose. From 1929 to 1941 he taught English at the University of Toronto, except for two years when he served as chairman of the English department at the University of Manitoba (1935–7). He was chairman of English at Cornell University from 1941 to 1944, when he moved to the University of Chicago, where he remained until his death. Brown published many articles and reviews dealing with British and American writers—he wrote more than fifty for the CANADIAN FORUM, of which he was an associate editor from 1930 to 1933. Northrop FRYE called him 'the first critic to bring Canadian literature into its proper context'. That context was one in which a national interest was not vitiated by the excesses of nationalism, and in which a cosmopolitan outlook never succumbed to the pressures of colonialism. From 1932 to 1941 Brown was one of the editors of the *University of Toronto Quarterly* and was instrumental in establishing its annual 'Letters in Canada' reviews. From 1936 to 1950 his judicious and perceptive articles on Canadian poetry exemplified his dedication to what he described as 'the raising of aesthetic and intellectual standards in Canada'. The early assessments—'The contemporary situation in Canadian literature' (1938) and 'The development of poetry in Canada, 1880–1940' (1941)—show Brown preparing himself for *On Canadian poetry* (1943, rpr. 1974), which incorporated the two articles and appeared in the same year as A.J.M. SMITH's *Book of Canadian poetry*. (These two works established the standards of excellence and many of the subsequent directions of Canadian criticism.) As a 'critical essay', *On Canadian poetry*—which received a GOVERNOR GENERAL'S AWARD and was reissued the following year in a revised and expanded version—was an advance on the tradition of mere historical enquiry. Brown's purpose in this lucid and cogently argued book was to show the difficulties of the Canadian writer in a colonial, materialistic, and puritanical society; to define the tradition of Canadian poetry by discovering what work 'remains alive and in some degree at least, formative'; and to describe and assess the poetry of those who were in Brown's view the 'masters': Archibald LAMPMAN, D.C. SCOTT, and E.J. PRATT. Brown insisted that 'careful interpretation, conducted with insight and a measure of sympathy, must precede judgment'. He was also the author of *Matthew Arnold—a study in conflict* (1948); *Rhythm in the novel* (1950, rpr. 1978), the published version of the Alexander Lectures given at the University of Toronto in 1949 and a valuable study of technique in the novel, with special reference to E.M. Forster; and *Willa Cather: a critical biography* (1953, rpr. 1980), which was completed for publication by his friend and colleague Leon EDEL and has not been superseded. In *Responses and evaluations: essays on Canada* (1977) David Staines gathered a selection of Brown's essays, including his annual surveys for the *U of T Quarterly*, and wrote a valuable introduction. See also Laura Groening, *E.K. Brown: a study in conflict* (1993).

Bruce, Charles (1906–71). Charles Tory Bruce was born of Scottish ancestry in Port Shoreham, Nova Scotia, and graduated from Mount Allison University in 1927. Joining the Canadian Press in Halifax, he later became a war correspondent and superintendent of the Canadian Press in London (England), and in 1945 was appointed general superintendent of the Canadian Press in Toronto. Bruce's first collection of verse, *Wild apples* (1927), introduced the concrete images, musical rhythms, and fascination with the sea that are characteristic of his later poetry and fiction. It was followed by *Tomorrow's tide* (1932), a collection of personal and descriptive lyrics; *Personal note* (1941), 'a statement of belief' in the midst of war about the spirit 'of mankind at its best'; and *Grey ship moving* (1945), a series of poems affirming the values of kinship and regional identity, especially in wartime. In the narrative poem *The flowing summer* (1947), an Ontario boy visiting Nova Scotian grandparents awakens to a sense of the land, the sea, and the traditions that are part of his heritage. These influences are further explored in *The Mulgrave Road* (1951, GGA). See *The Mulgrave Road: selected poems of Charles Bruce* (1985) edited by Andy Wainwright and Lesley CHOYCE. As a writer of fiction, Bruce published *The Channel Shore* (1954), a lyrical chronicle of three generations of family life in coastal Nova Scotia between 1919 and 1946. Similar in theme and in the skilful handling of time is *The township of time* (1959), a sequence of interrelated stories set along the Channel Shore between 1786 and 1950.

Bruce, Harry (b. 1934). Born in Toronto— son of the poet, novelist, and newspaperman Charles BRUCE—he grew up in Toronto, but was educated at Mount Allison University, New Brunswick (B.A., 1955) and the London School of Economics (1956–7). Harry Bruce moved from newspaper reporting in Ottawa and Toronto to *Maclean's*; in the 1960s he was

successively managing editor of *Saturday Night*, editor of *The Canadian*, and columnist for the *Star Weekly*. In 1971 he moved with his family to Halifax, where he became an impassioned advocate for the Maritimes and an essayist of great charm and perception. His move outside the usual confines of journalism had begun with a series of personal essays written under a pseudonym for the *Toronto Star* and then published as *The short happy walks of Max Macpherson* (1968), in which he transformed grimy beer parlours and back alleys into places of mystery and nostalgic beauty. Later, established in Nova Scotia (at Port Shoreham, Chedabucto Bay), he published a stream of pieces that made his reclaimed region and his own life into one subject. Bruce's essays can be read as an enactment of the romance of Canadian regional longing, the struggle of a central Canadian to reclaim parental roots in Nova Scotia. The best of these appeared in two collections, *Each moment as it flies* (1984) and *Movin' east* (1985). An original work, *Down home: notes of a Maritime son* (1988), is perhaps his best and best-received book. In 1992 he published *Maud: a life of L.M. Montgomery*. More recent books are *Illustrated history of Nova Scotia* (1997) and *The pig that flew: the battle to privatize Canadian National* (1997). In *Tall ships: an odyssey* (2000), with more than eighty colour illustrations and maps, Bruce's introduction and captions describe Tall Ships 2000, the spectacular transatlantic races organized by the International Sailing Association. *Never content: how mavericks and outsiders made a surprise winner of Maritime Life* (2002) is the lively success story of the Maritime Life Assurance Company which, while based in Halifax, expanded westward. Bruce established a parallel career as a biographer of business leaders with books about the entrepreneur R.A. Jodrey, the supermarket tycoon Frank Sobey, and the corporate lawyer Frank Manning Covert. In 2009 Bruce published *Page fright: foibles and fetishes of famous writers*, an extensive and entertaining book that was called before publication 'a writer's book about writing.'

Bucke, Richard Maurice (1837–1902). Born in Methwold, England, he was raised on a farm near London, Upper Canada (Ontario). Self-educated until he entered McGill University, he graduated in medicine in 1862 with a prize-winning dissertation. He studied abroad and practised in Sarnia and London (Ontario) before being appointed in 1877 superintendent of the Asylum for the Insane in London, a position he held until his death.

Bucke pursued two different careers: as the originator of occupational therapy, he was a world-renowned alienist, professor of mental and nervous diseases at the future University of Western Ontario, and president of both the American Medico-Psychological Association and the Psychological Section of the British Medical Association; and, as a mystic and an idolator of Walt Whitman, the famous poet's editor, official biographer, and literary executor. Whitman visited Bucke in London twice, the first time in the summer of 1880 when he travelled to Montreal and Quebec City, a trip that was recorded in *Walt Whitman's diary in Canada with extracts from other of his diaries and literary note-books* (1904). After reading Whitman's poetry one night in 1872, Bucke experienced a mystical illumination in which he saw that the cosmos promises man fulfilment in happiness, love, and immortality. He elaborated on this Utopian vision in *Man's moral nature: an essay* (New York, 1879), whose thesis is that if the world is steadily improving, then the most advanced example of a superior moral nature must be embodied in a contemporary. This was exemplified in his next work, *Walt Whitman* (Philadelphia, 1883), the first biographical study of the poet—whom Bucke saw as a paragon of moral nature—which incorporates revisions made by Whitman himself, some of which were directed at modifying Bucke's idolatrous tone. Bucke wrote Whitman several letters—the last written six days before the poet's death in 1892—about his theory of 'cosmic consciousness' (the omniscient, intuitional mind that transcends self-consciousness), but on this subject Whitman never replied. Out of Bucke's theories grew his most ambitious and enduring work, *Cosmic consciousness: a study of the evolution of the human mind* (Philadelphia, 1901), a major contribution to the field of mysticism that remains in print. Bucke edited several posthumous volumes of Whitman's writings, including *The wound dresser. A series of letters written from the hospitals of Washington during the War of Rebellion by Walt Whitman* (Boston, 1898), and was one of the editors of the *Complete writings of Walt Whitman* (10 vols, 1902). See *The new consciousness: selected papers of Richard Maurice Bucke: biography, medicine, Walt Whitman, literature, Cosmic consciousness* (2007), compiled by Cyril Greenland and John Robert COLOMBO. A significant volume, it can be ordered online at www.batteredbox. com. See also Artem Lozynsky, *Richard Maurice Bucke, medical mystic* (1977), both a critical biography and an edition of Bucke's letters to Whitman and his friends; and Peter

Rechnitzer, *A journey to cosmic consciousness: the life of Dr R.M. Bucke* (1993) and *R.M. Bucke* (1994). Colm Feore and Rip Torn starred as Bucke and Whitman in *Beautiful Dreamers* (1990), a feature film about Bucke's life, directed by John Harrison.

Buckler, Ernest (1908–84). Born in Dalhousie West, Nova Scotia, he was educated at Dalhousie University (B.A. in Mathematics) and the University of Toronto (M.A. in Philosophy). After working as an actuarial mathematician in Toronto, he was forced by ill health to return in 1936 to the family farm near Bridgetown, Nova Scotia, where he farmed, and wrote short stories during the forties and fifties that appeared in *Esquire, Collier's, Saturday Night, Maclean's*, and the *Atlantic Advocate*.

For the present writer Buckler was not the fine literary craftsman he was thought to be when his first novel was published (see below), and is still thought to be by some. His short stories have been collected in two volumes, beginning with *The rebellion of young David and other stories* (1975), edited by Robert D. Chambers. All but two of these fourteen stories are included in *Thanks for listening: stories and short fictions* (2004), selected and edited by Marta Dvořak. His stories are often reminiscences about childhood in which farm and family life, and Christmas, figure prominently, with plots that are banal, often sentimental—though sometimes, in their own way, fetching. They are, however, marred by narrative clumsiness and inappropriate diction ('It was the hypnotic week before Christmas and the children were languid and adventurous by turns.'—the opening sentence of 'Just like everyone else'). His metaphorical language has been praised, but the reader cannot respond favourably to the similes in 'The sun drowsed, like a kitten curled up on my shoulder. The deep flour-fine dust in the road puffed about my bare ankles, warm and soft as sleep.' ('Penny in the dust'.) Buckler's texts often refer to the difficulties of writing ('There were no ideas. Then there were too many ideas. It was all there, if I could get at it, how it is with everybody and everything, but the sentences for it were broken up, and stuck inside my head, and when I read over the words that did come, that was not it, or any part of it, at all.' The opening of 'It was always like that'.) Such passages might express his own frustration over the perceived gap between his intentions as a writer (and his ambition) and his limited, untrained ability. Once in a while, however, the reader is brought in touch with an able, unpretentious writer. 'The Christmas order' is unencumbered by the flaws mentioned above. Though the plot is commonplace, perfect for a magazine of the time, the narrative is believable, has suspense, and moves smoothly towards its satisfying surprise ending. It is about a family situation (the ten-year-old son's negative feelings for his stepfather), a snowstorm, and a crisis at Christmastime. Buckler's imagination and his devotion to the idea of family and to the agrarian way of life were positive attributes, but he was seriously handicapped as a writer. How one of today's creative-writing courses would have helped him!

Buckler's first novel and best-known publication is *The mountain. and the valley* (1952, NCL). It is about the Canaan family on their farm in the Annapolis Valley, and centres on David's short life from childhood (to his death at the age of thirty)—with his twin sister Anna, brother Chris, his parents, and his grandmother Ellen, who works on a rug made from pieces of old memory-laden family clothes—and on his growing desire to become a writer, which he hesitantly tries to fulfill. Buckler wished to convey the thoughts and intense feelings of inarticulate characters, their unexpressed tensions, quotidian activities, and significant episodes in their lives. Wanting very much to produce important fiction, he worked on this novel for some six years. Its complex, imaginative design, its deeply felt portrayal of farm and family life—and the intrusion of the war through the return of David's brother-in-law, who was in the navy—presumably attracted Holt's, Buckler's New York publisher. In a day when editorial assistance was not often given to authors, he received none. The basic dialogue and excess of descriptions (some apposite and vivid), the inappropriate metaphors and diction ('Their thoughts had an almost antiphonal, church sound in their heads, with the spell of the day.'), and the 'literary' language ('the still hypnotic air', 'the concatenation of the moment') work against Buckler's creating a lucid narrative that flows. Instead, the text descends often into wilful obscurity and creates a sad paradox when both characters and scenes are little more than lifeless constructs with strains of failed poetic prose. Many sentences and paragraphs demand a slow reading, often a second reading—not to savour the style, in the words of one critic, but to try to discern a meaning: 'He was alone now in this thing he'd got himself into.//He had the cold sensation he always felt when the time was now for a thing (no matter how unpleasant)

which had hitherto been left to lie in the comfortable realm of the any-moment-he-chose possible. The bushes and the long hills struck in his mind with an exacting emergence from background.' *Pace* Buckler's admirable determination to record things 'exactly' (David's word), his efforts tie him up in literary knots: too many things for him were inexpressible. In the conclusion, however, when David climbs the neighbouring mountain, reaches the top, and dies, Buckler redeemed himself: the ending of David's life is described beautifully. *The mountain and the valley* impressed reviewers, and later evoked long, laudatory critiques from at least two academics. The paperback sales, in both the US and Canada, were enormous (schoolbook sales presumably accounted for most of them). In the early 1950s, when it was published, there were virtually no other new Canadian novels that had anything like the ambitious intentions of this one. But it is surprising that in Canada the status of 'classic' was conferred on it, when it is so flawed and so boring. (THIS ICONOCLASTIC CRITIQUE IS BY WT.) In *The cruelest month* (1963)—the month of April—Paul Creed is a recluse who seasonally 'rents people'—renting out his rural retreat at Endlaw (an anagram of Thoreau's Walden) to city sophisticates and inviting his visitors to play dangerous intellectual parlour games in which they strip each others' personalities bare. The emotions released lead to unexpected rearrangements before, in the tradition of pastoral comedy, relations are re-established on a surer footing. Paul, too, needs rearranging; like David Canaan he is inwardly scarred. *Oxbells and fireflies* (1968), Buckler's most genial book, is in the tradition of the descriptive sketch and rural reminiscence, recreating a country childhood (based partly on his own) in a simpler era. There are affectionate details and whimsical anecdotes that one expects of the genre, but Buckler's intensity of descriptive simile—all phenomena are both exactly themselves and imaginatively something else—emphasizes his maladroit way of looking at things. The prose in *Oxbells*, and in *The mountain and the valley*, attempts to capture those moments of unity when, for Buckler, inside and outside become one. In the sense that he conceived moments of unified being (awkwardly described)—where the conscious and unconscious selves are united with each other, with others, and with the external environment—to be the essence of existence, Buckler was a romantic writer. He was also, however, a realist, aware of how rare, fleeting, and fragile such moments are. The much less serious *Whirligig: selected prose and verse* (1977) has an affectionate introduction by Buckler's friend Claude Bissell, former president of the University of Toronto. Humour (rather forced) rather than wit—e.g., Ann Landers' replies to letters from Moll Flanders, Ophelia, and Helen of Troy—pervades these journalistic pieces and Buckler's verse, which includes limericks. Buckler was made an Officer of the Order of Canada in 1974. See Alan R.Young, *Ernest Buckler* (1976); Claude Bissell, *Ernest Buckler remembered* (1989); John Orange, *Ernest Buckler and his works* (1990); and Marta Dvořak, *Ernest Buckler: rediscovery and reassessment* (2001).

Budd, Henry. See ABORIGINAL LITERATURE: 2.

Buell, John (b. 1927). Born in Montreal, he was educated at the Université de Montréal, where he received a Ph.D. with a thesis on form and craft in Shakespeare. He taught in the Communication Studies faculty at the Loyola campus of Concordia University, where he is now Professor Emeritus. The author of five suspense novels of unusual skill, he is somewhere between Graham Greene and Raymond Chandler in his mode, for his central theme is the mystery of good and evil in a decaying world. In *The pyx* (1959), filmed by Harvey Hart in 1973, the vulnerability and self-knowledge of Elizabeth Lucy, a high-class call girl and drug addict, operate as counterpoints to the destructive Montreal underworld—especially the demonic setting of Keerson's Black Mass rituals. Elizabeth despairs of the 'huge nothingness of evil confronting her', and, without benediction, falls victim to Keerson's criminal agents. In *Four days* (1962), ostensibly a chronicle of a young boy's fatal idealization of his criminal elder brother, reality is so perverted that life ultimately becomes an ambush. Buell's most disciplined novels are *The Shrewsdale exit* (1972), *Playground* (1976), and *A lot to make up for* (1990). In the first, the theme of unachieved retribution is worked out with relentless clarity as Joe Grant fails to obtain revenge against three motorcycle thugs who have murdered his wife and young daughter. *Playground* is an interior drama of a man trapped in a wilderness after a plane crash. The quietly unspectacular *A lot to make up for* is in the tradition of Georges Simenon as it follows two young people in trouble. Stan Hagan, once addicted to drugs and booze, turns up in Ashton, a small Canadian town, looking for Adele Symons, who has taken their baby girl (born addicted) and left him in order to make a new life for herself. Stan has a lot to make up for,

and so has Adele, who is victimized anew in the town where she seeks refuge; but with the help of some benevolent townspeople the two find absolution for their past errors and a new direction for themselves.

Buell has also written two books about spiritual matters: *Thinking about God: a very private matter* (2007) and *Travelling light: the way and life of Tony Walsh* (2004), about an English-born Roman Catholic religious figure known for teaching in an Aboriginal community, Inkameep, in British Columbia and later for founding Benedict Labre House, which serves the poor in the east end of Montreal.

Bugnet, Georges (1879–1981). He was born at Chalon-sur-Saône, Burgundy, France. He immigrated to Canada in 1905 and settled north of Edmonton after working briefly in France as a journalist. For fifty years he worked on the land, writing to while away the winter hours and to supplement the meagre earnings farming brought him. Of his three novels, two have been translated. In *Nipsya* (1924)—published under the pseudonym 'Henri Doutremont'—a young Métis has to make a choice between the white and Native ways of life; she compromises by marrying a man who is half-Native and by becoming a Christian. It at first passed unnoticed in French, but in an excellent translation (1929) by Constance Davies-Woodrow it was acclaimed by English-speaking readers. In *The forest* (1976)—David Carpenter's translation of *La forêt* (1935), Bugnet's masterpiece—the Bourgoins, a young French immigrant couple, are doomed, because instead of trying to live in harmony with nature, they struggle against it or mistrust it. Nature becomes a true protagonist, and Bugnet conveys its pervading, awesome presence in powerful yet restrained language. Long before ecology became a common concern, Bugnet, who was a distinguished horticulturist, chastised his fellow creatures for abusing the environment. Indeed, the primary theme of his *Journal, 1954–1971* (1984) is the weather and the effect it will have on his garden. See David Carpenter, 'Georges Bugnet: An Introduction', *Journal of Canadian Fiction* (Fall 1972)

Bullock, Michael (b. 1918). He was born in London, England, and educated at Stowe School, Buckinghamshire (one of his teachers was T.H. White, author of *The once and future king*), and at the Hornsey College of Art. He developed an early interest in languages and became an outstanding translator

Bullock

from German, French, and Italian. He arrived in Vancouver as a Commonwealth Fellow in 1968, and in 1969 became a member of the Department of Creative Writing at the University of British Columbia, remaining until his retirement in 1983. Bullock explored the possibilities of short fiction and prose poetry in a series of brilliant short pieces collected in *A savage darkness* (1969), *Sixteen stories as they happened* (1969), and *Green beginning, black ending* (1971). He is a master of the fragment, the fable, the nightmare, and the enigma. Everything in his fiction is fluid and changeable. Many of his pieces, however strange, are autobiographical at their source and deal with Bullock's concerns with evil, power, war, ecology, and immortality. The loose format of these collections became more developed and structured in *Randolph Cranstone and the pursuing river* (1975; UK title *Randolph Cranstone and the glass thimble*, 1977), an important collection of linked short stories in which dreamlike sequences unfold with their own fantastic logic, yet remain entirely convincing as the main character tries to achieve aesthetic distance in his life, though he is forever chased by a torrent of words that causes everything about him to become transformed. From 1978 to 2003—from *Black wings white dead* (1978) to *Erupting in flowers* (1999), *Nocturnes: poems of night* (2000), and *Colours* (2003)—Bullock published more than twenty collections of poetry as well as several volumes of short fiction, and the interconnected fables and fictions in *Randolph Cranstone and the veil of Maya* (1986) and *The story of Noire* (1987). Many of his poems were inspired by his family home in London, England, or his adopted home, Vancouver. Others use river and water imagery as symbols of creativity: depth, mirrors, and whatever is mysterious or unconscious. Bullock might be studied as a magic realist or fabulist; equally, he could be approached as a mystic or transcendental poet. See *Moons and mirrors* (1994), poems about the moon drawn from eighteen of his books, and *Michael Bullock: selected works 1936–1996* (1998), edited by Peter Loeffler and Jack Stewart, of which more than half is devoted to prose.

Burnard, Bonnie (b. 1945). Born in Petrolia, Ontario, she received a B.A. from the University of Western Ontario in London, where she lives. She spent some twenty years in the West, mostly in Regina, with her husband (they are divorced) and their three children. She began writing in the 1980s and her stories are collected in *Women of influence* (1988, rpr.

1991) and *Casino and other stories* (1994, rpr. 2000). The first book catalogues the intimate retrospections occasioned by deaths of siblings, parents, marriages, past relationships and past selves, bringing to the surface regrets and denials, but also tentative self-awareness and quiet self-assertion. The women of influence in the title story of the first collection are the narrator's mother and aunt, both dying in different hospitals. The aunt sends her sister a letter, recalling happily their 'young sisterhood'. The mother says to her daughter: "'I've wasted a lot of time believing that her beautiful face made mine uglier. Now I'm thinking what a pleasure it was to have her all those years. I should have taken her just the way I took a sunset, or a lace tablecloth.'" The daughter visits her aunt and this sentiment is conveyed. The narrator's last words: 'Good women, full of grace. Stay with me.' *Casino* is thematically more diverse and more loosely structured. In the title story, a popular dance hall overlooking Lake Huron (referred to in *A good house*, see below) is described with Burnard's sympathetic exactitude, as are the band and some of the people who go there to dance: Duncan, Jack, Grady, Norm—we also learn what happens to them later in life. (The casino itself comes to a band end.) 'Deer heart' begins with a woman's drive across the prairie with her daughter to have lunch with the Queen, in 'the small prairie city where the Queen was to lunch with her subjects'; on the drive home a deer 'dove for the headlights'. Burnard's novel *A good house* (1999, rpr. 2000) is about the Chambers family, Bill and Sylvia, and their three children, Paul, Patrick, and Daphne, who live in Stonebrook, a small town in southwestern Ontario near Lake Huron; it focuses on various years, heading ten chapters, from 1949 to 1997. Two early events have lasting importance: for Daphne—when she took part in some teenaged circus stunts in 1952 and broke her jaw, which became slightly disfigured, affecting her relationship with men; and for Bill, when the admirable Sylvia died in 1955 at the age of forty. The novel is a comfortable, authentically detailed account of family members through the years and the house they lived in—room after room is described—until the second generation acquires their own dwellings and additions to the family. These are intelligent people who have integrity, and their relationships are convincing. But for the most part they are little more than names—except when two prolonged conversations bring some of them to life. And except for Margaret, a family friend whom Bill marries after Sylvia dies and who proves to be the linchpin of the family, with always the right thing to say, the right attitude—especially about such things as divorces and misfortunes. All events are held together by Burnard's strong feeling for the family she created, and their bonds. *A good house* won the GILLER PRIZE. In *Suddenly* (2009) the twenty-five-year friendship of Sandra, Jude, and Colleen is galvanized by the fact that Sandra is dying of cancer, but their relationships past and present, their characterization, and Burnard's intelligence as a writer evoke admiration and ... enjoyment.

Burnard has also edited two collections of short stories: *The old dance: love stories of one kind and another* (1986) and *Stag line: stories by men* (1995).

Burwell, Adam Hood (1790–1849). Probably the best lyric poet Canada produced in the early nineteenth century, he was born of Loyalist parents near Fort Erie, Upper Canada, who raised him on the family farm in Welland County; he moved to the Talbot Settlement about 1817. He was ordained deacon in 1827 and in 1828 priest of the Church of England. By 1836 he had been expelled from the Anglican priesthood for doctrinal irregularity and spent the remainder of his life in Kingston (Ontario) as a minister of the Catholic Apostolic Church ('Irvingite'). Some of his poems appeared in *The Scribbler* between 1821 and 1823 and in *The Canadian Review and Literary and Historical Journal* in 1825. For one year (Sept. 1830–Sept. 1831) Burwell edited a religious weekly, *The Christian Sentinel*, in which a number of his works, literary and theological, appeared both under his own name and under several pseudonyms. Much of his early poetry was inspired either by nature or by love. Using a variety of forms, he is at his best when he escapes from the jogging rhythms of end-stopped lines; sometimes he achieves an almost mystic intensity. Of greatest interest today are the poems that describe specific Canadian scenes and events, such as 'The Battle of Lundy's Lane', 'Talbot Road', 'Farewell to the shores of Erie', and 'Journal of a day's journey in Upper Canada'. Burwell's late poetry combines his lifelong feeling for nature with his theological convictions—in it nature becomes a vehicle of revelation. See the selection of his poems in *Talbot Road* (1990), edited by Michael Williams.

Bush, Catherine (b. 1961). Born and raised in Toronto, she attended University of Toronto Schools. She completed a degree in comparative literature at Yale University, lived and worked in New York for five years, and spent a fellowship year at the Fine Arts Work Center in Provincetown, Massachusetts. She taught creative writing at Concordia University, Montreal (1997–90) and has also taught at the Humber School for Writers, Toronto, and in the University of Guelph's M.F.A. program. She lives in Toronto. Her first novel, *Minus time* (1993, rpr. 2000) begins when Helen and Paul Urie drive to Florida to witness the launch of the spaceship in which their mother, Barbara, is the Canadian astronaut who, with the American Peter Carter, is trying to set a record for human space habitation. 'Minus time' refers to those 'terrible, anticipatory moments just before the launch'. In the course of some nine months, Helen talks by phone to Barbara in the space station (while 'every ninety minutes her mother circled through the sky above her head'); but her mother's physical disappearance disturbs her, makes her changeable, given to capricious behaviour, such as allying herself with Foster (with whom she falls in love) and Elena, two radical environmental activists, and being chained to the arches over the Toronto City Hall. Barbara questions Helen about this and Helen becomes argumentative, accusatory, almost hysterical. Always calm, reasonable, and perceptive, Barbara comes across as a real, not invented, person and she is admirable. In many ways so is her husband David, a seismologist, though he has gone off to Los Angeles, then Mexico City, to attend the results of the earthquakes there; but he does reunite happily with his daughter and son. For the paperback edition, Bush revised the second half of the novel, reducing its length by thirty-four pages (a good thing). *The rules of engagement* (2000, rpr. 2001) is a complex postmodern novel that pleases with its energy and the clarity of its descriptions, and the brave attempt to use love and war/violence as parallel themes; and exasperates with its characters who are merely names, the coincidences that forward the plot, and the disruptive switching back and forth in time. The narrator is Arcadia Hearne—self-centered, flighty, perversely wrongheaded in most situations—who was born and educated in Toronto but leaves because of the central event in her life, when two fellow students fight a duel over her in which one is injured, not killed (several discussions of duelling). She lives in London, England (many descriptions of London districts and streets), and is a researcher for the Centre for

Contemporary War Studies (many digressions discussing war and interventionism). She has had several lovers, whom she leaves abruptly (one she marries but divorces). Her sister Lux passes on an envelope filled with $5000 to help Basra Alale, an escapee from Mogadishu, move on. When Arcadia learns from her latest lover—the Iranian Amir Barmour, whom she discovers is a passport forger—that Basra has reached Toronto, she follows her there. In *Claire's head* (2004, rpr. 2005) Claire and her sister Rachel, who lives in New York, both suffer from migraines. Rachel unaccountably disappears without leaving a message and the novel is an account of Claire's pursuing one clue after another—visiting Montreal, New York (twice), Amsterdam, Italy, Las Vegas, Mexico—eliciting countless interviews along the way. Vivid, informative descriptions of the painful migraine experience (known to the author) appear throughout. Like *Minus time*, *Claire's head* was revised for the paperback edition (though it is the same length): one wonders why Bush thought the slightly changed new ending was preferable to the first one. Bush is a dexterous, bountiful writer—generous with plot contrivances, characters, dialogue, descriptions, retrospections, and researched information. This reader, however, felt that a more disciplined, pared-down approach to the writing of these novels might have increased enjoyment.

Butala, Sharon (b. 1940). Sharon Le Blanc was born near the northern village of Nipawin, Sakatchewan. She was educated at the University of Saskatchewan (B.Ed., 1962; B.A., 1963) and became an educational psychologist, specializing in teaching children with learning disabilities. After her first marriage of fourteen years ended in 1975, she married Peter Butala and now lives on an isolated cattle ranch in southwest Saskatchewan, having written numerous books that identified her as an admirable writer. She was made an Officer of the Order of Canada in 2001.

Queen of the headaches (1985, rpr. 1994), nominated for a Governor General's Award, contains fourteen stories about ordinary men and women who suffer moral anxiety, many of them stubborn farm wives with a strong work ethic who believe in responsibility and self-reliance. In the title story, a woman with a headache finds solace in her pain as her family of overachievers find success in their various careers. The idea of succumbing to a physical illness appears in *Fever* (1991), sixteen highly

emotional stories mostly about middle-aged prairie people stoically wrestling with the bewildering complexities of their lives. The stories are linked by themes of illness, depression, or life-threatening physical ailments that are in turn connected to mid-life crises such as infidelity, guilt, and attempts to make sense of an unlived life. In the title story a woman has an affair while her husband lies in hospital with a fever. In the best story, 'The prize', a man deals with self-doubt and insecurity after winning a major literary award. Butala's first novel, *Country of the heart* (1984, rpr. 1999), was nominated for the W.H. Smith/Books in Canada First Novel Award. Her second, third, and fifth novels—*The gates of the sun* (1986, rpr. 1994), *Luna* (1988, rpr. 1994), and *The fourth archangel* (1993)—form a loosely linked trilogy. *The gates of the sun* is a traditional novel of education; it describes the life of Andrew Simpson from childhood to old age and death. His picaresque life is set against a mini-history of Saskatchewan, especially farm politics, the natural cycles of the moon and seasons, and the wind and grasslands, with the sun as a motif in Andrew's spiritual education. In *Luna* Butala describes wives, daughters, sisters, matriarchs, their lives, dreams, aspirations, and isolation, expertly contrasting the women's world indoors (and their inner world) with the outdoor world of ranchers and their struggles with weather and animals. For her women, the traditions of home, family, and hard work are the surest means of finding happiness. With *The fourth archangel* Butala created one of the finest portraits of a small Canadian town. An elegy for the passing of rural life, a deep lament for the lost wild grasslands that farming has destroyed, the novel describes the plight of the small western town of Ordeal and the turmoil of its inhabitants. A futuristic Depression—with bad weather, financial insecurity, creditors, and bankers—is set against a backdrop of history, memory, and dream. *Upstream: 'le pays d'en haut'* (1991, rpr. 1996) reclaims Butala's father's lost French-Canadian heritage. Possibly her most autobiographical novel, it uses the device of a diary to link past and present, language and culture, Saskatchewan and Québec, in the story of Chloe coming to terms with her estranged father in one of Saskatchewan's dwindling francophone villages. *The garden of Eden* (1998, rpr. 1999) is a sequel to *Country of the heart*, in which Iris, its protagonist, leaves Saskatchewan for the wider world, namely Ethiopia, which Butala visited in 1995. *The perfection of the morning: an apprenticeship in Nature* (1994, rpr. 2005) was begun after she moved to the ranch, in an extraordinary landscape, that is her home. It 'began as a small, impersonal book about building a relationship with Nature. As I wrote and rewrote, I began to see that there was no separating my spiritual journey, my life, from the reasons for and the effects of my daily contact with Nature.' So it is essentially an autobiography, but one 'in which I am torn between the facts and history and the truth of the imagination.' The twenty brief essays in *Coyote's morning cry: meditations and dreams from a life in nature* (1995) are on subjects as varied as old age, the beauty and awe of ancient petroglyphs, and 'the chorus of coyotes on a frosty morning'. A non-fiction trilogy was completed with *Wild stone heart: an apprentice in the fields* (2000, rpr. 2001), a meditation celebrating both natural and spiritual discoveries on a grass-covered field belonging to her husband that had never been ploughed, 'all of it strewn with stones of varying sizes and many colours, and having an air of wildness over and in it.' The title story of *Real life* (2002)—a collection of ten stories, many of them about some aspect of family life—is about the reunion of Dan and Edie, who had married almost thirty years before when they were students. They have a long conversation about the past, filled with mutual recriminations, calmly expressed. Towards the end, Dan says that he's thinking of marrying again 'a young woman'. 'There's not much demand for old women,' Edie says. In 'Saskatchewan' Jenna, a Saskatchewan writer, goes to Toronto to give a reading, after having been on a jury for Canada's top literary award: she was outvoted by the two other male jurors, so that Bella Griffin, the most deserving writer, didn't win it. On this visit she meets Griffin and is subjected to a distressing chat when she tries to explain why she allowed the award to go to the wrong person. The title of the story expresses the 'purest joy' she felt when, on her return home, her plane plunged 'through layers of resonant blue toward the vast, mysterious plains below'. The final story, 'Winterkill', portrays a tough, gruelling winter on a Saskatchewan farm. Farming is of course one of the subjects discussed in *Lilac moon: dreaming of he real West* (2005), Butala's exploration—through family reminiscences, memoirs, history, and a multitude of realistic descriptions—of the realities and myths of living in the Prairie provinces, notably Saskatchewan. Commentaries range from the provocative 'rural people speak a different language than urban people, one full of spaces and meaningful silences, where what is not said is often what carries the point, whereas urban people

seem to think that *everything* can and should be said.... ' to the commonplace observation that writers of today offer 'a much more varied, nuanced, and complex' picture of western society than Frederick Philip GROVE and Sinclair ROSS. In 2008 Butala published *The girl in Saskatoon: a meditation on friendship, memory and murder*—the murder, in 1961, being that of twenty-three-year-old Alexandra Wiwcharuk, who was a high-school friend.

Butler, Juan (1942–81). Born in London, England, the son of an English father and a Spanish mother, he came to Canada with his family in 1942 and grew up in Toronto. He dropped out of school after grade ten, travelled extensively in Europe and Morocco, than returned to Canada at the end of the sixties to reside at various times in Toronto and Montreal. In 1981 he hanged himself in a Toronto psychiatric hospital. Butler's three novels—*Cabbagetown diary: a documentary* (1970), *The garbageman* (1972), and *Canadian healing oil* (1974)—are impassioned indictments of a squalid world that robs men of dignity. Michael Armstrong Taylor, the young diarist of *Cabbagetown diary*, is an immigrant bartender whose callous eyes witness the stupidity and hypocrisy of his low-class associates and his high-class customers. Written from his slum apartment in downtown Toronto, the entries begin in July and end in October of one year—the length of an affair Michael abruptly ends when his girlfriend becomes pregnant. The first-person narrator of *The garbageman* is an insane writer from Toronto. Incapable of love yet anxious for human contact, he commits murders in France and Spain. An inmate of the mental institution where his story ends summarizes the novel's theme: 'Life killing itself because of its lack of pride in itself.' The first-person narrator of *Canadian healing oil*, set in a timeless surrealistic universe, becomes Jean Brébeuf, achieving salvation in a martyrdom of love. The artist-as-martyr theme became a sad prophecy of Butler's final years, when his psychological suffering prevented him from having peace.

By Grand Central Station I sat down and wept (1945, rpr. 1966, 1977). This novel by Elizabeth SMART—begun in 1940, while the author was living at a writers' colony in Big Sur, California, and completed in 1941 at Pender Harbour, British Columbia, where she was awaiting the birth of her first child—was published in 1945, in an edition of two thousand copies, by James Meary Tambimuttu of Editions Poetry, London, the imprint of his famous journal, *Poetry London*. A mass-paperback edition came out in England in 1966, and the first North American edition in 1977. Since then it has been recognized as a classic, which Brigid Brophy called one of 'half a dozen masterpieces of poetic prose in the world.... *By Grand Central Station* is one of the most shelled, skinned, nerve-exposed books ever written.' A love story written in the form of a rhapsodic prose-poem, it is quintessentially lyrical: sounding antiphonally throughout are rhythms, images, and refrains that echo the Song of Solomon. It takes its title from a play on the opening of Psalm 137 ('By the rivers of Babylon, there we sat down, yea, we wept, when we remembered Zion.') Set in North America in the early years of the Second World War, it is a type of interior monologue where all attention is focused on the narrator's intense and obsessive passion for a married man. There are few external events beyond a car journey through the western United States, the narrator's ultimate return alone to the west coast of

Canada to have her child, and a failed reunion of the lovers at Grant Central Station in New York. The book is haunting because Smart moves the story into mythological key. Behind the narrator's voice one hears the echoes of other passionate heroines from Homer's Helen, to Virgil's Dido, and Emily Brontë's Catherine. The story does not hide its autobiographical origins because one of Smart's themes is the interpenetration of life and literature—it is not simply that the narrator lives her life as a myth, but that the myths themselves have been rendered quotidian, and Dido walks living onto the book's stage. The erotic passion the narrator records with dazzling metaphoric exuberance infuses even the landscape with a kind of animistic intensity; few readers forget the famous passage: 'Under the waterfall he surprised me bathing and gave me what I could no more refuse than the earth can refuse the rain.' The book seduces the reader into identifying with its account of a hopelessly addictive, life-engrossing passion.

C

Callaghan, Barry (b. 1937). The son of Morley CALLAGHAN, he was born in Toronto, and educated at St Michael's College, University of Toronto (B.A., 1960; M.A., 1962), which he left in 1965 before completing his doctoral dissertation. From Sept. 1966 to Mar. 1971 Callaghan was literary editor of the Toronto *Telegram*; during and after this period he was a host and documentary producer for CBC-TV, and made some twenty short films. Since 1966 he was professor of English at York University, Toronto (he is now Professor Emeritus), where in 1972 he founded the literary magazine EXILE, and in 1976 EXILE EDITIONS. Callaghan's *The Hogg poems and drawings* (1978), reissued in 1997 as *Hogg: the poems and drawings*, is a sequence—supplemented by Callaghan's visual art—detailing the protagonist's semi-religious quest to Jerusalem in order to liberate himself from the stifling conventions of Hogtown (Toronto). Finding passion, history, and even absurdity at the end of his pilgrimage, he makes a descent into the underworld of the Toronto subway, emerging with a new awareness of his identity and an

acceptance of his roots. The sensuality, aloneness, and distrust of the 'thought-police' (any person or establishment that would identify the non-conformists with the criminal) that are apparent in the *Hogg poems* are also motifs in *The Black Queen stories* (1982, rpr. 1994), a collection of fourteen polished tales that range from vivid portraits of gamblers and gays to subtle explorations of their relationships. Evident throughout is Callaghan's compassion for his characters, despite their idiosyncrasies and occasional outrageousness. This was followed by two poetry collections: *As close as we came* (1982), a series of short, luminous, lyric poems, some of them love poems, that were seemingly inspired by the grim atmosphere of seventeenth-century Russia ('We atone and atone, persist/in the sin of doing nothing/but exist,/despise despair,/and innoculate our lives with alcohol'—'Carpe diem'); and *Stone blind love* (1987), a moving sequence inspired by the death of Callaghan's mother. In *Hogg: the seven last words* (2001), the persona that Callaghan has created is in Leningrad, in search of adventure and love. The 111 poems are accompanied by 'Hogg's notes', about Russian life, writers, and history. While not always germane to the respective poem—'Sky queen' merely mentions a Potemkin sailor, referring to the warship, and there are two-and-a-half pages on Potemkin, the lover of Catherine the Great—the notes are always informative and interesting. For 'Osip Mandelstam moves his lips' there is a long, eloquent letter by Mandelstam's widow, Nadezhda; for 'At Dostoievsky's grave', Hogg/Callaghan has reason to include a clever limerick. The 'Seven last words' are: 'Ice is only rain yielding life again.'

Callaghan's first novel, *The way the angel spreads her wings* (1989, rpr. 1995), is a profound and complex work in Joycean prose about a war photographer searching for a woman he loved and lost. His second novel, *When things get worst* (1993), is a compelling story of a strange woman who maintains her connection to the land in a farm community where most farmers have severed their ties. The stories collected in *A kiss is still a kiss* (1995) are linked by images of blindness, war, cemeteries, and decay. Some of the stories in *Between trains* (2007) are only a page or two long, but there are long stories that are very good. They are obviously the work of a Catholic writer—priests and spiritual matters appear in many of them, to say nothing of references to Augustine and Aquinas—but Callaghan is also skilled at portraying various ethnicities, such as the Jewish survivors of the Holocaust working on Toronto's Spadina Avenue in 'Drei alter kockers (Three old fogies)' and the speech of T-bone, the black lover of a blonde woman in 'A one-night stand'. In 'Dog days of love' Father Wilson 'was an old priest who led a quiet life. He said Mass every morning at the side altar of his church, read a short detective novel, had a light lunch, and went out walking with his dog', to which he was devoted. He was also devoted to the Shroud of Turin, of which he had a replica. When he dusted the Shroud and left it out to air and later was shocked to discover that the dog had destroyed it, 'He could not believe the look of terror, and at the same time, the look of complete love in the dog's eyes.' He took the dog's head in his arms to reassure him of his own love. 'Without shame' is about Lyle Kopff and his sister, plain Alice, who own a bakery—she is a pastry chef and is always happy. 'Lyle said, "Sometimes I think you must be one of those happiness flashers for Jesus." "Not likely," she laughed.' She became pregnant and never told the name of the father. '"I think I'll call the child Happy," she said.' He was born dead, but lived in her mind, giving her happiness.

Callaghan the storyteller, the raconteur with an unusual memory for dialogue, composed an entertaining long memoir, *Barrelhouse kings* (1998, rpr. 1999), that passes back and forth in time with anecdotes about his childhood, his family, his far-flung activities, his relationships with friends and people he has met, some of them famous; cumulatively he presents us—until the closing passages on Morley Callaghan's funeral and after—with a vivid, full, admiring portrait of his father. *Raise you five: volume one* (2005) and *Raise you ten: volume two* (2006)—both with the same subtitle, *Essays and encounters 1964–2004*—are two hefty, enjoyable collections of Callaghan's journalism that throw light on Callaghan himself and his varied interests. His accounts of literary figures are of particular interest; these include Auden, Updike, LEACOCK, Beckett, Mailer, LAYTON, Vonnegut, Claire MARTIN, and Nathanael West. Volume Two ends with a memorable, very personal portrait of the famous American literary critic Edmund Wilson, who had praised Morley Callaghan in his *O Canada: an American's notes on Canadian culture* (1964).

See *Barry Callaghan: essays on his works* (2007), edited by Priscila Uppal, in which the contributors include Margaret ATWOOD, Marie-Claire BLAIS, Joyce Carol Oates, Noah Richler, Timothy FINDLEY, Dennis LEE, and Anne MICHAELS.

Callaghan, Morley (1903–90). Born in Toronto, where he lived all his life, he was educated at St Michael's College, University of Toronto, from which he graduated in 1925, and at Osgoode Hall. He was called to the bar in 1928 but never practised law. As a student he had worked during summer vacations as a cub reporter on the Toronto *Daily Star* during Ernest Hemingway's short period there, and the American novelist showed an interest in his stories, encouraging Callaghan to pursue writing instead of law. Hemingway demonstrated the solidity of his interest by taking some of Callaghan's stories to France, where they were published in expatriate literary magazines; while in the United States, stories that Callaghan himself had sent out were accepted by *American Caravan* and noticed by F. Scott Fitzgerald, who showed them to his New York publisher, Scribner's. In 1928 Scribner's published Callaghan's first novel, *Strange fugitive*, and a year later his first volume of short stories, *A native argosy*. In the same year, 1929, Callaghan went to Paris, where he encountered Hemingway again, became friendly with James Joyce and

Fitzgerald, and was ironically observed by the young John GLASSCO (see his MEMOIRS OF MONTPARNASSE), about whom he wrote the story 'Now that April's here'. This brief Parisian interlude became the subject of one of Callaghan's most appealing books, *That summer in Paris* (1963, rpr. 2002). To this period belongs another collection of Callaghan's stories, *Now that April's here* (1936)—his two collections were brought together in *Morley Callaghan's stories* (1959, rpr. 1986)—and his Paris-printed novella, *No man's meat* (1931). Callaghan's three gauche and tentative early novels—*Strange fugitive* (1928, rpr. 2004), *It's never over* (1930, rpr. 2004), and *A broken journey* (1932)—are novels of consequences, in which the characters' acts shape their generally unhappy fates. *Strange fugitive* is a kind of Rake's Progress, whose central character graduates from a bullying lumberyard foreman into a bootlegger who dies under the sawed-off shotgun of his rivals. *It's never over* traces how the tangled emotions of the two people close to a man who is hanged for killing a policeman in a speakeasy raid by hitting him on the head with a chair bring them close to a second murder situation. *A broken journey* uses the rivalry between a mother and daughter to illuminate the problems of innocence and infidelity and the destructive aspects of love. In none of these melodramatic novels did Callaghan really find himself as a writer: the influence of both Hemingway and Fitzgerald is intermittently evident. A sudden sureness of tone appeared in Callaghan's fourth novel, *Such is my beloved* (1934) and continued through *They shall inherit the earth* (1935, NCL) and *MORE JOY IN HEAVEN* (1937, NCL), which have an economy of form and a lucidity of expression and feeling that make them the best of Callaghan's works, and perhaps the best novels written in Canada during the 1930s. They are moralist novels that bear a generic resemblance to the *récits* (or novellas) of French writers like Gide and Camus. Set in the Depression era, whose physical rigours their characters suffer, they avoid the political conclusions that so many novels of the era sought and offer the moral predicaments of their characters as routes to spiritual ends—which, however, they see only 'through a glass, darkly'. In 1948 Callaghan published a book for young people, *Luke Baldwin's vow* (rpr. 1974; reissued in 2005 as *The vow*). Callaghan's next three novels—*The LOVED AND THE LOST* (1951, GGA; rpr. 1994), *The many colored coat* (1960, rpr. 1988), and *A passion in Rome* (1961)—are all attempts to combine the moral searchings of the earlier novels with more ambitious formal structures of the classic realist novel, leading to a softening of style and a straining of credibility. The unity of conception and the force of moral passion that distinguished the novels of the 1930s are evident in neither of the first two novels; and *The many colored coat* is a moral tale that would have made an excellent novella, but was laboured into an overlong and over written full-length novel. *A fine and private place* (1975) may well be Callaghan's least effective novel, for it is the story of an unappreciated novelist that has personal implications and is used to present a flattering self-analysis and a contemptuous dismissal of the characters—clearly Callaghan's critics—who are blind to the worth of the novelist. Callaghan, however, redeemed his record with *Close to the sun again* (1977), in which he returns successfully to the terse novella form of his best period, evading the temptations of realism in favour of moral symbolism as he writes a strange story of how the will to power develops in men when their personal defeats dominate them and destroy their natural impulses. Of Callaghan's late fiction, *The enchanted pimp* (1978) is combined with his novella of the thirties, *No man's meat*, to provide a contrast in settings: downtown Toronto for the first and Muskoka cottage country for the second. The most admirable of the last novels—both daring and imaginative—is *A time for Judas* (1983, rpr. 2005), which is narrated by the fictitious Philo of Crete, secretary to Pontius Pilate and a friend of Judas, who is redeemed. *Our lady of the snows* (1985) is an expanded version of *The enchanted pimp*, and *A wild old man on the road* (1988), a novella, is thinly veiled autobiography set in the twenties in Toronto, Paris, and Rome. In 1982 Callaghan was made a Companion of the Order of Canada.

Barry CALLAGHAN edited *The lost and found stories of Morley Callaghan* (1985), which contains twenty-six of his father's stories that had never appeared in book form; *The Morley Callaghan reader* (1997); *The New Yorker stories* (2001), published in that magazine between 1928 and 1938; and the four volumes of *The complete stories* (2003). In Barry's own memoir, *Barrelhouse kings* (1998, rpr. 1999), he cumulatively fashions a vivid and of course admiring portrait of his father. See also *Morley Callaghan: reflections, reviews, and reminiscences of a literary life* (2008).

Callwood, June (1924–2007). Born in Chatham, Ontario, she became a much-respected journalist, publishing from the 1950s onward, especially in *Maclean's* and the Toronto *Globe and Mail*. She married the well-known sportswriter Trent Frayne in 1944. Beginning with *Love, fear, hate and anger* (1964), Callwood wrote some thirty books on a variety of subjects. As her writing career sharpened her awareness of social injustice, she became a civil libertarian and social activist who helped to bring social issues, such as homelessness among youth and drug addiction, into public consciousness. A good example of her social activism may be seen in *The right to have enough money: a straightforward guide to the disability income system in Canada* (1990). She also wrote on AIDS-related issues, for example *Jim: a life with AIDS* (1988) and *Trial without end: a shocking story of women and AIDS* (1995); in 1987–8 she founded Casey House (named after her son, Casey Robert, who died in 1982), a home for terminally ill AIDS patients. *Twelve days in spring* (1986, 3rd edn 2003) is her account of how she and a group of women banded together to care for sixty-eight-year-old Margareet Frazer as she was dying from cancer; half the royalties are donated to Casey House. Callwood addressed women's issues, either in the form of general treatises on certain areas of concern to women, such as *The law is not for women* (1976), with Marvin Zuker, or in such case studies as *The sleepwalker* (1990), on a specific criminal case. She wrote a biography of a woman spy, *Emma: Canada's unlikely spy* (1984), and ghostwrote numerous memoirs of American celebrities. *The man who lost himself: the Terry Evanshen story*, about the Canadian football star's loss of memory after a van ran into his jeep, was published in 2000. The recipient of more than a dozen honorary degrees, Callwood was on the executive of Amnesty International, Canada (1983), Chair of the WRITERS' UNION OF CANADA (1979–80), and Bencher of the Law Society of Upper Canada (1987–91)—among many other official positions. She was appointed a Companion of the Order of Canada in 2001.

Cameron, Anne (b. 1938). Born near Nanaimo, British Columbia, and living near Powell River, she has written some forty books (thirty titles were in print in 2006)—novels, children's books, and collections of poems. Her fiction for adults includes *Daughters of Copper Woman* (1981), *The journey* (1982), *Women, kids, and huckleberry wine* (1989), *South of an unnamed creek* (1989), *Bright's Crossing* (1990), *Escape to Beulah* (1990), *Kick the can* (1991), *Wedding cakes, rats, and rodeo queens*

(1994), *A whole brass band* (1992), *Dee Jay and Betty* (1994), *The whole fam damily* (1995), *Selkie* (1996), *Aftermath* (1998), *Those Lancasters* (2000), *Sarah's children* (2001), *Hardscrabble row* (2002), and *Dahlia Cassidy* (2004). Three of these novels are historical. *The journey* has the Klondike of the late 1890s as background, as does *South of an unnamed creek*, which is about a group of women who bond in Dawson City. In *Escape to Beulah* another group of women, both black and white, escape from Cassidy, a cruel plantation owner, in the pre–Civil War American South. Cameron's novels are often formulaic and contrived, with little delineation of character or background, but her British Columbia novels bespeak a serious concern with sexual abuse, women and children in isolation and at risk, cultural neglect, multiculturalism, and a society that turns its back on the impoverished or the sexually marginalized in working-class communities. They deal openly in colloquial language with situations of drunkenness, poverty, loneliness, failure, and violence—relieved by strong women who find solace, relief, or escape in their imagination, or in the world of Native fantasy and myth. *Daughters of Copper Woman*—which has been translated into several languages, with more than 200,000 copies in print—includes the story of an abused child who finds strength and trust with Native elders who introduce her to the powers of the spiritual world; Northwest myths and legends are woven into details of everyday life to create a message about the social and spiritual power of women. In 1988 Cameron was severely criticized by Lee MARACLE, who asked her to stop using Native stories in her work, which resulted in debates in the literary community over 'appropriation of voice' and led to new perspectives on writing out of one's own background. *A whole brass band*—the saga of an unconventional family led by a single mother and a fishboat captain, Jean Pritchard—while having an energetic but unbelievable plot, is at once funny, caustic, and thoughtful, with its commentaries on the difficulties of building and maintaining family bonds. *Aftermath*, about children taken from their homes by authorities, continues the theme of child abuse introduced in *Daughters of Copper Woman*. In the story collection *Bright's Crossing*, a fictional Vancouver Island industry town is seen through the eyes of eleven women. Cameron is praised for her easy narrative style, her skill with colloquial dialogue and her salty humour, and for her depiction of earth mothers who respond to family situations with exuberance and ribald wit.

Cameron

Cameron's poetry appears in *Earth witch* (1982) and *The Annie poems* (1987), which explores from a lesbian perspective imagery of Vancouver Island forests and seacoasts. The notable *Dreamspeaker* (1979, rpr. 2005), described as a juvenile, about an abused boy who is healed by village elders, began as the script for a television film (1977) directed by Claude Jutra. Among Cameron's other books for children are Native legends retold—including *How Raven freed the moon* (1985), *How the loon lost her voice* (1985), *Raven and Snipe* (1991), and *Raven goes berrypicking* (1991)—and *Orca's song* (1987) and *Lazy boy* (1988). *Dzelarhons: myths of the Northwest Coast* (1986) was written for adults.

Cameron, Elspeth (b. 1943). She was born in Toronto and educated at the University of British Columbia (B.A., 1964), the University of New Brunswick (M.A., 1965), and McGill University (Ph.D., 1970). She was professor of English at Concordia University, Montreal, from 1970 to 1977; taught at New College, University of Toronto, from 1980 to 1990, when she was made professor of English; and directed the Canadian Studies Program at University College from 1994 to 1997; she now teaches Canadian studies at Brock University. Cameron is the author of important and extensive biographies of three towering figures in modern Canadian literature. In undertaking *Hugh MacLennan: a writer's life* (1981, rpr. 1983) she was partly inspired to deal with and make sense of a dismissive attitude to MacLENNAN the writer: that he broke new ground with *Barometer rising* but was essentially a moralistic writer of fictional social history. Her penetrating study of the seven novels, and of the life, threw new light on MacLennan. Irving LAYTON asked Cameron to write his biography, *Irving Layton: a life* (1985), and co-operated in her research. But when her book—about the 'zig-zag' life of a poet who 'hated to be unmasked' and never wanted to be 'pinned down'—was published, his rage was widely expressed in newspapers. A responsible and carefully researched account of the poet's tumultuous life—including his treatment of many women, among them his wives, and of his children—that also discusses his poetry (both his best poems and his worst), it is perhaps not surprising that it gave offence. But the biography was admired and praised by others. *Earle Birney: a life* (1994) is very long—some 700 pages drawn from an enormous archive and including 100 pages of endnotes—but it is also highly readable and illuminating. For Cameron, BIRNEY 'resembles Loki, the Old Norse god, who represents the principle of change. Dynamic and unpredictable, exciting and mischievous.... Birney's unconventional craftsmanship, his penchant for playful satire, his Nordic appearance ... and his restless, predatory temperament all call to mind Loki. He loved poetry, but he loved much else, and lacked the single-mindedness to dedicate himself to it, or to anything else.' But in old age, 'Birney more and more resembled Don Quixote'. The biography is an impressive portrayal of a difficult subject. Cameron's latest substantial biography is *And beauty answers: the life of Frances Loring and Florence Wyle* (2007), about two sculptors who came to Toronto from New York in 1911 and 1912 respectively and became known for their public neoclassical sculptures and, personally and popularly, as 'the Girls'.

In 1997 Cameron surprised everyone with an autobiographical work, *No previous experience: a memoir of love and change* (rpr. 1998), about her subservience to her husbands, the break-up of her third marriage, and her lesbian relationship with a professor at the University of Calgary (which eventually ended). Cameron co-edited, with Janice Dickin, *Great dames* (1997), a collection of sixteen biographical pieces on Canadian women of accomplishment, including 'the REFUS GLOBAL women', Gwethalyn GRAHAM (by Cameron), and Dr Marion Hilliard.

Cameron, George Frederick (1854–85). Born in New Glasgow, Nova Scotia, he moved with his family to Boston in 1869 and in 1872 entered Boston University to study law. Later he worked with a law firm there. His early interest was in the classics and he is said to have read most of Virgil and Cicero in the original before he was fourteen. While articling in law he contributed poems and essays to several Boston newspapers. In 1882 he entered Queen's University, Kingston, and was named the prize poet in 1883, when he was made editor of the Kingston *News*, a position he held until his death. A selection of Cameron's poetry, *Lyrics on freedom, love and death* (Kingston, 1887), edited and published by his brother, Charles L. Cameron, was unlike other Canadian verse of the time. Displaying little effort to write about 'Canadian' subjects such as nature and patriotism, it reflects Cameron's strong interest in classical culture, and his wide political concerns in poems sympathetic to the independence of Cuba and in praise of the democratic aspirations of the United States—clouded by a prevailing pessimism.

Campbell, Maria (b. 1940). This Métis writer was born on a trapline in northwestern Saskatchewan, the eldest of eight children; she was raised in a road-allowance community and attended a one-room elementary country school in northern Saskatchewan. When her mother died, Campbell at twelve years of age had to leave school to look after the other children. She left home at fifteen and went to Vancouver. In her twenties she returned to the Prairies, where she was a community worker, activist, and organizer. She lives at Gabriel's Crossing, Batoche, Saskatchewan, and is an associate professor in the Department of English, University of Saskatchewan. With the help of a collective she wrote *Many laws* (1969), explaining the laws that confront Aboriginal people when they move to the city. Campbell's memoir *Halfbreed* (1973, rpr. 1983) is a daring account of a strong-willed woman who overcame poverty, alcoholism, drug addiction, sexual abuse, and prostitution by the age of thirty-three, because 'I had a whole lot of stuff inside me that I had to write to find out who I was, to heal myself.' It rises above the level of confessional biography because Campbell views her life in the larger context of a distinct Métis culture. She gives a mythic dimension to the story of her people, and a powerfully distinctive voice to a people with few illusions and even fewer realizable hopes, who had been ignored for too long. On school and university course lists across the country, *Halfbreed* became a watershed publication for the Aboriginal peoples of Canada and established Campbell as 'the Mother of us all', in the words of Daniel David MOSES. Campbell likes to explore theatre as a way of bringing her messages to Canadians, and has written four plays collectively. *Jessica*, written in collaboration with Linda Griffiths, portrays a young Métis woman's transformations from innocence to despair to self-discovery. It opened in 1986 at the Theatre Passe Muraille, Toronto, winning the Dora Mavor Moore Award for outstanding new play, and also played at the Quinzanne International Festival in Quebec City, when it was judged the Best Canadian Production. In 1989 it was published, along with the story of its turbulent creation, in *The book of Jessica: a theatrical transformation*. The eight stories in *Stories of the road-allowance people* (1995, rev. 2005), 'translated' by Campbell, are not written in standard English but 'in the dialect and rhythm of my village and my father's generation', with each paragraph reading like a poem in free verse; the illustrations in this large-format book are paintings by Sherry Farrell Racette. Campbell received two honorary doctorates in 1995: from the University of Regina and York University, Toronto. She was appointed an Officer of the Order of Canada in 2008.

Campbell, Wilfred (1860–1918). An Anglican clergyman's son, William Wilfred Campbell was born in Newmarket, Canada West (Ontario), and upon completing high school in Owen Sound taught for a year in a country school at Zion, near Wiarton, Ontario. He enrolled at University College, University of Toronto, in 1880, but in 1882 transferred to Wycliffe, the university's Anglican divinity school. The following year he transferred again, this time to the Episcopal Theological School in Cambridge, Massachusetts. Ordained in 1886, Campbell served various parishes before resigning from the ministry in 1891; for the rest of his life he worked in the Ottawa civil service. The poetry of Wilfred Campbell—who is sometimes included among the CONFEDERATION POETS—is to a large extent the chronicle of a sensitive man's struggle to find meaning in an age of shifting values. *Snowflakes and sunbeams* (St Stephen, N.B., 1888; rpr. 1974) is concerned chiefly with nature, and the influence of the English Romantics is apparent in almost every poem; the beauty of nature is glorified in his best-known and most-anthologized poem, 'Indian summer'. In *Lake lyrics and other poems* (Saint John, N.B., 1889) nature is perceived less as a manifestation of God's presence on earth than as a spiritual force in itself. Campbell's most significant nature poetry is stark and horrifying in its imagery. In 'The winter lakes' (*Lake lyrics*) the poet casts off the conventional nineteenth-century pose of being transported by nature's beauty and probes instead a profound sense of doubt in the face of a landscape unrelieved by hope. Similarly, in 'How one winter came in the lake region', in *The dread voyage* (Toronto, 1893), he paints a bleak portrait of a world untouched by God's grace. In winter lakes and landscapes Campbell found a metaphor for his despair over the religious doubt of the age. After the turn of the century, Campbell, for whom the monarchy and Empire provided a reassuring link between past and present, expressed his imperialist philosophy in verse, as in the elegiac 'Victoria', in *The poems of Wilfred Campbell*—also published under the title *The collected poems of Wilfred Campbell* (both 1905)—which laments her death. Campbell's final book, *Sagas of vaster Britain: poems of the race, the Empire and the divinity of man* (1914), argues for the imperialist cause at a time when the

Empire was going to war. Campbell saw in imperialism's idealism and continuity the potential for meaningful action in an age of uncertainty and flux. As a newspaper columnist, Campbell joined his fellow poets Archibald LAMPMAN and Duncan Campbell SCOTT to write the column 'AT THE MERMAID INN' for the Toronto *Globe* (1892–3). See *Vapour and blue: Souster selects Campbell* (1978), edited by Raymond SOUSTER. Carl F. KLINCK wrote a fine biography, *Wilfred Campbell: a study in late provincial Victorianism* (1942, rev. 1977), and an introduction to Campbell's *Selected poems* (1976).

Canada Council for the Arts, The. The 1951 report of the Royal Commission on National Development in the Arts, Letters and Sciences—popularly known as the Massey Commission Report after its chair, Vincent Massey—recommended to Parliament the creation of the Canada Council in order 'to foster and promote the study and enjoyment of, and the production in, the arts, humanities and social sciences.' Passage of the Canada Council Act by Parliament followed on 28 March 1957, with initial funding from an Endowment Fund of $100 million derived from the death duties of Nova Scotia industrialists Sir James Dunn and Izaak Walton Killam. In 1966 a Parliamentary grant of $16.9 million was approved, which grew annually to represent in the early 1990s 90 per cent of the Council's budget. In the first year of operation, 1957–8, the Council dispensed grants and awards in the value of $1.4 million. In 2007–8 the Council distributed more than $164.5 million in grants in the following areas: Music ($27,402,000), Theatre ($24,041,000), Writing and Publishing ($21,864,000), Visual Arts ($18,917,000), Dance ($16,405,000), Media Arts ($13,273,000), Integrated Arts ($2,247,000), and Public Lending Rights—payment to writers for the use of their books in Canadian libraries ($9,159,000). In 2007–8 the Council received a total of $182.5 million in parliamentary appropriation. See also GOVERNOR GENERAL'S LITERARY AWARDS.

Canadian Authors' Association. It was established in 1921 to lobby against proposed copyright legislation that threatened to discriminate against Canadian writers. Its founders—Stephen LEACOCK, Pelham Edgar, B.K. SANDWELL, and John Murray Gibbon, who became its first president—anticipated a bi-national literary association. The CAA, as it soon became known, worked to develop a sense of cultural and literary solidarity among writers throughout Canada. Composed of local branches across the country, it convened annually in the spring; its self-governing French Section lasted until 1936, when planning for the Société des Écrivains Canadiens (est. 1938) began. In the early 1920s it lobbied successfully for changes in copyright legislation and kept its members informed in the pages of the *Canadian Bookman* (1921–2), edited by Sandwell, and successively in the *Authors' Bulletin* (1922–33), the *Canadian Author* (1933–40), the *Canadian Author and Bookman* (1940–92), and the *Canadian Author* (1992–8). In an attempt to make Canadians more aware of the writers and books of their country, the CAA sponsored the first Canada Book Week in November 1921, which took place annually until 1957, and there were other literary initiatives. The poetry chapbooks of the different branches, privately printed in the late 1920s and early 1930s, culminated in the founding of *Canadian Poetry Magazine* (1936), which eventually merged with the *Canadian Author and Bookman* in 1968. The CAA was also responsible for the establishment in 1937 of the GOVERNOR GENERAL'S LITERARY AWARDS, whose administration by the CAA under a specially appointed Awards Board (est. 1944) lasted until 1959, when it was assumed by the CANADA COUNCIL. In 1946 the Awards Board was entrusted with the adjudication of the new Stephen Leacock Medal for Humour, which it administered until 1960, when responsibility for the award passed to the Stephen Leacock Society. In 1975 the Association established the Canadian Authors' Association literary Awards with the goal of proving that 'literary excellence and popular appeal are entirely compatible'. In 1963 the CAA initiated a campaign to bring to Canadian authors a public lending right, but although other writers' groups joined this movement the Public Lending Right program did not become a reality until 1986. The Association also successfully lobbied to have Canada join the Universal Copyright Convention and helped form the Canadian Writers' Foundation (1932), which continues to provide financial assistance to indigent authors and their families. The official handbook of the CAA, *The Canadian writer's guide*, was first published in 1962 (13th edn 2002). In 1964 the CAA reaffirmed the long-held policy of welcoming unpublished writers as associate members. The CAA, with its motto 'Writers helping writers', continues to provide opportunities for networking, professional development, and mentoring to emerging writers and in 2008 began building the foundation for a youth program. See also The WRITERS' UNION OF CANADA, The LEAGUE OF CANADIAN POETS, and the PLAYWRIGHTS UNION OF CANADA.

Canadian encyclopedia, The. This huge one-volume encyclopedia (more than 2500 pages) had its origins in the three-volume work commissioned by Mel Hurtig, edited by James MARSH, that was published by Hurtig Publishing of Edmonton in 1985; a second edition (four volumes) was published in 1988. Avie Bennett, having bought McCLELLAND & STEWART in 1986, was attracted by the possibility of acquiring The Canadian encyclopedia when it was announced in 1989 that Hurtig Publishing might be for sale. This transference took place, and the 'Year 2000 Edition' of the Encyclopedia (2000) was prepared, expanded and updated, still under the expert direction of editor-in-chief James Marsh. With 250 consultants, some 4000 contributors, and a staggering array of statistics, its more than 10,000 articles present a cornerstone of Canada's self-knowledge. CD-ROM versions of the Encyclopedia, first produced in 1991, sold over a quarter of a million copies. The Canadian encyclopedia 2001 (2000)—on four CD-ROMs or one DVD—was described as the World Edition, with more than 1000 new and updated articles; fully bilingual, it incorporates The Canadian Oxford dictionary. The full updated text and multimedia of The Canadian encyclopedia, along with The encyclopedia of music in Canada, are now available free of charge on the Internet at www.thecanadianencyclopedia.com. The online version now attracts some 2 million visitors each month.

Canadian Fiction Magazine (1971–98). Beginning as a student publication in the Creative Writing Department at the University of British Columbia, CFM grew into an independent national journal. Since its first gestetnered issue it has fostered a national and international awareness of contemporary Canadian short fiction in both English and French, and in translation from the unofficial languages of Canada. The first editor was R.W. Stedingh (1971–4). Since 1975 it was edited by Geoff Hancock, who became editor emeritus at the end of 1997 while continuing to work on the magazine. In 1991 it entered into partnership with QUARRY PRESS, Kingston, which became owners of the publication in 1996. Generous support from the Ontario Arts Council and The CANADA COUNCIL FOR THE ARTS (up to $50,000 annually) enabled

the magazine to continue publication for nearly three decades, until financial restraints led to a reformatting of the publication as a biannual anthology. It has published entire issues devoted to single authors (Robert HARLOW, Jane RULE, Leon ROOKE, Mavis GALLANT); and Canadian writers at work (1987), edited by Geoff Hancock, a selection of interviews. Among some ambitious 300-page issues were 'Writers from Ontario', 'A Decade of Quebec Fiction', 'Latin-American Writers in Canada', the fifteenth- and twentieth-anniversary issues, and the Silver-anniversary anthology of 1997 (more than 400 pages), which included many distinguished Canadian short-story writers, some who rose from obscurity to international prominence during the magazine's first twenty-five years.

Canadian Forum, The (1920–2000). This 'independent journal of opinion and the arts', as its masthead proclaimed, sprang from The Rebel, a periodical that had been started at the University of Toronto by students and professors—one of whom, Barker FAIRLEY, became the first literary editor of the Forum. While it has generally been on the left side of the political spectrum—its writers on political and social issues have included F.H. Underhill, Eugene FORSEY, and F.R. SCOTT—it always complied with its editorial stance of being an independent forum for ideas and opinions, while also devoting space to poetry, fiction, and book reviews.

Because the Forum published the first work of many Canadian poets as well as new work by established writers, the monthly was highly regarded by members of the Canadian literary community. In the early 1970s it started a policy of giving a double-page spread to new work by a different poet. Among its editors and literary editors have been such writers and critics as Earle BIRNEY, Northrop FRYE, Milton Wilson, Peter STEVENS, and Tom MARSHALL. The last editor was Robert Chodos. See J.L. GRANATSTEIN and Peter Stevens, eds., Forum: Canadian life and letters from 1920–70: selections from 'The Canadian Forum' (1972).

Canadian Literary Magazine, The (1833). An early cultural periodical, it was issued monthly between April and June 1833 in York (Toronto), Upper Canada. Its editor was John Kent, 'a gentleman recently arrived from England', its printer Thomas Dalton, and its publisher George Gurnett. Before the first number appeared on 6 April 1833, Gurnett included in his newspaper, The Courier of Upper Canada, a prospectus and several advertisements about the 'Journal'. They announced its contents as articles on such subjects as the 'U.E. Loyalists' and 'News of the Literary World', invited contributions from 'provincial authors', and promised sixty-four pages and a 'lithograph engraving' in each number. The April issue had all these features; its twenty items included an introductory editorial, a description of Niagara Falls, three poems and a tale by Susanna MOODIE, a 'prize poem' by Henry Scadding, a review of a recently published sermon on the cholera epidemic of 1832 by Archdeacon George Jehoshaphat Mountain, and a lithograph. The succeeding two issues contained items by William 'Tiger' Dunlop and W.F. HAWLEY, and more poems by Moodie. The magazine, distributed in both Upper and Lower Canada, was well reviewed by newspapers in both provinces. Still, it ceased publication after the third issue—perhaps because its editor miscalculated the financial resources of the recently arrived well-educated English immigrants towards whom it was at least partly aimed. Nevertheless it was significant. As one of the first cultural periodicals in Upper Canada it provided an early Canadian outlet for the works of its new settlers. Its formula of mixing several types of articles on various subjects and encouraging local authors was similar to that used a few years later by the first really successful Canadian periodical, *The LITERARY GARLAND*.

Canadian Literature (1959–). Founded by George WOODCOCK, it was the first quarterly devoted entirely to the criticism and discussion of Canadian writing, publishing poems, articles, and reviews in both English and French. It is published at the University of British Columbia. The introductory editorial of the first issue declared that 'it will not adopt a narrowly academic approach, nor will it try to restrict its pages to any school of criticism or class of writers.' This policy supported a wide variety of critical approaches, and led to contributions not only from the most distinguished Canadian critics, but also from important writers in other fields, notably fiction and poetry. The journal continues to publish poems in every issue and devotes a large amount of space to book reviews, which appear on the journal's website before print publication. It has produced important special issues on individual writers—for example Thomas KING, Gabrielle ROY, and Anne CARSON—as well as thematic issues, such as Native Writers and Canadian Writing, Asian-Canadian Writing, Black Writing, South Asian Diaspora, the Literature of

Atlantic Canada, and Francophone Writing Outside Québec. The journal can be searched on the website and is available online in most university libraries from issue 170–71 (Autumn 2001). W.H. NEW took over the editorship when Woodcock resigned in 1977 after producing seventy-three issues. New edited the journal until 1995, producing seventy-two issues. Subsequent editors have been Eva Marie Kröller (1995–2003) and Laurie Ricou (2003–7). The present editor is Margery Fee.

Canadian Mercury, The (1928–9). This was 'A Monthly Journal of Literature and Opinion', published in Montreal, that was national in outlook and international in standards; it offered the reader serious poetry, fiction, commentary, and criticism. Seven issues appeared between Dec. 1928 and June 1929, when it collapsed with the stock market. Among its founding editors were F.R. SCOTT and Leo KENNEDY, who were members of the so-called MONTREAL GROUP, which introduced literary Modernism to Canada. In spirit at least, *The Canadian Mercury* was an outlet for the writers who, as students at McGill University, had established the *Literary Supplement* (1924–5) to the *McGill Daily*, a student newspaper, and then its offshoot the *McGILL-FORTNIGHTLY REVIEW* (1925–7). Among its contributors were A.J.M. SMITH, A.M. KLEIN, John GLASSCO, and Leon EDEL.

Canadian Notes & Queries. See *CNQ: CANADIAN NOTES & QUERIES*.

Canadians of old (1890, 1995). This is the title of two translations of *Les anciens canadiens* (Quebec, 1863) by Philippe-Joseph AUBERT DE GASPÉ, a famous historical romance of the Seven Years' War. The best-known early translation, by Charles G.D. ROBERTS (1890), made the work very popular in English; in 1974 it was added to the NEW CANADIAN LIBRARY, where it remained for many years. A definitive modern translation by Jane Brierley was published in 1995; it includes an introduction by the translator and the extensive 'Notes and Clarifications', in translation, that appeared in the original French edition. In April 1757 two students at the Jesuit College in Quebec City are about to sail for Europe and enter the French and English armies. One is Jules d'Haberville, son of a *seigneur*; the other, Archibald Cameron of Locheil, is the son of a Scott killed at Culloden. When the war breaks out, the two friends find themselves back in Canada as officers in opposing forces. Arché is compelled by his superior to burn the farms on the South Shore, including the d'Haberville manor, where he had often been a guest. Subsequently he saves Jules' life, and after the war assists the ruined d'Haberville family, with whom he returns to live, although Jules' sister Blanche refuses to marry him. The novel is filled with the author's personal and family reminiscences—life at the d'Haberville manor is essentially that of Aubert de Gaspé's family, filtered through the memory of a lifetime reader of Sir Walter Scott—and with legends, anecdotes, and countless details of customs and daily life in the region at the end of the French regime. As a *seigneur*, Aubert de Gaspé regretted the abolition of seigneurial tenure in 1854 and attempted in his novel—which he called a potpourri of memories—a nostalgic reconstruction of seigneurial society in its ideal form; in it he also urged the need for greater integration with the English-speaking population. Rambling and at times repetitive, this early example of oral history affords an intimate and charming introduction to the cultural heritage and political disillusionment of French-Canadian landowners in mid-nineteenth-century Québec.

Cape, Judith. Pseudonym of P. K. PAGE.

Cappon, James (1854–1939). Born in Dundee, Scotland, and educated at the University of Glasgow, he taught literature for two years at Geneva and then at Glasgow, where he wrote his first critical study, *Victor Hugo* (1885). In 1888 he became professor of English language and literature at Queen's University, Kingston, Ontario, and contributed articles frequently to *Queen's Quarterly*. Cappon's pamphlet *Charles G.D. Roberts and the influence of his times* (1905) is a milestone in Canadian literary criticism in placing a Canadian poet in his context and giving an overview of modern literary trends. This pamphlet was expanded to *Charles G.D. Roberts* (1925), a volume in the Makers of Canadian Literature series. Cappon also wrote *Bliss Carman and the literary currents and influences of his time* (1930). His critical writing is distinguished by its engagingly familiar yet scholarly style.

Cardinal, Harold. See ABORIGINAL LITERATURE: 3.

Cardinal, Tantoo. SEE ABORIGINAL LITERATURE: 5.

Careless, J. M. S. (b. 1919–2009). James Maurice Stockford Careless was born in Toronto and educated at the University of Toronto (B.A., 1940) and Harvard University (A.M., 1941; Ph.D., 1950). He joined the history department at the University of Toronto in 1945; on his retirement in 1984 he was appointed University Professor Emeritus. He was made an Officer of the Order of Canada in 1981. After publishing *Canada: a story of challenge* (1953, GGA; rpr. 1991), Careless proceeded to suggest new lines for historical inquiry, including the ways in which metropolis and hinterland had interacted in Canada's past. The concluding volume of *Brown of the Globe* (1959; 1963, GGA; rpr. 1989) demonstrated that the origins of nineteenth-century Canadian liberalism owed much to British antecedents. *The union of the Canadas, 1841–1857* (1967) disentangles a complicated period fraught with conflicts. In advocating the intellectual pursuit of such concepts as region, class, and ethnicity, Careless opened the floodgates to a multiplicity of new historical approaches. Later he devoted himself to developing a sense of place in *Toronto to 1918* (1984, rpr. 2002), which won the City of Toronto Book Award, and *Frontier and metropolis* (1989). Careless has also published *Ontario: a celebration of heritage* (2 vols, 1991, 1992) and *Canada: a celebration of heritage* (2 vols, 1994, 1995). His essays are collected in *Careless at work* (1990). As adept at the podium as in print, Maurice Careless has reminded audiences that while they might consider his name unfortunate for someone who headed Toronto's history department (1959–67), one of his predecessors had been George Wrong.

Cariou, Warren. SEE ABORIGINAL LITERATURE: 5.

Carleton Library. A paperback reprint series aimed at the secondary and post-secondary school markets but also endeavouring to appeal to the general reader, the Carleton Library was launched on 25 May 1963 as a co-operative venture between Carleton University's Institute of Canadian Studies and MCCLELLAND & STEWART. The series' original objective was to make available inexpensive editions of texts in Canadian history and the social sciences, and volumes in the fields of history, politics, economics, sociology, geography, law, anthropology, business science, and media studies appeared. The Carleton Library was guided by a general editor, an associate editor, and an editorial board drawn from a variety of disciplines. MACMILLAN COMPANY OF CANADA and then Gage briefly took over as publisher in 1979 and 1980, producing about ten volumes before Carleton University Press assumed responsibility. From 1981 the list greatly expanded; but in April 1998 the CUP ceased operations and its list, including the Carleton Library, is now distributed by MCGILL-QUEEN'S UNIVERSITY PRESS.

Carman, Bliss (1861–1929). William Bliss Carman, a first cousin of Charles G.D. ROBERTS and a distant relation of Ralph Waldo Emerson, was born in Fredericton, New Brunswick, and educated at the University of New Brunswick. He spent an unhappy year at Oxford and Edinburgh in 1882–3 before attending Harvard University in 1886–8, where he met Richard Hovey (1864–1900), who later co-authored several books of poetry with him. At Harvard he attended the lectures of Josiah Royce and George Santayana, whose anti-materialistic philosophies he found congenial. He then became a literary journalist in New York. In 1896 he met Mary Perry King, who became his lifelong patron and companion, and after 1908 he settled near the Kings in Connecticut. Carman was a poet of the Maritime landscape, a blend of forest, field, and sea that he employed both realistically and symbolically. He was the first Canadian poet to transform the external world into an interior, psychic landscape that delineated his characteristic moods—yearning, loss of love, melancholy, grief, and, on occasion, rapture. His particular sensibility was nurtured by Wordsworthian 'pantheism' and Emersonian transcendentalism, both of which emphasized humanity's oneness with the universe. He borrowed the Pre-Raphaelites' fondness for associating colours and emotions. He was attracted to contemporary *fin-de-siècle* Romanticism, which rejected the scientific rationalism of the age and sought reality in a visionary dream world whose symbols were drawn from art and nature. Having drifted from the Anglican faith, Carman recognized Nature as the source of his creative power and spiritual consolation. His poetry celebrates the 'kinship' he felt with all living things, and his work, particularly up to 1910, records his quest for a philosophical system to underpin his emotional experiences. A mystical vision in 1886 sustained Carman in his earliest volumes: *Low tide on Grand Pré: a book of lyrics* (New York, 1893), *Behind the arras: a book of the unseen* (Boston, Toronto, 1895), and *Ballads of lost haven: a book of the sea* (Boston, 1897). This experience is at the centre of his finest poem, 'Low tide on Grand Pré', in which the grieving speaker recaptures the timelessness and ecstasy of what may have been a past love

affair. In these volumes Carman's voice, elegiac and gentle, observes the fragility of life, the passing of time, and the coming of death. In his collaboration with Hovey on *Songs from Vagabondia* (Boston, 1895; rpr. 1972, 1992), Carman found another 'voice', that of the literary vagrant whose back-to-nature heartiness and optimism had wide appeal and helped to initiate a revolt against the 'genteel tradition' that characterized much American poetry of the time. Hovey helped Carman to see how exaltation of the physical could lead to spiritual insights. The sequels include *More songs from Vagabondia* (Boston, 1896; rpr. 1972) and *Last songs from Vagabondia* (1901, rpr. 1972), and Carman by himself wrote *Echoes from Vagabondia* (1912). Turning to classical themes in the carefully organized *Sappho: one hundred lyrics* (1904), Carman produced several flawless and timeless songs, some of which are 'translations' and 'restorations' of Sappho, while others are Carman's original poems. The figure of Pan, the goat-god, traditionally associated with poetry and with the fusion of the earthly and the divine, becomes Carman's organizing symbol in the five volumes issued between 1902 and 1905 and reprinted as *The pipes of Pan: containing 'From the book of myths,' 'From the green book of the bards,' 'Songs of the sea children,' 'Songs from a northern garden,' 'From the book of valentines'* (1906). His intention was to trace the religious and philosophical evolution of man through Pan's music. In his later poetry the mystical and visionary characteristics became less prominent and his language and rhythms became closer to colloquial speech, but too often the sound is more important than the sense. In more than fifty volumes of poetry, Carman showed great versatility with musical cadences, and with poetic forms ranging from lyrics and dramatic monologues to meditations. Often accused of verbosity, he admitted his 'prolixity' and his problems in editing repetitive passages and trite language. Despite the early praise he received from poets such as Ezra Pound and Wallace Stevens, modernist poets and critics in Canada, particularly the MONTREAL GROUP, spent half a century torpedoing most of Carman's *oeuvre*. However, since the 1970s he has received more positive reappraisals. Contemporary poets such as Al PURDY, D.G. JONES, and Elizabeth BREWSTER have come to Carman's rescue, and recent critics have found much to admire in his poems. Carman also published several books of essays and 'talks' and edited three anthologies, including *The Oxford book of American verse* (1927, rpr. 1975). See *Windflower: selected poems of Bliss Carman*

(1985), edited by Raymond SOUSTER and Douglas LOCHHEAD; and *Bliss Carman: a reappraisal* (1990) edited with an introduction by Gerald Lynch.

Caron, Louis (b. 1942). Born in Sorel, Québec, he worked at several occupations—broadcasting, public relations, and journalism—and was the author of many radio and television plays for Radio-Canada before devoting his time fully to writing fiction. His prize-winning first novel, *L'emmitouflé* (Paris, 1977; rev., Seuil, 1982), is the only one that has so far been translated, by David Lobdell as *The draft-dodger* (1980). Caron convincingly recreates the atmosphere of the 1917 conscription crisis and offers a point of view rarely heard or accepted in English Canada: namely, a sympathetic portrayal of a French Canadian refusing to fight in a war he does not believe in. The juxtaposition of the elderly Nazaire's experiences with those of his nephew Jean-François, a Franco-American conscientious objector to the Vietnam War, provides an ideological continuity within the francophone community: the nephew's recollections of events in his grandfather's life enable the reader to understand Nazaire's flight from the law and his subsequent alienation.

Carr, Emily (1871–1945). Born in Victoria, British Columbia, she studied painting at the California School of Design in San Francisco (1891–3), in England (1899–1904), and Paris (1910–11); two of her paintings were hung in the prestigious Salon d'Automne in Paris in 1911. In the summer of 1898 she made the first of many trips to Native villages, travelling by steamer up the west coast of Vancouver Island to Ucluelet. Here the seed of what was to be a lifelong interest in West Coast Native people and culture germinated. In the summer of 1912 she made a highly productive trip to the remote Skeena River region and the Queen Charlotte Islands. In the Native villages there, Carr gathered a wealth of images and impressions that would be a recurring focus of varying intensity throughout her career as a painter. The bold colours and aggressive brush strokes that characterized her work when she returned from Europe, and her 'new' way of looking at things, were not well received by local people, who were unprepared for any deviation from the English landscape tradition. After 1913 she painted less and turned to other means of supporting herself, including running an apartment house, called Hill House, on her father's property in Victoria; raising sheepdogs; and

making pottery. A turning point came in 1927 when Carr received an invitation to be part of the National Gallery exhibition 'Canadian West Coast Art, Native and Modern' and travelled to Ottawa and Toronto, where she was greatly influenced by meeting Lawren Harris and other Group of Seven artists. She revisited the Skeena River region and the Queen Charlottes in 1928, but a year later she abandoned her Native themes and concentrated on the British Columbia forests, which held a particular mystery for her.

From her many trips to Native communities and the remote regions of British Columbia, Carr drew creative inspiration for powerful paintings—huge, pulsating skies bursting with light and energy and intense sculptural forests—and for the journals and notes that she later used for her published sketches and stories. She began keeping a journal in 1927, recording ideas, themes, or impressions that could be reworked in paint. Always a good storyteller, she enrolled in a short-story correspondence course in 1926 and in another course at Victoria College in the summer of 1934. Her first attempts at creative writing were aided by the constructive criticism of three 'literary' friends: Flora Burns, Ruth Humphrey, and Margaret Clay. After 1937, when Carr was often confined to bed as a result of several strokes and heart attacks, she turned seriously to writing. In 1940 some of her Native stories were read on the CBC—first by Dr Garnet Sedgewick, head of the English Department at the University of British Columbia, and then by Ira Dilworth, a regional director of the CBC in Vancouver. With Dilworth's encouragement and assistance she completed her first book, *Klee Wyck* (1941, GGA; rpr. 2003)—the title, meaning 'laughing one', is the name the Nuu-chah-nulth people gave her. This series of short stories, which won a Governor General's Award, describes with perception, warmth, wit, and originality aspects of British Columbia life, based on her visits to Native villages. The next year *The book of Small* (1942, rpr. 2004) was published. Like all Carr's books, it is autobiographical: describing her family life and nineteenth-century Victoria from the point of view of Emily Carr the child (nicknamed 'Small'). Her writing style—simple, clear, direct, gently humorous, and carefully pruned of all but essential elements, like her painting—was now clearly established. A few months after the publication of *The house of all sorts* (1944, rpr. 2004), which describes entertainingly her career as a landlady and raiser of bobtail sheepdogs, Carr died. *Growing pains* (1946, rpr. 2005) was written between 1939 and 1944 and, by her request, was published posthumously. This engaging account of her life highlights particularly her art-school days in San Francisco and London.

Other posthumous books followed: *Pause: a sketchbook* (1953, rpr. 2007) centres on Carr's fifteen-month convalescence in the East Anglia Sanatorium in Suffolk, England (1903–4). These humorous and sometimes poignant reminiscences of the people and events in the sanatorium, written thirty years later, are supplemented by drawings and doggerel verse. *The heart of a peacock* (1953, rpr. 2005) is a selection of stories and previously unpublished prose sketches edited by Ira Dilworth, whom she had made her literary trustee. Selections from Carr's journals, composed between 1927 and 1941, were combined in *Hundreds and thousands: the journals of Emily Carr* (1966, rpr. 2006), which, in recording her joys, challenges, disappointments, and her constant search for the means to understand and express the world around her, is marked by the vivid descriptions and touching honesty of her very personal style. Pieces by Carr about her dogs are collected in *Flirt, Punk and Loo: my dogs and I* (1997, rpr. 2005 as *Emily Carr and her dogs*). *An address* (1955), with an introduction by Ira Dilworth, contains a memorable speech Carr gave on 4 Mar. 1930 before the Victoria Women's Canadian Club, which was celebrating her first exhibition in her native city. See also *Fresh seeing: two addresses by Emily Carr* (1972), which has a preface by Doris Shadbolt and includes Dilworth's introduction to the 1930 speech. Most of these books are available in paperback and have been translated into several languages. *The Emily Carr omnibus* (1993) and *The complete writings of Emily Carr* (1993, rpr. 1997), both edited by Shadbolt, contain all Carr's writings. See also *Opposite contraries: the unknown journals of Emily Carr and other writings* (2003)—including letters from Sophie Frank who lived on the reserve called Squamish Mission and letters to Ira Dilworth—edited by Susan Crean, and *Corresponding influence: selected letters of Emily Carr and Ira Dilworth* (2006) edited by Linda M. Morra.

See Maria TIPPETT, *Emily Carr: a biography* (1979, GGA, rpr. 1982; rev. 1994, rpr. 2006), Doris Shadbolt, *The art of Emily Carr* (1979, rpr. 1987), Edythe Hembroff-Schleicher, *Emily Carr: the untold story* (1978), Paula Blanchard, *The life of Emily Carr* (1987, rpr. 2001), and Anne Newlands, *Emily Carr: an introduction to her life and art* (1996). Shadbolt

reasseses her earlier work in *Emily Carr* (1990) and edited *Seven journeys: the sketchbooks of Emily Carr* (2002). Susan Crean's illuminating *The laughing one: a journey to Emily Carr* (2001) is not strictly a biography but an extensive series of reflections (with Chronology, Notes, and Bibliography, nearly 500 pages), filled with insights on important periods and moments in Carr's life, the people she knew and various issues; it incorporates fictional passages that recreate events or are internal monologues, and the author sometimes introduces herself as she pursues her research. Penguin Canada's Extraordinary Canadians series includes *Emily Carr* (2008) by Lewis DeSota. Kerry Mason (Dodd) and the photographer Michael Breuer present excerpts from Carr's previously unpublished journals and letters, together with photographs of her sketching locations, in *Sunlight in the shadows: the landscape of Emily Carr* (1984). Letters from Carr have been edited by Doreen Walker in *Dear Nan: letters of Emily Carr, Nan Cheney and Humphrey Toms* (1990). *Emily Carr: new perspectives on a Canadian icon* (2006), published by the National Gallery of Canada in a large format, is a collection of essays with many colour reproductions and black-and-white photographs to accompany an exhibition touring to four other Canadian galleries in 2007 and 2008; there are two essays on Carr's writings. *The magnificent voyage of Emily Carr* (1992) is a play by Jovette MARCHESSAULT, translated by Linda Gaboriau. The bestselling American novelist Susan Vreeland is the author of *The forest lover* (2003), a novel based on Carr's life.

Carrier, Roch (b. 1937). Born in Sainte-Justine-de Dorchester, a village in the Beauce region of Québec, Carrier studied at the Université Saint-Louis in New Brunswick (B.A., 1957), the Université de Montréal (M.A., 1964), and the Université de Paris (D.ès. L, 1970). He was secretary-general of the Théâtre du Nouveau Monde (1970), taught at the Collège Militaire Royal de St-Jean (1964–70), was director of the CANADA COUNCIL (1994–7) and the National Librarian of Canada (1999–2004). He is a Fellow of the Royal Society of Canada (1987) and an Officer of the Order of Canada (1991).

With Michel TREMBLAY, Carrier is one of the two most widely read Québécois authors in English Canada. (In spite of the abundance of his diverse literary productions over more than thirty years, critical attention to the French editions of Carrier's books has sadly declined, presumably because of his federalist sympathies.) English translations of Carrier's work have been made by Sheila FISCHMAN. Carrier has moved through different narrative styles to develop his themes—nostalgia for Québec's rural past, the reality of the dream world, a diffuse nationalism—and often adopts the viewpoint of childhood. He came to prominence with his first three novels: *La guerre, yes sir!* (1968; trans. 1970; 4th Eng. edn 1998); *Floralie, where are you?* (1971; *Floralie, où es-tu?*, 1969); and *Is it the sun, Philibert?* (1972; *Il est par là le soleil*, 1970). *La guerre*, still Carrier's best-known and most popular work, is a post-colonial, decolonizing novel that dramatizes the linguistic and social violence of individuals and village life within the context of the conscription crisis of the Second World War. Carrier combines extreme bitterness against Les Anglais (who are uncomprehending and wooden British stereotypes) with the depiction of a warm and solid village life. A more dream-like *Floralie* goes back thirty years before this event to the wedding night of the parents of *La guerre*'s central character, combining a comic tale of religion and sex with nightmare. *Is it the sun, Philibert?* is the dark story of a French-Canadian village boy confronting the horrors and corruption of work in Montreal. One of the most important of Carrier's subsequent novels, *They won't demolish me!* (1974; *Le deux-millième étage*, 1973) is one of the few with an urban setting. This was followed by *The garden of delights* (1978; *Le jardin des délices*, 1975), one of his most successful works. It is a rather Rabelaisian, parodic story of the attempt by an unscrupulous profiteer to exploit the desires and credulity of a small town—but it is also a bitter exposé of the pettiness of those who would allow themselves to be exploited. *No country without grandfathers* (1981; *Il n'y a pas de pays sans grand-père*, 1979) is an extended fable whose meaning finally refers to the activity of the writer. More a statement of Carrier's literary and ideological affiliations than an original story, it is a kind of twentieth-century rewrite of Félix-Antoine SAVARD's *Menaud, Maître-draveur (Master of the river)*. *Lady with chains* (1984; *La dame qui avait des chaînes aux chevilles*, 1981) is an ambitious, dense story of a woman's dream of revenge; harsh, bare, and intense, it is weakened by the nature of the husband's unlikely crime—abandoning his baby in a snowstorm. *Heartbreaks along the road* (1987; rpr. 1990; *De l'amour dans la feraille*, 1984) is a powerful political satire of life in Québec under Premier Maurice Duplessis. Carrier's novels of the nineties are *The man in the closet* (1993; *L'homme dans le placard*, 1991);

The end (1994; *Fin*, 1992); and *The lament of Charlie Longsong* (1998; *Petit homme tornade*, 1996). *Prayers of a very wise child* (1992; *Prières d'un enfant très très sage*, 1988) and *Prayers of a young man* (1999; rpr. 2000; *Prières d'un adolescent très très sage*, 1988) are collections of stories. Among Carrier's other story collections, the best known is *The hockey sweater and other stories* (1979; *Les enfants du bonhomme dans la lune*, 1979). Its famous title story inspired *The sweater*, an animated NFB short subject by Sheldon Cohen, whose illustrations complement the story's publication as a popular children's book, *The hockey sweater* (1984). Carrier's other books for young people include *The longest home run* (1993; *Le plus long circuit*, 1993), which has become, like *The hockey sweater*, a children's classic.

Carrier made a stage adaptation of *La guerre, yes sir!* (1970)—an English translation was successfully produced at the Stratford Festival in 1972—and has written several other plays, including *Le celeste bicyclette* (1980), which, as *The celestial bicycle*, was produced in English at the Tarragon Theatre, Toronto, in 1982.

Carson, Anne (b. 1950). Born in Toronto, and educated at the University of Toronto (B.A., 1974; M.A., 1975; Ph.D., 1981), she was professor of classics at the University of Calgary (1979–80), at Princeton University (1980–7), and at Emory University, Atlanta, Georgia, from 1987 to 1988, when she became professor of classics at McGill University, Montreal. She is now professor of classics, comparative literature, and English at the University of Michigan (2003–). A poet and essayist as well as a classical scholar, Carson uses mixed genres, modernist fragment, and journal entry in an intensely personal quest to understand the nature and complexities of romantic love, family bonds, the self, and love of God. Her work has appeared widely in the United States and England in leading literary journals and anthologies. Four books indicate the unusual range of her writing: *Eros the bittersweet: an essay* (1986), a reading of Sappho that focuses on the meaning of erotic desire and its relation to pleasure and pain, a process that the English word 'bittersweet' inverts (*If not, winter* [2002] is subtitled *Fragments from Sappho*—Carson's translations in a bilingual edition); *Short talks* (1992), a collection of prose poems that were later included in *Plainwater: essays and poetry* (1995); and *Glass, irony and God: essays and poetry* (1995). For Carson, essays and poems may be written in either prose or verse. Her writing shows a wide range of influences: the Greek texts she has spent her life studying; experimental writers, including Gertrude Stein and Italo Calvino; European surrealism; the Catholic mystics; and Chinese poetry. Dense with literary and cultural allusions, her work creates a timeless space in which Carson's own spiritual and emotional concerns can exist along with the trials of Emily Brontë (in 'The glass essay', a long poem about a failed love affair) or against Bashō's retreats from the world, which gloss her own pilgrimage through Spain in the rhapsodic 'Kinds of water: an essay on the road to Compostela'. At heart an experimental religious writer, with a rich knowledge of the Christian mystic tradition as well as an interest in Eastern religions, metaphysics in general, and psychoanalysis, Carson addresses both worship and doubt, and the difficulties of living in a world of divine immanence. Her sympathies are for marginal figures—outsiders, *isolatos*, lovers, pilgrims, penitents, the ill, and the old. Whether she is recreating some of the violent contradictions in ancient Judaism in the powerful poem 'Book of Isaiah', or recounting her own dislocation during a trip to Rome in 'The fall of Rome: a traveller's guide', Carson remains a lapidary stylist, writing lyrical and reflective narratives of the pain of daily existence. *Autobiography of Red: a novel in verse* (1998), a tour de force, blends an original translation of fragments by the Greek poet Stesichoros (sixth century B.C.) with a mock interview with the writer and Carson's own retelling of the tale of Geryon, the redwinged monster boy who falls in love with Herakles. Set in contemporary North America and Peru, the novel is a meditation on the power of beauty and eros that mixes surrealist moments with strong narrative. *Man in the off hours* (2000, rpr. 2001), a collection of poems and essays, includes the surprising 'Irony is not enough: essay on my life as Catherine Deneuve', about the solitude of loving—a central and recurring subject is Carson's work. It won the GRIFFIN POETRY PRIZE. In *Economy of the unlost* (1999) Carson discusses the poets Simonides of Keos and Paul Celan, contrasting the work of the Greek writer (fifth century B.C.) with the poems of a Romanian-Jewish Holocaust survivor in a reading that ranges from the relation of poetry to money, to the connections between poetry and death, time, and the nature of language itself. *The beauty of the husband: a fictional essay in 29 tangos* (2001, rpr. 2002) is partly the story of a marriage ('So why did I love him from early girlhood to late middle age / and the divorce decree came in the mail? / Beauty.

No great secret.') and partly plays on John Keats's idea that beauty is truth—each 'tango' has an epigraph (one or more lines) by Keats.

Carson translated Sophocles's *Electra* for the Oxford series The Greek Tragedy in New Translations, rendered by translators who are poets themselves. The play is preceded by a long introduction by Michael Shaw and the Translator's Foreword, in which Carson discusses Electra's language and her screams, 'bursts of sound expressing strong emotion'.

Carson's most substantial volume is a miscellany, *Decreation: poetry, essays, opera* (2005, rpr. 2006), the title referring to an undoing of self, beginning with the undoing of various forms of writing as represented in this book. Fourteen approachable poems, the first one called 'Sleepchains', are followed by the essay 'Every exit is an entrance (a praise of sleep)', in which many well-known names and titles appear: Elizabeth Bishop and her poem 'The mammoth', Virginia Woolf and *To the lighthouse* and *The voyage out*, Homer and *The Odyssey*, et al. This is followed by an 'Ode to sleep'. The next thirty-nine pages of prose and poetry are devoted to 'Foam (essay with rhapsody): "On the sublime in Longinus and Antonioni"'—Cassius Longinus (c. 220–273) having written the treatise *On the sublime* and Michelangelo Antonioni (1912–2005) having directed the film *The red desert* with its star Monica Vitti—all of whom are mentioned in these passages. This is followed by 'Decreation', a short essay in three parts with love, and God, as the themes. It is about Sappho; Marguerite Porete, who was burned alive in 1310 because her book about the love of God was considered heretical; and Simone Weil, the twentieth-century French classicist and philosopher: 'Each of the three women we've been considering had the nerve to enter a zone of absolute spiritual daring. Each of them undergoes there an experience of decreation, or so she tells us.' The next section, 'Decreation (an opera in three parts)' is the libretto for an opera whose characters include Hephaistos and his wife Aphrodite, and Ares, her lover; Marguerite Porete; Simone Weil and her mother and father. Each part begins with an Argument; the playful verses that follow are revealing about the characters and their respective situations. There are seven other sections, including an 'oratorio' and a 'screenplay' involving Heloise and Abelard in modern times. *Grief lessons: four plays by Euripides* (2006, rpr. 2008) is Carson's translation of *Herakles, Hekabe, Hippolytos,* and *Alkestis*. Appearing in the spring of 2010, *Nox* (physically) is a publishing phenomenon: almost 200 pages printed on a very long strip of paper in accordion folds; they are folded into a carefully designed box made of heavy, handsomely covered board, on the back of which are Anne Carson's words: 'When my brother died I made an epigraph for him in the form of a book. This is a replica of it, as close as we could get.' She tells us about a poem Catullus wrote for his dead brother, which she tried to translate many times. 'No one (even in Latin) can approximate Catullan diction, which at its most sorrowful has an air of deep festivity, like one of those trees that turns all its leaves over, silver, in the wind.' The left-hand page of any two-page spread is an often long dictionary definition in English of one Latin word in Catullus's poem; the right-hand pages—which include photographic fragments such as postage stamps and snapshots of brother and younger sister as children—are mainly made up of stark, moving prose poems relating to brother Michael and his life: he ran away in 1978, barely communicated with his mother and sister, and died in Copenhagen in 2000, leaving a widow, whom Anne Carson visited. Published by New Directions, New York (Penguin Books Canada Limited), it is a beautiful work, exhibiting several kinds of creativity in honouring Carson's estranged, little-known brother. *Nox* is Latin for night—and death.

In 1996 Carson won the Lannan Literary Award, a $50,000 (US) prize given by the Lannan Foundation, Los Angeles (the only other Canadian to win this award is Alice MUNRO); and in June 2000 she won a MacArthur Foundation grant, the so-called genius grant, of $500,000 (US). She was made a Member of the Order of Canada in 2005.

Caswell, Edward (1861–1938). Born in Goderich, Canada West (Ontario), he joined the Methodist Book and Publishing House in 1881. In 1892 he was appointed manager of the book-publishing operation and became a force in the editing of manuscripts and in communications with authors at a time when the firm became committed to Canadian nationalism and increasingly promoted Canadian literature. Caswell was influential in the publication of works by Catharine Parr TRAILL, Nellie McCLUNG, Robert SERVICE, William Wilfred CAMPBELL, Charles G.D. ROBERTS, and Isabella Valancy CRAWFORD. Though he left the MBPH in 1908 for a better-paying position as assistant librarian and secretary-treasurer of the Toronto Public Library, his commitment to promoting and developing Canadian literature continued until his death. During these years he was co-publisher with Willet Haigt of editions of John RICHARDSON's *WACOUSTA* and *The war of 1812* and William Dunlop's *Recollections of the war of 1812*; the editor of the first Canadian edition (1929) of Traill's *The BACKWOODS OF CANADA*; and an essayist and active promoter of Canadian writing. He edited the anthology *Canadian singers and their songs* (1902; enlarged edition 1925).

CEECT. See CENTRE FOR EDITING EARLY CANADIAN TEXTS.

Centre for Editing Early Canadian Texts. A project begun at Carleton University, Ottawa, in 1979, whose objective has been to prepare and publish scholarly editions of major works of early Canadian prose that were either out of print or available only in corrupt editions. The general editor of the CEECT was Mary Jane Edwards, Carleton University, who was assisted by an editorial board and a team of distinguished advisers; the project received long-term funding from the Social Sciences and Humanities Research Council of Canada and from Carleton University. The CEECT series includes works by Frances BROOKE, James DE MILLE, Thomas Chandler HALIBURTON, Julia Catherine HART, Rosanna LEPROHON, Thomas McCULLOCH, Susanna MOODIE, John RICHARDSON, and Catharine Parr TRAILL. Early in 2007, however, the CEECT office was closed, and most of its papers were placed in the Carleton University Archives. Mary Jane Edwards' edition of William KIRBY's *The GOLDEN DOG* was published in 2008. The books are distributed by McGILL-QUEEN's UNIVERSITY PRESS.

Champlain, Samuel de. See Writing in NEW FRANCE.

Charivari, The. See George LONGMORE.

Charlesworth, Hector (1872–1945). Born in Hamilton, Ontario, he was trained as an accountant but instead became a renowned figure in Toronto journalism and a notable force in the arts. As a drama critic he survives only as a brief portrait in a Robertson DAVIES novel, *World of wonders* (1975), where his bearded resemblance to Edward VII is noted; but his criticism of the Group of Seven gave him a peculiar place in Canadian art history. Though he admired many of their paintings, he criticized them often enough ('the hot mush school') to become, in the 1920s, the new movement's most notorious enemy. Charlesworth put down his journalistic roots as a reporter and editor on the Toronto *Mail and Empire*, but his career flourished at *Saturday Night*, then a national weekly—first as a contributor, then associate editor (1910–25), finally editor (1925–32). He left three superb volumes of anecdotal memoirs—*Candid chronicles* (1925), *More candid chronicles* (1928), and *I'm telling you* (1937)—describing everything from famous murders he covered in his youth to the plagiarism suit against H.G. Wells that a Toronto woman pursued, relentlessly but unsuccessfully, for many years. He retreated to a twilight career as freelance music reviewer and died a critic's death at Toronto on December 30, 1945: a heart attack killed him after he received a telephone call from Duke Ellington angrily objecting to Charlesworth's *Globe and Mail* review of his concert ('jungle music à la Harlem').

Charlevoix, Pierre-François-Xavier de. See Writing in NEW FRANCE.

Charron, François (b. 1952). Born in Longueuil, Québec, he began writing in his teens, and soon became associated with various modernist magazines and writers, particularly those associated with the publishing house and periodical *Les Herbes Rouges*. Since 1972 he has published more than thirty-five works and won many literary prizes, yet his poetry is known in English only through the selections that appeared in *Ellipse 44* (1990) and in *After 10,000 years, desire: selected recent poems* (1995), translated by Bruce Whiteman and Francis Farley-Chevrier. The lyricism of the period between 1980 and 1995, the simplification and 'readability' of style, a contemplation of the sublime and concern with metaphysics and religion have steered Charron's work away from the formalism of his earlier writings into what some critics consider postmodernism.

Chaurette, Normand (b. 1954). Born in Montreal, he obtained a B.A. in literature from the Université de Montréal in 1976 and an M.A. in 1981. A skilled amateur musician, he is best known as a virtuoso dramatist, the author of many plays that have earned him an international reputation. Their subjects vary greatly, and the plots are secondary to the role of structure, but all the works are characterized by Chaurette's passion for language, form, and music. Only three of his plays are available in English. *Provincetown playhouse, July 1919, I was 19* (1986)—a translation by William Boulet of *Provincetown playhouse, juillet 1919, j'avais 19 ans* (1981)—is based on the destruction by fire in 1977 of the Provincetown Playhouse-on-the-Wharf. A play within a play, it takes place at several levels simultaneously in the mind of a thirty-eight-year-old playwright, interned for madness, whose career was interrupted abruptly by a death/murder nineteen years earlier. In nineteen tableaux—evoking youth, homosexual love, and beauty—Chaurette constructs an ambiguous and lyrical drama on the theme of the artist in society. His most enigmatic exercise in style, again without a plot in the conventional sense, is *Fragments of a farewell letter read by geologists* (1989, rpr. 1998)—a translation by Linda Gaboriau of *Fragments d'une lettre d'adieu lus par des géologues* (1986). A commission of inquiry is held into the mysterious death of a geologist who led an expedition to Cambodia. The search has metaphysical overtones, the fragments revealed are tantalizing, but nothing is resolved. The language—by turns technical, amusing, disquieting—constitutes a dialogue of the deaf. The primarily literary nature of Chaurette's theatrical writing places additional demands on staged productions. In *The queens* (1992, rpr. 1998)—the translation by Gaboriau of *Les reines* (1991)—the oratorical language is both a lyrical score for six women's voices and a dramatic text. With specific historical and literary references—Shakespearian rhythm without imitation, ironic humour with feminist implications—Chaurette debates the atemporal nature of power. The bizarre characteristics of the next two plays lend them a kind of metaphysical quality. *All the Verdis of Venice* (2000)—Gaboriau's translation of *Je vous écris du Caire*—is a farce that takes place in La Scala, Milan. Verdi is being forced to finish writing *Don Carlo,* though he'd rather be in Cairo finishing *Aida.* The characters are the prompter, the director, Verdi, and two opera singers. *The concise Köchel* (2005) is made up of the surreal conversation of the Motherwill sisters, pianists who spend all their time playing Mozart—the title refers to the numbering system the Austrian Köchel gave to all Mozart's compositions; it is mentioned only three times in the play and has little significance—and the Brunswick sisters, musicologists. 'Our son', who never appears, has submitted to 'many years of domination by Mozart. He wants reparation. He agrees to die on the condition that we prepare him, our child ... as an offering, and as the main course .... If we promise to eat him, then he will agree to hang himself, tonight, before midnight.'

Child, Philip (1898–1978). Son of a major figure in Ontario's steel industry, he attended schools in Germany and Switzerland, and was a student at Trinity College, University of Toronto, in 1917, when he enlisted in the army and served as an artillery officer during the Great War, an experience that marked his life. Returning to Trinity in 1919, he earned a B.A. in 1921 and proceeded to an affiliated B.A. at Christ's College, Cambridge, in the same year, and a Harvard M.A. in 1923. There followed a lectureship at Trinity, a Harvard doctorate, teaching at the University of British Columbia, and sustained work as a writer of fiction, until his return in 1942 to Trinity, where he eventually became Chancellor's Professor of English. Alongside the surface realism of Child's fiction rests his preoccupation with the visionary, the nightmarish, and the fabular as escape from the terrors of the everyday. Thus *The village of souls* (1933), set in New France, is in many ways a postwar novel. The hero, Jornay, struggles amid a modernist wasteland in his search for a ground of being. Torn between two women, Aboriginal (Anne) and European (Lys), Jornay unites himself with wilderness Canada when Lys dies of smallpox. In the manner of Adventure fiction, his endurance is tested during a visionary experience with his dead love. The novel concludes with a journey to the Mississippi with Anne. *God's sparrows* (1937) deals overtly with the Great War (as does the later narrative poem of 1965, *The wood of the nightingale*). Combining the family saga with the war novel, featuring its hero's reconciliation with a dead cousin through a dream, *God's sparrows* leaves David Thatcher (whose American-Canadian ancestry resembles Child's) shattered at the end. *Blow wind, come rack* (1954)—written under the pseudonym 'John Wentworth'—thrusts an academic into the violent world of the spy thriller. *Day of wrath* (1945) offers a grim account of a Jew's fate under Hitler. *Mr Ames against time* (1949, GGA) pits an old man against time in his efforts to save his son from a frame-up for murder. *The Victorian house* (1951), a long poem, funnels the break-up of Anglo-Canadian cultural values through its narrator's recollections of a property that he finally refuses to sell. Modernist in its themes of disintegration, though often old-fashioned in style, Child's fiction reflects his concern with the adaptation of the European newcomer to the Canadian wilderness (*The village of souls*) and with the loss of social coherence (*God's sparrows, The Victorian house*)—major cultural preoccupations in the southern Ontario of its time.

Chislett, Anne (b. 1942). Born in St John's, Newfoundland, she was educated at Memorial University (B.A., 1964) and studied theatre at the University of British Columbia. With her husband, James Roy, she founded in 1975 the Blyth Festival, in southwestern Ontario, and retired from teaching high-school English and drama in 1980 to become a full-time playwright. Most of Chislett's work has been successfully produced at the Blyth Festival, including her adaptation of Harry J. Boyle's 1964 novel, *A summer burning* (prod. 1977); *The tomorrow box* (1980, rpr. 1984); *Quiet in the land* (1983, rpr. 2003, GGA); *Another season's promise* (1988, co-authored with Keith Roulston); *Yankee notions* (1993); and her adaptation of Ralph Connor's 1902 GLENGARRY SCHOOL DAYS (prod. 1994). The principal recurring theme in Chislett's plays is the concept of change, with older generations often pitted against the young. For example, in *Quiet in the land* a rebellious Amish teenager comes into conflict with family traditions and religious conventions. A similar conflict is seen in *Another season's promise*, though here the younger generation (embodied by a farmer's city-dwelling son) is eager to return to a more traditional way of life that is being threatened by encroaching urbanization and capitalist values. Drawing on the conflict between rural and urban life as a dramatic framework, Chislett delves into more political territory in *The tomorrow box*, where the changing role and value of women in society is examined from differing perspectives. The layered, cycloramic structure of *Yankee notions*, which deals with the aftermath of the 1837 Upper Canada rebellion, is evidence of Chislett's flexibility as a playwright. Conventional dramatic structure, comedic undertones, and sensitive characterization are the hallmarks of all these plays.

Choy, Wayson (b. 1939). He was born in Vancouver and was educated at the University of British Columbia (B.A., 1961), majoring in creative writing under Earle BIRNEY, and teaches English at Humber College, Toronto. His novel *The jade peony* (1995, rpr. 2009), which became a national bestseller and shared the (Ontario) Trillium Book Award in 1996, won praise for its detailed and delicately cumulative account of the life (and the past) of one family in Vancouver's Chinatown in the 1930s and 1940s. It is narrated in three sections by Only Sister, Second Brother, and Third Brother, all of them young. Formalities and beliefs from Old China are very much present, but Canadian influences and experiences inevitably make their way, as young

Choy

Sekky (Third Brother) found in the classroom of Miss E. Doyle, whose announcement 'I am the General of this class' persuaded the pupils, her 'soldiers', to co-operate with her. In this last section, the friendship of Sekky with his older neighbour Meiying, in love with a Japanese boy, leads to a sad and dramatic wartime conclusion. The jade peony was a carved pendant Sekky's grandmother had left to him. 'In the centre of this semi-transluscent carving, no more than an inch wide, was a pool of pink light, its veins swirling out into the petals of the flower.' The colour, she told him, was the colour of her spirit. *Paper shadows: a Chinatown childhood* (1999, rpr. 2005) portrays a family's life in Vancouver's Chinatown with more intricacy and detail because it is a memoir and because the family is Choy's own: his father Toy, a chef on the CPR West Coast boats, and his mother Lilly. An extraordinary gift of total recall enables him to relate his life as Sonny, his childhood name, from the age of three through his early years in public school (while also being made to attend a Chinese school, an alien experience that was abruptly terminated). Brief narratives, with much convincing dialogue—among parents, Grandfather, and aunts—and interludes about forebears, create an endearing and vivid portrait of a family, a culture, a place, and a historical time. The book opens and closes with Choy's learning, at age fifty-six, that he had been adopted. No hint of this had ever been given to him, and his real parents remain paper shadows. A sequel to *The jade peony*, *All that matters* (2004, rpr. 2005) is narrated by Kiam-Kim (First Son) beginning in 1926 when, aged three, he arrives in Vancouver, from China, with Father and Poh-Poh, his grandmother (the Old One), at Gold Mountain (Vancouver), to join another 'paper family'—people who had arrived with false documents. There follows the interesting account of his growing up in the Chinese community of Vancouver, in the thirties and forties, and of the life of his family. Poh-Poh is dominant, though attached to myths of Old China; Father, a widower, who knows some English and becomes employed, agrees to receive 'a female helpmate and companion'. Thereupon the young and beautiful Chen Siu-Diep (Stepmother) comes from China to join Father and his family, and bears two siblings, one of them Sekky (Third Brother), friend of Meiying—whose relationship, and the jade peony, are both described in *The jade peony*. Liam's growing up, his friendship with neighbour Jack O'Connor, his romance with (and eventual marriage to) Jenny Chong, the

war, and the disclosure of some of the 'silences' of Old China, all drive this well-conceived and well-written novel to its subtle conclusion. The title comes from the Confucian epigraph: 'With words, all that matters is to express truth.' The novel won the (Ontario) Trillium Book Award.

In 2009 Choy published *Not yet: a memoir of living and almost dying*, a sensitive account of his having, and recovering from, an asthma–heart attack and four years later another heart attack. Choy was made a Member of the Order of Canada in 2005.

Choyce, Lesley (b. 1951). Born in Riverside, New Jersey, educated at Rutgers University (B.A., 1972), Montclair State College (M.A., 1974), and City University of New York (M.A., 1983), he settled in 1978 at East Lawrencetown, Nova Scotia, where he established Pottersfield Press (1979–). He became a Canadian citizen in 1984. A man of great spirit and many talents, he is a professor of English at Dalhousie University, has hosted a syndicated TV talk show in Halifax, surfs (year-round) in the North Atlantic, and has published a long list of books, only a few of which can be mentioned here. His first of many collections of lyrical poems was *Re-inventing the wheel* (1980) and his most recent is *Revenge of the optimist* (2004). His short stories, written in a variety of modes, are collected in *Dance the rocks ashore* (1997). He has written more than a dozen young-adult novels, including *Dark end of dream street* (1994) and *The summer of Apartment X* (1999), a humorous story about three high-school graduates who rent a horrible apartment near the beach and their attempts at romance; the most recent are *Smoke and mirrors* (2004), *Sudden impact* (2005), and *Deconstructing Dylan* (2006). *The trapdoor to heaven* (1996) is an ingenious science-fiction novel. *The second season of Jonas MacPherson* (1989) portrays the emotional life of an aging fisherman, *The republic of nothing* (1994) is an ambitious coming-of-age novel, and *World enough* (1998) is about a loser who finds himself in a rehab centre in Halifax, along with many engaging characters. Choyce has also written histories: *Nova Scotia: shaped by the sea* (1996) and *The coasts of Canada* (2002). *Transcendental anarchy* (1993) is a memoir.

CIV/n (1953–5). A Montreal little magazine nominally edited by Aileen Collins, it was heavily influenced by the editorial ideas of Louis DUDEK and Irving LAYTON, in whose home editorial meetings were held. The name was contributed by Dudek from a line about civilization in an Ezra Pound letter: 'CIV/n not a one man job.' The seven issues carried both poems and reviews, the latter nearly all by Dudek and Layton. Poets who contributed were mostly Canadian and included, as well as Dudek and Layton, Anne WILKINSON, Phyllis WEBB, Miriam WADDINGTON, Raymond SOUSTER, A.J.M. SMITH, Eli MANDEL, D.G. JONES, and Robert Currie. The seven issues have been reprinted in *CIV/n: a literary magazine of the 50's* (1983) edited by Aileen Collins, with the assistance of Simon Dardick.

Clark, Catherine Anthony (1892–1977). Born in London, England, Catherine Smith immigrated to Canada in 1914. In 1919 she married Leonard Clark and settled in the Kootenay Mountains of British Columbia, where she raised her family and wrote part time, not publishing her first book until she was fifty-eight. *The golden pine cone* (1950, rpr. 1994) chronicles the adventures of two children who abandon the security of their families and journey to the mysterious world of fantasy, called by Clark the 'inner world', to rescue their dog and return a magical pine cone to its rightful owner. This plot reappears in various guises in all of Clark's subsequent fantasies. *The sun horse* (1950), *The one-winged dragon* (1955), *The silver man* (1959), *The diamond feather* (1962), and *The hunter and the medicine man* (1966) are all quests set within the Kootenay wilderness so familiar to Clark. Her 'inner world' is not the never-never land of traditional fantasies but the quasi-magical world of Native lore, a world inhabited by the Glass-Witch, the Flame-lighter Woman, and other figures drawn from Aboriginal legends. In her Kootenay wilderness the natural and supernatural merge; there is no rigorous distinction between the real and the unreal. Similarly, Native legends influence Clark's presentation of moral values. Her fantasies present no absolute goodness or evil; rather, individuals are judged as either selfish or selfless. The true hero and heroine are judged not for their courage but for their ability to give to others; their identity is defined in terms of the community. All Clark's fantasies preach a common doctrine: humanity survives by acting, by confronting chaos, and by caring for each other. The re-publication of *The golden pine cone* in 1994, with an introduction by Sheila Egoff and Judith Saltman, and feminist critics' interest in Clark, suggest that there is a place for her unique approach to fantasy: a merging of traditional elements of fantasy and Native folklore that could provide the prototype for a distinctly Canadian fantasy.

Clark, Eliza (b. 1963). Born in Mississauga, Ontario, she graduated in 1985 from York University, Toronto, where she majored in creative writing. She has taught creative writing part-time at Ryerson Polytechnic University, the Humber School for Writers, and York University. Clark is a comic novelist who specializes in eccentric characters with dilemmas that often have an undercurrent of sadness. She sets her novels in the southern United States—especially Florida—which Clark often visited as a child. Her books are peppered with references to American popular culture, from Dean Martin, Taco Bell, and 'Let's Make a Deal' to Elvis in Graceland. In *Miss you like crazy* (1991, rpr. 1999) the heroine, Marylou, is torn between her philandering husband Zak and a graveyard flower vendor named Emmanuel. The novel's Florida trailer-park setting, where Marylou's mother dies, embodies Clark's quirky perspective on human relations. *What you need* (1994) continues Clark's comic exploration of the travails of New Age characters, and again demonstrates her flair for idiosyncratic voices. Buddy Whelper and his ex-wife Cheryl, 'out of stubborn habit', tended to shop at the same times. 'When Cheryl would catch him fondling a lush grapefruit or a hard cucumber, she'd undam a flood of curses that always seemed to be perched on the tip of her tongue.... "Cheryl," he'd yell, "we once had love in common. We were lit from inside like Japanese lanterns on a moony night." "That doesn't compute with me," his ex would holler back.' In *Bite the stars* (1999, rpr. 2000) Clark tells the story of Grace Larson, a single mother whose only son, Cole, is on death row. As his execution approaches, Grace looks back on Cole's difficult life, which began with a premature birth in church on Palm Sunday as a tornado struck the building and killed nineteen people. Clark is also the author of two picture books for children, both illustrated by Vladyana Krykorka—*Butterflies and bottlecaps* (1996) and *Seeing and believing* (1999)—and created *Writer's gym: exercises and training tips for writers* (2007), with contributions from numerous writers, some well known.

Clark, Joan (b. 1934). Born Joan MacDonald in Liverpool, Nova Scotia, she studied drama at Acadia University and education at the University of Alberta, and spent several years teaching. She married Jack Clark, an engineer with the Royal Canadian Air Force, and went with him to Winisk, Hudson Bay, later the inspiration for her novel *The victory of Geraldine Gull*. She lived for twenty years in Alberta

Clark

before moving to St John's, Newfoundland. Her first three books were children's stories: *Girl of the Rockies* (1968), *Thomasina and the trout tree* (1971), and *The hand of Robin Squires* (1977, rpr. 2005), which was translated into Swedish, Danish, and French. Her first adult book was a collection of short stories, *From a high thin wire* (1982, rpr. 2004), focusing on problems of adolescence and motherhood and the struggle for self-realization. Then came three more children's books: *The leopard and the lily* (1984), a poignant fable in the manner of Oscar Wilde, and a pair of coming-of-age stories, *Wild man of the woods* (1985) and *The moons of Madeleine* (1987, rpr. 1998), written from a male and then a female perspective respectively. A second book of short stories, *Swimming toward the light* (1990, rpr. 2002), was followed by four novels for adults, *The victory of Geraldine Gull* (1988, rpr. 1994), *Eiriksdottir: a tale of dreams and luck* (1994, rpr. 2003), *Latitudes of melt* (2000, rpr. 2001), and *An audience of chairs* (2005, rpr. 2006). *Eiriksdottir* shared the same historical material about the Vikings as her children's book *The dream carvers* (1995). *Latitudes of melt*—the title referring to where southward-moving icebergs start to melt—begins with the discovery off the coast of Newfoundland, in 1912 after the *Titanic* sank, of a child in a basket on a floating icepan. Named Aurora, she is 'grafted onto' the family of the fisherman who found her, and her life is described until old age, along with her granddaughter's research into her origins. On the first page of *An audience of chairs* Moranna MacKenzie, who lives in a Cape Breton farmhouse, is playing a Rachmaninov concerto on a piano board. The performance exhausts her, 'but not for long, and soon she is on her feet, bowing to an audience of chairs.' Known as Mad Mory, she makes the best of her disordered life, carving wooden figures of her ancestors to sell to tourists, writing unwanted sermons for the United Church minister, responding vocally to news she reads about. 'One of her ideas is to move the United Nations to Antarctica, where its members would be free from politics and outside influences.' She has a lover, Bun, who for part of the year helps to run a ferry between Cape Breton and Newfoundland. The novel interrelates details of this present, and the past, of the self-absorbed, eccentric, irresponsible Moranna: her childhood, her attempts as an actress, her happy marriage to Duncan Fraser, the birth of two daughters, Bonnie and Brianna, her neglect of them, the swift removal of the children from her life, being confined to an asylum (from which she escapes), and

the end of her marriage. Clark has drawn a believable portrait of a character whose willfulness and eccentric behaviour lead her into trouble and she becomes 'absolutely and impossibly mad, riding the ferries, hiding in the cellar, wandering around the island outlandishly dressed, shouting at people...'—always haunted by the loss of her daughters. The time comes when she never 'flipped' again, when self-control and reasonableness took over, both strengthened by an epiphany: on TV she sees Bonnie—Dr Fraser, a distinguished scientist—being interviewed. She goes to Halifax to hear her lecture, though she doesn't meet her, and learns Bonnie is going to be married. When the wedding is about to take place she sends both daughters bouquets of wildflowers; standing on the street, she watches them enter and leave the church.... (There is a promising resolution.) In Clark's skilful hands Moranna—the various shifts in her mind and behaviour, the details of her life, her relationship with other people—becomes memorable.

The places where Clark has lived have strongly influenced her fiction: a mining town in Nova Scotia, Alberta and the Rockies, and Newfoundland and the Viking site at L'Anse aux Meadows. A fascination with violence has disturbed some of her readers—the severing of the hero's hand in *The hand of Robin Squires*, for example, or Freydis's satisfaction in splitting the skulls of her fellow Vikings and watching the blood spurt in *Eiriksdottir*. Clark portrays strong female characters, like the rebellious and ungovernable Ojibwa Geraldine Gull, who commits terrorist acts against whites. Yet she can also write passages of delicate poetic beauty, as in a lyrical description of the moths in her story 'Luna moths'.

The word for home (2002, rpr. 2003) is a substantial novel for young girls, set in 1924 in Newfoundland. Sadie and her little sister Flora are living with their 'sharp-eyed landlady' Mrs Hatch because their mother has died and their father has gone prospecting for gold in the interior of Newfoundland. The very readable narrative incorporates everyday life in St John's, troubles at school, and suspense when their father's letters and the money he's been sending cease. *Snow* (2006) is a picture book for children. Joan Clark was appointed an Officer of the Order of Canada in 2008.

Clark, Sally (b. 1953). Born in Vancouver, she moved to Toronto in 1973 to study fine arts and theatre at York University, where she wrote a short story about a professor's middle-aged wife who disappears while the couple are on vacation. This became her first full-length play, *Lost souls and missing persons* (1985, rpr. 1998), a comedy that premiered at Theatre Passe Muraille in 1984. The production of *Moo* (1989) by the Factory Theatre, Toronto, won the 1989 Chalmers Canadian Play Award. In two acts comprised of forty-seven short scenes, it is the story of an eccentric, feisty woman and her romantic obsession with Harry, an exciting cad. Though her genteel family are appalled, chasing her evasive lover all over the world allows Moo an adventurous and highly unconventional life. Extremely funny in Act One, the play turns dark in Act Two when Moo is institutionalized by the family and abandoned. Harry finds her and the play concludes with a stunning finale. The Canadian Stage's 1989 production of Clark's *The trial of Judith K* (1991)—an earlier version was produced in 1985—was nominated for a Dora Award and for a 1991 Governor General's Award. In 1989 Toronto's Tarragon Theatre mounted *Jehanne of the witches* (1993), a dramatization of the story of Saint Joan and her friendship with Gilles de Rais. In 1991 Toronto's Theatre Plus mounted *Life without instruction* (1994), a revenge comedy based on the true story and real trial of Artemisia Gentileschi, the seventeenth-century Italian painter who charged her teacher with rape. *Saint Frances of Hollywood* (1996), produced in 1994, bears clear thematic and stylistic connections to her other plays. Based on the life of the glamorous movie star of the 1930s, Frances Farmer, Clark's play rejects a linear structure, employing instead a series of short scenes. Again, the play is a dramatization of a true story and the protagonist is an extraordinary woman in a power struggle with a society that has no place for her. Clark's characters are wilful heroines, and not simply victims: in their inevitable defeat they exhibit an admirable vitality. *Wasps* (1998), produced in 1996, is a frenetic social satire of manners, a 'drawing-room comedy for distempered times'. *Wanted* (2004) is a substantial, ambitious play about the Klondike Gold Rush of 1897. It begins with an announcer saying: 'WANTED: a young lady or widow, not over thirty, unencumbered and matrimonially inclined to accompany an able-bodied forty-year-old prospector to the Klondike.'

Clarke, Austin C. (b. 1934). Born and educated in Barbados, Austin Chesterfield Clarke became a schoolteacher there before moving to Canada in 1955 to study at Trinity College,

University of Toronto. In 1959–60 he worked as a reporter in Timmins and Kirkland Lake, Ontario, before joining the CBC and eventually becoming a freelance broadcaster. Between 1968 and 1974 he taught creative writing and was writer-in-residence at Yale, Brandeis, Williams, and Duke Universities and at the University of Texas. In 1974–5 he was appointed cultural attaché to the Barbadian embassy in Washington, followed by a year as general manager of the Caribbean Broadcasting Corporation and adviser to the prime minister of Barbados. An acknowledged spokesman for the black community in Toronto, Clarke served on the Metro Toronto Library Board from 1973 to 1976, and subsequently on the Ontario Board of Censors and the Canadian Immigration and Refugee Board (1988–93). He has been given honorary doctorates by Brock University and Trinity College and is a Member of the Order of Canada (2002).

A highly gifted writer, Clarke is the author of seventeen books. His first two works of fiction deal with life in Barbados. *Survivors of the crossing* (1964) and *Amongst thistles and thorns* (1965)—the latter a collection of short stories—present the island as economically bleak and impoverished, full of desperate people struggling for survival. For the ambitious individual, escape to North America is the only chance for prosperity. *The meeting point* (1967, rpr. 1998), the first novel in Clarke's trilogy about the lives of Caribbean immigrants in Toronto, explores what that chance means in human terms. Introducing a group of West Indian immigrants, it presents the underside of wealthy Toronto by revealing the racist exploitation of blacks. *Storm of fortune* (1971, rpr. 1998) and *The bigger light* (1975, rpr. 1998) chart their slow and eventful adaptation to Canadian social values and conventions. These novels are filled with bitterness and sadness, lightened by the indomitable humour and spirit of Clarke's characters. They are enriched by Clarke's mastery of dialogue, realism, and psychologically subtle and astute characterizations. *The prime minister* (1977, rpr. 1994) is an exposé of political corruption in a developing nation that grew out of Clarke's experiences as a civil servant in Barbados. His second collection of short stories, *When he was free and young and he used to wear silks* (1971), further elaborates the theme of blacks struggling to make good in Canada. Four other collections followed: *When women rule* (1985), *Nine men who laughed* (1986), *In this city* (1992, rpr. 2008), and *There are no elders* (1993, rpr. 2000). Throughout these works, which are about white and black Canadians at 'the meeting point', Clarke moves back and forth between 'Wessindian' and Anglo-Canadian English; but while the Caribbean dialect may be amusing at times, Clarke's themes are stringently tragic, as his characters and their language are swamped by a Puritan white Canada.

Of Clarke's more recent novels, *The origin of waves* (1997, rpr. 2003), begins with the reunion, after almost fifty years, of two Barbadians who exchange memories in a bar, providing a rich and vibrant narrative that reaches into the past and includes the cumulative histories of both men. *The question* (1999, rpr. 2004) is narrated by Malcolm, a judge in immigration court, who meets at an afternoon party a red-haired woman who mesmerizes him; they marry, and the novel is about the difficult terrain of their marriage. *The polished hoe* (2003, rpr. 2006) is a long, brilliant distillation of Clarke's knowledge of the past and present, the people and social customs, of an island called Bimshire (his native Barbados?), as told partly by Mary-Mathilda, who has killed Mr Bellfeels with her hoe and wants to make a statement to the police. Not only was Bellfeels her boss on the sugar-cane plantation she worked on as a field hand, but she was his mistress for some thirty years and bore him a son, Wilberforce. 'Mr. Bellfeels took her, as his right, in his natural arrogance of ownership, as part of the intricate ritual and arrangement of life on the Plantation—"if it wasn't you, Mary-girl," Ma told her, "it wouldda be somebody-else daughter. And even though it is what it is, I still feel more better to see that is you getting some o' the sweets that goes along with it, if you know what I mean!" Ma had told Mary-Mathilda this two years after she had introduced Mary girl to Mr. Bellfeels that Sunday morning in the Church Yard, when he towered over her [she was thirteen] from the saddle of his horse.//Mr. Bellfeels had had Ma, too, for years; "taking what he want"....' Mary lives in the Great House and was given a servant, Gertrude, and Bellfeels paid for the education of Wilberforce (he went to Oxford) until he became a much-respected doctor in the village. The driven, forward-moving, detailed narrative—over one long night Mary-Mathilda's recollections of her life are interrupted by the comments of a constable, then of a sargeant, Percy Stuart (she has known him all her life and he was in love with her), until she begins her 'statement' about the murder (on page 450)—is a virtuosic bringing to life of a West Indian community, with all its intricacies, combining the vernacular with passsages of educated diction, that is impressive not only in its detail but in its emotional richness. It won the GILLER PRIZE, shared (with Nino RICCI), the (Ontario) Trillium Award, and won the Commonwealth Writers Prize Best Book Award. *More* (2008), a Toronto novel, is mainly the monologue of Idora Morrison, a server at Trinity College, made up of tumbling thoughts about her past, her hardships, black violence, gun crimes (is her son involved?), and other aspects of the life of a poor black woman in a city edged in racism.

The final story in *Choosing his coffin: the best stories of Austin Clarke* (2003) is the title story—the only one that had not been published before—in which a Canadian son, the narrator, drives his West Indian mother, now an American, in New Jersey to choose a coffin for her husband (the son's stepfather), who is in a coma. The beautifully described details—realistic, though eccentric and tinged with humour—of their few hours together while on this mission end with a surprising phone call in the mother's house that is both funny and sad.

Although in the first volume of his autobiography, *Growing up stupid under the Union Jack* (1980, rpr. 1998), Clarke concentrates on his own childhood in Barbados, allusions to the larger framework of British colonialism expand his topic as he demonstrates what the British Empire meant to its non-white population. The novel *Proud empires* (1986) fictionalizes this same material, with a stronger cynicism concerning island politics, and a stronger tone about the frigidity of white Canadian life supplanting the *joie de vivre* of the Caribbean peoples. *Pig tails 'n breadfruit: rituals of slave food*, a Barbadian memoir was published in 1999 (rpr. 2000). See Barry CALLAGHAN ed., *The Austin Clarke reader* (1996), and Stella Algoo-Baksh, *Austin C. Clarke: a biography* (1994).

Clarke, George Elliott (b. 1960). Born in Windsor Plains, Nova Scotia, he grew up in Halifax and was educated at the University of Waterloo (B.A., 1984), Dalhousie University (M.A., 1989), and Queen's University (Ph.D., 1993). From 1994 he was assistant professor of English and Canadian Studies at Duke University, North Carolina, and in 1999 he joined the English department of the University of Toronto, where he was appointed E.J. Pratt Professor of Canadian Literature in 2003. He has received honorary doctorates from Dalhousie, New Brunswick, Alberta, and

Waterloo universities. A seventh-generation Canadian and a descendant of Black Loyalists who settled in Nova Scotia in 1783, Clarke has coined the term 'Africadian' to describe the black Nova Scotian experience that is central to his writing. Drawing upon abundant memories of childhood visits to his maternal grandparents' home in Three Mile Plains, N.S., his poetry celebrates the richness of life encountered in even the poorest rural black communities in his youth—the familiarity with Biblical stories, phrasing, and cadences, the emphasis on oral narrative, the vivacity of an everyday language enriched by metaphor, and above all the presence of music, from spirituals to jazz and the blues. *Saltwater spirituals and deeper blues* (1983) is animated by a powerful and convincing sense of racial injustice. Clarke prefers, however, to move beyond the simple contours of protest poetry to record the beauty as well as the pain that marks the Africadian experience. Convinced of the power of myth, and the epic scope available to twentieth-century poets in the form of the lyric sequence, he combines the elegance of certain European literary forms and traditions with the spikiness of local and popular idiom in his attempt to bring Black Nova Scotian experience to life. His most accomplished work, *Whylah Falls* (1990, rpr. 2000), is a tour de force in this regard. Mingling blank verse, traditional poetic forms (such as the aubade, distich, and idyll), prose poems, journalistic snippets, recipes, old photographs borrowed from Nova Scotian archives, and a lush language that is simultaneously arcane and richly contemporary, the cycle recreates African-Canadian life in a fictional village in Jarvis County, N.S., in the 1930s, as an educated black poet returns to woo his beloved Shelley. *Whylah Falls: the play* (1999) was produced by CBC Radio in 1996 and on the stage by the Eastern Front Theatre, Halifax, in 1997. *Lush dreams, blue exile: fugitive poems 1978–1993* (1994) includes a number of tightly constructed political poems, such as 'To Liu Chan, near Nanking' and 'November 22, 1963', but primarily features Africadian poems, in praise of landscape and elucidation of ancestry, that are marked by the bounteous language, insistent rhythms, and lively allusiveness that characterize Clarke's poetry at its best. *Beatrice Chancy* (1999) is Clarke's libretto for James Rolfe's opera of the same name, which was produced with great success in Toronto in June 1999. (Beatrice was sung brilliantly by the very young Measha Brueggergosman.) Set in the Annapolis Valley in 1801, it was inspired by *The Cenci*, Shelley's verse

tragedy of incestuous rape, murder, and execution. The Canadian tragedy unfolds when the sixteen-year-old slave Beatrice Chancy, daughter of a white slave owner and his black mistress, after returning from a convent school in Halifax, makes known her love for Lead, another slave. Her enraged father rapes her; Beatrice wreaks vengeance by stabbing her father to death; and she and Lead are hanged. The libretto, appearing overwritten in print, provides a heart-wrenching underpinning for the beautiful score of the opera. *Execution poems* (2000, GGA; rpr. 2001) is a collection inspired by the hanging for murder, in 1949, in Fredericton, New Brunswick, of Clarke's cousins (once removed), George and Rufus Hamilton. They 'smacked a white taxi driver, Silver, with a hammer to lift his silver'. '*Rue*: Here's how I justify my error:/The blow that slew Silver came from two centuries back./It took that much time and agony to turn a white man's whip/into a black man's hammer. *Geo*. No, we needed money....' Clarke imagines the pasts of these two men in his first novel, *George & Rue* (2005) and describes vividly, in 'blackened' English, their lives, the murder, the trial, and their deaths. In the poetry collection *Black* (2006)—which is adorned with black pages, striking photographs of nude black women on a black background, among other illustrations—the first poem is 'George & Rue: coda'. The last lines of Part I are: 'Rue ain't feel nothing bad or wrong or upset./A white man was dead, yes; but they had booze and cash.' Parts II and III, respectively, are 'Trials & convictions' and 'The hangings'.

Clarke's other collections of verse are *Blue* (2001), of which he says: 'Theses poems are black, profane, surly, *American*. Their bitterness came honestly. US-torched, I wept these lyrics twixt 1994 and 1999.' The poems are in five parts: Black Eclogues, Red Satires, Gold Sapphics, Blue Elegies, and Ashen Blues. In *Illuminated verses* (2005) Clarke and the photographer Ricardo Scipio—there are dramatic photographs of nudes on every other page—celebrate the beauty of young black women. *Blues and bliss: the poetry of George Elliott Clarke* (2008), selected and with an introduction by Jon Paul Fiorentino, appeared in the Laurier Poetry Series. *Québécité: a jazz fantasia in three cantos* is the libretto for a three-act dramatization of the multi-racial romance of two couples in Quebec City: a Hindu of Indian descent, a Chinese girl, a Haitian of black-and-white ancestry, and an Africadian of mixed background (African-American, Mi'kmaq, born in Halifax). This jazz opera—music by D.D. Jackson—was commissioned by the Guelph Jazz Festival, of which the artistic director is Ajay Heble, who in a 'Postlude' says that the plot exerts 'a necessary challenge to mainstream assumptions about Quebec as white.' It was first performed in September 2003. *Trudeau: long march, shining path* (2007) contains (among many descriptive passages and the author's introduction, with footnotes) the libretto—carefully researched but playfully inventive—for an opera by D.D. Jackson about the career of Pierre Elliott Trudeau. Clarke has been active as an editor. *Fire on the water: an anthology of black Nova Scotia writing* (2 vols, 1991, 1992) and *Eying the North Star: directions in African-Canadian literature* (1997) were followed by the hefty, large-format *Odysseys home: mapping African-Canadian literature* (2002), which is a selection of Clarke's essays—including 'A primer of African-Canadian literature'—reviews, and a 136-page bibliography. Clarke was appointed an Officer of the Order of Canada in 2008.

Clutesi, George (1905–88). Born at Port Alberni, British Columbia, he was among the first of the Native peoples to record in a popular way, and to interpret from a Native perspective, the culture of the indigenous peoples, notably that of the Nootka (Nuu-chah-nulth) nation of the Pacific Northwest coast. Clutesi worked as a fisherman and piledriver for more than twenty years. During convalescence from a back injury he began to teach the traditional ways. Emily CARR was impressed by his drawings and in 1945 bequeathed her artist's materials to him. Clutesi subsequently worked for CBC Radio and ran an art shop before his death in Victoria, B.C. He is the author of two illustrated books of traditional lore that proved to be popular and to have special appeal for young readers: *Son of Raven, son of Deer: fables of the Tse-shaht People* (1967) and *Potlatch* (1969).

CNQ: Canadian Notes & Queries was first published in 1968 by William Morley as a four-page supplement to *The Abacus*, the newsletter of the Antiquarian Bookseller's Association of Canada. Modelled on *British Notes & Queries*, it was a journal, Morley wrote, 'of little discoveries encountered, often by serendipity, in the course of scholarly investigation', and queries that often arise in the course of research that are beyond one's 'present resources to solve'. In 1990 Morely passed on the journal do Douglas (now George) FETHERLING, and he—sensing that

the Internet would soon take over *CN&Q*'s function as an academic bulletin, reconceived it as a journal of literary, cultural, and artistic history and criticism. Fetherling continued publishing *CN&Q*—depending on the issue, with either 'charming' or 'calculated irregularity'—until 1997, when he sold it to The PORCUPINE'S QUILL, where it first came under the editorial direction of John METCALF, the editor most responsible for the aesthetic and contrarian tone and vision it has taken on since. After publishing another eighteen issues over the next nine years, Porcupine's Quill passed *CN&Q* onto Dan Wells of BIBLIOASIS in Windsor, Ontario. The handsomely redesigned *CNQ: Canadian Notes & Queries* has continued with Metcalf's preoccupations. It has increased its frequency to three times a year. Almost by default, it has become one of the only venues in the country for lengthy non-academic critical reviews of Canadian literature. *CNQ*'s mission also includes the recording of literary and cultural history and the investigation of cultural infrastructure. Periodic features are published on unjustly neglected Canadian artists and writers, including, in recent years, Clark BLAISE, George JOHNSTON, Eric ORMSBY, and Mark Anthony JARMAN. Its Salon des Refusés issue (74, Summer/Fall 2008), alongside *The New Quarterly*, was a reaction to the recently published *Penguin book of Canadian short stories* edited by Jane URQUHART, highlighting the work of twenty writers that had been omitted, becoming, according to the *Toronto Star*, the flashpoint 'for one of the sharpest literary debates this country has ever seen.' Entering its forty-first year in 2009, *CNQ* remains one of the more respected critical journals in the country.

Coach House Press. Synonymous for most of its life with fine-crafted books and adventurous editorial policies, it was founded in Toronto in 1965 by Stan Bevington, with the editorial assistance of Wayne Clifford. Clifford was succeeded as editor in 1966 by Victor COLEMAN, who by 1973 had built Coach House into one of the three largest publishers in Canada of innovative literary titles. Coleman resigned in 1974, and between then and 1988 the list was edited by a collective, initially consisting of Bevington; writers bp NICHOL, Michael ONDAATJE, Frank DAVEY, and David Young; graphic artist Rick/Simon (who left the press in 1979); and lawyer Linda Davey. Other editors in this period included Martin Kinch, Val Frith, art historian Dennis Reid, novelist Sarah Sheard, drama critic Robert

Wallace, and poets David MCFADDEN and Christopher DEWDNEY. The press's early years, under Coleman's editorship, were characterized by hand-set type, multicoloured offset printing, fortuitous collaborations between author and designer, and titles by open-form writers from both the USA and Canada. These included Ondaatje, George BOWERING, Nichol, McFadden, Joe ROSENBLATT, Daphne MARLATT, Matt COHEN, Allen Ginsberg, and Robert Creeley. In many ways Coach House represented a continuation of CONTACT PRESS, extending Contact's welcome to new poets and supporting most of the writers in the Contact Press anthology *New wave Canada: the new explosion in Canadian poetry* (1966), edited by Raymond SOUSTER. In the 1974–88 period the interests of the press diversified to include the work of previously established writers like D.G. JONES, Phyllis WEBB, Louis DUDEK, Eli MANDEL, Sheila WATSON, John MARLYN, Dorothy LIVESAY, Gwendolyn MacEWEN, and Robert KROETSCH; numerous first books, including those of Paul QUARRINGTON, Gail SCOTT, Sharon THESEN, and Anne MICHAELS; textbooks such as Ondaatje's *The long poem anthology* (1979) and Bowering's *Fiction of contemporary Canada* (1980); plays by Kinch, George F. WALKER, and Ann-Marie MacDONALD; and a Québec translation series.

In 1987–8 Bevington's decision to withdraw from publishing in order to focus on his commercial printing business led to a crisis that saw several editors leave and others, notably David Young and Sarah Sheard, attempt to reorganize Coach House as a more mainstream and profitable enterprise. A limited company was formed to acquire the press from Bevington, with its board of directors including business people unfamiliar with Canadian small-press publishing. The death of bp Nichol in 1988 robbed the board of its strongest advocate of innovative writing and activist publishing. Because of the generous federal and provincial subsidies available to Ontario publishers in the early 1990s, however, the new Coach House grew rapidly, its distribution contracted to MCCLELLAND & STEWART, and most of its editorial work performed by employees rather than by its unpaid volunteer editors. In the fall of 1996, after federal subsidies to publishing had been cut by up to 60 per cent, and an Ontario loan guarantee program for publishers was cancelled, the directors voted to dissolve the press and return all copyrights to its authors. See Victor Coleman, *The day they stole the Coach House Press* (1993). In January 1997 Bevington announced the birth of Coach House Books,

with Hilary Clark as editor, located in the same old coach house on bpNichol Lane. The press's initial publications appeared both as expensive handmade limited-edition volumes and as online texts on the Internet. In 1999 Darren Wershler-Henry took over as editor, and the house began publishing trade editions of innovative poetry, fiction, and drama, all printed in-house on two old Heidelberg presses.

The reputation of the new Coach House has been growing steadily since its rebirth in 1997, but it skyrocketed with the publication in 2001 with the publication of Christian BÖK's *Eunoia*. This work of experimental poetry won the coveted GRIFFIN POETRY PRIZE in 2002 and has sold more than 19,000 copies. Other poetry highlights include Steve MCCAFFERY's *Seven pages missing*, Nicole BROSSARD's *Notebook of roses and civilization*, Di BRANDT's *Now you care*, Sylvia Legris's *Nerve squall*, and Sina Queyras's *Lemon hound*. In 2002 Alana Wilcox took over as editor and began publishing more fiction, including Golda Fried's *Nellcott is my darling*, which was a runner-up for the GGA, Claudia Dey's *Stunt*, Sean Dixon's *The girls who saw everything*, Maggie Helwig's *Girls fall down*, Andrew Kaufman's *All my friends are superheroes*, Andrew Wedderburn's *The milk chicken bomb*, and Howard Akler's *The city man*.

Coach House's non-fiction list has also enhanced the press's reputation. The uTOpia series—*uTOpia: towards a new Toronto* (2005) edited by Jason McBride and Alana Wilcox, *The state of the arts: living with culture in Toronto* (2006) and *GreenTOpia: towards a sustainable Toronto* (2007), both edited by Alana Wilcox, Christina Palassio, and Johnny Dovercourt—and its books on architecture in Toronto, including *Concrete Toronto: a guide to concrete architecture from the fifties to the seventies* (2007) edited by Michael McClelland and Graeme Stewart, have been celebrated for contributing to a renaissance of civic engagement in the city. Coach House's film list includes titles by Guy Maddin and Mike Hoolboom, and its drama list includes plays by Linda Griffiths, Claudia Dey, Karen Hines, and Darren O'Donnell.

Coach House has had dozens of awards and nominations. In 2008 it received the Province of Ontario's inaugural Premier's Award for Excellence in the Arts for Arts Organizations. The opening of the transformed Art Gallery of Ontario in November 2008 showcased, in the Signy Eaton Gallery, the work of various artists in an exhibit called 'Canadian Art in the 1960s & 1970s Through the Lens of the

Coach House Press

Coach House Press'. Stan Bevington was appointed a Member of the Order of Canada in 2009.

Cody, Hiram Alfred (1872–1948). Born in Cody's, New Brunswick, on the Canaan River north of Saint John, and educated at the Saint John Grammar School and King's College, Windsor, Nova Scotia, he was ordained in 1898 as an Anglican clergyman. During his career as a priest he served a number of parishes in his native province—he became rector of St James Church, Saint John, in 1910—and as far afield as the Yukon. He wrote twenty-three novels, published between 1910 and 1937, among them *The frontiersman: a tale of the Yukon* (1910), *The fourth watch* (1911), *The long patrol; a tale of the Mounted Police* (1912), *The king's arrow: a tale of United Empire Loyalists* (1922), and *The trail of the Golden Horn* (1923). Although Cody's fiction owes much to the boy's adventure-tale tradition of R.M. BALLANTYNE and Frederick Marryat, it attempted to reach beyond an all-male readership by providing both a 'romantic interest' and a Christian message. His novels are imbued with the 'muscular Christianity' that emerged in the latter part of the nineteenth century and flourished sporadically until the 1930s. In *The unknown wrestler* (1918), for example, the accomplished fighter who wins the respect of a tough rural community eventually reveals himself as their new Anglican minister. Cody's fiction typically owes more to his literary ancestors than to his own immediate observations and experiences.

Cogswell, Fred (1917–2004). Frederick William Cogswell was born in East Centreville, New Brunswick, where he grew up. After serving in the Canadian army (1940–5), he studied at the University of New Brunswick (B.A., 1949; M.A., 1950) and at Edinburgh University (Ph.D., 1952). He returned to the University of New Brunswick to teach in the Department of English, where he remained until his retirement, and his appointment as Professor Emeritus in 1983. He was a Member of the Order of Canada. Editor of *The FIDDLEHEAD* from 1952 to 1967, he inaugurated Fiddlehead Books, a publishing enterprise involving more than 300 titles that he continued until 1981. (See FIDDLEHEAD POETRY BOOKS.) Cogswell's poems—characterized by compression, wit, the use of a wide variety of both traditional and modern forms, and a gentle, ironic view of the world—appear in thirty volumes, from *The stunted strong* (1954), to *A long apprenticeship: the collected poems of Fred Cogswell* (1980)

and *Fred Cogswell: selected poems* (1983, edited with a preface by Antonio D'ALFONSO), followed by many other collections, including *As I see it* (1994), *In my own growing* (1995), *The trouble with light* (1995), *Folds* (1997), *Deeper than mind* (2002), *Dried flowers* (2002), *Ghosts* (2002), *Later in Chicago* (2003), and *The kindness of stars* (2004). Cogswell's strengths as a craftsman are evident in five books of translations: *One hundred poems of modern Quebec* (1970), *A second hundred poems of modern Quebec* (1971), *The poetry of modern Quebec* (1976), *The complete poems of Émile Nelligan* (1983), and *Unfinished dreams: contemporary poetry of Acadie* (1990), with Jo Anne Elder. As editor, publisher, poet, and critic, Cogswell maintained a broadly tolerant and humane stance, a disregard of fashion, and a wide eclecticism of taste. See *The vision of Fred: friend of poets—ami des poètes: conversations with Fred Cogswell on the nature and function of poetry* (2004) edited by Cogswell and Wendy Scott.

Cohen, Leonard (b. 1934). Born in Montreal, he grew up in its affluent Westmount district and attended McGill University. Shortly after graduating he published his first book of poetry, *Let us compare mythologies* (1956, rpr. 2006). After publishing a second book of poetry, *The spice-box of earth* (1961), and spending some time in England, he published a novel, *The favourite game* (1963, NCL; rpr. 2000). Since then he has lived intermittently on the Greek island of Hydra, in New York, Montreal, and Los Angeles, from which he once made monthly week-long visits to the Mount Baldy Zen Center to commune, as a Buddhist monk, with an aged Zen master. (Indifferent to his financial situation in this period, he was defrauded of a fortune by his former business manager.) In the 1960s he published the poetry collections *Flowers for Hitler* (1964); *Parasites of heaven* (1966); a second novel, *BEAUTIFUL LOSERS* (1966, NCL; rpr. 2004); *Selected poems* (1968), for which he declined a Governor General's Award; and began a career as an internationally successful songwriter-composer-singer. Later books of poetry include *The energy of slaves* (1972); *Death of a lady's man* (1978); *Book of mercy* (1984, rpr. 1994), a collection of contemporary Psalms; and *Stranger music: selected poems and songs* (1993). Among his albums are *Songs of Leonard Cohen* (1968), *Songs from a room* (1969), *Songs of love and hate* (1971), *Live songs* (1973), *New skins for the old ceremony* (1974), *The best of Leonard Cohen* (1975), *Death of a ladies' man* (1977), *Recent songs* (1979), *Various positions*

(1985), *I'm your man* (1988), and *The future* (1992). At the age of seventy-four Cohen revived his career as a singer with highly successful concerts in London and New York, and in April 2009 he embarked on a two-month tour of North America.

Throughout the sixties Cohen's poetry and fiction were extremely popular, particularly with high-school and college readers. The appeal of his poetry was based chiefly on a traditional and recognizably 'poetic' prosody, suggestive imagery that subjective readers could easily project themselves into, and a theme of moral non-responsibility. George WOODCOCK argued that Cohen was usually conservative in poetic craft and escapist in theme. The poetry of his first two books draws heavily on Greek and Hassidic mythologies—not to reveal them as alive in the present but to convert the present into the sepulchral figures of mythology. Cohen's language here is highly decorative, reminiscent of the early Yeats. While the poems of his third book, *Flowers for Hitler*, venture into both satire and experimental verse forms, those of the fourth, *Parasites of heaven*, return to the conventional and dispassionate measures of the earlier volumes.

A consistent theme in his books—the importance of reducing life to ceremony, of escaping from life by transmuting its slippery actualities into the reliable simplicities of myth and art—is developed most clearly in Cohen's novels. It is the lesson by which Breavman 'comes of age' in *The favourite game*. In *Beautiful losers* it is the lesson 'I' must learn from 'F', and includes not only the transmuting of object and event but the self-reduction of personal identity into the anonymity of sainthood. The loser triumphs by escaping the desire to win. A clear extension of this belief appears in *The energy of slaves*, a collection of fragments, failed poems, and anti-poems. On the surface its directness and self-deprecating cynicism appear to mark a repudiation of the earlier poetry; in fact, it represents a logical step in the saintly self-abnegation Cohen has always advocated: master becomes slave, poetic craftsman becomes his own beautiful loser— 'only a scribbler', in his words. Once again Cohen is working towards a kind of martyrdom. This opposition between decadent craftsman and beautiful loser reappears in *Death of a ladies' man*, which juxtaposes texts exemplifying a quest for beauty and sardonic commentaries. Here Cohen manages, simultaneously and with equal weight, to affirm his visions of ceremony and to deconstruct them. Thus the book becomes both his most traditional and most postmodern work. *Stranger music* (1993) was followed by *Book of longing* (2006, rpr. 2007), with Cohen's drawings and decorations appearing on almost every page—'Always after I tell him/what I intend to do next,/Layton solemnly inquires:/ Leonard, are you sure/you're doing the wrong thing?' ('Layton's question'). The distinguished American composer Philip Glass was inspired to write a musical accompaniment to twenty-two poems in this collection—performed in Toronto in June 2007 and released the same year as a CD: *Philip Glass: Book of longing. A song cycle based on the poetry and images of Leonard Cohen*. Cohen was appointed a Companion of the Order of Canada in 2002.

See Ira Bruce Nadel, *Various positions: a life of Leonard Cohen* (1996).

Cohen, Matt (1942–99). Born in Kingston, Ontario, he moved with his family to Ottawa, where he attended grade school and high school. Though his parents were Jewish, he has recorded that his upbringing was not religious. He went on to the University of Toronto (B.A., 1964; M.A., 1965); his postgraduate degree was in political theory. In 1968 he became a full-time writer of novels and short stories. *Korsoniloff* (1969) was followed shortly afterwards by a fantasy novella, *Johnny Crackle sings* (1971). These are both tales of inner alienation, of divisions within the consciousness that can end only in permanent loss and that hold the characters on the edge of madness. In *Korsoniloff* a schizoid teacher of philosophy tells the separate but inter-intrusive lives of the cold and analytical 'I' and the ineffectually passionate and amoral Korsoniloff, who seeks truths that would destroy him. *Johnny Crackle sings*—a freer fantasy that lacks the clinical verisimilitude of *Korsoniloff*—is the tale of a country boy ruined by an ambition to become a big-time folk singer. In its exploration of drug-created states of mind it moves constantly on the edge of surrealism, and has the kind of self-consciousness that shows a writer still searching for his appropriate form. While this novel was being written Cohen was already working on the stories included in *Columbus and the fat lady* (1972), which established the territory he would occupy in his later novels. *Night flights* (1978) includes some stories from *Columbus* and offers the same mixture of rural fantasy in stories that prefigure the larger novels and somewhat symbolic tales that explore the verges of psychological breakdown in a similar way to Cohen's earlier, smaller novels.

Cohen

The five novels published between 1974 and 1981—*The disinherited* (1974, rpr. 2000), *Wooden hunters* (1975), *The colours of war* (1977, rpr. 1993), *The sweet second summer of Kitty Malone* (1979, rpr. 2000), and *Flowers of darkness* (1981, rpr. 1993)—are at first glance more conventional than Cohen's earlier books, but they can be linked with the more obviously experimental novels because they work less by linear chronology than by a constant interpenetration of past and present. There is a disturbing sense of the provisional in the lives of all their characters, and ominous transitions that do not always turn out to be disastrous. All these novels—except for *Wooden hunters*, which takes place among deprived Natives and washed-up whites on an island resembling one of the Queen Charlottes in British Columbia—are set, or end, in the fictional Salem, in a southern-Ontario countryside, where the once-prosperous farming economy established by Loyalists and British immigrants is fast disintegrating. *The disinherited* is a chronicle novel that develops the theme of agrarian decline through the changes in the lives of a pioneering family. *The colours of war* seems at first to be a futurist novel as it describes a journey across a Canada riven by civil war; but the hero's journey through the future, and his destination in the heart of the Ontario countryside, which Cohen has made his special terrain, represents a flight into the protective past. *Kitty Malone* centres on two drunken, ugly, life-worn people and their eventual happiness, and gains its effect by inverting the pattern of the customary romance. *Flowers of darkness*, which shows the destruction by the consequences of his own hypocrisy of a demonic preacher, reads in many ways like a genial parody of William Faulkner, to whose Yoknapatawpha County Cohen's creation of his own country of the imagination has been compared.

The Spanish doctor (1984, rpr. 2000), Cohen's most commercial novel, is set in medieval Spain, a time of anti-Jewish pogroms. The main character, Avram Halevi (who came to Cohen in a dream), becomes a wandering Jew, a stranger and an outsider, moving east, not west, through the Renaissance medical centres, and eventually into the heart of Russia (where Cohen's ancestral roots lie). *Nadine* (1986) describes a woman's attempt to reconstruct herself physically and psychologically after throwing herself on a terrorist's grenade in front of a Jerusalem hotel. Born of Jewish parents during the German occupation of Paris, she was left in the care of her aunts while her parents tried to flee. *Emotional arithmetic* (1990, rpr. 2007) tells the harrowing story of a reunion of three survivors of a Nazi internment camp in France. A virtuoso performance, it began with Cohen wondering what it must have been like to have been on a train destined for Auschwitz. Here he explores 'love and hate, time passed and time remaining, injuries suffered, and revenge meted out.' The novel is linked to *Nadine*—Jakob Bronski, one of the three survivors, is Nadine's father. *Emotional arithmetic* was made into a film (released in 2008) directed by Paolo Barzman, starring Susan Sarandon, Christopher Plummer, Gabriel Byrne, Roy Dupuis, and Max von Sydow. *Freud: the Paris notebooks* (1991) is a slim, complex, somewhat mystifying three-part novella about expatriates. A humorous send-up of the myth of Sigmund Freud, the main character is not the famous doctor but a fictional nephew whose life parallels the real Freud with his injuries and solutions. *The bookseller* (1993, rpr. 1997) explores notions of obsessive love and revenge. A *roman à clef* set in Toronto's Annex (near the University of Toronto) in the 1970s, this fast-paced thriller has several strong scenes set in used-book stores, a pool hall, and seedy Yonge Street hotels that provide a subtle and poignant subtext of Toronto as a city of bleak subcultures. *Last seen* (1996), Cohen's most autobiographical novel, is about a writer, Alec, who copes with the death of his younger brother, Harold, from lung cancer (which, like his brother, Matt Cohen himself died of). It is narrated from the points of view of both the dying Harold and the grieving Alec. Unable to follow Harold into the grave, Alec finds healing in a fantasy about a club of Elvis Presley impersonators. In *Elizabeth and after* (1999, GGA; rpr. 2000), Elizabeth dies in a car crash at the beginning of the novel, but she is a ghostly presence in the lives of her son Carl, a young divorced man, when he returns to the fictional town of West Gull in the Kingston area where he grew up, of his daughter whom he wants to get to know, and of others who had been part of Elizabeth's life. Of Cohen's collections of stories, *The expatriate* (1982) and *Café le dog* (1983) were followed by *Living on water* (1988), a collection of moving, poetically acute, stories that include as subject matter cancer, infidelity, alchoholism, decay, and dread; there is a luminosity within the central characters, even at the moment of death. *Lives of the mind slaves* (1994) features often humorous stories of lonely, middle-class Jewish male intellectuals who despair of life's unfairness; every opportunity for success meets with even greater failure.

Cohen co-edited, with Wayne Grady, *The Quebec anthology 1830–1990* (1996), whose thirty-three stories attest to a wide-ranging and sympathetic knowledge of French-Canadian literature. Two books were published posthumously in 2000: *Getting lucky* (rpr. 2001), a collection of stories, and *Typing: a life in 26 keys* (rpr. 2001), an enjoyable memoir. In a two-paragraph preface to the latter book Patsy Aldana, Cohen's partner, says: 'Matt wrote *Typing* in five months after he was diagnosed with lung cancer and finished [it] three weeks before he died.' In the last paragraph of *Typing,* Cohen—the author of twenty-six books—mentions the novel he was working on: 'For the next several years I'll be inhabiting these people and this place, waiting for their secrets to be revealed. For me it is the very essence of writing, and what has made the writing life the only one I could live.'

See *Uncommon ground: a celebration of Matt Cohen* (2002), edited by Graeme GIBSON, Wayne Grady, Dennis LEE, Priscila Uppal—an informative and enjoyable festschrift of thirty-two pieces by writers including Margaret ATWOOD, George BOWERING, Greg HOLLINGSHEAD, Don MCKAY, Anna PORTER, Monique PROULX, Alan TWIGG, and Rachel WYATT.

Cohen, Nathan (1923–71). Born in Sydney, Nova Scotia, he attended Mount Allison University from 1939 to 1942. After obtaining his B.A. in English, he wrote for and edited the labour *Glace Bay Gazette* in Nova Scotia from 1944 to 1945. In Toronto he began to attract attention with his theatre reviews for the *Canadian Jewish Weekly* and *Wochenblatt* in 1946. He was the CBC's Toronto drama critic from 1948 to 1958, gaining national exposure on the programs 'Across the Footlights' and 'CJBC Views the Shows'. Besides editing his own publication, *The Critic,* from 1950 to 1953, and working as a CBC Television story editor from 1956 to 1958, Cohen chaired the CBC TV series 'Fighting Words' (also aired on CBC Radio) from 1953 to 1962, and appeared as theatre critic on the radio series 'Critically Speaking'. From 1959 until his death he was the drama critic of the *Toronto Star.* He saw the critic as the conscience of the theatre. Covering theatre in Toronto and nationally, he helped to guide the transformation of indigenous Canadian theatre from an amateur activity to fully professional status; in his *Star* columns—often controversial for their harsh critiques—he made Canadian theatre a matter of national interest. While he repeatedly called for the writing and production of Canadian plays, he demanded that Canadian theatres meet international professional production standards—an attitude that frequently caused unprecedented animosity. Philip Stratford, in the *CANADIAN FORUM* (Feb. 1960), declared that 'the Cohen mystique consists in bringing ultra-Broadway standards to bear on a sub-Broadway product, and the result is always dispiriting, often ludicrous.' See Wayne E. Edmonstone, *Nathan Cohen: the making of a critic* (1977, rpr. 1983).

Cole, Peter. See ABORIGINAL LITERATURE: 5.

Coleman, Victor (b. 1944). Born in Toronto, he grew up there and in Montreal and was a high-school drop-out. Living on Toronto's Ward's Island in 1965, he founded the magazine *Island* and Island Press, which helped to shift the avant-garde poetry centre from Vancouver to Toronto. He entered book publishing as a production assistant for the Oxford University Press, Toronto (1966–7), and in 1967 joined COACH HOUSE PRESS, where for nearly a decade he served as the major Coach House editor: his catholic tastes were reflected in the work of the new Canadian writers and the American poets published by Coach House. After discontinuing *Island* and Island Press, he founded the Coach House literary magazine *Is.* For two years Coleman was director of the Nightingale Arts Council, operating in Toronto as A Space, which sponsored literary readings and performance art. He taught CanLit and creative writing for the Toronto District School Board, and at York and Queen's Universities, was programmer for Queen's University's National Film Theatre, Kingston, Ontario, and is chief editor for the Centre for Contemporary Canadian Art's Canadian Art Database (www.ccca.ca). An important figure in Canadian avant-garde or postmodernist verse, Coleman believes poetic form to be the natural extension of content. Though influenced by many American poets—including Jack Spicer, Charles Olson, and Robert Creeley—he developed his own distinctive voice. His poems are usually short reflections that eschew any formal structure. His early volumes—*From Erik Satie's notes to the music* (1965), *One/eye/love* (1967), *Light verse* (1969), *Old friends' ghosts: poems 1963–68* (1970), *Back east* (1971), and *Some plays: on words* (1971)—are filled with idiosyncratic verses condensed almost to the point of impenetrability. Yet the poems are always playful and challenging: intoxicated with the limitless possibilities of imagery and thought existing as inseparable entities, they demand to be seen as moments of intuition or discovery. Five other volumes in the 1970s continued his experiments to shape language to its maximum force as he let sound and movement create the form of poetry. *Corrections* (1985) is a self-conscious and at times frustratingly disrespectful rewriting of six of the poet's first nine books of poetry. Shaped by a strategy that allows Coleman to foreground concerns both old (sex and the physicality of being) and new (theories of chaos and flux), the book implicates both the poet and his written word in the instability and relentlessly personal processes of creating poetry itself. Although a tenacious interest in things theoretical continued to shape to varying degrees such later collections as *Honeymoon suite* (1990), *Waiting for Alice* (1993), and the selected poems of *Lapsed W.A.S.P.* (1994), the fundamentals of Coleman's poetry remain for the most part unchanged. The clever and effective narrative title poem of *The day they stole the Coach House Press* (1993)—'The day they stole the Coach House Press/was sunny, a little hazy, warm & inviting,/but death was a cold shoulder against the wheel/of greed'—is included in *Icon tact: poems 1984–2001* (2006). A substantial book of 170 pages, it is well worth reading, and owning. It concludes with a short account of the author's career (which Coleman presumably wrote) that imparts the information—astonishing to anyone who remembers the young Victor Coleman in the 1960s—that he has five children and seven grandchildren. Missing is a series of 26 poems—with the letters of the alphabet as titles—that was published in an edition of 100 copies in 2005.

Coles, Don (b. 1928). Born in Woodstock, Ontario, he graduated from the University of Toronto (M.A., 1953), gained an M.A. in 1955 from Cambridge University, and spent 1952–65 travelling around Europe, an experience that profoundly influenced the content and tone of his subsequent poetry. He returned to Canada in 1965, where he became professor of humanities and creative writing at York University, Toronto, retiring in 1996. His poetry collections are *Sometimes all over* (1975); *Anniversaries* (1979); *The Prinzhorn collection* (1982); *Landslides: selected poems, 1975–1985* (1986), which includes new poems; *K. in love* (1987), a sequence based on the love letters of Franz Kafka; *Little bird* (1991), an extended verse-letter addressed to his dead father; *Forests of the medieval world* (1993, GGA); *Someone has stayed in Stockholm* (1994), a selection published in England; and *Kurgan* (2000). Coles served a long and rigorous poetic apprenticeship, moving from what he calls 'ornate stuff' to a crisp and chaste diction that can accommodate vernacular speech rhythms and subtle intellectual distinctions. While most of Coles' verse is technically 'free', it is carefully controlled by a fine ear for rhythm, cadence, and sonority. Many of his poems are devoted to the 'changeless, ordinary things' of everyday life (the satisfaction and anguish of love, the tensions of marriage, the ever-fluctuating relations between parents and children, our manifold human responses to 'the catastrophe of time'). Others represent a detached, resigned, yet profound brooding on the cultural monuments of the past. Unlike most of his Canadian contemporaries, Coles remains aloof from narrowly nationalistic concerns, and expects his readers to be conversant with the main traditions of Western civilization—his poems are full of references to such figures as Tolstoy, Ibsen, Kafka, Mann, Rilke, and Munch. At the same time, he consistently emphasizes the need for verbal clarity. A poem, he argues, 'should offer a comprehensive and usable piece of content', while employing a language 'accessible to serious readers'. All these characteristics are present in *Kurgan*, with the title poem (named for an ancient burial mound) memorably recounting the discovery of the remains of a Sarmatian princess. Other poems are about Hector, Samuel Beckett, the woman Pushkin married, Ibsen, and Tolstoy; and in such family poems as 'These photos of the children' Coles takes a commonplace subject and turns it into a long memory poem that is unsentimental, loving, and profound. *How we all swiftly: the first six books* (2005)—the title is that of the first poem in *Sometimes all over*—conveniently, for readers who don't know Coles' work, contains in one volume the significant collections he published until 1991, with a long, informative Introduction by W.J. KEITH. *The essential Don Coles* (2009), selected by Robyn SARAH—who contributed an interesting summary of Coles's life and career—was published by THE PORCUPINE'S QUILL in its Essential Poets series.

Don Coles surprised and impressed admirers of his poetry (and others) by publishing, at an advanced age, an original novel, *Doctor Bloom's story* (2004), narrated by the very tall Nicolaas Bloom, born in Amsterdam (family name Blom) of a Scottish mother, studied medicine and graduated from the University of Leiden as a doctor in 1973, became a cardiologist, and received a fellowship at Cambridge University. In Cambridge, his wife Saskia died of breast cancer. He then moved to Toronto, renting 'a small furnished house on a short street a little north of Eglinton, east of Mt. Pleasant'. (Among other things, this is an enjoyable Toronto novel, with many locations named.) Working halfheartedly in a medical clinic, he pursues his dream of becoming a writer by enrolling in a Thursday-night creative-writing course at Ryerson University, led by his neighbour Larry Logan, in which the young Swiss-born Sophie Führ is also a student. A complicated series of events transpires, which Bloom/Coles describes in a freewheeling narrative, filled with amusing turns of phrase, that intertwines memories of Bloom's early life and marriage, countless gratuitous but witty observations and literary references (to the Chekhov he reveres, Orwell, Strindberg, Iris Murdoch, the Austrian novelist Robert Musil, George Eliot, Simone Weil, Henry James, et al.), his falling in love with Larry's estranged wife, Marianne, a psychoanalytic psychotherapist—without neglecting the ongoing saga of Sophie's being physically abused (by her husband), once with Bloom as a distant witness. 'This woman, who would not defend herself and wanted no defender, needed one in spite of herself.' Should this be Bloom? Should he use his medical knowledge to affect the husband's heart condition fatally? Four people are concerned about Sophie, and are in different ways involved—Nik Bloom, Marianne, Larry, and Marianne's doctor friend Celia Coomaraswamy, who treats Sophie. The beginning of the end takes place at the Banff Centre for the Fine Arts, of which Larry is appointed senior fiction editor. He arranges for Sophie to be chosen as one of the five writers he is to supervise and Sophie accepts the invitation. A few weeks after she arrives in Banff her husband follows her there. Without once indulging in 'poetic' writing, poet Coles creates in Bloom a persona with whom the reader bonds, and gives him a quirky manner of expressing himself that is delightful.

Coles' *A dropped gloved on Regent Street: an autobiography by other means* (2007) is the kind of delightful literary miscellany, combining new pieces with previously published articles and book reviews on famous authors (Graham Greene, Mann, Tolstoy, Hugo, Brecht, Flaubert, among many others) that one associates with British rather than Canadian writers. The autobiographical element appears in 'Scenes from Cambridge life', 'A sentimental education: growing up in Woodstock, Toronto, London, Stockholm, Florence', and in the title piece: the twenty-three-year-old Don Coles connects with an older blonde

beauty in Florence without ever saying a word; she 'returned my look' and a few minutes later 'gazed directly across the street at me'—'I did and said nothing'; some months later in London, in Regent Street, a woman's glove was dropped, it was hers, 'Our eyes met'. Again he did nothing—'drowning in self-contempt'. Coles turns to literary biographies—having read 'all the major poems, all the classic novels, the plays'—and writes interestingly on works he liked, including Hermione Lee's *Virginia Woolf*, Victoria Glendinning's *Trollope*, and Claire Tomalin's *Pepys*. This is a book that rewards and entertains the reader in many different ways.

Colombo, John Robert (b. 1936). Born in Kitchener, Ontario, he studied at the University of Toronto (B.A., 1959), and while there he organized poetry readings at the Bohemian Embassy. In the almost five decades since he graduated—as in-house editor for various publishers, an associate editor of *The TAMARACK REVIEW*, teacher of creative writing, essayist and book reviewer, editor and anthologist, translator and poet, and most importantly as the man who collected Canadian quotations and many other examples of Canadian lore—he has become a national figure: John Robert Colombo, Man of Letters; or Master Gatherer, as Robin SKELTON named him in a review. He is a Member of the Order of Canada (2004).

Probably Canada's best-known maker of 'found poetry', or what he also calls 'redeemed prose', Colombo created in *The Mackenzie poems* (1966), *John Toronto: new poems by Dr Strachan* (1966), *The great wall of China* (1966), and *The great San Francisco earthquake and fire* (1971), pure examples of the genre. Perhaps most provocative is *The great cities of antiquity* (1979), a collection of found poems in a dizzying variety of modes, based on entries in the famous eleventh edition of the *Encyclopaedia Britannica*. It is Colombo's most extreme collage, a veritable textbook on the many formal experiments of modern and postmodern poetry. See also *Foundlings: uncollected found poetry* (2002). *Abracadabra* (1967) reveals a writer of larger ambitions, one who seeks the poem where previous texts and life collide. *Neo poems* (1970) is a paradigmatic example of his generous and open poetics, as are such later collections as *Off earth* (1987) and *Luna Park* (1994). Even when his poems do not clearly contain found prose, they still insist that almost everything we know or imagine depends upon some previous 'text'. A richly ironic, devious, and witty imagination drives these books. Colombo has managed to produce a book of original poems each year for the past twelve years. See *The poems of John Robert Colombo* (3 vols, 2005) and *The aphorisms of John Robert Colombo* (2006).

Collage, of course, is the great art of juxtaposition, and Colombo is a master of witty parataxis, as the whole of *Translations from the English: found poems* (1974) demonstrates. Basically the same impulse that led to the notes and commentaries of that book led to his vast collection, *Colombo's Canadian quotations* (1974), the first of many mass-market books that have followed. A critic can fit this reference work into Colombo's creative *oeuvre* with no trouble, for although Colombo has not 'redeemed' its prose, he has organized it so that the whole emerges as a massive hoard designed to show us what has been said of and in Canada throughout its history. Later versions—*The dictionary of Canadian quotations* (1991), *Colombo's all-time great Canadian quotations* (1994), *John Robert Colombo's famous lasting words* (2000), and *The Penguin dictionary of popular Canadian quotations* (2006)—cover a wider and more contemporary range, but they follow the basic paradigm of the original. Determined to do for general references what he had done for quoted matter, he wrote some 6,000 entries for *Colombo's Canadian references* (1976), *Colombo's book of Canada* (1978), *Colombo's names and nicknames* (1979), *Canadian literary landmarks* (1984), and *999 questions about Canada* (1989). These works, along with *The Penguin treasury of popular Canadian poems and songs* (2002), are manifestations of the same impulse to gather and collate various leaves of Canada's book.

Colombo's abiding interest in the weird and mysterious in Canadian folklore and experience has led to numerous compilations, notably the six-volume set called *The Native series: songs of the Indians* (2004), *Poems of the Inuit* (2004), *The mystery of the shaking tent* (1993), *Windigo: an anthology of fact and fantastic fiction* (1982), *Voices of Rama: traditional Ojibwa tales from the Rama reserve, Lake Couchiching* (2004), and *Songs of the great land* (2004). *Mysterious Canada: strange sights, extraordinary events, and peculiar places* (1988) is the first comprehensive, illustrated survey of supernatural and paranormal events and experiences. It was followed by thirty-six compilations of accounts that 'raise issues that vex and perplex the rational mind', which Colombo describes in folkloric terms as 'memorates'. The collections range from *Extraordinary experiences* (1989) to *Terrors of the night: Canadian accounts of eerie events and weird experiences* (2005) and

Strange but true: Canadian stories of horror and terror (2007). One of Colombo's most delightful books, *Mostly monsters* (1977), is both comic compilation and witty found poetry. It is a collage of the pop mythology of the past century in which pulp fiction, films, radio shows, comic strips, and much else are ransacked to create a vision of our dreams of good, nightmares of evil, and of our ambiguous awareness that real power lies somewhere between and cannot easily be identified or found on the 'right' side. The multitude of Colombo's publications as both writer and editor of anthologies is best accounted for in his *Self-Schrift* (1999), informal commentaries—some long, some short—on the background of 136 titles. Like his recent collections of poetry, it is one of the QuasiBooks (photocopied text, coil bound with clear plastic covers) appearing under the personal publishing imprint of Colombo & Company.

It is not well known that Colombo has written and published book-length monographs on four psychical researchers (R.S. Lambert, George and Iris Owen, James Webb) and *O rare Denis Saurat: an appreciation* (2003), about a French scholar of Milton and Blake, teacher, public speaker, literary critic, and theorist of the paranormal (1890–1958) who was head of the French department of King's College, London, from 1926 to 1950, and a spokesman for France in England and an apologist for England in France.

There are 187 separate publications listed on Colombo's website: www.colombo.ca.

Colony of unrequited dreams, The (1998, rpr. 1999). This novel by Wayne JOHNSTON is formally a fictional memoir of Joey Smallwood (1900–91), the first premier of Newfoundland when it became a province of Canada in 1949. But it is complex, interweaving personal history, Newfoundland history, politics, a blighted romance, a mystery, and above all the island itself and its people in a compelling narrative. The character Smallwood tells us that he was born into a poverty-stricken, dysfunctional, ever-growing family, but through his prosperous uncle was sent to the élite Bishop Feild School. An undernourished, skinny, unprepossessing boy, though he was a great reader and had wit, Smallwood was surprisingly taken up by Prowse, the captain of the school, for standing up to the scornful, sharp-tongued Sheilagh Fielding (called simply Fielding) from the nearby girls' school. He eventually did well in his studies, but the headmaster, who disliked him, while unavoidably recording his high standing in academic subjects, persistently marked his 'character' 45 out of 500. When a letter to a local paper denouncing the school was ascribed to him by the headmaster, even when Fielding said she had written it, Smallwood was demoted to the Commercial class, 'for those judged to be unsuitable to go on to university', and he quit. He became a court reporter for the *Telegram*, and then boarded the sealing ship *Newfoundland* to report on the seal hunters, a trying episode that culminated when some stranded hunters were found as 'a strange statuary of the dead.... Two men knelt side by side, one man with his arm around the other, whose head was resting on his shoulder in a pose of tenderness between two men that I had never seen in life.... Three men stood huddled in a circle, arms about each others' shoulders, heads held together like schoolboys conferring on a football field.' Smallwood became a convinced socialist and spent several years in New York, poverty stricken, working for a socialist paper, and returned to Newfoundland determined to organize the railway workers into a union, walking the entire length of the railway and its branches. Years later he tried to organize a fishermen's union along the south and southwest coast, leaving the schooner when it could go no further to walk on ice, with the rising and lowering waves beneath. 'I discovered that it was possible while walking on the ice to become seasick.' In 1937 he became a broadcaster, five days a week for fifteen minutes, to make Newfoundland better known to Newfoundlanders, thus becoming well known himself. When, in 1949, a majority of votes in a second referendum favoured Newfoundland's becoming a province of Canada, Smallwood was the obvious leader and its first premier. But Smallwood and Fielding, not politics, are at the centre of the novel. Fielding—the stronger and more perceptive figure, who appears throughout in almost always troubling scenes—was Smallwood's great love, though their relationship was platonic and adversarial. The narrative is frequently interrupted by 'Fielding's Condensed *History of Newfoundland*', a recounting of historical events in the form of brief, amusing summaries; by excerpts from her journal from 1916 to 1989 in the form of undelivered letters; and by her acerbic newspaper columns that often comment sardonically on Smallwood's activities ('an atom of dissent beneath my mattress')—in all of which her voice is unmistakable and consistent. She is a memorable (fictional) creation, like the novel itself.

In an endnote Johnston acknowledges his debt to Richard GWYN's *Smallwood: the unlikely revolutionary*.

Combustion (1957–60). Raymond SOUSTER's fourth little magazine (following *Direction*, 1943–6; *Enterprise*, 1948; and *CONTACT*, 1952–4), *Combustion* was probably begun to help replace the American magazine *Origin*, recently suspended by its editor, Souster's friend Cid Corman, who wrote weekly to Souster during the *Combustion* years, suggesting subscribers and contributors and offering manuscripts that might otherwise have been published in *Origin*. Initially the content of *Combustion*, which was mimeographed in editions of 100 to 125 copies, was balanced between Canadian and international material; but in the later issues international work predominated, including generous selections by American writers previously published in *Origin*: Robert Creeley, Gary Snyder, Robert Duncan, Fielding Dawson, and Louis Zukofsky. *Combustion* made a significant contribution to American literature, and a modest one to Canadian writing by keeping it informed of international accomplishments. Souster published fourteen issues, the last appearing in Aug. 1960, eight months before Corman's launching of the second series of *Origin*.

Compton, Anne (b.1947). Born in Bangor, Prince Edward Island (the eleventh child in a family of eleven—see her poems 'Convolvulus' and 'Waking'), she was educated at the University of Prince Edward Island (B.A., 1969), York University, Toronto (M.A., 1971), and the University of New Brunswick (Ph.D., 1988). Adjunct Professor at UNB Saint John and Honorary Research Associate at UNB Fredericton, she is also director of the Lorenzo Reading Series, considered the best university reading series (in 2007–8 it included WRIGHT, HILL, HAY, and GOWDY).

A disciplined and engaging poet, Compton embraced a range of subjects in her first collection, *Opening the Island* (2002), beginning (and ending—see below) with Prince Edward Island: 'Here is a place you live on/[everywhere else you live in] *in* Ontario they say,/she lives *on* the island./Alighted, they mean, but the locution is unfamiliar.' One of the delights of this collection are the the cultural ingredients, poems about famous writers, and their characters: John Milton 'When my father died I was born/into my own language' ('Amanuensis: John Milton's daughter'), Hawthorne's Hester Prynne ('Hester Prynne's letter to Surveyor Pue'), Eliot's Mr Prufrock ('The

Compton

mermaids singing'), Malory's Guenevere ('Guenevere writes to them who wrote of her'), Catharine Parr TRAILL ('Unreadable flowers'). And poems about famous painters: Vermeer: 'The windows of Vermeer open inward/letting eternity flow over a sill/in parody of earthlight' ('Lightwork in Vermeer'), 'Cézanne: still life', Renoir ('A thin woman looks at Renoir's *The Bathers* 1918–19'), and 'Claude Monet: Rouen Cathedral, early morning, 1894'. The final section of the book, 'Closing the Island', has an epigraph by John THOMPSON: 'When I meet you again I'll be all light....' The final poem is called 'Inherit the light': 'When we return to that island, words won't be necessary./There will be no signposts; getting lost will not be possible.' The final poem in Compton's second collection, *Processional* (2005, GGA) is followed by a page with two italicized lines on it: 'We're figures in a processional, we are. And above us, all around,/ the procession of the seasons accompanies us.' The poems are the calm, incisive recapturing of elements in the poet's life that imprinted themselves on her imagination, including houses, life in them, nature and the seasons, the past ('who can say how or why it all blazed away'), death and dying. 'The house after dark, winter': 'The book marked and put down for the night. The house/settling on its plot: midnight, a woman in conclusion.' 'Woman of a certain age, spring': 'The heart's arterial rage/ requires the surge of a river/flinging itself free.//We've wintered over, not seized up. I'm here to tell you/the blood acts up at any age.' 'What the dying talk about': 'Not forgiveness./ Pain, they know, has cleared all debts in that regard./The worth of work compels resistance to the dark.' 'The calling out of names': 'The place the dead go has hooded windows. No binoculars./There are not birds in the air or anything else worth watching…. Still, there's the tug of the familiar,/the familial—someone's habit here of singing out a name—that solicits//attention if only because touch was the last sensation/a hand brushing a forehead//and for a moment, they think our thoughts and our inarticulate arms/open and birds, with the most beautiful bodies, lift into the air.' Some lighthearted offerings include a letter to the English author Simon Winchester ('How to get to Saint John') and 'A schoolmaster lessons a scholar in figurative language', which begins 'Row four, seat six, how is the heart like a house?' Nature again: 'This air, early morning': 'This air is here every morning and we're not noticing/its osculatory offerings. Like partners in a waltz,/the lofty trees nod and stir. Threaten/to sweep us off our feet.'

The contributor of many refereed essays and many reviews to journals, Compton as a scholar distinguished herself with *A.J.M. Smith: Canadian metaphysical* (1994), among the best critical studies of a Canadian poet. She also made a selection of ACORN's poems for *The edge of home: Milton Acorn from the Island* (2002), in which her Preface and long Introduction—an essay called 'The ecological poetics of Milton Acorn's island poems'—are valuable commentaries on his work. *Meetings with Maritime poets: interviews* (2006) contains Compton's interviews with sixteen Maritime poets, only two of which—George Elliott CLARKE and Elizabeth HARVOR—are known in the rest of Canada. Compton co-edited, with three others, *The poetry of Atlantic Canada* (2002), a substantial anthology.

Conan, Laure. Pseudonym of Marie-Louise-Félicité ANGERS.

Confederation poets. Since the publication of Malcolm ROSS's influential anthology *Poets of the Confederation* (1960, NCL)—with selections from the poetry of Charles G.D. ROBERTS, Bliss CARMAN, Archibald LAMPMAN, and Duncan Campbell SCOTT—the term 'Confederation poets' has been generally taken to refer to these four writers, although others—such as William Wilfred CAMPBELL, George Frederick CAMERON, and Isabella Valancy CRAWFORD—are sometimes included under this rubric. Malcolm ROSS's retrospective application of the term 'Confederation poets' is a good example of canon making along national lines, in a cultural moment inspired by the founding of the Canada Council (1957), and the establishment of the NEW CANADIAN LIBRARY (NCL), with Ross himself as general editor (*Poets of the Confederation* was the first anthology in the series). Publishing their first volumes of verse in the 1880s and 1890s, Roberts, Lampman, Carman, and Scott were among the first really good poets writing in the recently formed Dominion of Canada. There are several good reasons for grouping them together. All were close contemporaries born in the early 1860s. Roberts and Carman were cousins; Roberts briefly edited *The WEEK*, in which Carman published his first poem. Lampman was encouraged in his poetic efforts by his reading of Roberts' *Orion and other poems* (Philadelphia, 1880). Lampman and Scott were close friends; with Wilfred Campbell they began the column 'AT THE MERMAID INN' in the Toronto *Globe*, in 1892; after Lampman died, Scott published a memorial edition of his poems in 1900. All four poets drew much of their inspiration from Canadian nature, but they were also trained in the classics and were cosmopolitan in their literary interests. All were serious craftsmen who assimilated their borrowings from English and American writing in a personal mode of expression, treating the important subjects and themes of their day, often in a Canadian setting. They have been aptly called the first distinctly Canadian school of writers.

Connor, Ralph. Pseudonym of Charles William GORDON.

Constantin-Weyer, Maurice (1881–1961). Born in Bourbonne-les-Bains, France, he immigrated to Canada in 1903 and settled in Saint-Claude, Manitoba, where he raised cattle and became a jack of all trades. In 1914, after an unsuccessful marriage to a Métisse, he returned to France to fight in the war and was gravely wounded. Contrary to what was long believed, he never returned to Canada. He spent the rest of his long life, mostly in Paris and Vichy, working as a newspaper editor, writing numerous articles, and about fifty books: novels, biographies, essays on a variety of subjects, translations, and even a play about Shakespeare, *Le grand Will* (Paris, 1945). In 1932 he received the Legion of Honour. Some fifteen books by Constantin-Weyer—including novels, story collections, biographies, and essays—have Canadian content and are grouped under the title *L'épopée canadienne*. In his first novel, *Vers l'ouest* (Paris, 1921), translated as *Towards the West* (1931)—the love story of two Métis set against the background of the war between the Sioux and the Métis—Louis Riel's father plays a minor role. *La bourrasque* (Paris, 1926)—the translation of which was called *The half-breed* (1930) in the USA and *A martyr's folly* (1930) in Canada—is a highly fictionalized treatment of Louis Riel's stormy career. Both works are marred by the extravagant liberties the author takes with history, especially in *La bourrasque*, where Riel becomes a grotesque figure. Constantin-Weyer was attacked by some writers for caricaturing the Métis, yet he was not devoid of sympathy for them. His best-known work, *Un homme se penche sur son passé* (Paris, 1928)—translated by Slater-Brown as *A man scans his past* (1929)—won him the Prix Goncourt and fame. The plot, partly autobiographical is a variation on the love triangle, and the characters are rather superficial; but one critic praised 'the atmosphere of the Prairies and the Forests, of the Great North and

Cold ... in this poem of Action' (Robert Garric). Even in his novels that take place in France, memories of Canada are often present. Of the francophones who have written novels about western Canada, he is certainly the most prolific, and the best painter of the western landscape.

Contact (1952–4). The third little magazine founded by Raymond SOUSTER, following *Direction* (1943–6) and *Enterprise* (1948), it was begun in Jan. 1952 in open discontent with the policies of John SUTHERLAND'S *NORTHERN REVIEW*. Souster's two principal advisers in this project were Louis DUDEK, who hoped it could be a 'workshop' for young Canadians, and the American poet and editor Cid Corman, who advocated high standards, even to the exclusion of Canadian contributors. For the most part Souster steered a middle course, although publishing many more American and international writers than Dudek liked. *Contact* was thus the first Canadian magazine to publish American poets of the Black Mountain school—among them Charles Olson, Robert Creeley, Paul Blackburn, Denise Levertov, and Vincent Ferrini. It led eventually to Souster's arranging public readings for both Olson and Creeley in Toronto, in his Contact Poetry Readings of 1959–62. Published in mimeograph format, *Contact* continued for ten issues until Mar. 1954. Despite its American and European contributors (among the latter were Octavio Paz, Jean Cocteau, Hugh McDiarmid, Jacques Prévert, and George Seferis), it never attracted more than fifty subscribers.

Contact Press (1952–67). Raymond SOUSTER'S small mimeographed magazines—*Direction* (1943), *Enterprise* (1948), *CONTACT* (1952–4), and Aileen Collins' *CIV/n* (1953–5), which advocated the new poetry of the 1950s, especially the Black Mountain poets, Cid Corman, and Ezra Pound—evolved into Canada's first major small press. With the guidance of Louis DUDEK, Souster—and, after 1959, with the financial support of Peter Miller—the press kept alive the tradition of artistic independent publishing that had begun with the *McGILL FORTNIGHTLY REVIEW*. The first title from Contact Press was *Cerberus* (1952)—poems by Irving LAYTON, Dudek, and Souster—whose title reference to the three-headed dog of myth, and guardian of the underworld, linked the three poets. The Contact Poetry Readings (1957–62), held in Toronto and organized by Souster, brought in such readers as Charles Olsen, Robert

Contact Press

Creeley, and Louis Zukowsky, and were well attended by up to a hundred patrons. *Contact* published early work by Eli MANDEL, Al PURDY, Milton ACORN, Gwendolyn MacEWEN, R.G. EVERSON, George BOWERING, Eldon GRIER, Robert HOGG, Daphne Buckle (MARLATT), Frank DAVEY, George JONAS, D.G. JONES, David McFADDEN, Fred WAH, Phyllis WEBB, and, in its final year of operation, the twenty-seven-year-old Margaret ATWOOD (*The circle game*, 1966, which won a Governor General's Award; the circles on the cover were done by Atwood with red stick-on dots from a stationery store). Dudek's decision not to reprint *The circle game* led in part to the formation of the House of ANANSI, which carried Atwood's book in its backlist. When Peter Miller withdrew financial support for family reasons, the press was discontinued. The last Contact title, *New Wave Canada: the new explosion in Canadian poetry* (1966)—edited by Souster, who was assisted in his editorial choices by Victor COLEMAN—was a symbolic passing of the torch to the newly formed COACH HOUSE PRESS. With poetry by George Bowering, Daphne Marlatt, bp NICHOL, Frank Davey, and David McFadden, the book was not an anthology of the past, but a prophecy of the future. By then the literary model of writer-editors and writer-publishers was established for other small presses, along with an enlarged perspective and important subsequent trends in Canadian literature.

Contemporary Verse (1941–52). An influential Canadian poetry magazine of its time, it was founded by Alan Crawley, who was variously assisted by Dorothy LIVESAY, Anne MARRI-OTT, Doris Ferne, and Floris Clarke McLaren. The first issue was published from North Vancouver in Sept. 1941; later the journal was edited from Victoria. *Contemporary Verse* played an important role at a time when there were few literary magazines in Canada. Crawley sought to maintain a high standard of writing, while keeping his pages open to poets of many inclinations. The criteria he announced in one of his editorials were that the work he published must be 'serious in thought and expression and contemporary in theme, treatment, and technique'. The more than 120 poets that appeared included virtually every important name in that vital era in the development of a Canadian tradition in poetry, as well as new talents; many of the best modern Canadian poets were first published in his magazine. Thirty-nine issues had appeared by the time Crawley felt he had completed his

task and ceased publication at the end of 1952. See *Alan Crawley and 'Contemporary Verse'* (1976) edited by Joan McCullagh, with a reminiscent introduction by Dorothy Livesay.

Contemporary Verse 2 (1975–). It was established by Dorothy LIVESAY—who had also co-founded *CONTEMPORARY VERSE*—as a periodical managed for its duration by editor Alan Crawley and devoted exclusively to contemporary Canadian poetry and poetry criticism. Canada's longest-running poetry quarterly, *CV2* continues to publish four times a year out of Winnipeg. In 1986 the magazine was redesigned to accommodate a feminist publishing mandate. In 2001, after nearly closing, the editorial and design formats of the magazine were completely overhauled under the direction of Clarise Foster, the editor, to become *Contemporary Verse 2: The Canadian Journal of Poetry and Critical Writing*. For most of its history all aspects of the publication were run by a collective management. Since 2001 *CV2* has operated under the governance of a board of directors. Operations continue to be managed by Clarise Foster, who publishes original verse, interviews, articles, essays, and reviews.

Cook, Michael (1933–94). Born in London, England, he joined the British army in 1949, serving for the next twelve years in Europe and the Far East. In 1962 he entered Nottingham University College of Education, where he trained as a teacher. In the mid-1960s he arrived in Newfoundland and was employed as a drama specialist in Memorial University's Extension Service. Subsequently he joined the university's English department and in 1979 was promoted to associate professor, retiring in 1993. He was active in Newfoundland as a critic, director, actor, and, after 1970, as a playwright. Cook's first published play, *Colour the flesh the colour of dust* (1972)—a historical drama set in St John's, Newfoundland, in 1762—is strongly influenced by Bertolt Brecht. The radio drama 'Tiln' (1973) perhaps showed too plainly the influence of Samuel Beckett. *The head, guts and sound bone dance* (1974) is an effort to evoke the antiquated attitudes of old-time Newfoundlanders as a bizarre contrast to the contemporary lifestyle on the island; it features the splitting and gutting of codfish on stage. *Jacob's wake* (1975) is an ambitious and occasionally powerful depiction of the disintegration of a Newfoundland outport family. *Quiller* (1975) and *Terese's creed*, which is included in *Tiln & other plays* (1976), are one-act plays, the latter a monologue in which Cook explores the inner life of outport characters. *Quiller*—a pathetic, sometimes tender, sometimes funny monologue by an outcast living on the fringe of a Newfoundland outport—is probably Cook's finest work. *The fisherman's revenge* (1976, rpr. 1985) treats the relationship between merchant and fisherman in comic fashion. *On the rim of the curve* (1977) is an attempt to dramatize the final days on earth of the Beothuks, newfoundland's Aboriginal people. *The Gayden chronicles* (1977, rpr. 1979) is a three-act play exploring the life of a rebel in the British navy who was hanged in St John's in 1812. Cook's plays celebrate the elemental and instinctive; they are harangues—assaults upon the audience's sense of decorum, and even upon intellect. Cook wrote: 'I've always had a deep distrust in my own head of intellectual responses.' His plays achieve few subtle effects, yet they are daring, passionate, and full of movement. They have been collected in *Tiln & other plays* and *Three plays* (1977). *The head, guts and sound bone dance* is included in *Major plays of the Canadian theatre 1934–1984* (1984), edited by Richard Perkins; *Jacob's wake* is in *Modern Canadian plays* (1985), edited by Jerry Wasserman.

Cook, Ramsay (b.1931). Born in Alameda, Saskatchewan, he attended schools there and in Manitoba, and the University of Manitoba (B.A., 1954); Queen's University, Kingston, Ontario, where he worked under A.R.M. Lower (M.A., 1955); and the University of Toronto, working under Donald CREIGHTON (Ph.D., 1960). In 1958 Cook was appointed to the history department of the University of Toronto, but a decade later he moved to York University, Toronto, as professor of history, retiring in 1996. General editor of the DIC-TIONARY OF CANADIAN BIOGRAPHY (1989–2004), he was made a Fellow of the Royal Society of Canada (1968), an Officer of the Order of Canada (1986), has received four honorary doctorates, and was awarded the Molson Prize (2005). After publishing *The politics of John W. Dafoe and the Free Press* (1963), Cook turned his back on the prevailing paradigms in his discipline so as to explore Canadian pluralism. A fine essayist who emerged as one of the principal interpreters of French-Canadian thought, he combined an interest in ideas with his knowledge of events and personalities. As the struggle of French Canadians to express themselves during the Quiet Revolution brought consternation to many confused English Canadians, Cook's explanations made sense of recent developments by linking them to history. Fascinated by Canadian nationalism in both its majority and minority expressions, he succeeded in revealing a variety of guises assumed by the French-Canadian sphinx in collections of essays such as *Canada and the French-Canadian question* (1966) and *The Maple Leaf forever* (1971) and in the series of articles in *French-Canadian nationalism* (1969). In *Canada 1896–1921: a nation transformed* (1974) in The Canadian Centenary Series, co-authored with Robert Craig Brown, the country's two solitudes disappeared into an account of the Laurier-Borden years that is magisterial in its sweep. Deepening an interest in cultural history, Cook provided a series of portraits of unconventional intellectuals in *The regenerators: social criticism in late Victorian English Canada* (1985, GGA). Essays in *Canada, Quebec and the uses of nationalism* (1986; 2nd edn 1995) update established themes, but also examine English-Canadian nationalism and cultural expression. The fifteen essays in *Watching Quebec: selected essays* (2005) were written over thirty years between the beginning of the Quiet Revolution and the failure of the Meech Lake Accord. *The teeth of time: remembering Pierre Elliott Trudeau* (2006)—a warm memoir of Cook's acquaintance, then friendship, with Trudeau over almost forty years (and a partial record of Cook's own career in the period)—is a graceful, incisive, illuminating addition to the many biographical portraits of a famous Canadian, the former prime minister.

Evidence of Cook's range is his long and important introduction to the reissue of H.P. Biggar's translation of *The voyages of Jacques Cartier* (1993, rpr. 2003).

Copeland, Ann (b. 1932), pseudonym of Virginia Ann Furtwangler (née Walsh). Born in Connecticut, USA, Copeland was educated in Catholic schools and New Rochelle College before entering the Ursuline Order as Sister John Bernard. She attended the Catholic University of America and Cornell University, where she completed a Ph.D. in English literature. She left the Ursulines after thirteen years, married, and moved in 1971 with her husband and two sons (one of whom was adopted) to Sackville, New Brunswick, where she began to write fiction. She now lives in Salem, Oregon. Her short stories have been collected in *At peace* (1978), *The back room* (1979), *Earthen vessels* (1984), *The golden thread* (1989, rpr. 1995), *Strange bodies on a stranger shore* (1994), and *Season of apples* (1996). Copeland's style is precise, understated, and often ironic.

Copeland

She frequently uses a central metaphor to create resonance among the images in her stories, such as the golden thread of Ariadne, which was used by Theseus to negotiate the labyrinth: the story (and book) of the same name suggests the delicate relations of faith, obedience, and friendship needed to negotiate the labyrinth of cloistered life in the time of Vatican II, the era in which Copeland sets many of her stories. She draws upon her experiences as a nun, a mother, and a teacher in convent schools and, later, at Dorchester Penitentiary. A key concept is commitment, uniting disparate experiences from a nun's vows to marriage vows, motherhood, education, and incarceration. Many of the stories in *At peace* are published in revised form in *The golden thread*, refocused on Sister Claire Delaney, who is also the central character of the stories in *Strange bodies on a stranger shore*. These are more ambitious structurally, blending past and present, as Claire negotiates middle age and memories of her former life as a nun.

Copway, George (Kahgegagahbowh, Standing Firm, 1818–69). An Ojibwa, born and raised near the mouth of the Trent River in the Rice Lake area of Upper Canada (Ontario), he was converted to Christianity at the age of twelve. In 1834 he began mission work as a teacher and interpreter with the American Methodist Episcopal Church among the Ojibwa on the south shore of Lake Superior. In 1836 he was sent to the Ebenezer Manual Labour School in Illinois, graduating in 1839. While on a visit to Rice Lake in the summer of 1840, he married a white woman, Elizabeth Howell, whom he met at the Credit River Mission. They immediately left for the American West, where they spent two years in the Upper Mississippi missions, returning to Canada in late 1842. Accepted as a preacher by the Wesleyan Methodist Canadian Conference, Copway left early in 1843 on a three-month missionary tour of Upper Canada with the Rev. William Ryerson. The next year he was sent to the Saugeen Mission on Lake Huron; he transferred in 1844 to Rice Lake, returning in 1845 to the Saugeen. The same year he was elected vice-president of the Grand Council of the Methodist Ojibwa of Canada West. Less than a year later the Saugeen band, and later the Rice Lake band, accused Copway of embezzlement. He spent a few months in prison and was expelled from the Methodist Conference. When he was released he moved back to the United States, where he became a literary celebrity and

popular public speaker as a result of his first book: *The life, history and travels of Kah-ge-ga-gah-bowh (George Copway), a young Indian chief of the Ojebwa Nation, a convert to the Christian Faith, and a missionary to his people for twelve years* (Philadelphia, 1847). A memoir of a childhood spent in the traditional migratory way, it provides a unique picture of growing up as a nineteenth-century woodland Ojibwa. So successful was the book, the first written by a Canadian Native, that it went through six editions by the end of the year and was republished in 1851 as *Recollections of a forest life*. Becoming a passionate advocate of Native rights, Copway toured the United States, delivering addresses from South Carolina to Massachusetts, pleading for support for his scheme of a large tract of land on the northeastern side of the Missouri River to be set aside as a permanent country for Natives of all tribes, to be known as Kahgega (Ever to be). His most famous work, *The traditional history and characteristic sketches of the Ojibwa nation* (London, 1850), was later published in the United States as *Indian life and Indian history by an Indian author…* (Boston, 1860; rpr. 1978). In it he praised the lyricism and bountiful vocabulary of the Ojibwa language and Ojibwa orators, hoping 'to awaken in the American heart a deeper feeling for the race of red men'. The book's success brought him international recognition and an invitation to speak at an important Peace Conference in Frankfurt, Germany, an experience he recorded in *Running sketches of men and places in England, France, Germany, Belgium and Scotland* (1851). Copway enjoyed the praise and friendship of such prominent literary figures as James Fennimore Cooper, Washington Irving, Henry Wadsworth Longfellow, Henry Rowe Schoolcraft, and Francis Parkman. But by late 1851 he was plagued by poverty, conflicting loyalties, and the desertion of many of his admirers. Parkman, for one, began to suspect Copway's sincerity and to resent his continuing requests 'for pecuniary aid'. Disillusioned and frustrated, but still enterprising and ever hopeful, Copway remained in the United States for at least another sixteen years, trying to earn a living as a lecturer. When that career failed, the once-celebrated writer and lecturer was forced to take a job as a Union Army recruiter. In the summer of 1868 he appeared, without his family, at the Algonkian-Iroquois mission at Lac-des-Deux Montagnes, northwest of Montreal, where he became involved in a dispute between the Sulpicians, who claimed ownership of the reserve, and the

Iroquois, who were threatening to convert to Methodism in protest. When a Methodist preacher arrived, Copway persuaded most of the Algonkians not to attend his service. He himself had converted to Roman Catholicism, but on the night before his first communion he suddenly died.

The writings of Canada's first Native author have been challenged for their authorship and reliability. No one can be certain whether or not Copway's educated wife collaborated in the writing of his books. George Harvey Genzmer, an American critic of the time, described Copway's writing style as 'an amalgam of Washington Irving, St Luke and elements derived from Methodist exhorters'. Copway's truth is in his understanding of his own history in the spirit of Aboriginal oral traditions.

Corbeil, Carole (1950–2000). Born in Montreal, she received her early education there and at Atlantic College, Wales, and graduated from Glendon College, York University, Toronto; she taught creative writing at York in 1998 and 1999. From 1979 to 1986 she wrote on cultural affairs for the Toronto *Globe and Mail* (she had a column called 'The Observer' during these years) and was a freelance columnist for the *Toronto Star* from 1994 to 1997. Corbeil wrote two novels. Their accomplished portrayal of character and fraught emotions, their easy movement back and forth in time, and their sharp and lucid language make one regret a literary career that was cut short by premature death. In *Voice over* (1992) we read about the Beaulieus from the 1950s to 1984: Claudine and Janine, in Montreal and Toronto, and their mother Odette, who was courted by, and married, Roger Beaulieu. He became an abusive alcoholic whom she had to support by modelling—their relationship culminated in Odette's attempted suicide. She obtains a divorce and later marries a well-to-do widower who lives in Westmount with two sons grieving for their mother. Odette and her new husband return from their honeymoon 'into a hormonal war zone with four teenagers riding around them like a posse, circling their intimacy and crushing it dead.' The girls suffer the rest of their growing up with the shock of two tormenting anglophone stepbrothers and of attending private English schools. Nevertheless they called that period their 'Cinderella time'. 'Claudine grabbed the language of their new house, said terribly, oddly, quite, of course, however, ate it all up.... The language in that house was the language of power, of the powerful, of reality ... of no to all the sadness that crept and seeped into the cracks of French.' Claudine and Janine move to Toronto, Claudine becoming a documentary filmmaker specializing in dark subjects, while living with Ben, then Colin; Janine marries Jim and has a daughter. The lives, relationships, various domiciles, and barely masked mutual alienation of mother and daughters are described with compelling immediacy. *Voice over* won the City of Toronto Book Award. The background of *In the wings* (1997) is theatre in Toronto, specifically a production of *Hamlet*, in which Alice Riverton is to play Gertrude; her younger lover Allan O'Reilly, a brilliant actor, later accepts the role of Hamlet. The critic Robert Pullwarden, obsessed with a young actress, also plays a key role in the plot. The human drama of mixed emotions moving towards a disastrous climax is set against Corbeil's fleeting discussions of *Hamlet*, and her convincing insights into interpretations. Allan in rehearsal 'was unwrapping himself before their eyes. It was a beautiful performance for being so hard won.' The novel too may have been hard won, but most difficulties were surmounted with apparent ease.

Coren, Michael (b. 1959). He was born in Walthamstow, Essex, England, and studied politics at the University of Nottingham (B.A., 1980) and then journalism at City University, London. He worked as a reporter for the *New Statesman* and a commentator for BBC Radio before moving to Canada in 1987. He became a jack of all writing trades in Toronto, reviewing books, writing articles, contributing columns, hosting a weekly evening talk show on CFRB Radio. Currently he is a radio and television broadcaster, advancing his conservative opinions on a daily CFRB Toronto talk show and hosting the daily weeknight discussion program *The Michael Coren Show*, which is available across the country on the Crossroads Television System. As a public personality his speciality is the expression of acerbic comment and sometimes polemical opinion on the issues and personalities of the day. The author of many books, he is particularly associated with biographies of famous British writers, including *Gilbert: the man who was G.K. Chesterton* (1989), *The invisible man: the life and politics of H.G. Wells* (1993, rpr. 2005), *The man who created Narnia: the story of C.S. Lewis* (1994, rpr. 2006), *J.R.R. Tolkien: the man who created The Lord of the Rings* (2001, rpr. 2004), and *R.L. Stevenson* (2004). There are three collections of his journalism: *Aesthete: the frank diaries of Michael Coren* (1993), satiric contributions to *Frank* magazine; *Setting it right* (1996), a gathering of newspaper and magazine columns; and *All things considered: collected columns and essays* (2001).

Cormorant Books Inc. The company was founded in 1986 in Dunvegan, Ontario, by Jan Geddes and Gary GEDDES (husband and wife, they later divorced). In 1989 Jan Geddes became the publisher and she concentrated on new fiction writers, including Nino RICCI's *Lives of the saints* and Charles FORAN's *Kitchen music*. In 1995 ownership changed: Jan Geddes retained 60 per cent of the shares and Stoddart Publishing, a subsidiary of General Publishing Company Ltd, acquired 40 per cent. In January 2001 Jan Geddes sold her shares, retired as publisher, and three new shareholders joined the company: Marc Côté, John Pugsley, and Susan Stewart. Marc Côté became the publisher. When, in August 2002, General Publishing collapsed into bankruptcy, Côté and Pugsley became the publisher. Côté now has that title. Since 2001 Cormorant has published numerous works of fiction, along with books on various subjects, that have made their mark in the press. These include Joseph BOYDEN's *Born with a tooth*, Sky GILBERT's *An English gentleman*, Neil BISSOONDATH's *The unyielding clamour of the night*, Elspeth CAMERON's *And beauty answers: the life of Frances Loring and Florence Wyle*, and Sally Gibson's *Inside Toronto: urban interiors 1880s to 1920s*. In recent years Cormorant has extended its range to publish gay and lesbian authors and to reissue some significant out-of-print books (e.g., *Earth and high heaven* by Gwethalyn GRAHAM).

In 2008 and 2009 Cormorant won the Canadian Booksellers' Association Libris Award as Small Press Publisher of the Year, and in 2009 Marc Côté was honoured in the same way as Editor of the Year. In 2010 the firm launched a new imprint, Dancing Cats, devoted to books for children and young adults, with Gail Winskill as publisher.

Costain, Thomas B. (1885–1965). Thomas Bertram Costain was born in Brantford, Ontario, and educated there. He began his journalistic career as a reporter for the Brantford *Expositor* and then worked in Guelph and for the Maclean-Hunter publications in Toronto. He became editor of *Maclean's* in 1914 and held that post until 1920, when he immigrated to the United States (he later became an American citizen) to be an associate editor of *The Saturday Evening Post*. In 1934 he became eastern story editor for Twentieth-Century Fox, and from 1939 to 1946 was advisory editor for Doubleday in New York. In this period he began to write historical fiction, and his first novel, *For my great folly* (1942), was a bestseller. This was followed by *Ride with me* (1944). In 1946 he began writing fiction full time. Costain's novels remain entertaining specimens of the historical-romance/adventure mode of popular fiction, and range in subject matter from the Cathay of Kubla Khan, to Napoleon's Europe, to New France. Fast-paced, exciting, stocked with easily understood characters, both fictional and historical, and employing complex, coincidence-packed plots, his works sold in the millions. *The black rose* (1945), for example, topped the 2-million mark in all editions and was made into a Hollywood spectacle film. Other novels include *The moneyman* (1947), *The silver chalice* (1952, rpr. 2006), *The tontine* (1955), *Below the salt* (1955), and *The darkness and the dawn* (1959). Costain's novels with Canadian settings are *High towers* (1949, rpr. 1993), a treatment of the Le Moyne family of New France that ranges from Hudson Bay to New Orleans; and *Son of a hundred kings* (1950), the rags-to-riches story of an orphaned immigrant boy in a Canadian small town in the 1890s. Costain also wrote a popular history of New France: *The white and the gold: the French régime in Canada* (1954). His career follows in some respects a pattern set by Gilbert PARKER and others, in which small-town Canadians made their way in the great metropolitan centres on the strength of their gifts as writers of popular fiction and romance. His success as a popular writer—his books sold nearly 12 million copies—was recognized by academe when he was given an honorary doctorate by the University of Western Ontario.

Coulter, John (1888–1980). Born in Belfast, he attended the School of Art and School of Technology there, and then won a scholarship to the University of Manchester. He returned to Belfast in 1912 and moved to Dublin in 1917, chiefly to be close to the leaders of the Irish literary renaissance and to the Abbey Theatre. Unable to establish his own theatre in Belfast, he moved to London to write and do freelance work for the BBC, for which he worked until 1936. In London, Coulter met Olive Clare Primrose, a Canadian writer whom he married in 1936 after settling in Toronto. Coulter published the story of their courtship in *Prologue to a* *marriage: letters and diaries of John Coulter and Olive Clare Primrose* (1979), a tribute to their happy life together until her death in 1971. They had two daughters: Primrose, a writer, and Clare, a distinguished Canadian actress. Coulter's early plays, reflecting his Irish background in setting and theme, are noteworthy for their local colour; but their lack of an element of surprise or dramatic reversal detracts from their overall effect. *The house in the quiet glen* (1937), which won several prizes at the Dominion Drama Festival in 1937, is a one-act comedy about an Irish girl whose parents arrange to marry her to a widower, not knowing she has designs on the widower's son. Another short folk drama, *Father Brady's new pig* (later retitled *Pigs*, then *Clogherbann Fair*—unpublished), concerns the struggle between a parish priest and his housekeeper over the purchase of a sow. Both a radio and a stage play, and the first play Coulter wrote in Canada, it was first produced by the Arts and Letters Club in Toronto in 1937. *The family portrait* (1937) is a full-length comedy—written for the Abbey Theatre, though not produced there—about the reactions of a Belfast family to its playwrighting son and his successful play; it mirrors the Coulter family. *The drums are out* (1971) treats a more serious theme: the effect of the Irish civil war on Protestants and Catholics alike. Set in Belfast in the early 1920s, it focuses on a family whose father is a policeman and whose daughter is secretly married to a member of the Irish Republican Army. It premiered at the Abbey Theatre on 12 July 1948, and played for five weeks to full houses. These plays of Coulter's, while reflecting life in northern Ireland, do not have the genuine Irish dialogue that O'Casey gave to his Dublin plays; with the exception of *The drums are out*, they also fail to develop the potential of their characters' situations. *The family portrait* was refused by the Abbey because Coulter could not rewrite the final scenes to the satisfaction of the director Lennox Robinson. Nevertheless it had a successful production by the Group Theatre in Belfast in 1948 and, under the title *The sponger*, was presented on CBC Television in 1956.

Coulter became fascinated with the Métis leader Louis Riel and wrote a RIEL TRILOGY. In 1949 he completed *Riel* (1962; 2nd edn 1972), a wide-ranging dramatization of events in Riel's life between the Red River Rebellion of 1870 and his hanging in 1885. According to the author's note, it was 'designed for presentation in the Elizabethan manner'—a farsighted step to take four years before the construction of Stratford's revolutionary thrust stage. In 1975 *Riel* received a production worthy of that design at the National Arts Centre, directed by Jean Gascon, with Albert Millaire as Riel. *The trial of Louis Riel* (1968), a courtroom drama and a much more limited play, uses transcripts from the trial and includes some French dialogue. Since its first production in Regina, where Riel was hanged, it has become an annual attraction there. *The crime of Louis Riel* (1976)—a revised version of *Riel* for theatre groups unable to meet the technical demands of the original—combines the expansiveness of *Riel* with the intensity of *The trial of Louis Riel*.

Coulter also wrote three opera librettos, all for the Canadian composer Healey Willan: *Transit through fire* (1942), a short verse-drama that concentrates on the bitter reflections of a young soldier on leave, and of his wife, about their society before the Second World War. This, and *Deirdre of the sorrows* (1944)—a retelling in verse and prose of the ancient Irish story of the foundling girl whose lovers are fated to die—were the first two Canadian operas commissioned and broadcast by the CBC. *Deirdre* (1965), a slightly revised version of the 1944 work, was first staged in 1965 at the MacMillan Theatre, Toronto, and was also the first Canadian opera to be produced, in 1967, by the Canadian Opera Company, at Toronto's O'Keefe Centre.

Coulter spent his last years writing his memoirs, *In my day* (1980), a long account of his life, career, and of people he knew in Canada and abroad. It was published the year he died in a signed limited edition of ninety-three copies—one for each year of the author's life. Coulter was active in the cultural life of Canada in other ways. In 1944 he had been among the artists who presented a brief to the Turgeon Committee of the House of Commons, which was responsible for the formation of the Massey Commission, and thus the CANADA COUNCIL; and in 1952 he persuaded his friend Tyrone Guthrie to come to Canada to direct the first production of the Stratford Festival. Coulter's preference for non-Canadian subjects, and in his Canadian plays for historical subjects with formal dialogue rather than contemporary topics and a Canadian idiom, suggests that he was not completely in touch with Canadian life. In fact his Irish plays were not Irish enough for the Irish, nor were his Canadian plays Canadian enough for Canada. Nevertheless Coulter showed younger writers that they must write from their own roots, and revealed the possibilities of Canadian history on stage.

Coupland

Coupland, Douglas (b. 1961). Born a Canadian citizen on a Canadian NATO base in Baden-Sollingen, Germany, he shortly afterward was brought by his family to West Vancouver, British Columbia, where he still lives. Both a trained sculptor and a novelist, he achieved near overnight success with his avant-garde first novel, *Generation X: tales for an accelerated culture* (1991, with many reprints). His nine succeeding novels—which continue his experiments in the literary avant-garde, expand the range and targets of his satire, and reaffirm his fundamentally ironic vision of contemporary culture—have consolidated his place as a writer of imagination, wit, and inventiveness who can also entertain. Though—particularly in his recent novels—his voluble, idiosyncratic protagonists are on the verge of being memorable, Coupland has not yet reached the point of creating rounded characters in works that will have a lasting place in literature. By its very title, *Generation X* became identified with the subculture of the late baby boomers, whose condition 'X' was the result of having been born too late to enjoy the postwar spoils of their forebears, but too soon after their early boomer confrères to be recognized as chronic have-nots. The novel's narrator-protagonist and two companions make their protest by opting out of mainstream North American society and maintaining an existential vigil while trading stories from the sidelines of the desert retirement community of Palm Springs, California. From such a setting—at once awesome and cliché-ridden—Coupland launches a grand satire in which the foibles and banality of a middle-class, consumer-driven culture are pitted against this more minimalist, thoughtful, if agonizingly self-ironic young threesome. Among Coupland's chief satiric devices are inventive marginalized glossings of his mottoes and neologisms (such as McJobs), and his elaborate metaphors and similes that yoke together, often in hyphenated form, strands of observed pedestrian life that instantly take on a comically pejorative incongruity. *Shampoo planet* (1992, rpr. 2005) continues the vein of satire with a street-smart twenty-year-old narrator-protagonist whose sense of irony is sharp enough to set him above the risible lifestyle of his Galiano Island hippie mother and the locals of his declining hometown of Lancaster, Washington, but is not quite sufficient to grant him a revelation of the transparency of his own wholesale belief in the future, good grooming, and corporate success. In short, he too emerges as an object of irony in his own account of what is objectionably ironic. *Life after God* (1994) moves out of comic satire and offers instead an elegaic confession from the viewpoint of a middle-aged Vancouverite travelling into the British Columbia interior. Images from the countryside's natural splendour provide points of departure for the narrator's nostalgic reminiscences of his childhood 'paradise lost' and of his generation's loss of God. Such a loss he attributes to his generation's ironic cast of mind, 'an irony that scorched everything it touched' and arguably amounted to the 'price paid for the loss of God'. Marking another radical shift in narrative strategies, *Microserfs* (1995, rpr. 2001) consists of an online diary of computer entries and in-coming email from the 'screen' of an erstwhile 'Microsoft' employee, Daniel Underhill. Thin on plot but thick with buzzwords, codewords, doodle pages, and idiosyncratic ramblings and rants, *Microserfs* critiques the malaise of high-tech corporate 'serfs' by juxtaposing the paralysing drudgery of Underhill's mechanistic workworld as a computer coder with the redemptive randomness of life itself. *Polaroids from the dead* (1996, rpr. 2003) collapses the border between fiction and history while sharpening the dialectic in our time between the iconographic and iconoclastic with a series of 'mini-stories'—illustrated throughout with full-page photographs taken from the annals of 'the early 1990s'—that bring full circle Coupland's central theme of the acceleration of history in the information age by serving as both mementoes for, and post-mortems on, recent select newsmaking events that so quickly become dated snapshots. Vancouver in the seventies, eighties, and nineties is the setting for *Girlfriend in a coma* (1998, rpr. 2001). On Grouse Mountain Richard and Karen make love, and at a party the next evening Karen falls into a coma, remaining in that state for nearly eighteen years, though she gives birth after nine months to a baby girl, Megan. Four others are part of the group and as the years pass we see their lives change, and Megan grow up, until Karen wakens and adjustments are forced on everyone. Richard, who has visited the hospital every week, still loves her. She becomes well enough to be interviewed on TV, and then the novel turns surreal. The last few chapters (and the first) are narrated by a seventh member of the group, Jared, a ghost, who died of leukemia as a teenager. Coupland the observer of pop, consumer/media-driven culture comes to the fore again in *Miss Wyoming* (1999, rpr. 2001), which begins when John Johnson, thirty-seven, finally meets Susan Colgate, twenty-eight, in a restaurant in Los

Angeles. He is a producer of inferior films who has become fixated on Susan, seen on TV while he was in hospital; she is a former teenaged beauty queen and an actress in a low-level TV sitcom and in movies. They take a long walk and share their dissatisfactions with their lives. John tells Susan he's scared when he thinks, *'Hey, John Johnson, you've pretty much felt all the emotions you're ever going to feel, and from here on it's reruns.'* They then separate. Their previous wanderings in search of some kind of metamorphosis after near-death experiences—John during a drug-related stay in hospital and Susan after surviving an air crash—and John's search for Susan makes up the bulk of the novel, which is enlivened by Coupland's portraits of the American environment and of Susan's monster mother. John and Susan come together at the end. The novel is rife with Coupland's wit and his familiar metaphorical and aphoristic language.

All families are psychotic (2001, rpr. 2002) is about the Drummond family of Vancouver who are meeting in Florida because daughter Sarah, an astronaut, is about to fly into outer-space from Cape Canaveral. Janet, the mother, is the most sensible and likeable member of the family. Ted is her ex-husband—'he dumped me for a trophy wife about four years ago'. Sarah was a thalidomide baby and has only one hand; she is having an affair with Gordon, her mission commander, and her husband is having an affair with Gordon's wife. The two sons are Wade, married to Beth, and Bryan, whose girlfriend calls herself Shw (*sic*). A shooting, cancer, adultery, AIDS, HIV (there is even the appearance of a purloined letter by Prince William, between two screwed-together sheets of clear plastic, that had been placed on Princess Diana's coffin) affect or complicate the lives of these people. But the soap-opera elements are redeemed by Coupland's typically fast-paced narrative, filled with lively, believable dialogue and uncritical descriptions of outrageous situations. *Hey Nostradamus!* (2003, rpr. 2004) is divided into four parts. The first, 1988: Cheryl, is the reminiscence of seventeen-year-old Cheryl Anway, who attends Delbrook Senior Secondary School in Vancouver and is religious—'I *did* discover religion during my campaign to catch Jason'. She tells of her secret marriage, over a one-night stay in Las Vegas, to Jason Klaasen, a fellow student: 'What appealed to me was that this marriage was something the two of us could have entirely to ourselves, like being the only two guests in a luxury hotel. I knew that if we got

engaged and waited until after high school to marry, our marriage would become something else—ours, yes, but not *quite* ours, either. There would be presents and sex lectures and unwanted intrusions. Who needs all that?' She then relates 'the step-by-step course of events in the cafeteria': 'After the first dozen shots, the fire alarm went off.' Fellow students Mitchell, Jeremy, and Duncan have guns and stage a high-school massacre, in which Cheryl herself is killed. The next section is 1999: Jason, who describes an awkward incident at his bank: 'I knew that they knew about me, about Cheryl, about 1988 and about my reputation as a borderline nutcase—*He never really got over it, you know.* I'm used to this.' This is the longest section (101 pages.) Next is 2002: Heather, narrated by Jason's girlfriend, followed by 2003: Reg, narrated by Jason's very religious father. While letting a human tragedy be the centre-piece of his novel, Coupland focuses not on the murderers but on one victim and the survivors, exploring the complexities of their lives and emotions with accuracy and (particularly in the case of Jason) even with humour. *Eleanor Rigby* (2004) is narrated by Liz Dunn—unmarried, has a good job, is fat, lonely, and considers herself invisible to others. 'Books always tell me to find "solitude".... "why be lonely when you can enjoy solitude?"' Her solitariness is changed when a young man, Jeremy, is brought to Lions Gate Hospital wearing a MedicAlert bracelet identifying Liz as the person to contact—he is her son. Jeremy has multiple sclerosis, is attractive, charming, and intelligent, though given to having visions. Of course he and his mother bond and he is soon able to take on a job, which he is good at. In one of many flashbacks we read of her high-school trip to Rome, and her homesickness and misery. The girls stay in a 'horrible little hostel', which Liz left one night to find, around the corner, an Elf gas station with a bathroom: '... its employees were the handsomest men any of us had ever seen, sculpted from gold, and with voices like songs. And there they were, in a gas station in the middle of nowhere, going to waste.... I'd never been flirted with before, nor has anybody flirted with me since.' Towards the end of the novel we learn how this led to the birth of Jeremy, and who his father is. This is an ingenious story, with many suprises, and Coupland's rendition of Liz's voice is always believable. The title is her email address (one word), as in the Beatles' song—it is mentioned only once.

The first sentence of *JPod* (2006) is 'Oh, God. I feel like a refugee from a Douglas

Coupland

Coupland novel.' The text is supplemented by countless (to this reader) meaningless Internet displays of random found texts and typography, including almost two pages of $ signs—which may be meant as visual jokes. The narrator is Ethan Jarlewski; he and five co-workers (whose names all start with a J)—all of them geeks—work in jPod, a Vancouver game-design company. The friendly, engaging dialogue of these people, which makes up most of the novel, takes the reader into such subjects as global piracy, people smuggling, the industrialization of China, marijuana grow ops—to say nothing of the dysfunctional family of Ethan and others. Ethan is told that pi 'is essentially a string of random numbers'. Mark locates the first hundred thousand digits of pi, on a pi website, and emails them to the others. 'Into this list I've inserted one incorrect digit. The first person to locate this rogue digit will win.' There follows forty-six pages of digits. Coupland himself becomes a (self-critical) character. *JPod* amounts to a readable, funny, overlong (516 pages) *jeu d'esprit*. Coupland, the lighthearted inventor of out-of-the-way, freewheeling novels, outdid himself with *The gum thief* (2007). It is made up of diary entries, and letters, mostly by Roger and Bethany, who work in a superstore selling office supplies (Staples). Roger is forty-three, his wife has left him. He is the same age as DeeDee (also heard from), the mother of Bethany, who wears black lipstick and 'swiped a pack of Wrigley's Orbit White chewing gum from the rack up front and then spent the morning chewing every piece, one by one, placing the resulting gum wads underneath the Bic Soft-Grip display racks'. In the first piece Roger says he's going to write a novel called *Glove Pond* ('What a name … the words have always sounded to me like the title of a novel or movie from England—like *Under Milk Wood*'). Extracts from *Glove Pond*, about Steve and Gloria, appear throughout *The gum thief* and the two are connected. The connections, and various complications, cannot be gone into here, but Coupland's fragmented text is amusing and, in its complex structure, accomplished. On the last page Roger's writing instructor gives *Glove Pond* a C- and offers him 'private editing at a rate of $40 per hour'. In 2009 Coupland published *Generation A*, set in the near future when bees may have become extinct and there is a 'pollination crisis.'

City of glass: Douglas Coupland's Vancouver (2000) is a highly personal and provocative illustrated portrait of his city; it was revised in 2009 for the Vancouver Olympics. *Souvenir of Canada* (2002) and *Souvenir of Canada 2* (2004) are Coupland's imaginative two-volume celebration of Canada combining many different kinds of evocative illustrations (not only of people and places) with his engaging, informative, sometimes loving and personal texts. *Terry* (2005) is a tribute to Terry Fox and his Marathon of Hope in 1980, when he ran 3,339 miles over 143 days to raise money for cancer research. It is in a large format, with many intimate photographs accompanied by Coupland's descriptive texts, which reveal that he himself was inspired by Fox, as so many others were. His royalties go to the Terry Fox Foundation. Coupland is also the author of *Marshall McLuhan* (2010), a brief biography in Penguin Canada's series Extraordinary Canadians.

Crawford, Isabella Valancy (1850–87). Born in Dublin of an educated and cultured family, she came to Canada in 1858, living first in Paisley, Canada West (Ontario), where her father, Dr Stephen Dennis Crawford, was the first doctor. He was township treasurer there and was convicted of misappropriation of public funds. This event—accounts of which Eric Parker uncovered in the *Paisley Advocate* (1865, 1866, and 1867)—provide a hitherto unsuspected explanation for the family's later reputation for being proud and keeping to themselves. They moved to Lakefield, staying initially in the house of Robert Strickland, nephew of Susanna MOODIE and Catherine Parr TRAILL; then to Peterborough, where Dr Crawford died in 1875 and Isabella's only surviving sister died in 1876; and finally to Toronto, where Isabella lived with her mother in several boarding houses before they settled in a building (that still stands) at the corner of John and King Streets, where she died from heart failure. Crawford was educated at home, where she studied the classical poets in English and French, while achieving an understanding of prosody; languages—while fluent in French, she also knew Latin; and the Bible. An energetic, determined woman, Crawford eked out an income by writing a great many short stories and novelettes, largely for American magazines and various newspapers, which also published her poems (at $1 to $3 apiece). Writing dense poetry in the Romantic tradition, and influenced by the Victorians, she nevertheless transcended them with her fantastic imagination and ardent dictioin, never lulling the reader with gentle, sonorous images. She published only one book in her lifetime, *Old Spookses' Pass, Malcolm's Katie, and other poems* (Toronto, 1884), 1,000 copies of which were printed at the author's expense. Despite generally favourable reviews in the English and Canadian publications to which she sent this 224-page volume, only 50 copies were sold. No definitive and complete edition of her poetry exists (many poems that appeared in newspapers have been uncollected), though there are the 1972 facsimile edition, with an Introduction by James REANEY, of *The collected poems of Isabella Valancy Crawford* (1905), edited by John Garvin and with an introduction by Ethelwyn WETHERALD; *Hugh and Ion* (1977), Glenn Clever's edition of the incomplete but powerful narrative poem found by Dorothy LIVESAY in the Lorne PIERCE Collection at Queen's University; and D.M.R. Bentley's scholarly edition, *Malcolm's Katie: a love story* (1987).

With her own life filled with tribulations, Crawford chose to make the dialogue of hope and despair, and the purgatorial role of suffering, the central themes of much of her work, including the narrative poems 'Malcolm's Katie' and *Hugh and Ion*. Written in blank verse, interspersed with lyrics of various metrical forms, they are early milestones in Canada's tradition of narrative poetry. In 'Malcolm's Katie' Crawford adapted to the setting of pioneer Canada the domestic idyll as she learned it from Tennyson. Striking and new, however, is Crawford's location of Max and Katie's conventional love story within a context of Native legends. In *Hugh and Ion* two friends who have fled the noxious city—presumably Toronto—for purification in the primal wilderness carry on a sustained dialogue, Hugh arguing for hope, light, and redemption and Ion pointing out examples of despair, darkness, and intractable human perversity. 'Old Spookses' Pass', a dialect poem set in the Rocky Mountains, concerns a dream vision of a midnight cattle stampede towards a black abyss that is stilled by a whirling lariat; 'The helot' makes use of the Spartans' practice of intoxicating their helots in order to teach their own children not to drink, as the starting point for a highly incantatory and hypnotic poem that ends in Bacchic possession and death; and 'Gisli the chieftain' fuses mythic elements, such as the Russian spring goddess Lada and the Icelandic Brynhild, into a narrative of love, betrayal, murder, and reconciliation. Some of Crawford's prose has been published: *Selected stories of Isabella Valancy Crawford* (1975) and *Fairy tales of Isabella Valancy Crawford* (1977), both edited by Penny Petrone, and *The Halton boys: a story for boys* (1979), edited by Frank M. Tierney. The

fiction displays a skilful and energetic use of literary conventions made popular by Dickens, such as twins and doubles, mysterious childhood disappearances, stony-hearted fathers, sacrificial daughters, wills and lost inheritances, and recognition scenes.

Crawford's novel *Winona; or, The foster-sisters* appeared serially in twelve instalments from 11 January to 29 March 1873 in *The Favorite*, a weekly 'story paper' owned by George-Édouard Desbarats and published in Montreal. It was not reprinted until 2007, in an edition—with a voluminous editorial accompaniment—edited by Len Early and Michael A. Peterman. An example of romantic 'sensation' novel that was so popular in the late nineteenth century, it is about Androsia Howard, daughter of a retired military officer, and Winona, daughter of a Huron chief. Other characters include Andrew Farmer, who proposes to Androsia but pursues Winona secretly, Archie Fraser, who takes the sisters to Toronto and then to his family's estate in the Thousand Islands region, where the climax occurs, and Jack Fennel, a Toronto detective. Professor D.M.R. Bentley says of this work: '*Winona* is sure to spark reconsideration of the achievements and trajectory of a writer who made a greater contribution than has hitherto been generally recognized to the literary culture that emerged in Canada during the post-Confederation period.'

See Dorothy Farmiloe, *Isabella Valancy Crawford: the life and the legends* (1983), and Elizabeth McNeill Galvin, *We scarcely knew her: Isabella Valancy Crawford* (1994).

Crawley, Alan. See CONTEMPORARY VERSE.

Creeps (1972). A long one-act play about the lives of men afflicted with cerebral palsy, its author, David FREEMAN, was born with this handicap. Director Bill Glassco encouraged him to develop 'The world of can't', an article Freeman had written for *Maclean's* in 1964 about workshops for CP victims, and the resulting play was produced by Toronto's Factory Theatre Lab on 5 Feb. 1971, directed by Glassco, to immediate acclaim; later in the year it opened Glassco's new Tarragon Theatre in Toronto. T.E. Kalem, writing in *Time* of a 1973 American production, called it 'powerful, harrowing, grimly humorous and altogether absorbing.' Its locale is the men's washroom of a workshop where five residents, all suffering from CP, argue about their lives and their mindless work (folding boxes, sanding blocks). The slight plot turns on the efforts of Tom, a would-be painter, to persuade Jim, a potential writer, to leave the shelter for the outside world (as Freeman did). The power of the play lies in its searing probing of the stricken men as they escape from their supervisor to the washroom, and from an outside world that treats them as objects of pity or ridicule. The contrast between the condition of these spastics and their constant talk of sex might be disturbing, but the play is surprisingly funny. The language of the play is brutal and obscene because Freeman's aim is to shock his audience into greater awareness of the common humanity that links the healthy and the disabled, and to suggest that freedom is essential to the health of body and mind.

Creighton, D.G. (1902–79). Donald Grant Creighton was born in Toronto and educated at the University of Toronto. He never lived for long away from his birthplace and its vicinity, except for a brief period at Oxford University, from which he returned in 1927 to teach in the department of history at Toronto. He remained there, acting as chairman from 1954 to 1959. He was appointed University Professor of History in 1968, and the year before was made a Companion of the Order of Canada. A historian who never lost his zest for teaching, Creighton was also a natural writer to a degree few historians attain. He was never merely an academic historian, for he placed a high value on literary style, writing in a craftsmanly prose and deliberately making his books accessible to a large public outside the universities. He wrote with great strength of opinion, so that his historical narratives are coloured by his conservative and nationalistic political attitudes. He always remained at heart an Upper Canadian, distrustful of the aspirations of Québec and unwilling to give importance to the regional differences between central and western Canada. He disputed freely with the liberal historians who, in his younger days, represented the dominant trend in his own discipline in Canada. But his controversial stance had its positive aspects, for he thought daringly, designed his books on a dramatic scale, and created some enduring Canadian myths. Like the Greeks, who assigned history to its muse Clio, Creighton regarded his discipline as a creative art.

Perhaps the most important formative influence on Creighton was that of Harold INNIS, who wrote as an economist but contributed much to our understanding of Canadian history through books like *The fur trade in Canada* (1930, rpr. 1999) and *The cod fisheries* (1940), in which he showed that Canada had an economic history before it had a political one. Creighton adopted and considerably adapted Innis's ideas, expressing them, in changed forms, in an attractively fluent prose that contrasted with the gnarled and obscure manner in which his mentor wrote. Creighton's first book, *The commercial empire of the St. Lawrence: 1760–1850* (1937)—reprinted in 1956, and as *The empire of the St. Lawrence: a study in commerce and politics* (2002)—showed how the fur-trading system of the St Lawrence and the Great Lakes created an east-west pattern of transport, occupation, and development that became an enduring historical factor, countering the geographical lines of the continent that run from north to south. In *Dominion of the North: a history of Canada* (1944), Creighton developed, on a much larger time scale, the insights projected in *The empire of the St. Lawrence*. Since he saw the process of early Canadian development as dependent on a single urge—that of fur trading and consequent exploration—lasting almost a century to the eve of Confederation, he tended to have a highly unified view of the history of Canada. He was not a regionalist, impressed by the historical differences between the various parts of Canada; nor was he a continentalist, impressed by the geographical urge that pointed towards a coalescence between Canada and the United States. *Dominion of the North* shows that he was an early Canadian nationalist, and he remained one to the end of his life. It demonstrated Creighton's conviction that Canada had its own manifest destiny, defined by the old trade routes that went east to west from Montreal to the Pacific, the routes that railways and highways would later follow. The combination of information and imagination resulted in a grand mythic view of Canadian history that the rest of Creighton's works developed. A myth requires a hero. The idea of Canada as a nation emerged in the movement towards Confederation that followed the decline of the fur traders, and Creighton saw the personification of that idea in Sir John A. Macdonald, the Dominion's founding prime minister, whose first adequate biography he wrote. The first volume, *John A. Macdonald: the young politician* (1952, GGA), takes Macdonald's career to the high point of Confederation; the second, *John A. Macdonald: the old chieftain* (1955, GGA), deals with the years of power and decline. (They were reissued in one volume, *John A. Macdonald: the young politician and the old chieftain*, in 1998.) Most political biographies submerge the man in the events, but in these two books Creighton sustained the biographical intent and produced a vital—if perhaps excessively heroic—portrait of Macdonald.

Among Creighton's other works are *The road to Confederation: the emergence of Canada, 1863–67* (1964), an account of how British North Americans, from Nova Scotia to Upper Canada, recognized that unity was the best way to solve their common economic problems, and perhaps the only way to protect themselves from the political danger posed by an America resurgent at the end of the Civil War. By 1970, when Creighton published *Canada's first century, 1867–1967*, he was considerably less confident about Canada's destiny than in his earlier books. He recognized that the north-south pull was stronger than he had thought, and that Canada's historic east-west ties were strained by the cultural and economic invasion from the United States. He also saw the trend to provincial autonomy and the rise of Québec separatism as elements weakening the Canadian political structure. He was unable to admit that stronger regions might build a new kind of confederalism, and as a result he felt a weakening confidence about the future of his country. This pessimistic mood was further developed in his last major work, *The forked road: Canada 1939–1957* (1976), in which Mackenzie King is cast—in contrast to John A. Macdonald—as the betrayer of Canada's future, the politician who sold the past to continentalism. The element of gloom does not lessen the power of Creighton's later and less hopeful books. Indeed, it provides the element of shadow that is perhaps necessary for a great myth.

Creighton has rarely been popular among other historians. But to imaginative writers—poets and novelists—he has offered a pattern within which they could shape their intuitions about Canadian life. On writers whose deep sense of history was modified by their awareness of place—like Hugh MacLENNAN, Margaret LAURENCE, Margaret ATWOOD, and Al PURDY—his glancing effect was evident.

Crozier, Lorna (b. 1948). Born and raised in Swift Current, Saskatchewan, she was educated at the University of Saskatchewan (B.A., 1969). She married, completed a teaching certificate, returned to Swift Current, and under her married name, Uher, taught high-school English (1972–7). Since 1996 she has been a professor in the Department of Writing, University of Victoria, becoming the Chair of Writing, and lives in Saanichton,

B.C. Her first poem was published in *GRAIN* in 1974. She then published two collections of poetry—*Inside is the sky* (1976) and *Crow's black joy* (1978)—before joining the poet Patrick LANE (to whom she is now married) in 1978 and completing an M.A. in English at the University of Alberta—her thesis being a collection of poems, *Humans and other beasts* (1980). *No longer two people* (1979), containing poems by both Uher and Lane, announced their creative and personal partnership and functioned as a pivotal turning point in Crozier's feminist poetics. But just as Crozier's reputation as a Prairie poet was firmly established, she began to move around the country so that Lane, and later she herself, could take up positions as writers in residence. They eventually settled in Saanichton, British Columbia, in 1991, when Crozier took up a full-time position in the Creative Writing Department of the University of Victoria. *The weather* (1981) was a watershed publication for Crozier. Dedicated to her family, whose name she 'reclaimed' and used for this and subsequent collections, it extended the range and tone of Crozier's poetry and displayed her increasing control and versatility. *The garden going on without us* (1985), new and selected poems, and her subsequent collection, *Angels of flesh, angels of silence* (1989), were nominated for a Governor General's Award—which she won for *Inventing the hawk* (1992). Crozier's *Everything arrives at the light* (1995) includes a sequence of ghazals (a form of Oriental lyric poetry) that had been published in a chapbook, *Eyewitness* (1993). *A saving grace: the collected poems of Mrs Bentley* (1996) is an imaginative and moving evocation of the narrator of Sinclair ROSS's novel *AS FOR ME AND MY HOUSE*.

There is an apparent paradox at the heart of Crozier's *oeuvre*: while often grounded in daily life, it increasingly gestures towards a world of myth and magic that lies both within and beyond that everyday world. Its central images (bread, hands, light, prairie, and sky), and figures (messenger angel, snake, horse, child, and fisherman), appear at the intersection of these two planes, in garden and prairie settings that are more figurative than earthly. In an ongoing project of feminist remythification, Crozier challenges inherited myths by allowing a silent female character to tell her side of the story. For example, 'On the seventh day' (*Inventing the hawk*) retells the creation story from the engagingly down-to-earth perspective of God's wife and combines humour with a distinctly feminist frame of reference that is crucial to Crozier's aesthetic. Her poetry can be bitingly funny, as in 'the sex lives of vegetables' (a series animating garden vegetables in *The garden going on without us*) and 'the penis poems' (in *Angels of flesh*), politically engaged (as in the challenge to Pinochet's regime in the Chilean sequence), and evocatively personal (as in the elegiac poems for the speaker's father in *Inventing the hawk*). *What the living won't let go* (1999), one of Crozier's best collections, is a gathering of luminous poems about family, childhood, and loss. The first section, called 'Names of loss and beauty'—the title of the first poem, which is followed by a poem (one of two) about her conception—includes a surprising poem narrated by the cat that swallowed Thomas Hardy's heart. In the second section are poems about 'another family': the younger sister, the older sister, the boy, his wife, their mother, the father. The third section is called 'Walking into the future': 'Away too long I carry/my bags up the four steps to our porch,/hesitate, as I've never done before./Sun-blind, I walk into the future,/see only shapes—a couch, a chair,/and someone rising, I don't know who/you will be.'

More recent collections are *Apocrypha of light* (2002), *Whetstone* (2005), and *Bones in their wings: ghazals* (2003), made up of forty-one ghazals and more than twenty pages of prose: one short essay describing her discovery of the ghazal (pronounced *guzzle*, as she tells us) in John THOMPSON's *Stilt Jack*, and a longer essay on the ghazal itself, which originated in Persia in the thirteenth century and is made up of couplets, a minimum of five, a maximum of twelve, with various 'rules' imposed. There are two recent Selected Poems. *Before the first word: the poetry of Lorna Crozier* (2005) is in a series intended to provide—as the general editor, Neil Besner, says in his Foreword—'thirty-five poems from across a poet's career', selected by a critic who writes an introduction (in this case Catherine Hunter), with an Afterword by the poet: Crozier's eloquent 'See how many ends this stick has: a reflection on poetry'. *The blue hour of the day: selected poems* (2007) is an uneven collection of Crozier's huge output of poems. In 2009 Crozier published *Small beneath the sky: a prairie memoir*, mainly about growing up in Swift Current.

Together Lorna Crozier and Patrick Lane edited *Addiction: notes from the belly of the beast* (2001)—in which alcoholism is prominent, as in pieces by Lane, Crozier (her father), David Adams RICHARDS, and John NEWLOVE—and the anthologies *Breathing fire* (1995) and *Breathing fire 2* (2004), both with the subtitle *Canada's new poets*.

Crummey, Michael (b. 1965). He was born in Buchans, Newfoundland, a small mining town near Red Indian Lake in central Newfoundland. In the late seventies he moved with his family to Wabush, Labrador. He was educated at Memorial University, St John's (B.A. in English, 1987), when he began to write poetry, and Queen's University, Kingston, Ontario (M.A.,1988)—dropping out of a Ph.D. program to concentrate on writing. His first novel is the much-praised *River thieves* (2001, rpr. 2002), set in 1810–20, and is about the Beothuk Indians—who became extinct some ten years after the end of the novel—and European settlers, with some of the action taking place on Red Indian Lake. The characters include David Buchan of the Royal Navy, who is determined to make contact with the Beothuk, called Red Indians by Europeans because they decorated their tools and even their bodies with powdered red ochre; John Peyton, who shares Buchan's interest in the Beothuk; his father, John Senior, who feels nothing but animus for them; and the old man's much younger housekeeper, the witty and intelligent Cassie. The Beothuks are a shadowy, evanescent presence in the novel (little is known about them)—except for a young woman, given the name Mary, who is captured after her husband and child are murdered, and is treated protectively. Two trips are made to the River of Exploits and Red Indian Lake, but murders occur each time—of two white men and then of two Beothuk. The novel is made of these events and memories of them, of the Europeans' fraught relations with each other, and moves back and forth in time, so that the story and somewhat lifeless characterizations build in a tortuous manner. Nevertheless, the novel is both a complex and an imaginative reconstruction of a little-known backwater of Newfoundland history. *The wreckage* (2005) is the fictional result of the cogent handling of period and foreign research, set in both Newfoundland and a prisoner of war camp in Japan during and after the Second World War. In the small community of Little Fogo Island in northeastern Newfoundland, Wish Furey falls in love with sixteen-year-old Mercedes Parsons, who returns his love; but because he's Catholic, rejection by her mother and even the townspeople follows. Subsequent narratives, headed 'Wish' or 'Mercedes', describe Wish's joining a British regiment and being shipped to Singapore, finding himself a POW in Japan and submitting to ordeals inflicted by Nishino (who speaks English and comes from

Kitsilano, British Columbia). Mercedes writes to him, hoping for an answer, is incorrectly informed that he has apparently died, marries, has two daughters—and she and Wish meet again in old age. These main events are imbued with many supplementary incidents and characters. Towards the end, an untoward prolongation attenuates the plot and undermines the two leading characters—but the ending itself is delicately handled, and satisfying. The rubric of the title applies to the destruction of Newfoundland houses by tidal waves, an extinguished love affair, Wish's half-lived life, the torture and death of prisoners, the bombing of Nagasaki. In 2009 Crummey published his third novel, *Galore* (page 3 of which describes a white-haired man being released from the belly of a beached whale). An epic multi-generational saga covering 100 years, it garnered reviews so enthusiastic that Crummey, already a singular Newfoudland novelist, became a distinguished one; it also confirmed the province's unique reputation for inspiring, over a very few years, so much impressive literature.

Crummey has published four collections of poetry—*Arguments with gravity* (1996), *Hard light* (1998), *Emergency roadside assistance* (2001), and *Salvage* (2002)—that are notable for their clarity, perceptiveness, and disciplined emotion. *Arguments with gravity* is a strong first poetry collection, with poems on diverse subjects, including Canadian writers. In 'Where the words come from' photographs of the poets Lorna CROZIER, Bronwen WALLACE, and Pat LOWTHER are described; in the sensuous 'Reading Ondaatje' a man describes a woman he is in bed with reading *In the Skin of a Lion* at 2 a.m. In 'News from home: metamorphosis' the poet's brother is confronted by the result of a plane crash and his mother starts thinking of her children: 'You can hear the difference in their voices when they call/how they have grown away from and toward me all at once/and I am changed too by this news from home/by the slow metamorphosis of the people I love'. 'Structural adjustment: an introduction' and 'Structural adjustment: the IMF representative's advice' are two salutary attacks on the International Monetary Fund. *Hard light*, combining brief prose narratives and poems, is, according to Crummey, 'a collaboration between myself and Newfoundlanders past and present [particularly his father]', evoking the physical activities of Newfoundlanders, particularly fishermen. It begins with 'Rust': 'The boy watches his father's hands.... They have a history the boy knows nothing of....

Twine knitted to mend the traps, the bodies of codfish opened with a blade, the red tangle of life pulled from their bellies.' A sequence of vivid poems with the overall title 'Discovering darkness' was inspired by the diary of Captain John Froude (1863–1939). In *Salvage*: 'Love and poetry, meaning–/ maybe it's just stubborn animal machinery/ manufacturing light for the mind/with darkness at the door' ('Naked'). 'Simmer': 'all her life my grandmother loved dusk,/the ambiguity of twilight,/how darkness seemed to seep/from the earth,/street lamps flickering/ to life while clouds shone/and blushed on the horizon/like apples ripening on a windowsill.'

Michael Crummey and Greg Locke collaborated on *Newfoundland: journey into a lost nation* (2004). Crummey contributes an introductory essay, partly drawing on his family's life in Newfoundland, and captions for Locke's photographs, which emphasize the (lost) cod fishery, suspended in 1992, and its fishermen. There is a photograph of John Crosbie announcing the moratorium on television. Crummey writes that Crosbie was the figurehead of 'a distant bureaucracy that had allowed the cod to be fished into near extinction by hundreds of Canadian and foreign factory trawlers, each of which took more cod in a day than an inshore fisherman could take in a season. And he was now ending the only way of life they and their families had ever known.'

For a writer in mid-career, Crummey was given by the WRITERS' TRUST, in 2008, The Timothy Findley Award ($15,000).

Culleton, Beatrice. See ABORIGINAL LITERATURE: 4.

Cumyn, Alan (b. 1960). Born in Ottawa, Ontario, he attended for one year Royal Roads Military College, Victoria, British Columbia; studied English and history at Queen's University, Kingston (B.A., 1983); and creative writing at the University of Windsor (M.A., 1984). In 1986–7 he taught English language and literature at Xuzhou Teachers College, Xuzhou City, People's Republic of China, and in the first half of 1994 in Salatiga, Indonesia. From 1991 to 1999 he was a writer, researcher, and editor on human-rights issues for the Immigration and Refugee Board of Canada.

In Cumyn's novel *Waiting for Li Ming* (1993), which draws on his time in China as a teacher, Rudy Seaborn arrives in Laozhu to teach English for a year and is met by his translator, the beautiful Oxford-accented (learned from the BBC) Li Ming. First-person narratives of Rudy's incomprehensible experiences as a complete outsider, knowing no Chinese, and of his forbidden love for Li Ming and hers for him, alternate with third-person accounts of his return to Canada a year later, where he is a student of creative writing and makes new friends—notably Louise (Lou), whom he attends while she gives difficult birth to a baby—while he waits to hear from Li Ming. She had been accepted as a teacher in his university at the time of the demonstration and massacre in Beijing's Tiananmen Square, when, to Rudy's horror, she appeared briefly in an interview on TV. The smooth depiction of both the present and the immediate past, and the realistic portrayal of the Chinese setting, and of character, emotion, and many moments of suspense, are remarkable in a first novel. *Between families and the sky* (1995) is a Canadian romance in two parts. 'The hole in the kitchen floor'—a metaphor for things that are not discussed—is about James Kinnell, whose father died young, his life as a teenager with his mother and his father's father, and his thwarted love affair with Mirele. In 'The memory holes of Garland Ross', Garland, a thirty-five-year-old virgin with 'winter inside', whose mother died soon after she was born, recalls her unsatisfactory childhood with her golf-obsessed father, becomes an architect, is attracted to a handsome young man, and is invited to suggest plans for changes in the house of his—Jim Kennell's—family. Jim's and Garland's lives within their respective families, their upsets, and Garland's slow submission to Jim's love and her eventual commitment to him, are described in an intricate narrative that is unsentimental, sensitive, and emotionally convincing. The hero of *Man of bone* (1998, rpr. 2002) is Bill Burridge, working in the Canadian foreign affairs department, who, with his wife and young son, accepts a deputy posting to 'Santa Irene, an island paradise' in the South China Sea. He is kidnapped by Kartouf terrorists and subjected to brutal torture that almost destroys his body and his mind as, shackled and hooded for much of the time, he agonizes over his pain and his physical state ('Bone. It's all I have left. Rigid, fleshless, jutting bone. Man of bone. Breathing bone. Breathing man of bone.'). He recalls his past (conveyed in interwoven sections), dreams, and hallucinates, during nine months of captivity. The story has its thriller aspects, but it is mainly a gripping account of Bill's moment-by-moment suffering, while

wanting to die, and his feeble attempts to survive—until he is rescued in a violent scene and taken home, an apparently ruined man. But in *Burridge unbound* (2000, rpr. 2002) his health has improved under medication, though remaining fragile, and he writes a book about his ordeal, becomes a celebrity, and founds with others Freedom International, 'processing misery for a lot of the world'. He unwillingly agrees to join a 'truth commission' in Santa Irene, set up by the interim president, Suli Nylioko (widow of a reformist who had been murdered by the regime), and flies back to the island with his nurse, Joanne. His time there, when he is far from his best—portrayed by recurring thoughts of his previous incarceration, his inability to communicate except through an interpreter, his contacts with suspicious people who appear to be his supporters, his attendance on the questionable and powerless truth commission, his growing love for Joanne, his surprising intimacy with the president—explodes in a suspenseful denouement that leaves no questions answered, and ends with his return to an anti-climactic family situation in Ottawa. Encompassing the deepest throes of suffering and suspense in the thriller genre, the two Burridge novels are interesting and complex narratives that have their grounding in Bill's family and emotional life, which are disrupted; at the end there is the suggestion that a happier life might lie ahead.

The comic novel *Losing it* (2001, rpr. 2002) opens with a quarrel between Lenore and her daughter Julia about throwing something out. (We learn later that Lenore has dementia.) Julia, the former student of English professor Bob Sterling, married him, and has an insistent two-year-old son, Matthew, who is still being breast-fed. Bob, fifty-four, is off-putting before he says a word, sleeping and snoring with his hairy back exposed (even when Julia pleads with him to put Matthew back to bed), then falling out of bed with a thump, taking the blankets with him and continuing to snore. Next morning he receives in the mail a brown-paper package before leaving for a conference in New York on Edgar Allan Poe, his specialty. At the airport he meets his beautiful twenty-one-year-old student, Sienna Chu. They sit together on the plane; he praises her incomprehensible poetry (thus mentally seducing her); then excuses himself to go to the washroom, where he opens the brown-paper parcel containing 'a portable vagina' and tries to put it on, which leads to extreme difficulties, even while the plane is landing. Unlike reviewers, this (elderly) reader was not amused. But what follows (the conference itself, Bob's dressing in women's clothers in his hotel room, Sienna's coming on to him in his room, their return to Ottawa, followed by many crises) provides some chuckles—though none in the many pages (including the first and last) devoted to the hallucinatory utterances of poor Lenore as she struggles to make sense of the images in her head. Admiration does come into play, however. After Cumyn's serious Burridge novels, this artfully contrived attempt at a comic extravaganza bespeaks a certain virtuosity, as does his Great War novel, *The sojourn* (2003, rpr. 2004). It is about Private Ramsay Crome of Victoria, B.C., in the second battle of Ypres (1915): 'The rain drips off the rims of our helmets, drums dolefully against any surface open to it: rubber, canvas, metal, mud. As luck would have it, I am on sentry while most of the platoon retreats to the relative shelter of dugouts. I survey the surroundings in snatches from the field periscope that has been set up close to the trench wall that collapsed in this morning's attack: tangles of barbed wire scratched across an ungodly expanse of blown-up field, the mud yellow in places, soupy, saucered with rain-filled ponds.' The complexities of the settings and of human relationships—life in the trenches with his comrades, many of whom are killed; life on leave in London with his uncle's family, including his cousin Margaret, with whom he falls in love; being taken prisoner in the Battle of Mount Sorrel (1916)—are portrayed with smooth narrative drive and believable battle and period detail. *The sojourn* has a sequel, *The famished lover* (2006), which interweaves Ramsay's marriage to, and life with, Lillian, a beautiful young farm girl, and the horrific experience of being a prisoner of war. Even in his worst trial as a prisoner, Ramsay imagines that Margaret (who has married) is with him, helping him to survive. And she continues to haunt him. His wife Lillian has simple desires and soon finds that her husband has closed off his past life to her; when she discovers his drawings of Margaret she considers her a rival. As a commercial artist Ramsay finds life difficult in Depression-era Montreal, but he manages to build a house in the country, only to have it burn down because of faulty wiring (he builds another), and falls in love, beginning an ardent affair with Dorothy, his boss. A vivid, well-handled family episode occurs towards the end of the novel when his brother Rufus and his wife, along with Margaret and her family, arrive from England to

stay for a short visit, a day and a night, in Ramsay's small house (the children sleep in tents); for all these people the furious, neglected Lillian provided good meals. When they depart, Ramsay is left with his small son Michael and an alienated wife, his future a question mark. The novel is shot through with good writing, but much of it—including the character of Ramsay, the wartime episodes, his working and married life—has somehow been drained of emotional depth and authenticity.

Cumyn has written three populart novels for young readers. In *The secret life of Owen Skye* (2002, rpr. 2008) Owen and his two brothers have adventures and Owen falls in love with Sylvia Tull, who moves away at the end. It has two sequels: *After Sylvia* (2004, rpr. 2008) was adapted by Cumyn for the stage in 2005—the play was performed by the Ottawa School of Speech and Drama at the University of Ottawa; *Dear Sylvia* (2008) is a funny epistolary novel that is not spoiled by Owen's poor spelling, which improves.

Curzon, Sarah Anne (1833–98). Born in Birmingham, England, the daughter of an affluent manufacturer, George Phillips Vincent, she received a private education and contributed prose and verse to family periodicals during her childhood and youth. She married Robert Curzon of Norfolk in 1858 and immigrated with him to Toronto in 1862. Her Canadian literary career included contributions of verse, essays, and fiction to the *Canadian Monthly*, the *Dominion Illustrated*, GRIP, *The WEEK*, *Evangelical Churchman*, and the *Canadian Magazine*. She also published women's-suffrage articles in British and American newspapers, and was a founding member in Nov. 1876 of the Toronto Women's Literary Club, which was based on the model of the American Society for the Advancement of Women. After her husband's death in 1878, she supported herself as a freelance journalist. In 1881 she was appointed associate editor of the *Canada Citizen*, the first Canadian prohibitionist paper, writing a regular column on women's suffrage. She is best known for her versedrama *Laura Secord, the heroine of 1812* (1887), a sentimental paean to Laura Secord's heroism in the War of 1812. Curzon's only other play, *The sweet girl graduate* (published in the periodical *Grip-Sack* in 1882), deals with the topical issue of women's higher education; it contributed to the passing of an Order in Council on 2 Oct. 1884 admitting women to University College, Toronto.

D

D&M Publishers Inc. Co-founded as Douglas & McIntyre in Vancouver in 1971 by Jim Douglas and Scott McIntyre, it grew from its inaugural two titles into one of Canada's largest Canadian-owned trade houses and the largest Canadian-owned English-language publishing house headquartered outside Toronto. With Scott McIntyre as its president, it proved to be something of a Canadian success story, having maintained a strong presence in British Columbia while expanding a national base in Toronto and an international export market that accounted for one third of its sales. There were originally three publishing divisions. The adult division's strengths included Canadian fiction, with an emphasis on Chinese-Canadian and Native authors, as well as French-Canadian literature in translation. Some notable works were Sky LEE's *Disappearing moon café* (1991), Bill Richardson's *Bachelor brothers' bed and breakfast* (1993), Wayson CHOY's *The jade peony* (1995), Monique PROULX's *The sex of the stars* (1996), and Fred Stenson's *The trade* (2000). Its strengths in non-fiction included Native studies, art and architecture, history, social/environmental issues, transportation, biography, and food and wine. Among the titles in two of these areas are Robert BRINGHURST's *A story as sharp as a knife: the classical Haida mythtellers and their world* (1999, rpr. 2000), Ingo Hessel's *Inuit art* (1998), Doris Shadbolt's *Bill Reid* (1998), and Dennis Reid's *Krieghoff: images of Canada* (2000). Monographs on architect Arthur Erickson and painters Patterson Ewan and Betty Goodwin, among other artists, have also been published. In 1993 the firm launched a new division out of Vancouver, Greystone Books, focusing on natural history, natural science, environmental issues, guidebooks, sports, health, popular culture, and the prairie interests of Western Producer Books acquired in 1992. The company's children's division, based in Toronto and overseen by Patsy Aldana, conjoined the well-established Groundwood Books with Douglas & McIntyre's own titles. (Groundwood was sold to Scott Griffin at the House of ANANSI in 2005.) Along with its own publications, the firm also distributed the books of a number of national and international publishers.

In May 2007 McIntyre sold a majority interest in the company to three British Columbia-based Canadian shareholders, retaining 25 per cent himself and becoming chairman and CEO of the company while remaining publisher of the Douglas & McIntyre division. Mark Scott, who holds the largest block of shares, is president and focuses on corporate acquisitions and developing a strategy for the digital future.

In September 2008 the company's legal name was changed from Douglas & McIntyre to D&M Publishers Inc., honouring the abbreviated name by which it has been best known. Three publishing divisions operate under the D&M rubric: Douglas & McIntyre, Greystone Books (David Suzuki's publisher), and New Society Publishers, which was acquired in June 2008 and is one of North America's leading publishers of environmental books; though based on Gabriola Island, B.C., its sales are mainly in the US. On the international distribution side, D&M will maintain the strong ten-year relationship with Farrar, Straus & Giroux. The company selectively buys Canadian rights to international books, notably Ishmael Beah's *A long way gone* (2007, rpr. 2008, 100,000 copies in print) and Karen Armstrong's *The Bible* (2007, rpr. 2008). Several exceptional books on Canadian art were published in 2007 and 2008 and D&M are keeping all Emily CARR's books in print. It is now a leading Canadian independent publisher.

D'Alfonso, Antonio (b. 1953). Born in Montreal to parents from Molise, Italy, he was educated at Loyala College (B.A., 1975) and the Université de Montréal (M.Sc., 1979). A publisher and writer, having founded GUERNICA EDITIONS in 1978, he expresses iconoclasm in both his creative and critical texts and a commitment to new ways of seeing reality. In *The other shore* (1986, rpr. 1988)—poetry and prose—and the poetry collection *Panick love* (1992)—first published in French—D'Alfonso explores the problems of living in several cultural environments, suggesting that change and contradiction embody ethnic subjectivity. In *The other shore*, a darkly passionate poetic figure meditates on the effects of cultural dislocation, questioning the success of immigration. Intense personal experience is interwoven with an ethnic community's anxiety and yearning. In *Panick love* the eroticism and treachery of sexual love is connected to the poet's view of the beauty and inaccessibility of Parisian/European society and to his own ambivalence towards Italian and Canadian cultures. Dream, passion, delirium, and alienation commingle, creating a world in which illusion is inseparable from reality. Both collections present a tortured and ongoing journey to self-discovery, unfulfilled sexual desire, and an open-ended life process. These motifs recur in the novel *Fabrizio's passion* (1995, rpr. 2000), which was also first published in French. Its realistic portrayal of an Italian family in Montreal is imbued with hallucinatory and nightmarish elements that capture the tragedy of immigration and the anguish of assimilation. D'Alfonso's books, which have a postmodern quality and defy standard expectations about closure, play with various forms that cut across genres, transgress aesthetic boundaries, and generate multiple, interconnecting themes. *Un vendredi du mois d'août* (2004), which won Ontario's Trillium Book Award, was translated by Jo-Anne Elder as *A day in August* (2005), the second volume of a trilogy about Fabrizio Notte, who has become a filmmaker who makes documentaries and attends a film festival in Montreal. The trilogy ends with *L'Aimé* (2007). D'Alfonso's multi-faceted mode of writing is itself emblematic of the complexities of ethnicity. As he states in his critical work *In italics: in defense of ethnicity* (1996), minority writing is not about defining territory but about paradoxical cultural processes. Ethnicity informs social reality and is part of Canadian cultural production. *Gambling with failure* (2006) is a collection of articles that includes four interviews with the author. D'Alfonso has published more than thirty titles in English and French.

Daniells, Roy (1902–79). Born in London, England, he came with his family in 1910 to Victoria, British Columbia. He was educated at the University of British Columbia, and the University of Toronto for graduate studies. He taught English at Victoria College, Toronto; at the University of Manitoba; and at UBC, where he became head of the English department in 1948, retiring in 1974. He was made a Companion of the Order of Canada in 1971. As a poet Daniells used traditional forms, particularly sonnet sequences linked by a common persona or an underlying theme, such as the sense of a quest or journey. His scholarly work on seventeenth-century poets influenced his technique, as well as his religious and philosophical thought. Technical skill, scrupulous phrasing, and a highly accomplished arrangement of effects, including dislocation and surprise, are always evident.

Clearly attracted by the new 'metaphysical' poets of the 1920s and 1930s, Daniells drew upon symbol and myth for ironic and witty counterpoint to images from contemporary life. Two sonnet sequences make up the major part of *Deeper into the forest* (1948). The 'Anthony' sequence centres on an ironic character, at the time of the Spanish Civil War, whose skepticism, rash impulses, and desire for action reflect that period's longing for belief and a sure cause. The twenty-one sonnets of the 'Forest' sequence are linked by the image of an emblematic forest drawn from folklore and legend, both frightening and enchanted. *The chequered shade* (1963), also chiefly a collection of sonnets, is arranged in three series. The first represents a pilgrimage across Europe by a travelling poet-humanist who is both vitally alive to landscape and works of art, and aware of the cruelties and triumphs of the past; the second group is a rewriting of Bible stories, psalms, and parables in which contemporary images and colloquial speech reflect the doubts and tensions of an individual seeking a lost faith. The third series, bringing the seeker back to Canada, asks insistently: What must the artist, the poet, do in this land and in this age? In her biography *Professing English: a life of Roy Daniells* (2002), Sandra DJWA portrays not only the man himself and his religious struggles, but the poet, and his life and influence in the world of academe.

Davey, Frank (b. 1940). Born in Vancouver and brought up in Abbotsford, British Columbia, he attended, in the early 1960s, the University of British Columbia (B.A., 1961; M.A., 1963). In 1961, in Vancouver, he was one of the founding editors of the influential poetry magazine *TISH*, and in 1965, in Victoria (where he was teaching), of *OPEN LETTER*. After doing graduate work at the University of Southern California (Ph.D., 1968, with a thesis on Black Mountain poetics), Davey taught in Montreal, Toronto, and London, Ontario, where in 1990 he was appointed the Carl F. KLINCK professor of Canadian literature at the University of Western Ontario (retired 2005). Davey's early books of poetry include *D-Day and after* (1963), *Bridge Force* (1965), and *The scarred hull* (1966); work from this period was collected in *L'an trentiesme: selected poems 1961–1970* (1972). Perhaps the most important period of Davey's writing as a poet occurred in the early 1970s, with *Weeds* (1970), *King of swords* (1972), *Arcana* (1973), and *The Clallam* (1974), which formed the basis for *Selected poems: the arches* (1980), edited with an important introduction by bp NICHOL. In the 1980s Davey published *Capitalistic affection* (1982), *Edward and Patricia* (1984), *The Louis Riel organ and piano company* (1985), and *The Abbotsford guide to India* (1986). Since then, he has been less prolific as a poet—though *Popular narratives* (1991) is an important collection. His poetry has been balanced between public and private themes, the public poems dealing mostly with Canadian history, and the private poems with family relationships. Stylistically, the early Davey was concerned with adapting Charles Olson's poetics into a Canadian context, while the later Davey has focused on what he himself has called 'the validity of fact': a strong distrust of metaphor is evident in both his poetry and his criticism. The historical poems, such as those on shipwrecks, reject the idea that the 'documentary' can confine itself to objective facts; rather, these facts fuel the poet's intense anger at the incompetence and arrogance of ships' captains, and at the imperialist habit of mind they represent. The more personal poems analyze the sterility of relationships based on false ideals of chivalric or imperialistic culture. *King of swords* and *Arcana* subject the material of the Arthurian legends to a ruthlessly contemporary criticism: 'the death of Arthur continues' in Belfast and in the suburbs of Vancouver. Davey's later poetry approaches 'the validity of fact' in the form of long, seemingly prosaic anecdotes characterized by tightness of form and control of language. *The Abbotsford guide to India* is at one and the same time a travel book, a parody of a travel book, and a brilliant poetic commentary on post-colonialism. The poem/essay 'Dead in France' (*Popular narratives*) moves flawlessly back and forth between history (the story of Héloïse and Abelard), cultural studies (the popular reception of a French film on Camille Claudel), and personal emotion (the poet's grief over the death of his friend bp Nichol). *Back to the war* (2005) is a straightforward, appealing collection of seventy-five poems that draw on Davey's childhood: '"I don't love you any more," I pout./ "As long as you don't love me any less," my mother says.' ('The bath'.)

As a critic and essayist Davey takes sometimes polemical positions that are exemplified in *From there to here: a guide to Canadian literature since 1960* (1974), and in the influential essay 'Surviving the paraphrase' (1976), later collected in a volume of the same title (1983). He subjected much of his own early work to a critical re-evaluation in *Reading Canadian reading* (1988). More recent collections include *Post-national arguments: the politics of the anglophone-Canadian novel since 1967* (1993), *Canadian literary power* (1994), and *Cultural mischief: a practical guide to multiculturalism* (1996). Always provocative, often uncomfortable, Davey's criticism is among the most individual and influential ever written in Canada.

In *How Linda died* (2001) Davey documents the last fifteen months of his wife's life—she died from a brain tumour in 2000—in detailed but interesting and poignant journal entries that describe Linda's steady decline and the matter of coping, not only on her part but on the part of her son and daughter and of Frank Davey himself, whose conflicting emotions he records openly in a moving family memoir. *Mr & Mrs G.G.: the media princess & the court philosopher* (2003) is about Adrienne Clarkson—particularly in the role of Governor General—and her husband John Ralston SAUL. Based on press clippings and Davey's reading of their respective books, it is an ambivalent portrait, focusing partly on Adrienne Poy's not being a typical immigrant, arriving in Canada at a young age with prosperous Chinese parents, speaking English, achieving a good education at Trinity College, University of Toronto, and the Sorbonne, and developing into a sophisticated woman. Thinly veiled racism and sexism in the criticism of Clarkson, and those issues themselves, are analyzed repeatedly, along with the suitability/unsuitability of Clarkson's governmental appointment; her successes are not ignored. On Saul, Davey is harder.

David, Jennifer. See ABORIGINAL LITERATURE: 5.

'David'. Earle BIRNEY's classic narrative poem, written in 1940, is about two students, Bob and David, who like mountain climbing in the Rockies. On their last climb, Bob loses his foothold; David stretches out his arm to steady him and loses *his* foothold. 'Without/ A gasp he was gone.' He fell to a ledge fifty feet below. Bob works his way down to him to find him alive, but pinned to an outcrop of rock that had pierced his back; he is paralysed. Emotional exchanges lead to David's pleading: 'For God's sake push me over!... I'd do it for you, Bob.' Bob gives in to him (this is not mentioned)—'That day, the last of my youth, on the last of our mountains.' 184 lines, in 4-line stanzas and nine sections, the poem was included in *David and other poems* (1942), which won a Governor General's Award. It captured the readers' imagination with its depiction of youthful excitement, physical adventure, suspense, tragedy, and guilt—all suffused with diction that encapsulates nature in the Rockies. The poem was inspired by the mountain-climbing death in 1927 of Birney's friend David Warden, a clever, handsome fellow-student of English literature at UBC.

Davies, Robertson (1913–95). William Robertson Davies was born in Thamesville, Ontario, and attended Queen's University, Kingston, and Balliol College, Oxford, where he took his B.Litt. in 1938. He then joined the Old Vic Company for two seasons of acting bit parts, teaching theatre history in its school, and doing literary work for Tyrone Guthrie, the director. Returning to Canada, Davies became literary editor of *Saturday Night* in Toronto from 1940 to 1942, then editor of the *Peterborough Examiner* (a paper his father owned), and in 1946 owner (with his two brothers). Until 1960 he threw his considerable 'leisure' energies into theatre, writing and directing plays for the Little Theatre and for several professional companies. He served on the board of the Stratford Festival from 1953 to 1971. He moved to Toronto in 1963 as Master of Massey College, University of Toronto, teaching in the English department and the Drama Centre until he retired in 1981. His many books encompass not only plays and the novels that have won him international renown, but criticism, belle lettres, stories, and speeches. He was made a Companion of the Order of Canada (1972), an honorary member of the American Academy and Institute of Arts and Letters (1980)—the first Canadian to be so honoured—and in 1986 Honorary Fellow of Balliol College. Among his many honorary degrees are a D. Litt. from Oxford (1991), and another from the University of Wales (1995).

Neither his journalism nor his drama is as important as the fiction that in the 1970s won Davies international recognition. Earlier he wrote *Tempest-tost* (1951, rpr. 2006), *Leaven of malice* (1954, rpr. 2006), and *A mixture of frailties* (1958, rpr. 2006), novels linked by their setting in the university town of Salterton (inspired by Kingston, Ontario) and by the recurrence of several characters. (All three novels are available in one volume as *The Salterton trilogy*, 1989.) They have rightly been called satiric romances, for their plots are romantic and their omniscient narrator observes the foibles of small-town Ontario sharply, but they are also nicely constructed comedies of manners. *Tempest-tost*, the slightest of the three, pursues the various stages of the local Little Theatre's production of Shakespeare's *The Tempest* and contains Davies' first examination of a crisis of middle age. In *Leaven of malice*, a false engagement notice in Salterton's *Evening Bellman* initiates a series of reactions that bring about the unmasking of the malicious prankster and the publication of a genuine engagement notice. *A mixture of frailties*, conceptually the most adventurous of the three, explores the transformation of an amateur into an internationally acclaimed singer and articulates Davies' deepest convictions about the nature of art. It includes the production of an opera called *The golden ass*, after Apuleius, described as 'one of the oldest and best stories in the world'. In the winter of 1999, Randolph Peters' opera *The golden ass*, for which Davies wrote the libretto, was given a highly praised premiere by the Canadian Opera Company.

Davies' reading of the works of C.G. Jung in the fifties and sixties had a strong impact on his writing. Where earlier he had turned away from images and ideas that rose unbidden in dream and vision, he now opened himself to them. He came to see the writer as giving shape to the archetypal material rising from the unconscious. As a result, in the Deptford trilogy—*FIFTH BUSINESS* (1970, rpr. 2005), *The manticore* (1972; rpr. 2005; GGA), and *World of wonders* (1975, rpr. 2005)—he wrote fictional autobiography or 'confession', in which the underlying presence of the archetypes is palpable. (Confession is one of the four categories of prose fiction Northrop FRYE defines in his 'Theory of genres', the fourth essay in his *Anatomy of criticism*.) This was a happy shift for Davies, since theoretical and intellectual interests (always an aspect of his writing) are as central to confession as presentation of character. In *Fifth business*, the master work of the trilogy, Dunstan Ramsay tells the story of his life as a memoir to be read after his death. He can thus speak frankly as he tells how ducking a stone-laden snowball—which stuns Mary Dempster, who gives premature birth to a son, Paul—resulted in his lifelong fascination with saints and his brush with the devil. Paul Dempster, who left his mother when he was young, enters Ramsay's life under another name, the world-famous magician Magnus Eisengrim. In *The manticore*, the story of Boy Staunton, thrower of the fateful snowball, the narrator is revealed indirectly as his son, the eminent lawyer David Staunton, who undergoes a Jungian analysis. David tells his (and his father's) story, in a series of notebooks as he enters, experiences, and finishes treatment. In *World of wonders* Davies supplies yet another context for his first-person narrative. As historian, creating a 'document' on a great man, Dunstan provides a verbatim record of Eisengrim's recounting, over a series of lunches and dinners, the surprising life that began prematurely as a result of his mother's being hit by the snowball. Eisengrim reveals himself broadly knowledgeable about carnivals, vaudeville, travelling theatre companies, mechanical toys, and the nineteenth-century illusions of Robert Houdin. *The Deptford trilogy* (1983) is available in one volume.

Davies' international reputation was confirmed and expanded by the Cornish trilogy. In *The REBEL ANGELS* (1981, rpr. 2008), *What's bred in the bone* (1985, rpr. 1997), and *The lyre of Orpheus* (1988) he considered the character and the underpinnings of the culture that had sustained him, and celebrated Canada's cultural coming of age with stories that present Canadians as full participants in Western civilization. The story of *The rebel angels* is unfolded by two narrators—Maria Magdalena Theotoky, a graduate student, and Simon Darcourt, a middle-aged priest and professor—and takes as its subject the nature of a university. In the remaining books of the trilogy Davies shifted his form once again, writing novels that have glints of romance and strong interests in art and in opera. In *What's bred in the bone*, the trilogy's fulcrum, the angel of biography reveals the life of the artist and collector Francis Cornish and, from time to time, discusses it with Francis's daimon from the chilly perspective of eternity. The record reveals how a boy born in Blairlogie, Ontario (which draws on Davies' painful recollections of Renfrew) became a master painter in the manner of the Renaissance, and it explores the subtle relationships between art, deception, and truth. *The lyre of Orpheus* is told omnisciently, but is centred, as was *The rebel angels*, in the perceptions of Maria Magdalena Theotoky and Simon Darcourt. As in *What's bred in the bone*, there is comment on events from the spirit world—this time by E.T.A. Hoffmann in Limbo. *Lyre* presents two intertwined stories—one concerning the creation and production of an opera from fragments left by Hoffmann, and the other about the researching and writing of the biography of Francis Cornish. *Lyre* also gathers, re-states, and expands many of the themes and ideas of the Salterton and Deptford trilogies. The one-volume *Cornish trilogy* was first published in 1992.

The linked series that began with *Murther and walking spirits* (1991, rpr. 1997) and *The cunning man* (1994, rpr. 1996), had Davies lived to write its third volume might well have been called his Canadian trilogy, for the two

completed books explore the roots of contemporary Canada. *Murther and walking spirits* is told by a ghost who finds himself coming to a fresh understanding of himself after death. He watches and learns and changes as events unfold in time present and as a series of films acquaints him with the lives of his forebears that shaped his own life in fundamental ways. These forebears were based on Davies' own, and, in his view, are characteristic of Canada's immigrants in that they were forced to leave lands they loved and to make their way in a place where life was limited and hard. *The cunning man* is a 'confession', telling the story of a doctor who chooses to treat both body and soul. Characteristically, Davies placed this life in the larger scheme of things through references to myth and to classical texts, here primarily Sir Thomas Browne's *Religio medici* and Robert Burton's *The anatomy of melancholy*. As in *Fifth business*, the story is concerned with the making of a saint, and, as in *The rebel angels* and *Murther and walking spirits*, with a murder. *The cunning man* also explores Toronto's cultural life from the 1930s to the 1970s—particularly as manifested in participants in the Hart House Theatre and in key (recognizable) musicians.

Davies' lively and topical plays of the forties and fifties made him Canada's most important playwright for a time. A recurrent theme is Canada's failure to see art as essential to its development into a civilized nation. *Overlaid* (1948)—which was reprinted in his one-act collection, *Eros at breakfast and other plays* (1949), along with the title play, *Hope deferred*, *The voice of the people*, and *At the gate of the righteous*—is deservedly his most frequently performed play. In it the life-enhancing force of art meets temporary defeat at the hands of respectability as 'Pop' relinquishes a cultural spree in New York to his daughter's yearning for a solid granite family tombstone. The full-length *Fortune, my foe* (1949)—which was reissued with *Eros at breakfast* in 1993—and *At my heart's core* (1950)—which was reissued with *Overlaid* in 1991—reveal Davies effectively manipulating his broader theatrical resources. Three plays are associated with the Crest Theatre, Toronto. *A jig for the gypsy* (1954) had its first production there, as did the specially commissioned *Hunting Stuart* the following year. *General confession*, also commissioned, was completed in 1958 but never produced. *Hunting Stuart* and *General confession* were published, along with the earlier *King phoenix*, in *Hunting Stuart and other plays* (1972); and *Hunting Stuart* was reissued with *The voice of the people* in 1994. In the Crest plays, art, magic, imagination, and love triumph. The highly theatrical Jungian play *General confession* is particularly wise in its depiction of the human condition. In it, the aged Casanova summons the spirits of Voltaire, the Ideal Beloved, and Cagliostro, and with them acts out key incidents in his life. The play ends with a trial in which the spirits accuse, defend, and try Casanova and through which he gains self-acceptance. Davies' adaptation of his novel *Leaven of malice*—titled *Love and libel* for its staging in 1960 and renamed *Leaven of malice* when he adapted it afresh for productions in 1973 and 1975—was published in *Canadian Drama* 7, no. 2 (1981). *Question time* (1975)—a Jungian play in which Canada's prime minister undergoes an identity crisis that has national implications—appeared in print soon after it was produced at the St Lawrence Centre, Toronto.

Davies had a distinctive career as a journalist. He made the *Examiner* one of the most frequently quoted papers in Canada. His weekly Saturday column of urbane and witty comment on the Canadian scene, written under the pseudonym 'Samuel Marchbanks' for the *Examiner* and for several other papers between 1943 and 1953, yielded four books: *The diary of Samuel Marchbanks* (1947), *The table talk of Samuel Marchbanks* (1949), *Marchbanks' almanack* (1967), and *The papers of Samuel Marchbanks* (1985), which gathers the earlier books into a 'scholarly edition', with explanatory notes by Marchbanks' old academic friend and look-alike, Robertson Davies. In *A voice from the attic* (1960), which includes some of the review articles Davies wrote for *Saturday Night* during his second stint as its literary editor from 1953 to 1959 along with fresh material, Davies argued that Canada needed intelligent, literate, general (as opposed to professional) readers as a stimulus to writers and as the basis of civilized life. The quality and range of his journalism are also evident in *One half of Robertson Davies: provocative pronouncements on a wide range of subjects* (1977), *The enthusiasms of Robertson Davies* (1979, rev. 1990), *The well-tempered critic: one man's view of theatre and letters in Canada* (1981), *The merry heart: selections 1980–1995* (1996, rpr. 1998), and *Happy alchemy: writings on the theatre and other lively arts* (1997, rpr. 1998). Not to be forgotten is *High spirits: a collection of ghost stories* (1982, rpr. 2007). See Judith Skelton Grant's selection of Davies' letters, *For your eyes alone: letters 1976–1995* (1999, rpr. 2000) and *Discoveries* (2002), covering the years 1938–75. See also Grant's magnificent biography, *Robertson Davies: man of myth* (1994),

which draws on a long series of interviews with Davies. *Robertson Davies: an appreciation* (1991) is a collection of essays edited by Elspeth CAMERON. James Channing compiled *The quotable Robertson Davies: the wit and wisdom of the Master* (2005). The late Val Ross's *Robertson Davies: a portrait in mosaic* (2008) is an oral biography incorporating the memories and comments of more than 100 people, including Davies' widow Brenda, their three daughters, many students, and Margaret ATWOOD and Alice MUNRO.

Day, Frank Parker (1881–1950). Born in Shubenacadie, Nova Scotia, and educated at Pictou Academy and Mount Allison University, he attended Oxford University as New Brunswick's second Rhodes Scholar and later studied at the University of Berlin. From 1909 to 1912 he was a professor of English at the University of New Brunswick. He then moved to the United States and taught English at the Institute of Technology, Swarthmore, and from 1929 to 1933 was president of Union College, Schenectady, N.Y. In the Great War he served in the Canadian army; he was promoted to the rank of colonel at Amiens and was commanding officer of the 25th Overseas Battalion. In middle life Day became a writer, the author of three novels and a work of non-fiction. In his best-known novel, *Rockbound* (1928; rpr. 1973; rev. edn 1989)—a realistic account of life in a primitive south-shore fishing community of Nova Scotia in the decade preceding the Great War—the passions of ambition, greed, and jealousy are exposed. Day depicts the narrow, harsh, and primitive life of the Rockbound Island fishermen and their families against the hostile and often violent background of the Atlantic. In *John Paul's rock* (1932) the central character is a Micmac (Mi'kmaq) who has run from the white man's law to live in isolation among the many lakes and barrens of inland Nova Scotia. In his solitude John Paul attempts to come to terms with God through the folklore of Glooscap and the morality of his Native background. In Day's *Autobiography of a fisherman* (1927, rpr. 2005) he demonstrates his deep knowledge of inland fishing and his close familiarity with nature.

Deacon, William Arthur (1890–1977). Born in Pembroke, Ontario, and raised in Stanstead, Québec, he was educated at Stanstead College and Victoria College, University of Toronto, which he left at the end of his second year. In 1918 he earned his LL.B. at the University of Manitoba and later joined the Pitblado law firm in Winnipeg. Meanwhile, he had developed an intense enthusiasm for literature and underwent years of rigorous self-training in writing, publishing essays and reviews in Canadian and American periodicals. In 1922 he left Winnipeg and went to Toronto, where he was hired as literary editor of *Saturday Night*. Deacon's six years there—which coincided with, and reflected, a period of buoyant Canadian nationalism—were stimulated by his enthusiastic commitment to the encouragement of Canadian writers, and to the building of a reading public for their work. He published two essay collections: *Pens and pirates* (1923), humorous and whimsical pieces on a wide range of topics; and *Poteen* (1926), essays on national themes and a lengthy critical discussion of Canadian literature. *The FOUR JAMESES* (1927) is a comic celebration of four of Canada's best bad poets—the work for which he is best remembered. All Deacon's writing in this decade was marked by an intense Canadian cultural nationalism (and some wit). Dismissed from *Saturday Night* in April 1928, after a series of disagreements over the editor Hector CHARLESWORTH's editorial policies, Deacon began syndicating book reviews in newspapers across Canada. Within a few months he was working almost exclusively for Toronto's *Mail and Empire*. When it was sold to the *Globe* in 1936, he became literary editor of the new *Globe and Mail*, a position he held until 1960.

Always active in the Toronto branch of the CANADIAN AUTHORS' ASSOCIATION, and becoming national president in 1946, he formed committees that produced a standard book contract and secured from the federal government special income tax provisions for Canadian writers. He had helped to establish the GOVERNOR GENERAL'S LITERARY AWARDS in 1937, under the aegis of the CAA, and served as chairman of the Awards Board from 1944 to 1949. Deacon's extensive papers, housed in the Thomas Fisher Rare Book Library of the University of Toronto, bear impressive testimony to his unstinting encouragement of Canadian writers, and to their eager and grateful response. See Clara THOMAS and John Lennox, *William Arthur Deacon: a Canadian literary life* (1982), and John Lennox and Michèle Lacombe, eds, *Dear Bill: The correspondence of William Arthur Deacon* (1988).

de la Roche, Mazo (1879–1961). She was born Maisie Roche in Newmarket, Ontario (though she invented a Toronto birthplace and name for herself) to lower middle-class parents who moved frequently in an unsuccessful search of economic betterment. Educated at various public schools, she began early to immerse herself in a world of fantastic invention that took the form of what she called 'the Play'. The entry into the family, when she was sixteen, of her younger cousin and lifelong companion, Caroline Clement, further enriched this activity. A fantasy narrative enacted daily by the two adolescents, and continued into old age, the Play nourished the writer's imagination ever after. Having published a short story in the *Atlantic Monthly* in 1915, de la Roche was more than halfway through her life before the appearance of her first book-length work, *Explorers of the dawn* (1922), a collection of stories about three boys set in the never-never land of Edwardian domesticity. *Possession* (1923) continued the search for a workable setting, as its opening idyll yields to the grim realism of the life she knew from her family's unsuccessful venture into fruit farming near Bronte, Ontario. *Delight* (1926) presented de la Roche's readers with her first memorable protagonist, Delight Mainprize, a passionate misfit harassed by her stodgy neighbours; it draws heavily on the time her family spent in Acton, Ontario. In 1927, in her late forties, de la Roche entered a long period of fame with the publication of *JALNA*, a novel about the Whiteoaks family, whose existence was centred on a house called 'Jalna', an amalgam of several grand houses the writer had observed in the neighbourhood of Clarkson, Ontario. (The Play provided many of its characters and situations.) *Jalna* won the *Atlantic Monthly's* highly publicized first-novel prize, and de la Roche was duly fêted and lauded—and prodded to produce more stories about the Whiteoaks family. She had not thought of producing serial fiction—her time frame in *Jalna* was too articulated to make such an enterprise a simple one. Nonetheless, encouraged mightily by her publisher, she wrote fifteen sequels (which provided her with an opulent lifestyle) that moved either backward or forward in time from the opening centre. After her death, Robertson DAVIES called the series 'the most protracted single feat of literary invention in the brief history of Canada's literature'. The titles are *Jalna* (1927, rpr. 2006), *Whiteoaks of Jalna* (1929, rpr. 2006), *Finch's fortune* (1931, rpr. 2007), *The master of Jalna* (1933, rpr. 2007), *Young Renny* (1935), *Whiteoak harvest* (1936), *Whiteoak heritage* (1940), *Wakefield's course* (1941), *The building of Jalna* (1944), *Return to Jalna* (1946), *Mary Wakefield* (1949), *Renny's* *daughter* (1951), *Whiteoak brothers* (1953), *Variable winds at Jalna* (1954), *Centenary at Jalna* (1958), and *Morning at Jalna* (1960). By 1966 the series had sold 11 million copies, with translations in nine languages. A dramatized version (*Whiteoaks*) of the first two novels played successfully in London from 1936 to 1939, and the film *Jalna* appeared in 1935. Various radio versions of the series appeared over the years. A 1972 CBC television production was a failure; yet a 1994 version on a French public channel, starring Danielle Darrieux as Gran, proved wildly popular and was televised on Radio-Canada.

Jalna and its successors concern themselves first of all with a house and an estate governed by Adeline Whiteoak (Gran), a vital, high-spirited, tyrannical Upper Canadian version of Victoria Regina. She and her grandson Renny, an Ontario Heathcliff, do not so much govern Jalna as power it. Their tempestuousness and anti-intellectualism are offset by the troubled Finch (named after the Toronto academic and poet Robert FINCH), the artistic brother whose temperament most resembles his creator's; his financial sacrifice saves Jalna at a crucial point. The many characters share an inexhaustible interest in each other's doings and passions, particularly the latter. Often quarrelsome, they remain loyal to each other. Credibility necessitated the death of Gran; the need for new material introduced a less-interesting generation (because less known to the author); and imagination waned, along with de la Roche's life. Still, an Upper Canadian myth of creation and decline articulates itself. The series epitomizes the colonial mentality in its unswerving allegiance to British institutions and mores, and conveys the Loyalist myth of a Canada redeemed by its British allegiance—and the myth of a humane, harmless gentry—though the author does not flinch from observing the ebbing of the material foundations for that cultural stance. By the series' conclusion, burgeoning modernity, American in origin, with television as its primary exemplar, has irrevocably altered the culture surrounding the property. Yet Jalna, the house, remains the great good place. The series is a soap opera in its narrative structure, but it is nonetheless ideologically weighted. Only within imperial-colonial arrangements could the obsessions about family and the often unconventional vitality sustaining the Whiteoaks be possible. Whether or not Jalna's Ontario ever existed is of less interest than the tightness with which de la Roche entwined strong colonial and familial values.

De la Roche wrote numerous other books. Her dateless autobiography, *Ringing the changes* (1957), in which fact and fiction combine, highlights her United Empire Loyalist ancestry. *Selected stories of Mazo de la Roche*, edited by Douglas Daymond, was published in 1979. See Joan GIVNER's *Mazo de la Roche: the hidden life* (1989), which boldly uses the fiction to illuminate many previously unrecorded details of the author's life, and Givner's novel *Playing Sarah Bernhardt* (2004), which focuses mainly on a play about Mazo de la Roche and Caroline.

de Lint, Charles (b. 1951). Born in Bussum, The Netherlands, and brought to Canada four months later, he grew up in a number of cities in Ontario and abroad; but from the age of eleven he has lived in the vicinity of Ottawa, where he now lives with his wife Maryanne Harris. Through the late 1970s and early 1980s he worked in record stores through the week and played with a Celtic band on weekends (he remains active as a musician), all the while writing urban fantasies about the work of magic in modern society. He sold three novels in 1983 and since then has been a full-time writer, publishing some sixty novels and story collections for an obviously loyal readership in North America. Many of his novels are set in Ottawa, but some take place in the fictional city of Newford. Among his major urban fantasies—or 'mythic fictions', as he calls them—are *Moonheart: a romance* (1984), *The wild wood* (1994, rpr. 2004), *Trader* (1996), *Forests of the heart* (2000), in which the Montreal ice storm of 1998 gives rise to the ancient Celtic Green Man, *The onion girl* (2001), and *Spirits in the wires* (2003). Jilly Coppercorn in *The onion girl* is very much present in *Widdershins* (2006), a huge novel (almost 500 pages)—we are told that to walk 'widdershins' is to walk counterclockwise or backward around something—and in *Promises to keep* (2007): Jilly—recovering from a troubled past—finds herself in an alternate world that offers the life she's always wanted. *The blue girl* (2004, rpr. 2006) is a novel for young adults. De Lint's short stories, characterized by Celtic lyricism and character analysis, are in his collections *Dreams underfoot* (1993) and *The ivory and the horn* (1995). He has also published three horror novels as Samuel M. Key.

De Lint won the World Fantasy Award for *Moonlight and vines* (1999) and *Little (grrl) lost* (2007). Seven of his novels are in the 'Reader's List' of the Modern Library's '100 Best Novels': *Yarrow: an autumn tale* (1986), *Greenmantle* (1988), *The little country* (1991), *Memory and dream* (1994), *Trader* (1996), *Someplace to be flying* (1998), and *Mulengro* (2003).

Delta (1957–66). Edited, printed, and published by Louis DUDEK in twenty-six issues between Oct. 1957 and Oct. 1966, *Delta* offered poems, mostly by younger Canadian writers, but also quotations from Dudek's personal readings in politics, science, and sociology, and occasionally poems, essays, and reviews by Dudek himself. Reflecting Dudek's conviction that poetry was an essential part of intellectual life, inseparable from the chief issues of its time, *Delta* was clearly a vehicle for his personal views of literature, but it also assisted younger writers and welcomed new developments.

De Mille, James (1833–80). Born in Saint John, New Brunswick, he was educated at the Horton Academy and Acadia College in Wolfville, and at Brown University, Providence, Rhode Island. In 1858 he married Elizabeth Ann Pryor, the daughter of the first president of Acadia University. He taught classics at Acadia from 1861 to 1865, and then taught history, rhetoric, and literature at Dalhousie College, Halifax, until his death.

De Mille was one of North America's most popular novelists in the last quarter of the nineteenth century. His intricate plots, deft handling of comedy and suspense, and gift for dialogue—the raciest and slangiest since T.C. HALIBURTON's Clockmaker stories—contributed to this popularity. In his haste to publish, De Mille padded excessively and occasionally left his plots with crude endings; yet his books reflected his own delight in linguistic puzzles and puns and his hatred of sham and humbug. Indeed, his 'potboilers' (as he called them) were often parodies of Victorian fictional realism through the use of narrative techniques now associated with postmodernist novels. He wrote historical romances, 'international' novels of manners and adventure, and sensational novels of mystery and ratiocination. His archetypal situation is a voyage, for pleasure or escape, by a group of men and women. Before the denouement the protagonist becomes increasingly obsessed, even temporarily insane, and each novel centres on one or more poetic scenes evoking terror. De Mille's questioning of traditional religious beliefs and contemporary values became an important motif underlying the surface humour and irony of his fiction. His first hit, *The dodge club; or, Italy in MDCCCLIX* (New York, 1869; rpr. 1981), a series of comic sketches about American tourists in war-torn Italy, spoofs national traits

and flatters De Mille's American readers with the first of his gallery of sharp-witted Yankees. The same setting reappears in *The American baron; a novel* (New York, 1872) and in *The babes in the wood: a tragic comedy; a tale of the Italian Revolution of 1848* (New York, 1875). *The lady of the ice; a novel* (New York, 1870; rpr. 1973), a first-person narrative about the foibles of two British garrison officers at Québec, contains a satiric explanation of the Fenian takeover of the United States and an Irish parody of Homer's *Iliad*. *A comedy of terrors* (New York, 1872) has a spectacular balloon escape from Paris during the Franco-Prussian war. De Mille's imitations of the mysteries popularized by Poe, Dickens, and Wilkie Collins—*Cord and creese; a novel* (New York, 1869), *The cryptogram; a novel* (New York, 1871; rpr. 1973), and *The living link, a novel* (New York, 1874)—are exciting, carefully convoluted stories of secret codes and assumed identities. The simpler plot of *The lily and the cross; a tale of Acadia* (Boston, 1874) deals with the rescue of a French woman from Louisbourg by an American-raised Frenchman—anticipating Charles G.D. ROBERTS' treatment of a similar theme. *A strange manuscript found in a copper cylinder* (New York, 1888; CEECT, 1986; rpr. 2000; Bakka Books edn 2001) is the most complex and philosophical nineteenth-century Canadian novel. Possibly written in the 1860s, it was published posthumously to cash in on the fashion for fantasy travels to imaginary societies—and anonymously, to protect its copyright. Adam More, a practical British seaman, narrates his experiences among the Kosekin of Antarctica, and his story is framed by the commentary of four yachtsmen on a pleasure cruise who discover a cylinder, floating in the sea, that contains the manuscript and take turns reading it aloud. In the tradition of Thomas More's *Utopia*, Swift's *Gulliver's travels*, and Poe's *Narrative of Arthur Gordon Pym*, De Mille organizes his double-edged satire around the Kosekins' worship of poverty, darkness, and death to present a mirror reflection of European values; but what first appears as superior to them is ultimately revealed as far worse.

One of the first Canadians to write for boys, De Mille avoided the overt didacticism commonly found in children's literature of the time. The Brethren of the White Cross series, drawing on the author's boyhood pranks around the Minas Basin, includes *The 'B.O.W.C.'* (Boston, 1869), *The boys of Grand Pré school* (Boston, 1870), *Lost in the fog* (Boston, 1870), *Fire in the woods* (Boston, 1872), *Picked up adrift* (Boston, 1872), and *The treasure of the seas* (Boston, 1873). The Young Dodge Club series, which includes *Among the brigands* (Boston, 1871), *The seven hills* (Boston, 1873), and *The winged lion; or, stories of Venice* (New York, 1877), recounts the European adventures of four teenaged boys. Other works by De Mille include the comic poem 'Sweet maiden of Passamaquoddy' ('... Shall we seek for communion of souls/Where the deep the Mississippi meanders,/Or the distant Saskatchewan rolls?...').

Denison, Merrill (1893–1975). Playwright, journalist, raconteur, broadcaster, historian, summer-resort owner (at Bon Echo, Ontario), conservationist, and man of many other interests and abilities, Denison was born in Detroit, Michigan, of a Canadian mother and an American father. His early training was in architecture at the universities of Toronto and Pennsylvania, but he soon turned to writing as his profession. Denison's output in many literary forms was prodigious; its quality, however, ranged from the first-rate to the embarrassing. His major contribution to Canadian letters was as a playwright. Throughout the 1920s he was at the forefront of Canada's Little Theatre movement as designer, actor, and playwright for Toronto's Hart House Theatre. Denison published some of his best work in *The unheroic North: four Canadian plays* (1923), containing *Brothers in arms, The weather breeder, From their own place,* and *MARSH HAY* (1973). Set in the backwoods of northern Ontario, the plays gently satirize the eccentricities and pretensions of backwoods people, astutely capturing their environment and the ironies of their various predicaments. Only *Marsh hay*, a full-length play, takes on a sombre note, illuminating what Denison saw as the tragic futility of his characters' lives. In all four plays Denison was in full command of structure and dialogue. *The prize winner* (1928) is an effective one-act comedy dealing with a down-at-heel carnival road show; and *Balm*, published in *Canadian plays from Hart House*, vol. 1 (1926), is a perfectly constructed and perceptive short piece on the foibles of old age. Denison made a significant contribution to radio-drama (then in its infancy), though his achievement in this medium is less memorable than his stage plays. As a historian of Canadian commerce, he wrote three commissioned books: *Harvest triumphant: the story of Massey-Harris, a footnote to Canadian history* (1948), *The barley and the stream: the Molson story* (1955), and *Canada's first bank: a history of the Bank of Montreal* (2 vols, 1966, 1967).

Denison's first wife, Muriel, was the author of the successful Susannah series of children's books. Dick MacDonald's *Mugwump Canadian: the Merrill Denison story* (1973) is a skimpy biography padded with lengthy excerpts by Denison.

Descant (1970–). It began as a literary supplement to the Newsletter of the Graduate English Association, University of Toronto. In 1974 the magazine left the university, and under the editorship of Karen MULHALLEN has become one of Canada's major literary quarterlies for poetry, fiction, interviews, visual arts, sculpture, photographs, and even music. Always distinguished by fine production values, it is published by the Descant Arts & Letters Foundation. The magazine has long had an interest in international authors, and has published special issues on Greece, Australia and New Zealand, India, China, Turkey, North Africa, Venice, Latvia, and Cuba. It published special issues—one on Dennis LEE (no. 39, 1982), which was simultaneously released as a hardcover book, and on composer R. Murray Schafer, 'The labyrinth and the thread' (no. 73, 1991). In the 1980s the magazine turned its attention to theme issues, such as Comedy and the Sporting Life, Memory Work/Dreams, Male Desire, Blood Relations, and more recently Music and Memoir (no. 107, 1999), A Museum of War (no. 108, 2000), Barbara GOWDY (2006), Hotels (2008), Cats (2008), as well as annual anthologies. See *Paper guitar: 27 writers celebrate 25 years of Descant magazine* (1995) edited by Mullhallen. An index to issues 1–50 appeared in no. 58 (Fall 1989) and there is an updated index in no.133 (Summer 2006): 'An index to 35 years of *Descant*'.

Desrosiers, Léo-Paul (1896–1967). Born in Berthier-en-Haut, Québec, he studied law at the Université de Montréal and worked as Ottawa parliamentary correspondent for *Le Devoir* before abandoning journalism to devote himself more fully to writing. He was employed as French editor of the *Proceedings and orders of the House of Commons* from 1928 until 1941, when he became librarian of the Montreal Municipal Library, from which he retired in 1953. Among his novels, only one, *Les engagés du Grand Portage* (1938), appeared in English, translated by Christina van Oordt as *The making of Nicolas Montour* (1978). It is an important historical novel about an unscrupulous *voyageur* who climbs to the upper echelons of the North West Company in the highly competitive fur trade of the early

1800s. The harsh environment forms a backdrop to the realities of bitter personal rivalries. Narrated in an epic present tense, it is enhanced by a descriptive power that Desrosiers was to consolidate in later work.

Deverell, Rex (b. 1941). Born in Toronto and raised in Orillia, Ontario, he graduated from McMaster University with a B.A. in Arts in 1963, and in Divinity in 1966 (submitting his first play, *The invitation*, as a thesis); in 1967 he earned a master's degree from Union Theological Seminary, New York City. He now lives in Coldwater, Ontario. In 1971 Deverell and his actor wife Rita began a long association with Regina's Globe Theatre (1975–90), which toured several of his plays for children, including *Shortshrift* (1972), *The Copetown City kite crisis* (1974), and *The Shinbone General Store caper* (1977). Set in small prairie towns, these plays frequently involve audience participation, although this is usually secondary to Deverell's playful treatment of serious social issues. Appointed writer-in-residence at the Globe in 1975, Deverell soon turned to adult plays with *Boiler room suite* (1978), which received numerous productions across Canada. Here fantasy brightens the lives of two homeless outcasts who, with compassion and humour, expose flaws in the powerful institutions that have failed them. In *Drift* (1981) and *Righteousness* (1983) action centres on an artist/prophet figure who recognizes that he has fallen short. In *Beyond Batoche* (1985), published also in *Deverell of the Globe* (1989) edited by Don Perkins, a playwright writing a documentary exposes the screens through which people filter history, especially that relating to Louis Riel. *Medicare!* (1981) investigates the Saskatchewan doctors' strike of 1962, while *Black powder: Estevan 1931* (1982) deals with riots arising from a miners' strike. See also *Plays of belonging: three plays* (1997). Deverell has written most of his more than thirty plays specifically for the Globe's theatre-in-the-round, which encourages episodic structure and cinematic techniques. Underlying his work is sympathy for the underdog and a strong spiritual conviction expressed as the need for communal effort.

Deverell, William (b. 1937). Born in Regina, and raised there and in Saskatoon, where his father was a newspaper editor, Deverell graduated from the law school at the University of Saskatchewan in 1963 and moved to Vancouver to establish a law practice specializing in civil-liberties cases. After the success of his novel *Needles* (1979, rpr. 2002), he gradually withdrew from the legal profession and is currently a full-time writer living on North Pender Island, British Columbia. Lawyers figure centrally in most of his crime novels and fast-paced thrillers. In *Needles* a Vancouver lawyer and addict is pitted against Dr Au P'Ang Wei, the ruthless drug lord responsible for shipping Southeast Asian heroin to Vancouver. *High crimes* (1981, rpr. 2005) also has to do with drug smuggling, this time marijuana, from Colombia to Newfoundland. *The dance of Shiva* (1984, rpr. 2004) presents another Vancouver case, about a massacre in a commune at Om Bay ('actual name O'Malley Bay'), where the leader is Shiva Ram Acharya, a.k.a. Matthew Bartholomew James. *Mecca* (1983) is a long novel in an expert thriller vein about a terrorist organization called the Rotkommando whose power-mad leader becomes the adversary of a revolutionary Québécois, Jacques Sawchuk, who had been expelled to Cuba and who acquires cartoon-like superhuman powers to defeat him. In *Platinum blues* (1988, rpr. 2003) a lawyer who is raising two teenaged daughters on his own is thrust into the criminal world as he opposes a large California recording company and its lawyers. *Mindfield* (1989, rpr. 2005) is one of several books (among them Timothy FINDLEY's *The telling of lies*) based on the disgraceful practice of Dr Ewen Cameron at McGill University, Montreal, who developed brainwashing techniques for the CIA. *Kill all the lawyers* (1994, rpr. 2001) is a mystery novel involving the various agendas of members of a Vancouver law firm that feminists are likely to view as a mere wimp's sexist fantasy. Deverell's *Street legal: the betrayal* (1995, rpr. 2004) is a prequel to his long-running TV series, set in Toronto in 1980. In *Trial of passion* (1997, rpr. 2002) a leading criminal lawyer, Arthur Beauchamp, comes out of retirement in the Gulf Islands to defend the acting dean of law at the University of British Columbia accused of the rape of one of his students. It won the Hammett Prize for literary excellence in crime writing and the Arthur Ellis Award for Best Crime Novel. In *Slander* (1999, rpr. 2003), set in Seattle and Vancouver and partly about relationships, lawyer Elizabeth Finnegan takes on Hugh Vandergraaf, a Supreme Court judge with whom she has always been at loggerheads and whom she forces to stand trial for rape. In *The laughing falcon* (2001, rpr. 2002), set in Costa Rica, a mixture of exciting and romantic episodes involve some disparate characters, including Maggie Schneider, a romance writer from Saskatoon; Slack Cardinal, a tour guide; Benito Madrigal, a revolutionary who has been committed to an insane asylum; Senator 'Chuck' Walker, who has his eyes on the US presidency as a republican candidate and his wife Gloria-May; and 'Halcón the Laughing Falcon' whose real name is Juan Santamaria Diego (Johnny Diego), a self-styled revolutionary with a colourful past. The ambiance of *Mind games* (2003) is entirely different as Deverell creates suspense in telling the story of Dr Tim Dare, a forensic psychiatrist for the criminal courts in Vancouver who has been in contact with many disturbed people and seems to be falling apart himself. *April fool* (2005) delightfully brings back Arthur Beauchamp, of *Trial of passion*—and Garibaldi Island—when he reads of the arrest for murder of one of his old clients, the famous jewel thief Nick 'The Owl' Faloon; it won for Deverell his second Arthur Ellis Award. The well-reviewed *Kill all the judges* was published in 2008.

Deverell's narrative skill has also lent itself to a work of non-fiction, *Fatal cruise: the trial of Robert Frisbee* (1991)—centred on the murder of a rich widow on board an Alaska cruise ship. An account of Deverell's unsuccessful defence of Robert Frisbee, a manservant, against a charge of murdering her, it also treats relevant details before and after the crime, about the trial itself, and almost amounts to another Deverell novel.

Dewart, Edward Hartley (1828–1903). Born in Stradone, County Cavan, Ireland, Dewart was six years old when his parents settled in Dummer Township, Upper Canada (Ontario). He attended local schools and the provincial Normal School, entered the Methodist ministry in 1851, and was ordained in 1855. In 1879 he received a D.D. from Victoria University, Toronto. He held various posts in Canada East (Québec) and West (Ontario) until 1869, when he became editor of the Toronto *Christian Guardian*, remaining in that position until 1894. Dewart compiled the first and last collection of Canadian poetry prior to Confederation, *Selections from Canadian poets; with occasional critical and biographical notes, and an introductory essay on Canadian poetry* (Montreal, 1864). He attempted to preserve poetry that he feared would be lost. In his introductory essay he attributed the lack of acceptance for Canadian poetry to a general preference among the educated for poems inspired by the romantic past of the countries in which they were born, and argued for the role of poetry in building a national spirit. Dewart marked out 'a future bright with promise' as the alternative inspiration for Canadian poets.

Dewdney, Christopher (b. 1951). Born in London, Ontario, into a family of scientists and artists, he received his education through local public schools, the Beal Art Annex School in London, and from his father, Selwyn, an anthropologist, ethno-archaeologist, writer, and teacher. (See *Daylight in the swamp: memoirs of Selwyn Dewdney* [1997], edited by Keewatin Dewdney.) His life partner is Barbara GOWDY. Though he moved to Toronto in 1980, Christopher Dewdney's poetic vision is partly inspired by the geology of the coves of the oxbow lakes in southwestern Ontario. An early collection of poems entitled *A palaeozoic geology of London, Ontario* (1973) was illustrated with his own collages. He served as poetry editor at COACH HOUSE PRESS in 1988, was appointed in 1993 Fellow to the McLuhan Program in Culture and Technology (University of Toronto), and taught creative writing at York University, Toronto. Dewdney is a leading avant-garde poet and thinker. His poetry, published in journals across North America and in Britain, features a unique scientific idiom and oscillates between science and myth, reason and intuition, the empirical and the surrealistic, in its quest for the 'secular grail'—or a scientific explanation of the mystery of being. In his preface to *Predators of the adoration: selected poems 1972–82* (1983) he describes his father's introducing him to limestone, 'almost entirely composed of the shells & skeletons of underwater creatures, millions of years old, compacted and turned to rock. His explanation transformed the rock into a miraculous substance....' As Dewdney grew older, the direct experiential knowledge he acquired from nature 'formed much of my sense of how the world was structured. I was more alert to the animal sense of territorial mapping than I was to the human. The forest was a silent theatre in which I learned perceptual dialogues independent of language.... In a sense, then, this book is the voice of the land and the creatures themselves, speaking from the inviolate fortress of a primaeval history uncorrupted by humans. It is a codex of the plants and animals whose technology is truly miraculous, and for whom I am merely a scribe.' It includes work from five collections, up to *Alter sublime* (1980). *The radiant inventory* (1988) is a collection of poems and prose-poems in which lyrics have a personal thrust, while also being informed by a bonding with nature and science, even neurophysiology ('Knowledge of neurophysiology as defence against attack'). Dewdney's love and knowledge of nature informs most of the beautiful lyrics, which include some fine love poems, in

Dewdney

Demon pond (1994). His interest in natural history, dreams, parallel worlds, and arcane vocabulary (of which there are only touches) is evident, but the poems about the natural environment—there are many about wind—have a kind of magic and raise the Canadian nature poem to a new level of sensibility and originality. The poems in *Signal fires* (2000)—which includes Books III and IV of 'A natural history of southwestern Ontario', the first two parts of which had been previously published, and incorporates an erudite scientific vocabulary that seems to fascinate Dewdney alone—are most enjoyed for those about love: not only sexual love, but love of nature, passing time, and even of cities. *The natural history* (2002) is also inspired by Dewdney's love and knowledge of nature and is replete with esoteric diction, ('Dactyl leaves of the white oak. The/white-tailed deer are melanized/thermograms of themselves. A consensual/domain in the summer wasteland. Giant/Haida eyes stare from beech trunks,/their rapt bliss.' p. 60); memorable images ('The anvil/tops of cumulonimbus graze/the stratosphere, moonlight high over/ the storm witnessed by a small passenger/airliner lost in the thirties.' p. 23), and sudden erotic interjections: 'We make love in the rush/ of warm rain. Orgasm-shivers flash/neuronal like foxfire through our single/body.' p. 67). In spite of much rich imagery inspired by phenomena of Nature, as imagined by a passionate devotee, incomprehensibility is unfortunately the rule: this is not a coherent work. *Children of the outer dark: the poetry of Christopher Dewdney* (2007) contains thirty-five poems from the above books, selected with an introduction by Karl E. Jirgens; in an Afterword Dewdney reviews his career as a poet.

The immaculate perception (1986) is a collection of aphorisms and brief essays that explore the mysteries of the brain and 'the spectacle of consciousness embracing its own materiality. It also deals with … consciousness being duplicated by technology, matter mimicking mind.' Another prose work, *The secular grail: paradigms of perception* (1993), explores the late twentieth century in a collection of *pensées* that are often poetic and have links with his poems—under such headings as 'City States' (on cities), 'Hostages of Culture' (on the telephone, the fax, etc.), 'Intimate Strangers' (on love and relationships), 'Sleights of Mind' (on dreams), and 'Shadows of Thought' (on language)—that illuminate and interpret a multitude of components related to Western culture. *Acquainted with the night: excursions through the world after dark* (2004, rpr. 2005) may be Dewdney's most enjoyable book. Taking its title from Robert Frost's poem, it celebrates nighttime and a multitude of things associated with night in twelve chapters from 6 p.m. to 5 a.m., followed by 'Night's last stand': 'As mysteriously and incrementally as night arrived, it begins to fade away.' Each chapter contains brief essays on often unexpected but relevant subjects, such as 'The physics of sunsets', 'Time travel, the international date line, and the progress of night across the world', 'The eyes of night', 'Vampire bats', 'The bridge of dreams: four children's night classics', 'Nightclubbing', 'Light pollution', 'The heart of darkness', 'The night sky'—among many other subtitles that draw on Dewdney's knowledge of nature, of literature (there are many quotations from poems), and of popular culture. All this is informed by both personal experience (Dewdney loves night) and meticulous research. Some 300 pages in length, this is an imaginative and wonderful book. A similarly brilliant meditation on time is *The soul of the world: unlocking the secrets of time* (2008).

Di Cicco, Pier Giorgio (b. 1949). Born in Arezzo, Italy, he was brought by his parents to Montreal in 1952 and lived briefly in Toronto before his family moved to Baltimore, where Di Cicco received his early education. He returned to Canada in 1968 to attend high school and then the University of Toronto, where he studied creative writing under F.W. Watt and received a B.A. in English (1973), a B.Ed. in 1976, and a M.Div. in 1990. A Brother in the Order of St Augustine (1983–8), he was named Deacon and the Priesthood, Archdiocese of Toronto, 1993, and is associate pastor of St Margaret Mary Church. He was Poet Laureate, City of Toronto, from 2004 to 2007.

His first collection of poetry, *We are the light turning*, was published in 1975; but his writing did not come to public attention until it was anthologized in Al PURDY's *Storm warning II* (1976). Thereafter his poems appeared in many literary magazines in Canada and abroad. Writing with originality and honesty about a wide range of interests—from the Italo-Canadian experience to neo-surrealism—and employing a variety of forms, including surrealism and 'deep images' (images in which the vehicle tends to be both archetypal and subconscious), Di Cicco is a prolific poet: *We are the light* turning (1975, rev. 1976), *The sad facts* (1977), *The circular dark* (1977), *Dancing in the house of cards* (1977), *A burning patience* (1978), *Dolce-Amaro* (1978), *The tough romance* (1979, rpr. 1990), *A straw hat for everything* (1981), *Flying deeper into* the century (1982), *Dark to light: reasons for humanness: poems 1976–1979* (1983), *Women we never see again* (1984), *Post-sixties nocturne* (1985), *Virgin science: hunting holistic paradigms* (1986), *The city of hurried dreams: poems 1977–1983* (1993), *The honeymoon wilderness* (2002, rpr. 2004), *The dark time of angels* (2003), *Dead men of the fifties* (2004), and *The visible world* (2006). *Living in paradise: new and selected poems* (2001) has a long Afterword by Dennis LEE, who says: 'One of the pleasures of a Selected Di Cicco is the chance to follow a recurrent pattern: to watch his headlong energies achieve a momentary stability in the pivotal books; to see subsequent collections repeat that coherence at a lower intensity, or fumble towards uncharted possibilities; and then to see him break through to some unexpected new voice and thematic focus…. this openness, this refusal to solidify, is part of the vitality that keeps his best work so fresh.' The last section of *Living in paradise* is devoted to 'New poems (1985–2001)'. In Lee's words: 'Even a quick scan of the new poems shows that Di Cicco has been reaching in two directions. One is expansive, conversational, riffling through memories and reflections. The other is brief, contractive, imagistic. There's a distinctive music in each mode; they convey the texture of contemplative experience in very different ways.'

Di Cicco is the author of *Municipal mind: manifestos for the creative city* (2007), a series of brief prose pieces on the soul of the city, the worth and meaning of cities.

Dickson, Lovat (1902–87). Horatio (Rache) Lovat Dickson was born in New South Wales, Australia, the son of a mining engineer, and was taken to South Africa at the age of seven. He attended school in England from 1913 to 1917 before coming to Canada. He graduated from the University of Alberta in 1927, winning the Governor General's Gold Medal, and stayed on to lecture for a year. (His romantic novel, *Out of the west land*, 1944, is based in part on his arrival in Canada as a youth and on his life as a student in Alberta.) He then accepted the offer of a wealthy Canadian, who had bought the *Fortnightly Review*, to edit that periodical, and thus entered the London publishing world. (He also edited *The Review of Reviews* from 1931 to 1934.) In 1932 he started his own publishing firm, Lovat Dickson Limited, and in 1933 launched *Lovat Dickson's Magazine* to establish his imprint in the literary world. One of his first publishing successes was *Pilgrims of the wild* (1935); he made its author, Grey Owl (Archibald

Stansfeld BELANEY), a celebrity in England by arranging highly successful lecture tours for him in 1936–7 and 1937–8. In 1938 Dickson sold his publishing list to Peter Davies and joined the Macmillan Company as assistant editor of general books, working under Harold Macmillan, the editor. He became chief editor, and then a director of the firm in 1941; when he retired in 1967 he moved with his wife Marguerite to Toronto. He was an Officer of the Order of Canada.

Unlike many editors, Dickson was a born writer, with the literary skill to master a variety of subjects and present them in a graceful narrative. The subject with whom he was most identified as a biographer was Grey Owl, who became his friend. In 1938, shortly after Grey Owl's death, Dickson published *A green leaf: a tribute to Grey Owl*, which includes an affectionate account of Grey Owl's two visits to England, press commentaries, and Grey Owl's letters. *Half-breed: the story of Grey Owl* (1939), a somewhat romantic portrait, with lyrical descriptions of Grey Owl's Canadian wilderness, is based partly on anecdotes told by Grey Owl to the author; it was coloured by the desire to defend him against the charge of being an impostor. It was superseded by *Wilderness man: the strange story of Grey Owl* (1973; rpr. 1991), the product of assiduous research and greater objectivity, in which a complex and well-rounded Grey Owl emerges. Dickson's other biographies were *Richard Hillary* (1950), about the author of a classic war memoir, *The last enemy*, who was disfigured in the Second World War and later killed in action at twenty-three; *H.G. Wells: his turbulent life and times* (1969; rpr. 1971), a study of the author, with an emphasis on his works, that was written with the permission of two of Wells's sons and the encouragement of Rebecca West; and *Radclyffe Hall and the well of loneliness: a Sapphic chronicle* (1975), a biography of the lesbian novelist that Dickson was asked to write by her companion, Una Troubridge. Dickson's flair for relating the influential events and atmosphere of a life (in this case his own) came together most successfully in two volumes of memoirs: *The ante room* (1959, rpr. 1975), and *The house of words* (1973, rpr. 1976), which took him into his early years with Macmillan. *The museum makers: the story of the Royal Ontario Museum* (1986, rpr. 1993) is a readable, informative, concise history of this great museum.

Dictionary of Canadian biography/Dictionnaire biographique du Canada. The *DCB/DBC* is a comprehensive national historical dictionary written by authors from across, and outside, Canada. The project was launched in 1959 after the University of Toronto received a bequest from James Nicholson (1861–1952), a Toronto businessman, to establish a Canadian version of Britain's *Dictionary of national biography*. Since 1961 research, editing, translation, and publication in English and French have been carried out in offices at the University of Toronto and Université Laval, overseen by the general editor (John English from 2006) and *directeur général adjoint* (Réal Bélanger from 1998). Over the years the project has received significant funding from the Social Sciences and Humanities Research Council, other federal and provincial government agencies, foundations, and private donations. The project is also supported by significant volunteer effort, considering that the honoraria paid to authors do not compensate them for their work.

Between 1966 and 2005, fifteen volumes were published in English and French by the presses of the two universities. Volumes are organized chronologically by death date. Volume I comprises biographies of people who flourished or died between 1000 and 1700, and Volume XV covers those who flourished or died between 1921 and 1930. The entries vary in length, from 500 to 18,000 words (the longest are Sir John A. Macdonald in XII, Sir Wilfrid Laurier in XIV, and William Lyon Mackenzie King, available online). From the outset the *DCB/DBC* has been distinguished by three critical attributes. First, it includes figures who did not belong to the elite. A work both of scholarship and popular interest, it tells the story of Canada through biographies of leaders, followers, and outsiders. In rediscovering and revealing the lives of ordinary people representing every walk of life, the *DCB/DBC* creates a history of Canadians against a social, cultural, economic, and political background. Second, biographies are based on primary sources, so that many articles shed new, often surprising light on their subjects. Third, the project's editorial standards are among the highest in the world. Biographies are extensively edited in their original language, then translated and carefully revised to ensure accuracy and readability in the other language. Works listed in bibliographies are comprehensively checked. The result is 'the single most indispensable research tool in Canadian historical studies', according to John FRASER.

For a scholarly work sales have exceeded expectations, with more than 100,000 copies

sold in English. Over the course of its almost fifty-year history, the project has dramatically extended its reach because of the exponential growth of electronic publication. The contents of all fifteen volumes, as well as biographies of eight twentieth-century prime ministers and fifteen other major figures, are now available on a website maintained by Library and Archives Canada (www.biographi.ca)

In 2000 the *DCB/DBC* published and distributed widely a CD-ROM version of the fourteen volumes then in print. The following year the Department of Canadian Heritage, in conjunction with Library and Archives Canada, approached the two universities about establishing a website. In some quarters there were serious reservations about the public's interest in an electronic version of text-based scholarship. Nevertheless the project went online in both official languages in October 2003. It was in that year that the Canadian Historical Association affirmed that 'The *DCB/DBC* is regarded as a fundamental tool of research and teaching in Canada.... Its ready accessibility on the Web will give it even greater influence than it has enjoyed in the past thirty years.' The results have been astonishing and bear out this prediction. During the first month there were 5486 visits to the site. Three years later, in October 2006, the number had soared to 84,420, and in Feb. 2008 the figure was 170,679. Between April 2007 and 31 March 2008 1,385,726 researchers viewed 4,634,380 'pages', and the average visit was fourteen minutes long.

In print and online the *DCB/DBC* has been recognized as one of the finest creations of its kind in the world. Freely accessible online, the *DCB/DBC* provides an invaluable point of entry into Canada's past. For English- and French-speaking Canadians it is not only a scholarly resource, but surely strengthens the Canadian identity by encouraging a continuing dialogue.   JOHN ENGLISH

Dimaline, Cherie. See ABORIGINAL LITERATURE: 5.

di Michele, Mary (b. 1949). Born in Lanciano, Italy, she came to Canada at the age of six. She completed a B.A. in English at the University of Toronto (1972), and an M.A. in English and creative writing at the University of Windsor (1974). Since 1991 she has been a professor in the creative-writing program of Concordia University, Montreal. Di Michele's collections of poetry include *Tree of August* (1978); *Bread and chocolate* (1980), printed together with a sequence of poems by

Bronwen WALLACE; *Mimosa and other poems* (1981), of which the title poem won first prize in the 1980 CBC Literary Competition; *Necessary sugar* (1984); *Immune to gravity* (1986); *Luminous emergencies* (1990), which contains a sequence of Chilean poems based on a 1987 tour with poets Patrick LANE, Lorna CROZIER, and Gary GEDDES; *Stranger in you* (1995), new and selected poems; and *Debriefing the rose* (1998). Vivid images and metaphysical intensity characterize her lyrical poems. The early works explore the poet's Italian-Canadian heritage, her family, and her coming of age. An independent young girl's ambivalence towards patriarchal authority, as characterized by the father figure, is the basis of many poems and central to 'Mimosa', a sequence of monologues spoken by a father and his two daughters. Even in her earliest work, the poet's awareness of the power dynamics inherent in the confessional act transforms personal lyrics into self-conscious meditations on the writer's craft. In her later work she increasingly situates herself within larger contexts of her literary legacies (as in 'My hart crane' and 'Rilke Sentiero'), and of her political responsibilities as a feminist poet (see especially the Chilean poems in *Luminous emergencies*). In the prefatory chapter of di Michele's novel, *Under my skin* (1994), Rita Latte, at the reception she has arranged after a screening, decides to press on her towering, handsome boss a novel, which she tells him has film possibilities and is about 'a serial rapist who is a Dr Jekyll and Mr Hyde type character.' It is the novel we then read, about another Rita, her friends, and her doctor and his wife, in which di Michele the poet transforms her gifts in a compelling work that is both a romance and a taut psychological thriller. *Tenor of love* (2004, rpr. 2005) is a well-told romance, based on secondary sources, about Enrico Caruso and the women in his life: the opera singer Ada Giachetti, by whom he had two sons; her sister Rina, whom he also loved; and the American Dorothy Benjamin, whom he married in New York three years before he died in 1921. The author's Italian background, and some knowledge of the world of opera, serve her dramatic portrayal of aspects of Caruso's life.

See *Mary di Michele essays on her works* (2007) edited by Joseph Pivato.

Diviners, The (1974, GGA; NCL). Margaret LAURENCE's last novel is linked to earlier ones in the Manawaka cycle by the inclusion of characters such as Stacey MacAindra of *The fire-dwellers*, events such as the fiery death of Piquette Tonnerre, and objects such as Hagar Shipley's plaid pin from *The STONE ANGEL*. As in the earlier novels, the main character is a woman, but unlike the others Morag Gunn grows up in the poorest section of town, looked down upon by most of the townspeople, and leaves it as soon as she can, only to find that she carries it always in her head. The narrative traces her life from childhood poverty to work as a local journalist, through her years at university, early marriage to and divorce from a professor of English, her career as a successful novelist, the birth of her daughter, life as a single mother in Vancouver and England, and her eventual return to claim Canada as her homeland—loosely paralleling Laurence's own life story. The resemblance is clearest in the setting of the present where, like Laurence, Morag is writing a novel in her cabin on the banks of Ontario's Otonabee River. The river that seems to flow both ways as the wind blows against its current provides a metaphor for the simultaneous backward flow of memory and forward flow of time. Among the novel's large and varied cast of characters, Christie Logan, the most original creation, is a natural poet and storyteller whose knowledge of society from analysis of its garbage leads to his socialist philosophy and uninhibited, often very funny, commentary. Scavenging serves as a correlative for the writer's hoarding of seemingly irrelevant material picked up in unlikely places; and water divining, as the title suggests, is the key metaphor in the novel's exploration of the nature of writing. To Laurence, the art of writing is a gift of grace, a mystery as impossible to fathom as is the power to locate underground water. A film version of *The diviners* (1992) was directed by Anne Wheeler.

Divisadero (2007, GGA; rpr. 2008) by Michael ONDAATJE begins in California with a father and his three unrelated children. Anna is his daughter whose mother died in childbirth; Claire, born in the same hospital in the same week when *her* mother also died, is adopted (Anna's father claimed the hospital 'owed him something'); the hired hand Coop, a few years older, whose parents were murdered, becomes part of the family and lives in the cabin of the girls' grandfather, which he rebuilt. When Anna is sixteen, in love with Coop, she paints a table blue for him. Her father, who had ridden up to the cabin, discovers them making love and nearly kills Coop. Everything changes: Anna and Coop never see each other again.

Coop becomes a gambler. In Tahoe, aged twenty-three, he falls in with Edward Dorn and his group. Anna, who had been living in Divisadero Street in San Francisco and has been educated as a scholar of French literature, is working on the manuscripts and journals of a French writer named Lucien Segura and is living in his house at Dému in Gascony, France. She is drawn to a man playing a guitar in a field, accompanying a woman singing; thus Rafael, whose mother (Aria) was a gypsy, enters her life and they fall in love. Claire works for a defence lawyer in San Francisco and spends an hour or two on Friday nights with her father. She is sent to Tahoe on a job and runs into Coop. He, however, is involved with Bridget, a drug addict, and with a threatening group of gamblers, who in time beat him nearly to death. Claire finds him, but he has lost his memory.

The last hundred pages of the novel are mostly about Lucien Segura in various stages of his life, beginning when he is an old man, having left his wife and daughters, to find a new place to live. He meets a man who calls himself an 'old thief', his gypsy wife Aria, and their young son Rafael. When Ariel and Rafael go south to retrieve their caravan, there is an astonishing description of Rafael's command of a runaway horse during an eclipse. We read about Lucien's childhood, the removal of an eye after splinters from a shattered window pierced it, the arrival at the neighbouring one-room farmhouse of Roman and his young wife Marie-Neige—a year older than sixteen-year-old Lucien—who was 'coaxed out of the quicksand of illiteracy by his mother.' She and Lucien read stories together, and she attends his wedding. (We never meet his wife.) We read about Lucien's middle age as a writer, his daughter Lucette's love affair—before and after she married—with her sister's suitor Pierre and his seeing them make love. 'There were nights when Lucien startled himself awake at his daughter's wildness.' Lucien buys the property Marie-Neige lives on and turns it over to her. To examine the papers 'He made her sit at the blue table. It was the table he would take away from that small farmhouse some years later, and it became his dearest possession of his life.' He takes part in the Great War, not as a soldier but as a volunteer assisting with a study of disease (he catches diphtheria, and a full description of that disease follows). Marie-Neige, the great love of his life, dies near the end of the war. Working in her farmhouse, Lucien begins to write stories about Roman and Marie-Neige and they are so successful that the central characters become famous. Rafael 'mentioned that he was

reading the series of adventures about Roman, but Lucien Segura said nothing.' The novel ends when Anna, briefly recalling, or recreating, events in the pasts of Lucien and Rafael, says: 'He does not feel this present life is real without the boy.'

Anna explains that Divisadero comes from the Spanish word for 'division'. 'Or it might derive from the word *divisar*, meaning "to gaze at something from a distance".' This could apply to the book as a whole—to the events referred to above and to the characters. They are all distant—the characters are really just names—but as this is Ondaatje's chosen mode of writing, it has to be accepted and adjusted to. Many readers, through reviews, have admitted that making one's way through the novel is rewarding, passages of poetic writing are enjoyed, but some have had to read it twice.

Djwa, Sandra (b. 1939). Sandra Drodge was born in St John's, Newfoundland, and educated at Memorial University and the University of British Columbia (B. Ed., 1964, Ph.D., 1968). She married Peter Djwa in 1958 (they divorced in 1987) and Lalit Srivastava in 1991. She joined the English department of Simon Fraser University in 1968 and became a full professor in 1980 (she was the first female chair of the department [1986–1994]); she retired in 2003 and is now Professor Emerita. In the 1960s, when Canadian literature was not yet established, Djwa's essays, public lectures, contributions to books, and organizational activities began making their enormous contribution to the understanding and knowledge of Canadian literature. A co-founder of the Association of Canadian and Québec Literatures (ACQL), 1973–4, and a former editor of the annual review of Canadian poetry for the *University of Toronto Quarterly*, she is best known as a poetry critic (Margaret ATWOOD, Leonard COHEN, A.J.M. SMITH) and as a biographer of Canadian poets. The Newfoundland poet E.J. PRATT, understandably, was her first specialty. She wrote *E.J. Pratt: the evolutionary vision* (1974) and the introductory essay for (while co-editing) the *Selected poems of E.J. Pratt* (2000). In preparation for a biography of F.R. SCOTT, she organized an interdisciplinary symposium of distinguished speakers, 'The Achievement of F.R. Scott', which took place in Vancouver over two days in February 1981. (Djwa co-edited the proceedings, *On F.R. Scott: essays on his contributions to law, literature, and politics* [1983].) The biography that resulted, *The politics of the imagination: a life of F.R. Scott* (1987, rpr. 1989) is a triumph. The highly intelligent and sensitive use Djwa made of the enormous amount of research that went into it—correlating the life of Scott himself and Canadian political and cultural life—is greatly enhanced by her skill in making a complicated and detailed text clear and readable. This biography is perhaps her most notable single achievement. (A French translation by Florence Bernard, *F.R. Scott: une vie*, was published in Montreal in 2001.) Roy DANIELLS—scholar, teacher, and poet, who taught in the Universities of Toronto and Manitoba, and for many years in the University of British Columbia—was the subject of another important Djwa biography, *Professing English: a life of Roy Daniells* (2002), in which she not only portrays the man himself and his religious struggles, but the poet, and his life and influence in the world of academe. It was awarded the Lorne Pierce Gold Medal of the Royal Society of Canada.

Djwa also edited a memoir by Carl F. KLINCK, *Giving Canada a literary history* (1991), and a collection of the poems of Charles HEAVYSEGE, another of her early specialties: *Saul and selected poetry of Charles Heavysege* (1976). (She wrote the entries in this *Companion* on EDEL, Heavysege, F.G. SCOTT, and F.R. Scott.) In 1994 Djwa was appointed a Fellow of the Royal Society of Canada. Her biography of P.K. PAGE, tentatively called *A journey without maps*, is a work-in-progress.

Dobbs, Kildare (b. 1923). He was born in Meerut, India, and educated at St Columba's College, Rathfarnum, Ireland, and Jesus College, Cambridge, from which he graduated in 1947. During the Second World War he served in the Royal Navy, first as an able seaman and later as a sub-lieutenant, before going into the commandos. He took a teaching diploma at London University before going in 1947 to what was then Tanganyika, where he served as a magistrate. After immigrating to Canada in 1952 he taught high school in Venice, Ontario. Thereafter he worked in Toronto as an editor for nearly ten years with the MACMILLAN COMPANY. It was at this time that he began writing and broadcasting radio scripts for the CBC, ranging from short talks and reviews to an impressive exploration of Joyce's *Finnegans Wake*. Through the 1960s and 1970s he was a regular contributor to the CBC's literary program, 'Anthology', produced for most of that time by Robert WEAVER, with whom, in 1956, he became one of the founding editors of the influential *TAMARACK REVIEW*. From 1965 to 1967 he was managing editor of *Saturday*

Night, and in 1968 he was a literary columnist for the *Toronto Star*. Now a freelance journalist, he is particularly known as a travel writer. George WOODCOCK called Dobbs's first book, *Running to paradise* (1962; GGA; rpr. 1974), 'a work of embroidered autobiography', and complimented its urbanity and wit, which he contrasted with the prevailing 'laboured Leacockian tradition of Canadian humour'. With photographer Peter Varley, Dobbs produced *Canada* (1964, rev. 1969), a celebration of the beauties of the country. *Reading the time* (1968), a collection of wise and quirky literary essays taken from his CBC and newspaper writings, invites the reader to 'see the house of mirrors [contemporary society] for what it is'. In quite another mood Dobbs produced, with the English artist Ronald Searle, *The great fur opera* (1970), a history of the Hudson's Bay Company that manages to be both good history and good fun. In *Pride and fall* (1981) he turned to fiction, looking back at his African experiences and hewing stories that touch many levels of the passion and ironies of colonial life. Dobbs has written about his travels in *Anatolian suite* (1989) and *Ribbon of highway* (1992), on a journey across Canada by Greyhound bus. Always fascinated by the ways of the rich, he has written articles in the *Financial Post* that were collected in *Smiles and chukkas* (1995), which explores the curiosities of affluence with wisdom and humour. At a time when most writers his age are slowing down, Dobbs produced his first volume of poetry, *The eleventh hour: poems for the third millennium* (1997), which combines the clarity, grace, and the comic touches of his prose, and reflects his diversity of interests in such poems as 'Berryman', about the American poet, 'Susanna and the elders', 'Memorial', about Dobbs' father, and the 'Dracula verses'. *Casablanca: the poem* (1999) is a sequence of poems—inspired by the celebrated film—that are imaginative meditations on the film's characters, on ideas and fantasies provoked by them, on the song 'As time goes by' (and the famous instruction, 'Play it, Sam'), in addition to the wartime political situation and some of its horrors. Stills, most of them artistically modified, enhance a little-known book that is a striking memento for readers who love the film. *Running the rapids: a writer's life* (2005) is an enjoyable autobiography.

Donnell, David (b. 1939). Born in St Mary's, Ontario, he was largely self-educated through his own reading and research in Montreal. Donnell moved to Toronto in 1958 and

Donnell

worked at a variety of jobs before publishing his first book, *Poems* (1961). During this early period he read his poems at the Bohemian Embassy, where Margaret ATWOOD, Gwendolyn MacEWEN, Milton ACORN, and other poets began to establish their reputations. With John Robert COLOMBO, he printed Atwood's first book, *Double Persephone* (1961), and then abruptly stopped writing between 1963 and 1974. The Donnell who re-emerged in 1977 with *The blue sky: poems 1974 to 1977* (illustrated by Joe ROSENBLATT) can be described as a 'spiritual surrealist' who examines the relationships of his life from a deliberately oblique perspective, as in the title poem or in the playfully moving 'Letter to the mountains', where he mixes the ironic and the deeply spiritual. In *Dangerous crossings* (1980) Donnell continued his growth and exploration of the ironic, against a backdrop of high culture, contemporary thought, and twentieth-century history, foreshadowing a major theme that evolves over the next several volumes: the individual placed in the psychological, moral, and imaginative fabric of the contemporary urban experience. *Settlements* (1983, GGA) includes work from his previous two volumes with some reworkings and new material, and in such poems as 'Strachan Avenue' blends his love for the urban landscapes of Toronto with his flair for expressing nostalgia. In *Water Street days* (1989) he examines his familial past and his childhood in St Mary's; the poems are simultaneously confessional and openly narrative in the voice of an ironic, self-critical raconteur. By contrast, *China blues* (1992) contains poems about the city and about the subtle tensions and ironies of contemporary urban life, the voice being that of one who is determined to find and mine stories from the realities of overlooked daily existence and the strange twists of perception that inhabit them. It won the City of Toronto Book Award. In a note at the end of *Sometimes a great notion* (2004), explaining that the words of the title come from a classic Leadbelly song, 'Goodnight, Irene' and were chosen because 'it's a great title', Donnell signals the relaxed, lucid nature of the poems contained therein: poems about writers ('Olson', 'What the Dickens?', 'Stephen Hawking and light', 'Proust was a master of sadness', 'Arendt', 'Nabokov'), Toronto ('Dupont Street in sunlight'), cooking ('Crab cakes w/blueberries'), flirtations ('Euclid')—'I said,/You look like the sort of girl/who probably knows a lot about Euclid's *Principles//of Geometry*'—and an institution ('CBC')—'Peter Tanye comes on

at 6 o'clock in the morning/& plays/a Celtic dance by some group from NFLD'. Imaginative and delightful, these poems play on Donnell's interests and on aspects of his life.

Donnell's fascination with prose fiction, evident in the final sections of *China blues* and *Water Street days*, is given fuller play in *Dancing in the dark* (1996), which concludes with stories about Tom Garrone—an Everyman for the nineties, a young urbanite searching for his identity in the labyrinthine world of contemporary pop culture and 'alternative lifestyles'. In *The blue Ontario Hemingway boat race* (1985) Donnell fictionalized the factual material he had gathered in *Hemingway in Toronto: a post-modern tribute* (1982). In both books Donnell strove not only to follow Hemingway through the events of the author's days in Toronto after the Great War, but to get inside his character's mind and look at the world through the vision of a figure totally immersed in the culture of his age.

Double hook, The. See Sheila WATSON.

Dougall, Lily (1858–1923). Born in Montreal and educated in New York, and at the University of Edinburgh and St Andrew's University, Scotland, she lived in Montreal from 1897 to 1903. By 1911 she had moved permanently to Cumnor, England, becoming the centre of a group dedicated to religious thought. Her first novel, *Beggars all*, appeared in 1892, and in all she published ten novels, one volume of short stories, and eight books of religious philosophy. Four of Dougall's novels have Canadian settings. *What necessity knows* (London, 1893; rpr. 1992) deals with British immigrants and religious conflict in eastern Québec, and focuses on rural Canada's challenge to imported hierarchies in terms of religion, class, and gender. In *The madonna of a day: a study* (New York, 1895), the heroine finds her attitudes and values are challenged when she experiences life in a mining camp in British Columbia. *The mermaid: a love tale* (New York, 1895), set on Prince Edward Island and the Magdalens, is about a doctor who is profoundly affected by a child murder he had witnessed in his youth. *The Zeit-Geist* (London, 1895) is the story of a young man's conversion from a life of dissolution to spirituality through non-dogmatic religious thought. Dougall's fiction is characterized by popular melodramatic conventions of her time such as coincidence, disguise, hidden identity, and thwarted love, but is noteworthy for its constant exploration of religious and philosophical themes, based on her own thorough knowledge of contemporary religious theories and sects, and for its portrayal of intelligent and spirited young women who are independent, morally reflective, and naturally drawn to the idea of egalitarian marriage.

Douglas & McIntyre Publishing Group. See D&M PUBLISHERS INC.

Doyle, Brian (b. 1935). Born in Ottawa and educated there at Carleton University (B.J., 1957; B.A., 1959), he became a high-school teacher and the author of outstanding fiction for young people. From his earliest novel, *Hey, Dad!* (1978, rpr. 2005), to his darkest, *Uncle Ronald* (1996, rpr. 1997), Doyle's subject matter is the city of Ottawa and the Gatineau hills, their streets and schools, topography, history, and eccentric residents. Doyle is known for his robust humour, his sensitivity to the rhythm and sound of words, his psychological penetration of young adulthood, and his detailed renderings of Irish-Canadian home life. His young-adult novels are populated by wildly comic caricatures and first-person (usually young male) narrators who distinctively combine strength and sensitivity: they are as comfortable reading poetry as playing hockey. His young adults are deliberately unprotected from the realities of sickness and death (*Up to low*, 1982, rpr. 1996), runaway fathers (*You can pick me up at Peggy's Cove*, 1979, rpr. 2005), racial and ethnic prejudice (*Angel Square*, 1984, rpr. 2004; *Spud Sweetgrass*, 1992), and wife and child abuse (*Uncle Ronald*). Recent titles include *Covered bridge* (2004), *Easy Avenue* (2004), and *Boy o'boy* (2005).

Doyle, Mike (b. 1928), who has also written under the name of 'Charles Doyle' was born in England of Irish parents. He lived in New Zealand from 1951 to 1966 and it was there that he first published his poetry. In 1967 he was a Visiting Fellow in American Studies at Yale University and decided to stay in North America. The next year he became a professor of English at the University of Victoria, British Columbia. Doyle's poetry has gone through several developments since his arrival in Canada, starting with the imagistic notations of *Preparing for the ark* (1973) through to more formally constructed poems in *Stonedancer* (1976). His straightforward approach appeared more succinctly in *A steady hand* (1982) and in the chapbooks *The urge to raise hats* (1989) and *Separate fidelities* (1991). In succeeding years he has sharpened his linguistic

responses, still keeping his concern for place and the relation of art and life, assuming a steadfastly honest and direct expression, often underpinned with clear-eyed irony and a deft satirical touch: see *Trout spawning at Lardeau River* (1997) and *Living ginger* (2004). See also *Intimate absences: selected poems 1954–1992* (1993) and *Where to begin: the selected letters of Mike Doyle and Cid Corman* (2000) edited by Kegan Doyle.

Drummond, William Henry (1854–1907). Born at Currawn House, near Mohill, County Leitrim, Ireland, he immigrated with his parents to Montreal at the age of ten. He attended Montreal High School, McGill University, and Bishop's University, Lennoxville, where he received an M.D. in 1884. He practised medicine in Montreal and died of a stroke in Cobalt, Ontario, after going there to help control a smallpox outbreak at a mine owned by his brothers. He is buried in Mount Royal Cemetery, Montreal.

Drummond's distinctive dialect verse, most of it dealing with French-Canadian *habitant* life and most of it amusing, was Canada's most popular poetry at the turn of the century. (His non-dialect verse did not have much appeal.) The popularity of *The habitant and other French-Canadian poems* (New York, 1897)—with an introduction by Louis FRÉCHETTE, the leading French-Canadian poet of the time—led to the publication of five other collections: two narrative poems in one volume, *Phil-o-Rum's canoe and Madeleine Verchères* (New York and London, 1898); *Johnnie Courteau, and other poems* (1901); *The voyageur and other poems* (1905); *The great fight* (1908), a posthumous collection containing a biographical sketch of Drummond by his wife; and *The poetical works of William Henry Drummond* (1912), again with an introduction by Fréchette. In her Introduction to *The new Oxford book of Canadian verse* (1982), Margaret ATWOOD wrote that Drummond's work 'is filled with creepy tales, heroic episodes, and a good deal of satire—most of it directed at "the English" as seen by the Québec *habitant*.' Although he professed to let his rustic Québécois 'tell their own stories in their own way' (Preface to *The habitant*), Drummond deliberately shaped his own mixture of French and English to provide animation, sentiment, and humour. Many anglophone readers in Canada, the United States, and England delighted in what they felt was a realistic insight into the voice and attitudes of the *habitant*. Nonetheless, as the *Montreal Star* (whose editor had been a friend of the poet) noted at the time of his death, Drummond's medical practice had been mostly in Montreal, and his country experience 'was not among the French-Canadians but among the Highland Scotch'. Drummond actually modelled the mischievous five-year-old in 'Leetle Bateese' and the wan mystic child in 'The last portage' on his own sons; and the title place of 'Little Lac Grenier' was his own favourite fishing spot. His exposure to the variety of broken English used by French-Canadian woodsmen and farmers occurred at Bord-à-Plouffe, where Drummond worked for six summers, from the age of fifteen, as a telegrapher. In his later poetry, however, the distinctive language of his *habitant* characters is more accurate as a measure of Drummond's artistic achievement than of Québécois utterance. Fréchette's introductory comments, though they express a general approval of Drummond's 'daring experiment', eventually praise only the poet's personal cultivation of his material 'with tools and means of his own invention'. That point is made more strongly in some observations at the time by the French-language press: 'This very special language is confined to a particular group in our population' and 'this bastard idiom ... has the attraction of the comedy of travesty' (translated from *La Patrie*, 15 Dec. 1901). *Le Journal de Françoise* referred to 'the bizarre language that he had created initially' (2 Nov. 1907, in translation). Critics agreed with Fréchette, however, in concluding that Drummond's *habitant* poems expressed a friendly spirit.

Dubé, Marcel (b. 1930). Born in Montreal, he attended the Jesuit Collège Saint-Marie and the Université de Montréal, and theatre schools in Paris in 1953–4. The most published and successful dramatist in Québec before Michel TREMBLAY, Dubé is possibly the best Canadian dramatist in English or French. His pre-eminence results from a highly poetic prose style, acute sensitivity to nuances of feeling and emotion, a classic sense of dramatic structure, and a tragic vision of life applied to contemporary situations in Québec society. Of Dubé's more than thirty plays, unfortunately few have been translated. He came to prominence with the successful production of *Zone* (1955), judged the best Canadian play at the Dominion Drama Festival. It is a realistic, if sometimes sentimental, story of a teenage gang of smugglers whose lives are restricted by the area or 'zone' in which they live. An English adaptation of the play (1982) was made by Aviva Ravel. *Le temps des lilas* (1958), a sad and moving play about a

group of people in a Montreal boarding-house, is reminiscent of Chekhov (Dubé's favourite playwright) in its sensitive portrayal of the disillusionment of the characters and the final quiet resignation of an old couple. An English translation by James Noonan, *Time of the lilacs,* was published in *Canadian drama/L'art dramatique canadien,* 16, 2 (1990). *Au retour des oies blanches* (1969), translated by Jean Remple as *The white geese* (1972) and considered by many to be Dubé's finest play, portrays an upper-class family in Quebec City and their gradual discovery of the truth about their relationships. Its plot, structure, and emotional impact, which resemble those of *Oedipus the king,* make it Dubé's closest approach to classical tragedy. *Jérémie* (1973) is a brief scenario for a ballet presented in 1973 by Les Ballets Jazz Contemporains at Sir George Williams University, Montreal (now Concordia University); the published version contains an English translation by Jean Remple. Dubé received the prestigious Prix Athanase-David in 1973, was made an Officer of the Order of Canada in 2000, and was given the Governor General's Performing Arts Award for lifetime artistic achievement in 2005.

Ducharme, Réjean (b. 1941). Born in Saint-Félix-de-Valois, Québec, he pursued various studies, always abandoning them, preferring to earn a living from small jobs, such as office clerk. He now lives in Montreal. He has neither been seen in public nor interviewed since Sept. 1966, when he stated in a brief interview with Gérald GODIN in *Le Magazine Maclean*: 'I don't want my face to be known. I don't want people to link me and my novel.... My novel is public, but I'm not.' The last statement alluded to his first novel, *L'avalée des avalés* (1966, GGA), which won immediate renown for being published by the distinguished Parisian firm of Gallimard (after having been rejected by a Montreal publisher). Ducharme's anonymity raised many rumours about his identity and made him a kind of celebrity. *L'avalée des avalés*—translated by Barbara Bray as *The swallower swallowed* (1968)—is one of the high points of modern French-Canadian fiction. Its half-Jewish, half-Catholic heroine, Bérénice Einberg, who transfers her love for the neglectful mother she adores to her brother, becomes manipulative (like her quarrelling parents) and callous to protect herself, choosing to hate whatever she cannot fully possess: she decides to 'swallow' the world in order not to be swallowed up by it. Her pain is brilliantly portrayed in farcical/comic terms as she rejects all traditional values and invents an anti-social and incomprehensible language, 'le bérénicien', to replace normal language that for her is based on illusion. Of Ducharme's many rich and innovative novels, only one other is available in English. Robert Guy Scully translated *Wild to mild* (1980), which was published in one volume with the French text, *L'hiver de force* (1973). André Ferron and his sister Nicole make their living as proofreaders but are 'drop outs' from society, determined to do literally nothing. The novel has the same vitality and poetry as *The swallower swallowed*, but is more realistic in its satire of the political and cultural milieu of Montreal in the 1970s. *Go figure* (2003)—the translation by Will Browning of *Va savoir* (1994)—creates an atmosphere in which emotion and affection emerge in a sumptuous writing style. Its main components are sporadic letters between the narrator, Rémi, and his wife, Mammy, who is travelling around the world (with her husband's former mistress) in an effort to regain her mental equilibrium after her miscarriage of twin girls; various encounters, touched with humour and love, between Rémi and his rural neighbours; detailed descriptions of the renovation of a ruined chalet, intended for Mammy if she ever comes back and into which the hero has just moved; and an intense friendship with a little girl, Famie, that gives rise to some dazzling passages.

Of Ducharme's plays, *Ha! Ha!* (1982, GGA) was translated by David Homel in 1986. *The daughter of Christopher Columbus* (2000)—the translation by Will Browning of *La fille de Christophe Colombe* (1969)—a mock epic written in determinedly ridiculous verse, is Ducharme's most radical attack on traditional literary structure and meaning. The wandering around the world of Columbus's daughter Colombia in a vain search for friendship is the pretext for a condemnation of civilization and of literature's pretense of transmitting meaning. Browning, an American, said in an interview (*Globe and Mail*, 7 Dec. 2000): 'If English Canada could understand the irreverent, passive-aggressive, "Pouf! Now you love me, now you don't" attitude of Ducharme, they might understand Quebec better.'

Dudek, Louis (1918–2001). Born in the east end of Montreal, of Polish immigrant parents, he attended McGill University and after graduating in 1940 worked as an advertising copywriter and freelance journalist. In 1943 he moved to New York and began graduate studies in journalism and history at Columbia University; shortly afterwards he changed his major from journalism to literature. On completion of his doctoral course work, he accepted an English appointment at City College, New York; he became acquainted with writers Paul Blackburn, Cid Corman, and Herbert Gold, and began a correspondence with Ezra Pound. In 1951 Dudek returned to Montreal, where he lectured at McGill in modern poetry, Canadian literature, the art of poetry, and European literature, until his retirement in 1982 He was made an Officer of the Order of Canada in 1983.

Dudek began his career as a poet in the 1936–40 period, publishing social-protest verse in the *McGill Daily*. In 1943 he joined John SUTHERLAND and Irving LAYTON in editing *FIRST STATEMENT*, which Sutherland had founded in 1942, and throughout his New York years Dudek contributed to it and to its successor, *NORTHERN REVIEW*. On his return to Canada he became immediately a major force in Canadian small-press publishing and influenced the development of Canadian poetry. Instructed by the editorial activities of Americans such as Pound and Corman, he was convinced of the necessity for poets to take their means of publication out of the hands of commercial publishers and into their own. In 1952–4 he was instrumental in shaping the editorial direction of Raymond SOUSTER's little magazine *CONTACT*. In 1952, together with Souster and Layton, he founded CONTACT PRESS, which, between 1952 and 1967, published early books by most of the major poets of the sixties and early seventies. (See Frank DAVEY, *Louis Dudek and Raymond Souster*, 1980.) In 1956 he began another publishing venture, the McGill Poetry Series, in which he published first poetry books by McGill students, beginning with Leonard COHEN's *Let us compare mythologies* (1956). Despite its name, the series was mostly financed and edited by Dudek. In 1957 he began *DELTA*, a personal literary magazine in which he attempted to promote further the urbane, realistic kind of writing his earlier editorial activities had encouraged. He terminated *Delta* in 1966; but the next year he co-founded, with Glen Siebrasse and Michael Gnarowski, the small press Delta Canada. On its dissolution in 1970 he co-founded, with his wife, Aileen Collins, yet another small press, D.C. Books.

Dudek's poetry collections are *East of the city* (1946), *Twenty-four poems* (1952), *The searching image* (1952), *Europe* (1955), *The transparent sea* (1956), *En Mexico* (1958), *Laughing stalks* (1958), *Atlantis* (1967), *Collected poetry* (1971), *Selected poems* (1979), *Poems from Atlantis*

Dudek

(1980), *Cross-section* (1980), *Continuation I* (1981), *Continuation II* (1990), *The caged tiger* (1997), *Reality games* (1998), and *The surface of time* (2000), which includes 'Sequence from "Continuation III"'. His selected poems were published as *Infinite worlds* (1988), edited by Robin BLASER. His early poems are mostly short lyrics that proceed from incidental observation and description towards a concluding insight or philosophical statement. Employing few metaphors or elaborate images, the descriptions are direct and realistic. Although many of the scenes are from ghetto and working-class life, and many of the sentiments are Marxist, a definite pessimism about human accomplishment pervades these poems. Optimism is usually reserved for nature's powers—'the soon-rampant seed', 'the great orchestrating principle of gravity'. With the publication of *Europe* and *En Mexico*, Dudek moved from short, incidentally related lyrics to book-length meditations with prose-like rhythms and a didactic tone. Unlike the lyrics, they interweave the general and particular so that their relationship is obscured; some passages seem to be illustrated sermons, while others offer flashes of inspiration gained from particulars. In *Europe, En Mexico*, and *Atlantis* Dudek attempts to be the morally responsible egoist, to make his self universal, to come to terms with 'the dichotomy of the self and the not-self, the I-myself and the man-kind-to-which-I-belong'; but he is still pessimistic about humanity's ability to reform and save itself. Joy, beauty, and eternity are certain residents only of nature. At the end of *Atlantis*, when the poet finally gains a vision of the lost continent, its 'palaces, and domes' are a North Atlantic iceberg—'a piece of eternity', 'a carved silent coffin', that promises only 'darkness' and 'infinite night'. In *The surface of time*, published the year before he died, Dudek writes 'I am nearly finished now/with what is probably my last word/in possibly my last line—in this happy poem.' A few lines above he had written 'I cannot tell you the full depth/of my indifference.' ('The last word')

Among Dudek's prose works are *1941 diary* (1996) and *Notebooks 1960–1994* (1995). See *Selected essays and criticism of Louis Dudek* (1978). See also *Louis Dudek: essays on his works* (2001) edited by George Hildebrand and *Eternal conversations: remembering Louis Dudek* (2003) edited by Aileen Collins, Michael Gnarowski, and Sonja A. Skarstedt, described on the front cover as 'A tribute anthology'. It is made up of tributes and reminiscences by many of Dudek's friends and acquaintances, and by his wife and son

Gregory (with some writings by Dudek), complemented by many snapshots.

Duley, Margaret (1894–1968). Born in St John's, Newfoundland, she was educated at the local Methodist College and in 1913 enrolled in the London Academy of Music and Dramatic Art in London, England. From 1918, until she began serious writing in the 1930s, her life was occupied with travel, reading, partying with the St John's elite, and local feminist agitation. She never married. In the Depression years her father's jewellery business declined and Duley began writing fiction, apparently to make money. Duley knew the Newfoundland outports only from a distance, from the perspective of an occasional summer visitor; yet it was to the outports that she turned for inspiration for her first novel, *The eyes of the gull* (1936), where outharbour existence is depicted as unremittingly stifling, condemning the heroine, Isabel Pyke, to a deprived and horrid round of loveless days. Real love is seen as something attainable only in the world of culture and sophistication outside Newfoundland. Duley's most snobbish novel, it is more carefully plotted and often more moving than the later books. *Cold pastoral* (1939) takes a similar outport heroine out of her native cove, now evoked in all its squalor and coarseness, and brings her to the greater world of St John's and, ultimately, London. Urban values are espoused until the end of the book, when she feels a sudden twinge of affection for her own 'bit of earth' in Newfoundland. This is the beginning of a reconciliation that is the theme of *Highway to valour* (1941), Duley's third and final novel with a Newfoundland setting. Her new heroine, after living through a number of grim episodes in a country that terrifies and dominates her, at length turns her face in acceptance 'towards the cold sea that was her heritage'. These books, showing a progressive deepening in the author's understanding of the nature of life in Newfoundland, appear to be stages in an odyssey of discovery and acceptance. While Duley never fully overcame a distaste for the jagged landscapes and stormy seas of her uncomfortable home, she portrayed Newfoundland with rare truthfulness and vividness. These three books dramatize encounters between a heroine and the inappropriate 'masculine' environment in which she had to function. The theme—women in pursuit of love—is examined with shrewd insight and, on occasion, humour. If we consider all four of Duley's novels, adding *Novelty on earth* (1942—published in England as *Green afternoon*, 1944), in which the Newfoundland setting is of no importance—we can see a theme emerging in her work that engrosses her even more than her connection with her homeland: she is struggling to define a feminist sensibility. She appears to have been torn between her desire to comment on the external world and her wish to explore the nature of her feminine sensitivity towards it, and towards men. In *Novelty on earth* Duley minutely chronicles a love affair between a twice-widowed woman and a married man. At the end her heroine rejects her lover because she 'couldn't be a squaw-woman and give him what he wanted.' We have a free modern woman before us. Duley thus transcended her provincial concerns to make a larger statement. See Alison Feder's *Margaret Duley: Newfoundland novelist, a biographical and critical study* (1983).

Dumont, Marilyn. See ABORIGINAL LITERATURE: 5.

Duncan, Norman (1871–1916). Born in North Norwich Township, Oxford County, Ontario, Norman McLean Duncan attended the University of Toronto (1891–4), but did not graduate. Soon afterwards he began a career as a journalist in the United States. In the summer of 1900 he went to Newfoundland to write articles for *McClure's Magazine*, a journal that specialized in geographical adventure. He returned to Newfoundland for other summer visits between 1901 and 1906, and again in 1910, forming a strong attachment to the Manuel family of Exploits Island in Notre Dame Bay. In an appreciation of Duncan, Wilfred GRENFELL noted that he had been 'a guest aboard our little hospital vessel' along the Labrador coast. Duncan also travelled farther afield, to the Near East and to Australia. From 1902 to 1908 he taught English and rhetoric at Washington and Jefferson College in Washington, Pennsylvania, and at the University of Kansas. During his last years drinking became a serious problem to him. He died suddenly, on a golf course, in Fredonia, New York.

Duncan was a prolific and popular author. His writings have been neglected by recent critics, perhaps because his defects—occasional sentimentality, a flowery, rhetorical style, and a liking for melodrama—are so apparent, and his subject matter is often so remote from ordinary North American experience. Yet his faults do not much detract from his considerable achievement. Like his contemporary, Jack London, Duncan went for literary inspiration to northern frontiers and to the lives of

forgotten people. His spirit was democratic, his writings affirmations of the imaginative possibilities inherent in common life. His first book, *The soul of the street: correlated stories of the New York Syrian quarter* (1900), reveals his familiarity with the legends and lives of Syrian immigrants, and his compassion and his interest in out-of-the-way modes of life. His experiences in Newfoundland stirred him deeply and provided material for ten works of fiction, much of it written for a juvenile audience: *The way of the sea* (1903, rpr. 1982), *Doctor Luke of the Labrador* (1904), *The adventures of Billy Topsail: a story for boys* (1906), *The cruise of the Shining Light* (1907), *Every man for himself* (1908), *Billy Topsail & Company: a story for boys* (1910), *The best of a bad job: a hearty tale of the sea* (1912), *Billy Topsail, M.D.: a tale of adventure with Doctor Luke of the Labrador* (1916), *Battles royal down north* (1918), and *Harbor tales down north* (1918). His collection of essays on Newfoundland, *Dr Grenfell's parish: the deep sea fishermen* (1905), expresses his admiration for Grenfell, who was undoubtedly the model for Dr Luke in his most popular novel. Of these works the most important is *The way of the sea*, reissued in 1982 and edited by John Coldwell Adams. It is a book of stories that explores the outharbour life of Newfoundland with profound understanding and sympathy. Duncan wrote eight other books, most of them novels, but nothing he experienced seems to have fired his imagination so strongly as Newfoundland. He was capable of sustained passages of exquisite, resonant prose. Writing about Newfoundland—the 'frayed edge' of North America where he found obscure inhabitants of a hidden world of adventure—he created an unwitting epic of outport life in stories showing the stamp of genius. John Coldwell Adams, in his Introduction to *Selected stories of Norman Duncan* (1988), writes that 'a little more time and effort' on Duncan's part might have put his stories 'in the front ranks'.

Duncan, Sara Jeannette (1861–1922). The daughter of a Scottish father and an Ulster Protestant mother, she was born and raised in Brantford, Canada West (Ontario). She attended the Toronto Normal School, but soon abandoned teaching for journalism. A high-spirited trip to the 1884 New Orleans Cotton Exposition as a freelance correspondent was followed by such substantial jobs as editorial writer and book reviewer for the *Washington Post* (1885–6), columnist for the Toronto *Globe* (1886–7), and finally columnist for the *Montreal Star* (1887–8). She also wrote extensively

Duncan

during this period for *The WEEK*. (See Thomas Tausky, ed., *Sarah Jeannette Duncan: selected journalism*, 1978.) In Sept. 1888 she set off with a fellow journalist, Lily Lewis, on an ambitious round-the-world tour. In Calcutta she met Everard Cotes, a museum official and subsequently a journalist. She married him in Dec. 1890 and lived with him in Calcutta and Simla (then the summer administrative capital of India) for most of the next three decades, though she spent large stretches of time alone in London. In the mid-1890s she wrote editorials for the *Indian Daily News*, a newspaper her husband edited. Early personal and professional fulfilment appears to have been followed by unhappiness in India and a nostalgic affection for Canada. The last few years of her life were spent in England, where she died.

Duncan's journalism comments with intelligence, vigour, and wit on an astonishing variety of Canadian social, political, and cultural questions. Her remarks on literary issues display a shrewd understanding of contemporary controversies, and she was keenly aware of developments in fiction—she even sought personal contact with William Dean Howells, E.M. Forster, and Henry James. (She knew Howells in Washington and Paris and entertained Forster in India; she sent James her novel *His honour and a lady*, which he acknowledged tardily and with elaborate, distancing graciousness, describing it as 'extraordinarily keen and delicate and able', before criticizing it gently but astutely.) Her first book, *A social departure: how Orthodocia and I went round the world by ourselves* (London and New York, 1890), is an edited version of her globe-trotting newspaper articles, unified by the invention of a naive young Englishwoman as the narrator's companion. The more inventive and polished *An American girl in London* (London and New York, 1891)—like its predecessor a collection of light sketches, which are here presented as a novel—concerns the adventures of a Chicago baking-powder heiress who is eagerly sought after by predatory Englishmen. Both books were favourably reviewed and appear to represent the height of Duncan's commercial success. In *A voyage of consolation* (London and New York, 1898) the heroine of *An American girl* ventures onto the Continent, and *Two girls on a barge* (London and New York, 1891) chronicles the self-conscious exploits of another unconventional heroine. Duncan takes her emancipated female protagonist much more seriously in *A daughter of to-day* (London and New York, 1894, rpr. 1988), a novel that ends with the heroine's

suicide. This ambitious work, set in the artist quarters of Paris and London, has admirable scenes but suffers from pretentiousness and an ultimate plunge into melodrama. Duncan's first outstanding literary achievement is *The simple adventures of a memsahib* (London and New York, 1893, rpr. 1986), an account of a conventional young Englishwoman's entry into Anglo-Indian society as narrated by a sophisticated veteran 'memsahib'. A subtle tragi-comedy, it reveals that in the years since Duncan's first sight of India, she had immeasurably deepened her understanding of the Anglo-Indian character. *His honour, and a lady* (London and New York, 1896), Duncan's first serious study of Indian politics, is an impressive work in which Duncan interweaves the fates of two women: the emancipated protagonist she so often portrayed, and a more conventional heroine. Her considerable powers of social observation are at their best in this novel, which also has a stylistic lightness and grace she was never quite able to recapture. *The path of a star* (American title, *Hilda: a story of Calcutta*; London and New York, 1899), like *A daughter of to-day*, has an artist protagonist—an actress this time—and strongly melodramatic elements. It widens the focus of Duncan's story of Calcutta society, taking in the religious, theatrical, and commercial communities as well as the civil servants; but it is flawed by a ponderous pseudo-Jamesian prose style.

It was not until 1902 that Duncan made North America a major setting for her fiction, in *Those delightful Americans* (1902), a light but entertaining story about a young English matron's discovery of American high society. Duncan's most Canadian novels—*The imperialist* (1904, NCL; rpr. 2005) and *Cousin Cinderella; or, A Canadian girl in London* (1908, rpr. 1994)—are also her best. *The imperialist* is a witty though balanced and sympathetic portrait of Brantford (called Elgin), a community in which 'nothing compared with religion but politics, and nothing compared with politics but religion' as sources of interest, and where a certain leading citizen was 'no more disposed to an extravagant opinion than to wear one side whisker longer than the other.' Advena Murchison, the novel's passionate, independent, and intellectual heroine, is the finest example of an autobiographical character type Duncan had depicted in several previous novels; the elder Murchisons are affectionate portraits of Duncan's own parents. The narrative ingeniously alternates parallel plots involving severe challenges to idealistic impulses in politics and love. Though Duncan insisted that 'my book offers only a picture of life and opinion, and attempts no argument', the title character's struggle to convert his stubbornly pragmatic fellow townsmen to the imperialist faith is presented sympathetically. *The imperialist* has been reprinted not only in the NEW CANADIAN LIBRARY, but in another reissue (1988, 2nd edn 1996) edited by Thomas E. Tausky, with notes, reviews, and Duncan's letters about the novel, and in a 2005 reprint edited by Misao Dean. *Cousin Cinderella*, an account of the efforts made by a Canadian brother and sister to gain social recognition for themselves and their country in London, is Duncan's most subtle and accomplished version of the international theme. Like *The imperialist*, it centres on an emerging sense of national consciousness and a struggle against lingering colonialism. As the narrator remarks in *The imperialist*, 'We are here at the making of a nation.'

Duncan's final two Indian novels, *Set in authority* (1906, rpr. 1996) and *The burnt offering* (1909, rpr. 1979), deal with imperialism on another front: the challenge to British rule created by the rise of militant Indian nationalism. Both books show increased sympathy towards the Indian character, and venture upon daring interracial subjects, though melodrama prevails in the end. *The consort* (1912, rpr. 1979), about British politics, is far less penetrating than its Canadian and Indian counterparts. Duncan's final novels—*His royal happiness* (1914), *Title clear* (1922), and *The gold cure* (1924)—rework the international theme in uninspired ways. The title story's theme in the collection of Duncan's short stories, *The pool in the desert* (1903, rpr. 1984, 2001), is the stultifying effect of a conformist society on the development of an artist.

See Thomas E. Tausky, *Sara Jeannette Duncan: novelist of empire* (1980) and Marian Fowler, *Redney: a life of Sara Jeannette Duncan* (1983).

Durkin, Douglas Leader (1884–1968). Raised on a farm in Ontario, he left with his family to homestead in the Swan River area of Manitoba. After studying philosophy and English at the University of Manitoba (B.A., 1908), he was a high-school principal in Carman, Manitoba, then taught for four years at Brandon College. He was with the English department of the University of Manitoba (1915–22), though on leave of absence from 1920 to 1922, before leaving Canada, probably in 1921, for New York, where Martha OSTENSO joined him. For three years he gave a course on 'The technique of the novel' at Columbia University. It is now thought that the novels published under Ostenso's name were co-authored by Durkin, although *Wild geese* is considered to be primarily Ostenso's work. In 1931 Durkin and Ostenso moved to Gull Lake, Minnesota; they married in 1945 and moved to Seattle in 1963. Writing both under his own name and under the pseudonym 'Conrad North', Durkin published poetry, novels, short stories, and serial novels, and co-authored a screenplay. His novel *The magpie* (1923, rpr. 1974) is set in Winnipeg and environs, opening in July 1919, the year of the Winnipeg General Strike. Its hero, nicknamed 'The magpie', has just returned from fighting in the Great War and has resumed working at the grain exchange, where his honesty is seen as something of an amusing quirk. The hero's initial desire for reform abates and then reasserts itself; he is finally driven temporarily to madness when his work and his marriage both fail. Regarded as a valuable depiction of post–Great War conditions, *The magpie* contributed to the movement towards realism, particularly urban realism, in Canadian fiction. Durkin's other novels include *The heart of Cherry McBain* (1919), a sentimental romance set in the Swan River area, and *The lobstick trail: a romance of Northern Manitoba* (1921), set in The Pas and environs, in which characters appreciate the land primarily either as a home or for the exploitation of its resources.

E

Eaton, Edith Maud (1865–1914). She was born in England, daughter of an English-educated Chinese mother, Grace Trefusius, and an English father, Edward Eaton. At the age of seven she immigrated with her family to Montreal. A stenographer, then a freelance writer for local newspapers, she moved in about 1900 to the West Coast, thereafter living in Los Angeles, San Francisco, and Seattle, with trips east to Montreal and Boston. Making the acquaintance of the Chinese communities, Eaton—using the pseudonym 'Sui Sin Far'—wrote articles and stories effectively criticizing social and political prejudice against Chinese immigrants and Eurasians. Her stories were collected in *Mrs Spring Fragrance* (1908). She may be considered the first North American of Chinese extraction to write realistically and convincingly of the difficulties and prejudices encountered by the Chinese in North America. On her death the Chinese community of Montreal erected a monument in her honour.

Eccles, W. J. (1917–98). William John Eccles was born in Thirsk, Yorkshire, England, and came to Canada in 1928. He served in the RCAF/RAF (1941–5) between attending MacDonald College and McGill University (B.A., 1949; M.A., 1951; Ph.D., 1955), and the Sorbonne, Paris (1951–2). After teaching at the Universities of Manitoba and Alberta, he joined the history department of the University of Toronto as professor in 1963, retiring in 1983. The foremost anglo-Canadian historian of the French regime in Canada, Eccles succeeded in breaking the grip on the anglophone imagination held by American romantic historian Francis Parkman. Iconoclasm, sometimes to the point of contrariness, and the ability to relate and describe vividly distant events and societies, brought attention to Eccles' writing. *Frontenac: the courtier governor* (1959), his revised doctoral dissertation, and the only modern biography in English of the famous governor of New France, met with acclaim because Eccles managed in lucid prose to overturn conventional portraits on every major interpretative point. *Canada under Louis XIV, 1663–1701* (1964) is one of the best titles in the Canada Centenary Series. *Canada during the French regime* (1968) comprises the E.R. Adair Memorial Lectures given at McGill University in 1967. *The Canadian frontier 1534–1760* (1969, rev. 1983)—in the Histories of the American Frontier Series—discusses the fur trade, imperial expansion, and military operations, with particular attention paid to the respective roles of merchants and Natives. *France in America* (1972, rev. 1990), in the New American Nation Series—reprinted as *The French in North America: 1500–1765* (1998)—is a compressed history of New France, the result of further research. The twelve important essays in *Essays on New France* (1987), written over twenty-five years, are preceded by an interesting memoir of Eccles' career as a scholar. Included is a critique of *The fur trade in Canada* (1930) by Harold INNIS, revealing its weaknesses.

Ecstasy of Rita Joe, The (1970, rpr. 1991). A landmark in modern Canadian theatre, George RYGA's drama was one of the first Canadian plays to win international recognition. Following the 1967 Vancouver Playhouse premiere, it was restaged in Ottawa two years later as the first English-language production at the National Arts Centre. It was performed in London, England, at the Hampstead Theatre Club; at the Kennedy Centre, Washington; and won an award for the best new production at the Edinburgh Fringe Festival in 1973. It also achieved considerable popularity as a 1971 ballet by the Royal Winnipeg Ballet (choreographed by Norbert Vesak).

Like much of Ryga's dramatic work, *Ecstasy* presents politics through a psychological perspective. Based on newspaper reports about the deaths of Native girls in Vancouver, it deals with a highly charged issue: the exploitation and degradation of the Amerindian by a supposedly liberal white society. The play presents the history of one such victim—from her childhood on a reserve, through her repeated arrests, to her murder by a gang of rapists—but the chronological sequence is fragmented. On a multiple set, past merges with present in episodic scenes framed by a recurrent courtroom trial. The brevity and dislocation of the episodes, and the juxtaposition of lyricism and brutality, mirror the protagonist's thought processes. The impression of a labyrinth, explicitly echoed in the setting, and the circular patterning of repeated actions, represent the status quo that imprisons Rita Joe. Social reality, transposed into psychological terms, demonstrates the effect of political oppression on the non-conforming individual in a way the audience can share emotionally. At the same time, the conventional liberal response is ruled out as self-indulgent romanticism through the figure of a singer, whose ballad rendering of the action is exposed as insensitive cliché. The interior nature of the drama and the repetitive trial sequences, in which all Rita Joe's court appearances merge into a composite image, universalize the action. The protagonist not only represents the plight of Native girls in general, but (in intention at least) of many other Natives exploited by the system. This archetypal quality gives the play considerable power.

ECW Press. It was founded in Toronto by Jack David and Robert Lecker in 1977, after

David had begun in 1974 publishing the journal *Essays on Canadian Writing* (also referred to as ECW); Lecker joined him a year later. ECW Press published primarily scholarly and academic books in the 1980s, reflecting its origins in the journal. Among the larger projects were *The annotated bibliography of Canada's major authors, Canadian writers and their works, Canadian fiction studies,* and *Canadian biography studies.* With the completion of these major works, the press shifted direction to publish more overtly trade titles, with a focus on the US market. Since 1995 pop culture, music, sports, and business titles have competed with poetry, fiction, and serious non-fiction. In 2003 David bought out Lecker, and in 2008 began the process of selling minority shares to some of the press's longtime employees.

Edel, Leon (1907–97). The son of immigrant parents, he was born in Pittsburgh, Pennsylvania, and raised in Yorkton, Saskatchewan. He attended McGill University—where, with A.J.M. SMITH and F.R. SCOTT, he became a founding member of the MCGILL FORTNIGHTLY REVIEW (1925–7)—and graduated with a B.A. (1927) and an M.A. (1928); his thesis was an early study of the experimental novel and Henry James, whose unpublished plays were the subject of his D.Litt. thesis at the Sorbonne (1932). In France, Edel held a three-year province of Québec scholarship and sent back 'Montparnasse letters'—redolent of modern music, the new art, and Paris—that were published in the CANADIAN MERCURY. He worked as a journalist for the *Montreal Star* (1927–9); the *Montreal Herald* (1932–34); Agence Havas, New York (1934–8); Canadian Press, N.Y. bureau (1939–41); *PM* (1942–3); and contributed reviews to the *CANADIAN FORUM* from 1930 to 1935. From 1937 to 1939, under a Guggenheim Fellowship, he edited James's plays in Paris. He was drafted into the US army in 1943 and served overseas as a French linguist until 1946. In 1947 Edel published *James Joyce: the last journey,* and, after the death of E.K. BROWN, the second half of Brown's *Willa Cather: a critical biography* (1953). In 1953 he was appointed associate professor of English at New York University and from 1966 to 1973 was the first Henry James Professor of English and American letters. From 1971 until 1978 he was Citizens Professor of English at the University of Hawaii. Edel received numerous awards, including both the Pulitzer Prize for biography and the National Book Award for non-fiction in 1963. Between 1953 and 1972 he published the five volumes of his biography of Henry James, later issuing a two-volume edition (1977) and a one-volume edition (1985). Widely recognized as one of the best biographies of our time, it demonstrates the application of theories put forward in his Alexander lectures, delivered at the University of Toronto in 1955–6, and first published as *Literary biography* (1957); this was later revised and remained in print as *Writing lives: principia biographica* (1984). Among Edel's many other publications, he edited James's most important works, including the ten-volume Bodley Head edition of selected novels (1967–74), four volumes of letters (1974–84), and *Selected letters* (1987).

Edel maintained a lifelong friendship with his fellow students at McGill who, along with him, were associated with the MONTREAL GROUP and became well-known writers. (Edel's 1984 Pratt Lecture at Memorial University, St John's, Newfoundland, was published in 1986 as *Memories of the Montreal Group.*) He has written occasional essays on Smith, Scott, Leo KENNEDY, and A.M. KLEIN. For the semi-fictional recollections of his friend John GLASSCO (a fellow expatriate in the 1920s), *MEMOIRS OF MONTPARNASSE* (1970), he wrote a warmly nostalgic introduction. After Glassco's death Edel published 'John Glassco (1909–1981) and his erotic muse' in *CANADIAN LITERATURE* 93 (Summer 1982). He also wrote an introduction to the 1975 reissue of Kennedy's *The shrouding* (1933) and contributed papers to the conferences honouring A.M. Klein (*The Klein symposium,* 1974), Smith ('The worldly muse of A.J.M. Smith', *University of Toronto Quarterly,* Spring 1978), Morley CALLAGHAN (*The Callaghan symposium, 1980*), and Scott ('F.R. Scott: Canadian', 1983). Following Smith's death, Edel's memorial address, 'Arthur and Jeannie: in memoriam'—read at Michigan State University on 11 Apr. 1981—was published in the last issue of *The TAMARACK REVIEW* (Winter, 1982). In 1989 Edel gave the first annual Frank Scott Memorial Lecture at McGill: 'Frank Scott and the Canadian Literary Renaissance' (*Fontanus* III, 1990).

Edge (1963–9). This literary and political magazine had nine issues and was founded in Edmonton, Alberta, by Henry BEISSEL, who continued it in Montreal when he moved there in 1966. While publishing many of the leading Canadian (including Québécois) poets and writers of fiction, it also ventured into politics in Alberta in its criticism of the Socred government there, which brought denunciation in the legislative assembly.

(A school teacher was fired for using *Edge* in class discussion.) It also included art, devoting two issues to Dennis Burton (no. 8) and Norman Yates (no. 9).

Edwards, Caterina (b. 1948). Born in Wellingford, England, she immigrated to Canada in 1956 with her English father and Italian mother and grew up in Calgary, Alberta, with many summers spent in Venice, Italy. Her education includes a B.A. (1970) and an M.A. (1973) from the University of Alberta, where she worked under Rudy WIEBE and Sheila WATSON. Some early short stories appeared under her married name, Caterina Lo Verso. She became the most important Italian-Canadian writer in western Canada with the publication of *The lion's mouth* (1982, rpr. 1993), the coming-of-age story of an Italian immigrant woman and one of the first Canadian novels to combine ethnicity with feminist questions. It is also a novel about the woman artist, for Bianca is not only trying to find her place between the culture of Italy and the geography of Canada, but is also learning how to become a writer. The clear, elegant prose of Edwards' fiction is evident in her drama *Terra straniera*, staged in 1986 at the Edmonton Fringe Festival and published as *Homeground* (1990); it is the first play to deal with the Italian immigrant experience on the Prairies. Her two novellas in one volume, *Whiter shade of pale, Becoming Emma* (1992), explore questions of ethnic identity for men and women in western Canada. Stories of women are collected in *Island of the nightingales* (2000). See *Caterina Edwards: essays on her works* (2000) edited by Joseph Pivato.

Eksteins, Modris (b. 1943). Born in Riga, Latvia, he was educated at Upper Canada College, Toronto, Trinity College, University of Toronto (B.A., 1965), and was a Rhodes Scholar at Oxford (B. Phil., 1967; D. Phil., 1970). He joined the history faculty of Scarborough College, University of Toronto, in 1970, and has been professor of history, University of Toronto at Scarborough, since 1980. Among his books are *The limits of reason: the German democratic press and the collapse of Weimar democracy* (1975) and *Rites of spring: the Great War and the birth of the modern age* (1989, rpr. 2004). This important work is a cultural history that synthesizes an enormous range of information, anecdotes, and reminiscences relating to European arts, customs, values, myths, manners, and morals before and after the Great War, and to the ravages and horrors

of trench warfare. It begins in Paris before the war and discusses Diaghilev's Ballets Russes, and particularly the opening night of Stravinsky's *Le Sacre du printemps* (*The Rite of Spring*) in May 1913, when pandemonium broke out shortly after it began. The audience was protesting their sudden confrontation with rebellion, liberation, and radical movement in the ballet (represented by the music, which spurned existing conventions of harmony, rhythm, and form, and by the graceless dancing), and with the brutal theme of the ballet, in which a chosen maiden dances to her death—all motifs that are considered to be emblematic of the age. The chapter on Berlin describes the advanced state of that city and the development of the idea of *Kultur* as being concerned with 'inner freedom' and a kind of mystical nationalism, and a national avant-garde free from outside influences. The long central section examines the conduct of the war in the trenches from the standpoint of the men, on both sides, who were so ruinously involved, and the bellicose attitudes expressed on the home fronts. The war's end, and its relegation 'to the realm of the unconscious or, more precisely, to that of the consciously repressed', are then discussed, followed by the celebrated 1927 flight to Paris by Lindbergh and the 1929 publication of Remarque's *All quiet on the western front*, and their significance; and a summary of the years 1933 to 1945, with portrayals of Nazism, and of Hitler and his version of reality, to his suicide. A beautifully written, richly enlightening study, *Rites of spring* is already a classic of history writing by a Canadian; it won the (Ontario) Trillium Book Award and has been translated into seven languages. *Walking since daybreak: a story of Eastern Europe, World War II, and the heart of our century* (1999) is a quasi-personal history that begins with Eksteins' maternal great-grandmother, a Latvian chambermaid to a Baltic-German baron in the middle of the nineteenth century. Focusing initially on his forebears in Latvia, it moves through the Great War and its disastrous effects on the Baltic states, to the Second World War, when his clergyman father, his mother, and their two young children become escapees, moving from place to place until they reach Berlin, where they survive the climactic bombings of 1945. It is a discursive history, whose chapters are made up of set-pieces, moving back and forth in time; among them are passages of autobiography, describing the plight of Eksteins' immediate family as DPs in Europe, their arrival in Winnipeg in 1949, in 'Toronto the Good' in 1952, his acceptance as a scholarship student at Upper Canada College in 1956, 'a mere six and a half years after leaving the refugee camps of Europe', and his time at Oxford University. (This episodic approach can be seen as an expression of the fragmentation of history in the twentieth century.) In conclusion, Eksteins looks at the devastating effects of the Second World War on Central and Eastern Europe—with 1.25 million tons of bombs dropped on German soil—and casts a salutary light on the evils of that war from the standpoint of a Canadian scholar whose family were once small figures surviving Allied attacks, and who has achieved a unique overview of the violence that led to the end of the war in 1945, a year that 'stands at the center of our century and our meaning.' *Walking since daybreak* won the first Pearson Writers' Trust Non-Fiction Award in 2000.

Elliott, George (1923–96). Born in London, Ontario, he spent his early childhood there, then moved with his family to Toronto, where he received his education and lived for a good part of his adult life. As a young man Elliott took a position for a year during the Second World War as editor of the local newspaper in Strathroy, a small town near London. The landscape, folklore, and ritual there coalesced with impressions Elliott had formed as a boy during summers on the farm owned by his mother's father in Bruce County, Ontario. The result—a magical world developed deftly and hauntingly by Elliott at intervals over nearly two decades—was his first book, *The kissing man* (1962, NCL; rpr.1998), a much-admired cycle of linked stories.

In 1948 Elliott joined MacLaren Advertising, Toronto, and eventually rose to the rank of vice-president. His business career at MacLaren's included a ten-year stint as a political adviser. Following a year as senior adviser in the Office of the Prime Minister in Ottawa, Elliott served as minister-counsellor for public affairs in the Canadian Embassy, Washington, then as manager of marketing services for the Export Development Corporation. His experiences and observations, during these and later years, of vastly different landscapes, folklore, and rituals provided material for *The bittersweet man* (1994), a second volume of stories—urban, urbane, and powerfully ironic. It contains stories written during the three decades after his first book, along with several new stories written once he had settled near Quebec City on Île d'Orléans. In what proved to be his final years, Elliott wrote the story cycle *Crazy*

water boys (1995), twenty-five very short, fiercely comic, and poignant stories set mainly in a fictitious semi-retirement home for elderly men somewhere in the Laurentian hills. An allegory of Canadian life in the last part of the twentieth century (as *The kissing man* can be seen as an allegory of Canadian life in the first part of the twentieth century), *Crazy water boys* begins with a memory of Expo 67 and ends some time in the future. Elliott also researched and wrote *God's big acre: life in 401 country* (1986), semi-fictional sketches about rural life, with photographs by John Reeves.

Ellis, Sarah (b. 1952). Born in Vancouver, British Columbia, she was educated at the University of British Columbia (B.A. Honours, 1973; M.L.S., 1975), and at the Centre for the Study of Children's Literature, Simmons College, Boston (M.A., 1980). In the eighties and nineties Ellis published four novels for children—*The baby project* (1986, rpr. 1994), *Next-door neighbours* (1989), *Pick-up sticks* (1991, GGA; rpr, 1992), *Out of the blue* (1994)—and a collection of short stories, *Back of beyond* (1996, rpr. 1999). The award-winning *The baby project* develops a theme common to all Ellis's fiction: that of the adolescent girl coming to terms with family change, in this case eleven-year-old Jessica's reaction to her family's new baby. *Next-door neighbour* is based on Ellis's own experience as the self-conscious daughter of a clergyman. *Pick-up sticks* was inspired by a radio broadcast in which a homeless woman recounted the series of bad breaks that forced her on to the street. *Out of the blue* concerns the feelings of a twelve-year-old girl who discovers that her mother had another daughter she gave up for adoption many years earlier. The stories in *Back of beyond* contain elements of the supernatural, and deal with such familiar themes as divorce and family violence with freshness and subtlety. Among the many books Ellis has published since that one are *A prairie as wide as the sea: the immigrant diary of Ivy Weatherall* (2001)—the first diary entry is dated 1 May 1926, when Ivy was eleven years old—and *The several lives of Orphan Jack* (2003). *Odd man out* (2006), which won the TD Canadian Children's Literature Award ($20,000), is about Kip, who spends the summer with his grandmother and five eccentric girl cousins. *Next stop!* (2000), about travelling on a bus, *Big Ben* (2001), *Ben over night* (2005), and *The queen's feet* 2006) are picture books. Ellis is also the author of *From reader to writer: teaching writing through classic children's books* (2000) and the editor of *Girls' own: an anthology of Canadian fiction for young readers* (2001).

Emblem Books (1954–62). Publication of this short-lived series of poetry booklets was begun in 1954 in Toronto by Jay MACPHERSON with her own collection *O earth return* and Daryl HINE's *Five poems* (1955). Although Macpherson's intention was to publish only these two brief works for private circulation by their authors, she agreed to publish a further booklet by Dorothy LIVESAY. The press's name was inspired by the emblems (originally linocuts by Macpherson, but redrawn for publication by Laurence Hyde) that appeared on the covers of the first two booklets. Macpherson undertook as ad hoc projects three more titles in the next few years: Heather SPEARS' *Asylum poems* (1958), Violet Anderson's *The ledge* (1958), and Dorothy Roberts' *In star and stalk* (1959). Like the earlier titles, each was professionally mimeographed, then hand-assembled by Macpherson. These would have been the final publications in the series had not Macpherson made contact in 1960 with Robert Rosewarne of Ottawa, who owned a manual letterpress and wished to attempt fine literary printing. A brief collaboration resulted in Emblem's two most attractive titles, each containing colour graphics by Rosewarne: Alden NOWLAN's *Wind in a rocky country* (1960) and Al PURDY's *The blur in between* (1962).

Emily Montague, The history of. See Frances BROOKE.

Encyclopedia of literature in Canada. See W.H. NEW.

Engel, Howard (b. 1931). He was born in Toronto and raised in St Catharines, Ontario, whose characteristics have taken root in the fictional community of Grantham in his crime novels. Engel graduated from McMaster University in 1955, and from the Ontario College of Education in 1956; he married his first wife, Marian Passmore (the novelist Marian ENGEL), in 1962. He became a producer of literary and cultural programs for CBC Radio and TV. As a writer of crime fiction, he helped found the Crime Writers' Association of Canada and received the Arthur Ellis Award in 1984. He became a Member of the Order of Canada in 2006.

Engel is credited with creating the first truly Canadian private investigator in the figure of Benny Cooperman, a dishevelled Jewish bachelor in his early thirties who lives in Grantham, eats chopped-egg sandwiches, pays weekly visits to his parents, and stumbles upon clues and culprits in a comical way that have led some reviewers to see Cooperman as a blend of Philip Marlowe and Woody Allen. The Cooperman novels are *The suicide murders* (1980), *The ransom game* (1981), *Murder on location* (1982), *Murder sees the light* (1984), *A city called July* (1986), *A victim must be found* (1988), *Dead and buried* (1990), *There was an old woman* (1993), *Getting away with murder* (1995), *The Cooperman variations* (2001), and *Memory book: a Benny Cooperman mystery* (2005)—see below. Actor Saul Rubinek played the 'gumshoe' in two CBC-TV specials based on the first and fourth novels. Other mystery novels are *Murder in Montparnasse* (1992), set in Paris in the 1920s and featuring a Toronto newspaper correspondent named Mike Ward, and the ingenious and entertaining *Mr Doyle and Dr Bell: a Victorian mystery* (1997, rpr. 1998). As this novel begins, in Edinburgh in 1879, Alan Lambert has been tried, convicted, and sentenced to hang for a double murder of which his brother is convinced he is innocent. He prevails upon Dr Joseph Bell, famous for his powers of observation and deduction, to find the real murderer and Bell asks his young student, Arthur Conan Doyle, to help him. Bell was indeed a professor of surgery at Edinburgh University and was the inspiration for Doyle's Sherlock Holmes.

Engel has also written a witty and interesting social history, *Lord high executioner: an unashamed look at hangmen, headsmen, and their kind* (1996), and *Crimes of passion: an unblinking look at murderous love* (2001), an expert account of some thirty cases. But his most significant work of non-fiction—because it is an accomplished, fascinating, medically revealing memoir—is *The man who forgot how to read* (2007), occasioned by an extraordinary event 'when I … was stricken with a sudden stroke in 2001, which put us [Engel and Benny Cooperman] out of the writing business by robbing me of the thing I loved above all things: the ability to read.' (The condition is called *alexia* [word-blindness] *sine agraphia*.) He could still write, but memory failed him, leading to all kinds of difficulties—even after several weeks in hospital and in rehabilitation—which he describes. He wrote to the famous neurologist and author, Dr Oliver Sacks, and visited him in New York (they became friends). The book, for which Dr Sacks wrote an informative Afterword, describes in compelling detail his gradual recovery—to the point of being able to compose the first draft of *Memory book* (published in 2005, two years earlier), which his editors helped him finalize. This Benny Cooperman novel is partially based on the condition he was recovering from, because Benny is also afflicted with *alexia* after receiving a serious blow on the head. Dr Sacks wrote the Afterword to the novel and also wrote an account of this episode in Engel's life in *The New Yorker*, 28 June 2010.

Engel, Marian (1933–85). Marian Passmore was born in Toronto and educated at McMaster and McGill universities. At McGill in the 1950s she had Hugh MacLENNAN as her M.A. thesis adviser, and this association led to a correspondence that lasted until shortly before her death (published—with most of the letters beginning 'Dear Marian'—as *Dear Marian, Dear Hugh: the MacLennan-Engel correspondence*, 1995, edited by Christl Verduyn). In 1960 Engel received a Rotary Foundation Scholarship that enabled her to study French literature at Aix-en-Provence; and she taught for a while in Cyprus. She returned to Canada in 1964, married Howard ENGEL, from whom she was later divorced, and made Toronto her home. She was the first chairperson of the WRITERS' UNION OF CANADA (1973–4) and was made an Officer of the Order of Canada in 1982.

Of Engel's eleven works of fiction, *Adventure at Moon Bay Towers* (1974) and *My name is not Odessa Yarker* (1977) are children's books. *Inside the easter egg* (1975) and the posthumous *The tattooed woman* (1985) are collections of short stories. Engel's novels are *No clouds of glory!* (1968), which was reissued in 1974 as *Sara Bastard's notebook*; *The Honeyman festival* (1970); *Monodromos* (1973), reissued in 1975 as *One way street*; *Joanne* (1975); *Bear* (1976, GGA; NCL); *The glassy sea* (1978); and *Lunatic villas* (1981, NCL), published in England as *The year of the child*. These novels are strongly concerned with the situation of women in society; yet they are not feminist so much as novels reflecting on the human condition from the point of view of women, with a woman in each case as the central character, and often as the narrator. Simply formed, deftly patterned, and clearly written, Engel's novels can be seen as presenting a gallery of feminine roles in contemporary Western society. *No clouds of glory*—her most irascible book—presents the woman as academic, challenging men in the career world, but also challenging women who take a traditional feminine role. *The Honeyman festival* (in which her economy of structure appears at its best) presents a kind of quintessential earth mother who has passed through a romantic period as actress and film director's lover to enter—loaded with her

memories—maternity and marriage. *Monodromos* is Engel's most elaborate novel, heavily decorated with background detail of life in Cyprus that satisfies sociological curiosity rather than one's aesthetic feelings. Here the woman is a divorced wife suddenly caught in a spin of insecurity, and moving back—through a surrogate sisterhood with her former husband—towards a renewed individuality. *Joanne*, a novel of less substance than the others—originally written in diary form to be read over CBC Radio—concerns the woman as wife and mother finding her way to stability through the ruins of a failing marriage. (There are no successful marriages in Engel's world.) *Bear*, which gained something of a *succès de scandale* for its daring plot of a woman enamoured of a pet bear, is really a fable rather than a novel in the ordinary sense, and presents the woman as a personification of humanity recognizing and uniting with its animal nature. *The glassy sea* presents the woman as nun, reentering the world and returning with new experience to the life of religious observance and service. If *Bear* shows humanity's need to recognize oneness with the natural world, *The glassy sea* shows how the spiritual life can give meaning to the brutal chaos of existence. It is perhaps Engel's best novel, beautifully concise, and the compassion, lyricism, and resonance of prose that underly all Engel's novels are here brought together in their most powerful expression. *Lunatic villas*—an 'entertainment' rather than a novel—is a vacation into farce, about the adventures of a haphazardly united family led by a single parent. Engel's talent was for *la comédie humaine*.

See *Marian Engel's notebooks: 'Ah, mon cahier, écoute...'* (1999), edited by Christl Verduyn, which presents the contents of the forty notebooks Engel kept from the age of sixteen until she died, and contains many entries that eloquently relate to her writing, her works in progress, and her personal life—to the very end of it. Verduyn also edited (with Kathleen Garay) *Marian Engel: life in letters* (2004). See also *Sunbeams from a golden machine: early poems and stories by Marian Engel* (2002) edited by Afra Kavanagh and Tammy MacNeil,

English patient, The (1992, rpr. 2006). Michael ONDAATJE's best-known novel secured his international reputation by being named co-winner of the Booker Prize. It also won a Governor General's Award (his third). Though not, strictly speaking, a sequel to *In the skin of a lion* (1987), it features two of its characters, Hana Lewis and the thief David Caravaggio, and refers to Clara and Patrick Lewis; the latter's death in wartime France is described near the end. It also resembles its predecessor by organizing its plot around a mystery story—the identity of the eponymous 'English patient'—and by being structured around two counterpointed and interwoven narratives. One is set in the novel's present, a Tuscan villa in the closing days of the Second World War; the other, a few years earlier in Cairo and the deserts of North Africa. In the former, Hana nurses a mysterious, severely burned pilot, meets the wounded Caravaggio, and has a love affair with the sapper Kirpal Singh, who is working in the area defusing bombs. In the temporally earlier narrative we see the patient, 'probably a Hungarian named Almasy', as a member of expeditions mapping the desert. More importantly, he is shown to be involved in an adulterous love affair with Katherine Clifton, the beautiful English wife of one of his colleagues. Her death as a result of a plane crash, deliberately caused by her husband, indirectly sets in motion the events that later lead to the patient's presence in a villa forty miles north of Florence.

The novel continues the engagement with history that was evident in its predecessor. The sensuous lyricism of the prose, tell-tale images, the understated, monotoned narrative voice, and temporally discontinuous structure relate *The English patient* to *In the skin of the lion*; but it surprises by the extent of its quotations, allusions, and references to the works of Homer, Herodotus, Piero della Francesca, Michelangelo, James Fenimore Cooper, and Kipling, providing a complex and sometimes obtrusive set of references that act as an indirect commentary on the two narratives. The use of della Francesca is particularly apt, because some of the novel's set pieces, though beautifully composed and evocatively described, have a static quality. *The English patient* was adapted as a film—directed by Anthony Minghella and released in 1996—that won an Academy Award as Best Picture.

Eskimo literature. See ABORIGINAL LITERATURE: INUIT LITERATURE.

Étienne, Gérard (b. 1936). Born in Haiti, and persecuted for his political ideas by the Duvalier regime, he came to Canada in 1969 and was professor of linguistics at the Université de Moncton, New Brunswick, until his retirement. Only Étienne's first novel, the bestseller *Le Nègre crucifié* (1974), has been translated, as *A shapely fire* (1987). Considered a canonic example of Caribbean literature, it was the

first novel to deal with all the forms of political cynicism and even cannibalism associated with Papa Doc Duvalier. The narrator forgets his own existence in a Haitian jail to analyze the situation of political prisoners and the depression and torture inflicted on them. Instead of resignation or suicide, he creates a form of ancestral language to build a strong resistance and a new hope for himself and his comrades. The novel *Crucified in Haiti* (2006)—the translation by Claudia W. Harris of *Monsieur le président* (2006), edited by Keith L. Walker—was unavailable at the time of writing and has not been examined.

Evangeline: a tale of Acadie (1847). This lengthy narrative poem by Henry Wadsworth Longfellow is based on a tale of hearsay (which the poet heard from a friend of Hawthorne, who had it from an Acadian woman). It is told against the historical background of the British expulsion in 1755 of the French-speaking Acadians from their lands along the shores of the Bay of Fundy, which had to do with the end of a 150-year struggle between France and England for possession of what is now Nova Scotia. *Evangeline* tells the story of an Acadian girl who is separated from her betrothed at the time of the expulsion and wanders in search of him throughout the American Midwest and the Atlantic states, only to find him years later on his deathbed. After he dies in her arms, Evangeline too dies, released from a life of exile and steadfast loyalty that has received no reward on earth. For background Longfellow drew partly on Thomas Chandler HALIBURTON's *An historical and statistical account of Nova Scotia* (Halifax, 1829). In his choice of hexameters, and in the characterization of his heroine, the poet was influenced by Goethe's *Hermann und Dorothea* (1797), a heartfelt depiction of a young woman's expulsion from her native soil. One of the most famous works in the English language, *Evangeline* appeared in some 270 editions and 130 translations between 1847 and 1947, including a notable translation into French by Pamphile Le May in 1865.

Evans, Allen Roy (1885–1965). Born in Napanee, Ontario, he grew up on a Manitoba farm, received a B.A. from the University of Manitoba and an M.A. from the University of Chicago, and did further graduate work at Columbia University, New York. Evans taught English in British Columbia high schools and by 1937 had organized an advisory and marketing service for writers in Vancouver. In addition to writing short stories for Canadian, American, and British magazines, he published one slim volume of poetry and four novels. His most significant novel, *Reindeer trek* (1935), a fictionalized account of the drive (1929–34) of 3000 Russian reindeer from Alaska to the Mackenzie delta, effectively sustains the suspense of a journey into the unknown, though characterization is slight and incidents are often implausible. It enjoyed wide popularity both in England, as *Meat: a tale of the reindeer trek (1929–35)* (1935), and when translated into several European languages. His final novel, *Dream out of dust: a tale of the Canadian Prairies* (1956), is a clear, cold account of a twenty-seven-year domestic war between a tyrannical prairie farmer and his young wife.

Evans, Hubert (1892–1986). He was born in Vankleek Hill, Ontario, and grew up in Galt. By 1910 he was a journalist in Toronto; he also worked for a time in British Columbia. In 1915 he joined the Canadian army and was wounded at Ypres in 1916. After the war Evans moved to British Columbia, finally settling on the coast. He supported himself and his family not only as a freelance writer but also as a fisherman, fisheries officer, logger, and beachcomber—activities that greatly influenced his literary subjects and brought him into contact with local Natives, for whom he expressed a strong sympathy in his writing. Evans wrote magazine serials; radio plays; short fiction, some of which was collected in *Forest friends* (1926) and *The silent call* (1930); and three novels. *The new front line* (1927) addresses the basic choices facing a soldier after the Great War; *Mist on the river* (1954), his best-known book, illustrates analogous choices facing Canada's Native peoples in their attempts to balance their heritage against an encroaching white society. Evans gave his Native characters strong, frequently anguished voices to express their often conflicting ideals of freedom and responsibility. *O time in your flight* (1979, rpr. 1994), an autobiographical novel, recounts the poignant, sometimes comic, clash between a young Ontario boy and his parents that finally confirms his belief that his freedom and future lie in far-off British Columbia. In late life Evans published two books of poetry, *Whittlings* (1976), which included most of the pamphlet *Bits and pieces* (1974), and *Endings* (1981). *Mostly coast people: the collected poetry of Hubert Evans* was published in 1982. Posthumous publications are two books published in 1991 and illustrated by Kim LaFave, *Bear stories* and *Silversides: the life of a sockeye*. See Alan TWIGG, *Hubert Evans: the first ninety-three years* (1984).

Everson, R.G. (1903–92). Born in Oshawa, Ontario, Ronald Gilmour Everson attended Victoria College, University of Toronto, and Osgoode Hall Law School. After practising law for several years, he took up public-relations work until his retirement in 1963. Everson started writing poetry in the late twenties, publishing then, and during the thirties and forties, in magazines in Canada and the United States. His first book, *Three dozen poems* (1957), initiated a series of volumes of carefully crafted descriptive and reflective verse: *A lattice for Momos* (1958), *Blind man's holiday* (1963), *Four poems* (1963), *Wrestle with an angel* (1965), *Incident on Côte des Neiges and other poems* (1966), *Raby Head* (1967, *The dark is not so dark* (1969), *Selected poems 1920/1970* (1970), *Indian summer* (1976), *Carnival* (1978), *Everson at eighty* (1983), and *Poems about me* (1990). Rooted in the Ontario and Québec landscapes he knew, Everson wrote short and gentle delineations of a horizon, a human being, or a limited action. He was a patient and loving observer of the human condition, while sometimes showing discomfort with the contemporary world. Though they abound in allusions to literary and historical personages, the poems seek to calm the reader by establishing a natural affinity and bond between the observing poet and the reader, who comes to see the scenes through the poet's understanding eyes. In his two final collections he balanced a deeply personal present with a sense of distance from which to consider the recollected past.

Exile: a literary quarterly (1972–). Founded by Barry CALLAGHAN with the support of Harry Crowe, dean of Atkinson College, York University, Toronto, the periodical was begun with the intention of making it 'one of the two best literary magazines in the world', according to Callaghan (the name of the other remained open for speculation). He brought with him many of the writers whose work he had supported during his tenure as editor of the *Toronto Telegram* book page: Marie-Claire BLAIS, Yehuda Amichai, Jerzy Kosinski, his father Morley CALLAGHAN, and Irish poet John Montague, to name a few. As a finely produced literary quarterly that has always sought to emphasize artistic content, from poems and short stories to avant-garde art work, *Exile* has consistently resisted the temptation to pad its pages with what Callaghan has termed 'factual filler', such as critical reviews, essays, and articles, and has focused on introducing leading-edge work by an array of international and Canadian, especially Québécois, writers. In 2000, vol. 24, no. 1 included prose

pieces by the French poet Emmanuel Hoc-
quard, the first chapter of Leon ROOKE's *The fall
of gravity*, five poems by Pablo Neruda, and six
poems by Daniel David MOSES.

Exile Editions. Founded by Barry CAL-
LAGHAN in 1976 as a book-publishing extension of the magazine *EXILE*, it has published
the work of many Canadian poets—including
The poetry of Gwendolyn MacEwan (two volumes, 1993), edited by Callaghan and Margaret
ATWOOD, and *The selected poems of Frank
PREWETT* (1987, rpr. 2000) edited by Callaghan and Bruce Meyer—but also, virtually
alone among Canadian publishers, a broad
range of books of poetry from languages other
than French: Serbian, Latvian, Ukrainian, Russian, Italian, Spanish, German, Croatian, Swedish, and Finnish. As a result, this small press is
no longer small, having well over 340 titles in
print. The broad range, and the literary depth
of its publications, reflect Callaghan's extensive
background and universal tastes.

Exploration literature in English.
I. INTRODUCTION. The early English-speaking explorers of Canada were assiduous writers. From the beginning their
superiors—whether mercantile or military—
required detailed reports on the new land,
and many of the explorers' letters and documents describe their attempts to preserve
these precious records while they travelled,
and to continue to write them despite great
deprivation and physical suffering. To 'write
down every occurrence', to describe 'everything as it is', was a duty that eighteenth-
century rationalism not only applauded but
considered a serious philosophical task. Yet
the explorers of Canada—men of the factual
world, with a great deal to attend to and little
time for the imaginative life—felt they had
literary skills sufficient only for 'a plain
unvarnished tale and unadorned language; all
matter of fact', in the words of John McDonald of Garth. Nevertheless, the texts that
record their experiences—fur-trade journals,
diaries, letters, scientific reports, autobiographies, and treatises—form the earliest record
in English-Canadian culture of the confrontation between the rationalist component of
the European imagination and a vast and
sensuous network of river valleys, lakes, and
heights of land that invited far more in the
way of interpretation than a strictly descriptive account.

The most interesting and imaginative literary phase of such writing is intimately associated with the exploration of the West and

North, after they had been penetrated by the
French, and with the great period of the fur
trade. Its typical published expression has been
the personal journal, mingling adventurous
narrative and scientific description. The European audience for such writings was a large
and well-informed one: readers abroad were as
likely to have perused Hearne and Mackenzie
and Henry on Canada as they were to have
read their fellow explorers in other unknown
lands. Many of these writings—for example,
those recording purely maritime exploration
and the search for a Northwest Passage—are
hard to associate with our imaginative literature because they really belong to the colonial
history of England. 'Exploration literature' is
here defined as those texts produced by an
observer who is describing and interpreting for
the first time Canadian regions unknown to
his own culture and that he experiences as a
sojourner rather than a settler. These interpretations, which naturally reflect the bias of the
writer's culture, became a part of the accumu-
lating body of explanation that entered into,
and shaped, the emerging consciousness of the
new English-Canadian culture and assumed an
imaginative role in our literary heritage.

Exploration writing is often classed with
'quest' literature; but quests tend to have a
mythic shape and a predetermined goal. In
exploration writing such a goal is usually
announced and may even be achieved, but the
shape of the adventure itself is not predetermined; literally anything may befall the
observer, and his obligation is less to mould the
account of it according to narrative conventions (though that, of course, sometimes happens, as in Alexander Henry's famous account
of the massacre at Fort Michilimackinac) than
to observe and record exactly what occurred,
usually on a day-to-day basis. There is a firm
rejection of everything 'poetic': all subjective,
metaphorical, and visionary perspectives are
treated with embarrassment or brisk skepticism;
and familiar literary devices such as structural
patterning, irony, and verbal play are almost
entirely absent. In a country without a genuine
native idiom, this evasion of the intimidating
example of polished literary models produced
a genuinely new form of discourse. While satu-
rated with empirical values both scientific and
historical, it was closely linked with autobiography and the first-person narrative, and indirectly produced some myth-making elements
of a new literature. The chronicle form, and the
factual language and open-ended vision of
these early writers, contributed to what
Northrop FRYE called the 'documentary tradition' in English-Canadian literature.

The explorer is uniquely a man of one book; the record of his experiences thus becomes a kind of heroic testimony, and was so perceived by his fellows. The man in the field—whether fur trader or scientific explorer—kept a daily log: a chronicle of events, natural observations, and astronomical measurements. This log he wrote up as often as he could into a journal that, if he were a fur trader, constituted his report to his masters. At the end of his posting the explorer looked forward to consulting his journals (as Samuel Hearne did) and turning them into a narrative that might gain him literary renown.

2. THE EXPLORER-WRITERS. Only five notable narratives of important explorations—by Hearne, Henry, Mackenzie, Thompson, and Franklin—will be mentioned here: all share the desire for a more general reading of nature and human experience, rather than the simple chronicle of daily events. Though this is how all these volumes originated, they are linked as well by the explorers' portrayal of a common world that, though still unexplored at its periphery, by now had evolved its own society, customs, and history. Samuel Hearne (1745–92) was a young Hudson's Bay Company man who, in 1770–2, on the instructions of his masters, travelled on foot from Fort Prince of Wales to the mouth of the Coppermine River on the Arctic Ocean. His *Journey from Prince of Wales's Fort in Hudson's Bay to the Northern Ocean...* (London, 1795; Richard Glover ed., 1958) is the first great classic of Canadian exploration. A straightforward account of events as they transpired, it nevertheless rises constantly to the challenge of generalization, as Hearne attempts both to report on scientifically, and to interpret, the meaning of the changing landscape and the Native life he experienced intimately—most memorably in his anguished account of the massacre at Bloody Fall, near the mouth of the Copper Mine River. Here the rigorously exact description of the empirical observer is coupled with the personal response of a man whose only language of feeling is that of the Age of Sensibility. See Farley MOWAT's treatment of Hearne's journals in *Coppermine journey: an account of a great adventure* (1958, rpr. 1990). Alexander Henry the Elder (1739–1824) represents the entrepreneurial spirit of the Scots and Americans who flooded the Northwest after the fall of Québec. His *Travels and adventures in Canada and in the Indian territories...* (New York, 1809; James Bain ed., 1901) covers fifteen years of trading and exploration around the Sault and on the Prairies from 1760 to 1776, and it too focuses on a famous massacre (which Henry barely escaped) at Fort

Michilimackinac in 1763. Like Henry, Sir Alexander Mackenzie (1763–1820), of the North West Company, was an entrepreneur, but one on a heroic scale. Grasping at once the nature of the interior as a mercantile problem, he made two brief, hard-driving journeys of immense importance: in 1789 down the river bearing his name to the Arctic Ocean; and in 1793 from Fort Chipewyan and across the Rockies to Bella Coola on the Pacific coast in 1793—the first white man to cross the continent of North America. His *Voyages ... through the continent of North America* (London, 1801) gained him immediate fame, and a knighthood; see the *Journals and letters* (1970), edited by W. Kaye Lamb. It was the imagination and aggressiveness of such Nor'Westers that drew to their ranks David Thompson (1770–1857), who in 1797 left the Hudson's Bay Company, where he had been an apprentice and trader since 1784, to become astronomer and surveyor for its rival—and 'the greatest practical land geographer who ever lived', mapping an area of the West stretching from Fort William to the interior of what is now British Columbia. Thompson's *Narrative of his explorations in western North America 1784–1812* (1916; Richard Glover ed., 1962) was compiled in his old age (1845–50) from nearly four dozen manuscript volumes of field journals, and, though unfinished, reveals a remarkable power of synthesis. Finally, there is the *Narrative of a journey to the shores of the Polar Sea...* (London, 1823) in which Captain John Franklin (1786–1847) describes the adventures of the British naval expedition under his command, which in 1819–22 returned, disastrously, to the Arctic Barrens, which Hearne had visited fifty years earlier. Franklin's *Narrative* strives for an objective effect, yet it is the most intensely dramatic of all these books. His death on another Arctic expedition thirty years later resulted in a mystery that gripped the European imagination for two decades. Of that tragic undertaking there is no narrative—only fragments of evidence to be pieced together slowly by others. These great explorations by Hearne, Mackenzie, Thompson, and Franklin were matched in grandeur by the brief but epic journey in 1808 down the near-impassable Fraser Canyon by Simon Fraser (1776–1862), recorded in his *Letters and journals 1806–1808* (1960) edited by W. Kaye Lamb. But Fraser has a different significance: he sought both to surpass Sir Alexander Mackenzie as an explorer and to write a journal that would bring him equal fame. The latter he did not do, but his extant log—a detailed factual and gripping record of one of the most hazardous and, ironically, least profitable of all expeditions of

Exploration literature in English

discovery—is perhaps the more interesting for its simplicity. Fraser marks a turning point in this account because he was strongly aware of his participation in a great tradition of exploration that had ideals of achievement and a conventional form of expression.

3. THE INFLUENCE OF EXPLORATION LIT-ERATURE. These and other texts hold the same place in our literary heritage as theological treatises and captivity narratives do in early American literature. Initially a subject for historical study, the explorers have emerged as writers in their own right with the proliferation of scholarly editions of their journals in the twentieth century. Such poets as John NEWLOVE and Don GUTTERIDGE have treated the men themselves as mythic figures; or, like George BOWERING and Mordecai RICHLER, have used them to ironize the very notion of myth. But few of the exploration narratives, save perhaps Hearne's, are securely situated in the evolving canon of Canadian literature. Yet with the evolution of the character of that literature—deeply committed to close observation, to local and individual circumstance, and to an ambiguous borderline between 'document' and 'literary work'—we increasingly see links between the imaginations of the explorers and of our contemporary writers, links that suggest how much both are the product of the practical, mercantile, and scientific culture of middle-class men in the Romantic age. Twentieth-century Canadian writing reflects some of the same deep inhibitions about language and metaphor, and shows the same abiding trust in the primacy of the document. The image of the log book or journal abounds, if not as a direct inheritance from the explorers, then as the result of a similar habit of mind that is reflected also in literary analysis, which often employs the image of 'map-making' as a term of critical discourse. The map itself has become a central metaphor of Canadian writing, as we can see in the hilarious map made of television sets in Thomas KING's *Green grass, running water* (1993), or in the 'great maps of art' in Michael ONDAATJE's *The ENGLISH PATIENT* (1992). And the explorer himself remains a powerful image, as the immense popularity of Stan Rogers' song 'Northwest passage' makes clear. Exploration discourse makes its modern appearance in the enthusiasm for autobiographical first-person novels and stories, in the poet's fascination with the image of the 'field note' or scientific observation (Robert KROETSCH, Christopher DEWDNEY); in the way novelist Timothy FINDLEY's narrators struggle to unearth from some infinitely

detailed but somehow unyielding documentary account the real significance of 'everything as it is'; or in Rudy WIEBE's attempt, as in *A discovery of strangers* (1994), to enter completely into the point of view of the world the explorers met with. It appears in the persistence with which English-Canadian writers adopt the metaphor of exploration to describe the very act of writing itself, a persistence that underlines the perceptiveness of Don Gutteridge when he calls the explorers 'our first philosophers'. Finally, in her poem 'The discovery', Gwendolyn MacEWAN reminds us that 'when you see the land naked, look again/ (burn your maps, that is not what I mean)/I mean the moment when it seems most plain/ is the moment when you must begin again'.

See Germaine Warkentin, ed., *Canadian exploration literature: an anthology* (1993). In her Preface to the Second Edition (2006), Professor Warkentin writes: 'Most noteworthy, the Native populations the explorers encountered have begun to speak vigorously in their own voices about how it feels to be explored. John Long (for James Bay) and Wendy Wickwire (for the West Coast) have studied the oral narratives—often transmitted over centuries— of the encounters of Natives with European explorers. Samuel Hearne's famous account of the massacre at Bloody Fall is now companioned by Robert McGrath's article on the numerous Inuit versions of that story. Jennifer Brown and Elizabeth Vibert's *Reading beyond words* and Laura Murray and Keren Rice's collection *Talking on the page: editing Aboriginal oral texts* have both adjusted the emphasis so as to focus on solely European discourse so as to focus on Native and Métis language and narrative. Today new critical editions of exploration texts, based not on out-dated printings but on fresh struggles with the original materials, are beginning to appear. W. Kaye Lamb's superb edition of *The journals and letters of Alexander Mackenzie* (1970) was available when [this] anthology was first published. Now we have editions by Barbara Belyea (Anthony Henday, and the *Columbia journals* of David Thompson), Laura Peers and Theresa Schenck (George Nelson), Richard Davis (Sir John Franklin), Lloyd Keith (North West Company documents), and Stuart Houston (Sir George Back). William E. Moreau's ground-breaking new text of David Thompson, in three volumes, will be published over the next few years, Conrad Heidenreich and Janet Ritch are re-editing Champlain, and I am producing a new edition of the narratives of Pierre-Esprit Radisson, scheduled for publication in the tercentenary year of his death, 2010.' GW

Fackenheim, Emil (1916–2003). Born in Halle, Germany, he came to maturity just as the Nazis were securing their hold on the country. He was interned in a concentration camp in 1938, but managed to escape Germany for Great Britain in 1939, and came to Canada in 1940. He took a doctorate in medieval philosophy at the University of Toronto, and in 1961 became a professor of philosophy there, focusing on metaphysics and especially Hegel, at the same time serving as a rabbi in Toronto's Holy Blossom Temple. After his retirement in 1981, when he was made Professor Emeritus, he moved with his family to Jerusalem, where he was appointed a Fellow in the Institute of Contemporary Jewry at Hebrew University.

In his teaching and writings Fackenheim treated the classic German philosophers, Kant, Schelling, and Hegel, as the culmination of the modern tradition of philosophy, and also as giving the intellectualized expression of Christianity. This interpretation appears in *The religious dimension in Hegel's thought* (1967) as well as in numerous articles and reviews of the 1950s and 1960s, some of which appeared in *The God within: Kant, Schelling, and historicity* (1996), edited by John Burbidge. The Hegel book treats Hegel's entire *oeuvre*, and instead of deflating Hegel's dialectical and speculative thought, Fackenheim emphasizes his success in mediating historical with logical thinking, surmounting Kant's division between the speculative and the practical, reconciling empiricism with rationalism, uniting moral with political thought, and overreaching the gulf that divides the religious from the secular. But Fackenheim shows that this philosophical success was predicated upon Hegel's conviction that, with the coming of Christ and the Spirit, all existence had been redeemed. Though he treats it with respect, Fackenheim could not endorse this conviction. And in most of the articles and reviews from that period, he shows the resistance offered by historical reality to the Christian idealism of the classic German thinkers. Fackenheim's challenge to that tradition had in part a specifically Jewish cast, and he made this element particularly clear in *Encounters between Judaism and modern philosophy* (1973), in which he grapples not only with Kant and Hegel, but with broader currents as well—empiricism and existentialism, for instance—from the point of view of Jewish thought. From the time of the Six-Day War in 1967, Fackenheim worried about the precarious position of the State of Israel, and his speeches and writings of the 1970s provoked great interest and controversy. He formulated what he called 'the 614th commandment'—that Jews are commanded to survive as Jews, forbidden 'to hand Hitler posthumous victories'; papers from this period appear in *The Jewish return into history* (1978). Fackenheim's thought became even more burdened by the memory of the Nazi Holocaust and he began to speak and write more and more about Auschwitz. *To mend the world: foundations of post-Holocaust Jewish thought* (1982)—as it is called in later editions—which he regarded as his *magnum opus*, reveals not only the world of horror in Auschwitz, but also the resistance offered there by faithful Jews, whose witness constitutes the true foundation of future Jewish thought. See 'A new commandment: Emil Fackenheim and the mystery of the Holocaust' by Theodore Plantinga, in *Myodicy*, issue 20, December 2003.

Fairley, Barker (1887–1986). Scholar, painter, poet, and teacher, he was born in Barnsley, Yorkshire, and won a county scholarship to Leeds University, graduating in 1907 with first-class honours in modern languages, with distinction in German. This led to his appointment the same year as Lektor in English literature at the University of Jena, where he obtained his Ph.D. An accidental meeting in his boarding house at Jena with a Canadian professor, who was scouting Europe for academic staff for the newly founded University of Alberta, resulted in his being offered a lectureship in German there. Five years later, in 1915, he was appointed associate professor of German at the University of Toronto. The painter J.E.H. MacDonald recognized in this shy young man of his own age an intellectual restlessness and dissatisfaction with the oppressive traditions of late Victorianism, and introduced him to the little group of artists— A.Y. Jackson, Arthur Lismer, Fred Varley, and others—who a few years later were to form the Group of Seven. Fairley became a close friend of the Group, and an early collector and champion of their paintings. (His collection may be seen in the Barker Fairley

Fairley

Lounge of the Faculty Club, University of Toronto.) At the same time he came under the influence of a lively figure on campus, Professor Sam Hooke of Victoria College, the editor of an undergraduate paper, *The Rebel*, whose views were very much those Fairley had inherited: a dissatisfaction with the social order and a conviction that it could be remedied. Fairley's wife, Margaret Keeling, shared and reinforced his radical sympathies, and *The Rebel* provided an opportunity to express their opinions. Fairley contributed poems, critical articles, and reviews to it, gradually assuming an influential position in shaping its policy. It was he who suggested that *The Rebel* should 'go to the country' with a new title: *The CANADIAN FORUM*. This was in 1920, the year the Group of Seven was officially formed. Fairley linked the two events. After four years at the University of Manchester, he returned in 1936 to the University of Toronto as head of the German department and set to work on the books that were to win him wide recognition as a German scholar. The first of these, *A study of Goethe* (1947), elicited an enthusiastic letter from Thomas Mann, and drew favourable notices in England, as did *Goethe's 'Faust': six essays* (1953). *Heinrich Heine: an interpretation* (1954) and *Wilhelm Raabe: an introduction to his novels* (1961) followed. Fairley's *Goethe as revealed in his poetry* (1963) and his authoritative translation of Goethe's *Faust* (1970) completed his canon on Goethe.

Painting had always been Fairley's passion and consolation. After his retirement from teaching in 1956, he turned for a time mostly to landscapes, but he also did many portraits, quickly executed, generally in a single sitting. In the 1970s the demand for his work accelerated sharply—exhibitions were sold out at high prices even before they opened. Fairley was also a poet; his publications in this area include *Poems of 1922, or soon after* (1972), *Poems* (1977), and *Wild geese and other poems* (1984).

Margaret Fairley—who edited *The selected writings of William Lyon MACKENZIE* (1960)—died in 1968. In 1978 Barker Fairley married Nan Purdy, who was the subject of some of his best late paintings.

Faludy, George (1910–2006). Born in Budapest, he was educated at universities in Berlin, Vienna, Graz, and Paris. He served in the Hungarian army, 1933–4, and was charged with anti-Nazi activities. In 1938 he immigrated to Paris and then to Morocco, where he was among those European intellectuals invited by President Roosevelt to enter the United States, which he did in 1941. He was appointed honorary secretary of the Free Hungary Movement and enlisted in the American army, serving in the South Pacific. Invited to return to Hungary in 1945, he settled in Budapest, where he worked as a journalist for five years until his arrest as a conspirator and an American spy. He was imprisoned for six months in the cellar of the secret-police headquarters in Budapest, then served three years of a twenty-five-year sentence at the forced-labour camp at Recsk (1950–3). During the 1956 Revolution, he escaped from Hungary and settled in London, England, where he served as editor-in-chief of the *Hungarian Literary Gazette* (1957–61) and as honorary secretary of PEN's Centre for Writers in Exile (1959–64). In 1967 he joined a circle of friends in Toronto and became a Canadian citizen in 1976. An occasional lecturer at North American universities, he was awarded a Doctor of Letters (*honoris causa*) by the University of Toronto in 1978.

Arthur Koestler once wrote: 'There is no doubt in my mind that Faludy belongs to the handful of contemporary Hungarian poets of international stature; and that among that handful he is *primus inter pares*.' Faludy had rocketed to fame with *Ballads of Villon* (Budapest, 1937), a collection of original poems written in the manner of the French troubadour, expressing disdain for authority—but the Nazis burnt the eleventh edition in 1943 and the Communists confiscated the fifteenth in 1947. Faludy published a dozen books in Hungarian between 1937 and 1980, the year his *Collected poems* appeared in New York. Five books of his prose have appeared in English: *My happy days in hell* (London, 1962; New York, 1963; Toronto, 1985), a meticulously observed and harrowing account of his three years at Recsk; *Karton* (London, 1966; a.k.a. *City of splintered gods*, New York, 1966), a historical novel set in Roman times; *Erasmus of Rotterdam* (London, 1970; New York, 1971), a sympathetic biography and study of humanism in action; and *Notes from the rainforest* (Toronto, 1988), a meditation, in the British Columbia interior, on human nature and inhumane society. Three collections of his poetry were published in Canada: *East and West* (1978), *Learn this poem of mine by heart* (1983), both compiled and largely translated by John Robert COLOMBO; and *Selected poems: 1933–80* (1985), compiled and largely translated by Robin SKELTON. The music of the original poems hardly survives the act of translation, but offsetting this loss are such strong features as the sense of locale (Budapest, Morocco, London, Philadelphia, Toronto, etc.); the feeling that love, though deep, is doomed; the belief that art ennobles and endures; the conviction that the Eastern European is sadistic and the Western world masochistic; the detestation of consumerism; and the abhorrence of autocratic authority.

Invited to return to Hungary, Faludy did so in 1989, and was immediately hailed as a long-lost hero; considered the leading poet of post-Communist Hungary, he was awarded the Kossuth Prize, the country's highest honour, in 1994. Old books were returned to print and new poetry collections were issued. He lived in Budapest until he died, though he retained his Canadian citizenship. George Faludy Place is the name of a parkette opposite the apartment at 25 St Mary Street, where he once lived.

Farm show, The (1976, rpr. 1997). The definitive example of the work of Toronto's Theatre Passe Muraille, this collective creation was first performed in a barn near Clinton, Ontario, in Aug. 1972, directed by Paul Thompson. After several weeks of immersion in the life of the farming community, the company created a series of monologues, sketches, songs, and visual images reflecting the vibrant yet vulnerable qualities of the community. In the tradition of Sunday School and Christmas concerts, skits at celebrations, parades and other festivities, *The farm show* spoke of and to a specific community—in its own patterns of speech and gesture—yet also succeeded in appealing to audiences throughout Canada and abroad, and it fused regionalism and nationalism in a powerful and exemplary fashion. It was influential in encouraging the participation of actors in script development, and in drawing attention to unconventional performance venues and non-traditional theatre audiences. Michael ONDAATJE's film, *The Clinton special* (1974), chronicles a tour in 1973. In 1985 the play returned to the Clinton area, where it was produced (with all but two of the original company) as part of Goderich Township's sesquicentennial celebrations. In the summer of 1996 it was recreated in a different form by the fourth Line Collective near Millbrook, Ontario. The published text was prepared by Ted Johns, a native of Clinton, whose conversations with Thompson in 1972 gave rise to the idea of the play.

Fawcett, Brian (b. 1944). Born and raised in Prince George, British Columbia, he graduated from Simon Fraser University, Vancouver, as a Woodrow Wilson scholar in 1969. He lives in Toronto. Though he published seven collections of poetry in the 1960s and 1970s, Fawcett is best known for his fiction and non-fiction. His strong social conscience is not at first apparent in *My career with the Leafs & other stories* (1982), nostalgic vignettes that include the narrator's charming account of a writer slipping into the starting lineup of the Toronto Maple Leafs. His tone darkens in the nineteen stories of *Capital tales* (1984), all revolving around the connotations of the word 'capital'; some are comic, some grotesque, some violent and disturbing. Many of the stories are quasi-autobiographical accounts of a boy whose illusions about life and love in a capitalistic society are painfully peeled away. The collection indicates the new direction Fawcett would take: the postmodern author often discourses with the reader about the writing of the tales, and announces 'that the job of literature is to keep the world going.' *The secret journal of Alexander Mackenzie* (1985) uses magic-realist devices to look at the demeaning spirit of capitalism. Narrated by self-proclaimed local historian Don Benson, the stories explore the conflicts between multinational corporations and small towns; the contradictions of fiction and history; and myth versus contemporary reality. The title story is a masterpiece: the eighteenth-century explorer, who was the first to reach the Pacific by land, discovers shamanism, hallucinogenic plants, and a talking bear in a consideration of such issues as how the past weighs on the present, social breakdown, and the threat of corporate culture.

A trilogy of controversial and provocative books—*Cambodia: a book for people who find television too slow* (1986), *Public eye: an investigation into the disappearance of the world* (1990), and *Gender wars: a novel and some conversation about sex and gender* (1994)—ask Where is civilization going? and combine text and subtext, flamboyant typefaces, and computer-page layouts: devices that allow Fawcett to hold contradictory opinions, to be ambivalent, and to have conflicting emotions. *Unusual circumstances, interesting times, and other impolite interventions* (1991) is a collection of revised newspaper and magazine articles on the arts and on crucial issues facing the Western world. This was followed by *The compact garden: discovering the pleasures of planting (a socialist garden book)* (1992), an amusing gardening book, and *The disbeliever's dictionary* (1997). *Local matters: a defence of Dooney's Café and other non-globalized people, places, and ideas* (2003), edited with an introduction by Stan Persky, is a series of essays (some previously published) on subjects that include the personal (his Toronto neighbourhood, off Bloor Street West, and the welcoming Dooney's Café, where he spends most mornings), literary ('Richler's end', 'A personal essay on the future of poetry': 'But poetry *is* an essential mode of human thought. It holds the technical protocols of metaphor, which is human language's most powerful but hardest-to-master instrument. Verse, on the other hand, is a temporary cultural expression of poetry, one that has been in a state of cognitive arrest for nearly eighty years.'); and ideas: 'Marshall McLuhan twenty years later', 'Aesthetics and environmentalism'. It is an enjoyable and enlightening book. Published in the same year, *Virtual clearcut: or, the way things are in my hometown* (2003), begins with Fawcett's Preface: 'In the Bowron River valley of northern British Columbia there is a clearcut so large that in the early 1980s, orbiting astronauts were able to see it during the daylight hours…. What they saw was the twentieth century's largest contiguous forestry clearcut, larger than any in the Amazon or the former Soviet Union.' The book presents four portraits of Fawcett's hometown, Prince George, some sixty kilometres northwest of the clearcut—set in 1990, 1993, 1996, and 2001—and includes personal reminiscences, accounts of how the town was affected by the clearcut, and protests the economic changes brought about by globalization and faceless corporations. 'Corporations are designed to make profits for their shareholders. That isn't negotiable. But there has to be a stronger local will than is here today if the corporations are to be given a rule book that makes them return equivalent value for what they're taking.' The clearcut is healing, but 'Prince George in the year 2001 is in deep trouble, like hundreds—or thousands—of other hinterland communities across North America.' This poignant, heartfelt depiction of the Prince George community is masterly.

Fennario, David (b.1947). Born David Wiper, he assumed the name Fennario, which a girlfriend gave him from a Bob Dylan song. He was raised in Pointe-Saint-Charles, a working-class district of Montreal, where most of his plays are set; he now lives in nearby Verdun. He left school at sixteen, worked at odd jobs, and was part of the hippie generation of the late 1960s, spending time in Montreal, Toronto, and New York. As a mature student at Dawson College, Montreal, he read widely, and became (and remains) a convinced Marxist. His first published work, *Without a parachute* (1974), is a straightforward, somewhat rambling record of his life and reflections as a blue-collar worker from Dec. 1969 to May 1971. It caught the interest of Maurice Podbrey, artistic director of Montreal's Centaur Theatre, who asked Fennario to write a play for Centaur and to become playwright-in-residence there, a position he held for several years. Fennario covered some of the same subject matter in another prose work, *Blue Mondays* (1984), based on further stories from his journals for the late 1960s. Fennario's career as a playwright was launched at the Centaur in 1975 with a production of *On the job* (1976), a one-act play about workers on Christmas Eve in the shipping room of a Montreal dress factory. Realistic, earthy, honest, and humorous, it depicts the plight of workers performing mindless jobs and finally rebelling against their employers. This same concern for the worker is shown in a longer one-act play, *Nothing to lose* (1977), produced in 1976 at the Centaur. Here Fennario introduces Jerry Nines, a character who plays himself—not very convincingly. *BALCONVILLE* (1980), Fennario's most successful and accomplished play, had its premiere at the Centaur in 1979. Set among the balconies of the tenement houses of Pointe-Saint-Charles where eight characters, English and French, live out the dog days of one summer, it is considered the first bilingual Canadian play and shows a genuine understanding and concern for the working poor who struggle to survive and fight for their dignity, often humorously, in a depressing social situation. The play has toured Canada and was performed at the Old Vic Theatre in London. Fennario's next work, produced at the Centaur in 1983, was *Moving*, a portrayal of the conflicts of a working-class, largely anglophone family, that surface when the family moves (as Fennario did) from Pointe-Saint-Charles to Verdun. There Fennario formed his own company, the Black Rock Community Group, which presented the first two of a trilogy of history plays. The first was *Joe Beef (A history of Pointe Saint Charles)* produced in Verdun in 1984 and in Toronto in 1986, and published in 1991. This musical drama is a comical and at times hard-hitting satire on the captains of industry who exploited the workers throughout Canadian history. These same captains of industry, as well as various political leaders, are the targets of *Doctor Thomas Neill Cream (mystery at McGill)* (1993), presented as *Doctor Neill Cream* by the Mixed Theatre Company in Toronto in 1988. The capitalist villains, many of whom were seen in *Joe Beef*, are shown as being more guilty of crimes against the working class of Montreal than the backstreet abortionist and brothel keeper Dr Cream. The third play in the trilogy, *The murder of Susan Parr*, marked the return of Fennario to the Centaur in 1989, following the closing of his theatre group in Verdun. Cast in the form of a murder mystery, the play presents a graphic picture of modern-day Pointe-Saint-Charles, where the condition of the working poor has barely improved since the nineteenth-century setting of the previous two plays. The controversial *The death of René Lévesque* (2003), produced at the Centaur in 1991, was an incomplete portrait of the former Parti Québécois leader, focusing on his betrayal of the working classes, a constant theme in Fennario's work. *Banana Boots* (1998) is a one-man show, a memoir narrated by the 'author' of the tour to Britain, notably Belfast, of the *Balconville* production. Banana Boots is the name of an Irish stand-up comedian who ridicules figures in Northern Ireland, including leaders of the Sinn Féin.

Ferguson, Trevor (b. 1947). Born in Seaforth, Ontario, he grew up in the tough Park Extension district of Montreal and spent part of his youth working on railways and building pipelines in remote parts of Canada. He now lives with his family in Hudson Heights, Québec. He was chair of the WRITERS' UNION OF CANADA in 1990–1. His six plot-driven novels, written with gusto, concern soul-searching men faced with extreme situations: *Highwater chants* (1977, rpr. 1997), *Onyx John* (1985, rpr. 1988), *The Kinkajou* (1989, rpr. 1990), *The true life adventures of Sparrow Drinkwater* (1993, rpr. 1994), *The fire line* (1995, rpr. 1996), and *The timekeeper* (1996). He made a fine debut with *Highwater chants*, about the pursuit through the B.C. forest of a mountain man who has lived in a cave for seventeen years; one of his brothers is among his pursuers. This suspenseful novel reveals, along with secrets of the past, various kinds of intelligence, understanding, and courage, and different responses to hatred, fear, and love. *The fire line* is about the disarming Reed Kitchen, a compulsive talker and storyteller who has the railway in his blood and is known throughout the Northwest for his inability to keep quiet. On his way to join a work gang hired to build a railway bridge in the Pacific northwest, he is accosted by a railway detective who wants him to keep an eye on a fellow worker who lied about his prison record on his job application. The ensuing adventure story—involving a run-in with vicious criminals illegally importing aliens from Asia—includes scenes of excruciating violence, but the character of Kitchen leavens the mix with charm and considerable guile. The narrative employs a form of scriptural diction as if to backlight the forces of good against the lowering presence of evil. Another page-turner, *The timekeeper*, concerns an orphan boy of sixteen who joins an unsavoury gang hired to build the Great Slave Lake railway, designed to haul zinc to Prince Rupert. Clever and indomitable, the boy witnesses unspeakable acts of violence within the gang, and endures beatings, near-starvation, and bitter cold. *Onyx John* features a young man—he and his siblings are all named after stones—who rebels against his father (a minister and an alchemist), enters into a life of crime, and lives in exile in Maine, a fugitive from the law. The novel is the journal he keeps about the search for his father, who has disappeared. 'I have spent my entire life trying to elude my father. Now I want to find him.' *Sparrow Drinkwater* is a picaresque tale about the life experiences of a lad born in a Mississippi madhouse to a charming schizophrenic teenager. Sparrow (his mother believes she was impregnated by a large bird) travels from Mississippi to Montreal (losing his mother on the way), where he is 'adopted' at the age of six by a bookkeeper and his family. Eventually he becomes a lawyer, a business tycoon, and a fugitive from charges of embezzlement. Aware from an early age that someone has arranged many events in his checkered career, Sparrow finally learns the identity, though not the name, of the mystery person. *The kinkajou* relates the adventures of Kyle Troy Elder, a devoted player of the dulcimer and a gifted singer of birdsongs. He leaves Montreal for Tennessee with his young pyromaniac girlfriend in search of artisans who make dulcimers, and remains for fifteen years, until he learns that he has inherited a Vermont inn from a father he has never seen. In Vermont he becomes involved with a strange group of nuns, a murder mystery, and a young woman who weeps tears of blood on Good Friday, and finds himself under suspicion for a mysterious poisoning. The theme of the absent father recurs in this novel, whose title is taken from a story written by Kyle's father.

Under the name John Sparrow, Ferguson entered the high-priced American publishing domain with *City of ice* (1999). This thriller, set in Montreal, centres on the detective Émile Cinq-Mars, who comes across the body of a boy, with a note attached to it bearing his name. The title *Ice lake* (2001) alludes to the frozen Lake of Two Mountains, northwest of Montreal, where Cinq-Mars is ice fishing in a hut until he hears a shriek: a women has discovered the head of a body in her fishing hole. Deciding that he had been lured to the ice lake to become involved in the murder investigation, he willingly takes his place at the centre of it; the case becomes interesting when he learns that the victim is connected with a drug company. With a complicated plot and satisfying characterizations, this long, well-written thriller is enjoyable.

Ferron, Jacques (1921–85). Born in Louiseville, Québec, he was educated at College Brébeuf, Trois-Rivières, and at Université Laval, where he graduated in medicine. Disheartened, while studying at Brébeuf, by the elitism of the French-Canadian upper class, he found himself turning more and more towards socialism. At the same time, discussions with Franco-Ontarians and Franco-Manitobans led him to think that Québécois alone had the opportunity to survive as a strong French-speaking nation in North America. He spent one year in the army, where he became convinced that Canada and Québec were incompatible solitudes, two nations that should be independent from each other. He first practised medicine on the Gaspé Peninsula, where he met several storytellers who became some of his most cherished characters. After eleven years as a general practitioner in working-class Montreal, he moved to Longueuil, where he practised as a family doctor. Well known for his political and social activities, Ferron founded in 1963 the Rhinoceros Party, a nonsense federalist party whose motto was 'From one pond to another'. After the murder of Pierre Laporte during the 1970 October Crisis, the FLQ requested that Ferron be the government negotiator. This was accepted by the Bourassa government, and Ferron played a key role in the surrender of the Rose brothers and François Simard. Between 1947 and 1963 Ferron published seven plays. But he is best known, particularly to English-speaking readers, for his fiction. *Contes du pays incertain* (1962, GGA), was Ferron's first major work, and stories from this and two later collections made up *Tales from the uncertain country* (1972), translated by Betty Bednarski. Using legends, fables, and tales to illustrate Québec's uncertain future, Ferron portrayed the land, formerly seen as a haven for survival, as being in

an advanced state of decay; life in the city, however, offered no viable alternative, for the tillers of the land found slavery as members of the exploited working class in the city. *Cotnoir* (1962)—translated by Pierre Cloutier as *Doctor Cotnoir* (1973)—is a novel that stylistically resembles a tale and presents one of Ferron's favourite themes: the necessity for a doctor to be both close to the people and a champion of freedom—which, in Québec, implied political independence. *La nuit* (1965)—translated by Ray Ellenwood as *Quince jam* (1977)—tells the story of François Ménard, a materialistic and bourgeois Québécois who, having lost contact with his heritage, gradually discovers a social order based on equality and historical awareness. *Papa Boss* (1966, rev. 1972)—translated with the same title by Ellenwood (1992)—describes the possession of an anonymous working-class woman by a capitalist angel, Papa Boss. *La charrette* (1968)—translated by Ellenwood as *The cart* (1981)—depicts a doctor who, like François Ménard, liberates himself from social 'deconditioning' (unawareness) and endeavours to help the 'cart-people' (workers) victimized by the diabolical boss. The young narrator of *L'amélanchier* (1970)—translated by Raymond Chamberlain as *The juneberry tree* (1975)—is initiated by her father into the 'good side of things': family and national history as indispensable tools for growing up, and the pressing need for the preservation of the flora, fauna, and historical landmarks of Québec. In *Les roses sauvages* (1971)—translated by Betty Bednarski as *Wild roses* (1976)—the businessman Baron learns the message of 'salvation' too late and joins the socially insane. *Le ciel de Québec*—translated by Ellenwood as *The penniless redeemer* (1984)—is Ferron's longest, most complex, and perhaps only true novel. It cleverly intertwines four main stories centred in Quebec City in 1937–8 (the centennial of the Patriote rebellion): clerics involve themselves in politics, politicians use patronage, western Québécois reveal their feelings of exile, and Métis are torn between the Prairies and Québec. In *Le Saint-Elias* (1972)—translated by Pierre Cloutier as *The Saint Elias* (1975)—the launching of a ship in 1896 parallels the launching, by Dr Fauteux, of the ideals of the Patriotes. A decisive battle ensues between the supporters of the zealous monarchist Monseigneur Laflèche and the devoted and patriotic Dr Fauteux. Most of Ferron's later novels display the same characteristics as *Tales from the uncertain country*: condensed plot; legend; parable; imaginative and fabulous atmosphere; animation of the animal and plant worlds; a surrealistic and fantastic vision; fantasy as seen through the eyes of a child; and irony, satire, and wordplay. His tales—translated by Betty Bednarski in *Selected tales of Jacques Ferron* (1984)—novels, and plays evoke both Lewis Carroll (*The juneberry tree* is a witty transposition of *Alice in Wonderland*) and *The thousand and one nights*. Ferron's father, who was a lawyer and political organizer, is a key antagonist in many of his novels. Ferron even claimed that he wanted to be a writer in order to denounce his conservative, elitist, and corrupt father; not surprisingly, biographical references were scattered throughout his works. There are also obvious links between Ferron's education and his writing. The tyranny and prejudices of religious communities encountered in his school life constituted one of his major themes.

Ferron's social and political ideas had considerable influence on modern Québec society. His thirty-odd works form a coherent system in which their predominant themes—justice; social concepts of love; the physical and psychological effects of capitalism; the doctor's role in society; religious excesses; the creation of new myths related to Québec history and politics; Québec and foreign writers in relation to Ferron's view of the world—are articulated in an original and esthetically pleasing setting. Ferron is in fact several writers in one: a *conteur*, a fabulist, a symbolist, and a creator of myths. In addition, as a literary geographer, historian, botanist, and folklorist of the 'uncertain country', Ferron, more than any other Québec writer, turned real people and real situations into literary beings and fictional places.

Fetherling, George (b. 1949). In 1999 Douglas (his first name) Fetherling changed his given name to George (his middle name) in honour of his father. Douglas / George Fetherling was saved, by an operation, from the genetic anomaly that killed his father, George Fetherling, and his father's father. Born to Jewish immigrants in Wheeling, West Virginia, though not a practising Jew, he came to Canada in 1966–7, becoming the first paid employee of the newly founded House of ANANSI and eventually establishing himself as a writer. Fetherling has written poetry, fiction, cultural history, art and film criticism, Canadian history, travel books, and memoirs, and edited many books, producing some sixty titles in all. Much of his adult life was spent in Toronto—with a stint in Kingston, Ontario, at the end of the 1980s and the beginning of the 1990s, when he was associated with the Kingston *Whig-Standard* as Literary Editor

(1988–92); he was Books & Ideas columnist for the *Ottawa Citizen* (1996–2000); and editor of *Canadian Notes & Queries* (1990–7). In 1995 he was awarded the Harbourfront Festival Prize (Toronto) 'for a substantial contribution to Canadian letters'. Fetherling has been writer-in-residence at Queen's University, Kingston (1993); the University of New Brunswick (2000–1); Berton House, Dawson City (2003); and Massey College, University of Toronto (2005). In 2000 he moved to Vancouver.

Fetherling's work as a poet is personal without being overtly emotional, witty at times, and often focused on social and political themes. He has himself described his poetry as 'a tool to see if I could register my experience in an accurate manner that might be accessible to others', and the precision of that statement is also characteristic of his poems. His poetry is most easily found in two selected volumes: *Variorum: new poems and old 1965–1985* (1989) and *Selected poems* (1994), and in *Madagascar: poems and translations* (1999)—the translations are from Martial. Other collections are *Rites of alienation* (1988), meditations on the urban experience in the form of 100 haiku, and *Singer, an elegy* (2004), a long series of couplets that pay tribute to his father, whose middle name was Singer: 'more of everything at the close than at the start, / though events and sensations were rushed // towards the end, as the day reached the point it reaches / and he thanked those who protected him until he died // and life for me began in earnest; / he passed it to me like a baton in a relay race'.

Fetherling has published two novels, *The file on Arthur Moss* (1994, rpr. 2005), about a journalist covering the Vietnam war, and *Jericho* (2005), set mainly in Vancouver. It is about Bishop, a brash marijuana dealer who is also a robber and is forever saying outrageous things ('All theatre has its origins in prostitution'); Beth from Alberta, a hairdresser who loses her job and is hired by Mr Steenrod, an undertaker ('After he had done his work, Mr Steenrod asked me to go style the deceased's hair while he ran an errand') and, as we learn at the end of the novel, has a great future in the undertaking business; and Theresa, a lesbian social worker ('What makes lesbians different from other persecuted groups is that we are discriminated against because of how we are supposed to look rather than on the basis of the way we're accused of talking.'). All three connect and end up stealing a postal van (arrest and imprisonment are in the offing) and head for the bush, near Williams Lake, where Bishop

Fetherling

has a hideaway, called Jericho, of some eight dilapidated buildings. Though it has attractions as a freewheeling work of fiction, *Jericho* is in some respects a self-indulgence that often tests the reader's patience, as when the sometimes mysterious narrator of a long passage in the first person is identified only by a minuscule typographic symbol before the first sentence. The novella in *Tales of two cities: a novella plus stories* (2006)—published under Fetherling's own imprint, Subway Books—is 'A tale of two cities', the two cities being *Toronto*—where the unnamed narrator, an authors' agent, was married to Faye, who at the beginning of the story takes part in this exchange: 'What do you want for your birthday? I asked. A divorce, she said.'—and *Vancouver*, where he begins an affair with Cynthia with whom he has an LDR (long-distance relationship), which is carried on by phone when he returns to Toronto ('we were doing much better on the phone than in person'). Reminiscing about his relationships and his two cities, the narrator includes little dialogue, though enough between him and Cynthia to reveal disagreements unfolding, egged on by Cynthia, who soon becomes furious (it is not clear why) and leaves him (to return briefly and unsatisfactorily). Unlike Faye and Cynthia, who never come to life—they are merely names—Eleanor Sim, one of his authors, is stylish, intelligent, and outspoken in her several brief appearances. At the end of the novella she gives the narrator news about Cynthia that shocks him. While Fetherling has claimed that 'A tale of two cities' is not autobiographical, there are many echoes of his own life in it: having Jewish parentage, a divorce, a connection with the publishing world, moving from Toronto to Vancouver, being an outsider (in a 2006 interview Fetherling says 'I am an outsider wherever I go.'). There is, of course, nothing wrong with any of this, and Fetherling is an expressive writer. But unfortunately, in 'A tale of two cities' the stream-of-consciousness account of a self-absorbed narrator who focuses on his relationships with two women that seem inexplicable never induces much sympathy or interest.

Fetherling has been deeply interested in the history, and especially the cultural history, of Canada, and this abiding obsession and affection has resulted in several important books, such as *The gold crusades: a social history of gold rushes, 1849–1929* (1988, rpr. 1997). *Gold diggers of 1929: Canada and the great stock market crash* (1989, rpr. 2004) is a fairly short (140 pages) but carefully researched treatment of the subject that is both illuminating and enjoyable to read. His interest in printing and publishing

resulted in two books on Canadian newspaper history, *The rise of the Canadian newspaper* (1990) and *A little bit of thunder: the strange inner life of the Kingston Whig-Standard* (1992). Some of his film criticism, much of it written for *The CANADIAN FORUM*, was collected in *The crowded darkness* (1988). Having edited *A George Woodcock reader* in 1980, Fetherling also wrote a percipient biography of WOODCOCK, *The gentle anarchist* (1998).

Fetherling is a reflective and attractively idiosyncratic travel writer, and has published four books in this genre: *Year of the horse: a journey through Russia and China* (1991), *The other China: journeys around Taiwan* (1995), *Running away to sea: round the world on a tramp freighter* (1998), and *Three Pagodas Pass: a roundabout journey to Burma* (2002). The third book is Fetherling's sometimes romantic and poetic, always informative, account of a four-month trip—to escape, to discover, to gain new insights—that took him from England to Panama, Tahiti, New Caledonia, New Zealand, New Guinea, Singapore, then through the Suez Canal and the Mediterranean, to Antwerp and back to England. Another extraordinary trip was documented in *Three Pagodas Pass*, the title referring to a pass through the mountains between Thailand and Burma, whose turbulent military regime Fetherling wanted to investigate. His book is a typically relaxed, informative account of an event-filled and geographically involved trip. His most accomplished and most moving book, however, is *Travels by night: a memoir of the sixties* (1994, rpr. 2000), a deeply personal and wonderfully realized account of his childhood and early manhood. *Way down deep in the belly of the beast: a memoir of the seventies* (1996), the second in what will eventually be a trilogy of autobiographical books, might better be described as a memoir of his twenties in Toronto, focusing on the friends, acquaintances, and others in the cultural world he inhabited. Fetherling's imagination burst forth with the idea for an unexpected reference book that is ingenious, informative, and gives much satisfaction: *A biographical dictionary of the world's assassins* (2001). Its seriousness of purpose is revealed in the Introduction, whose subheadings are: 'Assassinations in Different Cultures', 'The Nomenclature', 'The Typology', 'Archetypes and Stereotypes', and 'The Literature of Assassination': 'in terms of social class and position, an assassin must kill up and not down to distinguish himself from the common murderer.' The book is carefully researched, as usual—his references are clearly given. The biographical stories are of course well told and full of interest. To *The Vintage book of Canadian memoirs* (2001) Fetherling contributed an elegant Preface, and good introductions to the various extracts, for a well-chosen anthology of substantial pieces by many well-known modern writers (most of whom have entries in this *Companion*). In the spring of 2010 Fetherling published *The Sylvia Hotel poems*, in which he describes a failed love affair and the central place in his life of his favourite Vancouver hotel, and *Walt Whitman's secret*, in which his skills as a novelist are burnished to a high degree of effectiveness; it is narrated by young Horace Traubel—in real life the author of *With Walt Whitman in Camden* (nine volumes, 1905–96)—and the secret has to do with a historical event (it is not that Whitman was gay).

See *Jive talk: George Fetherling in interviews & documents* (2001). See also *George Fetherling and his work* (2005), edited by Linda ROGERS, who has written a sensitive and appreciative Introduction, calling Fetherling 'an enigma'. The book includes short pieces on his poetry by W.H. NEW and George Elliott CLARKE, an interview with John Clement Ball, and a reading of Fetherling's journals by Brian Busby.

Fiamengo, Maria (b. 1926). Born in Vancouver of Yugoslav parents from Dalmatia, she was educated at the University of British Columbia and received an M.A. in creative writing, under thesis director Earle BIRNEY, for her book of poems *The ikon: measured work*. For many years she taught in the English department at UBC. Fiamengo's other poetry collections—*Quality of halves* (1958), *Overheard at the oracle* (1969), *Silt of iron* (1971), and *In praise of old women* (1976), some poems of which were reprinted in *North of the cold star: new and selected poems* (1978), and *Patience after compline* (1989)—are reflective, intellectual, humorous, and passionate. In addition to writing about political repression and social injustice, she is especially effective in dealing with the oppression of women by themselves. Her ironic wit keeps her matter-of-fact imagery—which often draws upon her Slavic origins—from becoming forced and her poems from becoming mere tracts or polemics. The poems in *White linen remembered* (1996) have a lyrical intensity grounded in socio-political realities, childhood memories, and elegies for intimate friends.

Fiddlehead, The. A literary magazine published continuously at the University of New Brunswick since 1945. Founded as a poetry magazine by Alfred BAILEY and Desmond PACEY with a group of student writers, and modelled on *PREVIEW* and *FIRST STATEMENT*, it served until 1953 as a purely local magazine. Fred COGSWELL, who became chief editor in that year and held the job until 1967, expanded the magazine to include writers from across, and outside of, Canada, and to print stories and reviews as well as poems. The magazine has followed a widely eclectic policy, which allowed it to publish many young and relatively unknown writers. A number of these—such as Al PURDY, Milton ACORN, Jay MACPHERSON, Elizabeth BREWSTER, and Alden NOWLAN—became well established. Kent THOMPSON, Robert GIBBS, Roger Ploude, Peter Thomas, Donald Conway, and Michael Taylor were the magazine's editors from 1967 to 1991, when Don McKAY assumed the editorship.

The present editor is Ross Leckie. See *Fiddlehead gold: fifty years of the Fiddlehead* (1995) edited by Sabine Campbell, Roger Ploude, and Demetres Tryphonopoulos.

Fiddlehead Poetry Books. One of Canada's earliest small presses, Fiddlehead Poetry Books Series was an important outlet for Canadian poets from 1957 until 1983. Writers first published by Fiddlehead include Roo BORSON (*Landfall*, 1977), Don GUTTERIDGE (*Death at Quebec*, 1971), Joy KOGAWA (*The splintered moon*, 1967), and Alden NOWLAN (*The rose and the puritan*, 1958). Fiddlehead also published early work by M. Travis LANE, Norman LEVINE, Dorothy LIVESAY, and Al PURDY. The driving force behind Fiddlehead Books for twenty-five years was Fred COGSWELL, who took on editing and publishing duties when the University of New Brunswick withdrew its support in 1958. During his editorship he published 307 titles, many of them financed out of his own pocket. His self-declared policy of eclectic publication, internationalism (only one-fifth of the writers published by Cogswell had connections with Atlantic Canada), an avoidance of coteries, and the sheer number of titles he produced (forty-four in 1973 alone) earned Cogswell a national reputation as a mentor of young writers. Peter Thomas, who ran the company from 1981 to 1988, reduced the number of titles published and, under the name GOOSE LANE EDITIONS, added prose to its list. In 1983 the company was incorporated as Fiddlehead Poetry Books and Goose Lane Editions Ltd, and all books since then have been published under the Goose Lane imprint.

Fidler, Peter. See EXPLORATION LITERATURE IN ENGLISH: 2.

Fifth business

Fifth business (1970, rpr. 2005). The first novel in the Deptford trilogy by Robertson DAVIES (and translated into sixteen languages), it established his international standing as an important novelist. The story has a double focus. As the 'autobiography' of the schoolmaster Dunstan Ramsay it narrates key events in his life: his ducking of a stone-laden snowball—which stuns Mrs Dempster (who gives premature birth to a son), his boyhood love for the saintly Mary Dempster, his experiences in the Great War, his researches as a hagiographer, and his encounters with the business magnate Boy Staunton, the magician Magnus Eisengrim, and the fantastically ugly Liesl Naegeli. While Ramsay figures as hero in his own story, he plays quite a different part in the lives of Mary Dempster, her son Paul, Leola Cruikshank, and Boy Staunton: he is 'fifth business'—playing a subsidiary but essential role in the drama of their lives, and bringing the action to an appropriate conclusion. Ramsay's gradual achievement of self-knowledge can be compared to Jung's 'individuation', and characters and situations encountered along the way to Jungian archetypes. For Jung, coming to terms with oneself involves retrieving and facing the contents of the unconscious—which contains archetypes to which he gave appropriate names. He called a man's unconscious notion of woman the Anima; those elements rejected from the conscious personality the Shadow; the characters inherited in the collective unconscious memory, shared by all people, the Magus or Magician, the Devil, the Wise Old Man—and so on. One achieves self-mastery by recognizing that the unconscious may distort one's view of other people and by reclaiming the archetype that has been projected on another person. In *Fifth business* the archetypes are not only projections that must be recognized and recovered but elements in a story that has a fairy-tale or mythic quality. At one level we are persuaded to accept a romantic world where figures like a saint (Mary Dempster), and Magus (Magnus Eisengrim), and a Wise Old Man (Padré Blazon) act out their archetypical roles unrestrained by prosaic reality.

Finch, Robert (1900–95). He was born at Freeport, Long Island, New York; studied at University College, University of Toronto, and at the Sorbonne in Paris; and in 1928 joined the staff of the Department of French, University College, Toronto, where he was a full professor from 1952 until his retirement in 1968. A distinguished scholar, particularly of seventeenth- and eighteenth-century French poetry, Finch was also a painter and harpsichordist, but he was best known as a poet. He was one of six poets included in the anthology *NEW PROVINCES* (1936). From the beginning he was primarily a lyric poet. In *Poems* (1946, GGA), his skill with language and form gave his wit full scope in epigrams and satiric portraits. Like other poets reacting against the confessional poetry of the Romantic era, Finch treated emotional experience with reticence and allusiveness. *The strength of the hills* (1948) contains a sonnet sequence on mountains that develops moral and religious themes and a series on the transforming power of snow that uses images of beauty rather than the stereotyped symbol of a hostile force.

Acis in Oxford (1961, GGA) and *Dover Beach revisited* (1961) reveal new interests and a considerable extension of range. *Acis in Oxford* includes three poems linked by associations with an Oxford college, its gardens, a public park, and the river, that also draw easily on long traditions of myth and culture. The problem of faith is central to *Dover Beach revisited*, which begins with a reconsideration of Arnold's famous poem by eleven speakers who, though loosely associated with the poem's provenance, are themselves timeless. A second section, 'The place revisited', consists of nine vigorous blank-verse poems about 'Operation Dynamo', the battle of Dunkirk. In *Silverthorn bush* (1966) Finch ranges widely through Chinese calligraphy, ancient and modern Tibet, early Canadian history, and the Western literary tradition; but, wearing his learning lightly, he also records the small experiences of ordinary life. In *Variations and theme* (1980), reflections on the nature of poetry, evocative miniatures of particular times and places, witty epigrams, hints of the experience of old age and memory, are complemented by the title poem—fourteen variations about the moments of illumination when past experience enters the present, while each experience also opens towards the future, towards an infinity beyond guessing. Later collections—all urbane, elegant, and vigorous—are *Has and is and other poems* (1981), *Twelve for Christmas* (1982), twelve rondeaux on poets, *The Grand Duke of Moscow's favourite solo* (1983), *Double tuning* (1984), *For the back of a likeness* (1986), *Sail-boat and lake* (1988), *Miracle at the jetty* (1991), and the posthumous *Improvisations: the last poems of Robert Finch* (1996).

Findley, Timothy (1930–2002). Timothy Irving Frederick Findley—known to his friends by his initials, Tiff—was born in

Toronto. He attended St Andrew's College, Rosedale Public School, and Jarvis Collegiate until, at the age of sixteen, he finished with formal schooling. For some years he pursued a theatrical career; he participated in Ontario's Stratford Festival's first season in 1953, receiving some coaching from its star, Alec Guinness, who sponsored Findley's studies at the London Central School of Speech and Drama. He toured extensively in *The Matchmaker* by Thornton Wilder, who became an important mentor, largely through the intercession of the star of that play, Ruth Gordon, for whom Findley wrote his first short story, 'About Effie'; it was published in Issue One of *The TAMARACK REVIEW* (Autumn 1956) and reprinted in his first short-story collection, *Dinner along the Amazon* (1984, rpr. 1996). In 1962 Findley met his partner of forty years, William Whitehead, and through the years they lived at Stone Orchard, their farm near Cannington, Ontario, in the Provençal village of Cotignac, and in Stratford, Ontario. He became an Officer of the Order of Canada in 1985.

Findley has written plays: *Can you see me yet*, 1976; *Sir John A.—Himself!* 1978; *The stillborn lover*, 1993; *The trials of Ezra Pound*, 1995; and *Elizabeth Rex* (2000, GGA, rpr. 2003). His theatrical sensibility extends to his fiction: he is a master of the dramatic scene and tableau. His first novel, *The last of the crazy people* (1967, rpr. 1996), about a lonely young boy, trapped in a repressive household, who kills his mother, father, and aunt as a way of silencing their pain, was largely dismissed by Canadian critics. In the 1990s, however, some critics found in it the seeds of his later fiction's concerns with madness as social construct and with the fascistic intolerance of 'deviance'. *The butterfly plague* (1969, rpr. 1996) is explicitly located in the historico-political frame of Nazi ideology. Moving between the poles of Hollywood and Germany—between film's rage for 'perfection' and Hitler's—Findley produced a haunting parable whose surrealist method cannot obscure its historical referents. But again, Canadian critics barely acknowledged its existence, or saw it as a sprawling, oppressively symbolic work. In 1986 Findley issued a revised version (commenting on his publisher's pressuring him to 'explain' symbols like the ever-present butterflies).

After the publication of his third novel, *The WARS* (1977, GGA; rpr. 2005), Findley would never again need to make his artistic presence known to Canadians. (It also gained an international audience, translated into French, German, Dutch, Norwegian, and Spanish.) It

was the basis of a film (1983), directed by Robin Phillips. This tale of a young Canadian soldier of the Great War focuses on some by now recognizably 'Findleyan' concerns (defiance of authoritarian ideologies, the punishing of 'deviance'—homosexuality). But it also meditates on language and texts as constructions; a researcher-narrator leads readers through a conundrum: how should an act of defiance of authority, like Robert Ross's attempt to set horses free on the battlefield, be 'read'? Findley continued to muse on language and texts as constructions in *Famous last words* (1981, rpr. 2005) by having two reader figures, Freyberg and Quinn, offer competing 'readings' of the memoirs of fascist sympathizer Hugh Selwyn Mauberley (Ezra Pound's persona in his poem of that name), transcribed with a silver pencil on the walls of rooms of a hotel in the Tyrol while he was a prisoner. It recounts sensational events in the thirties and early forties, and many of the characters are historical figures: the Duke and Duchess of Windsor, Queen Mary, von Ribbentrop, Rudolf Hess, Charles Lindbergh, Sir Harry Oakes, and Pound himself, described as Mauberley's 'surrogate father'. But lest readers feel too lulled by the notion of history-as-text, Findley rudely undercuts the aestheticism of Quinn, the sympathetic reader, with the objections of Freyberg, who reminds him that Mauberley 'walked with Mussolini ... sat down with von Ribbentrop ... wrote Fascist garbage.' Findley's text now seems to interrogate the writer's craft itself as ideological project: if a writer creates worlds reminiscent of, but other than, the experiential world, is there a dangerous potential for that creativity to ally itself with another dream of world-making: fascism? In *Not wanted on the voyage* (1984, rpr. 1996) his intertextual study of fascism returns, but this time the intertexts reach back to Genesis and to medieval miracle plays. A spirited retelling of the story of Noah, the novel reconfigures the Ark as harbinger of the Holocaust; the humans and animals grouped in this ship's hold are 'not wanted on the voyage'—they are potential victims of a 'final solution'. In *The telling of lies* (1986, rpr. 1996) Findley adopted a first-person narrative mode; another departure was in his engaging the mystery story as a means of meditating on institutional 'lies', and the counter-lies or defiances, that he had conceptualized in previous fictions. In this novel, however, the counter-lies participate in the very economy of deception that they are supposedly set in opposition to. In keeping the identity of the killer of drugs magnate Calder Maddox a secret, Vanessa Van Horne acknowledges that she has started to play the same game as her enemies, the CIA and global capitalism.

In many ways Findley's *Headhunter* (1993, rpr. 2002) and *The piano man's daughter* (1995, rpr. 1996) form a duet on the theme of socially constructed notions of madness. In its dark, futuristic investigation of abuses of power at the 'Parkin Institute of Psychiatric Research', *Headhunter* is Findley's most sombre novel, in which a ring of pederasts is uncovered that preys on children, pandered to them by Rupert Kurtz, the power-obsessed psychiatrist-in-chief. (The novel incorporates an intertextual reading of Conrad's *Heart of darkness*, set in contemporary Rosedale, Toronto.) *The piano man's daughter* is something of an antidote to the despair of *Headhunter*. The madness of Lily Kilworth (the piano man's daughter and the protagonist) is both uncontrollable and strangely beautiful and healing. She is a rewriting of the 'mad' seer—the Cassandra—of the previous novel, the librarian Lilah Kemp. And Lily's son Charlie (another Marlow-type seeker), in his quest for the identity of his father, is searching, like so many of Findley's other male figures, for a way of being male that will not align him with the paternal authoritarianism of fascistic ideologies. His comments frame the events of the novel, which take place between the turn of the twentieth century and the end of the Second World War—which is also the background of *You went away: a novella* (1996, rpr. 2002). The settings here, however, are air force bases in Barrie and Trenton, Ontario, and it is a novella only in the sense that the plot is less complex than that of Findley's other novels—though the characters (husband, wife, son, lover) and situations are treated with the same patience and insight. As in *Famous last words*, actual historical figures pervade *Pilgrim* (1999, rpr. 2000), which opens in 1912 and is about an art historian named Pilgrim who, after the last of several attempts to commit suicide, allows himself to be committed to a psychiatric clinic outside Zurich and to be observed by Dr Carl Jung, who acquires his journals. These reveal Pilgrim's belief in his past lives (from his dreams?) that connect him with Leonardo da Vinci, his La Gioconda (the Mona Lisa), Saint Teresa of Avila and the crippled shepherd she befriended, and more briefly with Oscar Wilde, Rodin, Henry James, and Alice B. Toklas, among other famous names; they lead Jung to his theory of the collective unconscious. Besides being a novel of characters and events—in which

Jung's wife plays a part—*Pilgrim* also strives to be a novel of ideas and questions, discoursing on such things as identity, the power of the unconscious, and past and present. The composer Lloyd Burritt based his opera *The Dream Healer* on *Pilgrim*; it was premiered at the Chan Centre for the Performing Arts, Vancouver, in March 2008.

Spadework (2001, rpr. 2002), set in Stratford, Ontario and attracting the reader with its theatrical background, focuses on the complications—i.e. unreceived phone messages, a brutal murder—that result when a gardener cuts into a telephone line with a spade. But it is mainly about the disintegrating marriage of the Kincaids: the promising young actor Griff, who becomes sexually involved with his director to aid his career, the effect this has on his wife Jane (who develops a crush of her own) and on their son.

Findley produced two other short-story collections: *Stones* (1988, rpr. 1996) and *Dust to dust* (1997, rpr. 2002). He discusses the writing of short stories in *Inside memory: pages from a writer's workbook* (1990, rpr. 2002). A more straightforward memoir is *From Stone Orchard: a collection of memories* (1998, rpr. 1999). *Journeyman: travels of a writer* (2003), edited and introduced by William Whitehead, is a kind of memoir, composed mostly from articles, speeches, journal entries on the subject of travel. Though Findley never liked leaving home, wherever that was, he travelled a good deal: 'Many of these travels informed what he wrote—and how he wrote. Apprentice, journeyman or master, Tiff never stopped developing his craft—and these journeys were part of that process. We visited many countries, and some of these countries—along with some of the people we encountered along the way—were reinvented in Tiff's writings.' See Carol Roberts, *Timothy Findley: stories from a life* (1994). See also *Timothy Findley: an annotated bibliography* (1990), edited by Carol Roberts and Lynne Macdonald, and *Timothy Findley and the aesthetics of fascism* (1998) by Anne Geddes Bailey.

Fineberg, Larry (b. 1945). Born in Montreal and educated at McGill University, and Emerson College, Massachusetts (B.A., 1967), he began his theatrical career as an assistant director with Frank Loesser's production company in New York. In 1972 he moved to Toronto, where three of his plays were produced in twelve months: *The Stonehenge trilogy*, *Death*, and *Hope*. Fineberg's most characteristic and successful work explores the bleakness of family life, sometimes with unbroken realism, sometimes with a mixture of realism and fantasy. *Death* (1972) is an austere one-act play that shows the despair of a dying old man, and the emptiness of the lives that surround him, in a series of short scenes full of sternly economical dialogue. *Stonehenge trilogy* (1972), revised as *Stonehenge* (1978), includes some grimly witty social satire in its presentation of scenes in the life of a middle-class Jewish community. The macabre comic fantasy of *Hope* (1972) was inspired by the drawings of Edward Gorey. Fineberg's adaptation of Constance BERESFORD-HOWE's novel *The book of Eve*, commissioned by Robin Phillips, artistic director of the Stratford Festival, marked a turning-point in Fineberg's career: when it was produced at the Avon Theatre in 1976, starring Jessica Tandy, *Eve* (1977) not only set box-office records but won a Chalmer's Award for its run in Toronto. (It was also a success in London, starring Constance Cummings, and elsewhere.) Another adaptation, *Medea* (1978), played the Third Stage at Stratford in 1978. During this period Fineberg also wrote two musicals, *Waterfall* (1974) and an adaptation of Homer's *Odyssey, Fresh disasters* (unpublished), both for Toronto's Young People's Theatre, produced in 1973 and 1976 respectively. In *Human remains* (1976, prod. 1975) two bisexual men, sexually involved, and the woman they have shared, engage in a dissection of their relationships and family backgrounds. *Montreal* (1982, prod. 1981) presents a somewhat diffuse satire on corruption that, despite its local references, could really be set anywhere. *Devotion* (1987, prod. 1985) shows a tense family gathering in the wake of the mother's suicide; as relationships break and regroup, the mother herself, still on stage, contributes caustic asides. The play's bleakness is relieved by occasional gentleness and dour, low-key humour. The characters of *Tickle me* (1990)—a rich woman who is two-and-a-half centuries old, and a brilliant young man who has found a cure for AIDS—have a mythic quality. The cure involves the blood of gay men, and works only for heterosexuals; but the play is too sketchy to explore the symbolic power of this idea fully. *The clairvoyant*, which takes place in 'a large coastal city in 2038', ran for three months in the spring of 1999 in Los Angeles, where it won the L.A. Garland Award for Playwrighting; it was also produced by the University of Toronto's Graduate Centre for the Study of Drama in March 2000.

Stonehenge, Death, Hope, and *Human remains* are collected in *Four plays by Larry Fineberg* (1978). See also Robert Wallace and Cynthia Zimmerman, eds., *The work: conversations with English-Canadian playwrights* (1982).

Finnigan, Joan (1925–2007). Born in Ottawa, she attended Lisgar Collegiate, and her life, and the many books she wrote, were very much associated with the Ottawa Valley. She married Grant MacKenzie in 1949 and had three children; he died suddenly in 1965. After she attended Queen's University, Kingston (B.A., 1967), she began driving through the Valley with her children, interviewing people, recording their stories. She lived latterly in Hartington, Ontario. Finnigan's early poetry, from *Through the glass, darkly* (1957) to *It was warm and sunny when we set out* (1970), concentrated on personal relationships and was sometimes confessional in tone, with an elegaic note of loss—though *Entrance to the greenhouse* (1968) is a series of haiku-like lyrics, focusing on her response to the quick upsurge of life in nature. This movement in her poetry is reflected in a collection, *In the brown cottage on Loughborough Lake* (1970) with photographs by Erik Christensen, that underlines the poet's feelings about nature in relation to a 'limbo all summer long' as she reflects on the death of love. *Wintering over* (1992) contains four long poems arising from Finnigan's interest in the Ottawa Valley settlers. Other poems continue her fascination with voice and character, and some are dramatic monologues: the title poem has been presented on stage at the Canadian Museum of Civilization and been performed in many schools throughout the Valley. The verse-drama contained in this volume, 'Songs from Both Sides of the River', was commissioned by the National Arts Centre, Ottawa, and staged there in 1987. Finnigan wrote the script for the well-known National Film Board movie *The Best Damn Fiddler from Calabogie to Kaladar* (1968), for which she won a Genie Award. She has also written many books of prose recounting tall tales, local legends, oral histories, and straightforward historical accounts drawn from the Valley and its people: *I come from the Valley* (1976), *Some of the stories I told you were true* (1981, rpr. 1988), *Dancing at the crossroads* (1995), *Down the unmarked roads* (1997), *Tallying the tales of the oldtimers* (1998), and *Life along the Opeongo Line: the story of a Canadian colonization road* (2004). *Old scores, new goals: the story of the Ottawa Senators*, was published in 1992. *Looking for a turnout* (2007) was Finnigan's fourteenth book of poetry.

First Statement (1942–5). Founded in Montreal in Sept. 1942 by John SUTHERLAND—and his sister Betty, Robert Simpson, Keith MacLellan, and Audrey Aikman—*First Statement* was Sutherland's response to a rejection of his creative writing by the recently founded *PREVIEW*. Intended as a fortnightly, but appearing irregularly, the magazine averaged eight to ten mimeographed pages for its first fifteen issues, with a core circulation of seventy-five. By 1943 Simpson and MacLellan had dropped from the board, and were replaced by Irving LAYTON and Louis DUDEK, with Sutherland still editor-in-chief; a shift from eclecticism to a poetry that articulated the local and everyday experience in plain language, and from a North American perspective, now became more pronounced. Unlike its frequent editorial target, *Preview*—known for the wit, technical sophistication, and cosmopolitan concerns of its slightly older and more established contributors—*First Statement* disavowed any poetry that seemed 'colonial', favouring work that was influenced by American models, such as Ezra Pound and William Carlos Williams, over what was considered to be *Preview*'s British influences: W.H. Auden, T.S. Eliot, and Dylan Thomas. With the acquisition of a printing press, *First Statement* improved in appearance with vol. 2, no. 1 (Aug. 1943). It became an irregular monthly with more than double the number of pages and—in addition to the usual poetry, short stories, and criticism—offered book reviews. Because of financial constraints it became a bi-monthly in Oct.–Nov. 1944 and averaged thirty-five pages per issue.

In 1945 First Statement Press launched the important New Writers chapbook series with Layton's first collection, *Here and now*, which was followed later in the year by Patrick ANDERSON's *A tent for April* and Miriam WADDINGTON's *Green world*. In late 1945, after thirty-three issues, *First Statement* merged with *Preview* to become *NORTHERN REVIEW*, with Sutherland as managing editor. He maintained control of First Statement Press, publishing Raymond SOUSTER's *When we are young* (1946); *Other Canadians: an anthology of the new poetry in Canada, 1940–46* (1947), edited by Sutherland and compiled in reaction to A.J.M. SMITH's first anthology, *The book of Canadian poetry* (1943); Layton's *Now is the place* (1948); Anne WILKINSON's *Counterpoint to sleep* (1951); and Kay Smith's *Footnote to the Lord's Prayer* (1951).

Fischman, Sheila (b. 1937). She was born in Moose Jaw, Saskatchewan, educated at the University of Toronto (M.A. 1959) and, settling in Montreal, went on to translate some 125 books from French into English, including works by Marie-Claire BLAIS, Roch CARRIER, and Michel TREMBLAY. She won the GGA for translation in 1998 (for *Bambi and me* by Tremblay) and has been given honorary doctorates by the University of Ottawa (1999) and the University of Waterloo (2001). She is a Member of the Order of Canada (2000). In 2008 she was made a Chevalier of the Ordre national du Québec. Also in 2008 she was given the Molson Prize, receiving the jury's praise: 'Literary translation is an under-recognized art form, an act of creation in which the creator is often anonymous. Ms Fischman has perfected this art form and deserves to be applauded by all Canadians.'

Fitzgerald, Judith (b. 1952). Born in Toronto, she was educated at York University (B.A., 1976; M.A., 1977), and has been a teacher, journalist, and critic of poetry and popular music (*Toronto Star*, 1984–8, 1998–). Fitzgerald is a poet with many collections to her credit. These include *City Park* (1972), *Journal entries* (1975), *Victory* (1975), *Lacerating heartwood* (1977), *Easy over* (1981), *Split/Levels* (1983), *Heart attacks* (1984), *Beneath the skin of paradise* (1984), *Given names: new and selected poems 1972–1985* (1985), *Diary of desire* (1987), *Rapturous chronicles* (1991), *Ultimate midnight* (1992), *Rapturous chronicles II: Habit of blues* (1993), *walkin' wounded* (1993), *River* (1995), *26 ways out of this world* (1999), and *Bagne; or, Criteria for heaven* (2000). Frank DAVEY, who edited *Given names*, writes in his Introduction that the best poems to 1985 are her 'non-generic texts that play confidently with story, pun, found materials, ironic autobiography, as well as lyric', and succeed in 'decentering' the patriarchic lyric by subsuming it in 'autobiography, drama, fiction, gossip, verse, polemic, history.' In her later collections the emotions of passion, pain, love, and loss are somewhat deflected by a curtailment of meaning and significance, by what Davey called 'unorthodox syntax', and by wordplay ('Two hearts forever beating/up on each other, tearing/the lining of every silver promise'—from 'very much like singing' in *walkin' wounded*). The poems in *Rapturous chronicles*, written in memory of Juan BUTLER, are collectively a long and intricate prose love poem to him. *walkin' wounded* contains Fitzgerald's cycle of baseball haiku ('Haiku curve') and other light poems—but illness (schizophrenia) is seriously present (in 'How do you explain schizophrenia to a hostile neighbour?' and other poems). *River* (the Detroit River)—written when she was writer-in-residence at the University of Windsor—is a long, not easily comprehended poem, with a four-page Author's Note that does not really explain it. *26 ways out of this world*, a series of poems with modern colloquial locutions, accommodates the shifting viewpoints of Joan of Arc and Gilles de Laval, Baron de Rais, who was with Joan at Orléans and was later executed for kidnapping 100 children (mostly boys), and maltreating and murdering them. Fitzgerald has also written *Building a mystery: the story of Sarah McLachlan and Lilith Fair* (1997), an informal account of her research into the career and recordings of the popular Canadian-born singer and songwriter. It includes the 1997 Lilith Fair tour, the idiosyncrasies of a fan, reprinted interviews, and personal interventions; an updated edition, *Sarah McLachlan: building a mystery*, was published in 2000. To a series called The Quest Library, produced by XYZ Publishing in Montreal, Fitzgerald contributed *Marshall McLuhan: wise guy* (2001), an informal brief biography. Conscientiously researched, it is a kind of collage of short narratives and anecdotes, both with some fictional ingredients, that is an engaging introduction to McLuhan and (not to denigrate it) might well bring this important Canadian figure to the attention of young adults. Fitzgerald may be best known, at present, for what has been called a four-part epic poem with the overall title *Adagios—Iphigenia's song* (2003), *Orestes' lament* (2004), *Electra's benison* (2006), and *O Clytaemnestra!* (2007)—that draws on the Greek myths of the siblings Orestes, Iphigenia, and Electra. Their parents were Agamemnon and Clytamnestra, who (with her paramour) murdered Agamemnon when he returned from the Trojan war. Later (incited by Electra) Orestes kills his mother and her lover. With vague references to these events, the poems in these books are passionate effusions that express pain, grief, and loss in language that is sometimes arcane ('Deposition, exequies, inhumation, sepulture, funeration,/mausoleum, conflagration, all Holocaustic extirpation.') and sometimes bursts out with modern locutions ('Ditch the past.', 'What I feel is nobody's business.'). Also interwoven are subtle references to the poet's past as well as to what is seen as the wreckage of modern civilization. Fitzgerald's poems have been extravagantly praised.

Fleming, May Agnes (1840–80). Born in Saint John, New Brunswick, Mary Agnes Early became one of the first Canadians to pursue a highly successful career as a writer of popular fiction. She published her first story, 'The last of the Mountjoys', in the New York *Mercury* in 1857, while she was still attending the Convent of the Sacred Heart in Saint John. For the next decade, often as 'Cousin May Carleton', she sold short stories and serialized novels to newspapers in Boston and New York. From 1868 to 1871, Early, now May Agnes Fleming—she had married William John Fleming, a machinist, in Saint John in 1865—wrote exclusively for the *Philadelphia Saturday Night*. After their first appearance, her works were usually republished, often with a different title, in volume form; sometimes they were dramatized. From 1872 until her death Fleming benefited from an arrangement that allowed her stories to appear simultaneously in the New York *Weekly* and the London *Journal*, and then be republished in book form by G.W. Carleton of New York and Low of London. The *Weekly* paid $100 per instalment and the *Journal* £12; she received a 15 per cent royalty from Carleton. Since her annual output was at least one novel that ran to about thirty instalments, she became a wealthy woman. In 1875 Fleming moved—with her husband, from whom she later separated, and her four children—to Brooklyn, where she died at age thirty-nine. Her popularity was such that her stories, frequently retitled, were regularly republished for more than thirty years after her death.

In her novels Fleming was able to achieve a balance between the domestic and the exotic that chiefly accounted for their appeal to her largely urban, middle-class, married women readers. Much of the action of her later stories took place in New York City; but her settings also included London and Paris, large estates in the USA and Great Britain, and—because French Canada provided an exotic locale for American readers—Montreal and the villages of Québec. Her protagonists were often relatively poor working women, such as seamstresses and teachers, and her plots usually centred on marrying them to apparently good, prosperous men, preferably with connections to the British aristocracy. Complications arose from the greed and inexperience of the women, who often chose weak husbands, and the evil nature of the men.

Among Fleming's novels are *La Masque; or, The midnight queen* (1863), *A mad marriage* (1875), and *Kate Danton; or, Captain Danton's daughters* (1876).

Flood, Cynthia (b. 1940). Born in Toronto, she was educated at the University of Toronto (B.A., 1961) and the University of California, Berkeley (M.A., 1962). She worked in

Flood

publishing in the USA and Canada before moving in 1969 to Vancouver, where she teaches at Langara College and is an activist in feminist and leftist politics. Her stories are collected in *The animals in their elements* (1987) and *My father took a cake to France* (1992), the title story of which won the 1990 Journey Prize. Flood writes stories that deftly, and often shockingly, expose the emotional and psychological undercurrents of intergenerational lives; ordinary events resonate with devastating and scarring import when they are recognized as the source of old and new psychic wounds. Her narrative voices never judge the issues or people represented; rather, with honesty, irony, and sometimes bitter regret, her fiction's surface ordinariness gives way to mysteries and secrets otherwise obscured or repressed. Her stories often loosely parallel her autobiography as a student, married to (and divorced from) Maurice J. Flood, who had been an American conscientious objector; and as a writer, teacher, and political and social activist working through the inheritances of being the daughter of Canadian historian Donald G. CREIGHTON and novelist and children's writer Luella Creighton. Flood's first novel, *Making a stone of the heart* (2002), randomly documents the lives throughout the twentieth century—old age, deaths, school days, births, etc., never in chronological order, though always with the years indicated—of people who are either related, tenuously linked, or not known to each other at all, and none of whom lead happy, fulfilled lives. The book opens in July 1997 with Owen Jones, an obnoxious old man in the Bella Coola Long-Term Care Facility, a central character, not long before he dies. The year before, Dora Cowan Dow dies, the mother of three children and the ex-wife of Ned, who makes a self-interested complaint to son John about the divorce, saying, 'I was *robbed*.... She hardened her heart, hardened it to a stone.' We learn that Dora and Owen were schoolmates and she witnessed his strapping before 200 pupils: 'The gymnasium is quiet, even with all the breathing rows of children, quiet except for the *zing!* of leather rising in the air and the *zot!* as the strap bites Owen's flesh.' Long after she was married, in 1935, they had a tryst (though they never saw each other again) and she became pregnant with—a lithopedian, an unborn child, 'a stone baby', discovered in the autopsy. Her partner, however, fantasized about Jerry, the son he might have fathered, celebrating his birthday, when 'the stone inside Owen began to melt.' Incorporating these and other events, and many other characters, the somewhat clever, but irritating fragmented text makes one unhappily conscious of the

misguided employment of a promising novelist's skill.

Foran, Charles (b. 1960). Born in Toronto (North York), he received his B.A. from the University of Toronto (1983) and his M.A. in Irish literature from University College, Dublin (1984). He settled for three years in Amenia, New York, when he began to write and publish short fiction. He taught literature for two years in Beijing, China; he returned to Canada in 1990 and lives in Peterborough, Ontario. His *Sketches in winter: a Beijing postscript* (1992, rpr. 1993) put him in the first rank of Canadian travel writers. An account of his experiences during the late 1980s, the book is a sensitive and deeply personal glimpse at the lives of the people of Beijing in the wake of the Tiananmen Square demonstrations. Foran continued his unique combination of travelogue and memoir in *The last house of Ulster: a family in Belfast* (1995, new edn 2005), which deals with the unromantic, often arduous demands of daily life for the middle-class Catholic McNally family in whose Belfast home Foran spent much time over a period of years. He has also published two successful novels. *Kitchen music* (1994) evokes life in rural Ireland as a richly textured backdrop for the entwined stories of two Canadians—one a recent arrival from Vietnam, the other an established Torontonian of Irish descent—on journeys of personal reconciliation. Foran's *Butterfly lovers* (1996) locates his main character in the immediate aftermath of what one Chinese character refers to simply as 'the Turmoil', the 1989 massacre of hundreds of pro-democracy protesters. Accepting a teaching post in Beijing, the book's Montreal narrator, David LeClair, experiences first-hand the paranoia and terror that grip the culture and spirit of the city and hold sway over the lives and minds of its inhabitants. *The story of my life (so far): a happy childhood* (1998) is a delightful memoir.

The novel *House on fire* (2001) is centred on Canadian Dominic Wilson—president of WilCor Communications, Hong Kong—where his Filipina wife, Esther, and two children are living—who is in the (fictional) city of Bon in Gyatso (Tibet?), where he has gone in search of Tashi Delag, the author of a story, 'Ocean', that haunts him. He is soon detained, told that his flight has been cancelled, and submits to a form of house arrest. The characters he finds himself involved with—Sun Nanping; Anatman Sangmo (called Ant); and Paddy Chan, who has Asian features, bleached hair, and an Irish accent, having been raised in Belfast—are all mysterious (though the narrative fails to be a thriller, if that was intended). Another important character, twelve-year-old Kuno, suddenly appears and takes Dominic to Tashi Delag. In the last quarter of the book, the text of 'Ocean' is given in eighteen pages, satisfying the reader's curiosity. Thereafter the novel, focusing on Wilson and his wife and narrated in the first person, declines in interest. *Carolan's farewell* (2005) is a historical novel set in Ireland in 1737 and is about the legendary blind harper and composer Terence Carolan (better known in real life as Turlough O'Carolan) and his servant and guide, and friend, Owen Connor. Carolan became blind at eighteen from smallpox, married late and had seven children; his wife died four years before the narrative begins. Carolan's health is fading and he is on the way home on horseback, with Owen as his guide, to die. Great talkers, the Irish: the book is filled with dialogue—conversations with everyone they meet and visit on their journey, and particularly between Terence and Owen themselves. Terence exclaims: "'The glass has not been filled that I would refuse to empty. Company all day and night, why not? Better a brood of kicking children or a nagging guide than an empty bed. Better a hound with meaty breath." / "A hound?" Owen says through a yawn./ "Nor do I covet solitude for the creation of my music. Quite the opposite. I play the harp for how it gains me companionship. I play to be admired and loved as well as fed and watered. As well as to gratify the Lord, naturally." / "Naturally…"' Offering warmth and good feeling, witty exchanges, arguments, disagreements, the conversations overpower the narrative without advancing it much or creating tension and narrative interest, and a period flavour is absent from both the diction and descriptions of the Irish setting. The many characters who appear conduct themselves believably and sometimes amusingly, but they are little more than Irish names. *Carolan's farewell*, however, was devised and written with skill and it pleased many readers.

Ford, R.A.D. (1915–98). Robert Arthur Douglas Ford was born in Ottawa and educated at the University of Western Ontario, London, where he studied English literature and history. He did graduate work in history at Cornell University and this led to a brief appointment in the history department there (1938–40). He then joined the Canadian Department of External Affairs and pursued a diplomatic career, holding various positions at the ambassadorial level in different countries. In 1968 he was appointed Canadian ambassador to the USSR, and in 1971 was made dean of the diplomatic corps in Moscow, a rich experience that led him to write *Our man in Moscow: reflections on the Soviet Union from Stalin to Brezhnev* (1989), reissued in 1992 with the subtitle *A diplomat's reflections on the Soviet Union*, and *A Moscow literary memoir: among the great artists of Russia from 1946 to 1980* (1995), edited by Carole Jerome. He retired in Randan, France, where he died. Much of Ford's first collection of poetry, *A window on the North* (1956, GGA), as the title suggests, concentrates on northernness, climatic extremes often being used as a metaphor for the violent extremes in contemporary life. The poems generally offer a cold and bleak attitude to life, though this atmosphere is tempered by love poems and some meditative reminiscences of warmer places and times. Translations of the poems of some modern Russian poets are included. Ford always had a continuing interest in translation, considering his versions to be more like 'imitations' than literal translations. Other translated renderings appear in *The solitary city* (1969), but not just from the Russian: there are versions of Brazilian, Serbo-Croat, and French works. Ford's own poems continued to express a distanced bleakness, the studied objectivity and control of language emphasized by his frequent use of formal metrical structures—though there is some simplification of language and form in *Holes in space* (1979), *Needle in the eye: poems new and selected* (1984), and *Dostoyevsky and other poems* (1989). Ford's career as a poet is represented in *Coming from afar: selected poems 1940–1989* (1990), in which the final section is devoted to translations.

Forever yours, Marie-Lou (1975, rev. 1994). This is the translation by Bill Glassco and John Van Burek of Michel TREMBLAY's *À toi, pour toujours, ta Marie-Lou* (1971), which was first performed in English in November 1972 at the Tarragon Theatre, Toronto. Tremblay has considered this 'string quartet for four voices' his best play. At once the most sophisticated in dramatic structure and the most vitriolic in its attack on the family ('I want to put a bomb in the family cell'), it works on three levels: as a universal statement on the difficulties of communication between members of a family; as an indictment of socio-economic and clerical pressures that degraded the Québec family; and as a political allegory, the parents representing the past, one daughter (Manon) the status quo, the other (Carmen) liberation. A highly theatrical work, the play consists of two interwoven dialogues, one between Léopold and Marie-Lou, the parents, the other between Manon and Carmen. The parents' dialogue occurs just before their fatal 'accident', in which Léopold crashes the car against a cement wall, killing them both; the daughters' dialogue is set ten years after that event. The entire play occurs in one location, the kitchen of the parents' home; but only the daughters actually occupy this space, centre stage. The parents, now dead, are given symbolic locales representing their favourite spots, Léopold to one side, in front of a tavern table, Marie-Lou to the other, in front of the television. To stress the absence of communication, all four characters remain static, speaking straight to the audience. The play is composed along musical lines ('it is a purely aural thing for me,' says Tremblay), creating a strong sense of unity and harmony in spite of the harshness of the theme and language. Tremblay conveys the desperate state of Léopold's marriage and Marie-Lou's aversion to both sex and her husband through heavy irony and a number of key words; Léopold himself is caught in the 'engrenage' (cogwheels) of a monotonous job, and fears the onset of madness, which runs in his family, so that suicide is the only solution. The two daughters react in opposite ways to their parents' death. Manon remains in the house, her life patterned after her mother's prayerful resignation; Carmen moves out and becomes a sexually liberated singer of cowboy songs on the Main. Both women appear in subsequent plays: Carmen as the central martyr figure in *Sainte-Carmen of the Main*, Manon as the religious fanatic in *Damnée Manon, sacrée Sandra*.

Forsey, Eugene (1904–91). Born in Grand Bank, Newfoundland, he attended McGill University, Montreal, and Oxford University, where, as a Rhodes scholar, he studied philosophy, economics, and politics. Forsey was rooted on the left of the Canadian political landscape and several times ran unsuccessfully for public office under the banner of the Co-operative Commonwealth Federation (CCF). He was among those who helped frame the Regina Manifesto (1933), the founding document of the CCF. In addition to teaching as a sessional lecturer at McGill, Carleton University, Ottawa, and Queen's University, Kingston, Forsey was director of research for the Canadian Congress of Labour (CCL) for fourteen years. From 1956 to 1966 he served as director of research for the CCL's successor, the Canadian Labour Congress, and from 1966 to 1969 he was director of special projects. In 1970 he

was summoned to the Senate, where he remained for eight years; and he was sworn to the Privy Council in 1985. The recipient of many honorary degrees, Forsey was made a Companion of the Order of Canada in 1989. Among his many publications, his most important scholarly work was *The royal power of dissolution of Parliament in the British Commonwealth* (1943, rpr. 1968). Deeply read in every aspect of the Constitution, he became well known to newspaper readers for his many 'letters to the Editor', which severely but elegantly addressed errors on constitutional and other points. (See *The sound of one voice: Eugene Forsey and his letters to the press* [2000] edited by J.E. Hodgetts.) *Freedom and order* (1974) is a collection of twenty-four essays on Canadian constitutional matters, and *How Canadians govern themselves* (1979, 2nd edn 1988) is an informative and readable booklet. *A life on the fringe: the memoirs of Eugene Forsey* (1990) presents Forsey—the graceful and lucid writer, steeped in English literature, and the witty storyteller—at his eclectic best. He reveals with a candour that is not without humour how he left Canada for Oxford a Meighen conservative only to return a committed socialist, and how he managed to maintain that improbable balancing act throughout the rest of his long life. Critic Robert FULFORD called *A life on the fringe* 'an astonishing guided tour of our entire political horizon over three generations'. It was nominated for a Governor General's Award.

Fortune and men's eyes (1967; 2nd edn 1974). This prison drama by John HERBERT was first workshopped at the Stratford Festival in Oct. 1965, but was not produced because its subject and language were thought unsuitable for Stratford audiences. It premiered in a full production at the Actors Playhouse, New York, on 23 Feb. 1967; not until 1975 did it receive its first full professional Canadian production, at Toronto's Phoenix Theatre, when it won the Chalmers Award as best Canadian play of the Toronto season.

While it draws upon Herbert's openly professed homosexuality and on his experiences in a Canadian reformatory on a charge of gross indecency (a charge he always denied), its primary theme is human relationships and how denial of love can warp young lives. The play is about the 'education' of a new inmate, Smitty, whose 'teachers' are his fellow inmates: Rocky, a pimp and homosexual (who professes to hate homosexual behaviour); Queenie, a transvestite; and Mona, an eighteen-year-old boy, the victim of repeated gang rapes. In the course of the play Smitty is raped by Rocky, taught the politics and power structure of prison life by Queenie, and offered a redemptive love by the Christ-like Mona. Mona's 'quality of mercy' speech from *The merchant of Venice* trial scene, and the references to Shakespeare's sonnet 29 ('When in disgrace with fortune and men's eyes / ... Haply I think on thee...'), are balanced against the raw and obscene language of the other characters. The hope implied by the Shakespearean allusions is undercut, however, by the brutal whipping of Mona by the prison guards, and by the progressive moral degeneration of Smitty. At the play's close he has given himself over to violence and a criminal future. Although its subjects—homosexual gang rapes, physical abuse—are unpalatable, Herbert's play is leavened by humour and raw energy. Queenie's Christmas drag routine is a comic theatrical *tour de force*, and all the characters are compelling in their rage to survive. The play quickly became internationally famous—in its first ten years it was performed in more than 100 countries in some forty languages. There was a film adaptation (1971), directed by Harvey Hart.

Foster, Cecil (b. 1954). He was born in Barbados and educated at the University of West Indies, Jamaica, and York University, Toronto (B.A., 1983; M.A., 1985, 1999). He immigrated to Canada in 1979, and in Toronto became a journalist, writing for the *Toronto Star*, the *Globe and Mail*, numerous magazines, and for CBC Radio and TV; he also taught journalism at the Ryerson Polytechnic University. He now teaches at the University of Guelph. Foster made a successful debut as a novelist with *No man in the house* (1991, rpr. 1993), the title referring to the situation of Grandmother Howell, whose husband had left Barbados for England (she later obtained a divorce), and who struggles to manage an impoverished family of two daughters, and three grandsons whose parents had disappeared in England, and of whom Howard Prescod, from ages nine to eleven, is the second leading character and the narrator. His at first reluctant, then accelerating, contact with education and reading—unexpectedly supported by the headmaster of the Christ Church Boys' Elementary School, who guided him for the Common Entrance Examination—is at the centre of the novel. But many other characters move in and out of the story as it makes its way through strenuous electioneering in Barbados—with

independence being voted on—to the climactic results of the election and of Howard's final examination. Foster's second novel, *Sleep on, beloved* (1995), moves in and out of time and place as it tells the story of Ona Morgan, who left Jamaica at seventeen, leaving her baby daughter behind in the care of her mother, to find a better life in North America, in Toronto, where a bad marriage, pregnancy, racism, and ill luck postponed her reunion with her daughter for twelve years. When Suzanne finally arrives she becomes rebellious, owing to her well-meaning mother's inability to deal with the effects of her daughter's transference to an alien culture. Suzanne misbehaves at school, gets into trouble with the law, and her mother ejects her from her apartment—when things soon go from bad to worse for Suzanne. Much later, separately and unknown to each other, mother and daughter return briefly to Jamaica—Suzanne when Grandmother Nedd is dying, and Ona after she has died, when Ona decides she cannot stay to assume her mother's mantle, having been 'tainted by life abroad'. She returns to Toronto and in the end becomes mad. Suzanne shows signs of achieving stability, seeing her future role as assuming responsibility for her half-brother Telson. 'She realized that every immigrant must assume a different personality to survive.' Foster's third novel, *Slammin' tar* (1998), is about Johnny Franklin, who for twenty-five years left Barbados annually for ten months as part of the 'Program' to labour with other Bajuns on the Eckridge tobacco farm in southwestern Ontario, run by George Stewart. Johnny had become the leader. On this trip to 'cold-arse Canada' is a new member of the group, seventeen-year-old Winston, whose easy ways are resented and who has a fight with Johnny. The story is narrated by the supernatural storyteller-cum-spider, Brer Anancy ('Believe me, I was there when they took the first of our people from Africa'), the loquacious and ubiquitous commentator on the characters and events of this disastrous season, which resulted in the return to Barbados of all the men but three: Tommy, who had died; Johnny; and young Winston, who had previously shown leadership qualities. They both decided to run, slammin' tar. *Dry bone memories* (2001) is a long, complex novel that has, at its centre, the narrator Edmund, a preacher's son in Barbados, and his chum from early boyhood, Jeffrey Spencer, whose father is a gravedigger (the two fathers are close friends). Midway through the book Edmund remembers their boyhood and there

Foster

is a wonderful monologue from Thelma, Jeffrey's mother, as she talks about her past to Edmund's mother. As adults Jeffrey and Edmund had 'consciously chosen to be different.' Jeffrey longed to make money, which he would use to help his island. He gradually achieves wealth—from drug lords, 'beginning as a mule to carry some of the stuff into Toronto and ship it in courier envelopes across the border into New York and Boston'—and power: he is made chairman of Caribbean International Airlines and is close, in a sinister way, to the prime minister. He is also drawn into the Organization, led by Alberto Gomez in Bogotá, Colombia, and 'was now part of a power structure that the people who mattered to him would call the seat of corruption.' The Organization, 'with its tentacles reaching out almost everywhere around the globe, knows how to look after those betraying it.' Jeffery insists on keeping Edmund by his side: 'Who else has a conscience so pure, pure enough, if I may say so, for two people?' The novel begins with an italicized Prologue of more than fifteen pages that is a kind of intense prose poem conveying little meaning, a mode that is repeated occasionally throughout this overwritten novel. The author writes *around* events instead of describing them quickly, directly, vividly; the effect of the book is therefore blunted and its potential thriller qualities are dulled. But Foster's expressivity as a novelist is undeniable.

Foster's skills as a journalist and researcher are evident in *A place called heaven: the meaning of being black in Canada*. Published in 1996, and still a salutary and illuminating study of the troubling strains of the vulnerable black population in Canada, it is a readable anecdotal account of such things as the negative experiences of able black politicians in government; the treatment of blacks in the media, which focus on conflicts with the law, sports figures, and entertainers; a long anecdote about Foster, as a teacher of creative writing, dealing with an adult black student who skipped classes and handed in her inadequate assignment late and protested her low mark—and the later acrimonious session with the student's mother (it eventually ended well); the anger and alienation of black youth; and the necessity for black communities to share the responsibility for black violence. These and many other topics lead to such statements as 'the gap between the black experience and the wider Canadian society is widening', and 'Blacks and other minorities in Canada are now caught in the right-wing

backlash with no party to defend them.' The title is drawn from a speech Martin Luther King made in Canada in 1967, referring to the spirituals of the Negro slaves: 'We sang of "heaven" that awaited us, and the slave master listened in innocence, not realizing that we were not speaking of the hereafter. Heaven was the word for Canada and the Negro sang of the hope that his escape on the Underground Railway would carry him there.' Foster's memoir *Island wings* (1998) reveals how much in *No man in the house* was drawn from his own childhood. But Foster became a cub reporter for the Caribbean service of the Reuters News Agency; saved enough money to fly to London to visit his mother, who had five other children, and his father, from whom she was divorced (there are sad, memorable portraits of both); and went on to study at the University of the West Indies. His career as a political reporter in Bridgetown was cut short when he published what was actually said in the House of Assembly; feeling threatened, he left Barbados, taking 'my island wings' to Toronto. The memoir makes a particular contribution in describing the volatile political situation in the Caribbean of the 1970s, particularly in Jamaica, Barbados, and Grenada. The opening of Foster's Preface to *Where race does not matter: the new spirit of modernity* (2005) indicates its thrust, and its hope, when he says the book 'is my way of coming to terms with myself as a Black Canadian, and as an immigrant who feels blessed to be living in Canada at this time yet can imagine a society in which all citizens are genuinely equal and share the same rights and privileges.' He describes his book as 'a conversation. It is also a reflection. And it is an idealist dream, perhaps falling just short of a utopian one.' This is true. But in exploring aspects of what he calls Modernity—such as 'the white-state model for those who feared or disdained Black power or so-called mixed-race democracy where power is shared by ethnic groups. This model argued that Black-skinned people should have no meaningful role in society'—Foster refers to many objectionable examples of ethnic prejudice, without, overall, coming to terms intellectually with the realities that affect the thinking and behaviour of people today (both black and white). The book's long, challenging discourse ends by saying that in 'Greek and Hebrew mythology, there was something socially uplifting and meritorious about having a Black skin.... Black skin signified something important about the human condition. // This is the message that Black skin should still retain in a land where there is no *race*.'

Foster, Norm (b. 1949). Born in Newmarket, Ontario, he was educated in radio and television arts at Centennial College, Toronto, and Confederation College, Thunder Bay. He lives in Fredericton, New Brunswick. The author of many light plays, Foster is perhaps the most produced playwright in both professional and community / amateur theatre in Canada. *Sinners* (1983) and *The Melville boys* (1986) were very successful in productions by Theatre New Brunswick. The first is about a furniture-store owner who is found in the arms of a local minister's wife; the second is about the lakeside weekend of Owen and Lee Melville and what happens when they are joined by two sisters. Other plays include *Ethan Claymore* (1998, rpr. 2000), about a young widower whose life is transformed; *The foursome* (1998, rpr. 2000), set on a golf course, in which four chums at a class reunion play golf and reminisce; and *Office hours* (1998), *Small time* (2001), *The long weekend* (2002), *Wrong for each other* (2003), *Looking* (2006), *The love list* (2006), and *Bedtime stories* (2007). *Vintage Foster: six plays by Norm Foster* (2001) contains *The Melville boys*, *Opening night* (1989), *The motor trade* (1991), *Wrong for each other*, *Jupiter in July* (1997), and *Drinking alone* (1998). *Jenny's House of Joy* (2007), set in a small town in Kansas in 1871 in the whorehouse of the title, is a five-character play. Jenny is 'the boss', and the 'ladies' are sharp-tongued Frances, in her forties; Anita, in her twenties; and Natalie, also in her twenties, who has escaped from her husband, who abused her, and immediately becomes very successful. Clara Casey appears twice, protesting the visitation of *her* husband (who is dying)—the second time with a rifle. The dialogue and actions of these women create a skilful light play that is both sharp and amusing. It was first produced at the Lighthouse Festival Theatre, Port Dover, Ontario, in June 2006.

Four Horsemen, The. This sound-poetry performance group began in 1970 when, after a joint reading by bp NICHOL and Steve McCAFFERY, Rafael Barreto-Rivera proposed that they should get together, with Paul Dutton, and 'jam'. They quickly became the premier sound-poetry ensemble in Canada, and by the late 1970s had attained an international reputation, working within the traditions of sound poetry established by such early-twentieth-century pioneers as Hugo Ball and Kurt Schwitters.

They stressed the *sound* of language as the primary material of their work, using such techniques as chant, repetition, and counterpoint; and developed flexible notational systems to permit a more precise interaction of the four voices. Sometimes the effect was to emphasize meaning in new ways, but often their work tended towards a diminution or 'abstraction' of the semantic content, a celebration of pure vocal sound. While their later performances became more theatrical, laying greater stress on the physicality of the performing body on stage, they set a standard of inventiveness, energy, and exuberant delight in language that challenges all poets, at whatever edge of experimentation. After Nichol's untimely death in 1988, the group's activities tapered off, although they occasionally performed together as simply The Horsemen. The Four Horsemen made several recordings—*CaNADAda* (1973), *Live in the West* (1977), and *Bootleg* (1981). *The prose tattoo* (1982) is an important collection of their collaborative texts, while *Horse d'oeuvres* (1975) contains separate pieces by each member.

Four Jameses, The (1927). This literary satire by William Arthur DEACON consists of biographical and critical appreciations of four real-life but mercifully obscure Canadian poetasters whose only connection was their common Christian name, their lack of talent, and the mock admiration they aroused in Deacon. Of the four, three wrote their doggerel about rural Ontario: James Gay (who called himself the poet laureate of Canada), James McIntyre (author of the dreadful 'Ode on the mammoth cheese'), and James MacRae (less inherently offensive than the others, but still a poet whose rhymes make the fillings in one's teeth ache). The fourth James was James Gillis of Cape Breton, who was ambidextrous, being equally ungifted in prose. *The four Jameses*, which appeared in a revised edition in 1953 and was reprinted again in 1974, is distinguished both by Deacon's use of quotations to enhance the reputations of his subjects, and by the straightness of his face while doing so.

Fowke, Edith (1913–96). Edith Fulton was born in Lumsden, Saskatchewan, and educated at the provincial university (B.A., 1933; M.A., 1937). She married Franklin Fowke in 1938. In the late 1940s she began recording immigrant and lumbering ballads in central Ontario, and this interest and activity broadened until she became one of Canada's leading folklorists, dedicated to revealing 'the hidden submerged culture lying in the shadow of the official civilization about which historians write'. She joined the English Department of York University, Toronto, in 1971 to teach courses in folklore; became a full professor in 1977; and retired as Professor Emerita in 1984. Fowke received many honours, including honorary doctorates from four Canadian universities, and was a Companion of the Order of Canada.

Among Fowke's more than twenty publications were many on folksongs, including *Folksongs of Canada* (1954, with Richard Johnston), *Traditional singers and songs from Ontario* (1965), *Lumbering songs from the northern woods* (1970), *The Penguin book of Canadian folk songs* (1973), and *Sea songs and ballads from nineteenth-century Nova Scotia* (1982). On non-musical folklore she collected the chants and rhymes of children for the popular *Sally go round the sun* (1969), *Ring around the moon* (1972), and *Red rover! red rover!: children's games played in Canada* (1988). Her folklore collections include *Folklore of Canada* (1976), *Folktales of French Canada* (1979), *Tales told in Canada* (1986), and *Legends told in Canada* (1988, rpr. 1994). Fowke's *Canadian folklore* (1988), in Oxford's Perspectives on Canadian Culture series, is a brief but valuable and wide-ranging survey of the subject.

Francis, Marvin. See ABORIGINAL LITERATURE: 5.

Franklin, John. See EXPLORATION LITERATURE IN ENGLISH: 2.

Fraser, Brad (b.1959). Born and raised in Edmonton—and now dividing his time between Toronto and Los Angeles—he writes unconventional, often controversial, plays that recall traditions of horror, black comedy, and farce, dramatizing love, violence, identity, and homosexuality. His early plays include *Mutants* (produced in 1980); *Wolfboy* (prod. 1981), published in a revised form in *The wolf plays* (1993) with *Prom night of the living dead* (prod. 1991); *Chainsaw love* (prod. 1982); *Rude noises (for a blank generation)* (prod. 1982); and *Young Art* (prod. 1987). Fraser is perhaps best known for *Unidentified human remains and the true nature of love* (1990). Both romance and murder mystery, it moves with disturbing ease between the serious and the comic. Seven characters search for and avoid love and sex in Edmonton, in a world of tension, insecurity, and violence. The characters—including a psychic prostitute, an anorexic book reviewer, a gay waiter, and a secret serial killer—circle each other, unable or unwilling to

communicate meaningfully except on an answering machine. First produced by Alberta Theatre Projects, Calgary, in 1989, and by Crow's Theatre Group at the Poor Alex, Toronto, the play had a great success and has been staged in Japan, Mexico, Britain (where it won the *London Evening Standard*'s Most Promising Play Award), and throughout North America. For *Unidentified human remains* Fraser received the 1991 Floyd S. Chalmers Award and a Genie Award for Best Adapted Screenplay for the 1993 feature film of the play (1993), directed by Denys Arcand. Later theatre pieces by Fraser are *The ugly man* (1993, prod. 1992); the book and lyrics of a musical based on the Craig Russell film *Outrageous* (1994), which was produced by CanStage, Toronto, in the fall of 2000; and *Poor super man: a play with captions* (1995), which was produced in Cincinnati, Edmonton, and Edinburgh in 1994 and in Toronto in 1995. *Martin yesterday* (1999, prod. 1997) is drawn from a personal experience when Fraser became involved with 'an older, well-established man' who had a guilty secret and was also HIV positive. As in other of his published plays, there is a long introduction about the genesis of the play, and about some of his other plays. *Snake in fridge* (2000) is about eight misfits who live in the same house. *Cold meat party* (2003), set in Manchester, England—its first production was in Manchester in 2003 and its second at Factory Theatre, Toronto, in 2004—dramatizes the reunion of former friends (middle-aged, straight and gay, one homophobic) at a funeral. While the witty dialogue hits amusingly on such subjects as love, death, aging, and sexual uncertainty, painfulness is not excluded as the play ends.

Fraser, D.M. (1946–85). Donald Murray Fraser was born in Stellarton, Nova Scotia, and grew up in Glace Bay. He was educated at Acadia University (B.A.), and did postgraduate work at the University of British Columbia. He remained in Vancouver for the rest of his life, becoming involved with Pulp Press, which published three of his books, and living in an apartment, over a store, that became a gathering place for readings and was called the Vancouver Least Cultural Centre (a parody of the Vancouver East Cultural Centre). Two collections of Fraser's stories were published in his lifetime: *Class warfare* (1974, 2nd edn 1976) and *The voice of Emma Sachs* (1983). These were followed by two posthumous publications: *D.M. Fraser: The collected works Volume I: Prelude* (1987), which includes all but one of the stories in these books, in addition to pieces found in Fraser's archives, and *Volume 2: Theme* (1989). *Ignorant armies* (1990) is a novel Fraser had been working on since 1978, and was compiled from his archive by Bryan Carson. Fraser was a writer whose imagination, sophistication, self-conscious but playful use of language, sly humour, and idiosyncratic perspective on ordinary events, or matter-of-fact treatment of the extraordinary—as when Clara, who wanted an elephant 'as an exercise in faith', acquired one and put it in the family room ('Elephantiasis' in *Emma Sachs*)—earned for him a reputation as a prose stylist. Two-thirds of *Class warfare* is made up of two long stories, the title story and 'Lonesome town'. In the latter a man Jamie McIvor meets in a pub says to him: "'I'll say one thing for you, you sure know a lot of words.'' 'I just wish I could figure out what to use them for,' Jamie says. ''That's always been the problem. The words have to add up to something, you see.''' This may or may not be the self-mockery of an author whose words do not always create a coherent narrative. A strong narrative prevails, however, in 'Class warfare', about a revolutionary group: 'At present, there are five of us active in the collective; until recently, there were six, but it became expedient to eliminate the sixth. That was Alex, whom we executed.... Alex made no protest. His defence was listless, perfunctory (*Do as you see fit, you will anyway*); had he argued, had he only resisted us, we would have found it easier to spare him. But he left us no choice.' *Ignorant armies* is a novel about the writer Gus Asher, the composer (and murderer) Devon, and the Marxist philosopher Petrov (among others)—all of whom appear in some of the stories (a chapter entitled 'Prelude and Theme' is also a story in *Emma Sachs*)—and relates, among other things, the disastrous result of Asher's love of both Joan and Devon, and of Johnny Girardi, who ends the novel. A chapter towards the end, called 'No', is Asher's long confessional meditation on his relationships and on Joan's suicide, concluding with 'May all our sins be forgiven.' The title is that of an opera by Devon, for which Asher wrote the libretto.

Fraser, John (b. 1944). Educated at Upper Canada College, Toronto, and Lakefield College School (Ontario), at Memorial University of Newfoundland (B.A., 1969) and the University of East Anglia (M.A., 1971), he began a distinguished and varied career as a journalist. For the Toronto *Globe and Mail* he was dance critic and feature writer (1972–5),

drama critic (1975–7), Peking correspondent (1977–9), and held other important appointments until 1987, when he became editor of *Saturday Night*, a post he held until 1994, when he became Master of Massey College in the University of Toronto. He has received three honorary degrees and is a Member of the Order of Canada (2001). Fraser's engaging literary facility and wit, and his ability to connect with people and even one culture that was far removed from his own, are evident in his books. His career as a dance and ballet reviewer served him well when he wrote the texts for two photographic studies of the ballet world: *Kain and Augustyn* (1977) and *Private view: inside Baryshnikov's American Ballet Theatre* (1988). *The Chinese: portrait of a people* (1980) is a long and illuminating record of Fraser's time in Peking and China. In the novel that grew out of this period, *Stolen china* (1996), James Halpert, at the end of four years as the Peking correspondent for a Toronto paper, is inadvertently drawn into a sinister and corrupt world having to do with the illegal export of Chinese antiquities. *Saturday night lives: selected diaries* (1994) contains many of the 'Diaries' Fraser wrote for each issue of *Saturday Night* while he was editor—mini-essays on a wide range of subjects, all of them interesting. His love of anecdote, and his grace and style, are well displayed in *Telling tales* (1986), a series of brief, light pieces on fourty-four Canadian 'names' that include his own self-deprecating contacts with many of them; and in *Eminent Canadians: candid tales of then and now* (2000), which ostensibly examines two bishops (Strachan and Finlay), two editors of the Toronto *Globe* (Brown and Thorsell), two prime ministers (Laurier and Chrétien), and two queens (Victoria and Elizabeth), but is enjoyably discursive and again includes personal anecdotes relating to some of his subjects.

Fraser, Keath (b. 1944). Born in Vancouver, where he lives, he was educated at the University of British Columbia (B.A., 1966; M.A., 1969) and the University of London (Ph.D., 1973). He has travelled widely in Asia, Europe, and Australia, and his travel experiences, especially in India and Cambodia, are prominent in his fiction. After teaching for five years at the University of Calgary, Fraser abandoned his career as a tenured English professor to write full time. He lives in Vancouver.

Fraser's startling imagery, rich ideas, textured language, and astonishing range of characters (especially new immigrants to Canada: he suggests that we are all foreigners to each other) are remarkable. *Taking cover* (1982), a collection of eight stories, is about love, loss, and the uses and abuses of language—one story is titled 'Roget's Thesaurus'. In 'This is what you were born for' a character suddenly struck deaf can only communicate through handwriting. The title story consists of instructions, in every cliché and banality imaginable, to people who enter a bomb shelter after a nuclear war has begun. Two of the most eloquent and disturbing stories in *Foreign affairs* (1985, rpr.1986) are 'The history of Cambodia' and 'Foreign affairs'. The former is about a female newspaper correspondent held prisoner by the Khmer Rouge for five years around the ruined temples of Angkor Wat; it is a story of horror, violence, and atrocity in which the dying woman is sustained by childhood memories of Vancouver. In 'Foreign affairs' a promising diplomat has his career cut short by multiple sclerosis; the story stands comparison with Margaret LAURENCE's *The STONE ANGEL* in its use of broken thought patterns and shattered dreams.

The four interconnected novellas of Fraser's highly original 600-page novel, *Popular anatomy* (1995)—written over a ten-year period—are a brave attempt to challenge the nature of storytelling. It is an X-ray of contemporary society as seen from a global perspective, with Vancouver as the fulcrum of the characters. Part one, 'Against nature', is about Dwight Irving, a travel agent who dislikes travel; on a trip to settle a dispute against a hotel that had scammed a group of tourists, he is imprisoned in a Latin American jail and slowly succumbs to the loss of his business and decay of his body; part two, 'The life of a tuxedo', is a long first-person soliloquy delivered by Dwight's foster child, an East Indian punk rocker in Vancouver who smuggles refugees; part three, 'Bones', is about Dwight's roommate, an unhappy chiropractor, Bartlett Day, who buys skeletons of slaughtered people in Uganda, Cambodia, and Peru to sell to medical schools; part four is a science-fiction memoir written chronologically backwards from 2091 to 1886 by a former mayor of Vancouver and details incidents of racism and intolerance. Overlong and unwieldy, and striving for a tension between multiple perspectives rather than dramatic conflict, *Popular anatomy* nevertheless won the Chapters / Books in Canada First Novel Award. The subtitle of *Telling my love lies* (1996, rpr.1997) is 'A book club's collection of stories and comments by...' and there follows a list of fictional names that appear as the authors of ten stories listed on the title page; each story is preceded by an uninteresting commentary whose connection with the story is not clear. Fraser's reason for imposing this pointless stratagem on his collection is mysterious. The title story is narrated by an opera singer of thirty-three, called Fin by his parents, who visits them for a week and finds that his father is losing his memory. His mother says: 'I'm telling my love lies.... Wouldn't you want a little filler in your life, if you'd had your memory neutered?' Deception in this story, about the past and the present in a small family, also enters Fin's relationship with his mother and his correspondence with her (it turns out that he's gay and lives with a partner in San Francisco), and the remembered accounts of the death of his Chinese friend Michael Wing when they were teenagers. The version given at the autopsy by his father, who 'could forgive everything but the truth', was accepted—drowning by misadventure—but 'The truth is Michael couldn't make up his mind about me.' In the end, the random moments that shape 'Telling my love lies' come together in one's mind as a coherent, resonant narrative. This story and four others are included in *13 ways of listening to a stranger: the best stories* (2005), which begins delightfully with 'Roget's Thesaurus', a tiny memoir that begins 'I had begun my lists. Mother was always saying, "Peter, why not play outside like other boys?"' On page 3, the last page, Roget / Fraser writes: 'Men are odd animals. I have never felt as at home around *them* as around their words; without these they're monkeys. (See TRUISM.) The other day I was going through my book and it struck me I have more words for Disapprobation than Approbation. Why is that?' In the title story (the title brings to mind Wallace Stevens' poem '13 ways of looking at a blackbird', in 13 numbered stanzas) six indigent, mostly young men are living in the Carlins' boarding house and we witness their good-natured kibitzing. When artist Colin designs a Father's Day card that is accepted by a chain of drugstores, Mrs Carlin, to celebrate, gives a Father's Day dinner to which they all contribute. At the dinner Gerry is given a telegram that is said to be from his son and Andrew reads it aloud. The ending, while sentimental, is touching and entirely persuasive. 'Flight' is in three sections (it is not clear why)—Grandson, Son, Father—the third of which describes Father and his wife having a 'champagne breakfast in the sky' in a rented balloon over the Gulf of Thailand.

The short *As for me and my body: a memoir of Sinclair Ross* (1997) is the result of Fraser's twenty-six-year friendship with ROSS (whom he calls Jim); in Ross's later years, in Vancouver, he often brought up in their conversations his homosexuality. *The voice gallery: travels with a glass throat* (2002), an extensive and eloquent meditation on the human voice, begins with a shocking scene when, beside him in bed, his wife had died in her sleep while he was awake. Suffering from a rare vocal disorder, he hardly had a voice: his eight-year-old son had to dial 911 at 4 a.m. and speak into the receiver. He later learned that he was suffering from laryngeal dystonia. With the help of the drug Botox his voice became more or less normal, temporarily; it took a few years for it to be restored to normal use. The book is mainly about his desire to meet others who had lost their voice and treats the reader to a fascinating series of anecdotes gathered from people he met as he travelled around the world.

Keath, a great traveller, edited the terrific anthology *Bad trips* (1991), made up of pieces and extracts by famous and not-so-famous writer/travellers, ten of them Canadian. This was followed by *Worst journeys: Volume 1* (1992, rpr. 1994) and *Volume 2* (1992, rpr. 1994).

Fraser, Simon. See EXPLORATION LITERATURE IN ENGLISH: 2.

Fraser, Sylvia (b. 1935). Sylvia Meyers was born and raised in a working-class district of Hamilton, Ontario. Her mother was a church and community worker and president of a temperance group, her father an inspector for a steel company. She has described her early life as 'Gothic' and 'emotionally disturbed'. Educated at the University of Western Ontario, she obtained a B.A. in English and philosophy in 1957. She became a successful journalist, with five years as a feature writer for the *Star Weekly* before she began writing fiction. Fraser's early fictions have been reframed in postmodernist readings by the publication of her moving and disturbing autobiographical account of a sexually abusive father in *My father's house: a memoir of incest and healing* (1987). The incest, from her earliest childhood until her teens, led to a split personality. Her stark, yet often lyrical book is written in two typefaces. Bold and italic (for the crime) confront the reader with recovered memories and give a sense of both the secrecy of incest, within the family and even the community, and the split that takes place within the child and later young adult who uncovers the mystery of her life, and finally her personal and family healing. She also describes the emotional beginning and end of her long

marriage. Fraser's first non-fiction work became a rallying point in the growing community of women who recalled the abuse they suffered. *The book of strange: a journey* (1992), which was published in the UK and in paperback as *The quest for the fourth monkey: a thinking person's guide to psychic and spiritual phenomena* (1994), continues her need to explore her incestuous past and that of other family members through 'strange' things that happened to her, including 'out of body' experiences. She describes her personal journey and speculations with the mystical side of life: telepathy, premonition, coincidence, prophetic dreams, reincarnation, and death. The impressively researched book is also a comprehensive study of particle physics, paranormal phenomena, the occult, and what she describes as the split in Western society between mysticism and materialism. The title refers to the Victorian knick-knack of china monkeys covering their eyes, ears, and mouth: the fourth monkey covers its genitals and was often removed from the group—Fraser uses this image to refer to sexual repression.

Fraser's early fictions, which frequently explore tormented sexual encounters, are now seen as symbolically representing Fraser's life. Her autobiographical first novel, *Pandora* (1972, NCL), with lyrical line drawings by Harold Town, is a backward look from an adult viewpoint at an imaginative journey in the life and mind of seven-year-old Pandora, who was raised to hate Germans and fear authority; she has a submissive mother and a cruel father with a hook for a hand. *The candy factory* (1975) is a powerful and lusty mystery novel. The factory of the title is both setting and metaphor for society and the fundamental theme of male/female relationships. The lives of several characters are examined, including a scatological tramp who lives in an abandoned drainage system and an elderly spinster who occupies a loft. *A casual affair: a modern fairytale* (1978) is an ingenious, sometimes flatly written novel about a failed love affair; fairy tales comment on and explain the characters—a beautiful blonde artist and a handsome diplomat. Fraser's occasionally overwritten and steamy novel *The Emperor's virgin* (1980) is about a vestal virgin in A.D. 81–96 who is buried alive by a king for breaking her vow of chastity. The painstakingly detailed research suggests parallels between ancient Rome and modern North America, especially in corruption and the loss of interest in traditional religion paralleled by interest in Eastern religion and the occult, ideas further developed in her later nonfiction. In her fast-paced and well-researched modern-day historical novel, *Berlin solstice* (1984, rpr. 1989), set against the rise and fall of the Third Reich, Fraser follows a group of characters from various classes. More importantly for Fraser, who is of German ancestry, the writing of this novel began the realization of what happened to her in her own life—she has said that Nazism represented her father the abuser, and that the collaborators represented her collaboration in her father's crime. *The ancestral suitcase* (1996) fictionalizes ideas from *The book of strange*. Nora Locke experiences many coincidences following the death of her mother. A suitcase in the attic and a fall downstairs transport her back to Victorian England before the First World War to unravel intrigue, passion, and murder in her family past. The heroine ponders 'the impossible possibilities' of synchronicity, karma, and reincarnation in this entertaining adventure.

Fraser has written two highly eventful travel books. *The rope in the water a pilgrimage to India* (2001) describes a journey of three months (and 12,000 kilometres), her purpose 'to spiritually transform myself.' She visits ashrams, including that of the late, famous Maharishi Mahesh Yogi, who taught Transcendental Meditation; takes yoga classes; fictionalizes and transcribes conversations with her personal guru; and is invited to stay, free of charge, at Mount Abu in the state of Rajasthan, southwest of Delhi, the headquarters of the Brahma Kumaris World Spiritual University—where, after seven days, she is 'spiritually, emotionally, and physically nourished.' She spends ten days at a Buddhist retreat outside Bangalore to take part in *vipassana*, meditating eleven (broken up) hours a day, after which Fraser says the experience would 'affect the rest of my life'. Travel is not neglected, and India itself is vividly brought to life in many places, but the centre of the book, symbolized by the title, is when she's saved by a miracle. She goes swimming, at Kovalam Beach on the Arabian Sea, and, without realizing it, is carried out by the riptide. She is struck on the leg by what she takes to be a rope from a floating net; she keeps swimming, but is struck again. She sees lifeguards whistling and desperately waving at her and swims towards them without making any progress—she's being carried out to sea. 'Suddenly I remember: *the rope!* At that instant, I felt it slash my thigh. Snatching it, I pull myself handhold by handhold toward shore....' There is much more to the episode. But it was not until she got home that she realized '*There was no rope.*' This book was followed by *The green labyrinth: exploring the mysteries of the*

Amazon (2003), which begins with her flight from Lima, Peru, to Iquitos on the Amazon River because 'I wish to drink ayahuasca—pronounced eye-a-waska—a highly visionary, psychoactive medicine whose name means "vine of the dead"' (described later as existing 'in a twilight zone of legality'). The first ayahuasca ceremony she experienced made her realize that 'this fall from rationality into meaninglessness was as hellish an ordeal as jaguars and anacondas might be to an Amazonian tribesman'—but there were seven others while she was in Peru ('I'm grateful for the insights I received into my own psyche'). Fraser's descriptions of subsequent trips to Cuzco, Machu Picchu, Arequipa, Nazca, and to Iquitos again are typically filled with countless incidents, many people met and connected with, and a spirited bringing to life of the huge region she visited. In 2008 Fraser was awarded the Matt COHEN Award in Celebration of a Writing Life ($20,000).

Tom and Francine: a love story (1998) is a picture book for children about two cats (and other animals). Fraser edited *A woman's place: seventy years in the lives of Canadian women* (1997), a large-format anthology of articles drawn from the pages of *Chatelaine*, with of course many illustrations from the magazine.

Fraser, William Alexander (1859–1933). Born in River John, Nova Scotia, he was educated in New York and Boston. After many years as an engineer in the oil districts of western Ontario, Burma, India, and western Canada, he began his writing career with stories published in the *Detroit Free Press*. Most of his writing life was spent in Georgetown, Ontario, and Toronto, where he died. Fraser made a substantial reputation as a writer of popular fiction, using the various locales in which he had lived in short stories and novels: the Far East in story collections such as *The eye of a god: and other tales of East and West* (New York, 1899) and *The Sa'Zada tales* (1905); the Canadian West in *Mooswa and others of the boundaries* (New York, 1900) and *The blood lilies* (1903); Ontario in *The lone furrow* (1907); and New York State in *Thoroughbreds* (1902), about horse racing, a favourite subject. He created a literary curiosity (recalling Kipling's *Jungle Book*) in *Mooswa*, which employs a large cast of animals who converse intelligently, have their own laws, and discipline each other; but the western forest setting and animal characteristics are carefully observed. Fraser, who also treated such issues as drug taking and drug trafficking in his fiction (*The lone furrow*, 1907, *Bulldog Carney*,

1919), wrote with a strong air of moral didacticism, though he was not always supportive of formal law-enforcement agencies, such as the Royal Canadian Mounted Police, which he satirized in *Bulldog Carney*. *The lone furrow* is perhaps his best novel. Set in western Ontario and Montreal, it uses intrigues and motifs of murder fiction, and demonstrates a not entirely conventional concern with moral and religious issues.

Fréchette, Louis (1839–1908). He was born at Hadlow Cove near Lévis, Québec, a seventh-generation Canadian. Graduating from the college of Nicolet in 1859, he began to study law at the newly established (1852) Université Laval the following year. In 1863 he published, at his own expense, a collection of his Romantic verse, *Mes loisirs*, the first volume of lyric poetry to appear in Québec. Having published three collections of poetry by 1879, Fréchette hurriedly assembled a new volume of verse under the double title *Les fleurs boréales. Les oiseaux de neige* (Quebec, 1879) and entered it in the annual competition of the Académie française. On 5 Aug. 1880, at the annual public session of the Académie in Paris, he received a Prix Montyon of 2,500 francs. On his return to Canada he was feted at a huge public banquet and was henceforth considered the unofficial poet laureate of French Canada. During the 1880s Fréchette composed a number of long historical poems for his major work, *La légende d'un peuple* (Paris, 1887), a collection of forty-seven tableaux arranged in three chronological sequences covering the seventeenth, eighteenth, and nineteenth centuries of Québec's history. Despite its lack of unity and the unevenness of its execution, this was his greatest achievement; its grandiose conception and its stirring passages make it the most important volume of poetry published in nineteenth-century Québec. After 1890 Fréchette wrote chiefly in prose, producing his only work available in English: a volume of romantic short stories published in both English and French under the titles *Christmas in French Canada* (Toronto, 1899) and *La Noël au Canada* (1900). He also wrote an introduction for William Henry DRUMMOND's *The habitant and other French-Canadian poems* (New York, 1897).

Freeman, David (b. 1947). Born in Toronto, a victim of cerebral palsy caused by brain damage at birth, he attended Toronto's Sunnyview School for the Handicapped until he was seventeen and began writing short stories and poetry there. An article by him, 'The world of can't'—an indictment of sheltered workshops like the one Freeman had attended—was published in *Maclean's* in 1964. The CBC commissioned him to write a play based on it and he did; but the producer, who thought Freeman's script would make unpleasant viewing on the national TV network, turned it down. In 1966 Freeman enrolled at McMaster University and graduated with a B.A. in political science in 1971. By that time he had shown his script to Bill Glassco, who encouraged him to rewrite it. Glassco directed CREEPS (1972), a long one-act play, at the Factory Theatre Lab in Toronto early in 1971. It was an instant success. Set in the men's washroom of a workshop for CP victims, *Creeps* dramatizes, not without humour, the anger and inner rebellion these victims feel towards a society that looks down on them and will not let them forget that they are different. Later in 1971 Glassco made *Creeps* the opening play at his new Tarragon Theatre in Toronto. It won the first Chalmers Award for the outstanding Canadian play produced in the Toronto area, and a New York production won Freeman a New York Critics Drama Desk Award for the outstanding new playwright of the 1973–4 season; it also played for two years in Los Angeles, where it won three Los Angeles Critics' Circle Awards. In 1981 it made a successful seven-week tour of Britain. *Creeps* may be found in two major anthologies, *The Penguin book of modern Canadian drama* (1984), edited by Richard Plant, and *Modern Canadian plays* (1993), 3rd edn vol. 1, edited by Jerry Wasserman.

Freeman's next play, *Battering ram* (1972), is longer and more complex. The central character, Virgil, is a cripple who is taken into the home of a middle-aged woman and her nubile daughter. In portraying the mutual exploitation of the emotions and sexual needs of all three characters, it shows Freeman's ability to go beyond the concerns of the handicapped to explore explosive situations between the sexes. With *You're gonna be alright, Jamie boy* (1974) Freeman moved away from the world of the physically handicapped. Jamie Dinsdale returns home from the Clarke Institute of Psychiatry in Toronto to realize painfully how his family—father, mother, daughter, and son-in-law—are addicted to television and derive their life values from it. Structured as a situation comedy, it reflects the dehumanizing qualities of TV-centred lives. *Flytrap* (1980), produced at Montreal's Saidye Bronfman

Centre in 1976, is about a husband and wife, in a floundering marriage, who invite a young man to live with them; Freeman attempted a more sophisticated humour here than in his previous plays. In 1975 Freeman moved to Montreal and still resides there, continuing to defend the rights of the disabled.

French, David (b. 1939). Born in Coley's Point, Newfoundland, he moved with his family to Toronto in 1945 and graduated from Toronto's Oakwood Collegiate. He then studied acting, first in Toronto and then at the Pasadena Playhouse in California. In 1960 he returned to Toronto and worked as an actor in CBC television drama. He then went on to become one of Canada's leading playwrights. He is an Officer of the Order of Canada (2001).

Leaving home (1972, rpr. 2001)—the first of French's MERCER PLAYS—was produced at the Tarragon Theatre, Toronto, in 1972 under the direction of Bill Glassco, who directed the first production of all French's plays (except *The forest*). The subject came from French's own experience: the breakup of a Newfoundland family, the Mercers, who have settled in Toronto. In the course of the play Jacob, the carpenter father, is forced to face his insecurities and his need for his children when both sons, Ben and Billy, decide to leave at the same time. The play's mixture of pathos and comedy, its convincing and lovable characters, and distinctively Canadian flavour, made it one of the most popular and widely produced Canadian plays. In *Of the fields, lately* (1973, rpr. 1991) Ben Mercer returns from Saskatchewan hoping for a reconciliation with his father; finding that the hostilities between them cannot be resolved, he leaves again. It won the Chalmers Award for 1973 and confirmed French as one of the few Canadian playwrights able to support himself by playwrighting alone. *Salt-water moon* (1985, rpr. 1988) premiered at the Tarragon in October 1984 and, after a very successful run there, transferred to the Bayview Playhouse, Toronto, in November. It is a two-character play in one act that dramatizes the courtship of Jacob and Mary Mercer in 1926 in the place where French was born. The romance, warm humour, and rich tapestry of the play give an authentic picture of Newfoundland life before Confederation. It won the Dora Mavor Moore Award for Outstanding New Play in 1984 and the *Hollywood Drama-Logue* Critics Award in 1987. *1949* (1989), a co-production of the Centre-Stage Company, Toronto, and the Manitoba Theatre Centre, opened in Toronto in 1988. It is set on the three days preceding the

referendum that would make Newfoundland a province of Canada, and brings together at their Toronto home—with the warmth and humour characteristic of the other Mercer plays—several Newfoundlanders with often bitterly opposed views on the fate of the province. Set in 1924, *Soldier's heart* (2002)—produced at Tarragon in 2001—is a three-character play, two of them Mercers, sixteen-year-old Jacob and his father Esau; the other character is Bert Taylor, the station master at Bay Roberts, Newfoundland. Jacob is leaving home, waiting for the train to St John's; Esau and Bert were in the same regiment at the Somme in the Great War, 'eight years ago tonight'. An effective and skilful play, it encapsulates deep emotions, as Jacob deals with his alienation from his father. Esau recollects war experiences with Bert, encouraged by Jacob, who leads him on until he describe the climactic, tragic war experience that has damaged him for life. Jacob then bonds with his father.

In *One crack out* (1976, rev. edn 2003)—produced by Tarragon in 1975, and by the Phoenix Theatre, New York, in 1978—French explores the world of gamblers, pool sharks, pimps, prostitutes, and strippers, capturing their distinctive, often brutal jargon and the precarious nature of their lives. *Jitters* (1980, rev. 1986), first produced at the Tarragon in 1979, is set in a Canadian theatre like the Tarragon and portrays a group—author, director, actors, stage people—before, during, and after the opening night of a new play. As they await a prospective New York producer (who fails to arrive) the play becomes a perceptive commentary on the hopes and insecurities of the Canadian theatre community. It is at once satiric, sad, sophisticated, and even farcical—the French work that is most pervaded by comedy. It has had widespread success on the stage, including the South Coast Repertory Theatre in Costa Mesa, California, in 1986, and the National Arts Centre in 1991. *The silver dagger* (1993), a mystery thriller, was a co-production in 1993 of the CentreStage Company, Toronto, and the National Arts Centre. But the genre does not mesh easily with French's comic send-up of it, and the play left audiences laughing but confused. In the summer of 1999 French's *That summer* (2000), about a young romance in 1958, was produced at the Blyth Festival in Ontario. *The riddle of the world* (2003), first produced at Tarragon in 1981, is a comedy about two men, Ron and Steve, and four young women who come and go (French says 'it might be interesting to see one actress playing all four parts.'). Ron has been abandoned by Beth, whom he loves, and Steve by his wife Greta; he sleeps on a couch in Ron's flat. Though friends, they have a stormy relationship—their dialogue is amusing—and their attempts to deal with their respective dissatisfactions, which they argue about, are played out in five scenes, in the last of which Steve leaves to spend a weekend at the Muskoka cottage of his lawyer, Terry (a male), and Ron is visited by a new neighbour, Jenny, who arrives to borrow a cup of sugar and invites him for dinner.

French worked closely with Donna Orwin, a scholar of Russian literature, in preparing a successful translation of Chekhov's *The seagull* (1978), which was produced at Tarragon in 1977 and on Broadway in 1992. In 1987 his adaptation of Alexander Ostrovsky's *The forest* (unpublished), based on Russian scholar Samuel Cioran's translation of the play, received a major production at the St Lawrence Centre in Toronto. French's adaptation of August Strindberg's play *Miss Julie* (2006), about the affair of the daughter of a count and the count's manservant, was produced by the Festival Antigonish Summer Theatre in 2005.

French, William (b. 1926). Born in London, Ontario, he graduated from the University of Western Ontario in 1948, when he joined the Toronto *Globe and Mail* as a general reporter. In 1954 he held a Nieman Fellowship to Harvard, and in 1960, with the retirement of William Arthur DEACON, he became the *Globe's* literary editor. From 1971 until his retirement in 1988, he wrote a perceptive, influential, and often witty literary column in the *Globe* devoted to serious book reviews and publishing news. He won the President's Medal of the University of Western Ontario for the best general-magazine article (1965) and National Newspaper Awards for critical writing (1978, 1979). From 1955 to 1983 he was an instructor in journalism at Ryerson Polytechnical Institute (now University) and a CBC radio journalist; in 1991 he was awarded an honorary D.Litt. by the University of Western Ontario. He is the author of *A most unlikely village: a history of Forest Hill* (1964).

Friesen, Patrick (b. 1946). Born in Steinbach, Manitoba, he graduated from the University of Manitoba with a B.A. in English (1969) and is a freelance filmmaker. He now lives in Vancouver. His first poetry collections, *the lands i am* (1976) and *bluebottle* (1978), contain many of the themes, motifs, and images that have continued to resonate throughout his work, which frequently explores the meaning and legacy of his Mennonite heritage. *The shunning* (1980), a powerful and multi-voiced book-length poem about two brothers and the struggle between individual faith and authoritarian community, is his fullest treatment of Mennonite culture. Later successfully adapted for the stage (1985) and for CBC Radio (1990), it also examines the passage of time and the relationship between spirit and flesh, two dominant concerns of Friesen's poetry. Peter Neufeld, the shunned brother in the poem, recognizes that 'memories can kill'. Resurrecting the past in the present is central to *Unearthly horses* (1984), a collection of poems that dramatizes how 'it's the living/that harrow the dead and rehearse their lives' and lead to a vital examination of grief, love, tradition, and family. In *Flicker and hawk* (1987) and *You don't get to be a saint* (1992), Friesen continues to examine the human condition in poems that wrestle with death, silence, and the 'several sides to love', while developing a longer line influenced by biblical prosody. These poems struggle with the inadequacy of language to 'speak once more about the flesh and spirit/the red heart and the blue wind'. *Blasphemer's wheel: selected poems, 1980–1994* (1994) was followed by the collections *A broken bowl* (1997), *St. Mary at Main* (1998), and *Carrying the shadow* (1999). *A broken bowl* is a series of untitled poems that make up one long poem, documenting at the end of the millennium a plethora of images— horrific, sad, always negative, often beautiful— and raising in conclusion the question of hope 'because we are what we are / and we look ahead and talk / because we are mistaken / and blunder on'. *St. Mary at Main* brings to imaginative life aspects of Winnipeg, and Friesen's bond with the city where he lived for thirty years, in strong poems that create for readers a bond of their own. Appearing off and on throughout the poems in *Carrying the shadow* are delicately expressed, never dispiriting references to death, dying, and the dead: 'we miss them all / and they tug at us / with a thread / we wipe our eyes / and tug back / the umbilical / never goes slack'. In the first poem of *The breath you take from the lord* (2002), a collection of spiritual poems about nature and family—in the first section of twenty-six poems called 'clearing poems'— we read: 'you are a man you don't know how else to say it you are a man who / has always sought god'. Some of the eloquent poems in *The earth's crude gravities* (2007) form a kind of spiritual autobiography, as in the poem 'god': 'god is the name I learned / the name of the light that followed me everywhere / god is the name // god is the name I turned from / because it wasn't god at all / but human terror / god is the name I turned from / because it lied'. And in 'going to church (a last time)': 'I want departure simple and ravenous / I want all props to collapse... I want it all to fall away leaving / only the smoke of the oldest story / and the story before that / the time of no story / now'. And in 'body of my death': 'how shall I live well / in the body of my death? // so asks the spirit/moving through all / and burning the body alive ... how shall I live well // how?' *Interim: essays & meditations* (2006) is a collection of early writings that attest to Friesen's effectiveness as a writer of prose. In the short final piece he describes witnessing the birth of his daughter in 1973, and of his son in 1977; and the death of his father in 1971. 'Three moments of wonder. The certainties of those moments and, in between, what we call our lives. While the births were amazing experiences, they weren't as astonishing as the death. I have a sense of where the child comes from, how it was created, but I haven't any notion of where a human goes when the last breath is lost.'

Frobisher, Benjamin. See EXPLORATION LITERATURE IN ENGLISH: 2.

Frye, Northrop (1912–91). Herman Northrop Frye was born in Sherbrooke, Québec, and attended primary and high schools in Moncton, New Brunswick—where, after leaving school, he took a course in a business college, becoming an exemplary typist. In 1929 he enrolled in Victoria College, University of Toronto, from which he graduated in 1933, standing first in the Honours course in Philosophy and English. He went on to study theology at Emmanuel College, Toronto, and in 1936 was ordained to the ministry of the United Church, serving briefly as a preacher in Saskatchewan, before attending Merton College, Oxford (M.A., 1940). Already, in 1939, he had started teaching as a lecturer in English at Victoria College; he became a professor in 1947, chair of the English department in 1952, principal (1959–66), and chancellor in 1978. Frye became the first University Professor of English at the University of Toronto in 1967, received the Molson Prize in 1971, was made a Companion of the Order of Canada in 1972, and received the Royal Bank Award in 1978. Apart from the books that will be discussed below, Frye's extra-academic activities included editorship of the CANADIAN FORUM (1948–52), when he encouraged the new poets who began to emerge in Canada during the later 1960s by publishing their works.

Frye's interests led him to combine several roles in a single career. As an academic, he sought to sustain a scholarly community that would play an active role in the national intellectual life, and Frye played his part in the development of a Canadian tradition of public as well as academic criticism. In 1950 he began to write the section on Canadian poetry in English for the *University of Toronto Quarterly's* annual critical roundup, 'Letters in Canada'. His surveys of current verse continued from 1950 to 1960, and in writing them Frye contributed more than any other critic to establishing the criteria by which Canadian writing might be judged. His chronicles in 'Letters in Canada' form the core of *The bush garden: essays on the Canadian imagination* (1971, rpr. 1995), in which he collected what he had written, over a quarter of a century, on Canadian literature and its creators. With its penetrating but endlessly patient judgements on individual writers, and its development of seminal attitudes to the function of a writer in a society emerging from colonialism, *The bush garden* helps to explain the influence Frye wielded, not only on academic and public critics alike but also, in a much more direct way, on Canadian poets. *The bush garden* includes the Conclusion that Frye wrote for the first edition of the *Literary history of Canada* (1965), in which he traced the liberation of Canadian culture from the 'garrison mentality' of colonial days. Frye was one of the editors of the *Literary history*, and to its second edition (1976) he wrote a further Conclusion, reflecting on the later richness of Canadian literary production and commenting that, despite the accompanying 'misery, injustice and savagery' in the world, what may 'matter more, eventually, is what man can create in the face of the chaos he also creates'. *Divisions on a ground: essays on Canadian culture* (1982) is a collection of writings and addresses on subjects of particular Canadian interest.

In Frye's many books of general relevance, he proceeds from an awareness of the essential universality of intellectual pursuits to develop theories of the function of criticism, of the character of literary genres, and of the nature of the myths that inspire the culture of the West. Frye's earliest work of major stature is *Fearful symmetry: a study of William Blake* (1947, rpr. 1990), his first book, which goes far beyond studying Blake himself to examine in depth the role of myth and symbol in the various literary genres. In *Anatomy of criticism* (1957) Frye analyzed the principles and techniques of criticism, isolating its various modes: the historical, the ethical, the archetypal or mythopoeic, and the rhetorical or classificatory. It is an impressive structure of prose and thought that often seems to stand in splendid independence of the literature that is its nominal reason for existence. *The great code: the Bible and literature* (1982, rpr. 1990) and *Words with power* (1990, rpr. 2007) bring together all that Frye learned—not only from literature, but also from his study of the anthropologist James Fraser, the psychologist Carl Jung, and the King James Bible—to consider how much the Bible itself may be considered a work of literature and how far it has been the source of Western literature as we know it. These two volumes, in which he plays somewhat cavalierly with the role of earlier mythological traditions, from the Homeric to the Ovidian, Frye clearly regarded as the destination of his career. All four works are Frye's masterpieces, monumentally self-contained and self-consistent in their systematization of literary and cultural history. His many other books reflect the essential division between Frye the writer and Frye the teacher, since they are mainly collections of lectures and articles, gathered in such ways as to illuminate rather unevenly certain common themes. They include *The educated imagination* (1963, rpr. 2002), the Massey Lectures; *The well-tempered critic* (1963); *Fables of identity: studies in poetic mythology* (1963); *The modern century* (1967); *The double vision: language and meaning in religion* (1991, rpr. 1995); *Fools of time: studies in Shakespearean tragedy* (1973), the Alexander Lectures; *Spiritus mundi: essays on literature, myth and society* (1976, rpr. 2006); *Northrop Frye on Shakespeare* (1986, GGA, rpr. 1988); and *The myth of deliverance: reflections on Shakespeare's problem comedies* (1993).

Northrop Frye: myth and metaphor, selected essays 1974–1988 (1990, rpr, 2000) was edited by Robert D. Denham. *Biblical and classical myth: the mythological framework of Western culture* (2004), by Frye and Jay MACPHERSON, contains a series of Frye's lectures entitled 'Symbolism in the Bible' and Macpherson's *Four ages of man: the classical myths*, first published in 1962.

See John Ayre, *Northrop Frye: a biography* (1989), and the interesting two-volume publication of the letters between Frye and his wife-to-be: *The correspondence of Northrop Frye & Helen Kemp, 1932–1939* (2 vols, 1996) edited by Robert D. Denham; a one-volume edition is *A glorious and terrible life with you: selected correspondence of Northrop Frye and Helen Kemp 1932–1939* (2007) selected and edited by

Margaret Burgess. See also David Cayley, *Northrop Frye in conversation* (1992); *Rereading Frye: the published and unpublished works* (1999) edited by David Boyd and Imre Salusinszky, eight essays, most of which developed out of a research seminar held at the University of Newcastle, Australia, in July 1994; and *Northrop Frye unbuttoned: wit and wisdom from the notebooks and diaries* (2004) selected by Robert D. Denham.

A continuing publishing project of the UNIVERSITY OF TORONTO PRESS is *The collected works of Northrop Frye*, to be published in 33 volumes; as of February 2008, 25 volumes had been published between 1996 and 2007. According to subject and volume(s), these include the *Frye-Kemp correspondence* (volumes 1 and 2), *On religion* (4), *Late notebooks* (5, 6), *Diaries* (8), *On literature and society* (10), *On Canada* (12), *Fearful symmetry* (14), *On Milton and Blake* (16), *The great code* (19), *Anatomy of criticism* (22).

Fulford, Robert (b. 1932). Born in Ottawa, he is descended from several generations of Canadian newspapermen and began his journalistic career as a teenager with the Toronto *Globe and Mail*. Later he moved to the *Toronto Star*, where he wrote a daily or weekly column on cultural questions for almost twenty years. He has also been on the staffs of several Canadian magazines, including *Maclean's*, but is most thoroughly identified with *Saturday Night*, which he edited from 1968 to 1987. Although mainly a periodical writer, he has also published books reflecting the politics that lie at the heart of his work and his transition from reporter to literary observer to social critic. *This was Expo* (1968), a work of almost instant reporting, nonetheless betrays a deep concern with the role of ideas in the national spectacle. *Crisis at the Victory Burlesk: culture, politics, and other diversions* (1968) is mainly a collection of *Toronto Star* columns about popular culture in the broadest sense. In *Marshall Delaney at the movies: the contemporary world as seen on film* (1974), he publicly revealed the identity behind the 'Marshall Delaney' pseudonym he used for cinema reviews in *Saturday Night*. Although he has continued to range widely over cultural matters—*An introduction to the arts in Canada* (1977) was an overview for students and new Canadians—after 1970 he became more concerned with the supposed failure of liberal ideology in society generally, as evidenced in *The Fulford file* (1980), an olio of his *Saturday Night* editorials. The transition, which followed his all-too-brief embrace of a more nationalistic viewpoint, also suggested a reversion to the natural concerns of a writer shaped by the cultural environment of the 1950s—with its agonized debate on psychoanalysis, communism, sexual repression, and the application of those topics to virtually every other subject. By the 1990s Fulford had more or less abandoned several of his early public interests, particularly fine art and jazz, gaining a new reputation as a cogent political commentator, public scold, and wit—as, for example, in his popular weekly column in the Toronto *Globe and Mail* (a return full-circle to his first home); he now writes a weekly column for the *National Post*. His most recent books are *Best seat in the house: memoirs of a lucky man* (1988), at once the liveliest and most elegant Canadian journalist's memoirs since those of Sir John Willison or Hector CHARLESWORTH several generations earlier; *Accidental city: the*

transformation of Toronto (1995), an affectionate but anti-nostalgic study of politics, development, and culture in the metropolis with which he is so thoroughly associated; *Toronto discovered* (1998), a large-format book in which Fulford's evocative and informative account of the city is supplemented by colour photographs; and *The triumph of narrative: storytelling in the age of mass culture* (1999), based on the Massey Lectures he gave in 1999, a series of reflections on such subjects as 'master narratives', including those of Gibbon, Macaulay, and Parkman, and on the stories in the Bible, the journalistic narrator (Orwell), the 'unreliable narrator' in literature, and the postmodernist view of narrative. Fulford appears as a character in works of fiction and non-fiction, including Douglas (George) FETHERLING's *Way down deep in the belly of the beast* (1996).

G

Gallant, Mavis (b. 1922). Born Mavis de Trafford Young in Montreal, she attended seventeen different schools there and in the eastern United States. She left Canada for Europe in 1950, after a short period working for the National Film Board and as a writer for the Montreal *Standard*, and after a brief marriage to John Gallant. Since then, living in Paris, she was remarkably dedicated to imaginative writing, maintaining a long connection with *The New Yorker*; most of her short stories have appeared there, the first in the issue of 1 Sept. 1951. Made a Companion of the Order of Canada in 1993, she is an Honorary Member of the American Academy and Institute of Arts and Letters, and a Fellow of the Royal Society of Literature. In 1983–4 she was writer-in-residence at the University of Toronto, which awarded her an honorary doctorate in 1994, one of her many honorary degrees. She was awarded the Molson Prize in 1997. In the fall of 2006 the government of Québec awarded Gallant the Prix Athanase David for literary excellence, the first time an English-language author had been so honoured. At almost the same time she was 'celebrated' at an event in New York's Symphonyspace, co-sponsored by New York Review Books, which she attended, assisted

by a friend who accompanied her from, and returned with her to, Paris.

Gallant has published two novels: *Green water, green sky* (1959, rpr. 1983) and *A fairly good time* (1970, rpr. 1983); and fourteen collections of shorter fiction: *The other Paris* (1956); *My heart is broken* (1964, rpr. 1993; British title *An unmarried man's summer*, 1964); *The Pegnitz Junction: a novella and five short stories* (1973, rpr. 2002); *The end of the world and other stories* (1973, NCL), selected and edited by Robert WEAVER; *From the Fifteenth District: a novella and eight short stories* (1979, rpr. 2001); *Home truths: selected Canadian stories* (1981, GGA; rpr. 2001); *Overhead in a balloon: stories of Paris* (1985, rpr. 2002); *In transit* (1988, rpr. 1997); *Across the bridge* (1993); and *The selected stories* (1996, rpr. 1997). There are also three collections of Gallant's stories selected by well-known writers: *The Moslem wife and other stories* (1994, NCL), selected by Mordecai RICHLER; *Paris stories* (2002), selected by Michael ONDAATJE; and *Montreal stories* (2004), selected by the American novelist Russell Banks, which contains three stories— 'Let it pass', 'In a war', and 'The concert party'—that had never appeared in a book. Many of these collections have been published in French, and some in German, Spanish, and

Dutch. Gallant has written trenchant book reviews for the *New York Times*, the *New York Review of Books*, and *The Times Literary Supplement*, and eleven are included in *Paris notebooks: essays and reviews* (1986, rpr. 1997).

The first of Gallant's two novels, *Green water, green sky*, is about the moral destruction of a girl by her foolish, protective mother. *A fairly good time* uses, with great skill, a variety of devices—journals, letters, interior monologues, recollective flashbacks—to illuminate the central story of the failure of a marriage between a Canadian girl and a member of a stuffy French family.

The difficulty of entering an alien culture is a theme that runs through many of Gallant's stories. Frequently they are about Anglo-Saxons—British as well as Canadians—leading empty and often spiteful lives in France or Italy. *The Pegnitz Junction* deals with the alienation of a whole people, the post-1945 Germans, from the past they seek desperately to forget. Even in *Home truths*, Canadians are shown as 'foreigners' not merely when they are abroad. Perhaps the most impressive cycle in that collection, the Linnet Muir stories, concerns the failure of a young returning Montrealer to find her bearings even in the city where she was born and spent her childhood. It is perilous to generalize about well over 100 stories that show a great variety of situation, characterization, and approach; but most concern people who have built up a protection from the world, and who in the end have been made to realize how precarious such defences are, and how hiding from life has only increased their vulnerability. Gallant's stories are witty and often humorous in their manner of expression, yet pathetic in their ultimate effect; detached and sharp in viewpoint—at times seeming to verge on callousness—they are nevertheless so involving that the final emotion is always nearer compassion than contempt. Gallant seems to conclude, sadly, that the people she writes of cannot be changed. Among the recent collections, *Across the bridge* includes some memorable stories about Canadians: '1933', 'The chosen husband', 'From cloud to cloud', 'Florida'—about the Larette sisters—and 'The Fenton child'. *The selected stories* (American title: *The collected stories*) is a monumental collection, containing fifty-two stories selected by Gallant herself. Her Preface may well become a classic capsule memoir of the childhood and early writing years of a literary artist—who, here, describes the impulse to write as 'a jolt that unbolts the door between perception and imagination and leaves it ajar

for life, or that fuses memory and language and waking dreams.' In 2009 MCCLELLAND & STEWART published a collection of thirty-one of her early and unfamiliar stories, *Going ashore* (rpr. 2010); the shorter American edition, *The cost of living: early and uncollected stories* containing twenty stories, was published by New York Review Books.

Gallant's play *What is to be done?* (1984)—bearing the title of Lenin's pamphlet—takes place in Montreal between 1942 and 1945, and is an ironic and vivid treatment of one strain of left-wing thinking while the war on fascism in Europe continued. It was produced at the Tarragon Theatre, Toronto, in November 1982 (and later televised). Gallant's nonfiction writings include her account of experiences and observations during the abortive revolutionary situation in France during 1968, 'The events in May: a Paris notebook' (*New Yorker*, 14 Sept., 21 Sept. 1968), in which she gives a rare personal assessment of the country she has so long inhabited, and her long introduction to *The affair of Gabriel Russier* (1971), describing the ordeal of a thirty-year-old French schoolteacher who had a love affair with an adolescent student—both works are included in *Paris notebooks*. See *Mavis Gallant: narrative patterns and devices* (1978) by Grazia Merler, *Reading Mavis Gallant* (1989) by Janice Kulyk Keefer, and *Transient questions: new essays on Mavis Gallant* (2005) edited by Kristjana GUNNARS. See also two of the many interviews Gallant has given: in *CANADIAN FICTION MAGAZINE* (1978, no. 28) and *BRICK* (2007, no. 80).

Galt, John (1779–1839). Born in Irvine, Ayrshire, Scotland, he combined business and literary careers before coming to Canada. By 1820 he had travelled through Europe and had worked as a political lobbyist, first for the promoters of a Glasgow-Edinburgh Canal and then for the United Empire Loyalists who sought redress for losses during the War of 1812. In 1820 Galt suggested a way to satisfy UEL claimants: the Canada Company, organized to raise funds by purchasing Crown lands and selling them to immigrants, hired him as secretary and sent him to Upper Canada (Ontario) in 1825. Meanwhile he was adding to his work as biographer, dramatist, historian, and as the author of a series of novels that rivalled Walter Scott's in popularity, writing eleven between 1820 and 1825. Galt's *Autobiography* (London, 1833), and to a lesser extent his *Literary life and miscellanies* (London, 1834), present vivid details of his Canadian experiences: dashing travels with 'Tiger'

Galt

Dunlop, political clashes with Bishop Strachan and Governor Maitland, the ritualistic founding of Guelph. There are also sharp speculations about the future of the colony. (The city of Galt, now Cambridge, was named after him.) Traces of these ideas and experiences appear also in fictional form in *Lawrie Todd; or, The settlers in the woods* (London, 1830), a novel set partly in upstate New York, and in the third volume of *Bogle Corbet; or, The emigrants* (London, 1831; rpr. 1977); both novels were published during the period of reversal and imprisonment that followed Galt's return to Britain in 1829. *Bogle Corbet* and *Lawrie Todd* are rightly seen as a pair—not so much because they deal with the same experience (immigration) at the same time (around 1825), and in roughly the same place (north and south of Lake Ontario), as because they discriminate carefully between group settlement and independent settlement. Of the two books, *Lawrie Todd* was more popular, partly because of its more varied descriptions of bush and river, roads and settlements.

By the time Galt died, his three sons—John, Thomas, and Alexander Tilloch Galt—had returned to Canada, where they would contribute to political, judicial, and financial development. See Ian Gordon, *John Galt: the life of a writer* (1972).

Garneau, Michel (b. 1939). Radio announcer, important poet and playwright, singer, and writer-celebrity, he is a one-man band and a one-man show. His *Poésies complètes, 1955–1987* was published in 1988; and he has been professor of improvisation (since 1972), writer-in-residence and *animateur* of writing workshops at the National Theatre School. But of his many publications, only three have been translated. *Four to four* (1978), the translation by Christian Bédard and Keith Turnbull of *Quatre à quatre* (1974), is a feminist verse-play about four generations of Québécois women and was produced at the Tarragon theatre in Toronto in 1974. It is one of his strongest plays. In another verse-play, *Warriors* (1990), the translation by Linda Gaboriau of *Les guerriers* (1989), two ad men get 'the contract of our lives', to create a slogan for the Canadian army, and their aimless chit-chat often segues into brief discourses on war and even warlike sentiments. *Small horses and intimate beasts* (1985) is the translation by Robert McGee of selections from *Les petits chevals amoureux* (1977), and is a collection of mostly untitled lyrics, with the French text on the opposite page, that celebrate his love of life, of humans and beasts: 'personally / i never knew a zebra / but i would like to / terribly'.

Garner, Hugh (1913–79). He was born in Batley, Yorkshire, England. In 1919 his father, who had worked briefly in Ontario before the First World War, moved his family to Toronto, settling in Cabbagetown, an east-central downtown area that Garner later described as 'a sociological phenomenon, the largest Anglo-Saxon slum in North America'. The father deserted his family, and Hugh Garner, a brother, and two step-sisters were brought up by their hardworking mother. Garner attended public school and a technical high school, and after graduation was briefly a copy boy on the *Toronto Star*. In 1933, one of the worst years of the Depression, he went on the road, stooking wheat in Saskatchewan, working for 20 cents a day in a relief camp in Kamloops, British Columbia, jailed as a vagrant in West Virginia. This itinerant life came to an end when he enlisted in the Abraham Lincoln Brigade to fight for the Loyalists in the Spanish Civil War. During the Second World War he served on a corvette in the Canadian navy.

After the war Garner set out to make his living as a writer. His first published novel, *Storm below* (1949), which drew on his wartime naval experience, has been described by the critic Hugo McPherson as 'an unheroic but oddly warming record of an encounter of nature, fate and man during six days at sea in 1943.' In 1950 a butchered version of Garner's earlier novel *Cabbagetown* appeared in paperback. When the complete text was finally published in 1968 (rpr. 2003), this story of the painful and sometimes melodramatic coming-of-age of Ken Tilling and his friends, with its description of working-class life in Toronto in the 1930s, was seen to be a major social novel by a Canadian. Garner's other novels include *The silence on the shore* (1962), a multi-character study set in a Toronto rooming house; *A nice place to visit* (1970), in which an aging writer-journalist investigates a sensational criminal case in a small town not far from Toronto; and *The intruders* (1976), about trendy members of the middle class who have moved into the former Cabbagetown slum area. In the 1970s Garner wrote three police novels, all set in Toronto, about Inspector Walter McDumont: *The sin sniper* (1970), *Death in Don Mills* (1975), and *Murder has your number* (1978). A fourth novel about Inspector McDumont, *Don't deal with five deuces* (1992), left unfinished when Garner died, was completed by Paul Stuewe. Having published more than fifty short stories, Garner won a Governor General's Award for *Hugh Garner's best stories* (1963); *The legs of the lame and other stories* (1976) is another collection. In his most successful fiction he was 'the loser's advocate ... Garner's people are life's outsiders, and this is consistent because he himself is an outsider....' (Robert FULFORD). To the end of his life Garner's spirit never really left Toronto's Cabbagetown, and it seems fitting that in 1982 the Hugh Garner Co-operative, a housing development, was built on Cabbagetown's Ontario Street, a few blocks north of the place where the Garners first lived in Toronto. See Paul Stuewe, *The storms below: the turbulent life and times of Hugh Garner* (1988).

Gatenby, Greg (b. 1950). Born in Toronto, educated at York University (B.A., 1972), a former editor at MCCLELLAND & STEWART (1973–5), he joined Toronto's Harbourfront Centre as its literary co-ordinator in 1975. In 1976 Gatenby became artistic director of the weekly Harbourfront Reading Series (see AUTHORS AT HARBOURFRONT CENTRE) and founder of the famous International Festival of Authors, held annually. He was replaced in 2003. Among his many honours, he was made a Member of the Order of Canada in 2000.

Gatenby is an anthologist and proficient poet. He combined literary nationalism with cosmopolitanism in two anthologies that bear the subtitle 'Canada through the eyes of foreign writers': *The wild is always there* (1993, rpr. 1994) and *The very richness of that past* (1995, rpr. 1996). Canada's scenery, society, and spirit are caught in the public and private words from the pens of dozens of sojourning writers ranging from Charles Dickens to Ernest Hemingway. He also compiled *Whale sound: an anthology of poems about whales and dolphins* (1977) and *Whales: a celebration* (1983), which includes prose, art, and music. As a writer of prose Gatenby produced *Toronto: a literary guide* (1999), an exhaustive and illuminating anecdotal account, by neighbourhood and streets, of addresses associated with writers. His achievement as a poet is the least noted of his endeavours. Two slight collections of occasional poems, *Rondeaus for Erica* (1976) and *Adrienne's blessing* (1976), were followed by two notable collections, *The salmon country* (1978) and *Growing still: poems* (1981). His poetry, always witty, is sometimes gruff and outspoken. 'Academic report on Literature III' is an extended comparison of Canadian writing with the stock market: 'Major US indicators continue to outstrip Canadian futures ... the interest rate in academia continued to decline....' But there are surprisingly graceful passages, as in the poem 'Screen siren', which recounts the chance encounter in New York City with a favourite movie star, Québec actress Carole Laure: 'I made her / hear my love for dolphins, talked of books still to come—/ any nonsense to protract her present, to let me / repose fluid kite tail dancing and happy.'

Gauvreau, Claude (1925–71). Born in Montreal, he attended the Collège Ste-Marie, then studied philosophy at the Université de Montréal. During the forties he became friendly with Paul-Emile Borduas, through whom he acquainted himself with Dadaism, Surrealism, Automatism, and the artists, journalists, and essayists who gravitated towards this important figure of the Montreal artistic community; he co-signed Borduas's famous manifesto, *REFUS GLOBAL*. As an avant-garde poet and playwright (and author of radio plays), his fame has increased with the passage of time, so that he is now considered to be one of Québec's most celebrated writers. Gauvreau's *Oeuvres créatices complètes* was published in 1977. Only two books present his work in English. *Entrails* (1981, rpr. 1992) is a translation by Ray Ellenwood of what he calls in his Introduction '26 dramatic objects' drawn from the *Oeuvres créatices*. Avant-garde in their 'stubborn non-realism', these 'objects' are poetic dialogues that 'deliberately affront every convention of the stage, showing us a world of intransigent fantasy, symbolic and mysterious, funny at times, often horrific, always disturbing.' *The charge of the expormyable moose* (1996) is Ellenwood's translation of *La charge de l'orignal épormyable* (1977). Set in a futuristic world, it deals powerfully with alienation, psychological torture, and physical brutality in a non-naturalistic manner. Gauvreau was very much against the realistic theatre of GÉLINAS, saying that 'the avant-garde must begin in the non-figurative and go beyond; anyone who doesn't move in this direction risks obsolescence.' Ellenwood tells us that when the play was first performed in May 1970, 'on the fifth night, according to the playwright's own account, there were only sixteen people in the audience and, after the intermission, four of the eight actors refused to continue the performance.' However, it has been produced several times since then.

Geddes, Gary (b. 1940). Born in Vancouver, British Columbia, he attended the University of British Columbia and the University of Toronto, where he obtained a Ph.D. in 1975. After retiring from the English department of Concordia University, Montreal, he returned to British Colmbia and lives in

Geddes

Sooke. In 2008 he received an important B.C. honour, the Lieutenant-Governor's Award for Literary Excellence.

Geddes's early collections of verse—*Poems* (1971), *Rivers inlet* (1971), and *Snakeroot* (1973)—reveal a sharp eye for physical detail, a keen and uncompromising intellect, and a poetic sensibility that balances subjectivity and objectivity, the personal and the impersonal, criticism and compassion. The lyric sequence of *Rivers inlet* moves from external descriptions to internal parallels, the British Columbia coastal landscape becoming a map of the poet's ancestry that explains the relationship of past to present. *War and other measures* (1976) is another long suite of poems. Paul Joseph Chartier died on 18 May 1966 in the men's washroom of the House of Commons when a bomb he was carrying accidentally exploded. Through the mind of Chartier the poetic sequence mirrors the society that resorts to violence and destruction, and becomes a scathing portrait and an impassioned indictment, a fable of contemporary Canada. Its violence and insanity surface again in *The acid test* (1981), though the setting expands to include the entire world: political tyranny, the arms race, and environmental ravage are but a few of its themes that reflect the absurd inhumanity of people; included is a revised version of *Letter of the master of horse*, a narrative poem first published in 1973.

Geddes's later interest in such ideologically charged geographies as China, Latin America, and Hong Kong is fuelled both by questions about aesthetics and the crucibles in which art and politics intermingle and by narrowly topical politics. His much-acclaimed *The terracotta army* (1984) is a blending of twenty-six poems inspired by the 1974 chance discovery in China of 8000 life-size terracotta soldiers and horses from 300 B.C., sculpted on the order of the emperor Ch'in Shi Huang and intended to serve as an imperial bodyguard in his afterlife. Threaded throughout the poems are meditations on the passion and fears of the men who 'created' the statues and their stories: the potter Bi, the tyrant Huang, the calligrapher Shuai Lizhi, and the poet Geddes. *Hong Kong poems* (1987) again reveals Geddes's ability to balance the immensity of historical events (in this case the experiences of two Canadian battalions during the Pacific campaign) with the idiosyncrasies and sufferings of individuals on both 'sides' of the tragic encounter. Turning to Latin America, Geddes produced a co-operative, bilingual collection with the Chilean poet Gonzalo Millan: *No easy exit / Salida difícil* (1989), a

record of his experiences and reflections during a troubling reading tour of Chile in 1987. There followed a collection of new and selected poems, *Light of burning towers* (1990), *Girl by the water* (1994), and *The perfect cold warrior* (1995). The latter volume has three distinct groupings of poems that speak through disparate voices: 'The Drive', a sequence of intense first-person narratives about growing up poor in Vancouver's Commercial Drive area; a section of poems set in and about Palestine, including the award-winning 'What does a house want?', which recounts the demolition of Palestinian houses by the Israeli army; and 'Norwegian Rabbit', subtitled 'The Trotsky poems'. Many of these poems reappeared in *Active trading: selected poems, 1970–1995* (1996). Blindness in different forms is the theme of the poems in the opening title section of *Flying blind* (1998), which were inspired by a trip Geddes made in 1993 through Israel and Palestine with the blind poet John Asfour. The polished, enjoyable poems and prose poems of *Skaldance* (2004) are full of stories and characters. Geddes was inspired by the skald, an Old Norse composer and reciter of poems. References to the Orkney Islands begin to appear: 'My grandfather // emigrated in 1907 from the Orkneys' ('Down for the Count') and 'Mother was a McGregor from Inverness,... / My father was a short almost comic / figure from Exmoor whom she had met / while stationed in the Orkneys.' ('How I was launched') The final section, 'The zeno transplant', is made up of parallel prose poems on alternate pages: e.g. the affair of Nicholas Zend and Dora in the 1990s faces a page about Orcadian Antonio Zen, a lover of birds, sailing with a crew in the Orkneys in the fourteenth century with Henry St. Clair, Earl of Orkney, and Father Odred. 'The priest was a lover of anything that floats and considered ships the perfect afterlife for trees.' These Orkney passages are narrative gems. *Falsework* (2007) is a book-length sequence of poetry and prose about the collapse, in mid-construction in 1958, of Vancouver's Second Narrows Bridge ('No warning, unless you / count vibrations'). Geddes's father searched for bodies in the wreckage and young Gary was an observer. Researching victims and interviewing survivors, the much older Gary produced a work that revives an important and little-known event and contains several outstanding poems. There are photographs.

Geddes proved himself as an engaging writer of non-fiction in two travel books: *Sailing home: a journey through time, place and memory* (2001, rpr. 2002) and *Kingdom of ten thousand things: an impossible journey from Kabul to Chiapas* (2005). The opening of the Preface to *Sailing home* sums it up: 'In the summer of 1998 I came back to the coast in search of my origins, looking for the mythical home-place…. My marriage had collapsed and I had chucked my tenured teaching job in Montreal to move west. I intended to structure my return around a book, writing my way home, using the day-to-day events of sailing up the coast (weather, reefs, people, errant Chilean submarines and, of course, sirens) as the narrative thread on which to hang my watery reminiscences of growing up out here.' This is an absorbing, delightful West Coast book. The trip described in *Kingdom* (the full title is a Chinese expression for life itself) was inspired by Geddes's fascination with Huishen, a monk from Kabul, who fled to China to the Americas in 458 and returned in 499. Geddes left for Afghanistan in August 2001 and–'on a caval-cade of jets, buses, taxis, pickup trucks, trains, donkeys, camels, and ferries, a container ship, and several small river launches, through twelve countries and through war zones, desert, jungle, mountain passes, muskeg, ancient ruins, floods'—travelled from Kabul to China, and from the South China Sea to Mexico. A superb travel book.

As an editor Geddes has produced two anthologies that have been the mainstay of many college English departments in Canada for some 40 years: *Twentieth-century poetry and poetics* (5th edn 2006) and *15 Canadian poets x 3* (4th edn 2001). He also edited *The art of short fiction* (1993) and *Skookum wawa: writings of the Canadian Northwest* (1975).

Geddes has also written a play, *Les maudits anglais* (1984). A bilingual political farce about French-English relations in Canada, it was produced in 1978 and 1983.

Gedge, Pauline (b. 1945). Born in Auckland, New Zealand, she spent part of her life in Oxfordshire, England, before moving to Alberta. This midwestern writer made a startling debut with the bestselling *Child of the morning* (1977, rpr. 2009), the first of nine novels about ancient Egypt. Set in the time of Thothmes I and II, it focuses on a female Pharaoh inspired by the historically androgynous figure of Hatshepsut. This was followed by *The twelfth transforming* (1985, rpr. 2007), *Scroll of Saqqara* (1990, rpr. 2007), *House of dreams* (1994, rpr. 2007), and its sequel *House of illusions* (1996, rpr. 2007). *The hippopotamus marsh* (1998, rpr. 2007) is the first volume of a trilogy called Lords of the Two Lands, about the reign of Prince Komose, of which *The*

oasis (1999, rpr. 2007) and *The Horus road* (2000, rpr. 2007) are sequels. *The twice born* (2007) is a long novel (554 pages) about the early life of Huy son of Hapu, who grew up to be Amunhotep son of Hapu, the revered Royal Scribe for Amunhotep III; he lived to the age of eighty and became a god of healing. He was responsible for erecting the two statues of Amunhotep that became known as the Colossi of Memnon. Gedge's other historical novels are *The eagle and the raven* (1978, rpr. 2003), a long work that is partly about the warrior-queen Boudicca (Boadicea), set in Celtic Britain and Rome; *Stargate* (1982, rpr. 1997), a fantasy about the early years of the history of the universe when each solar system was ruled by a sun lord; and *The covenant* (1992, rpr. 1993), a Gothic mystery. Gedge's novels are scrupulously researched and as historically accurate as any recognized historiographic text. While her writing is considered 'popular' in North America (less so in Europe, where her Egyptian novels interest Egyptologists), her plots are uncomplicated and her narratives are passionate, convincing, and written with exquisite detail that includes vivid descriptions of landscapes, architecture, and people. They are persuasive interpretations of the distant past that fascinate and delight a large international readership. The novels have sold 250,000 copies in Canada alone and 6 million copies worldwide.

Gélinas, Gratien (1909–99). Born in Saint-Tite-de-Champlain, Québec, he moved with his family shortly afterwards to Montreal, and was educated at the Collège de Montréal, where he completed the program in classical studies and was active in the school's dramatic society. Forced to leave school in 1929 because of the Depression, he worked at various jobs while continuing his involvement in theatre by founding the Troupe des Anciens du Collège de Montréal and acting with the Montreal Repertory Theatre in both English and French and on radio. In 1935 he married Simone Lalonde, with whom he had six children. After her death he married in 1973 the distinguished French-Canadian actress Huguette Oligny. The first important figure in modern Québec theatre, Gélinas and his work as actor, playwright, and administrator were recognized in many ways. He assumed chairmanship of the Canadian Film Development Corporation (1969–77); received, among many other awards, honorary doctorates from twelve Canadian universities; and was made a Companion of the Order of Canada in 1990.

Gélinas

Gélinas's early work on radio, beginning in 1934, prepared him for a series of his own in which he played a simple, sensitive, Chaplinesque character named Fridolin, a role he played on radio from 1937 to 1941. In 1938 he began an annual stage revue at the Théâtre Monument National, *Fridolinons*, based on the same character; it played annually until 1946, with a retrospective revue in 1956. *(Les Fridolinades*, drawn from the revues, was produced at the National Arts Centre, Ottawa, in 1987 and in Toronto in 1989.) Two of the skits and monologues from *Fridolinons* became the basis of his first full-length play, *TIT-COQ* (1950, rpr. 1994; English translation by William Johnstone, 1967). Its opening night at Montreal's Monument National on 22 May 1948 was a landmark in the history of popular theatre in Québec. In the summer it moved to the Théâtre du Gésu and played—in both French and English, with Gélinas in both versions—more than 500 performances until 1951 and made Gélinas the best-known and best-loved actor and playwright in the province.

Gélinas wrote and played the leading role in *Bousille et les justes* (1960, rpr. 1987), portraying a simple-minded and honest man victimized by the intrigues of relatives wanting to avoid a family scandal. A type of modern morality play—raising the issue of moral honesty versus family pride, and satirizing some traditional religious practices in Québec, and their failure to sensitize people to moral concerns—it has been performed in many parts of Canada in an English translation, *Bousille and the just* (1961), by Kenneth Johnstone and Joffre Miville-Dechêne; and in 1996 it was successfully revived with more than 100 performances.

Meanwhile in 1954 Gélinas wrote and starred in a weekly comedy, *Les quat'fers en l'air*, and in 1956 he played leading roles in Stratford, Ontario, productions of *Henry V* and *The merry wives of Windsor*; he was also named vice-president of the Greater Montreal Arts Council, a post he held until 1963. In 1958 he founded in Montreal the Comédie-canadienne, which was both a theatrical company and a theatre. That same year Gélinas was elected president of the Canadian Theatre Centre, and in 1960 he was one of the founders of the National Theatre School in Montreal.

Gélinas's third play, *Hier, les enfants dansaient* (1968), which was published in an English translation by Mavor MOORE as *Yesterday the children were dancing* (1967), is about a family divided by the issues of federalism and separatism in Québec; it was first produced in

1966 at the Comédie-canadienne, and in 1967 in English at the Charlottetown Festival. Though Gélinas insisted 'This isn't a political manifesto, it's a love story', it was still a powerful presentation of the political issues that divided Québécois. *La passion de Narcisse Mondoux* (1987), a two-character play—translated by Linda Gaboriau as *The passion of Narcisse Mondoux* (1992)—is the story of a retired plumber who seizes the opportunity to woo, after her husband's death, the well-off woman he has loved for forty years. Unapologetically romantic and sentimental, and a success wherever it has been performed, the play starred Gélinas and his wife Huguette Oligny, and premiered at Toronto's French theatre, Le Théâtre du P'tit Bonheur, in the fall of 1986. In 1988 it opened in English at the Piggery Theatre in North Hatley, Québec, where English and French performances alternated. It travelled successfully across Canada in English and French, and to parts of the United States, including a five-week run off-Broadway in 1989, always with Gélinas and Oligny performing.

For his theatre activities over almost seventy years and his dramatic works—which prepared the way for later playwrights in giving an authentic and memorable picture of Québec life—Gélinas was an influential figure in the cultural life of Québec and the whole of Canada. The only biography is in French, *Gratien Gélinas: la ferveur et le doute* (2 vols, 1995–6) by Anne-Marie Sicotte, one of his granddaughters (another is the famous Mitsou).

Generals die in bed. See Charles Yale HARRISON.

Gervais, Marty (C.H.) (b. 1946). Charles Henry Martin ('Marty') Gervais was born in Windsor, Ontario (where he still lives) and received his B.A. (1971) from the University of Guelph and his M.A. (1972) from the University of Windsor before embarking on a career as a journalist with the *Globe and Mail*, Toronto, Canadian Press, and the *Windsor Star*, where he has been entertainment editor, religions editor, and book editor. In 1969, encouraged by James REANEY, with whom he co-authored the play *Baldoon* (1976), Gervais founded the literary publishing house Black Moss Press (1969–). As a historian of Essex County and the Windsor area who has worked on Reaney's principle that lively history and literary material can be found in any region of Canada, Gervais produced several notable histories of the area, including *The* *rumrunners: a prohibition scrapbook* (1980, rev. 2008), a bestseller (25,000 copies) that chronicled the illicit liquor trade of the Prohibition era in Detroit, and the documentary drama *The fighting parson* (1983), about the Prohibition crusades of the tragic and fated Reverend J.O.L. Spracklin, whose zeal against alcohol led to murder. As a literary critic, Gervais wrote *The writing life: historical and critical views of the TISH movement* (1976), an interest that is reflected in the Black Mountain overtones and stylistics of his early poetry. Gervais went through several phases and changes in his poetry, which has seen a transformation from the satirical voice of the early volumes—*Sister Saint Anne* (1968), *Something* (1969), *Other marriage vows* (1969), *A sympathy orchestra* (1970), *Bittersweet* (1972), *The believable body* (1979), and *Public fantasy: The Maggie T poems* (1983), a thinly veiled satire on Margaret Trudeau—to the serious interim volumes *Poems for American daughters* (1976) and *Into a blue morning* (1982). In his introduction to the latter book, Al PURDY noted that Gervais was 'pushing against his limitations, trying to shove the barriers in his mind a little farther ahead; snatching spare moments from being a husband and father and wage earner to write poems'. What may have proved to be a barrier to Gervais, in mid-career, became the strength and substance of *Autobiographies* (1989) and *Tearing into a summer day: prose poems* (1996), where he writes about his life and family with joyful celebration, expressing reverence for the beauties and revelations that daily life offers him. In *Autobiographies*, observances of the commonplace become moments of transcendent epiphany and insight. For Gervais, the personal is invested with the same qualities as the sacred, a carry-over from his renewed spirituality, his travels and self-discoveries in South America, and his profound interest in American poet and monk Thomas Merton and the monastery in Gethsemane, Kentucky. *Letters from the equator* (1986), *Playing God: new poems* (1994), and *Tearing into a summer day* (1996) contain exquisite expressions of humane spirituality. See also *Scenes from the present: new selected poems* (1991). *The science of nothing* (2000), *To be now: new & selected poems, 1989–2003* (2003), and *Wait for me: new poems* (2006),

Gervais's work as a journalist led to the publication of *Seeds in the wilderness: profiles of world religious leaders* (1994), a collection of articles and interviews. *From America sent: letters to Henry Miller* (1995) was inspired by Miller's visits to Windsor in the 1940s, where he stayed at the old British American Hotel.

A chambermaid was fascinated by his apparent sexuality and these are the delightful letters (unmailed) she supposedly wrote him. Gervais describes the book as 'largely a work of fiction'; it is 'dedicated to Marie-Anne Mineau whose own words are written here as I remembered them and as I imagined them.' *A show of hands: boxing on the border* (2004) is filled with Gervais's photographs of young teenagers, in the regions of Detroit and Windsor, boxing; the photos are interspersed with the young peoples' journal entries about boxing ('Once you get boxing in your blood, it never leaves ....') *My town: faces of Windsor* (2006) is a selection of ten years of Gervais's 'My Town' columns in the *Windsor Star* in which he portrays amusingly and vividly some of Windsor's most colourful characters—as well as, towards the end of the book, some well-known writers: Alistair MacLEOD, Marshall McLUHAN, Miriam WADDINGTON, Margaret ATWOOD, and W.O. MITCHELL.

The novella *Reno* (2005)—written in Windsor for The 3-Day Writing Contest (it won third prize)—demonstrates, for the first time, Gervais's ability as a writer of fiction. It is narrated by twelve-year-old Henry, who is confined to his house as he recovers from polio. He changes his name to Reno: the central figure is Reno Bertoia, a real-life baseball player who played for the Detroit Tigers and led the American League in batting. A smoothly written and interesting story, *Reno* skilfully describes a young man's interests and fixations in the 1950s, and ends with his meeting (as a doctor) Reno Butoia thirty years later.

GGA. See GOVERNOR GENERAL'S LITERARY AWARDS.

Gibb, Camilla (b. 1968). Born in London, England, she was brought to Canada and educated at North Toronto and Jarvis Collegiates, the University of Toronto (B.A., 1991), and Oxford University (D. Phil., 1997). In doing research for her doctorate in social anthropology she spent one-and-a-half years in Harar, Ethiopia, an experience that informed her third novel. She is adjunct faculty member of the U of T's English department's M.A. program in Creative Writing.

Gibb's first novel, *Mouthing the words* (1999), displays technical dexterity as Thelma Barley discloses—from the time she is a little girl in England until adulthood in Canada—her inner life, which has been forever affected by her father's abuse of her. 'We all sought salvation through imaginary friends. Daddy's was a secretary named Teresa. I knew, because sometimes he would come into my room at bedtime and say, "Let's play a game. Let's pretend we are at work, and I am your boss and you are my secretary named Teresa." He'd sit on my bed and I would pretend that I was typing.... "And what does Teresa do when the boss comes into the room?" he'd ask me. "That's right," he'd say. "She closes her eyes and opens her mouth and the boss gives her a nice kiss." And he'd stick his smoky tongue in my mouth and I would feel his bristly face. I didn't like that part....' Thelma had her own imaginary friends: Ginniger, Janawee, and Heroin. She tells Aunt Esme about them and about being Daddy's secretary and his kiss for a job well done. '"But what happens if you don't do a good job?" [Esme] asked. "Well, sometimes he says, Miss so-and-so, I think you've made an error in typing this correspondence. I think you'll have to lie down while I discipline you."' When this happens, she tells her aunt, she dreams: '"About a flying insect.... I feel very high because I'm only a tiny insect and I am afraid of being so high and my bed and the room look so big. And when the noise gets too loud I just suck in my breath really hard and my eyes turn inside my head and all I see is big red."' Esme tells her sister, who throws plates and a chair at her husband—who leaves for Canada. In the following twenty-three chapters we read sometimes casual and witty, sometimes dismaying accounts of Thelma's life, her alienation from her difficult mother, becoming crazed and institutionalized, recovering, and achieving a brilliant law degree in Toronto and a scholarship to Oxford. She has an affair with Patrick, who loves her and whom she loves. But at the end of the book he's seeing someone else, though he's not in love with her. 'I'm comfortable. It's nice. Pleasant. Uncomplicated. Easy.' Thelma can only say to herself: 'Oh. So it's better to be comfortable.... all I have is a lumpy futon beneath me and a heart breaking in the hands of a man who loves me. He is comfortable. I am not.' *Mouthing the words* won the ($8000) Toronto Book Award in 2000. In *The petty details of so-and-so's life* (2002) Emma and Llewellyn Taylor, brother and sister—Em and Blue for short—live in a dysfunctional family and share a deep bond from early childhood. Their father Oliver, a failed architect who decides to become an inventor, turns crazy and leaves the family; their mother Elaine becomes an alcoholic. Em's life, though not straightforward, leads her to a satisfying lesbian relationship with Nina; while Blue, who becomes a tattoo

artist, is forever in search of his father, and is imprisoned for attempted murder—of an old man he thought was his father. Em and Blue never come together again.

Gibb's unusual style in these novels—her breezy, conversational, perceptive treatment of taboo themes (child abuse, the desertion of a father, mental illness, violence etc.) in a succession of easy, sometimes humorous dialogues—is transformed for her third novel, *Sweetness in the belly* (2005). It is a dense, structured narrative of Lilly's life, latterly as a nurse in London, England, in the 1980s (and in 1990–1 at the end) and in Harar, Ethiopia, in the early 1970s. Lilly had vagabond parents who lived in one country after another (she was born in Yugoslavia) until they ended up in Morocco and were mysteriously killed there, leaving their eight-year-old daughter in the charge of the Great Abdul, a Sufi sheikh, and Muhammed Bruce Mahmoud ('a large English convert with a white beard'). 'The Great Abdul would be my teacher, my guide, my father in senses both spiritual and mundane. Muhammed Bruce would be my guardian, visiting me regularly and paying for my keep.' The Great Abdul teaches her the Qur'an. ('I was not always a Muslim, but once I was led into the absorbtion of prayer and the mysteries of the Qur'an, something troubled in me became still.') When she is sixteen she is sent to the ancient Ethiopian city of Harar, where she lives, in abject poverty (vividly described) with Nouria and her four children, whom she teaches the Qur'an, along with the neighbours' children. Learning the language, she becomes accepted as a teacher in the community, though she is very much an outsider, a *farenji* (foreigner), a white Muslim who speaks Harari but is horrified by the ritual circumcision of Nouria's two young daughters. One of them is infected and Dr Aziz Abdulnasser arrives to treat her. He is a wise, attractive, liberal, half-Sudanese black man with whom, in time, Lilly falls in love. He is clearly drawn to Lilly, though he challenges her strict Muslim beliefs, calling them an escape from the modern world. When Haile Selassi is deposed and civil chaos is expected, she leaves for London and they are separated forever. In Lilly's life as a hospital nurse she makes friends with a refugee from Ethiopia, Amina, with whom she forms a community association to reunite refugees; Amina's husband Yusuf eventually arrives in London; but not Lilly's Aziz, though we learn what happened to him. Quite apart from the descriptions of Ethiopia, particularly of Harar in a time of famine, Gibb's portrayal of Lilly and

Aziz, both unusual and memorable characters, invests this novel with distinction. It won the (Ontario) Trillium Award.

Gibbs, Robert (b. 1930). Born in Saint John, New Brunswick, he was educated at the University of New Brunswick and at Cambridge University, receiving his Ph.D. from UNB, where he taught English until his retirement; he is now Professor Emeritus. He lives in Fredericton, N.B.

Gibbs has long been associated with *The FIDDLEHEAD* and the Maritime Writers' Workshop. Since some of his poems were included in Fred COGSWELL's *Five New Brunswick poets* (1962), Gibbs has published numerous collections of poetry: *The road from here* (1968), *Earth charms heard so early* (1970), *A dog in a dream* (1971), *A kind of wakefulness* (1973), *All this night long* (1978), *The tongue still dances: poems new and selected* (1985), *Earth aches* (1991), and *Angels watch do keep* (1997). *A space to play in* (1981) is a selection published in pamphlet form by the LEAGUE OF CANADIAN POETS. Gibbs's poems contain sensual and witty descriptions of human and non-human landscapes, subtle insights into relationships, a sophisticated understanding of the workings of the mind, the mutterings of dream, and the interworkings of conscience, the subconscious, grief, and nostalgia. His rhythms give a sense of sustaining—and detaining—energy; his language combines the melodic with the colloquial. *Driving to our edge* (2003) is a collection of enjoyable poems revealing a writer, and the things that strike his imagination, that are both appealing. One reads with particular pleasure poems about three writers who have entries in this *Companion*: 'AGB' (Gibbs's teacher, Alfred Goldsworthy BAILEY), 'Alden and Robbie's day' and 'A one-sided call to a many-sided man' (Alden NOWLAN), and 'RG' (Ralph GUSTAFSON).

Gibbs has also written highly effective fiction. In his collection of short stories, *I've always felt sorry for decimals* (1978), he recreates, through the mind of the same observant and imaginative child, a provincial society just now fading into history: New Brunswick in the late 1930s and early 1940s. Gibbs's child narrator combines the role of author/creator with that of the innocent rememberer of things past, a 'petit Marcel', through whose purer, simpler eyes an adult world of anxiety and dread is faintly hinted. Gibbs's fantasy novel *A mouth-organ for angels* (1984) has been described by Martin Waxman (*Quill and Quire*, October 1984) as an 'intricate dream sequence, part fairy tale, part Oz, part Alice in Wonderland, and part Huck Finn'. In *Kindly light* (2007) Frank MacBean of Saint John tells the story of much of his life, beginning when he's twelve. He ends by saying: 'So my past and my present reach to touch hands. Between them lay my own wooing and wedding of Ursula, her two miscarriages with their attendant hopes and terrible letdowns, and the bright fulfillment that came with Cecily. The years following, like all years, checkered with light and shade, teem with events too many and too new for me to want to relive.' In both his poetry and fiction Gibbs shows a delicate ear for the nuances of Maritime speech and decorum, and a gentle savouring humour.

Gibson, Douglas. See MCCLELLAND & STEWART

Gibson, Graeme (b. 1934). Born in London in the southern Ontario he would so ably chronicle, explore, and interrogate, Gibson attended Upper Canada College, Toronto, and the University of Western Ontario (B.A., 1958). He has been both a novelist and a galvanizing force in Canadian cultural politics from the early 1970s, serving as a much-respected chairman of The WRITERS' UNION OF CANADA and of The WRITERS' TRUST OF CANADA, and as president of Canadian PEN. As a long-standing volunteer of the Writers' Trust of Canada, he was given in 2008 the Writers' Trust Award for Distinguished Contribution. He lives in Toronto with Margaret ATWOOD, with whom he has a daughter, Jess. He was made a Member of the Order of Canada in 1992. Gibson's first novel, *Five legs* (1969, rpr. 2003), voices with poetic impact concerns that are prominent in his subsequent fiction: personal and cultural paralysis, death in all its guises, blocked creativity, the grieving process, and father-son entanglements. Ingeniously refracted through the opposing yet complementary sensibilities of its two main characters, this 'stream-of-consciousness' novel details a winter journey through the stricken heart of WASP Ontario. Occasioned by the funeral of a student, Martin Baillie, who succumbed to the same repressive, conventional, and puritanical forces that warped the life of his professor, Dr Crackell, the trip pits a harried Crackell against his unwanted travelling companion, Felix Oswald, Baillie's roommate and best friend. Felix—equally tormented, crippled, and haunted, feeling cornered by the deadening pressures of conformity and respectability deforming Crackell—manages a temporary escape. *Five legs* was hailed on publication as avant-garde and a stylistic tour de force—it was the impressive first novel published by the House of ANANSI. *Communion* (1971) continues and darkens the fractured, feverish story of self-mocking Felix Oswald, deepening the themes of cultural malaise, of maiming, strangled articulateness and psychological survival. Though seeking refuge in a flight to the northern wilds, Felix, an obsessive veterinarian's assistant, is unable to evolve beyond a futile identity with animal victims and entrapment in his own neuroses; the sick husky he befriends is run down by Felix's own car, choosing to be a victim—like Bailie, the hit-and-run casualty of *Five legs*, and Felix himself, who perishes at a southern border crossing that was nightmarishly set ablaze by American street kids. (*Five legs* and *Communion* were published in one volume in 1979.) As in all Gibson's fiction, characters overlap, coalesce, and reduplicate one another, giving rise to an eerie sense of doubleness, of mirrors mirroring mirrors—the hallmark of SOUTHERN ONTARIO GOTHIC. *Perpetual motion* (1982, NCL; rpr. 2003), perhaps Gibson's best and most accessible novel, churns up nineteenth-century rural Ontario in a rich, Gothic outpouring of eccentric characters colliding around fictional Mad River. Robert Fraser, a technology-intoxicated inventor of overbearing rationality fatally obsessed with power, control, and dynastic grandeur, violently pursues perfection through a perpetual-motion machine that promises triumph over the elements. Yet he brings destruction not only on his family but also on the vibrant natural world he wars against. Again, Gibson structures this marvellous epic, enlivened by local colour and folklore, around parallel characters and doubles, especially 'the man of reason' and 'the wild man'. The powerful, moving *Gentleman Death* (1993, rpr. 2002), as with his first two linked novels, complements *Perpetual motion*, with which it shares a like-named protagonist. Set mainly in Toronto in the late 1980s, it presents an engaging portrayal of fifty-six-year-old novelist Robert Fraser as he encounters death the leveller, and painfully yet resolutely—and not without humour and moments of serenity—comes to terms with his own aging and mortality, and his grief, from a series of unsettling losses: of parents, a brother, friends, wilderness areas and entire ecosystems, of a recognizable Canada dismantled during the Mulroney regime. But slowly and honestly, Fraser perseveres, keeping what is genuine, socially committed, and 'wild' in himself and in the dance of life and death. *The bedside book of birds: an avian miscellany* (2005) is an anthology of memorable writings about birds throughout the ages—with more than 100 stunning illustrations in colour—enhanced by the eloquent introduction to the book, and introductions to the nine sections, by the avid and knowledgeable birdwatcher Gibson himself. Extravagantly beautiful in appearance (designed by Scott Richardson) and published internationally, this is a superb book. Giving up novel writing in the mid-nineties because 'I discovered I had nothing more to say as a novelist', Gibson (in a 2006 interview), thinking of the *Bedside book* as an alternative novel, went on to say: 'Each of my novels was concerned with everything that was singularly important to my life at the time. And that's the same with this book. Inside of me, it has the same weight.'

Gibson, Margaret (1948–2006). Born and raised in Toronto, her formal education ending with grade ten, she suffered from mental illness for most of her life: she was hospitalized the first time at fifteen and for several years thereafter was a voluntary mute. Marrying in the early 1970s Stuart Gilboord, with whom she had a son Aaron, they divorced and she moved in with her friend Craig Russell, the talented female impersonator who played a leading role in the Canadian film *Outrageous*, adapted from Gibson's story 'Making it'. This was in her first collection of stories, *The butterfly ward* (1976), which was a critical success: she was co-winner (with Margaret ATWOOD) of the City of Toronto Book Award. *Considering her condition* (1978), Gibson's second collection, was somewhat less successful; its title is that of a story in *The butterfly ward. Sweet poison* (1993, rpr. 1994) presents seven confessional stories about abused women who find refuge in various kinds of oblivion, even madness. The title story in *The fear room and other stories* (1996) is partly told from the standpoint of a boy of two-and-a-half years who had been beaten by his mother's boyfriend; other stories treat obsession, memory, and mental illness. Among the best of Gibson's stories are 'Ada', 'Making it', 'Considering her condition', 'Brian Tattoo', 'Still life', 'Sweet poison', and 'The fear room'. *Opium dreams* (1997, rpr. 1999)—winner of the Chapters / *Books in Canada* First Novel Award—eloquently and lyrically describes the lives of Maggie (who had suffered from mental illness) and her father, a victim of Alzheimer's disease whose mind has been reduced to jumbled memories. In *Desert thirst* (1997), a collection of five long stories, the mental stress, or delusions, of the main characters is conveyed by three of the titles: 'A slipping away kind of life', 'Stalker', and 'Empty'.

With mental illness as Gibson's central theme, her protagonists are often shown 'functioning' outside of institutions, disguising themselves, walking 'the fine line between reality and fantasy'; but reality—which cannot simply be equated with normalcy or its opposite—can be the hideousness of the world, from which the narrator tries to avert her gaze, as well as those rare moments of innocence when delight takes over. Although in both perceptions of reality Gibson's beautiful losers are more 'real' than her normal people, madness is no escape. 'Sometimes it can be beautiful inside this space', but more often it feels like being damned. Violence is everywhere—much of it directed against women. But there is also tenderness, especially for small children and for others who suffer alongside Gibson's protagonists. And there is sometimes a lovely gallantry in all the pain.

Gibson, William (b. 1948). Born in Conway, South Carolina, he visited Toronto in 1967 and remained in Canada to avoid being drafted into the US army. He married a teacher and settled in Vancouver, where he earned a B.A. (1977) from the University of British Columbia. During his studies Gibson began writing science-fiction short stories, which he published in numerous SF journals and magazines. His first novel, *Neuromancer* (1984), is credited with launching the cyberpunk movement. An immediate success, it was the first novel to win, in the same year, three prestigious SF awards: the Hugo, the Nebula, and the Philip K. Dick. It was also the first volume of his Cyberspace trilogy, the others being *Count Zero* (1986) and *Mona Lisa overdrive* (1988). In his fiction Gibson situates our contemporary relation to a high-tech environment in an SF context in order to push the implications of that relationship to their extremes. As a result of his early novels and stories, 'cyberspace', 'netsurfing', 'ICE', 'jacking in', and 'neural implants' entered popular usage, as did 'net consciousness', 'virtual interaction', and 'the matrix'. His stories and novels focus, in general, less on plot than on creating vivid descriptions of techno-scenarios, although in *Virtual light* (1993) character is important, and the techno-scenarios serve to move its plot along, rather than merely indulge Gibson's descriptive powers. *Idoru* (1996) is probably Gibson's most interesting and enjoyable novel from a literary standpoint, and the most wide-ranging in the territory it covers—Japan, Hong Kong (Kowloon), and

Russia (the underworld of Moscow)—and in the characters and situations it embraces, as well as in its mordant satire of present Western mores, translated into the early twenty-first century, which is filled with high technology. An *idoru* is a transient pop star in Japan, and one of the novel's events (a satire on celebrity) is the engagement of Rez, the lead singer in a Japanese group, to an *idoru* named Rel Toei—who turns out to have been created by a computer! In a 1996 interview Gibson said: 'I don't [i.e., no longer] feel like I'm being chased by technological change. I just sort of surf along on its spume.' *All tomorrow's parties* (1999) follows *Virtual light* and *Idoru* to form the Bridge trilogy, with some of the same characters.

Taking place in 2002, *Pattern recognition* (2003, rpr. 2005) centres on Cayce Pollard, a thirty-two-year-old New Yorker who is an unusually astute marketing consultant, very sensitive to logos and advertising, and works only for fees. The novel begins when she has been flown to London, staying in her absent friend Damien's apartment, to advise the marketing firm Blue Ant about a proposed logo for a shoe company (she says no). The head of Blue Ant, Hubertus Bigbend, then hires Cayce to find out who is responsible for releasing a series of film clips on the Internet. Her Chicago friend Peter Gilbert, named Parkaboy, tells her by email that one of the clips has an uncrypted watermark. There follows a complicated, suspenseful narrative, involving many other characters, and moving to Tokyo, then Moscow (and the Russian Mafia). The attacks of 11 September 2001 occurred while Gibson was writing his novel, and this horrific event, which becomes a breaking point from the past, is seen on TV by Cayce in Tokyo ('An experience outside of culture') and is connected with Cayce's father's disappearance; at the end of the novel Cayce reads about his last moments in New York. Much praised by reviewers and many readers, *Pattern recognition* was given the front page of *The New York Times Book Review*, and was briefly #4 in the *Times*'s bestseller list; but the 'cool' argot, the constant name-dropping of businesses and new and fashionable products, characters of many nationalities who don't seem to have any identity and are merely names, all interfered with this reader's enjoyment. In the opening lines of *Spook country* (2007) Hollis Henry receives a phone call from Rausch, of *Node*: 'She turned on the bedside lamp, illuminating the previous evening's empty can of Asahi Draft, from the Pink Dot, and her sticker-encrusted PowerBook, closed and sleeping. She envied it.' *Node* is a magazine that has not yet been published and Hollis is hired to report on locative art, what one character calls 'spatially tagged hypermedia', and this turns out to involve her in a dangerous scenario, with many characters, that includes global money laundering. It leads to three different storylines—unfolding (ineffectively) in eighty-four brief chapters—in which (as in *Pattern recognition*) Hubertus Bigend eventually appears and many brand names are mentioned. For the first time in a Gibson novel both New York City (where there is a terrific chase scene) and Vancouver are significant.

Gibson wrote the script for the film *Johnny Mnemonic* (1995), based on his short story of the same title.

Giguère, Roland (b. 1929). Born in Montreal, he trained as a printer at the École des Arts Graphiques there and at the École Estienne in Paris. In 1949 he founded Éditions Erta in Montreal, which published books of poems and prints by Québécois writers and artists until 1978. Giguère has long been an important figure in the literary and artistic life of Québec, publishing collections of poetry from the forties to the eighties. There are only two collections available in English, both of them selections from several of his books: *Mirror and letters to an escapee* (1977), translated by Sheila FISCHMAN, and *Rose and thorn* (1988), a more comprehensive collection translated by Donald Winkler. His early work was inspired by the purest spirit of surrealism. His care for form and structure as a poet, reminiscent of his discipline as a printer, was at the service of an ever-springing flow of dream-like imagery whose power derives from an authentic inner exploration of the individual and collective unconscious. His later poems, including love poems, are notable for their beauty and clarity of language and imagery, their wordplay—and not a little surrealism.

Gilbert, Sky (b. 1952). Born Schyler Lee Gilbert in Norwich, Connecticut, and raised in Buffalo, New York, he graduated from York University, Toronto, with a B.A. in 1977, influenced strongly by the avant-garde work of Robert Benedetti. He left graduate studies at the University of Toronto (M.A., 1999; he earned a Ph.D. there in 2006) to found Buddies in Bad Times Theatre, Toronto, with Matt Walsh and Gerrard Ciccoritti. Under Gilbert's long and productive leadership (1979–97), Buddies developed a mandate to encourage innovative and gay or lesbian artists, creating a space for alternative theatre that challenged mainstream assumptions about both gender and staging. Gilbert now holds the University Research Chair in Creative Writing and Theatre Studies at Guelph University, and lives in Hamilton, Ontario.

In 1994 Buddies acquired a permanent home in the former Toronto Workshop Productions theatre, making it the largest gay and lesbian theatre in North America. After the success of early plays such as the 1980s *Lana Turner has collapsed*, about poet Frank O'Hara, Gilbert wrote, directed, and/or acted in several colourful, extravagantly theatrical plays that treated gender issues with farcical and joyful irreverence. Gilbert has published three collections of plays—*This unknown flesh* (1995), *Painted, tainted, sainted: four plays* (1996), and *Avoidance tactics: three* plays (2001)—as well as individual works, including *The dressing gown* (1989) and *Play murder* (1995), whose main characters are the torch singer Libby Holman and the young heir to a tobacco fortune, Smith Reynolds, her husband, who died in a shooting. *Rope enough* (2005) is a psychological mystery in which Ichabod and Dylan are charged with the murder of Ichabod's parents. Honours include Dora Awards for *The whore's revenge* (1990) and *Suzie Goo* (1992). *Digressions of a naked party girl* (1998) and *Temptations for a juvenile delinquent* (2003) are collections of pseudo-poems that read like gay monologues. The two novels *Guilty* (1998) and *St. Stephen's* (1999) are both about Jack: in *Guilty* he's a gay actor who becomes involved with an ex-hustler who is trouble (and is killed), and in *St. Stephen's* he's a professor, attracted to younger men, in a small university where there are many of them—in denial, he has an affair with the dean of arts who hired him. *I am Kasper Klotz* (2001)—'My name has been changed to protect the innocent.'—opens with his confession: 'I kill people. Innocent people. I make them die….' HIV-positive, he infects Aaron, a 'beautiful' young midwesterner and is accused of assault and attempted murder. The novel is a memoir, a 'morbidly funny' exploration of the AIDS world and people who are dominated by it. *Brother Dumb* (2007) is a different kind of memoir, that of a famous American writer who published a bestseller in 1951. He is a recluse, lives in New Hampshire, and is (unconvincingly, in Gilbert's hands) straight, with two offspring. He wants to find love with a very beautiful woman—one, then another, enters his life—but he seems incapable of love and ends up a cranky old man who is on his third, much younger, wife. As a memoirist he has logorrhea and will discourse on just about anything—writing, critics, Orson Welles, Bette

Davis in *Now Voyager*—and revels in his misanthropy, 'I mean my hatred for ordinary people, for the people that you meet at the store. Yes, the fact that I hate on a regular basis is a problem. The anger I feel towards my ex-wife, for example—that definitely has a pathological aspect to it.' He is without a name—he refers to himself as Brother Dumb—but he seems to be impersonating J.D. Salinger. (There are numerous echoes of Salinger's life.) If so, the effort appears to be pointless and the loquacious narrator seems fraudulent, though his narrative is entertaining at times. Gilbert's best novel is *An English gentleman* (2004). James Barrie, the author of *Peter Pan*, became a close friend of the beautiful Sylvia Llewelyn Davies and her husband Arthur, who had five sons whom Barrie used to take to Kensington Gardens, London, where a statue of Peter Pan was erected in 1912. Peter was inspired by the eldest Llewelyn Davies boy, George (one of his brothers was called Peter). When their father died, followed three years later by their mother, Barrie adopted them. He was especially attached to Michael and they exchanged some 2000 letters from 1905 and 1921 when Michael was at Eton, then Oxford University. (Peter eventually burned them.) For his novel Sky Gilbert cleverly invented more than fifty letters, giving each correspondent his own believable voice; the last one is supposed to have been written on the day Michael drowned (aged twenty) in the River Thames, in the treacherous Sandford Pool, Oxford. Michael couldn't swim. He was with his close friend Rupert Buxton (twenty-two). Were they lovers? Possibly. Was this a mutual suicide? His brothers Peter and Nico thought it might have been. Can one read anything improper in the loving letters written to Michael? No. But these concerns attracted Gilbert's imagination. (He wrote his M.A. thesis on Sir James Barrie; the 1979 publication *J.M. Barrie & the lost boys* by Andrew Birkin was another source for his text.) His imagination was given full play in the last hundred pages, narrated by Manny Masters—a contented but lonely gay high-school teacher who had acquired the letters—in which he describes harbouring a nineteen-year-old boy, Alan Peche, who wants to be a writer, in his apartment so that he can help him with his writing. A bond develops (nothing sexual) but Manny's obsessive feelings towards Alan, and his obtuseness about his real nature, are meant to echo those of Barrie towards Michael. Admitting the thread of homosexuality that runs through these pages—implicit in the Barrie section, explicit in an Epilogue by Alan Peche—Gilbert has

said that he was most interested in 'two much more important issues: love and death'—thinking, one supposes, of Michael and Rupert. Journal entries make up the novel *Wit in love* (2008), about a philosopher in love; it is loosely based on the life and loves of Ludwig Wittgenstein.

An outspoken gay activist with a flamboyant alter ego 'Jane', Sky Gilbert frequently rouses the ire of conservative factions in government and the press, expressing through his lifestyle the process of confrontation seen in his plays. In 1997 he resigned his post as Artistic Director of Buddies to concentrate on writing. In 2000 his play *The emotionalists* (2000) was produced in Toronto and praised for its relatively true and comical portrait of Ayn Rand, the American writer whose polemical and melodramatic novels and other books became bestsellers for advancing the idea of self-interest, and for opposing all inhibiting controls, such as government. *Ejaculations from the charm factory* (2000) is a memoir that covers the years 1979 to 1997, when both theatre and sexual politics filled his life. Gilbert edited *Perfectly abnormal: seven gay plays* (2006) and *Gay monologues and scenes: an anthology* (2007).

Giller Prize, now called the Scotiabank Giller Prize. This was inaugurated in 1994 by Toronto businessman Jack Rabinovitch in honour of his late wife, literary journalist Doris Giller; it awarded $25,000 to the author of the best Canadian novel or short-story collection. In September 2005 it was announced that Scotiabank would co-sponsor the award, increasing it to $40,000 for the winner and $2500 for each of the finalists, and in April 2008 the total amount of the prize money rose to $70,000, with $50,000 going to the winner and $5000 to each runner-up The presentation—for which CTV is the exclusive broadcast partner—takes place at a gala black-tie dinner in November. Winners to 2009 are:

1994
M.G. VASSANJI. *The book of secrets.*

1995
Rohinton MISTRY. *A fine balance.*

1996
Margaret ATWOOD. *Alias Grace.*

1997
Mordecai RICHLER. *Barney's version.*

1998
Alice MUNRO. *The love of a good woman.*

Giller Prize

Gilmour, David (b. 1949). Born in London, Ontario, he grew up in Toronto and attended Upper Canada College (1959–67) and the University of Toronto, studying French literature (B.A., 1972; B. Ed., 1978), and doing graduate work on comparative literature at Victoria College, U of T, under Northrop FRYE. (He is currently Pelham Edgar Visiting Professor at Victoria College.) He was managing editor of the Toronto Film Festival (1980–4) and became a film critic for CBC's *The Journal* and *The National* (1986–97). He was the popular host of 'Gilmour on the Arts' (*Newsworld*, 1994–7) while also becoming a screenwriter and novelist. His novels are *Back on Tuesday* (1986, rpr. 2006), *How boys see girls* (1991, rpr. 1992), *An affair with the moon* (1993, rpr. 1994), *Lost between houses* (1999, rpr. 2000), *Sparrow nights* (2001, rpr. 2002), and *A perfect night to go to China* (2005, rpr. 2006, GGA). Many readers welcome the first-person narratives of Gilmour's novels—which have elements of autobiography—because they demonstrate agreeable fluency in combining lively dialogue and vivid descriptions as they convey the travails of a heavy-drinking, narcissistic narrator who is usually girl-crazy: ('Before too long she was in your bed and then in your heart.'—*Back on Tuesday*). The fact that one often wonders what is really being written about in these discursive narratives is an anomaly. For example, in *Back on Tuesday* Gene has an angry disagreement with his ex-wife J. and flees with his five-year-old daughter Franny to Jamaica—in effect kidnapping her. Every detail is described, from the arrival at the airport and the hotel, putting Fran to bed, and his descent to the hotel bar and the people he meets there (including Lily, whom he's attracted to, who has a husband) and spends time with until, some eighteen hours later, he comes to his senses on Tuesday and phones J., who arrives at the airport to collect Fran. In *How boys see girls* the woman Bix is obsessed with, called Holly, is bad news—though on the last page of the book he receives a phone call from her, pedals his daughter's bike over to Holly's house, enters through an open front window, tumbles into bed with her, has sex, then dresses and departs, all without saying a word. (The title is that of a book his young daughter is reading.) *An affair with the moon* is about Harrow Winncup and Christian Blackwood who are school chums and drift in and out of each other's lives into middle age. Harrow, an alcoholic and drug addict who becomes a bandleader, often desires Christian's company, once pleading with him to go to his house, where Harrow tells him that he's killed Pascal, his tenor saxophonist. Christian becomes involved in the legal proceedings that follow, as does Harrow's malevolent mother. Did *she* kill Pascal? Who is telling the truth? The award-winning *A perfect night to go to China* begins with every parent's nightmare, when Roman (implausibly) leaves his six-year-old son Simon behind an unlocked door while he goes to a bar down the street for fifteen minutes and reurns to find that Simon is gone. The novel recounts—in simple, clear, lyrical prose—the effect this has on Roman's life and mind, as he loses his job, is tormented by guilt, brings Simon to life in dreams and converses with him, robs a bank and uses the money to go to an island in the Caribbean, where his mother died. (On the way to the airport he suddenly says 'God, it's a beautiful day.' And the taxi driver responds with what his mother used to say after such an exclamation: 'A perfect day to go to China.'). At the end of the book Roman is in a canoe, has taken handfuls of pills, falls asleep, wakes up—and who knows what is happening? He sees a yellow house and 'a small boy was standing on the porch.... I waved, I hurried, shoeless, toward him, but he went inside.' After the suspense caused by Simon's disappearance—very much felt by the reader—the ambiguous ending is a sad anticlimax. *The film club: a true story of a father and son* (2007) tells of Gilmour's decision, when his son Jesse has apparently given up on high school at sixteen, to allow him to leave school as long as he sees three films a week with his father—'It's the only education you're going to get.... But no drugs. Any drugs and the deal's off.' Countless films are described and briefly discussed (fun for any reader who's a film buff). Drug-taking makes an appearance, but not disastrously, and Jesse's love affairs, and then their dissolution, first with Rebecca, then with Chloë, continually transfix him. When the three years are up, Jesse takes a crash high-school course that qualifies him for university, which he proceeds to attend. The book is an unusual, endearing record of the strong relationship between a father and son ... until Gilmour the father realizes 'that he'll never come back in the same form again.' He himself has become 'A visitor from now on. But what a strange, miraculous, unexpected gift, those three years in the life of a young man at a time when normally he begins to shut the door on his parent.'

Givner, Joan (b. 1936). Born Joan Mary Parker Short in Manchester, England, Givner took an honours degree in English at the University of London in 1958, married David Givner in 1965, and returned to London for a Ph.D. (1972), following teaching and graduate study in the USA. In 1972 she resumed teaching in the English department of the University of Regina, where she remained until taking early retirement in 1995 and moving to British Columbia to write full time. She lives on Vancouver Island. Between 1984 and 1992 she edited the *Wascana Review*. Her first book was *Katherine Anne Porter: a life* (1982, rev. 1991), which established her as a feminist biographer. This was followed by *Katherine Anne Porter: conversations* (1987), a collection of interviews. In *Mazo de la Roche: the hidden life* (1989) Givner communicates her fascination with DE LA ROCHE's multiple ambivalences—'sexual, national, racial, and religious'—and with her need to 'inscribe her own female desire obliquely' within the conventions of the novel.

Givner's first collection of short fiction, *Tentacles of unreason* (1985), is pleasing apprentice work that shows her exploration of the notion of 'fictional fictions' and 'fictions of autobiography', finding the female presence in the 'intertext between the two'. For example, in the title story of her second collection, *Unfortunate incidents* (1988), a literary biographer at work on the life of 'Rachel de la Warr' meets Rachel's adopted daughter Aiméee, in a sophisticated reminder of de la Roche and her adopted daughter Esmée. The

stories in *Scenes from provincial life* (1991) demonstrate a similar wilful assault on the sort of criticism that finds women's writing merely autobiographical. The title story of *In the garden of Henry James* (1996) is about Libby, from Canada, visiting her mother in southern England, and their trip to James's Lamb House in Rye, which gives rise to thoughts about William and Alice James, and *The turn of the screw*, that are interrupted by trivial, dutiful exchanges between mother and daughter. Givner's husband once asked her: 'Suppose you wrote a novel, what would it be about?' Her immediate answer: 'It would be about a man who got pregnant', which is indeed the subject of her first novel, *Half known lives* (2000). This satire, based on so-called advances in biotechnology, was partly inspired by a famous Regina anti-abortion case and its all-male participants. *Playing Sarah Bernhardt* (2004) is an agreeable novel about acting that draws on Givner's biography of Mazo de la Roche. Harriet was playing Bernhardt in a play, with a cast of two, when she got stage fright, repeatedly, and left it—only to be called to audition for a play about Mazo de la Roche. She won the part and became friends with the author, Hope Prince, who described Mazo as someone 'so out of sync with the real world'that she 'could lead her own inner life, keeping it absolutely intact, and yet appear before the world in a disguise that made her completely—or almost completely—acceptable.... she led a double life, and she twisted that other life into fictional currency, and used it to conquer the world. It was an incredible feat.' The text includes brief passages from the play, which in an author's note Givner says are adapted from her play *Mazo and Caroline*, performed in Saskatchewan in 1992. The novel itself, with its ingenious combination of various characters and subjects, certainly engages the reader's interest.

Givner turned her life-writing talents on her own experience with *The self-portrait of a literary biographer* (1993), focusing on her grammar-school beginnings and her growth into her own writing. *Thirty-four ways of looking at Jane Eyre* (1998) is a collection of essays—including one on researching the life of Katherine Anne Porter and two on Eudora Welty—and short stories. The title piece is a tour de force that employs elements of memoir, essay, and fiction to portray a lifelong devotion to Charlotte Brontë's famous novel.

Givner has published in Canada and the US three novels for girls around the age of eleven: *Ellen Fremedon* (2004, rpr. 2006), *Ellen Fremedon, journalist* (2005), and *Ellen Fremedon, volunteer* (2007).

Glass, Joanna McClelland (b. 1936). Born Joan Ruth McClelland in Saskatoon, Saskatchewan, she developed an interest in theatre as a high-school student. After graduation in 1955 she performed with the Saskatoon Community Players while working as an ad writer and broadcaster at a local radio station. She soon moved to Calgary, Alberta, to join Betty Mitchell's Workshop 14. Her lead role in Maxwell Anderson's *Anne of the thousand days*, the Calgary entry in the 1957 Dominion Drama Festival, won her a scholarship from the Alberta Cultural Activities Branch to study acting for the summer at the Pasadena Playhouse, California. She next enrolled in Warner Brothers Drama School, but soon left for New York. There she met physicist Alexander Glass, whom she married in 1959; they divorced in 1976. After thirty years of residence in the United States (latterly, Guilford, Connecticut), she now makes her home in Toronto.

In the early 1960s Glass acted at Yale, where her husband was a student, but once her three children were in school she turned to writing. In 1966 she completed an early version of the play that was eventually become *Artichoke*. A second work, *Santacqua*, was accepted at the Herbert Berghof Studio, New York, for workshop production in Dec. 1969. Glass's breakthrough as a professional dramatist came in Nov. 1972 with the production of the companion one-act pieces *Canadian Gothic* and *American modern* (published jointly in 1977) at the off-Broadway Manhattan Theatre Club, with a revival the following spring. Set in a small prairie city and a New York suburb respectively (and usually produced together), the one is a sombre study of a failing struggle against emotional repression, the other a tragicomic sketch of eccentric accommodation to marriage breakdown. The first of many Canadian productions followed in Nov. 1973 at the Pleiades Theatre, Calgary. *Canadian Gothic* appeared in *Best short plays of 1978* (1980) and in *Prairie performance* (1980) edited by Diane Bessai. Glass's full-length play *Artichoke* (1979), a comedy with a Saskatchewan farm setting, was premiered at the Long Wharf Theatre, New Haven, Conn., in Oct. 1975, starring Colleen Dewhurst; Bill Glassco mounted the first Canadian production at Tarragon Theatre, Toronto, in Oct. 1976. Glass's witty dialogue and sharp-eyed view of western Canadian rural society enliven this play about a middle-aged wife who astonishes her family by deciding to take a lover for the summer. Glass developed a similar theme in her first novel, *Reflections of a mountain summer*

(1974). Set alternately in the Canadian Rockies and Grosse Point, Mich., it combines the author's perceptions of Canadian and American personality and her response to the traumas of modern living. Glass's next two plays premiered on Broadway: *To grandmother's house we go* (1981), starring Eva Le Gallienne, in Jan. 1981; and *Play memory* (1984), directed by Harold Prince, in Apr. 1984. Although the latter earned a Tony nomination, critical response to both plays was lukewarm. The former, in a contemporary American setting, reverses the usual generational conflict in its comic-ironic exploration of the question, 'Is there life after children?' *Play memory*, set in the Saskatoon of the playwright's youth, is a largely autobiographical study of the decline of a proudly unrepentant alcoholic as recollected years later by his daughter, and has its origins in a short story, 'At the King Edward Hotel', written in 1975 and published in *Winter's tales* 22 (1976); its first dramatic version, entitled *The last chalice*, was commissioned by the Manitoba Theatre Centre for its twentieth-anniversary season in 1977. Glass was awarded a Guggenheim Fellowship in 1981 for the extensive revision of the play, which had its Canadian premiere at the 25th Street Theatre, Saskatoon, in Jan. 1986; it was published in *NeWest plays by women* (1987) edited by Diane Bessai and Don Kerr. As playwright-in-residence at the Canadian Stage Company, Toronto (1987–8) Glass completed a new prairie comedy, *Yesteryear*, premiered at the St Lawrence Centre, Toronto, in Jan. 1989. The Canadian premiere of *If we are women* (1994), a co-production of the Canadian Stage Company and Vancouver Playhouse, opened at the St Lawrence Centre in Jan. 1994; the American premiere had taken place the previous July at Williamstown Theatre Festival, Williamstown, Mass. (A London, England production, directed by Richard Olivier, starred Joan Plowright.) Whereas in *Yesteryear* Glass explores a light side to the Saskatoon of her youth, in *If we are women* she forwards the lives of *Play memory's* mother and daughter into the contemporary setting of a Connecticut beach house. The four women of this play—two widowed grandmothers, a divorced daughter, and an ebullient granddaughter—having determined to make their own choices, exchange the stories, regrets, angers, and hopes of their lives. Once more the playwright's unflagging gift for character delineation through vigorous patterns of speech, in both monologue and dialogue, serves her well. In 1967 Glass was secretary to eighty-one-year-old Francis Biddle—who had an illustrious career, having been Attorney General under Franklin Roosevelt and Chief American Judge of the International Military Tribunal at the Nuremberg Trials—in Georgetown, Washington until he died in less than a year. Her skilful and effective two-character play *Trying* (2004) dramatizes the experience, having the curmudgeonly, oh-so-critical Judge Biddle pit himself against the spirited and plain-spoken Glass character, called Sarah Schorr. Without being in the least sentimental, it shows truthfully, often amusingly, how two people, through 'trying', negotiate extreme differences—in age, background, intellect—and quietly bond. The play was first produced in Chicago in March 2004; at the National Arts Centre, Ottawa, in Sept. 2004; and twice in New York in Oct. 2004—always to good reviews. *Palmer Park*—about racial integration in the upper-middle-class Detroit neighbourhood of that name in 1968—was produced in the Studio Theatre of the Stratford Festival in 2008.

Glass's second novel, *Woman wanted* (1985), is a type of play-novel that skilfully integrates and expands thematic, narrational, and dramatic features of her plays. It was filmed in 1998, starring and directed by Kiefer Sutherland, also starring Holly Hunter and Michael Moriarty.

Glassco, John (1909–81). Born in Montreal of a merchant family, John Glassco, known to his friends as Buffy, entered McGill University in 1925, but left without graduating. Defying his father's displeasure, he preferred to complete his education in sensibility in Paris. He stayed in France for more than two years, frequenting expatriate and artistic circles, living often in deep poverty, and finally contracting tuberculosis, which forced him to return to Montreal for treatment. His account of this early part of his life, MEMOIRS OF MONTPARNASSE (1970; 2nd edn 1995; reissued by New York Review Books in 2007), was immediately recognized as one of the finest Canadian autobiographies when it was published forty years later—though it was later discovered to be fiction, based on fact. Indeed, in the Introduction to the Second Edition of the *Memoirs* (1995) edited by Michael Gnarowski, we read that Glassco himself thought of it—privately, not publicly—as fiction. (See Philip Kokotailo, *John Glassco's richer world: Memoirs of Montparnasse* [1988]). In 1935, having survived the removal of a lung, Glassco retired to Foster, in the Eastern Townships of Québec, and immersed himself in the local life, running the rural mail route, founding the

Foster Horse Show in 1951, and acting as mayor of Foster from 1952 to 1954. During his later decades he divided his time between Montreal and Foster.

Glassco once remarked that he was 'as much a novelist, anthologist, translator and pornographer' as he was a poet or a memoirist. His early publication, a surrealist poem called 'Conan's Fig', appeared in *transition* in 1928, and he first became known to Canadians as a poet through *The deficit made flesh* (1958). His later books of verse are *A point of sky* (1964); *Selected poems* (1971, GGA); and the long satiric-parodic poem, *Montreal* (1973). His prose works, besides *Memoirs of Montparnasse*, are the three novellas in *The fatal woman* (1974), or appeared under a variety of *noms de plume*. 'A season in limbo' by 'Silas M. Gooch', a fictional treatment of a later stay in hospital, appeared in *The TAMARACK REVIEW* 23 (1962). Other pseudonymous works are largely exercises in mannered pornography: *Contes en crinoline* (1930) by 'Jean de Saint-Luc'; *The English governess* (1960) by 'Miles Underwood'; *The temple of pederasty* (1970) 'after Ihara Saikaku'; and *Fetish girl* (1972) by 'Sylvia Beyer'. *The English governess* was eventually republished under Glassco's name as *Harriet Marwood, governess* in 1976 and with the original title in 2000. 'I came'—he wrote in the *Memoirs*—'under the renewed influence of Huysmans, Pater, Villiers, Barbey d'Aurevilly and others of the so-called Decadents, and decided to write books utterly divorced from reality, stories where nothing happened.' Following this direction, Glassco wrote not only the pseudonymous novels and novellas listed above, but also completed *Under the hill* (1959), Aubrey Beardsley's unfinished erotic story of Venus and Tannhäuser.

As a poet John Glassco is in the classic tradition; his combination of the bucolic and elegiac modes links him to the Augustans as well as to the decadent writers of the 1890s, while also owing much to his familiarity with the poetry of both France and Québec. His poems are largely concerned with the simple actualities of life in the Eastern Townships, full of images of derelict farmhouses and decaying roads that peter out in the bush; but reflections on the human condition are never far away from descriptions of the countryside, so that the life of the land and the lives of people are woven together. In such poems, whose sensitivity towards the natural world strangely balances the deliberate artificiality of his fiction, Glassco combines a true joy in beauty with a sense of the pathetic in human existence—a sense of loss stirred by his reading of history and literature and of his experience of a rural Québec that time had passed over and left neglected. Some poems are a link with his prose by moving into the mythology of literature and history: 'The death of Don Quixote' and 'Brummel at Calais' show Glassco as a master of echoes, and of parody and pastiche in the best sense; they evoke the philosophy of the nineteenth-century dandy and decadent (Brummel, Baudelaire, Wilde) that is also evident in his prose writings. An important recent publication of Glassco's poetry is *John Glassco: Selected poems with three notes on the poetic process* (1997), arranged with an informed biographical Introduction and Notes by Michael Gnarowski. Glassco's excellent translations of the poems of SAINT-DENYS-GARNEAU, and other Québec writers, should be considered a part of his poetic *oeuvre*, for he achieved the rare feat of writing fine English poetry while translating from the French. His translations can be found in *The poetry of French Canada in translation* (1970), which he edited, and in the *Complete poems of Hector de Saint-Denys-Garneau* (1962), whose *Journal* he also translated (1962). Brian Busby's biography of Glassco, *A gentleman of pleasure*, will be published in 2011.

Glengarry school days (1902, NCL). A perennially popular collection of loosely interrelated sketches by Charles William GORDON, who used the pseudonym 'Ralph Connor', *Glengarry school days: a story of early days in Glengarry* is memorable for its depiction of typical one-room-schoolhouse events—a spelling bee, the annual examination, a game of shinny—drawn from Gordon's childhood memories of Glengarry, Ontario's easternmost county, in the 1860s. In the opening sketches we meet Archie Munro, teacher at the 'Twentieth' school, a man who daily conquers the physical pain of an old injury, and is an uplifting example of self-mastery. The teachers who succeed him—a brutal bully, several weaklings, and a cynical occasional drunk—fail to stir the students to do their best academically and morally. But the last teacher, John Craven, gradually becomes a worthy successor to Munro under the influence of the book's powerful inculcator of moral values, the Presbyterian minister's wife, Mrs Murray. Her example, and that of Mrs Finch, civilize boys and men alike.

Glover, Douglas (b. 1948). Born in Simcoe, Ontario, he studied at York University, Toronto (B.A., 1969), and the University of Edinburgh (M. Litt., 1971), and obtained an M.F.A. at the Iowa Writers' Workshop in 1982.

He has taught at Vermont College since 1995 and lives in Wilton, N.Y., near Saratoga Springs. In 1986 four of his stories appeared in *First fictions*, Faber & Faber's prestigious anthology. *The mad river* (1981) contains seven stories in a variety of settings, ranging from contemporary Greece to ancient Rome; exploring notions of good and evil, Glover has each of his characters come face to face with a moment of destiny. In *Dog attempts to drown man in Saskatoon* (1985) the title story, about a man and his marital separation, is a postmodern metafiction of confused identities. *A guide to animal behaviour* (1991) shows even greater breadth of imagination in its eleven stories. Glover's penetrating insight, inventiveness, and quick mood changes explore the ephemeral nature of the self, often in danger of disintegrating in the reality of human suffering. His character studies include gay women, a seventeenth-century missionary artist, and a mentally-ill homeless man who lives in a box on the street. In *16 categories of desire* (2000) the title story is about a young woman, caring for her dying mother and longing for a sexual adventure, who recalls Sister Mary Buntline's far from reverent 'categories of desire'. The title of Glover's *Precious* (1984, rpr. 2005) is the nickname of Moss Claude Elliott, given to him when, as a young man at an air base, he had a blind date with the colonel's niece (ten years older and fat) who tried to seduce him with baby talk, calling him 'pwecious', until the colonel appeared to break them up. Word soon got round. In the novel, Precious is a middle-aged, thrice-married, hard-drinking man who takes a job on a small newspaper in a town on Lake Ontario called Ockenden, where there's a murder. Immensely readable with racy dialogue, it belongs among the best-written mystery novels and was a finalist for the W.H. Smith / Books in Canada First Novel Award. His second novel, *The south will rise at noon* (1988, 2nd edn 2004), is an unconvincing, though often entertaining, comic novel set in Florida about a drug addict and an anti-intellectual drifter on the set of a Hollywood film epic about the Civil War. *The life and times of Captain N.* (1993, rpr. 2001) is a triumph of energetic and visual prose. Glover's short-story experiments with historical settings, the dislocated sense of self, and the emphasis on myth over reason all appear in this dark, funny, violent, historical novel that teems with twentieth-century anxieties. Set on the Niagara frontier in the later years (1779–80) of the American Revolution, it uses several voices to tell the story of Captain

Hendrick Nellis, his son Oskar, and Mary Hunsraker, a German immigrant girl kidnapped by the Mississauga Amerindians who embraces their lifestyle, eventually becoming a medicine woman. The shifting narratives, dreamlike visions, and different voices eventually merge as one to capture brilliantly different ways of looking at the world, one's place in it, and especially the conflict between European and Native viewpoints. *Elle* (2003, GGA) is a highly imaginative (though basically accurate) fantasy that elaborates ingeniously and with much detail on a historical event. When the Sieur de Roberval left France to start a colony in New France in 1542–with Jacques Cartier, who had preceded him the year before but gave up; Cartier met Roberval on the shores of Newfoundland on his way back to France. On board Roberval's ship was his niece Marguerite, her lover Richard, and her nurse. To punish the headstrong Marguerite for her affair with Richard, he deposited her, with her nurse, on an island in the Gulf of St Lawrence; Richard jumped into the ocean and followed them. André Thevet (1502–90) left a record of this in his *Cosmologie Universelle* (1575): 'Poor Marguerite—who eventually returned to France after two years and five months on that island—has told me the story of all the things that happened to her there.' Her lover dies, and so does her nurse. Impressively, and with responsible artifice in this re-creation of history, Glover invented Thevet's 'things'—including many dreams, in one of which Marguerite turns into a bear. She gives birth: 'it has a face like my own, but ... there is nothing else human about it. It is strangely deformed and sexless, and for arms and legs there are tiny appendages like fins. It breaths in gasps like a drowning fish and gazes at me with wise eyes as blue as the sea.' It is cuddled, spoken to, loved, but dies. 'The air is so cold it seems solid; it would freeze these words were I to speak them. I am languid from starvation and cold. I cannot imagine why I am still alive.' Briefly, late in the book, Marguerite speaks in a different voice: 'I tell you now I am very old and writing this memoir in secret ... as a protest against all the uplifting, inspirational and exemplary texts claiming to be about my life. I am myself, not what they have written. M. Thevet, in his *Cosmologie Universelle*, was the only one to mention that after I was rescued I suddenly thought better of it and wished to remain.' *Elle* has been described as Rabelasian. When Marguerite returns to France we find her living on the estate of M. Cartier at Limoilou, near Saint Malo, with her much

older lover—referred to occasionally in the text as F.—who turns out to be François Rabelais. 'I study F.'s books, following the words with my finger, teaching myself to read again. What I love about his stories: He writes as if he is never afraid of what he might say next.' (This is true of Glover's Marguerite.) F. took Marguerite to Paris before he died and there, as a bereft old woman: 'I am far gone in self-pity, melancholy, misanthropy and other words ending in -y.... I have told my story over and over to anyone who will listen.... In Canada I was, briefly, next thing to a god (an ambiguous and confusing state), but now I am perceived as a liar, a madwoman and, worst of all, a bore. (Weep, weep.) No one believes a word I say, either that I once went to the New World or knew the celebrated F.'

Notes home from a prodigal son (1999)—made up of essays written from 1988 to 1999, three interviews, and a memoir—is a lively and outspoken collection that contains wide-ranging critical discussions. Glover's essays are mainly on literary subjects, including point of view ('The masks of I') and humour ('Laughter and anxiety'), the works of Hubert AQUIN, and admiring reviews of ATWOOD's *Cat's eye* and Leonard COHEN's *Beautiful losers*. 'Nihilism and hairspray' is an iconoclastic discussion of literary Canada. *The enamoured knight* (2004) is a brilliant, illuminating study of the complexities of Cervantes' *Don Quixote*. Glover's Introduction begins: '*Don Quixote* is an extraordinarily contemporary story because it's about two pillars of modern life, love and books. To be precise, it's about an impossibly romantic love and bad books. It's that paradoxical thing, a book against books. The narrator's avowed purpose is "'no other than to inspire mankind with an abhorrence of the false and improbable stories recounted in books of chivalry."'

Glover edited OBERON's annual series *Best Canadian stories* from 1996 to 2006. See *The art of desire: the fiction of Douglas Glover* (2004) edited by Bruce Stone.

Godbout, Jacques (b. 1933). Born in Montreal, he was educated at the Université de Montréal. After obtaining an M.A. in French literature (with a thesis on Arthur Rimbaud), he taught from 1954 to 1957 at the University College of Addis Ababa, Ethiopia, returning to Montreal to work as film director and scriptwriter for the National Film Board, where he remained. The author of three volumes of poetry between 1956 and 1960, he is best known as a novelist. Of his translated novels, Godbout's second novel, *Le couteau sur*

Godbout

la table (1965)—translated by Penny Williams as *Knife on the table* (1968)—recounts the outer and inner journeys through Canada and the United States of a nameless Québécois narrator as he seeks to link his identity with the garish artificiality of Disneyland decors and the repressed puritanical atmosphere of the CPR towns of western Canada. These journeys lead finally to a break with his English-Canadian mistress, Patricia, and to a suggestion that Québec's identity may perhaps be achieved only through violence. Godbout claimed that the novel was conceived as a love story, but changed direction when the FLQ bombings began in 1963. *Hail Galarneau!* (1970) is Alan Brown's translation of *Salut Galarneau!* (1967, GGA), his most successful novel, largely because of the irrepressible humour and humanity of its central character, who provides a satiric and immensely funny view of Québec's economic and language problems and its domination by an America that it loves. In *Dragon Island* (1978), the translation by David Ellis of *L'île au dragon* (1976), the central images are of global pollution and destruction that threaten the mind as well as the planet, and of a Québec that is slowly succumbing to the vulgarities of the American way of life. Michel Beauparlant, a writer and a modern version of Saint Michael the Archangel, confronts his dragon in the form of William T. Shaheen, Jr, an American capitalist who has bought the island Beauparlant lives on in order to use it as a site for atomic waste. *An American story* (1988), the translation by Yves Saint-Pierre of *Une histoire américaine* (1986), refocuses attention on the pervasiveness of American culture, and on the marginalization of the French language in North America in the aftermath of the 1980 Referendum. Godbout employs parallel narratives: a lengthy written deposition in journal style by Gregory Francoeur (son of an Irish tennis star and a Québécois Larousse salesman), and a third-person narrative that fills in the missing information. While this is Godbout's most serious novel since *Knife on the table*, it also revisits many themes, including the search for happiness, the reconciliation of First and Third World realities, and the threat of apocalypse. The tight and entertaining short novel *The golden Galarneaus* (1995), a sequel to *Hail Galarneau!*, is Patricia Claxton's translation of *Le temps des Galarneau* (1993), about the Galarneau brothers: the modest and appealing François, a reader who is satisfied to be a security guard; the intellectual Jacques; and Arthur, a revolutionary. The eventful narrative is recounted by

François, who in the end steals a collection of eastern erotica to pay for a new life in French Guiana. In 2008 *Operation Rimbaud* was published, Claxton's translation of *Opération Rimbaud* (1999). Michel Larochelle—a Jesuit, an agnostic, and a spy—meets Haile Selassie in Montreal's Windsor Hotel in 1967. The Emperor of Ethiopia wants him to steal the Tablets of the Law, bearing the Ten Commandments—a secret mission called 'Operation Rimbaud'.

Godfrey, Dave (b. 1938). Born in Winnipeg, he spent most of his early years in rural Ontario. He was educated at the University of Iowa (B.A., 1960; M.F.A. in creative writing, 1963; Ph.D., 1967). Under the auspices of the Canadian University Service Overseas (CUSO), Godfrey served as acting head of the English department of Adisadel College, Cape Coast, Ghana, from 1963 to 1965. After teaching at the University of Toronto, he was chair from 1978 of the creative-writing department of the University of Victoria, British Columbia, until he decided to devote full time to his software development company, Softwords. He has been a major force in Canadian publishing and a strong advocate of nationalist policies. With Dennis LEE he co-founded in 1967 the important literary press, House of ANANSI. In 1969, hoping that a broad spectrum of Canadian titles might have a larger cultural impact than the purely literary, he joined with James BACQUE and Roy MacSkimming to found another Toronto publishing house, New Press. In 1973, having separated himself from both House of Anansi and New Press, he founded PRESS PORCÉPIC, a literary press that he and his wife Ellen GODFREY continued to operate until the early 1990s, when it merged with Beach Holme Publishing.

As significant and valuable as his teaching and publishing activities have been, Godfrey's fiction—his first story 'River two blind Jacks' was published in Issue 19 of *The TAMARACK REVIEW* (1961)—has been an even greater accomplishment. *Death goes better with Coca-Cola* (1967), his first collection of stories, is notable for its subtle techniques of juxtaposed narratives and its symbolic use of the kitsch of American popular culture to depict the greed and latent violence of twentieth-century people. His only novel, *The new ancestors* (1970, GGA), juxtaposes four different temporal perspectives of the same events to create an Einsteinian vision of relative values. Although set in Ghana, its principal content is its depiction of human experience as relative, non-linear, and atemporal. Godfrey moved even further from conventional realism in *I Ching Kanada* (1976) and *Dark must yield* (1978), a collection of fifteen stories. *I Ching Kanada*—a prose meditation that takes the hexagrams of the traditional *I Ching* as its starting point—is composed in images, often merely noun phrases: each meditation focuses on culture, showing how culture, born of mother and hearth, grows to become country. *Dark must yield* offers stories that blend different voices and blur expected distinctions between story and essay, story and autobiography. Their effect resides not in narrative or characterization but in the inferences a reader can draw from the juxtapositions and contrasts of voice; these stories insist that the ultimate ground of political sovereignty lies in individual consciousness.

Godfrey, Ellen (b. 1942). Ellen Swartz was born in Chicago and received a B.A. from Stanford University, California, where she met Dave GODFREY, whom she married. They live in Victoria, British Columbia, where she is President of Softwords Research International, a computer software firm. Ellen Godfrey has written four mystery novels. *Murder among the well to do* (1976) and *The case of the cold murderer* (1978) feature Rebecca Rosenthal, a dauntless Jewish widow who in her early seventies solves family-related murders in Toronto and environs with vigour and a certain valiant élan. While somewhat forced at times and overly dependent on the mechanics of the 'locked room' syndrome, these novels are interesting for their portrayal of a gallant, aged detective figure who does yoga for fitness and mental health, shops for expensive clothes when stressed, and observes those younger with mordant wit—as well as for the somewhat acerbic portrayal in the second novel of the start-up of a small publishing house in Toronto in the early 1970s. *Murder behind locked doors* (1988), a classic puzzler in which an executive is cleverly murdered in a locked computer room, and *Georgia disappeared* (1992), involving the murder of a friend in a client firm, feature Jane Tregar, a corporate headhunter in the computer software industry. *Murder on the loose* (1999) and *Murder on the Lovers' Bridge* (1999) are notable for their realistic treatment of Canadian corporate life and competitiveness, as well as for their depiction of the insecurities and costs associated with life at the executive level for single urban career women who fear they may lose the very jobs they have sacrificed so much to attain. Godfrey also wrote *By reason of doubt:*

the Belshaw case (1982), which won an Edgar award from the Mystery Writers of America and is the non-fiction account of the murder of Betty Belshaw (wife of world-renowned University of British Columbia anthropology professor Cyril Belshaw), who disappeared in Paris and was found dead in the Swiss Alps.

Godin, Gérald (1938–94). Born in Trois-Rivières, Québec, he dropped out of school to work as a proof-reader for the newspaper *La Nouvelliste*. Later he was employed as a reporter for *Le Nouveau Journal* in Montreal and as a researcher for the Radio-Canada daily news-commentary program *Aujourd'hui*. An early contributor to *PARTI PRIS*, he was for a time editor of the magazine and director of Les Editions Parti Pris. In the Parti Québécois sweep of 1976 he was elected to the Québec National Assembly in Robert Bourassa's old riding of Mercier. Re-elected in 1981, he became Minister of Cultural Communities and Immigration, with responsibility for all aspects, except education, of Bill 101, Québec's language law. Godin published eight volumes of poetry, only one of which has been translated: *Soirs sans atout* (1986), translated by Judith Cowan as *Evenings at loose ends* (1991), a bilingual edition: 'What, you've forgotten my telephone number?' 'Listen, old friend, I think you know / they removed a tumour from my brain / as big as a mandarin orange / and I'm afraid / your telephone number was in it.' ('Your phone number'). As a poet Godin made considerable use of *JOUAL*, calling this 'a sort of literary sit-in'—a way of using what he saw as the degradation of the French language in Canada as an instrument of revolution. Most of his poetry, however, is personal rather than political in the narrow sense. There are ironic or wryly tender love poems, mocking glances at some of his fellow-revolutionaries and at the contradictions in his own mental processes, much gaiety and exuberance, and a sheer delight in words. A true poet with a marvellous sense of language and its possibilities, Godin was unique among younger French-Canadian writers for his balance and good humour. He also published a novel, *Ange exterminé* (1991), which was translated by Cowan as *Exterminated angel* (1992). It is a bogus detective story with political overtones, set in Montreal of the 1970s, that is also a high-spirited romp full of jokes and word-plays but in no way equal to the poetry.

Golden Dog, The (1877, abr. 1989, NCL). William KIRBY's historical romance, set in New

France in 1748, first appeared in the United States (Rouses Point, New York, 1877) without copyright and was pirated a year later by a New York publisher. An 'authorized' edition, with corrections and changes by Kirby and some cutting by the publisher, appeared in Boston in 1896 and was reprinted frequently, its title *The Golden Dog (Le Chien d'or): a romance of the days of Louis Quinze in Quebec*. The plot's romantic entanglements involve the passion of the hot-headed seigneur and army officer Le Gardeur de Repentigny for the faithless Angélique, who is bent on seducing the corrupt Intendant Bigot and thus becoming the most powerful woman in the colony. Another affair involves the love of Le Gardeur's virtuous sister Amélie for Pierre Philibert, son of the honest proprietor of the Golden Dog trading firm. A chronicle in the tradition of Scott and Dumas *père*, Kirby's novel includes ambition, greed, deception, passion, and murder within a Gothic setting, and in a New France that here seems more European than North American. It is a historical romance of its time: the setting is idealized, the dialogue high-flown, the sentiments inflated, its plot fraught with coincidence. The historical Angélique Péan, wife of the adjutant and mistress of Bigot, suggested Kirby's temptress. The criminal known as 'La Corriveau', hanged in 1763 for murdering her husband, becomes a professional poisoner in Kirby. Le Gardeur and the bourgeois Philibert were historical figures. The title comes from a stone bas-relief that appeared on the front of Philibert's house: a dog with a bone in its paws sits above the motto that Kirby translates as: 'I am a dog that gnaws his bone,/I couch and gnaw it all alone—/A time will come, which is not yet,/When I'll bite him by whom I'm bit!' The stonework can still be found on a post office that now commands the corner of Côte de la Montagne and rue Buade in Quebec City. It was probably put there long before Philibert's time, and may be a copy of a French original; for Kirby its promise of retribution conveniently epitomized the fate that overtakes all in his story.

Goldsmith, Oliver (1794–1861). Born in Saint Andrews, New Brunswick, he grew up in the Annapolis Valley and subsequently worked for the commissariat of the British army in Halifax (1810–33), Saint John (1833–44), Hong Kong (1844–8), and Newfoundland (1848–53). He retired to England and died at his sister's home in Liverpool. Goldsmith's literary career was brief and limited: his narrative poem, *The rising village*, was published in London in 1825 and reprinted in Saint John in 1834 with some revisions and a few additional short lyrics; an *Autobiography*, found in family papers, was edited by W.E. Myatt and published in 1943 (2nd edn 1985). The narrative of *The rising village* describes the stages of growth in frontier life: the first building, the coming of other settlers, the addition of communal institutions and occupations that shape village life, and the emotional conflicts that come with social interaction and that form the folk history of the settlement. Goldsmith has been acclaimed as the first native-born poet to publish a volume of verse; but the fact that he was the grandnephew of the popular Irish novelist, dramatist, and poet Oliver Goldsmith, author of *The vicar of Wakefield* (1766) and *The deserted village* (1770), has tended to deflect critical attention from the poem itself. Both British and colonial readers would have grasped that its central subject was the settlement and civilizing of a wilderness area, that the heart of this experience lay in nurturing right human values (virtue) in a physical environment that was ill-suited and even hostile to their sustenance, and that the virtue invested in communal life was always vulnerable to corruption, not only from external circumstances but from internal weakness as well. Striving for civilized life while recognizing its essential vulnerability was elemental to appreciating the drama of colonial experience and is, not surprisingly, a deep-rooted theme in colonial Canadian literature. Gerald Lynch edited a modern reprint of *The rising village* (1989).

Goose Lane Editions was founded in 1954 by the *Fiddlehead* magazine as FIDDLEHEAD POETRY BOOKS, becoming its prose imprint in 1981. In 1983 the company was incorporated as Fiddlehead Poetry Books & Goose Lane Editions Ltd, and all books since then have been published under the Goose Lane imprint. With a mandate that includes publishing books of high literary and cultural significance, regardless of genre (for example, poetry and literary fiction, art, biography, history, and travel), Goose Lane employs nine people at its office in Fredericton, New Brunswick, and the publisher is Susanne Alexander. Among its authors are Shauna Singh Baldwin, Lynn Coady, Alan CUMYN, Douglas GLOVER, George Elliott CLARKE, Kathryn Kudenbroawer, the late Alden NOWLAN, and the late John THOMPSON. In 1997 Goose Lane became Canada's first publisher of literary fiction in audiobook format, as a result of the launch of the Between the

Covers Collection, a collaborative venture with CBC Radio and some of Canada's best actors and writers.

Gordon, Alison (b. 1943). She was born in New York City, the daughter of pioneering socialist and international-relations expert King Gordon and granddaughter of the well-known novelist Charles GORDON (Ralph Connor). She attended Queen's University from 1960 to 1965, leaving without a degree, and spent many years working for CBC Radio and Television as a program assistant, producer, and host. In 1979 she joined the *Toronto Star* as a sportswriter. Her experiences covering the Toronto Blue Jays between 1979 and 1983 are recounted in her first book, *Foul balls: five years in the American League* (1984), a perceptive work that reveals the author's passionate knowledge of baseball and much about the Jays during their formative years. Gordon has also written a series of mystery novels featuring sportswriter and amateur sleuth Kate Henry. In the first of these, *The dead pull hitter* (1988), Henry investigates murder, drugs, and blackmail surrounding the fictional Toronto Titans in the heat of a pennant race. It has been followed by four other baseball novels: *Safe at home* (1990), *Night game* (1992), *Striking out* (1995), and *Prairie hardball* (1997). While Gordon's novels lack the intricate plots of classic whodunits, they skilfully evoke the sometimes clashing worlds of journalism and baseball.

Gordon, Charles William (1860–1937). Canada's first bestselling author, who published under the pseudonym 'Ralph Connor', was born in Glengarry County, Canada West (now Ontario), the son of a Presbyterian minister. He completed a B.A. in classics and English at the University of Toronto (1883), graduated from Knox College in 1887, spent a year at the University of Edinburgh, and was ordained in the Presbyterian ministry in 1890. At a loss after his mother's death in 1890, he found his feet during nearly four years as a missionary to the miners, lumbermen, and ranchers around Banff, Alberta. In 1894 he accepted a call from the west-end mission in Winnipeg, which became St Stephen's Church the following year and was his charge until he retired in 1924. He accompanied the 43rd Cameron Highlanders to war in 1915 as their chaplain (some 350 of them were from his own congregation); he then became senior Protestant chaplain to the Canadian forces. Generously unsectarian in his views, as moderator of the Presbyterian Church in 1921–2

he helped move the Presbyterians towards union with the Methodists and Congregationalists: this was realized in 1925 by the creation of the United Church of Canada.

Seeking support for the church's western missions, Gordon wrote several fictional sketches drawing on his missionary experience for the Toronto-based Presbyterian magazine *The Westminster*. They so delighted editor and readers that he was asked for more, and again more. The series was collected as *Black Rock: a tale of the Selkirks* (Toronto, 1898); its immediate success in Canada and the United States established him as an author. The pattern thus set—a serial run in *The Westminster*, followed by a book for the Christmas market—continued through the publication in 1912 of *Corporal Cameron of the North West Mounted Police: a tale of the Macleod Trail*. Gordon had intended to use 'Cannor' (the middle syllables of Brit. Can. Nor. West Mission) as his pseudonym, but the telegraph operator who forwarded the name to *The Westminster* changed it to 'Connor'.

In Gordon's stories principle always wins through in the end. And although he often refers to God and Providence, his religion is human-centred, dependent on the ability of the individual to master his will. For Gordon, 'good' meant acting in the interests of family and community; 'evil' is, at base, a selfish disregard of others. To live fruitful lives, individuals must find the will to control their personal desires (for wealth, alcohol, violence) and withstand temptations to act selfishly. Often his characters endure physical pain silently and continue to remain effective in the role assigned to them in the community: self-control and self-abnegation are their chief virtues. However, Gordon's action-packed plots also allow ample opportunity for the display of physical courage, as much a part of a Connor hero as the more important moral courage. Like many earlier Victorian writers, Gordon deliberately stirred his readers' softer emotions with scenes of pathos; like them, he appeared to find these morally valuable. Connor wrote for the many readers who liked their fiction to combine adventure, lively characterization, and Christian uplift.

Gordon's popularity as a writer peaked early. His publishers sold five million copies of his first three books—*Black Rock, The sky pilot: a tale of the foothills* (Toronto, 1899), and *The man from Glengarry: a tale of the Ottawa* (1901, NCL); while the quarter-million first edition of his minor classic, GLENGARRY SCHOOL DAYS: *a story of early days in Glengarry* (1902, NCL), was followed by immediate reprintings in Canada, the United States, and Britain. Though his later novels sold well, their sales never achieved the heady heights of those early volumes.

In *Black Rock* and *The sky pilot* Gordon discovered the subject that focused his energies as a novelist until the Great War (and in two later books): the frontier. This provided colourful figures—cowboys, ranchers, shantymen, who were involved in drinking, gambling, and fighting. He typically confronts them with a civilizing agent—a minister (a 'sky pilot'), a doctor, schoolmaster, policeman, or good woman—who returns them to the structures and controls of civilization. The anarchy that is brought within bounds is both within and without, and each story climaxes in both self-mastery and the creation of a stable, caring community. The battle is bodied forth at least once in each story in a game or contest demanding skill, courage, and principle. Of the remaining western books—*The pilot at Swan Creek and other stories* (1905), *The doctor: a tale of the Rockies* (1906), *The foreigner: a tale of Saskatchewan* (1909), *Corporal Cameron of the North West Mounted Police*, its lacklustre sequel *The patrol of the Sun Dance Trail* (1914), and *The Gaspards of Pine Croft: a romance of the Windermere* (1923)—only *The foreigner* has any distinction. Powerfully portraying the sordid boarding-house life of Slavic immigrants on the outskirts of Winnipeg in the 1880s, it then follows a lad to a farm in Saskatchewan, where he gradually substitutes a 'Canadian' (orderly, socially responsible, abstemious, patient, tolerant) for an 'Old World' (disorderly, exploitative, drunken, violent, wildly passionate) conception of manhood. Gordon's three remaining frontier books are set in the East and draw on his experience as a young boy in Glengarry, the easternmost county in Ontario, and on his parents' earlier experience ministering to pioneers. *The man from Glengarry* traces the development of Ranald Macdonald into a man of self-control and principle whose energies are thrown into the struggle to civilize the West and make it part of Canada. It describes such pioneer rituals as a sugaring off, a wake, and a logging bee, and like Gordon's other frontier stories, makes lively use of the dialect of his French-Canadian, Irish, and Scots characters. *Glengarry school days* is about the teaching of self-mastery, while the later and slighter *Torches through the bush* (1934) focuses on a Presbyterian revival in the early 1860s. Gordon's mother appears in all three Glengarry books, disguised as the saintly Mrs Murray; and judging by his portrait of her in *Postscript to adventure: the autobiography of Ralph Connor* (1938; revised and introduced by Gordon's son, J. King Gordon), she is the informing spirit behind many other idealized women in his early books.

The Great War redirected Gordon's energies. Fearing that the fight for freedom might be lost because of the apathy he found at home when on leave, he wrote *The major* (1917) to stimulate afresh the enthusiasm that carried men overseas in 1914. But his most emotionally powerful war book is *The sky pilot in no man's land* (1919). It begins with a vivid description of the beauty of a young, fit male body as the novel's young padre, Barry Dunbar, dives nude from a rock during a camping trip. The meaning of this scene becomes clear during the book's keynote sermon, in which Dunbar, taking as his text Romans 12:1, tells a battalion of soldiers that their role is to offer clean, fit bodies as a sacrifice to God. Between 1919 and 1936 Gordon published many other books—novels, some historical, short-story collections, nonfiction—but all are forgotten, except for his posthumously published autobiography.

Most of the novels of 'Ralph Connor' are available in the US from various obscure American publishers: Amereon Limited, Classic Books, Dodo Press, Echo Library, 1st World Library-Literary Society, IndyPublish, Kessinger Publishing, Lerner Publishing Group, and Lightyear Press.

The short biography, *Charles William Gordon* (1981), by Keith Wilson, is authoritative; see also John Lennox, *Charles W. Gordon ('Ralph Connor') and his works* (1988).

Gotlieb, Phyllis (1926–2009). Born in Toronto, Phyllis Fay Bloom was educated at the University of Toronto (B.A., 1948; M.A., 1950) and married Calvin (Kelly) Gotlieb, who taught computer science at the university. Her poetry, verse-dramas, short stories, and novels (mostly science fiction) demonstrate a strong interest in family relationships, historical roots, and the cultural implications of biological or technological possibilities. Gotlieb's chapbook, *Who knows one* (1961), was followed by the collection *Within the Zodiac* (1964), which reprinted some of the earlier poems and announced Gotlieb's developed style: musicality, colloquialism, relish for detail, and affirmation of her Jewish heritage. In *Ordinary, moving* (1969) the title sequence, which ends the book, is constructed from folk verse, game songs, and jump-rope ditties; its locale is the school play-yard of all time and space; its subject the human child, fortunate, suffering; it ends, as does the children's game, with *'and* begin again'. It was shortlisted for a Governor General's Award. *Doctor Umlaut's earthly kingdom* (1974) includes not only shorter poems (of which the elegy 'Jennie Gotlieb Bardikoff' is perhaps the most touching), but also most of the verse-drama commissioned by the CBC, 'Doctor Umlaut's earthly kingdom' (1966), 'Silent movie days' (1971), and 'Garden varieties' (1972), a 'miracle' play on the Creation and Noah's flood, with nuances of the music hall, Don Marquis, and Thornton Wilder. Another verse-drama, 'The contract', is included in the collected poetry *The Works* (1978), which does not, however, include a later verse-drama, also commissioned by the CBC: 'God on trial before Rabbi Ovadia' (1976). *Red blood, black ink, white paper: new and selected poems 1961–2001* (2002)—demonstrating that Gotlieb's poetic energy and imagination did not diminish in old age—includes such later poems as 'Red black white' ('blood ink paper have been my life I bore/children in a slush of blood/dreamed in a scratch of ink/and that damned white paper/with words to be written everywhere'); and three long poems: 'Mother', 'Thirty-six ways of looking at Toronto, Ontario', and 'Geffen and Ravna: four sestinas'.

Gotlieb's first novel is as richly moving as her poetry. *Why should I have all the grief?* (1969) portrays an Auschwitz survivor coping with a painful return to the contingencies of ordinary family life, while recalling and re-understanding his own father. Her other novels, and her short stories, are science fiction. Both *Sunburst* (1964, rev. edn 2001), and *O Master Caliban!* (1976) have been published internationally and translated into several languages. *Sunburst* deals with the problems for family and community of handling juvenile delinquents genetically cursed with telekinetic and telepathic powers. *O Master Caliban!* explores 'Dahlgren's world' of genetic mutation and semi-human machines in terms of the problems of adolescence and maturation. In *A judgement of dragons* (1980), a pair of telepathic cat Candides become educated in the ways of the past and present other worlds (beginning with the ancestral village of the hero of *Why should I have all the grief?*). *Emperor, swords, pentacles* (1982) and *The Kingdom of the cats* (1985) continue the cat saga. 'Dahlgren's world' is revisited in *Heart of red iron* (1989). It was followed by *Flesh and gold* (1998), the related *Violent stars* (1999), *Mindworlds* (2002). Gotlieb's final novel was *Birthstones* (2007), published by Robert J. SAWYER Books. *Son of the Morning and other stories*

(1983) and *Blue apes* (1995) are SF story collections. In June 2008 the organization SF Canada presented Gotlieb with the first Lifetime Achievement Award.

Ethical concern and an interest in psychology and the effects on culture of environmental contingency fuel Gotlieb's plots, but her novels, like her poetry, are primarily memorable for the colour and charm of their personae: the avuncular Montaigne-quoting goat and the huge red cats in *A judgement of dragons*, the floating genius *enfant terrible* in *O Master Caliban!* Her imagery is as magical as that of Chagall or Tchelitchew, and combines the fantastic and the mundane with Dickensian vigour. Gotlieb's primary effect is an expression of joy in the created universe.

Gough, Laurence (b. 1953). Laurence Gordon John Gough was born in Vancouver, where he lives with his family. He is in the front rank of the ever-growing coterie of crime writers resident in British Columbia. Canadians don't believe in entrepreneurs as lawmen, in the hard-boiled private eye; they don't believe in privatizing justice. Hence, Canadian crime writers have tended towards the *roman policier*, the novel with the professional public eye, as exemplified by Gough's Vancouver police officers Jack Willows and Claire Parker. Gough won two Arthur Ellis Awards from the Crime Writers of Canada for *The goldfish bowl* (1987) and *Hot shots* (1990). Between these two novels he published *Death on a #8 hook* (1988, rpr. 2001; American title *Silent knives*). Other titles are *Serious crimes* (1990, rpr. 2002); *Accidental deaths* (1991); *Fall down easy* (1992); *Killers* (1993, rpr. 1995), in which a prominent marine biologist is found afloat in the killer-whale pool at the Vancouver civic aquarium; *Heartbreaker* (1995, rpr. 1996), with the detectives pitted against a pretty-boy petty thief and a beach bunny with some very nasty friends; *Memory lane* (1996), in which the partners race to prevent a death, while an ex-convict develops a relationship with the girlfriend of a dead former fellow inmate. Succeeding novels are *Shutterbug* (1998, rpr. 1999), *Funny money* (2000), *Serious crimes* (2002), and *Cloud of suspects* (2003). Gough has also written one out-of-series international thriller, *Sandstorm* (1991), set in Egypt. Translated into fifteen languages, his books are sold in eighteen countries.

Governor General's Literary Awards. In 1937, with the approval of the Governor General, Lord Tweedsmuir (the novelist John Buchan), the CANADIAN AUTHORS'

Governor General's Literary Awards

ASSOCIATION launched the Governor General's Literary Awards, which have evolved into Canada's premier awards. The first prizes were awarded in the spring of 1937 for two books published in 1936. Subsequently prizes were awarded for the best books of fiction, non-fiction, poetry, or drama published by a Canadian writer in the previous year. Only books in English (or translated from French) were eligible. The CAA's National Executive took on the judging themselves; but in 1944 an autonomous standing committee of judges from across Canada was set up, known as the Governor General's Awards Board. The awards were usually presented at an Awards Dinner, the finale of the CAA annual convention which occurred in the spring in various cities across the country. The prize consisted of a bronze medal, but in 1942 silver medals began to be awarded. In 1951 the Association of Canadian Magazine Publishers donated $250 to accompany each medal. During the early period three changes were made in the award categories. In 1942 the drama category was dropped, and non-fiction was split into two categories: creative and academic. In 1949 an award for juveniles was added.

In 1959 The CANADA COUNCIL (created in 1957) agreed to administer the awards and to provide at least six prizes of $1,000 each for awards in both French and English in poetry or drama, fiction, and non-fiction. It also agreed to pay the costs for winners attending the presentation ceremony, and hosted a dinner following the Governor General's reception. By 1971, it had assumed the entire responsibility for organizing the French- and English-language juries, which were composed of experienced writers, scholars, and literary critics. The awards board was reorganized into two nine-person juries (one for French works and one for English) divided into three sub-committees—one each for fiction, non-fiction, and poetry and drama. In 1981 a separate category for drama was inaugurated to recognize the best published play in English and French of the year. In 1987, the Canada Council Prizes for Children's Literature (text and illustration) and Translation (English to French and French to English) were integrated into the awards. There are currently fourteen Governor General's Literary Awards, seven in English and seven in French, in the following categories: fiction, poetry, drama, non-fiction, children's literature text, illustrations, and translation (French to English and English to French). There is a separate jury for each category.

The value of the prizes was increased in 1966 to $2500, in 1975 to $5000, in 1989 to $10,000, in 2000 to $15,000, and in 2007 to $25,000 in commemoration of the Canada Council's fiftieth anniversary. Since 1964 winners have received a copy of their award-winning book specially bound by a prominent Canadian bookbinder; until 2004 the bound books were created by Pierre Ouvrard, master bookbinder, of Saint-Paul-de-l'Île-aux-Noix, Québec; upon his retirement in 2005 Lise Dubois of Montreal was selected as the bookbinder.

In 2000 the Council began awarding $1000 to non-winning finalists in all categories. The publishers of winning books also receive a $3000 grant for promotion of the winners. As of 2007 the total value of the prize money distributed by the Canada Council for the Arts to GG winners and their publishers amounted to approximately $450,000.

In 1980, with the agreement of Governor General Edward Schryer, the presentation of the awards was moved outside Government House and ceremonies were held in different cities. At the same time, to better publicize the prizes and the work of Canadian writers, the Canada Council began announcing the names of finalists in all the categories in the weeks preceding the presentation. In 1990, to increase opportunities for publishers and booksellers to promote the finalists and winning books, the Council began to make substantial changes to submission procedures and the timing of the announcement of the awards. In 1992 the Council began announcing the award-winners in November to coincide with the major book-buying season. For English-language books this meant that books published between 1 Sept. and 30 Sept. could be eligible for an award either in the year they were published or in the following year's competition. The eligibility period for French-language books is from 1 July, or the previous year to 30 June of the year of the awards, which better coincides with the publishing schedules of French-language publishers.

Also in 1992 the National Library of Canada (now Library and Archives Canada) initiated an annual gala reading by inviting the award winners to read from their works in the Library's auditorium during the week of the awards ceremony. Since 1988 BMO Financial Group (formerly Bank of Montreal) has contributed to the awards by sponsoring various promotional activities, including the production of finalists' and winners' bookmarks, which are distributed to bookstores and libraries across the country.

In 1997 the official awards ceremony returned to Ottawa, with a black-tie reception and dinner at Rideau Hall, hosted by the Governor General and attended by members of the literary community from across Canada. Efforts to increase the reading public's awareness of the Governor General's Literary Awards continue.

A list of winners to 2009 follows:

1936
Bertram BROOKER. *Think of the earth*. Fiction.
T.B. Robertson. *T.B.R.—newspaper pieces*. Non-fiction.

1937
Laura G. SALVERSON. *The dark weaver*. Fiction.
E.J. PRATT. *The fables of the goats*. Poetry.
Stephen LEACOCK. *My discovery of the West*. Non-fiction.

1938
Gwethalyn GRAHAM. *Swiss sonata*. Fiction.
Kenneth LESLIE. *By stubborn stars*. Poetry.
John Murray Gibbon. *Canadian mosaic*. Non-fiction.

1939
Franklin Davey McDowell. *The Champlain Road*. Fiction.
Arthur S. BOURINOT. *Under the sun*. Poetry.
Laura G. SALVERSON. *Confessions of an immigrant's daughter*. Non-fiction.

1940
Ringuet (Philippe PANNETON). *Thirty acres*. Fiction.
E.J. PRATT. *Brébeuf and his brethren*. Poetry.
J.F.C. Wright. *Slava Bohu*. Non-fiction.

1941
Alan SULLIVAN. *Three came to Ville Marie*. Fiction.
Anne MARRIOTT. *Calling adventurers*. Poetry.
Emily CARR. *Klee Wyck*. Non-fiction.

1942
G. Herbert Sallans. *Little man*. Fiction.
Earle BIRNEY. *David and other poems*. Poetry.
Bruce HUTCHISON. *The unknown country*. Non-fiction.
Edgar McInnes. *The unguarded frontier*. Non-fiction.

1943
Thomas H. RADDALL. *The pied piper of Dipper Creek*. Fiction.
A.J.M. SMITH. *News of the phoenix*. Poetry.
John D. Robins. *The incomplete anglers*. Non-fiction.

E.K. BROWN. *On Canadian poetry*. Non-fiction.

1944
Gwethalyn GRAHAM. *Earth and high heaven*. Fiction.
Dorothy LIVESAY. *Day and night*. Poetry.
Dorothy Duncan. *Partner in three worlds*. Non-fiction.
Edgar McInnes. *The war: fourth year*. Non-fiction.

1945
Hugh MacLENNAN. *TWO SOLITUDES*. Fiction.
Earle BIRNEY. *Now is time*. Poetry.
Evelyn M. Richardson. *We keep a light*. Non-fiction.
Ross Munro. *Gauntlet to Overlord*. Non-fiction.

1946
Winifred Bambrick. *Continental revue*. Fiction.
Robert FINCH. *Poems*. Poetry.
Frederick Philip GROVE. *In search of myself*. Non-fiction.
A.R.M. Lower. *Colony to nation*. Non-fiction.

1947
Gabrielle ROY. *The tin flute*. Fiction.
Dorothy LIVESAY. *Poems for people*. Poetry.
William Sclater. *Haida*. Non-fiction.
R. MacGregor Dawson. *The Government of Canada*. Non-fiction.

1948
Hugh MacLENNAN. *The precipice*. Fiction.
A.M. KLEIN. *The rocking chair and other poems*. Poetry.
Thomas H. RADDALL. *Halifax: warden of the north*. Non-fiction.
C.P. STACEY. *The Canadian Army, 1939–1945*. Non-fiction.

1949
Philip CHILD. *Mr Ames against time*. Fiction.
James REANEY. *The red heart*. Poetry.
Hugh MacLENNAN. *Cross-country*. Non-fiction.
R. MacGregor Dawson. *Democratic government in Canada*. Non-fiction.
R.S. Lambert. *Franklin of the Arctic*. Juvenile.

1950
Germaine GUÈVERNMONT. *The outlander*. Fiction.
James Wreford Watson. *Of time and the lover*. Poetry.
Marjorie Wilkins Campbell. *The Saskatchewan*. Non-fiction.
W.L. MORTON. *The Progressive Party in Canada*. Non-fiction.

Donalda Dickie. *The great adventure.* Juvenile.

1951

Morley CALLAGHAN. *The LOVED AND THE LOST.* Fiction.

Charles BRUCE. *The Mulgrave Road.* Poetry.

Josephine Phelan. *The ardent exile.* Non-fiction.

Frank MacKinnon. *The Government of Prince Edward Island.* Non-fiction.

John F. Hayes. *A land divided.* Juvenile.

1952

David WALKER. *The pillar.* Fiction.

E.J. PRATT. *Towards the last spike.* Poetry.

Bruce HUTCHISON. *The incredible Canadian.* Non-fiction.

Donald G. CREIGHTON. *John A. Macdonald: the young politician.* Non-fiction.

Marie McPhedran. *Cargoes on the Great Lakes.* Juvenile.

1953

David WALKER. *Digby.* Fiction.

Douglas LePAN. *The net and the sword.* Poetry.

N.J. Berrill. *Sex and the nature of things.* Non-fiction.

J.M.S. CARELESS. *Canada: a story of challenge.* Non-fiction.

John F. Hayes. *Rebels ride at night.* Juvenile.

1954

Igor Gouzenko. *The fall of a titan.* Fiction.

P.K. PAGE. *The metal and the flower.* Poetry.

Hugh MacLENNAN. *Thirty and three.* Non-fiction.

A.R.M. Lower. *This most famous stream.* Non-fiction.

Marjorie Wilkins Campbell. *The Nor'westers.* Juvenile.

1955

Lionel Shapiro. *The sixth of June.* Fiction.

Wilfred WATSON. *Friday's child.* Poetry.

N.J. Berrill. *Man's emerging mind.* Non-fiction.

Donald G. CREIGHTON. *John A. Macdonald: the old chieftain.* Non-fiction.

Kerry Wood. *The map-maker.* Juvenile.

1956

Adele WISEMAN. *The sacrifice.* Fiction.

Robert A.D. FORD. *A window on the north.* Poetry.

Pierre BERTON. *The mysterious North.* Non-fiction.

Joseph Lister Rutledge. *Century of conflict.* Non-fiction.

Farley MOWAT. *Lost in the barrens.* Juvenile.

1957

Gabrielle ROY. *Street of riches.* Fiction.

Jay MACPHERSON. *The BOATMAN.* Poetry.

Bruce HUTCHISON. *Canada: tomorrow's giant.* Non-fiction.

Thomas H. RADDALL. *The path of destiny.* Non-fiction.

Kerry Wood. *The great chief.* Juvenile.

1958

Colin McDougall. *Execution.* Fiction.

James REANEY. *A suit of nettles.* Poetry.

Pierre BERTON. *Klondike.* Non-fiction.

Joyce Hemlow. *The history of Fanny Burney.* Non-fiction.

Edith L. Sharp. *Nkwala.* Juvenile.

1959

Hugh MacLENNAN. *The watch that ends the night.* Fiction.

Irving LAYTON. *A red carpet for the sun.* Poetry.

André Giroux. *Malgré tout, la joie.* Fiction.

Félix-Antoine SAVARD. *Le barachois.* Non-fiction.

1960

Brian MOORE. *The luck of Ginger Coffey.* Fiction.

Frank Underhill. *In search of Canadian liberalism.* Non-fiction.

Margaret AVISON. *Winter sun.* Poetry.

Paul Toupin. *Souvenirs pour demain.* Non-fiction.

Anne HÉBERT. *Poèmes.* Poetry.

1961

Malcolm LOWRY. *Hear us O Lord from heaven thy dwelling place.* Fiction.

T.A. Goudge. *The ascent of life.* Non-fiction.

Robert FINCH. *Acis in Oxford.* Poetry.

Yves THERIAULT. *Ashini.* Fiction.

Jean LE MOYNE. *Convergences.* Non-fiction.

1962

Kildare DOBBS. *Running to paradise.* Fiction and autobiographical writing.

Marshall McLUHAN. *The Gutenberg galaxy.* Non-fiction.

James REANEY. *Twelve letters to a small town* and *The killdeer and other plays.* Poetry and drama.

Jacques FERRON. *Contes du pays incertain.* Fiction.

Gilles Marcotte. *Une littérature qui se fait.* Non-fiction.

Jacques Languirand. *Les insolites et les violins de l'automne.* Drama.

1963

Hugh GARNER. *Hugh Garner's best stories.* Fiction.

J.M.S. CARELESS. *Brown of The Globe.* Non-fiction.

Gatien Lapointe. *Ode au Saint-Laurent*. Poetry.

Gustave Lanctot. *Histoire du Canada*. Non-fiction.

1964

Douglas LePAN. *The deserter*. Fiction.

Phyllis GROSSKURTH. *John Addington Symonds*. Non-fiction.

Raymond SOUSTER. *The colour of the times*. Poetry.

Jean-Paul Pinsonneault. *Les terres sèches*. Fiction.

Réjean Robidoux. *Roger Martin du Gard et la religion*. Non-fiction.

Pierre Perrault. *Au coeur de la rose*. Poetry.

1965

Alfred PURDY. *The cariboo horses*. Poetry.

James Eayrs. *In defence of Canada*. Non-fiction.

Gilles Vigneault. *Quand les bateaux s'en vont*. Poetry.

Gérard BESSETTE. *L'incubation*. Fiction.

André S. Vachon. *Le temps et l'espace dans l'oeuvre de Paul Claudel*. Non-fiction.

1966

Margaret LAURENCE. *A jest of God*. Fiction.

George WOODCOCK. *The crystal spirit: a study of George Orwell*. Non-fiction.

Margaret ATWOOD. *The circle game*. Poetry.

Claire MARTIN. *La joue droite*. Fiction.

Marcel TRUDEL. *Histoire de la Nouvelle-France: vol. II., Le comptoir, 1604–1627*. Non-fiction.

Réjean DUCHARME. *L'avalée des avalés*. Poetry and theatre.

1967

Eli MANDEL. *An idiot joy*. Poetry.

Alden A. NOWLAN. *Bread, wine and salt*. Poetry.

Norah Story. *The Oxford companion to Canadian history and literature*. Non-fiction.

Jacques GODBOUT. *Salut Galarneau!* Fiction.

Robert-Lionel Séguin. *La civilisation traditionelle de 'l'habitant' aux XVIIe et XVIIIe siècles*. Non-fiction.

Françoise Loranger. *Encore cinq minutes*. Drama.

1968

Alice MUNRO. *Dance of the happy shades*. Fiction.

Mordecai RICHLER. *Cocksure and Hunting tigers under glass*. Fiction and essays.

Leonard COHEN. *Selected Poems 1956–68* (declined).

Hubert AQUIN. *Trou de mémoire*. Fiction (declined).

Marie-Claire BLAIS. *Les manuscrits de Pauline Archange*. Fiction.

Fernand Dumont. *Le lieu de l'homme*. Non-fiction.

1969

Robert KROETSCH. *The studhorse man*. Fiction.

George BOWERING. *Rocky Mountain foot* and *The gangs of Kosmos*. Poetry.

Gwendolyn MacEWEN. *The shadow-maker*. Poetry.

Louise MAHEUX-FORCIER. *Une forêt pour Zoé*. Fiction.

Jean-Guy Pilon. *Comme eau retenue*. Poetry.

Michel Brunet. *Les Canadiens après la conquête*. Non-fiction.

1970

Dave GODFREY. *The new ancestors*. Fiction.

Michael ONDAATJE. *The collected works of Billy the Kid*. Prose and poetry.

bp NICHOL. *Still water, The true eventual story of Billy the Kid, Beach head, The cosmic chef: an evening of concrete*. Poetry.

Monique BOSCO. *La femme de Loth*. Fiction.

Jacques BRAULT. *Quand nous serons heureux*. Drama.

Fernand OUELLETTE. *Les actes retrouvés*. Non-fiction (declined).

1971

Mordecai RICHLER. *St Urbain's horseman*. Fiction.

John GLASSCO. *Selected poems*. Poetry.

Pierre BERTON. *The last spike*. Non-fiction.

Gérard BESSETTE. *Le cycle*. Fiction.

Paul-Marie LAPOINTE. *Le réel absolu*. Poetry.

Gérald Fortin. *La fin d'un règne*. Non-fiction.

1972

Robertson DAVIES. *The manticore*. Fiction.

Dennis LEE. *Civil elegies*. Poetry.

John NEWLOVE. *Lies*. Poetry.

Antonine MAILLET. *Don l'Orignal*. Fiction.

Gilles Hénault. *Signaux pour les voyants*. Poetry.

Jean Hamelin and Yves Roby. *Histoire économique du Québec 1851–1896*. Non-fiction.

1973

Rudy WIEBE. *The temptations of Big Bear*. Fiction.

Miriam Mandel. *Lions at her face*. Poetry.

Michael Bell. *Painters in a new land*. Non-fiction.

Réjean DUCHARME. *L'hiver de force*. Fiction.

Albert Faucher. *Québec en Amérique au dix-neuvième siècle*. Non-fiction.

Roland GIGUÈRE. *La main au feu*. Special Award (declined).

Governor General's Literary Awards

1974

Margaret LAURENCE. *The DIVINERS*. Fiction.

Ralph GUSTAFSON. *Fire on stone: a collection of poetry*. Poetry.

Charles RITCHIE. *The siren years*. Non-fiction.

Victor-Lévy BEAULIEU. *Don Quichotte de la démanche*. Fiction.

Nicole BROSSARD. *Mécanique jongleuse suivi de Masculin grammaticale*. Poetry.

Louise Déchêne. *Habitants et marchands de Montréal au dix-septième siècle*. Non-fiction.

1975

Brian MOORE. *The great Victorian collection*. Fiction.

Milton ACORN. *The island means Minago*. Poetry.

Anthony Adamson, Marion MacRae. *Hallowed walls*. Non-fiction.

Anne HÉBERT. *Les enfants du sabbat*. Fiction.

Pierre Perrault. *Chouennes*. Poetry.

Louis-Edmond Hamelin. *Nordicité canadienne*. Non-fiction.

1976

Marian ENGEL. *Bear*. Fiction.

Joe ROSENBLATT. *Top soil*. Poetry.

Carl BERGER. *The writing of Canadian history*. Non-fiction.

André MAJOR. *Les rescapés*. Fiction.

Alphonse Piché. *Poèmes 1946–68*. Poetry.

Fernand OUELLET. *Le Bas Canada 1791–1840 changements structureux et crise*. Non-fiction.

1977

Timothy FINDLEY. *The WARS*. Fiction.

D.G. JONES. *Under the thunder the flowers light up the earth*. Poetry and drama.

Frank SCOTT. *Essays on the Constitution*. Non-fiction.

Gabrielle ROY. *Ces enfants de ma vie*. Fiction.

Michel GARNEAU. *Les célébrations suivie de Adidou Adidouce*. Poetry and drama. (declined).

Denis Monière. *Le développement des idéologies au Québec des origines à nos jours*. Non-fiction.

1978

Alice MUNRO. *Who do you think you are?* Fiction.

Patrick LANE. *Poems new and selected*. Poetry.

Roger Caron. *Go boy*. Non-fiction.

Jacques POULIN. *Les grandes marées*. Fiction.

Gilbert LANGEVIN. *Mon refuge est un volcan*. Poetry.

François-Marc Gagnon. *Paul-Émile Borduas*. Non-fiction.

1979

Jack HODGINS. *The resurrection of Joseph Bourne*. Fiction.

Michael ONDAATJE. *There's a trick with a knife I'm learning to do*. Poetry.

Maria TIPPETT. *Emily Carr*. Non-fiction.

Marie-Claire BLAIS. *Le sourd dans la ville*. Fiction.

Robert Melançon. *Peinture aveugle*. Poetry.

D. Clift and S. McLeod Arnopoulos. *Le fait anglais au Québec*. Non-fiction.

1980

George BOWERING. *Burning water*. Fiction.

Stephen SCOBIE. *McAlmon's Chinese opera*. Poetry.

Jeffrey Simpson. *Discipline of power*. Non-fiction.

Pierre Turgeon. *La première personne*. Fiction.

Michel Van Schendel. *De l'oeil et de l'écoute*. Poetry.

Maurice Champagne-Gilbert. *La famille et l'homme à délivrer du pouvoir*. Non-fiction.

1981

Mavis GALLANT. *Home truths*. Fiction.

F.R. SCOTT. *The collected poems of F.R. Scott*. Poetry.

George Calef. *Caribou and the barren-lands*. Non-fiction.

Sharon POLLOCK. *Blood relations and other plays*. Drama.

Denys Chabot. *La province lunaire*. Fiction.

Michel BEAULIEU. *Visages*. Poetry.

Madeleine OUELLETTE-MICHALSKA. *L'échappée des discours de l'oeil*. Non-fiction.

Marie LABERGE. *C'était avant la guerre à l'Anse à Gilles*. Drama.

1982

Guy VANDERHAEGHE. *Man descending*. Fiction.

Phyllis WEBB. *The vision tree: selected poems*. Poetry.

Christopher MOORE. *Louisbourg portraits: life in an eighteenth-century garrison town*. Non-fiction.

John GRAY. *Billy Bishop goes to war, a play by John Gray with Eric Peterson*. Drama.

Roger Fournier. *Le cercle des arènes*. Fiction.

Michel Savard. *Forages*. Poetry.

Maurice Lagueux. *Le Marxisme des années soixante: une saison dans l'histoire de la pensée critique*. Non-fiction.

Réjean DUCHARME. *Ha! Ha!...* Drama.

1983

Leon ROOKE. *Shakespeare's dog*. Fiction.

David DONNELL. *Settlements*. Poetry.

Anne CHISLETT. *Quiet in the land*. Drama.

Jeffery Williams. *Byng of Vimy: General and Governor General*. Non-fiction.

Suzanne Jacob. *Laura Laur*. Fiction.

Suzanne Paradis. *Un goût de sel*. Poetry.

René Gingras. *Syncope*. Drama.

Maurice Cusson. *Le contrôle social du crime*. Non-fiction.

1984

Josef SKVORECKY. *The engineer of human souls*. Fiction.

Paulette JILES. *Celestial navigation*. Poetry.

Judith THOMPSON. *White biting dog*. Drama.

Sandra GWYN. *The private capital: ambition and love in the age of Macdonald and Laurier*. Non-fiction.

Jacques BRAULT. *Agonie*. Fiction.

Nicole BROSSARD. *Double impression*. Poetry.

René-Daniel Dubois. *Ne blâmez jamais les Bédouins*. Drama.

Jean Hamelin and Nicole Gagnon. *Le XXe siècle: histoire du catholicisme québécois*. Non-fiction.

1985

Margaret ATWOOD. *The HANDMAID'S TALE*. Fiction.

Fred WAH. *Waiting for Saskatchewan*. Poetry.

George F. WALKER. *Criminals in love*. Drama.

Ramsay COOK. *The regenerators: social criticism in late Victorian English Canada*. Non-fiction.

Fernand OUELLETTE. *Lucie; ou Un midi en novembre*. Fiction.

André ROY. *Action writing*. Poetry.

Maryse Pelletier. *Duo pour voix obstinées*. Drama.

François Ricard. *La littérature contre elle-même*. Non-fiction.

1986

Alice MUNRO. *The progress of love*. Fiction.

Al PURDY. *The collected poems of Al Purdy*. Poetry.

Sharon POLLOCK. *Doc*. Drama.

Northrop FRYE. *Northrop Frye on Shakespeare*. Non-fiction.

Yvon Rivard. *Les silences du corbeau*. Fiction.

Cécile Cloutier. *L'écouté*. Poetry.

Anne Legault. *La visite des sauvages*. Drama.

Régine ROBIN. *Le réalisme socialiste: une esthétique impossible*. Non-fiction.

1987

M.T. KELLY. *A dream like mine*. Fiction.

Gwendolyn MacEWEN. *Afterworlds*. Poetry.

John Krizanc. *Prague*. Drama.

Michael IGNATIEFF. *The Russian album*. Non-fiction.

Morgan Nyberg. *Galahad Schwartz and the cockroach army*. Juvenile (text).

Marie-Louise Gay. *Rainy day magic*. Juvenile (illust.).

Patricia Claxton. *Enchantment and sorrow: the autobiography of Gabrielle Roy*. Trans. (Fr.–Eng.) by Gabrielle ROY.

Gilles ARCHAMBAULT. *L'obsédante obèse et autres agressions*. Fiction.

Fernand OUELLETTE. *Les heures*. Poetry.

Jeanne-Mance Delisle. *Un oiseau vivant dans la gueule*. Drama.

Jean Larose. *La petite noirceur*. Non-fiction.

David Schinkel and Yves Beauchesne. *Le Don*. Juvenile (text).

Darcia Labrosse. *Venir au monde*. Juvenile (illust.).

Ivan Steenhout and Christiane Teasdale. *L'homme qui se croyait aimé; ou La vie secrète d'un premier ministre* by Heather Robertson. Trans. (Eng.-Fr.).

1988

David Adams RICHARDS. *Nights below Station Street*. Fiction.

Erin MOURÉ. *Furious*. Poetry.

George F. WALKER. *Nothing sacred*. Drama.

Anne Collins. *In the sleep room*. Non-fiction.

Welwyn Wilton KATZ. *The third magic*. Juvenile (text).

Kim LaFave. *Amos's sweater*. Juvenile (illust.).

Philip Stratford. *Second chance* by Diane Hébert. Trans. (Fr.-Eng.).

Jacques Folch-Ribas. *Le silence; ou Le parfait bonheur*. Fiction.

Marcel Labine. *Papiers d'épidémie*. Poetry.

Jean Marc Dalpé. *Le chien*. Drama.

Patricia Smart. *Écrire dans la maison du père*. Non-fiction.

Michèle Marineau. *Cassiopée; ou L'été polonais*. Juvenile (text).

Philippe Béha. *Les jeux de pic-mots*. Juvenile (illust.).

Didier Holtzwarth. *Nucléus* by Robert Bothwell. Trans. (Eng.-Fr.).

1989

Paul QUARRINGTON. *Whale music*. Fiction.

Heather SPEARS. *The word for sand*. Poetry.

Judith THOMPSON. *The other side of the dark: four plays*. Drama.

Robert Calder. *Willie: the life of W. Somerset Maugham*. Non-fiction.

Diana Wieler. *Bad boy*. Juvenile (text).

Robin Muller. *The magic paintbrush*. Juvenile (illust.).

Wayne Grady. *On the eighth day* by Antonine MAILLET. Trans. (Fr.-Eng.).

Louis Hamelin. *La rage*. Fiction.

Pierre Desruisseaux. *Monème*. Poetry.

Governor General's Literary Awards

Michel GARNEAU. *Mademoiselle Rouge*. Drama.

Lise Noël. *L'intolérance: une problématique générale*. Non-fiction.

Charles Montpetit. *Temps mort*. Juvenile (text).

Stéphane Poulin. *Benjamin et la saga des oreillers*. Juvenile (illust.).

Jean Antonin Billard. *Les âges de l'amour* by Dorothy LIVESAY. Trans. (Eng.-Fr.).

1990

Nino RICCI. *Lives of the saints*. Fiction.

Margaret AVISON. *No time*. Poetry.

Ann-Marie MacDONALD. *Goodnight Desdemona (Good morning Juliet)*. Drama.

Stephen Clarkson and Christina McCALL. *Trudeau and our times*. Non-fiction.

Michael BEDARD. *Redwork*. Juvenile (text).

Paul Morin. *The orphan boy*. Juvenile (illust.).

Jane Brierley. *Yellow-Wolf and other tales of the Saint Lawrence* by Philippe-Joseph AUBERT DE GASPÉ. Trans. (Fr.-Eng.).

Gérald Tougas. *La mauvaise foi*. Fiction.

Jean-Paul Daoust. *Les cendres bleues*. Poetry.

Jovette MARCHESSAULT. *Le voyage magnifique d'Émily Carr*. Drama.

Jean-François Lisée. *Dans l'oeil de l'aigle*. Non-fiction.

Christiane Duchesne. *La vraie histoire du chien de Clara Vic*. Juvenile (text).

Pierre Pratt. *Les fantaisies de l'oncle Henri*. Juvenile (illust.).

Charlotte and Robert Melançon. *Le second rouleau* by A.M. KLEIN. Trans. (Eng.-Fr.).

1991

Rohinton MISTRY. *Such a long journey*. Fiction.

Don McKAY. *Night field*. Poetry.

Joan MacLEOD. *Amigo's blue guitar*. Drama.

Robert Hunter and Robert Calihoo. *Occupied Canada: a young white man discovers his unsuspected past*. Non-fiction.

Sarah ELLIS. *Pick-up sticks*. Juvenile (text).

Joanne Fitzgerald. *Doctor Kiss says yes*. Juvenile (illust.).

Albert W. Halsall. *A dictionary of literary devices: gradus, A–Z* by Bernard Dupriez. Trans. (Fr.-Eng.).

André Brochu. *La croix du nord*. Fiction.

Madeleine Gagnon. *Chant pour un Québec lointain*. Poetry.

Gilbert Dupuis. *Mon oncle Marcel qui vague vague près du métro Berri*. Drama.

Bernard Arcand. *Le jaguar et le tamanoir*. Non-fiction.

François Gravel. *Deux heures et demie avant Jasmine*. Juvenile (text).

Sheldon Cohen. *Un champion*. Juvenile (illust.).

Jean-Paul Sainte-Marie and Brigitte Chabert Hacikyan. *Les enfants d'Aataentsic: l'histoire du peuple Huron* by Bruce G. Trigger. Trans. (Eng.-Fr.).

1992

Michael ONDAATJE. *The ENGLISH PATIENT*. Fiction.

Lorna CROZIER. *Inventing the hawk*. Poetry.

John Mighton. *Possible worlds and a short history of night*. Drama.

Maggie Siggins. *Revenge of the land: a century of greed, tragedy and murder on a Saskatchewan farm*. Non-fiction.

Julie JOHNSTON. *Hero of lesser causes*. Juvenile (text).

Ron Lightburn. *Waiting for the whales*. Juvenile (illust.).

Fred A. Reed. *Imagining the Middle East* by Thierry Hentsch. Trans. (Fr.-Eng.).

Anne HÉBERT. *L'enfant chargé de songes*. Fiction.

Gilles Cyr. *Andromède attendra*. Poetry.

Louis-Dominique Lavigne. *Les petits orteils*. Drama.

Pierre Turgeon. *La Radissonie: le pays de la baie James*. Non-fiction.

Christiane Duchesne. *Victor*. Juvenile (text).

Gilles Tibo. *Simon et la ville de carton*. Juvenile (illust.).

Jean Papineau. *La mémoire postmoderne: essai sur l'art canadien contemporain* by Mark A. Cheetham. Trans. (Eng.-Fr.).

1993

Carol SHIELDS. *The stone diaries*. Fiction.

Don COLES. *Forests of the medieval world*. Poetry.

Guillermo Verdecchia. *Fronteras Americanas*. Drama.

Karen Connelly. *Touch the dragon*. Non-fiction.

Tim WYNNE-JONES. *Some of the kinder planets*. Juvenile (text).

Mireille Levert. *Sleep tight, Mrs Ming*. Juvenile (illust.).

D.G. JONES. *Categories one, two and three* by Normand de Bellefeuille. Trans. (Fr.-Eng.).

Nancy HUSTON. *Cantique des plaines*. Fiction.

Denise Desautels. *Le saut de l'ange*. Poetry.

Daniel Danis. *Cella-là*. Drama.

François Paré. *Les littératures de l'exiguïté*. Non-fiction.

Michèle Marineau. *La route de Chlifa*. Juvenile (text).

Stéphane Jorisch. *Le monde selon Jean de…* Juvenile (illust.).

Marie José Thériault. *L'oeuvre du Gallois* by Robert Walshe. Trans. (Eng.-Fr.).

1994

Rudy WIEBE. *A discovery of strangers.* Fiction.

Robert Hilles. *Cantos from a small room.* Poetry.

Morris PANYCH. *The ends of the earth.* Drama.

John A. Livingston. *Rogue primate.* Non-fiction.

Julie JOHNSTON. *Adam and Eve and Pinch-me.* Juvenile (text).

Murray Kimber. *Josepha: a prairie boy's story.* Juvenile (illust.).

Donald Winkler. *The lyric generation: the life and times of the baby boomers* by François Ricard. Trans. (Fr.-Eng.).

Robert Lalonde. *Le petit aigle à tête blanche.* Fiction.

Fulvio Caccia. *Aknos.* Poetry.

Michel Ouellette. *French town.* Drama.

Chantal Saint-Jarre. *Du sida.* Non-fiction.

Suzanne Martel. *Une belle journée pour mourir.* Juvenile (text).

Pierre Pratt. *Mon chien est un éléphant.* Juvenile (illust.).

Jude Des Chênes. *Le mythe du sauvage* by Olive Patricia Dickason. Trans. (Eng.-Fr.).

1995

Greg HOLLINGSHEAD. *The roaring girl.* Fiction.

Anne SZUMIGALSKI. *Voice.* Poetry.

Jason SHERMAN. *Three in the back, two in the head.* Drama.

Rosemary SULLIVAN. *Shadow maker: the life of Gwendolyn MacEwen.* Non-fiction.

Tim WYNNE-JONES. *The maestro.* Juvenile (text).

Ludmilla Zeman. *The last quest of Gilgamesh.* Juvenile (illust.).

David Homel. *Why must a black writer write about sex?* by Dany LAFERRIÈRE. Trans. (Fr.-Eng.).

Nicole Houde. *Les oiseaux de Saint-John Perse.* Fiction.

Émile Martel. *Pour orchestre et poète seul.* Poetry.

Carol Fréchette. *Les quatre morts de Marie.* Drama.

Yvan Lamonde. *Louis-Antoine Dessaulles: un seigneur libéral et anticlérical.* Non-fiction.

Sonia Sarfati. *Comme une peau de chagrin.* Juvenile (text).

Annouchka Gravel Galouchko. *Sh, et les dragons d'eau.* Juvenile (illust.).

Hervé Juste. *Entre l'ordre et la liberté* by Gérald Bernier and Daniel Salée. Trans. (Eng.-Fr.).

1996

Guy VANDERHAEGHE. *The Englishman's boy.* Fiction.

E.D. Blodgett. *Apostrophes: woman at a piano.* Poetry.

Colleen Wagner. *The monument.* Drama.

John Ralston SAUL. *The unconscious civilization.* Non-fiction.

Paul YEE. *Ghost train.* Juvenile (text).

Eric Beddows. *The rooster's gift.* Juvenile (illust.).

Linda Gaboriau. *Stone and ashes* by Daniel Danis. Trans. (Fr.-Eng.).

Marie-Claire BLAIS. *Soifs.* Fiction.

Serge Patrice Thibodeau. *Le quatuor de l'errance* followed by *La traversée du désert.* Poetry.

Normand CHAURETTE. *Le passage de l'Indiana.* Drama.

Michel Freitag. *Le naufrage de l'université—et autres essais d'épistémologie politique.* Non-fiction.

Gilles Tibo. *Noémie—le secret de Madame Lumbago.* Juvenile (text).

The French-language jury gave no award for juvenile illustration.

Christiane Teasdale. *Systèmes de survie—dialogue sur les fondements moraux du commerce et de la politique* by Jane Jacobs. Trans. (Eng.-Fr.).

1997

Jane URQUHART. *The underpainter.* Fiction.

Dionne BRAND. *Land to light on.* Poetry.

Ian Ross. *fareWel.* Drama.

Rachel Manley. *Drumblair—Memories of a Jamaican childhood.* Non-fiction.

Kit PEARSON. *Awake and dreaming.* Juvenile (text).

Barbara Reid. *The party.* Juvenile (illust.).

Howard Scott. *The Euguelion* by Louky BERSIANIK. Trans. (Fr.-Eng.)

Aude. *Cet imperceptible mouvement.* Fiction.

Pierre Nepveu. *Romans-fleuves.* Poetry.

Yvan Bienvenue. *Dits et inédits.* Drama.

Roland Viau. *Enfants du néant et mangeurs d'âmes—guerre, culture et société en Iroquoisie ancienne.* Non-fiction.

Michel Noël. *Pien.* Juvenile (text).

Stéphane Poulin. *Poil de serpent, dent d'araignée.* Juvenile (illust.).

Marie José Thériault. *Arracher les montagnes* by Neil BISSOONDATH. Trans. (Eng.-Fr.).

1998

Diane SCHOEMPERLEN. *Forms of devotion.* Fiction.

Stephanie BOLSTER. *White stone: the Alice poems.* Poetry.

Djanet Sears. *Harlem duet.* Drama.

Governor General's Literary Awards

David Adams RICHARDS. *Lines on the water—a fisherman's life on the Miramichi.* Non-fiction.

Janet LUNN. *The hollow tree.* Juvenile (text).

Kady MacDonald Denton. *A child's treasury of nursery rhymes.* Juvenile (illust.).

Sheila FISCHMAN. *Bambi and me* by Michel TREMBLAY. Trans. (Fr.-Eng.).

Christiane Frenette. *La terre ferme.* Fiction.

Suzanne Jacob. *La part de feu* précédé de *Le deuil de la rancune.* Poetry.

François Archambault. *15 secondes.* Drama.

Pierre Nepveu. *Intérieurs du Nouveau Monde: essais sur les littératures du Québec et des Amériques.* Non-fiction.

Angèle Delaunois. *Variations sur un même 't'aime'.* Juvenile (text).

Pierre Pratt. *Monsieur Ilétaitunefois.* Juvenile (illust.).

Charlotte Melançon. *Les sources du moi—la formation de l'identité moderne* by Charles Taylor. Trans. (Eng.-Fr.).

1999

Matt COHEN. *Elizabeth and after.* Fiction.

Jan ZWICKY. *Song for relinquishing the earth.* Poetry.

Michael Healey. *The drawer boy.* Drama.

Marq de Villiers. *Water.* Non-fiction.

Rachna Gilmore. *A screaming kind of day.* Juvenile (text).

Gary Clement. *The great Poochini.* Juvenile (illust.).

Patricia Claxton. *Gabrielle Roy: a life* by François Ricard. Trans. (Fr.-Eng.).

Lise Tremblay. *La danse juive.* Fiction.

Herménégilde Chiasson. *Conversations.* Poetry.

Jean Marc Dalpé. *Il n'y a que l'amour.* Drama.

Pierre Perrault. *La mal du Nord.* Non-fiction.

Charlotte Gingras. *La liberté? Connais pas....* Juvenile (text).

Stéphane Jorisch. *Charlotte et l'Île du destin.* Juvenile (illust.).

Jacques BRAULT. *Transfiguration* by E.D. Blodgett and Jacques Brault. Trans. (Eng.-Fr.).

2000

Michael ONDAATJE. *Anil's ghost.* Fiction.

Don MCKAY. *Another gravity.* Poetry.

Timothy FINDLEY. *Elizabeth Rex.* Drama.

Nega Mezlekia. *Notes from the hyena's belly.* Non-fiction.

Deborah Ellis. *Looking for X.* Juvenile (text).

Marie-Louise Gay. *Yuck, a love story.* Juvenile (illust.).

Robert Majzels. *Just fine* by France Daigle. Trans. (Fr.-Eng.).

Jean-Marc Dalpé. *Un vent se lève qui éparpille.* Fiction.

Normand de Bellefeuille. *La marche de l'aveugle sans son chien.* Poetry.

Wajdi Mouawad. *Littoral.* Drama.

Gérard Bouchard. *Genèse des nations et cultures du Nouveau Monde.* Non-fiction.

Charlotte Gingras. *Un été de Jade.* Juvenile (text).

Anne Villeneuve. *L'écharpe rouge.* Juvenile (illust.).

Lori Saint-Martin and Paul Gagné, *Un parfum de cèdre* by Ann-Marie MacDONALD. Trans. (Eng.-Fr.).

2001

Richard B. WRIGHT. *Clara Callan.* Fiction.

George Elliott CLARKE. *Execution poems.* Poetry.

Kent Stetson. *The harps of God.* Drama.

Thomas Homer-Dixon. *The ingenuity gap.* Non-fiction.

Arthur Slade. *Dust.* Juvenile (text).

Mireille Levert. *An island in the soup.* Juvenile (illust.).

Fred A. Reed and David Homel. *Fairy ring* by Martine Desjardins. Trans. (Fr.-Eng.).

Andrée A. Michaud. *Le ravissement.* Fiction.

Paul Chanel Malenfant. *Des ombres portées.* Poetry.

Normand Chaurette. *Le petit Köchel.* Drama.

Renée Dupuis. *Quel Canada pour les autochtones? La fin de l'exclusion.* Non-fiction.

Christiane Duchesne. *Jomusch et le troll des cuisines.* Juvenile (text).

Bruce Roberts. *Fidèles éléphants.* Juvenile (illust.).

Michel Saint-Germain. *No logo: la tyrannie des marques* by Naomi Klein. Trans. (Eng.-Fr.)

2002

Gloria Sawai. *A song for Nettie Johnson.* Fiction.

Roy Miki. *Surrender.* Poetry.

Kevin Kerr. *Unity (1918).* Drama.

Andrew Nikiforuk. *Saboteurs: Wiebo Ludwig's war against big oil.* Non-fiction.

Martha Brooks. *True confessions of a heartless girl.* Juvenile (text).

Wallace Edwards. *Alphabeasts.* Juvenile (illust.).

Nigel Spencer. *Thunder and light* by Marie-Claire BLAIS. Trans. (Fr.-Eng.)

Monique LaRue. *La gloire de Cassiodore.* Fiction.

Robert Dickson. *Humains paysages en temps de paix relative.* Poetry.

Daniel Danis. *La langue-à-langue des chiens de roche*. Drama.

Judith Lavoie. *Mark Twain et la parole noire*. Non-fiction.

Hélène Vachon. *L'oiseau de passage*. Juvenile (text).

Luc Melanson. *Le grand voyage de Monsieur*. Juvenile (illust.)

Paule Pierre-Noyart. *Histoire universelle de la chasteté et du célibat* by Elizabeth Abbott. Trans. (Eng.-Fr.).

2003

Douglas GLOVER. *Elle*. Fiction.

Tim Lilburn. *Kill-site*. Poetry.

Vern Thiessen. *Einstein's gift*. Drama.

Margaret MacMILLAN. *Paris 1919: six months that changed the world*. Non-fiction.

Glen Huser. *Stitches*. Juvenile (text).

Allen Sapp. *The song within my heart*. Juvenile (illust.).

Jane Brierly. *Memoirs of a less travelled road: a historian's life* by Marcel TRUDEL. Trans. (Fr.-Eng.).

Élise Turcotte. *La maison étrangère*. Fiction.

Pierre Nepveu. *Lignes aériennes*. Poetry.

Jean-Rock Gaudreault. *Deux pas vers les étoiles*. Drama.

Thierry Hentsch. *Raconter et mourir: aux sources narratives de l'imagination occidental*. Non-fiction.

Danielle Simard. *J'ai vendu ma soeur*. Juvenile (text).

Virginie Egger. *Recette d'éléphant à la sauce vieux pneu*. Juvenile (illust.).

Agnès Guitard. *Un amour de Salomé* by Linda Leith. Trans. (Eng.-Fr.).

2004

Miriam TOEWS. *A complicated kindness*. Fiction.

Roo BORSON. *Short journey upriver toward ōishida*. Poetry.

Morris PANYCH. *Girl in the goldfish bowl*. Drama.

Lt.-Gen. Roméo Dallaire. *Shake hands with the devil: the failure of humanity in Rwanda*. Non-fiction.

Kenneth OPPEL. *Airborn*. Juvenile (text).

Stéphane Jorisch. *Jabberwocky*. Juvenile (illust.).

Judith Cowan. *Mirabel* by Pierre Nepveu. Trans. (Fr.-Eng.).

Pascale Quiviger. *Le cercle parfait*. Fiction.

André Brochu. *Les jours à vif*. Poetry.

Emma Haché. *L'intimité*. Drama.

Jean-Jacques Simard. *La réduction: l'autochtone inventé et les Amérindiens d'aujourd'hui*. Non-fiction.

Nicole Leroux. *L'hiver de Léo Polatouche*. Juvenile (text).

Janice Nadeau. *Nul poisson où aller*. Juvenile (illust.).

Ivan Steenhout. *Les andes accidentelles* by Robert Finlay. Trans.(Eng.-Fr.).

2005

David GILMOUR. *A perfect night to go to China*. Fiction.

Anne COMPTON. *Processional*. Poetry.

John Mighton. *Half life*. Drama.

John Vaillant. *The golden spruce: a true story of myth, madness and greed*. Non-fiction.

Pamela Porter. *The crazy man*. Juvenile (text).

Rob Gonsalves. *Imagine a day*. Juvenile (illust.).

Fred A. Reed. *Truth: the quest for immortality in the Western narrative tradition* by Thierry Hentisch. Trans. (Fr.-Eng.).

Aki Shimazaki. *Hotaru*. Fiction.

Jean-Marc Desgent. *Vingtième siècles*. Poetry.

Geneviève Billette. *Le pays des genoux*. Drama.

Michel Bock. *Quand la nation débordait les frontières: les minorités françaises dans la pensée de Lionel Groulx*. Non-fiction.

Camille Bouchard. *Le ricanement des hyènes*. Juvenile (text).

Isabelle Arsenault. *Le coeur de monsieur Gaugin*. Juvenile (illust.).

Rachel Martinez. *Glenn Gould: une vie* by Kevin Bazzana. Trans. (Eng.-Fr.).

2006

Peter Behrens. *The law of dreams*. Fiction.

John Pass. *Stumbling in the Bloom*. Poetry.

Daniel MacIvor. *I still love you*. Drama.

Ross King. *The judgment of Paris: the revolutionary decade that gave the world Impressionism*. Non-fiction.

William Gilkerson. *Pirate's passage*. Juvenile (text).

Leo Yerxa. *Ancient thunder*. Juvenile (illust.).

Hugh Hazelton. *Vetiver* by Joël Des Rosiers. Trans. (Fr.-Eng.)

Andrée Laberge. *La rivière du loup*. Novel.

Hélène Dorion. *Ravir: les lieux*. Poetry.

Évelyne de la Chenelière. *Désordre public*. Drama.

Dany LAFERRIÈRE. *Je suis fou de Vava*. Juvenile (text).

Rogé (Roger Girard). *Le gros monstre qui aimait trop lire*. Juvenile (illust.).

Sophie Voillot. *Un jardin de papier* by Thomas Wharton. Trans. (Eng.-Fr.)

2007

Michael ONDAATJE. *DIVISADERO*. Fiction.

Don Domanski. *All our wonder unavenged*. Poetry.

Governor General's Literary Awards

Karolyn Smardz Frost. *I've got a home in glory land: a lost tale of the Underground Railroad*. Non-fiction.

Colleen Murphy. *The December man (L'homme de décembre)*. Drama.

Iain Lawrence. *Gemini summer*. Juvenile (text).

Duncan Weller. *The boy from the sun*. Juvenile (illust.).

Nigel Spencer. *Augustino and the choir of destruction* by Marie-Clair BLAIS. Trans. (Fr.-Eng.).

Sylvain Trudel. *La mer de la tranquillité*. Fiction.

Annette Hayward. *La querelle du régionalisme au Québec (1904–1931): vers l'autonomisation de la littérature québécoise*. Non-fiction.

Serge Patrice Thibodeau. *Seul on est*. Poetry.

Daniel Danis. *Le chant du dire-dire*. Drama.

François Barcelo. *La fatigante et le faineant*. Juvenile (text).

Geneviève Coté. *La petite rapporteuse de mots* by Denielle Simard. Juvenile (illust.).

Lori Saint-Martin and Paul Gagné, *Dernières notes* by Tamas Dobozy. Trans. (Eng.–Fr.)

2008

Nino RICCI. *The origin of species*. Fiction.

Jacob Scheier. *More to keep us warm*. Poetry.

Catherine Banks. *Bone cage*. Drama.

Christie Blatchford. *Fifteen days: stories of bravery, friendship, life and death from inside the new Canadian army*. Non-fiction.

John Ibbetson. *The landing*. Juvenile (text).

Stéphane Jorisch. *The owl and the pussycat* by Edward Lear (illust.).

Lazer Lederhendler. *Nikolski* by Nicolas Dickner. Trans. (Fr.-Eng.).

Marie-Claire BLAIS. *Naissance de Rebecca à l'ère des tourments*. Fiction.

Michel Pleau. *La lenteur du monde*. Poetry.

Jennifer Tremblay. *La liste*. Drama.

Pierre Ouellet. *Hors-temps: poétique de la posthistoire*. Non-fiction.

Sylvie Desrosiers. *Les trois lieues*. Juvenile (text).

Janice Nadeau. *Ma meilleure amie*. Juvenile (illust.).

Claire Chabalier and Louise Chabalier. *Tracey en mille morceaux* by Maureen Medved. Trans. (Eng.-Fr.).

2009

Kate Pullinger. *The mistress of nothing*. Fiction.

David ZIEROTH. *The fly in autumn*. Poetry.

Kevin Loring. *Where the blood mixes*. Drama.

M.G. VASSANJI. *A place within: rediscovering India*. Non-fiction.

Caroline Pignat. *Greener grass: The famine years*. Juvenile (text).

Jirina Marton. *Bella's tree*. Juvenile (illust.).

Susan Ouriou. *Pieces of me* by Charlotte Gingras. Trans. (Fr.-Eng.).

Julie Mazzieri. *Le discourse sur la tombe de l'idiot*. Fiction.

Hélène Monette. *Thérèse pour joie et orchestre*. Poetry.

Suzanne Lebeau. *Le bruit des os qui craquent*. Drama.

Nicole V. Champeau. *Pointe Maligne: l'infiniment oubliée*. Non-fiction.

Hervé Bouchard. *Harvey*. Juvenile (text).

Janice Nadeau. *Harvey*. Juvenile (illust.).

Paule Noyart. *Le miel d'Harar* by Camilla GIBB. Trans. (Eng.-Fr.).

Govier, Katherine (b. 1948). Born in Edmonton, she studied at the University of Alberta (B.A., 1970) and York University, Toronto (M.A., 1972), and taught creative writing at York University from 1982 to 1986. She was a founder of the Writers in Electronic Residence program, an initiative of The WRITERS' DEVELOPMENT TRUST, a program that links professional writers and students via telecommunications. She has lived in Toronto since 1971.

Govier has published nine novels: *Random descent* (1979), *Going through the motions* (1982), *Between men* (1987, rpr. 1988), *Hearts of flame* (1991, rpr. 1992), *Angel walk* (1996), *The truth teller* (2000, rpr. 2001), *Creation* (2002. rpr. 2003), *Three views of crystal water* (2005), and *The ghost brush* (2010); and three collections of short stories: *Fables of Brunswick Avenue* (1985), *Before and after* (1989), and *The immaculate conception photography gallery* (1994). Of the early books, it was the short stories in *Fables* that deservedly won most notice: clear-eyed glances into the lives of young women (and here and there a young man) making it, not always by choice, on their own in Toronto's lower Annex in the early 1980s. *Random descent* is a generational story, altogether admirable in its detail but ponderous in movement; *Going through the motions* is better paced, shedding some of *Random descent's* careful canvas en route. Many interesting developments are noticeable in the books that follow, but *Angel walk* is Govier's first fine work. The story portrays a young Canadian woman arriving in pre–Second World War Britain, picking up, almost casually at first, an interest in photography, credibly meeting a few of London's *illuminati* (most usefully, the ex-Maritimer press lord, Lord Beaverbrook), and then, without hurry, flowering into a rich and several-dimensioned life as apprentice and an ultimately internationally celebrated photographer, and the decades-long lover of a much older, consistently selfish, and minor painter. The presentation of this relationship—a complex and minutely reported-upon affair that by sheer intelligence escapes every one of a thousand clichés—is a triumph. The title of *The truth teller* refers to Cassie (Cassandra), a student at the Manor School for Classical Studies in Wychwood Park, Toronto, run by the charismatic partnership of Dugald Laird and his (second) wife Francesca Morrow, both elderly. Cassie develops a 'blind certainty about what was to come', and the narrative includes the activities of the unruly students who called themselves the 'Dead Ladies', in Toronto and during a ten-student tour to Athens and Delphi.

By means of fiction, *Creation*—about John James Audubon, the naturalist and artist of *Birds of America* fame—fills in a gap in Audubon's biography when he spent the summer of 1833, with a crew and his son Johnny and other young men, sailing off the coast of Labrador in search of new species of birds to paint. Also sailing these waters was Captain Henry Wolsey Bayfield, who was surveying the coast for the Royal Navy. The two men meet occasionally on board one or the other's ship and strike up a friendship. The title *Creation* of course refers to Audubon's work on his paintings, but it could also pay tribute to Govier's creativity in a novel that adroitly combines fact and fiction and displays an extraordinary command of unlikely subjects (for Govier), such as nature and weather, sailing, surveyors' tools, the appearance of birds and their habits, killing them to make them models, wiring their bodies so that Audubon can paint them in a natural position. Some quotations from the text: 'Past the Île d'Orléans. Past the Île-aux-Coudres. [Bayfield] avoids the south channel and the lesser-known channel on the north side, and takes the middle, which was his own discovery. // Past the mouth of the Saguenay, where the water is half brine, half fresh, and hovers at the freezing point. // He can taste the salt in the air. The schooner leaps to the wind and it is like his own body.' 'The sea is calm and the sun is brilliant. These little islands, not far off the coast of the north shore of the Gulf, are of a peculiar limestone quite separate from that of the mainland. The shores have been pounded, worn to a fantasy of shapes. They are a little Egypt with their soft stone figures standing like bottles and whistling as the air moves through and around them. Standing trees that have died and dried in the sea wind rattle like white china. Even in rigor mortis, nothing has broken them.' 'The hold [of Bayfield's ship] is very clean and heated by the stove. The tools of the surveyor are here, the chains and lead plumbs, the theodite with its gleaming half circle, various compasses and arcs.' 'The little warbler alights on a bush within shot. [Tom] raises his gun and, with his usual accuracy, hits it. // The body is there, in the moss. In a moment Audubon is holding it in his hand, its wings spread open in his palm.' 'He knows the bird [a white-winged crossbill] when Johnny brings it in, a beautiful male, its red back, head and chest gleaming against the white patches on its wings, and its sharp curved beak giving it the look of a Renaissance cleric... He wires it, quickly, in profile, with wings down and half outspread to best show the lovely egg-shaped white patch on the top of the wings.... And he paints, mixing the watercolours he has brought with local tinctures from berries.... Drawing is a meditation to him. His hand imitates every line of the posture in which he has arranged the bird's wings, tarsis, bill and feet; he outlines each feather fastidiously.' The novel incorporates Audubon's memories of his young life and his thoughts about his devoted wife and a young woman he has fallen in love with, achieving a believable, engrossing narrative that combines the imaginary and the factual with great adroitness—indeed, with artistry. The Epilogue of this accomplished novel, relying on facts, describes the remainder of the life of each main character. *Three views of crystal water* (2005) is a generational saga covering almost a hundred years, set chiefly in Vancouver and Japan, and divided into three sections called 'Views'. It opens in 1934, with thirteen-year-old Vera—her mother dead, her father sojourning in far places—waiting for the arrival on the *Empress of Japan* of James Lowinger, her beloved grandfather, a pearl merchant. (We read that he had his first experience of the pearl fishery in the 1860s as a boy in Ceylon.) He descends from the ship with his much younger Japanese mistress, Keiko, and the three of them live together in Vancouver. At one point Lowinger takes three woodcut prints out of their folder—they have the same name as the title of the book—and leaves them for Vera to examine. In each one there are people, and also water, and the hint of a story. (Late in the book Vera rearranges them and creates a story for herself.) In 1936 Grandfather dies and Keiko takes Vera to Japan, where they settle off the coast on 'summer island', where pearl fishing is central. Keiko is an *ama*, 'born of the sea'—a diver; and Vera learns to become a diver. Life in Japan and with Keiko, Vera's dives, her Japanese friends, her love affair with

Tamio, pearl lore and pearl fishing, the oncoming war, Vera's connecting with her father, who takes her back to Vancouver, where she marries a much older man—these events fill out this long, studiously faithful portrayal of a different time, a different place, and an exotic goal for many of the characters: pearls. Vera eventually returns to Japan (in the last few pages), finds Tamio, and is about to be reunited with Keiko.

Govier has edited two anthologies about travel: *Without a guide: contemporary women's travel adventures* (1994) and *Solo: writers on pilgrimage* (2004). Pieces by Margaret ATWOOD and Govier herself appear in both.

Gowdy, Barbara (b. 1950). She was born and raised in Windsor, Ontario, educated in Toronto schools, and studied theatre arts for a year at York University, Toronto. Active in literary publishing from 1974 to 1979, she worked for Lester & Orpen Dennys, Toronto, eventually becoming managing editor. She is a Member of the Order of Canada (2007).

Gowdy has been called the most fearless black humorist in Canada. In her insistence that we can find grace and redemption only in accepting our bodies as they are, even if deformed, she has brought to mind the works of the photographer Diane Arbus and the short-story writer Flannery O'Connor. Some of Gowdy's fiction reflects an obsession with the body, the freaky, the extreme, the grotesque. In stories that are metaphors for spiritual crises, she reveals how spirit transcends the body. Her writing is innovative and unique, her language precise, her material unusual, and often funny. Gowdy's first collection of poems and stories was *The rabbit and the hare* (1982). She then spent a year in the UK researching her historical novel *Through the green valley* (1988), a lyrical story of a poor Irish boy and his three sisters swept up in a war that eventually brings them to America. With *Falling angels* (1989, rpr. 2003), which was translated into six languages, Gowdy began to explore her major concerns, the metamorphosis of the flesh, and tolerance within the family. In this black comic study of a dysfunctional urban family, a father forces his family to spend a vacation in a bomb shelter, while three adolescent girls come to terms with their bodies, their family, and their lives. The eight startling, sometimes amusing, stories in *We so seldom look on love* (1992, rpr. 2006) feature such subjects as necrophilia, exhibitionism, transvestism, Siamese twins with warring heads, a woman with two sets of reproductive organs, and a woman with an extra pair of

legs. The stories, based on fact, are written with convincing detail in spare and elegant language, and the characters are portrayed sympathetically. The title story, about necrophilia, was successfully adapted as a prizewinning feature film, *Kissed*, directed by Lynne Stopkewich. Gowdy's third novel, *Mister Sandman* (1995, rpr. 2007), explores preconceptions of what constitutes a happy family. The parents are closet homosexuals, which neither knows about the other; other characters include an obese sister, a speechless autistic dwarf, and an 'idiot savant' to whom the others confess their anxieties, as if at prayer. Because Gowdy sees tolerance as a form of love, the centre of this daring and witty novel has a visionary calm. Even more surprising than her previous two books, *The white bone* (1998, rpr. 2007) is a tour de force whose characters are African elephants, all of whom talk, most believably, and have names and distinctive identities. Mud, the central character, her friend Date Bed, and the young male Tall Time search for a White Bone—the bone of a newborn baby elephant 'bleached to a blinding whiteness'—that is believed to appear 'in times of darkness' to guide elephants to a Safe Place, far from humans, whom they call 'Hindleggers'. The elephants have beliefs and feelings, even a religion—they worship the She, the mother of all elephants—and, though humanized, inhabit a world of their own that is unlike the world of humans, who slaughter them for ivory. As imagined by Gowdy—in a novel that combines a form of social comedy with tragedy—both this world and the characters are convincing and compelling. *The romantic* (2003, rpr. 2007) is narrated by Louise Kirk, whose mother, a former beauty queen, leaves her husband and daughter, aged nine, putting a note on the fridge: 'I have gone. I am not coming back. Louise knows how to work the washing machine [not true].' Shortly afterwards the German Richters move onto their street, with their adopted son Abel (short for Abelard), a clever, handsome boy of Louise's age with whom she falls in love: she is obsessed with him throughout his short life. Abel returns her love, but without Louise's passion. While going to high school they have sex and Louise becomes pregnant (unbeknownst to Abel) and has an abortion. While never ceasing to love Abel, jealousy makes her angry with him and they go their different ways, coming together again, only to separate—until his last days. On page 1 we are told that Abel is dead—his actual death in his 20s (he's an alcoholic, though he never behaves like one) occurs at the end of the book. Highly fluent and down-to-earth recollections of the minutiae of Louise's early life, this is an unstructured novel of memories—moving backwards and forwards in time, sometimes confusingly—of Louise's memories of her mother (her mother reappears, as ashes in an urn) and of her conversations with Abel. One thinks of Abélard and Héloïse (Abel calls her Hell-Louise), the renowned French romantic couple of the twelfth century. Louise thinks: 'We're not them. Abélard and Héloïse's love was indestructible, and everything they suffered came from outside that love. With Abel and me, the assault came from within. From him.' The story of *Helpless* (2007, rpr. 2008) is told from the viewpoints of Celia and her stunning mixed-race nine-year-old daughter Rachel, who live with their gay landlord and friend Mika; and Ron, a pudgy appliance repairman and his girlfriend Nancy. Once Ron sees Rachel he is entranced, and stalks her outside her school and home, convinced that she is in harm's way because her mother lets her visit the nightclub where she sings on weekends and the landlord is possibly abusing her. Ron will rescue her and attractively furnishes for her a room in his basement. During a summer blackout, when Rachel, in a panic, runs out of the house (Mika has had an accident and she thinks he's dead), Ron abducts her. The bulk of the narrative focuses on the captivity of Rachel, who slowly warms to the kindly attentions of Nancy, who herself is a helpless accessory to the kidnapping she knew nothing about; on Ron's joy from having Rachel in his house, mixed with fear of frightening her by his presence—Nancy tells him to say away from the room until Rachel calms down; and on Celia's grief, and her desperation when it becomes clear that the police have no clue about where Rachel could be. The suspense accruing from the isolation of Ron and his captive—there is no way of finding out where she is—is palpable. The characterizations are rounded and convincing. Rachel is resourceful, though delusional about being threatened by what she calls slave-drivers. She eventually lets Ron share her supper with Nancy, and looks up to him as a protector; she pleads with Nancy to phone her mother and tell her she's all right, which Nancy does—she also mails a brief letter Rachel has written to Celia. Ron's growing closeness to Rachel turns into something else in his mind—he loves her, but does not believe in 'crossing the line'. This stressful narrative, interweaving complex characters—Ron may be somewhat crazy, but he's not a monster—and a multitude of episodes, has a

delicately rendered conclusion that is satisfying. It is a testament to Gowdy's taste and skill. In 2008 *Helpless* won for her the Ontario Trillium Book Award.

Graham, Gwethalyn (1913–65). Gwethalyn Graham Erichsen-Brown was born in Toronto, attending Rosedale Public School and Havergal College there. She was educated at the Pensionnat des Allières in Lausanne, Switzerland; and Smith College, Massachusetts. A novelist and journalist, her writing most often dealt with the need for justice, tolerance, and international understanding. Her first novel, *Swiss sonata* (1938, GGA; rpr. 2005), explores the interwoven stories of twenty-seven residents at a Swiss boarding school on the eve of the Second World War. Although somewhat awkward because of its many characters and implausible time frame (all events take place during a single day), it represents a timely appeal for international empathy and understanding. Graham's second and stronger novel, *Earth and high heaven* (1944, GGA; rpr. 2004), set in Montreal during the Second World War, is the story of Erica Drake, a journalist from an affluent Westmount family who falls in love with a Jewish lawyer. The novel focuses on the blatant anti-Semitism of her socially prominent family, especially her father, and is an unsparing portrait of upper-class anti-Semitism in Canada during the war. The novel, which draws upon Graham's own experience in wishing to marry a Jewish-Canadian lawyer to whom her father was unalterably opposed, was a popular and critical success in Canada and abroad and was translated into nine languages. While somewhat dated and frequently awkward in its use of excessively expository dialogue, the novel is nonetheless notable for the sharpness of its deeply felt attack on covert racism in Canada. *Dear enemy: a dialogue on French and English Canada* (1963), which Graham wrote in collaboration with Solange Chaput-Rolland, is an exchange of letters exploring the conflicts between English and French Canadians. At her death she was at work on a novel about English-Canadian and Québécois relations.

Graham, Ron (b. 1948). Born in Ottawa, he grew up in Montreal and was educated at McGill University (B.A., 1968) and the Institute of Canadian Studies, Carleton University (M.A., 1971). His first book was a short novel, *Naughts and crosses* (1980), a surrealistic murder story set in Montreal during the October Crisis of 1970. He was associate producer of a much-admired TV series, 'The Canadian Establishment', which led to his first appearance as a national journalist with a 1980 *Saturday Night* article about the making of the series. For the next seven years he was closely identified with that magazine, where his prize-winning articles won him a reputation for resourceful reporting, excellent storytelling, and the ability to make unexpected leaps of insight in order to explain how his subjects fit into Canadian society. Much of *One-eyed kings: promise and illusion in Canadian politics* (1986) is based on his magazine profiles of Joe Clark, John Turner, and others. Pursuing his own deepest interests, he next turned to the condition of religion in Canada and wrote the remarkably broad-ranging and original *God's dominion: a skeptic's quest* (1990), in which he discerned patterns of faith in religious communities as different as the Tibetan Buddhists of Halifax and the Sikhs of British Columbia. (Conrad Black sued M&S and Graham for a passage in the book that he claimed was libellous; the book was not withdrawn, nor was the passage deleted, and the suit was finally settled out of court.) The persistent Canadian constitutional crisis encouraged Graham to explore, in *The French quarter: the epic struggle of a family—and a nation—divided* (1992), his own ancestral francophone connections, reaching back to Zacherie Cloutier, a master carpenter who crossed the Atlantic in 1634. In *All the king's horses: politics among the ruins* (1995) Graham discusses Canadian politics in the nineties, focusing on Kim Campbell's five-month tenure as prime minister, Jean Chrétien, Paul Martin, and others. In the last chapter he summarizes the country's 'great fall', to which the book's title alludes. Ron Graham edited *The essential Trudeau* (1998), made up of 258 brief extracts from the great man's writings. 'My role as an editor was to go through Trudeau's writings and speeches, extract the essence from them, and order them according to theme, logic, and number.' Graham added introductory commentaries of his own.

Grain. See Robert STEAD.

Grainger, Martin Allerdale (1874–1941). Born in London, England, he spent most of his childhood in Australia. In 1893 he won a scholarship to Cambridge University, where he excelled in mathematics. Upon graduating in 1896 he spent several adventurous years in northern British Columbia, then fought in the Boer War; he returned to B.C., trying his hand at placer-mining, logging, and some journalism. In 1910 he began his career in the British Columbia forest industry, first as secretary of the Royal Commission on Forestry (writing most of the report that led to the establishment of the B.C. Forest Service) and rose to the position of chief forester in 1917. In 1908, while in England, he wrote *Woodsmen of the West* (1908, NCL) to raise enough money on which to marry. It was based on Grainger's letters to his future wife. Less a novel than a sequence of realistic, dramatized personal observations, it is recounted by a first-person narrator who retains the author's name and identity. Enthralled by the challenge of a frontier environment and intrigued by the individualism and initiative of the western logger, Mart recounts incidents illustrating the character type he most frequently encountered: men who were enterprising yet foolhardy, pragmatically shrewd yet financially naive, physically fearless yet emotionally undisciplined. The rather spare plot centres on Mart's conflicts with his boss, Carter, who personifies the raw spirit of free enterprise. Despite his personal distaste for the man, Mart remains in his employ, held by his fascination with Carter's ruthless and single-minded exploitation of both the land and his men. Carter emerges as a villain in his relations with human beings, but as a hero in his determination to conquer both an inhospitable environment and the vagaries of the anonymous world of big business. Grainger's detailed descriptions of the unromantic life of the West Coast handlogger, and of the climate and terrain of northern British Columbia, make *Woodsmen of the West* one of the best examples of early-Canadian literary realism.

Granatstein, J.L. (b. 1939). Jack Lawrence Granatstein was born in Toronto and educated at the Royal Military College, Kingston (B.A., 1961), the University of Toronto (M.A., 1962), and Duke University, North Carolina (Ph.D., 1966). He was a historian in the Directorate of History, National Defence Headquarters, Ottawa, from 1964 to 1966, when he became professor of history at York University, Toronto; after early retirement, he was appointed in 1995 Distinguished Research Professor of History Emeritus. He was made an Officer of the Order of Canada in 1997, and in 1998 was appointed Director of the Canadian War Museum, a post that he gave up in 2000 in order to write. He is senior research fellow at the Canadian Defence and Foreign Affairs Institute and lives in Toronto.

The most prolific historian of twentieth-century Canada, Granatstein supplanted, in his many books, the themes of an earlier generation of historians who had been interested in the emergence of the country from colony to nation, from a British world to American influence. Political and military history, and occasionally foreign affairs, have been Granatstein's principal interests in his more than three dozen books and one dozen edited volumes. Asking the right questions, prodigious in research to discern the answers, and able to communicate, Granatstein altered one's understanding of Canada's history. The political and military experiences and the top brass of the Second World War fascinated him: *Canada's war: the politics of the Mackenzie King government* (1975, rpr. 1990), *Broken promises: a history of conscription in Canada* (1977), *Bloody victory: Canadians and the D-Day campaign 1944* (1984), and *The generals: the Canadian Army's senior commanders in the Second World War* (1993; rev. 2005). He also wrote *War and peacekeeping* (1991) and co-authored *Mutual hostages: Canadians and Japanese during the Second World War* (1990). The movement of Canada away from Britain and closer to the USA was explained with dispassion and balance, supported with sound evidence culled from North American and British archives, in *For better or for worse: Canada and the United States to the 1990s* (with Norman Hillmer, 1991), and *Yankee go home? Canadians and anti-Americans* (1996). But Granatstein did not ignore the importance of individuals, writing *Mackenzie King: his life and world* (1977), *The Ottawa men: the civil service mandarins 1935–1957* (1982, rpr. 1998), and a study of one of the mandarins, *A man of influence: Norman Robertson and Canadian statecraft 1929–68* (1981). Other Granatstein publications include a criticism of universities, *The great brain robbery* (1984), and *Sacred trust? Brian Mulroney and the Conservatives in power* (1986), which were both polemical, while in *Canada 1957–1967: the years of uncertainty and innovation* (1986), written for the Canadian Centenary Series, Granatstein entered the arena of cultural history. *Who killed Canadian history?* (1998, 2nd edn 2007), an eloquent essay protesting the disappearance of Canadian history studies in schools, or their subordination into topics of political correctness, and the harmful effects of this—ending with suggestions for their resurrection. *Prime ministers: ranking Canada's leaders* (with Norman Hillmer, 1999) is a collection of succinct, clear portraits of twenty prime ministers, Mackenzie King ranking no. 1, Macdonald no. 2, Laurier no. 3, St Laurent no. 4, and Trudeau no. 5. *Our century: how Canada became the best place on earth* (2000) was followed by *Canada's army: waging war and keeping the peace* (2002), a long, monumental work,

described by the author as 'a history of the Canadian army, of organized bodies of Canadians fighting, training, and serving their nation in peace and war.' In the same year Granatstein published *W.L. Mackenzie King* (2002), a good paperback mini-biography (sixty-four pages) in the long Fitzhenry and Whiteside series The Canadians. Amazingly, from the standpoint of abundant productivity, Granatstein went on to publish *Canada and the two world wars* (with Desmond Morton, 2003); *Who killed the Canadian military?* (2004), in which the last two chapters are headed 'Last rites: Jean Chrétien finishes off the Canadian Forces' and 'The way ahead: resurrecting the Canadian military'; *Hell's corner: an illustrated of Canada's Great War 1914–1918* (2004), a large-format book with extraordinary photographs, and paintings and sketches, from the collections of the Canadian War Museum, many of them never published before, and a companion volume, *The last good war: an illustrated history of Canada in the Second World War 1939–1945* (2005); and *Whose war is it? how Canada can survive in the post-9/11 world* (2007), the war being 'the war against terror that will affect us even as Canadians hope in vain that it will not.' *The importance of being less earnest: promoting Canada's national interests through tighter ties with the U.S.* (2003) is the C.D. Howe Institute's Benefactors Lecture given in Oct. 2003. Granatstein edited, with Norman Hillmer, *First drafts: eyewitness accounts from Canada's past* (2002), a long and fascinating anthology of the first-hand reports of observers covering more than 500 years; modern times are of course given much space, with a salutary emphasis on the writings of the brilliant reporter Matthew Halton (1906–56). With David J. Bercuson, Granatstein wrote the *Dictionary of Canadian military history* (1992).

Grandbois, Alain (1900–75). Born in Saint-Casimir de Portneuf, Québec, he studied law at Université Laval; though admitted to the bar in 1925, he never practised. A considerable inheritance allowed him to travel abroad almost continuously between 1918 and 1938. Based in Paris—where he met fellow-expatriates Ernest Hemingway, Blaise Cendrars, and Jules Supervielle—he travelled extensively in Europe, Africa, India, Russia, China, and Japan. After his return to Canada he wrote steadily, earning his living by giving many radio talks on his travels, lecturing, and writing articles, as well as working as bibliographer at the Bibliothèque Saint-Sulpice. (In this period he translated Merrill DENISON's *The barley and the stream: the Molson story*, under the title *Au pied* *du courant*, 1955.) In 1956 he took up residence in Mont Rolland, north of Montreal. Grandbois was renowned as a poet. His collections of poems, published between 1944 and 1957, are admired for the sonorous harmonies and exotic colours of their language and for their impelling, incantatory rhetoric. His prose writings, close in theme to his poetry, reflect his love of travel, and include biographies of explorers who, on their journeys in search of the earth's *éblouissants secrets* (dazzling secrets), courted danger and death. *Né à Québec: Louis Jolliet* (Paris, 1933; Montreal, 1949, 1969) was published in an English translation by Evelyn Brown as *Born in Quebec* (1964). A bilingual collection of Grandbois's poetry, *Selected poems* (1964), contains translations by Peter Miller with the French originals. Grandbois became a Companion of the Order of Canada in 1967.

Grant, George (1918–88). George Parkin Grant was born in Toronto and educated at Upper Canada College; Queen's University, Kingston; and Oxford University, where he was a Rhodes Scholar. His paternal grandfather, George Monro Grant (author of OCEAN TO OCEAN), had been a principal of Queen's, and his maternal grandfather, Sir George Parkin—who, like his father, had been a principal of Upper Canada College—had headed the Rhodes Trust. From 1947 to 1960 George Grant taught philosophy at Dalhousie University, Halifax, becoming head of the department; he was then chairman of the department of religion at McMaster University, Hamilton, Ontario, until 1980, when he returned to Dalhousie as Killam Professor.

Grant's writings have occupied a major place in Canadian intellectual life since the appearance of *Philosophy in the mass age* (1959, rpr. 1995). His influence has been significant in literature, political theory, and religious thinking, though he has remained outside the bounds of most professional philosophers. Christianity had always been central to his thought. He was influenced for a time by Hegel; but his strongest philosophical inclinations were generally Platonic, though both Simone Weil and Martin Heidegger influenced his later thought. *Philosophy in the mass age* sought to establish the importance of the Judaeo-Christian tradition as a major element in the understanding of human freedom and the transcendence of nature, while seeking to retain the relevance of the classical notion of a natural order that sets limits to human behaviour. *Lament for a nation: the defeat of Canadian Nationalism* (1965; 2nd edn 1970, with a new introduction by the author, rpr.

2005) had a wide influence on proponents of Canadian economic nationalism, with its thesis that Canada had been destroyed as a viable nation by the ideology of American liberalism backed by technology and corporate capitalism. Grant's nostalgia for the values expounded by John G. Diefenbaker (Conservative prime minister of Canada, 1957–63) suggests a strong conservative strand in his thought, which he described as occurring when the New Democratic Party supported the official (Liberal) Opposition in a vote critical of Diefenbaker's position on the stationing of American nuclear missiles in Canada. Grant's conservatism was of the sort that figures in Canadian politics as 'red Toryism', having little to do with the support of 'free enterprise' but emphasizing social responsibility, the duties of the strong to the weak, and the sense of continuing community. The theses in *Lament for a nation* were extended somewhat in *Technology and empire: perspectives on North America* (1969), essays that clearly associated Grant's thought with that of Leo Strauss and Jacques Ellul. Grant's writings emphasize tradition, and are a severe critique of the notion that the primary meaning of human life is to be found in history that exemplifies continuous progress. His CBC Massey Lectures, published as *Time as history* (1969, rpr. 1995) and focusing on an examination of Nietzsche, insist that there are eternal values, and that basic Christian notions soundly limit what can be done to, and with, human beings. In *English-speaking justice* (1974; rev. 1985; rpr. 1998) Grant returned to criticizing liberal ideology with a cutting analysis of the philosophy of John Rawls, and of other recent forms of the social-contract theory. While Grant's philosophical interests changed and developed considerably over the years, the centre of his political thought continued, to the end of his life, to reflect clearly his original Platonism, with its insistence on stability rather than change, eternal values rather than temporal pleasures, and community rather than individuality. *Technology and justice* (1986) is made up of six essays that discuss the various ways in which technology has influenced society. Grant's writings have been brought together in the *Collected works of George Grant* edited by Arthur Davis and Peter C. Emberley: *Volume I 1933–1950* (2000), *Volume II 1951–1959* (2002), and *Volume III* (2005).

See William Christian, *George Grant: a biography* (1993); David Cayley, *Conversations with George Grant* (1995); *George Grant: selected letters* (1996) and *The George Grant reader* (1997), both edited by Christian (the latter with

Sheila Grant); *George Grant and the subversion of modernity: art, philosophy, politics, religion, and education* (1996) edited by Arthur Davis; T.F. Rigelhof's short biography, *George Grant: redefining Canada* (2001); *Athens and Jerusalem: George Grant's theology, philosophy, and politics* (2006) edited by Ian Angus, Ron Dart, and Randy Peg Peters; and *George Grant: a guide to his thought* (2007) by Hugh Donald Forbes.

Grant, George Monro. See OCEAN TO OCEAN.

Graphic Publishers (1925–32). Founded by Henry C. Miller, an Ottawa printer, and incorporated on 6 July 1926 with Miller as president, the Graphic Publishers, also referred to as Graphic Press, was an Ottawa-based publisher that sought, in the words of its founder, 'to handle nothing but Canadian books by Canadians and for Canadians'. Graphic's first book was Madge MACBETH's *The land of afternoon* (1926), a satire on social and political life in Ottawa, published under the pseudonym 'Gilbert Knox'. The book was an instant success and launched the press. Although in its seven years Graphic was seldom free from financial difficulties or infighting, it published no less than eighty-three titles under various imprints before it succumbed to the Depression. Graphic's publications included fiction, poetry, plays, essays, history, and criticism. Macbeth's other titles included the feminist satire *Shackles* (1926). Another early success for the press was Frederick Philip GROVE's *A search for America* (1927), which had two printings. In 1929 Grove joined Graphic as head of its subsidiary, Ariston Publishers Limited. Other well-known Canadian authors published by the press included William Arthur DEACON, Merrill DENISON, and Watson KIRKCONNELL. Raymond KNISTER won first prize in the Graphic Publishers' Canadian Novel contest for his manuscript *My star predominant*; however, the press failed before the book could be printed: it was published by the RYERSON PRESS in 1934.

Gray, Charlotte (b. 1948). Born in Sheffield, England, she graduated with a B.A. from Oxford University (1969) and with a diploma in social administration from the London School of Economics and Political Science (1970). She is married to George R.M. Anderson, president and CEO, Forum of Federations, and has three sons. Coming to Canada with her family in 1978, she was the Ottawa editor, then a contributing editor, of *Saturday Night* (1986–2001). Since then she has made her name as a biographer and social historian who can transform an immense amount of research on aspects of Canadian history into works of strong narrative interest. She was appointed a Member of the Order of Canada in 2007.

The idea for Gray's first book was inspired. *Mrs King: the life and times of Isabel Mackenzie King* (1997, rpr. 2008) brings to life a hitherto little-known woman who was both the daughter of William Lyon MACKENZIE and the mother of William Lyon Mackenzie King, who held power longer than any other Canadian prime minister. Isabel Mackenzie (called Bell as a girl) married John King, a lawyer who had graduated from Osgoode Hall, Toronto; but when he turned down a clerkship offered by the premier and attorney-general of Ontario in favour of practising law in his hometown of Berlin (later Kitchener), Ontario, he made a mistake that imposed a lifelong condition of impoverishment on the couple, and on their four children: Belle, Willie, Jennie, Max—among whom only Willie (WLMK) would eventually provide, on request, financial aid for his indigent parents. The biography is a skilful blending of accounts of each member of the King family, their relationships, and portraits of places (Berlin, Toronto at the turn of the century). Gray's vivid portrait of Isabel herself—physically attractive, sometimes charming and fun-loving, attached to all her children, but constantly showing angry resentment over the privations her marriage created for her—pays special attention to the mutual dependence that developed between Isabel and the mature Mackenzie King. Gray says in her Preface: 'I could almost feel her hunger for a passionate, romantic attachment that her husband could never satisfy, and that her elder son rushed to fill.' Late in the book there are many passages such as the following: 'After Willie had seen his mother off at the train station, he allowed himself to wallow in abject adoration: "She is, I think, the purest and sweetest soul that God ever made."' His obsession with his mother lasted until the day he died. The book is marred by the hopelessly indistinct reproductions of many potentially interesting illustrations.

The individual biographies of the Strickland sisters, Susanna MOODIE and Catharine Parr TRAILL, born at the beginning of the nineteenth century, are familiar in general terms. But Gray's double biography, *Sisters in the wilderness: the lives of Susanna Moodie and Catharine Parr Traill* (1999, rpr. 2008)—describing their early life at Reydon Hall, Suffolk, and in London as beginning writers; their marriage to two ineffective men, whom they loved; a terrible Atlantic crossing and their disagreeable trip overland from Montreal to Upper Canada;

Gray

the trials of being inexperienced farming pioneers in a hostile environment, and their different ways of coping, while both pursued their ambitions as writers—amplifies their lives to the very end with a wonderful accretion of detail, and in an enjoyable narrative. The sisters lived for a long time. Susanna died first, in 1885, and Catharine died fourteen years later, in 1899. Gray amassed a great deal of information about Pauline JOHNSON for her long, definitive biography *Flint & feather: the life and times of E. Pauline Johnson, Tekahionwake* (2002). The book describes Johnson's parentage—she was the daughter of an attractive, cultivated man, a Mohawk chief who married an English gentlewoman; her youth in the family home Chiefswood, which her father had built in 1855; and Pauline herself, the budding writer of lyric poetry, and her debut as a performer, reciting her verse for the first time on Saturday evening, 16 January 1892 in Toronto, enchanting her audience. Peforming in both evening dress and Indian costume, Johnson crossed the country nineteen times, and the Atlantic—performing in London—three times, always with the praise and endorsement of personages. It was a strange life, but in the context of the last forty years of the nineteenth century and the first decade or so of the twentieth, the author captures it well. Charlotte Gray is also the editor of *Canada: a portrait in letters 1800–2000* (2003). A mammoth (more than 500 pages) collection of letters—chosen with imagination and discernment—with illuminating long introductions to the periods and short introductions to many letters, it is a rich resource and a great book to read. Next was her biography of Alexander Graham Bell, born in Edinburgh in 1847, whose father, Professor Melville Bell, left Scotland with his family in 1870 and settled in Brantford, Ontario. *Reluctant genius: the passionate life and inventive mind of Alexander Graham Bell* (2006) is perhaps Gray's most demanding biography, because of the scientific intricacies of Bell's development of the telephone in Boston (and of his other inventions), which she succeeds in explaining to the enlightenment, without perhaps the full understanding, of the unscientific reader: 'Suddenly the idea struck him that it might be possible to create an undulating electric current that could carry sound along a telegraph wire in the same way that air carried sound waves from the speaker to the hearer. The telephone receiver, pressed to a human ear, could act like an electrical mouth. Current flowing through an electromagnet would cause the receiver's membrane to vibrate. The vibration, reasoned Alec, would then hit the listener's eardrum, making it vibrate too. The listener's ear would interpret these vibrations as the sounds spoken by the person at the other end of the wire.' A year and a half later: 'On the evening of March 10, 1876, Alec and Watson [his assistant] set up a receiver on the bureau in Alec's bedroom, then took the transmitter with its battery connected to the cup of sulfuric acid into the room next door. Watson barely had time to return to the bedroom before he heard Alec's voice emanating from the receiver, saying, quite clearly, "Mr. Watson, come here, I want you!"' Alec's popular telephone lectures and demonstrations; his marriage to Mabel Hubbard (who had been deaf since childhood) in 1877 when he was thirty—she was twenty and the mainstay of his life; his fame and contacts with famous people, including Queen Victoria and Helen Keller; the building of a house and research laboratory on Cape Breton Island at Baddeck, Nova Scotia (now the Alexander Graham Bell National Historic Site)—all this and much more has been subsumed in the absorbing text of this definitive biography. For Penguin Canada's series of brief biographies, Extraordinary Canadians, Gray wrote *Nellie McClung* (2008), a perceptive and well-researched biography.

Gray, James H. (1906–98). He grew up and was educated in Winnipeg during its boom years. After a succession of jobs at the Winnipeg Grain Exchange and with stockbrokers, he was forced to go on relief during the Depression. He took to writing articles, and as a result was engaged in 1935 as a reporter on the *Winnipeg Free Press*, becoming an editorial writer in 1941, and Ottawa correspondent in 1946. From 1947 to 1955 he edited the *Farm and Ranch Review*, and from 1955 to 1958 the *Western Oil Examiner*. He fought against domination of oil exploration by American multinationals, eventually moving to the Home Oil Company in Calgary to promote an all-Canadian pipeline to Montreal.

After his early retirement in 1963, Gray began to write the vivid, unconventional social histories of the Prairies that made him one of Canada's leading popular historians. Three books are chiefly autobiographical: *The boy from Winnipeg* (1970, 2nd edn 1996), captures the atmosphere of his childhood; *The winter years* (1966, rpr. 2003), of which he was most proud, describes how the Prairies survived the Depression with such expedients as food vouchers and 'boondoggling' work projects; and *Troublemaker!* (1978, rpr. 1983) tells of

Gray's career as a journalist and the causes that engaged him, from the politics of the oil patch to the marketing of western grain. Other works, drawing on oral history and personal knowledge as well as archival sources, investigate aspects of daily life on the Prairies that until then had received scant documentation. *Men against the desert* (1967, 2nd edn 1996) celebrates the success of the Dominion Experimental Farms and the Prairie Farm Rehabilitation Administration in helping farmers to combat the drought, dust, and insect infestations of the thirties. *Red lights on the Prairies* (1971, rev. 1995) is a history of prostitution in prairie towns before the Depression, grimly revealing the lack of social amenities in early settlements. *Booze: when whisky ruled the West* (1972, rev. 1995), about the tradition of heavy drinking on the Prairies, throws cold water on the received liberal view that prohibition was a disaster, and argues that life improved when the bars were closed. *Bacchanalia revisited* (1982), pursuing the theme in the modern era, reveals its attitude in the subtitle *Western Canada's boozy skid to social disaster.* Gray also wrote *The roar of the twenties* (1975); *Boomtime* (1979), a lavishly illustrated record of immigration up to the First World War; *A brand of its own* (1985), a history of the Calgary Stampede; *Talk to my lawyer!* (1987), an anecdotal history of the Calgary bar; and *R.B. Bennett: the Calgary years* (1991). Gray was appointed a Member of the Order of Canada in 1988.

Gray, John MacLachlan (b. 1946). Born in Ottawa, he was raised in Truro, Nova Scotia, and attended Mount Allison University (B.A., 1968) and the University of British Columbia (M.A., 1972). Active in Vancouver theatre, Gray founded Tamahnous Theatre. In the mid-1970s he moved to Toronto and became involved with Theatre Passe Muraille, composing music for a number of productions including Rick SALUTIN's *1837: the farmers' revolt* (1976) and *The false messiah* (1982), and Herschel Hardin's *The great wave of civilization* (1976). These early theatrical endeavours led to the aspect of Gray's career for which he is most recognized: a playwright committed to forging a uniquely Canadian sense of the musical. Gray now lives in Vancouver where he wrote a weekly column, called 'Gray's Anatomy', for the Toronto *Globe and Mail*, 2000–3. He was made an Officer of the Order of Canada in 2000.

Gray's first musical to gain national attention was *18 wheels* (1987), which premiered at Theatre Passe Muraille in 1977 and was produced across Canada. Portraying Canadian truckers whose musical influences are country and western music from the USA, Gray established in this early piece his recurrent interest in defining Canadian identity in the face of an array of international influences.

Billy Bishop goes to war (1978), written in collaboration with Eric Peterson (and winner, in 1982, of a Governor General's Award), is a work for two performers. In the original production, Peterson played Billy Bishop, with Gray providing musical accompaniment as the Piano Player: it was well acted, well produced, and popular. In many ways the play is a coming-of-age story in which Bishop recounts incidents from his life, and in the process performs a range of characters. The question haunting the end of *Billy Bishop*–'Makes you wonder what it was all for?'—could usefully serve as the question raised by *Rock and roll* (1982). This semi-autobiographical piece dramatizes the reunion of a rock band, the Monarchs, in the fictionalized locale of Mushaboom, Nova Scotia. Here, using rock and roll (which developed in Canada with heavy debts to influences from the USA), Gray seems to suggest that Canadian appropriations of artistic forms leads to a uniquely Canadian vital expression of local culture.

Both plays deal with the experiences of aging protagonists, for whom authentic identity seems to be associated with past glories; and, in some sense, they deal also with memory and identity. In *Don Messer's jubilee* (1985) Gray tackled issues of national nostalgia. In 1969 the Canadian Broadcasting Corporation cancelled a popular Canadian television show featuring Messer, a fiddler, to make way for programming aimed at a younger audience who were culturally predisposed to the musical genres that Gray had used in *Rock and roll*. In writing *Don Messer's jubilee* Gray sought to immerse himself in the local musical idioms of the Maritimes and recover a part of Canadian musical heritage that was disowned by the CBC's cancellation of Messer's long-running show.

Local boy makes good: three musicals by John Gray (1987) contains *18 wheels, Rock and roll*, and *Don Messer's jubilee*.

Other books by Gray include *I love Mom: an irreverant history of the tattoo* (1994), *Lost in North America: the imaginary Canadian in the American dream* (1995), and *Men, women and relationships: making peace with the opposite sex* (1996). His first novel, *Dazzled* (1984), is a satiric tale of marital breakdown in which the protagonist, Willard, sets aside his idealism and enters the world of business. *A gift for the little master* (2000) is a thriller/murder mystery/stalker tale set in a West Coast city (Vancouver?) that is impelled by fast, tough dialogue and the characters themselves: Delores Gunn, who runs freelance TV crews that stick to the police; Eli, a bicycle courier; and the cop Turner, 'who views the civilian world in tiers of contempt'.

Gray then submerged himself in the Victorian period, writing two highly praised novels set in London. *The fiend in human* (2003), a thriller set in 1852, focuses on Edmund Whitty, a correspondent for a tabloid, *The falcon*—the novel begins with his description of the hanging at Newgate Prison of William Ryan (whom he calls Chokee Bill, 'The Fiend in Human Form') for a series of murders of prostitutes with a white silk scarf. The stranglings continue, however, and Whitty turns detective. *The fiend* is an entertaining attempt at a Dickensian novel—though the language, and the thrust of the narrative, are not in the least Dickensian. *White stone day* (2005) ('A Good Read Guaranteed Or Your Money Back', so says the publisher, Random House Canada) again features Edmund Whitty in 1858. Like Charles Dodgson (Lewis Carroll)—'whose life and work inspired this entirely fictional account', in the author's words—the Reverend Boltbyn, we are told, began as a child 'his lifelong habit of marking significant days by pasting a small, smooth white stone … in his diary, as a sign of special happiness.' He loves spending time with two young sisters, Emma and Lydia Lambert, telling them stories and photographing them. 'They posed as wood nymphs in white dresses with garlands in their hair; as country maids with bare shoulders and impish visages; and as the most charming beggar girls ever.' In this intricate novel, filled with descriptions of London, many events transpire, including a seance in which Whitty appears to receive a message about his brother's death, the murder of the fraudulent psychic responsible—for which Whitty is arrested—and a secret pornographic ring. These and many other crises are overwhelmed by the abundance of detailed descriptions; though the novel is described as a thriller, suspense evaporates. *Not quite dead* (2007) is a complicated entertainment—set in Philadelphia and Baltimore in 1849—that involves the writers Edgar Allan Poe and Charles Dickens (their 'sensibilites' rather than the facts of their lives, according to the author), along with Dr William Chivers, 'the best friend of Eddie Poe'. Finn Devlin, a defeated Irishman abroad' who hates the English and becomes a Fenian, and numerous other male and female characters, surround a grisly murder and a kidnapping. The facts of the lives of Poe and Dickens

are disregarded on the whole—Dickens visited the US in 1842 and Poe died in 1849—but they come to life as characters. For Dickens, responding to all the events that were arranged to welcome him, 'It was a level of scrutiny he had not experienced since his birth. At first, the fuss over him pleasurably inflated his self-regard; but it was not long before he realized, to his puzzlement and hurt, that to be famous is not the same as to be admired, or even liked.' Poe asks his old friend Willie Chivers to stage his death, because he feels he's being persecuted, and Dr Chivers does this; so it is Poe who is 'not quite dead'.

Gray, John Morgan (1907–78). Born in Toronto, publisher and author John Gray was educated at Lakefield College and Upper Canada College and the University of Toronto, where he did not take his degree. Following a year as an assistant master at Lakefield, an introduction to Hugh Eayrs, the unpredictable but brilliant president of the MACMILLAN COMPANY OF CANADA—whose exasperating qualities and mannerisms are drawn with a novelist's skill in Gray's memoir *Fun tomorrow* (1978)—procured him a job as an educational representative. The years of crossing and recrossing the continent in the Depression gave Gray a knowledge of book publishing, and of people in hard times. This was to serve him well when, after four years' active service in Europe—during which he rose to become GSO(2) in the Intelligence Corps of the First Canadian army in Holland—he returned somewhat reluctantly to publishing. Eayrs died in 1940 and—the appointment of his successor having been postponed until after the war—Gray was made manager in 1946 and within a year president. He retired in 1973.

This was a propitious time to take charge of a Canadian publishing company. The long servitude of the industry to its British and American overlords, which had made many publishers no more than importing agencies, was about to be transformed. Given full powers and resources, limited only by British Exchange Control restrictions, Gray was provided with an opportunity to become not only a leader but, by virtue of his partnership in a worldwide publishing organization, a spokesman for the trade. With the Massey Report (1951) pointing the way, and the CANADA COUNCIL (1957) providing both publishers and authors with the backing they needed, the Canadian publishing industry was about to mature. Many leading Canadian authors joined the Macmillan list, and the evidence of how well Gray served them as editor is preserved in the Macmillan archives, now at McMaster University. Gray's part in this period of growth in Canadian publishing can be traced in the numerous papers he gave at conferences and in public addresses, and in an article he wrote for CANADIAN LITERATURE 33 (Spring 1967). Master of a simple, unadorned style with humorous undertones, he had always wanted to be a writer. His chief interest was in Canadian history, and his *Lord Selkirk of Red River* (1963) won the University of British Columbia medal for best biography of the year. *Fun tomorrow*, published a few weeks after his death from cancer, was to have been part of a two-volume memoir and ends at the point where he took over command of Macmillan Canada. Gray was a founding member of the Board of Governors of York University from 1960 to 1970, was appointed an Officer of the Order of Canada in 1975, and received many honorary degrees.

Green, Terence M. (b. 1947). A science-fiction and fantasy writer, Terence Michael Green was born in Toronto. He has a B.A. (1967) in English and a B.Ed. (1973) from the University of Toronto, and an M.A. (1972) in Anglo-Irish Studies from University College, Dublin. He taught English at East York Collegiate Institute, Toronto, from 1968 to 1999 and has been a lecturer at the University of Western Ontario since 2005. Green is the author of a trio of increasingly accomplished SF novels. *Barking dogs* (1988)—expanding a previously published short story of the same name—is a tale of vigilantism and psychological breakdown in a future Toronto, in which perfect, portable lie detectors—'barking dogs'—change both interpersonal relationships and criminal justice. The anthology *Ark of ice* (1992), edited by Lesley CHOYCE, contains a novelette entitled 'Blue limbo' that was later developed and published as *Blue limbo* (1997). *Children of the rainbow* (1992) displaces a variety of characters through time, with the author undertaking to combine the *Mutiny on the Bounty* story, the anti-nuclear protests of Greenpeace, and an Inca religious revival. This was republished in 2006 under the title *Sailing time's ocean*, which bears the imprint Robert J. SAWYER Books. Green's third novel, the slim *Shadow of Ashland* (1996)—the beginning of a trilogy—is again an expansion of a short story, in this case 'Ashland, Kentucky' (first published in *Isaac Asimov's Science Fiction Magazine*, Nov. 1985). About a son's search for his dying mother's brother who had disappeared

decades ago, it is highly autobiographical, with real relatives of Green appearing under their own names. *A witness to life* (1999, rpr. 2000) is not science fiction—though the narrator, Martin Radey (1880–1950), the grandfather of Leo Nolan, the narrator of *Shadow of Ashland*, is dead—but a family chronicle in which Martin explores and questions his relationships to his two wives and his children. His story, set in old Toronto, of one man's life is told in spare, imaginatively realized episodes. Completing the trilogy is *St Patrick's bed* (2001)—which is actually a sequel to *Shadow of Ashland* and is also a novel about family. Leo Nolan and his wife Jeanne want to have a child, though Jeanne has a teenaged son, Adam, who says he would like to see his biological father. Leo drives into the US in search of him—reliving his own family's past in the process—and accidentally meets Adam's father in Dayton, Ohio. Later Adam himself meets him and returns to tell Leo and his mother about the visit. At the end of the novel Leo and Jeanne spend a week in Ireland and a young man talks to them about St Patrick's Well—a symbol of fertility—and Bed, a long stone concave rectangle wide enough to hold one person. He tells them how to get there. 'Barking dogs' and 'Ashland, Kentucky', plus eight other stories by Green, are collected in *The woman who is the midnight wind* (1987).

Grenfell, Wilfred Thomason (1865–1940). Born at Parkgate, Cheshire, England, he attended Marlborough College in Wiltshire. In 1883 he entered medical school in the London Hospital, and in 1888 became a member of the Royal College of Surgeons and the Royal College of Physicians. While a medical student he wandered one evening into a meeting conducted by the American preacher D.L. Moody and came away 'feeling that I had crossed the Rubicon'. Determining on a life of service, in 1888 he started work with the medical section of the Nation Mission to Deep Sea Fishermen, serving in the North Atlantic from Iceland to the Bay of Biscay and becoming an expert sailor. In 1892 he travelled to Newfoundland to assess the need for medical services in the northern regions of the colony. He returned the following year with two doctors and two nurses and established at Battle Harbour the first hospital of what would be called the Labrador Medical Mission. His life thereafter was devoted to the advancement of his medical work in Newfoundland and Labrador. In 1912 the International Grenfell Association was formed to co-ordinate and promote Grenfell's activities. Grenfell also experimented with ways to improve the Newfoundland economy, emphasizing self-help, home industries, co-operatives, and a diversified approach to the development of resources. He was the recipient of many honours, including an honorary M.D. from Oxford University in 1907, and was knighted in 1927.

Grenfell was a brilliant publicist, and his numerous speeches, magazine articles, and books were part of his favourite activity of promoting and financing his mission. His books are somewhat repetitive and opinionated, but they are not without a certain liveliness and power, and their number reflects his popularity as a writer and the fame that came to surround him. Grenfell's books fall into three main categories. First, there are his factual, scientific, and promotional accounts of Labrador that include *Vikings of to-day; or, Life and medical work among the fishermen of Labrador* (London, 1895); *The romance of Labrador* (1934), an eloquent statement of his love for his adopted homeland; and *A Labrador logbook* (1938), one of his most engaging books, revealing Grenfell's idiosyncratic opinions and the extent of his miscellaneous reading. Second is the Labrador storybook—true tales of the people and of his experiences among them. The best, among many books, is *Adrift on an ice-pan* (1909, rpr. 1998)—first published as *A voyage on a pan of ice* (1908)—a hair-raising account of a brush with death that first brought Grenfell's name to the attention of the world; it can be read with genuine pleasure today. A third group of books by Grenfell comprises his many religious and autobiographical works. Though born an Anglican, Grenfell had been brought to something close to an evangelical conversion by Moody, and his religion was an untroubled, wholehearted commitment to a life of Christian action; he wrote many books displaying an unshakeable and simple faith.

See *The best of Wilfred Grenfell* (1990, rpr. 2001) and Ronald Rompkey, *Grenfell of Labrador: a biography* (1991).

Grey, Francis William (1860–1939). Born in England, he was the son of the Hon. Jane Stuart and Admiral the Hon. George Grey, grandson of Charles, the second Earl Grey, prime minister of England when the Reform Bill of 1831 was passed, and first cousin of the fourth Earl Grey, governor general of Canada from 1904 to 1911. It is not known when he came to North America, but he was teaching at Manhattan College, New York, in 1885 when

he married Jessie, daughter of Charles Octave Rolland, seigneur of Ste Marie de Monnoir in the Richelieu district; at this time he had probably converted to Roman Catholicism. From 1903 to 1904 he taught English literature and elocution at the University of Ottawa, from which he received in 1908 the degree of Doctor of Letters for his 'many literary productions ... in both prose and verse'. In 1905 he joined the Dominion Archives in a clerical position that was made permanent in 1908, and in 1912 he was appointed translator. He resigned in 1913 on a pension of $500 a year. In later years Grey lived in Edinburgh, Scotland, where he died. At the time of his death Grey was heir presumptive to the fifth Earl Grey (his great-grandson succeeded to the title in 1963). He is best remembered for his novel, *The curé of St. Philippe: a story of French-Canadian politics* (London, 1899), a realistic and entertaining portrait of a small Québec community, based on the Rolland seigneury, at the end of the nineteenth century. Wide-ranging in theme and characterization in the tradition of the nineteenth-century English novel, it incorporates the religious and political interests evident in Grey's later plays and essays. The establishment of a new parish in the Richelieu district, and events surrounding the 1896 federal election—in which, for the first time in Québec, the Rouges (Liberals) overcame the Bleus (Conservatives)—provide the central issues. English- and French-speaking Catholics and Protestants, clergymen, landowners, and local politicians all become involved. Religion, romance, and business intrigues are interwoven with English-French relations, the clergy's role in the community, and political corruption. An intrusive narrator—citing numerous literary figures (of whom Carlyle is the favourite) and maintaining a low-key and lightly humorous tone—fills in the background and comments on the issues. This light, ironic tone, along with the novel's accurate portrayal of the intricacies of the political and religious issues of late nineteenth-century Québec, recommend the novel to us today. See Rupert Schieder's introduction to the NEW CANADIAN LIBRARY edition of 1970.

Grey Owl. See Archibald Stansfeld BELANEY.

Grier, Eldon (b. 1917). Born in London, England, of Canadian parents (his father was a captain in the Canadian army), he was raised in Montreal and began his professional career as a painter. In 1945 he went to Mexico to study fresco painting with Alfredo Zalce, and was later apprenticed to Diego Rivera as a plasterer.

On his return to Montreal he became a teacher under Arthur Lismer at the Montreal Museum of Fine Arts. Between 1955 and 1965 he travelled extensively in Europe—he began to write poetry while living in Spain—and spent a number of winters in Mexico. His poetry collections include *A morning from scraps* (1955), *The year of the sun: poems* (1956), *The ring of ice* (1957), *Manzanillo & other poems* (1958), *A friction of lights* (1963), *Pictures on the skin* (1967), *The women of Quebec* (1969), *Selected poems: 1955–1970* (1971), *The assassination of colour* (1978), and *Collected poems* (2000). Grier—who in 1997 was made a Life Member of the LEAGUE OF CANADIAN POETS in recognition of his contribution to Canadian poetry—seemed to find his voice immediately, writing poems in the tradition of Modernism that were the product of critical intelligence and a highly visual imagination. Pleasure in language is the centre of his aesthetic experience, and his reflective poems are infused with the colloquial. He wrote many travel poems, of which those on Mexico are exceptionally powerful. The enormous impact of painting on his work is evident, not only in the numerous poems to painters and sculptors (Morandi, Marini, Picasso, Modigliani, Morrice, Giacometti) but in the frequency with which he approaches a poem like a still life: a 'ceramic' of images, light, and colour. Many poems are anecdotal, focusing on an emotionally fraught moment in which a character is deftly portrayed in a phrase or two, and there is a commitment to a belief in the will's capacity to reassert human values: tenderness, simplicity, beauty. Reading his work, one encounters a sensibility of deep generosity and compassion—a writer committed to new explorations of creativity as an antidote to the modern temptation to nostalgia. Grier now lives in Vancouver.

Griffin Poetry Prize. Canada's most generous poetry award was founded in 2000 by Scott Griffin, a wealthy automotive-parts manufacturer, who also started the Griffin Trust to raise public awareness of poetry's cultural importance (among the Trustees are Margaret ATWOOD, Michael ONDAATJE, and Carolyn Forché). The awards go to one Canadian and one international poet who writes in English, with each winner now receiving $75,000 and the nominees receiving $10,000. The Canadian winners to 2010 are:

2001
Anne CARSON. *Men in the off hours.*

2002
Christian BÖK. *Eunoia*

2003
Margaret AVISON. *Concrete and wild carrot.*

2004
Anne Simpson. *Loop.*

2005
Roo BORSON. *Short journey upriver toward Oishida.*

2006
Sylvia Legris. *Nerve squall.*

2007
Don MCKAY. *Strike / slip.*

2008
Robin BLASER. *The holy forest.*

2009
A.F. MORITZ. *The sentinel.*

2010
Karen Solie. *Pigeon.*

Grignon, Claude-Henri (1894–1976), who used the pseudonym 'Valdombre', was born in Sainte-Adèle, Québec. After being educated partly at the Collège Saint-Laurent, Montreal, and partly at home, he moved to Montreal and became a civil servant. From 1916 to 1939 he wrote articles for various newspapers, but returned to the Laurentians in 1936 and started a second career as a radio writer. As a journalist Grignon was a well-known polemicist and an earnest nationalist. But he is best known as the author of *Un homme et son péché* (1933), which was reprinted many times and translated by Yves Brunelle as *The woman and the miser* (1978). This novel represents, within a sociological perspective, the consequences in Québec of the economic crisis of the thirties, symbolized by the selfish miser, Séraphin Poudrier, and male domination of women, symbolized by the cruel treatment and ensuing death of Séraphin's wife. Its strength lies in its realistic style and in the portrayal of the sado-masochistic relationship of the lustful husband and the submissive wife. In 1936 Grignon published a bitter reply to those who saw only the sordid aspects of his novel, explaining how his book was based on actual events and real characters and scolding his contemporaries for their lack of imagination and their failure to write good 'regional' novels. Its plot was the basis of a highly successful radio series (1939–65) and television serial (1956–70) in Québec, and two motion pictures (1948 and 1950). Grignon became an Officer of the Order of Canada in 1969.

Grip (1873–94). A comic and satirical weekly published in Toronto between May 1873 and

Grip

December 1894, it was initiated by cartoonist John Wilson Bengough, with the financial support of publisher-bookseller Andrew Scott Irving. Beginning as a five-page weekly, of which two pages were advertisements, it eventually increased to eight pages. Bengough continued as editor and chief illustrator, with the exception of one year beginning 1892 when John Phillips Thompson took over; the weekly was then suspended for a year, after which Bengough resumed editorship.

With its humorous and satirical cartoons and writings on politics—local, provincial, and national—and on religion, literature, and society, *Grip* became Canada's *Punch*. It also published satiric verses, witty pseudonymous letters, columns such as 'Pen, Pencil, and Press' on writers and writing, and essays of social satire. While sometimes deriding aspects of the women's movement, *Grip* published Sarah Anne CURZON's blank-verse comedy *The sweet girl graduate* (1882), in which—although women were forbidden entry to university—a cross-dressing young woman graduates with top honours. Although purporting to be politically independent, *Grip* usually supported the Whig or reformist view. Its ridicule, through cartoons, of Sir John A. Macdonald and the Pacific Scandal, in its first years of publication, helped establish its popularity. In fact, so successful were these early satirical cartoons that in 1875 Bengough published *The Grip cartoons.... May 1873 to May 1874.* Although he remained *Grip's* main illustrator, sometimes providing illustrations under pseudonyms, other illustrators in later years included Charles W. Jeffreys, Tom Thomson, Arthur Lismer, and J.E.H. MacDonald. Stephen LEACOCK was a contributor in the paper's final year.

Grosskurth, Phyllis (b. 1924). Born Phyllis Langstaff in Toronto, Grosskurth was educated at the University of Toronto (B.A., 1946), the University of Ottawa (M.A., 1960), and the University of London (Ph.D., 1962). Combining in this period marriage, child-rearing, and a return to academic studies, in 1965 she joined the English department of the University of Toronto, of which she is now Professor Emeritus, and where she was appointed to the Humanities and Psychoanalytic Thought program in 1986. She is an Officer of the Order of Canada.

Grosskurth's dissertation for her Ph.D. was on 'The literary criticism of John Addington Symonds'; within two years she had published *John Addington Symonds: a biography* (1964, GGA; American title, *The woeful Victorian: a biography of John Addington Symonds*). Grosskurth returned to Symonds in her edition of *The memoirs of John Addington Symonds* (1984). Symonds' circle included Leslie Stephen, about whom she published a monograph, *Leslie Stephen* (1968), one of the Writers and Their Work series sponsored by the British Council. Grosskurth has also written two other brief monographs, *Gabrielle Roy* (1969) and *Margaret Mead: a life of controversy* (1989), among countless articles, reviews, and journalistic pieces that have appeared internationally. Her principal works, however, are dense, carefully researched and argued, indeed monumental biographical studies of three titans of psychoanalytic thought. In *Havelock Ellis: a biography* (1980) Grosskurth explored the life and writings of the famous Victorian sexologist, and makes clear that Ellis's first important work, *Sexual inversion*, included parts of two pamphlets by Symonds, a homosexual, that strove to eradicate cruel prejudices towards, and misinformation about, homosexuality (the two authors originally planned to collaborate). In *Melanie Klein: her world and her work* (1986), the first biography of Klein, the author of *The psychoanalysis of children* emerges in Grosskurth's view as *the* figure in child psychoanalysis, far eclipsing Anna Freud in theoretical vision and practice. (Nicholas Wright's play, *Mrs Klein*, which opened in London in 1988 and in New York in 1995, is based on Grosskurth's biography.) *The secret ring: Freud's inner circle and the politics of psychoanalysis* (1991, rpr. 1993) is a portrait of Freud's 'secret committee', which included, among others, Sandor Ferenczi, the great Hungarian who both encouraged and analyzed Melanie Klein; Karl Abraham, whose analysand she was in Berlin; and Ernest Jones. Grosskurth's position is that the 'subtext of psychoanalytic history is the story of how Freud manipulated and influenced his followers and successors', binding them to him in a secret society, and privileging each with the gift of a ring, making Freud indeed the 'ringmaster'. Yet for all Freud's undoubted power, the secret circle petered out in the 1920s amid acrimonious disputes. Grosskurth associates Freud with the tradition of nineteenth-century Romanticism, as if he saw himself as a Wagnerian hero. In *Byron: the flawed angel* (1997, rpr. 1998) she portrayed perhaps the greatest Romantic, returning to a life in literature with a portrait of a man who, like Freud, 'undid the values of the Enlightenment'. See Grosskurth's memoir, *Elusive subject: a biographer's life* (1999).

Groulx, Lionel-Adolphe (1878–1967). Born in Vaudreuil, Québec, Groulx was ordained a priest in 1903 and completed a doctorate in theology in Rome five years later. His appointment in 1915 to the chair of Canadian history at Université Laval (Montreal) launched him on a lifetime career of writing, speaking, and lecturing, during the course of which he became a major intellectual figure in Québec. Topics such as the linguistic rights of French-Canadian minorities, their role within Confederation, the importance to them of a 'homeland', and the essential differences between the two 'races' of Canada caused Groulx to be praised by some, denounced by others (including Louis Saint-Laurent and *Time*), and to be widely read. When he died, the Québec government proclaimed a day of national mourning and honoured him with a state funeral. Groulx's efforts to promote a 'national consciousness' among his compatriots led to controversy: at the height of the Conscription Crisis of 1917, his course on the origins of Confederation, which harshly criticized the founding fathers, brought demands from the university administration for an oath of loyalty to the Crown. As editor from 1921 to 1928 of a monthly review, *L'Action française* (which continued to be published under the title *L'Action nationale*), Groulx the polemicist remained in the vanguard of French-Canadian nationalism. As a historian Groulx was intensely interested in the French presence in North America and the lessons it could draw from the past in order to survive as a culturally autonomous group within the Canadian political reality. This preoccupation led to the publication of numerous books between 1918 and 1964. He wrote two novels, of which the best known is *L'appel de la race* (1922), translated as *The iron wedge* (1986) by J.S. Wood. Becoming a *cause célèbre* on publication, it is one of the rare Québécois novels to be set in Ontario, and reflects the tensions aroused in the French-Canadian community by Ontario's Regulation Seventeen (1912), which limited French instruction in francophone schools to one hour per day. For its apparently racist arguments and vocabulary, the novel seems shocking; but compared with the bitter and frequently specious arguments for eliminating French as the language of instruction in Franco-Ontarian schools that appeared in the Ontario press of the period, its language and rhetoric are quite restrained. Susan Mann Trofimenkoff's *Variations on a nationalist theme* (1973) offers a broad selection of

excerpts from Groulx's writings in English translation.

Grove, Frederick Philip (1879–1948). Born Felix Paul Greve in Radomno, Prussia, he was raised in Hamburg where his parents, Carl Edward and Bertha (Reichentrog) Greve, settled in 1881. He attended the Lutheran parish school at St Pauli, and later the classical Gymnasium in preparation for university. Family life apparently was not happy; his parents divorced. Early in Felix's first university year, at Bonn, his mother died and his life became unsettled. He lived extravagantly, borrowing large sums on various pretexts, mostly from a well-to-do fellow student named Herman Kilian. Greve left Bonn without graduating and spent a *Wanderjahr* in Italy. In 1902 he resumed his studies, this time at Munich, but again failed to complete his degree. That same year his first two books were privately published: *Wanderungen* (poems) and *Helena and Damon* (a verse-drama). To earn a precarious living, he began translating English authors, including Oscar Wilde, into German, and he wrote some impressionistic criticism, mostly on Oscar Wilde. Moving to Berlin, Greve formed a liaison with Elsa (Else) Plötz, wife of an architect; the two spent the winter of 1902–3 in Italy, again largely on money borrowed from Kilian under false pretences. On his return to Germany in 1903 Felix was charged by Kilian with fraud and spent a year in prison. Immediately on his release in June 1904 he travelled to Paris to meet André Gide, to whom he had previously written and whose works he was then translating. Gide's record of this first meeting—published as '*Conversation avec un Allemand*' in his *Oeuvres complètes* (1935)—portrays an elegant young man who, while confessing to compulsive mendacity (he was frank about his imprisonment), seemed at the same time to be soliciting some sort of encouragement from Gide. For the next five years—living with Elsa, first on the French coast at Étaples and later in Berlin—Greve worked feverishly to pay off his debts translating, from English to German, Wilde, Pater, Dowson, Browning, Wells, Meredith, and Swift; and Gide, Murger, Flaubert, Balzac, and LeSage from the French. His translations of Cervantes, supposedly from the Spanish, apparently used English models, as did his major project, a translation of the *Thousand and one nights*, which remained popular in Germany for half a century. Greve's original works from this period included at least one play, some pamphlets and articles on Oscar Wilde, a few poems and reviews, and two novels: *Fanny Essler* (1905), based on Elsa's sexually explicit letters, and *Maurermeister Ihles Haus* (1906). In the English translation of *Fanny Essler* (2 vols, 1984) by Christine Helmers, A.W. Riley, and Douglas O. Spettigue, Riley and Spettigue say in their introduction that the novel 'is very much of a piece with all of Grove's work'.

In 1907 Greve and Elsa marry in Berlin-Wilmersdorf. Despite this great productivity, Greve's effort to free himself from debt and make a living by his pen failed. He was in financial difficulties when, late in 1909, he faked his suicide and fled to the USA, where he was subsequently joined by Elsa. According to Elsa's autobiography, Greve attempted to farm in Kentucky for almost two years, when he abandoned her. He probably spent the next year as an itinerant labourer in the USA and Canada, a life he graphically described in *A search for America: an odyssey of an immigrant* (1927, NCL). Under the name Fred Grove he then became a schoolteacher in Manitoba, initially at Haskett and Winkler in German-speaking Mennonite districts. In 1914 he married Catherine Wiens (1892–1972). Their only daughter, Phyllis May, born in 1915, died in 1927. A son, Leonard Grove, was born in 1930. After teaching in several Manitoba communities, Grove retired in 1923 to devote himself to writing.

Grove's first book in English, *Over prairie trails* (1922, NCL), grew directly out of his weekend commutings in 1917, when he taught at Gladstone, Manitoba, and Catherine had a small school in the bush some thirty-five miles north. Though not entirely free of Grove's rather pedantic, amateur scientific observations, *Over prairie trails* is for many readers his most engaging and confident book. Along with *The turn of the year* (1923), it attracted critical attention for its loving descriptions of nature sustained by the narrative of his almost epic weekend struggles through fog and winter storms to reach home and the longed-for 'domestic island'. His first Canadian novel, *Settlers of the marsh* (1925, NCL), was considered too frank for public taste in the 1920s and did not sell well. It has gradually won recognition, however, as one of the first works of Prairie realism. A critical edition edited by Alison Calder was published in 2005. A measure of financial success came with publication of the partly autobiographical *A search for America*—one of the most compelling of many North American quasi-novels that record the suffering and disillusionment, as well as the idealism, of the immigrant—and of the naturalistic novel *Our*

daily bread (1928). Three cross-country tours under Canadian Club auspices in 1928 and 1929 brought Grove to prominence, and at the end of 1929 he moved to Ottawa as president of Ariston Press, a subsidiary of GRAPHIC PUBLISHERS. Selected addresses were published as *It needs to be said* (1929, rpr. 1982 edited by W.J. KEITH).

The Graphic venture was not successful. Grove believed that the true circumstances of the company, and the fact that he had no real control, had been concealed from him. (The experience was to bear fruit in *The master of the mill*, in which Sam Clark makes a similar discovery.) Grove left Ottawa after a year, bought a farm near Simcoe, Ontario, and tried raising dairy cattle. In the deepening economic depression of the thirties, the attempt failed. Forced to sell most of his land, Grove lived in near poverty for a decade, supported by his wife's private teaching. After *The yoke of life* (1930) and *Fruits of the earth* (1933, NCL) there were no books published until *Two generations* (1939). Sub-titled *A story of present-day Ontario*, this novel drew on Grove's dairying experience, but the triumph of Phil and Alice Patterson revealed a new buoyancy. Grove's last years brought belated recognition and the publication of his most thoughtful works: *The master of the mill* (1944, rpr. 1961), Grove's second Ontario novel, which records the growth of monopoly capitalism in the story of the Clark dynasty; *In search of myself* (1946, GGA), a fictionalized autobiography; and *Consider her ways* (1947, rpr. 2001), a sometimes pedantic, often humorous, surprisingly human, satire in which a colony of ants undertakes a study of mankind. Grove's novels—which abound in detail that is often maddeningly trivial and whose language is often stilted—are cumulatively effective in creating a sense of character in relation to milieu. This, rather than their larger purposes—what he called 'the tragic interpretation of life'—led critics to label Grove a 'naturalist' or 'realist'. Most of the novels portray dynamic, creative, but limited pioneer figures whose possessions turn to ashes with the alienation of family and community. In the two set in the Big Grassy Marsh district near Lake Manitoba, the young Swede Niels Lindstedt in *Settlers of the marsh* becomes a successful pioneer only to be ruined by a disastrous marriage, while *The yoke of life* (once described as 'a Canadian *Jude the Obscure*') records the early idealism, disillusionment, and suicide of Len Sterner. In Grove's two prairie novels the patriarch John Elliot of *Our daily bread* escapes being cared for by his unsympathetic children by returning to the abandoned homestead to die; *Fruits of the earth* chronicles Abe Spalding's rise to power and the resultant alienation of his family. Many of the Canadian protagonists—John Elliot, Abe Spalding, Sam Clark, Ralph Patterson, and the narrator of *In searth of myself*—are older men whose failures may be predetermined, but who nevertheless are driven to try to understand. In their recurrent phrase, 'I am I', character is seen as fate: these men are what they are, and at their best they are heroic and universal. Facing death, or watching their achievements slip away from them, they challenge the illusion of human progress, question the values of society, and ask where mankind has failed. Projecting himself in them, Grove transcended his own failures. In the emotional confrontations of *Settlers of the marsh* and *The yoke of life*, in the balanced complexities of *The master of the mill*, even in the allegorical *Consider her ways*, Grove wrestled with manifestations of his own psyche that may account for much in his work that earlier critics found unconvincing—such as the unexpectedly romantic elements that sometimes appear, like the unicorn Len Sterner fancies he sees in the Manitoba bush in *The yoke of life*.

Many of Grove's short stories were first published in a series in the Winnipeg *Tribune* (1926–7); some of them were closely related to, or excerpted from, the material of the western novels. 'Snow', first published in *Queen's Quarterly* (Spring, 1932), has been much anthologized. Though Grove was seldom happy in the shorter form, the Grove canon was expanded with the publication of a selection of the short stories, *Tales from the margin* (1971), edited by Desmond PACEY. In 1939, while he was writing *The master of the mill*, Grove amused himself by writing a lively novella for boys called *The adventure of Leonard Broadus*, for which he drew on his young son, himself, his family life, and the Ontario setting in which he was living. It was published in twelve instalments in *The Golden Boy*, a United Church journal, beginning in April 1940; and was republished in *Canadian Children's Literature: A Journal of Criticism and Review*, no. 27/28, 1982, with two articles, and a note on the manuscript, by Mary Rubio.

Scrutinizing Grove's past in order to date the Grove canon, D.O. Spettigue could find no foundation for either the European childhood or the American years as Grove had described them, and this insight led to a

period of research and the publication by Spettigue of *FPG: the European years* (1973), which revealed Grove as Greve, and Grove's autobiography *In search of myself* as a curious blend of fiction and distorted fact. Margaret Stobie's *Frederick Philip Grove* (1973) examined critically the teacher/author as he had appeared to his Manitoba contemporaries. Despite gaps, these books—together with the *Letters* (1976) edited by Desmond Pacey (which includes the German correspondence)—made it possible thirty-odd years ago to relate Grove/Greve the man to the writings, both late and early. A significant biography published in 2001 is *F.P. Grove in Europe and Canada: translated lives* by Klaus Martens, which has many unfamiliar illustrations. See also Paul I. Hjartarson and D.O. Spettigue, eds, *Baroness Elsa* (1992) and *Baroness Elsa: gender, Dada, and everyday modernity: a cultural biography* (2002) by Irene Gammel, a professor of English at the University of Prince Edward Island. This is a long biography of Greve's Elsa Plötz, an eccentric and colourful woman who was a painter and sculptor—in the US she fell in love with Marcel Duchamp and was part of the New York Dada scene—who in 1913 married a German baron, Leopold von Freytag-Loringhoven (he fought in the First World War and later committed suicide).

Guernica Editions. Founded in Montreal, by Antonio D'ALFONSO in 1978, Guernica Editions has been committed to giving voice to issues and questions about ethnicity, identity, and the politics of ethnicity and gender, both French and English. The press has published the work of well-known Québécois writers, both in French and in English translation, and especially writers of Italian origin, including Marco Fraticelli, Filippo Salvatore, Marco MICONE, Fulvio Caccia, Mary MELFI, Pasquale Verdicchio, and Penny Petrone. Literary and cultural critics—such as Joseph Pivato, Francesco Loriggio, Enoch Padolsky, and D'Alfonso—have examined the significance of identity and ethnicity, and of minority writing in Canada. In 2008 Guernica published their substantial thirtieth-anniversary catalogue—which includes three indexes: of yearly publications, authors, and titles—a period in which they published 'over 450 titles and 1000 authors'.

Guèvremont, Germaine (1893–1968). Germaine Grignon was born in Saint-Jérôme, Québec, and educated there and in Lachine and Toronto. She married Hyacinthe

Guèvremont

Guèvremont in 1916 and moved to Sorel, Québec, where she started her career as a journalist on the staff of *Le Courrier de Sorel* (1928–35); after she moved to Montreal in 1935 she worked for the Montreal *Gazette*. With the publication of her first novel, *Le survenant*, in Québec (1945) and Paris (1947), Guèvremont became well known. Her second novel, *Marie-Didace* (1947), was to form part of a trilogy (the third was never completed). Both novels were translated into English by Eric Sutton and published together as *The outlanders* (Toronto, 1950, GGA; rpr. 1978, NCL) and *Monk's reach* (London, 1950). The novels concern the Beauchemin family and depict the disintegrating rural world in a spare, highly realistic manner. *Le survenant* recounts the sudden intrusion of a stranger into a tight family circle and the consequences upon the social organization of the community. *Marie-Didace* deals with the extinction of the male line of the family by the birth of the title character.

Gunnars, Kristjana (b. 1948). Born in Reykjavik, Iceland, Gunnars has lived in Canada since 1969. She holds a B.A. from Oregon State University (1972) and an M.A. from the University of Regina (1977); she was professor of English at the University of Alberta from 1996 to 2003. Gunnars has published seven books of poetry—*Settlement poems*, I and II (1980, 1981), *One-eyed moon maps* (1981), *Wake-pick poems* (1982), *The night workers of Ragnarök* (1985), *Carnival of longing* (1989), *Exiles among you* (1996)—and three short-story collections: *The axe's edge* (1983), *The guest house and other stories* (1992), and *Any day but this* (2004). Her publications also include four novels: *The prowler* (1989), *The substance of forgetting* (1992), *The rose garden: reading Marcel Proust* (1996), and *Night train to Nykobing* (1998). *Zero hour* (1991) is a compact and poetic account of Gunnars' grief over her father's death.

Postmodern theories of literature and storytelling are often explored in Gunnars' fiction, and all her writing probes the ambiguities of meaning, the problems and process of memory, and the character of truth and reality. Gunnars is known primarily as a poet, but she struggles against the boundaries of genre. In fact, classification of her work into distinct genres like novel/poem/autobiography is not entirely convincing. Gunnars' books of poetry are collections of poem cycles—carefully arranged groups of poems relating to the same topic; and most of her novels are really prose poems, written in stark, elliptical language with a rich layering

of image. *The prowler*, which has 167 chapters, most shorter than one page, tells the story of a nameless girl growing up in Iceland, Denmark, and North America, struggling with an identity crisis brought on by internal and external repression. *The substance of forgetting* is about a woman living alone in the Okanagan Valley who has embarked on the process of recreating her world and herself. *The rose garden* was published as non-fiction, but is in fact an amalgam of memoir, theory, and fiction, outlining the personal and scholarly insights gleaned by a Canadian literary scholar during a study leave in Germany. *Night train to Nykobing* begins when a love-lorn woman boards the night train in Denmark and begins a letter to her lover she does not intend to send, while at the same time reflecting on her affair and her love. A hard book to relate to is *Any day but this* (2004), a collection of twelve short stories. To begin with, there is no story with the book's title. The first one, 'Directions in which we move', is about Arne Ibsen, a Norwegian who teaches sociology at the University of Alberta. We read about his first house, his wife Gro, who hated being in Edmonton, about two childhood traumas, when he had an eardrum pierced and when he had his adenoids removed. Gro leaves him for Norway and at the end Arne watches her plane fly away. In 'Dreaming of the Coliseum' Karl is a poet about to give a reading in the Vancouver Public Library. His family background and interests are described while he's waiting for the reading to begin, along with the dress of every woman in the audience of ten. The description of the reading itself is a mild satire. 'Code pink and denim' is about Elly, who teaches in a university, her conversations with her colleague Anthony Felix (who is operated on for prostate cancer, whose wife dies), and about her short day, Wednesday, when she ruminates about herself, the quiet life, and reads poems by her beloved poet George Herbert. 'She had come to a point in life where things were not connecting. She had to work on it.' Many pages pass about books she's read when—with the phone beside her—'She reached for the receiver.' 'Pleasures liberty cannot know', more of a story, begins with an amusing episode when five-year-old Carla George falls several times while playing hopscotch on the broken concrete of the sidewalk—the last time she injured her arm and blood flowed. She insisted that her mother phone the mayor's office. Her mother got a secretary; Carla spoke to her and was given an appointment the next day. She went to the mayor's office with her brother and mother, the mayor greeted her warmly (photographers were present), and, at Carla's insistence, phoned the works department to have the pavement fixed. 'You'll go far, Carla' was the response of friends and neighbours: in the following descriptions of Carla's life we see that she did not go far. But at the end, when she's living with the much older Don, a carpenter, she pulls out a scrapbook with a clipping in the *Vancouver Sun* about her visit to the mayor's office. Laughing, Don reads aloud the exchange between the child Carla and the mayor. 'Don said, shaking her shoulders affectionately, "You sure haven't changed much."' The titles of these four stories mysteriously bear no apparent relation to the texts. (In the second story the word Coliseum appears once in a parenthesis, referring to the architecture of the Vancouver Public Library.) And the word 'stories' does not strictly apply to these narratives—made up of a loose series of arbitrary descriptions; they lack a *line* that clearly relates the beginning and the ensuing text with the end, as in a real story.

The eight essays in *Strangers at the door: writers and the act of writing* (2004) grew out of the decade Gunnars spent teaching creative writing at the University of Alberta. She edited *Transient questions: new essays on Mavis Gallant* (2005).

See *Kristjana Gunnars: essays on her works* (2004) by Monique Tschofen.

Gurik, Robert (b. 1932). Born in Paris of Hungarian parents, he came to Canada in 1951, and in 1957 received his professional engineer's certification from the Institut Polytechnique de Montréal. While working as an engineer in and around Montreal, he had his first plays produced by little theatres and in regional competitions of the Dominion Drama Festival. In 1967 *Le pendu* was judged the best play and the best Canadian play at the Dominion Drama Festival finals held in Newfoundland. He left engineering work in 1972 to devote himself to the theatre, and became one of the most prolific and most produced Québec playwrights in the 1960s and 1970s. Only three of his plays are available in English. *Api 2967* (1967), *Le pendu* (1967), and *Le procès de Jean Baptiste M.* (1972), which have been particularly popular both in Québec and abroad, were translated as *Api 2967* (1974) by Marc F. Gélinas, *The hanged man* (1972) by Philip London and Laurence Bérard, and *The trial of Jean-Baptiste M.* (1974) by Alan Van Meer. These three plays illustrate Gurik's preoccupation with runaway technology and

consumerism, authoritarian regimes, the hardships of the poor, and the naivety of those who either refuse to accept the status quo or actively try to change it. *Api 2967* is a clever and amusing play set in a futuristic world of test-tube babies, food in capsule form, long but sterile and perfectly controlled life, television monitors watching everyone, and dictionaries from which words describing such outmoded concepts as love and passion have been removed. Only the two main characters, the professor and his female research assistant, resist the system and discover and enjoy some hitherto unknown and forbidden pleasures before they perish. The hero of *The hanged man*, Yonel, is a poor young beggar and former miner who is apparently, but not really, blind. With his father's help he devises a money-making scheme: he will pretend to plan to hang himself and then try to sell a piece of 'hangman's rope'—a popular if somewhat macabre good-luck charm. At first he makes money and seems to help luckless members of his entourage; but when they learn that the hanging is not to occur and that he means to establish organizations to help the world's poor, they force him to hang himself. The play ends with a chorus, sung by a group of children playing in the background, telling how nothing has improved in the village since Yonel's death. Gurik's plays not only criticize those who would impose their will on society; they also offer little hope for those who conform to, and profit from, the consumer society, as in *The trial of Jean-Baptiste M.*: the name, which evokes '*Monsieur tout le monde*' and Québec's patron saint, suggests a Québécois Everyman, in this case one hoping to get and keep a steady job. Though handicapped by lack of education and an unwarranted prison record, he is finally hired by a big industrial firm in Montreal, but his efficiency and inventiveness create unrest and jealousies and he is eventually fired. Frustrated by the injustice, he shoots and kills several of his former bosses. The events leading up to the shooting alternate with scenes of Jean-Baptiste's grotesque trial in which witness, judge, and jury are played by the same group of unfeeling and hysterical individuals. In the end Jean-Baptiste is convicted of both the murder and the more serious crime, in the jury's eyes, of disobeying society's laws, thereby interfering with orderly production and consumption.

Gustafson, Ralph (1909–95). Ralph Barker Gustafson was born in Lime Ridge, in the Eastern Townships of Québec, to a Swedish father and an English mother. After graduating

Gustafson

in 1929 from Bishop's University he stayed on to do an M.A., writing a thesis on Keats and Shelley, before going to Keble College, Oxford, where he took a second B.A. in 1933. After a short period of teaching at a private school in Brockville, Ontario, he went back to England, where he published his first two collections of poetry. With the approach of war Gustafson returned to Canada, and then moved on to New York City, where he spent the war years working for the British Information Services. After the war he continued to live in New York, where he freelanced as a writer and music critic. In 1963 he accepted an offer to return to Bishop's University as a professor of English and poet in residence. He and his wife moved to North Hatley, Québec, where he spent the remainder of his life. He retired from teaching in 1979.

Gustafson's first important book of poetry was *Rivers among rocks* (1960), the first of his books to be published in Canada. *Rocky Mountain poems* (1960) introduced his longlasting passion for travel. In *Sift in a hourglass* (1966) and *Ixion's wheel* (1969) the language of his poetry becomes increasingly simplified and colloquial, to its great benefit, though it remains highly allusive. His command of cultural reference is always impressive, and a close reading inevitably discovers the influence of music in his formal procedures. *Selected poems* (1972) was followed by *Fire on stone* (1974, GGA). Although already sixty-five years old at that time, Gustafson was not only entering on the most productive twenty years of his career, he was also only at the mid-point in his development as a poet. *Gradations of grandeur* (1982) is a book-length work, and *Directives of autumn* (1984) is the first of four final collections that contain some of Gustafson's most moving and accomplished poetry. *Configurations at midnight* (1992) is a poetic autobiography. Two versions of a reworked selected poems appeared in the 1980s, *The moment is all: selected poems 1944–83* (1983) and *At the ocean's verge* (1984), which was published in the United States. The *Collected poems* appeared initially in two volumes in 1987, to which a third volume was added in 1994. *Visions fugitive* (1996), a collection of new poems, was a posthumous publication, as was *Selected poems* (2001), which is a new version of his selected poems made by Gustafson himself; it has an introduction by Bruce Whiteman.

The poetry is identifiably modernist in tone and form, and the influence of Ezra Pound and Wallace Stevens is evident in Gustafson's mature work. He had close ties to John SUTHERLAND and the group of poets who published in FIRST STATEMENT and NORTHERN REVIEW, but he felt most akin to poets like Robert FINCH, Robert FORD, and others whose formal affinities were more conservative than those of the *First Statement* group. Gustafson's poetry ultimately stands somewhat apart from the recognized strains of modernist and postmodern Canadian poetry, perhaps because of his long residence outside the country.

Gustafson was the editor of one of the first critical anthologies of Canadian poetry, the *Anthology of Canadian poetry (English)* (1942), which he compiled for Penguin Books during the war. Out of this came the larger and largely rethought *Penguin book of Canadian verse* (1958), which was several times revised and reissued and contributed to the formation of a canon of good and great poets that had a long and important influence. Gustafson's correspondence with poet W.W.E. ROSS, edited by Bruce Whiteman and published in 1984 as *A literary friendship*, documents the editing of the anthologies and contains much insightful criticism. His light verse, collected in *The celestial corkscrew and other strategies* (1979), also contains literary and social criticism obliquely rendered. Gustafson's short stories were collected in *Vivid air* (1980) and his selected essays in *Plummets* (1986). He was made a Member of the Order of Canada in 1992. See Dermot McCarthy, *Ralph Gustafson and his works* (1989).

Gutteridge, Don (b. 1937). Donald George Gutteridge was born in the village of Point Edward, Lambton County, Ontario, and in 1960 graduated in English from the University of Western Ontario. After teaching high school for seven years, he became assistant professor of education at Western, where he is now Professor Emeritus of Education. He won the President's Medal of the University of Western Ontario for *Death at Quebec* (1971), a poetry collection of monologues by historical figures (including the Jesuits in Huronia) and village poems. This work came between *The village within: poems towards a biography* (1970) and *Saying grace: an elegy* (1972), both of which show his inclination to stitch together his own life with that of his village and country. His talent for mythologizing history shows best in *Riel: a poem for voices* (1968) that is in part a documentary collage in which letters, newspaper and diary entries, political proclamations, and posters are mixed with long-lined monologues and welded into a single metaphor. In *Coppermine: the quest for North* (1973), Samuel Hearne's journals are the source for a horrific, sometimes surreal, Canadian version of the El Dorado myth. *Borderlands* (1975) uses violence, irony, and a skilful interplay of voices to recreate John Jewitt's two-year enslavement by the Nootka. More political is *Tecumseh* (1976). The first two parts of the poetry collection *Something more miraculous* (2004) are described as the life of the poet as grandfather. The title poem, contained in the miscellany of the third part, begins 'When I was seven and a bit,/ furious in the fever that shook/me like Pentecost palsy/and woke, later, lucky/to be Lazarus.... Something more miraculous/than me' brought him back.

Gutteridge passed to personal themes in a series of works entitled Time is the Metaphor, written in a demotic style and beginning with the comic and sometimes poignant novel *Bus-ride* (1974), set in a small Ontario town in March 1939, which focuses on a Junior B hockey player bewildered by the process of growing up. In *The true history of Lambton County* (1977), a long poem with multiple voices, the poet assembles an album of his own history and childhood memories that are droll, romantic, and tragic. *All in good time* (1981), a small-scale comic novel, takes up some of the characters from *Bus-ride* at a later period, and, using sports, politics, and sex, tells a touching and ironic story of a people on the edge of winter and war. *God's geography* (1982), a collection of poems that juxtapose village memories and childhood with later experience and world events, shows that *Time is the metaphor* forms a narrative of the past from which the poet evolved. The novels *St. Vitus dance* (1987) and *Shaman's ground* (1988), subtitled Volumes One and Two of *Lily's story*, explore with conviction and humour the impact of historical events on the individual fortunes of the protagonist, Lily Fairchild, and the evolving communities of Point Edward and Sarnia between 1840 and 1922. The struggles of a working-class family in Point Edward in 1936 are portrayed in *Bewilderment: a novel of the Great Depression* (2000). *How the world began* (1991) concludes *Time is the metaphor* and provides a foundation for earlier books in the series through a fictional representation of Lambton County pioneers buffeted by the War of 1812. *The exiled heart (selected narratives 1968–1982)* (1986) documents exploration and exile in poems and journal entries from five earlier collections. In *Love in the wintertime* (1990) and *Flute music in the cello's belly* (1997), richly allusive poems celebrate connection in family, friendship, and creativity. *Still magical*

(2007) pays a graceful tribute to old age: 'beholding the manger and the Son,/as the Three Kings did,/believing, like me,/in a world still magical. ('Morning'). A profound shift to the personal, with a focus on intense and immediate aspects of experience, marks Gutteridge's recent poetry and fiction. The paired novels *Summer idyll* (1993) and *Winter's descent* (1996) recreate with precision and evocative physicality the worlds of absence and discovery that mark a boy's transition from childhood to adolescence in the fatherless years of the Second World War in south-western Ontario.

Gutteridge combines wit and history—his knowledge of Toronto and surroundings in 1837, the year of the Rebellion—in his three absorbing Marc Edwards mysteries. In *Turncoat* (2003) Edwards, an ensign in the British army posted to Toronto, is accustoming himself to the coarse ways there when Lieutenant Governor John Colborne sends him to a hamlet on Lake Ontario to investigate the murder of Colborne's personal spy. This was followed by *Solemn vows* (2003) and *Vital secrets* (2007), set in Toronto when Marc's friend and colleague Rick Hilliard is accused of murder.

Gutteridge is also the author of *Teaching English: theory and practice from kindergarten to grade twelve* (2000).

Guy, Ray (b. 1939). Raymond Guy was born in Come By Chance, Newfoundland, and spent his childhood in nearby Arnold's Cove; he was educated there, did a final year of high school on Bell Island, then a major mining town, and went on to Memorial University of Newfoundland ('one of the most sickening experiences of my life') and Ryerson Polytechnical Institute in Toronto. He graduated from Ryerson in 1963 with a diploma in journalism and began writing for the St John's *Evening Telegram*, first as a reporter and latterly as a daily columnist. It was in the *Telegram*, which he quit in 1973 but to which Guy returned sporadically in subsequent years, that his best-known pieces were published—brilliant, scorching attacks on the faltering Liberal administration of Premier J.R. Smallwood and nostalgic items on his own early years in Arnold's Cove, termed by Guy 'Juvenile outharbour delights'—these personal columns have a charm and warmth that set them apart from Guy's other work. Watching Smallwood operate appears to have permanently soured him on politics, but he continued to write mordantly and fearlessly on the subject, and became more and more

Guy

outspoken. His *Telegram* columns in 1995–6 featured bitter, though not undeserved, assaults on the Roman Catholic church. One of the best-known and most widely admired Newfoundland writers, Guy lived on his wits in St John's: as a journalist, freelance columnist, radio and TV commentator, and principal actor (Jack, the crotchety boarder) in the local CBC-TV series 'Up at Ours' (1978–80). His columns have been collected in: *You may know them as sea urchins, ma'am* (1975; six printings by 1978; rev. edn 1985)—the joke is that sea urchins are sometimes called whore's eggs in Newfoundland; *That far greater bay* (1976; rev. edn 1985)—the bay is Placentia Bay, the location of Arnold's Cove; *Beneficial vapours* (1981); *This dear and fine country* (1985)—the country is Newfoundland; and *Ray Guy's best* (1987).

Gwyn, Richard (b. 1934). Richard John Philip Jermy Gwyn was born in Bury St Edmunds, England, raised in China and India, and educated at Stonyhurst College and the Royal Military Academy, Sandhurst. Gwyn immigrated to Canada in 1954; four years later he married the writer Sandra Fraser. (Sandra GWYN died in 2000 and he married Carol Bishop in 2005.) He worked as a journalist with United Press International, Thomson Newspapers, Maclean-Hunter Business Publications, *Time*, and the Canadian Broadcasting Corporation; subsequently he served as assistant to federal minister Eric Kierans and as a divisional director in the federal Department of Communications. From 1973 to the present he has been a nationally syndicated columnist for the *Toronto Star*, based in Ottawa (1973–85), London (1986–92), and Toronto (from 1992); for TVOntario's program *Studio 2* he has been a longtime foreign-affairs panelist. Gwyn was made Chancellor of St Jerome's University, University of Waterloo, and was appointed an Officer of the Order of Canada in 2002.

All Gwyn's bestselling books are informed about Canadian political matters, concerned with social issues, abreast of developments in philosophical thought, and are serious contributions to their subjects. Their sense of nationalism is tempered by a pragmatism in keeping with the times. Gwyn's first book was *The shape of scandal: a study of a government in crisis* (1965), an examination of the Lucien Rivard affair, concerning a convicted drug smuggler whose escape from prison created a scandal for the Liberal government, with charges of bribery being made; there was a Royal Commission and the Minister of Justice resigned. This was followed by *Smallwood: the unlikely revolutionary* (1968; rev. edn 1972), *The northern magus: Pierre Elliott Trudeau and Canadians* (1980), *The 49th paradox: Canada in North America* (1985), and *Nationalism without walls: the unbearable lightness of being Canadian* (1995; rev. edn 1996). *John A. The man who made us: the life and times of John A. Macdonald: Volume One 1815–1967* (2007, rpr. 2008) in 2008 won the ($25,000) Charles Taylor Prize for excellence in literary non-fiction. Gwyn said he wanted to write this biography because 'there had been no biography for over half a century', alluding to Donald CREIGHTON's two-volume work. Gwyn's jurors lauded Gwyn's writing from a twenty-first-century perspective 'while painting for his readers a vivid image of nineteenth-century Canada: its society, customs, character and politics.' He has received numerous other awards, including a 1985 National Magazine Award shared jointly with Sandra Gwyn. For Fitzhenry & Whiteside's long series of very short biographies (eighty pages) *The Canadians*, Gwyn wrote *Pierre Elliott Trudeau* (2006).

Gwyn, Sandra (1935–2000). Born Alexandra Fraser in St John's, Newfoundland, she graduated from Dalhousie University, Halifax (B.A., 1955) and three years later married the journalist Richard GWYN. She served as an information officer with the National Gallery of Canada, as an editor of *Canadian Art*, and as a freelance writer and researcher for *Time*, *Maclean's*, the Canadian Broadcasting Corporation, the Royal Commission on the Status of Women, and the Federal Task Force on Information. She worked as Ottawa editor of *Saturday Night* (1975–80), and then as contributing editor (1980–7). While living in Ottawa she did considerable research at the National Archives to write two remarkable historical studies that are rich in social and personal detail. *The private capital: ambition and love in the age of Macdonald and Laurier* (1984, GGA) was dramatized by CBC-TV and shown in Jan. 1990. Its successor, *Tapestry of war: a private view of Canadians in the Great War* (1992, rpr. 1993), was written with passion and compassion. Gwyn received other awards, sharing a 1985 National Magazine Award jointly with Richard Gwyn, and was appointed an Officer of the Order of Canada in May 2000. The Winterset Award for Newfoundland writers, named for her childhood home, has been established in her honour.

H

Hacking, Ian (b. 1936). Born in Vancouver, he was educated at the University of British Columbia (B.A., 1956), and at Cambridge University (B.A., 1958, Ph.D., 1962). He taught philosophy at UBC (1964–9); at Cambridge (1969–74)—he is an honorary Fellow of Trinity College; at Princeton University (1974–82); and was a professor at the University of Toronto from 1983, teaching in the philosophy department and in its Institute for History and Philosophy of Science and Technology. Since 2003 he has been University Professor Emeritus. In the spring of 2000 Hacking became the first English-speaking scholar to be elected to the Collège de France, Paris (founded in 1529)—which, in a 1995 publication (below) he refers to in passing as 'the most prestigious academic site in France'—with the requirement an inaugural address and thirteen weekly lectures (in French) in the spring of 2001. He now holds the chair of philosophy and history of scientific concepts at the Collège. In 2004 he was made a Companion of the Order of Canada.

Over more than three decades Hacking has written numerous books, covering many fields and disciplines, that have been influential and are widely cited. In describing his 'great project'—'How We Make Up People', how humans categorize and see themselves—in an interview (*Toronto Star*, 21 May 2000), he said: 'I'm unusual in that I move from subject to subject. Most [philosophers] don't. I have this extraordinary curiosity about all aspects of the natural and human world, the interaction between physical sciences and the social sciences.' His books include *Logic of statistical inference* (1965); *A concise introduction to logic* (1972); *Leibnitz and Descartes: proof and eternal truths* (1973); *The emergence of probability: a philosophical study of early ideas about probability, induction and statistical inference* (1975, 2nd edn 2006); *Why does language matter in philosophy?* (1975), based on lectures he gave at Cambridge in 1972 and repeated in 1973; *Representing and intervening: introductory topics in the philosophy of natural science* (1983); *The taming of chance* (1990); *Rewriting the soul: multiple personality and the sciences of memory* (1995, rpr. 1998); *Mad travellers: reflections on the reality of mental illness* (1998); and *The social construction of what?* (1999). As an example of his philosophical investigations of far-reaching subjects, *Rewriting the soul* is an erudite (but clear and readable) examination of the concept of multiple personality and its claimed origin in child abuse (we are reminded that in earlier centuries there was 'not much of an idea of the child, and still less of child abuse'), mostly among women, and of the prime role of memory, 'a key to the soul'—which is 'an idea that involves character, reflective choice, and self-understanding, among much else.' ('A soul is a pilgrimage through life.') Among his final thoughts, about memory and sexual harassment, is the statement: 'As a cautious philosopher, I am inclined to say that many retroactive redescriptions are neither definitely correct nor definitely incorrect.' The four lectures and supplementary material in *Mad travellers* discuss a long-forgotten psychiatric epidemic—that of fugueurs, people (mostly men) who are impelled to travel obsessively and uncontrollably—and focus on the first fugueur, Albert Dadas, who in the 1880s travelled to Algeria, Moscow, and Constantinople, remembering nothing of these journeys. Doctors' reports on Dadas's case when he was admitted into a Bordeaux hospital in 1886 (notably the records of Dr Philippe Tissié, who published a thesis, *Les aliénés voyageurs* in 1887), set off an epidemic of similar cases, until 1909. It became known as a transient mental illness, 'an illness that appears at a time, in a place, and later fades away.' 'When is traveling mad? When do the mad express their insanity by travel? When is the madness of travellers taken to be a kind of madness in its own right?' And was this a real disorder? These are a few of the questions taken up in this thought-provoking work, which provides rich historical background for an obscure outbreak of bizarre behaviour, the fugue, sheds light on the nature of hysterical fugue (it is not considered a real mental illness), and includes passages from Tissié's writings, among them his observations of Albert. In *Mad travellers* Hacking refers to the 'fashionable phrase' social construction, and says in passing: 'In a forthcoming set of lectures, *The social construction of what?* I state what, in my opinion, is useful and what is deplorable in the idea of social construction.' The book of this title, partly based on these lectures, is grounded in the much-discussed conflict between social constructionists who see knowledge as a product of society, and the scientific view of knowledge as quite distinct

Hacking

from the social domain; it upholds the balanced view that recognizes the importance of historical and cultural settings in interpreting subjects and discoveries, while emphasizing the obvious validity of underlying scientific truths. To clarify the meaning of construction, it begins with a long list of things that have been said to be socially constructed (among them emotions, homosexual culture, mind, nature, technological systems, women refugees), and addresses in some detail the subjects of madness (biological or constructed?), child abuse, weapons research, rocks (dolomite, touching on the philosophy of science), and interpretations of Captain Cook. These chapters also look at issues surrounding the debate about constructionism. The *what* of the book's title is applied to applications of the concept of social construction. For example, it is the *idea* of child abuse, and of women refugees, that is socially constructed. Under the heading Women Refugees, Hacking asks: '*What* is said to be constructed, if someone speaks of the social construction of gender?' This is discussed, along with the shorthand word 'idea' and different forms and notions of constructionism. The book is a philosopher's informal (sometimes chatty) and illuminating discourse on the nature of knowledge. *An introduction to probability and inductive logic* (2001) is a highly praised textbook, published in a large format, that considers such topics as decision theory, Bayesianism, frequency ideas, and the philosophical problem of induction. About the essays in *Historical ontology* (2002), written between 1993 and 2001, Hacking says: 'Two closely connected themes predominate: some novel ways in which a philosopher can make use of history, and my uses of the early "archaeological" work of Michel Foucault.'

In August 2009 Hacking learned that the parliament of Norway had awarded him the Holberg International Memorial Prize ($750,000), honouring his achievement in changing human understanding of key concepts and their implications in the natural and social sciences.

Haig-Brown, Roderick (1908–76). Born in Lansing, Sussex, England, Roderick Langmore Haig-Brown was educated at Charterhouse, where his grandfather had been headmaster. He left school and immigrated to Washington State in 1926. The next year he moved to British Columbia, where he worked as a logger, trapper—he sometimes shot cougars for bounty money—fisherman, and tourist guide. He went to England in 1929

and wrote his first novel there; homesick for B.C., he returned in 1931. Appointed magistrate in the village of Campbell River on Vancouver Island in 1934, he served as a provincial court judge for thirty-three years, retiring the year before his death. During the Second World War he was a captain, then major, in the Canadian army, and was briefly on loan to the RCMP. Haig-Brown was director of the National and Provincial Parks Association of Canada, a member of the International Pacific Salmon Commission, served on three federal electoral boundaries commissions, and was chancellor of the University of Victoria. He also fought publicly, and often with little support, against hydro and industrial development in B.C. for harming the natural environment. His home, Above Tide, on a twenty-acre farm near Campbell River, is now a Heritage House.

Haig-Brown wrote twenty-five books—including adult novels, essay collections, and children's books—but he is best known as a nature writer, specializing in fishing and natural history. As an outdoorsman who was also a fine prose stylist, he was skilled at observing creatures in natural settings, especially 'the strangeness and beauty of the fish, their often visible remoteness, their ease in another world, the mystery of their movements and habits and whims.' He wrote the first item in the first issue of CANADIAN LITERATURE, about the writer in isolation. His first publications were *Silver: the life story of an Atlantic salmon* (1931, rpr. 1989), written when he was twenty-three; *Pool and rapid: the story of a river* (1932, rpr. with illustrations in a limited edn, 1997); *Panther* (1934; rpr. 2007. American title, *Ki-yu: story of a panther*); *The western angler* (1939), which describes the Pacific salmon and western trout and established Haig-Brown as a fishing authority; and *Timber* (1942, rpr. 1993), a novel about unionizing a lumber camp (English edn, *The tall trees fall*, 1943). *Return to the river* (1941) is about a Chinook salmon in the Columbia river. These were followed by some of his best books: *A river never sleeps* (1946, rpr. 1991); two outstanding novels for young people, *Starbuck Valley winter* (1946, rpr. 2002), and its sequel *Saltwater summer* (1948, rpr. 2000); and *Measure of the year* (1950, rpr. 1991), an evocative book of essays describing the cycle of Haig-Brown's year as writer, magistrate, fisherman, and community leader. He then began his best-known work, a tetralogy: *Fisherman's spring* (1951, rpr. 1988), *Fisherman's winter* (1954, rpr. 1990), *Fisherman's summer* (1959), and *Fisherman's fall* (1964, rpr. 1987). *Winter* is perhaps the best, combining satisfying descriptive writing with practical information for anglers, as he describes a three-month fishing trip to Chile and Argentina in 1950. *Summer*, a collection of angling adventures, stresses conservation. *Spring*, which is about the essence of sport angling and the fisherman's relationship to the fish, the river, and the natural world, captures the quiet philosophy of Walton's *Compleat angler*. *Fall*, about Haig-Brown's favourite angling season, gives an excellent account of the migratory cycles of the Pacific salmon and steelhead trout; in the remarkable final chapter, scuba diving in his river, he identifies himself too strongly with the fish to catch and kill them. This is probably his last important book. The four books have been combined in one volume, *The seasons of a fisherman* (2000).

Other works include *On the highest hill* (1955), a novel; *Captain of the Discovery* (1959), a biography of Captain George Vancouver; *The farthest shores* (1960), a history of B.C. that began as a series of radio dramatizations; and *The whale people* (1962, rpr. 2003), a juvenile portraying the life and hunting methods of the Nootka (Nuu-chah-nulth) who went out in canoes to hunt whales. Haig-Brown's daughter, Valerie, edited a three-volume collection, *The world of Haig-Brown*, made up of *Woods and river tales* (1980), mostly unpublished stories dating from the 1930s and 1950s; *The master and his fish* (1981); and *Writings and reflections* (1982), drawing on Haig-Brown's papers in the archives of the University of British Columbia. She also edited, with Thomas McGuane, *To know a river: a Haig-Brown reader* (1996, rpr. 2000).

Halfe, Louise. See ABORIGINAL LITERATURE: 5.

Haliburton, T.C. (1796–1865). Born in Windsor, Nova Scotia, of New England stock, Thomas Chandler Haliburton was educated at King's College and was called to the bar in 1820. He practised law in Annapolis Royal, representing that constituency in the provincial assembly from 1826 to 1829, when he was appointed a judge of the Inferior Court of Common Pleas. He was promoted to the Supreme Court of Nova Scotia in 1841. In 1856 he retired and went to live in England, where he held a seat in the House of Commons from 1859 until just before his death in Isleworth, Middlesex.

During his life and ever since, Haliburton has been the subject of many controversies, namely his apparent transformation from a political moderate to an inflexible Tory, his love-hate for Nova Scotia, his ambivalence towards the United States; and in modern criticism there have been disagreements about his place in the Canadian tradition of humour and satire and the significance of his political vision. In the 1820s, for example, he advocated the removal of legal disabilities against Roman Catholics; a provincial grant to Pictou Academy, Pictou, N.S., which had been founded by the Presbyterian minister, the Rev. Thomas McCULLOCH; and a system of common schools—all of which his party regarded as radical and progressive measures. In fact, he was always a Tory; he emphasized the British heritage and envisaged Nova Scotia—and all of British North America—flourishing under a monarchical system, governed by an educated elite and guided by a state church. In the 1840s, when his fellow Nova Scotians rejected government by the predominantly Loyalist, Anglican 'family compact' in favour of a more democratic system of responsible government, Haliburton could hardly contain his contempt for them behind his good-humoured satire. His disappointment undoubtedly contributed to his decision to forsake Nova Scotia and go 'home' to England to pursue his literary and political ambitions. Yet the tensions created by his praise and criticism of Nova Scotia resulted in his most enduring writings.

His first literary effort, the historical pamphlet *A general description of Nova Scotia, illustrated by a new and correct map* (Halifax, 1823), appeared anonymously. Encouraged by the interest in local history, and hoping to raise the status of Nova Scotia in the eyes of the world, Haliburton enlarged it into *An historical and statistical account of Nova-Scotia* (2 vols, Halifax, 1829). From the emphasis in this account on romantic highlights like the expulsion of the Acadians, Henry Wadsworth Longfellow drew background for EVANGELINE (1847). Although Haliburton's access to documents was limited, his history, which ends in 1763, was a major piece of historical writing in nineteenth-century Canada. This book did not allow him to criticize contemporary events, so Haliburton turned to satiric sketches, contributing—with his friends, who included the reformer Joseph HOWE and journalist Beamish Murdoch—to 'The Club' papers (1828–31) in *The Novascotian*. Most of his fictions involve a journey into a new country and a first-person narrator (a mouthpiece for Haliburton), who investigates the new society. At times he uses several narrators or 'voices' in order to milk humour from the clash of perspectives between his characters, the author, and the reader. In 1835–6 he wrote twenty-one sketches entitled 'Recollections of Nova Scotia' for *The Novascotian*, and they proved so popular that Haliburton enlarged them into *The clockmaker; or The sayings and doings of Samuel Slick, of Slickville* (First series, Halifax, 1836; London, 1837; NCL). His satiric purpose was to show that actions, not complaints, were the only way to improve local conditions, and each sketch—composed mainly of dialogue—begins with an entertaining incident and ends with a pithy moral observation. Haliburton drew on his own experiences as a judge to send his fictional squire around Nova Scotia in company with Sam Slick, the brash Yankee clock pedlar whose aggressive salesmanship is a compound of 'soft sawder' and 'human natur'. Conveying Haliburton's own ambivalent attitudes towards Maritimers and, in later books, towards the British, and his reservations about the directions of American society, Slick praises American commercial know-how and attacks Nova Scotian apathy, yet he is suspicious of American demagoguery and praises Nova Scotia's natural resources and its hardy inhabitants. But readers could ignore Haliburton's message because Slick's energetic high spirits and his Yankee dialect—an unceasing flow of homely aphorisms and epigrams—charmed audiences everywhere: Slick, the archetypal swaggering and sharp American trader, became one of the most popular comic figures of the century and turned the first series of *The clockmaker* into the first Canadian bestseller. The literary influences on Haliburton's humour have been attributed to Thomas McCulloch's 'Letters of Mephibosheth Stepsure' in *The Acadian Recorder* (Halifax) in 1821–3 and to Seba Smith's *Life and writings of Major Jack Downing; of Downingville, away down east in the state of Maine* (Boston, 1833).

An extended trip to Britain in 1838–9, when he was lionized, changed the direction of his literary career, for Haliburton undertook the re-invention of the British North American colonies, addressing British readers in two sequels: *The clockmaker; or, The sayings and doings of Samuel Slick, of Slickville, Second series* (London, Halifax, 1838) and *Third series* (London, 1840). He now believed that Nova Scotia's economic problems and the political troubles that erupted in the 1837 Rebellion in Upper and Lower Canada could not be solved by the provinces themselves but only by changes in Colonial Office policy, and he introduced scenes in which North Americans and British personages clashed. He also enlarged the role of Slick's Episcopal

clergyman, the Rev. Hopewell, to articulate a conservative American vision. After the 1837 Rebellion, Haliburton's hardening Tory attitudes caused a rift with Howe and frequently marred the artistry of his books. His savage attacks on Lord Durham's *Report* (1838) in *The bubbles of Canada* (London, 1839), and in a series of letters to the London *Times*—reprinted as *A reply to the report of the Earl of Durham* (London, 1840)—arose from Haliburton's anger at the British abandonment of British North America and his contempt for the liberals and reformers who were gaining influence in British affairs. He was opposed to a union of the Maritime Provinces and the Canadas because he believed it would lead to independence and even annexation to the United States, and he attacked responsible government because he thought it would lead to mob rule and party factions. Even after the British North American provinces had achieved responsible government, Haliburton argued against it in *The English in America* (2 vols, London, 1851), which was republished as *Rule and misrule of the English in America* (2 vols, New York, 1851). This work traces the origins of American democracy from its beginnings in Massachusetts, and is Haliburton's most extended criticism of the ideals and institutions of the United States, as well as an attack on two centuries of British 'misrule' on the American continent. However, in *An address on the present condition, resources and prospects of British North America* (London, 1857) he grudgingly accepted the notion of a colonial federation, although he preferred an imperial federation in which the colonies would be represented at Westminster.

Among Haliburton's other books, *The old judge; or, Life in a colony* (2 vols, London, 1849), is a sympathetic and rich portrait of Nova Scotia, delineating vice-regal rituals, country picnics, and village court trials, along with folklore, legends, and ghost tales, of which 'The witch of Inky Dell' is one of the most evocative stories in nineteenth-century Canada. Haliburton uses three narrators to give coherence to the loosely structured sketches and stories.

Long recognized as one of the founders of American humour, although he is hardly mentioned in twentieth-century American studies of humour, Haliburton is rightly regarded as the last and best in the Loyalist Tory satiric tradition of Canada. The first Canadian writer to use roads, railways, and steamships as literary devices, he was also the first fiction writer to employ regional dialects, and the first to create dialogue that is colloquial and racy. Above all, he gave Nova Scotians an imaginative and mythic map based on their roots in the Old and New Worlds, which gave them a vital sense of identity and community.

Modern editions of some of Haliburton's works include the NEW CANADIAN LIBRARY edition of *The clockmaker*, First series (1993); the Tecumseh Press edition of *Recollections of Nova Scotia: The clockmaker; or The sayings and doings of Samuel Slick, of Slickville (First series, numbers 1–21)* (1984), edited by Bruce Nesbitt; the CENTRE FOR EDITING EARLY CANADIAN TEXTS edition of *The clockmaker: Series one, two, and three* (1995), edited by George L. Parker; and *The old judge; or, Life in a colony* (1978), edited by M.G. Parks.

See *Inventing Sam Slick: a biography of Thomas Chandler Haliburton* (2005) by Richard A. Davies.

Handmaid's tale, The (1985, GGA; rpr. 1999). This novel by Margaret ATWOOD is in the tradition of the dystopian novel. Using a quotation from Jonathan Swift's *A modest proposal* as an epigraph, Atwood signals that she is writing satire and not science fiction. The novel is set in the near future in the United States, in a location that is recognizably Cambridge, Massachusetts. A bloody *coup d'état* has installed a neo-Puritan dictatorship whose governing class, the 'Commanders of the Faithful', has established a fundamentalist theocracy that calls itself Gilead. Atwood's premise is that this might happen were certain trends, evident in the mid-1980s, pushed to their logical conclusion: the rise of right-wing fundamentalism as a political force in the USA, the decline in the Caucasian birth rate in North America and northern Europe, and the rise in infertility in the First World as a consequence of chemical pollution, excessive levels of radiation, sexually transmitted diseases, and other factors. Threatened by an epidemic of infertility, the government of Gilead has made abortion, birth control, and homosexuality crimes punishable by hanging. In this nightmare society, woman's highest purpose is only to breed—fertile women, commandeered into producing babies for the state, are forced into a harem-like seclusion, while the rich and powerful male elite practise polygamy. The regime creates an 'instant pool' of women by declaring second marriages and non-marital liaisons adulterous. Such women are arrested as morally unfit and confined to 'Rachael and Leah Re-education Centers', where they must service Gilead as surrogate breeders or and aids. (Genesis 30: 1–3.

provides the state's theological justification for this control of women. Jacob's wife Rachael, unable to conceive, used the services of her handmaid, Bilhah, as a surrogate: 'Go in unto her; and she shall bear upon my knees, that I may also have children by her.') To create this world, Atwood drew on her own knowledge of fundamentalism: from her reading of the Bible to her deep knowledge of American history and particularly of the seventeenth-century witch burnings of her own Puritan ancestors, to her travels in Iran and Afghanistan and her interest in military tactics. Politically astute, the novel provides a disturbing and convincing portrait of how a totalitarian system functions: how such a regime might grow out of the failure of modern democracies to deal with environmental pollution, biological weaponry, etc., by perverting the public nostalgia for 'traditional values'. The story is narrated as a chilling personal account by a handmaid called Offred. An Afterword closes the novel: 'Historical Notes on The Handmaid's Tale', parodying an academic conference, is a partial transcript from the Twelfth Symposium on Gilead Studies, from the year 2195, in which a Native American anthropologist, discoursing on the document that is Atwood's novel, looks back on this obscure moment in history and provides an explanation of the various stages of the Gilead regime, and hypothesizes about the characters' fates.

On publication the novel was not considered far-fetched, but rather a disturbingly prophetic analysis of the consequences of religious fundamentalism pushed to extremes. *The handmaid's tale* was the source of a film (1990), directed by Volker Schlorndorf, with a screenplay by Harold Pinter; and of an opera by Poul Ruders (libretto by Paul Bentley), first produced to great success by Copenhagen's Royal Opera in Mar. 2000, and by the Canadian Opera Company in the autumn of 2004.

Harbourfront Reading Series. See AUTHORS AT HARBOURFRONT CENTRE.

Harbour Publishing. One of British Columbia's major publishing houses, it was founded in 1974 by Howard WHITE. He had had great success with a community newspaper, *The Peninsula Voice*, and with *Raincoast chronicles* (1972–), a magazine-format series featuring stories and articles about the B.C. coast; in Harbour's first year *Raincoast chronicles first five*, a hardcover book, began its sale of 50,000 copies. Books on a wide variety of subjects have followed, all emphasizing a West Coast sensibility and West Coast authors. Among its literary authors have been Anne CAMERON, Hubert EVANS, Edith IGLAUER, Patrick LANE, John Pass, and Tom WAYMAN. Though not originally associated with the West Coast, Al PURDY had several books published by Harbour, and *Beyond remembering: the collected poems of Al Purdy*, selected and edited by Purdy and Sam Solecki, appeared in 2000. The monumental *Encyclopedia of British Columbia*, edited by Daniel Francis, was also published in 2000.

Harlow, Robert (b. 1923). Born in Prince Rupert, British Columbia, he was moved in 1926 with his family to Prince George, where his father was a roadmaster with the CNR. After serving in the RCAF (he was a Lancaster bomber pilot), he earned a B.A. (1948) from the University of British Columbia, where he was a member of one of Earle BIRNEY's first creative-writing workshops, and he was the first Canadian to attend Paul Engle's Writers' Workshop at the University of Iowa, where he received an M.F.A. in 1950. Harlow joined the Canadian Broadcasting Corporation as a public-affairs producer and in 1953, with Robert WEAVER, was instrumental in planning and inaugurating the literary program 'Anthology'. He was appointed director of radio, B.C. region, for the CBC in 1955. In 1959 he joined with Birney and others to found the literary magazine *Prism International*. In 1965 he was appointed founding head of the newly accredited Department of Creative Writing at UBC, a position he held until 1977, and from then until 1988 he was Professor of Creative Writing; he is now Professor Emeritus. A sophisticated writer, with a careful sense of style, he was a major influence on a generation of B.C. and Canadian writers. Harlow likes 'big books' that span space, time, and generations of British Columbians. His taste runs to rich prose, and he often calls attention to the artifice of fiction: his narrative voice frequently appears as a counterpoint or subtext. Harlow's first three novels—*Royal Murdoch* (1962), *A gift of echoes* (1965), and *Scann* (1972)—form a trilogy about the fictional town of Linden, B.C., modelled on Prince George. Connected by the maturing of relationships among generations, they feature grotesque characters, lavish metaphors, and sudden bursts of violence. *Royal Murdoch*, the most traditional, tells the story of an old man, Royal Murdoch, who gathers his friends and family about him to witness his final days. *A gift of echoes* concentrates more on commentary than on plot as the protagonist, John Grandy, contemplates the passage of time and sees that the 'structure of his history was dismembered'. *Scann*, Harlow's major novel, interlocks five novellas about Amory Scann, editor of the Linden newspaper. Supposedly writing a special issue about the fiftieth anniversary of the town, he actually writes about his faltering marriage, his Second World War experiences, an epidemic, and chronicles the saga of trapper Linden and settler Thrain, two men central to the history of the town. Their epic struggle in the wilderness against a wolverine (modelled on a story in Howard O'HAGEN's *Wilderness men*, 1958) is one of the great set-pieces in western Canadian fiction. *Making arrangements* (1978), a comic novel about horse racing, portrays a group of hangers-on in a cheap Vancouver hotel attempting to raise enough money for a once-in-a-lifetime bet on a horse race; it involves drugs, the kidnapping of an industrialist, and Pay-TV sex. *Paul Nolan* (1983) describes a few days in the restless life of the forty-nine-year-old main character who is driven by sexual conquest, but is without morality and love. With complex time shifts, Harlow expertly traces the emotional contours of a failed marriage, affinity with a homosexual friend, and Nolan's failure as a parent, and makes good use of Vancouver as a setting. *Felice: a travelogue* (1985) explores the theme of liberation as Felice Gentry breaks away from domestic responsibilities when she discovers she has a cancerous tumour; she travels to Poland at a time of political turmoil associated with Lech Walesa and the Solidarity movement. Adolescent sexuality is explored in *The saxophone winter* (1988). Set in 1938, in the fictional small town of Long River, B.C., it is the perceptive and compassionate story of five months in the life of fourteen-year-old Christopher Waterton that include his first romance with a thirteen-year-old. The boy's passion is for big-band jazz; like Joseph SKVORECKY's alter ego, Danny, he dreams of finding freedom as a jazz musician and his parents, with difficulty, buy him an alto saxophone for Christmas. Harlow's protagonist learns of scandal and injustice in a novel that begins with a fire and ends with a flood. *Necessary dark* (2002) describes the life of eighteen-year-old Howard Tate when he becomes a bomber pilot for three years during the Second World War, in a narrative that is often exciting and eventually sad, and is clearly based on Harlow's own wartime experience.

Harris, Christie (1907–2002). Lucy Christie Irwin was born in New Jersey, USA, and was moved as a small child to British Columbia. Married in 1931 to an immigration officer, Thomas Harris, she became the mother of five children, and lived in Vancouver. In the 1960s she established a reputation as a writer of children's books, in which her major contribution was her presentation, in fantasies and other stories, of Northwest Coast Native material and her retellings of Native legends and folktales, beginning with *Once upon a totem* (1963). She wrote historical fiction in *Raven's cry* (1966, rpr. 1992), a well-researched but weakly fictionalized account of the tragic treatment of the Haida by traders, missionaries, and government officials; a crime novel in *Mystery at the edge of two worlds* (1978), about the theft of Native artifacts; fantasies, based partly upon Indian folk material, in *Secret in the Stlalakum wild* (1972), and *Sky man on the totem pole?* (1975), which borders on science fiction; and retellings of Native tales and legends in *Once more upon a totem* (1973), *Mouse woman and the vanished princesses* (1976, rpr. 2005), *Mouse woman and the mischief-makers* (1977, rpr. 2004), *Mouse woman and the muddleheads* (1979), *The trouble with princesses* (1980), and *The trouble with adventuring* (1982). Harris's stories—written before Native people wrote and published stories from their own knowledge—created a link with another culture and age and asked us to see ourselves in a significantly 'other' way. Her creative powers were most fully realized in attempting to provide the non-Native reader with the Native world-view, for Harris went beyond simply retelling legends and tales to reinvent them so that readers are encouraged to examine their own culture in an entirely different context. Her last novel, *Something weird is going on* (1994), set in Vancouver, is a novel for girls in which Xandra Warwick is shaken by the feeling that she's being watched and is haunted by uncomfortable memories. Christie Harris was appointed a Member of the Order of Canada in 1980.

Harris, Claire (b. 1937). Born in Port-of-Spain, Trinidad, she was educated at University College, Dublin (B.A., 1961), and the University of the West Indies (Dip. Ed., 1963) before immigrating to Canada in 1966, and the University of Lagos (Dip. Media, 1975). She taught at the secondary-school level in Calgary, Alberta, until her retirement in 1994. She began to write for publication in 1975 while on study leave in Lagos, where she was encouraged by Nigerian poet John Pepper

Clark, and has produced eight collections of poetry: *Fables from the women's quarters* (1984, rpr. 1995), which won the Commonwealth Award for Poetry for the Americas Region; *Translation into fiction* (1984); *Travelling to find a remedy* (1986); *The conception of winter* (1989. rpr. 1995); *Drawing down a daughter* (1992), which was nominated for a Governor General's Award; *Dipped in shadow* (1996); *Under black light: new and selected poems* (1999); and *She* (2000). Many of Harris's longer poems bear witness to injustice, and experiments with typography and page arrangement draw attention to the voices of those who cannot speak for themselves. In 'Where the sky is a pitiful tent' each page is divided horizontally, a contrapuntal arrangement through which a poetic narrative of terrorism in Guatemala is underscored by the real-life documentary testimony of Rigoberta Manchu, a victim of that regime. 'Nude on a pale staircase' portrays the colonization of women by male-dominated social institutions, including Western systems of aesthetic representation. Closer to home, Harris censures Canadians who tolerate evil in the form of social injustice, as in the poem 'Policeman cleared in jaywalking case', which documents public indifference to a real-life incident in which a black Albertan schoolgirl was arrested and strip-searched for an alleged misdemeanour. In her shorter poems Harris often writes of Caribbean women exiled from their African roots by British colonial policy in the West Indies. While mourning the irrecoverable loss of her own African heritage, since all experience for her must be mediated through the English language in which she was educated, she insists nonetheless on the power of the African-Canadian poet to use English as an instrument for inscribing 'A Black reading' (to quote the title of another of her poems) upon the 'white space' that is North America's idea of itself. Indeed, Harris's faith in the power of lyric poetry and standard English (although she employs dialect at times), along with her humanist tendency to speak in terms of general truths and shared values, sets her somewhat apart from the more radical poetics of other African-Canadian writers such as M. Nourbese PHILIP and Dionne BRAND—with whom she co-authored *Grammar of dissent* (2005). Clearly, however, she is no less committed to matters of social redress. Harris has also written poems that are personal in tone and portray friendship, and maternal and erotic love. *Drawing down a daughter* is an ambitious book-length narrative in which a woman addresses her unborn child in poetry and prose, through a vibrant collage of stories, songs, recipes, and historical details that signify the richness of the heritage into which the child will be born. *She* is a series of poems, many in dialect, and prose pieces made up of the letters of Penelope-Marie Lancet, living in Calgary, to her sister Jasmine in Trinidad. They reveal Penny's fragmented personality, and while meaning is often hermetic, the passion and vivid imagery are not.

Harrison, Charles Yale (1898–1954). Born in Philadelphia, Pennsylvania, he left school in grade four—over a dispute, it is said, with a teacher about *The merchant of Venice*—and at sixteen was working for the *Montreal Star*. Soon after the outset of the Great War he enlisted in the Royal Montreal Regiment and was a machine gunner in Belgium and France; he was wounded at Amiens in 1918. He returned to Montreal and worked as a theatre manager, a real-estate salesman, and newspaper reporter before moving to New York, where he worked as a public-relations consultant, radio commentator, and writer.

Harrison's contribution to Canadian literature was a powerful war novel based on his experiences with his Canadian regiment: *Generals die in bed*, which was published in England and the USA in 1930, and reprinted in 1975 with an Introduction by Robert F. Nielsen. Parts had appeared in magazines—some German—by 1928, the year before publication of Erich Maria Remarque's *All quiet on the Western Front*, Ernest Hemingway's *A farewell to arms*, and Robert Graves' *Goodbye to all that*. (Nielsen suggests that Remarque may have been influenced by these extracts while writing his novel.) Ford Madox Ford praised *Generals* and it was translated into Spanish, French, and Russian. Beginning in Montreal, the setting quickly changes to Europe and trench warfare, moving briefly (and terrifyingly) to no man's land, behind the trenches, and to London. The narrator, an eighteen-year-old Canadian soldier, relates his experiences in a deceptively simple style, describing explicitly and objectively the relentless horrors of trench warfare. Fighting is not romanticized, compassion for the soldier's plight is not restricted by nationality, and war is depicted as a brutalizing process. The narrator concludes that the enemies are 'the lice, some of our officers and Death'. Nielsen compares the memorable scene in which the narrator kills a soldier at close range and has difficulty in removing the bayonet from the body to a similar scene in Remarque's novel. *Generals die in bed* is characterized by its strength and simplicity of diction, unifying motifs, cutting irony, and black humour. It is an outstanding novel about the Great War.

Harrison wrote several other novels, and *Clarence Darrow* (1931), the first book-length biography of the famous lawyer.

Harrison, Keith. See Pat LOWTHER.

Harrison, Susie Frances (1859–1935). Susie Frances Riley, who often used the pseudonym 'Seranus', was born in Toronto and educated there at a private school for girls, and for two years in Montreal. While living in Québec she developed a keen interest in French-Canadian culture that would become evident in her writing. In 1879 she married John W.F. Harrison, a professional musician, and they had two children. After living in Ottawa until 1887, she made Toronto her permanent home. There she became well known as a professional pianist and vocalist, an authority on French-Canadian folksongs, and was principal of the Rosedale Branch of the Toronto Conservatory of Music for twenty years. Beginning to write when she was sixteen, she contributed literary and musical reviews, articles, essays, short stories, and poetry to Canadian, British, and American newspapers and literary magazines. She was a regular correspondent for the Detroit *Free Press* and the Toronto *Globe*, and was editor of *The WEEK* for nine months. She is significant as a minor novelist and poet who, as a member of the Confederation generation, attempted to identify and express a distinct Canadian voice and character. Her first book, *Crowded out! and other sketches* (Ottawa, 1886), is a collection of stories, most of which attempt to capture particular characteristics of Canadians. The title story depicts, with psychological intensity, the frustrations of a Canadian writer who tries in London, England, to publish works with Canadian content. There are several stories whose haunted, disturbed characters, first-person narrative, and weird events show the influence of Edgar Allan Poe. Many of the stories contain French-Canadian characters and settings. Harrison wrote two novels: *The forest of Bourg-Marie* (London, 1898), a mythic study of the disintegration of French-Canadian society as the younger generation leave their native land and tradition for the wealth of the United States, and *Ringfield* (1914), a melodrama in which an idealistic Methodist minister is corrupted by a bohemian French-Canadian actress and her English poet-lover. But Harrison was best known in her day as a poet. Her most ambitious poetry collection is *Pine, rose and fleur de lis* (Toronto, 1891), a collection of lyrical verse organized in sections that include a long travel sequence, 'Down the river', consisting mostly of villanelles, a form appropriate to its subject—a fancy-free boat ride through French Canada; a monody on Isabella Valancy CRAWFORD; several poems on England; and a miscellany of nature and love poetry. Conventional in language and form, these poems are of interest mainly for their celebration of the people and landscape of Canada and the point of view of Canadians. Six other poetry collections followed. In the late nineteenth century Harrison enjoyed a favourable critical reception in Canada, and her work was reviewed not only there but in England and the United States—in *The Week*, the *Canadian Magazine, Literary World, London Spectator, Saturday Review*, and *Critic*—where she was praised for her knowledge of French Canada, her 'new world conceits', and her gift of song.

Hart, Julia Catherine (1796–1867). Julia Catherine Beckwith was born in Fredericton, New Brunswick, of New England and French ancestry, and gathered many stories and travel impressions on her childhood visits to relatives in Québec and Nova Scotia. A number of these were incorporated into ST URSULA'S CONVENT; or, The nun of Canada (Kingston, 1824; rpr. 1991), the first novel published in British North America written by a native-born author; edited by Douglas LOCHHEAD, it was reissued in 1991 by the CENTRE FOR EDITING EARLY CANADIAN TEXTS. In 1820 she moved from Fredericton to Kingston, Upper Canada, where she lived with her aunt, the mother of Québec historian Abbé Ferland. Between 1822 and 1824 she married George Henry Hart; conducted a girls' boarding school in Kingston; and moved to the United States with her husband. In 1831 the Harts settled in Fredericton, where George Hart held a position in the Crown Lands office. Mrs Hart remained in her native city for the rest of her life, contributing short fiction to the *New Brunswick Reporter and Fredericton Advertiser* and working on an unpublished novel, *Edith; or, The doom*, which focuses on a family curse and its expiation during the time of the American Revolution. In all her writing she revealed a heightened romantic sensibility and a strict adherence to the conventions of popular fiction. *St Ursula's Convent* is therefore typical in introducing shipwrecks, kidnappers, exchanged babies, and a false priest into a sentimental story of Québec seigneurial and convent life. A less sensational novel is *Tonnewonte; or The adopted son of America* (Watertown, N.Y., 1824–5), a two-volume romance published in three different editions in the United States after the Harts had moved there in 1824. Set in France and in upper-state New York, it appealed to American patriotic feelings by contrasting the democratic opportunities and naturalness of American life with the chaos and class-consciousness of France during the Napoleonic era.

Harvey, Kenneth J. (b. 1962). Born in St John's, Newfoundland, he was president (1981–9) of Offshore Promotions/Image Design Ltd and newspaper columnist until he embarked on a career as an author—the voluminous author of sixteen books since 1990, many of them published internationally. His novels include *Brud* (1992), *Stalkers* (1994, a thriller), *Nine-tenths unseen: a psychological mystery* (1996), *The woman in the closet: a mystery* (1998), *Skin hound (there are no words): a trans-composite novel* (2000), *The town that forgot how to breath* (2003), *Inside* (2006), and *Blackstrap Hawco* (2008). His short-story collections are *Directions for an opened body* (1990), *The hole that must be filled* (1994), *The great misogynist* (1996), *The flesh so close* (1998), and *Shack: the Cutland Junction stories* (2004), Harvey has also written a book of essays, *Everybody hates a beauty queen* (1998) and a collection of poetry, *Kill the poets* (1996). He lives in Burnt Head, Cupids, Newfoundland and Labrador.

Among Harvey's novels, the text of *Skin hound* alternates between the interviews of a psychiatrist and police detective with an English professor (Patient X), who has confessed to murdering his family, and passages from the journal Patient X is asked to write, in which his friend Cassandra has a leading role. In spite of the subject matter, the narrative is not tense but casual in tone as the author displays his ingenuity. Harvey's imagination took a leap when he embarked on the writing of *The town that forgot how to breathe* (2003), in which the town of Bareneed and its people are afflicted with strange happenings, including fish flying out of the ocean onto land; fully dressed drowned bodies floating ashore—from the past (as far back as the 1700s) and the present; ghosts; and a widespread breathing disorder, 'some sort of virus that interfered with people's breathing and resulted in an inexplicable form of amnesia', leading in some cases to death. The novel's long chapters—with headings alluding to times of day from Thursday until Tuesday night—are divided into disconnected episodes, each describing an incident pertaining to one of the many characters. These include the toothless old Miss Laracy, who believes in spirits, has second sight, speaks in a disagreeable (hard to interpret) Newfoundland dialect, and appears throughout the novel; Joseph Blackwood and his young daughter Robin; his estranged wife Kim; Dr Thompson, who is forever being called upon to deal with health emergencies; old Doug Blackwood, Joseph's uncle, who remembered 'the creature he had seen out on the water. He refused to call it a mermaid, because that would be fairy tale foolishness; yet he assumed that was exactly what the creature was'; a neighbour of Joseph's, Claudia, whose daughter Jessica has died and whose ghost only Robin can see: they spend time together and one high point of the novel occurs when Jessica may be leading Robin to *her* death (the aftermath is suspenseful). Miss Laracy was called upon to identify, in the fish plant, the many corpses that had been thrown up by the ocean: she gasps 'at the spectacle of what plainly lingered above—amber spirits shredded to tatters. Each disjointed apparition, drifting like a fluttering sheet of cobwebs, resembled the body beneath it.' Incorporating one serious family relationship (Joseph, Robin, Kim) and the responses of many other characters to unfathomable uprisings from the sea, and to the breathing disorder, the novel is an unusual achievement—though it is weakened by the episodic form of the narrative. *Inside* (2006) is about a man found to be wrongfully convicted of murder who is released from prison, from 'inside', after fourteen years. Short sentences, sometimes one word long, convey his traumatized response to a new reality (a device that becomes wearying): 'His daughter, Jackie, mother of his granddaughter, had been worried. She feared him. She did not want his granddaughter near him because she feared him. That was what had made him angry.... Then the talk of the man who had been seeing his wife. Fourteen years. What's it like to be out? What's it like to be free?.... What are your plans? You'll get a million bucks now.' Myrden, the former prisoner, is opaque as a character, as is the alienation of his wife and daughter. And who killed the girlfriend he was accused of murdering? One positive aspect of the novel is the happy reunion with Ruth, a former lover. When Myrden and Ruth return from a trip to Spain he finds that his daughter and granddaughter have been beaten by Willis, Jackie's partner. He takes them out of the house and puts them in

Ruth's car. The last word of the ominous last sentence repeats the title: 'Then he went back inside.' The novel won the 2006 Roberts Writers' Trust Fiction Prize. In 2008 Harvey published *Blackstrap Hawco: said to be about a Newfoundland family*, a huge (and heavy) 829-page novel that centres on the Hawco family, begins with Blackstrap's father in Bareneed in 1953, and is the result of Harvey's inimitable, often eccentric way with fiction, drawing on an endless fund of details and incidents (some actually transcribed from short stories he's published, as he admits) to create a kind of epic celebration of the history of Newfoundland that mythologizes a people who have endured untold miseries.

Harvey's many stories often include incidents that administer little shocks. In the first paragraph of a story in *The great misogynist*, set in Africa, the white narrator kneels over Nuba (the story's title) and carves 'the pattern that will mark her as mine. I drew the nail upward across her oiled ebony belly, my hand steadily guiding the diagonal gouges into her flesh. Streams of sheening deep-red fluid spilled along her black skin....' The story called 'Suhad' is made up of letters Norman Bruff, a journalist in Tehran, writes to his girlfriend Gail in Canada. They are readable accounts of their troubled relationship leading to descriptions of life in Tehran, and of Suhad, a young woman he meets who is a devoted Muslim—he transcribes two interviews with her about her beliefs: 'Suhad is an extremely intelligent woman. Stern, late-twenties, passionate, attractive ... I admire her more and more each day.' He eventually tells Gail that 'I plan to stay here.' And in his next letter: 'I have become a Muslim.' Suhad, whom he marries, prays for him. 'Such devotion. One day she might approach a priest and, while kissing his hand, pull the pin on one of the twenty hand grenades strapped to her body beneath her *chadour*. The destruction of a priest is a glorious blow against the government.' His final letter is signed Ali Rajavi. In 'The muffled drum' (*Shack*) Hedley Thistle has died and the boy Whitey transports his frozen body on a snowmobile to his cabin 'where he was leaned up against the birch tree alongside the shack. Hedley's mouth open as though trying to say something and Whitey knowing that the mouth had not been open when he first set the body down. Stepping closer, he saw a furry clump of brown jerking out from the mouth. The fur did not move for a moment and then it nudged out further, showing itself to be a squirrel.... The first sentence of 'The broken earth' (in both *Shack* and *The flesh too close*) is: 'The baby' first three teeth grew out black and rotted and she suffered greatly and died with a screech.' The story ends when the father carries the body to the grave he has just dug—and finds that his baby is living. The voluble descriptions in Harvey's stories displace a narrative line that would strengthen them and compel the reader's attention.

Harvey, Jean-Charles (1891–1967). Born at La Malbaie (Murray Bay), Québec, Harvey took the traditional *cours classique* at the Petit Séminaire de Chicoutimi (1905–8), then spent seven years as a Jesuit scholastic (1908–15). A reporter with *La Presse* (1915) and *La Patrie* (1916–18), he was subsequently hired by La Machine agricole nationale in Montmagny to handle the firm's public relations. In 1922 he moved to *Le Soleil* in Quebec City, acting as editor-in-chief from 1927 until Apr. 1934, when he was relieved of this position the day after the Archbishop of Québec condemned his novel *Les demi-civilisés*. Premier Taschereau appointed Harvey director of the Office of Statistics for Québec, but after Maurice Duplessis's election in Aug. 1936 he was fired a second time. For nine years Harvey published his own weekly newspaper, *Le Jour* (1937–46). After the war he lectured widely, worked as a radio commentator (with CBC International and CKAC), and edited two papers, *Le Petit Journal* and *Le Photo Journal* (1953–66). During the unsettled 1960s, Harvey defended both federalism and bilingualism and spoke out against separatism—warning his anglophone friends, however, that Québécois would need constitutional changes guaranteeing the survival of their language and culture if they were to realize their full potential as North American francophones within a federalist state. He was the author of three novels, three collections of short stories, and six books of essays. His best-known novel, *Les demi-civilisés* (1934; 2nd edn 1962)—translated by John GLASSCO as *Fear's folly* (1982)—marked a turning-point in the liberation of Québec fiction from unrealistic and socially irrelevant depictions of life and morality. Here he condemned the control of Québec's economy by the English community and, more significantly, scathingly denounced the power of the Québec clergy in all spheres, attacking in particular their betrayal of the spirit of the Gospel message. Through the sexual liaison of Max Hubert and Dorothée Meunier, and the free-thinking ideas of their revolutionary magazine, Harvey criticized the lack of intellectual and moral freedom in Québec during the 1920s. His anti-clericalism was harshly expressed through Hermann Lillois, who wonders what Christ would think of 'the triple alliance of capital, civil power and the Church' that keeps his people in fear and 'servile silence'. This attack on the political, economic, and religious status quo brought a swift public condemnation of the book by Cardinal Villeneuve, and Harvey was for many years a pariah; but he is now recognized in Québec as a defender of intellectual, moral, and artistic freedom.

Harvey, Moses (1820–1901). An Irishman of Scottish descent, Harvey was born in Armagh, Ireland, and educated in Belfast, where he was ordained a Presbyterian minister in 1844. In 1852 he became pastor of St Andrew's Free Presbyterian Church in St John's, Newfoundland, and was soon prominent as a lecturer on biblical and scientific subjects. In 1878 he retired from the active ministry, apparently because his voice failed him, and dedicated himself to the profession of letters. In 1891 he was awarded an honorary LL.D. by McGill University. He committed suicide in St John's.

Harvey was a writer of wide interests, great industry, and enthusiasm—a Victorian polymath who ranged in subject matter over history, science, poetry, religion, and contemporary society. The author of many books, including collections of lectures and four theological tracts, he began in the late 1860s what might be described as a massive publicity campaign on behalf of the colony, becoming the most relentless, and possibly the most gifted, of a generation of literary boosters of Newfoundland in books such as *Newfoundland; its history, its present condition, and its prospects in the future* (Boston, 1883), written with the English novelist and journalist Joseph Hatton, and reissued in London as *A short history of Newfoundland: England's oldest colony* (1883); *Newfoundland as it is in 1894: a handbook and tourist's guide* (St John's and London, 1894); *Newfoundland in 1897; being Queen Victoria's diamond jubilee year and the four hundredth anniversary of the discovery of the island by John Cabot* (London, 1897); and *Newfoundland in 1900; a treatise of the geography, natural resources and history of the island...* (New York and St John's, 1900). Harvey's burning message about the island's resources possibly had incalculable effects upon generations of Newfoundland writers.

Harvor, Elisabeth (b. 1936). Born Erica Elisabeth Arendt Deichmann in Saint John, New Brunswick—the daughter of the famous

Harvor

potters Erica and Kjeld Deichmann—she started nurse's training in 1954 at Saint John General Hospital but left nine months before graduation, married Stig Harvor in 1957 and, after a year-and-a-half in Europe, settled with him in Ottawa. They had two sons and were divorced in 1977. In 1983 she enrolled at Concordia University; after a qualifying year in lieu of a B.A., she obtained an M.A. in 1986. She lives in Ottawa. Harvor has published four volumes of short fiction: *Women and children* (1973), which was reprinted with slight revisions as *Our lady of all the distances* (1991); *If only we could drive like this forever* (1988); and *Let me be the one* (1996), which was nominated for a Governor General's Award. As a poet, the winner of several awards, she has published two collections: *Fortress of chairs* (1992) and *The long cold evenings of spring* (1997). Harvor writes of women—women in marriage and out of marriage, as mothers, as student nurses—with a style that is at once subtle and wry, shrewd and ironic. By a deft and vivid use of detail, and with a detached but not uncompassionate eye for human nature and its foibles and credulities, she is able to give overtones and undertones to even the simplest and lightest events and material. Harvor's frank and often humorous first novel, *Excessive joy injures the heart* (2000)—the title is a statement made by a Chinese acupuncturist in a lecture—displays her gift for conveying rigorous self-analysis in this story about Claire Vornova, thirty-seven and separated from her husband, whose life and work become charged by a painful love affair with her holistic therapist that mainly lies in her imagination, and by the complexities of this obsession. On the first page of *All times have been modern* (2004, rpr. 2005) thirteen-year-old Kay is on a boat in New Brunswick and receives a harmless come-on from a soldier when he asks her to light his cigarette; she doesn't respond ('Because I don't want to')—but she likes being close to him. When she's twenty she meets Alexander Olenski and a beautifully described interlude precedes his making love to her. After a courtship by mail, they marry, have two sons, and after fifteen years the marriage ends (it is not clear why). She is a writer, has published a novel, and one story has appeared in *The New Yorker*, but she needs a job and finds one in an architects' office, where she meets Michael Galbraith. There is a mutual attraction (though he is married, with children), they fall in love, and this relationship dominates Kay's life—until the end, when he is asleep with a cold and she is lying beside him, thinking that 'their good years together

could just be beginning. Could be, but won't be, because as I'm drifting off to sleep another voice makes its own dark pronouncement. These are the last days of your happiness.' This much-praised novel is a first-person narrative of one woman's life, filled with good dialogue and believable descriptions of people and places that blend with an unconventional love story—in which, unfortunately, characterizations and emotion have been dampened by Harvor's detached literary facility.

Hay, Elizabeth (b. 1951). Born in Owen Sound, Ontario, she was educated at the University of Toronto (B.A., 1973). She has taught creative writing at New York University and the University of Ottawa (1991–4), and worked as broadcaster and documentary producer for CBC Radio in Yellowknife (from 1974 to 1978—see her novel *Late nights on air*, described below), Winnipeg, Toronto, and Latin America. She now lives, with her family, in Ottawa. *Crossing the snow line* (1989) is described as a collection of stories—taking place in Canada with Keith, whom the narrator married, and in New Orleans and Mexico, where she fell in love with Alec. In all these settings the images of snow, white, and coldness appear and reappear; and of warmth—of climate and 'the generosity of melting, which, of course, is the generosity of love.' The stories are made up of conversations, episodes, and aphoristic statements ('In love everything rises—our anxiety and our bodies, and afterwards the bed is white, blankets are thrown back, clothes scattered like crumbs.') that, in spite of their brevity, collectively achieve the effect of a striking novel. Two other early books, *The only snow in Havana* (1992) and *Captivity tales: Canadians in New York* (1993), are free-and-easy but engaging memoirs that set down brief experiences amid discussions that look at things through the lens of history and recall historical characters, who usually have to do with the North. In *Havana* Beth and Alec are living and travelling together, and Beth gives birth to a baby girl in that city. Fur and snow are constant images (the first 'story', though set in Mexico, is called 'Fur and snow counterpoint'); other settings are Salem, Boston, Yellowknife, New York (Brooklyn), and Toronto. The apparently random short narratives about the present and the past make up a text that seems, poetically, to provide both the satisfaction and interest of fact—i.e., information—and the enjoyment of a fictional creation. *Captivity tales*, again containing images of fur and snow, interweaves living in New York, with Alec and two children, with anecdotal accounts of the residence there of famous Canadians (Snow, Wieland, CARR, Stratas, MCLUHAN, SETON, Gould, among others). 'In my mind I change the map of New York from one of a city where I continually get lost to a place with Canadian landmarks, orienting me, shoring me up; invisible anchors, where other Canadians have stayed and suffered and been happy. A new sort of mapmaking....' *Small change* (1997) is made up of Beth's stories about friendship, realistic and far from sentimental, that also portray her everyday life and her character—her self-examinations, her pithy observations about friendships, her and her friends' responses to them, and the reasons for their eventual dissolution. In the end, Beth sadly decides that 'The pattern leads here. To a woman past forty counting up friendships and arriving at small change.' Standing apart in this collection is 'Hand games', a chilling story of the 'friendship' of Beth's daughter Annie with cruel little Joyce, both aged five. In time '[Joyce's family] moved. And just before moving Joyce took pains to remind Annie of who was boss. Don't ever think you don't need me, and don't ever think I need you.'

These books were written in the first person. *A student of weather* (2000), Hay's first novel, written in the third person, is about Norma Joyce Hardy—homely, wilful, capable of deceit, but strong, in many ways admirable—and her much older sister Lucinda, beautiful, industrious, and responsible for the well-being of her widowed father and Norma Joyce. But 'Two sisters fell down the same well, and the well was Maurice Dove'—an attractive, educated, entirely agreeable man from Ontario, who began to visit Saskatchewan, where the Hardys lived, to study the weather there. The sister who fell the hardest was Norma Joyce; she was eight, he was twenty-three, the year was 1938. Steeped in love and loss, weather and flora, the novel describes these people with cool objectivity and careful language, particularly the life of Norma Joyce. She moved with her family to a house left to them in Ottawa—close to that of the Doves—and we read about her until she is in her forties. Maurice, meanwhile, became a well-known writer and married twice. Norma Joyce bore a son who gave her great happiness and matured well, but Maurice remained the centre of her life, their paths crossing occasionally. Looking at a photograph of Maurice when he was twenty-three, she thinks: 'A child falls in love with a man, and the man is attracted by the intensity he has generated. Then his attention shifts to something else.

End of story.' But there is much more. *Garbo laughs* (2003, rpr. 2004), is a delight for movie-lovers, though it's enjoyable on several levels. Writer Harriet Browning, denied movies as a child, is seduced by them as an adult and can't get enough of them. She often writes letters to Pauline Kael that she never sends. Her architect husband, the admirable Lew Gold, puts up with her obsession, struck 'by the contradiction in her, the contradiction between her old-fashioned scruples and her licentious ease with movies: she was a puritan addicted to Hollywood, and she was leading their kids down the same brainless path.' Her son, ten-year-old Kenny, is also addicted, and knowledgeable (his specialty is Frank Sinatra) and his sister Jane plays along. A bright journalist neighbour with silver hair, Diana Bloom, meets Kenny accidentally, is bowled over by his friendly outspokenness and his love of movies, which she shares, and visits his family, whose 'easy company' she enjoys; she becomes a special friend of Harriet's. They talk about movies and form a Friday-night movie club. The frequent interruptions of movie or movie-star appraisals and gossip are a fillip, but the novel is also about many other things: family relationships—cold Harriet's with her loving husband, with her difficult Aunt Leah, Lew's with Dinah, the children's with their parents—the city of Ottawa and the ice storm of 1998, illness and death. The narrative is made up of telling episodes, some of them merely brief dialogues—the dialogue throughout is engaging, often witty—that coalesce in a warm portrait of people one likes reading about. The title is from the ad for the film *Ninotchka* (though MGM forgot that Garbo also laughs in the early scenes of *Camille*). Serious Harriet ('I have no sense of humour') eventually laughs. In *Late nights on air* (2007, rpr. 2008)—winner of the GILLER PRIZE—Hay has skilfully interwoven a wide range of topics with smoothness and narrative appeal: a radio station in Yellowknife, its broadcasters and other employees, the intimacy of radio, the city itself, Justice Berger's Mackenzie Pipeline Inquiry of the mid-seventies; the disastrous trip to the Barrens in 1926–7 of John Hornby, his seventeen-year-old cousin Edgar Christian (who left a diary, later published as *Unflinching*), and Harold Adlard—they all starved to death; and the six-week canoe trip into the Barrens, inspired by Hornby, undertaken by four colleagues. A stunning new arrival at the station, Dido Paris, who immediately becomes a successful broadcaster, is struck by the beauty of the North: 'Overhead were ravens and lake gulls, all around were low hills made of the oldest rock in the world bathed by the most beautiful light on earth, and lovely miniature birches and small flowers clinging and spreading.' The interrelationships at the radio station—involving middle-aged Eleanor, the receptionist; young Gwen, who drove all the way from Ontario to experience the North and is given a midnight program of her own, in which she becomes more and more proficient; Harry, the acting head of the station; and Ralph, another broadcaster—become central for much of the book. Harry falls in love with Dido and they have an affair—but she suddenly disappears, leaving for California with the unpopular technician Eddy. The highlight of the novel is the six-week canoe trip of Eleanor, Harry, Gwen, and Ralph into the Barrens and along the Thelon River to reach Hornby's hut, which the victims lived in, and their graves. This is an engrossing narrative about the extreme physical strain of carrying heavy packs, pushing canoes over frozen lakes, the relief experienced by periods of relaxation (and by sleep), being ravished by the beauty of the Far North, and by the sudden appearance of herds of caribou: 'Black antlers above the greenery, the willows, the water.... The ripples of movement that occurred when one animal started and the rest followed. They were like camels in the sand dunes, beautiful on the blond hills, moving and gathering, arranging themselves in small, elegant groups around the willows....' The activities and thoughts of the four canoeists and their easy dialogue provide reading pleasure; but the trip is interrupted by three highly suspenseful episodes, one of them a tragedy—only three are flown back to Yellowknife. The novel ends eight years later.

Hayman, Robert (1575–1629). Reared in Devon, England, he was a graduate of Exeter College, Oxford, and a student at Lincoln's Inn, London. During his stay at Lincoln's Inn, 'his geny being well known to be poetical', he became acquainted with Michael Drayton, Ben Jonson, George Withers, and other poets. Around 1618 he became governor of the Bristol merchants' plantation at Bristol's Hope in Conception Bay, Newfoundland. His initial visit to the colony was for fifteen months; he returned in successive summers until around 1628. In an address to Charles I in 1628 Hayman admitted that the commodities so far received from Newfoundland 'are in their particulars base, and meane'; yet, he added, 'they honestly imploye many people'. He proposed that Charles rename the island Britaniola. Hayman died while on an expedition up the Oyapock River in South America. He was the author of *Quodlibets, lately come over from New Britaniola, old Newfound-land. Epigrams and other small parcels, both morall and divine.... All of them composed and done at Harbor-Grace in Britaniola, anciently called Newfound-land* (London, 1628). The first book of English poetry to be written in what is now Canada, it contains much uncritical praise of the climate and resources of Newfoundland. As poetry, *Quodlibets* (i.e., 'What you will') is rough, homely verse, with here and there a touch of irony or a compelling phrase. Hayman knew his book consisted of 'bad unripe Rimes', but he apparently published it to make a point about the literary potential of the new colony: 'For if I now growne dull and aged, could doe somewhat, what will not sharper, younger, freer inventions performe there?' He was thus a conscious pioneer—not just as a colonist, but also as a poet.

Hearne, Samuel. See EXPLORATION LITERATURE IN ENGLISH: 2.

Heavysege, Charles (1816–76). His birthplace has been given as Huddersfield, England; but in letters to the London critic Charles Lanman, Heavysege claimed only that his 'ancestors on the paternal side' were from Yorkshire, and that Bayard Taylor's article in the *Atlantic Monthly* (Oct. 1865), which gave Liverpool as his birthplace, was 'generally correct'. He immigrated to Canada in 1853 and settled in Montreal, where he was employed as a woodcarver in a cabinet works. He later became a journalist on the staff of the *Transcript* and the *Daily Witness*. After the publication of his first dramatic poem, *The revolt of Tartarus* (London and Liverpool, 1852), a six-book epic in blank verse, his successive poems and dramas drew from the Bible, Shakespeare, Byron's *Cain* and 'Hebrew melodies', and the popular dramas *Saul* and *Filippo* by Vittorio Alfieri. Heavysege's protagonists are typically romantic rebels ruled by a dominant passion: Saul is proud, Jephthah rash, and Jezebel concupiscent. However, each is placed within the old Shakespearean world of order and universal degree where spiritual revolt is inevitably followed by punishment. In *Saul: a drama in three parts* (Montreal, 1857), Saul's character is developed to show a growing hubris that ultimately becomes satanic. Coventry Patmore, in an unsigned review in the *British North American*, praised it as 'indubitably the best poem ever written out of Great Britain'. Much of

Heavysege's subsequent literary effort was dedicated to the rewriting of *Saul*, his best work: a second edition was published in London and Montreal in 1859, a third in Boston in 1859, reprinted in 1876; in 1967 it was reprinted in *Saul and selected poems*, with an introduction and review of criticism by Sandra DJWA. The verbal wit and sustained eroticism of the tragicomedy *Count Filippo; or The unequal marriage* (Montreal, 1860; rpr. 1973) made the drama unpalatable to Victorian Canada. In *Jephthah's daughter* (Montreal, London, 1865) Heavysege turned to the Bible for its saga of the great but rash Israelite leader who sacrifices his daughter to keep his vow to God; he included some sonnets, four of which are reprinted in *Saul and selected poems*. 'Jezebel'—a poem that appeared in the *New Dominion Monthly* (Jan. 1868) and was reprinted by Golden Dog Press, Ottawa, in 1972—contains a description of the death of Jezebel, her bones licked by dogs, which has a macabre vitality. Heavysege also published a novel, *The advocate* (Montreal, 1865; rpr. 1973), a potboiler of unassimilated Gothic elements. Overvalued during his lifetime by critics wishing to assert the existence of a Canadian literature, Heavysege has been undervalued since his death, largely because of the wave of revisionist criticism in the 1920s that dismissed him as British rather than Canadian, partly because much of his work is closet drama, and also because his surname encourages easy satire. Robertson DAVIES in *Leaven of Malice* puns on the 'heavy' aspects of *Saul* and dubs his fictional critic, Solly Bridgetower, the Heavysege man in 'Amcan'. Yet Heavysege was an examplar to Charles SANGSTER, Charles G.D. ROBERTS, and W.D. LIGHTHALL, and was admired by the moderns W.W.E. ROSS and A.J.M. SMITH. George WOODCOCK—writing on Heavysege in *Canadian writers and their works* (1988) and developing much of his interpretation from the Introduction and summary of criticism appended to Djwa's edition of Heavysege—characterizes him as a 'good bad poet', states that Heavysege had a 'natural power and obsessive preoccupation with the conflict between human and divine justice', and accepts her judgement regarding his placement as a major poet in relation to his time, composing passages of genuine poetic vigour and psychological insight. Handicapped by limitations in his literary background and by the lack of a supportive Canadian culture, Heavysege's considerable achievements in his best works, *Saul* and *Jephthah's daughter*, are all the more impressive. He is the major figure in the Canadian literary world up to 1870.

Hébert, Anne (1916–2000). Born at Sainte-Catherine-de-Fossambault, Québec, she spent her childhood and adolescence in Quebec City and from the mid-1950s lived in Paris, making frequent visits to Canada. In the late nineties she moved back to Québec, to Montreal, where she died from bone cancer on 22 Jan. 2000. For her distinguished poetry and fiction she was awarded three Governor General's Awards (in 1960 for poetry, in 1975 and 1992 for fiction), the Molson Prize in 1967, the Académie française award in 1976, and in 1982 the Prix Fémina for her novel *Les fous de Bassan*. She was appointed a Companion of the Order of Canada in 1968.

A considerable influence on the content of her writing was that of her cousin, Hector de SAINT-DENYS-GARNEAU. A privileged witness to the development of his poetry, Hébert assimilated some of his major symbols (hand, heart, bone, the word, etc.), while modifying them considerably. His death in 1943 shattered all Hébert's tranquil notions, and her own writing was henceforth marked by revolt. Beginning with the short story 'Le torrent' (written in 1945), her characters would be rebellious, in open revolt against their fate as Québécois. Overly cautious publishers would delay until 1950 the appearance of her collection of short stories *Le torrent*; the title story, about repression, has a powerful explosive charge that was, for informed readers, a symbolic depiction of the French Canadian's inner deprivation. *Le torrent* was reissued with four new stories in 1963; *The torrent* (1967) is the English translation by Gwendolyn Moore.

Meanwhile Hébert was working on a collection of poems, *Le tombeau des rois* (1953), in which harsh revolt is given a highly personal expression and an ultimately liberating outcome. The title poem, a classic of modern Québécois literature, is an exploration of the unconscious filled with symbols: a bird (the poet), kings (the voices of the past), jewels and flowers (the allurements of the dead), water (dread), closed chambers (tombs), bones (death), and light (an awakening). Here liberation is as much psychological as poetic and consists in mentally expelling the figures of dead kings—those master images, with civil as well as religious significance, that had for so long dominated the colonized, clericalized minds of the Québécois. See 'The art of translation' in *The TAMARACK REVIEW* 24 (Summer 1962), which contains letters, and a dialogue, between F.R. SCOTT and Hébert about Scott's translation of her poem, which is included in *The collected poems of F.R. Scott* (1981). Other poetry collections followed, including *Le jour n'a d'égal que la nuit* (1992), translated by Lola Lemire Tostevin as *Day has no equal but the night* (1997). Hébert's poems have also been translated by Alan Brown in *Poems* (1975) and by A. Poulin in *Anne Hébert: selected poems* (1988).

Hébert's plays—*Le temps sauvage, La mercière assassinée*, and *Les invités au procès*, published in a single volume under the title *Le temps sauvage* (1967)—transpose into dramatic terms her progression from dream to language. In *Le temps de sauvage*, her major play, she describes the progress of Québec from rural and silent to urban and dynamic. The central character, Agnès, would like to keep her children 'outside of time', in her own silent, maternal night; the children grow impatient, force destiny, and in the end Agnès agrees to live in a world of speech and communication. The three plays have been translated by Eugene Benson and Renate Benson in the journal *Canadian Drama/L'Art dramatique canadien*, vol. 9, no. 1 (1983), vol. 10, no. 2 (1984), and vol. 14, no. 2 (1988).

A liberation similar to that expressed in *Le tombeau des rois* appeared in the rather static novel *Les chambres de bois* (1958), translated by Kathy Mezei as *The silent rooms* (1974). Catherine marries Michael, whose life is dominated by dreams. He forces his young wife to live shut away in their Paris rooms, then leads her to the gates of death. Catherine revolts, and in the last part of the novel we see her in a situation of light and love. In the late 1960s Hébert commenced work on a novel-cycle that begins in the nineteenth century and gradually moves into recent times. *KAMOURASKA* (1970, rpr. 2000), her most important and best-known novel, was based on an actual murder committed in nineteenth-century Québec. The 1974 translation was by Norman Shapiro; a new translation by Sheila FISCHMAN was published in 2000. *Les enfants du sabbat* (1975, GGA) was translated as *Children of the Black Sabbath* (1978) by Carol Dunlop-Hébert. Set in the 1930s and 1940s, it is a story of sorcery based on rigorous research into ancient and local witchcraft. The central character, Julie, and her brother Joseph are the children of parents who live on the fringes of society and engage in secret practices in the countryside outside Quebec City. Hébert uses the technique of flashback, but with a twist: Sister Julie of the Trinity, who is gifted with vision into the past, mentally leaves her convent and is literally transported to her birthplace in her parents' shanty. The main action is set in the convent, where the nuns and church authorities are increasingly scandalized by the peculiar behaviour of Sister Julie, the daughter of a sorcerer, who is dedicated to sorcery through an initiatory rape by her father. She is submitted to divine exorcism, without result. Even worse, she finds herself mysteriously pregnant and gives birth to a baby that the authorities leave to die in the snow. The rebellious Julie, however, runs away from the convent to join a waiting lover. The third novel in this cycle, *Héloïse* (1980)—translated with the same title by Sheila Fischman (1982), who translated all the succeeding novels—is no less astonishing. Here the action is set in modern Paris and the author uses the devices of fantasy and somnambulism to show how a young man, Bernard, succumbs to the lure of death and the past as embodied in a dead woman who has become a vampire named Héloïse and wanders day and night through the Paris Métro sucking people's blood. In *Les fous de Bassan* (1982)—*In the shadow of the wind* (1983, rpr. 1994)—Hébert skilfully blends the voices of the wind, the sea, and the birds (les fous de Bassan) with those of six narrators who try to reconstruct the dark events that occurred one August night in 1936 in the little English-speaking village of Griffin Creek in the Gaspé, when two young girls, Nora and Olivia, were raped and murdered on the beach. In *Le premier jardin* (1988)—*The first garden* (1990)—the central character, Flora Fantanges, who has made her career as an actor in France, returns to her native Quebec City in the summer of 1976 to play the role of Winnie in Samuel Beckett's *Oh les beaux jours (Happy days)*. Overwhelmed by memories, she relives her dispossessed childhood (the first garden), the scenes and street names of the city reminding her not only of her own past but of the historical exploitation of women in the past. In *L'enfant chargé de songes* (1992, GGA)—*Burden of dreams* (1994)—the central character, Julien Vallières, while travelling to Paris in 1946, relives memories focused on his mother and his lover. A letter announcing the birth of his child returns him to Québec, possessed of greater insight and understanding. *Aurélien, Clara, Mademoiselle et le lieutenant anglais* (1995)—*Aurélien, Clara, Mademoiselle and the English lieutenant* (1996)—is a slight piece, a *récit*. Although its protagonist, Clara, is only fifteen, she takes stock of the past as she prepares to enter into marriage with the English lieutenant. But as is so often the case when Hébert contrasts reality and dream, Clara's wedding night pales in comparison with her idealized vision of it. *Est-ce que je te dérange?* (1998)—*Am I disturbing you?* (1998)—is about the young Québécois Delphine, adrift in Paris and obsessed by a married lover whom she thought had made her pregnant. She is taken up by Stéphane and Edouard, the narrator, who describes his acquaintance with her until her death; it was nominated for the Giller Prize. *Un habit de lumière* (1999)—*A suit of light* (2000)—is made up brief, luminous, sometimes mordant monologues by Rose-Alba Almevida, a Spanish concierge working in Paris; her young son Miguel, who for her is 'like some unbearable dazzle of light. A real little torero in his suit of light'; her husband Pedro; Jean-Ephrem de la Tour, a black dancer at the Paradis perdu nightclub who is adored by both mother and son; and a neighbour. The monologues express the mother's daydreaming 'until a gnawing hatred for the life given to her sweeps over her like an equinoctial tide', in the words of the neighbour; the love and rage she elicits in her husband; and the boy's fantasies as he puts on makeup and a dress, or as he becomes obsessed with Jean-Ephrem and is finally rejected, with tragic consequences. These last four novels make up *Anne Hébert: collected later novels* (2003), with an interesting Introduction by Hébert's friend, Mavis GALLANT.

The astonishing violence of Hébert's plots, the rigour of her vocabulary, the sureness of her craft, and her intense dramatic sense have brought her an enviable reputation as a novelist that extends beyond her native Québec to an international readership. See *Anne Hébert: essays on her works* (2007) edited by Lee Skallerup.

Heighton, Steven (b. 1961). Born in Toronto, he grew up in Northern Ontario, and has lived in several places in Western Canada, and in Red Lake, Japan. He attended Queen's University, Kingston, Ontario (B.A., 1985; M.A., 1986). Inspired by Victor COLEMAN's creative-writing class at Queen's, he turned his attention to writing poems, some of which are distinctive and memorable, and highly poetic prose. He lives in Kingston and was editor of *Quarry* magazine (1988–94). The centre section of Heighton's first collection of poems, *Stalin's carnival* (1989), is presented as translations of poems written by the Russian dictator. One long sequence in *The ecstacy of skeptics: poems* (1994) explores the Apollonian and Dionysian poles of experience, using theories of the left and right brain hemispheres. Heighton's most accomplished (and most enjoyable) poetry collection is *The address book* (2004). The first poem, 'Address book', of the first section (called 'Fourteen Addresses') is about starting a new address book, noting the names of 'every friend / you buried or let drift, those Home for the Aged / maiden relations, who never raged / against the dying of anything, and in the end / just died.' The fourth and last section, 'Fifteen approximations', contains striking translations of poems by Rimbaud, NELLIGAN, Homer, Rilke, Dante, Baudelaire, and others. Heighton's most recent poetry collection is *Patient frame* (2010). His first collection of stories, *Flight paths of the emperor* (1992, rpr. 2001), explores the intersection of Japanese and Western cultures and the theme of change and turmoil.

On earth as it is (1995, rpr. 2001) is made up of eleven stories in the forms of elegies, confessions, and memories that range from Kingston to Kathmandu; in the novella 'Translation of April', the narrator recalls moods and moments of a deceased lover. Heighton's ambitious first novel, *The shadow boxer* (2000, rpr. 2001)—set in northern Ontario, Toronto, and Cairo—is about young Sevigne Torrins, who lives with his father in Sault Ste Marie (his mother has gone to Cairo with his older brother and her lover), and takes up boxing to impress his father, who has also infected him with a passion to become a writer. *Foreign ghosts* (1989) is made up of poetic journal entries of a trip to Japan written in the style of Basho's *Narrow road to the deep north*. In *The admen move on Lhasa: writing and culture in a virtual world* (1997), an extended essay, Heighton expresses his dislike of corporate culture, advertising, and tourism; the argument is sketchy, but the prose is elegant and poetic.

Afterlands (2005), which has been published internationally, is an accomplished novel that brings to life an extraordinary event in the Far North. In 1871 the US navy sent the USS *Polaris* to the Arctic to plant the American flag at the North Pole. Trapped in ice for a whole winter, it turned back. During a storm off Ellesmere Island nineteen members of the crew and six dogs climb onto an ice floe, taking two large rowboats with them. The castaways were a white American (George Tyson, the senior officer, who takes command); a black American, the chef; five Germans (including Roland Kruger, a prominent character); plus a Dane, a Swede, an Englishman, and two Inuit families—notably Tukulito (Hanna), her husband Ebierbing (Joe), and their young daughter Punni. For more than six months they were lodged on a shrinking ice floe drifting south—amid many crises, including shortage of food (killing dogs to eat their meat) and animosities (though much bad behaviour is mixed with noble, heroic behaviour). Out hunting, Ebierbing (Joe) has lost his Inuit companion, Hans Christian, and when Joe comes back to the group only Kruger offers to help: 'Ebierbing takes Kruger's mitten firmly in his own and they push into the white-out, hand in hand like schoolchildren lost in a forest.... Snow burns into Kruger's eyes like whipped sand on a beach, then freezes on his lashes, sealing them shut. He staggers blindly, still pulled by Ebierbing. After a moment the healing pressure of a warm, bare palm over his eyes, patiently thawing them open.' (Hans turns up and is saved.) The castaways are finally discovered by a steamer. While there is much more in the novel—such as Kruger's later life in Mexico and his meeting again with George Tyson in Washington in 1889—Heighton's extraordinary reconstruction of human beings at the mercy of Nature at its most extreme (supplemented by numerous extracts from George Tyson's 1874 book, *Arctic Experiences*) is a distinct literary success. *Every lost country* (2010)—in which Heighton engaged his considerable talent as a writer of fiction in a distant, exotic location, Nepal and China—is about Lewis Book, a former *Médecins sans frontiers* doctor, and his teenaged daughter Sophie, who are on a climbing expedition in Nepal led by Wade Lawson, and become involved in the Chinese pursuit of Tibetan refugees; the doctor and Amaris, a Chinese-Canadian filmmaker who is Lawson's cinematographer, are captured. The characterizations, and the action that unfolds, blend in an accomplished, even thrilling novel.

Helwig, David (b. 1938). Born in Toronto, he lived there, then in Hamilton, Ontario, and Niagara-on-the-Lake before attending the University of Toronto (B.A, 1960) and the University of Liverpool (M.A., 1962). He then taught at Queen's University, Kingston, Ontario (1962–74). He also taught at the penitentiary near Kingston, an experience that led to his non-fiction work, *A book about Billie* (1972), created from taped interviews with a habitual offender and revealing the author's fascination with criminal cleverness and cunning. Helwig gave up teaching in 1974 to become the literary manager of CBC-TV (until 1980); since than he has devoted himself to writing full time. He now lives in Prince Edward Island. In 2008 he received the $20,000 Matt Cohen Award: In Celebration of a Writing Life. He was made a Member of the Order of Canada in 2009.

Helwig's first collection of poems, *Figures in a landscape* (1967), delineated with clarity and directness ordinary domestic events, as well as artistic figures such as Canaletto, Matisse, Gordon Craig, and Bunyan. Many of the poems were reprinted in *The sign of the gunman* (1969)—the title sequence indicating how his work had begun to turn to darker, violent themes. *The best name of silence* (1972) has poems, many narratives, and dramatic monologues whose characters struggle with spiritual crises involving risk and danger. The narrative poems in *Atlantic crossings* (1974) focus on four travellers making the ocean journey, meditating on the paradoxes of human behaviour and the struggle between evil and violence and decency, even elaborating on the polarities of morality and intelligence opposed to creative inventiveness or even madness. These conflicts surface in the opening poem of *A book of the hours* (1979), based on the relationship between the scholar Thomas Bullfinch and his ward. Poems from these books—along with new poems—were collected in *The rain falls from rain* (1982). *Catchpenny poems* (1983) contains poems arising from nineteenth-century prints. The title poem of *The hundred old names* (1988) proclaims, on Chinese nights, that 'The vanished/ come here and speak/in ancient insect voices./We of the Hundred Old Names are still always among you'. *The beloved* (1992) traces the interconnected lives of David and Goliath, Saul and Jonathon, and Absolom and Bathsheba; in the title poem of *A random gospel* (1996), each part has a Biblical epigraph. *Telling stories* (2000) contains *Atlantic crossings, Catchpenny poems, The beloved,* and begins with 'The boy inventor', based on 'a story I found in the introduction to a copy of Bulfinch's mythology'. The enjoyable poems in *The human day* (2000) make up a variegated collection, beginning with a poem entitled 'Montreal' and ending with a poem about the Picasso Museum in Paris—with poems about Al Purdy ('Al on the Island') music ('Sonata for the other hand'), and the hottest day of the year ('16 July 1998'), among many others, in between. *The year one* (2004) is a collection of long poems, one for every month of the year; they are narratives that draw on memories of his life.

Helwig's first collection of short stories, *The streets of summer,* was published in 1969. He went on to write novels with a wide range of themes and subjects, from the domestic to the religious and musical. His interest in the ordinary is at the centre of his sequence of four novels set in Kingston: *The glass knight* (1976), *Jennifer* (1979), *It is always summer* (1982), and *A sound like laughter* (1983). The bishop (1986) is about the dying Henry, an Anglican bishop, to whom the people he was most touched by—including his Inuit charges in the Arctic—come back in memory. *A postcard from Rome* (1988, rpr. 1989), about a Canadian opera singer, has a strong operatic thrust, with scenes from *Der Rosenkavalier* occurring throughout as a leitmotif. *The time of her life* (2000), set in North America and France, is about the long and multi-faceted life of Jean Dunphy. Some of the characters and ideas in his ambitious novel *Just say the words* (1994) appeared in *The blueberry cliffs* (1993), a collection of short prose pieces that are poetic 'takes' on relationships and people. The novel *Saltsea* (2006) tests Helwig's ability to handle a range of characters connected with the hotel called Saltsea on Prince Edward Island—previous owners, caretakers, and guests.

Four novellas attest to Helwig's irrepressibility as a writer. In the discursive, playful *Close to the fire* (1999) the lawyer-narrator, who refers to himself as 'the wicked uncle', takes Meg away from her much older husband, Orland ('a lovely man whose wife I would steal away'), and marries her. He calls Meg (Marijke) the Dutchess because she's Dutch; her two daughters are 'the little Dutchesses'. Many years later she learns that Orland is dying and says to her husband: 'I want him to come here.' 'There were girls who wanted friendship or a little fun, but I wanted a straight train to heaven. I was always disappointed until the adventure of my first adultery, insatiable upon the rich flesh of Orland's naughty wife. It was forbidden, and it was perfect. I swore I couldn't live without her, made her leave him, and now here we were, facing the dark days of the year, and she said she wanted to bring him back. Time foreshortened, and the years that had gone by, second by second, had turned themselves into bits of memory….' Orland is met at the bus station (he has one leg) and is given a bedroom, in which he eventually dies. Some time before this event—witnessed only by the narrator—Jane the Carpenter constructs his coffin. *The stand-in* (2002) begins 'It is death brought me here, ladies and gentlemen. I am not the man you wanted, but Denman Tarrington, who had been invited to deliver this first set of Jackson lectures, is no longer with us. A week ago he was found dead on a green tile floor in front of a mirror covered with steam in a hotel near Lincoln Centre.' The novella is made up of the stand-in's three lectures, in which he discusses all kinds of things, including (in the first lecture) his meetings with Tarrington in Paris, the Canadian painter

James Wilson Morrice, and Somerset Maugham's and Arnold Bennett's acquaintance with Morrice (both writers used him in their novels). *Stand-in* is a *jeu d'esprit*. *Duet* (2004) brings two cranky oldsters together—Carmen, a retired Toronto policeman whose wife has died, and Norma who has a junk shop—and sensitively describes a gradual change in their relationship. In *Smuggling donkeys* (2007) the life of Warren Thouless, a retired teacher (and actor) whose wife has left him to go to India, is changed by a former student, Tessa Niles, who talks him into buying a deconsecrated church and turning it into a theatre.

The child of someone (1997) is a collection of autobiographical pieces that includes 'The garden of the gods', a brief memoir of Helwig's friend Tom MARSHALL. *Living here* (2001) is a collection of essays about Helwig's various interests, beginning with an illuminating and little-known account of two poets, Robert FINCH and Edward LACEY. Two other Canadian writers are the subjects of 'A walk round Hugh MacLennan' and 'Al' [Purdy]. Helwig edited *A magic prison: letters from Edward Lacey* (1995).

The names of things: a memoir (2006) is an informal autobiography that discursively, but enjoyably, recalls not only Helwig's family life but his life as a writer and his many relationships in the world of Canadian literature and publishing, notably the OBERON PRESS.

Hémon, Louis (1880–1913). Born in Brest, France, he moved to Paris with his family when he was still young. His father, Félix Hémon, was a university instructor and France's inspector-general of public education. Louis took courses in oriental languages at the Sorbonne and received a law degree. After finishing his military service at Chartres (1901–2), he went to England (1903) and made his home for eight years in London, where he honed his writing skills as correspondent for a French sports magazine. During that period he married Lydia O'Kelly, with whom he had a daughter, Lydia Kathleen. Leaving both wife and daughter with her family in England, he set sail for Canada in 1911. Hémon spent short periods in Quebec City and Montreal—he worked briefly as a bilingual stenographer for a Montreal insurance company—and then went north, living at Péribonka in the Lac Saint-Jean area, working on the farm of Samuel Bédard. It was there that he wrote his now-famous MARIA CHAPDELAINE: *récit du Canada français*. After sending the manuscript to France, he set out for western Canada, but was killed in a train mishap at Chapleau, Ontario, at the age of thirty-three. *Maria Chapdelaine* appeared in serial form in *Le Temps* (Jan.–Feb. 1914), but was not published in book form in Canada until 1916. Criticized by some French Canadians for the unromantic view it presented of life among the *habitants*, it was nevertheless quickly recognized as an important work of fiction and has achieved the status of a classic. An English translation by William Hume BLAKE, with the subtitle *A tale of the Lake St. John country*, was published in 1921 and remains the standard one, with reprints in 1984, 1985, 1992, 2004, and 2005. Alan Brown produced a new translation for a large-format limited edition—illustrated by Gilles Tibo, with an introduction by Roch CARRIER—that was published in 1989 (rpr. 1992). Hémon wrote other fiction: *Colin-Maillard* (1924), translated by Arthur Richmond as *Blind man's buff* (1924); *Battling Malone, pugiliste* (1925), translated by W.A. Bradley as *Battling Malone and other stories* (1925); and *Monsieur Ripois and nemesis* (1925), translated by W.A. Bradley—the French text, *Monsieur Ripois et la némésis*, was not published until 1950. A collection of short stories, *La belle que voilà* (1923), was translated by W.A. Bradley as *My fair lady* (1923). All Hémon's works were published posthumously. Hémon's fascinating life and death have been the subject of much speculation in several publications. But all that may be said with certainty about this extraordinary man is that his life and work provoked French Canadians to scrutinize their own culture in a way they had never done before. For this reason alone, if for no other, Canadians may claim Hémon as their own.

Hendry, Tom (b. 1929). Born in Winnipeg, he started his practice there as a chartered accountant in 1955 when he was also writing short stories for the Canadian Broadcasting Corporation and acting in television and radio productions. His first play, *Do you remember?* (unpublished), originally produced by CBC Winnipeg in 1954, was directed by John Hirsch for the Rainbow Stage in the summer of 1957. That same year Hirsch and Hendry co-founded Theatre 77, which, in 1958, merged with the Winnipeg Little Theatre and became the Manitoba Theatre Centre. Giving up accounting in 1960 to work in theatre full time, Hendry was the first manager/producer of Winnipeg's Rainbow Stage, while also serving as administrator of the Manitoba Theatre Centre. The Centre produced his plays *Trapped* (unpublished) in 1961 and in 1964 *All*

about us, a Brechtian musical co-written with Len PETERSON and Alan Lang that toured the country before becoming CTV's first dramatic production. From 1964 to 1969 Hendry was secretary-general of the Canadian Theatre Centre. He served as literary manager for the Stratford Festival for two years; co-founded in 1971 Playwrights Co-op and Toronto Free Theatre; and in 1974 co-founded (with Douglas Riske) the Banff Playwrights Colony and the Banff Playwriting Department, directing the Banff programs for three years. From 1972 to 1982 he was alternately treasurer and chair of Playwrights Canada (now PLAYWRIGHTS GUILD OF CANADA) and president of Toronto Free Theatre. He was policy director of the Toronto Arts Council from 1985 to 1994 and was made an Officer of the Order of Canada in 1995.

In Hendry's *Fifteen miles of broken glass* (1972), produced by CBC-TV in 1967 and CBC Radio in 1968 and adapted for the stage in 1969, the central character, Alec McNabb, is a passionately committed air cadet who despairs when the Second World War ends three months before he comes of age. Some people were outraged by Hendry's musical *Gravediggers of 1942* (1973)—with music by Steven Jack—which contrasts the facts of the Dieppe disaster with the youthful enthusiasm of a group of kids trying to raise money for War Bonds. In both works the idealistic and romantic yearning to participate in a great conflict is set against the harsh realities the young characters must later face. *Satyricon* (unpublished, produced in 1969) was the first big-budget Canadian theatre piece performed at the Stratford Festival. It is a satire on middle-class values and vulgarity based on the satirical romance by Nero's arbiter of elegance, Petronius. (Hendry's songs, set to music by Stanley Silverman, became the basis for Richard Foreman's off-Broadway production *Doctor Selavy's magic theatre* [unpublished, produced in 1972], the United Artists recording of which is now a collector's item.) Hendry's *How are things with the walking wounded?* (1972), set in Montreal during Expo 67, opens with Willy, an affluent English-Canadian businessman, hosting a party for his young French-Canadian lover, René, in celebration of their two-year relationship. Much to his dismay Willy discovers that his fortune is not enough to keep René, and he is left to rearrange his alliances. In *Finger of fate* (2006), a five-character play set in a café in a small Ontario town north of London, the easy—sometimes amusing, sometimes bickering—exchange of dialogue among four of the characters carries the play along successfully until the newly widowed Grace Oakley appears towards the end. She, a former friend of Melvin's, is the finger of fate, and all ends happily. *Byron* (unpublished, produced in 1976), based on Harriet Beecher Stowe's *Lady Byron Vindicated* (1870), with music by Steven Jack, and *Hogtown: Toronto the Good* (unpublished, produced in 1981), with music by Paul Hoffert, both present imagined meetings and struggles between historic figures. In *Byron*, Stowe, a friend of Lady Byron in real life, visits Lord Byron in Italy and, with puritanical zeal, rails against his aristocratic humanitarian stance, demanding from him heroic action. The central characters in *Hogtown*, a musical about the legislation of civic morality, are taken from local history: vice-busting Toronto mayor William Howland and the madam of a brothel, Belle Howard. The use of serious subject matter, plus the inclusion of a musical score that is intended to widen the work's popular appeal, are characteristic of most of Hendry's plays.

Hennepin, Louis. See Writing in NEW FRANCE.

Henry, Alexander, the Elder. See EXPLORATION LITERATURE IN ENGLISH: 2.

Henry, George (Maungwudaus, 1811–after 1855). Born at the Forty-Mile Creek in the Credit River area (in present-day Ontario) to Mesquacosy and Tubinaniqua (the mother of Peter JONES), Henry was an Ojibwa who converted to Christianity in 1824 and became one of the most promising Aboriginal candidates for the Methodist ministry. Along with Peter Jones, John Sunday, and Peter JACOBS, he was considered one of the foremost members of the Methodist Church in Canada, devoting fifteen years to the conversion of his people to Christianity, travelling long distances, teaching, interpreting, preaching, and enjoying great respect among his own people and his Methodist superiors. In the late 1830s he helped James Evans write an Ojibwa hymn book and regularly sent letters to the *Christian Guardian*, the Methodist newspaper. In 1840 he suddenly left the ministry. For the next three years he worked as the government interpreter at the St Clair Mission; and in 1843, to his half-brother Peter Jones's horror, he organized a dance troupe to tour the United States and Europe. Wherever they stopped, they were entertained and honoured as celebrities by royalty and high society alike. Henry's reminiscences and impressions of his experiences overseas appeared in three pamphlets, of which *An account of the Chippewa Indians, who have been travelling among the whites in the United States, England, Ireland, Scotland, France and Belgium* (Boston, 1848) is his most detailed literary effort. It records his impressions of persons and places in London, Paris, Dublin, Edinburgh, and Glasgow, as well as shrewd comments on the contemporary scene and amusing anecdotes. His perceptive and amusing impressions are the first of few Aboriginal testimonials regarding Europeans that survive.

Herbert, John (1926–2001). Born John Herbert Brundage, he was educated in Toronto until age seventeen, when he went to work, first in the advertising department of Eaton's. Following a six-month sentence in the Guelph Reformatory in 1947—the outcome of being harassed by local toughs who tried to rob him and who accused him of homosexuality at a time when it was illegal—he worked at a variety of jobs. In 1955 he began to study ballet and theatre in Toronto, and during the 1960s he served successively as artistic director for three Toronto theatre companies, including his own Garret Theatre Studio. He was also a teacher of drama and writing. Of Herbert's published dramas, the most famous is *FORTUNE AND MEN'S EYES* (1967; 2nd edn 1974). Set in a Canadian reformatory, it explicitly derives from, but does not duplicate, his own crucial experience of incarceration. (A cross-dresser, even in prison, Herbert based the rebellious 'Queenie' on himself.) It was given a workshop at the Stratford Festival in 1965 and received its first commercial production at the Actors' Playhouse, New York, in Feb. 1967; the film adaptation (1971) was directed by Harvey Hart. *Omphale and the hero* (1974) is reminiscent of, but does not imitate, the style and technique of Tennessee Williams. Melodramatic in situation and dialogue, it calls for expressionism in its set design and in the character's personalities; but it is also implicitly allegorical, offering the audience an opportunity to equate the characters and their predicaments with cultural, political, economic, and moral circumstances in Canada. In a town on the border between two French- and English-speaking provinces a drifter, Mac, and a prostitute, Antoinette, become lovers out of loneliness and the need for comfort. Partly because of greed, partly under pressure from the mayor and policeman, Mac deserts Antoinette for a rich Italian widow. Four short plays published together as *Some angry summer songs* (1976)—*Pearl divers, Beer room, Close friends,* and *The dinosaurs*—also deal with varieties of relationship and betrayal, further exploring the frequent emphasis in Herbert's work on the desperate need people have for human contact, the desperate measures they will take to achieve it, and the even more despairing retreats they will often ultimately choose in favour of personal security and safety. Herbert, who lived in Toronto, was writer-in-residence and associate director of The Smile Company, beginning in 1984.

Highway, Tomson (b. 1951). Born on a trapline in northern Manitoba, he spoke only Cree until at age six he was separated from his family (of twelve children) to attend a Roman Catholic boarding school in The Pas, and when he was fifteen a high school in Winnipeg. A gifted pianist, he studied with William Aide at the University of Manitoba; he spent a year in London, England, before graduating from the University of Western Ontario in London, Ontario in 1976 with a B.Mus. and a B.A. in English. While at Western, Highway worked with, and was influenced by, James REANEY. Highway then rejected what he termed 'the white man's game', and worked with various Native organizations across Canada for seven years. In 1985 he wrote and directed *A ridiculous spectacle in one act* with the De-ba-jeh-mu-jig Theatre on Manitoulin Island, Ontario. This Native theatre company also workshopped *The Rez sisters* (1988), which catapulted Highway to national recognition when it was produced in Toronto by Act IV Theatre Company and Native Earth Performing Arts. Touring across Canada and to the Edinburgh Festival in 1993, it was produced in New York and translated into French. Irreverent, exuberant, touching, and broadly humorous, the play features a trickster figure, Nanabush, as a positive healing force who effects magical transformations in the lives of seven women on a reserve (the Rez) as they make an epic journey to the Biggest Bingo in the World. The cultural collision between Native and non-Native societies is given a darker, more violent treatment in the second play in a projected Rez series, *Dry Lips oughta move to Kapuskasing* (1990), which focuses on seven eccentric men on the reserve. Following its premiere, co-produced by Theatre Passe Muraille and Native Earth, *Dry Lips* transferred to the Royal Alexandra Theatre, Toronto, for an unprecedented run in a commercial theatre. The third play in the Rez series, *Rose* (2003), is very long (138 pages), is in 3 acts and 37 scenes, and has 17 characters.

Starting off as a cabaret of songs, produced by Native Earth Performing Arts, the play was work shopped by the Canadian Stage Company and produced once in 1999 by the University College Drama Programme, University of Toronto. Rose of the title—Chief Big Rose, aged fifty-nine—is chief of the Wasaychigan Hill Reserve in 1992 and must constantly defend her position, particularly against Big Joey, who wants to open an extravagant casino in the women's Community Hall. The published edition of the play ends with a personal essay by Highway, 'Should only Native actors have the right to play Native roles?' *Ernestine Shuswap gets her trout: a 'string quartet' for four female actors* (2005) centres on the Native peoples of British Columbia realizing that they had lost their lands and on the grievances of fourteen chiefs of the Thompson River basin listed in a signed document that was presented to Prime Minister Sir Wilfrid Laurier in Kamloops on 25 August 1910. He never appears, of course, since this is a play for four women whose exchanges dramatize not only the tragedy but the comedy implicit in the theme. *Comparing mythologies* (2003) is Highway's Charles R. Bronfman Lecture in Canadian Studies, a public lecture delivered on 23 September 2002 at the University of Ottawa. It is prefaced by 'The opposite of prayer: an introduction to Tomson Highway' by John Moss.

Between 1986 and 1992 Highway was artistic director of Native Earth Performing Arts, nurturing other Native playwrights such as Daniel David MOSES and Monique Mojica, as well as staging his own plays. Among his seven unpublished plays are *Aria*, a series of twenty-two monologues about Native womanhood first performed in Toronto in 1987. *New song ... new dance* (performed 1988), preceded *The sage, the dancer, and the fool* (performed 1989), about a young male Native's day in Toronto (played by three actors symbolizing the three nouns of the title). In 1993 Centaur Theatre, Montreal, premiered *Annie and the Old One*. Highway enhanced his reputation as a writer by publishing a successful novel, *Kiss of the Fur Queen* (1998, rpr. 1999), about the Cree brothers Jeremiah and Gabriel Okimasis, one a pianist, the other a dancer; elements of Native folklore have been seamlessly woven into the dramatic and moving narrative. Though the characters have been described by the author as fictitious, Tomson and his late brother René cannot help but come to mind. Highway was given honorary degrees (D.Litt.) by the University of Winnipeg (1993), the University of Western Ontario (1993), the University of Brandon (1996),

Laurentian University (2000), and Université de Montréal (2005); he became a Member of the Order of Canada in 1994.

Highway wrote the bilingual texts (English and Cree) for three large-format picture books for children, beautifully illustrated by Brian Deines: *Caribou song* (2001), *Dragonfly kites* (2002), and *Fox on the ice* (2003).

Hill, Lawrence (b. 1957). He was born in Oakville, Ontario, and educated at Université Laval, Quebec City (B.A. in economics, 1980), and the Johns Hopkins University, Baltimore (M.A. in writing, 1993). He taught creative writing at Ryerson Polytechnic University, Toronto, and now writes full time; he lives in Burlington, Ontario. The author of three highly readable novels, Hill is especially adept at blending the lives and activities of many characters in a forward-moving narrative. The protagonist of *Some great thing* (1992) is twenty-six-year-old Mahatma Grafton, born in Winnipeg, whose father Ben, a railway porter, wanted him to bear the first name of a great figure in history and settled on the name given to Gandhi (Great Soul). Mahatma (sometimes called Hat) is well educated—he is conversant in French and Spanish—and his up-and-down career as a black reporter with the fictional *Winnipeg Herald* is central. The newsroom, the subversion of Mahatma's gifts as a reporter by a man senior to him, the 'stories'—including a killing in the St Albert-Princeton hockey arena while an English- and a French-speaking team were playing, and the issue of French language rights in Manitoba—give life to the novel, and the relationships of the characters, some of them colourful, give it emotional depth. *Any known blood* (1997, rpr. 1998) is a long, accomplished novel about five generations of Langston Canes. The family history (based, the author says, on that of his own family, though 'almost all of this book is invented') is pieced together by Langston Cane the Fifth in the present day. His father is a prominent Oakville doctor and civil-rights activist, happily married for many years to Dorothy Perkins of Winnipeg, a white woman—the narrator's mother. His grandfather, Langston Cane III, was educated at Lincoln University in Pennsylvania, and eloped with Rose Bridges, of a well-to-do black Baltimore family, to the consternation of her mother; in Oakville he became a highly respected minister in the African Methodist Episcopal Church. His great-grandfather was born in Oakville and grew up in Baltimore, where he was raised by Nathan Shoemaker, a Quaker, and graduated from college to become a minister, in Baltimore, of the A.M.E. Church. His great-great-grandfather, Langston Grafton I, born in Virginia in 1828, escaped from Maryland and landed in Oakville in 1850 on the Underground Railway. He left Oakville with John Brown who, determined to destroy slavery, two months later fatally attacked the US weapons arsenal at Harpers Ferry, Virginia, in 1859. Hill skilfully combines the details of a long family history, which opens up gradually and not in chronological order, in an intimate account of the Canes' joys and sufferings. Some of the characters in his first novel, among them Mahatma Grafton, appear in this one. *The book of Negroes* (2007)—its American title is *Someone knows my name*—is impressive for the depiction of its main character and for its masterly interweaving of different times, places, ways of life, and many secondary characters in a smooth narrative that captivates the reader. It begins in London in 1802, with the words of the narrator Aminata Diallo: 'I seem to have trouble dying. By all rights I should not have lived this long.' The second chapter is dated Bayo, 1745. Aminata is eleven and living happily with her parents in a village in West Africa; she has learned birthing from her mother, who is a skilled midwife. Suddenly many villagers are abducted by African slavers, her parents are killed, and Aminata is attached by rope to a long line of captives being taken to a slave ship. The narrative that follows—beginning with the terrible voyage across the Atlantic, described in great detail—is an epic story. Aminata learns to read and eventually becomes fluent in English and a lover of books. ('Reading felt like a daytime dream in a secret land.') In 1757, on an island off North Carolina, she is a slave on the indigo plantation of Robinson Appleby, who rapes her. (This event, and the attempt of the cook, Happy Jack, to comfort her and take her away, are sensitively described.) Two years later her lover Chekura makes her pregnant and they marry; when Appleby sees her dressed in finery, and expecting, he tears the dress off her and shaves her head. She is sixteen when her son is born and Appleby sells the baby, and he sells Aminata too to Solomon Lindo, who lives in Charles Town (Charleston), South Carolina, where her life improves greatly. Lindo goes to Manhattan in 1775 and takes Aminata with him. She escapes and attains her freedom. It is there that she is asked to list, in the 'Book of Negroes', all the black Loyalists who will be going to Nova Scotia. She herself goes there in 1783, to Birchtown and Shelburne, and gives birth to a daughter, May, who three years later is abducted by Meena's employers, the

Witherspoons, and taken on a ship to Boston. Poor treatment 'of the landless Black Loyalists and the perpetuation of slavery' in Nova Scotia lead to an exodus by many Negroes, including Aminata, back to Africa—under the leadership of the abolitionist John Clarkson—to Freetown, Sierra Leone. Finally, in 1802, Aminata is in London and John Clarkson and his brother Thomas are taking her to the offices of the Committee for the Abolition of the Slave Trade. (Among its members was William Wilberforce, who in 1807 secured passage of a bill abolishing the slave trade.) The abolitionists said they would interview her, 'with delicacy and all meticulous care', and write a short account of her life, 'including the abuses you suffered in the slave trade.' Aminata told them vehemently that she would write her own story, 'on my terms and my terms only'. She gave William Wilberforce fifty pages to be used for his report to the parliamentary committee, before which she appeared. This appearance, and her account of being branded, was in all the newspapers the next day and resulted in an invitation to have tea with the Queen and the mad King George III—as well as, miraculously, in a reunion with her eighteen-year-old daughter May. In the last few pages of the novel Aminata says 'I am finally done. My story is told'—the story we have of her life—and the ending is a happy one. In 2008 *The book of Negroes* won the $15,000 Rogers Writers' Trust Fiction Prize and the Commonwealth Writers' Prize for Best Book, and Hill was chosen the Canadian Booksellers' Association's author of the year. An illustrated edition of *The book of Negroes* was published in 2009.

The deserter's tale: the story of an ordinary soldier who walked away from the war in Iraq (2007) by Joshua Key as told to Lawrence Hill is about the American family man who joined the US army, spent nine months in Iraq, and while home on leave refused to go back; he is seeking asylum in Canada and his case is before the Canadian courts.

Hillen, Ernest (b. 1934). Born of a Dutch father and a Canadian mother, Anna Watson, he moved when he was three with his parents and brother to Indonesia, where his father worked on a tea plantation, and where they lived during the Second World War in extremely difficult circumstances, described in his first book. He immigrated to Canada with his family in 1952 and wrote for many newspapers and magazines, including *Saturday Night*, of which he was a contributing editor. *The way of a boy: a memoir of Java* (1993, rpr.

2008) describes the effects on Hillen as a boy, and on his family, of the Japanese occupation of Java. In 1942 his father was sent to a camp; and when Jerry, his brother, was thirteen he too was sent off (to his father's camp, as Ernest and his mother later learned). Unimaginable privations; brutal treatment witnessed; the endurance by Ernest and his mother of ever-smaller living spaces, under horrible conditions in four camps; portrayals of other people in the camps, some young friends of Ernest, and of his strong, quiet, sensitive mother, who tried always to use her common sense ('This'll be over one day, you know', she'd say, and 'Try to be true to yourself')—all are contained in this mesmerizing narrative. Gentle, warm, childlike in the drift of subjects, yet never skirting the most repugnant details, it is an exceptional example of literary craft. This was followed by a happy, and equally skilled, family chronicle, *Small mercies: a boy after war* (1997, rpr. 2008), which focuses on the ocean voyage to Canada in 1946 and the return after sixteen years of Anna, with her sons, to her parents in Toronto and their 'normal' life there, during which Ernest attended public school. They eventually rejoined his father in Java. In 2009 Hillen published *A weekend memoir*, a collection of travel pieces he published in *Weekend* magazine as a result of travelling across Canada in the 1970s.

Hilles, Robert (b. 1951). Born in Kenora, Ontario, he was educated at the University of Calgary (B.A. in psychology and English, 1976; M.Sc. in educational psychology and computer-assisted instruction, 1984). For ten years he was managing editor of the literary magazine *Dandelion*. From 1983 to 2001 he was professor of computer programming at the DeVry Institute of Technology, Calgary. He lives on Salt Spring Island, B.C.

Hilles won a Governor General's Award for his poetry collection *Cantos from a small room* (1993), moving meditative poems about losing a loved one to cancer. His other collections are *Look the lovely animal speaks* (1980), simple, restrained poems about his childhood and his father; *The surprise element* (1981); *An angel in the works* (1983), which questions love and its limits; *Outlasting the landscape* (1989), lyrical meditations on his daughter, sleep, dreams, family, and time; *Finding the lights on* (1991), *A breath at a time* (1992), *Nothing vanishes* (1996), *Breathing distance* (1997), *Somewhere betweens obstacles and pleasure* (1999), *Higher ground* (2001), *Wrapped within again: new and selected poems* (2003), and *Slow ascent* (2006).

Raising of voices (1993) is a harrowing novel that portrays a family enduring madness and alcoholism in Northern Ontario. *A gradual ruin* (2004), a much more accomplished novel, presents a succession of emotional or striking scenes in two narratives, in more or less alternate chapters, one set in northern Ontario and Winnipeg and the other at the end of the Second World War in Germany, then Russia. We read about Shirley and Alice, unhappy daughters of Wendell in Dryden, Ontario. Shirley leaves home first, for Winnipeg; and Alice follows her. Shirley lives with Rudy, who makes her pregnant; Rudy seduces Alice and makes *her* pregnant with Judith. Alice meets Peter, loves and marries him and Peter adores Judith, who is devastated when he dies. When she hears gossip that Peter was not her real father she turns against her mother, takes to shoplifting, is put in a foster home on a farm, which she leaves in horrendous circumstances. In March 1945, a few weeks before Germany surrendered, paratrooper Tommy Armstrong (from Kenora, Ontario) was part of an Allied operation to capture Berlin before the Russians did, but is in a low-flying glider, which is shot by German ground fire. Tommy bails out, and from then on he is on his own. We read about his travails; his bonding with a suffering German girl (Freda), who eventually dies; his capture by Russians, his imprisonment and torture; his escape and amazing journey by horse to a mansion not far from Moscow, lived in by the beautiful Oksana Yerenko, the unwilling mistress of the colonel-general, who is driven weekly from Moscow to see her. (Her life story as she tells it is a creative marvel in the novel.) Tommy falls in love with Oksana and the two of them manage to reach the Canadian Embassy; there is a chance that they might escape Russia together—but she is taken off the plane. Tommy, heartbroken, returns to Canada alone. (Only here, towards the end of the novel, do the two stories converge.) After teenaged Judith runs from her foster parents' farm, she tries to hitchhike and is picked up by Tommy in his Chrysler New Yorker. 'I can take you as far as Winnipeg,' he says. But as she gets to know him in the car she accepts his invitation to stay in the little house in his back yard. He becomes her support and protector and she quietly assists him domestically. At the end of the novel he drives her to meet Alice, her mother.

Near morning (1995) is a collection of short stories. *Kissing the smoke* (1996) and *Calling the wild* (2005) are family memoirs, the first book focusing on Hilles' grandfather and father, along with an extended meditation on

work; the second is made up of stories about his father.

Hill-Tout, Charles. See ABORIGINAL LEGENDS AND TALES: BIBLIOGRAPHY

Hind, Henry Yule. See EXPLORATION LITERATURE IN ENGLISH: 2.

Hine, Daryl (b. 1936). Born in Vancouver, he studied classics and philosophy at McGill University, Montreal (1954–8), failing to get a degree. In 1958 he received a Canada Foundation-Rockefeller fellowship and travelled to Europe, living in France until 1962. Between 1963 and 1967 he completed his M.A. and Ph.D. degrees in comparative literature at the University of Chicago, and in 1967 joined the English department at Chicago. From 1968 to 1978 he edited the prestigious magazine *Poetry*.

Hine is the author of thirteen books of poetry: *Five poems* (1955); *The carnal and the crane* (1957); *The devil's picture book* (1961); *The wooden horse* (1965); *Minutes* (1968); *In and out: a confessional poem* (privately printed, 1975; rpr. 1989); *Resident alien* (1975); *Daylight saving* (1978); *Selected poems* (1980); *Academic festival overtures* (1985); *Arrondissements* (1988, rev. 1989); *Postscripts* (1991); and *Recollected poems 1951–2004* (2007). His poetic gift was recognized early. He published his first poems in CONTEMPORARY VERSE at the age of fifteen, and *The carnal and the crane* at the age of twenty-one. Northrop FRYE described the experience of reading its long, meditative lines as being 'like watching heavy traffic at night: a brilliant series of phrases moves across a mysteriously dark background.' *Selected poems* presents a good cross-section of themes and styles. His poems are complex, intellectual, and technically sophisticated. Hines delights in traditional forms, experimenting with villanelles, satires, sestinas, and metrical patterns such as iambic pentameter with complicated rhyme schemes. Yet his tone and themes are modern, his voice is intensely personal, and he creates startling colloquial metaphors. The tension between his extraordinary technical mastery and an anguished exploration of the chaos of personal life—as in 'Aftermath'—lends some of his poetry considerable power. A repeated strategy in his poetry is to reinterpret classical mythology in the light of contemporary experience. Most of Hine's poetry, however, is remarkable for the wit, candour, and intelligence with which he explores the range of emotions from lust to love. Hine's two book-length poems—*Academic festival overtures*, written in a modern adaptation of Homeric style, and *In and out*—are moving autobiographical reminiscences of student life, with its homoerotic love affairs; but it is the technical tour de force that impresses. The substantial *Recollected poems 1951–2004* must stand as Hine's most important collection, as it contains his own choice of poems that cover his whole career. In his Introduction he says that while he has attempted free verse 'I have always returned to the metred and rhymed forms with which I am most comfortable.'

The hero of Hine's novel *The prince of darkness and Co.* (1961), British poet Philip Sparrow, author of *A guide to witchcraft*, lives on an island called Xanadu. An elaborate parody of mythology, the book has a climax that occurs on Midsummer Night in an adolescent orgy of sacrifice—the novel's purpose being to contrast those who play intellectually with the 'powers of darkness' and those for whom such forces are real. Hine has also written a travel book, *Polish subtitles: impressions from a journey* (1962), after living briefly in Warsaw to edit English subtitles for a Polish film; and several plays, including *Defunctive music* (1961), *The death of Seneca* (1968), and, for radio, *Alcestis* (1972). Hine has received three Canada Council grants, a Guggenheim Fellowship, a MacArthur Fellowship, and a medal from the American Academy of Arts and Letters.

Hodgins, Jack (b. 1938). Born in Comox, British Columbia, he grew up in the logging and farming settlement of Merville on Vancouver Island and studied creative writing under Earle BIRNEY at the University of British Columbia, from which he received a B.Ed. in 1961. He taught high school in Nanaimo from 1961 to 1980, when he undertook two visiting professorships, the latter at the University of Victoria, where from 1985 to 2002 he was a professor in the Creative Writing Department. In 2006 he received an award for literary excellence by the Lieutenant-Governor of British Columbia. He was made a Member of the Order of Canada in 2009.

Vancouver Island, particularly the Comox Valley where Hodgins was born, has been the setting for most of his books. His first major work was the short-story collection *Spit Delaney's island* (1976), which introduced the recurrent theme that imagination can redeem or transcend the physical. The stories focus either on unhappy characters, limited by their belief that they can 'know' only what they see, or on dreamers, like Spit Delaney himself, who are notable for their shocking, unconventional

behaviour. Structurally unremarkable, the stories feature eccentric characterizations and a pervasive fusion of realism and parable. This collection was quickly followed by two immensely good-humoured and formally innovative novels, *The invention of the world* (1977, NCL, rpr. 2010) and *The resurrection of Joseph Bourne* (1979, GGA, NCL), and by the collection of stories *The Barclay family theatre* (1981, rpr. 1991). Figuring in all these books are the seven daughters of the Barclay family, together with their husbands and children, who first appeared in a story in *Spit Delaney's island* ('Other people's troubles'). *The invention of the world* and *The resurrection of Joseph Bourne* achieve remarkable structural and linguistic adventurousness that parallels that of the main characters: Maggie Kyle (daughter of Christina Barclay) and the poet Joseph Bourne. In the first novel, larger-than-life characters—an evangelist who has beguiled an entire Irish village into coming to Vancouver Island to serve him at his personal colony, an old woman who has spent her life combing the island with donkey and manure spreader in an unsuccessful search for her birthplace, loggers whose Bunyanesque loves and brawls culminate in a wedding that is both feast and battle—are presented in a style that moves easily from fable to interior monologue to fantastic list. In *The resurrection of Joseph Bourne*, Hodgins' contention that the human spirit can 'invent' the world is manifested in the surprising changes brought about in Port Annie, an isolated Vancouver Island community, by a tidal wave that bears both a Peruvian ship and an ostensibly magical young woman of quintessential grace and beauty. Consciously defying the tradition of 'modern novels' in which 'believers were always made to look like fools', Hodgins creates an extravagant, life-affirming book that encompasses parody, romance, mystery, biblical allegory, and backwoods humour. *The Barclay family theatre* illuminates the background of various Barclay characters, and extends, often in discontinuous narratives, Hodgins' investigation of the contrast between the local, with its ambiguous pleasures of repetition and domesticity, and the risks and large vistas of the surrounding world. *The honorary patron* (1987) and *Innocent cities* (1990, rpr. 2000) further contrast the local and the cosmopolitan. *The Macken charm* (1995, rpr. 2000) returned to the up-island locale and extravagant style of Hodgins' early fiction. Although lacking the narrative complexity of the two earlier up-island novels, it reasserts their emphasis on vision and imagination, and their complex and entertaining mock-epic interpretations of working-class lives. Here the son of another Barclay sister narrates his teenage struggle to believe in his dream of being an internationally successful filmmaker when the only world he has experienced is that of the narrow but energetically procreative Mackens and Barclays, whose triumphs and failures have been legendary in the Comox Valley but have never survived contact with a larger world. *Broken ground* (1998, rpr. 1999) is an ambitious and moving novel set in the pioneering settlement at Portuguese Creek on Vancouver Island, created by ex-soldiers returned from the Great War. The long first section, dated 1922, is called 'Voices from Portuguese Creek', the voices being those of half-a-dozen settlers who speak in separate narratives; the last section is dated 1996. Linking the two is the theme, discreetly conveyed, of how lives in the present were coloured and affected by the war and its horrors, evoked by memories and in letters. *Distance* (2003), highly praised when it was published, centres on Sonny Aalto, a successful businessman (whose wife left him, then died) who lives in Ottawa, which is described as he thinks about it on his flight to Vancouver Island to see his father Timo, who was reportedly dying. Of Finnish heritage, Timo had been a failed logger; never much for work, he is a drinker and reads Russian novels; he had been deserted by his wife, who left him with young Sonny, to return to Australia, her homeland. When Sonny meets his father in hospital, Timo seems to be recovering and is cantankerous, resenting the fact, as his friends do, that his son has seen little of him over the years. Distance exists in the relationship of Sonny with his father, in that of Sonny with his difficult daughter Charlotte, and in the trip Sonny, Timo, and Charlotte take to Australia after Sonny received a letter from his mother that was an invitation (she has a new family and a very large property). They experience Sydney, and are then driven to Queensland to visit Sonny's mother, Virra Hawkins, and her estate at Kalevan Station. But they never meet her. The land is flooded and Sonny only receives a message from her lawyer about the sale of her property to the state government (she is described as a tyrant), which throws into disarray her two sons, half-brothers of Sonny, who removes himself from this event. He and his father (but not Charlotte) fly back to Vancouver Island and, it is suggested, to a permanent relationship with Holly Fitzgerald, who had entered his life in B.C. 'He can't imagine the rest of his life without Holly, but the surprise is that he cannot imagine the rest of his life without his father, either.' For one reader

this long, overwritten novel would have been more enjoyable without the intrusion of the conversations of so many uninteresting secondary characters—names only—that weaken the portrayal of the Aaltos themselves and their immediate relationships. The much more focused treatment of characters and events recommends Hodgins' stories in *Damage done by the storm* (2004). 'Balance' is a surprising and amusing story narrated by a man who helps to make orthotics, moulded inserts for shoes that he calls 'feet', and who falls in love with the feet of Donna Rossini. 'Balancing the foot in my palm, I felt the warmth of her flesh.' He writes to her. Hodgins is good at describing the warmth of family life. In 'This summer's house' Nathan and Astrid Wagner are waiting for their family to arrive at the summer house they've rented, 'their parents, their children, their grandchildren. Four carloads of them.' They 'missed the three o'clock sailing', but there follows a narrative that interweaves incidents in the present, family memories, and repeated appearances of Freddie, who had vacated the house to make room for them and returns to find things he had left behind. Finally the ferry is about to arrive with the family: '… the commotion would likely scare [Freddie] off. And if it did not, Nathan Wagner, who'd had plenty of practice, would just have to find a way to help him fit in.' In the title story retired Senator Alfred Buckle is preparing to attend the opening of the shop of his grandson Warren, whom he and his wife Judith had raised. But there has been a dreadful snowstorm around Ottawa and the train trip was halted by a tree falling over the track. The Senator, despairing, after all the events of the trip, prepares himself to arrive at Warren's party very late. There are seven other stories in this collection, all of them interesting. Hodgins's *The master of happy endings*, published in 2010, is an affecting novel about what may be the final adventure in the life of Axel Thorstad, a former schoolteacher aged seventy-seven and a recent widower living on a remote island off the British Columbia coast, when he places a want ad in a newspaper offering himself as a tutor for a young student. Mrs Montana answers and Axel finds himself driving to Los Angeles with her teenaged son, Travis, an actor who is on his way to a TV engagement in Hollywood and whom Axel coaches.

Hodgins edited *A passion for narrative: a guide for writing fiction* (1993; rpr. 1995; rev. 2001), an ingenious combination of Hodgins' illuminating commentaries on various pointers illustrated by brief quotations from the works of many famous writers.

Hollingshead

Hollingshead, Greg (b. 1947). Gregory Albert Frank Hollingshead was born in Toronto and raised in Woodbridge; Ontario; he attended Victoria College, University of Toronto (B.A., 1968; M.A., 1970), and the University of London (Ph.D., 1974). Beginning to teach at the University of Alberta in 1975, he was Professor of English there from 1993 and in 2005 was appointed Professor Emeritus; he is also Director of the Writing Programs at the Banff Centre for the Arts. The stories in his *Famous players* (1982) owe much to the surrealism of the early lyrics of Bob Dylan and the fiction of Samuel Beckett and William Burroughs. While characters can be outwardly conventional, their lives are tumultuous with irrational events, unexplained violence, and reverses of fortune. The narratives are often so compressed they sometimes require repeated readings to sort out details. In the further stories collected in *White Buick* (1992), Hollingshead loosens his style but not the message, which, as in 'When she was gone', explores the deepest reaches of the macabre. His novel *Spin dry* (1992), 'written very much in the shadow of Pynchon's *Crying of Lot 49*', is focused on the lives of suburbanites holding their lives together with dream therapy and eccentric encounter groups. Despite its jaunty comic tone, it failed to capture much of an audience. Hollingshead's strong third collection of stories, *The roaring girl* (1995, GGA; rpr. 2004), became a bestseller for twenty weeks in Canada, with editions in the USA and Britain. Reflecting a more subtle image of middle-class life than his previous work, most of the stories show an affinity with Hollingshead's earliest writing, embedding illogical and unsettling events in what appears to be perfectly ordinary life. *The healer* (1998, rpr. 2004) is about Tim Wakelin, a journalist who goes to the pre-Cambrian country of northern Ontario to meet Carolyn Troyer, said to be a healer through whom forces of nature work on human situations; strange events follow from his romantic relationship with her and from violence induced by her parents. *Bedlam* (2004) is a long historical novel (1797–1818) based on the true story of James Tilly Matthews who was confined in London's oldest hospital for the insane, called Bethlem (known as Bedlam). It begins with a letter he wrote in 1818 to his beloved wife Margaret, who had just visited him, in which he reminisces about the beginning of his trials, saying that she once blamed the Revolution in France for drawing him from her side. 'But that, my love, was only me saving England from the bloody contagion. It was not my two

years as secret emissary between nations nor my three in French gaols that doomed us but a fateful encounter on the last ship to carry me home.' Margaret—who spent twenty years demanding to be given reasons for his incarceration and arguing with the authorities—is the second main character in the novel; the third is the apothecary, John Haslam, who is in charge of him. He tells Margaret on their first meeting: 'As to your husband, I would say he's a republican—in a condition of nervous collapse. Unable to vent his politics for risk of being hanged, he talks nonsense. Whatever the particulars of his initial admission, he's hied himself back to safety [after escaping, Matthews returned] inside the finest madhouse in the world. He's a lunatic, who knows exactly what he's doing....' Margaret's assiduous attempts to free her husband, claiming he's not a lunatic, and Haslam's justifications for holding him, doubts about Haslam's veracity and about the true state of Jamie Matthews' mental health—combined with insights into the separate lives of all three (including Margaret's with her son Jim)—feed into a complex novel that is not all that easy to read. The attempt at late-eighteenth-century language is awkward and inconsistent; and Jamie, Margaret, and Haslam—all three expressing literacy and intelligence in speech and (the Matthews') letters—sound the same. One appreciates, however, the abundant research that went into the novel. For example, as the real John Haslam wrote numerous books—including *Observations on insanity* (1798) and *Illustrations of madness* (1810, rpr. 1988)—Hollingshead sometimes used Haslam's 'own words and phrases'; and Bethlem itself, including its patients and staff, is vividly described, along with the city of London.

Hollingsworth, Margaret (b. 1942). Born in Sheffield, England, she grew up in London and trained as a librarian at Loughborough College; she completed her education in Canada, with a B.A. (1971) in psychology from Lakehead University and an M.F.A. (1974) in theatre and creative writing from the University of British Columbia. From 1992 to 2003 she taught creative writing at the University of Victoria, where she is now Professor Emerita.

A prolific writer of radio and television drama, Hollingsworth has also written many stage plays, including one-act plays that excel at conveying the gist of a lifetime in a brief episode of the present. *Bushed* (1973, rpr. 1981) is set in the laundromat of a northern town; it is used as shelter and meeting place by two retired workers whose exclusion from the world of action, except in fantasy and memory, is reflected in women's mimed sheet-folding and the relentless turning of the machines. *Alli alli oh* (1979) is virtually the monologue of a woman retreating to insanity from two contrasting lifestyles, neither of whose demands she is willing or able to fulfil. The companion play *Islands* (1983) focuses on a second character from the earlier play, a woman who finds freedom in her unconventional choice of life as a farmer and a lesbian. *Operators* (1975, rev. 1981) is a more complex one-act play that deals with the friendship of two women, night-workers in a northern Ontario factory, who have used games and fantasies to ward off boredom, frustration, and dangerous self-knowledge. An intrusion by a third woman threatens their relationship, but this episode leads to new awareness and a positive, if ambiguous, conclusion. Hollingsworth's most frequently produced work, *Ever loving* (1982), is a multi-scene play that uses techniques of simultaneous action, flashback, 'freezing', and includes popular songs for ironic effect in a story of three war brides of the 1940s—English, Scottish, and Italian—and their difficulties in adapting to Canada and to their husbands' lives. *Mother country* (1980) is set on an island off the British Columbia coast and captures the eccentricities of Canadians who are more English than the English. Through three adult daughters it comically portrays the attempt to break ties with both England and the mother, who embodies qualities traditionally associated with England.

War babies was published with four earlier plays in a collection entitled *Wilful acts* (1985, rev. 1998), introduced by Ann Saddlemyer. This multi-layered drama presents a play within a play, the revealed subconscious of a forty-two-year-old pregnant writer who fears entrapment in domesticity and resents her war-correspondent husband's relative freedom. At the other extreme from the sprawling complexity of this play is the spare economy of *Diving* (1985), where a woman diver, literally on the edge, suggests through her brief monologue the entire scope of woman's lot in a male-dominated society, represented by an insistent male 'voice off'. A second collection, *Endangered species* (1988), contains four highly experimental one-act plays where the surrealism verges on nightmare. For example, *It's only hot for two months in Kapuskasing* has a woman answering an urgent summons to the apartment of an old acquaintance where, in the middle of the

night, she encounters a frightening, bizarre, and inexplicable situation. Hollingsworth returned to the monologue form in the tragi-comic play *In confidence* (1995). Exploring the sexuality of two middle-aged women who, without speaking to one another, hold a kind of intimate mental conversation across three thousand miles, the play re-examines many of her early themes: the immigrant experience, alienation and loneliness, the importance of home, the delicate balance of male/female relations, the range of sexual tastes and the potential violence in them, the subversive strategies women adopt to counteract the narrowness of their worlds, and above all, the power of women's friendships. *Numbrains* (1995) captures contemporary idiom in the short monologue of a teenage boy as he keeps vigil over a dying whale on the beach. His social alienation is counterpointed by his deep knowledge of, and sympathy for, other forms of life.

Be quiet (2003), Hollingsworth's hefty first novel in which Emily CARR is a prominent character, is set not only in Canada but in France in 1911 where Carr met the New Zealand painter Frances Hodgkins, and in England where she was treated for eighteen months in a sanatorium in East Anglia. These two successful painters are contrasted, in present time, with Catherine Van Duren, who is also a painter but who married, had a daughter, Kit, and became an academic in order to support her family. On her retirement she looks forward to resuming her life as a painter. Kit travels to England to find her father, Roger Rintoul. He has a young wife, Ilona, who owns the diary of her great-great-aunt, Winnifred Church, who was in Brittany in 1911 and wrote remorselessly about Emily Carr and Frances Hodgkins. (Ilona dies in childbirth, leaving a twin, whom Kit takes charge of.) Catherine is beset by many problems. In comparison Emily Carr, who gave up everything for her art, lives a relatively stable and contented life in the decade before it ends.

Hollingsworth's short stories, collected in *Swimming under water* (1989), explore similar social and psychological themes as the plays, especially relations between the sexes and the search for home.

Hollingsworth, Michael (b. 1950). Born in Swansea, Wales, he immigrated to Canada with his parents in 1956 and now lives in Toronto. He is both a playwright and a musician, primarily interested in integrating rock music, video, and live theatre. Since his first play, *Strawberry fields* (1973)—inspired by John

Lennon's lyrics and focusing on the aftermath of a rock concert—premiered at Toronto's Factory Theatre Lab in 1973, his work has become exceedingly complex. Hollingsworth's other plays include *Clear light* (1973), based on transcripts of the Watergate trials and bad LSD experiences. The Metropolitan Toronto Police Morality squad closed the production for alleged obscenity in film sequences featuring pornographic clips. *Transworld* (1979), like all his plays, deals with psychotics, madness, drug abuse, and political repression—representing the collective psychosis of society. In the 1980s and early 1990s Hollingsworth created an eight-part play, *The history of the village of small huts: parts 1–8* (1994). This work is a monumental, ironic, and unique vision of Canada's past, described by *Maclean's* as 'Pierre BERTON meets Monty Python'. Based on the idea that the word 'Canada' comes from an Iroquois word loosely translated as 'village of small huts', Hollingsworth created a satire of various colonial periods of Canadian history. Using events from the past to illuminate the difficulties of today, he re-invented Canadian history through the French and British colonial periods, from Jacques Cartier and Champlain to the end of the Second World War. The play includes 19 separate stories, 914 scenes, more than 400 characters, and a veritable encyclopedia of theatrical styles, from burlesque and comedy of manners, to puppets, masks, and computer-generated imagery. Hollingsworth sees the visual image as more natural than the word to an audience raised on television, and feels that the results of his experimentation will lead to a redefinition of drama.

Hood, Hugh (1928–2000). Born in Toronto of an English-Canadian father and a French-Canadian mother, Hugh John Blagdon Hood was educated at the University of Toronto (B.A., 1950; M.A., 1952; Ph.D., 1955), and spent his academic career largely at the Université de Montréal. Academic interests—his dissertation examined the psychology behind the poetry of the English Romantics—and religious convictions combined in his presenting, in many books, a fictional view of Canadian experience in this century that is realistic in detail and emblematic in intent.

Three distinguishing characteristics of Hood's fiction are: 1. An unobtrusive but discernible Roman Catholic perspective on experience: earthly affairs convey the symbolic weight of the spiritual. 2. A close acquaintance with popular culture, the technical aspects of jobs, the inner workings of the bureaucracies shaping contemporary life. 3. A concern with placing Canada's history and culture within the broader frame of Western culture. First recognized for his often superb short fiction, Hood produced eight collections of stories: *Flying a red kite* (1962, rev. 1987), *Around the mountain: scenes from Montreal life* (1967, rpr. 1994), *The fruit man, the meat man and the manager* (1971), *Dark glasses* (1976), *None genuine without this signature* (1980), *August nights* (1985), *A short walk in the rain* (1989), and *You'll catch your death* (1992). The five volumes of Hood's *Collected stories* are: I—*Flying a red kite* (1987), II—*A short walk in the rain* (1989), III—*The isolation booth* (1991), IV—*Around the mountain: scenes from Montreal life* (1994), and V—*After all!* (2003), which contains seventeen stories Hood wrote in the last decade of his life, between September 1991 and December 1994. W.J. KEITH's Foreword to *After all!* pays tribute to Hood as 'One of the most skilful and probing Canadian practitioners of the short story as a subtle and concentrated literary form.' Perhaps the most widely anthologized of his stories are 'Flying a red kite' and 'Recollections of the works department', based on a summer job experience in Toronto, which first published in *The TAMARACK REVIEW* in 1962 (Issue 22). *Light shining out of the darkness and other stories* (2001) was published posthumously in the NEW CANADIAN LIBRARY but is now out of print.

Among Hood's novels, *White figure, white ground* (1964, rpr. 1983), *The camera always lies* (1967), *A game of touch* (1970), and *You can't get there from here* (1972, rpr. 1984), the first three deal with figures within what we now term the cultural industries (painting, film, cartooning), while the last presents a satirical portrait of the corporate forces (economic, philanthropic) unleashed upon a developing African country resembling Canada.

The twelve volumes in *The New Age/Nouveau siècle* series have occupied a major share of Hood's writer's energies (though the novella *Five new facts about Giorgione* was published in 1987). *The swing in the garden* (1975, rpr. 1993), *A new Athens* (1977, rpr. 1984), *Reservoir ravine* (1979, rpr. 1985), *Black and white keys* (1982), *The scenic art* (1984), *The motor boys in Ottawa* (1986), *Tony's book* (1988), *Property and value* (1990), *Be sure to close your eyes* (1993), *Dead men's watches* (1995), *Great realizations* (1997), and *Near water* (2000) form a *roman fleuve* narrated by Matthew Goderich, who has a stroke in *Near water*, but his mind ranges over details of his past. His ancestral memories stretch back to the 1880s, and the series concludes with sci-fi projections of the world to come. (*Near water* was published shortly after Hood's death.) The New Age series, then, has a Genesis-to-Revelations scope—though the narrator's response to historical shifts in the experience of central Canada during his lifetime is featured. Each volume contains a number of epiphanic visionary scenes, counterbalanced by the doings of an extensive cast of characters and the narrator's frequent meditations on various aspects of his culture. Hood once compared his project to Proust's *À la recherche du temps perdu*, having sought to duplicate his formidable predecessor's 'narrative technique, the appeal to the philosophy of time'. Hood's aim in the series was to represent 'historical mythology, the articulation of the past, the articulation of the meaning of our society in terms of the way we live our lives'. No project that ambitious, and so boldly put, will elude detraction. The narrator's unengaging personality, the Laurentian viewpoint inflating itself into an all-Canadian perspective, Goderich's village-explainer disquisitions, have all attracted unfriendly notice. Its defenders point to the sheer bravado of the enterprise, the richness of its moments of visionary recollection, and the deftness with which the narrative relates the experience of the wide world to our national one. Hood's large concerns and wide vision render his writings unique among imaginative preoccupations in current Canadian fiction. See W.J. Keith, *Canadian odyssey: a reading of Hugh Hood's* The New Age (2002).

Hood also published three essay collections: *The Governor's Bridge is closed* (1973), *Trusting the tale* (1983), and *Unsupported assertions* (1991); and a sports biography, *Strength down centre: the Jean Beliveau story* (1970). He was made an Officer of the Order of Canada in 1988.

Horwood, Harold (b. 1923). He was born in St John's, Newfoundland, and received his formal education at Prince of Wales College there. In 1945, with his brother Charles, he founded *Protocol*, a journal that published experimental writing. From 1949 to 1951 Horwood was a Liberal member of the Newfoundland legislature. His important column in the St John's *Evening Telegram*—'Political notebook' (1952–8)—was at first conciliatory in its attitude towards the administration of J.R. Smallwood, but eventually became harshly critical of its policies. Horwood thus provided a voice of dissent in a decade of political domination by the Liberal party in

Newfoundland. In 1958 he turned to freelance writing, a move that appears to have coincided with a growing radicalism in political outlook. In the sixties and seventies he became an apologist for the 'counterculture' and adopted, to some extent, the hippie lifestyle. A founding member of the WRITERS' UNION OF CANADA, he was its chairman in 1980–1. He now lives in Nova Scotia's Annapolis Valley and is a Member of the Order of Canada (1979).

The author of twenty-six books, Horwood is perhaps at his best as a writer when he simply observes the natural environment and displays his sensitivity to the normally unnoticed world of flora and fauna—though he is rarely content to do just that. Typically he wishes to promote what he regards as enlightened notions, while jettisoning and denouncing the old. The setting of his first novel, *Tomorrow will be Sunday* (1966, rpr. 1992), is an isolated Newfoundland outport, home to forty-six families, most of them belonging to the fundamentalist Church of the Firstborn, ruled by the tyrannical precepts the church espoused. (The outport is richly portrayed, and there are passages of lyrical and dramatic power.) The novel is about the intellectual and physical coming-of-age of Eli Palisher, in his middle teens and an unusually mature and well-spoken boy for his age and background; he is naturally alienated from the rigid piety of his parents and neighbours and the harsh treatment that results. When young Christopher Simms, who left the outport at sixteen to attend school and go to university, returns as the new teacher, he spots Eli's intelligence immediately. There follows Eli's 'great awakening, colored with hero worship and the strange excitement of a boy's first adventure of the mind and the heart.' At the centre of the novel is the strong and blameless relationship of Eli and Christopher; the iniquitous influence of Brother John, the pastor, and its effect on their lives; and the flouting of taboos against sex in both homosexual activity instigated by an unexpected person and Christopher's and Eli's love for Virginia. In *The foxes of Beachy Cove* (1967), a work of meditation and observation that invites comparison with Thoreau's *Walden*, Horwood takes us on walks through the Newfoundland countryside and on canoe trips up its rivers, impressing us with the thoroughness of his knowledge of external nature and making us see what we had not before learned to look for. This is Horwood at his best. In his second novel, *White Eskimo: a novel of Labrador* (1972), he plunges into romantic excess about the Inuit of Labrador, who are seen as noble savages exploited by the 'white racist' Moravians and the meddling Dr GRENFELL (disguised as 'Dr. Tocsin')—extreme judgements that are hard to accept, even from a novelist. This was followed by a collection of short stories, *Only the gods speak* (1979); they convey, in Horwood's words, some of his 'deepest concerns, from the need for closer communion between people to the fear that white civilization has shot its bolt.' Horwood's propagandizing reached its peak in the novel *Remembering summer* (1987, rev. 1997), featuring the return of an unrecognizable Eli Palisher. In *Dancing on the shore* (1987), a work of reflection on the environment at Annapolis Basin, Nova Scotia, Horwood wrote that he 'had absorbed an exaggerated view of the importance of the novel'. In 1997, however, he published another novel, *Evening light*, the life story of Jonathon, from his boyhood in a Newfoundland outport until he is an old man, that draws on Horwood's affection for the island and its ways—which is also very much part of his memoir, *A walk in the dream time: growing up in old St John's* (1997, rpr. 1998). A second memoir, *Among the lions: a lamb in the literary jungle* (2000) includes the founding of the Writers' Union, in some detail, and Horwood's relationships, or contacts, with others Canadian writers.

The flight from fiction is borne out by *The magic ground* (1996), a treatise on the natural world. Among Horwood's early books is a fine biography of Captain Bob Bartlett, *Bartlett: the great Canadian explorer* (1977, rpr. 1989), and the second volume in the Canada's Illustrated History series, *The colonial dream 1497/1760* (1978). *Joey* (1989, rpr. 1990) is a stimulating biography of J.R. Smallwood.

Hospital, Janette Turner (b. 1942). Born in Melbourne, Australia, Janette Turner moved with her family at the age of seven to Brisbane where, in 1965, she graduated with a B.A. in English from the University of Queensland, worked as a high-school teacher, and married Clifford George Hospital. In 1967 they moved to the USA, where she worked as a librarian at Harvard University and had two children. In 1971 they moved to Kingston, Ontario, where her husband became a professor at Queen's University. In 2003 she was appointed Carolina Distinguished Professor of Literature, University of South Carolina, and lives in Columbia, S.C. This is where she began her studies in medieval literature, receiving an M.A. in 1973. As a writer of fiction she has been the recipient of numerous awards; has been twice nominated

for Britain's Booker Prize; and her books have been published in many languages.

Hospital has published seven novels: *The ivory swing* (1982), *The tiger in the tiger pit* (1983, rpr.1987), *Borderline* (1985), *Charades* (1988), *The last magician* (1992), *Oyster* (1996, rpr. 1997), and *Orpheus lost* (2007); four collections of short stories: *Dislocations* (1986), *Isobars* (1991), *Collected stories* (1995), and *North of Nowhere South of Loss* (2004); a crime thriller, *A very proper death* (1990), published under the pseudonyn 'Alex Juniper'; and a novella, *L'Envolée* (1995), commissioned by Myriam Solal and published in French. An essential feature of Hospital's fiction has to do with characters who straddle several countries and several kinds of cultural perceptions, and do so in a way that brings to critical scrutiny the codes of knowledge and systems of order by which, and in which, people make and find themselves at home. In *The ivory swing*—set in South India, where she and her family lived in 1977—Hospital documents cultural nuances while exploring their complexities, discovering that there remain certain incommensurable differences resulting from distinct world views in spite of attempts at mutual understanding. She moved to the disjunction between 'reality' and one's perception of reality in *The tiger in the tiger pit*, in which the Carpenter family crosses borders of geography, memory, and emotion as they reunite for their parents' fiftieth wedding anniversary. Adopting the musical structure of a fugue, Hospital experiments with conventional narrative by shifting the narrative point of view with each chapter, revealing multiple perspectives of various past events. How even the most philanthropic acts are subject to political consequences is demonstrated in *Borderline*, which challenges the difficulty of separating the imaginary from the real as apolitical characters become implicated in the lives and consequences of illegal Salvadorean immigrants who attempt to cross the American/Canadian border. Both medieval literature and the indeterminacies of twentieth-century quantum physics provide the narrative and metaphoric structures for *Charades* and *The last magician*. In the former the narrative parallels that of *The thousand and one nights*, but with a feminist, revisionist twist. With its metaphors of sub-atomic particle theory, this quest narrative shifts and turns as the protagonist, Charade Ryan, probes the mysteries of the origins of the universe, of matter, and of Charade herself. In *The last magician* the principles of quantum physics are used to reveal how two contradictory states and contestant worlds coexist simultaneously. Using familiar images and simple detail drawn from Dante's *Inferno*, Hospital exposes the subterranean world beneath the respectability of the city and reveals how the two prey on one another. Like *Borderline*, *The last magician* invites critical reflection on contemporary moral, political, and economic issues that are relevant to any metropolitan centre. *Oyster*—set in Outer Maroo, a small opal-mining town in the Australian Outback—is an exploration of the complex philosophical and metaphysical issues surrounding the tremendous power and seductiveness held by a religious cult leader over his followers, and probes their psychology. Powerful in its evocation of a mirage-ridden landscape that is as insubstantial and unreliable as its guru cult figure, the novel also invokes the contentious debate surrounding white Australian cattle ranchers and opal miners who are contemptuous of government accommodation to Aboriginal land-claim issues. *Orpheus lost* (2007) is an intricate novel involving Mishka Bartok, a gifted violinist, the grandson of Hungarian Jews (whose father was Lebanese) who settled in Queensland after the Second World War. He wins a scholarship to study in Boston and falls in love with Leela (his Eurydice), a musicologist whose former lover in the American South was a brilliant mathematician who now works for a government organization in search of suspected terrorists. The plot has a political-thriller aspect, but there are various other elements—meditations on music and numbers, religious fanaticism, the legend of Orpheus, the opposition of Jews and Muslims—that, however unevenly treated, convince one of the author's imagination and expertise.

Hospital is also an accomplished short-story writer. *Dislocations* is a collection of stories structured thematically around characters who experience a form of dislocation, be it geographic, cultural, or personal. The settings are diverse (ranging across three continents), and while loneliness, fear, and death are present in many of the stories, the end result is triumph. In the interrelated narratives comprising *Isobars*, her characters are not the detached observers of realism but appear fragmented and discontinuous as they are positioned in a larger field of events where past and present are simultaneous. *North of Nowhere South of Loss* (2004) is a collection of fourteen stories set in Australia, Canada, the US, Japan, and France.

Houston, James (1921–2005). Born in Toronto, he attended the Ontario College of Art. After serving with the Toronto Scottish Regiment during the Second World War, he went north to Baffin Island, where for nine of his twelve years there he was the region's first civil administrator. He is generally credited with the initial development of Inuit art in Canada. Houston was made an Officer of the Order of Canada in 1972 for his work as an administrator, artist, and writer. In 1988 he was appointed Master Designer of Steuben Glass, and his later career as a glass-maker is the basis for *Frozen fire* (1986) and *Fire into ice: adventures in glass making* (1988).

Beginning with *Tikta' liktak: an Eskimo legend* (1965) and ending with *Drifting snow: an Arctic search* (1992), Houston has written sixteen books for children and young adults, often with his own illustrations, all full of factual information about Native customs woven into the action of the stories. Two of these novels, *The white archer: an Eskimo legend* (1967) and *Akavak: an Eskimo journey* (1968), centre on journeys in which physical courage parallels moral development. Houston's plotting is generally very loose, his emphasis being on events rather than character development; the protagonist is most often a child or young adult who, through a series of crises, grows to maturity. The omnibus collection *James Houston's treasury of Inui legends* (2006) contains four of his retellings: 'Tiktaliktak' (1965), 'The white archer' (1967), 'Akavak' (1968), and 'Wolf run' (1971), illustrated by Houston's drawings. In *Frozen fire: a tale of courage* (1977, rpr. 1986) and *River runners: a tale of hardship and bravery* (1979) he moved away from traditional themes and began dealing with problems in the modern Inuit world. In *Long claws: an Arctic adventure* (1981) he makes good use of the bear as a visible sign of terror. Having spent considerable time living in a cabin in the Queen Charlotte Islands, Houston also wrote *Eagle mask: a West Coast Indian tale* (1966) and *Ghost paddle: a North West Coast Indian tale* (1972).

Houston's adult novels, like many of his children's books, draw on true stories of Native contact with Europeans. *The white dawn: an Eskimo saga* (1971) was based on an incident in 1896 when three New England whalers were first rescued and then killed by Inuit. Houston heard of these men from Inuit friends on Baffin Island and was later able to confirm parts of the story from the ship's log of the *Abbey Bradford*. (He wrote the screenplay for the 1974 film.) *Ghost fox* (1977), about the abduction of a New England farm girl by Abenaki Natives in the 1750s, has the historical and anthropological accuracy of his other works. *Spirit wrestler* (1980, rpr. 1997) is a fictional examination of the spirituality and chicanery of shamanism. For *Eagle song* (1983) Houston consulted the journal of John R. Jewitt, of the American brig *Boston*, who was captured by the Nootka chief Maquinna in 1803. The story is told by Maquinna's brother-in-law. His other two novels are *Whiteout* (1988, rpr. 1991) and *Running West* (1989).

Confessions of an igloo dweller (1995) is an account of Houston's years in the Canadian Arctic; *Zigzag: a life on the move* (1998) is a continuation of his autobiography, recounting in 100 stories his many 'lives' since then, including that of a glass sculptor; and *Hideaway: life on the Queen Charlottes* (2000) celebrates his residence on one of these British Columbia islands.

Howe, Joseph (1804–73). Born in Halifax, he received some formal schooling, but at the age of thirteen was taken as an apprentice into the family printing and newspaper business, the same office that had earlier published the first literary journal, *The NOVA-SCOTIA MAGAZINE*. He went on to a brilliant career as an author and journalist, establishing his newspaper *The Novascotian* as the leading journal in nineteenth-century Halifax; but he is best remembered as the pre-eminent politician of nineteenth-century Nova Scotia. He was elected to the legislative assembly in 1836, and for the next twelve years fought for responsible government. He reached the peak of his provincial political career as premier from 1860 to 1863. In the Confederation debate of the mid-1860s Howe led the opposition forces in Nova Scotia and ran as an Opposition candidate in the first federal election in 1867. He won, but by 1869 became convinced that opposing Confederation was futile. He accepted an appointment to the federal cabinet as secretary of state for the provinces, and served as minister until appointed lieutenant governor of Nova Scotia in Apr. 1873, two months before his death at Government House, Halifax.

In the 1820s and 1830s Howe wrote a lot of verse, most of which was published in local newspapers. It was later collected and posthumously published in *Poems and essays* (Montreal, 1874), in which there are two poems of more than passing interest: 'Melville Island', which was first published in 1825, and 'Acadia'. In the first Howe uses a description of a former military prison near Halifax as a point of departure for philosophic observations on human experience. 'Acadia' (probably written

in the early 1830s) contains a rather vague vision of a bright social, political, and economic future for the people of Nova Scotia.

Some of Howe's early journalistic pieces have a vivacity and sharpness of observation that make them a continuing delight to read. Of particular note are his 'Western rambles' and 'Eastern rambles'—which ran serially in *The Novascotian* between 1828 and 1831—where he describes two journeys in Nova Scotia employing anecdotes, commentary, and observation, in the manner of William Cobbett's 'Rural rides'. At the same time Howe contributed (as T.C. HALIBURTON did) to 'The club papers', a series of satiric and witty dialogue discussions of people and events by an ostensibly fictitious group of Halifax gentlemen. Through the 'Rambles' and 'The club papers' in the 1820s and 1830s, Howe helped to set the literary tone of the times and to nurture the confidence that Nova Scotian writers developed in themselves and in the cultural potential of colonial society. Howe's greatest contribution as a cultural figure, however, lay in his lifelong belief in the necessity of developing a local literature and in the encouragement he gave to those around him to write and publish. After purchasing *The Novascotian* (1824–1826) from George Renny Young in Jan. 1828, he (and, later, with John Sparrow THOMPSON) turned the paper into a cultural and intellectual vehicle in the community, opening its weekly columns to local essayists, fiction writers, and poets.

M.G. Parks edited *Poems and essays* (1973), *Western and eastern rambles: travel sketches of Nova Scotia* (1973), and *Acadia* (rev. edn 1989). See J. Murray Beck, *Joseph Howe: conservative reformer, 1804–1848*, vol. 1 (1982) and *The Briton becomes Canadian, 1848–1873*, vol. 2 (1983).

Huggan, Isabel (b. 1943). Born Jean Isabel Howey in Kitchener, Ontario, she grew up in nearby Elmira, studied at the University of Western Ontario (B.A., 1965), and spent time in Kenya, the Philippines, and France, where she lives in Tornac. She married Bob Huggan in 1970. She is best known for her first collection of short fiction, *The Elizabeth stories* (1984, rpr. 1990). The setting is the fictional small Ontario town of Garten, and the stories chart the development of Elizabeth Kessler from pre-school to her imminent departure for university. Elizabeth is intellectually precocious but emotionally cowardly, both qualities captured in the constant references to her parents as 'Frank' and 'Mavis': the distance built into familial relations in this upper-middle-class background functions as an ironic device for revealing how Elizabeth's desire to escape Garten's various claustrophobias is simultaneously underwritten by her saturation in Garten's (and her parents') ways. Subtle forms of unearned snobbery, ethnic and class prejudice, sexual repression, and an unreflective sense of self and others constitute Elizabeth's difficult inheritance. Despite her attempts to escape, she unconsciously lives by these forms and is frequently the sometimes witting agent of malicious practices. The stories in *You never know* (1993, rpr. 1996) are set in such diverse places as Scotland, Canada, Kenya, and France, and are mostly told through the perspective of adult women. They immerse us in relationships that test, through carefully controlled ironies, the limits of self-awareness, especially in upper-middle-class protagonists whose liberal aspirations tend to be exposed in quiet but nevertheless disturbing ways. Although these stories reflect the various adults that Elizabeth Kessler might have become, the link between the volumes is the more broadly thematic one specified by the closing lines of the second collection: 'Why we enter each other's lives and how we are meant to fit together is more than is given us to know. And yet that's what we want, isn't it? That's what we want to understand.' Huggan's stories are careful tracings of this multifaceted desire to understand how people are meant to fit together and why we often fail to do so. They have been included in many anthologies. *Belonging: home away from home* (2003, rpr. 2004)—a gathering of essays/memoirs and stories—offers Huggan the writer in full: her warmth, elegance, lucidity, and her ability to convey sudden illuminations. In the first piece, 'There is no word for home'—home is where she lives with her husband in the Cévennes mountains of southern France-'you cannot say *home*' in French, and she gives variants, including *notre maison*. It was her husband who first fell in love with the region when they were hiking 'more than a decade ago ... he said immediately, that he knew he was *chez lui dans les Cévennes*.... When it happens, this carnal knowledge of landscape, it is very like falling in love without knowing why, the plunge into desire and longing made all the more intense by being so utterly irrational, inexplicable. The feel of the air, the lay of the land, the colour and shape of the horizon, who knows? There are places on the planet [where] we belong and they are not necessarily where we are born.' What follows is a brief memoir of the discovery of a new place to live and the creation of a new home, of the people who became part of this, and meditations on the past that all these things aroused—a smooth, sometimes lyrical narrative that has depth and meaning. In 'Saving stones' Huggan writes 'I still collect stones and shells, for it seems I am not myself unless I have a few pieces of the planet close at hand. They are needed as reminders, as mnemonic objects that, in their own mute way, prompt me to look for stories and then to tell them. Stones are cues, leading me back and forth in time until I am here, putting words on the page.' One of three stories in the book, 'The window', evokes the happy marriage of John and Lila (surely that of Bob and Isabel) as it centres on their house and the window facing their front terrace. John calls Lila down to look back into the house 'through the oblong eight-paned window that gives a view of the dining-room inside. The room is golden and glowing, lit in some way that makes it seem something other than reality: a painting, a photograph.' John says this was why he called her down. 'I thought it looked like a painting too.... Dutch, do you think? Maybe seventeenth century?' There are yellow tulips loosely arranged in a pottery jug in the centre of a cedar table. She thinks about the jug and how she acquired it (a gift from a former lover who had been to Italy). There are other things in the story—there is a phone call to his father from John's son—but one is mainly left with the memory of having been privy to an hour or so in a happy marriage. *Belonging* was awarded the Charles Taylor Prize for Literary Non-Fiction.

Hughes, Monica (1925–2003). Born Monica Ince in Liverpool, England, she had lived in Egypt, England, Scotland, and Zimbabwe before coming to Canada in 1952. She married Glen Hughes in 1957 and lived in Edmonton. Hughes speaks of the shock she felt upon entering the Canadian landscape, of the fear and loneliness created by the Laurentian Shield and the Prairies. This sense of alienation, imposed by a setting, recurs in her novels for young people, especially in *Earthdark* (1977), the Isis trilogy (*Guardian of Isis*, 1981, rpr. 2000; *Keeper of the Isis light*, 1982, rpr. 2000; *The Isis pedlar*, 1982, rpr. 2000), and *Beyond the dark river* (1979, rpr. 1992). One of the most important and talented writers for adolescents of the present day, known in both North America and Europe, Hughes produced historical fiction (*The gold-fever trail*, 1974, rpr. 1990; *The treasure of the Long Sault*, 1982, rpr. 1990) and realistic novels; but she is best known for her science fiction (*The Isis trilogy*, 2000, rpr. 2006; *Crisis on Conshelf Ten*,

1975; *The tomorrow city*, 1978). The teenage heroes/heroines in Hughes' novels become isolated by circumstances, which force them to make choices that define their character and identity. They face the universal adolescent difficulties of parental short-sightedness, the fear and hostility aroused by being 'different', the loneliness of isolation, and the need for close friendships. Hughes insists upon a character's search for truth and humanistic values. Presented as a saving remnant against the dehumanization of modern or future mass cultures, and usually caught in a web of intolerance and power, her main characters undergo a struggle that is of importance to the survival of their civilization. Two major themes permeate Hughes' fiction: the conflict of cultures and respect for the power and beauty of nature. In the conflict of cultures, those who survive do so because of their deep fidelity to the traditional humanistic values of courage, tolerance, and individual choice; and as in most important children's literature, the value of revering nature is closely associated with development of self and respect of others.

Hughes wrote some forty books, primarily focusing her talents on science fiction, which always contains a bedrock of realism— what she calls 'scientific facts', or perhaps simply the facts of reality. *Sandwriter* (1986, rpr. 2003), and its sequel *The promise* (1989, rpr. 2004), provide strong female heroes who experience rebirth into a new, fuller existence by being willing to accept their responsibility to a larger world than one they have felt 'safe' and comfortable in. In *Where have you been, Billy Boy?* (1995, rpr. 2005) she cleverly uses the situation of the *Wizard of Oz* to show us the hero's choice of returning to an impoverished past (the Kansas of 1908, in fact) after seeing the world of eighty-five years later and rejecting the glitter and technological glow of 1993. He chooses to return because of his attachment to the old carousel operator, Johannes (the Wizard?). For Hughes, character is always determined by such choices and the power of choice is fundamental.

One of Hughes' most popular novels for young readers is *Invitation to the game* (1990, rpr. 2004), a powerful book that once again pits individual choice against a technologically closed universe (the image of enclosure, or being trapped, is one that recurs in Hughes—see *The refuge* [1989, rpr. 1992], with its fenced-in 'garden'). *Invitation* offers us a futuristic world (twenty-second century) so dehumanized that even individual choice is almost impossible. The unemployed youth we

follow here ironically show us that when technology becomes so overwhelmingly anti-human, there is almost no such thing as individual choice—there can only be a shared co-operation that can act to break through the prison. Settings can be realistic, as in *Blaine's way* (1986, rpr. 2005), set in southwestern Ontario during the Depression and the Second World War; they can be futuristic as in *Beckoning lights* (1990), where the theme of prejudice is probed by using 'aliens' as 'others' who are feared, even hated by the antagonist, Barry Trevor, whose drive for wealth makes it impossible for him to accept the Other as just as human as he is. In *The golden Aquarians* (1994), the planet Aqua is the setting for a battle between son, Walter, and father, Colonel Elliott, who has control of Aqua and is destroying it. A poet and musician, Walter overcomes the Colonel's attempt to make him into 'a man'. Ironically, back on earth, Walter and his father (who has amnesia and forgets his Colonel past) are reunited, and we experience one of those ambiguous endings Hughes is noted for: will the Colonel remember and return to his past? *The maze* (2002), a fantasy adventure, begins with Andrea Austin's being viciously persecuted by Crystal, a fellow student at Abbotsford High; a mysterious black box Andrea is given, with a maze inlaid in it, provides the fantastic element of this gripping story.

Having become Canada's foremost science-fiction writer for young adults, Hughes also became one of our finest realistic writers, with *Hunter in the dark* (1982, rpr. 2003), *My name is Paula Popowich!* (1983), *The ghost dance caper* (1993), and *The faces of fear* (1997, rpr. 1998). She was a Member of the Order of Canada (2001).

Published posthumously in the US in 2004 are two series of informative books for children illustrated with full-colour photographs, for which Hughes wrote the brief texts, on Nature Patterns (*Migration, Weather patterns, Water cycle*) and Festivals (*My Divali, My Id-al-Fitr, My Hanukkah, My Rosh Hashanah, My Chinese New Year, 2006*).

Humphreys, Helen (b. 1961). Born in Kingston, England, she lives in Kingston, Ontario. She began her distinguished writing career as a poet, publishing *Gods and other mortals* (1986), *Nuns looking anxious, listening to radios* (1990, rpr. 2004), *The perils of geography* (1995), and *Anthem* (1999), which capture the reader's interest with vivid metaphors and imagery and a precise and disciplined use of language. The first poem of *Gods and other* *mortals* ('Somewhere in the night') begins: 'Outside the window the city becomes/a string of coloured beads pulled tight/across the dark, damp throat of the night.' Part 2 is a group of poems for voices ('The dinner', 'I have a photograph', 'Being away', 'I was there, I saw it happen', 'Dialogue of the psyche'). The poems in the final group are named for figures in classical mythology: Epimetheus, Atalanta, Patroclus, Thetis, Bellerophon, Cassandra. The title of the title poem in *Nuns looking anxious* is the caption of a photograph: 'There is only one radio,/ And the nuns are actually smiling.//They seem happy.//Perhaps the person who wrote that/hated nuns. Or gave up religion/because it wasn't any fun.' The title poem of *The perils of geography* ends: 'The pulse of sunlight/sliding along train track,/shunting your heart into/sidings of loss, bumping/don't go don't go don't go/against the barricade.//Every misted hollow folds/words over on your tongue./Like time travel gone wrong,/ the perils of geography./All that old cartography./O, the New World.' In *Anthem* 'Climatology' is a delicate memory of her father's 'weather diary' in which he makes perfunctory remarks ('*Rain heavy*') and on 8 May 1945 '*Rain early* and then *Crowds/ cheering. The war is over.*' It ends: '*Never seen anything,* writes my father,/*so pretty as the sun rising/on snow and ice covered trees.*' The treatment of nature is pleasingly singular: 'What can't be seen at night: the pale/pink of roses. Anything blue.//Colour is not constant. Nothing/that holds colour can be relied on./ At night what is distinguished is not light/or dark, but lighter or darker' ('The anatomy of trees'). Three of the poems are transpositions of poems by Elizabeth Bishop, Louise Bogan, and Sylvia Plath. 'Through a mesh of kisses, falling rain/on the roof. The clear feel of this minute,/electric and sudden, air hissing with light./To wake together, the same rain, what/ our bodies hear' ('After a Poem by Elizabeth Bishop'). Every once in a while an aphorism delights: 'I'm reading poems by a woman who wrote about/her death before she knew she was dying. Poetry/rises as memory, comes down as prophesy' ('Foxes').

Humphreys has said that she gave up writing poetry (for now, perhaps?) in favour of fiction, and has proved that she is an extremely able practitioner of that genre. Her career as a novelist began with *Ethel on fire* (1991), a novella that is a subtle attempt to make fun of heritage interests focused on Ontario pioneers. The setting is a little log cabin with one window, the home of the pioneer MacLeod family called the MacLeod Heritage Museum. Mary, the curator, is assisted by Christine and Michael (who is building a boat in the barn, even though he hates sailing and the water). Joanne is a student worker keen on pioneer history, and Gavin is the site manager. They are forever telling stories, to each other and particularly to Joanne, about the various pioneer objects on display. Some stories are obviously fanciful. Other may or may not be true: the butter churn was used as a washer to churn the dirt out of clothes; the washboard was used as a meat tenderizer; the bellows was filled with fruit and used to expel pits—once a pit hit an eye of the MacLeods' dog Oedipus. Christine says to Joanne: 'See that lamp? That's an Ethel lamp. It was named after a woman who was, of course, called Ethel.' When cooking over the fire, alone in the house, her skirts caught fire and she burned to death. Her distraught husband, who devised a lamp that lasted longer than a candle because it burned animal fat, put it in the window 'so she would find her way back.' (This title episode is never referred to again.) A meeting is held, described in amusing detail, at which it is decided to hold a costume party to celebrate 'the MacLeods' 150th anniversary'. The visitors to the museum, who have been kept in the background, now turn out in numbers. *Ethel on fire* is a striking preview of Humphreys' narrative skill, as she adroitly handles dialogue, characters, episodes—and, in this case, humour.

As a novelist Humphreys writes about the past and takes on specialized subjects, researching them thoroughly—the research filters naturally into her narratives. *Leaving earth* (1997, rpr. 1998) takes place in Toronto in August 1933 when Grace O'Gorman, a famous flyer, with the inexperienced Willa Briggs, takes off in Grace's Moth biplane to break an endurance record by flying over the Toronto shoreline and harbour for twenty-five days. Minute-by-minute actions by the flyers—and the periodic transfers of fuel and food, crises (such as the loss of paper in a rainstorm, making communication by notes impossible), the sign language they invented for themselves—offer a gripping narrative. This is combined with chapters on land that mostly have to do with teenaged Maddy, who lives with her parents on the islands, on Hanlan's Point. Employed in the entertainment area, her father Fram runs the carousel and Del, her mother, is a fortune teller. The renowned Grace O'Gorman is a kind of goddess for Maddy and she is transfixed by the plane as it flies overhead. On the plane, Willa can't get over the appearance of the lake: 'The infinite gradations of shading, notching the colour blue a little this way towards grey, a little that way towards green. The lighter aureole around the deeper dark of land.' 'To hang in the sky a plane moves towards a horizon it can never enter, a line that just keeps receding.' About the sign language: 'Grace first showing the sign for *day*— her closed right fist arcing from east to west to demonstrate the sun moving across the sky....' There comes a time when Willa 'exists in a state that's somehow between waking and sleeping....' We read also about many things that are happening at ground level. The novel is an absorbing achievement in which love, betrayal, and history (the Depression, Toronto Nazis, the oncoming war) are interwoven. It won the City of Toronto Book Award. The research that went into *Afterimage* (2000, rpr. 2009) was devoted to Victorian photography, and particularly photographs taken by the famous Julia Margaret Cameron, especially those of her maid Mary Hillier. In 1865 teen-aged Annie Phelan arrives at Middle Road Farm in Sussex to be a maid in the household of Isabelle and Eldon Dashell. 'Born Irish, raised English,' she tells Mrs Dashell. 'My family died in the hunger.' A bright young woman, she has been taught to read by her previous employer and has just finished *Jane Eyre*. She has nothing in common with Tess, the illiterate laundry-maid with whom she shares an attic bedroom. (Tess lets Wilks, the driver, make love to her, with the expected result, and her carelessness brings about a devastating event.) After Isabelle had given birth to the third of her stillborn babies, Eldon gave her a camera. Photography then engrossed her (her hands were black from the silver nitrate she used). She liked to create scenes with children, and then photograph them. The beauty of Annie soon caught her attention and Isabelle persuaded her to pose—as Guinevere, Ophelia, Sappho, the three Virtues (Grace, Humility, Faith), and Mary Madonna—and Annie was the perfect model. In this rich novel, filled with episodes, much more happens. The social background is interwoven subtly. Eldon comes to life in his fixation with maps, with the three expeditions to the Arctic of Sir John Franklin, and in his interest in Annie, whom he encourages to use his library. There is the mere hint of feelings of desire and love shared by Isabelle and Annie (and by Grace and Willa in *Leaving earth*). An unforgettable episode occurs near the end of the book when a five-year-old boy model, dressed as an angel, his wings on fire, is thrown out of

a window by Annie, landing on a mattress (described also in the novel's first two pages.) *Afterimage* won the WRITERS' TRUST Fiction Prize. *The lost garden* (2002, rpr. 2009) is impressive partly because it brings to life both London during the blitz in 1941, twenty years before the author was born, and the gardens in a neglected Devonshire estate, the plots and growths of which had to be researched from scratch (the author is not a gardener). Plain, lonely Gwen Davis, a young horticulturalist, leaves her beloved (war-torn) London for the countryside to supervise a small group of the Women's Land Army—the Land Girls—as they plant potatoes in some of the gardens of Mosel. At the train station she is met by David and Captain Raley, both in the Canadian army, who figure prominently. There unfolds an absorbing, sensitively written account of Gwen's winning over the Land Girls, each one of whom she has given the name of a potato. Their leader Jane (who is haunted by her fiancé's being posted as missing) befriends Gwen and is a constant companion. Gwen discovers hidden gardens of the estate, which she wants to keep secret, cultivating them for herself. 'I rub the dirt between my fingers. The red earth of Devon is thick and full of texture. I put a little on the tip of my tongue and taste the wormy, metallic tang of soil choked with nutrients. It will be fine.' Throughout the book we read of Gwen's devotion to Virginia Woolf (who died in 1941)—whom she may or may not have followed seven years before in the streets of London—and to *To the lighthouse*. At Gwen's suggestion Jane reads the novel to her friend David, and Gwen listens, thinking: 'The heart is a river. The act of writing is the moving water that holds the banks apart, keeps the muscle of words flexing so that that the reader can be carried along by this movement. To be given space and the chance to leave one's earthly world. Is there any greater freedom than this?' Humphreys' imagination, research, and often lyrical prose were next trained on animal lore in *Wild dogs* (2004, rpr. 2005), about six people who for one reason or another have submitted to having their dogs removed from their lives. The dogs have formed a feral pack—called 'wild dogs'—and their owners band together each evening near the woods, hoping that their dogs will appear. Strangers to each other at first, they gradually form tentative relationships. Alice, the narrator, lost her dog Hawk when her boyfriend got tired of it and took it away from her. In addition there is strange Malcolm in his forties, who lets Alice live in a cabin near his farmhouse, whose dog is Sydney; Lily in her twenties, brain-damaged, whose dog she calls Dog; thirteen-year-old Jamie whose stepfather not only beats him but deprived him of his dog Scout—Alice and he become friends; Walter, a middle-aged man who lives with his daughter and son-in-law whose dog is Georgie; and there is 'you', unnamed until towards the end of the book (her name is Rachel), a wildlife biologist with whom Alice falls in love and whose pet is a wolf she calls Lopez. ('You show slides of the wolves in the pack you're studying ... The wolves gaze balefully out at us, yellow eyes shrewd and cold. their scrawny frames matted with knots of fur.' 'I had never felt with anyone what I felt with you, and I still believe in that, despite all that's happened.') The voices of these characters, in separate monologues, make up part two (ending with Rachel and Alice) in which elements of the story are rounded out—a sad event is caused by a hunter—and lead to a kind of resolution. Alice, whose dog Hawk returns to her, says at the end: 'Your leaving will not be solved by your coming back.' And 'The heart is a wild and fugitive creature.//The heart is a dog who comes home.' In 2008 Humphreys published *Coventry* (rpr. 2009), which begins on the night of 14 Nov. 1940, when there is a 'bomber's moon'. Harriet Marsh is on the roof of Coventry Cathedral acting as a fire watcher when a bombing raid destroys Coventry—she saves herself just as a bomb hits the Cathedral. The novel is an acclaimed portrayal of the blitz.

The River Thames froze solid forty times between 1142 and 1895. Humphreys has written a delightful brief narrative for each of the frozen-river years in *The frozen Thames* (2007, rpr. 2008). With a small page size (5 x 6 inches), printed on stiff coated paper, and with period illustrations in colour, it is a gem of a book. **1434**. 'Moving the wine by barge was a peaceful slow drift up the Thames.... Now that the whole length of the river has frozen, all the way from London Bridge to Gravesend, John must make the journey overland.' **1565**. 'The Queen shoots at prickes set upon the ice. She has done this every morning since the river froze.' **1691**. 'But I am learning that each ice, each freeze, is different from the one before. That freeze was hard and smooth. This one is uneven, spongy underfoot, covered with snow. I cannot even see the ice itself, and so only half believe that it is there. But when I turned and saw my footprint filling with water, I knew that not only is the ice there, but the water is there as well.' **1814**. 'The river Thames froze solid and a

Frost Fair was once again set up on the ice. The public way constructed between Blackfriars and London Bridge was named 'City Road' and soon became choked with booths and amusements, and taverns.'

In 2009 Humphreys was awarded the HARBOURFRONT Festival Prize ($10,000).

Huston, Nancy (b. 1953). Born in Calgary, she grew up there and in Edmonton. Her mother suddenly left the family when Huston was six, and her relationship to her mother tongue is related, in her accounts, to that early abandonment. Her family moved to New Hampshire when she was in her teens and she attended Sarah Lawrence College in Bronxville, New York (B.A., 1975). She moved to Paris, where she still lives, and received an M.A. (1977) from the École des hautes études en sciences sociales, studying with the leaders of post-structuralism, including Roland Barthes (her M.A. thesis, published as *Dire et interdire*, 1980, dealt with profanity). A sometime teacher—she has been visiting professor and guest lecturer at numerous universities and institutions in North America and Europe—she is also a harpsichordist and flutist. She is married to the Bulgarian-born writer Tzvetan Todorov and they have a daughter and son. Huston has received honorary doctorates from the Université de Montréal (2000), the University of Guelph (2003), and McGill University (2006), and is an Officer of the Order of Canada (2005).

Huston has published nine novels in English (translated by herself). *The Goldberg Variations* (1996)—translated from *Les variations Goldberg* (1981)—is a tour de force; published after Barthes' death, it was dedicated to him. The novel's action lasts exactly an hour and a half, the time it takes Liliane Kulainn to play Bach's *Goldberg Variations* on the harpsichord before thirty friends and acquaintances in her Paris apartment; thirty-two inner monologues give voice to Liliane and her guests. Most of Huston's key themes—music, words, writing, passion, sex, the body, food, the passage of time, and the relationship between time and space—are launched here. *The story of Omaya* (1997)—a translation of *Histoire d'Omaya* (1985), with its ironic reference to *L'histoire d'O*, the classic pornographic novel of a woman in love with her own abasement—presents, through fragment and collage, the psychic collapse of an already fragile young actress who was abducted and abused by a group of men and, having pressed charges against them, found herself on trial. For *Plainsong* (1993) Huston drew for the first time on her childhood experiences of life in western Canada and found herself writing, also for the first time, fiction in English. This lyrical and desperate novel relates the narrator's attempts to reconstruct imaginatively her grandfather's life: an aspiring writer-philosopher who found himself trapped in the role of husband, breadwinner, father who lost the ability, but not the longing, to make an intellectual contribution. Huston rewrote the novel in French, and *Cantique des plaines* (1993) won a Governor General's Award. The prize sparked a controversy in Québec literary circles—because it was a translation, because the author was not a Québécoise. The angry protests from five Québécois publishers ironically gave the novel heightened visibility and won Huston many new readers. The lapidary and intense *Slow emergencies* (1996) was also first written in English, but was published after the French version, *La virevolte* (1994). It is the story of mother-daughter love and abandonment across three generations and a meditation on the relationship between art (dance) and life. The same metamorphosis of the everyday into literature, pain into transcendence, is at the heart of *Instruments of darkness* (1997), a translation of *Instruments des ténèbres* (1996). The narrator, Nadia (Nada), alternately reflects on her own troubled past and present and writes a novel, inserted in the text, about a young servant girl who killed her newborn child in eighteenth-century France. The French edition was nominated for the Prix Goncourt and was chosen by the Paris magazine *Lire* as one of the twelve best books of 1996. *The mark of the angel* (1999)—Huston's translation of *L'impreinte de l'ange* (1998)—is about Raphael, a noted flutist; the affectless German girl, Saffie, he hires as his maid and falls in love with and marries; their son Émil; and András, a Hungarian Jew who repairs musical instruments, whom Saffie falls in love with (undisclosed to each other is the fact that both had known horror, Saffie in Germany and András in Budapest). Set in Paris and beginning in May 1957, with the Algerian war as an unsettling, violent background, the novel is an intimate narrative (Huston, jarringly, sometimes uses the second person to draw the reader closer to details) describing people, in some ways innocent, caught up in an irresistible train of events. *Prodigy: a novella* (2000), set in the south of France with alternating points of view, is about Lara, a piano teacher; her brilliantly gifted daughter Maya, a happy piano prodigy; and Lara's Russian mother Sofia. It is a translation of *Prodige: polyphonie* (1999).

We learn in the first pages of *Dolce agonia* (2001)—entitled 'Prologue from Heaven'—that God is observing and commenting on what follows. Sean Farrell, poet and academic (terminally ill), is about to give a Thanksgiving dinner party in a wintry New Hampshire for twelve guests, including fellow academics and former lovers. and their spouses. (God reappears several times to tell of the deaths of certain characters.) '"Hey, Charles," says Sean…. This man Sean clasps willingly and warmly to his body—Charles Jackson, a tense and elegant black man, barely forty, new to the department, to whom he'd taken an instant liking because, though celebrated from coast to coast for a sizzling collection of essays titled *Black on White*, he'd refused to teach a course on African American poetry. Insisted on teaching the poets he loved, from Catullus to Césaire, and from Whitman to Walcott.' A brilliant text that seamlessly unfolds the lives and thoughts of all the guests—and of Sean himself—magically blends comedy and sadness.

To her English translation of *Lignes de faille* (2006)—which sold more than 400,000 copies in France and won the Prix Femina—Huston gave the title *Fault lines* (2006). It is a family history narrated backwards, first in 2004 by Sol (Solomon), Kristina's great-grandson in California; then in 1982 by her grandson Randall in New York and Haifa; then in 1962 by her daughter Sadie in Toronto and New York; and finally in 1944–5 by Kristina herself (Klarysa, Erra), in Germany during the catastrophic end of the Nazi years, when she learns that she was one of the two hundred thousand non-German children stolen in a 'Germanization' program initiated by Himmler to compensate for German losses. A singular conceit of the novel is that all four narrators are six years old! Despite combining the occasional injection of sophisticated diction and adult concepts with childish misconceptions and the subservience of childhood, the narratives are very readable (one soon accepts the anomaly). Here is Sadie practising the piano: 'And then gradually the piece was spoiled by my learning it—by the mistakes I made, causing Miss Kelly to scribble purple comments all over the page including the illustration—so now when I try to play the song it just falls apart in my hands. Every bar is a hurdle to be gotten over. I'm so scared of making a mistake that I stare at the bar as if my eyes would pop out of my head and when it's time to go on to the next bar my eyes jump to the right but it's too late, I've already made a mistake and Gran calls out to me from the kitchen "*F*-sharp, Sadie!"' The narratives are remarkable literary constructs, conveying both complex family relationships and the stark influences of wars—in Lebanon and Israel and in Germany—paradoxically in the manner of easy-going precocious six-year-olds.

Huston has published two collections of essays in English. *Losing north: musings on land, tongue and self* (2002) was originally published as *Nord perdu*. She tells us on the first page that the title means 'forgetting what you were going to say. *Losing track of what's going on. Losing your marbles.*' *Longings and belonging* (2005) is a more substantial collection of essays written over twenty-five years. Some are about writers (Simone de Beauvoir, Sylvia Plath and Ted Hughes, Simone Weil, Milan Kundera, Christian Bobin, Peter Handke, Marguerite Duras, Tolstoy and Sartre, Elfriede Jelinek). One essay is entitled 'On being beautiful' and begins: 'I am beautiful.' In a note at the end Huston says: 'Of all my essays, this is the one that has been the most widely translated—it exists in thirteen languages including Hebrew and Japanese and was even published in Braille; it sparked off violent controversies in Italy and Spain.... I should add that, a decade having passed since I wrote it, my daughter is now more beautiful than I am, and that is fine with me.'

Although writing in two languages, Huston has said that she is not at home in either of them. She has written movingly of her self-translations, a kind of bilingual writing and rewriting with no true source or target language. It is precisely this in-between, uncomfortable, and yet vital position that is the source of her considerable creative energy.

Hutcheon, Linda (b. 1947). Born Linda Bortolotti in Toronto, and educated at the University of Toronto (B.A., 1969; Ph.D., 1975), and Cornell University (M.A., 1971), she taught at McMaster University, Hamilton, from 1976 to 1988, the year she became University Professor of English and comparative literatures at the University of Toronto. One of Canada's best-known and most frequently cited literary critics as well as an influential teacher and editor, Hutcheon has popularized post-structuralist theories among the academic community and its students, and shown their relevance to contemporary Canadian concerns with identity, history, and community in her many books, including *Narcissistic narratives* (1980), *A theory of parody: the teachings of twentieth-century art forms* (1985), *A poetics of postmodernism: history, theory, fiction* (1988), *The Canadian postmodern: a study of contemporary English-Canadian fiction*

(1988), *The politics of postmodernism* (1989), *Splitting images: contemporary Canadian ironies* (1991), and *Irony's edge: the theory and politics of irony* (1995). They have influenced the field of postmodern theory, cultural studies, and Canadian literary and cultural studies as they are practised in Canada and elsewhere. Hutcheon's clear style and breadth of reference across various fields of cultural representation (notably architecture, literature, painting, and opera) provide a synthesizing overview of culture as a system governed by representation conventions that rivals Northrop FRYE's. Unlike Frye, however, Hutcheon increasingly brought formalist readings into contact with political questions, particularly those involved in the representation of history, gender, and race. Each of her books contributes a new angle to what is now emerging as the governing goal of her work: the anatomization and investigation of complicitous critique. From her earliest work on what she calls 'narcissistic narrative' to later considerations of postmodern aesthetics, parody, and irony, Hutcheon has wrestled with her desire to celebrate self-reflexivity in contemporary art as a liberating strategy even as she recognized the limitations of this stance. With her husband, Dr Michael Hutcheon, she also wrote *Opera: desire, disease, death* (1996), an entertaining discussion of some famous operas in the contexts of the subtitle, *Bodily charm: living opera* (2000), and *Opera: the art of dying* (2004).

Hutchison, Bruce (1901–92). Born in Prescott, Ontario, he was taken to British Columbia as an infant and grew up in Victoria. He became a high-school journalist for the Victoria *Times* in 1918 and a political reporter in Ottawa in 1925; he returned to the *Times*, also reporting on the provincial legislature for the Vancouver *Province*. He was an editorial writer and columnist for the Vancouver *Sun* (1938), assistant editor on the Winnipeg *Free Press* (1944–50), and then returned to the Victoria *Times*, where he served as editor from 1950 to 1963, establishing his reputation as a leading political journalist and commentator. In 1963 he became editorial director of the Vancouver *Sun* and in 1979 editor emeritus; he wrote a weekly column for the *Sun* until his death. By the end of his career he had received many honours, including three Governor General's Awards. He was made an Officer of the Order of Canada in 1967.

In nearly seventy-five years of political reporting, spanning the careers of ten prime ministers, Hutchison developed friendships

Hutchison

with political personalities ranging from Louis St Laurent and Lester Pearson to Pierre Elliott Trudeau and Jean Chrétien. His writings on Canada and its political figures were characterized by the confidential vignette, but he was criticized for partisan loyalty to the Liberal party—a charge he always denied. His best-known book, *The unknown country: Canada and her people* (1943, GGA), is a delightful panorama of Canada, containing vivid descriptions of place and personality, with short lyrical vignettes between chapters. Hutchison also dealt successfully with the larger movements of politics and economics. His novel *The hollow men* (1944), the story of a newspaper correspondent disillusioned by world war, combines subtle political satire with sympathy for wilderness life. Hutchison's other titles include *The Fraser* (1950) in the 'Rivers of America' series; *The incredible Canadian: a candid portrait of Mackenzie King, his works, his times, and his nation* (1952, GGA); *Canada's lonely neighbour* (1954); *The struggle for the border* (1955); *Canada: tomorrow's giant* (1957, GGA); and *Mr Prime Minister 1867–1964* (1964), which was condensed as *Macdonald to Pearson: the prime ministers of Canada* (1967). Hutchison also wrote *Western window* (1967), a collection of essays, as well as the text for *Canada: the year of the land* (1967), a lavish picture book on Canada produced by the National Film Board. At the age of eighty Hutchison published *Uncle Percy's wonderful town* (1981), a dozen fictional and nostalgic accounts of life in Emerald Vale, B.C., a town with the features of Merrit, Cranbrook, and Nelson in British Columbia. While short on emotional range, these stories—narrated by a fourteen-year-old boy—evoke a vanished time and place. *A life in the country* (1988) is both a memoir and a meditation on country life. Hutchison's autobiography, *The far side of the street* (1976), expressed a highly personal view of the growth of his generation, and reaffirmed his vision of a modern and responsible Canada. See *To Canada with love and some misgivings: the best of Bruce Hutchison* (1991) edited by Vaughn Palmer.

Huyghue, Douglas Smith (1816–91). He was born in Charlottetown, Prince Edward Island, while his father was stationed there with the military, and was educated in Saint John, New Brunswick. In 1840–1 he was living in Halifax and contributing poetry to *The Halifax Morning Post* under his pseudonym 'Eugene'. A year later he was again resident in Saint John and had become a regular contributor of poetry, fiction, and prose to the literary periodical *The Amaranth*. His activities between 1841 and 1844 include co-hosting an exhibition of Native artifacts in Saint John with New Brunswick's Indian commissioner, Moses Perley, and working with the Boundary Commission settling the border between Maine and New Brunswick after the Aroostook War. His novel *Argimou: a legend of the Micmac* (Halifax, 1847) first appeared as a serial in *The Amaranth* in 1842. Two years later he left the Maritimes and moved to London, England, where he contributed descriptive sketches to *Bentley's Miscellany* and published a second novel, *The nomades of the West; or Ellen Clayton* (London, 1850). In 1852 Huyghue immigrated to Australia, where he held various government posts until his retirement in 1878. Huyghue's poems and stories reflected his lifelong interest in the culture and society of Native peoples. Although *Argimou* purports to be a romance set in Acadia in 1755, it is in reality an impassioned novel of conscience exploring the disintegration of Mi'kmaq culture under the influence of European settlement; it is also one of the first Canadian novels to describe the Expulsion of the Acadians, and was popular enough to be re-serialized in Saint John as late as 1860. Its successor, *Nomades of the West*, never achieved the same reputation, although it too reflected the author's intimate understanding of Native people 'before their ranks were thinned, or their spirit broken by aggression.

I

Iglauer, Edith (b. 1917). Born in Cleveland, Ohio, she received her B.A. from Wellesley College (1938) and the next year obtained a graduate degree in journalism from Columbia University, New York. During the Second World War she worked for the Office of War Information in Washington, was a war correspondent for *The Cleveland News*, and married the well-known writer Philip Hamburger (divorced 1966). After writing as a freelance journalist, she became in 1961 a staff writer for *The New Yorker*, a venue that paradoxically led her into the Canadian North. Her first two books, *The new people: the Eskimo's journey into our time* (1966)—revised in 1979 and retitled *Inuit journey* (rev. edn 2000)—and *Denison's Ice Road* (1975, rpr. 2005), developed out of articles she wrote for *The New Yorker* and *Maclean's*. The first describes the meetings that led to the founding of the Inuit co-operatives for marketing goods to the south, particularly crafts; and the second describes her experience of accompanying John Denison and his crew while they built the ice road from Yellowknife across northern lakes to a silver mine. These glimpses of Canadian life led Iglauer to move in the early 1970s to Vancouver, where she met John Heywood Daly, a commercial fisherman, whom she married in 1976. Iglauer brought to her new life the same intense curiosity that characterizes her writing on other subjects. After Daly's death in 1978, she wrote a memoir about accompanying him during the fishing season that was published as *Fishing with John* (1988, rpr. 2000), which documents the fishing season off the British Columbia coast and bears many of the marks that make Iglauer's writing memorable. She is drawn to stories of energy, enterprise, and vision: both the Inuit co-operative initiative and the ice-road construction reflect these qualities, as do the subjects of other *New Yorker* pieces, such as *Seven stones: a portrait of Arthur Erickson* (1981, rpr. 1982), her famous profile of Pierre Elliott Trudeau (July 1969), and her 1972 article describing the construction of the World Trade Centre's massive foundation, which took seven years to write (since the foundation took seven years to complete): that investment of time, and degree of perseverance, characterize Iglauer's approach to her subjects. *The strangers next door* (1991), selected articles and excerpts from Iglauer's writings, illustrates her documentary impulse, her ability to catch emotional and sensory nuance, and her willingness to embrace exhausting, demanding circumstances to satisfy her desire to know. She lives in Garden Bay, B.C.

Ignatieff, Michael (b. 1947). Born in Toronto—the son of the distinguished Canadian diplomat George Ignatieff and the former Alison Grant, a painter—he lived in many different locations as a child, including Yugoslavia, Geneva, and Paris. He was educated at Trinity College, University of Toronto (B.A., 1969),

Harvard University (Ph.D., 1975), and Cambridge University (M.A., 1978). He taught history at Harvard (1971–4) and the University of British Columbia (1976–8), and was Senior Research fellow at King's College, Cambridge (1978–84). In 1985 he was visiting professor at the École des Hautes Études, Paris. He then, in his own words, 'climbed the monastery wall', becoming a television host for the BBC and writing the script for *Nineteen nineteen* (1985), a film whose subject was the last two surviving patients of Sigmund Freud. Ignatieff is a man for all media, bringing intelligence, warmth, urbanity, and verbal facility to everything he undertakes. He was editorial columnist for *The Observer* (London) from 1990 to 1993 and from 2000 to 2005 was Director of the Carr Centre for Human Rights Policy, Kennedy School of Government, Harvard University. In 2006 he returned to Canada and became a Member of Parliament, House of Commons, and is now Leader of the Liberal Party. He has received seven honorary degrees.

Ignatieff's writing career began with a history, *A just measure of pain: the penitentiary in the Industrial Revolution* (1978). He began to write for a broader audience with *The needs of strangers* (1984), a meditation on individualism in Western states, and on the attempts to institutionalize mechanisms that respond to human needs. *The Russian album* (1987, GGA; rpr. 2009) is an intensely personal look at Russian history of the last century through four generations of his own aristocratic family. Family members included Count Paul, an education minister to Czar Nicholas, who was saved from a Bolshevik execution by admiring students. The family escaped abroad, with some difficulty, to the home of an English nanny, and from there the Ignatieffs moved to Canada. The appeal of the book lies in the combination of facts and personalized history that has been characteristic of Ignatieff's writing since then. (Just as distinguished, in Canadian terms, was his mother's side of the family—including his uncle George Parkin GRANT—which he wrote about in *True patriot love: four generations in search of Canada* (2009, rpr. 2010). His forays into fiction met with a mixed response. *Asya* (1991, rpr. 1992) describes the life of a Russian emigré, Princess Anastasia Vladimirova Galitzine, an aristocrat who flees the revolution to Paris, where she is finally joined by her husband, a Red spy. A failed romance, it was vilified in Britain, though less harshly treated in Canada. *Scar tissue* (1993, rpr. 2002), the story of a man who watches his mother die of Alzheimer's disease, poses questions about sentience and the self.

Ignatieff

Now came accolades in Britain—it was nominated for the Booker Prize—but Canadian reviewers were uncomfortable with it, being unpersuaded that the novel could properly be called fiction, since Ignatieff's mother had died from the same disease. Ignatieff himself said that he wanted to write 'on the edge [of non-fiction]'. *Charlie Johnson in the flames* (2003), a short novel (158 pages) that draws on the author's experience of war in the Balkans, is about the war correspondent of the title who, with his photographer Jacek, witnesses a woman known to them being set on fire. 'She was screaming at the commander, fists raised, when the gasoline arced over her and the lighter touched her hem.... As she ran, her arms were like wings of flame, and she blundered into [Charlie] in an embrace of fire—and you were both down, in the dusty road, rolling over and over.' The woman dies, but Charlie is left only with bandaged hands and his determination to find the woman's killer. His wounds heal in the home of Jacek and his wife; he goes back to England and his wife but rejects both, returning to the Balkans to pursue his manhunt—self-destructively. Present and past appear in the novel confusingly, and the characters are merely names; but wartime colour, emotion, and suspense, though shallowly rendered, contribute to an entertaining read.

Isaiah Berlin: a life (1998, rpr. 2000) is an engrossing biography of the great liberal philosopher and thinker—who was also connected with several crucial events and the friend of many other famous people—based on interviews with Berlin over almost ten years and on access to his papers.

Ignatieff's reporting, in his words, 'on ethnic war, the collapse of old states and the fiery birth of new ones' leading to travels in various war zones, produced four books. *Blood and belonging: journeying into the New Nationalism* (1993, rpr. 1994) accompanied a series of BBC documentaries examining various 'new' nationalisms in Yugoslavia, Québec, Germany, and elsewhere. Here Ignatieff examines the tension between 'civic nationalism', based on consensus, and 'ethnic nationalism', based on blood. The great strength in this collection of essays is the sense of Ignatieff's own anguish and outrage as a self-avowed liberal and cosmopolitan facing the violent and irrational 'call of the blood' of drunken young soldiers on the rampage. *The warrior's honour: ethnic war and the modern conscience* (1998) is made up of five thoughtful and eloquent essays that examine the ethics of television; intolerance; 'our fumbled and ambiguous interventions in

the affairs of states', particularly in the Balkans; the position of the Red Cross in modern war; and the 'nightmare of history from which we are trying to awake'. Ignatieff's *Virtual war: Kosovo and beyond*, made up partly of previously published (or sections of) articles defending NATO's bombing, was published in 2000. *Empire lite: nation-building, in Bosnia, Kosovo and Afghanistan* (2003) focuses on 'the dynamics of ethnic conflict and the dilemmas of intervention ... the imperial struggle to impose order once intervention has occurred.' It is made up of four essays, three of which appeared in the *New York Times Magazine*. In his Preface, Ignatieff says that 'The essential paradox of nation-building is that temporary imperialism—empire lite—has become the necessary condition for democracy in countries torn apart by civil war.' These essays by a prospective politician were criticized for 'spin-doctoring': for example, while supporting the neoconservative defenders of the invasion of Iraq and the depiction of UN administrators as incompetents, Ignatieff also favours humanitarian interventions. *The lesser evil: political ethics in the age of terror* (2004) is composed of six Gifford Lectures delivered at the University of Edinburgh in January 2003—eloquent and persuasive discussions of evil and terrorism—that tacitly amount to a justification of America's draconian war against terror, the 'morally problematic character of necessary measures'—the lesser evil. Missing is an examination of the formidable theme of finding an effective means of treating the political causes of terrorism. The CBC Massey Lectures, *The rights revolution* (2000), discuss the subject of the title particularly as it is affecting Canada and Aboriginal rights. Ignatieff edited *American exceptionalism and human rights* (2005), a substantial book of essays. In the long essay that comprises his Introduction—which carries the book's title—Ignatieff says: 'The American creed itself—because it speaks so eloquently of the equality of all peoples—enjoins Americans to deliberate, to listen, to engage with other citizens of other cultures.... The critical cost that America pays for exceptionalism is that this stance gives the country convincing reasons not to listen and learn. Nations that find reasons not to listen and learn end up losing.'

Incubation (1967, rpr. 1986). This is the English translation, by Glen Shortliffe, of Gérard BESSETTE's *L'incubation* (1965, GGA), which is important in modern Québec fiction for its exploration of the depths of the human psyche—symbolized by the labyrinthine basements of the library where the narrator, Legarde, works—and for its innovative, frequently imitated, style: the text is an implosive and introspective first-person narration in one long paragraph. Legarde strives to say afloat in a world that continually threatens to drown him, and expresses despair at the degeneration of the relationships that surround him. Long, unpunctuated sentences record the stream of his ideas and emotions. He accompanies his dissolute friend Gordon to Montreal, where Gordon meets his former lover, Néa, after twenty years. They are both guilt-ridden for having wished the death of Néa's husband—a wish that was fulfilled. Because of Néa, Gordon's wife leaves him, but Néa, realizing that Gordon no longer cares for her, commits suicide. Néa is the novel's only passionate character: the men are rendered helpless by acute neurosis. Bessette was quoted as saying: 'With a great many distortions and changes, *L'incubation* recounts a drama that I have experienced, both in reality and in fantasy.'

'In Flanders Fields'. See John MCCRAE.

Influence of a book, The (1993). This is the English translation, by Claire Rothman, of the first French-Canadian novel, *L'influence d'un livre: roman historique* (Quebec, 1837) by Philippe-Ignace-François Aubert de Gaspé, son of Philippe-Joseph AUBERT DE GASPÉ. Born in Quebec City in 1814, Aubert de Gaspé Jr took part of his classical secondary course at the Séminaire de Nicolet before becoming a stenographer and journalist. Imprisoned for a month in 1835 following an altercation with a member of the legislative assembly, he avenged himself by planting a stinkpot in the vestibule of the assembly. He was then obliged to take refuge in the family manor-house at Saint-Jean-Port-Joli, where he amused himself by reading fiction and composing his novel, which was published by subscription in Sept. 1837. He subsequently worked as a journalist in Halifax, where he died in his twenties in 1841. His novel is a pre-Romantic work of mystery, adventure, and love. The title refers to *Le Petit Albert*, a popular manual of superstitious recipes that encouraged Charles Amand, an eccentric amateur alchemist living on the shores of the St Lawrence River, to seek the philosopher's stone. One of his macabre experiments requires the use of a black hen stolen at the full moon; another involves a *main de gloire*, the dried arm of a hanged man, which Amand removes from the dissection room after the execution of a murderer. Duped by practical jokers

and shipwrecked off Anticosti Island, Amand suffers one disappointment after another until, after five years' absence, he finds a modest treasure of $500. The lover in the tale is an elegant young student, Saint-Céran, who becomes a doctor and wins the hand of Amand's daughter Amélie. At least one chapter of the novel (the legend of Rose Latulippe in Chapter V) appears to have been written by Aubert de Gaspé's father, who later composed *Les anciens canadiens* (*CANADIANS OF OLD*). Published just as the Rebellion of 1837 was beginning, *L'influence d'un livre* received little attention, although one 'letter to the editor' criticized its lack of realism. Aubert de Gaspé retorted that Amand was modelled on a person he had known, and historians have since shown that certain of the events and characters are based on reality: the murder actually took place at Saint-Jean-Port-Joli in Aug. 1829, and some of the secondary characters (the giant Capistrau, la mère Nolet) are drawn from persons known in the district.

Innis, Harold Adams (1894–1952). Born on a farm near Otterville, Ontario, he was a scholarship student in political science at McMaster University (then in Toronto). Upon graduating in 1916 he enlisted in the army, took part in the attack on Vimy Ridge in Apr. 1917, and was wounded in the leg a few months later. He received an M.A. from McMaster and a Ph.D. from the University of Chicago with a thesis that was published as *A history of the Canadian Pacific Railway* (1923). In Chicago he met and married Mary Quayle, who later became a writer and economic historian. In 1920 he was appointed to the department of political economy in the University of Toronto, where he remained for the rest of his life. Simultaneously involved in research, teaching, compilation, travel, and publication, Innis became the driving force behind the intellectual development of political economy specifically, and of social science generally, in the university and throughout Canada. He devised 'a philosophy of economic history applicable to new countries' that for Canada has come to be known as the 'staple approach': an analytical method that stresses the dominance of a succession of export commodities, or staples, in Canadian development; the subordination of other activities to the production of staples; the vulnerability of an economy that grows around staples in a dependent relation with centres of Western civilization; and the political repercussions that were a consequence of that vulnerability. *The fur trade in Canada: an* *introduction to Canadian economic history* (1930, rpr. 1999) is his best-known publication using this methodology, but he pursued this approach with a major study of Canada's earliest staple, *The cod fisheries: the history of an international economy* (1940). Innis's disillusionment with the rising irrationality expressed in world events of the 1930s and 1940s, and with the inadequate approach for understanding such complexities, led him to consider the study of empires. Aware that the severest difficulty with this undertaking was the scholar's problem with bias, he proceeded to address 'bias' by focusing on various empirical communications systems and analyzing their impact on the nature and structure of society. Two important books emerged from this field of study: *Empire and communications* (1950, 3rd edn 1986) and *The bias of communication* (1951, rev. edn 2003). Though Innis was not a talented writer—he often overwhelms or confuses his readers with a sometimes cryptic prose that tends to be swamped with unnecessary detail—he was one of Canada's most prolific and influential scholarly authors. He transformed Canadians' awareness of the source and basis of their nationhood, and contributed—as no other Canadian scholar has—to the discussion of important philosophical questions dealing with the human condition and survival. His creative ideas have influenced a succession of Canadian scholars (including Donald CREIGHTON and Marshall McLUHAN) and a variety of disciplines in the social sciences. After Innis's death Mary Quayle Innis edited his *Essays in Canadian economic history* (1956). See also D.G. Creighton, *Harold Adams Innis: portrait of a scholar* (1957, 2nd edn 1978); the chapter on Innis in Carl BERGER, *The writing of Canadian history: aspects of Canadian historical writing: 1900–1970* (1976; 2nd edn 1986); and Daniel Drache, ed., *Staples, markets and cultural change: selected essays* (1995). See also *Harold Innis in the new century: reflections and refractions* (1999) edited by Charles R. Acland and William J. Buxton, reissued in 2000 under the title *Harold Innis in the new century: a history of the telecommunications industry in Canada, 1846–1956*.

International Festival of Authors. See AUTHORS AT HARBOURFRONT CENTRE.

Inuit literature. See ABORIGINAL LITERATURE.

Itani, Frances (b. 1942). Frances Hill was born in Belleville, Ontario, and attended the Montreal General Hospital School of Nursing (R.N, 1963). Changing careers, she attended the University of Alberta (B.A., 1974), where she studied with W.O. MITCHELL, and the University of New Brunswick (B.A., 1980). Married to Tetsuo Itani, she has a son and a daughter and lives in Ottawa. Her early books are collections of poetry: *No other lodgings* (1978), *Rentee Bay* (1983), and *A season of mourning* (1988), which is the most interesting; the poems, about memories and everyday life, are haunted by two deaths—that of her sister Marilyn and her friend Helen. These were followed by two collections of short stories published in the same year, *Truth or lies* (1989) and *Pack ice* (1989), and *Man without face* (1994)—the man of the title appearing in one of the narrator's childhood comics, which makes her think how she constantly observed the behaviour of her alcoholic father (who sometimes fell flat on his face) until his death. Itani then graduated to a prominent commercial publisher, HarperCollins, with *Leaning, leaning over the water: a novel in ten stories* (1998, rpr. 2003), about a family in the 1950s: Maura, her husband Jock, and their three children. Their house, in the beginning, is 'A long narrow bungalow [the title of the first story] in a tiny village at the end of a dirt road beside the swiftest portion of the Ottawa River.' The chapters (stories) render a child's view of life, and the changes in a family over a relatively short period, memorably. *Poached egg on toast* (2004, rpr. 2005) contains many of Itani's early stories plus seven new ones.

Two novels attracted a good deal of attention. *Deafening* (2003, rpr. 2004) is a remarkably controlled, eloquent historical novel that begins in 1902 and encompasses disability, romance, and war. It is about Grania O'Neill, who becomes totally deaf when she has scarlet fever at the age of five. Her father runs a hotel in Deseronto, Ontario, for which her mother superintends the preparation of meals, so it is her grandmother, Mamo, who begins to teach Grania: how to read, how to say words. She attends public school, to little effect. 'You should be in a proper school for deaf children,' Mamo tells her. 'You're losing time. You would learn new things. There is a special school in Belleville.' She goes there for ninth months in the year and and at first it's a shock. But she grows to like it, makes friends, and learns a lot. Her learning experience through seeing—and feeling lips as words are uttered, until she becomes fluent in sign language and lip-reading—is described by Itani interestingly, not at all boringly. In 1915 Grania meets and falls in love with Jim Boyd, a hearing man, and marries him. He soon departs for wartime

Europe in the Ambulance Corps as a stretcher-bearer, and his travails are vividly described. Grania's making him particularly conscious of sound, and of hands (her sign language), sharpens his responses. Itani's handling of a plot notable for its diversity is accomplished. *Remembering the bones* (2007, rpr. 2008) is narrated by eighty-year-old Georgina Danforth Witley who, when she's driving to the airport to fly to England to attend Queen Elizabeth's birthday lunch—she [and ninety-nine other invited guests) shares the same birthday—she drives the car off the road. 'The car lands in the top branches of a large tree and then flips, and flips again, and brushes past another tree, and down and down…. Her scapula is stabbed by a lightning edge of rock. Root or rock, her flight has ended. Georgie has sunk to the bottom of Spinney's Ravine.' The rest of the narrative is made up of her memories. 'The shoulder. Scapula! What a splendid boost is memory.' She tells herself how pleased Grandfather Danforth (a doctor) would have been, if he'd returned from the war, 'that she had memorized the bones.' 'My life unknits as I lie here. How many days? How many nights?…' Itani was made a Member of the Order of Canada in 2006.

Iwaniuk, Waclaw (b. 1915). Born in Chelm in eastern Poland, he studied at the Free University of Warsaw and contributed prose and poetry to avant-garde literary periodicals. During the Second World War he enlisted with the Polish Mountain Brigade, was captured and imprisoned in Spain, escaped, and made his way to England, where he joined the British First Armoured Division and fought in Europe. After the war he studied at Cambridge University and in 1948 immigrated to Canada, becoming a citizen in 1953. He worked as a court-room translator in Toronto until retirement in 1978. Iwaniuk wrote close to two dozen Polish-language books between 1936 and 1997, most of them volumes of poetry. The earliest and latest books appeared in Poland; the ones in between were issued by émigré houses in London, Paris, Brussels, and Toronto, where two books were issued in English. *Dark times: selected poems of Waclaw Iwaniuk* (1979), edited by John Robert COLOMBO, offers poems translated by Vancouver translator Jagna Boraks and others. The stark poem 'Carthage' talks of Poland ('A strange land/a sad land/this dark foyer/to Asia'); Canada is the subject of the magnificent 'Elegy in a Toronto cemetery' ('I was not born here,/I was not bequeathed this parcel of land,/yet my voice quivers as I speak of it'). *Evenings on Lake Ontario: from my Canadian diary* (1981) consists of meditations written in English on the cycles of impersonal history and the continuity of private life in Toronto. One poem expresses the sense of ambivalence found in a city of defiant exile and personal renewal: 'Toronto became my many graveyards/and my painful redemption./I have never danced to music I did not like.' The poems are characterized by intellectual imagery, measured emotion, and ironic comment in free-verse forms.

J

Jacobs, Peter (Pahtahsega, He who comes shining, Ojibwa, 1805–90). Born near Rice Lake in Upper Canada, Jacobs was trained as a Methodist missionary by William Case, superintendent of Native missions and schools in Upper Canada, and worked among the tribes on Lake Superior, Rainy Lake, Norway House, and Fort Alexander (Manitoba) until he left for England in 1842 for his ordination. He returned to the Rainy River region in 1844–9, and in 1852 made a tour from Rice Lake to York Factory, recorded in *Journal of the Reverend Peter Jacobs, Indian Wesleyan missionary,* *from Rice Lake to the Hudson's Bay territory, and returning … with a brief account of his life; and a short history of the Wesleyan mission to that country* (Toronto 1853; 2nd edn, Boston, 1853; 3rd edn, New York, 1858), which provides a valuable account of the mission field. A dynamic orator, who drew large crowds wherever he spoke, Jacobs lectured in Canada, the United States, and England. He died at the Rama Indian Reserve, near Orillia, Ontario.

Jalna (1927). Mazo DE LA ROCHE's novel was entered by the author in the $10,000 *Atlantic*

Monthly prize competition for a first novel. *Jalna*'s victory in the highly publicized event led its publisher, Little Brown, to order an initial printing of 45,000 copies in October. By Christmas sales had approached 100,000. It initiated a series of fifteen sequels, which the author had not planned, that created international bestsellers (11 million copies by 1966) and ended a year before her death. A stage dramatization, a film, and a radio series were created in de la Roche's lifetime. Since then, two television series have appeared, one of them originating in France. Jalna is the name of a house and property located within the Toronto region in Clarkson, Ontario (a number of residences claim to be its original). It is named after the Indian hill station where the soldier Philip Whiteoak and his bride Adeline passed the early years of their marriage. As the novel opens, Adeline has been transformed into the peppery matriarch Gran, who rules a household consisting of her sons and their attachments, and a parrot who swears in Hindi. Among her offspring are Renny, her headstrong likeness who will reign after her death at the age of 100, and Finch, a troubled artist who most resembles his creator. A series of sexual intrigues preoccupies the novel. Renny falls in love with the American bride of his brother Eden, who, in turn, enjoys a fling with a neighbour's daughter, who later elopes with Piers, another Whiteoak brother. Such soap-opera formulas underlie the rest of the series. It is the house that remains central. Enduring, expandable, accommodating, it survives even when American materialism (embodied in the arrival of TV) undermines the foundations of the Whiteoaks' colonial culture. Old World graciousness, New World informality and drive, the unending tensions of family life—all these forces are reconciled within Jalna's magic walls.

Janes, Percy (1922–99). Born in St John's, Newfoundland, Percy Maxwell Janes moved in 1929 with his family to Corner Brook—where his father, Eli Janes, a blacksmith, had found work in the new pulp-and-paper mill—and passed his formative years in this frontier boom town. From 1938 to 1940 he attended Memorial University College, St John's, but at eighteen he left for Montreal and enlisted in the Canadian navy, serving for nearly four years in the medical corps. He then enrolled in Victoria College, University of Toronto, and became acquainted with modern literature. Graduating in 1949, he worked as a tutor, principally at Grove School in Lakefield, Ontario, and as a carpenter. In the early 1960s he dedicated his life to writing. He travelled widely, living for many years in England, and died in Newfoundland.

Janes' first book was the self-published *So young and beautiful* (1958), a novel set in small-town Ontario that reveals the stirrings of a real talent and the germs of ideas and characters that would emerge fully in *House of hate* (1970, rpr. 1992). Begun in the mid-1960s, following the death of his father, when Janes decided to write about the life of his family in Corner Brook, this is a brilliant, obsessive, bleak novel about the corrosive effects of a cantankerous father, Saul Stone, upon his wife and children. Janes takes us into the lives of Saul's children to show how each in turn was twisted and coarsened by the atmosphere of recrimination, suspicion, and violence that Saul created in his home. Janes rivets our attention upon domestic scenes of frightening rawness; analyzes with brutal frankness, yet with some compassion, the motives of the central character; and accurately conveys Newfoundland habits of speech. We feel that we are on the delicate boundary between autobiography and fiction and are witnessing the rare phenomenon of a man telling the whole truth about himself, his family, and his society. Janes continued to write both fiction and poetry. *Light and dark: poems* (1980) contains poems on Newfoundland themes that reveal an alert, ironic sensibility affectionately bemused by what was happening in his native province, and more personal poems in which he broods over his craft and middle age. *Newfoundlanders: short stories* (1981)—three more stories are added in *A collection of short stories* (1987)—is often lighthearted and whimsical, while the novel *Eastmall* (1981), a far less impressive work than *House of hate*, focuses on local concern over large-scale municipal development in St John's. *Requiem for a faith* (1984), and *Requiem for a faith II: the rebels and the renegades* (1984), and *No cage for conquerors* (1984) show a further falling off from *House of hate*; but *The picture on the wall* (1985)—which ends with a scene of unpunished, stomach-turning violence, the like of which is rarely found in literature—has in it something of the anger and grit of his best novel.

Jarman, Mark Anthony (b. 1955). Born in Edmonton, Alberta, he was educated at the University of Victoria (B.A., 1980), and the University of Iowa (M.F.A., 1983), where he was a member of the Iowa Writers' Workshop; he was an instructor in the English department at Iowa in 1982–3. He has also taught creative writing at Mount Royal College,

Calgary (1984–7), was a visiting lecturer at the University of Victoria (1997–9), and is now professor of creative writing and English at the University of New Brunswick.

Jarman's career as an innovative writer of short stories began with his collection *Dancing nightly in the tavern* (1984, rpr. 2007), which introduces a writer who only occasionally produces straightforward stories: he writes as people think, letting all kinds of unrelated thoughts and images intrude, never mind if his narrative is thrown into disarray. With 'Cowboys Inc.', written while Jarman was at the Iowa Writers' Workshop, he felt he had 'broken through to a new way for me to smash together matters of head and heart.' He liked its 'jagged edges. The story wasn't easy to digest, was not A to B, and not tied up with [a] pretty bow, but I realized I liked it that way. It had the power of pastiche, or collage, a quality that was accidental and brutal, but attractive to my eye and ear.' (*CANADIAN NOTES & QUERIES*, Issue 74, page 27.) This admission does not alleviate the let-down feeling one has about sentences and actions that are not always comprehensible and characters that are little more than names. One is not let down, however, by surprising juxtapositions of incidents, sudden shots of humour, nor by the words themselves—diction is significant. Jankovitch—driving across the US westward in flight from a warrant for his arrest in Missouri—we first meet in the washroom of an Interstate rest area, 'slouched at the sink in shorts.' The other character, Ironchild, is sitting on a toilet. Jankovitch sees him, 'closes the cubicle door behind him, grunting as he maneuvers Ironchild's now-heavy body, propping his paratrooper boots inside the toilet bowl, the dead man's armpits damp, his skinhead cut bristling at Jankovitch's face, breath gone, skin white, clammy....' (Ironchild keeps reappearing, always referred to as 'the dead man'.) The third character is Virginia—there is a sex scene on an ironing board, until it 'crashes down'. (Jarman: 'I wanted to make use of a guy I worked with as a janitor.... I also wanted a dead man as an ongoing character, and I wanted a sex scene on an ironing board.' *CNQ*, p. 27.) The story ends when the car turns over in a storm. 'Virginia's face is a strange ... star, her ruined mouth leaking blood into a spreading stain over his clothes'. Jankovitch 'wants a bus to the clean coast, to start over, away from the binges of deceit and drinking, the trail of abortions and carwashes, mescal and frozen grins, reckless driving, drinking.... He swears he's going to change. Starting Monday.' Jarmon has a fondness for derelict, marginal characters, struggling to make ends meet and drinking a lot, as in the title story—which at no point accounts for dancing nightly in the tavern. It is about Luke and Woody and their confabulations, their drinking, and a last fight: 'Luke stands shouting and Woody shoves him once more and Luke's boot breaks through his father's gut-string guitar, Woody stomping out to the car with Luke after him trying to shake the splintered guitar from his foot.... Luke watches the slate-blue car disappear.' The opening story in *New Orleans is sinking* (1998), 'California cancer journeys', appears to have an autobiographical component as the narrator, with his wife Sharon and three very young children (describing Jarman's real-life family) motor across the US to California because Sharon's mother is dying of cancer. The short narrative describes mortgaging their house to buy a new car, the children's response to the trip and to the motels they stay in, and includes the narrator's thoughts about his best friend, Levi; their arrival, the gruff nature of mother-in-law Gladys; thoughts about death ('My father died last year in California on Valentine's Day. He had a heart attack while walking out for a copy of *The San Diego Union*.'); and the news that Levi has died. 'After a fortnight of sunny chaos ... Sharon and I just want to get the hell out.... And escape exactly what? Escaping escape?' The British Columbian title story, having nothing to do with New Orleans, is narrated by a waitress at the Orca Hotel; at the shift's end she is approached by Barbara: 'Would I keep an eye out for a pocket watch she had lost among the cracked lobster and pint glasses? Because of this I remembered Barbara later, when things happened, when Barbara was found under the government wharf.' Her friend Treeface 'went on a binge after Barbara drowned... blowing wads of money'. The time came when Treeface was seen pissing at the end of the wharf, in a heavy wind, and he 'tumbled over the edge of the pier, pants trapping his ankles... and then the waves lifted and broke over him.' *19 knives* (2000, rpr. 2001) is a highly praised collection of fourteen stories among which is a humorous fantasy, 'Love is all around us'. The first sentence is 'My close personal friend Kurt Waldheim phones me up—*lonely*, everyone's ostracizing Kurt in his bunker aerie in Alberta's foothills, not as many Nazis as he thought....' In what follows every character—a stewardess, a performer who makes out with kd lang, a hockey referee et al.—is Margaret ATWOOD. The last words are '*Without you we are lost.*' The collection contains the extraordinary 'Burn Man on a Texas porch', which opens with an eleven-line one-sentence paragraph, beginning with 'Propane slept in the tank and propane leaked while I slept, blew the camper door off and split the tin walls ... blew the camper door like a safe and I sprang from sleep into my new life on my feet in front of a befuddled crowd, my new life on fire....' Towards the end, Burn Man says: 'I still have that shy desire for the right fire to twist me back just as easily to what was: milky youth and a mysterious person falling towards me on a Texas porch with her tongue rearranging hope in my mouth.' In the title story the narrator, a recovering heroin addict, is sent home with methodone, which he mixes with 'the sweetest orange juice I can find, because the meth is so bitter.' He puts a sign on it, DO NOT DRINK; and his boy, who loves orange juice, gets up in the middle of the night and drinks it, with tragic results. After many digressions we read that the narrator recognizes the hospital the ambulance takes them to because 'three years ago a policeman shot me in someone else's backyard', thinking he had pulled a knife—he had no knife. The police sealed the yard and looked for a knife as evidence. 'Next morning nineteen knives lay in the grass of that small yard. Every cop in town must have driven by and flipped a knife over the fence.' In 'Cougar' the narrator is going into the woods 'to chop us a free Christmas tree' when he is attacked by a cougar. 'The cat eyed me, ears pinned back, small lower jaw dropped in a snarl, springing at my shoulders. I felt naked even with my folding saw and hardware-store gloves and heavy coat and boots. I ducked and turned but still got knocked over from the cat's force.' The encounter—suspensefully described, with the narrator's thoughts and recollections providing an unwelcome counterpoint—continues for almost five more pages; but all ends well. In 2008 Jarman published another collections of fourteen stories, *My white planet*.

The novel *Salvage king, ya!: a herky-jerky picaresque* (1997, rpr. 2003)—named after the family junkyard. of Drinkwater, the narrator—is metafiction, a fragmented narrative that is an amiably digressive account of the interactions of Drinkwater; Waitress X (whom we meet on the first page and with whom he is having an affair), who has a violent boyfriend; Kathy, his ex-wife; 'my Intended'; and two men called Shirt Is Blue and Neon. There are vivid, intermittent scenes from Drinkwater's past as a minor-league hockey player. Along the way we read about a player's losing his left eye because of Drinkwater's slap shot. 'The forward's eye

collapsed like an egg and I didn't want to look. No one wanted to look.' And about a fight on the rink: 'I take the puck away and skate up ice. Never Pass hooks me in the stomach but I move the puck over the blue line where he hooks me again. I shove him quickly and keep going and he hits me on the back of the head as I'm leaving, says to me, Fuck off old man.' Disparate episodes that contribute to the narrative include how Shirt Is Blue's Alsatian dog died and her burial, and Marilyn Munroe's making *River of No Return* in Alberta in the company of Joe DiMaggio. Focusing on Drinkwater's love life is the scene where he's sleeping and 'Blinds crash open and I wake up confused, expecting Waitress X's boyfriend wanting to kill. Instead my Intended is staring at me like a shirtless vampire. / "I dreamed you had an affair. The little slut."/"What was she like?" I'm truly interested and apprehensive.' His Intended (in her dream) had a. 22 and was going to use it—on him. As one reviewer said: 'No one writes quite like this.' *Killing the swan* (1986), published by PRESS PORCÉPIC, is a collections of poems in which stanzas offer striking imagery ('Salmon curl around rock/Spawn eggs in a tern's beak / Birds tear at the fish as they swim/Then sated, gulls eat only the pupils'—'Scissorbills with Jaegers'), with meaning being resistant collectively.

Ireland's eye (2002) is an engaging travel book. Jarman's mother was born in Dublin and his grandfather drowned in a Dublin canal in 1922 on the day of Michael Collins' funeral. The book depicts a changing Ireland, first visited in 1981; and twenty years later, when his mother is slipping into Alzheimer's dementia. Jarman edited *Ounce of cure: alcohol in the Canadian short story* (1992) when he became interested in the subject; it includes twenty-three stories by VANDERHAEGHE, MUNRO, ROOKE, FINDLEY, GARNER, VALGARDSON, TREMBLAY, KROETSCH, RULE, COHEN, and HODGINS, among lesser-known writers.

Jarvis, William Henry Pope (1876–1944). Born in Summerside, Prince Edward Island, he was a journalist in western and central Canada and died in Canton, Ontario. His three volumes of fiction are of interest mainly for their re-creations of local colour. *The letters of a remittance man to his mother* (1908), set in Winnipeg and on Manitoba farms, sketches with comic hyperbole the practical education of a supercilious young Englishman. *Trails and tales in Cobalt* (1908) is a collection of anecdotes from western and northern mining camps drawn loosely together within the framework of a prospecting adventure in northern Ontario. In the preface Jarvis claims to have known the mining regions of British Columbia and to have spent five years prospecting and mining in Alaska and the Yukon. His tales are heavy with particulars of the principles and processes of prospecting, mining, and wilderness living that continually overcome his uncertain grasp of fictional form and technique. *The great Gold Rush* (1913) follows a group of Klondike stampeders through the hardships of the wilderness and of dealing with corrupt officials and noble but inflexible Mounted Policemen.

Jasmin, Claude (b. 1930). Born in Montreal, he studied at the Collège Grasset and the École des Arts appliqués. He has been a ceramist, actor, art teacher and critic, a television designer at Radio-Canada, and director of the literary and art pages of the *Journal de Montréal*. Jasmin has published numerous novels, plays, collections of short stories for adults and children, and autobiographical sketches and journals. Revolt and violence, some of it politically motivated, are recurring features of his fiction. His best-known novel, *Ethel et le terroriste* (1964)—translated by David Walker as *Ethel and the terrorist* (1965)—is a transposition of the first fatal FLQ incident in Apr. 1963, when night watchman William O'Neill (of French-Canadian descent) was killed by a bomb at a Montreal armoury. In *Ethel* the event takes place in Feb. at a post office. Paul, who placed the bomb, flees to New York, according to his nationalist group's instructions, with his mistress Ethel Rosensweig, whose immediate family had survived the Holocaust. During their six days there he is obliged to take part in another violent episode at the Canadian consulate. Paul's fear of the consequence of his acts and Ethel's preoccupation with possible victims of violence are relieved by escapist dreams and love making. Ethel, who had lost many relatives in Europe, prods the conscience of her lover and influences him towards pacifism. Though she threatens to leave him over the death of the night watchman, she is faithful to the end and returns with him to Montreal, where he is summoned. *Mario* (1985)—the translation by David Lobdell of *La sablière* (1979)—is an ambiguous, powerful novel about the relationship of fifteen-year-old Clovis and his younger brother Mario, who has a brain disorder.

Jeanneret, Marsh (1917–90). Born in Toronto, he graduated from the University of Toronto in 1938 and entered publishing as a traveller in textbooks for Copp Clark Co. Ltd, rising to a senior position before joining the UNIVERSITY OF TORONTO PRESS in 1953 as its director. During the next twenty-four years, until his retirement from that position, he built the Press from modest stature to its present status as one of the largest and most respected university presses in North America. Jeanneret was the first Canadian elected president of the Association of American University Presses (1970) and was founding president of both the bilingual Association of Canadian University Presses (1972) and the International Association of Scholarly Publishers (1976). His impact on Canadian publishing extended well beyond the academic field. He served as president of the Canadian Copyright Institute (1965–7), and of the Canadian Book Publishers' Council (1968), bringing to these offices characteristic concentration, energy, and imagination. In 1970 he was appointed one of three members (and the only publisher) of the Ontario Royal Commission on Book Publishing, and was the principal author of its final report, *Canadian publishers and Canadian publishing* (1973), which offered broad recommendations to encourage Canadian publishing in its English-language centre. As head of the University of Toronto Press, Jeanneret stressed the importance of international distribution and international standards in this country's scholarly publishing, and under his leadership the Press pioneered Canadian participation at the Frankfurt International Book Fair and opened its own offices in Buffalo, New York, and London, England. He also frequently stressed the importance of university publishing to Canadian self-understanding. To this end he encouraged the development of university presses, publishing in both official languages, on campuses other than his own. Jeanneret was the author of three high-school history texts—*Story of Canada* (1947), *Notre histoire* (1949), and *Canada in North America* (1961)—as well as of numerous articles on publishing and education. In 1989 he published his memoirs, *God and Mammon*.

Jenness, Diamond. See ABORIGINAL LEGENDS AND TALES: BIBLIOGRAPHY.

Jesuit Relations. This is the collective name given to a series of reports sent from Québec to the Provincial Father of the Society of Jesus in Paris and signed by the Québec Superior. '*Relation de voyage*' is a standard phrase in French and is found in other writings on

New France. What makes the *Jesuit Relations* original is their sustained and relatively standardized serial character. Each annual '*Relation de ce qui s'est passé en la Nouvelle France*' in the main series addresses the reader in a personal manner and gives an agreeable, often humorous, account of matters great and small in a curious, distant land. An official optimism sustains even the most discouraging accounts, as if to encourage the admiration and support of sponsors in France and maintain the good social tone of letters that might be read aloud in company. The first collective edition (Quebec, 1858) was superseded by the scholarly work of Reuben Gold Thwaites, who added to these *Relations* a mass of personal letters, memoirs, journals, and other documents. His monumental edition, the 73 volumes of *The Jesuit Relations and allied documents; travels and exploration of the Jesuit missionaries, in New France 1610–1791*, heavily annotated and with page-for-page translation, was published in Cleveland from 1896 to 1901 in an edition of 750 sets. Combining a wealth of minutiae about life in New France, and the customs of the Native population, with dramatic narratives of travel, exploration, and adventure, and written by educated Europeans, these materials have provided rich source material for historians, geographers, philologists, and ethnologists—as well as for writers of creative literature. The best sustained passages of the *Relations* are in the central early reports (Thwaites, vols 5 to 35), from Paul Le Jeune's in 1632 to Paul Ragueneau's in 1650. Le Jeune lands at Québec on 5 July, and after two months of domestic administration records a curious decision: the major victories for God are to take place elsewhere. While all '*sauvages*' are eager to be rescued from their misery, the stable Huron population, in a fertile area east of Georgian Bay (southern Ontario), offers the best chance of conversion. Hereafter the Huron missions occupy an increasing portion of the annual Relations until, in 1650, Ragueneau writes of the destruction by Iroquois in 1649 of Saint Marie (near Midland, Ontario), where he had been superior for four years, struggling against odds and witnessing the martyrdom of his brethren. From Le Jeune to Ragueneau—via Fathers Brébeuf, Jérôme Lalemant, Garnier, Vimont, Chaumont, Lemercier, and Dablon, among others—the heroic rhetoric of conversion is mixed with the determined application of spiritual exercises. One modern critic has described this series of the *Relations*—with its exotic characters, grotesque details, and miraculous events—as a baroque drama with, at its centre,

paradox and inversion of values. The *Relations* can also be read as a record of day-to-day happenings, ranging from minute episodes to personal accounts of major events in the colony, of the daily routines and spiritual discipline of the Jesuits themselves and the many accounts of Amerindian life, with emphasis on an edifying and exaggerated portrayal of the Native response to the Christian message—all narrated with elegance and charm.

The Jesuit Relations and allied documents is the title of abridged and selected editions by Edna Kenton (1954) and S.R. Mealing (Carleton Library, 1990).

Jiles, Paulette (b. 1943). Born in Salem, Missouri, she grew up in the Ozarks and obtained a B.A. in Spanish literature from the University of Missouri. She lived in the Canary Islands and North Africa before arriving in Canada in 1969. *Waterloo Express: poems from a journey* (1973), her first collection of poetry, was followed by *Celestial navigation* (1984, GGA; rpr. 2004) and the vigorous *The Jesse James poems* (1988). *Blackwater* (1988) represents a cross-section of prose and poetry. Her drama scripts for radio were adapted for *Song to the rising sun: a collection* (1989). *Flying lessons: selected poems* (1995) draws from *Celestial navigation*, *The Jesse James poems*, and *Song to the rising sun*, and adds 'Ragtime', a suite of poems about Scott Joplin. Especially in her poetry, Jiles' persona is partly that of a sardonic, streetwise pulp-fiction detective, partly a romantic drawn to violent events and oversized myths. Always, her darting imagination is yoked to shrewd observation. Jiles spent seven years as a media correspondent and consultant among the Cree and Ojibwa of northern Ontario, the latter experience vividly recounted in *North Spirit: travels among the Cree and Ojibway nations and their star maps* (1995, rpr. 2003). She has also written fiction, including a science-fiction novel, *The late great human road show* (1986), and the racy, more successful *Sitting in the club car drinking rum and Karma-Cola* (1986, rpr. 2003; its subtitle the US title, *A manual of etiquette for ladies crossing Canada by train*). In the new millennium Jiles surprised her readers by producing two novels that are powerful and were highly acclaimed. The protagonist of *Enemy women* (2002)—a Civil War novel imbued with poetic lyricism, set partly in the Missouri Ozarks—is eighteen-year-old Adair Colley. When the Colley house is destroyed and her father is captured by lawless Union militiamen, Adair (with two young sisters) determines to walk 120 miles north, thus embarking on a series of trials that are softened only by Adair's meeting—in the St Louis prison where she has been incarcerated—a Union soldier, Major William Neumann. He falls in love with her, as she does with him. He helps her escape, but they come together in the end. *Stormy weather* (2007, rpr. 2008) is about another ordeal, the Great Depression and the Texas Dust Bowl in the 1930s, and about the Stoddard family, Jack and Elizabeth and their three daughters, Mayme, Jeanine, and Bea. Jack's work keeps him on the road; he takes Jeanine with him to convince his wife that he is no longer drinking and carrying-on (these activities continue)—until he dies in prison. The four women, Elizabeth and her daughters, along with Jack's racehorse Smoky Joe, return to Elizabeth's derelict family farm in central Texas, and the novel becomes a dramatic account of a small family's efforts to survive under dire circumstances. The non-fiction *Cousins* (1991)—part love story, part family saga—is Jiles' first return to her Missouri roots and to her far-flung relatives. She now lives in Texas, the setting of her 2009 novel *The color of lightning*.

Joe, Rita (1932–2007). A Mi'kmaq, Rita Bernard was born in Whycocomagh, Cape Breton Island. From the age of five, when her mother died, until she was twelve she lived with a series of foster parents. From 1944 to 1948 she attended the Indian Residential School in Shubenacadie, Nova Scotia, and in 1954 she married Frank Joe. She began writing in 1969 with a column, 'Here and There in Eskasoni', in the *Micmac News*. In 1974 she won the Nova Scotia Writer's Federation poetry competition with her collection *The valiant race*. Four years later, *Poems of Rita Joe* (1978), a collection of twenty-six untitled poems, a few with Mi'kmaq translations, was published. Joe then went back to school, graduating with her Grade XII certificate and a diploma in business education. She made numerous personal appearances across Canada and parts of the United States, giving workshops, seminars, lectures, poetry readings, and radio/television interviews about her Mi'kmaq culture and heritage. Three more collections are *Song of Eskasoni: more poems of Rita Joe* (1989), *Lnu and Indians we're called* (1991), and *We are the dreamers: recent and early poetry* (2000). Joe's poems range gracefully across many subjects from Native residential schools, battered women, the Ksan Dancers of British Columbia, to Donald Marshall Jr, the Mi'kmaq who spent eleven years in prison for a crime he did not commit. Joe writes with spareness and dignity, gentle candour, and quiet humour as she protests past injustices and pleads for understanding and compassion for her people. Her poem 'When I was small' hangs in the Museum of Civilization, Hull, Québec. In 1989 Joe was made a Member of the Order of Canada and in 1993 she received an Honorary Doctor of Laws degree from Dalhousie University. Spending her whole life in Nova Scotia, living in Eskasoni, she died in Sydney. See *Song of Rita Joe: autobiography of a Mi'kmaq poet* (1997).

Johnson, Pauline (1861–1913). Born on the Six Nations Reserve near Brantford, Canada West (Ontario), she was the daughter of a Mohawk father and an English mother, Emily Susanna Howells (a relative of William Dean Howells). Her education was for the most part informal, but she very early became familiar with the poetry of Byron, Scott, Longfellow, Tennyson, and Keats. Her Native background was less influential than popular tradition would have it, although she knew the history of her father's family and listened as a child to tales and legends told by her grandfather. Johnson's poems first appeared in the New York magazine *Gems of Poetry* in 1884, and thereafter in several British and North American magazines, including *The WEEK*. Two of her poems were included by W.D. LIGHTHALL in his anthology *Songs of the Great Dominion* (London, 1889), and they were praised by Theodore Watts-Dunton in his review of the book, creating Johnson's reputation as an authentic 'Indian' voice in poetry. This reputation was firmly established by her public readings, particularly after she adopted Native dress (which she wore when she recited Native poems; otherwise she wore evening dress). From 1892 until her retirement to Vancouver in 1909, Johnson was an extremely popular and compelling performer, touring not only Canada but parts of the United States; she also visited London, attracting favourable public attention there in 1894, and again in 1906. Johnson's abilities as a performer gave her poetry much of the high reputation it enjoyed during her lifetime.

Johnson's first collection, *The white wampum* (London, 1895), was published by the Bodley Head in London. Other volumes were *Canadian born* (1903) and *Flint and feather* (1912, rpr. 1997), misleadingly described as 'the complete poems'. After her retirement she produced *Legends of Vancouver* (1911, rpr. 1997), a collection of short pieces inspired by the tales and

legends she heard from her friend Joe Capilano, a Squamish chief. *The Shagganappi*
(1912) and *The moccasin maker* (1913) appeared
posthumously: both are primarily collections
of short sentimental and didactic fictions,
including some previously published boys'
adventure stories. *The moccasin maker* contains
'My mother', Johnson's fictionalized and
romantic account of her parents' courtship
and her own early years. Today the bulk of
Johnson's poetry appears derivative and shallow, echoing the styles and themes of Romantic and Victorian writers, and of such Canadian
poets as Charles G.D. ROBERTS and Bliss CAR-
MAN. The Native qualities of the verse were
exaggerated, because Johnson most often used
Native materials that for the most part lent
themselves to conventional poetic expression.
At times, however, she did speak for the
Native in 'Ojistoh', 'The corn husker', and
'Silhouette', and she was influential in her use
of Native legends. Johnson's attitude to her
heritage was ambiguous. She insisted with
pride and conviction on its importance—in
1886 she adopted the name 'Tekahionwake'
(although not legally entitled to it), and she
knew and resented the bigoted treatment the
Native peoples often endured—yet she also
wrote poems and stories that celebrated
European culture, and often presented the
Native in picturesque and conventional terms.
Feeling the claims of both cultures, she never
resolved them—a tension that occasionally
found poetic expression, as in 'The idlers' and
'Re-voyage'.

See *E. Pauline Johnson, Tekahionwake: collected poems and selected prose* (2002) edited by
Carole Gerson and Veronica Strong-Boag.
Numerous recent biographies have been
written about Pauline Johnson, notably
Charlotte GRAY's *Flint & feather; the life and
times of E. Pauline Johnson, Tekahionwake*
(2002). There are also Betty Keller's two
biographies: *Pauline* (1987), which includes
some of the uncollected and unpublished
poems, and *Pauline Johnson: first Aboriginal
voice of Canada* (2000); and *Paddling her own
canoe: the times and texts of E. Pauline Johnson
(Tekahionwake)* (2000) by Veronica Strong-
Boag and Carole Gerson.

Johnston, Basil H. (b. 1929). An Ojibwa
(Anishinaube) born on the Parry Island
Indian Reserve, Ontario, he received his early
education at the Cape Croker Indian Reserve
Public School. At the age of ten he entered
the Spanish Indian Residential School in
northern Ontario, graduating with his high-
school diploma in 1950. In 1954 he received

a B.A. from Loyola College, Montreal, and in
1962 his secondary-school teaching certificate from the Ontario College of Education,
going on to teach history at Earl Haig Collegiate, Toronto, from 1962 to 1969. He then
joined the Department of Ethnology at the
Royal Ontario Museum, Toronto, where he
worked for twenty-five years. To reclaim and
regenerate Anishinaubaek culture—its values,
beliefs, customs, wisdom, and language—has
been Johnston's chief occupation. He has
produced the most extensive Anishinaubaek
language courses on tape and in print.
Although Johnston writes in both English
and Ojibwa, only his works in English have
been published. The majority of his books—
Ojibway heritage (1976, rpr. 1988), *How the
birds got their colours* (1978), *Tales the elders told:
Ojibway legends* (1981), *Ojibway ceremonies*
(1982, rpr. 1987), *By canoe & moccasin: some
Native place names of the Great Lakes* (1986),
Tales of the Anishinaubaek (1993), *The Manitous: the spiritual world of the Ojibway* (1995),
*Mermaids and medicine women: Native myths
and legends* (1997)—record and enlarge the
literary canon of the Anishinaubaek. His
most popular book, *Moose meat and wild rice*
(1978, rpr. 1987), a collection of twenty-two
stories about reserve life, focuses on the
humorous situations in Native-white relations. His ear for Native/English oral speech
patterns and vocabulary is marvellously accurate, though enthusiasm can lead to excess—
we are at times overpowered by the sheer
surfeit of words. In his memoir *Indian school
days* (1988, rpr. 1991) Johnston recalls his
experiences as a young student during the
1940s at the Spanish Indian Residential
School. Rather than attacking government
policy that regulated the Native residential
school system, which was rooted in racism
and ethno-centrism, Johnston writes with
vigour and humour about the mischievous
antics and amusing adventures of the students. *Crazy Dave* (1999) is made up of stories
about Johnston's grandmother, Rosa, and her
five sons, including Uncle Dave, who was
born with Down's syndrome—on the Cape
Croker Reserve. Johnston writes: 'the more I
thought about [Uncle Dave], the more he
reminded me, in certain respects, of the place
and the situation of the North American
Indian in Canadian society.' *Honour Earth
Mother: Mino-Audjaudauh Mizzu-Kummik-
Quae* (2003) is a celebration of the wonders
of nature, seen through the eyes and stories of
a Native: 'The earth is a book, alive with
events that occur over and over for our benefit. Mother Earth has formed our beliefs,

attitudes, insights, outlooks, values and institutions.' *Anishinaubae thesaurus* (2007) is an impressive guide to the language, containing sections on parts of speech and 'A few common verb roots'. In 1994 Johnston received an Honorary Doctor of Laws degree from the University of Toronto. He is a Member of the Order of Canada.

Johnston, George (1913–2004). George Benson Johnston was born in Hamilton, Ontario, and educated at the University of Toronto (B.A., 1936). After several years as a freelance writer in England, he joined the RCAF at the outbreak of the Second World War and served as a reconnaissance pilot in Africa. He returned to the University of Toronto (M.A., 1945) and taught at Mount Allison University, Sackville, New Brunswick, from 1947 to 1949. He then joined the staff of Carleton College (later University) in Ottawa, where he became a popular teacher of Anglo-Saxon and Old Norse and an internationally known scholar of the Icelandic sagas.

All of Johnston's poetry is informed by his intelligence, warm personality, sense of absurdity and compassion, from the serious light verse of his early poems to the plain speech, austere forms, and sometimes complex rhythms of his later work. Many of the poems in his first collection, *The cruising auk* (1959), seem to belong to a complete and self-sufficient world that unifies the book: a small city like Ottawa that has not yet acquired the anonymity of a huge metropolis is viewed as if through reflecting mirrors that distort and change perspectives. The poems combine fantasy with direct simplicity, and comment on the desires and illusions of ordinary people, observed with affection and ironic amusement. The wit and satiric edge of the poems are sharpened by the apparently simple stanzaic forms, playful metres, and rhyme. *Home free* (1966) includes several poems involving the same characters and displaying similar qualities of lively wit and fluent movement. Two long poems have public themes. 'Under the tree' is a passionate poem about the effects of capital punishment upon the hangman, the hanging judge, and the whole community involved in an execution. 'Love in high places', a narrative and reflective poem, concerns the transformation over two generations of love into an obsession with worldly success. *Happy enough: poems 1935–1972* (1972) contains the two earlier collections and a number of new poems that include lyrics or brief narratives about

farm, sea, or rock-bound coast and poems celebrating personal affection or reflecting wryly and humorously on domestic occasions. The title poem of *Taking a grip* (1979) suggests the need for maintaining some kind of order—in ordinary things or in the whole threatened world—in the face of possible chaos. In several poems there is an elegiac quality, but Johnston's wit and humour are still evident. Most of the poems in *Ask again* (1984) are occasional in the sense of being written for specific occasions, some public ('Convocation address', 'A celebration of Northrop Frye'), others private, most of them notable for employing unusual and intricate metres and verse-forms often derived from Johnston's study of early languages. *Auk redivivus: selected poems* appeared in 1981, and *Endeared by dark: the collected poems* in 1990. The latter contains a group of new poems, as does *What is to come: selected and new poems* (1996)—all marked by Johnston's characteristic mixture of technical deftness with a relaxed, seemingly casual tone. *The essential George Johnston* (2007), selected by Robyn SARAH, is a delightful, slender, attractive memento of Johnston's poetry—beginning with nine poems from *The cruising auk*—published by The PORCUPINE'S QUILL.

Two of Johnston's translations from Old Norse, *The Faroe Islanders' saga* (1975) and *The Greenlanders' saga* (1976), were revised and reprinted, with a new introduction and notes, as *Thrand of Gotu* (1994).

Johnston, Julie (b. 1941). Born in Smiths Falls, Ontario, she studied physiotherapy and occupational therapy at the University of Toronto, graduating in 1963, and worked as a physiotherapist until 1967, when the first of her four daughters was born. After moving to Peterborough, Ontario, in 1970, Johnston obtained an honours degree in English (1984) from Trent University. Using her knowledge of physiotherapy, she began writing a novel set in the Ottawa Valley in the 1946–7 period when polio was epidemic, and could kill or cripple healthy children in a matter of hours or days. This novel, *Hero of lesser causes* (1992; rpr. 1996; GGA), was published to acclaim. She made history by winning a second Governor General's Award with her second novel, *Adam and Eve and Pinch-me* (1994, rpr. 1996), a story about a Children's Aid ward who, angry and estranged, confides her thoughts to her computer.

Based on the diary of Fred Dickinson, written in 1904, *The only outcast* (1998) is about a boy, called Fred Dickinson, whose mother has just died unexpectedly and whose sense of loss and physical awkwardness, and his stuttering, make him feel like an outsider; life changes when he bonds with a girl and makes a macabre discovery that is related to stories his grandfather told him. Johnston has related accurately the life of Susanna MOODIE in an effective novel, *Susanna's quill* (2004), that should be of great interest to teenaged girls who enjoy reading about the Canadian past.

Johnston, Wayne (b. 1958). Born in St John's, he was taken at the age of one to Goulds, Newfoundland, on the Avalon Peninsula and raised there. He was educated at Memorial University of Newfoundland (B.A., 1978)—he was a reporter for the St John's *Daily Times* from 1978 to 1980—and the University of New Brunswick (M.A., 1984). He now lives in Toronto. Johnston has written five novels of increasing accomplishment; they are all written in the first person. The first four novels are recollections of boyhood and family life, three of them set in Newfoundland and coloured by its speech and ways. (*Human amusements* is set in Toronto.) The skilful narratives offer soberly perceptive, tender, detailed accounts of families, boys' lives, and daily events that blend genuinely funny moments and outrageous eccentricity with informative, even mundane descriptions that never lose the reader's interest. In *The story of Bobby O'Malley* (1985) Bobby's ill-matched parents—he's a TV newscaster with a crazy sense of humour, she's a schoolteacher, staunchly Roman Catholic—are observed as Bobby grows from eight to sixteen, marked for the priesthood, and relates to new friends as his parents move from house to house; he describes a shocking episode in his childhood at the end of the novel. *The time of their lives* (1987, rpr. 1991) is the chronicle of three generations of the Dunne family, headed by Dad, whose tyrannical and stubborn ways affect his children, for the most part adversely, but whose dying in hospital they all loyally attend as the novel ends. The story—told by Johnny, a grandson—draws the reader into the web of cruelties and wayward behaviour of this large family of failures. The Newfoundland Ryans of *The divine Ryans* (1990, rpr. 1998) acquired that name because 'there were so many priests and nuns in the family'—so says Draper Doyle ('my name is Draper, not Draper Doyle'), the narrator, looking back on his life when he was nine years old. It had been a locally important family, but all that was left of its 'empire' was the *Daily Chronicle*—called by everyone 'The Word of God', the heading over the scriptural quotation that was

in the upper right-hand corner of the front page of every issue—and the funeral home called Reg Ryan's. The heterogeneous family of Ryans living under one roof was headed by the domineering Aunt Phil (Philomena)—who, when they watched Saturday-night hockey games on TV, insisted on calling the Leafs (despised because she thought of them as Protestants) 'the Leaves'. The vagaries of the family are well described by Draper Doyle, whose own young life, with its many tribulations, is punctuated by repeated sightings of the ghost of his dead father, for which he is ridiculed until he keeps them to himself. Again, a shocking episode occurs at the end of the novel. Johnston wrote the screenplay for the film that was released in 2000. The tight family in *Human amusements* (1994, rpr. 2002) is made up of three: the witty father, a teacher and failed writer; the mother, who as a scriptwriter for TV in the 1950s created two hugely successful series for children, in the first of which she stars as Miss Mary; and their son the narrator, Henry Prendergast, who from the ages of seven to eighteen appears in both series and achieves celebrity in the second, about Philo Farnsworth, the very young inventor of television. The novel is partly a satire of early television and its development of fan worship, and partly Johnston's typically searching (and endearing) probe of the interaction of members of a small, self-enclosed family unit. His first three novels clearly brought to a peak his mastery of a great subject, Newfoundland, enabling him to produce the quintessential Newfoundland novel, *The COLONY OF UNREQUITED DREAMS* (1998, rpr. 1999), a fictional memoir of Joey Smallwood (1900–91), who was the first premier when Newfoundland became a province of Canada in 1949. The island—its bleak beauties, its fierce winter weather, its clusters of isolated people verging on starvation—and weedy, ill-educated Smallwood's ambitions for it underpin the entire novel; but the eventful, compelling narrative also combines personal history, Newfoundland history, and politics with (blighted) romance and mystery. Smallwood is a distant, hated name in *Baltimore's mansion: a memoir* (1999, rpr. 2000), which shares with Johnston's novels the technique of looking back on childhood and family. But it is grounded in the reality of Wayne Johnston's grandfather, a blacksmith who sees the days of blacksmithing ending; of his father, an agricultural technologist who works for the Department of Fisheries, grading fish and making three-week trips by boat on often stormy seas to inspect fish plants; and of the two men's despair over Confederation.

Their lives blend with an unsentimental but deeply felt and lyrical portrayal of Newfoundland itself—the customs, the landscape, the weather—and their particular experience of it, and love for it. In May 2000 *Baltimore's mansion* won the first $25,000 Charles Taylor Prize for Literary Non-Fiction. The title is an allusion to Sir George Calvert, first Baron Baltimore, and the Mansion House that was built for him and his family at Ferryland on the Avalon Peninsula, though he spent only one disastrous winter there in 1628–9 (he was then granted a Royal Charter to settle the colony of Maryland, which was founded by his son, the second Lord Baltimore).

The navigator of New York (2002, rpr. 2003) is a historical novel set in the period 1881–1909, when Americans were fascinated with explorers. It is epic in scope, taking the reader from St John's, Newfoundland, to Brooklyn and Manhattan, to Antarctica and the Arctic—including a tortuous search for the North Pole—all described with admirable exactitude. It is human relationships, however, that are central to the novel. The narrator is Devlin Stead, whose doctor father, Francis, abandoned his wife, Amelia, and very young son to pursue Arctic exploration—he participated in a Greenland expedition of Robert Edwin Peary (1856–1920) and Dr Frederick Albert Cook (1865–1940). Devlin's mother dies mysteriously, having apparently drowned off Signal Hill near St John's. Then, in 1892, Francis disappears in the Arctic. Devlin's life changes when, as a teenager in 1897, he receives letters—sent to his Uncle Edward and given to him unopened—from Dr Cook, revealing that Cook, when a teenager himself, had met Amelia in Manhattan—she was visiting her cousin Lily. They fell in love and had a brief affair, of which Devlin was the result; Dr Francis Stead of St John's, whom Amelia was engaged to and married, was not his father. Devlin leaves Newfoundland for America, and locates the address in Brooklyn of Dr Cook, his father, who gives him quarters in his large house—Devlin's home for the next ten years. Though Cook shared with Peary a determination to be the first to reach the North Pole (the two were not at all friendly), he was sent by the Peary Arctic Club to rescue Peary, who had been away for almost thirty months—and bring him, or at least his wife and daughter, back. Devlin accompanies him and they find Peary at Etah in North Greenland. When he deigns to visit their ship, he faints and nearly falls overboard—Devlin saves his life (which made him a celebrity when he got home).

Devlin later accompanies Cook on his two-year expedition to and from the North Pole, which Cook claimed to have reached in 1908 (Peary in 1909). The novel gradually uncovers secrets that link Francis Stead, Devlin, Amelia, Dr Cook, Peary, Lily, and Kristina Sumner—whom Devlin meets in New York and marries. Ingeniously plotted (the final revelations make one rethink the whole novel), incorporating two real people and some real events—and with vivid descriptions of various settings as an absorbing counterpoint—the novel is an impressive achievement. While a student at Bishop Feild's in St John's, Devlin reads Richard Hakluyt's classic *Principal navigations* (1589) and discovers that 'explorers were referred to as navigators'. The navigator of the title is surely Devlin himself, who explored both New York and, to some degree, the Arctic. *The custodian of paradise* (2007) is about the life of Sheilagh Fielding—beginning before her appearance in *The colony of unrequited dreams*. Built on layers of time, it interweaves several narratives, beginning in the 1940s when Fielding (as she is called), also in her forties, settles in an abandoned community on a deserted island, Loreburn, off the south coast of Newfoundland in order to write a book. Journal entries and letters fill in the details of her life. When she is six her mother leaves her husband and daughter for no known reason. Sheilagh attends Bishop Spencer School for girls, adjacent to Bishop Feilds, attended by Daniel Prowse, the grandson of a famous Newfoundland historian, and Joe Smallwood. Prowse invites her to meet his grandfather, who likes her, and whom she sees several times; after one of these visits Prowse seduces her and, at fifteen, Fielding is pregnant. Her father—though hating his former wife for leaving him—takes Fielding to New York in 1916 and leaves her in the house of her mother, who is now the wife of Dr Breen; the arrangement is that the resulting twins, Sarah and David, will be known as the natural offspring of the Breens and raised by them. The novel describes Fielding's life after this event. Lame, using a cane, and never getting over the loss of her children, she becomes a witty, devastating journalist, making enemies and having virtually no friends except for Smallwood; but all this time she is observed by an unknown man (and his 'delegate'), who comments on her life in letters, signed as 'Your Provider'. At the end of the book the two meet on Loreburn and his identity in disclosed. A masterly writer, Johnston handles the complexities of the novel magnificently, though he indulges himself with an over-abundance of episodes and descriptions, making the book too long.

Jonas, George (b. 1935). Born in Budapest, he came to Canada in 1956. Since that time he has written poetry, fiction, and non-fiction, and produced and directed for radio and television in Toronto, where he was for many years a producer with the Canadian Broadcasting Corporation. He writes weekly columns for the *National Post* and CanWest News Service.

In Jonas's three volumes of new poetry— *The absolute smile* (1967), *The happy hungry man* (1970), and *Cities* (1973)—an ironic wit offers the only relief to the monotonous vacuum of people's lives depicted in sparse and spare verse. In the first volume the protagonist leads an empty life in poems of unhappiness and alienation. Little levity or optimism appears in *The happy hungry man*, where the narrator's cynicism distances himself and his reader from the human scene. *Cities* is a suite of poems that journeys from contemporary Toronto, the poet's adopted city, back through urban haunts in New York, London, and Vienna to his Hungarian birthplace. The prevailing self-absorption causes the poet himself and his interests to be evoked rather than the world's great cities. *The east wind blows west* (1993) is a collection of new and selected poems.

The undecorated style of Jonas's verse often borders on the prosaic, and it is no coincidence that he later turned almost completely to prose. With Barbara Amiel (to whom he was married from 1974 to 1979) he wrote *By persons unknown: the strange death of Christine Demeter* (1977), an exhaustive prose account of the murder of a Toronto woman and the conviction of her wealthy Hungarian-born developer husband. Behind the facts is the authors' analysis of the social and ethnic backgrounds of the main characters and a scathing dissection of the complex legal processes involved in the trial. *Vengeance* (1984; rpr. 1985; new edn 2005) is a well-written, suspenseful account of the aftermath of the Munich Massacre of 1972—when Palestinian terrorists entered the Olympic Village and captured and later killed eleven Israeli athletes. Israel dispatched 'Avner' and four others to find and execute those who enabled the massacre. Jonas travelled far and worked hard to verify the information he compiled, using the means at his disposal with their attendant limitations. When published the book aroused criticism on various fronts (improving its bestseller status); but its 2005 edition has a Foreword by

'Avner', a Preface by Jonas, and an Introduction by the Pulitzer Prizewinner Richard Ben Cramer that authenticate the book. *Vengeance* was partly the source for Steven Spielberg's film *Munich* (2005). With two exceptions, the pieces in *Reflections on Islam: ideas, opinions, arguments* (2007) appeared in the *National Post* between 2001 and 2006. Over a relatively long but recent period this provocative subject is discussed from a right-wing standpoint. Jonas supports the war in Iraq and attacks 'liberalism' and its immigration practices, free-wheeling multicultural policies, and criticisms of Israel and the US government—while clouding his arguments with misconceptions and omissions, such as reducing Islam to an abstract name for a faith in which fanaticism and violence predominate, and confusing Islam and Arabs, Islam and Islamism. These columns contained arguments that turned out to be wrong and were not corrected for book publication, e.g., Jonas's belief in the weapons of mass destruction, and that in Afghanistan 'the terrorists are virtually powerless against the forces arrayed against them'. The writing, however, is witty and insightful, and it is hard to disagree with his disdain for politically correct pieties about respecting cultural sensitivities and for the silence of Muslim leaders—and Muslims in the West—when one atrocity is followed by another.

In Jonas's novel *Final decree* (1982, rpr. 2000) a Hungarian-born carpenter who lives in Toronto arrives home one day to find his wife and two children gone, as his wife begins her search for personal fulfilment. Costly and inhumane legal machinations unfold once she files for divorce. The novel's compelling structure, weaving back and forth in time through the carpenter's mind, propels the plot relentlessly and naturally to a violent climax in which the hero, now the victim of a seemingly inexorable legal network, takes the law into his own hands.

Jonas's play *Pushkin*, a dramatization in three acts of Aleksandr Pushkin's life (1799–1837) and the conflict between romanticism and idealism, was commissioned by Theatre Plus, Toronto, and produced in May 1978. Jonas has also published collections of selected essays and short journalistic pieces: *Crocodiles in the bathtub* (1987) and *Politically incorrect* (1991). The title of his substantial and provocative memoir, *Beethoven's mask: notes on my life and times* (2005) alludes to his father's saying late in life that the whole world reminded him of a masked ball (he was once a baritone who sang a leading role in Verdi's *Un Ballo in Maschera* with the Vienna State Opera):

'Europe is a carnival in Venice, with assassins dressed up as lyric poets. Butchers lurk in ducal palaces wearing Beethoven's mask. The voice is Beethoven's, but the hand is Beria's.' For a Hungarian born in 1935, the dehumanization of Europe—to which he remains devoted—haunts Jonas and underlies the remarkable account of his early life in Hungary, his arrival of Canada halfway through the book (page 207), forty-five years spent here and his successful career. All this—presented in seventy short chapter plus an Epilogue—is enlivened by many choice anecdotes.

Jonas edited *The scales of justice: seven famous criminal cases recreated* (1983) and *Volume II: Ten famous criminal cases recreated* (1986), containing the scripts—by writers including Guy Gavriel KAY, Ellen GODFREY, Jack BATTEN, William DEVERELL, and Jonas himself—for the very popular CBC Radio series 'The Scales of Justice'.

Jones, Alice (1853–1933). The daughter of Lieutenant-Governor Alfred Gilpin Jones of Nova Scotia, she was born and educated in Halifax. In the 1880s and 1890s she travelled extensively; her visits to Algeria, Brittany, Venice, London, and various European centres led to a series of travel essays in *The WEEK* in the 1890s, and later informed her novels with an intimate understanding of continental settings, customs, and social expectations. *The Night-Hawk: a romance of the '60s* (1901) appeared in New York under her sometime pseudonym 'Alix John' and is set in Paris, Halifax, and the Confederacy during the American Civil War. Incorporating a thinly disguised version of the famed 'Tallahassee' episode into its tale of blockade running, it introduced the strong female figure common to all Jones' fiction. *Bubbles we buy* (1903)—reprinted in England as *Isobel Broderick* (1904)—developed a plot of international intrigue against a backdrop of Europe's fashionable society and Nova Scotia's age of sail. Successful in Britain as well as in North America, it resembled three subsequent novels—*Gabriel Praed's castle* (1904), *Marcus Holbeach's daughter* (1912), and *Flame of frost* (1914)—in counterpointing the shallowness of the international set against the vitality of Canada's less tradition-bound society. Like *Gabriel Praed's castle*, *Bubbles we buy* is also a story of young North American artists struggling to achieve recognition at the Salon in Paris. While both novels introduced strong 'new woman' figures into this environment, *Gabriel Praed's castle* expanded the international theme by exploring the vulnerability of a forthright Canadian businessman when confronted with European decadence and corruption. Jones invites comparison with Sara Jeannette DUNCAN in her emphasis on strong woman characters and in her treatment of international themes. She moved to Menton, France, in 1905 and remained there until her death.

Jones, D.G. (b. 1929). Douglas Gordon Jones was born in Bancroft, Ontario, and educated at McGill University (B.A., 1952), and Queen's University (M.A., 1954), and the University of Guelph (D.Litt., 1982). After teaching English literature at the Royal Military College (1954–5), Kingston, and the Ontario Agricultural College (1955–61), Guelph, he moved to Québec and taught at Bishop's University (1961–3) before moving to the Université de Sherbrooke (1963–94). He lives in North Hatley, Québec.

In 1969 he founded *Ellipse*, the only Canadian magazine in which poetry in English and French were reciprocally translated. As an anglophone teaching in a French-language university, and as an editor of a bilingual journal, he and his writings have reflected an openness to both Canadian and French-Canadian cultures. His translations of poems by Paul-Marie LAPOINTE, *The terror of the snows* (1976), was followed by an enlarged edition, *The fifth season* (1985); he edited Gaston MIRON's *The march to love: selected poems by Gaston Miron* (1986), of which he translated the title suite and other poems; and was the translator of Normand de Bellefeuille's *Categories, one, two, & three* (1992), which won a Governor General's Award for translation, and Émile Martel's *For orchestra and solo poet* (1996).

Jones first became known as a poet of unusual, if rather unfashionable, lyrical clarity and philosophic intensity. His first collection, *Frost on the sun* (1957), was followed by *The sun is axeman* (1961), *Phrases from Orpheus* (1967), *Under the thunder the flowers light up the earth* (1977, GGA), and *A throw of particles: the new and selected poetry of D.G. Jones* (1983). As the title *Phrases from Orpheus* suggests, Jones has tended to see his larger, more embracing forms in mythological terms, though he has been saved from the amorphous vagueness of much mythopoetic poetry by an aesthetic precision, an economy of language, and a neo-imagistic sharpness of outline. The neo-imagism is perhaps most apparent in *Under the thunder*, but the empathies of this book range more widely than those of the earlier volumes. The myths have not departed from the poet's vision, but they have changed their forms. The gods come this time in other guises, and often as painters, for two of the five sections of the book are devoted to poems inspired by David Milne and Alex Colville. Jones matches an appreciation of the lyrical qualities of these painters with a strong visual and 'painterly' element in his own verse. His later collections are *Balthazar and other poems* (1988); *The floating garden* (1995), which includes five interesting suites of poems and a group of shorter poems that show Jones at his best and most enjoyable; *Wild asterisks in cloud* (1997), a collection that ends with 'Saint Martins/Sint Maartens', a long poem sequence whose vivid lyrics draw the reader into a tourist's seductive experience of the Caribbean island; and *Grounding sight* (1999). *The stream exposed with all its stone: collected poems* was published in 2008.

Jones is also the author of an important work of criticism, *Butterfly on rock: a study of themes and images in Canadian literature* (1970), in which he sees the dominant themes and images in the literature of Canada as emanations of the mythical and moral structure of our society when, at a critical changing point, it ceased to be the garrison society described by Northrop FRYE and entered into a dialogue with the natural world it had formerly rejected in fear.

Jones, Peter (Kahkewaquonaby or Sacred Feathers, 1802–56). The son of Augustus Jones, a Welsh land surveyor, and Tuhbenahneequay, daughter of Mississauga Chief Waubanasay, he grew up among his mother's people on the northwestern shore of Lake Ontario where Hamilton now stands. When he was fourteen his father took him to his farm on the Grand River and he was sent to school. He was converted to Christianity at the age of twenty-one and nearly two years later began his missionary career as an itinerant Methodist preacher, converting his own Ojibwa band and other Ojibwa-speaking bands around Lakes Huron and Superior. So successful was his mission work that in 1833 Jones was ordained and became the first Native Methodist missionary in Canada. He preached at numerous missionary meetings in what is now Ontario and Québec, and in the United States, where his Native and non-Native listeners were awed by his eloquence. He soon became the influential leader of a group of remarkable young Ojibwa—George COPWAY, George HENRY, Peter JACOBS, John Sunday, Allen Salt, and Henry Steinhauer—who were trained by the Wesleyan Methodist Missionary Society to become teachers, interpreters, and missionaries. Three times he visited Great Britain, where he spoke on behalf of the rapidly growing Canadian missions, delighting large audiences and fêted by royalty and distinguished men and women of the realm. In 1833, in New York, despite much opposition, he married Eliza Field, the accomplished daughter of a prominent London merchant. Jones was a prolific writer. Many of his sermons, speeches, and articles appeared in missionary publications, local newspapers, journals, and in pamphlet form in Great Britain and the United States. He is remembered principally for two books published after his death: *Life and journals of Kah-ke-wa-quo-na-by (Rev. Peter Jones) Wesleyan minister* (Toronto, 1860) and *History of the Ojebway Indians: with especial reference to their conversion to Christianity* (London, 1861; rpr. 1970). Numerous letters, briefs, reports, and petitions to government officials survive that attest to Jones' unrelenting labours as spokesman on behalf of his people, as he tried to help them gain legal title to their land and to have their injustices redressed. He established a model agricultural settlement along the Credit River, where the Mississauga hunters became self-supporting Christian farmers. In his *History* he wrote: 'Oh, what an awful account at the day of judgment must the unprincipled white man give, who has been an agent of Satan in the extermination of the original proprietors of the American soil.'

Joual. Literary *joual* came into prominence in Québec in 1964 and was of major interest for about ten years. Before 1964 the word *joual* had been used pejoratively: its existence as a dialect pronunciation of *cheval* is well attested in rural Québec, Normandy, and other parts of France. Claude-Henri GRIGNON and André Laurendeau had referred to it to denote not only a corrupt speech but the deprived culture that went with it. Émile Coderre ('Jean Narrache') had developed in his poetry an orthographic and lexical style to record the resentment and frustration of the down-and-out Montrealer of the Depression years, admitting a certain sympathy and even sentimentality. Jean-Paul Desbiens drew widespread attention to the use of *joual*, particularly in the lower-class districts of Montreal, in his *Les insolences du Frère Untel* (1960; translated by Miriam Chapin as *The impertinences of Brother Anonymous*, 1962), in which he regarded it as a disease like malnutrition. The year 1964 saw the publication of *Le cassé—Flat broke and beat* (1968)—a novella by Jacques RENAUD, and in the following year a short novel, *Pleure pas,*

Germaine!, by Claude JASMIN; in 1968 Michel TREMBLAY's *Les BELLES SOEURS* (1968) was performed. For all three works the authors chose a literary form that could fully exploit the novelty of making uneducated speech the main medium of expression and standard French a marginal, usually comic, intrusion. The popularity of these works in *joual* had a major impact on Québec letters. Among the features of *joual* are anglicisms and barely assimilated English words; obscenities and picturesque blasphemies; and non-standard syntax and orthography that often imply an erosion of basic grammar. The thematic correlatives are violence and alienation; murder, rape, abortion, perversion, and prostitution; the boredom of factory work and the hopelessness of the unemployed; unsupportive relations with family, friends, and sexual partners; lack of direction or positive awareness of social goals; and resentment, vituperation, and an inability to communicate—all are found, in different mixes, in *joual* works. Marie-Claire BLAIS's *Un joualonais, sa joualonie* (1973)—*St. Lawrence blues* (1974)—mocked the literary affectation of proletarian language, which by that time had become repetitious. Her bitter parody marked the beginning of the end of the literary use of *joual*, but its influence remains in a less-intensive cult of oral style.

Journals of Susanna Moodie, The (1970, 24th rpr. 2007). This sequence of poems by Margaret ATWOOD, which has never been out of print, is one of the most important efforts to create a Canadian myth of the wilderness. It is based on the life of Susanna MOODIE, an English gentlewoman who immigrated in 1832 to Upper Canada (Ontario). Journal I describes Moodie's arrival in Canada and her experiences during seven years of settlement in the Ontario bush. Her efforts as a pioneer failed, and Journal II records her escape to Belleville, Ontario, where her husband had been made sheriff. Journal III describes her as an old woman living in estrangement from the artificial civility of a Canadian Victorian town. In the last poems of the cycle she is resurrected as a spirit haunting the twentieth-century Canadian mind with accusations of its betrayal of its historical traditions. From the first poem ('Disembarking at Quebec'), through 'The wereman', a poem about Moodie's husband, 'Departure from the bush', 'Death of a young son by drowning', the 'Dream' poems (which include 'The bush garden' and 'Brian the stillhunter'), and 'Thoughts from underground', this collection is one of the most memorable literary evocations of immigrant experience in modern Canadian literature. Moodie provided Atwood with a Canadian archetype that enabled her to explore what was, in 1970, an obsession with the moral and psychological problems of colonialism and with the issues of cultural identity. As Atwood explains in her Afterword: 'We are all immigrants to this place even if we were born here: the country is too big for anyone to inhabit completely, and in the parts unknown to us we move in fear, exiles and invaders.' The Canadian psyche, Atwood felt, was schizophrenic, split by a deep ambivalence: while we preached ardent affection for Canada, we remained detached and critical observers. Moodie becomes in these poems a heroic figure struggling to 'unlearn' old European codes of behaviour in order to speak a new language. At the end of the cycle she is the spirit of the land, accusing Canadians of erecting a garrison mentality: alienated in a world of concrete and glass, they remain ignorant of the wilderness that surrounds them. A lavish limited edition (120 numbered copies) of *The journals*, illustrated by Charles Pachter and published in 1980, was issued in a smaller-format trade edition in 1997.

Justice, Daniel Heath. See ABORIGINAL LITERATURE: 5.

K

Kamouraska (1973, rpr. 2000). Anne HÉBERT's most successful novel, *Kamouraska*—published in French in 1970 and translated by Norman Shapiro in 1973—skilfully combines two plots. The first, based on an actual murder case in nineteenth-century Québec, takes place during the Rebellion of the Patriotes in Lower Canada: in 1839 a young woman, Elisabeth, induces her American lover, Doctor Nelson, to kill her husband, a violent man who is seigneur of Kamouraska. Nelson accomplishes the dreadful deed, then flees to the USA. Elisabeth is arrested, imprisoned, and finally released. She assumes the obligatory mask of bourgeois respectability, marrying a Quebec City notary named Roland. The second plot, which reinterprets the first, is set some twenty years later. Elisabeth's second husband, gravely ill, is about to die. She will soon be free again, but what will she do with that freedom? Remain faithful to her honourable role of widow and mother, or try to rejoin her American lover? As she contemplates these choices she sees again, in the course of a single night of terrifying lucidity, all her violent past. Arriving at a dreadful realization of her sealed fate, she decides to cling to her false respectability. This devastating portrait of a woman in anguish, consumed by passion, is written in broken, telegraphic sentences that give the novel a breathlessly romantic style. It is also studded with details about the manners, dress, and customs of nineteenth-century Québec. A visually beautiful film directed by Claude Jutra, *Kamouraska* (1973), captures the dramatic subtleties of the novel.

Kane, Paul (1810–71). Born in Ireland, he came to York (Toronto) about 1819 (subsequently he claimed to have been born in York). He studied portrait painting as a young man, and lived and worked in Toronto, Cobourg, Detroit, and Mobile, Alabama. He toured Europe in 1841–2 and spent time in London in 1842–3, where he became a friend of the American artist George Catlin, who had lived and painted among forty-eight Amerindian tribes in the United States. Kane left London in 1843, determined to paint the Native peoples of Canada. His three-year western journey began from Toronto on 17 June 1845, and took him to Georgian Bay and thence, by way of a number of Hudson's Bay Company posts, to Fort Vancouver. From there he made sketching trips to Oregon, to the north-west region then known as New Caledonia, and to the southern part of Vancouver Island. Kane's best-known works are the 100 canvases he painted largely from sketches made during his travels; several hundred surviving sketches are important not only for their documentary value but also for their freshness and immediacy. Kane wrote *Wanderings of an artist among the Indians of North America...* (London, 1859), a classic of Canadian travel literature. Based on his diary—expanded with extracts from field logs, stories, and legends about the Native peoples he encountered—it provides extensive and careful information and description in a narrative that is free of the heavy embellishment that was characteristic of other Victorian writing. It was illustrated with reproductions of a number of Kane's sketches and paintings. The English-language edition sold out; French, Danish, and German editions appeared between 1860 and 1863, and a second English edition appeared in 1925. See *Paul Kane's frontier: including 'Wanderings of an artist among the Indians of North America' by Paul Kane* (1971), edited with a catalogue raisonné by J. Russell Harper—a large, lavishly illustrated volume that contains a definitive biographical study by the late Dr Harper.

Kattan, Naim (b. 1928). Born in Bagdad, Iraq, of Jewish parents, he attended a Hebrew school, where he learned Arabic, French, and English in preparation for his studies in the law faculty of the University of Bagdad. Because of the unfavourable political climate he left Iraq at the end of the Second World War for Paris, where he studied literature at the Sorbonne before coming to Montreal in 1954. He was head of the literary section of the Canada Council from 1967 to 1990, and in 1994 was appointed associate professor at the Université du Québec. He is an Officer of the Order of Canada.

The three worlds Kattan has lived in (the Middle East, Europe, and North America), and the cultures he has immersed himself in (Jewish, Arabic, French, and North American), inform his essays, novels, and short stories with an unusually wide range of perceptions, which he conveys with remarkable clarity. Only four of his books are available in English. His first book of essays, *Le réel et le théâtral* (1970)—which was translated by Alan Brown as *Reality and theatre* (1972)—combines informal autobiography with formal speculation on the cultural, religious, and linguistic differences between the occidental and oriental ways of perceiving reality: the latter confronts reality directly, while the former resorts to theatrical mediation. In the tradition of the French structuralists, Kattan operates through a series of binary oppositions: the image and the unseen, object and shadow, groups and communities, actors and dictators, word and place. His interest in such dichotomies as occident and orient, Arabic and French, Jew and Arab, male and female found their way into Kattan's first autobiographical novel *Adieu, babylone* (1975), translated by Sheila FISCHMAN as *Farewell, Babylon* (1976), which was reissued in 2005 as *Farewell, Babylon: coming of age in Jewish Baghdad*. The nameless narrator recounts his childhood experiences in Bagdad during the Second World War, describing his family's fear of the Germans and the Farhoud, a pogrom-like attack by the Bedouins against the Jewish population. The narrator's sexual and literary apprenticeship is described with very little dialogue to interfere with the discursive narration. In *Les fruits arrachés* (1977)—*Paris interlude* (1979) in Fischman's English translation—the protagonist Méir has a much smaller narrative role, as Kattan shifts to a more dramatic form where dialogue predominates. Having left Iraq, Méir studies literature at the Sorbonne at a time when France is recovering from the trauma of the Second World War. His alternating affairs with a French, a Polish, and a Dutch lover symbolize the instability of postwar Europe. As in the first novel, this one ends with a departure—for North America. Three other novels followed. Some of Kattan's stories were translated into English by Judith Madley and Patricia Claxton and collected in *The neighbour and other stories* (1982). Kattan also wrote *A.M. Klein: poet and prophet* (2001), translated by Edward Baxter.

Katz, Welwyn Wilton (b. 1948). Born in London, Ontario, she received a B.Sc. in Mathematics (1969) from the University of Western Ontario and a Diploma in Education (1970) from Althouse Teachers College. She taught mathematics at South Secondary School, London, for seven years, turning to full-time writing in 1977. Her first published novel for children, *The prophecy of Tau Ridoo* (1982), was her entrance into fantasy, a genre she would continue to develop in original ways, combining with the supernatural elements real-life issues such as moral choices, effects of divorce on children, and male-female relationships. Both *Witchery Hill* (1984, rpr. 1995) and *Sun god, moon witch* (1986, rpr. 1995) are set in England and blend the fantasy of pagan magic with realistic adolescent dilemmas. The award-winning *False face* (1987), set in Katz's hometown, is a story of a daughter of divorced parents who finds a dangerous set of Native false-face masks. *The third magic* (1988, GGA; rpr. 1990; 2nd edn 1999) is a time fantasy using Arthurian material. *Whalesinger* (1990), set on the California coast, explores adolescent emotions surrounding death and sexuality, as well as the thoughts of a mother whale with a sick calf. *Come like shadows* (1993, ror, 2000), set in Stratford, Ontario, and in Scotland, aligns past with present, Scotland with Canada, as real witches from the past enter a production of Shakespeare's *Macbeth* that emphasizes

Québec, as well as Scottish, nationalism. *Time ghost* (1994), another time-shift story, is set in the future (and our present) through the agency of the 'timeless' location of the North Pole. In *Out of the dark* (1995), a boy's fascination with Vikings helps him adjust to the death of his mother. With each book, Katz has enriched her style, further complicated her structure, and delved more deeply into character. Some controversy has attached to her works—over her appropriation of voice and revelation of the ceremonies of Native peoples in *False face*, her evil and unpleasant mother figures, and her sometimes violent expressions of the darkness in the human psyche. She is, however, a talented writer whose books have value for young adults in not avoiding reality even while entering fantasy worlds. *Beowulf* (1999, new edn 2007), beautifully illustrated in colour by Laszlo Gal, is a fine retelling in prose, intended for young people, of the famous Old English epic.

Katzmann, Mary Jane (1828–90). Born in Preston, Nova Scotia, she showed exceptional intelligence at an early age, but because she was female she was not given the benefit of a formal education. In 1845 her poetry came to the attention of Joseph HOWE, who praised it in 'Nights with the muses', a series of articles on Nova Scotia writers in *The Novascotian*. In 1852, at the age of twenty-four, she became editor of a new literary magazine, the *Provincial* (Jan. 1852–Dec. 1853). As the foremost female editor of her time, she encouraged other women writers to project a humanistic vision of society through writing. From 1848 to 1851 Katzmann published a large amount of verse in the *Guardian* (Halifax), and in the late fifties and sixties her verse appeared frequently in local newspapers. A collection, *Frankincense and myrrh* (Halifax, 1893), was published posthumously, as was her *History of the townships of Dartmouth, Preston, and Lawrencetown* (Halifax, 1893). As a poet Katzmann was prone to generalities, melodramatic effects, and dull religious and moral didacticism—characteristics that mark the verse of contemporary 'female poets' in Britain and the United States upon whom she patterned herself—but she was always technically competent, at her best when writing descriptive verse or charming song-like lyrics. She married William Lawson in 1869 and died of cancer in Halifax.

Kay, Guy Gavriel (b. 1954). Born in Weyburn, Saskatchewan, he grew up in Winnipeg, where he gained a B.A. (1975) in philosophy

Kay

from the University of Manitoba. He also has an LL.B. degree (1978) from the University of Toronto, and was called to the Ontario Bar in 1981. Kay first entered the world of high fantasy when he assisted Christopher Tolkien with the editorial construction of his father J.R.R. Tolkien's *The Silmarillion* (1977). Disagreeing with the son's decision to publish all of the elder Tolkien's writings, Kay turned his hand to writing his own trilogy, *The Fionavar tapestry*: the first volume, *The summer tree* (1984, rpr. 1987), was followed by *The wandering fire* (1986, rpr. 1987) and *The darkest road* (1986). This is a truly post-Tolkien fantasy that builds on, rather than simply copying, its great original; with its creation of a 'first' universe of Fionavar, from which all others depend, and with its adult approach to sexuality it lifts fantasy to a new level of psychological complexity. As Neil Randall has pointed out, Kay developed a complex form of shifting focalization in *The Fionavar tapestry*, which has a more complicated narrative strategy than most fantasies. Kay has said that one of his influences was the great historical novelist Dorothy Dunnett, and his three later novels reveal how much he learned from her. They are set in another world, in another universe, yet they carefully play off European history in fascinating ways, exploring human problems in a world lacking our exact religious and tribal affiliations. They also slowly rejected all the usual 'magic' associated with fantasy. Kay improved on his method of deepening characterization throughout *Tigana* (1990, rpr. 1999), *A song for Arbonne* (1992, rpr. 2000), and *The lions of Al-Rassan* (1995, rpr. 2000). The first alludes to Renaissance Italy, the second to Troubadour-era France, and the third to the end of the multicultural experiment in Spain in the fourteenth century. *Sailing to Sarantium* (1998, rpr. 2003), Book One of *The Sarantine mosaic*, is a long fantasy on themes of Byzantium (meditations on which, by W.B. Yeats, inspired the author) that offers political intrigue, danger, and romance. The artisan Caius Crispus (Crispin) finds that he has been chosen to design the mosaics for the dome of the new sanctuary in the golden city of Sarantium, towards which he travels while confronting his feelings about love and loyalty amid an interesting array of characters and events. In the sequel, *Lord of emperors* (1999, rpr. 2003), work on the dome is undertaken against a background of political machinations. By placing these stories in another world, Kay interrogates questions of faith, philosophy, race, and culture—without necessarily offending readers' biases. As a result, he

has enlarged the range of epic fantasy. His novels have been translated into sixteen languages.

Set in Vinmark (Scandinavia) 1000 years ago, *The last light of the sun* (2004) is a 500-page historical saga that draws on Celtic, Anglo-Saxon, and Norse myths and begins with a partial list of characters strangely named according to their nationality: Anglcyn (English), Erling (Viking), Cyngael (Welsh). *Ysabel* (2007) is another departure, beginning with Ned Marriner and his father at Aix-en-Provence in modern times and taking us into the distant past. Kay's career as a novelist who blends history and fantasy may have reached a climax with *Under heaven* (2010)—very long (567 pages) and richly inventive—which draws on China's Tang dynasty in the eighth century and describes the many-faceted life and adventures of young Shen Tai, son of the now-deceased great military leader of the Kitan Empire.

Readers of these fantasies should know that *Beyond this dark house: poems* (2003) reveals Kay as an interesting poet. With clear diction and a true feeling for rhythm and line-length, he addresses a range of subjects, including Winnipeg, his past (including his loves), foreign places (e.g., Crete, London), the classics ('Being Orpheus', 'Medea'), and myth ('Guinevere at Almesbury', 'At the death of Pan'). The collection opens with 'Night drive: elegy', a longish narrative poem that is a moving reminiscence and begins 'Driving through Winnipeg this autumn / twilight, a sensation has lodged / somewhere behind my breastbone / (impossible to be more precise).' The beauty of nature is recorded in 'A carpet', a short poem: 'Always something new. / Above the cliff tonight / the moon, two days from full, / glimpsed through traceries / of cirrus cloud, / laid down a diffusion / of woven light on the sea.'

Kearns, Lionel (b. 1937). He was born and raised in the Kootenay region of British Columbia, where he was an enthusiastic student, musician, and athlete. In the early 1960s, while studying at the University of British Columbia, Kearns became a close friend of George BOWERING, Frank DAVY, and Fred WAH and contributed significantly to the development of their magazine TISH. Exposed to the ideas of both Marshall McLUHAN and the Russian Formalists, he began an investigation of modern prosody that led to his proposal for 'stacked verse'—a page notation system for oral poetry that featured a 'stress axis' running vertically down the page through the most heavily accented syllable of each phrase of the poem. He set out the theory of stacked verse in his M.A. thesis, and illustrated the notation in *Songs of circumstance*, published by Tishbooks in 1962 (republished in conventional notation by the RYERSON PRESS in 1967 as *Pointing*). These well-crafted poems, marked by irony and understated humour, were followed by *Listen, George* (1964), a free-flowing, long-line verse-letter recalling his youth, which Kearns wrote while studying structural and generative linguistics at the School of Oriental and African Studies, University of London. Active in the British poetry scene, Kearns came under the influence of the European concrete- and sound-poetry movements, creating the first version of his much-published mathematical mandela 'The birth of God'. In 1966 he returned to Canada to take up a position in the English department at Simon Fraser University. *By the light of the silvery McLune: media parables, poems, signs, gestures, and other assaults on the interface* (1968) is a book of celebration and social protest rooted in the preoccupations of the 1960s. *Practicing up to be human* (1978) marked a return to the rhythmically crafted, intellectually intense poems of his early work. *Ignoring the bomb* (1982) is a collection of new and selected poems. His finest work, *Convergences* (1984), is a book-length poem for voices that explores the impact of the arrival of Captain Cook's two ships on the Native people of Nootka Sound, British Columbia. It exemplifies Kearns' continuing fascination with the idea of text (context, subtext, hypertext) and his interest in West Coast history. Kearns' latest collection, *A few words will do* (2007)—described on the back cover by his friend George BOWERING as a 'selected poems'—is a collection of light-hearted/serious poems that are clear, concentrated reflections on his life ('Michelle in Trois Pistoles'), his family ('Dorothy' [his mother], 'With my daughter'), poetry ('Vocations: One of the poets/became a carpenter./Began building houses/instead of poems.//At least you can/live in them/he explained.'), and literary interests ('Birneyland'); there are also prose poems and effective typographic stunts. It is a lively, energetic collection.

Since retiring from Simon Fraser in 1986 Kearns became increasingly interested in the literary potential of digital media, pioneering online education by teaching, from his home in Vancouver, a continent-wide graduate course, 'The Cybernetics of Poetry', for ConnecEd, the distance educational facility of the New School for Social Research, New York. In 1988 he became the first writer-in-electronic-residence, helping Trevor Owen establish an online creative writing program that has since flourished across Canada as the 'wier' project.

Keeshig-Tobias, Lenore (b. 1950). Born in Wiarton, Ontario, to Keitha (Johnston) and Donald Keeshig, the eldest of ten children, she is a member of the Chippewa of Nawash First Nation on the Bruce Peninsula. She attended elementary school on the Cape Croker Reserve and received her high-school education at Loretto Academy, Niagara Falls, and the Wiarton District High School. In 1983 she received a Bachelor of Fine Arts degree from York University, Toronto. She was the founding chair for the Racial Minority Writers' Committee in the WRITERS' UNION OF CANADA. In her poetry—which has appeared in journals and anthologies—Keeshig-Tobias tends to express herself with delicate simplicity, a gentle humour, and unpretentiousness. Much of it draws on the realities of the life of Native people and the mythological icons and symbols of the Chipewa. One of her favourite symbols is the trickster, considered by Canadian Aboriginal writers to be a symbol of cultural rebirth. In a long poem that is characterized by an untypical coarse virility of phrase and is divided into sixteen sections, entitled 'Trickster beyond 1992: our relationship' in *Indigena: contemporary Native perspectives* (1992), written to be performed, her narrative has a surprising twist, for it is the white man who is the trickster, from whom it is learned what not to do. Keeshig-Tobias has written two bilingual (English/Ojibwa) children's books illustrated by her daughter Polly, *Emma and the trees* (1996) and *Bird talk* (1991), as well as *Into the moon* (1996) and *The truth about Nibbles* (2005)—Nibbles is a hamster. She has been instrumental in bringing the issue of cultural appropriation to public attention (causing much controversy in academic circles and the media). Strongly committed to the oral storytelling tradition, she has been untiring in encouraging First Nation writers to reclaim their own stories and myths. In her essay 'Not just entertainment' in *Through Indian eyes: the Native experience in books for children* (1992), edited by Beverly Slapin and Doris Seale, she says: 'The issue is about culture theft, the theft of voice. It's about power.'

Keith, Marian. Pseudonym of Mary Esther MacGREGOR.

Keith, W.J. (b. 1934). William John Keith was born in London, England, and educated at

Keith

Jesus College, Cambridge University (B.A., 1958) and the University of Toronto (M.A., 1959; Ph.D., 1961). He taught in the English department of McMaster University, Hamilton, Ontario, from 1961 to 1966, when he moved to the University of Toronto, where in 1995 he was appointed Emeritus Professor of English, University College. He was editor of the *University of Toronto Quarterly* from 1976 to 1985 and contributed many reviews to its annual 'Letters in Canada' issues. Apart from a brief study of Charles G.D. ROBERTS (1969), Keith's early books were on English literature: *Richard Jefferies: a critical study* (1965), *The rural tradition* (1974); these were followed by *The poetry of nature* (1980) and *Regions of the imagination: the development of British rural fiction* (1987). As a critic trained in the 'practical criticism' of the fifties and sixties, he avoided methodologies, and over some twenty-five years wrote books of criticism on Canadian literature that are unusual and salutary for their clarity and unpretentiousness. His close readings of texts illuminate works discussed while also offering striking perceptions. These qualities are apparent in his authoritative *Canadian literature in English* (1985) in the Longman Literature in English Series, which was reissued in a revised and expanded edition (2 vols, 2006), the second volume of which ends with two essays: 'Twenty years after' and 'Polemical conclusion'. Other critical volumes are *A sense of style: studies in the art of fiction in English-speaking Canada* (1989), which includes chapters on ten writers, among them DAVIES, GALLANT, LAURENCE, MUNRO, and ATWOOD; *An independent stance: essays on English-Canadian criticism and fiction* (1991) in the series Critical Directions published by The PORCUPINE'S QUILL; and *Literary images of Ontario* (1992) in the Ontario Historical Studies Series. His books on individual Canadian authors include *Epic fiction: the art of Rudy Wiebe* (1981), *Introducing Margaret Atwood's the edible woman* (1990), and *Frederick Philip Grove and his works* (1990). Keith has also published two collections of poems: *Echoes in silence* (1992) and *In the beginning and other poems* (1999).

Kelley, Thomas P. (1905–82). Born at Campbellford, Ontario, he travelled as a youngster with his father's medicine show, then boxed professionally in the United States. His career as a pulp writer began in 1937, when he sold the first of three fantasy adventure serials to *Weird Tales*. Using various pseudonyms, he filled many an issue of *Uncanny Tales*, the leading Canadian pulp magazine published during the Second World War. Thereafter he churned out some two-dozen paperback books, largely of the true-crime variety. *The black Donnellys* (1954, rpr. 1993) and *Vengeance of the black Donnellys* (1969, rpr. 1995)—his lurid accounts of the Irish blood feud and its aftermath that took place in the 1880s in Lucan, Ontario—have sold hundreds of thousands of copies. *The fabulous Kelley* (1968, rev. 1974) is a surprisingly sensitive evocation of the life and times of his father, known as 'Doc Kelley, Canada's King of the Medicine Men'. A lively character, Thomas Kelley claimed to be 'king of the Canadian pulp writers' and 'the fastest author in the East'. He died in Toronto, leaving unpublished a fantasy-adventure novel set in A.D. 7109.

Kelly, M.T. (b. 1946). Born in Toronto, Milton Terrence Kelly was educated at York University (B.A., 1970) and the University of Toronto (B. Ed., 1976). He has lived in Edinburgh, Scotland; has been a high-school teacher in Levack, Ontario; a city-hall reporter in Moose Jaw, Saskatchewan; and a freelance writer and newspaper columnist in Toronto. Constant in Kelly's fiction has been a Celtic lyricism (though in a progressively simpler style), sensitivity to landscape and weather, and characters who are profoundly uncomfortable with each other. Women are ambivalent goddesses, deeply troubling to men, but also rendered with great empathy. In the title novella of *The more loving one* (1980), a collection of stories set in Toronto, the protagonist dabbles in psychodrama, shucks off his wife for a new woman, but finds that the latter can live only in his mind's eye. In such stories, sensations tell painful truths. In his first novel, the often hilarious *I do remember the fall* (1977, rpr. 1989), the self-mocking Randy Gogarty moves towards a better understanding of himself amid vocational intrigues, poignant domestic politics, and low comedy in a small city called Elk Brain, Saskatchewan. Kelly's play *The green dolphin* (1982) and the stories in *Breath dances between them* (1990, rpr. 1992) return Kelly to Toronto. The viewpoint Kelly adopts for settings outside Toronto is typically that of someone lost in alien physical and psychological terrain. For Michael Leary, the protagonist of *The ruined season* (1982), northern Ontario is 'the empty country of his imagination', an ominously enigmatic landscape. This unresolvable love and hate is reiterated in Kelly's poetry collection *Country you can't walk in* (1979, rpr. 1984). Kelly's popular and critically acclaimed novel, *A dream like* *mine* (1987, GGA; rpr. 2009), which was filmed in 1991 as *Clearcut*, puts the outsider on a reserve in northwestern Ontario, bewildered by the violent retribution that followed a pulp mill's pollution, and by the even more confounding world of the spirituality of Natives. Readers who take the sparse plotting and rudimentary character development of *Out of the whirlwind* (1995, rpr. 1996) as flaws miss the point of this novel. Kelly uses the parable form to tell of an ill-fated canoe expedition of three Torontonians and a northern-Alberta teenager to depict, powerfully and poetically, claustrophobic human conflict and the otherness of nature. *Save me, Joe Louis* (1998, rpr. 2000) is a novel about Robbie Blackstone, a talented boxer, aged sixteen, and the people in his life who envisage a big-time career for him—his mother, her boyfriend, and two handlers—and his growth towards self-assertion and independence. In 2009 Kelly published *Downriver: poems with a prose memoir and a story*.

Kennedy, Leo (1907–2000). Born in Liverpool, England, he moved with his family to Montreal in 1912. Though he had left school after repeating grade six, he was admitted to the Montreal campus of Laval (now the Université de Montréal), where he studied English for two years and became closely associated with F.R. SCOTT and A.J.M. SMITH of the *McGILL FORTNIGHTLY REVIEW* after they discovered Kennedy to be the pseudonymous 'Helen Lawrence' in the lonely-hearts column of the Montreal *Star*. In 1928, with Scott, he founded and edited the short-lived *CANADIAN MERCURY*. In 1933 his only collection of poetry, *The shrouding*, was published by Macmillan at the urging of E.J. PRATT. Kennedy was a modernist who sought to replace the sentimental romanticism of the 'Maple Leaf school' with objective craftsmanship. Under the influence of the metaphysical and mythic sensibilities of T.S. Eliot and Sir James Frazer, he wrote poems that sought salvation from the winter wasteland of death and oblivion by fusing Christian faith in the resurrection with the myth of renewal found in the order of nature: buried bones are like crocus bulbs awaiting the spring to sprout heavenward. By 1936, when his poems were included in the modernist anthology *NEW PROVINCES*, he was already turning his back on much of his early work, writing committed criticism of social realities for radical periodicals like *New Frontier*. Some of his socialist writings were published pseudonymously, for he was working throughout the 1930s for advertising agencies in Montreal,

Toronto, and Detroit. In 1942 he moved to a Chicago agency and freelanced as a book reviewer for the *Chicago Sun*. He eventually settled in Norwalk, Connecticut, as a staff writer for *Reader's Digest*. In 1976 he returned to his literary friends in Montreal, living for ten years with his daughter-in-law, before retiring to a hotel in Pasadena, California. *The shrouding* was reprinted in 1975 with an introduction by Leon EDEL, who described Kennedy as the sprightly leader of Canada's 'graveyard school' of metaphysical poetry. His short story 'A priest in the family', first published in *The CANADIAN FORUM* (April 1933), was reprinted in *Great stories of the world* (1972). See Patricia Morley, *As though life mattered: Leo Kennedy's story* (1994).

Kertes, Joseph (b. 1951). Born in Budapest, he was educated at York University, Toronto (B.A., 1975) and the University of Toronto (M.A., 1976). At Humber College, Toronto, he has been professor of English (1980–91), chair of applied arts (1991–2), and director of the innovative year-round writing and comedy programs. He is now dean, School of Creative and Performing Arts, Humber College (2000–). Kertes has written three novels. The narrator of *Winter tulips* (1988) is Ben Beck, a young Jewish music student—he plays the viola—who leaves Montreal to study at the University of Toronto. He lives over the Blue Sky restaurant, owned by friendly Stavro Dioskouri. (Ben's mother thinks the name is Italian. 'It's Greek. Nana Mouskouri, Melina Mercouri, Stavro Dioskouri.') Ben becomes friends with the wayward Dioskouri son, John, and falls in love with his attractive and intelligent sister, Diane, to his mother's chagrin. In the conversations and exchanges of the two ethnic families, the dialogue of the generous, warmhearted Greek parents is sparse, rendered in phonetic English; that of the wary Becks is argumentative and emotional, with Mrs Beck protesting Ben's growing fondness for Diane, having mortified him at the beginning of the book by pronouncing firmly, when she meets an acquaintance of his in his apartment, 'Intermarriage doesn't work' and leaving the room. *Winter tulips*—the title refers to plastic tulips in front of the Dioskouri house—won the Leacock Medal for Humour. The title of *Boardwalk* (1998) refers to the one in Atlantic City, to which Clyde, a successful broker with a wife and son, takes his innocent younger brother Eddie, the narrator, for a few days' entertainment. For Clyde this means gambling and giving a lounge singer he had met in Toronto 'a little dingle'—though it is Eddie who becomes smitten with the singer, called Bunny. While Clyde carries on in the background, Eddie has a series of hapless experiences that exclude an affair with Bunny. In 2008 Kertes published *Gratitude*, an ambitious novel (in which Raoul Wallenberg appears) set in Budapest in 1944 that deals vividly with the various kinds of devastation produced by the Nazi occupation, beginning with young Lili's loss of her Jewish family—she goes to Budapest and is taken in by the Beck family (see *Winter tulips*), who offer their protection. Kertes has also written two successful children's books: *The gift* (1995) and *The red corduroy suit* (1998), both illustrated by Peter Perko.

Kidd, Adam (1802–31). Of the many early Canadian writers who produced a single volume of poetry, Adam Kidd has received more attention from modern critics than the quality of his work merits. Many others wrote equally well, on similar themes, but Kidd's flamboyant personality, and his early death, make him a sympathetic subject for study. Born in Ireland, he settled in Québec with his family while in his teens. Sometime in the mid-1820s he was considered as a candidate for the Church of England priesthood, but having displeased Bishop Mountain for an undocumented reason he was rejected as unsuitable. He travelled in Upper Canada in 1828, but late in that year was living in Montreal and publishing poetry in the local radical newspaper, *The Irish Vindicator*, as well as in *The Irish Shield* (Philadelphia), both under his own name and under the pseudonym 'Slievegallin'. His poetry collection, *The Huron chief, and other poems* (1830), demonstrates the nobility of the Native people in their natural state and the perfidy of the whites who attempt to convert them while seizing their land. The central figure is the chief Skenandow, a wise and peaceful man, ultimately murdered by whites whose release from captivity he has effected. Kidd, as narrator, spends much time recording details of the Aboriginal way of life and describing the scenery of the Great Lakes region. A number of shorter poems complete the volume. After its publication he set off on a journey through Upper Canada, publicizing his book and gathering material and subscriptions for a new one on a similar theme. He seems to have spent the winter of 1830–1 with friends in Kingston. Aware that he was dying—he published a farewell poem, 'Impromptu', in the *Kingston Chronicle* (12 Mar. 1831)—he returned to Québec, where he died four months later.

Another Montreal poet, W.F. HAWLEY, had also published many poems in the *Vindicator*. When Hawley's book, *Quebec, the harp, and other poems*, appeared in 1829, several courteous mentions in that newspaper were followed by a savage review, which one suspects was written by Kidd. *The Huron chief*'s publication in Montreal a little later provided occasion for critical revenge. The book was mockingly dissected in the *Gazette* and spiritedly defended by the author in the *Vindicator*. The *Gazette* correspondent also told of Kidd's selling subscriptions for his book from door to door. If Kidd did indeed sell 1500 copies of *The Huron chief* as he claimed, that number is more than double the recorded sales of any other pre-Confederation literary work. Criticism of *The Huron chief* was not confined to the pages of local newspapers. Taking exception to a footnote that attacked Mr Buchanan, the British Consul in New York, for policies he advocated with regard to navigation in the St Lawrence, Buchanan's sons and a 'friend' attacked Kidd on a Montreal street and subjected him to a public thrashing. There are two versions of the story: one by Kidd in which he emerges triumphant; the other by the 'friend', which portrays the poet as beneath the notice of a gentleman. It appears that only Kidd's dignity was hurt, but the incident is a striking indication of the status of poets in early Canadian society. A modern annotated edition of *The Huron chief*, edited by D.M.R. Bentley, was published by Canadian Poetry Press at the University of Western Ontario in 1987.

Kilbourn, William (1926–95). Born in Toronto, he was educated at Trinity College, University of Toronto (B.A., 1948); Harvard University (A.M., 1949; Ph.D., 1957); and Oxford University (B.A., 1952; M.A., 1956). He taught at McMaster University, Ontario (1951–3, 1955–62), and from 1962 was professor of humanities and history at York University, Toronto. He was a Member of the Order of Canada. A passionate lover of his country and his city, and a political activist (he served on the committee that led to Pierre Elliott Trudeau's being chosen as leader of the Liberal Party, and in Toronto he was both a reform alderman, 1970–6, and a Metro councillor, 1973–6), Kilbourn wrote and edited books that grew out of both these interests—all of whose texts were informed by a historian's knowledge and made readable by literary grace, wit, irony, and the infusion of drama and significance. His first book was *The firebrand: William Lyon Mackenzie and the rebellion* *in Upper Canada* (1956; 2nd edn 1960), a memorable characterization of MACKENZIE. Other books relating to Toronto were *Toronto in pictures and words* (with photographs by Rudi Christl, 1977, rpr. 1983); *Toronto observed: its architecture, patrons, and history* (with William Dendy, 1986); *Intimate grandeur: one hundred years at Massey Hall* (1993); and two anthologies: *The Toronto book* (1976) and *Toronto remembered: a celebration of the city* (1984), containing pieces by himself and others. Kilbourn's books of more national interest were *The making of the nation: a century of challenge* (1966; rev. 1973), a picture-history in the Canadian Centennial Library; *Pipeline: Trans-Canada and the great debate: a history of business and politics* (1970); *C.D. Howe: a biography* (with Robert Bothwell, 1979); and the anthology *Canada: a guide to the peaceable kingdom* (1970), sixty-two pieces portraying Canada at the end of the 1960s. An Anglican, Kilbourn was co-author (with A.C. Forrest and Patrick Watson) of *Religion in Canada: the spiritual development of a nation* (1968) in the Canadian Illustrated Library.

King, Basil (1859–1928). Born in Charlottetown, Prince Edward Island, William Benjamin Basil King was educated locally and at King's College, Windsor, Nova Scotia. He was ordained an Anglican priest and served St Luke's Pro-cathedral, Halifax, as rector from 1884. In 1892 he became rector of Christ Church, Cambridge, Massachusetts. Failing eyesight forced him to resign his charge in 1900 and he devoted the rest of his life to travel and writing. He wrote more than twenty novels, beginning with *Griselda* (1900), in which he worked within the conventions of popular moral fiction. Disparagement of divorce is evident in his second title, *Let no man put asunder* (1901). *In the garden of Charity* (1903), his only digression from Boston-New York settings and from his portrayal of the international world of wealthy Americans, is set among Nova Scotia fisherfolk. Its themes of love, betrayal, and marital fidelity are worked out with compelling vigour. Two other novels followed, but King's early novels did not reach a wide audience until they were reprinted after two successive bestsellers made him famous. These were *The inner shrine* (1909), a trite exercise in the Howells-James international mould, and *The wild olive* (1910), a more interesting drama of moral crisis. King used his fiction to promote understanding across class, sex, and international barriers. But in his later work he over-exploited popular themes about the crossing of class boundaries,

especially through marriage, though he was adept at portraying capable women, and was eager to explain the social background of the many Canadian characters who appear in about half of his twenty-two novels—the last of which was published in 1930. In the 1920s King became a kind of popular sage with several books. Thirty thousand copies of his religious-philosophical work, *The conquest of fear* (1921), were sold in 1930 alone.

King, James (b. 1942). He was born in Springfield, Massachusetts, and educated at the University of Toronto (B.A., 1967) and Princeton University (M.A., 1969; Ph.D., 1970). He joined the English department of McMaster University, Hamilton, Ontario, in 1971, becoming a full professor in 1983 and University Professor in 1996. He is a prolific and proficient biographer, specializing initially in English subjects—William Cowper (1986), Paul Nash (1987), Herbert Read (1990), William Blake (1991), Virginia Woolf (1994)—until he embarked on three important, very readable Canadian biographies. *The life of Margaret Laurence* (1997, rpr. 1998) is a substantial overview of LAURENCE's life that deals openly and sensitively with the personal side and casts penetrating insights on her various writings, particularly her novels. *Jack, a life with writers: the story of Jack McClelland* (1999, rpr. 2000) includes details of MCCLELLAND's life story, his warm, sometimes unconventional personality, his gift for friendship, his loyalty to his authors, and his editorial instinct; in focusing on his career as president of MCCLELLAND & STEWART and the vicissitudes of that firm, it is a valuable addition to the history of Canadian book publishing. *Farley: the life of Farley Mowat* (2003) reveals a conflict between MOWAT's gregarious, fun-loving public persona and a nature described by King as 'melancholic' and 'tormented'. There was another conflict with his demanding father, librarian Angus Mowat, who imposed a goal of literary success on his son, which Farley, in his own eyes, failed to fulfill. *Telling lives or telling lies? Biography and fiction* (1997) is King's F.E.L. Priestly lecture.

Of his four absorbing, carefully crafted novels, three are based on real people. *Faking* (1999) is an ingenious treatment of the career of Thomas Wainewright (1794–1847)—art critic, painter, fraud, and poisoner, who was also a 'copyist', forging works by some famous painters. The story unfolds in the conflicting accounts of Tom, his wife, his sister-in-law, and his son, and gives rise to considerations of truth and untruth, the real and the fake.

(The character of Wainewright was also used in a novel by Bulwer-Lytton, a story by Dickens, and an essay by Wilde.) *Blue moon* (2000) is about a celebrated novelist who, before she dies, asks her therapist to oversee the publication of her last book, which turns out to be a memoir that identifies her as the notorious Evelyn Dick, who was convicted of the murders of her husband and infant son in 1946, and here is convicted only of the latter crime and disappears after serving a twelve-year prison sentence. *Transformations* (2003)—set in the 1850s in London and Florence and (in the last forty-four pages) in Washington, D.C. in 1863—is, in the author's words, loosely based on some incidents in the early life of Daniel Home (1833–1886), a Victorian medium. He is derided by some (notably the poet Robert Browning) and praised and honoured by others (notably Abraham Lincoln). In a smooth narrative, couched in the suggestion of formal Victorian diction, King introduces, and relates the stories of, the many men and women who have reason to request Home's services, or are otherwise connected with each other, unfolding along the way the crimes of a serial killer, the manipulation of fake works of art, and supernatural concerns aroused, inevitably, by Home himself. Adding to the interest of the novel is King's inclusion of such famous people as Elizabeth Barrett Browning and her husband Robert, Walt Whitman, Jenny Lind, and Mary Todd Lincoln and her husband. For perhaps his best novel, *Pure inventions* (2006), King immersed himself in the culture of Japan, experiencing the country at first-hand and informing himself on the subject of woodblock prints and their leading artists. The book opens with Yoshiko, her adult son Hiroshi, and Mrs Eliot attending a performance, in 1905 in London's Covent Garden, of *Madama Butterfly*, 'which bore such a strong resemblance to [Yoshiko's] own unhappy history. Unlike Cio-Cio San, Yoshiko did not take her own life, but she did have a child—Hiroshi—conceived during a brief liaison and then marriage to Lieutenant Eliot of the American navy. Yoshiko and Butterfly did share one trait: although they had been courtesans, they had experienced love only once in their lives.' The plot of the novel focuses on Hiroshi, his childhood and wayward youth (he's a thief), his love of artists' prints, his training as a printmaker by a Master and becoming wealthy, not only as a forger but as a dealer of classical prints. When the law is about to descend on him, Mrs Eliot, the widow of his father, appears. She takes him and his mother to London. Yoshiko returns to Japan and Kate Eliot takes Hiroshi to Boston. There, with his socially prominent stepmother's encouragement, he succeeds as an authority on Japanese prints in the Boston Museum of Fine Art, is befriended by the wealthy Isabella Stewart Gardner, is often invited to her fabulous home, and becomes a respected artist. When Hiroshi is in his fifties his desire to return to Japan overcomes him. 'Kate observes that they have become close, very much mother and son, in the nineteen years they have known each other.' Hiroshi tells her that under her influence he has become 'a better man than he ever hoped to be.'

King, Thomas (b. 1943). Of Cherokee and Greek ancestry, King was raised in the central valley of California. He has held positions in Native Studies programs in the universities of Utah (where he obtained his Ph.D.), California, and Minnesota, and for ten years at the University of Lethbridge. He now teaches at the University of Guelph. King's short stories, some of which are collected in *One good story, that one* (1993), distil the concerns, characters, and wit of all his work: they show Native people and tricksters making life out of old and new stories and undermining outsiders' expectations of them. In the title story, anthropologists listen to an old grandmother (or maybe a grandfather, or maybe a coyote) tell a 'traditional' creation story that turns out to be a hilariously cockeyed version of the account in Genesis. In 'Joe the painter and the Deer Island massacre' a town pageant goes awry when the Native narrator and his oddball white friend present a different perspective on history than that anticipated.

King's first novel, *Medicine River* (1990, rpr. 1996), concerns a Toronto photographer who goes home to Alberta for his mother's funeral, whereupon his old friend Harlen Big Bear conspires to keep him there. Will, the protagonist, plays the alienated intellectual to Harlen's amusing bungling and scheming. A second novel, *Green grass, running water* (1993, rpr. 1994), is wider in scope, couching stories of domestic life, political resistance, and Native community within a coyote story of the creation of the world. The title of *Truth and Bright Water* (1999, rpr. 2000) refers to a small town in Montana and to a reserve across the river (and the Canadian border in Alberta), almost joined by a bridge that was never completed. Young Tecumseh, the narrator, lives in Truth and his cousin Lum, whose only goal is to win the Indian Days race, lives in Bright Water. Tecumseh's relations with his remarkable dog Soldier, with the eccentric Monroe Swimmer, a successful painter who has come home, and with his family, and his account of his friendship with Lum unfold in a narrative of mystery, comedy, and drama that ends in tragedy. In his fiction King draws on the oral traditions of many different Native Peoples, bringing various trickster traditions together to challenge entrenched stereotypes; one of his greatest talents is in creating a laconic but effective spoken language. As well, his writing shows Native people living their lives with a matter-of-fact quirkiness, wrapped up in each other rather than in their relations with non-Native people. *A short history of Indians in Canada* (2005) is a collection of twenty humorous short stories. In the title story the doorman of the King Edward Hotel tells Bob Haynie, who complains that he can't sleep, to go to Bay Street for some excitement. Bob arrives there at 3 a.m. and 'looks up just in time to see a flock of Indians fly into the side of the building./Smack!' King's 2003 CBC Massey Lectures, *The truth about stories: a Native narrative* (2003), is an exploration of the Native storytelling tradition and won the Trillium (Ontario) Book Award. King has written three picture books for children about Coyote: *A Coyote Columbus story* (1992, rpr. 2002), illustrated by William Kent Monkman, *Coyote sings to the moon* (1998, rpr. 2001) and *Coyote's new suit* (2004), the latter two illustrated by Johnny Wales. King was made a Member of the Order of Canada in 2004.

Kinsella, W.P. (b. 1935). William Patrick Kinsella was born in Edmonton, Alberta, and spent nearly two decades in business before earning a B.A. in creative writing (1974) at the University of Victoria and an M.F.A. (1978) at the University of Iowa, where he was enrolled in the Writer's Workshop. He was made an Officer of the Order of Canada in 1994 and in 2009 received the George WOODCOCK Lifetime Achievement Award.

Kinsella's fiction—which for the most part celebrates two worlds, the Ermineskin reserve he places near Hobbema in southern Alberta, and the American mid-West, where his baseball-inspired semi-fantasies are set—is marked by humour, sentiment, and compassion, with touches of mythic resonance and euphoric anti-authoritarianism. In both the Native stories and the baseball fantasies Kinsella attacks vice, prejudice, dullness, and rampant absurdity, his constant touchstones being a good heart endowed with the ability to dream.

Kinsella's Native stories, many of which feature young Silas Ermineskin and his friend Frank Fencepost, are knitted together by recurring motifs and familiar characters into a unified fictional tapestry. Ermineskin's spare but vivid idiom deftly expresses his mingled naivety and shrewdness. Seen through his eyes, the white world is repressive, humourless, moralistic, theoretical, and legalistic; its excessive rationalism and materialism have left it loveless and sterile. By contrast the Native world is frankly sexual, pragmatic, and spontaneous, drawing its strength from joyous and resilient anarchy. Kinsella's style is primarily humorous, but he is equally adept at portraying the darker side of human nature and life on a reserve. These stories are in the collections *Dance me outside* (1977, rpr. 1987), *Scars* (1978), *Born Indian* (1981), *The moccasin telegraph* (1983), *The Fencepost chronicles* (1986, rpr. 1996), *The Miss Hobbema pageant* (1989, rpr. 1995), *Brother Frank's Gospel Hour* (1994)—the last three were reissued together in *The Silas stories* (1998) then in *The W. P. Kinsella omnibus*—and *The secret of the Northern Lights* (1998). While his Amerindian stories—which are very much like Native 'tall tales'—have won Kinsella high praise, they have also led to accusations by some Native critics of appropriation of voice. But this has not stopped him from writing about these characters, who are so close to his heart, nor has it stopped readers from enjoying them.

Kinsella's baseball fiction includes the story collections *Shoeless Joe Jackson comes to Iowa* (1980); *The thrill of the grass* (1984); *The further adventures of Slugger McBatt* (1988), reissued as *Go the distance* (1995); *The Dixon Cornbelt League* (1993); *Magic time* (1998, rpr. 1999); *Japanese baseball and other stories* (2000); and *Baseball fantastic: stories* (2001)—all of which display imaginative and manic verve. In the title story of *Shoeless Joe Jackson comes to Iowa*, a high-spirited blend of 'fact and fantasy, magic and reality', a Kinsella-like narrator obeys a mysterious voice that bids him construct a backyard left field as a shrine to his father's hero, Shoeless Joe Jackson, unjustly disgraced in the 1919 White Sox scandal. This touching and liberating fantasy about love, innocence, the land, and the mystique of baseball later became the novel *Shoeless Joe* (1982), in which Joe redeems himself. Other novels that are baseball connected are *The Iowa baseball confederacy* (1986), *Box socials* (1991), and *If wishes were horses* (1996). All these books, as well as the film adaptation of *Shoeless Joe* (*Field of Dreams*, 1989), made Kinsella a leading writer of baseball lore. See also Kinsella's *Diamonds forever: reflections from the field, the dugout and the bleachers* (1997).

Three works of fiction outside the above subject categories are the story collections *The alligator report* (1985) and *Red wolf, red wolf* (1987, rpr. 1997), containing the story 'Lieberman in love', which was made into a live-action short film that won an Academy Award in 1996; and the novel *The winter Helen dropped by* (1995).

Kirby, William (1817–1906). Grandson of United Empire Loyalists and the voice of Loyalism in his day, Kirby was born a tanner's son in Kingston-upon-Hull, England. His family immigrated to the United States in 1832, and Kirby to Upper Canada in 1839, settling in Niagara-on-the-Lake, Ontario (where his house still stands). Kirby practised as a tanner until he married Eliza Madeline Whitmore, one of the extensive Servos clan of Niagara Loyalists. He was editor of the *Niagara Mail*, collector of customs from 1871 to 1895, and became a charter member of the Royal Society of Canada in 1882. Kirby's literary importance rests largely on his authorship of *The GOLDEN DOG* (Rouses Point, New York, 1877; abridged 1989, NCL), which was reprinted frequently. It is set in New France in 1748, its characters based on historical figures, its usage of Gothic conventions highly romantic. Weighted (as its Epilogue reveals) with the ideology of a One Canada that fuses both English and French portions, attributing loyalty to British institutions as the chief characteristic of both segments, the novel's conception is ambitious. Kirby's lesser works display the contours of an Upper Canadian Tory mentality. *The U.E.: a tale of Upper Canada* (Niagara, 1859) is an epic in twelve cantos written in heroic couplets. Of minor formal interest, it displays the primary assumptions of the Loyalist mythology that was influential in the culture of Victorian Ontario: melding the 1837 Rebellion to the cycle of Loyalist challenges in 1776 and 1812; warning that Upper Canada is an Eden constantly threatened by marauders and traitors both inside and out; and stretching the historical limits of United Empire Loyalism to include anyone defending British-Canadian institutions and territory. The forest, so grim in the writings of John RICHARDSON, is here a plantation for producing the Royal Navy's masts. *Annals of Niagara* (Welland, 1896) is a shapeless historical narrative of the barbarities accompanying the desultory border warfare after the battle of Queenston Heights in the War of 1812. The writings and career of Kirby reveal the extent to which the concept of loyalty in his time changed into a rhetorical epithet expressing Tory approbation. Lorne PIERCE's *William Kirby: the portrait of a Tory Loyalist* (1929) notes how Kirby relished a souvenir that his son sent him from Regina: a piece of the rope that had hanged Riel.

Kirkconnell, Watson (1895–1977). Born in Port Hope, Ontario, he was educated at Queen's University, the Toronto Conservatory of Music, and Oxford University. From 1922 to 1940 he taught English, and later classics, at Wesley College, Winnipeg. From 1940 to 1948 he was head of the English department at McMaster University, and from 1948, until his retirement in 1964, he was president of Acadia University. In 1966 he came out of retirement for two years as head of Acadia's English department. A founding member of the CANADIAN AUTHORS' ASSOCIATION, he served two terms as national president (1942–4, 1956–8). During the Second World War he chaired the Writers' War Committee and was active in the creation of the Humanities Research Council, which led to the writing, with A.S.P. Woodhouse, of *The humanities in Canada* (1947). Kirkconnell was doubtless Canada's most prolific and industrious scholar, producing more than 150 books and booklets and over 1000 published articles. A tireless linguist, he translated poetry from more than fifty languages, in collections that included *European elegies: one hundred poems chosen and translated from European literature in fifty languages* (1928); *The Magyar muse: an anthology of Hungarian poetry, 1400–1932* (1933); *Canadian overtones: an anthology of Canadian poetry written originally in Icelandic, Swedish, Hungarian, Italian, Greek, and Ukrainian* (1935); and, in collaboration with Séraphin Marion, *Tradition du Québec/The Quebec tradition* (1946). He also wrote three critical aids to Milton's poetry. Kirkconnell's major contribution to Canadian scholarship was his annual comprehensive review of Canadian writing in languages other than English and French for the 'Letters in Canada' survey in the *University of Toronto Quarterly*. Between 1938 and 1965 he supplied twenty-eight such annual reviews, which evaluated specific works and commented on trends and themes peculiar to the ethnic press. His promotion of the literature of immigrant groups within their Old World traditions, as well as his massive translations of European poetry, and his constant championing of immigrants in the face of prejudice, were warmly appreciated by many groups. His own poetry incongruously mixed classical forms with modern themes, as in *The tide of life* (1930) and *The eternal quest* (1934). *The flying* *bull and other tales* (1940) forces a series of western 'tall tales' into the form of the Canterbury tales. More poems were collected in *Manitoba symphony* (1937), *Lycra sacra: four occasional hymns* (1939), *Western idyll* (1940), *The flavour of Nova Scotia* (1976), and *The coronary muse* (1977), written in hospital. *Centennial tales and selected poems* (1965) contains narrative poems on historical themes. Kirkconnell's autobiography, *A slice of Canada* (1967), links many of his varied concerns, revealing the intellectual integrity, Christian faith, and wide knowledge of world literature that informed them. *The undoing of Babel: Watson Kirkconnell—the man and his work* (1975), edited by J.R.C. Perkin, contains six essays in honour, particularly, of his linguistic skills. Perkin wrote *Morning in his heart* (1985), a short biography, which includes a selective bibliography.

Kiyooka, Roy (1926–94). Born in Moose Jaw, Saskatchewan, he was a second-generation Canadian-born Japanese Canadian who became a singular and perhaps the most important figure in the history of Japanese-Canadian art, writing, and culture. He studied art with J.E.H. MacDonald of the Group of Seven. He then studied abstract expressionism with Will Barnet, Barnett Newman, and Clement Greenburg. (His elegant abstracts hang in many major galleries and private collections.) In 1960 he began teaching at the Vancouver School of Art, and his teachings inspired many local artists. As a creative artist who was at home in a variety of disciplines—painter, poet, sculptor, photographer, filmmaker—Kiyooka was a primal force in the artistic renaissance of Vancouver in the 1960s. He organized many poetry readings, and was a key link between the avant-garde poets of Vancouver and the COACH HOUSE PRESS group of Toronto; for many years his partner was poet Daphne MARLATT. Although better known as an artist, Kiyooka transformed language with precision; words, syntax, and space were used as instruments of artistic expression. His poetry collections include *Kyoto airs* (1964), *The unquiet bed* (1967), *Nevertheless these eyes* (1967), *Stoned gloves* (1970), *The Fontainbleau dream machine: 18 frames from a book* (1977), and *Of seasonal pleasures and small hindrances* (1978). His *Transcanada letters* (1975) contains verbal snippets of everyday life, notes to his children, and reflections on art. These uncensored, unedited, free-flowing disclosures are playful and undisciplined, and celebrate the joy of making something—a picture, a poem, or a living. Kiyooka's free-form style

fell out of favour with more controlled poets of the 1980s and 1990s. A decade later his *Pear tree poems* (1988) were complex poems of mortality, imagination, lost love, and failed marriage; the central image of the book is a pear tree that embodies the stability of which Kiyooka was deprived. But the tree is also a muse that embraces the earth and gives him peace with 'a small garden'. A complete collection of Kiyooka's writings—including biography, bibliography, and explication of the poems—is *Pacific windows: collected poems of Roy Kiyooka* (1997) edited by Roy Miki. *All amazed: for Roy Kiyooka* (2002)—edited by John O'Brian, Naomi Sawada, and Scott Watson—is a celebration of Kiyooka that grew out of the conference held in his honour in October 1999. The transcript of the conference, curated by Daphne MARLATT and Michael ONDAATJE, precedes five essays. *Pacific rim letter* (2004) is a substantial collection of letters Kiyooka wrote between 1975 and 1985 that throw light on the artistic and literary community he was involved in.

Klein, A.M. (1909–72). Abraham Moses Klein was born in Ratno, Ukraine, and in 1910 his family moved to Montreal, where he spent the rest of his life. His background was orthodox and he received a solid Jewish education in Hebrew, the Bible, and the Talmud. Although Klein's Jewish teachers encouraged him to enter the rabbinate, by his high-school years he had abandoned strict religious orthodoxy, acquiring in its stead his lifelong commitment to Zionism and to his vocation as a poet. In 1926 he entered McGill University, where he met the *McGILL FORTNIGHTLY REVIEW*: Leon EDEL, Leo KENNEDY, F.R. SCOTT, and A.J.M. SMITH. Klein never published in the *Review*; his one submission was rejected because he refused to change the word 'soul', which the editors considered insufficiently modern. However, about this time he began to publish in Canadian and American periodicals, both Jewish and non-Jewish: *Menorah Journal* in 1927; *Poetry* in 1928; *The CANADIAN FORUM* and *CANADIAN MERCURY* in 1929. (Klein continued this practice throughout his career, publishing as well in *The Canadian Jewish Chronicle*, *The Canadian Zionist*, *The Jewish Standard*, *Opinion*, *CONTEMPORARY VERSE*, *FIRST STATEMENT*, *PREVIEW*, *NORTHERN REVIEW*, and *New Directions*.) About this time he first read James Joyce's *Ulysses*, which was to influence his poetry and prose throughout his career. In 1930 he graduated from McGill and enrolled as a law student in the Université de Montréal, graduating in

1933 to practise law, a profession he never found very satisfying or remunerative. In 1936 a highly laudatory account of his work appeared in W.E. Collin's pioneering study of Canadian literature, The WHITE SAVANNAHS, and in the same year two of his poems, 'Out of the pulver and the polished lens' and 'Soirée of Velvel Kleinburger', were included in the anthology NEW PROVINCES. In 1938, to supplement his income as a lawyer, Klein took on the editorship of a Montreal weekly, The Canadian Jewish Chronicle, which he held until the end of his career in 1955. In 1939 Klein became speech writer and public-relations adviser to Samuel Bronfman, president of Seagram's and, as head of the Canadian Jewish Congress, the most powerful leader of the Jewish-Canadian community for over thirty years. (Mordecai RICHLER, who owes much to Klein's groundbreaking achievement—compare, for example, Klein's The second scroll and Richler's St Urbain's horseman—presents a cruelly satirical portrait of the relationship between Bronfman and Klein in Solomon Gursky was here.) Klein published his first volume of poetry, Hath not a Jew..., in 1940. In the early forties he came in contact with a number of younger writers involved in Preview and First Statement who encouraged his interest in modern poetry: Patrick ANDERSON, P.K. PAGE, Louis DUDEK, John SUTHERLAND, and Irving LAYTON (whom he had known for some years). In 1944 he published Poems and The Hitleriad, and in 1948 The rocking chair and other poems, which won a Governor General's Award. From 1945 to 1948 he was a lecturer in the English Department of McGill, an appointment made possible by Bronfman, a prominent financial supporter of McGill, who was concerned that Klein might leave Montreal to take up an offer of employment in New York. The following year he ran for the CCF in the federal riding of Cartier, where he suffered a personally devastating defeat. Soon after this he was sent by the Canadian Jewish Congress, again with the support of Bronfman, on a fact-finding trip to Israel and to Jewish refugee camps in Europe and North Africa. The SECOND SCROLL (1951, NCL; rpr. 2000) is a novel inspired by that trip. Not long after its publication Klein began to show signs of psychological distress, leading to several suicide attempts in 1954. After a partial recovery he became increasingly reclusive, giving up his law practice and his editorship of the Chronicle, avoiding contact with anyone but his immediate family, and ceasing to write altogether. The short story 'The almost meeting', by Henry KREISEL, testifies to the devastating effect of Klein's premature silence on a generation of younger Jewish-Canadian writers.

In an article reprinted as the preface to Hath not a Jew..., the prominent Jewish-American writer Ludwig Lewisohn described Klein as 'the first contributor of authentic Jewish poetry to the English language'. Although in his later poetry, especially the poems collected in The rocking chair, Klein leaves explicitly Jewish themes behind, Klein did form an important link to the vital Yiddish culture of Montreal. He was particularly close to the Montreal Yiddish poet Y.Y. SEGAL, and his translations of the poetry of Segal and of a number of other Yiddish and Hebrew writers make up a substantial and often impressive body of work. Even more important, Klein's distinctly Jewish perspective provided a stimulus to many younger Jewish writers in Montreal and elsewhere in Canada, such as Layton, Leonard COHEN, Richler, Miriam WADDINGTON, Eli MANDEL, Henry Kreisel, and Seymour MAYNE. Hath not a Jew..., consisting almost entirely of poems from the late twenties and early thirties, most fully explores Klein's relationship to his Jewish heritage, whose rich diversity is the keynote of the volume (see the manifesto poem, 'Ave atque vale'). Klein's celebration of the unity underlying this diversity, of the One in the many, is the theme of the volume's finest poem, 'Out of the pulver and the polished lens', and has many parallels in Klein's later works. This collection contains some of Klein's most beloved poems, but there is often a quaint folkloric quality about them, reflecting the fact that most of them celebrate a way of life based in the shtetl of Eastern Europe, which had almost disappeared by the time most of the poems were written and which Klein never knew at first hand. The essentially celebratory and optimistic vision of Hath not a Jew... did not survive the thirties. The Depression, the rise of Nazism, and Klein's own difficult personal circumstances seemed to overwhelm him: in this period he wrote relatively little (apart from journalism)—a few satirical poems and short stories in which he appears to be groping, unsuccessfully, for a tenable point of view, and a number of translations. It was only with the outbreak of the Second World War that he returned to serious sustained creative writing. The Hitleriad, an attack on Hitler that reflected Klein's interest in eighteenth-century satire, especially Pope's Dunciad, falls flat as a whole, despite some witty passages. Klein the satirist is at his best when he can recognize in the object of his satire genuine human qualities, however distorted. Understandably he could not achieve this perspective on Hitler, and as a result was often reduced to bombast and trivial abuse. Much more impressive are the anguished, prophetic psalms that were gathered together, along with some earlier works, to form 'The psalter of Avram Haktani', the most important section of *Poems*. A note of forced rhetoric mars several of them, but in the best the immediacy of Klein's confrontation with evil gives rise to a sense of pathos and intensity that is missing in most of his earlier work.

In the early forties Klein also produced a substantial body of prose works that remained unpublished during his lifetime. They attest to a growing sense of despair, and are characterized by a disturbing, almost obsessive, emphasis on isolation, futility, and self-disgust (often of a sexual nature). Klein was not able to bring any of the works of this period to completion. However by the mid-forties, beginning with 'Sestina on the dialectic' and 'Portrait of the poet as landscape', Klein's work takes on a more positive note as he begins to explore dialectical modes of thought, owing more to the Kabbalah, to which he had been introduced by Gershom Scholem's *Major trends in Jewish mysticism* (1954), than to Marx or Hegel. The negative aspects of experience, which he had been forced to acknowledge in the thirties and early forties, and which had nearly silenced him as a creative writer, now gave rise to a dialectical vision in which negation, in the form of social and spiritual fragmentation, is seen to lead inevitably to the eventual achievement of a higher unity. The most moving statement of this vision occurs in the final poem of *The rocking chair*, 'Portrait of the poet as landscape' (which precedes the other poems in the volume chronologically), in which the poet's isolation from his community comes to be seen as a temporary stage in a process of self-transformation ('he makes of his status as zero a rich garland'). The Québec poems in *The rocking chair* are a profoundly dialectical study of the power of community for both good and evil (see especially 'The rocking chair' and 'Political meeting'). This is Klein's finest collection. Stimulated by modern poets such as T.S. Eliot, W.H. Auden, Dylan Thomas, and Karl Shapiro—as well as by the metaphysicals, G.M. Hopkins, and Joyce—Klein developed a striking idiom of his own, by turns highly allusive and startlingly direct, coolly ironical and warmly sympathetic, and marked by great flexibility and subtlety of rhythm. Although there are striking differences between early and late

Klein, certain features are constant: a kaleidoscopic profusion of metaphors; puns, often multilingual; a richly varied vocabulary making substantial use of foreign loanwords, archaisms, and, especially in the later Klein, Joycean neologisms; and non-linear 'spatial' structures that work through a mosaic-like accumulation of varied perspectives. These aspects of Klein's poetic technique seem most closely related to his central vision of a unity achieved through the greatest possible diversity.

The second scroll is Klein's most complex and ambitious work, both formally and conceptually, and the most important expression of his Zionism. While writing it Klein was deeply involved in a massive, never-to-be-completed commentary on Joyce's *Ulysses*, and Joyce's influence is everywhere apparent in the novel: the structural principle of parallels between its five chapters (and glosses) and the five books of the Pentateuch recalls Joyce's extensive use of Homeric parallels; and Klein's highly wrought polyphonic prose (see especially 'Gloss gimel') owes much to Joyce's example. Like *Ulysses*, *The second scroll* is an essentially optimistic work: it celebrates the human capacity for self-renewal, especially through language, even in the face of the apparently overwhelming evil of the Holocaust. The influence of Scholem's book is also evident in the novel, which draws heavily on Kabbalistic myths of creation stressing the interdependence of evil and good, exile and redemption. Uncle Melech, the object of the narrator's search throughout the novel, embodies the Messianic yearning of the exiled many for the ideal One; but, as Melech's story and the history of his people illustrate, it is only through the dialectical process of affirmation through negation, summed up by the Kabbalistic phrase 'Aught from Naught', that this ideal is achieved. But the celebration of 'Aught from Naught' is marked by a certain skepticism. This is present from the very beginning of Klein's attempts to interpret experience dialectically, and intensifies until it becomes the dominant note of his writings, both published and unpublished, in his final years. The short stories 'Letter from afar' and 'The bells of Sobor Spasitula', for example, present the Marxist version of the dialectic as a destructive self-delusion; and 'The Bible's archetypical poet' recasts 'Portrait of the poet as landscape' as a grim allegory of the poet's fate. Even more radical in its questioning of the attempt to impose a dialectical model—or any model, for that matter—on experience are the two completed chapters of a projected novel on the theme of the Jewish legend of the golem; their ironic exploration of the nature of creativity and the limits of art, which grew out of Klein's personal agony and self-doubt, foreshadows central concerns of much of the postmodernism of recent years. Klein wrote very few new poems during this period and no major ones, but some of the revisions of his earlier poems that he undertook in the fifties, and some of his translations of the Ukrainian poet H.N. Bialik who wrote mostly in Hebrew, also of this period, are among his finest creations.

The following volumes have so far appeared in the *Collected works* published by the University of Toronto Press: *Beyond Sambation: selected essays and editorials 1928–1953* (1982) edited by M.W. Steinberg and Usher Caplan; *The short stories of A.M. Klein* (1983) edited with an introduction by Steinberg; *Literary essays and reviews* (1987) edited by Caplan and Steinberg; *The complete poems* (2 vols, 1990)— *Part 1, 1926–1934; Part 2, 1937–1955*—edited with an Introduction by Zailig Pollock; *Notebooks: selections from the A.M. Klein Papers* (1994) edited by Pollock and Caplan; and *Selected poems* (1997), edited by Caplan et al. Caplan's *Like one that dreamed: a portrait of A.M. Klein* (1982) is an excellent biography, with many photographs of Klein and his milieu and excerpts from his work, many previously unpublished. Pollock's *A.M. Klein: the story of the poet* (1994) surveys the entire body of Klein's writing.

Klinck, Carl F. (1908–90). Born in Elmira, Ontario, he held a B.A. from Waterloo College (1927), Waterloo, Ontario, and an M.A. (1929) and Ph.D. (1943) from Columbia University. From 1928 to 1947 he taught at Waterloo, where he became dean of arts. In 1947 he began a distinguished career at the University of Western Ontario, London, where he became head of the English department (1948), professor of Canadian literature (1955), and Professor Emeritus on his retirement in 1973, the year he was made an Officer of the Order of Canada. Klinck became a scholar-adventurer in the field of Canadian literature—as editor, biographer, critic, and bibliographer—long before this discipline had any academic stature. His personal bibliography is substantial. He edited or wrote on books by many nineteenth-century writers, but was best known as general editor of the *Literary history of Canada* (1956, 2nd edn 1976), to which he contributed two chapters on literary activity in the Canadas from 1812 to 1880. His longtime importance as a senior statesman of Canadian letters rested on his making accessible much early writing long before it was regarded as important to the national literary consciousness. Approaching this literature and its authors in a spirit of modest proselytizing and thorough scholarship, Klinck made contributions to the advancement, breadth, and maturity of Canadian studies that were an enduring and major academic achievement. A posthumous memoir edited by Sandra DJWA, *Giving Canada a literary history* (1991), is a characteristically modest testimony to his pivotal role in the consolidation of Canadian literary history.

Knister, Raymond (1899–1932). He was born in Ruscomb, near Stoney Point, Essex County, Ontario, and attended Victoria College, University of Toronto, and Iowa State University. He worked on his father's farm near Blenheim, Ont., from 1920 to 1923, when he moved to Iowa City to become associate editor of an avant-garde literary magazine *The Midland*. In 1924 he lived in Chicago briefly before returning to Canada in the autumn. In 1925 his poem 'A row of horse stalls', and his stories 'Elaine' and 'The fate of Mrs Lucier', appeared in *This Quarter*, the literary magazine published in Paris. In 1926 he moved to Toronto, where he freelanced; his work appeared in the *Toronto Star Weekly* and *Saturday Night*. The next year Knister married Myrtle Gamble and for the summer they moved to Hanlan's Point, Toronto Island, where Knister completed his first published novel, *White narcissus* (1929, NCL). He edited the anthology *Canadian short stories* (1928), considered to be the first anthology of its kind; his introduction to it is still of critical interest. In 1929 the Knisters moved to a farmhouse near Port Dover, Ont., where Knister wrote *My star predominant* (1934); a daughter, Imogen, was born in 1930. Frederick Philip GROVE encouraged Knister to submit *My star predominant* to GRAPHIC PUBLISHERS' Canadian Novel Contest, and in 1931 it won the $2500 first prize. In 1931–2 he lived in and near Montreal, returning to Ontario after Lorne PIERCE had offered him a job on the editorial staff of the RYERSON PRESS that would allow him time to write. While swimming off Stoney Point, Lake St Clair, in Aug. 1932, Knister drowned. ('Raymond Knister—man or myth?', in *Essays on Canadian writing* 16 (1979–80)—edited by Imogen Givens, Knister's daughter—includes a diary account by her mother about the day of Knister's drowning.) At the time of his death a number of his stories and poems, and two novels, were unpublished; a good deal of this material has since been published.

White narcissus was published in Toronto, London, and New York. Set in rural south-western Ontario, it concerns a writer, Richard Milne, who returns home in order to make a final attempt to convince his childhood sweetheart, Ada Lethen, to marry him. Ada feels it is her duty to stay at home because for years, as a consequence of a quarrel, her parents have communicated only through her. The white narcissus of the title becomes a symbol of obsession, a subject given serial exploration in the course of the novel. While the novel is usually and justly considered a work of realism, the lyricism of some passages approaches prose poetry. *My star predominant* is a well-researched novel based on the last years of the life of John Keats, in which the poet's social milieu is vividly conveyed. Of Knister's many short stories, probably the best known is 'Mist-green oats', about a young man's break with his life on the family farm. His stories recurrently focus on some form of psychological initiation. Knister also wrote novellas. In 'Innocent man' the story of a man's wedding frames the tale of his false arrest and wedding night spent in a Chicago jail. During the night each prisoner tells the story not of his guilt but of his innocence; the tension between black and white prisoners, and between inmates and guards, threatens to explode in violence. 'Peaches, peaches' is set on a fruit farm; as an overabundant crop of peaches ripens, a young man first encounters sexual politics. A strength of these two novellas—both of which are included in *The first day of spring: stories and other prose* (1976) edited by Peter STEVENS—is the power with which atmosphere is evoked. Other stories, as well as essays, appear in *Raymond Knister: poems, stories, and essays* (1975) edited by David Arnason et al., and six stories are included in *Selected stories of Raymond Knister* (1972) edited by Michael Gnarowski. Knister's poetry, which contains powerful descriptions of nature, is usually associated with the imagist school, although Knister also employed the forms of the prose poem ('Poisons'), the serial poem ('A row of horse stalls'), and the longer poem ('Corn husking'). Dorothy LIVESAY edited, with a memoir, the *Collected poems* (1949), which is actually a selection: more poems are found in *Raymond Knister: poems, stories and essays*. See *After exile: a Raymond Knister poetry reader* (2003) edited by Gregory Betts.

Knowles, R.E. (1868–1946). Robert Edward Knowles was born in Maxwell, Ontario, the son of an Irish Presbyterian minister. Educated at Peterborough Collegiate, Queen's University, and Manitoba College, he was ordained in 1891 and served as pastor of Stewarton Presbyterian Church, Ottawa. In 1898 he became minister of one of Ontario's largest Presbyterian churches, Knox's in Galt. Between 1905 and 1911 Knowles wrote seven novels—*St Cuthbert's* (1905), *The undertow* (1906), *The dawn at Shanty Bay* (1907), *The web of time* (1908), *The attic quest* (1909), *The handicap* (1910), and *The singer of the Kootenay* (1911)—published by the evangelical publisher Fleming H. Revell in New York and reissued in Toronto, Edinburgh, and London. They gained considerable popularity— Ontario sales of *The attic quest* rivalled those of works by Ralph Connor (C.W. GORDON) and L.M. MONTGOMERY. These novels Knowles regarded frankly as an extension of his ministry. Their style owes much to biblical rhythms and phraseology and to the rhetoric of Knowles' impassioned, crowd-pleasing sermons. Interest centres on the moral crises and religious experiences of the characters. The didactic plots, relying heavily on coincidence, echo biblical parables of admonitions such as 'your sin will find you out', while deathbed scenes and symbolic patterns point frequently to an extra-temporal world. Less dated is Knowles' humour and sometimes shrewd insight into character. The novels also provide a realistic glimpse of life in the villages and towns of Ontario. Difficulties probably related to alcoholism put an end to Knowles' career as a novelist and resulted in his formal retirement from his ministry in Jan. 1915. He began to work as a journalist: starting with mainly religious reporting for the *Toronto Star* in the early twenties, he soon became that paper's special writer sent to interview celebrities—including Albert Einstein, Franklin D. Roosevelt, William Butler Yeats, and Thomas Mann—besides providing many short opinion pieces in his familiar rhetorical and humorous style. See *Famous people who have met me: the life and interviews of R.E. Knowles* (1999), edited and introduced by Jean O'Grady.

Koch, Eric (b. 1919). Born in Frankfurt, Germany, to a well-to-do Jewish bourgeois family, he was lucky enough to get out of the country in 1935 to continue his schooling in England. He attended Cambridge University (1937–40), but was arrested in 1940 as an enemy alien and deported to Canada. He was released from detention camp in 1941 and continued his education at the University of Toronto

(1942–3). In 1944 he joined the Canadian Broadcasting Corporation, where he was a producer from 1953 to 1971 and then regional director (Montreal) until 1977. He retired from the CBC in 1979 and for fifteen years was a course director at York University in the Social Science Division, teaching a course on the politics of Canadian broadcasting.

Koch's first novel was *The French kiss* (1969), a brilliant comic version of the cause and consequences of General de Gaulle's famous 1967 '*Québec libre!*' speech in Montreal. The first-person narrator of the novel, the fat, vain Jo-Jo, is a history professor at Université de Montréal and also a secret agent for de Gaulle. Jo-Jo parallels the story about de Gaulle's attempt to aid the Québec independence movement with a narrative about Napoleon III's endeavour to help Italy throw off the yoke of Austrian domination during the 1860s. Both men fail in their ambitions to extend French influence through intervention in other nations' affairs. The disillusioned Jo-Jo, writing in 1977 (eight years after the publication of the novel and a year after the triumph of the Parti Québécois at the polls), concludes that the Québec separatist movement is dying. Though wrong about the future of Québec separatism—at least in the short term—*The French kiss* remains a tour de force both about history and the future: charming, funny, and pathetic by turns. Koch's next two novels are set in the future. *Leisure riots* (1973) is narrated by a director of a think-tank, Diedrich Bierbaum, who is asked by the president to investigate and find remedies for a series of apparently random acts of violence that break out across the USA in 1979. In *The last thing you'd want to know* (1976), Bierbaum reappears as the narrator. This time—it's 1984—he is asked by the president to find out why a number of people in the criminal class have reformed their lives on being told by a mysterious woman the date of their death. In both novels Koch pits rational, problem-solving methods against the powers of the irrational. The struggles and the intrigues provide admirable arenas for him to demonstrate his talent for urbane satire. In *Goodnight, little spy* (1979) Koch invents a small African country, Lalonga, and sends there Monty Haynes, who is supposed to give a western spin to a pr firm that is counselling the corrupt President. This is a neat, satiric, funny look at a developing nation. *Icon in love: a novel about Goethe* (1998) is based on Goethe's last romantic passion, when he was seventy-two, for seventeen-year-old Ulrike von Levetzow over three summers at Marienbad (1821–3)—but it takes place in 1992, in Stockholm, where the famous writer (and television performer), Goethe, goes to receive the Nobel Prize and meets Ulrike. It is an ingenious novel, accommodating actual Goethe lore, transposing some of it to the amusingly portrayed modern Stockholm setting—and including a murder to be resolved. *The man who knew Charlie Chaplin: a novel about the Weimar republic* (2000) is prefaced by the author's saying '… a few readers with long memories may note a resemblance between my invented central figure, Peter Hammersmith (a Wall Street millionaire and philanthropist), and a real person, the financier and philanthropist Otto H. Kahn (1867–1934).' The short Preface in the novel *Earrings: Baden-Baden, 1883* (2002) tells us that 'In 1883, my grandfather Robert Koch won the favour of the elderly Duchess of Hamilton on a visit to Baden-Baden, the summer capital of Europe. She launched him on his way to become one of the most eminent jewelers of Europe.' Not knowing how this happened, 'I had no choice but to embroider established historical facts about time and place with the way I wanted it to have happened.' *Arabian nights, 1914: a novel about Kaiser Wilhelm II* (2003) opens with the premise that in Ouda, 'an imaginary desert kingdom not far from Mesopotamia', Sharazad, the Grand Vizier's beautiful daughter, 'volunteered for service in the King's bed'. 'After their lovemaking, she told the King a magnificent story, open-ended so as to leave him in suspense'—Kaiser Wilhelm II is the subject of all the stories, which precede the onset of the Great War. Perhaps because Koch's inventive, highly readable fiction—with its grounding in European, especially German, culture and events—fits into no acknowledged category of Canadian literature, his novels are not as well known as they should be.

Koch's non-fiction includes *Inside Seven Days: the show that shook the nation* (1986), a detailed examination of the rise, decline, and fall of the CBC-TV program *This Hour Has Seven Days* and *Deemed suspect: a wartime blunder* (1980), an autobiographical account of Koch's early years as an 'enemy alien' when he was deported to Canada, along with a number of Jewish compatriots, many of whom later played an influential role in the artistic and intellectual life of Canada. *Hilmer and Odette: two stories from the Nazi era* (1995) is about two of Koch's German relatives who stayed behind in Germany. Both were illegitimate children who were unknown to Koch until the 1980s. When informed of their lives, he set out to discover what happened to them. Hilmar died in Auschwitz; Odette, unaware of her Jewishness, spent the war in affluence, hobnobbing with the Nazi elite. *The brothers Hambourg* (1997), of particular interest to Torontonians, offers separate biographies of the four Hambourg brothers—Mark, a well-known pianist; violinist and Bach scholar Jan; Boris, director of the Hambourg Conservatory in Toronto who played cello in the Hart House String Quartet for twenty-two years; and Clement, a pianist who loved jazz and who founded the House of Hambourg, a club where Toronto musicians could perform progressive jazz. *I remember the occasion exactly* (2006) is an interesting and enjoyable informal memoir that takes Koch from 1919 (the first chapter is called 'My Conception') to 1941, when he left the internment camp and found himself living in the Montreal home of the elderly Gerald Birks (the son of the jeweler Henry Birks) and his wife Phyllis.

Kogawa, Joy (b. 1935). Born in Vancouver, she was moved with her family to the interior of the province during the evacuation of Japanese-Canadians from the West Coast during the Second World War. She has also lived in Saskatoon and Ottawa, where she worked as a writer in the prime minister's office (1974–6), and now lives in Toronto. Kogawa's first volume of poetry, *The splintered moon* (1967), established her direct, often understated voice in short-lined pieces relying on epigrammatic tightness, a transliteration of her Japanese heritage in the way these short poems express a moment's experience without comment; yet they do not, like haiku, summarize the transitory quality of the experience through a tight focus on one image, but rather state the experience directly in pared-down phrasing. The first half of *A choice of dreams* (1974) details a visit to Japan, but the poems often shift away from oriental feeling to a clear-eyed, undramatic sensibility. The tones and moods in this collection continue in *Jericho Road* (1977), though the language is more thoroughly metaphorical, a development that continued in her later poetry in *Woman in the woods* (1985). The poems in *A song of Lilith* (2000) tone down the story of the woman who, according to Hebrew mythology, was created with Adam, was his first wife, rejected her inferior status, and was expelled from Eden—and became vengeful and dangerous, threatening all children. *A garden of anchors: selected poems* (2003) is made up of poems 'written mostly in the 60's and 70's', in the author's words.

Kogawa, however, is best known as a novelist, particularly for her award-winning *Obasan* (1983), which has its source her experience of the wartime evacuation of the Japanese, and derives its power from the same direct and sober language of her poetry, avoiding any excesses of bitterness or resentment. (Kogawa's children's book, *Naomi's road* [1986; rpr. 1995; rev. 2005], was based on *Obasan*.) The same is true of *Itsuka* (1992, rpr. 1993), a sequel that follows the life of one of the younger characters in *Obasan*. In Toronto Naomi, the protagonist, involves herself in the struggle for recognition and redress for those Japanese-Canadians who were evacuated. Life on the Prairies is featured in *The rain ascends* (1995, rev. 2003), which recounts the struggle of a young woman whose father, a minister—a man she has been overly devoted to—is discovered to have been a child molester.

Naomi's tree (2008), based on *Naomi's road,* is a picture book, illustrated by Ruth Ohi, about a cherry tree that grew in Naomi's backyard—that of the Kogawa family's Vancouver house. In an Afterword, Kogawa thanks the Save Joy Kogawa House Committee for purchasing the house as a writers' centre. The recipient of honorary degrees from three Canadian universities, Kogawa is a Member of the Order of Canada (1986).

Kokis, Sergio (b. 1944). Born in Rio de Janeiro, he developed a strong interest in fine arts and philosophy as a young student. Involved in clandestine political activities protesting Brazil's dictatorship (sketching caricatures and political posters), he was arrested by the military police, who accused him of 'crimes against national security'. A scholarship to study in France enabled him to leave Brazil discreetly and complete a master's degree in psychology at Université de Strasbourg in 1969. The same year he was offered a post as psychologist at the Gaspé Psychiatric Hospital before completing a doctorate in clinical psychology at Université de Montréal in 1973. Teaching psychology briefly at Université du Québec à Montréal, he accepted another position as psychologist at Sainte-Justine childrens' hospital, where he spent twenty years before devoting himself in 1995 entirely to painting and writing. Kokis published eight novels, but only two have been translated. In his award-winning first novel, *Le pavillon des miroirs* (1994), translated by David Homel and Fred Reed as *Funhouse* (1999), the narrator relives, in his new homeland, Québec (never mentioned specifically), in a series of flashbacks, various stages of his life before immigration: a childhood raised in a bordello in the company of prostitutes, their clients, drunks, and the terminally ill;

Kokis

adolescence in a boarding school with young people from mixed social backgrounds; and, finally, a study tour to the northeastern State of Bahia, where the horrifying living condition of the peasants make the slums of Rio look attractive. The shocking contrasts of Brazil are re-created with powerful imagery and psychological realism. Though many events parallel those in Kokis's own life, he insists that this is not an autobiographical novel, but rather an exploration of art and creativity seen through the memories of a painter who recalls the colours and forms of his childhood and tries to integrate them into his present work and thinking, while sharing the psychological disruption of the immigrant torn between the new cultural necessities of the present and vivid memories of his past. In *The art of deception* (2002), a translation by W. Donald Wilson of *L'art du maquillage*, Max Willem, a Montreal art student in the 1960s who is obsessed by outward appearances and by the fact that reality can be obscured by illusion and artifice, turns himself into an outstanding art forger... subjecting himself to the demands of an international forged-art conspiracy.

Korn, Rokhl (Rachel) H. (1898–1982). A major poet of the modern Yiddish literature that flourished in eastern Europe before the Holocaust, she was brought up on a farm and educated in Galicia, part of the Austrian Empire annexed by Poland in 1919, the year she began writing in Yiddish instead of Polish. When the Germans invaded Poland in 1939, Korn fled to the Soviet Union, where she spent the war years making her way from the refugee camps in Tashkent and Uzbekistan to Moscow. There she was welcomed and assisted by the Yiddish writers' community. After the war she returned to Poland and resumed her literary activities in Lodz, where she was elected to the executive of the Yiddish writers union. Subsequently she represented the union at a PEN Congress in Stockholm; from there she immigrated to Canada, settling in 1948 in Montreal, where she lived until her death. Korn was the author of nine books of poetry and one collection of short stories. She remained, throughout her life, a frequent and influential contributor of essays, poems, and stories to every prestigious Yiddish journal in America, Israel, and Europe, and was awarded nearly all the existing literary prizes for Yiddish literature. Korn's poems are beloved and celebrated for their lyrical vision and realistic depiction of country life and landscape, and her stories are famous for their profound

psychological penetration and dense, complex, and unsentimental style. A volume of her selected poems has appeared in English translation: *Generations* (1982), edited by Seymour MAYNE. *Paper roses* (1986) is a bilingual edition of Korn's poems, selected and translated by Seymour Levitan. See Korn's story 'Earth', translated by Miriam WADDINGTON and included in the anthology she edited, *Canadian Jewish short stories* (1990), and Waddington's memoir 'Rachel Korn: remembering a poet' in her *Apartment Seven* (1989). Korn's story 'The road of no return', translated by Waddington, is in the anthology *Found treasures: stories by Yiddish women writers* (1994) edited by Margie Wolfe, Frieda Forman, and Sarah Swartz.

Kostash, Myrna (b. 1944). Born in Edmonton of Ukrainian parents, and educated at the University of Alberta (B.A.), the universities of Washington, Seattle (graduate studies), and Toronto (M.A.), Kostash has been a freelance writer, an instructor in Women's Studies, and an associate film producer at the National Film Board. She was Chair of the WRITERS' UNION OF CANADA in 1993–4.

Kostash is the author of numerous books of non-fiction in which she examines her subjects with the same relentlessly honest gaze that she trains on her own beliefs. In *All of Baba's children* (1977, 3rd edn 1992), about the lives of Ukrainian immigrants in Two Hills, Alberta, Kostash explodes the myth of immigrant Ukrainians as docile, religious peasants and reveals the complexity of the world the immigrants left behind and the one they came to. *Long way from home* (1980) treats politics of the 1960s and the student movement in Canada. In *No kidding* (1987), an examination of the lives of teenage girls, Kostash as a feminist looks back at a younger generation to see what gains had been made for women, and finds the experience brutally sobering. The girls were often harsh with one another, locked in cruel relationships, and ignorant of basic information on sex. *Bloodlines: a journey into eastern Europe* (1993) is a study of eastern-European Slavic nations based on several years of travels in those countries shortly before the collapse of the Soviet Union and the dramatic changes that swept through the area. It is therefore a series of impressionistic snapshots of the region in the final days of Communism that includes the narrator, her relatives, hotel clerks, and various conformists and non-conformists. As in her previous books, Kostash reveals complexity without ever slipping into easy generalities. *The doomed bridegroom: a memoir* (1998) focuses on the connection between 'political and sexual arousal' and the author's desire 'to narrate a personal history of arousal by transgressive men, alive and dead', in Greece and Ukraine, Warsaw and Belgrade, though the memoir begins in Mississippi. Portraying herself and others, Kostash blends social history and politics with emotional bonding and coupling, while also drawing the reader into life in eastern Europe from the seventies to the nineties. For *The next Canada: in search of our future nation* (2000, rpr. 2001) Kostash travelled across Canada and, focusing on a multitude of subjects, interviewed under-thirty-five-year-olds to find out how *they* thought of Canada. *Reading the river: a traveller's companion to the North Saskatchewan River* (2006), written and compiled with researcher Duane Burton, is an excellent history of the river, which runs from Saskatchewan River Crossing in Alberta to Grand Rapids, Manitoba. There are many quotations from historical and modern writers.

Kreisel, Henry (1922–91). He was born in Vienna and left Austria for England in 1938 after the Nazi takeover. Sent to Canada by the British authorities in 1940, he was interned for eighteen months. He then attended Jarvis Collegiate, Toronto; the University of Toronto (B.A., 1946; M.A., 1947); and the University of London (Ph.D., 1954). Kreisel began teaching at the University of Alberta in 1947, and had a distinguished career there. He described himself as being 'one of the first people probably to bring to modern Canadian literature the experience of the immigrant.' Both of his novels have as protagonists men who find it difficult to come to terms with the contrast between the 'hell' of Austria in the 1930s and the bland, but more secure, character of Canadian life. In *The rich man* (1948) Jacob Grossman, a presser in a Toronto clothing factory, returns to Europe after more than three decades in North America. His seemingly innocent decision to 'throw money around like a rich man' becomes a trap when his Viennese relatives, in the anti-Semitic and repressive climate of 1935, turn to him for financial help he cannot provide. Grossman's growing awareness of the moral blunder into which vanity and lack of self-knowledge have led him is effectively presented, as is the tension created within a family of strong-minded individuals who are sometimes bound together and sometimes thrown apart by adverse circumstances. *The betrayal* (1964, rpr. 1971) deals with moral irresponsibility in a more dramatic, less atmospheric, way.

Theodore Stappler, a young Austrian seeking with his mother to escape the Nazis, is paralysed by fear when he realizes that both of them have been betrayed by a fellow Jew. Stappler survives, ultimately to confront his enemy in Edmonton. The troubled consciences of both Stappler and his betrayer, who has plausible self-justifications to offer, are powerfully rendered. The characterization of Mark Lerner, the Jewish-Canadian professor who narrates the story, is a convincing study of North American naivety attempting to comprehend the dark European heritage. *Klanak islands: eight short stories* (1959), edited by William C. and Alice McConnell, and *The almost meeting and other stories* (1981, rpr. 2004) bring together stories with both European and western-Canadian settings that Kreisel wrote over more than two decades. In the latter category is the much-admired and widely reprinted 'The broken globe', and the charmingly wry 'The travelling nude'. Kreisel's essay, 'The prairie: a state of mind' (1968), a seminal study of the literary implications of the prairie sensibility, has been reprinted several times (see Donna Bennett and Russell Brown, eds, *An anthology of Canadian literature in English: Volume II*, 1983). *Another country: writings by and about Henry Kreisel* (1985), edited by Shirley Neuman, includes interviews given by Kreisel, his letters, creative work, and a diary of his 1941 internment, along with ten critical essays about him and a bibliography of his writings. Kreisel was made an Officer of the Order of Canada in 1987.

Kroetsch, Robert (1927–2011). Born and raised in Heisler, Alberta, he attended the University of Alberta (B.A., 1948), then spent the next six years working in various parts of the Canadian North as a labourer, and as a civilian information officer for the US Air Force in Labrador. In 1954 he attended McGill University for a year to study under Hugh MacLENNAN, and in 1956 completed an M.A. at Middlebury College, Vermont. He later attended the Writers' Workshop at the University of Iowa, earning a Ph.D. in creative writing in 1961. He remained in the USA, teaching English at the State University of New York at Binghamton until 1978, when he became professor of English at the University of Manitoba, while pursuing his career as a prolific writer, and was made Distinguished Professor in 1985. He retired in 1995 and makes his home in Winnipeg, Manitoba.

Kroetsch's *But we are exiles* (1965) is based on his experiences working on Mackenzie River riverboats. While this novel is written in a realist manner, the epigraph from Ovid that originally appeared on its title page calls attention to parallels between the protagonist's story and the Greek myth of Narcissus; as well, some elements of the book recall Conrad's *Heart of darkness*, the most important of Kroetsch's early influences. This 'layering' of extended mythic and literary allusions to give saliency to narrative events, although rooted in well-established conventions of 'International Modernism', made the novel a departure in Canadian fiction. In the novels that followed, Kroetsch's interest in myth became progressively more evident in the surface of his texts, moving his writing beyond modernism's use of myth and towards the 'fabulations' that have been an important strand in English-language fiction since the 1960s. Structured by comic and surreal episodes, his *Out West* triptych—*The words of my roaring* (1966, rpr. 2000), *The studhorse man* (1969, GGA; rpr. 2004), and *Gone Indian* (1973, rpr. 1999)—is an extended investigation of the fabulous and mythic implications of rural life on the Prairies. Beneath the surface of *The words of my roaring*—a historically based account of Alberta in the 1930s—Kroetsch creates an elaborate structure of myth, blending the tale of Pluto's abduction of Persephone with Christian allusions, and introducing extensive patterning derived from Frazer's *The golden bough*, the Babylonian-Assyrian mythologies of Marduk and *The epic of Gilgamesh*, and other narratives to provide a complex (if to some extent invisible) grounding for this Depression-era story of John Judas Backstrom, a small-town undertaker running for office in the Alberta general election of 1935. Though a follower of a political leader named Applecart, a man who uses the Book of Revelation to turn Westerners against the East (an allusion to William 'Bible Bill' Aberhart, the evangelical founder of the Social Credit Party in Canada), Backstrom bases his campaign on a whimsical promise to bring rain in a way that recalls Frazer's belief that all ancient rulers were first of all rainmakers. In *The words of my roaring*, and in the novels that followed, Kroetsch's use of myth is also postmodern, in that there is such a superfluity of allusions and echoes that they resist a single, coherent reading. In *The studhorse man* Kroetsch uses not only Old World myths—in particular, parallels to, and parodies of, Homer's *Odyssey* and the myths of Poseidon and Demeter—but also introduces North American mythology, setting up extensive resonances with Native trickster tales. He became attracted to

the trickster figure after encountering Sheila WATSON's use of Coyote in *The double hook*, and it has continued to fascinate him throughout his career. *Gone Indian* is the tale of an American graduate student, Jeremy Sadness, who is fascinated by Archibald Stansfeld BELANEY (the British immigrant who deceived the public in his guise as Grey Owl). Jeremy comes to the Canadian West seeking a vanished American frontier but finds instead a winter-carnival celebration in which he has a series of dreamlike adventures. Containing allusions to several myths of Native people, to the Funeral Games section of Virgil's *Aeneid*, to Dante's *La vita nuova*, and to the Norse myth of Ragnarok, *Gone Indian* ends with its hero, mounted on a snowmobile and accompanied by a beautiful woman, ambiguously disappearing into the North. Kroetsch's fifth novel, *Badlands* (1975, rpr. 1999), also generally parodies the male adventure quest: its river-raft journey into the Alberta Badlands variously recalls and inverts a number of tales, including the underworld descents made by both Orpheus and Coyote, the gathering of troops for the final siege of Troy, and Mark Twain's *Huckleberry Finn*. Its story of William Dawe, a paleontologist who leads an expedition in search of dinosaur bones, is reconstructed by Anna Dawe, who uses her father's field notes to recreate, a generation later, his journey of exploration. Her discovery that 'There are no truths, only correspondences' suggests much about the way Kroetsch's fiction makes it impossible to feel that any interpretation is ever final. *What the crow said* (1978, rpr. 1998)—with its play with ideas about language and its tale of prairie people who begin a War Against the Sky—continues Kroetsch's investigations of myth and his ironic reconsiderations of his literary and intellectual tradition. Located more clearly in the realm of the fantastic than any previous work, this novel shows the impact on Kroetsch of Latin American writers such as Gabriel García Márquez. (In 1980 Kroetsch published *The 'Crow' journals*, selections from the journal he kept while working on the novel.) *Alibi* (1983) and *The puppeteer* (1992, rpr. 1993) represent two-thirds of a trilogy Kroetsch decided not to finish. In *Alibi*—a novel about gender, desire, and guilt that plays with patterns of death and rebirth, fall and regeneration—William William Dorfendorf is on a quest that carries him from the New World to the Old. In the employ of a wealthy collector, the mysterious and god-like Jack Deemer, he must find the perfect spa. (Water—and wasteland imagery—recur throughout Kroetsch's fiction.) In *The puppeteer* Deemer becomes the framing narrator of a complex story that plays with the borderlines between life and art and between metaphysics and fiction. The movement of the previous novel is reversed, so that the detective-like 'Dorf' is now accused of a crime and finds himself in flight rather than in quest, his freedom growing ever more limited. *The man from the creeks* (1998, NCL) is an entertaining novel about the Klondike Goldrush in which 'the lady that's known as Lou' and Dan McGrew are among the characters.

In the seventies and eighties Kroetsch emerged as an important poet, working chiefly with the long poem. (*The stone hammer poems*, [1975], collects his earlier, shorter, poems.) *The ledger* (1975, 2nd edn 1979) and *Seed catalogue* (1977, rpr. 2004) attracted special interest for his creation of a palimpsest, in which his poem is superimposed onto found documents of an earlier era. These two poems, along with *The sad Phoenician* (1979), *The criminal intensities of love as paradise* (1981), *Letters to Salonika* (1983), *Advice to my friends* (1985), *Excerpts from the real world* (1986), and others are collected in *Completed field notes: the long poems of Robert Kroetsch* (1989, rpr. 2000), a long poem made out of long poems, unified not by content but through juxtaposition, repetition, permutation, and voice. *The hornbooks of Rita K* (2001) and *The Snowbird poems* (2004) are two playful collections. Rita Kleinhart is said to have disappeared in 1992 from the Museum of Modern Art in Frankfurt, leaving behind poems and fragments of poems, some of which are presented and commented on by her lover Raymond. He himself is often heard from: 'I am, as it were, half technician, half lover of the plain truth.' The Snowbird travels south in search of warmth: 'Never mind the water, just keep an eye on the sky/for falling objects. And I'm not talking meteors here./You could get hit on the head by a large rubber ball.' ('Beached 3').

Kroetsch has also been an influential critic and theorist who helped provoke Canadian interest in postmodernism as a literary and intellectual movement. In *Labyrinths of voice* (1981), a book-length interview with Shirley Neuman and Robert Wilson, he drew heavily on post-structuralist and other contemporary criticism to contextualize his ideas about writing. Many of the critical essays he published between 1971 to 1989 may be found, often extensively revised, in *The lovely treachery of words: essays selected and new* (1989).

A likely story: the writing life (1995) is a series of sketches that blend autobiographical reminiscences with reflections on writing and on his reading of Margaret LAURENCE, Rudy WIEBE, and Wallace Stegner.

Kulyk Keefer, Janice (b. 1952). Born Janice Kulyk and raised in Toronto, the child of a Ukrainian father and a Polish immigrant mother, she draws upon the experience of inhabiting more than one cultural world in her poetry, fiction, and critical writing. A graduate of the University of Toronto (B.A., 1974), she completed an M.A. (1976) and a Ph.D. (1983) in modern English literature as a Commonwealth Scholar at the University of Sussex, England. After a year in France, she and her husband, Michael Keefer, moved to Nova Scotia, where both taught at the Université Sainte-Anne from 1982 to 1986. In 1990–2 she was associate professor of English at the University of Guelph, Ontario, and is now professor, School of English and Theatre Studies (1992–).

After winning the CBC short-story competition for two consecutive years, Kulyk Keefer published three books of short stories, *The Paris-Napoli express* (1986), *Transfigurations* (1987), and *Travelling ladies* (1990, rpr. 1992), which uses the motif of journeying to explore her female protagonists' lives, families, and relations to culture at crucial points of transition; and five novels, *Constellations* (1988), *Rest Harrow* (1992), *The green library* (1996), *Thieves* (2004), and *The ladies' lending library* (2007). Kulyk Keefer's fiction is written with clean, precise control. Many of her short stories, as well as her novels, are set on the French shore of Nova Scotia and explore the tensions and limitations within a society defined by language, history, and geography and that regards outsiders with suspicion. In *Rest Harrow* the Canadian protagonist, Anna, escapes her lover for a year's research in England, only to find new demands upon her fragile self-containment. Similarly, in *The green library* the stability of the heroine, Eva, is irrevocably altered when her Ukrainian heritage is revealed to her, causing her to visit Kiev and revisit a past that is foreign. While Kulyk Keefer has often created immigrant characters, this is the first novel to use her own ethnic heritage, and the result is a powerful look at the divided experience of one world that demands conformity as the price of acceptance and another that equally demands loyalty and silence about the darker elements of its culture and history. Ukrainian women (and some of their children) are very much at the centre of *The ladies' lending*

Kulyk Keefer

library, in which seven women—including Lesia Baziuk, Nettie Shkurka, Nadia Senchenko ('wife of the only millionaire they are ever likely to know'), Sonia Martyn (whose husband Max changed his last name from Martyniuk)—meet for gin and gossip at Sasha Plotsky's cottage at Kalyna Beach (an imaginary location on Georgian Bay) 'every Friday afternoon, as their husbands are starting the long drive up from the city' and to discuss the books they've been reading and exchanging. Taking place in 1963, the year the Taylor/Burton film *Cleopatra* was released (gossip about this recurs), the narrative is a skilled amalgam of the histories of these first-generation immigrants, past the prime of youth, and their relationships with their spouses and children, and with each other. Some of the children appear in little sub-plots, along with Sonia's outrageous sister-in-law, Marta, who was emotionally damaged by a terrible past in Ukraine. To say that it is a woman's novel is not to denigrate it—it is a rich evocation of a time, a place, and of a particular group of people. *Thieves: a novel of Katherine Mansfield* (2004) adheres closely to the published evidence of the biographical details—provided by Mansfield's journals and letters—and fills in the 'blanks' of the life with Kulyk Keefer's own inventions. She has produced a plausible narrative without, however, capturing the 'rawness of pain' and 'dazzling delight of being alive in the world' that she says, in an addendum, she was struck by in the journals. (One longs to read a biography instead, with quotations from the letters and journals.) Mansfield's life story is interspersed with a succession of chapters entitled 'Roger' and 'Monty'. The Australians Roger Mills—whose book *Beyond the Blue Mountains* Kulyk Keefer acknowledges as a source of information—and his son Montgomery are both obsessed with Katherine Mansfield, writing about her and researching her life. Monty steals a letter addressed to his father that takes him to Chicago, then Windsor, Ontario, in search of Mansfield lore (other thefts of letters come to light, thus the title). These extensive father/son intrusions lack the interest of those chapters, entitled 'Beyond the Blue Mountains' devoted to Mansfield herself.

Kulyk Keefer has published three books of poems, *White of the lesser angels* (1986), *Marrying the sea* (1998), and *Midnight stroll* (2006). The wide range of subjects in *Marrying the sea* include 'Elizabeth Smart, 70' ('Remembering that girl, her hair as soft as butter,/you say it hurts to look at me.'), 'Katherine

Mansfield to Middleton Murry' ('I have no language left. No one here/can pronounce my name. Everyone knows/I'm about to die.'), and a group of thirteen poems, with the overall title 'The Isle of Demons', narrated by Roberval's niece, the subject of Douglas GLOVER's novel *Elle* ('I have been here as long/as it takes black hair/to become its own ghost.') *Midnight stroll* is divided into three sections. The first, bearing the book's title, is inspired by young Ukrainian women living in suburbia; the second is a collection of verse drawn from the vivid descriptions recorded in *Etty: the letters and diaries of Etty Hillesum 1941–1943*, a Jewish writer and mystic who died in Auschwitz, aged twenty-nine; the third (followed by ten pages of illustrated notes) is entitled 'The waste zone', which was suggested 'both by T.S. Eliot's *The Waste Land*, and the Summit of the Americas held April 19–21, 2001, in Quebec City to agree to the creation, by 2005, of a $17 trillion trade bloc: the Free Trade Area of the Americas ....' The title 'Waste zone' refers to 'the cityscape of Québec, poisoned by clouds of chemicals used to separate witnesses and protesters from the thirty-four Heads of State ... participating in the summit; allegorically it is the entire global zone now open to unregulated commercial exploitation.' The three sections of *Midnight stroll*—which record significant moments, in strikingly different settings, in poems that are concise and clear but strangely unpoetic—are accompanied, respectively, by paintings by Natalka Husar, drawings by Claire Weissman Wilks, and photographs by Goran Petkovski.

Kulyk Keefer has also written two valuable books of literary criticism. In *Under eastern eyes: a critical reading of Maritime fiction* (1987) her thesis is that the fiction of this region has its own themes and traditions, generated by its distinct cultural history, and she supports her claims with engaging discussions of writers from Thomas Chandler HALIBURTON to David Adams RICHARDS. *Reading Mavis Gallant* (1989) is a critical study of the works of GALLANT, which influenced Kulyk Keefer's own literary development. Kulyk Keefer co-edited (with Solomea Pavlychko) *Two lands new visions: stories from Canada and Ukraine* (1998), an anthology containing ten stories each by Ukrainian writers in translation and by Ukrainian-Canadians. *Honey and ashes: a story of family* (1998) is an eloquent memoir of her forebears in Staromischyna (the Old Place), Ukraine, and Toronto. *Anna's goat* (2000) is a picture book for children illustrated by Janet Wilson.

L

Laberge, Albert (1877–1960). He was born in Beauharnois, Québec, where his family had occupied the same land since 1659. While attending the Collège Sainte-Marie in Montreal, apparently expecting to prepare for the priesthood after his *cours classique*, he occasionally visited the library of an uncle who was a doctor and avidly read the French Naturalists. A confession of this 'sin' led to his expulsion from the Collège and, so far as we can judge from his story 'La vocation manquée', to his lifelong anti-clericalism. For four difficult years Laberge held odd jobs and studied law—feeling an aversion, one presumes, to returning to the family farm. In 1896 he began to work for *La Presse*, where he continued for thirty-six years, mainly as sports writer but also as art critic. In 1932 he retired to Châteauguay, where he was able to give more time to writing. Laberge was the author of thirteen published volumes of stories and sketches and an unpublished novel, as well as of poems and literary articles published in periodicals; but he is best known for his novel *La Scouine* (1918), translated as *Bitter bread* (1977) by Conrad Dion. Because Laberge was aware of the misfortunes of his friend Rodolphe Girard (author of the scandalous MARIE CALUMET), he allowed his novel to appear in an edition of only sixty copies. (Girard, after a much milder show of disrespect for the clergy in his 1904 novel, was dismissed by *La Presse*.) It is set in the farming region of Beauharnois, where the author grew up, and appears to cover some fifty years from 1813. The title is a meaningless nickname made up by children for the smelly, mean, disagreeable Paulina Deschamps, the principal character. Closeness to the land has a brutalizing effect, and religion has little recognizable place, apart from the ritual marking of the bread with a cross (a refrain in the novel, compressing all Laberge's feelings about traditional rural life into one haunting symbol, clearly a parody of the Communion). The novel is most enjoyed for its short, finely pointed sketches, written in hard, polished prose; and many details are memorable, not only for their visual and aural clarity but also for their symbolic overtones. Because of its attention to detail and its deterministic view of life, it has been considered the first realistic novel in Canada.

Laberge, Marie (b. 1950). Born in Quebec City, she received her early education there and entered the École de journalisme et d'information of Université Laval in 1970, studying in several faculties; she took part as well in collective productions of the local Troupe des Treize. From 1972 to 1975 she studied acting at the Conservatoire d'art dramatique de Québec, then taught theatre at the Université du Québec à Chicoutimi and developed theatre courses for Danse-Partout. She earned an enviable reputation as actress, producer, and educationalist before launching her career as dramatist. The plays of Laberge are characterized by their intensity, emotion, and often violence: some become melodramatic; others depict human distress with convincing realism. She develops plot and structure—generally linear—with great skill, and excels in the psychological delineation of character, especially that of women, who occupy the foreground of her work. Her plays in translation include *Before the war, down at l'Anse à Gilles* (1986), Alan Brown's translation of *C'était avant la guerre à l'Anse à Gilles* (1981, GGA). It is the sympathetic tale of a young widow who decides to free herself and an abused friend from the oppressiveness of their Québec village life in 1936. In *Forgetting* (1988), Rina Fraticelli's translation of *Oublier* (1987), the four daughters of a woman dying of Alzheimer's disease are briefly reunited on a stormy winter night; each has suppressed memories that have warped their lives. *Aurélie, my sister* (1989), Fraticelli's translation of *Aurélie, ma soeur* (1988), is set against a sombre background of complex family relations, but the figure of Aurélie stands out as a model of understanding and generosity. Virtually all Laberge's plays have proved popular with the Québec public. Her first play to attract international attention was *L'homme gris* (1986)—translated by Fraticelli as *Night* (1988)—in which a middle-aged man harangues his victimized daughter until she rebels in a gesture of ultimate violence. The play was largely responsible for Laberge's receiving the award of the Croix de Chevalier de l'ordre des Arts et des Lettres in France in 1989. At least four other plays have been staged successfully in Europe. Beginning in 1989 Laberge also published four successful novels about self-knowledge and sexual passion.

Lacey, E. A. (1937–95). Edward Allan Lacey was born in Lindsay, Ontario, and was

Lacey

educated at University College, University of Toronto, where he studied modern languages and literature (majoring in French and German), graduating in 1959. Among his friends were Henry BEISSEL, David HELWIG, and John Robert COLOMBO. He attended the University of Texas on a Woodrow-Wilson Fellowship and achieved an M.A. in linguistics in 1961. Thereafter his promising future was ruined by his self-destructive impulses—aided by alcoholism and the way he experienced his homosexuality (picking up rough trade, often exposing himself to abuse and robbery). He may have been a manic-depressive. In 1960, coming from Mexico, at the Nuevo Laredo border crossing, the customs officer told him to sit in the waiting room until he sobered up and he quite needlessly shouted at him, 'I know what you're looking for!' and pulled out a bag of marijuana. He was, of course, arrested and spent two months in prison; he was barred permanently from entering the US. In 1961–83 he worked as a translator, or taught English, in Mexico, Trinidad, Brazil, Greece, and Thailand—where he lived until 1987. He inherited an estate from his parents that would have made him financially independent but he ran through the money. In 1991, in Bangkok, in a drunken stupor, he was run over by a car and was not only injured severely but suffered brain damage. He returned to Canada, which he 'hated', and lived in various homes in Toronto until he died. Lacey had a brilliant mind and was fluent in at least four languages. He was well acquainted with Canadian poetry—he could quote whole poems—and contributed poetry reviews to Beissel's magazine EDGE. His poetry collections are *Forms of loss* (1965)—perhaps the first openly gay Canadian book of any kind; *Path of snow: poems 1951–1973* (1974), *Later: poems 1973–1978* (1978), and *Third world: travel poems* (1994). *Path of snow* contains many poems drawn from his life, including the long poem 'Stroke' about his mother's fatal illness; 'Les visites interprovinciales', about his first sexual experience—when, at the age of fourteen, he spent a night in the same bed with his French-Canadian friend Michel ('going on sixteen'), who later married 'and occasionally sends me a Christmas card'; and 'Laws—for Dr Timothy Leary', addressed to 'Judge Ben Connelly/(Houston, Texas)': 'I remember / standing before you / in your dark courtroom / years ago / December 16/1960 ..../Ordinary case./Ordinary criminal./Pot possession./College kid./Border crossing/at Laredo./Drunk or stoned/at time of arrest.'The last poem is called 'The Lindsayite': 'For many years I lived in Lindsay./Most important, I was born in Lindsay. / That's why I'm cold and proud: I am made of snow.' The poems are followed by nine pages of notes ('Some explanations'—many of them very long), three pages of passport stamps, and photos of his boyfriends.

Lacey's poems—which emphasize the themes of exile and alienation and are strongly autobiographical in their often prose-like narratives—are not outstanding. They are very readable, however, because of their lucid and exotic content and the poems' sensitivity to nature, and to revelations of life in the Third World; in addition, they display a degree of metrical and lyrical skill. Lacey was a brilliant translator. *The collected poems and translations of Edward A. Lacey* (2000), edited with an introduction by Fraser SUTHERLAND, brings his work together in a huge volume published by Colombo & Company. See also *A magic prison: letters from Edward Lacey* (1995), edited by David Helwig, with an Introduction by Henry Beissel—the letters were to him.

La Corne, Luc de (known as La Corne Saint-Luc). See Writing in NEW FRANCE.

Ladoo, Harold Sonny (1945–73). Born in Couva, Trinidad, he came to Toronto in 1968 and received a B.A. in English from Erindale College, University of Toronto. He died in Trinidad under mysterious circumstances—he was presumably murdered. Ladoo's talent as a novelist was recognized and encouraged by Peter SUCH and Dennis LEE, but Ladoo found no popular acceptance as a writer while he lived. Before he left Toronto for the last time he was working as a dishwasher at a restaurant. Lee's long poem, 'On the death of Harold Ladoo', is a meditation on a talent destroyed prematurely. Although Ladoo's estate includes fragments from nine uncompleted novels, only two have been published: *No pain like this body* (1972, rpr. 2003) and *Yesterdays* (1974). Ladoo intended these works to form part of a Faulknerian cycle, encompassing the history of the West Indies, his own biography, a history of Canada in the Caribbean, and slavery. *No pain* is a plotless novel about a family of East Indian rice-growers in 1905, on an imaginary Carib island. Written in dialect, and incorporating poetic imagery as if perceived from the point of view of a child terrified by a rainstorm, the novel treats, with an engaging lyricism, brutality, death, insanity, and sickness. *Yesterdays* is about a Hindu in Trinidad in 1955 who wants to come to Canada and convert Canadians to Hinduism, in the same way Canadian missionaries went to Trinidad to convert the people there. Under a simple plot lies a fine comic sense, often bawdy or scatological, and beneath that is a bitter indictment of colonialism, poverty, and enforced religion.

Laferrière, Dany (b. 1953). Born in Port-au-Prince, Haiti, where he practised journalism, he was the co-founder of the weekly journal *Le Petit Samedi Soir*. When his colleague, Gasner Raymond, was found murdered during Duvalier's regime, Laferrière moved to Montreal in 1978. He then embarked, not without difficulty, on a career as a writer. In less than ten years he published the first of nine books, all of them grounded in his own life and including fictionalized memoirs of his childhood and wise and amusing takes on life as a black in a mainly white environment. They feature a well-tuned ear for language and dialogue and an easy narrative style. The English translations of his fiction have all been made by David Homel. Laferrière achieved celebrity with the publication of his first book, *How to make love to a Negro* (1987)—*Comment faire l'amour avec un Nègre sans se fatiguer* (1985). Called a novel, it is made up of fictionalized autobiographical episodes, each with a colourful title, narrated by a young black immigrant who lives near Montreal's Carré St-Louis and takes pleasure from being desired by white women. While humorous, the novel also attacks racism, stereotypes, and other negative portrayals of human beings. It was the basis of a film (1988) directed by Jacques W. Benoît. *Eroshima* (1991)—*Éroshima* (1987)—is a novel with international settings, made up of brief *pensées*, episodes, dialogues, in which the names of John Lennon and Rita Hayworth are mentioned, and Norman Mailer, Alberto Moravia, V.S. Naipaul, and the black painter Jean-Michel Basquiet make appearances. Love affairs with the Japanese-Canadian Hoki, and her friend Keiko and others, are central. The idea for this book was the image of a young couple making love in Hiroshima on the morning of the dropping of the atom bomb, which is a recurring image that fascinates the narrator, suggesting both sexual energy and 'a kind of ecstasy brought on by evil'. In *An aroma of coffee* (1993)—*L'odeur du café* (1991)—the narrator is a ten-year-old boy who describes his childhood and his relationship with his grandmother, Da, who is the centre of life in a Haitian village. For its sensitivity and lyricism, this is Laferrière's masterpiece. The sequel, *Dining with the dictator* (1994)—*Le gout des jeunes filles* (1992)—is also a lyrical novel. After a dispute with one of the dictator

Duvalier's *tontons macoutes* in Port-au-Prince, an adolescent boy takes refuge in Miki's house across the street, where he discovers the power of words (represented by the poetry of the Haitian Magloire Saint-Aude) and contemplates the beauty of the girls living in the house (the power of sex). This initiation into the world of women makes him feel that he has discovered the secret of life. *Why must a black writer write about sex?* (1994)—*Cette grenade dans la main du jeune Nègre est-elle une arme ou un fruit?* (1993)—is called a novel on the cover of the English edition, but the first sentence says 'This is not a novel.' It is a series of chapters—conversations, anecdotes, mini-essays, portraits of black celebrities—drawn from a well-informed black writer's experiences of the 1990s. *Down among the dead men* (1997)—*Pays sans chapeau* (1996)—is another novel of episodes with headings, about a return to Haiti, that often feature his mother and his Aunt Renée and are lightened by Laferrière's gift for dialogue. In *A drifting year* (1997)—*Chronique de la dérive douce* (1994)—Laferrière describes both lightly and sadly, mostly in verse, his first year in Montreal. Since then he has published several books in French that have not been translated, including *Je suis fou de Vava* (2006), a book for children that won a Governor General's Award.

Lahontan, Louis-Armand de Lom d'Arce de. See Writing in NEW FRANCE.

Lampman, Archibald (1861–99). He was born in Morpeth, Canada West (Ontario), where his father was an Anglican clergyman. His family moved to Parrytown in 1866 and the next year to Gore's Landing in the Rice Lake district, where the Strickland sisters, Susanna MOODIE and Catharine Parr TRAILL, knew the young Lampman. In 1868 he contracted rheumatic fever, which contributed to his early death. In 1874 his family moved to Cobourg and from 1876 to 1879 he attended Trinity College School, Port Hope, and then Trinity College, Toronto. In the spring of 1880 he read, 'in a state of wildest excitement', a new book of poems, *Orion* (1880), by Charles G.D. ROBERTS, whom he would later know. In 1883, after a brief and unsuccessful attempt at teaching in Orangeville High School, he became a clerk in the Post Office Department, Ottawa, a position he held for the rest of his life. From Ottawa he made walking tours of the surrounding countryside—which he loved, and loved to describe in verse—and with his friend Duncan Campbell SCOTT (also a government employee) canoeing expeditions into the wilderness. From 1883 until the last year of his life Lampman's poems appeared frequently in Canadian, American, and British periodicals, notably *The WEEK* and the Toronto *Globe* and, in the United States, *Harper's*, *Scribner's*, and *Youth's Companion*, a Boston magazine edited by his friend E.W. THOMSON. In 1887 Lampman married Maud Playter, and with the help of a small legacy he provided, he published privately *Among the millet and other poems* (Ottawa, 1888). From 6 Feb. 1892 to 1 July 1893 he joined Scott and Wilfred CAMPBELL in writing 'AT THE MERMAID INN', a weekly column of literary and social comment that appeared in the Toronto *Globe*. Lampman was elected to the Royal Society of Canada in 1895 and that same year *Lyrics of earth* was published by Copeland and Day, Boston.

In 1889 Lampman fell in love with Katharine Waddell, a fellow clerk. The exact nature of their relationship is still unclear, but they may have lived together for a time. This attachment was a source of great distress for Lampman in his last years. He was at work on the proofs of *Alcyone*, which he intended to have published in Edinburgh, when he died. Scott, as Lampman's literary executor, ordered a printing of twelve copies (Ottawa, 1899). This was the first of several editions of Lampman's poems edited by Scott, who endeavoured, all his life, to keep his friend's reputation alive. Scott also edited *The poems of Archibald Lampman* (1900), for which he provided a memoir; *Lyrics of earth: songs and ballads* (1925); *At the Long Sault and other new poems* (1943, with E.K. BROWN); and *Selected poems of Archibald Lampman* (1947). Lampman's reputation as the finest of the CONFEDERATION POETS is largely based on a small body of nature poetry written, for the most part, relatively early in his brief career. In recent years, however, critical emphasis has shifted from Lampman as a gently melancholic heir of the Romantics and Victorians to Lampman as alienated precursor of modernism, leading to a new interest in his more obviously troubled later works and to new ways of looking at many of the justly admired nature poems. Like Keats and Tennyson, the two greatest influences on his diction, Lampman was a master of sonority with few, if any, rivals in Canadian literature. Rhythmically he is sometimes fluent to the point of monotony, but he is capable of creating, through slight rhythmic variation, the impression of an immediate notation of moment-to-moment sensation. Lampman's later poetry was often experimental in its rhythms. 'At the Long Sault', reflecting the striking contrast between the very free iambs of the main narrative and the much more regular anapests of the lyrical ending, is one of the finest rhythmic effects in Canadian poetry. At least as important as the music of Lampman's verse is its pictorial quality. Lampman's nature poems abound in vivid pictures of the Canadian landscape that are both objective in their precise descriptiveness and subjective in their evocation of the intensely felt essence of the scene. Lampman's ability to express his vision with great immediacy through the accumulation and arrangement of musical and pictorial effects is at its best in his sonnets (e.g., 'In November', 'Solitude', 'Among the orchards', 'Sunset at Les Eboulements', 'Winter uplands'). His vision owes much to Wordsworth in particular and to the Romantics in general. Humanity, spiritually exhausted by an unhealthy existence in the city, must renew itself through a solitary communion with nature that in its exalted state is usually described by Lampman as a 'dream', the most charged word in his vocabulary. However, the Romantic influence on Lampman is undercut by other elements, to the ultimate enrichment of the poetry. In many of Lampman's finest poems (e.g., 'April', 'Heat', 'In November', 'Winter uplands') the celebration of nature is touched by unease, even fear. In particular the passivity involved in communion with nature comes to be seen as threatening, with its final end not a higher vision but death ('Death', 'A summer evening', 'The frost elves'). The narrative poems (apart from 'At the Long Sault', which is in a mixed lyric-narrative mode) are less successful. With his meditative cast of mind, Lampman shows little skill in the creation of plot or character, and his gift for capturing immediate sensations finds no scope in these poems, with their heightened rhetoric and bookishly exotic settings. One partial exception is 'A story of an affinity', his only narrative set in nineteenth-century Canada, which seems to reflect Lampman's painful relationship with Katherine Waddell. His earlier love poems, little more than sentimental literary exercises, are less interesting than the poems inspired by Waddell, published posthumously in *At the Long Sault and other new poems* ('A portrait in six sonnets'), and later in *Lampman's Kate: late love poems of Archibald Lampman* (1975) edited by Margaret Coulby Whitridge. Lampman's strong-minded 'friend', as he calls her, is a more convincing and challenging presence than the shadowy beloved of the earlier lyrics. Even these poems, however, lack passion or sensuality, for Lampman shared the prudery of his age with regard to 'uninnocent emotion' (see his essay, 'The modern school of poetry in England'). The most intense note in the late love lyrics is of frustration and despair, as in 'Man', one of his finest and most painful poems.

The darkness of Lampman's late love lyrics typifies much of the poetry of his last years where passive acceptance of nature's healing power is rejected as Lampman becomes increasingly concerned with the value of decisive action. This development is probably a response to his growing sense of helplessness in the face of unrewarding work at the post office, his agonizing relationship with Katherine Waddell, the deaths of his son and father, and his own failing health. His espousal of socialism in these years (see 'The land of Pallas') seems diametrically opposed to his earlier praise of the solitary dream of nature far from the world of men: there is nothing dreamy about the powerful and sometimes strident invective in much of the later verse ('To a millionaire', 'The modern politician', 'Liberty'). In most of this poetry, with the exception of some excellent sonnets, the freshness of the earlier work tends to be sacrificed for larger, more abstract effects. But Lampman's new directions lead to successes that could never have been predicted on the basis of his earlier work. One of the most impressive of these is 'The city of the end of things', a visionary poem in which industrial society is presented in nightmarish terms: the 'grim idiot at the gate', with which the poem ends, is Lampman's most powerful evocation of the deathlike passivity to which his society threatened to reduce man's creative powers. The finest of the late poems is the unfinished 'At the Long Sault: May 1660', which, in the version edited by Scott, has become a Canadian classic. The poem describes the successful but suicidal attempt of Adam Dollard (called Daulac) and his company to save Ville-Marie against an Iroquois attack. Even in its imperfect state the poem is outstanding, not only for its formal boldness but also for its breadth of vision. Nature here is a source of both good and evil; humanity must choose to make of the world what it can. 'Dream' is once more a key word, but there is nothing passive about the dreaming of Daulac and his men. The lyric at the close, in which a harmony between humanity and nature has been achieved through active struggle and sacrifice, is a touching statement of the vision towards which Lampman had been moving in his later years.

Much of Lampman's previously inaccessible prose has been published in recent decades. The *Selected prose* (1975), edited by Barrie Davies, contains a number of pieces that throw important light on the poetry. His most intrinsically valuable prose is to be found in his letters to Edward Thomson edited by Arthur Bourinot (1956) and, in more complete form, by Helen Lynn (1980); in his contributions to 'At the Mermaid Inn' (see *At the Mermaid Inn...*, 1979, with an Introduction by Barrie Davies); and in *Essays and reviews* (1996) edited by D.M.R. Bentley. The Lampman of these writings is more varied and attractive than we might suspect from his poetry. *Lyrics of earth* and the Scott edition of *The poems* are available in recent reprints: the first (1978) edited by D.M.R. Bentley; the second (1974), including 'At the Long Sault', with an Introduction by Margaret Coulby Whitridge, who also edited *Lampman's sonnets, 1884–1899* (1976). See also *Comfort of the fields: the best-known poems of Archibald Lampman* (1979), a selection by Raymond SOUSTER, and *Archibald Lampman: selected poetry* (1980, rpr. 1990) edited by Michael Gnarowski.

Lane, M. Travis (b. 1934). She was born Millicent Travis in San Antonio, Texas. She received a B.A. from Vassar, and an M.A. (1957) and a Ph.D. (1967) from Cornell University. She moved with her husband, Lauriat Lane, Jr (who died in 2005) to New Brunswick in 1960 and they became Canadian citizens in 1973. She has taught in the Department of English of the University of New Brunswick and was appointed Honorary Research Professor. She lives in Fredericton. From 1970 until the 1990s she was the principal poetry reviewer for *The FIDDLEHEAD*. Lane's first book of poems, *An inch or so of garden* (1969), was published by New Brunswick Chapbooks. This was followed by several larger volumes: *Poems 1968–1972* (1973), *Homecomings* (1977), and *Divinations and shorter poems* (1980), all published by FIDDLEHEAD POETRY BOOKS. Other volumes include *Reckonings: poems 1979–1985* (1988), *Solid things: poems new and selected* (1993), *Temporary shelter: poems 1986–1990* (1993), *Night physics* (1994), *Keeping afloat* (2001), and *Touch earth* (2006). Lane's long poems and lyrics range over many subjects—place, home, landscape, ecology, war, etc.; and are endowed with her care for language—her sensitivity and intelligence in its use. See *The crisp day closing on my hand: the poetry of M. Travis Lane* (2007), a collection in the Laurier Poetry Series of thirty-five of Lane's best poems, selected by Jeanette Lynes (whose long introduction is an interesting summary of her work), with an Afterword by the author.

Lane

Lane, Patrick (b. 1939). Born in Nelson, British Columbia, and educated at the University of British Columbia, Lane has lived mostly in the West and on the West Coast, supporting himself by working in the logging, mining, and construction industries and, later, by teaching. With bill BISSETT and Seymour MAYNE, he established the small press, Very Stone House, in the early 1960s. His poetry collections include *Letters from the savage mind* (1966); *Separations* (1969); *Mountain oysters* (1971); *The sun has begun to eat the mountain* (1972); *Passing into storm* (1973); *Beware the months of fire* (1974); *Unborn things: South American poems* (1975); *Albino pheasants* (1977); *Poems new and selected* (1979, GGA); *The measure* (1980); *Old mother* (1982); *Woman in the dust* (1983), illustrated with Lane's own drawings; *Linen crow, a caftan magpie* (1984); *Poems selected and new* (1987); *Winter* (1991); *Mortal remains* (1992); *Too spare, too fierce* (1995); *Selected poems: 1978–1997* (1997); and *The bare plum of winter rain* (2000). In 1979 he published a collection with his then partner, now his wife, Lorna (CROZIER) Uher, called *No longer two people*. He also edited the work of his brother (q.v.), who died in 1964: *Collected poems of Red Lane* (1968).

The locus of much of Lane's early poetry—particularly in *Mountain oysters* and *The sun has begun to eat the mountains*—is the West Coast and the Prairies, as he writes of logging camps and forests, Native people, hunting, and bush farming. The poems are tough-minded and anecdotal, full of narratives about working-class people; they show a remarkable and moving empathy for lives that are hard, painful, and vulnerable. Lane has a fine gift for image, and writes of the tragic not histrionically but in understatement, often deflecting attention in a poem to some small detail that is made to carry the full horror of a situation. His genuine understanding of violence—the woman who aborts herself in a dingy hotel ('There was a woman bending'); the pregnant cat dipped in gasoline and set alight ('Last night in darkness')—challenges the reader's complacency. In later books—like *Unborn things* and *Albino pheasants*—Lane's language and imagery developed in subtlety, and there is a more reflective voice, with a broader historical and literary reference. *Poems selected and new* demonstrates the evolution of his work from a poetry that relied on narrative impact for its effects to one that expresses a painfully achieved personal vision, in passages of lyrical beauty. In *Old mother* he grieves in sombre, elegiac poems for the violations of history and human disorder. Life is a brutal pantomime of sexual conquest and deadly combat. In allegories of slaughter and bestial rapacity, such as 'The young man' and 'All my pretty ones', Lane explores the grotesque monsters that live 'below the mind', and concludes that the atavistic root of the psyche is the lust for death. Lane's talent is multifaceted. He has often illustrated his poetry with his own drawings—stark, haunting images that seem to proceed from a nightmare vision. In 1991 Lane published *Winter*, perhaps his most powerful sequence, forty-five poems on the theme of winter that begins: 'The generosity of snow, the way it forgives/ transgression, filling in the many betrayals.' The poems show the mature Lane, still haunted by loss and violence, but with an uncanny gentleness and grace located in the desolate landscapes. In 1992, ready to exorcise some of his ghosts, he published *Mortal remains*, poems about the death of his brother and his father's murder, twenty-five years later. 'Poetry cannot save us,' he explains, 'but it can provide us with some small redemption.' *Go leaving strange* (2004) also draws from his own life: the longer of two sections is called 'The Addiction Poems': 'The truth is I saw what I saw. / I did what I did. So what do I feel? / I feel sometimes my heart in its cage / not screaming, just going on steady, / one beat and one beat going on' ('The truth'). When Lane—a keen gardener and naturalist—freed himself from alcohol and drug addiction, he not only gained strength from gardening but this occupation released a flood of memories that found their way into a fascinating and poignant work, *There is a season: a memoir in a garden* (2004): 'A year ago I lay on the floor in the front hall having a seizure, my stomach heaving, my muscles in spasms, blood in the back of my throat. I had been drinking forty or fifty ounces of vodka a day for months....Today I picked the last fruit in the garden. My hands remember apples. They feel their own way to the hidden fruit in the leaves, take the plump weight and twist or bend it so the stem breaks away.' With Lorna Crozier, Lane edited *Addiction: notes from the belly of the beast* (2001), in which alcoholism is prominent, as in pieces by Lane, Crozier (her father), David Adams RICHARDS, and John NEWLOVE. The Mocambo Café in Victoria, B.C. gave birth to the Mocambopo Reading Series, started by Jim Andrews in 1995. Lane edited *Mocambo nights: poetry from the Mocambopo poetry reading series* (2001), an anthology of poems mainly by B.C. writers and some from elsewhere.

Lane has also published a collection of stories, *How do you spell beautiful? And other stories* (1992), most of which are located in the working-class communities of small company towns. He captures these dying towns and their impoverished inhabitants with a precise realism; but it is his lyric images that stay in the mind. In 2008 Lane published his first novel, *Red dog, red dog*—a family drama set in the Okanagan Valley in 1958, but recalling life on the prairies in the twenties and thirties and as far back as the 1880s—to good reviews.

Over three decades Patrick Lane's work has made him central to the Canadian writing community. On the occasion of his fifty-fifth birthday Susan MUSGRAVE compiled and edited *Because you loved being a stranger: 55 poets celebrate Patrick Lane* (1994). A collection of poems written about or dedicated to Lane, it is a moving tribute to one of Canada's most gifted poets.

Lane, Red (1936–64). Richard Stanley 'Red' Lane, the elder brother of Patrick LANE, was born in Nelson, British Columbia, and died in Vancouver of a cerebral hemorrhage. During his short life he lived in various parts of western Canada and worked at jobs that accommodated the 'maverick' wanderings recorded in his poems. Although most of his work appeared posthumously, Lane's poems were published in little magazines in the early 1960s. The Toronto journal *Ganglia* devoted its second issue to his book *1962: poems of Red Lane*, which brought him to the attention of poets such as Milton ACORN, who later lamented Lane's untimely death in the elegiac poem 'Words said sitting on a rock sitting on a saint'. In 1968 Seymour MAYNE and Patrick Lane (who cites his brother as an important influence on his decision to write) published *Collected poems of Red Lane* under their imprint, Very Stone House. (It was reprinted in 1978 by Black Moss Press.) The poems in the first section, 'The surprise sandwich', were written for children and are statements of feelings, experiences, and observations that conclude with questions involving the reader in a game of self-reflection and response. The core of the book, however, lies in the later sections, which chronicle Lane's experiences in a manner that, although not yet fully developed, is crisp and visually powerful and sometimes experimental. The book concludes with a haunting poem, 'Death of a poet (for Milton Acorn, ultimately)', that eerily foreshadows Lane's sudden death at twenty-eight. Like Acorn, Lane viewed the world from a populist standpoint: his poems portray incidents—on street corners, in beer parlours, and cheap hotels—in detailed observations that grow out of the poet's participation in these events. *War-cry* (1973) is a long anti-war poem dedicated to Lane's father and edited from manuscripts by

his brother Patrick. Much of Red Lane's poetry bears marks of the uneasiness and lack of polish of the developing poet; but his work is significant for its controlled use of colloquial speech, and its strong and direct treatment of unadorned reality.

Langevin, André (b. 1927). Born in Montreal, he lost both his father and mother by the age of seven. His next five years were spent in an institution that he later described as 'asylum-like', a 'locked-in world', worse than the Saint-Vincent-de-Paul penitentiary. He later enrolled in the Collège de Montréal, pursuing his studies to the level of belles lettres. After a series of odd jobs, his first regular employment was in 1945 as a messenger for *Le Devoir* where, six months later, he was made responsible for the paper's literary section. He remained in that position for three years, reading voraciously and 're-educating' himself: he was influenced by the writings of Camus and Sartre, and particularly by Gabrielle ROY's *Bonheur d'occasion* (1945)—*The TIN FLUTE* (1947). He published many articles, mostly on literary or artistic subjects, in *Le Devoir* and *Notre Temps*, as well as literary criticism for the Canadian Broadcasting Corporation. In 1948 he joined the information staff of Radio-Canada, becoming a producer there. Langevin was awarded a Guggenheim fellowship in 1955. A frequent contributor of articles on subjects of political or social interest to periodicals, he was awarded the 1967 Prix Liberté for his articles in *Le Magazine Maclean*. In 1978 he was voted 'Grand Montréalais' of the preceding two decades in the field of literature. Langevin wrote five novels that established him as an important contemporary Québec writer. The only novel translated into English is *Poussière sur la ville* (1953), translated by John Latrobe and Robert Gottlieb as *Dust over the city* (1955). Considered one of the classics of French-Canadian literature, it is about a doctor, Alain Dubois—the narrator—and his wife Madeleine, who is the mainspring of the plot, which concerns her infidelity with Richard Hétu and its consequences. Dubois's initial rage and humiliation culminate in his half-drunk delivery of a hydrocephalic child whom he is obliged to kill to save the mother's life—an incident that affects him profoundly. When the curé attempts to ruin Dubois's practice and arrange to have Hétu married off to the niece of the town's leading businessman, Madeleine tries unsuccessfully to shoot her lover and then dies by turning the revolver on herself. This short novel, which has all the elements of classical tragedy, is written in a beautifully simple style.

Langevin

Langevin, Gilbert (1938–95). Born in La Dorée, Québec, in the Haut-Saguenay, where he received his early schooling, he went to Montreal in 1958 for further studies but did not complete them. In 1959 he founded Éditions Atys, which he directed until 1965. Around 1960 Langevin began organizing poetry recitals throughout Québec, but particularly in Montreal at the Bar des Arts and the Perchoir d'Haïti. Later he became active in the Atelier d'expression multidisciplinaire. He worked at the Bibliothèque Sulpice, the press of Université de Montréal, and Radio-Canada. In the 1980s he mounted and starred in several shows, for example, in *Comme il parle, comme il chante*, in 1982 and 1984. For many years Langevin's name was associated with Montreal's alcoholic counterculture. He wrote numerous songs, published in two collections, that he described as 'much rougher and more compact' than his poems—some were recorded by Pauline Julien—and publishing over thirty collections of poetry, receiving a Governor General's Award for *Mon refuge est un volcan* (1978): Langevin expressed his intention to donate part of the award towards the 'defence of political prisoners in Québec'. Selected poems translated by Marc Plourde were published in *Body of night* (1987), a bilingual edition. Langevin's corpus constitutes a sort of inner autobiography; infused with a vibrant indignation, his poetry is distinguished by its extreme conciseness and sobriety of form, simplicity of phrase, verbal inventiveness, and a tragic tone. His usual themes are those of love, anguish, dream, the opposition between light and dark, sweetness and bitterness, with the poems of his last years often haunted by the idea of illness. Langevin was made an Officer of the Order of Canada in 1980.

Language (English). For much of its history, Canadian English has been described as if either British English or American English was the norm from which it was the deviation. Textbooks, dictionaries, usage and style guides were either British or American, some merely 'Canadianized'. However, scholarly work of the last fifty years has led to a better understanding of the distinctive features of Canadian English. Those who worry about Canadians 'Americanizing' under the influence of US media assume, often incorrectly, that Canadians are aware of where the forms they use or adopt come from. In fact, the Canadian use of variants from both British and American English is one of Canadian English's distinctive features.

Accent / Phonology. The English spoken by second-generation middle-class urban Canadians (the majority of the population) is remarkably uniform from the Québec-Ontario border to British Columbia. Settlement history explains this uniformity, as the movement of Loyalists from the northern US (Pennsylvania, New York, New Jersey, and western Vermont) after the end of the American War of Independence in 1783 populated Ontario; and after 1870 the west of Canada was populated from Ontario. Subsequent immigration and educational practices affected attitudes (often south-eastern standard British English was held up as a prestige norm) and added some minor features, but the main features of Canadian English were in place before the first surge of British English speakers arrived in central Canada after the end of the Napoleonic Wars in 1815. Some studies have been done of distinctive rural accents (for example, of the Ottawa Valley), but many of these accents are disappearing.

Canadian English shares many features with the English of the northern American states that differ from Standard Southern British English—most prominently:

the loss of the palatal glide in words like *news, student, tune* (i.e., the pronunciation of *news* moves from nyooz to nooz)

t-flapping: When a *t* appears between vowels, most Northern American English speakers change the *t* sound to a *d* sound, and thus *metal* and *medal* will both sound like *medal*. This shift also occurs in words where the *t* appears after *r* and before a vowel sound (*hearty* and *hardy*—both sound like *hardy*)

merged low back vowels: Canadians pronounce *cot* the same way they say *caught* (other examples, *Don/dawn, tot/taught, hock/hawk*), a feature that is shared with the northern American regions from which the Loyalists came, although it is now spreading in the US

the use of *r* after vowel sounds. Unlike southern British English and the English spoken on the Atlantic coast of the US, Canadian English retains the *r* sound in words such as *car* and *farther*. Unlike Americans, Canadians tend not to lower the vowel sound before an *r* in words such as *borrow* and *sorry*

Canadians differ from northern Americans in that they usually pronounce the *a* sound in foreign loan words—such as *drama,*

Mazda, Datsun, and *pasta*—like *a* in *bat*, not the *a* in *father.*

Canadian Shift. Canadian English speakers pronounce the vowel in *cot/caught* farther back than American speakers, which appears to have triggered a vowel shift. The shift involves the front lax vowels: the short *a* of *trap*, the short *e* of *bet*, and the short *i* of *sit*. This shift, first described in 1995, is a change that is in progress, moving in the opposite direction from the Northern Cities Shift in the northern US, thus differentiating the two dialects.

Canadian Raising. The term refers to the raised beginning sound of two diphthongs, the vowel sound in *house* and the vowel sound in *knife*, before voiceless consonants (such as *p, t, k, s, f*). Thus, in Canadian Raising the diphthong in the first word in the following pairs has a raised beginning sound, while the diphthong in the second does not (because the consonant is voiced in the second word): *lout/loud, bout/bowed, house/houses, mouth* (n.), *mouth* (v.), *spouse/espouse, bite/bide, fife/five, site/side, tripe/tribe, knife/knives.* These phonetic variations are recognized as a marker of Canadian speech because some (but not all) appear in dialects of US English, Irish English, and Scottish English. Disagreements persist about the origin of the feature (is it derived from Scottish English, a conservative retention of an older distinction, or a unique feature of dialect mix in Canada?), and whether or not it is declining.

Accents in Québec and Atlantic Canada. Most English-speakers in Québec live in Montreal. The passing of the Charter of the French Language in 1977 mandated French as the sole official language of the province, and most workplaces require the use of French. Thus bilingualism is rising in Montreal. Because English-speakers have been in the minority in Montreal since 1867 and tend to live in ethnic enclaves, some distinctive pronunciations have been discovered in Jewish and Italian ethnic groups. English-speakers in the Maritimes are distinguished primarily by their pronunciation of the low back vowel before *r* in words such as *car*, and *hardy*, as well as by the distinctive pronunciation of some words—e.g., *aunt* rhymes with *jaunt*, not *ant*. The distinctiveness of the Newfoundland accent is accounted for by its isolation from the mainland, its early settlement (early sixteenth century), primarily from the west of England and southern Ireland, and its late entry into Confederation (1949); however, its speakers are moving towards continental North American English norms.

Vocabulary. The editors of the work-in-progress revision of the *Dictionary of Canadianisms on historical principals* (Avis et al., 1967), still the best source for Canadian vocabulary, have defined a Canadianism as falling into one of four categories: forms originating in Canada (neologisms), such as *gas bar*; forms preserved in Canada that have fallen into (relative) disuse elsewhere, such as *riding* for electoral district; forms that have undergone a change of meaning in Canada, such as *glory hole* (a rich fishing area); and culturally significant terms, such as *green paper* (which is also used in other parliamentary democracies).

Spelling. Spelling varies across Canada between British and American norms in part because textbook and dictionary use has varied in each province's educational system. Some British spellings have come to be seen as symbolically Canadian; for example, use of *centre* and *theatre* in the names of institutions, and *-our* endings in words such as *honour*.

Syntax. A very few minor differences between Canadian English and other varieties have been identified. Although the use of *eh* at the end of sentences is used in many varieties, it is becoming a marker of Canadian identity.

Scholarly Work on Canadian English. In the past few decades new interest in world varieties of English and improved computer technology have facilitated research into Canadian English, demonstrated by the appearance of reference books, such as historical and desk dictionaries, and usage and style guides. Linguists and lexicographers have assembled corpora of Canadian English for a variety of purposes and have also produced systematic surveys. Canadian English has been included in many important guides to world English and series on world Englishes, as well as special issues of journals (most recently *Anglistik: International journal of English Studies*, 2008). The Strathy Language Unit's Occasional Paper series has published the results of surveys of Vancouver, Québec, and Ottawa English. Canada is included in projects on North American English. Only a few monographs have appeared on Canadian English so far. For an overview, see Laurel Brinton and Margery Fee, 'Canadian English', *North American English*, edited by John Algewo, volume 6 of *History of the English Language* (2001), general editor Richard Hogg, Cambridge University Press, pp.422–40.

MARGERY FEE

Lanigan

Lanigan, George T. See 'The AHKOOND OF SWAT'.

Lapointe, Paul-Marie (b. 1929). Born in Saint-Félicien, Québec, he studied at Collége St Laurent and the École des Beaux-Arts in Montreal before becoming a journalist with *L'Événement-Journal* (1950–4) and *La Presse* (1954–60) and co-founding, with Jean-Louis Gagnon, *Le Nouveau Journal* (1961). A free-lance writer and journalist for Radio-Canada in 1962–3, and editor-in-chief of *Le Magazine Maclean* (1964–8), he joined Radio-Canada in 1968 as radio-program director in the French Services division. From 1948 to 1979 Lapointe published seven collections of poetry, beginning with *La vierge incendié*—produced in the true spirit of automatic writing and containing poems that were in time received with enthusiasm for their glorification of revolt and the provocative mixture of the sacred and profane—and including *Le réel absolu: poèmes, 1948–1963* (1971), which won a Governor General's Award and contained 'Arbres', Lapointe's best-known work, a magnificent litany expressing the will to retrieve one's heritage that coincided with the new socio-political climate of Québec in the 1960s. A selection of his poems translated by D.G. JONES was published in *The terror of the snows* (1976), of which *The 5th season* (1986) is a revised and enlarged edition.

LaRue, Monique (b. 1948). Born in Montreal, she received her B.Ph. from the Université de Montréal (1970) and earned her master's degree in philosophy from the Sorbonne in the Université de Paris (1971), and in 1976 her Doctorat de troisième cycle en Lettres. Since 1974 she has been a member of the French department of the Collège Edouard Montpetit, Montreal. Between 1979 and 1995 LaRue published four novels. Her third novel, *Copies conformes* (1989)—translated by Lucie Ranger as *True copies* (1996)—earned her the Grand Prix du livre de Montréal in 1990 and remains the best known and most studied of her books. The line between fiction and reality, truth and lies, the illusions created by fictive space, the tyranny of the image, Plato's hierarchy between the original and its copy in art, and *la paternite* of ideas—all converge in this postmodern detective story. The plot, derived from Dashiell Hammett's *The Maltese falcon*, was rewritten by LaRue with a female protagonist, a young Montreal mother in search of her husband's lost research diskette in San Francisco.

Lau, Evelyn (b. 1971). Born in Vancouver to Chinese immigrants, she achieved a precocious *succès de scandale* with her first book, *Runaway: diary of a street kid* (1989, rpr. 1996), containing diary entries from Mar. 1986 to Jan. 1988 chronicling her escape from her screaming mother and her alienated father to fend for herself at age fourteen. She began writing stories and poems as a child and became addicted to writing. The selections from her diary are remarkable for their mature verbal facility, and her self-knowledge about her inability to control her wayward behaviour, including drug taking and suicide attempts; her acceptance/rejection of the many people who tried to help her; and her resort, mid-way in her diary, to prostitution—all of which she describes in an Epilogue as 'one phase of my life'. After one of her suicide attempts, she writes: 'I'm not going to die, because I've decided to shape a book out of this journal.... The book that will redeem me, justify my existence.' In Lau's first short-story collection, *Fresh girls and other stories* (1993, rpr. 2001), the call girls undergo various encounters that lead to joyless sex. The novel *Other women* (1995, rpr. 1996) begins when Raymond, an older man, tells Fiona that, for love of his wife, he is putting an end to their fifteen-month friendship; for Fiona he was the first love of her life and he obsessed her, though the relationship was unconsummated, as we read in the ensuing chapters, which include other couples in relationships. Lau published in 1999 *Choose me* (rpr. 2000), a collection of longer stories that, while they continue to focus mainly on unattached, available young women, cynical but always hopeful about love and attachment, have more depth, sophistication, and variety. One story is about a middle-aged woman's troubled relationship with her impotent husband; another is about Melody, married to a much older man, who has a fling in Rome with the young, attractive Stephen, whom she cannot forget—though she returns to her unsatisfactory marriage. The frequent relationships with much older men are summarized in 'Suburbia', about Belinda, who observes her lover's 'clumsy, eager lovemaking, as if he were a boy at the start of his sexual career, rather than a man caught in the physical limitations of its decline.' Lau's sharp observations and narrative skill create smooth, anti-romantic stories that have a subdued erotic pulse.

Lau made her mark as a poet in the collections *You are not who you claim* (1990), *Oedipal dreams* (1992), which was nominated for a Governor General's Award, and *In the house of slaves* (1994, rpr. 1999). As a poet she is affectless, all-seeing, employing striking images; and while joyless experiences of sex, such as sadomasochism in *Slaves*, colour many of her poems, they tend to focus on other things, such as her surroundings: 'I am ready to snap the birch switch/offer you an opened mouth/close my eyes against your oils and watercolours,/let me know when it's over'—but she has already described the paintings ('Adult Entertainment'). *Slaves* includes poems without sexual content, such as 'The monks' song' about her father's hearing Buddhist monks sing: 'I remember their song, he hummed it for days after-wards,/it was one of the last times/his eyes were shiny as bells, ringing/from some region around the heart.' A detached and even treatment of the sexual and non-sexual is also evident in *Oedipal dreams*, in which a poem such as 'Night after night' and its horrific conclusion ('I dream about cutting you up/and stuffing you into the garbage chute/after following the instructions on the door:/drain all garbage, wrap and tie tightly, no bottles/please because they might break/on their way down') is in the same company as a poem about her visit to Freud's house in Hampstead, London, 'Freud, At 20 Maresfield Gardens': '... then your study, the spread over the couch/patterned like jewels, a scarlet cushion in the centre/like an eye set in a forehead'. The taut, controlled poems in *Treble* (2005)—perhaps Lau's strongest collection—draw you in and satisfy your interest in the way she honours its many themes: *personal*—'Small', 'Laughing in My Sleep', 'Migraine' ('... the sweet nothing/sleep of codeine./In the absence of feeling,/an angel's chorus'); *other places*—'Varadero—Havana', Toronto ('Osgoode Hall'), Montana, Wyoming ('Travelling nowhere'); *love*—'Infidelity: a love poem', 'I love you' ('Fifty times a day you said it./Anyone else would have died of boredom,/but for me it was the hook that slid under the skin,/buried itself in bone.'); *divorce*—'The divorce house'; and *suicide*—'The rainbow wasn't enough', 'Christ Church Cathedral'.

The long central chapter of *Inside out: reflections on a life so far* (2001), entitled 'Anatomy of a Libel Lawsuit', arose from a 'memoir', 'Me and W.P.', that Lau published in a magazine about her two-year affair, when she was twenty-four, with W.P. KINSELLA, who was sixty. Kinsella sued. The suit was eventually resolved by a published apology.

Laurence, Margaret (1926–87). Jean Margaret Wemys was born in the Prairie town of Neepawa, Manitoba, which inspired her fictional 'Manawaka'. Her parents, of Scots and Irish descent, died when she was young and she was brought up by an aunt who had become her stepmother. Having decided as a child on a career as a writer, she contributed to school and college magazines and as early as 1939 used the invented name 'Manawaka' in a story for a *Winnipeg Free Press* contest. After graduating (1947) in Honours English from United College, Winnipeg, she worked as a reporter for the *Winnipeg Citizen*. In 1947 she married Jack Laurence, a civil engineer, and in 1949 moved with him to England. From 1950 to 1957 they lived in Africa, for the first two years in the British Protectorate of Somaliland (now Somalia), then in Ghana just before its independence. Laurence's experience of these countries led to a variety of writings on African subjects over a period of some sixteen years: the first of these was *A tree for poverty* (1954, rpr. 1993), an essay and a collection of Somali poetry and prose, which she completed while in Somaliland. Two children, Jocelyn and David, were born to the Laurences before their return to Canada in 1957. While living in Vancouver from 1957 to 1962 Laurence saw the appearance in Canadian journals of her African short stories, later collected in *The tomorrow-tamer* (1963, NCL), and the publication of her African novel, *This side Jordan* (1960, NCL). At the same time she was writing a first draft of a novel set in Canada, which would eventually be rewritten and published as *The STONE ANGEL* (1964, NCL; rpr. 2004). After separating from her husband in 1962 (the Laurences were divorced in 1969), she moved with her children to England, where she lived for ten years. In this prolific decade she published a memoir of her life in Somaliland, *The prophet's camel bell* (1963, NCL); three of the four Manawaka novels: *The stone angel*, *A jest of God* (1966, GGA, NCL), *The fire-dwellers* (1969, NCL); *A bird in the house* (1970, NCL), a collection of linked stories, also set in Manawaka; a children's book, *Jason's quest* (1970); and *Long drums and cannons* (1968), a critical study of Nigerian writing in English during a fifteen-year period of cultural renaissance that was ended by the tribal warfare of the mid-1960s. This period also saw the publication of several magazine articles, which were later collected in *Heart of a stranger* (1976, rpr, 2003). From 1974 she made her home in Lakefield, Ontario, spending summers at her cottage on the Otanabee River, near Peterborough,

Laurence

where most of the fourth Manawaka novel, *The DIVINERS* (1974, GGA, NCL), was written. She wrote three more children's books: *Six darn cows* (1979, rpr. 1986); *The olden days coat* (1979, rpr. 1998), which was made into an award-winning television drama in 1981; and *The Christmas birthday story* (1980). Laurence was Chancellor of Trent University, Ontario, from 1980 to 1983. Her memoir, *Dance on the earth* (1989, rpr. 1990), was completed by her daughter after Laurence's death; it celebrates motherhood and friendship, and includes letters to her lifelong friend Adele WISEMAN. She was made a Companion of the Order of Canada in 1971 and received the Molson Prize in 1975.

Laurence's African writings introduce the themes of survival, freedom, and individual dignity that dominate her major novels. In the deserts of Somaliland she translated and paraphrased the oral poems and stories of the Somali nomads, to form the first collection in English of this material. Her introduction to *A tree for poverty* tells of the harsh, drought-ridden lives and compensatory culture of the nomads. The best of Laurence's African books, *The prophet's camel bell*, written a decade after she left Somaliland, is a vivid travelogue based on her diaries and records the author's spiritual journey from naive enthusiasm and hasty judgement to a respect for the privacy and dignity of others. The two books dealing with Ghana, the novel *This side Jordan* and *The tomorrow-tamer*, are more overtly political; set in the period when the country faced its independence, they give full rein to Laurence's anti-imperialist, anti-colonial views. In *This side Jordan* Laurence sometimes attempts to see through African eyes, but is less successful in this novel than in the semi-allegorical story 'Godman's master', which appears in *The tomorrow-tamer*. Stories in this collection examine closely, and often ironically, the nature of freedom, and show special sympathy for those, both African and European, who no longer fully belong anywhere. The title story illustrates the book's main concern, the conflict between old and new ways.

Laurence's greatest achievement lies in the four Canadian novels dominated by the town of Manawaka, which is not simply a fictional version of Neepawa, though similar in many details, but an amalgam of all prairie small towns infused with the spirit of their Scots-Presbyterian founders. Although only *A jest of God* is set entirely in Manawaka, the town—with its paralysing, often hypocritical, respectability and harsh social divisions—represents in each novel a constricting force to be overcome by the main characters, while also becoming an emblem of life itself. Laurence's chief concern as novelist is the depiction of character, and at the centre of each novel is a powerfully realized woman. Ninety-year-old Hagar in *The stone angel* tries to stave off physical disintegration and death with all the dignity she can. She acquires a measure of grace in acknowledging the pride that, though it has been her strength, has shackled her emotions and stopped her from loving freely. (Kari Skogland's film, starring Ellen Burstyn, was released in 2008.) Unlike Hagar, who has a rich and humorous zest for life, Rachel, the unmarried school-teacher in *A jest of God*, endures a sterile, introverted living death; but is able to break away from Manawaka after a sexual affair—its traumatic consequences bring her a liberating self-knowledge. Rachel's sister Stacey, the protagonist of *The fire-dwellers*, is a spiritually isolated housewife and mother threatened by domestic and social chaos, which she fears. Experience of real tragedies and near-disasters, together with the help of a stranger (as in Hagar's case), result in a hopeful conclusion that offers the possibility of communication with others. Morag in *The diviners* faces the dilemma of trying to live her own life as a writer, while coping with the emotional and physical demands of being wife and mother. Unlike the three previous heroines, she was not brought up in a middle-class family but in the haphazard environment of the garbage-collector's unconventional home. She thus understands social ostracism, so familiar to the Métis, who are powerfully represented here, as elsewhere in the cycle, by the Tonnerre family. Morag's liaison with Jules Tonnerre produces a daughter whose consciousness of her mixed heritage, painful though it is, holds promise of a better future. Of the four novels, *The diviners* deals most richly with their shared themes of ancestral heritage and the relation of past to present. Laurence had a rich ear for nuances of speech, ranging from everyday slang to the colourful, oracular poetry of chanted myth. There is much humour in her work and a strong sense of irony. Depth is given to the prose by a wide range of metaphorical and symbolic allusion, notably to the Bible and to the natural world. Each of the Manawaka novels is dominated by imagery associated with one of the four elements; and this, together with numerous cross-references and the unifying presence of the town itself, justifies the reading of the four works as a unit, a tetralogy expressing Laurence's view of the human condition where grace, symbolized by water, may ultimately be offered to those who endure.

A bird in the house stands slightly apart from the four novels in that it is, as Laurence said, 'semi-autobiographical'. The short stories about the girlhood of Vanessa MacLeod recreate some of the experiences of the young Margaret Laurence, especially in facing the death of a parent and coming to terms with the autocratic spirit of a stern grandfather. The narrator is the adult Vanessa, but her voice belongs simultaneously to the young Vanessa who, as an apprentice writer, makes a point of listening and observing and so has much to report. Through her we encounter the tensions and consolations of family life and, in the later stories, social issues with the particular flavour of small-town and rural life during the Depression.

Laurence's work has been published in several languages. In their English and American editions some of the books are differently titled: *The prophet's camel bell* appeared in New York as *New wind in a dry land* (1964); the English paperback of *A jest of God* was entitled *Now I lay me down* (1968), and the Warner Brothers film of this novel—directed by Paul Newman and starring Joanne Woodward—was called *Rachel, Rachel* (1968).

The first draft of *Dance on the earth: a memoir* (1989) was completed, Jocelyn Laurence tells us in her Preface, a month before her mother was told she had terminal cancer. In spite of her growing weakness she continued to work on subsequent drafts, off and on, and discussed the book with her daughter, who edited it for publication after her mother died. There are collections of letters between Laurence and Al PURDY, Adele WISEMAN, and Gabrielle ROY. See *A very large soul: selected letters from Margaret Laurence to Canadian writers* (1995) edited by J.A. Wainwright. See also *A place to stand on: essays by and about Margaret Laurence* (1983) edited by George WOODCOCK; James KING, *Margaret Laurence: a life* (1997, rpr. 1998); *Margaret Laurence: critical reflections* (2001) by David Staines; *Margaret Laurence's epic imagination* (2005) by Paul Comeau; *Alien heart: the life and work of Margaret Laurence* (2005) by Lyall Powers; and *Margaret Laurence: the making of a writer* (2005) by Donez Xiques.

Laut, Agnes Christina (1871–1936). Born in Stanley Township, Huron County, Ontario, she was two when the family moved to Winnipeg, then a frontier town. Upon graduating

from the University of Manitoba, she wrote for the *Manitoba Free Press*. When ill health caused her to spend a summer in the mountains of British Columbia, she conceived a lifelong love for the wilderness, feeling a special affinity for those who opened up the Canadian North and the Canadian and American West. She moved to the United States, where she pursued these interests in many publications. Her novel *Lords of the North* (1900), a historically accurate and action-filled story of the rivalry of the North West and Hudson's Bay Companies, inaugurated her successful career as a writer, and was the first of her five novels on Canadian subjects. Among her many works of historical nonfiction, the earliest and perhaps best known is *Pathfinders of the West: being the thrilling story of the adventures of the men who discovered the great Northwest* (1904). Laut also wrote three volumes in the Chronicles of Canada series—on the northern fur trade, the pioneers on the Pacific coast, and the gold fields of British Columbia respectively—published between 1914 and 1916. Laut was the first writer permitted by the Hudson's Bay Company to use diaries and photographs from their archives in her works. She died on her estate in Wassaic, New York.

Lawson, Mary (b. 1946). Growing up near Sarnia in southwestern Ontario, she attended McGill University, graduated with a degree in psychology, went to England in 1968, met the man who became her husband, and has lived there ever since, raising two sons and returning to Canada once a year. Lawson has written two memorable, acclaimed novels—set at the northern edge of the Canadian Shield in Northern Ontario—that are old-fashioned in that they are straightforward, clear, emotionally direct; with mostly good people as characters, and events that are entirely persuasive and hold the reader's interest from beginning to end. *Crow Lake* (2002, rpr. 2003) is where the Morrison family have their house: the parents and Luke, nineteen, Matt, seventeen, Kate, seven, and eighteen-month-old 'Elizabeth known as Bo'. At dinner one night it is announced that Luke, who had passed his senior matriculation, had been accepted at teachers' college in Toronto, an important event in the parents' lives. The next day they were driving to Struan, twenty miles away, to buy Luke a suitcase when their car was hit by a fully loaded logging truck whose brakes had failed; they were killed. In spite of all opposition, Luke and Matt are determined to take charge of their sisters. The narrator is Kate as an adult, a twenty-six-year-old university professor of invertebrate ecology in Toronto, and the chapters alternate between memories of her childhood and the growing love she has for Daniel, a brilliant young full professor in her zoology department. Characters in the childhood chapters include the neighbours Pye—Calvin Pye, a farmer, who has a temper and mistreats his children (and whose violence leads to a killing); the Morrisons' doctor ('in fact the only doctor for about a hundred miles'), Dr Christopherson, who lives in Struan; Miss Carrington, the teacher in a one-room schoolhouse; and Mrs Stanovich, 'a large soft lady who looked as if she didn't have any bones and who talked to the Lord all day'. As a child Kate, who was almost preternaturally close to Matt, treasured their time together at 'the ponds', in one of which, 'our pond', there was a shelf where the water was shallow 'and many of the pond dwellers congregated there, and of course you could see right to the bottom.' Matt, who is brilliant, describes what they are looking at as they lie on their stomachs. 'Sticklebats were drifting aimlessly about…. Matt had told me … that the male Sticklebats did all the work. They made the nests and courted the females and fanned the nests to keep the eggs supplied with oxygen.' Thus Kate was led to her later career. Years later Matt's son Simon invites Kate to his eighteenth birthday party, and Matt adds a note: 'Bring someone if you want to.' Driving the 400 miles to Crow Lake with Daniel sitting beside her, Kate is overwhelmed, thinking about what lies ahead: introducing Daniel to her family, her estrangement from Matt after he married Marie Pye and became a farmer, not a university professor who would have magnetized students, not bored them as she thinks she does. When they arrive at the house, Daniel is welcomed warmly and he takes to them all. Young Simon is charming, intelligent, affectionate. Matt hugs Kate. Luke, who makes rustic furniture, comes with Bo, who has become a chef. The next day a picnic is held, attended by neighbours who have become friends. There are two emotional high points. In the kitchen Marie says to Kate: 'If you only knew how much your opinion matters to [Matt]…. Luke forgave him years ago…. But your disappointment—you thinking his whole life is a failure, feeling so sorry for him for the way he let himself down—that's been so hard for him to bear. That's been the hardest thing. Everything else that's happened to him has been easy compared to that.' Kate is shocked; she denies feeling this way. She tells Daniel: '… she

thinks I think what happened to Matt is a tragedy.' Daniel's reply: '… from what I've seen of him, my guess is that he came to terms with it a long time ago. The problem is you didn't. And as a consequence, he's lost what he had with you. That's the real tragedy.' Again she's astonished and upset. But not long after, she sees Matt and Daniel talking about something seriously: 'Two remarkable men, deep in conversation, walking slowly across the dust of the farmyard. It was not a tragic picture…. I suppose the real question is not why I saw it then, but why I didn't see it years ago.' In the last few lines of the novel a resolution is delicately suggested when Matt, Daniel, and Kate visit the ponds together.

Each chapter in *The other side of the bridge* (2006, rpr. 2007) opens with an epigraph in the form of two headlines from the *Temiskaming speaker* dated (in alternate chapters) in the 1930s and 1940s or the 1950s and 1960s. So we read about Arthur Dunn as a dependable, trustworthy youth—whose handsome younger brother Jake is an unreliable, selfish, lazy troublemaker who plays on women and doesn't hesitate to seduce young Laura, the minister's daughter, with whom Arthur is in love. Large of frame and hardworking, Arthur grows into an adult who takes over his father's farm. Other leading characters are the sterling doctor of the town (who appears in *Crow Lake*) and in the later period his son Ian Christopherson, a teenager who works part-time on Arthur's farm and adores Laura, now his wife. Pete is Ian's Ojibway friend whom he loves fishing with in his handsome canoe, a gift from his father. There are intermittent crises of gripping suspense, such as when young Jake and Art (as Jake called him) are on a bridge and to Art's disgust Jake tries a daredevil trick with a pole, falls into the river on his back and nearly drowns—Art saves him, though he is forever haunted by the thought that he had wished he would drown. Fifteen years later Jake returns, stays with Art's family, only to arouse his brother's anger in a shattering climax, unwittingly brought about by Ian. In retrospect the reader is impressed by how this quiet, smooth narrative contains a complicated interweaving of believable characterizations, emotional connections, wartime deaths (neighbours' sons), a tortured relationship (the two brothers), abortive romance (Laura/Jake), and love (Laura/Arthur)—all infused with the command of a gifted novelist.

Layton, Irving (1912–2006). Born in Romania, he came to Montreal with his parents (Lazarovitch) at the age of one, and was educated at Baron Byng High School and Macdonald College, where he earned a B.Sc. in agriculture. After brief service in the Canadian army (1942–3), he did postgraduate work in economics and political science at McGill University, obtaining an M.A. in 1946. He taught English at a parochial school in Montreal, while also teaching part-time at Sir George Williams College (now Concordia University). He was appointed writer-in-residence at Sir George in 1965, and to a similar post at the University of Guelph in the winter of 1969. That year he was appointed professor of English at York University, Toronto, from which post he retired in 1978. He was awarded a Doctor of Civil Laws by Bishop's University in 1970 and a D.Litt. from Concordia in 1976, the year he was made an Officer of the Order of Canada.

Layton was a member of the active group of young poets in Montreal who contributed to *FIRST STATEMENT*, founded by John SUTHERLAND in 1942. With Louis DUDEK in 1943 he joined Sutherland in editing the magazine and remained an editor until it merged with *PREVIEW* in 1945 to become *NORTHERN REVIEW*. He resigned in the 1950s when new editorial policies were adopted by Sutherland. In 1952 he was associated with Dudek and Raymond SOUSTER in founding CONTACT PRESS, a co-operative venture to publish the work of Canadian poets. Together with Dudek, he was instrumental in shaping the editorial policy of Aileen Collins' magazine *CIV/n* (1953–5). In 1955 he declined an invitation by Charles Olson to join the faculty of Black Mountain College, North Carolina, and the editorial board of the *Black Mountain Review*. However, he was in close contact with the American poets Robert Creeley, Cid Corman, and Jonathan Williams throughout the 1950s, and in 1956 edited a Canadian issue of Corman's magazine *Origin*. His extensive correspondence with Creeley was published in 1990 as *Irving Layton and Robert Creeley: the complete correspondence, 1953–1978*.

Layton's poetry has dazzled, puzzled, angered, and astonished its readers since its first publication. He vigorously opposed the aestheticist concept of the poem as a paradigm of the beautiful. To Layton the poem must convey truth, which can reside in the most ignoble and 'unpoetic' subjects and be expressed in blatantly non-poetic forms. The craft of poetry lies in finding the words, however unconventional, to manifest the poet's vision. Many of Layton's early collections were prefaced by attacks on alleged restricters of the freedom of the poet's imagination—professors, critics, clergymen, rationalist poets, puritan editors—who were, in Layton's view, abetted by women in attempting to confine the poet's Apollonian spirit to a world of comfort, convention, and predictability. In these collections Layton presented himself as defiantly breaking a puritan embargo on image, magic, and sexuality, and as making the irrational an accepted part of Canadian poetry for the first time since LAMPMAN and CARMAN. In his rehabilitation of the irrational, however, he invariably included himself among the liars, hypocrites, yahoos, and philistines of whom he wrote. His voice thus appeared to come from inside the primal energy and vileness of our world, as a presumably 'honest' testimony to its dangers and powers. The most impressive of Layton's poems have captured the poet's own extravagance, as 'The day Aviva came to Paris', 'Shakespeare', and 'Keine Lazarovitch', and revealed a wit that can astonish with both appropriateness and reach. Layton's voice in such poems has been confident, bawdy, and at times hyperbolic, yet capable of discerning self-perception.

From the 1940s until the early 1980s he was extraordinarily productive, publishing an average of one book a year. Layton's publications in the first two decades of his career are: *Here and now* (1945), *Now is the place* (1948), *The black huntsman* (1951), *Love the conqueror worm* (1953), *In the midst of my fever* (published in Mallorca by Robert Creeley, 1954), *The long pea-shooter* (1954), *The cold green element* (1955), *The blue propeller* (1955), *The bull calf and other poems* (1956), *The improved binoculars* (published in North Carolina by Jonathan Williams, with an introduction by William Carlos Williams, 1956; rpr. 1991), *Music on a kazoo* (1956), *A laughter in the mind* (also published by Jonathan Williams, 1958), and *A red carpet for the sun* (1959, GGA). They establish the underlying dichotomies of his vision: poet v. society, poetry v. literature, the individual v. the state, passion v. reason, creativity v. order, sacrifice v. rationalization, rudeness v. decorum, imperfection v. perfection, life v. art. The later poems continually expand the amount of the ostensibly horrific, trivial, or crude that this life-affirming vision must necessarily and paradoxically include. The collections of his middle years—*The swinging flesh* (1961), *Balls for a one-armed juggler* (1963), *The laughing rooster* (1964), *Collected poems* (1965), *Periods of the moon* (1967), *The shattered plinths* (1968), *The whole bloody bird: obs, alphs, and poems* (1969), *Nail polish* (1971), and *Lovers and lesser* men (1973)—are increasingly angry and strident in tone. In later collections—*The pole vaulter* (1974), *For my brother Jesus* (1976), *The covenant* (1977), *The tightrope dancer* (1978), *Droppings from heaven* (1979), *For my neighbours in hell* (1980), *Europe and other bad news* (1981), *The Gucci bag* (1983), and *Fortunate exiles* (1987)—Layton gave renewed emphasis to anti-Christian themes and to his Jewishness, using the latter as a symbol of passion, dignity, and truth. His poetry can be examined in depth in *The collected poems of Irving Layton* (1971), in several volumes of selected poems, including *The darkening fire: selected poems, 1945–68* (1975), *The unwavering eye: selected poems, 1969–75* (1975), *A wild peculiar joy: selected poems 1945–1982* (1982)—reissued in 2004 with an introduction by Sam Solecki, *Final reckoning: poems 1982–1986* (1987), and *Fornaluxt: selected poems 1928–1990* (1992). His other publications included *Engagements: the prose of Irving Layton* (1972), a collection of ten short stories, articles, prefaces, and reviews; *Taking sides: the collected social and political writings* (1977); *Waiting for the Messiah: a memoir* (1985); and *Wild gooseberries: the selected letters of Irving Layton* (1989) edited by Francis Mansbridge. Other books are *Uncollected poems 1935–59* (1976), *The love poems of Irving Layton: with reverence & delight* (1984). *Dance with desire: the love poems of Irving Layton* (1986, rev. 1992), and another collection of letters, *An unlikely affair: the Layton-Rath correspondence* (1980, with Dorothy Rath).

See Elspeth CAMERON, *Irving Layton: a portrait* (1985); and Henry BEISSEL and Joy Bennett, eds, *Raging like a fire: a celebration of Irving Layton* (1993).

Leacock, Stephen (1869–1944). Stephen Butler Leacock was born in Swanmore, England. His father, after failing at farming in South Africa and Kansas, took his family in 1876 to Canada, where they settled on a farm in the Lake Simcoe district of Ontario. It was never a success, and the father eventually abandoned his wife, leaving her to raise the family of eleven children (of whom Stephen was the third). Leacock was educated locally and then at Upper Canada College, Toronto. After a year at the University of Toronto he became an unenthusiastic schoolteacher in 1888; from 1889 to 1899 he taught at Upper Canada College, finding time to complete a degree in modern languages at the University of Toronto in 1891. In 1899, inspired by Thorstein Veblen's *Theory of the leisure class*, he enrolled at the University of Chicago, where he did graduate work in political economy

under Veblen. He married Beatrix Hamilton in 1900, and upon receiving his Ph.D. in 1903 was appointed lecturer in the Department of Economics and Political Science at McGill University. In 1906 he published his first and most profitable book: *Elements of political science* (rev. 1921), a college textbook. In 1907–8 he went on a lecture tour of the British Empire to promote Imperial Federation, and when he returned to McGill he became head of his department, helped found the University Club, and built a summer home on Lake Couchiching near Orillia, Ontario. McGill, the University Club, and the home in Orillia became the focal points of his existence. In 1910 the first of his many books of humour was published, *Literary lapses* (NCL). Elected to the Royal Society of Canada in 1919, Leacock became a charter member of the CANADIAN AUTHORS'ASSOCIATION in 1921, and that year went on a lecture tour of England. He remained head of his department until his enforced retirement in 1936, after which he made a triumphant lecture tour of western Canada that resulted in *My discovery of the West: a discussion of East and West in Canada* (1937, GGA). He continued to write prolifically until his final illness.

Leacock's humorous books usually gathered together, in time for the Christmas trade, miscellaneous pieces that had appeared previously in various magazines. As a result, most of them have little or no overall unifying structure. The mix in *Literary lapses* is typical: funny stories, some little more than anecdotes, others more extended; monologues and dialogues; parodies ranging from fashionable romantic novels to Euclid; humorous reflections and essays on a wide variety of topics. Much of Leacock's humour, in this book and others, is exuberant nonsense that, like Lewis Carroll's, sometimes breaks out into a violence that would be disturbing if it were not so obviously in fun. Modern parallels might be the Marx Brothers or *Monty Python's Flying Circus*. Leacock's parodies (see especially *Nonsense novels*, 1911; *Frenzied fiction*, 1918; and *Winsome Winnie, and other new nonsense novels*, 1920), which are undervalued today, offered him an excellent opportunity to give vent to this strain of irresponsible anarchy. Lord Ronald in 'Gertrude the governess; or simple seventeen', who 'flung himself upon his horse and rode madly off in all directions', is the most famous example of this strain of Leacock's humour. Often, however, a more serious note mingles with the humour, and some of Leacock's funniest pieces—such as 'My financial career', 'Hoodoo McFiggin's Christmas', or any of the sketches from *ARCADIAN ADVENTURES WITH THE IDLE RICH* (1914, rpr. 2002, NCL)—show genuine sympathy for decent but ineffectual victims of a coldly indifferent or actively hostile world. It is clear from pieces such as these why Leacock considered Mr Pickwick and Huckleberry Finn to be the two greatest creations of comic literature, and why he was approached to write a screenplay for Charlie Chaplin.

The most striking aspect of Leacock's style is the illusion of a speaking voice, which is so strong in all his works. Like his masters, Dickens and Mark Twain, Leacock was a great lecturer and raconteur, and many of his pieces must be read aloud or recited for their full effect. But much of the humour of his best pieces comes from their modesty of tone. They seem to be recounted, as simply and straightforwardly as possible, by someone who is not intending to amuse us and would probably find our amusement puzzling. Leacock's finest achievement in this respect is the naively self-revealing narrator of *SUNSHINE SKETCHES OF A LITTLE TOWN* (1912, rpr. 1995, 1996, 2002, NCL). Another aspect of Leacock's humour that may also owe something to the oral tradition is the way in which he elaborates a single idea, capping one ingenuity with another until he reaches an inevitable but absurd climax (the final irrational act of the narrator that follows a crescendo of humiliations in 'My financial career') or collapses into an equally inevitable but absurd anticlimax (as in the apparent tragedy turned farce of 'The marine excursion of the Knights of Pythias' or 'The Mariposa bank mystery' in *Sunshine sketches*).

Leacock's two most important books are *Sunshine sketches* and *Arcadian adventures*—the first a regional idyll portraying the essentially good-natured follies of Mariposa, a small Ontario town based on Orillia; the second, set in an American city, presenting a much harsher criticism of a hypocritical and destructive plutocracy. These two books stand apart from the rest of Leacock's humorous writings in their artistic unity and seriousness of purpose. Leacock's thirty-odd books of humour include *Behind the beyond, and other contributions to human knowledge* (1913), *Moonbeams from the larger lunacy* (1915), *My remarkable uncle, and other sketches* (1942, NCL), and *Last leaves* (1945). See also *The Penguin book of Stephen Leacock* (1981, 25th anniversary edn 2006) selected and introduced by Robertson DAVIES; *Feast of Stephen: an anthology of some of the less familiar writings of Stephen Leacock* (1990) edited

by Robertson Davies; the stories and two essays on humour in *My financial career and other follies* (1993, NCL) selected by David Staines; *The Stephen Leacock quote book* (1996) edited by John Robert COLOMBO; *Leacock on life* (2002) edited by Gerald Lynch; and *On the front line of life: Stephen Leacock: memories and reflections* (2004), a collection of Leacock's essays selected and edited by Alan Bowker.

Leacock also produced some twenty-seven non-humorous books, most of which are of little lasting interest. Two exceptions are *My discovery of England* (1922) and *The boy I left behind me* (1946). The first is based on Leacock's 1921 lecture tour of England and contains two of his best pieces: 'We have with us to-night', a hilarious account of the tribulations of a public lecturer, and 'Oxford as I see it', a powerful defence of the ideal of education as a humane experience. *The boy I left behind me* consists of the opening chapters of an autobiography that was interrupted by Leacock's death. It is shrewd and unsentimental but evocative, and even in its truncated form is one of Leacock's finest sustained pieces of writing. Some of Leacock's other non-humorous books, while skilful and sometimes genuinely eloquent, provide important insights into the issues that concerned Leacock all his life and that underlie much of his best humour. His most dearly held belief, which links him to the Victorian age in which he spent his formative years, was in progress, which he saw as culminating in the achievements of Anglo-Saxon civilization. This belief underlies his many works of history, political science, and economics, such as *Baldwin, Lafontaine, Hincks: responsible government* (1907), *Economic prosperity in the British Empire* (1930), *Canada: the foundations of its future* (1941), and *Montreal: seaport and city* (1942), among many others. For Leacock the essence of progress was an ever-increasing capacity for human kindness, which found its highest artistic expression in Anglo-Saxon humour, especially as it is reflected in the works of Twain and Dickens. He argued this thesis most notably in *Mark Twain* (1932), *Charles Dickens, his life and work* (1933), *Humour: its theory and technique* (1935), and *Humour and humanity* (1937). Throughout his life there was a tension between his proclaimed optimism about the continuing progress of humanity and his feeling of unease (expressed most forcefully in *The unsolved riddle of social justice*, 1920) about the triumph of materialism, with its exaltation of *laissez-faire* individualism and its undermining of traditional social ties —a particularly Canadian stance of Tory

Leacock

humanism that Leacock shares to some extent with other Canadian social satirists such as Haliburton, Sarah Jeannette DUNCAN, and Robertson Davies, and with philosophers such as Charles TAYLOR and George GRANT. Leacock's hostility to the chaotic forces that he saw threatening human progress was reflected in his views on imperialism. Like many of the Canadian imperialists of his day (again Haliburton and Duncan come to mind), Leacock saw the British Empire, for all its failings, as a humane alternative, rooted in tradition and community, to the unfettered materialism of the American capitalist juggernaut—a kind of Mariposa writ large. To be sure, Leacock's imperialism often came out in unpleasant ways, as in his unyielding opposition to non-Anglo-Saxon immigration to Canada; but whatever the forms his world view sometimes took, it was deeply rooted in a genuine desire that the gradual progress of humanity not be brought to a halt.

Most readers of Leacock agree that his writing career shows little sign of development, either intellectual or artistic. He did, however, continue to produce excellent pieces, such as 'My remarkable uncle' (1942); and in his last years he wrote some fine essays, essentially serious but leavened with humour, among the best of which are the final chapter of *Humour: its theory and technique*, with its vision of the universe as a great cosmic joke, and two meditations on old age: 'When men retire' (1939), and 'Three score and ten—the business of growing old' (1942). Nonetheless there remains a sense of disappointment, of unfulfilled potential, in his career. It has been argued, notably by Robertson Davies, that, perhaps because of his impoverished and unstable childhood, Leacock craved the reassurance that fame and money brought, and that this led him to fall back uncritically on successful formulas. This is undoubtedly true; but another reason may be that the kindly view of an ever-progressing world that Leacock wished to maintain was at odds with his gift. Leacock's insistence that humour should be kindly is clearly wrong-headed when tested against the world's great humour, including his own, especially *Sunshine sketches* and *Arcadian adventures*, with their critique—implicit in the former and bitterly explicit in the latter—of 'money-getting in the city'. It is hard to see how Leacock could have continued in the far from kindly direction that seemed to lie ahead of him after *Arcadian adventures* if he were to maintain his faith in progress. His emphasis on the need for kindliness in humour seems, then, a rationalization

for his pulling back from the fullest implications of his essentially pessimistic vision of man in the modern industrial age. Ironically, it may have been Leacock's need to maintain his faith in the progress of humanity that thwarted his own progress as an artist and the fullest development of the gifts with which he was so generously endowed.

The letters of Stephen Leacock (2006), containing more than 800 letters, was selected and edited by David Staines with Barbara Nimmo (Leacock's niece and literary executor). See also Robertson Davies, *Stephen Leacock* (1970); Gerald Lynch, *Stephen Leacock: humour and humanity* (1988); and Albert MORITZ and Theresa Moritz, *Stephen Leacock: his remarkable life* (2001).

League of Canadian Poets, The. A non-profit arts service organization, the League is the national association of professional publishing and spoken-word poets in Canada. Its purpose is to enhance the status of poets and nurture a professional community to facilitate the teaching of Canadian poetry at all levels of education and to develop the audience for poetry by encouraging the publication, performance, and recognition of Canadian poetry nationally and internationally. As well as providing members and the public with many benefits and services, the League speaks for poets on many issues, including freedom of expression, Public Lending Rights, CanCopy, contract advice, and grievance. It is actively involved with other arts and literary organizations in discussion with government bodies on matters that affect writers. A bimonthly newsletter keeps members informed of both political and professional matters and provides a common voice for a collective response to important issues. Founded in 1966 by a group of five poets, the League now serves almost 600 members whose work reflects the regional and cultural diversity of this country.

Lee, Dennis (b. 1939). Born in Toronto, he attended the University of Toronto Schools and Victoria College, University of Toronto (B.A., 1962; M.A., 1965), where he taught for several years. He was a founder of the experimental Rochdale College, Toronto, and co-founder (with Dave GODFREY) of the House of ANANSI Press, of which he was editorial director (1967–72). After his association with Anansi ended, Lee embarked on a varied career, writing poems for children and song-lyrics for the television program *Fraggle Rock*, and serving as a literary consultant for

MCCLELLAND & STEWART (1981–4). He was Scottish-Canadian Exchange Fellow at the University of Edinburgh (1980–1). Lee has received honorary degrees from Trent University, Victoria University (2002), and the University of Toronto (2009); is an Officer of the Order of Canada (1993); and was the first poet laureate of Toronto (2001–4).

A central concern in Lee's critical work *Savage fields: an essay on literature and cosmology* (1977) is to define both the creative and critical acts as fundamentally religious in nature. In his first book of poems, *Kingdom of absence* (1967), he explores 'a cosmos gone askew' in a sequence of sonnets that abound in images of alienation, absence, loss, and disinheritance. He comes armed in his next book, *Civil elegies* (1968)—and in the revised and enlarged *Civil elegies and other poems* (1972, GGA; rpr. 1994)—with the pessimism of George GRANT's *Lament for a nation*, and with his own sense of disappointment and complicity in charting his country's 'failures of nerve and its sellouts'. The elegies expand beyond Canada to encompass the history of material interests, imperialism, and war. Lee's dialogue of self and soul continues through his next two works: *The death of Harold Ladoo* (1976), an elegy in which the poet examines the cultural and spiritual currents surrounding the death of his friend and fellow writer (q.v.) and declares that the notion of art as an absolute brings only 'redemptive lunacy' or 'bush league paranoia'; and *The gods* (1978), a meditation on life in the uncivil, technological space we inhabit, where, despite the absence of values and signposts, we should 'honour the gods in their former selves,/albeit obscurely, at a distance, unable/to speak the older tongue; and to wait/till their fury is spent and they call on us again/for passionate awe in our lives, and a clean high style.' These two long poems, and the earlier *Not abstract harmonies but* (1974), were revised and published together in *The gods* (1979). His later works include *Riffs* (1993), a Dantean-jazz mini-novel in verse, cast as an excursion from spiritual and erotic ecstasy to rejection and solitude; and *Nightwatch: new and selected poems 1968–1996* (1996). We are told in the blurb for *un* (2003) that 'Lee is exploring the catastrophic new reality we have made of our planet' but this is expressed in short poems in which diction and syllabification are themselves disintegrating. It begins 'In wreck, in dearth, in neckson,/godnexus gone to fat of the land,/into the wordy disyllabification of evil—small/crawlspace for plegics, 4, 3, 2, 1, un.' ('inwreck'—alluding to the term *inscape* coined by Gerard Manley

Hopkins?).This reader is oblivious of the erudition and subtlety that have been said to inform this collection. For the publisher, ANANSI, Don MCKAY edited the book and Robert BRINGHURST did the typography. Lee's *yesno* (2007) is dedicated to them. Lee has said about this collection—described as a companion volume to *un*—'to articulate a world in which the demolition derby and the possibility of living more constructively in the natural order are both real. And at once. So, not just no; not just yes; but yesno.' *Body music* (1998) is a collection of essays.

Lee became famous for his books of poetry for children: *Wiggle to the laundromat* (1970), *Alligator pie* (1974), *Nicholas Knock and other people* (1974), *Garbage delight* (1977), *The ordinary bath* (1979), *Jelly belly* (1983), *Lizzy's lion* (1984), *The ice cream store* (1991), *Ping and Pong* (1993), *Bubblegum delicious* (2000), and *The cat and the wizard* (2001), in which Toronto's Casa Loma figures prominently, and *SoCool* (2004). Tributes to Lee's talents as an editor and essays on his writing appear in *Task of passion: Dennis Lee at mid-career* (1982). See also Tom Middlebro, *Dennis Lee and his works* (1984).

Lee, SKY (b. 1950). Born in Port Alberni, British Columbia, she received a Fine Arts Degree from the University of British Columbia and worked as an artist on the feminist magazine *Makaral*. Her first novel, *Disappearing Moon Café* (1990), is a multigenerational saga that illuminates the dilemma of being Chinese in this century. Fifteen years in the writing, the novel describes a young Chinese woman investigating her past across five generations as it illuminates the history of the Chinese in Canada and the growth of Vancouver's Chinatown with both historical fact and elements of magic realism, and addresses, sometimes in a lecturing tone, issues of racism and cultural isolation. Her collection of four stories, *Bellydancer* (1994), is at once despairing and humorous. The stories describe a young woman who learns the art of belly dancing from an older woman; themes include how women are abused by men, but find love and healing in the company of women.

Lemelin, Roger (1919–92). Born in a working-class district of Quebec City, the eldest of ten children, he left school in eighth grade during the Depression—starting to work at fourteen, and reading and studying independently. Beginning in 1961 he was a full-time businessman, first in Quebec City, where he managed advertising, food-processing, and lumber firms, then in Montreal, where he was publisher and president of *La Presse*. Lemelin's first novel, *Au pied de la pente douce* (1944)—translated by Samuel Putnam as *The town below* (1948)—was a pioneer novel of the urban working class in Québec; its widely read translation provided English-speaking readers with their first insight into that milieu. His second novel, *Les Plouffe* (1948), translated by Mary Finch as *The Plouffe family* (1950), became the basis for a popular TV series on the French and English networks of the Canadian Broadcasting Corporation, beginning in 1952, the year Lemelin published *Pierre le magnifique*, translated by Harry Binsse as *In quest of splendour* (1955). The dominant theme of these three novels—all set in Quebec City and linked thematically and chronologically—is the stifling of ambition in the most gifted young people from the poor sections of the city who are frustrated in their desire to rise above their milieu (the passage upward is represented symbolically in the first two novels by the staircases and roads leading from Lower to Upper Town) and to secure a place in the prosperous secular world. The first novel treats the last years of the Depression; the second starts from that point and continues until the spring of 1945; and the third takes place between the summer of 1949 and the spring of 1950. The working-class family is dominated by the mother. The father—when he exists—is in the background, timid, crushed, passive, but often breaking out into fits of anger to compensate for his lack of authority. The 'couple'—as a sharing, consultative unit—is often the mother and the priest. A keen observer of French-Canadian life, Lemelin portrayed strains and conflicts between the poor and those who are somewhat better off, and sometimes between the poor and the wealthy. The suffering of the poor—who must work for well-to-do '*étrangers*'—is sometimes increased by their sense of cultural alienation, symbolized in the first two novels by allusions to a people without a flag.

A critic of the *ancien régime* and of the right-wing nationalism that held sway for so long in Québec, Lemelin castigated the narrowness and backwardness of the traditional rural parish transplanted into the city, and its spiritual leaders, the clergy. His social satire not only reflected the growing Americanization of Québec and the abrupt end of its isolationism with the advent of the Second World War, but announced the modern, secular, liberal era that was to come to fruition with the Quiet Revolution in the sixties. These three novels display verve, spontaneity, humour, and satire (sometimes diminished by Lemelin's penchant for melodrama). With

them Lemelin became, along with Ringuet (Philippe PANNETON) and Gabrielle ROY, an initiator of social realism in French-Canadian fiction. Lemelin wrote the scripts for the TV version of *Les Plouffe* and for the film (1981) directed by Gilles Carle. He was made a Companion of the Order of Canada in 1980.

Le Moyne, Jean (1913–96). Born in Montreal, he almost completed a classical education under the Jesuits at Collège Sainte-Marie, but the onset of deafness obliged him to interrupt his studies. With the encouragement of his father, a physician, who fostered in him an interest in Greek culture and the Bible, Le Moyne undertook to educate himself, including in his reading not only French, but English, Spanish, Russian, and American literatures. With the international perspective thus acquired, Le Moyne was not affected by the nationalism of his era. He learned from Henry James, however, to identify himself as a North American without forgetting his European heritage. In 1929 he became associated with a group of dynamic young intellectuals who were to influence the literary and intellectual life of Québec: Robert Charbonneau, Claude Hurtubise, Paul Beaulieu, and the man responsible for directing the evolution of French-Canadian poetry towards modernism, Hector de SAINT-DENYS-GARNEAU. With them, and with Robert Élie, he was active in founding, in 1934, the periodical *La Relève*. The articles by this group—and contributions by the French writers Maritain, Daniel-Rops, and Emmanuel Mounier—helped to free Québec from its clerical restraints and to open it to the outside world. Le Moyne published many pieces in *La Relève*; however, while his associates became increasingly interested in literature and social and political problems, he became more preoccupied with religious questions, though not to the exclusion of poetry and music. He joined the Canadian Broadcasting Corporation in 1951 and was managing editor of *La Revue moderne* from 1953 until 1959, when he became a writer and researcher for the National Film Board. In 1969 he joined the prime minister's office in Ottawa, where he remained until his retirement in 1978. In 1968 Le Moyne received the Molson Prize for his unique contribution to Canadian arts and letters. He was made an Officer of the Order of Canada in 1982, when he was appointed to the Senate of Canada, retiring in 1988. His *Convergences* (1961, GGA), a collection of essays that first appeared between

1941 and 1961, was one of the notable French-Canadian publications of its time. In a translation by Philip Stratford—with some essays deleted and replaced by others—it was published as *Convergence: essays from Quebec* (1966). It is remarkable not only for being a masterpiece of essay writing, but these writings were the contribution to the Quiet Revolution of a unique French Canadian: a penetrating thinker and polished literary stylist whose intellectual roots were international rather than provincial. The topics discussed include the author's early intellectual development, theology (a subject that permeates his writing), Saint-Denys-Garneau, Teilhard de Chardin, Rabelais, Pickwick, Henry James, and some great composers. But it is his aphoristic essays on aspects of French Canada—focusing on the role of religion and of women—that make the strongest impression. 'Our education', he wrote, 'was a long soak in the high water of clericalism.' Ecclesiastical authority, 'having once saved us from the peril of extinction ... kept up the habit but thereafter tended to save us from life.' A major preoccupation of Le Moyne was the problem of dualism—the relation between the spirit and the flesh—which implies 'a defective attitude toward matter and toward the flesh', engendering guilt, fear, alienation, and accounting for a morbid, neurotic strain in French Canada. 'Two signs suffice to identify this dualism: it ignores Easter and it hates women.' In the French-Canadian society of which he wrote, women were relegated to fulfilling the myth of the French-Canadian mother. 'We multiplied greatly through rejecting the flesh ... we deceived ourselves by entering into a union in which the wife was the mother.' These neuroses had two main effects on French-Canadian fiction over a long period, from Laure Conan (Félicité ANGERS) to Marie-Claire BLAIS, sister-novelists who 'share the same psychological heredity': true women were absent from it, and it had a common subtext: 'It is forbidden to love and be happy because—guess why—because it is a sin.' Such ideas, which ran counter to the current ideology, were those of a deeply religious man who criticized the Church from within; of a committed French Canadian who, dismissing nationalism as 'a kind of folklore', aspired to be a total man, while seeing for French Canada a destiny and culture of its own.

LePan, Douglas (1914–98). Douglas Valentine LePan was born in Toronto. After obtaining degrees from the universities of Toronto and Oxford, he served as instructor and tutor in English literature at Harvard University (1938–41), leaving to become personal adviser on army education to General McNaughton. From 1943 to 1945 he served as a gunner with the First Canadian Field Regiment in Italy. At the end of the war he entered the diplomatic service as first secretary on the staff of the High Commissioner's Office in London. It was during these years that he completed and published his first volume of poems, *The wounded prince* (1948). LePan remained with the Department of External Affairs until 1959, holding various appointments, including that of counsellor and later minister counsellor at the Canadian Embassy in Washington (1951–5) and assistant undersecretary of state for external affairs (1958–9). After five years as professor of English at Queen's University (1959–64), LePan served as principal of University College, University of Toronto (1964–70), and as University Professor (1970–9). He was appointed senior fellow of Massey College in 1970 and an Officer of the Order of Canada in 1998.

LePan's poetry, from *The wounded prince* to his last works, is notable for its formal purity and its immaculate ordering of sight, sound, and sense. In poems like 'A country without a mythology' and 'Canoe-trip' he makes us see Canada as an outsider might see it, and for the first time. But the insider with second-sight hints at the riddle of a hidden landscape of the mind, and we come to know our land as no outsider ever could. *The net and the sword* (1953, GGA) expresses the experience of transplanted Canadian men in a world of war and desolation in which young Canadian soldiers, homesick for their own distant landscape, aliens in a world they cannot fully comprehend, live and die, brave in their fears and with compassion in their bones. As no other Canadian has done, LePan in this book gave us in a mighty paradox the utter meaninglessness of war and the indestructible meaning of the intrinsically human. In *Something still to find* (1982) LePan continued his quest for meaning and order. There are poems of savage irony—like 'Hideout' and 'Crackup'—in which a world 'at peace' seems more terrible than the world at war in *The net and the sword*. There are sensitive, personal poems of loss and dissolution and poems of the land like 'The green man', which gives to this country its mythology and its meaning. Midway in this volume is a cluster of love poems that might have been the poems of a man in the summer of his life. They would reappear as prelude to

Far voyages (1990), poems addressed to a young man who in 1985 died agonizingly of cancer. *Weathering it: complete poems, 1948–1987* (1987) is prefaced by a set of fifty new poems (*Weathering it*) that serve as a kind of summing up, a valediction in which old, far-off things were not forgotten, and old triumphs and sorrows are recollected sometimes in tranquillity, sometimes in pain and dark foreboding. In *Far voyages* we are given the love story that had ended before the 'weathering' poems were written, and was announced in the puzzling cluster of poems in *Something still to find*. In what seems a second spring the poet exults in a burst of new energy, an exuberant lyricism shadowed at times by self-doubt and the awareness of his own mortality. When his lover is at last stricken, the poet 'goes down into dread' with him and comes to know the very taste of death. *Macalister, or Dying in the dark* (1995), a verse-drama based on what is known of the life and fate of John Kenneth Macalister, brings into play the author as poet, novelist, and dramatist. In an imaginative and experimental meta-realism LePan tells us of a young Canadian soldier who was parachuted behind enemy lines in France as a secret agent. With his comrade, Frank Pickersgill, Macalister is captured by the Nazis, tortured, and executed. The author who appears in the poem as questioner, double, and poet puts on the stage of our mind Macalister, his mother, his wife, and a military historian who gives a documentary dimension to the action. As he awaits certain death, Macalister wonders if his fate can be reconciled with any notion of faith, meaning, or purpose. Might he at least die in the light of the answers? Just before his obscene and lingering death on a meat-hook, he has a brief vision of the greenery of his home town and the church of his boyhood. But he dies in the dark, no answers given.

LePan's novel *The deserter* (1964, GGA) is a quest for a sustaining faith among the broken shards of values at war's end. Pursued by the military police and by gangs of criminals, haunted by the memory of a perfect moment of love (a paradise not to be regained), the protagonist Rusty is 'away without leave' and seemingly without hope. In this nightmare underworld of pursuit and flight, evidences of simple human courage and sacrifice bring Rusty at last to the realization, in a kind of epiphany, that the rock upon which he must build his faith and rest his hope is not made from a dream of the perfect but instead, as D.G. JONES puts it (in *Butterfly on rock*), from 'the love of persons' and 'of a perishing imperfect world'. *Bright glass of memory* (1979) is

LePan's recollection of some of the central moments in his career as a public servant. The novelist is at work here in vivid sketches of General McNaughton, Lord Keynes, and Vincent Massey; and we are aware of the poet in the insets and miniatures, and in the reflective moments of insights and self-scrutiny set down in quiet between the fusillades of politicians.

Leprohon, Rosanna (1829–79). Rosanna Eleanora Mullins was born in Montreal, where her Irish-born father was a prosperous merchant. She attended the Convent of the Congregation of Notre Dame and, encouraged to write by the nuns who educated her, she began publishing in *The* LITERARY GARLAND: under the initials R.E.M. two poems appeared in Nov. 1846, and a story, 'The stepmother', was serialized in the spring of 1847. As Rosanna Mullins she continued to contribute to the *Garland* until it ceased publication in 1851. In that year she married Jean-Baptiste-Lucain Leprohon, a medical doctor whose ancestors had come to New France in the eighteenth century. They lived in Montreal, except for a few years after their marriage, when they resided in Saint-Charles, Québec; they had thirteen children.

Leprohon's most significant novels appeared in the 1860s: 'The manor house of De Villerai: a tale of Canada under the French dominion', which was serialized in *The Family Herald* from 16 Nov. 1859 to 8 Feb. 1860; *Antoinette de Mirecourt; or Secret marrying and secret sorrowing: a Canadian tale* (Montreal, 1864, NCL; scholarly edition, 1989); and *Armand Durand; or, A promise fulfilled* (Montreal, 1868; rpr. and rev. 1994). Using conventional patterns of nineteenth-century fiction, each story focuses on aspects of French-Canadian society, with French Canadians as the chief characters. 'The manor house of De Villerai' is set in Canada in the years immediately preceding the Conquest, and *Antoinette de Mirecourt* in Canada shortly 'after the royal standard of England had replaced the fleurs-de-lys of France'. Both novels explore such themes as the psychological problems facing the 'old French' who stayed in 'their country' after 'it had passed under a foreign rule', and love between people of different national, religious, and social backgrounds. Using as her main plot the 'secret marriage' of Antoinette, a French Roman Catholic, to a Protestant English army officer, Leprohon developed these themes with some complexity. *Armand Durand*, set in the nineteenth century, traces what in many ways is a typical French-Canadian career: that of a bright young farmer's son who becomes a lawyer and then a politician. These works were well reviewed at the time of their first publication in both the English- and French-Canadian press, and a French translation of each was published. Leprohon has never been entirely forgotten, but since the 1970s there has been renewed interest in her works in both English and French Canada. The English and French versions of each of her three Canadian novels have been reproduced on microfiche by the Canadian Institute for Historical Microreproduction. A scholarly edition of *Antoinette de Mirecourt*, prepared by John C. Stockdale, was published by the CENTRE FOR EDITING EARLY CANADIAN TEXTS in 1989. An edition of *Armand Durand*, introduced by Lorraine McMullen and Elizabeth Waterston, appeared in 1994. Modern critics have pointed to Leprohon's gifts as a storyteller, her realistic portrayal of French-Canadian life and French-English relations, and her conservative but nevertheless feminist views on the education of women and on marriage as a partnership. She has also been recognized as one of the first English-Canadian writers to depict French Canada in a way that earned the praise of, and resulted in her novels being read by, both anglophone and francophone Canadians.

Leslie, Kenneth (1892–1974). Born in Pictou, Nova Scotia, he was educated at Dalhousie (B.A., 1912), Nebraska (M.A., 1914), and Harvard Universities, where he continued graduate studies in philosophy and mysticism. His marriage to Elizabeth Moir, daughter of the wealthy Halifax candy merchant, enabled him to pursue such literary interests as the Song Fishermen—a Nova Scotia literary group he formed with Charles G.D. ROBERTS, Bliss CARMAN, Charles BRUCE, and Robert NORWOOD. This period of his life saw the publication of *Windward rock* (1934), *Lowlands low* (1935), *Such a din!* (1936), and *By stubborn stars and other poems* (1938, GGA), his best collection of poems. As a crusading journalist, Leslie moved to New York, where he edited the radical *Protestant Digest* (later called *Protestant*) from 1938 to 1949. After Senator Joseph McCarthy and Bishop Fulton Sheen implicated him as a Communist (*Life* magazine included him with Charlie Chaplin, Albert Einstein, and Thomas Mann in a group of fifty suspected 'fellow travellers'), he returned to Halifax, where he continued to edit *Protestant* until 1953. As the editor of *Man and New man* from 1957 to 1972, he was subjected to RCMP surveillance. Leslie once cited Christ and the First Baptist Church as the sources for his commitment to social reform; such poems

as 'O'Malley to the Reds' (inspired by Father Moses Coady of the co-operative self-help Antigonish Movement) suggests his preference for Christian socialism motivated by love, over Marxist violence motivated by rhetoric.

Leslie's best poems are steeped in the imagery of the sea. In 'Cape Breton lullaby', for which he wrote a haunting melody, the lost lambs in a shepherd's pasture remind a mother of her husband spending the night at sea. 'Halibut cove harvest' is a lament for the heroic toil of fishermen who have been replaced by sea-raping trawlers. In 'By stubborn stars', a sonnet-sequence like George Meredith's 'Modern love', Leslie charts the course of a tempest-tost love affair. After a defiant vow to go his own way—'I sail by stubborn stars, let rocks take heed,/and should I sink … then sinking be my creed'—he grows to realize that he will find consolation only through song, by which he recognizes his personal experience as archetypal. Sean Haldane's curiously edited selection *The poems of Kenneth Leslie* (1971) led Leslie to make his own selection: *O'Malley to the Reds and other poems* (1972).

Levine, Norman (1923–2005). Born and brought up in Ottawa, he served in the RCAF during the Second World War and afterwards studied at McGill University (B.A, 1948; M.A., 1949). He served overseas in the RCAF (1942–5), went to England in the late 1940s, and lived there for most of the time in St Ives, Cornwall until his return to Toronto in 1980. Later he moved to France, and died in Darlington, England.

Levine's first two books were poetry collections: *Myssium* (1948) and *The tightrope walker* (1950), in which many of the poems are about the physical presence of St Ives. *I walk by the harbour* (1976) was mostly written in St Ives in 1949. His war novel, *The angled road* (1952), was small in size and scope, sensitive and personal—the story of the coming-of-age of David Wrixon, who is commissioned in the RCAF and has two youthful love affairs in England; the dramatic events of life in wartime usually take place offstage. The autobiographical *Canada made me* (1958) sets out to examine Canadian society from the underside as Levine observed life in Canada in the 1950s from a consistent if unfashionable point of view. 'I like the lower towns,' he wrote, 'the place across the tracks, the poorer streets not far from the river. They represent failure, and for me failure here has a strong appeal.' Setting out on his journey of rediscovery with very little money, he lived in cheap hotels and rooming houses, waiting anxiously for small cheques to reach him, eating in greasy spoons and drinking beer in barren beverage rooms. By the time his journey ended in Quebec City, both the book and its author seem to have been nearly overcome by exhaustion. Levine's portrait of the optimistic and often complacent society of Canada in the 1950s offended some Canadians. Though both English and American editions of *Canada made me* were published in 1958, only a few copies of the English edition were distributed in Canada. The first Canadian edition didn't appear until 1979, when his own country, in which profound changes had taken place, finally caught up with Levine; it was reissued by PORCUPINE'S QUILL in 1993.

In his fiction Levine was preoccupied with what he described as 'the precarious existence' of the wrote, with the abrasions and the loving closeness of marriage and family life, and the need to come to terms with the past. He wrote autobiographical fiction in the modern manner—examining the details and the repetitions of daily life in an often deliberately fragmentary prose. His novel *From a seaside town* (1970, rpr. 1993) is about Joseph Grand, who was born in Canada, served in the RCAF during the Second World War, and lives in England with a wife and children while he pursues a precarious career as a travel writer. Levine is best known for his short stories, published over thirty years in eight collections: *One way ticket* (1961), *I don't want to know anyone too well* (1972), *Selected stories* (1975), *Thin ice* (1979), *Champagne barn* (1984), *Something happened here* (1991), and *The ability to forget* (2003), in which the stories that have the most life seem to be autobiographical, set in St Ives, though they are impaired by an underlying flatness and inconsequentiality. See also *By a frozen river: the short stories of Norman Levine* (2000). His collections have been translated in The Netherlands, Switzerland, and Germany. In 2002 Levine received the Matt COHEN Award: In Celebration of a Writing Life.

Lighthall, William Douw (1857–1954). Although he was born in Hamilton, Ontario, Lighthall's career was closely associated with Montreal and the province of Québec. Educated at the Montreal High School and McGill University (B.A., 1879; B.C.L., 1881; M.A., 1885), he practised law in that city until 1944 and held offices in local historical and literary societies and on municipal commissions and military bodies. Mayor of

Westmount from 1900 to 1903, he helped to found the Union of Canadian Municipalities. As a productive author, he wrote three historical sketches of Montreal between 1898 and 1907, and two novels about French Canadians (1888, 1898) and another about Natives (1908). Lighthall was elected to the Royal Society of Canada in 1905 and became its president in 1918. He is remembered today as editor of the second major anthology of Canadian poetry (the first being that by Edward Hartley DEWART)—*Songs of the great Dominion: voices from the forests and waters, the settlements and cities of Canada* (London, 1889; rpr. 1971), which highlighted the new tone of national confidence. Including poets of the time who are still respected, and many others now forgotten, it enjoyed some success—affirming many of the humanistic ideals of late nineteenth-century Canada—and was reissued in a reduced form in 'The Canterbury poets' as *Canadian poems and lays: selections of native verse, reflecting the seasons, legends, and life of the Dominion* (London and New York, 1893).

Lill, Wendy (b. 1950). Born in Vancouver, she grew up in London, Ontario, and in 1971 graduated from York University, Toronto, with a degree in political science. In 1977 she moved to Kenora, Ontario, working as a consultant for the Canadian Mental Health Association, and then as a reporter for a Native newspaper and writing radio documentaries for the Canadian Broadcasting Corporation. Moved by what she learned and experienced, she committed herself to telling the stories 'that are already out there', to fictionalizing real incidents and events. In 1979 she moved to Winnipeg, where for four years she worked as a freelance broadcaster and journalist. She moved to Dartmouth, Nova Scotia in 1984 and became a Member of Parliament (NDP) for Dartmouth in the 1997 federal election, to be re-elected (2000–4).

Lill's first stage play, *On the line* (produced in 1982), is agitprop, a theatre piece dramatizing the exploitation of immigrant women in the Winnipeg garment industry. *The fighting days* (1985), spanning the years 1910 to 1917, tells the story of the idealistic Manitoba journalist Frances Beynon, who held some prominence in the suffragist movement until she broke with her famous colleague Nellie McCLUNG over the issues of pacifism and immigrants' rights. *The occupation of Heather Rose* (1987) is a monodrama that relates the psychic journey of a cheerfully naive and altruistic white nurse while on the Snake

Lake Reservation, and how the isolation, her alien sensibility, and her own irrelevance overwhelm her. Toronto's Tarragon Theatre produced a revised version in 1988. *Memories of you* (1989, rpr. 2003) focuses on the controversial life of the writer Elizabeth SMART, in which Smart is confronted by her enraged daughter, Rosie, who accuses her of having lived a vacuous and selfish life. Smart's own version of her romantic obsession with poet George Barker alternates with scenes in the present. A play based on the 1972 burning of a Shubenacadie residential school for Native children, *Sisters* (1991), presents the story through the memories of Sister Mary, a nun who admitted to committing arson. Lill has said: 'I wanted to tell the story from the other side.' Here, as in her earlier plays, she uses history and memory to allow the necessary distance that permits reflection, doubt, and revisionist thinking. *All fall down* (1994) dramatizes the escalation of hysteria that occurs when a daycare worker is charged with sexual abuse. The accused never appears on stage, but Lill's point is the damage such occurrences do to the entire community. *Corker* (1998) is 'all about making sure that there is a place in our communities for the mentally disabled', in Lill's words. *The Glace Bay Miners' Museum*, based on Sheldon Currie's novel, was produced at the Factory Theatre, Toronto, in Nov. 1999. *Chimera* (2007) has both a parliamentary and scientific background (the title alludes to the possible result of cross-species research) that focuses on efforts to regulate genetic engineering. The characters are a reporter, two MPs, the executive assistant of one of them, a much-admired elderly scientist, and a lawyer/lobbyist. Their discussions and disagreements are effectively portrayed. *Chimera* was first produced at the Tarragon Theatre, Toronto, in January 2007. Lill has won praise for her courageous exploration of the emotional truths that drive ideological positions, and for the political commitment at the heart of her work.

Lillard, Charles (1944–97). Born in Long Beach, California, he was educated at the University of Alaska and the University of British Columbia. He lived in dozens of locations in Alaska and B.C., working in the bush and on the water. His poems, essays, and numerous books about B.C. history were attempts to understand what he called the last frontier of the Pacific Northwest. As a poet, Lillard wrote out of a strong sense of place, combining regionalism and Native mythology, and a link with European classicism, so he was not a typical bush poet celebrating the lonely life of a man in the wilderness: his poems are neither romantic nor understated. Lillard's mature collections—*Drunk on wood* (1973), *Voice, my shaman* (1976), *Coastal sanctus* (1983), *A coastal range* (1984), and *An early morning fragment* (1993)—found a balance between Native mythology and the poetic lessons learned from classical European literature. His major long poem, *Jabble* (1976)—privately printed—was followed by other privately printed collections: *Poems (mythistoria-1)* (1979) and *Green weather country: dramatis personae* (1991). The imagery of his poems—which are often evocations of rugged landscape—includes rivers, logging trucks, ravens, and totems. Myths intersect with reality as he writes about the wildness of landscape, the wildness within men and women, and the wildness of mythology. Lillard's seventh collection, *Circling worth* (1988), won the fifth annual Dorothy LIVESAY Poetry Prize. *Shadow weather: poems new and selected* (1996) contains powerful evocations of the wilderness—especially in poems such as 'Petroglyph at tidemark', 'Encounter, Waldron Island', and 'Closing down Kah Shakes Creek'. A serious West Coast historian, Lillard also wrote *Warriors of the north Pacific* (1984), *Seven shillings a year: the history of Vancouver Island* (1986), *The ghostland people: early explorations of the Queen Charlotte Islands* (1989), and *Just east of sundown: the Queen Charlotte Islands* (1995).

Literary Garland, The (1838–51). This monthly magazine was begun in Dec. 1838 by Montreal publisher John Lovell—an Irishman who came to Canada in 1820 and later made a reputation as a publisher of directories, school texts, and gazetteers—and his brother-in-law, John Gibson, who served initially as editor and after 1842 as co-publisher. For its time the *Garland* was the leading literary journal in British North America, and had the longest lifespan. Taking seriously James Holmes' assertion that 'the literature of a country is the *measure* of its progress towards refinement' (Aug. 1840), it set about providing, in the early numbers, a mix of poetry, book reviews, essays, prose, fiction, news of the arts, jokes, anecdotes, helpful household hints ('make your own catsup'), and music scores designed to appeal to a wide range of readers. Eventually the *Garland*'s pages were filled with essays on linguistics, dramatic sketches (often with a biblical setting), poems of Victorian gift-book calibre, and a plethora of formulaic romantic-historic fiction—material that appealed only to a small coterie of readers and contributors who saw themselves as upholders and promoters of a genteel tradition. Parts of John RICHARDSON's *The Canadian brothers* appeared in the *Garland* (1839); Rosanna Mullins LEPROHON contributed poetry and prose from an early age; and Charles SANGSTER contributed poems. But apparently few Canadian writers could produce what the *Garland* thought to be worthy of publication: too rarely did such material as Susanna MOODIE's five sketches—published in 1847 (Jan., Mar., June, Aug., Oct.), and later to reappear in ROUGHING IT IN THE BUSH—find its way there. Many of its writers, not surprisingly, had cultural allegiances and values that were located elsewhere, and they were not interested in making the *Garland* a vehicle of Canadian literary expression, which was one of its declared aims. There was, finally, little to distinguish the *Garland* from its American competitors. With John Gibson's death in the fall of 1850, it lost its chief moving force. There were simply not enough subscribers who shared, and were willing to pay for, the cultural values evidenced by the *Garland's* principal contributors, and the financial problems became too daunting. With no. 12 of vol. IX (Dec. 1851) it succumbed to the indifference of those for whom it was to have been a voice, and to foreign competition—a pattern that was to be repeated again and again in Canadian periodical publishing.

Little, Jean (b. 1932). Born in Taiwan to parents who were both Canadian medical doctors serving as missionaries for the United Church, she returned to Canada shortly before the Second World War erupted. Almost blind since birth, Little was educated in Guelph, Ontario, and at Victoria College, University of Toronto, receiving an Honours B.A. in English (1955). After training as a 'Special Education' teacher in the USA, she combined teaching and writing until royalties made full-time writing possible. She has lectured widely in the USA, the UK, and across Canada, usually accompanied by a Labrador guide dog—first Zephyr and then Ritz, both essential elements of her public persona. She was made a Member of the Order of Canada in 1992 and lives in Elora, Ont. By 1998 Little had published eleven novels, two books of autobiography and two of historical fiction, two books of poetry, and numerous picture books. Her publications, grounded in the emotional and psychological lives of children, explore both self-defeating and successful ways of coping with threatening events. Little's novels include *Mine for keeps* (1962, rpr. 1994), *Home from far* (1965), *Take wing* (1968), *One to grow on* (1969, rpr. 1991), *Listen for the singing* (1977, rpr. 1989), and *Mama's going to buy you a mockingbird* (1984). Her autobiographies are *Little by Little* (1987) and *Stars come out within* (1990); the two books of historical fiction are *His banner over me* (1995, rpr. 1996), based on her mother's life as a daughter of foreign missionaries, and *The belonging place* (1997), based partly on her own Scottish ancestors. Several short novels and picture books include *Lost and found* (1986), *Different dragons* (1986), *Emma's magic winter* (1998), and *What will the robin do then?* (1998). The thirteen books she has published since 1998 include *Somebody else's summer* (2005), about Samantha and Alexis, who meet on a flight from Vancouver to Toronto and decide that they want to trade places for the summer, exchanging each other's job; *Forward, Shakespeare* (2005)—Shakespeare is a seeing-eye pup; and *Dancing through snow* (2007), about Min Randall who, without any family background, has been subjected to four foster homes. Little's books, which have won many awards, have been translated into French, German, Danish, Dutch, Japanese, Greek, Welsh, and Norwegian, and are available in Braille.

Livesay, Dorothy (1909–96). Born in Winnipeg, she came to Toronto in 1920 when her father, J.F.B. Livesay, became manager of the Canadian Press. She attended Glen Mawr private school for girls, where she met women teachers who—together with her father—encouraged her to consider questions of atheism and socialism. Influenced by Shaw, Ibsen, and Emma Goldman, whose lecture series in Toronto she attended early in 1926, she enrolled in the fall of that year in French and Italian at Trinity College, University of Toronto, where her evolving ideas about socialism and women's rights led her to study privately Emily Dickinson, H.D., Katharine Mansfield, and the sociological writings of Friedrich Engels. When only eighteen she published her first poetry collection, *Green pitcher* (1928), which Livesay later criticized for not dealing openly with social issues. Nevertheless these were well-crafted poems that showed skilled use of the imagist technique. On graduation (B.A., 1931) Livesay went to Paris to study at the Sorbonne (Diplôme d'études supérieures, 1932). Deeply moved by the poverty and violence created by the Depression, she returned in 1932 to the

University of Toronto, where she entered the School of Social Work and shortly after joined the Communist Party. But her second book, *Signpost* (1932), reflected few of these interests; rather it showed the increasing sophistication of her imagist skills, as in 'Green rain', and an original sense of feminine sexuality. As is now well documented in her retrospective collection of essays, poems, letters, and reminiscences, *Right hand left hand* (1977), Livesay spent the thirties organizing for the Party; employed as a social worker in Montreal, in Englewood, New Jersey, and in Vancouver; writing for the Marxist news magazine *New Frontier*; and learning from Auden, Spender, and C. Day Lewis how to marry political ideas to poetic craftsmanship. Although Livesay's powerful poems from this period, focusing on Depression conditions and the Spanish Civil War, did not see book publication until *Selected poems* (1957) and *Collected poems: the two seasons* (1972), they appeared throughout the thirties in periodicals. In the 1940s Livesay continued to publish overtly political poetry: *Day and night* (1944, GGA), concerning workers' contributions to wartime industry; *Poems for people* (1947, GGA); and *Call my people home and other poems* (1950)—the title verse-play for radio dramatizes the persecution of Japanese-Canadians during the Second World War. Most of this work was marred by unconvincing dramatic voices and simplistic political diction.

After an extended residence in Vancouver, where she married Duncan Macnair and raised two children, Livesay travelled to Zambia, where she taught English for UNESCO from 1960 to 1963. Stimulated by the rapidly evolving Vancouver poetry scene and by her study of linguistics while earning an M.Ed. (1966) from the University of British Columbia, Livesay began writing a new kind of poetry, concrete and phenomenological in style, and in content centring on womanhood and physical love. These changes resulted in her two finest books: *The unquiet bed* (1967) and *Plainsongs* (1969). A new concern to give voice to vigorous old age appeared in *Ice age* (1975) and *The woman I am* (1977; rev. 1991; rpr. 2000). Livesay's other poetry collections include the long-poem collection *The documentaries* (1968), *Plainsongs extended* (1971), *Nine poems of farewell* (1973), *The raw edges: voices from our time* (1981), *Phases of love* (1983), *Feeling the worlds* (1984), and *The self-completing tree: selected poems* (1986). *Archive for our times: the previously uncollected and unpublished poems of Dorothy Livesay* (1998), edited by Dean J. Irvine, was published posthumously. Prose

writings include *A Winnipeg childhood* (1973), fictionalized reminiscences expanded in *Beginnings* (1988), and *The husband: a novella* (1990). Livesay was appointed an Officer of the Order of Canada in 1986.

See *Journey with my selves: a memoir 1909–1963* (1991) and Lee Briscoe Thompson, *Dorothy Livesay* (1987).

Lochhead, Douglas (1922–2011). He was born in Guelph, Ontario, and raised for the most part in Ottawa, where his father was Dominion Agricultural Bacteriologist. Through his New Brunswick mother, Lochhead's childhood was also shaped by the experience of Canadian Maritime rural life. He received a B.A. (1943) and a B.L.S. (1951) from McGill University and an M.A. (1947) from the University of Toronto. Between 1943 and 1945 he served in the Canadian army, achieving the rank of lieutenant. His marriage in 1949 to the late Jean St Clair of Sydney, Nova Scotia, further deepened and extended Lochhead's personal and imaginative associations with the Maritimes. He was Librarian at Victoria College, British Columbia (1951); Cornell University (1952–3); Dalhousie University, Halifax (1953–60); York University, Toronto (1960–63); and Massey College (1963–75), University of Toronto, where he was Founding Librarian and Professor of English at University College. From 1975 until 1987, when he retired and became Professor Emeritus, Lochhead was Davidson Professor of Canadian Studies and Director of the Centre for Canadian Studies at Mount Allison University, Sackville, New Brunswick.

Lochhead has written many books of poetry. *The full furnace: collected poems* (1975) and *Tiger in the skull: new and selected poems: 1959–1985* (1986) offer similar and representative selections of Lochhead's first poems, followed by differing selections of his later, steadily maturing work. In *Millwood Road poems* (1970), whose contents are fully reprinted in the collected volume of 1975, Lochhead found the voice of his early maturity. Set in his Toronto home of the 1960s and 1970s, on Millwood Road, his poems here are understated, gentle, frequently comic vignettes of domestic life, animated by the unpredictable presences of two very young daughters and assorted suburban flora and fauna. Lochhead's move to Sackville in 1975 and the self-renewal he experienced in its surroundings helped to impel the prolific poetic activity that followed. A close friendship with the poet John THOMPSON also had an immediate effect on his work. Thompson's attritional dedication to poetry, the circumstances of his death, and the stylistic example of his posthumously published poetry collection, *Stilt Jack* (1978)—a typescript copy of which Thompson entrusted to Lochhead to ensure its survival—all left their mark on Lochhead's *High Marsh Road* (1980, rpr. 1996), a series of prose poem journal entries, whose setting is the Tantramar Marshes, that reveal the writer deeply conscious of personal loss, missed opportunities for love, self-betrayal, and guilt. Written in free-verse tercets, *A & E* (1980) is a six-part monologue delivered by 'A' to his wife 'E'—the subject is love and its evanescent revelation in the natural order of the cosmos. *Battle sequence* (1980), a chapbook, is by contrast a collection of eight semi–prose poems, voiced by a poetic persona more bitter and despairing than the one in *High Marsh Road*. This voice speaks also in many prose poems in *The panic field* (1984), particularly in the book's title sequence, which is a meditation on Lochhead's wartime experiences, and in 'In a winter apartment', where the protagonist tries and fails to recover the kind of balance *A & E* enacts. *Upper Cape poems* (1989) is a reflective and miscellaneous collection that is notable for the elegy 'John Thompson' and for a lyrical sequence 'Words in winter—six poems'. The elaborate *Dykelands* (1989) contains a sequence of twenty-six poems written to accompany photographs by the landscape photographer Thaddeus Holownia. The poems, written in free-verse couplets, succinctly celebrate the immense openness and layered natural and human history of the Tantramar Marshes. The privately printed *Black festival: a long poem* (1991) is a fifty-three part elegy for Lochhead's wife. Few of its lines are more than three words and few of its stanzas are longer than six lines—its diction is of the utmost simplicity. In the late 1980s Lochhead worked on a sequence of prose poems devoted to the Nova Scotia Baptist preacher and visionary, Henry Alline (1748–84). *Homage to Henry Alline & other poems* (1992) contains not only the thirty-part main title sequence but also a related work of equal complexity, 'Vigils & mercies 1–30'. The sequence 'Homage to Henry Alline', while taking into account the ambiguities and limitations of its protagonist, including the unintentional comedy of some situations Alline himself contrived, presents Alline as a Blakean force of positive energy and imagination. In the sequence 'Vigils & mercies' Lochhead drops the mask of Alline, depicting himself overtly as a pilgrim undergoing an explicitly Dantean journey in which he is his 'own Virgil', finding and feeling his way into the balanced

cosmos improvisationally. Although *Breakfast at Mel's and other poems of love and places* (1997) contains several sequences that are as concerned with baffled relationships as the ones depicted in 'In a winter apartment' and in parts of *High Marsh Road*, its dominant tone is celebratory. *All things do continue: poems of celebration* was published in the same year. The title *Midgic: a place, a poem* (2003)—a small book of short poems handsomely produced by Gaspereau Press in Kentville, Nova Scotia—is of Mi'kmaq origin, the name of a village 'on the edge of the great Tantramar Marsh not far from the sea', Lochhead says in a prefatory note, which begins: 'This is a love story.'—'a day of sun/Midgic melts/into itself//wetlands/with new waters/the slow green/beginning'.

Lodge, Rupert C. (1886–1961). Born in Manchester, England (a nephew of Sir Oliver Lodge, the physicist and spiritualist), Rupert Clendon Lodge came to North America in 1914 and taught at the University of Minnesota and the University of Alberta, before moving in 1920 to the University of Manitoba, where he remained (apart from a year as visiting professor at Harvard, and other occasional absences) until he retired in 1947. Later he taught at Queen's University, Kingston, Ontario, and at Long Island University, New York. He died in St Petersburg, Florida.

Probably the most widely read philosopher to work in Canada, Lodge played an important role in the development of pluralist ideas, in bringing philosophy to the Canadian West, and in the development of the 'philosophical federalism' that characterized Canadian thought in the inter-war years. His *Introduction to modern logic* (1920) shows the influence of the British idealists. Thereafter he pursued his own ideas, maintaining that philosophy was irreducibly pluralistic, and that every philosophical question could be answered from the viewpoint of a realist, an idealist, and a pragmatist: one may view the world either as a collection of objects that is simply 'there', as a system of experiences, or as something whose nature cannot be objectively defined but can be used in the furtherance of one's goals. His books—beginning with *The questioning mind* (1937) and *The philosophy of education* (1937)—develop this theme across a wide range of philosophical issues. *The philosophy of business* (1945) applies this trichotomy to practical life and to the theory of business, and *Applying philosophy* (1951) extends the thesis to other workaday domains. Lodge wrote with great clarity and simplicity and conveyed ideas to a wide audience; his books achieved a popularity that is rare in modern books in philosophy. *The philosophy of education* was widely consulted in colleges and faculties of education, especially in the United States. *The great thinkers* (1949), in which Lodge discussed the major philosophers from the past in an easy-going style almost wholly without technical jargon (though with a good deal of scholarly acumen), continues to be widely read. It illustrates Lodge's thesis that philosophy is a continuing enterprise whose past actively influences its present. This belief was widely criticized (especially by G.S. BRETT), but Lodge defended it with skill and persistence.

Lonergan, Bernard, J.F. (1904–84). Born in Buckingham, Québec, he taught at Jesuit seminaries in Montreal and Toronto, at the Gregorian University, Rome (1953–65), Harvard University (1971–2), and Boston College (1975–83). He is thought by some enthusiasts to be among the greatest philosophers of the twentieth century: the Lonergan Research Institute at Regis College, Toronto, is one of many such institutions throughout the world that study his work. Lonergan had a lifelong ambition to provide an up-to-date and comprehensively critical method for Catholic theology that culminated in *Method in theology* (1971). In *Insight: a study of human understanding* (1957, 2nd edn 1992), he prepared the way with a study of the mind when it attains moments of understanding in mathematics, natural science, the realm of common sense, psychotherapy, political theory, epistemology, metaphysics, hermeneutics, ethics, and natural theology. This study had been preceded by two sets of articles on the work of Thomas Aquinas, one concerned with his theory of grace, the other with his notion of the 'inner word' as applicable both to human psychology and to Trinitarian theory. (Both were later published in book form as *Grace and freedom*, 1971 and *Verbum, word and idea in Aquinas*, 1967, rpr. 1997.) Lonergan considered the experience of seeing into the nature of things as the ultimate experience of God, understood as an intelligent will underlying world process. Four basic types of activity are involved in human knowing and doing, described in his later writings as 'four transcendental precepts': 'Be attentive, be intelligent, be reasonable, be responsible.' The foundation of his thought is thought itself: we get at the truth about things by applying our minds correctly. 'This man does not think, therefore this man is not to be listened to.' The

intellect is superior to the will (Thomas Aquinas) and God is the source of understanding: it is reasonable to believe that God exists in order fully to explain our universe, divine intelligence accounting for its intelligibility, divine will for its having the particular kind of intelligibility that science progressively finds it to have. It is to be admitted, too, that God is revealed more or less directly in other religions, and is active in the hearts of all those who love truth and justice, whether acknowledged explicitly or not.

See F.E. Crowe, *Lonergan* (1992); H.A. Meynell, *An introduction to the philosophy of Bernard Lonergan* (2nd edn 1992); *The Lonergan reader* (1996) edited by Mark D. Morelli and Elizabeth A. Morelli; and the multi-volume *Collected works of Bernard Lonergan*, published for the Lonergan Research Institute of Regis College, Toronto, by the UNIVERSITY OF TORONTO PRESS.

Longfellow, Henry Wadsworth. See *EVANGELINE: a tale of Acadie*.

Longmore, George (1793–1867). Born in Quebec City, the son of a British army doctor stationed there, he spent part of his youth in Québec before he was commissioned ensign in the Royal Staff Corps, a military engineering unit, at Hythe, England, in 1809. He served in the Peninsular War and in 1820 was posted to Montreal, where he was engaged in supervising construction of the Lachine Canal, and the Grenville Canal on the Ottawa River. He returned to England in 1824 and never again resided in his native land, although a younger brother settled, and both his parents died, in Canada. Before going on half-pay with the rank of major in 1832, he had been acting surveyor-general of Mauritius for three years. In 1834 he received an appointment in Cape Colony, where he was appointed to various official positions and published many uncollected poems and stories in periodicals, in addition to seven volumes of poetry. While he was in Montreal, Longmore published *The charivari; or Canadian poetics: a tale after the manner of Beppo* (Montreal, 1824), by 'Launcelot Longstaff'. A humorous poem in 179 *ottava rima* stanzas, it is modelled on Byron's *Beppo* (1818) and tells of the courtship and marriage-day of an old bachelor, Baptisto, and the young widow of his choice, Annette. The protagonists were said, at the time, to be well-known Montreal residents, and the work itself comments satirically on many aspects of Montreal life. A charivari—in its earliest form the noisy serenading of a newly married couple on their wedding night—had become in Montreal the means by which mobs, not always good-humoured, extorted funds for drink or charity from well-to-do bridegrooms. During a riotous charivari in 1823 a passerby had been shot, a house destroyed, and participants on both sides were forced to flee the country. There were public demands that charivaris be outlawed. Longmore's portrayal of a charivari with a happy ending was intended to suggest that the custom was an innocent one that did not necessarily lead to riot and destruction. (Before Longmore's identity as the author was established, an attribution of the work to Levi ADAMS was long accepted.) Another work of Canadian interest by Longmore is 'Tecumthé', which appeared in *The Canadian Review and Literary and Historical Journal* (Dec. 1824). An account of the great chief's life and death, and of the early years of the War of 1812, 'Tecumthé' focuses principally on its hero and his life—unlike John RICHARDSON's *Tecumseh*, published four years later, in which the events of the war have as much prominence as the life of Tecumseh. It was included in the anonymous *Tales of chivalry and romance* (Edinburgh and London, 1826), along with other long and short poems, many of which had been published in Montreal periodicals. Longmore, who also published other works, was at his best when writing about people, places, and events of which he had first-hand knowledge, sometimes showing flashes of wit. He was an amateur versifier, but an unusually competent one: rough metre or awkward rhymes are rare in his poetry. The Canadian Poetry Press at the University of Western Ontario has published modern annotated editions of *The charivari* (1991), edited by D.M.R. Bentley, and *Tecumthé* (1993), edited by Mary Lu MacDonald.

Loved and the lost, The (1951, rpr. 1994). One of Morley CALLAGHAN's most successful novels, *The loved and the lost* is set in downtown Montreal: the Ritz.Carlton Hotel, the Montreal Forum where the Canadiens play, the night clubs and restaurants of the inner city, and the grand residences of upper Westmount. Jim McAlpine, an ambitious former university professor who is hoping to become a political columnist on the Montreal *Sun*, has come to the city at the invitation of the newspaper's publisher Joseph Carver. He is attracted to Carver's wealth and power and by his daughter Catherine. But he also becomes involved with another woman, Peggy Sanderson, who has dropped out of middle-class society (long

before that became a lifestyle) and spends much of her time in the city's small black community. Trying at one point to explain herself to McAlpine, Peggy says that 'all kinds of people walk in on me.' Finally the wrong person walks in and she is brutally murdered. McAlpine's involvement with her destroys his prospects at the *Sun*, but he has already been destroyed by her death, and by his conviction that he has betrayed her by not being constant. Admired and enjoyed for its elements of an urban thriller, for its affecting love story and the subtle exploration of Peggy Sanderson, *The loved and the lost* won a Governor General's Award, and a paperback edition sold half a million copies in Canada and the United States. It was in large part because of reading this book that the American critic Edmund Wilson described Callaghan in *The New Yorker* as 'perhaps the most unjustly neglected novelist in the English-speaking world ... a writer whose work may be mentioned without absurdity in association with Chekhov's and Turgenev's.'

Lowry, Malcolm (1909–57). He was born in Birkenhead, England, where his father was a wealthy cotton broker. His inclination to escape the business life his family assumed he would follow was first expressed actively when, in 1928, Lowry signed on as a cabin-boy on a freighter bound for the China coast, an experience whose more harrowing aspects found a place in his first novel, *Ultramarine* (1933); however, it did not prevent him from sailing two years later as deckhand on a ship bound for Oslo, where he sought out the Norwegian writer Nordahl Grieg, whose novel *The ship sails on* (1927) greatly influenced Lowry's early work. Already Lowry's growing enthusiasm for literature had led him into a correspondence with the American poet and novelist Conrad Aiken, who took him as a paying guest in the summer of 1929 and whose *Blue voyage* (1927) impressed Lowry and finds an echo in *Ultramarine*. In the autumn of 1929 Lowry entered St Catherine's College, Cambridge, graduating in 1932; but his encounters with Aiken, Grieg, and with younger writers he met at Cambridge contributed far more to his literary persona than did his academic studies. At Cambridge, Lowry began seriously to write. *Ultramarine* was completed in 1932; rewritten after the manuscript had been stolen from the car of a publisher's reader, it finally appeared in 1933. This was the unusual beginning of a strange literary career that was marked by intense industry and little apparent production. Lowry published only two books during his lifetime: *Ultramarine* (which he later rejected as immature) and *Under the volcano* (1947, rpr. 1994). But his scanty publication was due mainly to an obsessional inability to complete to his own satisfaction any work longer than a short story. During the years following the completion of *Under the volcano* in 1945, he worked on a whole cycle of novels, of which it would form part: this was to be entitled *The voyage that never ends*. Two of the novels intended for inclusion in this cycle—*Dark as the grave wherein my friend is laid* and *October ferry to Gabriola*—were published posthumously, in 1968 and 1988 respectively; but in neither case was the final form Lowry's own, for the editors (Margerie Lowry, his wife, and Douglas Day in the first case, and Margerie Lowry in the second) had to deal with chaotic manuscripts offering alternative versions of many passages. *The voyage that never ends: fictions, poems, fragments, letters* (2007), edited with an introduction by Michael Hofmann, is a kind of self-portrait that has been described as 'magnificent'; it includes fragments from the unfinished novels Lowry worked on during the last ten years of his life. Other works by Lowry published after his death are *Lunar caustic* (1963), a novella; *Hear us O Lord from heaven Thy dwelling place* (1961; rpr. 1987; rpr. 2009 edited by Nicholas Bradley), a collection of short stories; *Selected poems* (1962), edited by Lowry's friend Earle BIRNEY; *Selected letters* (1965), edited by Harvey Breit and Margerie Lowry; and *Psalms and songs* (1975), edited by Margerie Lowry, a miscellany bringing together some early and late stories, most of them previously uncollected, with a few recollections by friends and acquaintances. *La mordida* (1996), a scholarly edition prepared by Patrick A. McCarthy, was meant to be part of *The voyage that never ends* cycle. In these works one can trace Lowry's physical journey through life, shadowed by alcoholism and paranoia, and an inner journey marked by spiritual hopes and terrors. His life, between leaving Cambridge and his death twenty-five years later, falls into three periods. First was the time of wandering, in Spain and France, Mexico, and the United States. During this period he married his first wife, Jan Gabrial, in 1933; went to Hollywood in 1935; and in 1936 travelled to Mexico, which made a profound and morbid impression on him and inspired *Under the volcano*, the first draft of which he completed in 1937. In 1938—his first marriage having foundered—he left Mexico for the United States and in 1939 reached Canada, where he married Margerie

Bonner in 1940 and lived until 1954, mainly in a beach shack at Dollarton. The profound impression his Canadian years made on him is shown not only in the stories contained in *Hear us O Lord*, but also in *October ferry to Gabriola*. There were interludes spent in Oakville and Niagara-on-the-Lake, Ontario, and again in Mexico (a disastrous second journey that was the basis of *La mordida*) and in Haiti, before he left Canada in 1954. He died—apparently of a combined overdose of alcohol and barbiturates—at Ripe, Sussex, in the summer of 1957. The coroner's verdict was 'Death by misadventure'.

Under the volcano has often been treated as Lowry's only successful work; it is without doubt his best. In this story of the murder of an alcoholic British consul, the human drama is integrated in a closely knit formal and metaphorical structure, and the sinister aspects of Mexico are used admirably to symbolize the metaphysical overtones; the strong autobiographical element is admirably subsumed in the fiction. In none of the other novels is the structural integration so complete. The facts and preoccupations of Lowry's life are insistently obvious in all, though *October ferry to Gabriola* presents a deeply moving, if imperfect, counterpart to *Under the volcano* and represents Lowry's Paradiso as compared with his Inferno. Lowry was also a considerable poet. See *The collected poetry of Malcolm Lowry* (1991) edited by Kathleen Scherf. See also Douglas Day, *A biography of Malcolm Lowry* (1973); Sheryl Salloum, *Malcolm Lowry: Vancouver days* (1987); and Gordon Bowker, *Pursued by furies: a life of Malcolm Lowry* (1993). See in addition *The collected poetry of Malcolm Lowry* (1992) edited by K.D. Scherf and C.J. Ackerley; *Sursum corda! the collected letters of Malcolm Lowry* (2 vols, 1995, 1996) edited by Sherill E. Grace; and *Inside the volcano: my life with Malcolm Lowry* (2000) by Jan Gabriel. See also Sherrill Grace, *Strange comfort: essays on the work of Malcolm Lowry* (2009).

Lowther, Pat (1935–75). Born in Vancouver, Patricia Tinmuth came from a working-class background. She left school at sixteen and took office jobs to support her writing. At eighteen she married Bill Domphousse, a fellow worker at the North Vancouver Shipbuilding Company, with whom she had a daughter and son. They were divorced, and in 1963 she married Roy Lowther; they had two daughters. Roy was a public-school teacher and activist who was eventually dismissed for his radical politics. Before her untimely death, Pat Lowther had been elected president of

The LEAGUE OF CANADIAN POETS and was teaching creative writing at the University of British Columbia. In 1977 her husband was convicted of her murder (he died in prison in 1985).

Pat Lowther published three books of poetry in her lifetime: *This difficult flowering* (1968), *The age of the bird* (1972), and *Milk stone* (1974). *A stone diary* (1977) was accepted for publication by Oxford University Press Canada before she died and was published posthumously. *Time capsule: new and selected poems* (1996)—with two Introductions, by her daughters Beth Lowther and Christine Lowther respectively—contains poems from these books; four early poems from *Final Instructions*, published in 1980 in an issue of *West Coast Review*; and a final section of poems found by Beth Lowther in parts of a manuscript her mother was writing at the time of her death, and that was mentioned in a cassette recording in which she named several poems in the manuscript as part of a conceptual work called *Time Capsule,* which she 'envisioned as a complex kind of witness ... that starts off as a physical description of human beings ... and eventually gets into things like history, context, and continuity.'

The poems in *This difficult flowering* explore varieties of female experience, and include convincing poems about motherhood—the body occupied by new life as the mind is by the poem. They try to make sense out of the pain, and normalcy, of private domestic life. Deeply influenced by the Chilean poet Pablo Neruda, Lowther had a political motive: the poems search for a new celebratory attitude to the body, to oppose the chameleon-like conformity that defines modern social life. Their directive cry is 'Be human'. In her later books Lowther discovered her enduring obsessions: life juxtaposed with the natural cycle; atavistic relations between man and woman as primitive giants trapped in the 'Janus-pain' of love. West-coast Native mythology provided metaphors for her themes; animals become spirit symbols of an elemental liberty that is destroyed by domestic rituals. *A stone diary* contains Lowther's best work. Here the poems have the directness and authority of an assured and sophisticated voice; they are simpler in style, and more anecdotal and personal. Their controlling metaphor is the quest for a symbiotic relationship with the landscape, where psyche and landscape engage in a fluid interchange as the poet aligns herself with nature's resistance to the encroachments of technology and mechanism. A sequence dedicated to the

memory of Pablo Neruda identifies Lowther's need to assert the poet's political voice. The poems are also preoccupied with pain and violence, and inevitably have a prophetic, elegiac tone: 'Love is an intersection / where I have chosen / unwittingly to die.' Although silenced prematurely, Lowther achieved in this book a range and depth that will give her work a permanent place in Canadian poetry. See Toby Brooks, *Pat Lowther's continent: her life and work* (2000). See also Keith Harrison's *Furry Creek* (1999), which he calls a 'non-fiction novel', mainly about Lowther's death. It incorporates fictional chapters, with echoes of Lowther's life, about people connected with the discovery of her body in Furry Creek and about a lover, alternating with poems by Lowther, and includes testimony from trial transcripts. Harrison provides at the end of the book his (previously published) 'Notes' on Lowther's poem 'Notes from Furry Creek', which appears in *A stone diary*. *The collected poems of Pat Lowther,* edited by Christine Wiesenthal, was published in 2010.

Ludwig, Jack (b. 1922). A native of Winnipeg, he graduated from the University of Manitoba in 1944 and moved to California to pursue a career as a writer. He later took a Ph.D. in English at UCLA (1953) and taught at Williams College (Mass.), Bard College (N.Y.), the University of Minnesota, and the State University of New York at Stony Brook. (While at Bard he co-founded, with colleagues Saul Bellow and Keith Botsford, the little magazine *The Noble Savage.*) Ludwig first attracted attention as a writer in 1959, with his brilliant story 'A woman of her age' in *The TAMARACK REVIEW* 12, an affecting portrait of Doba Goffman, a wealthy old woman in the Montreal Jewish community. In his first two novels he brought a ribald tall-tale quality to the mordant, self-ironizing tradition of social satire also visible in work of such Jewish contemporaries as Bellow, Philip Roth, and Mordecai RICHLER. The first of these, *Confusions* (1967), is a comedy of manners and academic satire that details the confusion and cultural dislocation of an American Jew who tries to master the 'Ivy League mythology' of Harvard, only to wind up on the faculty of a California university for which neither his working-class Jewish background nor his Harvard-acquired credentials and style have prepared him. *Above ground* (1968, NCL 1974) is another story of confusion and constant change, the semi-autobiographic account of a boy who, despite a childhood injury that hospitalizes him for an extended period and leaves him permanently lame, pursues the 'bait of life' and grows into a man who falls into love with one woman after another. As in his first novel, *Above ground* is a comic monologue delivered by a man trying to sort out the dark and consuming reality that he believes lurks behind life's everyday appearances. Although this novel is partly, in the modernist tradition, a descent beneath the surfaces of life, it also anticipates the pattern of Margaret ATWOOD's *Surfacing* by showing its protagonist's struggle to emerge back into a daylight world 'above ground'. (Ludwig's title responds to Dostoyevsky's 'Notes from underground'. In an early critical monograph, *Recent American novelists* (1962), Ludwig wrote that the novelists of his generation were 'turning from the Kafkaesque "Underground Man" towards an "Aboveground Man"', the hero who breaks out of his real, or symbolic, sealed-off room to re-enter the world of action and history. In the novella *A woman of her age* (1973)—an expansion of the 1959 story—the central character makes just such a re-entry, in her eighty-fifth year. Here the 'confusions' of Ludwig's earlier novel recur as Doba Goffman tries to understand her perplexing metamorphosis from youthful radical to wealthy matron.

Lunn, Janet (b. 1928). Born Janet Louise Swoboda in Dallas, Texas, she attended high school in Ottawa, and Queen's University, Kingston, Ontario. In 1950 she married Richard Lunn (deceased). For many years she lived in Ontario's Prince Edward County, a location that provides the background for her many books written for young people and children (she now lives in Ottawa). Her first novel, *Double spell* (1968, rpr. 2003), is the story of twin girls who find an antique doll that leads them into the past, to 1840s Toronto. A highly readable, neatly constructed tale, it combines elements of traditional domestic fiction—big, happy family, rambling ramshackle house, rambunctious dog—with conventions of the ghost story: unseen forces and psychic disturbances. More ambitious in narrative and emotional scope are the two novels set in Lunn's home territory. *The root cellar* (1981, rpr. 2001) is a time-travel narrative in which young Rose travels geographically from southern Ontario to Washington, D.C., and historically from the present to the period just after the American Civil War. Rose, a neglected orphan, finds in her journey a sense of companionship, a realization of her own strengths, and the means to integrate facets of her fragile personality. Lunn's able

manipulation of the mechanics of time travel and her confident use of historical detail add up to a suspenseful narrative exploring time, continuity, and change. In *Shadow in Hawthorn Bay* (1986, rpr. 2001) Lunn creates a passionate, almost gothic tale of a young woman, a Scottish immigrant, who travels to Canada in pursuit of her one true love. Lunn's re-creation of life in the period around 1815 and her powerful evocation of a malevolent landscape provide a vivid background for this story of longing and redemption. Lunn's gift for presenting the past to young people is also shown in her pioneer story *One hundred shining candles* (1990, rpr. 1994); in a collection of historical vignettes, *Larger than life* (1979); and in *The story of Canada* (1992, rev. 2000), a lively and substantial illustrated history, written with Christopher MOORE and illustrated by Alan Daniel. *The hollow tree* (1997, GGA), set in 1775, begins in New Hampshire, where Phoebe Olcott's cousin Gideon has been hanged as a British spy, leaving behind a secret message for Phoebe to deliver; her actions become entwined with those of young Jem Moorrassy, an escaping Loyalist. *A rebel's daughter: the 1837 Rebellion diary of Arabella Stevenson* (2006), in the Dear Canada series, is a compelling evocation for young people of the period and its events, with illustrations and maps.

Lunn's picture-book stories—including *The twelve dancing princesses* (1979), *Amos's sweater* (1988, rpr. 2007), *Duck cakes for sale* (1989), *The umbrella party* (1998), and *Laura Secord: a story of courage* (2001)—reveal a pawky wit and expertise in the highly patterned rhythmical prose of children's tales. Lunn was Chair of The WRITERS' UNION OF CANADA for 1984–5 and was appointed a Member of the Order of Canada in 1997.

Lyall, William (1811–90). Born in Paisley, Scotland, and educated at the Universities of Glasgow and Edinburgh, he was ordained into the Church of Scotland and took the part of the Free Church in the Great Disruption of 1843. He came to Toronto as a tutor at Knox College in 1848. In 1850 he moved to Halifax, Nova Scotia, and apart from three years in Truro, N.S., remained there for the rest of his life. After a decade at the Free Church College, he taught philosophy at Dalhousie University until his death. Lyall's major work, *Intellect, the emotions and the moral life* (Edinburgh, 1855)—which was widely read and used in colleges of the Maritime Provinces for half a century—attempts to bridge the gap between the intellect and the emotions that had played a central role in philosophy since Plato. Weaving a complex synthesis of common-sense realism, and Augustinian neo-Platonism, Lyall argued that the emotions in general, and love in particular, were crucial sources of knowledge and formed an essential basis for action. In Lyall's theory the direct object of an emotion (the source of joy or anger, or the object or person loved or hated) affects the indirect object—the state of mind and character of the person who has that emotion. With the education of the emotions and the imagination, the individual may become aware of more appropriate direct objects; sexual love, for instance, may develop into love of God.

Lyall's Augustinian political thesis—that the state, though necessary to human beings in their fallen condition, is to be regarded with a measure of suspicion—contrasts sharply with that of his predecessor at Dalhousie, Thomas McCULLOCH, who sought a political order based on a natural relation between human beings and their physical environment. Lyall saw fallen humanity as needing an elaborate political organization, and the isolated communities of the Maritimes in the context of a larger world. His ideas thus mark a passage in political thought in the Maritime Provinces towards the era of compromise and negotiation that led to Confederation.

M

McArthur, Peter (1866–1924). He was born in Ekfrid Township, Middlesex County, Canada West, in a log house now standing in Doon, Ontario, and attended public schools; in 1887 he received a teacher's certificate at the Strathroy Model School. In 1888, after teaching for six months, he entered the University of Toronto—to make ends meet he contributed pieces to *Grip*—but in 1889 he became a reporter for the *Toronto Mail*. From 1890 to 1895 he freelanced in New York, largely as a jokesmith for *Judge, Life*, and *Town Topics*, and then became editor of *Truth* (1895–7). After another period of freelancing in New York, he went to England (1902), where he wrote for *Punch* and worked on W.T. Stead's *Review of Reviews* and *Daily Paper*. He returned to New York (1904) and opened an advertising agency. It failed, and in 1909, without work or funds, he had to take refuge on the Ekfrid homestead. While in New York, McArthur had written short stories for *Truth*; a book, *The prodigal and other poems* (1907); various articles for American magazines; and in England, a satire on Canadian-British relationships, *To be taken with salt; being an essay on teaching one's grandmother to suck eggs* (1903). At Ekfrid, however, McArthur made his name with articles for the Toronto *Globe* (1909–24) and the *Farmer's Advocate* (1910–22). From these journalistic activities were drawn *In pastures green* (1915), *The red cow and her friends* (1919), *Around home* (1925), and *Friendly acres*

(1927). Centring on pioneers and the simple life, farm activities, and farm animals (treated mainly as comic characters), the delight of nature and an almost messianic 'back-to-the-land' message, these essays made him the leading Canadian writer in the rural tradition. They also revealed his gift for humour, which gave him special insight for his critical study *Stephen Leacock* (1923).

Macbeth, Madge (1881–1965). Born in Philadelphia, Madge Hamilton Lyons was educated at Hellmuth Ladies' College, London, Ontario. She then married Charles Macbeth and moved in 1904 to Ottawa, where she supported her two young sons as a writer when she became a widow, and where she remained until her death. She began working as an Ottawa journalist in 1908, writing several regular columns in magazines and newspapers, including 'Over my shoulder' for the *Ottawa Citizen* throughout the 1950s. 'Frieda's engagement' (1908)—included in *New women: short stories by Canadian women, 1900–1920* (1991), edited by Sandra Campbell and Lorraine McMullen—was Macbeth's first short story published in Canada. Hundreds of magazine articles, stories, and twenty novels appeared between 1910 and 1965. Among her early works are the novels *The changeling* (1909), *The winning game* (1910), and *The Patterson limit* (1923). Macbeth used various pseudonyms, notably 'Gilbert Knox' for her satires *The land of afternoon* (1924), a scathing and controversial commentary on political and social intrigue at Government House, Ottawa, and *The kinder bees* (1935), also about life in Ottawa. She created controversy through her frank discussions of sexuality, particularly in *Shackles* (1926), *Lost: a cavalier* (1947), and *Shreds of circumstance* (1947). Macbeth was a key figure behind the establishment of what would become the Canadian Broadcasting Corporation, and was instrumental in the creation of the CANADIAN AUTHORS' ASSOCIATION (of which she was the first female, and only three-time, national president). She published two autobiographies, *Over my shoulder* (1953) and *Boulevard career* (1957).

McCaffery, Steve (b. 1947). Born in Sheffield, England, he became interested in alternative poetry while studying at the University of Hull (B.A., 1968). Immigrating to Canada in 1968, and specializing in linguistics, epistemology, and literary criticism, he undertook graduate studies at York University, Toronto (M.A., 1969) and at the State University of New York, Buffalo (Ph.D., 1998), where in 2004 he was appointed David Gray Professor of Poetry and Letters. McCaffery previously taught in the Department of English at York University, where he was made professor in 2003. Early in his career as a writer he moved from text to performance as a condition of writing beyond the book. His collaboration with the sound-poetry group the FOUR HORSEMEN began in 1970. He has published some twenty books, however, including *The black debt* (1989), *Theory of sediment* (1991), and *The cheat of words* (1996), which exemplifies Umberto Eco's innovative notion of the open text by illustrating how layers of surprisingly ironic meanings are generated when the conventional meaning of language is unsettled. Influenced by Dadaism, Surrealism, and 'pataphysics (a late nineteenth-century absurdist movement initiated by the French dramatist Alfred Jarry—see Christian BÖK), and applying theories of Wittgenstein, Barthes, Derrida, Bataille, Deleuze, and Guattari, McCaffery abandoned mainstream conventions of genre and logic. In his often satiric performances at international festivals of poetry, he dislocates narrative through multiple perspectives and shifting voices—redefining boundaries between artist and audience through sound poetry, video, film, audio-recording, choreography, and performance art. More recent books include *Seven pages missing: Volume One: selected texts*

1969–1999 (2000), *Volume Two: previously uncollected texts 1968–2000* (2002), poetry and prose; *Prior to meaning* (2000), criticism; and two collections of poetry, *Bouma shapes* (2002), *Crime scenes* (2006). *The Basho variations* (published by Book Thug, Toronto, in 2007) is his typographically imponderable tribute to the Japanese poet Basho Matsuo (1644–94). McCaffery is documented in Michael ONDAATJE's film *Sons of Captain Poetry* (1971). In the mid-1970s and early 1980s, with Charles Bernstein and others, he developed the L=A=N=G=U=A=G=E school of writing, which investigates connections between cognition and linguistics. His *Rational geomancy: the kids of the book machine* (1992), a collection of reports, essays, and manifestos co-written with bp NICHOL under the name TRG (Toronto Research Group), is both a logical and intuitive inquiry into the multiple forms of postmodern writing. Partly in response to McLUHAN's notion that 'the medium is the message', McCaffery engages the reader in a satiric, self-reflexive, and often parodic loop through his analyses of performance, 'pataphysics, the book as machine, visual and sound poetry, anti-narrative, and a host of contemporary writers and theoreticians. In 2008 McCaffery published *Every way Oakly: homolinguistic translations of Gertrude Stein's* Tender Buttons—i.e., translation within the same language.

McCall, Christina (1935–2005). Born in Toronto, she graduated in English Language and Literature from Victoria College, University of Toronto (1956), where her professors included Northrop FRYE, E.J. PRATT, and Kathleen Coburn (English); Donald CREIGHTON and Bertie Wilkinson (history); and C.B. Macpherson (political science). During her marriage (1959–77) to Peter NEWMAN, she pursued a career as an increasingly influential political journalist known for the grace and clarity of her writing and for her skill as a researcher and analyst. She was associate editor, then Ottawa editor, of *Chatelaine* (1958–62); Ottawa columnist for *Saturday Night* (1967–9) and executive editor (1976–80); associate editor of *Maclean's* (1971–3); and National Reporter for Toronto's *Globe and Mail* (1975–6). From 1962 to 1975 she was a researcher and creative editor for her husband, contributing substantially to his articles and books, and was under contract to co-author with him a work to be called *The anatomy of Canada*, which was later published in two volumes by Newman as *The Canadian establishment* (1975, 1981). She spent two years writing *Grits: an intimate* *portrait of the Liberal party* (1983), the 'intimate portrait' of the subtitle having been made possible by the author's first-hand acquaintance with Ottawa in the Lester Pearson/early Trudeau years, her skilled use of 174 interviews, and her gift for weaving subtle political analyses, probing character sketches, and memorable anecdotes into a compelling narrative. In 1978 McCall married Stephen Clarkson (b. 1937), professor of political science in the University of Toronto, and from 1984 to 1994 she collaborated with him on *Trudeau and our times*, a masterly two-volume study of the Trudeau era that is partly a political/intellectual biography of Pierre Elliott Trudeau. Volume 1, *The magnificent obsession* (1990, GGA; rpr. 1997) covers the Trudeau ministry from 1968 to 1979 and describes his prolonged effort to fulfill his obsession for patriating the Canadian constitution and entrenching within it a charter of rights and freedoms. Volume 2, *The heroic delusion* (1994, rpr. 1997), in which this goal was achieved, deals mainly with his ministry from 1980 to 1984, which reflected his mistaken belief that Canada could remain both liberal and autonomous in an increasingly integrated North America. Illuminating their eminent subject and those who served him, and clarifying political intricacies—and the impact on Canadians of the Trudeau era—the authors elevated the writing of Canadian political history by combining literary distinction, original perceptions, and unimpeachable scholarship. *My life as a dame: the personal and the political in the writings of Christina McCall* (2008)—edited by Stephen Clarkson, with a Foreword by Eleanor WACHTEL—is a superb anthology of her journalistic writings that records her distinction in this genre.

McClelland, Jack (1922–2004). John Gordon McClelland was born in Toronto, the only son of John McClelland, who owned and ran the publishing firm MCCLELLAND & STEWART. After attending the University of Toronto Schools and St Andrew's College, he enrolled in math and physics at the University of Toronto in 1940 and the next year enlisted as a commissioned officer in the Royal Canadian navy, serving as captain on a motor torpedo boat 747; he rose to the rank of lieutenant commander. In 1946 he completed a B.A. at Trinity College, University of Toronto, and joined his father's firm. Early on he pressed his father to rely less on the distribution of British and American books and to work towards establishing a solid list of Canadian authors. In 1952, when he had become

familiar with all aspects of the business, he became president. His intuitive sense of what makes a good manuscript, his formidable energy, and his genius for friendship enabled him to enlist many of the best Canadian authors of his time: Irving LAYTON, Earle BIRNEY, Gabrielle ROY, Leonard COHEN, Sheila WATSON, Roger LEMELIN, Mordecai RICHLER, Margaret LAURENCE, Margaret ATWOOD, and Michael ONDAATJE, to name but a few. With some authors, such as Pierre BERTON and Farley MOWAT, he formed enduring friendships. His motto was 'McClelland and Stewart publish authors, not books.' His 1982 Molson Prize attested to the enormous contribution he made not only to Canadian publishing, but to Canadian culture in producing a large and diverse list of books that collectively represent the cornerstone of Canadian literature. He was named a Companion of the Order of Canada in 2001 and received eleven honorary degrees. In 1982 McClelland appointed his former vice-president of publishing, Linda McKnight, president of the firm, and he became chairman of the board and president of Seal Books, a collaborative paperback venture between McClelland & Stewart and Bantam Books. Even for a man once described as 'the mercurial helmsman' of Canada's most influential publisher, the year 1985 can be best described as volatile. Beginning with the sudden resignation of McKnight, the year ended with the sale of the company, which had been in the McClelland family for almost eighty years. Plagued in the previous year by financial difficulties that had precipitated a twenty-one-member consortium of investors stepping forward with $1 million in rescue capital, McClelland & Stewart was purchased by Toronto real-estate developer Avram (Avie) Bennett at the end of 1985. Although he extended to McClelland a five-year consultancy contract, the full term of this agreement was never realized: McClelland severed all ties with the company after only two years. In 1987 McClelland sold his controlling interest in Seal Books to Anna PORTER, a former M&S executive. Criticized at times for his almost fearless disregard for public decorum, Jack McClelland is remembered by many for a lifelong dedication to Canadian writing that Farley and Claire Mowat once described as fuelled by 'faith and conviction and pizzazz'. See Sam Solecki, ed., *Imagining Canadian literature: the selected letters of Jack McClelland* (1998), and James KING, *Jack, a life with writers: the story of Jack McClelland* (1999, rpr. 2000).

McClelland & Stewart. Founded in 1906 by John McClelland, formerly manager of the library department of the Methodist Book Room (later the RYERSON PRESS), in partnership with Frederick Goodchild from the same company, it began as a library supply house selling books secured from foreign publishers. The imprint McClelland and Goodchild was initiated three years later. In 1910, L.M. MONTGOMERY's *Kilmeny of the orchard*—her first Canadian publication—appeared. Three years after the firm was incorporated in 1911, George Stewart, a Bible salesman from the Methodist Book Room, joined it. In 1918 Goodchild formed his own company (Frederick D. Goodchild) and the firm became McClelland & Stewart Ltd. Before the First World War, M&S expanded its activities as agents for British and American firms by starting to build a list of Canadian publications. In 1917 it became the publisher of Ralph Connor (Charles William GORDON); its other Canadian authors at that time included Bliss CARMAN, Marjorie PICKTHALL, Marshall SAUNDERS, Duncan Campbell SCOTT, Isabel Ecclestone MacKay, and Marian Keith (Mary Esther MacGREGOR). Between the wars, books by Stephen LEACOCK, Arthur STRINGER, Frederick Philip GROVE, Laura Goodman SALVERSON, and Thomas H. RADDALL were added to its list. After the Second World War—under the direction of John (Jack) McCLELLAND, who joined his father's firm in 1946 and became president in 1952—M&S began its steady shift away from handling agencies to concentrate on its Canadian publishing. Three celebrated Québec novels were published in translation: Gabrielle ROY's *The TIN FLUTE* (*Bonheur d'occasion*), which appeared in 1947, and Roger LEMELIN's *The town below* (*Au pied de la pente douce*) and *The PLOUFFE FAMILY* (*Les Plouffe*), which appeared in 1948 and 1951 respectively. In the late forties, the beautifully designed Indian File Series of poetry books—including collections by James REANEY, Robert FINCH, and Phyllis WEBB—began the strong commitment of M&S to poetry publishing. By 1954 40 per cent of the firm's revenues came from Canadian publications. In 1958 the NEW CANADIAN LIBRARY reprint series of major Canadian works was started, and the following year M&S published Irving LAYTON's *A red carpet for the sun*, Mordecai RICHLER's *The APPRENTICESHIP OF DUDDY KRAVITZ*, and Sheila WATSON's *The double hook*. By 1962 it had dropped most of its foreign agencies, a decision that seemed well justified by the commercial success of books by Pierre BERTON, Farley MOWAT, of Peter NEWMAN's *Renegade in power* (1963), Margaret LAURENCE's *The STONE ANGEL* (1964); and, in the years that followed, of subsequent works by these authors and books by Margaret ATWOOD, Earle BIRNEY, Marie-Claire BLAIS, and Leonard COHEN, among other well-known writers. In the area of scholarship, M&S published in 1963 the first two volumes in its eighteen-volume history of Canada, The Canadian Centenary Series, under the editorship of W.L. MORTON and Donald CREIGHTON. Despite severe financial difficulties (government grants had been successfully sought in 1970 and 1978 to keep the company from folding), there is now hardly an area of literature, and of Canadian life, that is not represented by M&S books—which include not only fiction and poetry and a wide range of non-fiction, but children's literature.

In 1982 McClelland appointed his vice-president of publishing, Linda McKnight, president of the firm, and became chairman of the board. He also became president of Seal Books, a collaborative paperback venture between M&S and Bantam Books. Three years later McKnight resigned over a dispute with McClelland, and in December of the same year the company was purchased by Avram (Avie) Bennett, a Toronto real-estate developer whose company had been part of a consortium of twenty-one investors that had raised more than $1 million to save M&S from financial collapse a year earlier. Although Bennett signed McClelland to a five-year consultancy contract, they parted after only two years. Early in 1987 Bennett named former television journalist Adrienne Clarkson as the company's president and publisher. It was during her tenure that M&S's flagship New Canadian Library series was redesigned and reset after thirty years; most significantly, a new general editor, David Staines, and an advisory board were brought in, most of the old titles were allowed to go out of print, and a new format was introduced for the new series, launched in October 1988, that included Afterwords by distinguished writers, critics, and scholars. In 1989 the company announced its purchase of the prized Canadian rights to James Michener's novel *Journey*. The much-publicized signing included Michener's promise to donate royalties from the Canadian edition to a fund for promising new writers; these proceeds were used to establish *The Journey Prize anthology*, an annual M&S collection of short fiction by young Canadian writers.

McClelland & Stewart

September 1988 saw another major redistribution of power within M&S, with Clarkson relinquishing her dual role after only eighteen months. Bennett subsequently resumed the presidency and named Douglas Gibson as his publisher. Following success in various editorial and publishing capacities at Doubleday (1968–74) and MACMILLAN's (1974–86), Gibson maintained his own banner under the M&S imprint from 1986. During those early years he attracted so many former Macmillan authors to M&S (including Robertson DAVIES, Mavis GALLANT, Jack HODGINS, W.O. MITCHELL, and Alice MUNRO) that Macmillan ceased publishing fiction, and the M&S list was able to offer the best of two venerable publishing houses combined. Even after he became publisher, Gibson continued to look after major authors under his editorial imprint Douglas Gibson Books.

While in years of change M&S continued to publish such high-profile non-fiction writers as Pierre Berton, Farley Mowat, and Peter Newman—along with new stars such as the CBC's Peter Gzowski and political memoirists such as René Lévesque—the company was quickly establishing itself as the pre-eminent publisher of Canadian fiction; indeed, many of Canada's best-known writers have attained international distinction under the M&S banner, including Margaret Atwood and Michael ONDAATJE. Ellen Seligman, who joined the firm full-time in 1977, rising to the position of editorial director of fiction, provided editorial guidance to a new generation of exceptional fiction writers, including David Adams RICHARDS (*Nights below Station Street*, 1988), Nino RICCI (*Lives of the saints*, 1990), Michael Ondaatje (*The English patient*, 1992), Jane URQUHART (*Away*, 1993), Shyam SELVADURAI (*Funny boy*, 1994), Rohinton MISTRY (*A fine balance*, 1995), Anne MICHAELS (*Fugitive pieces*, 1996), and André ALEXIS (*Childhood*, 1998)—all of whom garnered prestigious national and international awards for their writing.

The 1990s began at M&S with a high-profile $1.5 million libel suit launched against the company and author Ron GRAHAM by Canadian media mogul Conrad Black for a passage in Graham's book, *God's dominion*, that Black claimed was libellous; in a much-publicized stand, Bennett refused to withdraw copies of the book or delete the passage in question. The suit was finally settled out of court in February 1992. In May 1991, Bennett ended months of speculation by announcing the purchase of the financially troubled Hurtig Publishers of Edmonton—home to such publishing megaprojects as The CANADIAN ENCYCLOPEDIA,

which M&S continued to develop, using CD-ROM technology. Other moves included the 1995 purchase of Montreal-based Tundra Books, a small but prestigious Montreal publisher specializing in beautifully illustrated children's books, and the acquisition of Reed Books Canada in 1996, adding a strong international agency list that includes such luminaries as Roddy Doyle. No success comes without stumbles. Some once-durable relationships proved difficult to maintain: Pierre Berton, for example, broke his almost four-decades-long association with the company in 1995. But as Margaret Atwood said, in a speech given to mark the company's ninetieth year: 'That any business has lasted this long is astounding; that the business is a Canadian publishing house is more astounding still.'

In June 2000 it was announced that Bennett—in order to safeguard the firm's future—had donated 75 per cent of the shares of McClelland & Stewart to the University of Toronto and sold the remaining 25 per cent to Random House Canada, which would provide expertise in sales, marketing, and electronic books. The university would hold five of the seven seats and Random House the other two on the board of directors, of which Bennett would be chairman. Gibson was appointed president and publisher, and Seligman publisher, fiction. Under the new arrangement M&S, aware of the need for independence, retained its own editorial, design, production, rights, and publicity departments. All the other business services were to be provided by Random House—namely sales, marketing, warehousing, distribution, and over-all financial management. Industry observers watched to see how the power-sharing arrangement would evolve.

M&S continued to enjoy public success, its authors winning prizes at home and abroad (for example in Dublin, where Alistair MacLEOD won the international IMPAC award for *No great mischief*). Seligman's fiction program claimed a majority of GILLER PRIZES over the years; star authors such as Atwood, Munro, and Ondaatje remained loyal to the company; and there were rising stars such as Rohinton Mistry, Jane Urquhart, and Guy VANDERHAEGHE, to be bolstered in time by David BERGEN, Elizabeth HAY, and Madeleine Thien.

Problems in the retail trade, however—such as excessive chain returns of unsold books far above the agreed limits—hit M&S hard, and in 2003 the company reluctantly offered Mac-farlane Walter and Ross for sale, after owning it for only three years. In the difficult climate

McClung

for even fine Canadian non-fiction publishing there were no takers and the company folded, though all its contracts were duly honoured.

In 2004 Gibson moved sideways to concentrate solely on his imprint, looking after fiction writers such as Mavis Gallant and Alice Munro, and political memoirists such as Brian Mulroney and Paul Martin. To replace him as president and publisher the Board brought in Douglas Pepper, a Canadian schooled in publishing in the Random House system, most recently as an executive editor at Crown in New York. He soon appointed Susan Renouf, formerly of Key Porter, as his vice-president. The new regime made a decision to cut staff, to cut the number of books published each year, and to try to secure a stable of younger non-fiction writers likely to appeal to a more urbane reading audience, a decision emphasized by the company's move into a restored former piano factory building on Sherbourne Street in downtown Toronto.

The years since have been marked by what observers see as a steady increase in the role of Random House. The separate M&S design department has been folded into the overarching Random House design group, sales conferences are now held in the Random House offices, and in 2008 the last of the distinct M&S sales force members were let go, leaving M&S books to be sold by the regular Random House sales force. These, and other similar changes, are publicly defended on the grounds of economy in difficult times in the perennially challenging business of Canadian publishing.

In 2008 Gibson left the company, planning to maintain his imprint on a freelance basis. Meanwhile M&S, despite publishing a much smaller list, continues to produce a wide range of fiction and non-fiction, and poetry, while remaining committed to the Journey Prize competition and to maintaining the New Canadian Library series, which in 2008 was redesigned yet again.

McClung, Nellie L. (1873–1951). Nellie Letitia Mooney was born on a farm near Chatsworth, Grey County, Ontario, of Methodist Scotch-Irish parentage. The family moved to Manitoba in 1880 and took up homestead land on the Souris River. Attending school for the first time at age ten, Nellie was enrolled in Winnipeg's Normal School within six years. She taught at rural schools in Manitoba, returning to Winnipeg in 1893–5 to complete high school at the Collegiate Institute. In 1896, having picked out her mother-in-law several years before, she married pharmacist Wesley McClung. An avid reader of fiction, with a lively imagination and easily stirred sympathies for the voiceless, downtrodden, and unfortunate, Nellie was caught up by the novels of Charles Dickens and the serials in the weekly *Family Herald*. Early ambitions to write stories about the Manitoba country people she lived among were sidetracked by the responsibilities of her growing family and by her widening activism in temperance and suffrage organizations. She achieved commercial success as a writer with her first book, *Sowing seeds in Danny* (1908, rpr. 1965), which sold more than 100,000 copies and helped pave the way for her rise soon afterwards to political prominence. Her political achievements were numerous: she was a front-line campaigner in the Manitoba elections of 1914 and 1915 that led to the enfranchisement of the province's women in 1916. She gave equally effective leadership in the Alberta suffrage cause after the McClung family's removal to Edmonton (1914), and unrelenting platform service in the campaign for prohibition; was elected to the Alberta legislature as a Liberal in 1921 (she was defeated in 1925); and was one of the 'famous five' who pursued the Persons Case to its successful conclusion in 1930. Her classic statement of Canadian feminism, *In times like these* (1915), was reprinted in 1972 by the UNIVERSITY OF TORONTO PRESS with an Introduction by Veronica Strong-Boag. On her husband's retirement in 1935 the McClungs moved from Calgary, where they had lived since 1923, to Gordonhead, near Victoria, B.C.

McClung published sixteen books, including several collections of short stories, and numerous uncollected stories and articles for newspapers and magazines. Her dramatic flair, charisma, and wit reached large audiences across Canada and the USA through her public readings from *Sowing seeds in Danny*. Two later novels, *The second chance* (1910) and *Purple springs* (1921, rpr. 1992), take Pearlie Watson, Danny's sister—whose temperament, philosophy, and adventures closely matched McClung's—through an independent young womanhood as a teacher and a campaigner for temperance and suffrage, ending with her marriage to an idealistic, progressive doctor. *Painted fires* (1925), McClung's last full-scale novel, showed her lifelong concern for immigrant groups in Canada through the trials of Helmi, a young Finnish girl. In 1996 the University of Toronto Press published a collection of McClung's short fiction: *Stories subversive: through the field with gloves off* edited by Marilyn I. Davis. Although McClung's penchant for pathos and moral uplift dates her fiction, her epigrammatic wit, and the humour and sprightliness of her stories and characters can still offer amusement. McClung effectively punctured stuffiness and pretension, and she had an ear for the colloquial rhythms and usages of turn-of-the-century westerners. She wrote two fine volumes of autobiography, *Clearing in the West: my own story* (1935, rpr. 2005) and *The stream runs fast* (1945, rpr. 2007). They were published together in one volume: *Nellie McClung: the complete autobiography: A clearing in the West* and *The stream runs fast* (2003) edited by Veronica Strong-Boag and Michelle Rosa . See Mary E. Hallett, *Firing the heather: the life and times of Nellie McClung* (1993) and R.R. Warne, *Literature as pulpit: the Christian social activism of Nellie L. McClung* (1993). In 2008 Charlotte GRAY published a brief but excellent biography, *Nellie McClung,* in Penguin's Extraordinary Canadians series.

McCourt, Edward (1907–72). Edward Alexander McCourt was born in Mullinger, Ireland, and brought to Canada in 1909; he grew up on a farm outside Kitscoty, Alberta. After taking his high-school education by correspondence, he studied English literature at the University of Alberta and, as a Rhodes Scholar, at Oxford University, from which he received an M.A. in 1937. On returning to Canada he taught English at Ridley College and Upper Canada College in Ontario, at the University of New Brunswick, and Queen's University, Ontario, before accepting a position at the University of Saskatoon, where he taught from 1944 until his death. McCourt's novels, rooted in the Prairies, are character studies that test the truth of Dr Fotheringham's declaration in *The wooden sword* (1956) that 'The life of everyman is no more than a succession of disillusionments. Each disillusionment constitutes a crisis. And a man's happiness—a relative term only—depends on the success or otherwise with which he meets each crisis.' McCourt's first and best-known novel, *Music at the close* (1947, rpr. 1979), traces the progressive disillusionment of Neil Fraser, an orphan given to romantic dreams, from his arrival on his great-uncle's prairie farm at the age of twelve until his death in the Second World War. *Home is the stranger* (1950) focuses on Norah Armstrong, an Irish war bride struggling to make a new life for herself in a small prairie farming community; disillusioned by her failure as wife and mother, she attempts suicide. A prairie university is the setting of *The wooden sword*, a psychological case study of Stephen Veneer, a professor of English whose adolescent dreams of heroism have been shattered by his war experiences, and whose unwillingness to come to terms with those experiences has driven him to the verge of a mental breakdown. *Walk through the valley* (1958) focuses on fourteen-year-old Michael Troy, whose faith in his father, Dermot, and in the romantic tales of adventure with which his father regales him, are all but destroyed when the police close in on Dermot's whiskey-running operation. In *Fasting friar* (1963), published in England as *The Ettinger affair*, the process of disillusionment is reversed: Walter Ackroyd, an aging, fastidious, and ascetic professor of English at a prairie university, finds new hope and courage when he falls in love with Marion Ettinger, wife of a colleague dismissed for writing a racy novel. In addition to these five novels, McCourt published forty-three stories, most of which are set in western Canada. None of his novels are currently in print. Among his other books is a biography of the author of *The great lone land* (1872), *Remember Butler: the story of Sir William Butler* (1967), and an important work of literary criticism, *The Canadian West in fiction* (1949, rev. 1970), a pioneering study of prairie writers that focuses on Ralph Connor (Charles W. GORDON), Frederick NIVEN, and Frederick Philip GROVE, but also includes discussions of Nellie McCLUNG, Sinclair ROSS, and W.O. MITCHELL.

McCrae, John (1872–1918). Born in Guelph, Ontario, he grew up under the influence of his military-minded father, and as an adolescent belonged to the Guelph Highland Cadets. His poems began to appear in periodicals as early as 1894. Graduating in medicine from the University of Toronto in 1898, he worked during that year at the Toronto General Hospital, and spent part of 1899 at Johns Hopkins University, Baltimore. After serving in South Africa (1899–1900), McCrae became a pathologist at McGill University; he was later associated in Montreal with the General Hospital, the Alexandra Hospital, and the Royal Victoria Hospital. (He published several medical publications.) In Sept. 1914 he embarked as a medical officer for the European theatre of war. His best-known poem, 'In Flanders fields', was written during the second battle of Ypres in the spring of 1915 and first appeared in *Punch* in Dec. 1915. In June 1915 McCrae left the front for the military General Hospital in Boulogne, where he died of pneumonia in Jan. 1918. Sir Andrew MACPHAIL published twenty-nine of McCrae's poems, which had appeared in periodicals during 1894–1917, as *In Flanders fields* and other poems (1919), which concludes with a memorial tract by Macphail, 'An essay in character', that includes biographical information as well as extracts from McCrae's journal and letters. The poems demonstrate McCrae's careful attention to poetic craft, his commitment to fruitful labour, and his profound concern for the fellowship of the dead, whom he portrays as wakeful and anxious lest their labours have been in vain. In his later poems these labours specifically include British Imperial military service. Only rarely, as in 'Flanders fields', does McCrae fuse his craft and concern for worthwhile service into an evocative statement on sacrifice for a higher principle. See John F. Prescott, *In Flanders fields: the story of John McCrae* (1985). The text of *In Flanders fields: the story of the poem by John McCrae* (1985)—a picture book for young readers—by Linda Granfield, illustrated by Janet Wilson, describes the wartime background of the poem and includes biographical details; this is supplemented by paintings, drawings, and photographs.

McCulloch, Thomas (1776–1843). Born in Ferenze, Renfrewshire, Scotland, he was educated at the University of Glasgow and at Divinity Hall, Whitburn. A member of the secession branch of the Presbyterian Church, he was ordained in 1799 and in 1803 was sent to Prince Edward Island. Unable to reach his destination, he stopped in Pictou, Nova Scotia. After a year, despite entreaties to move to P.E.I., McCulloch accepted a call to remain there. He soon became involved in many activities outside his ministry. He founded Pictou Academy (incorporated 1816) and became caught up in the Anglican Church's endeavours to dominate education in the province: he was unable to obtain funds for the academy or the power to grant degrees. McCulloch was a natural reformer, and under his leadership Pictou became a centre of protest against the Establishment. In 1838 he became the first president of Dalhousie University, a non-sectarian institution of higher learning in Halifax, and remained in this post until his death. He founded a theological seminary at West River, Pictou County, which was moved after his death to Truro in 1858 and two years later joined with the Free Church Seminary to form the Halifax Presbyterian College. In 1925 this institution amalgamated with the Mount Allison Faculty of Theology to form Pine Hill Divinity Hall of the United Church of Canada. McCulloch was also a naturalist in the nineteenth-century tradition. His collection of bird specimens

attracted the attention of John James Audubon, who visited him in 1833.

McCulloch was a prodigious letter-writer and pamphleteer on a wide range of subjects who managed also to write books of general as well as educational and theological interest, often driving himself to the point of exhaustion. As a writer he is best known for his *Letters of Mephibosheth Stepsure*, which first appeared in serial form in the *Acadian Recorder* between 22 Dec. 1821 and 11 May 1822 and in Jan. and Mar. 1823. The letters were printed in book form in 1862 and, as *The Stepsure letters*, reprinted in 1960 (NCL), with an Introduction by Northrop FRYE (this edition is no longer in print). A superb edition of this work, *The Mephibosheth Stepsure letters* (1990, CEECT), edited by Gwendolyn Davies, contains considerable material about McCulloch's life as a clergyman and writer in nineteenth-century Nova Scotia, and is the most detailed and scholarly study of McCulloch to date. McCulloch's satiric and humorous account of the rural life of Pictou County in the 1820s created a furore in the newspaper columns of the time. Northrop Frye describes McCulloch as 'the founder of genuine Canadian humour; that is, of the humour which is based on a vision of society and not merely a series of wisecracks on a single theme.' The *Stepsure letters* had a strong influence on HALIBURTON's Sam Slick sketches, and it is clear that McCulloch wrote in the tradition that had its flowering in LEACOCK. In 1824 McCulloch published in *The NOVASCOTIAN* the moral tale 'William', depicting the fortunes of an emigrant and the difficulties awaiting those who were not prepared to work hard in the New World. 'William' was joined with a similar work and reprinted as *Colonial gleanings: William and Melville* (Edinburgh, 1826). McCulloch also wrote books on education and religion.

MacDonald, Ann-Marie (b. 1959). An actor, playwright, television writer, and novelist, she was born on a Canadian Air Force base in West Germany; the family moved frequently during her childhood, but their roots are in Cape Breton Island. MacDonald attended high school in Ottawa, studied a year at Carleton University, and then enrolled at the National Theatre School, graduating in 1980, when she moved to Toronto to begin her acting career. She has performed in films and on the stage. The transition to writing for the stage happened naturally through her involvement with Toronto's feminist fringe theatre. She was an actor/writer of *This is for you, Anna* (1985), a collective creation that is an imagistic political performance piece revolving around a mother's actual revenge for her daughter's murderer; it toured provincially in 1984, in Britain in 1986, and nationally in 1990. *Clue in the fast lane* (produced in 1984) was co-written and co-performed with Beverley Cooper. A spoof on the Nancy Drew detective genre, it began as a series of late-night performances before its production at Theatre Passe Muraille, Toronto, in 1985. *The road shows* (produced in 1986), a satirical spin on regular 'road movies' featuring a pair of wily and witty sisters, was also co-written and co-performed with Cooper. *Goodnight Desdemona (Good morning Juliet)* (1990, GGA; rpr. 1998) is an ingenious piece, written entirely in blank verse, in which a beleaguered academic literally falls into the worlds of Othello and Romeo and Juliet, altering their stories and her sense of herself. Revised and remounted for a national tour in 1990, it has had over fifty productions worldwide. *The Arab's mouth* (1995) is an amalgam of Gothic mystery, Freudianism, feminism, myth, magic, and nineteenth-century rationalism. *Belle Moral: a natural history* (2005)—produced at the Shaw Festival in 2005—had its origins in *The Arab's mouth*. It takes place in 1899 on the east coast of Scotland, not far from Edinburgh. The title is the name of the large stone house the MacIsaacs live in: Pearl, an amateur scientist; her aunt Flora; her emotional brother Victor, who returns after the death of his father and is haunted by the fact that his mother died after giving birth to him. Other characters include two servants; Dr Seamus Reid, the father's friend; and Mr Abbot, who has come to read the father's will. The entertaining play is about family secrets and is a comedy, even though MacDonald has woven into it some speechifying from Pearl and Dr Reid as they argue about natural history, ideas and morals, art versus science, truth and lies.

MacDonald's first novel, *Fall on your knees* (1996, rpr. 1997), was published to great praise (it was nominated for the Giller Prize and was Oprah's Book Club selection in 2002, which made it a bestseller). Her experience as a playwright and an actor may have given her the compelling, intimate narrative voice that recounts an epic family history, set mostly in New Waterford, Cape Breton Island. The family is Scottish-Lebanese: in 1898 thirteen-year-old Materia Mahmoud elopes with eighteen-year-old James Piper, a piano tuner, and they have four daughters. The novel is an emotionally rich, often surprising and disturbing saga of four generations. It has brilliant surfaces, is adventurous in its plotting

and characterization and filled with energy. The intricate plot is advanced steadily and clearly, satisfying a reader's desire for stories in both countless little narratives and in the collective family saga. The first sentence of MacDonald's second novel, *The way the crow flies* (2003, rpr. 2004), is 'The birds saw the murder.' Extraordinary and very long (811 pages in its paperback edition), it was inspired by an event well known to older Canadians when fourteen-year-old Steven Truscott was found guilty of the murder of a twelve-year-old girl in 1959 and sentenced to life imprisonment (paroled in 1969, he was exonerated in 2007). The novel opens in 1962 when a happy family heads by car for the air-force base at Centralia, in southwestern Ontario. Having served the RCAF in Germany, Wing Commander Jack McCarthy—accompanied by his Acadian wife Mimi, and their two children, Michel (Mike), aged eleven, and Madeleine, aged eight—is about to become director of the Central Officers' School. When they arrive they meet their neighbours, particularly the Froelichs, who live across the street: the German Henry Froelich, who is teaching math (a specialist in engineering physics, he has numbers tattooed on his arm), and his wife Karen and their five adopted children, good-looking Richard (Ricky, Rick), Colleen, Elizabeth (in a wheelchair—she has cerebral palsy), and twin baby boys. (One mother describes Ricky as 'so responsible and well adjusted'; some of Madeleine's friends have a crush on him, but at fifteen he is too old for them.) Jack accidentally meets his former flight instructor, Squadron Leader Simon Crawford, who describes himself as a diplomat, based in Berlin, and asks Jack for a 'favour': a defector—a scientist on his way to the US—'needs a safe place to live for six months or so'. Thus Oskar Fried (whom Henry Froelich identifies from a distance as a former Nazi) enters Jack's life, secretly, and complicates it. There are many episodes describing Madeleine at school, in the Grade Four class of Mr March. (He abuses Marjorie, Grace, and Madeleine—'the following little girls will remain after the bell'—who tell no one about it. This has a pernicious impact late in the novel). These scenes alternate with McCarthy family episodes and Oskar Fried episodes. Everything changes, however, when Claire McCarroll is strangled—she is one of Madeleine's classmates and the daughter of the American placed at the station to escort Oskar Fried to the US Ricky Froelich, who discovers the body when he is out in woods with his dog Rex, informs the police, is accused of the murder, and arrested. On that Wednesday afternoon Jack had passed him in Fried's car and waved to him—but Rick was sun-blinded and didn't recognize him, though he saw his air-force cap. Jack was Ricky's only alibi because he saw him pushing his sister's wheelchair in the opposite direction of the murder; but his oath of secrecy forbad him, in his mind, from admitting this. (Poor Elizabeth Froelich uttered a few incomprehensible words that only her mother knew identified the direction Ricky was going in, but the police ignored her.) At the trial Marjorie, Grace, and Madeleine are questioned, and their answers—the first two lie; Madeleine's answers are accurate but misleading—lead to Ricky's conviction and sentence, which is commuted in November 1963 from hanging to life imprisonment, until 1973, when he is paroled and resumes life under a different name. This intricate novel is vivid, sometimes eloquent, but it is overwritten, lacking a disciplined shape—it is far too long. The last 200 pages of the paperback—about the adult Madeline's successful career as a comedienne (though as a character she has no sense of humour), her lesbian relationships, many sessions with a therapist—extend the novel by far too many pages, leading to a disengagement from the compelling and often suspenseful main narrative. The conclusion, however, is gripping. We are told what the crows saw—the murder is described in detail. Then: 'The sun is halfway down the sky when Madeleine puts her car into first and rocks up the stony track toward a log house just coming into view.' This is where Colleen lives, with her brother Rick. He is cheerful and welcomes her, though he is in a wheelchair: he has muscular dystrophy.

MacDonald, D.R. (b.1939). Born on Cape Breton Island, in Boularderie Centre, David R. MacDonald is the great-grandson of Gaelic-speaking Scottish Highlanders who settled the land in the early 1800s. His father was a sailor who moved the family to Ohio to be closer to his work as an officer on the Great Lakes ore freighters. MacDonald (who has a seaman's license) received an A.B. degree from Ohio University and an M.A. from Ohio State University. In 1969 he received a Stegner Fellowship in Fiction at Stanford University, California, where he teaches creative writing, while spending every summer in Boularderie Centre, writing in a renovated barn on family property. As a writer he is powerfully attuned—like his friend Alistair MacLEOD—to the landscape and people of Cape Breton, their language and culture. A people who are dignified, resourceful, often drunken and intolerant, Cape Bretoners' lives unfold and their endeavours are examined, in MacDonald's slow, detailed narratives, through conversational exchanges, recollections, obsessions, accompanied by many intense, vivid descriptions of nature. His literary debut was as a gifted wrier of short stories, the author of *Eyestone* (published in the US in 1988, reprinted by Penguin Books in 1989). The title story is about Royce Simmons, a painter who moves from Boston with his new wife and buys a house and farm on Cape Breton from Mr Corbett, who requests that he and his wife live in it until they both die. Ill, he eventually hangs himself. Royce is then haunted by white-haired Mrs Corbett. 'Sometimes in the woods he glimpses her as she forages for plants: suddenly she is there, and then not. She is a folk healer, or was. She takes her clothesbasket into the house, looking his way once before she closes the door.' After a branch strikes him and injures his eye, he sees her in the distance and staggers towards her. 'What is it you want?' / 'The house. My wife went back to Boston, as you know, this spring. She can't live in the cottage. I ... to get her back, I must have the house ... .' / 'If it's the house you want, you shall have it. All of it.... You've hurt your eye, have you? Come down to me after dinner. We have a cure for that.' Her cure was an eyestone, which looked like a small white pebble. She placed it under his eyelid. 'Lie still. You mustn't move about. Let the stone move. It's very old in my family, the stone, very old.' 'The Flowers of Bermuda' is not about Bermuda at all, but about Bilkie Sutherland, a lobster fisherman who lives on Cape Breton. Bilkie was no longer a regular churchgoer after his nine-year-old son Torquil was killed in a tragic accident. 'God had taken away his only boy, and Bilkie could not fathom that even yet.' But a sermon delivered by the new minister, Gordon MacLean, impresses him and he receives a postcard from him when he is visiting the Hebrides Islands off Scotland. Suddenly his wife tells him: 'Rev. MacLean's been stabbed in Oban ... .' Two thugs tried to steal his wife's purse and while he attacked one, the other knifed his back. MacLean dies. When Bilkie hears this he goes to a tavern and sings 'Oh there be flowers in Bermuda ... .' Rather than attend the wake, he goes out in his boat: '"Ah!" was all Bilkie said when the wave rose under him, lifting the boat high like an offering.' These two stories and others are included in *All the men are sleeping* (2002, rpr. 2003), a distinguished collection that should be better known. The title story is about Dr Blair MacKenna, who takes Isobel, visiting from Halifax (and who loves him), across a frozen lake by a horse-driven sleigh to visit a patient. 'Through the dizzying snow the horse's black rump, straining against its fear, against Blair's grip on the reins, disappeared again and again. Its instincts might or might not keep the sleigh clear of what they all were afraid of, she, Blair, the horse: tender ice, a wide crack of open water.' They arrive at the farm and Isobel sees its 'huddled, darkened outbuildings, cowering in deep snow. The wind thrashed about, powdery, stinging'—and there they spend the night, with Josie, the sick man's wife, Jack, and the fiddler Angus Ban, and in these hours the feelings of Blair and Isabel are explored. They leave when Hector, the patient, dies of pleurisy. In the sleigh 'Isobel turned and saw water, the awful color of it seeping into snow like blood in a cut, into the thin grooves playing out behind them, but she said nothing.' MacDonald has received two Pushcart Prizes and one O. Henry Award for his stories.

The central character of MacDonald's first novel, *Cape Breton Road* (2000, rpr. 2001), is nineteen-year-old Innis Corbett, born on Cape Breton, who was carelessly raised by a widowed mother in Boston, took to stealing cars, and is deported , returning unwillingly to Cape Breton to live for a year with Starr, his uncle. The fairly even tenor of his life as a loner with an active mind, willing to do odd jobs, and devoted to a secret project—growing marijuana seedlings to earn money to travel west—is disrupted when Starr brings home the beautiful Claire. The relationship of all three, who are powerless to resist dead-end situations, is conveyed in expert dialogue. Innes's prolonged and unresolved drama—he falls in love with Claire—is firmly rooted in the setting, which is described in minute and poetic detail: 'Wind came through the clearing in soft, calming sweeps through grass and ferns. The leaves of his cannabis shivered, turned like feathers and flashed the paler green beneath. The hardy young spruce, the fir, the dead pines barely moved.' In *Lauchlin of the bad heart* (2007), Lauchlin MacLean is of course the central character and is in his fifties when the novel—which goes back and forth in time—begins. His promising career as a boxer in his youth is cut short by his bad heart (there is far too much about boxing in the novel). The bad heart—nitroglycerine pills are a help—might be considered a metaphor for his uncommitted romantic and sexual attachments to married women, among whom Morag's is the most lasting relationship in his life. He becomes obsessed, however, by the beautiful but blind Tena MacTavish, the wife of his friend Clement, when she enters his mother's store, where he is storekeeper. Always with Clement's permission he visits her and reads to her, takes her out for drives and walks. Clement has an unsavoury business partner called Ged Cooper, whom he sues for money owing to him. Cooper vows to take revenge. On the first page of the novel we learn that Clement has disappeared. Its climax a great many pages later—the search for Clement, the discovery of his body, Lauchlin's tracking down Cooper, the prime suspect, in an old house in the woods, and his entrapment by Cooper—contribute to a suspenseful, satisfying conclusion.

MacDonald, Wilson (1880–1967). Wilson Pugsley MacDonald was born in Cheapside, Ontario, and educated at Woodstock College and McMaster University, Hamilton. A minor poet who satisfied public taste with his 'romantic sensibility' and simplistic ideas, MacDonald came into prominence just after the First World War, and appears today as the last Canadian writer of a brand of romantic verse—with its musical quality and abundance of colour—that was rooted in the nineteenth century. But he also drew upon his Christian beliefs to expose hypocrisy and smugness—the marks, in his view, of twentieth-century humankind. For him, civilization was essentially evil; life had been made a mockery of in art, religion, and education, and people must return to the soil if they were not to be destroyed by their own vanity. *Comber Cove* (1937) reflects his disappointment in society and in those who corrupt it. Towards the end of his life he became known as a satirist, but much of what he wrote was petulant and bitter; he held strong, frequently unpopular, opinions, and did not care what others thought of him. He attained a popular following in Canada and abroad, but received no critical acclaim from those, in the 1930s, who preferred F.R. SCOTT, A.J.M. SMITH, Dorothy LIVESAY, and considered MacDonald a versifier. Among his collections are *The song of the prairie land, and other poems* (1918), *Out of the wilderness* (1926), *A flagon of beauty* (1931), *The song of the undertow, and other poems* (1935), and *Comber Cove*. Beginning in the early twenties, he went across the country reading his poetry to audiences in large cities and small towns. His personal shyness disappeared on stage, where he became dynamic; humming, chanting, and singing; he synchronized his whole performance to make poems come alive for his audience. On one of his tours he kept a notebook record of his journey, embellished with drawings. See Stan Dragland, *Wilson MacDonald's western tour, 1923–24* (1976).

McDougall, John (1842–1917). Born in Owen Sound, Canada West (Ontario), John Chantler McDougall grew up on the Methodist mission stations conducted by his father, the Rev. George Millward McDougall, among the Ojibwa of the Great Lakes. His formal education was limited to backwoods schools and two terms at Victoria College, Cobourg. The eldest of eight children, he left college at sixteen to accompany the mission family to Norway House on Lake Winnipeg. There he served as schoolteacher to the Native children, becoming fluent in Swampy Cree. Beginning in 1862 he worked for ten years as translator, provisioner, and apprentice missionary in the McDougall mission network, now moved inland to stations on the North Saskatchewan River. Whitefish, Victoria (Pakan), Edmonton, and Pigeon Lake were his homes, but he led a life of constant travel, following the Native camps as they in turn followed the buffalo. He was ordained as a Methodist minister in 1872. John McDougall is known for six books that made him a favourite with the turn-of-the-century Canadian reading public. A biography of his father, *George Millward McDougall: pioneer, patriot and missionary* (Toronto, 1888), was followed by five books of memoirs detailing his own adventurous life on the frontier among the Natives. The entire series is marked by surprising consistency of tone and freshness of recall. *Forest, lake and prairie: twenty years of frontier life in western Canada, 1842–62* (Toronto, 1895) describes his boyhood and youth; *Saddle, sled and showshoe: pioneering on the Saskatchewan in the sixties* (Toronto, 1896) covers the years from 1862 to McDougall's first marriage in 1865. *Pathfinding on plain and prairie: stirring scenes of life in the Canadian North-west* (Toronto, 1898, rpr. 1971), which recounts events from 1865 to 1868, went into several printings and was given a facsimile reprint. The most consciously structured and most satisfying of the series, *In the days of the Red River rebellion: life and adventure in the far west of Canada (1862–1872)* (1903, rpr. 1983), tells of the mounting strains on the interior region's residents during the period of unrest and uprising at Fort Garry. *On western trails in the early seventies: frontier life in the Canadian North-west* (1911) carries the story to 1875. J.E. Nix edited a sixth volume of memoirs, *Opening the great West* (1970), which had been left in manuscript at McDougall's death. It describes the events of 1876, chief among which was the death of his father on the plains near Calgary.

MacEwen, Gwendolyn (1941–87). Born in Toronto, she attended schools there and in Winnipeg. She published her first poem in *The CANADIAN FORUM* when she was seventeen, and left school at eighteen to pursue a literary career. She taught herself Hebrew, Arabic, Greek, and French, translating writers from each of these languages. She published over twenty books, in a variety of genres, and also wrote numerous radio docudramas for the Canadian Broadcasting Corporation. She had a surprising five-month marriage to the much older poet Milton ACORN; and later married, for six years, the Greek singer Nikos Tsingos; in 1972 they operated the Trojan Horse, a Toronto coffee house. Her links with Greece led her to write a volume of travel recollections, *Mermaids and ikons: a Greek summer* (1978, rpr.1984), and to translate with Tsingos two long poems of the contemporary Greek writer Yannis Ritsos. These were published in *Trojan women* (1981), which included MacEwen's version of Euripides' *The Trojan women*. Her modern adaptation of Aristophanes' *The birds* appeared in 1983.

MacEwen published two novels, *Julian the magician* (1963, rpr. 2004) and *King of Egypt, king of dreams* (1971, rpr. 2004), as well as two collections of short stories, *Noman* (1972), and *Noman's land* (1985), and three children's books: *The chocolate moose* (1979), *The honeydrum: seven tales from Arab lands* (1983), and *Dragon sandwiches* (1987). Her collections of verse include *The rising fire* (1963), *A breakfast for barbarians* (1966), *The shadow-maker* (1969, GGA), *The armies of the moon* (1972), *Magic animals: selected poems old and new* (1974), *The fire-eaters* (1976), *The T.E. Lawrence poems* (1982), *Earthlight: selected poetry 1963–1982* (1982), and *Afterworlds* (1987, GGA). Two volumes of *The poetry of Gwendolyn MacEwen*, edited by Margaret ATWOOD and Barry CALLAGHAN, appeared posthumously: *Vol. 1: The early years* (1993) and *Vol. 2: The later years (1994)*. See also *The selected Gwendolyn MacEwen* (2008) edited by Meaghan Strimas, with an introduction by Rosemary SULLIVAN.

In approaching MacEwen's verse and prose alike, the reader is tempted, as Margaret Atwood has said, 'to become preoccupied with the brilliant and original verbal surfaces she creates'. But this bright enamel of words and images, which woos the reader's initial pleasure, overlies profundities of thought and feeling. The extraordinary feat of empathy represented by *The T.E. Lawrence poems*—the voice seems to be Lawrence's own—suggests the oracular seriousness in her verse, and a growing inclination to move away from the elusive introspection of the early poems. This development can be seen by comparing the selections included in *Magic animals* with those in *Earthlight*, published seven years later. The poems in the latter volume have a greater solidity of texture and concreteness of imagery, a sharper visualness; they reveal a preoccupation with time and its multiple meanings, with the ambivalences of existence, with the archetypal patterns that emerge and re-emerge from ancient times to now, but also with the actual human lives that carry on in their mundane way within such patterns. There are few Canadian poets with a grasp as broad as MacEwen's of the poetic dimensions of history—the realm of the muse Clio—and of its necessarily Zoroastrian duality, expressed in the last line of *The T.E. Lawrence poems*: as T.E. Lawrence dies, his mind exclaims, 'Night comes and the stars are out. Salaam.' Light lives in darkness; darkness nurtures light.

Such concerns, recurring throughout her poetry, take personified form in MacEwen's novels that blend fantasy with history: *Julian the magician*, with its early-Renaissance preoccupation with hermetic quasi-philosophies and their ambiguous relationship to Christianity; *King of Egypt, king of dreams*, with its imaginative reconstruction of the gallant and eventually futile life of the heterodox pharaoh, Akhnaton. The stories in *Noman* are united by the central enigmatic character who names the book, and here the protean quality of MacEwen's talent takes full flight as her vision of 'Kanada' whirls in a mythological carousel whose turning unites us with every temporal past and every spatial present.

MacEwen's last book, *Afterworlds*—published in the year of her death—seems, uncannily, to be a summing-up of her work. It includes her much-admired radio drama, *Terror and Erebus*, written in 1965; poems to lost lovers; and political poems lamenting the nuclear terror into which the world was plunging. And yet she seemed to have found a new affirmative direction for her work through her reading of modern physics, which confirmed her sense of the mystery inherent in the material world. This is evident in her last poem, 'The Tao of physics', which concludes with the remarkable challenge: 'Here where events have a tendency to occur / My chair and all its myriad inner worlds / Whirl

around in the carousel of space; I hurl / Breathless poems against my lord Death, send these / words, these words / Careening into the beautiful darkness.'

See Rosemary Sullivan, *Shadow maker: the life of Gwendolyn MacEwen* (1995).

McFadden, David (b. 1940). Noted for his poetry of pop-art image and ironic ingenuousness, he lived his first thirty-nine years in Hamilton, Ontario. In 1962 he joined the staff of the *Hamilton Spectator* as a proofreader, became a reporter for the paper in 1970, and resigned in 1976 to take up freelance writing and editing. McFadden's poetry appeared first in *TISH, IS, Evidence, Weed, Talon*, and in his own mimeographed magazine *Mountain* (1962). The poems of McFadden's first major collections—*Letters from the earth to the earth* (1968), *Poems worth knowing* (1971), and *Intense pleasure* (1972)—use his family life with his wife and two daughters as their central symbol. Details about cooking meals or repairing toys are affirmed as important, despite the larger twentieth-century context of brutality and commercial exploitation. McFadden personified this conflict between family life and North American media advertising in his characterization of Ricky Wayne, the protagonist of his first novel, *The great Canadian sonnet* (1970). In the seventies his writing shifted its focus from the family home to the family's exploration of the outside world. The major poems of *A knight in dried plums* (1975) are the marvellously comic tourist poems 'Somewhere south of Springhill' and 'A typical Canadian family visits Disneyworld', in which an ostensibly naive narrator satirizes both the conventional expectations of the tourist and the outside world's eager fulfilment of these expectations. *On the road again* (1978) continued this exploration, although without the family as a central image.

McFadden followed these books with three comic 'novels': *A trip around Lake Erie* (1980), *A trip around Lake Huron* (1980), and *A trip around Lake Ontario* (1988). In exceedingly brief, discontinuous chapters, these picaresque works illustrate the struggle of the small man to make sense of an increasingly surreal and commercialized century. Updated and somewhat reworked, the texts of these three books make up *Great Lakes suite* (1997). The subtitle *Curious rambles and singular encounters* is an apt description of his delightfully whimsical *An innocent in Ireland* (1995), which was followed by *An innocent in Scotland: more curious rambles and singular encounters* (1999), plus *An innocent in Newfoundland* (2003) and *An innocent in*

Cuba (2005), both with similar subtitles. *Animal spirits: stories to live by* (1983), published with drawings by Greg Curnoe, is a retrospective collection of McFadden's short stories. Other books by McFadden are *The poem poem* (1967); *The saladmaker* (1968); *The ova yogas* (1972); *The poet's progress* (1977); *I don't know* (1978); *A new romance* (1979); *My body was eaten by dogs* (1981), selected poems edited and introduced by George BOWERING; *Country of the open heart* (1982), a book-length poem; *Three stories and ten poems* (1982); *A pair of baby lambs* (1983)—which contains two long, charming, funny poems, 'The cow that swam Lake Ontario' (published as a book in 2003) and 'Stormy January'; *The art of darkness* (1984); *Gypsy guitar: one hundred poems of romance and betrayal* (1987); *Anonymity suite* (1992); *There'll be another.* (1995), which begins with a moving remembrance of the painter Greg Curnoe, his close friend; and *Five star planet* (2002). *Why are you so sad? Selected poems* (2008) and *Be calm, Honey: 129 sonnets* (2008) are lighthearted collections, often humorous.

Macfarlane, David (b. 1952). Born in Hamilton, Ontario, and educated at the University of Toronto, he is a freelance journalist who has contributed to many Canadian and American magazines, for several years writing a weekly column for the Toronto *Globe and Mail* and winning ten National Magazine Awards. The family described in *The danger tree: memory, war, and the search for a family's past* (1991, rpr. 2000) is that of the author's mother, the prominent but never truly prosperous Goodyears of Newfoundland, beginning with her grandfather and grandmother, Josiah and Louisa Goodyear, and their six sons and one daughter—Macfarlane's great-aunt Kate, whom Louisa 'never forgave for being a girl and denying a mother her seven sons'. Three of the sons were killed in the Great War. The actions they and the Newfoundland Regiment were part of, described in vivid detail, and their deaths, make up a poignant and horrific narrative thread through the whole book. At the worst moment of the Somme offensive on 1 July 1916, the surviving Newfoundlanders 'found themselves only as far forward as a single, gnarled tree.... It was a landmark the Newfoundlanders used to mark the beginning of No Man's Land. They called it the Danger Tree.' The book also encompasses the author's boyhood discovery of his grandfather Joe, and his great-uncles Ken and Roland; his adult connections with the surviving Goodyears; and some highlights of Newfoundland history. All is smoothly interwoven with many good family and Newfoundland stories. In Macfarlane's first novel, *Summer gone* (1999, rpr. 2000), Bay Newling, divorced, takes his twelve-year-old son Caz—who lives with his mother, Sarah—on a canoe trip in northern Ontario and tells him stories by the campfire about his life, dwelling particularly on his memorable and only experience of a summer camp for boys in 1964. 'Bay told Caz that he had never seen anything as beautiful as his first glimpse of the water, the rock, the pines, and the windy blue sky of the Waubano Reaches.' But he was intensely homesick 'in the most beautiful place he knew. Sadness and beauty. He had never, in his life, separated the two.' The beauties of summer in the north had been enjoyed previously when Bay, Sarah, and six-year-old Caz rented the cottage of the family of Peter Larkin, the idolized camp counsellor who had disappeared from Bay's life. These events are central, but *Summer gone* is also a lyrical evocation of cottage country, of canoeing, of memory, and unfolds in a continuous flow without regard for time or place, portraying in sharp detail Bay's childhood, schooling, and later professional life as a magazine editor; the director of the camp; Bay's father; Sarah's stepfather; Peter Larkin's sister; and the blissful summer days at the Larkin cottage that lead to an event that causes the end of Bay's marriage. The reader's interest in *Summer gone* as a literary work is divided between its beautiful construction and language, the author's rendering of the powerful hold of memory, and the layers of narrative that make up the novel as it wends its way to a haunting conclusion. It was a co-winner in 2000 of the Chapters/Books in Canada First Novel Award. Macfarlane wrote the text for *At the Ojibway: 100 summers on Georgian Bay* (2006), a large-format picturebook, filled with photographs, that celebrates the enjoyments of the Ojibway Hotel, built in 1906 on Ojibway Island, one of many islands in Georgian Bay, Ontario. Macfarlane also edited, and wrote a long introductory essay for, *Toronto: a city becoming* (2008), containing twenty-two other essays and a lavish array of photographs.

McFarlane, Leslie (1903–1977). Born in Carleton Place, Ontario, and raised in Haileybury, he worked as a reporter on the Cobalt Nugget and other newspapers before contributing to American pulp magazines under such pseudonyms as 'Roy Rockwood' (for juveniles), 'James Cody Ferris' (westerns), and 'Bert Standish' (general articles). In 1926, answering an advertisement ('Experienced Fiction Writer Wanted to Work from Publisher's

Outlines'), placed in an American trade paper by the Stratemeyer Syndicate, he commenced two decades of ghostwriting. In his lively autobiography, *Ghost of the Hardy Boys* (1976), he explained how he wrote the first Hardy Boy book under the house name 'Franklin W. Dixon' in his room above a bank in Hailey-bury. He began with *The tower treasure* (1926) and completed twenty volumes in the popular boys' adventure series. As well, he was the first writer to use the name 'Carolyn Keene', the byline later identified with the Nancy Drew detective books for young girls. Under his own name he wrote *Streets of shadow* (1930), a romantic novel, and *McGonigle scores!* (1966), a hockey juvenile that continues to find readers. *A kid in Haileybury* (1975, rpr. 1996) is a brief memoir of his boyhood. McFarlane scripted documentary films for the National Film Board and contributed dramatic scripts to CBC-TV, serving as the Corporation's chief drama editor in 1958–60. He retains a secure place in the affections of three generations of North American young-sters from the moment they opened the first of the Hardy Boy books and began to read: 'Two bright-eyed boys on motorcycles were speeding along a shore road.'

McGill Fortnightly Review (1925–7). Founded by A.J.M. SMITH and F.R. SCOTT, then graduate students at McGill University, Montreal, it was described by Leon EDEL, a contributing editor, as representing 'the innovative spirit of the 1920s in Canada'. Other writers associated with the journal were A.M. KLEIN and Leo KENNEDY. It developed out of the modernist movement of the early twentieth century, associated primarily with James Joyce and T.S. Eliot—Smith's second article in the *Review* was an analysis of Eliot's *The waste land* (1922). In various editorials, Smith argued that Cana-dian poets must go beyond the 'maple-leaf school' of Bliss CARMAN, Archibald LAMPMAN, Duncan Campbell SCOTT, and Charles G.D. ROBERTS in favour of free verse, imagistic treatment, displacement, complexity, and a leaner diction free of Victorian mannerisms. One target of the *McGill Fortnightly Review* was the CANADIAN AUTHORS' ASSOCIA-TION, founded in 1921. The last issue of the journal included F.R. Scott's much-antholo-gized satirical poem 'The Canadian authors meet', which pilloried the Association as representing amateurism in art. While short-lived, the journal was important in first articulating the new ideas of modernism that were to influence Canadian literature beginning in the 1940s.

McGill Poetry Series. See Louis DUDEK.

McGill-Queen's University Press. The venture of two Canadian universities, McGill-Queen's University Press (MQUP) was estab-lished in 1969 and has always sought to attract a broad cross-section of Canadian academics in focusing on publications in the humanities and social sciences. In 2008 it originated 130 titles, distributing them world wide, with the bulk of the sales in Canada and the United States. The executive director and senior editor is Philip Cercone. MQUP publishes numerous series, including Studies in the History of Ideas, Studies in the History of Religion, Native and Northern Series, Footprint Series, Arts Insights, and the MQUP/Beaverbrook Foundations Art History Series. In 1999 it launched the Hugh MacLellan Poetry Series and now publishes at least two books of poetry annually. As an offshoot of this series it pub-lished its first book of fiction in 2000—*The Accidental Indies* (2000) by Robert Finley, which landed on *Maclean's* bestseller list. MQUP's titles in fiction and literary criticism include new editions of Phyllis Brett Young's *The Torontonians* (2007) and *Psyche* (2008), and Wendy Davis's *Dal and Rice* (2008), Alan H. Adamson's *Mr Charlotte Brontë: the life of Arthur Bell Nichols* (2008), Mary Ann Gillies and Aurelea Mahood's *Modernist literature* (2007), Priscilla Uppal's *We are what we mourn: the con-temporary English-Canadian elegy* (2008), Rein-hold Kramer's *Mordecai Richler: leaving St Urbain* (2008), and Nora Foster Stovel's *Divining Margaret Laurence* (2008). When the Carleton University Press closed in 2000, MQUP took over the CARLETON LIBRARY series and CUP's backlist; it also distributes the books of the CENTRE FOR EDITING EARLY CANADIAN TEXTS.

MacGregor, Mary Esther (1876–1961). Born Mary Esther Miller in Rugby, Ontario, she was educated in Orillia and at the Toronto Normal School. She married a Presbyterian minister, the Rev. Donald MacGregor, in 1909, residing first in London, Ont., then in Brantford and Owen Sound, where they retired. Under the pseudonym 'Marian Keith', MacGregor was a prolific writer of popular fiction. Most of her stories depict rural life, particularly in predominantly Scottish settle-ments in Ontario in the 1880s, where con-flicts among English, Irish, and Scottish settlers, and between Methodists and Presby-terians, served as her focus. *Duncan Polite, the watchman of Glenoro* (1905) is about a minister whose desire to install an organ in the church causes a furore. It was followed by *Treasure Valley* (1908), *Lizbeth of the Dale* (1910), *The end of the rainbow* (1913), *In orchard glen* (1918), *Little Miss Melody* (1921), *The bells of St Stephen's* (1922), and *The forest barrier* (1930). Her trilogy—*As a watered garden* (1947), *Yonder shining light* (1948), and *Lilacs in the dooryard* (1952)—set in a community near Georgian Bay, continued to stress her central themes of goodwill and community co-operation. *The silver maple* (1906), depicting a Canadian expedition to rescue General Charles Gordon at Khartoum, and *A gentleman adventurer: a story of the Hudson's Bay Company* (1924), have a broader focus. In all, MacGregor wrote fourteen novels—the last, *A grand lady* (1960), was published a year before her death. Although overly didactic, sentimental by modern standards, and slim and formulaic in plot, her books retain some value as regional idylls rich in quotidian detail regarding life in small Ontario communities before the turn of the century.

MacInnes, Tom (1867–1951). Born in Dresden, Ontario, Thomas Robert Edward MacInnes was a son of Thomas McInnes, a lieutenant-governor of British Columbia (1897–1902): he changed the spelling of his family name. He went with his family to New Westminster, British Columbia, in 1881, was educated at the University of Toronto, and was called to the bar in 1893. He was secretary to the Bering Sea Commission (1896–7) and helped supervise the importation of goods to Skagway (1897) for members of the Klondike Gold Rush. He practised law in Vancouver and was involved with the drafting of immigration laws in 1910, and with import regulations and the control of narcotics. From 1916 to 1927 MacInnes spent long periods in China, where he had business interests. As a result he developed a sympathy for the treatment of Orientals living in British Columbia; his views of British Columbia prejudice appeared in the pamphlet *Oriental occupation of British Columbia* (1927). MacInnes's autobiographical *Chinook days* (1926) contains his impressions of people, places, and events in British Columbia history. His narrative poems—concerned with adventure or dramatic situations in strange environments (his attitude is bohemian), and expressing his enjoyment of life—were highly popular in his lifetime. He wrote light, easy verse that dismissed smugness and respectability with unconcerned humour. Even when MacInnes is sometimes serious, an amused detachment underlies his work, as though

poetry were merely one form of expression, as good as any other. He felt that any subject was appropriate for poetry and was especially interested in examining people within a natural landscape, on the fringes of society. Though uninterested in poetic subtleties—his rhythms are often forced and pedantic, his rhyme schemes careless and rough—he was intrigued with elaborate poetic forms, such as the villanelle, and with a five-line stanza of his own he called the 'mirelle'. His belief that joy and delight, rather than the prevalent melancholic outpourings of the soul, were essential to poetry was expressed in one of his later and best-known poems, 'The tiger of desire', which fits an allusion to the past (Blake) and to contemporary concerns (a type of Darwin-mysticism) into his usual structure, the villanelle. His collections are *A romance of the lost* (1908), reprinted with other poems in *Lonesome bar, A romance of the lost, and other poems* (1909); *In amber lands* (1910), *Rhymes of a rounder* (1913), *The fool of joy* (1918), *Roundabout rhymes* (with a Foreword by Charles G.D. ROBERTS, 1923), *Complete poems of Tom MacInnes* (1923), *High low along: a didactic poem* (1934), and *In the old of my age* (1947).

McKay, Don (b. 1942). Donald Fleming McKay was born in Owen Sound, Ontario, and raised in Cornwall. He was educated at Bishop's University, Lennoxville, Québec, the University of Western Ontario (B.A., 1965; M.A., 1966), and the University of Wales (Ph.D., 1971). He has taught Canadian literature and creative writing at the University of Western Ontario and, from 1990 to 1996, at the University of New Brunswick, where he was editor of The FIDDLEHEAD (1991–7); he has also been an editor and co-publisher of BRICK BOOKS since 1976. He now lives in Victoria, B.C. McKay has written eleven books of poetry: *Air occupies space* (1973); *Long Sault* (1975), a long poem; *Lependu* (1978); *Lightning ball bait* (1980); *Birding, or Desire* (1983); *Sanding down this rocking chair on a windy night* (1987); *Night field* (1991, GGA); *Apparatus* (1997); *Another gravity* (2000, GGA); *Camber: selected poems 1983–2000* (2004), the title poem of which refers to 'That rising curve, the fine line / between craft and magic where we / travel uphill without effort, where anticipation, / slipping into eros, / summons the skin.' *Strike / Slip* (2006) won the GRIFFIN POETRY PRIZE, for which the jury citation declared that 'His gift, it seems, is as natural as the living world he so frequently chooses to write of, and his poems as airborne and acrobatic as the birds which populate the vast skies and landscapes of his imagination.' McKay explains the title in a note: 'A strike/ slip fault ... is a high-angle fault along which rocks on the one side move horizontally in relation to rocks on the other side with a shearing motion.' One example is the Loss Creek–Leech River Fault on southern Vancouver Island. *Field marks: the poetry of Don McKay* (2006) is a brief collection in the Laurier Poetry Series, selected with an introduction by Méira Cook. *Vis à vis: fields notes on poetry & wilderness* (2001) and *Deactivated West 100* (2006) contain variations, in both prose and poetry, on a poetics of place. McKay's gift for metaphor—which he calls 'anthropomorphic play'—produces in his work delightful and startling portraits of familiar objects, rivers, trees, and small creatures, birds especially. His poetry is informed by his concern for the natural environment—for the ways in which wilderness co-exists with us, teasing and frustrating our need for firm understanding, or for knowledge as a kind of ownership. McKay conceives of 'wilderness' not solely as threatening ecosphere but as the elusive quality of otherness in all things, even tools: the things we have our hands on, but cannot grasp in the full sense. His ironic sense of humour, deadpan delivery, and knack for overturning clichés give some of his work a deceptively light tone.

Mackenzie, Sir Alexander. See EXPLORATION LITERATURE IN ENGLISH:1.

Mackenzie, William Lyon (1795–1861). Born in Scotland, where both his grandfathers had fought for the rebel cause at Culloden, Mackenzie immigrated to Upper Canada in 1820. He founded *The Colonial Advocate* (Queenston, 1824; York, 1824–34) and a succession of other newspapers, which he edited, published, and wrote much of the copy for: *The Correspondent and Advocate* (Toronto, 1834–6); *The Constitution* (Toronto, 1836–Nov. 1837); *Mackenzie's Gazette* (New York 1838–9; Rochester, 1839–40); *The Volunteer* (Rochester, 1841–42); *The New York Examiner* (New York, 1843); *Mackenzie's Weekly Message* (Toronto, 1852–6); and *The Toronto Weekly Message* (1856–60). In his career as a radical politician and agitator, Mackenzie was elected to—and expelled from—the Upper Canada House of Assembly several times, and was the first mayor of Toronto for nine months in 1834–5. A leader in the 1837 Rebellion, which collapsed following skirmishes with government forces near and in

Toronto on Dec. 7, Mackenzie escaped to the United States, where he felt the influence of the editor and journalist Horace Greeley. He returned to Canada under the Amnesty Act of 1849, was re-elected to the Assembly in 1851, and resigned in 1858. During a lifelong messianic quest to make of his nation a genuinely charitable community, his reckless, impulsive, opinionated personality became itself a main cause of the controversies that surrounded him.

Mackenzie published many books and his interests were wide-ranging; for example, *Essay on canals and inland navigation* (Queenston, 1824), *Catechism of education* (York, 1830), *Sketches of Canada and the United* States (London, 1833). All his writing was in large part polemical, and the following titles indicate the prevailing tone: *The legislative black list of Upper Canada; or, Official corruption and hypocrisy unmasked* (York, 1828), *Celebrated letter of Joseph Hume, esq., M.P., to William Lyon Mackenzie* (Toronto, 1834), *The seventh report from the select committee of the House of Assembly of Upper Canada on grievances* (Toronto, 1835). He was also a raconteur: of tales of war and intrigue (*Head's flag of truce*, Toronto, 1853?); of frontier rowdiness (*The history of the destruction of the 'Colonial Advocate' press*, York, 1826); of escape and adventure (*Mackenzie's own narrative of the late rebellion*, Toronto, 1838). He wrote memorable character studies (*Life and opinions of Andrew Jackson*, York, 1829; and *The sons of the Emerald Isle; or Lives of one thousand remarkable Irishmen*, New York, 1845). He also wrote vivid, concrete, observant accounts of Upper and Lower Canada, its scenes and people, that earn him a place among significant travel writers of Canada. He was a puritan moralizer—and a furious, chronic, Juvenalian satirist—of the 'family compact' of Upper Canada, and of several Americans (*The life and times of Martin van Buren*, Boston, 1846; *The lives and opinions of Benjamin Franklin Butler, United States district attorney, and Jesse Hoyt, counsellor at law, formerly collector of customs for the port of New York*, Boston, 1845). Mackenzie's writing mixes shrill invective with a prophet's exalted visions and a Calvinist sense of good v. evil—which, for Mackenzie, meant poor v. established rich. Wide reading enabled him to mix homely similes from Scottish folklore, poetic quotations, rustic-frontier anecdotes, Biblical analogies, with elevated declarations of abstract political principle. His expository and polemical pieces, at their best, proceed via methodical arguments buttressed with fact, example, and illustration; long periodic sentences build in rhythm and sound towards conclusions as climactic in cadence as in meaning.

Some of Mackenzie's writing has the quality of poetry. See John Robert COLOMBO's selection of 'redeemed prose', *The Mackenzie poems* (1960): 'We have often repeated / that we want more legislators / who are able to sign their own names, / and write three words following each other / without misspelling, / and we must allow them / to get an education somewhere.' And the 'found poem' from Mackenzie's 1837 Navy Island proclamation in Raymond SOUSTER's *Hanging in* (1979). The colourfully heroic Mackenzie often appears as a character in Canadian literature. See, for example, Rick SALUTIN's drama *1837: the farmer's revolt* (1975); James REANEY's children's novel *The boy with an R in his hand* (1965); and William KILBOURN's *The firebrand* (1956), a biography that, like the writings of its subject, often achieves literary stature. In Dale Hamilton's 1990 agit-prop community play *The spirit of Shivaree*, Mackenzie inspires a 1980s farmers' revolt against a modern oligarchy turning farm land into suburban real-estate. However controversial, Mackenzie will always be needed (as Dennis LEE writes in *Nicholas Knock and other people*, 1974), in the way that every nation needs its millennialists.

See *The selected writings of William Mackenzie: 1824–1837* (1960) edited by Margaret Fairley, and the passages by Mackenzie in A.J.M. SMITH's *The book of Canadian prose, vol. 1: early beginnings to Confederation* (1965).

McLachlan, Alexander (1818–96). Born in Johnstone, Scotland, he worked in a cotton factory until he was apprenticed to a tailor in Glasgow. In 1840 he immigrated to Caledon, Upper Canada (Ontario), to take possession of the farm of his father, who had died. He sold it the next year and cleared land for three other farms before moving in 1850 to Erin Township, where he worked as a tailor to support his family of eleven children; achieving a reputation as a speaker, he also gave lectures for the Mechanics' Institute. Through his friendship with D'Arcy McGee, he was made immigration agent for Canada in Scotland in 1862. In 1877 he moved to a farm in Amaranth Township, Ontario, where he lived until he retired to a house in nearby Orangeville in 1895. For his idylls about log houses, 'hosses', and oxen in the bush, McLachlan is the poet of the backwoods pioneers; in his time he was known as 'the Burns of Canada' for his celebration of the democratic spirit of brotherhood and the toil of the common man. 'A backwoods hero' celebrates the steadfast work

of the pioneer—'he chopped, he logg'd, he cleared his lot'—who turns the backwoods into a prosperous and charitable farming community. McLachlan was at his best in light lyrics that document the customs of country life, as in 'Sparking' (the pioneers' slang for courtship). Like Burns, he complements his reverence for the common man with kindly humour, satirizing skinflints and mistreaters of oxen. Occasionally, as in 'We live in a rickety house', he rises to the ironic pitch of a Blakean nursery song in condemning the naivety of pious charity workers who fail to recognize the church's responsibility for the ignorance and crime that exist among the poor. Of his five volumes of verse—*The spirit of love and other poems* (Toronto, 1846), *Poems* (Toronto 1856), *Lyrics* (Toronto, 1858), *The emigrant and other poems* (Toronto, 1861), and *Poems and songs* (Toronto, 1874)—the 1874 volume is his best collection, while 'The emigrant' is his most ambitious single poem, an unfinished epic in narrative couplets and songs telling of the Scottish immigrants who sailed across the ocean to clear land for a home in the backwoods of Upper Canada. As E.H. DEWART noted in his introduction to the posthumous collection *The poetical works of Alexander McLachlan* (Toronto, 1900; rpr. 1974 with an Introduction by E. Margaret Fulton), McLachlan 'was too often satisfied with putting the passing thoughts that occupied his mind into easy, homely rimes.' For his scholarly edition of *The emigrant* (1990), D.M.R. Bentley wrote a detailed introduction.

Maclennan, Hugh (1907–90). Born in Glace Bay, Nova Scotia, the son of a medical doctor, he grew up in Halifax, was educated at Dalhousie University and, as a Rhodes Scholar, at Oxford, and travelled in Europe before taking his doctoral degree in classical studies at Princeton University. His dissertation, published as *Oxyrhynchus: an economic and social study* (1935, rpr. 1968), showed a leftist bias that was later cured by MacLennan's visit to Russia in 1937; but some critics point to the relevance for his fiction of its analysis of the decay of a Roman colony cut off from its roots in the parent civilization. While at Princeton, MacLennan also began writing fiction, but, out of economic necessity, turned to the teaching of Latin and history at Lower Canada College, Montreal, in 1935. Originally encouraged to write by the American writer Dorothy Duncan, whom he married in 1936, he made two abortive attempts at novels with international settings. According to MacLennan, Dorothy directed him to the national theme and setting that he knew, and the result was BAROMETER RISING (1941, NCL), which drew on his boyhood experience of the Halifax explosion of 1917. On the strength of its *succès d'estime* he spent a year in New York on a Guggenheim Fellowship. He returned reluctantly to Lower Canada College, but then TWO SOLITUDES (1945, rpr. 1993, NCL) became a commercial success and won a Governor General's Award, as did *The precipice* (1947) and his first volume of essays, *Cross-country* (1949). MacLennan was now a celebrity, writing regularly for *Maclean's* and other national magazines. His second volume of essays, *Thirty and three* (1954), brought him a fourth Governor General's Award; but by this time financial pressure and Dorothy's chronic illness obliged him to seek academic security, and he began lecturing part-time in the English Department of McGill University. The impact on MacLennan of Dorothy's death is apparent in the emotional intensity of *The watch that ends the night* (1959, rpr. 1991), the novel—for many readers his best—that brought him a record fifth Governor General's Award. He followed it the next year with a third volume of essays, *Scotchman's return and other essays* (1960). In 1967 he became a Companion of the Order of Canada; in 1968 he was made a full professor at McGill and received his seventh honorary degree. He retired as Professor Emeritus in 1979 and lived until his death with his second wife, Frances Walker, at North Hatley, Québec.

Though MacLennan's public honours were closely associated with his reputation as a nationalist, his larger subject was Graeco-Roman civilization and its long decline to the present. This Spenglerian view—in which the key to survival and to more fulfilling lives may be found in learning the lessons of history and the wisdom taught by both classical and Judaeo-Christian writers—accounted for MacLennan's vision, in the early novels, of Canada, heir of European culture, as a mediator between the crude, vital New World and an Old World informed by classical ideals; and it justified his use of classical models, particularly the Homeric epic. George WOODCOCK and others have pointed to the prominence in MacLennan's fiction of the Odyssean archetype—a figure that is often not simply a home-seeker but an emissary of civilization to an increasingly indifferent world.

MacLennan's deliberate choice of Canadian concerns for his subjects, and his early view of Canada as mediating between an inherited culture and North American obsessive materialism, earned him a too-facile reputation as a crusading nationalist. Of course he was a nationalist. Neil Macrae of *Barometer rising* could have no identity until the colonial past, engendered in violence, had been violently destroyed. As Neil's identity is acknowledged, so is that of the nation: it has earned the right to be itself. In *Two solitudes* Paul Tallard and Heather Methuen combine artistic creativity with a symbolic marriage of the two founding peoples, and Paul determines to write a novel about Canada. In *Each man's son* (1951, NCL), which features the Cape Breton of MacLennan's childhood, Alan Mac-Neil is saved from the crippling life of the mines and taught the privilege of belonging to civilization, especially in Canada, as respected honest broker of the postwar world, where the past can meet the energy of the future. But the optimism inherent in MacLennan's early nationalism soon soured. In *The precipice* there is already a sense of dismay at the destructive power of American industry and less confidence in Canada's ability to meliorate it. The small Ontario town in which the action begins has only potential; not even the Second World War can arouse it until American energy, in the person of Stephen Lassiter, invades it. In *The watch that ends the night* it is openly acknowledged that scientific, military, economic, and even political power ultimately reside outside Canada; salvation is not national but an individual and a personal dream. Jerome Martel—doctor, saviour, man of violence—returns, almost from the grave, to threaten the happiness of timid, bourgeois George Stewart and his sick wife Catherine, who was once married to Jerome. But through him, George and Catherine—who represents what is gracious and civilized in a declining world—learn to accept her death.

The tone of MacLennan's last two novels is much darker. *Return of the sphinx* (1967, rpr. 1986) deals with the nation's failure to heal the rift between French- and English-speaking Canadians, and with the perpetuation in the New World not of the values but the hatreds of the Old. With this novel MacLennan conceded that Canada's future, like its politics and economics, was beyond our control: everything the protagonist, Alan, had stood for seemed lost, the only hope being represented by a rural French-Canadian wedding and Alan's awareness of love for his children. *Voices in time* (1980, rpr. 1993), set in Montreal fifty years after it was destroyed by a nuclear holocaust, portrays a world like that of Orwell's *1984* as John Wellfleet, like Orwell's Winston, finds and puzzles over the evidence of his family's past and a former civilization: decline and fall are here complete. MacLennan moved back and forth in time and space to repeat his major theme: that the failures to learn the lessons of the past and to guarantee civilized values make the destruction of the West—like the destruction of the classical world—inevitable.

MacLennan's novels have been criticized for their didacticism, the tendency to tell rather than show. Too often the author stops to reflect on national and historical issues or to explain in laboured dialogue or monologue what his characters are supposed to mean. Though MacLennan can be sensitive, he sometimes becomes embarrassed and rhetorical in intimate scenes, especially sexual ones. Generally well within the realistic mode, his protagonists (notably Jerome Martell) sometimes seem more romantic than real. Some of them, however—George Stewart, Athanase Tallard—are memorable as well as representative. There are fine set pieces in some of the novels. The Halifax explosion in *Barometer rising*, Jerome's recollection of his escape from the lumber camp in *The watch*, and Archie MacNeil's decline in *Each man's son* show MacLennan's gift for fast-paced, exciting narrative. With *The precipice* the characterization becomes more overtly psychological, and in all the novels a sustained structure of imagery reinforces character and theme.

Related to the three volumes of essays, most of which are journalistic and occasional pieces, are the texts for *The colour of Canada* (1967); *McGill: the story of a university* (1961); and *The rivers of Canada* (1974), which is a much-revised version of *Seven rivers of Canada* (1961). Its introductory essay, 'Thinking like a river', acknowledges the 'watershed of the '60s' that changed the writer's, and our, world: MacLennan's realization that for Canada and the Western world a cycle of civilization, or order and human values, was ending, to be replaced by the violent era of the 'rough beast'. This realization informed the fiction and the non-fiction alike and gave unity to MacLennan's work. His essays on the rivers, like those on Canadian cities, effectively personify characteristics of the landscape he loved. *The other side of Hugh MacLennan* (1978), essays edited by Elspeth CAMERON, selects the best of the non-fiction and testifies to MacLennan's skill in the shorter form. See also *Hugh MacLennan's best* (1991) edited by Douglas Gibson. *Dear Marian, Dear Hugh: the MacLennan-Engel correspondence* (1995), edited by Christi Verduyn, contains mostly letters from MacLennan to Marian ENGEL.

See Elspeth Cameron's *Hugh MacLennan: a writer's life* (1981), which provides a wealth of personal data and anecdotes with careful documentation.

MacLeod, Alistair (b. 1936). Born in North Battleford, Saskatchewan, he grew up in Alberta until he was ten. In 1946 his parents took their family back to their Cape Breton ancestral farm. Macleod studied at the Nova Scotia Teacher's College, St Francis Xavier University (B.A., B. Ed., 1960), the University of New Brunswick (M.A., 1961), and Notre Dame University (Ph.D., 1968). He taught English at the University of Indiana for three years and then moved in 1969 to the University of Windsor, Ontario, where he taught English and creative writing, and was appointed University Professor in 1993; he is now Professor Emeritus. He was the fiction editor of *The University of Windsor Review* for some twenty-five years.

MacLeod began publishing short stories in Canadian and American journals in the 1960s and 1970s, and his stories 'The boat' and 'The lost salt gift of blood' were included in *Best American short stories* in 1969 and 1975 respectively. His collections *The lost salt gift of blood* (1976, NCL) and *As birds bring forth the sun and other stories* (1986, NCL) both received critical praise. Joyce Carol Oates introduced MacLeod's work to a larger American audience with her selection of his stories, *The lost salt gift of blood: new and selected stories* (1989), which includes four of the *Blood* stories, six of the *Sun* stories, and a long story, 'Island'. One senses—as Oates points out—that MacLeod's intensely compacted stories 'might have been expanded into novels'. This was followed by *Island: the collected stories of Alistair MacLeod* (2000, rpr. 2001), which contains two new stories. His deep identification with the geography and culture of Cape Breton—its Gaelic heritage, the working life of the farm, mine, bush, and sea—lies at the centre of his stories, which draw on the oral tradition of storytelling. MacLeod's narrators are also haunted by their pasts, immediate and ancestral, and they elegiacally reflect on their pasts in what appears to be the immediate present, in a kind of eternal 'nowness' in which their pasts bleed persistently into their present. Many of his narrators attempt to free themselves from their families, from the traditional island professions of mining, farming, and fishing, and from the close-knit Cape Breton culture, by leaving for eastern or mid-western cities. In these stories ('The vastness of the dark', 'The lost salt gift of blood', 'The boat', 'The return',

MacLeod

'The road to Rankin's Point') MacLeod explores a kind of triple-paradox: you have to leave home, but you can never leave home, and when you leave home you cannot come back. In his highly praised first novel, *No great mischief* (1999), MacLeod's Cape Breton heritage and his gift for storytelling are reflected in the anecdotes that fill the family history of the Cape Breton MacDonalds. The narrator is Alexander MacDonald, a successful orthodontist in southwestern Ontario who, as the novel begins, is driving to see his alcoholic brother, Calum, in Toronto, a meeting that arouses memories and stories, beginning in 1779, when the first of the Highland MacDonald clan immigrated to Cape Breton. Having themes of loss—of the parents of the narrator (his name is seldom mentioned) and his twin sister when they were three, and of the Gaelic linguistic heritage—and history, the novel is carried from beginning to end by memories of the past, sometimes achingly described. Grandpa and Grandma, who raised the two young orphans, and their other Grandfather, all happy and admirable people, are at its centre—with the two grandfathers, old friends, often talking about ancient Highland battles (Grandpa would say, 'Never was a MacDonald afraid', and quote, 'My hope is constant in thee, Clan MacDonald'). But family reminiscences also abound among the narrator's three much older brothers, and when the narrator visits his sister, married and living in Calgary. Music is important in their lives, and the text is often interrupted by songs sung in Gaelic, and by fiddling. In 1968, immediately after he graduated in dentistry, the narrator had joined for a summer his brothers working in the uranium mine at Elliot Lake, replacing a cousin killed in an underground accident. Between the MacDonalds and the French-Canadian mineworkers there is conflict—an ironic subversion of the mutual loyalty that existed between the French and the Scots in the historical past (about Culloden, 'If only the ships had come from France!' is a cherished refrain)—and a murder ensues, involving Calum. At the end of the novel the narrator visits Grandma, now 110, who does not recognize him and whose memories of the past overtake the present, as they do in the novel—though their hands finally join in a Gaelic song. The title comes from James Wolfe's saying, in a letter mentioning his Highlanders, that there would be 'no great mischief if they fall'. The novel won the IMPAC Dublin Literary Award in 2001. MacLeod's *To everything there is a season: a Cape Breton Christmas story* (2004), is a beautiful and charming short book illustrated by Peter Rankin. He was appointed an Officer of the Order of Canada in 2007.

MacLeod, Joan (b. 1954). Born in Vancouver, she has creative-writing degrees from the University of Victoria (B.A., 1978) and the University of British Columbia (M.F.A., 1981). Her entrance into the world of theatre began when she wrote the libretto for *The Secret Garden* (prod. 1985 by Comus Music Theatre), an opera adaptation by Stephen MacNeff of the classic Victorian novel. She moved to Toronto in 1985 to join Tarragon Theatre's Six Playwrights Unit and then became playwright-in-residence until 1992, when she returned to British Columbia. In 1987 Tarragon premiered *Jewel* and *Toronto, Mississippi*, which were published in one volume in 1989—both plays have had many productions. The former (rpr. 2002) is the poignant 'conversation' that a young widow has with her husband, a casualty of Newfoundland's 1984 Ocean Ranger oil-rig disaster. *Toronto, Mississippi* (rpr. 2008) is about Maddie, a single mom trying to raise mentally handicapped daughter Jhana, and Maddie's boarder Bill. The crisis occurs when Jhana's flamboyant father, an Elvis Presley impersonator, shows up and decides not to leave, eventually misinterpreting the relationship of Jhana and Bill. *Amigo's blue guitar* (1992, GGA; 3rd edn 1997) juxtaposes cultures and complicates personal motives while dealing with the consequences for a Gulf Island (British Columbia) family when they sponsor a Salvadorean refugee. *The hope slide* (1994, 2nd edn 1999)—published with *Little sister*—returns to the monologue form, but this time the speaker plays not only herself but other characters: embarked on a tour of her one-person show about the Doukhobors, an actress experiences a dark night of the soul. The controlling metaphor is loss, but her reverie weaves together memories of coming of age in the 1960s, the famous landslide outside Hope, British Columbia, untimely deaths by AIDS, and persecution of the Doukhobor community. The subject of *Little sister*, written for teenage audiences, is self-image, body image, and eating disorders. MacLeod's *2000* (1997), produced in 1996, is less about particular issues than about a general anxiety for the future. Living on the edge of a century, on the edge of a ravine, a middle-aged couple are totally immersed in their own hectic present as urban planners—but various intruders make them painfully aware of their own estrangement. *The shape of a girl*, based on the horrifying killing of the Victoria schoolgirl Reena Virk, is a one-act, one-character play commissioned by Green Thumb Theatre and first produced in Calgary in 2001. It was published with *Jewel*, in one volume, by TALON-BOOKS in 2002. In 2008 MacLeod published *Homechild*, a play first produced by the Canadian Stage Company in Toronto in January 2006 (and, in a revised form, in Victoria in 2007), which centres on Alistair, a retired farmer, who had come from Scotland to Canada in 1922 as a 'home child', part of an officially sanctioned child migration from Britain to Canada that separated children from their families, often forever, and sometimes allowed them to be employed as child labourers. *Another home invasion* (2009) is a new play: who is robbing a home's elderly occupants?

McLuhan, Marshall (1911–80). Herbert Marshall McLuhan was born in Edmonton, and spent his youth in Winnipeg. He graduated from the University of Manitoba (B.A., 1933; M.A., 1934) and received a doctorate in English literature from Cambridge University in 1943. In 1944, after teaching English at Saint Louis University, a Jesuit institution in St Louis, Missouri, he returned to Canada to teach at Assumption College (now the University of Windsor). From 1946 until 1979 he taught English at St Michael's College, University of Toronto, where he became interested in media of communication, culture, and technology, organizing an interdisciplinary seminar in 1953–4 under the sponsorship of the Ford Foundation. Outgrowths of this project included the innovative periodical *Explorations*, which he co-edited with Edmund (Ted) Carpenter from 1953 to 1959, and the Centre of Culture and Technology (1963–81), at the University of Toronto, of which he was founding director. One of the first scholars to occupy the Albert Schweitzer Chair at Fordham University, New York, in 1967, he was named a Companion of the Order of Canada in 1970.

Although usually described as a communications scholar, McLuhan made major contributions to literary and cultural studies, and to the understanding of the role of media and the effects of technology in society. His first work, *The mechanical bride: folklore of industrial man* (1951, rpr. 2003), applied the strategies of a satirically focused critical interpretation to products of popular culture and the media industries. As early as 1959 (writing presciently about the 1990s), he said in a letter that in the electronic age 'we are returning to

the old tribal patterns, abandoning the highly individualistic ways of the Western World.... The tribe is a unit, which, extending the boundaries of the family to include the whole society, becomes the only way of organizing society when it exists in a kind of Global Village pattern ... caused by the instantaneous movement of information from every quarter to every point at the same time. Tribal man, or family man, is characterized by certain basic outlooks and strategies, of which perhaps the most obvious is a deep sense of togetherness, a strong resistance to change.'

McLuhan's international reputation was established by two works bridging historical and theoretical problems. *The Gutenberg galaxy: the making of typographic man* (1962, rpr. 2000) analyzes the pre-print, oral/aural culture and the cultural changes brought about by Gutenberg's invention of movable type and the mass production of books; it introduced publicly one of McLuhan's most famous phrases in stating that the world had become a 'global village' in its electronic interdependence. *Understanding media: the extensions of man* (1964, rpr. 1971) examines the radical changes in man's responses caused by electronic communications and contains one of his most celebrated aphorisms, 'the medium is the message'. After the publication of these books McLuhan's name became a word in itself, such as *mcluhanisme* in France. His work paralleled the interests of other Canadian scholars, particularly H.A. INNIS—who has often been described, erroneously, as his mentor. (McLuhan did share with Innis a realization of the importance of technology in shaping human cultural development.) While McLuhan, like Northrop FRYE, was interested in problems of interpretation and symbolism, he had a broader scope, seeking a total cultural criticism. He emphasized the way polysemy in language (e.g., puns, ambiguity, metaphor) reveals the continuum between all orders of cultural expression.

Influenced by the work of avant-garde writers such as Wyndham Lewis and James Joyce, McLuhan created, with Quentin Fiore, a series of *essais concrètes* combining photography, layout, advertising techniques, headlines, typography, and visual arrangement: e.g., *The medium is the massage* (1967) and *War and peace in the global village* (1968). Other books by McLuhan include *Counterblast* (1969); *Culture is our business* (1970); *Take today: the executive as dropout* (with Barrington Nevitt, 1972); *The city as classroom* (1977); and *Verbi-voco-visual* (1967), which was originally Issue 8 of *Explorations*. He co-authored (with Wilfred WATSON) *From cliché to archetype* (1970), and (with Harley Parker) *Through the vanishing point* (1968), a study of the contemporary revolution by media and the avant-garde against the assumptions of Renaissance perspective and print culture. In addition to *Explorations*, McLuhan co-edited with his son, Eric, *The Dew Line*, an important information letter for those involved in government, business, and academia. Eugene McNAMARA edited *The interior landscape: the literary criticism of Marshall McLuhan 1943–62* (1969, rpr. 1971). Two posthumous publications are *Laws of the media: the new science* (1988), co-authored with Eric McLuhan, and *The global village: transformation in world life and media in the 21st century* (1989), co-authored with Bruce Powers. *Letters of Marshall McLuhan* (1987)— selected and edited by Matie Molinari, Corinne McLuhan, and William Toye—contains important biographical and critical commentary, and annotations, by Toye.

McLuhan conceived of himself as a 'poet *manqué*' who produced do-it-yourself creativity kits. Despite obvious weaknesses in his writings (such as a tendency towards technological determinism), their perceptions, theoretical suggestivity, and paradoxes are distinctive, inventive, and very much a product of his having pursued his career in Canada. Possessing a typical Canadian sensitivity to the way in which technology, cultural products, and media affect the quality of life, McLuhan was one of the first scholars to recognize that technology had become a major factor in human evolution and in the changing shape of modern culture. As his literary criticism and concern with history suggest, his thought was rooted in humanism, modernist art, and literature, and in an avant-garde version of Thomism that grew out of his conversion to Catholicism. While in the late 1970s and the 1980s there was a decline of interest in McLuhan (though his name never ceased to be mentioned in print media), his influence among artists, filmmakers, and multimedia artists persisted. In *The media lab* (1987) Stuart Brand first called attention to McLuhan's important influence among researchers at the MIT Media Lab—such as its former director, Nicholas Negroponte. In the 1990s McLuhan re-emerged as a major influence with the appearance of the new cyberworld of the Internet and virtual reality: the first issue of the magazine *Wired* opened with five pages of elaborate visual display incorporating quotations from McLuhan, and on the masthead he was named the magazine's 'patron saint'; in early 1994 a miniature photo with a short aphorism was added. *Mondo 2000* has declared him to be 'a man for all media', and an article in the second issue of *Post-modern culture* linked McLuhan to James Joyce and modernist art as an important figure in the pre-history of cyberspace. McLuhan's works continue to assist us in understanding the global technoculture of computers and telecommunications: his theoretical contributions to the interface between rapidly evolving technology and human culture have been recognized by the McLuhan Teleglobe Canada Award sponsored by UNESCO.

See *Essential McLuhan* (1995) edited by Eric McLuhan and Frank Zingrone; *McLuhan, or modernism in reverse* (1996) by Glenn Wilmott; *Marshall McLuhan: the medium and the light: reflections on religion* (1999) edited by Eric McLuhan and Jack Szklarek; *McLuhan in space: a cultural geography* (2002) by Richard Cavell; *Understanding me: lectures and interviews* (2003) edited by Stephanie McLuhan and David Staines, with an Introduction by Tom Wolfe; *McLuhan for managers: new tools for thinking* (2003) by Mark Federman and Derrick De Kerckhove; and the biographies *McLuhan: the medium and the messenger* (1989, rpr. 1990; rev. 1998) by Philip MARCHAND, *Marshall McLuhan: escape into understanding* (1997) by W. Terrance Gordon, and *Marshall McLuhan* (2010) by Douglas COUPLAND in Penguin Canada's series Extraordinary Canadians.

MacMechan, Archibald (1862–1933). Born in Berlin (Kitchener), Ontario, he was educated at the University of Toronto and Johns Hopkins University, and was professor of English at Dalhousie University, Halifax, from 1889 until two years before his death.

MacMechan published many books—including collections of engaging familiar essays, and of writings about the sea—but he is especially remembered for his critical survey of the principal works of English- and French-Canadian authors, *Headwaters of Canadian literature* (1924, NCL 1974), which sets forth his strongly held views concerning the need for a native literature worthy of international recognition. His adherence to idiosyncratic standards, and his recognition of the dual national culture, make this book an important contribution to early Canadian literary criticism.

MacMillan, Margaret (b. 1943) was educated at the University of Toronto (B.A., 1962) and Oxford University (B. Phil., 1968; D. Phil., 1974). She was professor of history at Ryerson University, Toronto, until 2002, when she became provost of Trinity College, University of Toronto, and professor of history. An Officer of the Order of Canada (2006), she is Warden of St Antony's College, Oxford (2007–). Her important scholarly books are distinguished for their narrative interest— MacMillan is a good storyteller. Growing out of a thesis on the British in India between 1880 and 1920, *Women of the Raj* (1988, rpr. 2005), concentrating on the 1850s to 1947, describes the experiences of British wives exiled to India and its alien ways, and draws on letters, memoirs, and interviews with relatives, including her own grandmother. A great Canadian scholarly work of recent years, and (more unusually) one published internationally that sold well, is *Paris 1919: six months that changed the world* (2001, rpr. 2003, GGA), a very long (more than 500 pages) but fascinating account (it won not only the Governor General's Award but the Duff Cooper Prize and the Samuel Johnson Prize) of the famous peace conference when President Woodrow Wilson, British prime minister David Lloyd George—MacMillan's great-grandfather— and French premier Georges Clemenceau met in Paris. The signing ceremony that officially ended the First World War took place in the Hall of Mirrors at the Palace of Versailles. *Nixon and Mao: the week that changed the world* (2007) has as its subtitle (echoing that of Mac-Millan's previous book) what Nixon said at the end of his trip to China in February 1972. MacMillan's narrative skills are again used to great advantage to describe, in the first half of the book, Nixon's first day in Beijing and his first meeting with Mao Tse-tung; and, in the second half, how the visit was secretly arranged by Nixon and Kissinger (in many ways two adversaries), leading to descriptions of the actual visit. In *The use and abuses of history* (2008), which began as a series of lectures, one 'abuse' is George W. Bush's and Tony Blair's drawing on false historical parallels for vindication of the war in Iraq. Margaret MacMillan is also co-author—with Marjorie Harris and Anne Desjardins—of the well illustrated *Canada's house: Rideau Hall and the invention of a Canadian home* (2004). She has also written *Stephen Leacock* (2008) in Penguin's Extraordinary Canadians series.

Macmillan Company of Canada, The.
The Canadian Macmillan Company was incorporated in 1905, as one of a chain of branches and depots of the London company then being established around the Empire. The New York company, which had been working the Canadian territory, because of its size was permitted to hold an interest in it.

Macmillan of Canada took off well, and within two years had put up a building at 70 Bond Street, where it was to remain until 1980. During the First World War the management under Frank Wise had become slack. In 1917 a young Yorkshireman, Hugh Eayrs (1894–1940), who had been in Canada for five years with Maclean-Hunter, joined Macmillan, and in 1921 he succeeded Wise as president. Eayrs had youthful vigour, brilliant, though sometimes impractical, plans, and an evangelistic belief in the future of Canada. Within two years he had published W.H. BLAKE's translation of Louis HÉMON's *MARIA CHAPDELAINE*, which became a great success in Britain and the USA, as well as in Canada. Eayrs acquired the agency for Cambridge Bibles and prayerbooks as well as for a whole group of British medical publishers. When, in 1950, the London partners decided to sell the Macmillan Company, New York—now a giant bigger than themselves and impossible to control—they bought back, as part of the deal, the interest the American company had been allowed to have in the Canadian company. Eayrs had died during the war and was succeeded in 1946 by John GRAY. From that point on, until Gray's retirement in 1973, Macmillan Canada, riding the crest of the wave of Canada's postwar publishing expansion under Gray's expert leadership, became one of the largest and most successful publishing companies in Canada. Its impressive list of Canadian authors included Mazo DE LA ROCHE, Morley CALLAGHAN, Hugh MacLENNAN, Robertson DAVIES, and Donald CREIGHTON. Difficulty in finding a suitable successor to John Gray caused the London partners to sell the Macmillan Company of Canada to Maclean-Hunter in 1973. In 1980 it was taken over by Gage Publishing Limited, who retained the imprint, but made the trade publishing activities of Macmillan a division of its largely educational business. In 1999 Macmillan Canada became an imprint of the newly founded CDG Books, which was purchased by John Wiley & Sons in 2002, when Macmillan Canada ceased as an imprint and a publishing house.

McNamara, Eugene (b. 1930). Born in Oak Park, Illinois, and educated in the Chicago area, he came to Canada in 1959 to teach English at the University of Windsor (then Assumption University), where he was instrumental, in 1967, in starting the Creative Writing Program, of which he was director until his retirement in 1995. He is now Professor Emeritus. He has long been associated with the academic and cultural life of Windsor, editing *The University of Windsor Review* for many years from its inception in 1965, and co-founding Sesame Press in 1973 with Peter STEVENS and Dorothy Farmiloe. But McNamara is generally known as a poet. The dominant mood of McNamara's poetry in *For the mean time* (1965), *Passages* (1972), *Hard words* (1972), and *In transit* (1975) is one of gently brooding melancholy about the passage of time, though this overall tone does not preclude tough irony and satire. Other poems concentrate on external reality, both on and below the surface, often centring on the joys and pains of family and human love, as the titles of some volumes suggest: *Love scenes* (1970), *Diving for the body* (1974), and *Forcing the field* (1981). For many years McNamara was a film critic, writing a weekly column for the *Windsor Star* and reviewing movies for CBC Radio. *Dillinger poems* (1971) and *Screens* (1977), which show both a fondness for the movie vision and a perception of film's romantic expression and falsifications, are full of clear, direct imagery that have a filmic sharpness; even when the poems are grounded in a documentary realism, they take on some of the glamour associated with movies. His later poetry is pervasively personal, while continuing with early themes—as in *The moving light* (1986)—though *Call it a day* (1984) concentrates on the depiction of physical labour and work in factories. An abundance of McNamara's poetry appears in *Keeping in touch: new and selected poems* (1998) and *Grace notes: new and selected poems* (2004).

McNamara's early fiction was collected in two volumes—*Salt: short stories* (1975) and *The search for Sarah Grace and other stories* (1977). His fiction has the same clarity as his poetry, though often his stories veer off into mysteries and ambiguities of character and event. *Spectral evidence* (1985) and *Fox trot* (1994) contain stories that are fictional extrapolations from various factual events and characters—he calls them 'factions'. The disparities between facts and fiction allow the stories to expand those ironic shifts and ambiguities that are present in the earlier work, as well as to undermine the nature of both fact and fiction with parodic patterns. The title story of *Waterfalls* (2000), a collection of fourteen engaging stories, is agreeably discursive and narrated by a university professor who is preparing to give a lecture in Chicago about Walt Whitman and Dr Richard BUCKE. He reminisces about Chicago, where he was born, and remembers being taken by his father when he was a boy to see the Olson Rug Company Waterfall, 'on the northwest side of the city.... At one side of the building an artificial waterfall had been constructed three or four stories high. There were plants and rocks and perpetually falling water.' The memory of this amazing sight, within the city, lasted and came to the fore again when the narrator visits Chicago as an elderly man to give his lecture, which includes a description of Whitman's visiting Niagara Falls with Bucke: 'They walked out on the suspension bridge, their white beards streaming in the wind.' The narrator doesn't hesitate to veer off into describing, among other things, the two men's association when Whitman spent one summer visiting Bucke at the Asylum for the Insane in London, Ontario, of which he was superintendent.

McNeil, Florence (b. 1937). Born in Vancouver, she was educated at the University of British Columbia (B.A., 1960) and the University of Alberta, where she met Eli MANDEL and Rudy WIEBE; she returned to UBC, studying under Earle BIRNEY, and received an M.A in English and creative writing in 1965. She taught English at Western Washington State College until 1968 and at the University of Calgary until 1973. The poems in McNeil's collections—such as *Walhachin* (1972), *Ghost towns* (1975), *Emily* (1975), and *Barkerville* (1984)—often take the form of linked sequences, typically grounded in a historical person, tribe, place, or event. *Walhachin* and *Barkerville* (later adapted as a stage production and radio play) deal with specific extinct communities in the British Columbia interior; the title of *Ghost towns* is self-explanatory; and *Emily* is based on the life of Emily CARR. The *overlanders* (1982) is based on the trek of settlers from Canada West (Ontario) to the B.C. interior in 1862. The documentary impulse even extends to *The rim of the park* (1972), drawn from her own life. Besides the sense of historical wonder, her work is marked by imagistic incisiveness and, in later collections, by fluid diction and increased openness of form. *Swimming out of history* (1991) gathers selections from six previous collections and adds new poems. *Breathing each other's air* (1994) is something of a mystery novel in which Elizabeth Morrison, an academic and biographer, tries to unravel the life of a woman with several pasts and names, one of them Ursula La Fontaine, who died when her yacht sank near the entrance to Vancouver harbour. She explores the shipwreck: underwater imagery and scuba diving and its necessary interdependence (thus the title) are important in the novel. Elizabeth's investigation of Ursula's death and life blends with a memoir of her own life and relationships as she tries to discover the truth in them. McNeil has also published two novels for young people: *Miss P. and me* (1982) and *All kinds of magic* (1984).

Macphail, Sir Andrew (1864–1938). Born John Andrew McPhail in Orwell, Prince Edward Island, he received a B.A. (1888) and an M.D. (1891) from McGill University. He practised medicine for about ten years, while also teaching in the medical faculty of the University of Bishop's College, Montreal, from 1893 to 1905. In 1907 he was appointed McGill's first professor of the history of medicine, a chair he held for thirty years. He had become editor of the monthly *Montreal Medical Journal* in 1903; when it merged with another medical periodical eight years later to establish the *Canadian Medical Association Journal*, Macphail was made editor of the new monthly. Serving overseas in the Canadian Army Medical Services (1915–19), he attained the rank of major. He was knighted in 1918. A prolific and forceful writer and an accomplished stylist, Macphail was the best Canadian personification of the nineteenth-century ideal of the non-specialist man-of-letters who wrote in a confident tone on a wide range of subjects—he published more than ten books and scores of shorter pieces. His favourite and most successful medium was the essay. Many of his essays appeared, in whole or in part, in *The* UNIVERSITY MAGAZINE, a quarterly Macphail edited from 1907 to 1920, with the exception of the time he spent overseas. In many respects this magazine was his most remarkable achievement. The book to which Macphail devoted most care, and which he considered his best, was published posthumously: *The master's wife* (1939, rpr. 1977, 1994). An autobiographical reminiscence of Prince Edward Island, it focuses particularly on his father, who was a school inspector ('the master' of the title), on his mother, and on Orwell. The characters in the book are real: as well as his parents and local people, they include literary and academic figures like Edward William THOMSON (disguised as 'the Old Gentleman'), and James Mavor, professor of political economy at the University of Toronto. For Macphail, his native province represented a way of life that emphasized stability and traditional ties, and a relative lack of materialism. For many years this book was a hidden treasure of Canadian writing. His two children published the novel through a private arrangement with a printer, and this method, with its lack of linkage to a system of distribution, combined with the outbreak of war in 1939 to make it virtually unknown. It was not until 1977, when it appeared in the NEW CANADIAN LIBRARY, that it received national distribution and the recognition and praise it deserved. In 1994 the Institute of Island Studies at the University of Prince Edward Island published a facsimile reprint of the original edition, including the same photographs of the main characters, and an expanded introduction. With its power, its rich texture, and its complexity, *The master's wife*, in the view of Janice KULYK KEEFER, is 'one of the finest and oddest pieces of prose to be found in Maritime, or Canadian literature as a whole' (*Under eastern eyes*). The 'Friends of Macphail' established the 'Sir Andrew Macphail (of Orwell, P.E.I.) Foundation Inc.' and have beautifully restored the Macphail house in Orwell.

Macpherson, Jay (b. 1931). Born in England, she came to Newfoundland with her mother and brother at the age of nine, and in 1944 the family settled in Ottawa. She studied at Carleton College (B.A., 1952), McGill University (B.L.S., 1953), and the University of Toronto (M.A., 1955; Ph.D., 1964), where she took courses from Northrop FRYE. She became a colleague in the English Department of Victoria College and eventually a full professor. For several years she combined her teaching duties with work as Frye's research assistant and taught a course with Frye on the Bible and mythology. She retired in 1996. Her first poems were published by Alan Crawley in CONTEMPORARY VERSE when she was eighteen. Her first poetry collection, *Nineteen poems* (1952), was published by Robert Graves' Seizin Press in Majorca. *O earth return* (later to become section two of *The boatman*) came out in 1954 under the imprint of her own small press, EMBLEM BOOKS.

Macpherson has not published a great deal of poetry, yet her reputation as an important Canadian poet was firmly established with her first commercially published book, *The BOATMAN* (1957, GGA). In this collection she was revealed as a poet of wit and erudition who—influenced by Northrop FRYE's theory of mythic displacement—rewrote mythological themes in colloquial style. *The boatman* was reissued in 1968 with sixteen new poems. Her next book, *Welcoming disaster* (1974 *sic*, actually 1975) was privately published. Both volumes were reissued in 1981 under the title *Poems twice told* (rpr. 2006), with decorative line drawings by the author. The poems in *The boatman*, and some of Macpherson's later poems, have the resonance of archetypal experience in the manner of William Blake's more epigrammatic pieces. In *Welcoming disaster*, a complex and difficult work, the poems record a psychological struggle against poetic silence in a personal wasteland. Composed of five parts plus an epilogue, the book follows a traditional mystical pattern: the way up and the way down are the same. The sequence begins in a dark night of the soul, with the poet metaphorically orphaned. The controlling symbol, a child's teddy bear called Tedward, functions as a substitute for 'Him not there' (father, lover, God), an embodiment of a childish need in the adult psyche and of a metaphysical longing. The struggle towards 'Recognitions' (Section IV) is realized when the child's bear is transformed into the constellation Ursa Major. The poet recognizes that direction can be found only when the dark impulses in the self are acknowledged and explored. As the critic Sherrill Grace has made clear, the poems achieve a profound cultural and archetypal resonance by their allusions to Sumerian and Babylonian myth. The female persona is identified with the goddess Inanna who, in the tradition of fertility cults, must annually search the underworld for the lost god, Dumuzi or Tammuz. But the peculiar originality and poignancy of the poems come from a second level of allusion: to the world of fairy tale and nursery rhyme. Grace suggests convincingly that Tedward can be associated with the Teddy Bear of A.A. Milne's *When we were very young*. Macpherson's extraordinary gnomic gifts are demonstrated by the way that even her Notes and Acknowledgements at the end of *Poems twice told* are rendered wittily and humorously in rhyme. *Four ages of man: the classical myths* (1962) is Macpherson's retelling of Greek myths for young people. In 1982 she published a scholarly study, *The spirit of solitude: conventions and continuities in late romance*, in which she examines traditional pastoral romance conventions in nineteenth- and twentieth-century narratives, including Mary Shelley's *Frankenstein*, and explores their evolution in Canadian literature from Oliver Goldsmith to James REANEY.

McWhirter, George (b. 1939). Born in Belfast, Northern Ireland, he was educated at Queen's University, Belfast (B.A.). After teaching at the Berlitz School in Barcelona, he immigrated to Canada in 1966 and attended the University of British Columbia (M.A.). From 1970 he taught at the University of British Columbia, becoming Professor in the Department of Creative Writing, and Head (1983–93), retiring in 2005. In 2007 he was appointed the first Poet Laureate for the City of Vancouver. His poems and stories are characterized by strongly textured detail, alien or grotesque characters, and the surreal influences of Spain and Latin America. His viewpoint is always unexpected. McWhirter's first book, *Catalan poems* (1971), was deeply immersed in his Spanish experiences; the poems work backward from the deathbed of Eduardo Valls to his marriage bed, in sometimes oblique language. In the partly autobiographical cycle of fifty-two poems, *Queen of the sea* (1976), the technology of the shipbuilding trades in his native Belfast, where the ill-fated *Titanic* and the *Reina del Mar* were built, provides extended metaphors. *Twenty-five* (1978) is a small collection of twenty-nine free-verse poems on the central theme of village life and Catholicism in Mexico. *The island man* (1981) is a poem-cycle set on Vancouver Island in the 1930s and based on motifs derived from *The odyssey* and the Spanish explorers of early British Columbia. *Fire before dark* (1984) examines an Irish childhood and the Canadian landscape, character, and identity. The longest section describes the experience of Greek, Vietnamese, Japanese, and Irish immigrants learning both a new language and adapting to the new world of Canada. More recent collections are *A staircase for all souls* (*the British Columbia suite*): *a wooded masque for readers and listeners* (1992), *Incubus: the dark side of the light* (1995), and *Ovid in Saskatchewan* (1998). *The incorrections* (2007)—a substantial collection of nearly 200 pages of poems that treat a huge array of McWhirter's interests—has an epigraph: 'In trying to correct an old wrong / I seem to create a new one / And find myself arraigned / by a hapless incorrection.' He edited with Betty Ferber a bilingual edition of the selected poems of the great Mexican poet Homero Aridjis, *Eyes to see otherwise* (2001).

McWhirter's fiction is innovative and sometimes experimental. The nineteen poetic, occasionally obscure, stories in *Bodyworks* (1974)—about a character named Hermione who lives in a mythological country, Sarne—are enriched by water imagery, an Irish comic vision, heroic gods, as well as scatological and sexual humour. *God's eye* (1981) contains eleven stories set in Mexico. *Coming to grips with Lucy* (1982) is a series of reminiscences about the perils of growing up in Ireland and growing old in B.C. The Irish stories are poetic, textured, and use intercut storylines, while the B.C. stories are often hard-edged and brutal, with an emotional undercurrent suggested by animal imagery. *A bad day to be winning* (1991) is a self-conscious poetic collection of character sketches set in Northern Ireland. The stories in *Musical dogs* (1996) are by an owner of dogs. Of McWhirter's novels, *Paula Lake* (1984) is a stylish novella set in B.C. with an unsympathetic main character—a disturbed lifeguard who kidnaps a Japanese boy; the story is told with complex time shifts, striking imagery and metaphor, and surreal incident. McWhirter's masterpiece, *Cage* (1987), refers to the moral dilemma of the Reverend Benjamin Carragher, assigned to a parish in a superstitious Mexican town. To overcome the poverty, he works with his parishioners to build bird cages for tourists; but he has also built a cage for himself. In this difficult novel, dreamscape and reality intermingle, as do past and present. *The listeners* (1991) tells the story of two musicians—a lute-playing father and a tuba-playing son, the Kerrs—in a series of flashbacks as they watch the parade that marks the Belfast celebration of the twelfth of July. McWhirter coined the word that gave the title to *The anachronicles* (2008), which he says 'takes its name from a combination of the words anachronism and chronicle.' The collection contains several long poems, including 'A journal for Don Caamaño' and 'Hops: a trans-Atlantic argument for two voices'—the voices are from Canada and Ireland.

Mad shadows (1960, NCL). This is the translation by Merloyd Lawrence of the first novel by Marie-Claire BLAIS, *La belle bête* (1959), which was published to mingled astonishment and acclaim when she was only twenty. Striking in its macabre intensity, its denial of pure realism, and in the boldness of its imagery and sheer headlong force, it presents characters less as individualized human beings than as raw essences—embodiments of evil, narcissism, jealousy, and greed. Against an almost featureless background, a frivolous mother, a beautiful imbecile boy, a jealous sister, a blind youth, enact a nightmare ritual of envy, murder, betrayal, and disfigurement. The novel is a hallucinatory moral fable, an examination of pure evil in a society torn from its roots.

Maheux-Forcier, Louise (b. 1929). Born in Montreal, she studied at the École supérieure Sainte-Croix and at the Conservatoire de musique et d'art dramatique de Québec, and spent two years studying music in Paris on a Québec government scholarship (1952–4). After taking courses in art history at the Université de Montréal, and another brief period in Europe in 1959, she abandoned music for

writing. Most of Maheux-Forcier's novels, and her one collection of stories, have been translated by David Lobdell. Her three novels of the 1960s, *Amadou* (1963), *L'île joyeuse* (1964), and *Une forêt pour Zoé* (1969, GGA)—translated as *Amadou* (1987), *Isle of joy* (1987), and *A Forest for Zoe* (1986)—form a triptych evoking a gradual move from paralysis and violence to the discovery of a sacred woman-centred world. The opening line of *Amadou*—in which the narrator, symbolically isolated in a house in the Québec countryside, announces she has killed her husband—signifies a violent rejection of the traditional patriarchal value system and inaugurates a process of birth that will continue throughout the triptych. Although the nostalgia for a childhood paradise, symbolized by the sandy island of Isle of Joy, remains a constant in Maheux-Forcier's work, the succession of goddess figures in *A forest for Zoe* marks a reconciliation with time and process and an ever-more joyous rejection of traditional societal structures. In the 1970s Maheux-Forcier became more explicitly concerned with her own art and its relation to life. In *Paroles et musiques* (1973)—translated as *Words and music* (1990)—a woman writer facing death attempts to evaluate her life and finds its meaning in her loves, her refusal to compromise, and above all in her writing. *En toutes lettres* (1980)—translated as *Letter by letter* (1982)—is a collection of wry, anecdotal, elegant short stories (whose titles follow the letters of the alphabet) that treat different facets, and different relationships, in the lives of women. Maheux-Forcier was made a Member of the Order of Canada in 1985.

Maillard, Keith (b. 1942). Born in Wheeling, West Virginia, he studied at West Virginia University and Vancouver Community College, graduating with a degree in music (1977). After travelling extensively in North America and working in the anti-Vietnam War movement, he immigrated to Canada in 1970. He is a professor in the Department of Theatre, Film, and Creative Writing, University of British Columbia (1989–). Heavily influenced by Henry Miller and Jack Kerouac, Maillard is a sensual writer, with great storytelling skills and lucidly expressed emotions—though his fiction has suggested that of the magic realists. He is especially interested in the coming-of-age novel, with emotionally crippled parents and distorted memories; his books challenge the meaning of 'autobiography', since they are fictionalized accounts of his own experiences. His first novel, *Two Strand River* (1976, rpr. 1996), is an adult fairy tale with the theme of androgyny on British Columbia's west coast. *Alex driving south* (1980, rpr. 1997) tells the story of a man coming to Canada to escape the draft. A long manuscript tentatively entitled *Difficult beginnings* became two novels: *The knife in my hands* (1981) describes five years in the life of John Dupre up to 1963 as he deals with his androgyny, American violence, and arcane spirituality; and *Cutting through* (1982) is the sequel, as Dupre searches for his ancestral roots, comes to terms with his sexuality and US politics, and moves to Toronto to work on an underground paper. *Motet* (1989, rpr. 1997) was the first of a planned series of five novels (a motet is a sacred choral improvisation with several voices). Its complex plot tells the story of Paul Crane, a classical-music teacher, his family, and his mid-life crisis; it has the psychedelic 1960s in Vancouver as background. Three novels are set in the fictional steel-mill town of Raysburg, West Virginia. *Light in the company of women* (1993) is a superbly researched, meticulously plotted tour de force, written in the style of a nineteenth-century historical novel, that tells the story of an aristocratic family and their submerged traumas. The sequel, *Hazard zones* (1995), describes a contemporary researcher in areas subject to floods, which become a metaphor for a destructive past filled with alcoholism, self-defeat, and suppressed sexuality. There is an emotional resolution helped by therapy, and what could have been clichéd becomes a vital and absorbing narrative of redemption and inspiration. *Gloria* (1999) is a long, dense family novel that captures the period of the 1950s, when young Gloria Cotter is torn between the conventional mores of Raysburg society, which include early marriage, and graduate school at Columbia University, which her strong literary interests and Professor Trevor Bolton lead her to—Gloria and Bolton are both memorable characters.

Maillard's most singular accomplishment is his four-part novel, with the overall title *Difficulty at the beginning*, that is a wonderful evocation of life in Raysburg from the late fifties to the seventies, focusing on John Dupre. The first novel, *Running* (2005), covering 1958–60, begins with his high-school years at Raysburg Military Academy and ends with his sexual fusion with Cassandra: 'I couldn't imagine anything more perfect than her long-legged coltish adolescent body, anything more beautiful than her concentrated Athena-gray eyes and face as strong as a hawk's. And then, with our

mouths screwed tight together, our legs intertwined, the impossible began to happen: all of me, from my toes to my eyeballs, seemed to be draining to a single point.' The uninhibited Maillard lets his freewheeling narrative skill take him where it may. In *Morgantown* (2006) Dupre is a junior at West Virginia University experiencing the complications caused by his many eccentric friends, members of the 'out crowd'. *Lyndon Johnson and the majorettes* (2006) takes place in 1965, though the first sentence reads: 'I was hurrying to the afternoon shift when I heard that Jack Kennedy was dead. [He died in 1963.] My first thought was, Jesus Christ, now we've got *Lyndon Baines Johnson*.' In time LBJ calls up the reserves. John had been living a happy life as a student in Toronto when, in *Looking good* (2006) he moves to Boston—living under an alias because he's wanted by the FBI as a draft-dodger—because he wishes to take part in what he and his friends call the REVOLUTION. When he and his best friend Tom Parker, now a drug dealer, and Pam Zalman seize control of an underground newspaper, they're in real trouble. The long novel is a vivid account of aspects of the counterculture in the US in the late 1960s. In its four volumes, *Difficulty at the beginning* offers a social history of the disorderly, tumultuous America of the 1960s in the form of a gifted writer's outpouring of vivid narrative, believable characters, and feisty dialogue. *The clarinet polka* (2002) is a rich and delightful long novel (nearly 500 pages) about Polish Americans in South Raysburg—a carefully researched tribute to the Polish-Americans Maillard grew up with in his hometown. As the narrative races along, it becomes a warmhearted, highly readable portrait of a community. Jimmy Koprowski, the narrator (now elderly), leaves the US Air Force in 1969—he had been in Vietnam—and finds himself living again with his family, notably his demanding father ('I don't know when I started calling him Old Bullet Head—probably in high school and never to his face.') Like his father, Jimmy's maternal grandfather, Dziadzio Wojtkiewicz, worked in a steel mill. Many workers were killed. 'Hey, you know what I seen, Jimmy? The tap hole. They didn't pack her right. Steel come down in the pit, kill fourteen, fifteen guys. You know what they do? Melt 'em back in the steel.' But resonating throughout the novel is not the steel mill, or the recent war, but Jimmy's love life and Polish music. At the very beginning of the book he receives the unexpected and repeated attentions of Connie, a beautiful young woman who claims she is happily married to a doctor and has three children. In addition Janice, who plays the clarinet, affects him seriously (along with drink); he eventually achieves a happy marriage. Jimmy's sister Linda is musical, plays the trumpet, and starts an all-girl polka band. In Jimmy's words, 'So you've got weird peasant music from Poland, and it mixes up with American popular music and you start to get something brand new, something that's not like anything they've got back in Poland—the Polish-American polka.' Linda plays him a tape that's over sixty years old, of 'this dumb old tune I've known my whole life.' It's 'Dziadunio', 'The Clarinet Polka'. Linda says: 'Don't you see, Jimmy? It's *ours*.'

Maillard's poetry collection, *Dementia Americana* (1994), won the Gerald Lampert Award for best first book of poetry.

Maillet, Antonine (b. 1929). Born in Bouctouche, New Brunswick, she was educated at the Universités de Moncton, N.B., and Montréal and Université Laval, where she received a Doctorat ès Lettres in 1970. She has taught literature and folklore at many universities, including Montréal and Laval, and is the recipient of many honorary degrees and awards. She is a Companion of the Order of Canada and a member of the Queen's Privy Council for Canada.

The leading writer of Acadia, Maillet has published many books; only those available in English translation are discussed here. She has revealed to a large public—through her books, and particularly through many performances (in both French and English) by Viola Léger of *La SAGOUINE* (1971)—the striking character of Acadian oral culture and language, which is a version of the sixteenth-century French of her ancestors. Maillet learned her craft as a storyteller from her pioneer relatives, from rural folklore, village entertainers, and at election meetings and social gatherings. Her language is not *chiac* (from Shediac, a small fishing port near Moncton)—the equivalent of the most anglicized urban *JOUAL*—but an old domestic French, coloured (and somewhat gratingly roughened, coarsened) by her personal touch and a special local intonation and accent. *La Sagouine* (freely translated as 'The Slattern')—of which an English translation by Luis de Céspedes was published in 1979—is a series of sixteen monologues that offer the reminiscences, grievances, anecdotes, and homilies of a seventy-two-year-old charwoman, a former prostitute, the wife of an Acadian fisherman. In the fantasy *Don l'Orignal* (1972, GGA), translated as *The tale of Don l'Original* (1978, rpr. 2004) by Barbara Godard, the *gens d'En-bas* (those who live on the other

side of the tracks) fight with the big shots, the powerful, who are named for their occupations—the Mayoress, the Barber, the Milliner, the Playboy—while Noume, Citrouille, General Michel-Archange, La Sainte, La Cruche, and other 'Sagouins' are given nicknames. These actor-storytellers appear in one work after another—indestructible, welcomed, having echoes of Homer, Rabelais, Balzac, and of characters in a picaresque novel, while remaining Acadians, a minority within a minority. The play *Gapi et Sullivan* (1973), retitled *Gapi* (1976)—translated as *Gapi and Sullivan* (1986) by Luis de Cespedes—portrays two contrasting characters: the settled Acadian, a former fisherman who is now a lighthouse keeper, and the wandering Irishman, a sailor with exotic memories and imagination. In the novel *Mariaagélas* (1973—translated as *Mariaagélas: Maria, daughter of Gélas* (1986) by Ben-Z. Shek—and in the play *Evangéline Deusse* (1975)—translated by Luis de Cespedes in 1986—Maillet again creates indomitable, marginal women, who remain upright and haughty despite their illegal traffic in alcohol and flesh: they sell, but they never truly sell themselves. Maillet undertook the ambitious task of chronicling the return of the Acadians—French settlers of what is now Nova Scotia who were expelled by British troops in the 1750s and scattered through British colonies in America and the West Indies. *Pélagie-la-Charette* (1979)—translated by Philip Stratford as *Pélagie: the return to a homeland* (1982, rpr. 2004)—recounts the odyssey and tribulations of one woman and a small group of outcasts who, picking up scores of other displaced Acadians, make their way over a period of ten years from the southern United States towards their ancestral homeland. It won the 1979 Prix Goncourt, the first time this prize had been awarded to an author who is not a native of France. Her picaresque and picturesque novels include *Crache-à-Pic* (1984), translated as *The devil is loose* (1986) by Philip Stratford, and *Le huitième jour* (1986), translated as *On the eighth day* (1989) by Wayne Grady. Always lively and engaging, Maillet has become a personality, an institution. A street (where she lives) has been named after her in the Outremont district of Montreal.

Mair, Charles (1838–1927). Born in Lanark, Upper Canada (Ontario), a timber town in the Ottawa valley, Mair began medical studies in 1856 at Queen's University, Kingston, but left in 1857 to work for ten years in his family's timber business. In 1868, after another year at Queen's, he went to Ottawa, where he became

Mair

one of the founders of the Canada First movement. He then accepted a job as paymaster to a government road party at the Red River Settlement (present-day Winnipeg). His vividly descriptive letters to his brother, who forwarded them to the Toronto *Globe*, praised the Northwest but insulted the Métis, particularly the women, and caused a furore in the Settlement. In Dec. 1869, during the Red River Rebellion, Mair was imprisoned and sentenced to death by Louis Riel. Escaping from Fort Garry, he later made his way east, to Toronto, where he roused Ontario's Orangemen over Riel's execution of Thomas Scott. Angry over Riel's confiscation of his poems, Mair returned to the West to join the suppression of Riel's Northwest Rebellion of 1885. Back in Toronto, he received a medal of honour and was proclaimed the 'warrior bard'.

Dreamland and other poems (Montreal, 1868), written before Mair joined Canada First, reveals a conventional imitator of Keats. Its preface, asking for guidance through candid criticism, is the first indication of Mair's method of composing poetry—creativity through consensus. R.G. Haliburton urged Mair to Canadianize his subject matter, to look to the Prairie buffalo rather than to Milton's 'Comus' for inspiration. Leaving the Northwest, where he had been a storekeeper in Portage la Prairie and Prince Albert, Mair moved in 1882 to Windsor, Ontario, to do research for *Tecumseh: a drama* (Toronto, 1886), a verse-play based on a central event for nineteenth-century writers, the War of 1812. This work (which benefited from the advice of George Denison, Goldwin SMITH, Daniel Wilson, Charles G.D. ROBERTS, and even Matthew Arnold) contrasts what Mair saw as the Canadian tradition of co-operative self-sacrifice with the American tradition of divisive self-interest. He identifies both Tecumseh and Isaac Brock as exemplars of self-sacrifice— 'the spirit and springs of actions which have made Canada what she is.' A Shakespearean model is effective in Mair's description of the Northwest as being vast as an ocean, with its shoreless prairies and roaring waves of earth-rumbling bison, and as he depicts low Yankee ruffians using slang mimicked from T.C. HALIBURTON's Yankee pedlar. The play's central metaphors are the axe as both tool and weapon, and water as both redemptive stream and drowning flood. All of Mair's other poems repeat the flaws rather than the epic strengths of *Tecumseh*. The revisions recorded in *Tecumseh: a drama, and Canadian poems* (1901) reveal his effort to Canadianize his earliest poems by replacing medieval knights with the warriors

and heroines of 1812. 'The last bison' presents a hermaphrodite bison singing a conservationist song before it dies. Mair supported the concern of this poem with an essay, 'The American bison', that led to the federal government's establishment of a sanctuary for the world's last bison herd. See Norman Shrive's introduction to *Dreamland and other poems / Tecumseh: a drama* (1974). See also Shrive's biography, *Charles Mair: literary nationalist* (1965) and its revised edition, *The voice of the burdash: Charles Mair and the divided mind in Canadian literature* (1995).

Major, André (b. 1942). Born in Montreal, he became interested at an early age in separatist politics and was expelled from the Collège des Eudistes for his writings in leftist student publications. He was a founder of PARTI PRIS, but broke with the group in 1965, after an ideological quarrel, to become editor of the literary section of *L'Action nationale*, the organ of the older Catholic nationalists of the right. He has been an arts editor of the weekly tabloid *Le Petit Journal*, a theatre and book critic for *Le Devoir*, and a radio producer. A precocious poet, Major published his first collection when he was nineteen, two other collections followed in the 1960s. But he is best known as a writer of short stories and novels. *La folle d'Elvis* (1981)—translated by David Lobdell as *Hooked on Elvis* (1983)—is a collection of wry, often slight stories about possible encounters that fail to take place, or when they do take place are merely tentative or disillusioning. In Major's most mature and ambitious work, a trilogy subtitled *Histoires des déserteurs*, he makes nominal and somewhat eccentric use of the classic police-chase form to express a sociological and psychological statement about rural Québec life. In three novels—*L'épouvantail* (1974), *L'épidémie* (1975), and *Les rescapés* (1976, GGA)—he weaves a tale of lust, murder, suicide, and violence of every sort to depict a society severed from its roots and yet still obsessed by a past that is at once too distant and too close. *L'épouvantail* has been translated by Sheila FISCHMAN as *The scarecrow of Saint-Emmanuel* (1977) and *L'épidémie* by Mark Czarnecki as *Inspector Therrien* (1980). *L'hiver au coeur* (1987), translated by David Lobdell as *Winter of the heart* (1989), tells a rather simple story, which manages to escape sentimentality, about a man who leaves his wife and his job in publishing, settles into a furnished room, encounters his childhood sweetheart and finds happiness with her. *La vie provisoire* (1995), translated by Fischman as *A provisional life* (1997), is a more complex account of disillusionment and attempted escape. Flee as he may, the protagonist is never able to achieve more than provisional freedom from an unhappy marriage and a sense of emptiness.

Major, Kevin (b. 1949). Born in Stephenville, Newfoundland, a small coastal outport with its local dialect and way of life, he graduated with a B.Sc. (1972) from Memorial University, St John's. An awareness of the dearth of literature for young people set in Newfoundland resulted in his becoming one of Canada's foremost authors of books for adolescents. As a high-school teacher he learned the idiom and perspectives of teenagers, qualities that characterize his novels, beginning with *Hold fast* (1978, GGA; rpr. 2003), *Far from shore* (1980, rpr. 2004), and *Thirty-six exposures* (1984, rpr. 1994). To reveal the intense feelings of a lonely teenage boy, he used fictitious letters to 'The Boss' in *Dear Spruce Springsteen* (1987, rpr. 1994). They all reflect Major's own memories of his confusing, perplexing teenage years, and those of his friends. In *Blood red ochre* (1989, rpr. 1996) Major used a literary time-slip device to take the reader back to Newfoundland's Beothuk, who were annihilated by white settlers through starvation, disease, and murder. Another tragic historical event is the focus of his powerful adult novel *No man's land* (1995, rpr. 2005), about the Battle of the Somme in the Great War. Describing it as a battle that should never have happened, he reconstructs the events and human emotions that climaxed in the slaughter of the Newfoundland regiment. In the fatal misty dawn of July 1st ('vapour oozing from the scarred fields ... undraping a battleground that seemed reluctant to show itself') and before the disaster that follows, they listen to the captain's pep-talk: 'Before today is out you shall be part of the greatest show of the war and by this time tomorrow a part of our greatest victory.' In 2005 Major published a play based on the novel, with the same title, that was commissioned by Rising Tide Theatre and first produced in Trinity, Newfoundland, in July 2001. Incidents of censorship in Newfoundland involving his first three novels led to Major's comic fantasy *Eating between the lines* (1991, rpr. 1995), in which the young protagonist finds himself physically projected into the book he is currently reading. Humour also characterizes *Diana: my autobiography* (1993), a parody of people's obsession with royalty that introduces his first female protagonist and fictional daughter,

Diana (named after 'Princess Di'), who contrives to realize her imagined royal connections. *Ann and Seamus* (2003) is based on the enthralling true story—told in verse, with illustrations by the well-known Newfoundland artist David Blackwood—of the rescue by the Harvey family, notably Ann, of 163 people—including Seamus, a young Irishman—shipwrecked off Newfoundland's south coast in 1828. *Gaffer: a novel of Newfoundland* (1997) is an imaginative, surreal story for adults about a boy and the sea. *As near to heaven by sea: a history of Newfoundland & Labrador* (2001, rpr. 2002) is a long (more than 400 pages) informal history, filled with anecdotes, that is enjoyable to read. In *Aunt Olga's Christmas postcards* (2005) great-greataunt Olga is ninety-five and collects very old Christmas postcards, which revive memories when her niece Anna visits her. This large-format picture book, illustrated by Bruce Roberts, is also illustrated by charming old Christmas cards from Major's own collection. Books by Major have been translated into French, Spanish, German, and Danish.

Malahat Review, The: Essential Poetry & Fiction (1967–). Conceived in 1965 by Robin SKELTON and John Peter (1921–83) as an international quarterly of life and letters, the first issue—published under the auspices of the University of Victoria—appeared in 1967. The title suggests the regional basis that complements Malahat's cosmopolitan ambitions (the Malahat is a mountain near Victoria, British Columbia, over whose slopes the main road runs northward up Vancouver Island). Skelton and Peter shared the editorship until the nineteenth issue (1971), when Skelton became editor (assisted at times by Derk WYNAND, Charles LILLARD, and William David Thomas). When the university nearly withdrew its support—a Committee to Disband *The Malahat Review* was actually struck—Skelton resigned and was succeeded in 1982 by Constance Rooke (1942–2008), who brought the magazine to the University of Guelph for part of her tenure there. With the 100th issue the magazine returned to the University of Victoria. Derk Wynand was editor from 1992 to 1998, succeeded by Marlene Cookshaw (1998–2003), then by John Barton (2004–).

What made *The Malahat Review* exceptional initially, and important among Canadian magazines, was its policy of printing the best of Canadian writing alongside the best that could be obtained internationally. Equally important was its publication of English versions of foreign works never before translated, and of special book-length issues relating to specific authors or areas of literature. These included the Herbert Read memorial symposium (no. 9, 1969; reprinted as a book, 1970); the Friedrich Nietzsche symposium (no. 24, 1972); the Gathering in celebration of the eightieth birthday of Robert Graves (no. 35, 1975); Austrian writing today (no. 37, 1976); and an issue on the famous Spanish poet Rafael Alberti (no. 47, 1979), with a specially designed cover by Miró. Skelton was often criticized for featuring English writers (e.g., Durell, Burgess, Lawrence, Graves, and Read, whose papers were in the University of Victoria's Special Collections). But he also published complete issues devoted to Canadian writing (no. 26, April 1970; no. 31, July 1974). The tenth-anniversary Margaret ATWOOD Symposium (no. 41, 1977) marked a turning point, when the magazine began to focus on Canadian writing. Up to that point the publication of the magazine three times a year was funded totally by the University. From then on it sought out grants, increased subscriptions, and acquired funding for special issues. The most ambitious special project was a group of three issues (nearly 900 pages) devoted to the West Coast Renaissance (no. 45, 1978, no. 50, 1979, and no. 60, 1981). Other special issues have featured the work of John METCALF, Sharon THESEN, Paulette JILES, and P.K. PAGE (no. 117). The subject of the September 2003 issue is Reviewing and the September 2007 issue is a Celebration of Robin Skelton. The magazine became a quarterly publication in 1985.

Mandel, Eli (1922–92). Elias Wolf Mandel, born in Estevan, Saskatchewan, left the University of Saskatchewan to serve in the Army Medical Corps during the Second World War. He then studied at the Universities of Saskatchewan (B.A., 1949; M.A., 1950) and Toronto (Ph.D., 1957), and taught English at the Collège Militaire Royal de St Jean, the University of Alberta, and York University, Toronto.

Mandel's first significant collection of poetry, 'Minotaur poems', appeared (together with poems by Phyllis WEBB and Gael Turnbull) in the CONTACT PRESS anthology *Trio* (1954). His first book was *Fuseli poems* (1960); this was followed by *Black and secret man* (1964); *An idiot joy* (1967, GGA); *Stony plain* (1973); *Crusoe* (1973), selected poems; *Out of place* (1977); *Mary Midnight* (1979) *Life sentence* (1981); and *Dreaming backwards: selected poems* (1981). The Second World War, and the horrors of the Jewish concentration camps in particular, appear to have profoundly affected

Mandel's poetry. Although specific references to the war do not occur until 1973 and *Stony plain*, all of his work is characterized by macabre images of suffering and destruction, and by a pervasive pessimism. The 'Minotaur poems' of *Trio* are concerned with the brutality of the western Canadian landscape, a land of 'sharp rocks ... / cold air where birds fell like rocks / and screams, hawks, kites and cranes.' *Fuseli poems* is titled in honour of the eighteenth-century Swiss-born English painter Henry Fuseli, whose work frequently depicted tragic subjects fantastically contorted by desperation, isolated in wildly Gothic backgrounds. The poems here speak of horrifying violence, despair, self-accusation, 'fables of indifferent rape / and children slain indifferently / and daily blood'. The three volumes that followed suggest little change in this bleak outlook. *Out of place*, a long meditative poem that focuses on failed Jewish settlements in Saskatchewan, and *Life sentence*, a collection of travel poems and journal entries largely set in India, Peru, and Ecuador, while less dramatic in their presentation of human misfortune, sustain a quietly pessimistic vision. For Mandel the world was static, an arena of eternal and meaningless persecution. In Germany there is Auschwitz; in Estevan, Saskatchewan, a sun that kills 'cattle and rabbis ... in the poisoned slow air'. Mandel's style was intellectual and contemplative—he was an ironic poet rather than an angry one. A central feature of his work is a deliberate lack of emotion, which amplifies the stark hopelessness of his outlook. His early work, exceedingly complex in syntax, formal in prosody, and literary in references, appears written for a scholarly rather than a public audience. Here, as in most of his poetry, Mandel saw ancient myths and literary stories as being alive in contemporary actuality, but obscuring the actual and personal. Because the poems lack a strong sense of the actual events that brought the particular myths to the poet's attention, many of the myths seem arbitrarily applied. However, beginning with the poetry of *Black and secret man*, Mandel enriched his work by introducing open verse-forms, spare but colloquial language, simplified syntax, and reportorial detail. While the meditative style remained, a resourceful, witty tone replaced the earlier sombreness. Mandel's later poetry became increasingly experimental: prose poems, concrete poems, and found poems can be seen in both *An idiot joy* and *Stony plain*; lists and found materials punctuate the intentionally flat tones of *Out of place*. Mandel maintained his black and mythological vision of the present, but the mythology was now rooted in anecdotal actuality.

In editing several influential anthologies, Mandel was instrumental in shaping the canon of Canadian poetry. *Another time* (1977) and *The family romance* (1986) are collections of essays that assert the fictive nature of literary reality and explore the nature and origin of writing.

Manguel, Alberto (b. 1948). Born in Buenos Aires, Argentina, he spent his childhood in Israel, where his father was the Argentine ambassador. He was educated at Colegio nacional de Buenos Aires (A.S., 1966) and as a student fell under the sway of the blind Jorge Luis Borges, to whom he read, and was influenced by the Argentine poet's personal charm, multilingualism, love of reading, sense of style, and fantastic imagination. He worked as a writer and editor in Milan and Tahiti before moving in 1982 to Toronto—where he was active as a reviewer, writer, and editor—and became a Canadian citizen in 1985. Since 1992, when he moved to Switzerland, he has lived in various places, including Canada—where he was writer-in-residence at the University of Calgary from 1998 to 2000—and now lives in France at Mondion, south of the Loire Valley.

A polymath and bibliophile, familiar with five languages, Manguel has published many books, including (besides his anthologies) essays, fiction, a memoir, a biography, and readers' guides to various subjects. With Gianni Guadalupi he composed *The dictionary of imaginary places* (1980, rev. edn 1999), a reader's guide to realms of the fantastic imagination. His internationally acclaimed anthologies *Black water: the book of fantastic literature* (1983, rpr. 1992) and *Black water 2: more tales of the fantastic* (1990, rpr. 1992) include stories written by some Canadian writers and a good many writers from Latin America. His theme anthologies include *The Oxford book of Canadian ghost stories* (1990), *Canadian mystery stories* (1991), *Fathers and sons* (1998), *Mothers and daughters* (1998), and *The ark in the garden: and other fables for our time* (1998). Other anthologies are *God's spies: stories in defiance of oppression* (1993), *The Penguin book of Christmas stories* (2005), and *The Penguin book of summer stories* (2007)—as well as collections of erotic and homosexual fiction. His novel *News from a foreign country came* (1991), set largely on the Gaspé Peninsula of Québec, reveals how a man's actions in Algeria and Argentina affected him and his wife and daughter in later years. His elegant

novella *Stevenson under the palm trees* (2002) is a fantasy, portraying the short last period of the life of Robert Louis Stevenson in Samoa, that interweaves the famous writer's early life in Edinburgh, his present life with his wife Fanny and his love of Samoa and its people, his precarious health, storytelling and dreams—plus the murder of a young girl that affects him and introduces echoes of *Dr Jekyll and Mr Hyde*. The book is decorated with woodcuts by Stevenson himself, made when he was convalescing in Switzerland. Manguel devoted seven years to the research and writing of *A history of reading* (1996, rpr. 1998), a work of considerable elegance and erudition. Related to this subject is *Into the looking-glass wood: essays on words and the world* (1998), a collection of essays—some hortatory, some personal—that have a strong narrative thrust and are informed by 'a lifetime addiction to the printed page' and by the belief that literature is the only consolation 'in our passage through the dark and nameless wood' that is life. At the beginning of *Reading pictures: a history of love and hate* (2000) Manguel says: 'Much as I love reading words, I love reading pictures, and I enjoy finding the stories explicitly or secretly woven into all kinds of works of art.' This substantial book, in a large format, is of course well illustrated (though it, and the next book cited, both printed in Canada, suffer visually from the choice of paper, which does not do justice to the illustrations). The fifteen chapters of *The library at night* (2006)—with uniform headings, from: 'The Library as Myth, ... as Order, ... as Space, ... as Power' to '... as Imagination, ... as Identity, ... as Home'—grew out of his own recently established library in a barn next to his fifteenth-century house in France. He describes his library at night, 'when the library lamps are lit, the outside world disappears and nothing but this space of books remains in existence. To someone standing outside, in the garden, the library at night appears like a vast vessel of some sort....'

With Borges (2004) is a brief memoir of Manguel's acquaintance with the famous Argentine writer, Jorge Luis Borges, referred to at the beginning of this entry. *A reading diary* (2004)—celebrating the rereading of favourite books, one per month over twelve months in 2002–3—records a series of notes for each month on the book being read, and related or unrelated observations, some having to do with Manguel's own life at the time; of the twelve books chosen, *Surfacing* by Margaret ATWOOD is the only Canadian one. A related publication, *A reader on reading*, appeared in

2010. *The city of words* (2007) is his 2007 CBC Massey Lectures, in which he confronts divisions in the world caused by differences in culture and people, and learning to live with them: 'Why do we seek definitions of identity in words, and what is, in such a quest, the storyteller's role? ... How do stories we tell help us perceive ourselves and others? Can such stories lend a whole society an identity, whether true or false? And to conclude, is it possible for stories to change us and the world we live in?' *Homer's 'The Iliad' and 'The Odyssey': a biography* (2007), in the excellent Books That Shook the World series, begins with brief summaries of the twenty-four books of each epic, followed by a discussion of Homer's identity and the probability that the works began as compilations of the 'songs' of many different storytellers. Most of the book, however, discusses various literary aspects of the works and their powerful influence on individual writers and on literature. It is a wonderful, highly readable disquisition. Manguel is also the author of *Kipling: a brief biography for young adults* (2002).

Maracle, Brian. See ABORIGINAL LITERATURE: 4.

Maracle, Lee (b. 1950). A member of the Sto:loh Nation of British Columbia, Lee Maracle grew up in a poor working-class district adjacent to the Burrard Reserve in North Vancouver and attended local elementary schools and Argyle Secondary School. But her education was obtained, she says 'from lots of books, dictionaries and talking to my elders'. She spent a difficult adolescence and youth filled with frustration, anger, and hatred towards whites, drifting from California's world of itinerant farm workers to Toronto's hippy/drug scene. She chronicled the injuries of these times in *Bobbi Lee: Indian rebel* (1975, rev. 1990). Shrill and shocking, this searing memoir became a popular social document of the period for students of contemporary Native issues. In *I am woman* (1988, rpr. 1996), a collection of autobiographical essays, her suffering and pain do not mean hopeless doom, for her resilience and tenacity enable her to emerge free and triumphant. Unapologetic in her wrath, Maracle subjects her readers to a remorseless exposé of the contemporary state of Native women. From 1989 to 1990 Maracle worked at the En'owkin Centre in Penticton, B.C., as a teacher of creative writing. In *Sojourner's truth and other stories* (1990), she tries to integrate two mediums, 'oratory and European story', in

narratives and essays that depict the plight of Native children in school, and Native women (doubly victimized as Natives and women); but she also portrays cross-cultural relationships. Her novel *Sundogs* (1991, rpr. 1992) focuses on the effect on Canada's Aboriginal people of two events that happened in 1990: Elijah Harper's filibuster in the Manitoba legislature and the Oka crisis in Québec. The novel is written from the point of view of a naive Native college student, living with her mother in Vancouver, who joins the Run for Peace that crosses Canada in support of the Oka freedom-fighters: within the space of a year she experiences a virtual rebirth as a Native. In *Ravensong* (1993) Maracle portrays the lives of Natives in a West Coast village during the 1950s where a flu epidemic devastates their community—while doctors in a nearby white village do nothing because the Native village is outside their jurisdiction. The novel explores the guilt and shame of both her white and Native characters. Maracle believes implicitly that words are a form of empowerment, and in her idiosyncratic style and language, writing outside the literary mainstream, she condemns inequities that go deeper than immediate quarrels and grievances, providing insights into Canada's dilemmas of race and culture. *Daughters are forever* (2002) and *Will's garden* (2002) are warm, believable re-creations of Salish / Sto:loh family life. *Daughters* is Marilyn's account of her alienation from her culture and her daughters, in an innovative narrative reflecting Salish storytelling, which, thanks partly to the influences of nature (and Westwind), leads to a transformed life. The second novel is not only about Will, in his second year of high school, and his relationship with his school friends, but his family's preparation for his Coming of Age Ceremony—as well as their confrontation with the crisis caused by his ruptured appendix and hospitalization. The garden is a beaded garden on a cape, made by Will: 'All of us are looking at the garden of roses on the cape. I'm seeing it like someone else did it. Two full roses on each lapel area of the cape jump up at you, trailing from them are leaves....' *Bent box* (2000) is a collection of poems. *My home as I remember* (2000), which Maracle edited with Sandra Laronde, is an anthology of poetry, fiction, and art work by First Nations, Inuit, and Métis women.

Marchand, Philip (b. 1946). Born in Pittsfield, Massachusetts, he came to Canada in 1964 to study at St Michael's College, University of Toronto (B.A., 1969; M.A., 1970), and is now a permanent Canadian resident. In 1974 he became a full-time freelance magazine writer, producing work for all the leading Canadian general-interest magazines, including *Saturday Night, Toronto Life, Chatelaine,* and *Maclean's*. A collection of his magazine pieces was published in *Just looking, thank you* (1976). He has been books columnist for the *Toronto Star* (1989–2008) and now writes a book column for the *National Post*. As an author he is best known for his widely praised *Marshall McLuhan: the medium and the messenger* (1989, rpr. 1990; rev. 1998), the first biography of MCLUHAN, whom he first heard speak on the opening day of McLuhan's modern-poetry course at St Michael's College in the fall of 1968. It is a lucid, perceptive, and comprehensive portrait of the man and his work; its 1998 edition has a Foreword by Neil Postman. *Ripostes: reflections on Canadian literature* (1998), nineteen essays that 'arose, in one form or another, from my work at the *Toronto Star*', opens with 'Confessions of a Book Columnist', in which Marchand describes the qualifications of a book reviewer as being well read, intelligent, and a lover of literature—qualities that have informed Marchand's weekly book reviews from the beginning. Removing himself from all forms of cultural hype, he is not afraid to embark on a well-considered, respectful dismantling of a reputation (for example, that of Margaret LAURENCE) or a book (*The ENGLISH PATIENT*), or to offer the occasional salutary pronouncement: 'Canadian literature is beginning to flower in an age overwhelmingly unfavourable to great art. The signs are obvious that we are in a decadent literary and cultural period—overemphasis on technique being one of the clearest of these signs. It is part of this decadence that we, in Canada, possess a very small, very sophisticated audience for serious literature, which is sufficient to call forth some remarkable, if minor, accomplishments in fiction.' *Ghost empire: how the French almost conquered North America* (2005) is an unusual example of popular history—it is both imaginative and informative—that focuses on the explorations of La Salle and the large part of North America he claimed for France. Marchand travelled over La Salle's route by car and plane—talking along the way to countless local-history enthusiasts who sometimes revived La Salle's persona in their area—while reflecting on his past, on the Catholic church, and on his own Catholicism. Marchand has also published a crime novel, *Deadly spirits* (1994), about a newspaper reporter, Heywood Murphy, who befriends LeRoy in a clinic for alcoholics; when LeRoy is murdered, Murphy becomes embroiled in nefarious activities and brutal treatment in trying to clear himself as the murder suspect.

Marchbanks, Samuel. See Robertson DAVIES.

Marchessault, Jovette (b. 1938). Born in Montreal, she was obliged to leave school at thirteen and go to work in a textile factory. Self-taught, she is a visual artist, novelist, and playwright. Her paintings, sculptures, and masks of telluric women have been widely shown in Toronto, Montreal, New York, Paris, and Brussels. A radical lesbian feminist, proud of her Aboriginal heritage and of the spiritual traditions on which it is based, she produced during a long creative period a multi-faceted and highly original body of novels and plays evoking a world in which divine and human power is predominantly female and bonds among women exist across time and space, whether these be personal, social, or cosmic. Her focus was on matrilinear bonds and women's culture, including women's knowledge, vision, energy, memory, and all women's production: in kitchens, salons, schools, hospitals, factories, offices, or in birthing and painting. The desire to achieve a visionary, utopian project, as well as trenchant social commentary, is evident in all of her work.

All Marchessault's fiction has been translated by Yvonne M. Klein. Her three-volume autobiographical novel, *Comme une enfant de la terre*, is based on the theme and structure of a quest or initiatory journey and is an exploration of human relations and of the bonds linking humans to spiritual, animal, vegetable, and mineral worlds. The autobiographical exploration undertaken occurs not only in the past and the present, but also in the future of a world that does not yet exist, but that can be made to exist through human creativity in mystical union with cosmic forces Marchessault's narrators relate the odyssey through evocations of events in her life, that of her family, and of Amerindian societies and their cultures. The first volume, *Le crachat solaire* (1975)—*Like a child of the earth* (1988)—recounts metaphorically and allegorically the birth and the memories of the narrator, whose origins are in 'solar spittle' and in the stars. *La mère des herbes* (1980)—*Mother of the grass* (1989)—combines the poetic qualities of the mystic quest with explicit and angry social commentary. In the third volume, *Les cailloux blancs pour les forêts obscures* (1987)—*White pebbles in the dark forests* (1990)—the narrator, a writer, and her visionary companion, an aviatrix, continue in dialogue the cosmic quest for mystic union and for understanding human existence, death, and evil. It opens a new dimension through a question, 'What about the Fathers?': by the end of the novel, the terrible gulfs between men and women are seen to render impossible personal and spiritual fulfilment for either sex. The trilogy is a rich exploration of women's experience, community, tradition, vision, spirituality, suffering, and solitude. In another work of fiction, *Triptyque lesbien* (1980)—*Lesbian triptych* (1985)—the first text is structured around a genealogy of generations of women, celebrating women's power and vehemently denouncing destructive forces in a male-dominated society. The second text, 'Les vaches de nuit', now well known as a dramatic monologue, is an extended metaphor in which the narrator identifies herself as a calf and her mother as a milk cow. This has been performed to powerful effect in French and English ('Night cows') by Pol Pelletier in Montreal, New York, Paris, Italy, Toronto, and Vancouver. The theme of the third text, 'Les faiseuses d'anges' (Backstreet abortionist), which has also been performed in Montreal as a dramatic monologue, is abortion: the narrator's mother is an abortionist, or 'angel-maker', who expresses her creative energy in knitting as well as in using her needles to produce abortions. Through an original use of extended paradox, Marchessault argues poetically in favour of women's rights to control their own bodies.

Marchessault's plays frequently offer fictional re-creations of real, historical women, particularly of authors, whose texts she cites extensively while situating them in the context of her dramatic universe. As a result of this original strategy, works from the past that were poorly read by critics are received in surprisingly fresh and new perspectives. The four protagonists of *La saga des poules mouillées* (1981, rpr.1989), which had a successful 1981 run at Montreal's Théâtre du Nouveau Monde—and, as *Saga of the wet hens* (1983) in a translation by Linda Gaboriau, at Toronto's Tarragon Theatre in 1982—are dramatizations of four of Québec's best-known writers: Laure Conan (Félicité ANGERS), Germaine GUÈVREMONT, Gabrielle ROY, and Anne HÉBERT. They meet in a mythic space where each assumes a poetically established totemic identity. The play offers an imaginative reading of their works, conversations between them, and a reinterpretation in a feminist frame of their creative experience. *Le voyage magnifique d'Emily Carr* (1990, GGA)—translated by Linda Gaboriau as *The magnificent voyage of Emily Carr* (1992)—is a homage to the cosmic vision of the painter (q.v.) and a dramatic reflection on life, creativity, solitude, and death. While Emily's sister seeks to restrain Emily within the norms of Victorian family and society, the voices of an Aboriginal friend, of the Aboriginal goddess D'Sonoqua, of a young Lawren Harris, and of the Soul Tuner support her in her struggle to share nature's secrets and to make her art.

Marie Chapdelaine (1921, rpr. 2005). A widely read classic of world literature, this novel by Louis HÉMON was published first in France in serial form in 1914, then in Montreal as a book in 1916. An English translation of 1921 by William Hume BLAKE, with the subtitle *A tale of the Lake St John country*, remains the standard one—there have been many reprints—but a translation by Alan Brown was published in 1989 (rpr. 1992). It is set in the Lac Saint-Jean region of Québec and portrays the farmers' attempts to tame the harsh land. On the death of the man she loves, and to whom she was betrothed, Maria is faced with the choice of marrying Lorenzo Surprenant, who would take her to a much easier life in the United States, or Eutrope Gagnon, who can offer her nothing better than the same difficult life she and her family have always known. In rejecting the opportunity to flee, she sacrifices herself in order that the values of her family and her community may be safeguarded. This devotion symbolizes Québec's determined struggle to secure a foothold for rural, Catholic, French society away from the onslaught of modern, urban, English-dominated life. Although Hémon had been living in Canada for less than three years when he began to write the novel, he succeeded in capturing the essence of Québec's cultural ideal as it was promoted at the beginning of the twentieth century. *Maria Chapdelaine: récit du Canada français* is a masterpiece that belongs solidly within the tradition of the *roman de la terre* or 'novel of the land', and may even be said to represent its perfected form. Among its many literary qualities are its range of styles, from the lyrical prose describing springtime and Maria's exchange of vows, to the muscular, spare accounts of the harsh winter and the death it brings; its sharply drawn characters; and its convincingly rendered scenes. The novel has been transformed into a political football, first by ideologues anxious to celebrate the characters' fidelity and to propose this as an ideal worthy of emulation, and more recently by critics intent on proving that the characters' submissiveness only enslaved them. *Maria Chapdelaine* may indeed crystallize, as Nicole Deschamps has suggested, 'a moment in the collective history of French Canada and thereby have become inseparable from the debate on that history.' What has been sacrificed during the heated 'political' debate is an appreciation of it as a work of art, an aspect that one presumes has not eluded its readers in more than twenty languages. There is a 2005 reprint of *Maria* published by Golden Dog and an edition for young people, published in the same year, translated by Hélène Rioux and illustrated by Rajka Kupesic.

Marie Calumet (1976). This is Irène Currie's translation of a satirical novel by Rodolphe Girard (1879–1956), published in French with the same title in 1904 and reprinted in 1946. Father Lefranc, the parish priest of St-Apollinaire in 1860, visits his neighbour, Father Flavel, the pastor of St-Ildefonse, whose rectory is in chaos. Lefranc sends him Marie Calumet, a still-comely forty-year-old woman who is a remarkable housekeeper. She soon has the presbytery running like clockwork, while unwittingly attracting the romantic interest of Narcisse, the hired man, and Zéphirin, the verger. Narcisse wins her hand and Zéphirin avenges himself by pouring a laxative into one of the dishes at the wedding feast. Most of the characters are naive, but sensitive and warmhearted. Marie has an exaggerated admiration for all things connected with the Church and its priests. During the bishop's pastoral visit she asks where to put Monsignor's 'holy piss', after pondering whether to save it; and wearing a crinoline and no underwear at the harvest feast, she trips on a walnut-tree root and scandalizes the pastor, who threatens excommunication. Another scandalous episode occurs when the pastor's teenage niece reads the most sensual verses (taking up thirteen pages in the novel) from J.F. Ostervald's version of the 'Song of Songs', which had been forbidden to the masses. These and other scenes are described by Girard both satirically and humorously. When the novel was published in 1904, 1000 copies were sold almost immediately; but it was condemned by the Church as 'gross, immoral and impious'. For the 1946 edition (on which the translation is based), Girard, in addition to making many stylistic improvements, modified many irreverent religious references and omitted the final chapter, with its scatological description of the consequences produced by the laxative. Even in the revised version, however, the novel conveys a realistic depiction of the customs, language, and morality of Québec around 1860. *Marie Calumet* is the first major French-Canadian novel to treat the Church and clergy in a humorous way.

Marie de l'Incarnation (1599–1672). Born Marie Guyart in Tours, France, she was married at eighteen and widowed two years later. In 1633 she entered the Ursuline monastery of Tours and in 1639 sailed for Québec, with three other Ursulines and Madame de la Peltrie, to found a 'seminary' for Native children and a boarding school for French girls. For more than thirty years, while she alternated as head of the monastery, she wrote thousands of letters to her son, Claude Martin, a Benedictine priest, and to various benefactors in France. Though a cloistered nun, Marie de l'Incarnation was in touch with everyone in the colony—the Jesuits, the governors and other notables, the Native converts, and common people. Her letters rank with the *JESUIT RELATIONS* as source material for the period. Because not intended for publication, they are more personal and informal and cover not only the triumphs and tragedies of the Jesuit mission but such mundane matters as the earthquake of 1663, the weather, the crops, the coming of the king's girls, and the fire that destroyed the Ursuline monastery in 1650. The style is lively, at times hasty and even breathless, shrewd and often tart in its observations, by turns practical and high-minded. Marie de l'Incarnation was the first social historian of Canada, and the breadth and vividness of the picture provided is remarkable in view of the fact that she frequently wrote of events she had not personally witnessed. *Word from New France: the selected letters of Marie de l'Incarnation* (1967), Joyce MARSHALL's translation of sixty-six letters, included a complete biography and a historical introduction. A classic work, it is unfortunately out of print.

Marlatt, Daphne (b. 1942). Born Daphne Buckle in Melbourne, Australia, to English parents who had been evacuated from Penang, Malaya, in advance of the Japanese occupation, she spent six postwar years in Penang before her family moved to North Vancouver in 1951. She enrolled in English at the University of British Columbia in 1960, and on graduation in 1964 went to the University of Indiana, where she completed an M.A. (1968) in comparative literature. Following the breakup of her marriage to G. Alan Marlatt (1963–71), she returned to British Columbia. She has been writer-in-residence at several universities and is a Member of the Order of Canada (2005). Marlatt's earliest works are the long poems *Frame of a story* (1968) and *leaf/leaf/s* (1969), which are highly contrasting experiments in language and form. *Frame*, written in a long prose line, retells Hans Christian Andersen's 'The snow queen', using the tale to reinterpret events in the author's life. *leaf/leaf/s*, written in lines of single words and syllables, accentuates minute fragmentary features of syntax and morphology so that at times they become the writing's primary content. While one work engages language at the level of sentence rhythm and narrative voice, and the other at that of phoneme and syntactic connection, each uses language to divine meaning through recurrence and resemblance. These tentative and visibly technical works were succeeded in the next decade by a number of long poems and related texts that explored phenomenology, autobiography, and the politics of the local—*Rings* (1971), *Vancouver poems* (1972), *Steveston* (1974), *Our lives* (1975), *Zócalo* (1977), and *What matters* (1980)—and culminated in *Selected writing: net work* (1980), edited by Fred WAH. While the texts in all of these—except the journal *Zócalo*—are presented as 'poems', their dominant feature is the long verse line, minutely punctuated, which suggests both the linguistic precision of poetry and the sequential motion of prose. All were written from inside a single consciousness and used linguistic structure to map perceptual processes in detail. *Rings* presents the images and fragmentary reflections in the mind of a woman whose marriage is crumbling and whose first child is about to be born. Puns, shards of words, metaphors, enigmatic images, and broken sentences combine to give a dense physical rendering of her simultaneous experience of pregnancy, memory, her husband's hostility, and her physical surroundings. *Vancouver poems* encounters that city through the subjective vision of someone freshly experiencing its geography, climate, and historical and political documents as interwoven, nearly co-present, phenomena. Marlatt's major work of this period, *Steveston*, presents the history and present of this Japanese-Canadian fish-cannery town as alive in the 'net' of consciousness cast by the writer. *Zócalo's* very different images and denser, more extended prose line give form to the intense experiences of a woman travelling in Yucatan (Mexico) who is separated by language, race,

gender, and class, yet not by eye or ear, from the scenes she witnesses.

In the 1980s Marlatt's public affiliation with lesbian communities marked a sharp change in the political perspectives and implied readership of her writing. The long poem/journal *How hug a stone* (1983) announced Marlatt's new interest in various feminisms and was quickly followed by the lyrical lesbian love texts of *Touch to my tongue* (1984), and its accompanying essay/meditation on feminist theorists Julia Kristeva and Mary Daly, 'Musing with mother tongue'. Marlatt published, with Betsy WARLAND, *Double negative* (1988), a collaborative long poem/journal about two lesbians crossing Australia's Nullarbor Desert that draws comparisons between the theft of Aboriginal lands and the denial of space to women who are lesbians. Later that year she published her best-received work to date, the novel *Ana Historic* (1988, rpr. 1997), which continued Marlatt's autobiographical investigations and linked semi-fictionalized accounts of her early family life to the erasure of women from the official early history of Vancouver. *Salvage* (1991) is a collection of texts 'salvaged' and expanded from those she had deleted more than a decade earlier from *Steveston*—which would have given it a more feminist emphasis. *Ghost works* (1993)—a collection that recasts *Zócalo*, *How hug a stone*, and her 1976 Penang journal 'Month of hungry ghosts'—illuminates, as Marlatt's introduction argues, the extreme difficulty of women's autobiography in cultures where the systemic erasing of women's activities leaves them only the ghosts of lives to reclaim or imagine. *This tremor love is* (2001) is a collection of love poems spanning twenty-five years. The theme that women, lacking documentary accounts of their own or their mothers' lives, must re-imagine or fictionalize their pasts is central to Marlatt's second novel, *Taken* (1996), which focuses on characters who strongly resemble Marlatt's parents during their Penang and Australian years. In 2008 Marlatt published *The given*, a long series of prose poem fragments (some entirely in lower case) that cohere in a memorable treatment of family, home, memory (the present is interwoven with the past), beginning with her mother's death 'when my father's call came. I can't wake her up, his voice like a child's, crushed, lost. I've tried, she won't wake up.' The first section of *The given*, 'Seven Glass Bowls'—where it is subtitled '[Overture]'—was published separately in 2003.

Readings from the labyrinth (1998) is a series of feminist 'musings', talks, letters, and notes, on topics that include writing and reading,

Marsh

the immigrant imagination, the lesbian tradition, women's autobiography and feminism, and the 'labyrinthine' structure of the text. Marlatt published in 2009 *The gull*, a play that dramatizes the link between the people of Steveston and the village of Mio in Japan; it contains a Japanese translation by Toyoshi Yoshihara.

Marlyn, John (1912–2005). Born in Hungary (family name: Mihaelovitcz), he came to Canada as an infant and grew up in Winnipeg's North End. He attended secondary school in Winnipeg, leaving at the age of fourteen, and beginning in 1930 studied literature at the University of Manitoba for a short period. Unable to find employment in Canada during the Depression, he moved to England where he became a script reader for a film company, Gainsborough Studios. He returned to Canada just before the Second World War and worked as a writer for various government departments in Ottawa, where he also taught creative-writing courses. He lived for many years on Gran Canaria, Canary Islands, and died there. Marlyn's *Under the ribs of death* (1957, NCL) is one of the earliest Canadian novels to deal with what has been called the 'third solitude'—life within ethnic cultures outside the Canadian mainstream. It is the story of Sandor Hunyadi, the son of an idealistic Hungarian immigrant, who is determined to escape the poverty and humiliation he associates with his immigrant background. Changing his name to Alex Hunter, he becomes a successful and ruthless businessman, only to be ruined in the Depression, a reversal that forces him to return to his family and the humanistic values he had earlier rejected. The novel is a powerful portrait of the hardships endured by immigrants, and of the driving ambition and susceptibility to materialistic values that can be triggered by such an experience. *Putzi, I love you, you little square* (1981) is a surrealistic satire set in the 1970s dealing, once again, with Hungarian immigrants in a city resembling Winnipeg. It is about a precocious fetus who speaks from his virgin mother's womb, advising her on the unworthiness of her suitors, quoting Shakespeare, Donne, Wordsworth, and other classical writers at length, and commenting tartly on life in the world beyond the womb, with special attention to the threat of technological incursions upon human privacy. While slight, *Putzi* is nonetheless a witty fable that argues for the same humanistic values (here personified in the character of Julian, a doctor), as did Marlyn's earlier novel.

Marriot, Anne (1913–97). Born in Vancouver, she was educated at The Poplars and at the Norfolk House School for Girls in Victoria, and took summer courses in creative writing at the University of British Columbia. She was encouraged in her poetry by Alan Crawley, and was on the founding committee of Crawley's CONTEMPORARY VERSE in 1941. She wrote dozens of school broadcasts for CBC Radio and the B.C. Department of Education, largely on creative writing or historical subjects. From 1945 to 1949 she was a script editor for the National Film Board in Ottawa. Marriot's best-known work is the long narrative poem, 'The wind, our enemy', which describes drought on the Prairies during the 1930s and was the title poem in a Ryerson Poetry Chapbook (1939). Subsequent early collections were *Calling adventurers* (1941, GGA). *Salt marsh* (1942), and *Sandstone and other poems* (1945). After a long silence, Marriot published *Countries* (1971), a series of moving poems in which the narrator, confined by a serious illness, investigates the memories of countries she has known; then, working with the materials of everyday life as Marriot travels about in her mental landscape, she discovers the heart of love. *The circular coast: new and selected poems* (1981) and *Letters from some island: new poems* (1985) include the best poems from the earlier collections and new works that reveal a unified whole in which Marriot seeks, with complex imagery and perfectly observed detail, the core of stability within a changing world. Her subjects are time, youth, and fulfilling dreams; aging and death are also prominent—she speaks a mantra to death: 'That is the timeless clock / that tells no hours / set to its / certain time.' *Aqua* (1991) also presents meditations on death, and a celebration of water as a spiritual force; the poems at the same time sparkle with vitality, courage, and strength. This last collection includes 'The rose and the dagger: stories from the island of Rhodes', poems for four speakers. Marriot's short stories were collected in *A long way to Oregon: selected stories* (1984).

Marsh, James (b. 1943). Born in Toronto, he was educated at Oakwood Collegiate and Carleton University, Ottawa (B.A., 1974). His prominent career as an editor began early, unconventionally, for after his second year at Waterloo Lutheran University (now Wilfrid Laurier) he was hired as an education editor at Holt Rinehart Winston, Toronto (1965–7), where he learned all aspects of the publishing business; and in 1970 he was made editor of the CARLETON LIBRARY series, editing sixty volumes over ten years. In 1980 Mel Hurtig made him editor-in-chief of *The CANADIAN ENCYCLOPEDIA* (for which he wrote 352 entries), a huge enterprise that involved some 40 staff, 200 consultants, and thousands of contributors; it has had three editions: 1985, 1988, and 1999. He is editor-in-chief of the online versions of *The Canadian encyclopedia* and *The encyclopedia of music in Canada*. Since 2000 Marsh has been Director of Content Development at the Historica Foundation. His books include *The fishermen of Lunenburg* (1968), *The fur trade in Canada* (1969), and *The exploration of Canada* (1970); he has also contributed chapters to several history books. Marsh was awarded the Centenary Medal of the Royal Society of Canada in recognition of his editing *The Canadian encyclopedia*, and is a Member of the Order of Canada. He lives in Edmonton.

Marsh hay (1923, rpr. 1973). A four-act play by Merrill DENISON, first published in his *The unheroic north: four Canadian plays* (1923), it was not produced until 1974 (Hart House Theatre, Toronto), directed by Richard Plant. Set in the dirty kitchen of a backwoods Ontario farmhouse, it depicts the aimless existence of the Serang family. The parents, Lena and John, in their early forties, are worn out, crushed by their hopeless twenty-year struggle with poor land. Lena blames John for not going west; John blames Lena for not wanting to leave relatives and friends. Of their twelve children, five are dead and three have run away. Those remaining are intent only on avoiding work. The neighbours are narrow-minded and uneducated—with the exception of Andrew Barnood, a placid, kindly man. He and William Thompson, an elderly lawyer who comes for the hunting season, are foils against which the family's deterioration is emphasized. Naturalism, in which heredity and environment so determine life that nothing one can do can alleviate or change the pattern, is clearly the philosophy behind *Marsh hay*. There is no hope for the future. The misery of the Serang family is climaxed by the pregnancy of fifteen-year-old Sarilin, a subsequent abortion, and her return to sexual promiscuity. The title of the play is symbolic of destitution: the wild marsh hay growing in the cedar swamps, so vital for the cattle's winter fodder, is often destroyed by beavers building their dams. A powerful statement of the ills of Ontario farmers in the early 1920s, *Marsh hay* is a tightly constructed play with sharp dialogue and powerful characterization in the portrait of John Serang. That it had to wait fifty years for its premiere is probably explained by the reluctance of the country's amateur theatres to promote such a bitter and bleak view of Canadian rural society. But it did receive a much-praised production in the summer of 1996 at the Shaw Festival, Niagara-on-the-Lake, Ontario.

Marshall, Joyce (1913–2005). Born in Montreal and educated at McGill University, she lived and died in Toronto. Her first novel, *Presently tomorrow* (1946), is set in the Eastern Townships of Québec, in an English-speaking enclave in the southwest corner of the province. The story takes place in the early 1930s when the Depression has caused political and social turmoil throughout Canada. Craig Everett, an idealistic but naive Anglican priest, whose social conscience has become an irritant to his superiors, has been sent from Montreal to conduct a retreat at St Ursula's, a boarding school for girls. Before the retreat has ended he is seduced by one of the students, a schoolgirl who is already more knowing than Craig will ever be. The fine prose and subtle exploration of character and motivations that distinguish this novel—which achieved some notoriety on publication because of its subject matter—are noticeable once again in *Lovers and strangers* (1957), which takes place in the latter half of the 1940s in Toronto. Katherine, a diffident young woman who bears the faint after-effects of polio, impulsively marries Roger Haines, an architect who seems to be already launched on a successful career. But although he appears to be outgoing, busy, and affluent, Roger suffers from his own insecurities, and the novel becomes a study of marriage and a career that are both going badly. Marshall's short-story collection, *A private place* (1975), brings together seven stories that appeared in magazines or were broadcast by the CBC at various times from the early 1950s to the 1970s. One story is set in Norway, another in Mexico; a third story, about childhood, takes place in the Eastern Townships; Marshall's best-known story, 'The old woman', is a study of an obsession that ends in madness, having as its background a remote village in northern Québec. But the tone of *A private place* is really established by the three remaining stories—'The enemy', 'Salvage', and 'So many have died'— about urban life in North America in the second half of the twentieth century; they are also stories about the lives that women lead who must live alone in big cities, solitary, vulnerable, sometimes physically endangered. *Any time at all and other stories* (1993) was selected for the NEW CANADIAN LIBRARY by

Timothy FINDLEY, who wrote an Afterword. The twelve stories include 'The old woman'; 'So many have died'; and five Martha stories, perceptive and tough-minded short fictions about childhood and growing up, written between the 1970s and the 1990s, with two of them published here for the first time—they are linked to three summers spent 'on one of the English streets at the edge of that French-Canadian village on the Ottawa River', not a welcoming place to be. *Blood and bone / En chair et en os* (1995) contains seven stories in English and their French versions, each by a different translator.

Marshall edited and translated *Word from New France: the selected letters of Marie de l'Incarnation* (1967), sixty-six letters by the famous cloistered nun (q.v.) for which she wrote a lengthy and important historical introduction. Her translations of three books by Gabrielle ROY—*The road past Altamont* (1966), *Wildflower* (1970), and *Enchanted summer* (1976)—involved her in a close and sympathetic collaboration with the author. See *In translation: the Gabrielle Roy–Joyce Marshall correspondence* (2006) edited by Jane Everett.

Marshall, Tom (1938–93). Born in Niagara Falls, Ontario, he was educated at Queen's University, Kingston, where he obtained a B.A. in history, and wrote an M.A. thesis on A.M. KLEIN. In 1964 he became a member of the English department at Queen's. Marshall's first four mature poetry collections—which form an interlocking cycle of earth, air, fire, and water imagery—were *The silences of fire* (1969), *Magic water* (1971), *The earthbook* (1974), and *The white city* (1976); selections from these make up *The elements: poems 1960–75* (1980). Marshall explores history, pain, and the human condition against a backdrop of the history, artists, and historical figures of Canada, a country that Marshall regards as 'a second chance' for humanity to redeem itself, since that opportunity was lost by Europeans: 'the garden of the gods is here'. Marshall moved easily 'between two worlds, the ordinary and the cosmic'. *Playing with fire* (1984) and *Dance of the particles* (1984) are lyrical longer poems that elaborate his established themes. Marshall's literary executor, David HELWIG, compiled *Some impossible heaven of the senses: last poems of Tom Marshall* (1994), which frequently shows the poet at his best.

Much of Marshall's fiction, and many of his essays, celebrate collective heroes and a sense of community. In his early fiction he often gently satirized inadequate academics and Toronto artsy types. He moved on to provocative character studies and complex narrative structures in his final works. His style was gentle, in the comic burlesque tradition. He explored sadness and loss in his quiet lyrical tone. Later fictions show a concern with spiritual and ecological issues. Marshall's first novel, *Rosemary Gaol* (1978), is a flawed though interesting comedy of manners about men and women in their early thirties making a bid for career and personal fulfilment before the onslaught of middle age. His protagonist is a teacher and amateur novelist who is writing a dull novel within the novel. Marshall wittily juxtaposes narrative styles to portray the pretensions of the university milieu. The five stories in *Glass houses* (1985) represent a serio-comic examination of characters going through upheavals in relationships. Two of the stories feature characters from *Rosemary Gaol*, and were intended to be part of a sequel. The most memorable stories are about a mildly disturbed child and a man with an obsession for the movie star Elizabeth Taylor. *Adele at the end of the day* (1987), a psychological novel, is a bittersweet masterpiece about an older woman, Adele Driscoll, who fades in and out of reverie. The past events of her life are seen from the point of view of Barney, her estranged son, a middle-aged man disappointed by his life and career. Marshall effortlessly handles shifting points of consciousness. *Voices on the brink: a border tale* (1989), set in Niagara Falls, is a combination of fiction, essay, poetry, and drama, with a narrator who muses on the death of his father, the murder of a friend, and ills of the USA and American pop culture, represented by Marilyn Monroe, who is in Canada to make a film. Its complex structure includes alternating chapters told in the first person by the middle-aged narrator and the third-person point of view of his younger self, as the narrative moves from disillusionment to tragedy. *Changelings: a double fugue* (1991) is a provocative psychological study of multiple personalities in a brother and sister. The novel unfolds like a fugue as the various characters overlap and move towards a brilliant resolution. In *Goddess disclosing* (1992) Marshall continued to explore the female voice. A loosely structured novel, with flashes of brilliance and an unsuccessful plot, the book blends ecological and feminist themes in his study of a small-time movie actress who could be Gaia, the female spirit of earth. The opening chapter, 'The other Mexico', is a splendid, haunting, and melancholy plea for the earth. Marshall's posthumously published postmodern novel, *The adventures of*

Marshall

John Montgomery (1995), tells an amusing story of Canada from the War of 1812 and the Rebellion of 1837 to the flag crisis of 1970 and the Oka crisis of 1990, through the central character and his descendants (including Lucy Maud MONTGOMERY and the author of the novel in hand), all of whom happen to become distinguished Canadian writers.

Marshall's prolific critical writings include *Harsh and lovely land: the major Canadian poets and the making of a Canadian tradition* (1979). His collection of essays, *Ghost safari* (1991), reflects on his literary friendships with Margaret ATWOOD, David HELWIG, Gwendolyn MacEWEN, and Bronwen WALLACE. *Multiple exposures, promised lands; essays on Canadian fiction & poetry* (1992) is a series of reflections on the lives and work of Atwood, Michael ONDAATJE, Al PURDY, Margaret LAURENCE, Leonard COHEN, Mordecai RICHLER, and other writers.

Martel, Yann (b.1963). Born in Salamanca, Spain, he spent his childhood in many different countries—his father was a diplomat. His French-Canadian parents settled in Montreal, but he attended high school at Trinity College School, Port Hope, Ontario, and studied philosophy at Trent University, Peterborough, Ontario (B.A., 1985). A skilled writer of fiction, he combines enthusiasm, narrative drive, and an innovative writing style—that can include offbeat prose forms—in such a way that the reader is immediately drawn into the text and gladly remains with it to the end. *The facts behind the Helsinki Roccamatios* (1993, rev. 2004) is a collection of four stories. The title story, which won the 1991 Journey Prize, is the narrator's description of his college friend Paul's contracting AIDS, the result of a blood transfusion he received in Jamaica. The narrator gives up his academic year and devotes himself to his friend. He decides that they should tell stories to pass the time—'to meet as storytellers to embrace the world—there, that's how Paul and I would destroy the void.' Thus the Italian-Finnish Roccamatio family, living in Helsinki, was invented; the stories would be about them. We don't read the stories told but only brief historical highlights of many years, from 1901 to 1961. The bulk of the text is a clear, delicate, moving description of the devastation of Paul's body, and the narrator's (and Paul's parents') response to this. Paul leaves the narrator a dictated note, dated 2001, giving a few lines of narrative and ending: 'Sorry, it's the best I could do. The story is yours.' 'Manners of dying' is a series of letters from the warden of the Cantos Correctional Institution to Mrs Barlow, describing her son Kevin's execution by hanging, each one describing differently Kevin's attitude, emotion, behaviour—evoking, briefly, different people, different lives, without ever evading the horror of the execution. The text of 'The Via Aeterna Mirror Company', about the making of a mirror, and about memory, is frequently set on the left side of the page and is interrupted by lines of nothing but *blah-blah-blah-blah-*; the rest of the text is in parentheses—but you want to read it to the end. A Canadian university student visiting a friend in Washington has a strange musical experience in a story whose title is also strange (but true): 'The time I heard the Private Donald J. Rankin String Concerto with one discordant violin, by the American composer John Morton'. A moving story is created from the strong impression the music made on the narrator, along with echoes of the Vietnam War when he sees the grave of Donald J. Rankin. *Self* (1996, rpr. 1997), Martel's first novel, is the narrator's breezy account of his life—beginning when his mother 'sat me on my potty on the dining-room table and set herself in front of me. She began to coo and urge me on, running her fingers up and down my back'—until he is thirty. The last page of the text is headed CHAPTER TWO, which is four lines long; the first sentence reads: 'I am thirty years old.' Everything is gone into as he grows up. He takes weight training. 'I must say that I never regretted these hours of slow sweaty exertion. I forgot my acne and my other woes and I looked down on my body that felt to me lean and nimble, strong and supple. There's a tightness of frame, a lightness of foot, that you feel when you are fit—it's wonderful.' Without any ado—this in not a traumatic event—he turns into a woman when he's eighteen and that, of course, colours the years that follow. The only traumatic events he / she experiences are the deaths of his parents in a plane crash and her rape, when the text turns into double columns: the words 'fear ...   fear ... fear ... / pain ... pain ... pain ...' alternate in their own column. Before the end of the novel, in which the theme of selfhood is memorably explored, the narrator turns back into a man. 'It didn't fare well,' Martel says in an Author's Note prefacing his next novel. 'Reviewers were puzzled, or damned it with faint praise. Then readers ignored it.'

Martel's second novel, *Life of Pi* (2001, rpr. 2002, 2004), which won the British Mann Booker Prize in 2002, was and still is extremely popular. It became better known for the central feature of the plot than for its literary quality: a sixteen-year-old Indian boy is marooned in a lifeboat with a Bengal tiger. In the first hundred pages Pi tells us about his early life. He was named after a swimming pool; his full name is Piscine Moltor Patel. His schoolmates abbreviated 'Piscine' unpleasantly until he insisted on being called Pi, the sixteenth letter of the Greek alphabet. He adheres to three religions. 'I was fourteen years old—and a well-content Hindu—when I met Jesus Christ on a holiday' and he is baptized. He also becomes a Muslim ('I just wanted to love God,' he says.) His father is director of the Pondicherry Zoo and Pi absorbs animal lore: an enclosure like a zoo can work well, but everything 'must be just right—in other words, within the limits of the animals' capacity to adapt.' Pi's father gives up on the dictatorial prime minister Mrs Ghandi and decides to migrate to Canada, boarding a Japanese ship with his wife, two sons, and various animals intended for other zoos. But the ship sinks in the Pacific and Pi is thrown into a lifeboat, which 'fell through the air and we hit the seething water.' His companions are the tiger Richard Parker (the name a registrar's mistake), a wounded zebra and a hyena hiding under a tarpaulin, and an orangutan called Orange Juice that floated to the lifeboat on an island of bananas held together by a nylon net. Among the things described in compelling, vivid prose are the following: the zebra being eaten alive by the hyena, who then eats the orangutan; the hyena being eaten by the tiger; forty-five survival items in a locker; thirst and its surcease ('to the gurgling beat of my greedy throat, pure, delicious, beautiful, crystalline water flowed into my system. Liquid life, it was.'); and being heaved up by a mountainous wave in a convulsive storm ('But the mountain would shift, and the ground beneath us would start sinking in a most stomach-turning way. In no time we would be sitting once again at the bottom of a dark valley.') The passage of time—227 days—unfolds with exact descriptions that lend plausibility to fantastic events, large and small. Salvation comes with a landing on the shore of Mexico. God, though often mentioned, does not weigh heavily in the book, and any allegorical intent implied by Pi's ruminations about religion is not fulfilled. The literary stature of Life of Pi lies instead in its exemplifying the potent attractions of storytelling in the hands of an expert: the reader willingly submits to Martel's creation of a magical paradox, making the incredible credible. A large-format edition of the book,

illustrated by the Croatian artist Tomislav Torjanac, was published in 2007.

In a pointless and oddly self-indulgent exercise, Martel—beginning on 16 April 2007—began sending the prime minister, every two weeks, a book to read, with a letter inserted discussing the book, often with comments on reading and writing. The letters accompanying the fifty-five books—mostly of international origin, with some Canadian titles—are collected in *What is Stephen Harper reading? Yann Martel's recommended reading for a prime minister and book lovers of all stripes* (2009). Martel received advances totalling $3 million for his next novel, *Beatrice & Virgil* (2010), about a donkey and monkey (named in the title), a writer called Henri, the narrator, and a taxidermist.

Martin, Claire (b. 1914), the pseudonym of Claire Montreuil. Born in Quebec City, she was educated by the Ursuline nuns and the Sisters of the Congrégation Notre-Dame. After a career as a radio announcer, first in Quebec City and then with Radio-Canada in Montreal, she married Roland Faucher, a chemist with the ministry of health in Ottawa and, while living there, began to write, producing a distinguished series of books. She was appointed an Officer of the Order of Canada in 1984 and a Companion in 2001.

Martin's first work was a collection of stories, *Avec ou sans amour* (1958), translated by David Lobdell as *Love me, love me not* (1987). From the outset Martin's writing has focused on brief depictions of love, always shown to be fragile, threatened, ephemeral: her gift is for the bold stroke, for precise observation, and for fusing irony with tenderness. Her best work was published during the sixties. *Douxamer* (1960)—translated by David Lobdell as *Best man* (1983)—portrays a writer who lays claim to her right to freedom by putting her career before love, by allowing herself to be unfaithful, and by marrying a man younger than herself—all time-honoured actions and privileges reserved for men. As traditional roles are reversed, abilities and temperaments—rather than gender—govern behaviour: the male protagonist, the writer's lover and editor, plays the role usually played by women, that of the Other—submissive, faithful, devoted. He is the narrator, the one who confides his suffering, openly pouring out his feelings about being a too-frequently obliging victim. The emphasis on individual confrontation and on subjectivism is even more apparent in *Quand j'aura payé ton visage* (1962), translated by David Lobdell as *The legacy*

(1986). About a love triangle involving two brothers and the wife of one of them, it reveals a tangle of family relations that touches on incest and other taboos, giving the author an opportunity to criticize the family and society. The narrative unfolds in the words of Catherine, Robert, and Jeanne Ferny respectively, providing a compressed and varied perspective, and throwing into relief the profound isolation of each person locked into his or her own world. Martin's major work is indisputably her books of memoirs, *Dans un gant de fer* (1965) and *La joue droite* (1966, GGA—for fiction!). Translated by Philip Stratford and first published in one volume, *In an iron glove* (1968), and later separately as *In an iron glove* (1973) and *The right cheek* (1975), they are two powerful and frank re-creations of a painful and oppressive childhood and adolescence in which Martin was exposed to violence and every kind of humiliation. The maleficent and terrifying figure of a despotic father can be seen as embodying the paralysing monolithic structure that for so long tyrannized Québec society and prevented its flowering. The books also expose, with merciless clarity, the situation of women—treated as inferior, incompetent, enslaved—and provide the key to the relentless quest for love that governs all Martin's work. Both in her fiction and her autobiographies Martin relentlessly pursued topics that were traditionally proscribed for Québec literature: extramarital love and the demythologizing of the sacrosanct image of the father as noble and good, the rightful holder of authority and knowledge. She showed a preference for the first-person narrative and for presenting multiple viewpoints, techniques that enabled her to probe the inner depths of human nature, bringing to light its complexity and giving the individual primacy over the group.

From 1972 Martin devoted herself to translating. Among the works she translated are Margaret LAURENCE's *The STONE ANGEL* (*L'ange de pierre*, 1976), Robertson DAVIES' *The manticore* (*Le lion avait un visage d'homme*, 1978), *World of wonders* (*Le monde des merveilles*, 1979), and Clark BLAISE's *Tribal justice* (*Le justice tribale*, 1985).

Marty, Sid (b. 1944). Born in South Shields, England, he was raised in Medicine Hat, Alberta, and educated in Calgary at Mount Royal Junior College. His grandparents were homesteaders of Swiss stock from Minnesota who were lured to Canada by the Canadian Pacific Railway and by useless promises of good farmland in the arid Palliser Triangle of southern Alberta—a background that inspired his best work. Marty received an honours degree in English from Sir George Williams University, Montreal, before deciding to work full-time as a park warden and writer. He was a season ranger in Yoho and Jasper National Parks from 1966 to 1973 and went on to become a park warden in Banff National Park. He now lives in the foothills of southwestern Alberta.

The poems in *Headwaters* (1973) draw upon Marty's Rocky Mountain experiences to remind readers that loneliness, death, and madness are part of the accepted life cycle. A deceptively simple stylist, Marty sees love, death, forest, fires, children—whether in urban or wilderness settings—as occurrences in a natural cycle. He developed these themes in *Nobody danced with Miss Rodeo* (1981), a three-part collection that again captures the sounds and elements of the Rocky Mountains. In the first sequence he contemplates the technological invasion of the wilderness by search and rescue aircraft, chainsaws, power boats, ski-lift operators, and helicopters. The title sequence includes bittersweet or humorous accounts of urban dwellers misplaced in a mountain setting. *Men for the mountains* (1978, rpr. 2000) is a prose documentary about the wardens in Canada's national parks, drawing on Marty's work in Banff. He eloquently describes his aesthetic of the intimate, ancient, and still oessential interdependence between humanity and the natural world, while also discussing isolation, grizzly bears, forest fires, tourists, the negative effects of the Trans-Canada Highway, the hunting season, and certain park-administration policies. *A grand and fabulous notion: the first century of Canada's parks* (1984), with a preface by Earle BIRNEY, is a large-format book with many illustrations that is a centenary (1885–1985) celebration of National Parks. *Leaning on the wind: under the spell of the Great Chinook* (1995, rpr. 2000), describing Marty's passion for southern Alberta, is a chronicle of its history and a plea for its future. The gripping, interconnected stories in *Switchbacks: true tales from the Canadian Rockies* (1999) were inspired by his life in the mountains. Marty outdid himself with the *The black grizzly of Whiskey Creek* (2008), a compelling narrative describing the hunt for, and eventual capture and shooting of a killer bear in Banff National Park in 1980. Marty says in an Author's Note: 'I have tried to tell part of the story from a bear's point of view', basing his interpretation on his knowledge of bears.

Master's wife, The. See Sir William MACPHAIL.

Matrix (1975–). This magazine of critical and creative writing was first published by the Champlain College Department of English in Lennoxville, Québec. Under editor Philip Lanthier, it was a biannual publication of poetry, short fiction, essays, and reviews. In 1988 co-editors Linda Leith and Kenneth RADU moved the magazine from Lennoxville to John Abbot College, Sainte-Anne-de-Bellevue. Matrix was enlarged, broadened, and modernized as a three-times-a-year glossy publication focusing on a revival of writing by English and non-francophone writers in Québec, for a community that felt cut off as a result of the 1980 referendum and the language laws. In 1995 the magazine relocated to Concordia University, Montreal, under editor-in-chief R.E.N. Allen. Its present editor is Jon Paul Fiorentino.

Mayne, Seymour (b. 1944). Born in Montreal, he was educated at McGill University (B.A., 1965) and the University of British Columbia (M.A., 1966; Ph.D., 1972). He taught briefly at UBC before joining the faculty of the University of Ottawa (1973), where he has been Professor of English since 1985. In his earliest collections of poetry— *That monocycle the moon* (1964), *Tiptoeing on the mount* (1965), *From the portals of mouseholes* (1966), and *I am still the boy* (1967)—Mayne is a frequently lighthearted explorer of human passion and sensuality. Discipline and intelligence stand behind his carefully controlled poems. *Manimals* (1969) is a comic diversion in poetry and prose. In later volumes—*Mouth* (1970), *For stems of light* (1971), *Face* (1971), and especially *Name* (1975)—the celebratory exploration in the earlier collections gives way to a more personal and painful probing. His poetry reveals a new consciousness of his Jewishness and a concern with social issues that always focuses on the human dimension. The sexuality of the early romantic poetry is replaced by pain and melancholy about the transience and mortality of the human condition. *Diasporas* (1977) and *The impossible promised land: poems new and selected* (1981) herald the secure voice of a mature poet, conscious of his heritage and his calling. Here Mayne is the literary descendant of A.M. KLEIN, the friend of Irving LAYTON and Leonard COHEN—the youngest poet of this quartet from the Montreal Jewish community. Though a bleak and pessimistic vision of life now permeates his poetry, Mayne finds hope in his commitment to Jewish traditions and in an awareness and acceptance of the cycle of time. As impassioned and indignant about the Holocaust as Layton, he never indulges in the 'gorgeous rant and offensive irony' that characterize much of Layton's later verse. The disciplined control of Mayne's poetry is reminiscent of Klein's later verse, though the increase in Jewish allusions and terminology in Mayne's recent volumes recalls Klein's early work. Visiting and revisiting biblical sources and stories in such collections as *Neighbour praying* (1984), *Crazy Leonithas* (1985), *Children of Abel* (1986), and *Killing time* (1992), Mayne wrote poems that increasingly dealt with the paradoxes that have long troubled people of deep faith: the coexistence of a benevolent God and the legacy of violence informing almost all world religions; ideas of innocence and evil; and, of course, the tensions between common language and the Word. Mayne's more recent books of poems are *The song of Moses and other poems* (1995), illustrated by Sharon Katz; the chapbook *Dragon trees* (1997); and *City of the hidden* (1998).

Melfi, Mary (b. 1951). Born near Rome, Italy, she immigrated to Montreal with her family at the age of six. She obtained a B.A. in English from Concordia University and a Master of Library Sciences from McGill University. Her writings are characterized by an avant-garde sensibility that transgresses the conventions of a given literary form (whether it is poetry, drama, or fiction). In each of her works poetry verges on prose, fiction is penetrated by poetic and dramatic devices, and a play has poetic and narrative elements— though the distinctiveness of the given form is not erased. Ideas about identity and culture that flow out of English-Canadian and Italian-Canadian / Québécois experiences interpenetrate each other. Melfi is interested in the metaphysical side of human existence, the difficulties of establishing a coherent feminine identity, cultural dislocation, and the artist's attempt to create a new reality. She has published six books of poetry. These include *A bride in three acts* (1983), a sardonically humorous long poem that looks at the private realm of heterosexual relations, relying on parody, the use of prose, and the intermixing of voices, and surreal imagery that veers towards the grotesque and the violent. Not only a tirade against the oppressiveness of patriarchy, it is a metaphysical view of the impossibility of fulfilling one's desire and the delusions that arise as a result. The *O Canada poems* (1986) and *A season in Beware* (1989) preceded the publication of *Stages: selected poems* (1998). *Infertility* *rites* (1991), a novel about a woman's obsession with having a child, replays in different ways the formal and thematic preoccupations of *A bride*. Driven to motherhood by her need to construct a world where she feels at home, the central character accepts ideas of traditional womanhood that come out of her ethnic background and are reinforced by patriarchal mainstream society. The juxtaposition of styles and the self-consciousness of the writing mirror the unreality of the protagonist's life and her obsessive self-awareness. This sensibility recurs in *Sex therapy: a black comedy* (1996), a play that verges on absurdist drama in which the roles of therapist and patient are continually subverted and inverted.

Memoirs of Montparnasse (1970; 2nd edn 1995; rpr. 2007). This famous work by John GLASSCO, which was published as an autobiography but was later discovered to be fiction, is based on the young Glassco's stay in Paris from 1927 to 1929, when he contracted tuberculosis. He says in a prefatory note that he wrote all but the first three chapters while in a Montreal hospital in 1932–3 before a critical operation. Patricia Whitney, in doing research for a literary biography of Glassco, discovered in the National Archives the text of all but the first chapter (which had been published in *This Quarter* in 1929) handwritten with a ballpoint pen in six scribblers dated 1964. The book that resulted is a remarkably vivid account of what it was like to be young in the Paris of the late 1920s. Glassco profited by the opportunity to meet, and had the sharp eye and clear memory to characterize, such writers as George Moore (whose *Confessions of a young man* [1888], he said, was a model for the *Memoirs*), James Joyce, Ford Madox Ford, Robert McAlmon, Gertrude Stein, and a score of others. All is recorded with a freshness of prose that gives the book a sense of contemporaneity with its succession of scenes and their inhabitants; in addition, the controlled ordering of happenings, and the vitality of the dialogue, lend the flavour of fiction to the narrative. Indeed, in the introduction to the second edition of the *Memoirs* (1995), edited by Michael Gnarowski, we read that Glassco himself thought of it, privately, as fiction. In a letter of 1968 to the American writer Kay Boyle, whom he knew in Paris in 1928 (she appears as Diana Tree in the *Memoirs*), he wrote: 'It's really fiction. I was trying to re-create the atmosphere and spirit of Paris in those days as it was for me. The way George Moore and Casanova did for the worlds of their youth'—who, he wrote in

another letter the next year, did not feel 'tied to historical truth; they were … liars and produced works of art by invention. Who cares about their lies now?' The second edition throws a new light on the *Memoirs*, with its Critical Introduction by Gnarowski, notes on the text, and brief accounts of people and places. In the recent reprint by New York Review Books, much of this additional material has been included.

Mercer plays. The importance and influence of David FRENCH's Mercer plays as a body of connected works has few rivals in Canadian drama. The first play, *Leaving home* (1972, rpr. 2001), is credited with consolidating the reputation of the Tarragon Theatre, Toronto—where it opened on 16 May 1972—in raising the credibility of Canadian drama, and encouraging the development of a Canadian neo-realistic 'school'. As a whole, the Mercer plays document a Canadian social phenomenon, the culture shock experienced by people moving within Canada from one region (Newfoundland) to another. Set in a Toronto working-class household in the late 1950s, *Leaving home* pits Jacob Mercer, the patriarch carpenter, against his eldest son, Ben, while the long-suffering mother, Mary, tries to keep the peace. The Mercers had moved to Ontario from Newfoundland when their sons were small, and the father/son conflict is both extended and localized by the clash between the values of outport Newfoundland and those of Toronto. The boys have grown up as urban North Americans and resent Jacob's old outport standards, especially those that define a 'man'. Most of the characters 'leave home' in the course of the play. Billy and Ben leave physically: Billy to marry a girl made pregnant by him, Ben to escape his father's tyranny. Jacob leaves home spiritually in abandoning the values of the fishing village he had left many years before—with his sons gone, there was no one to whom he could pass them on. Father/son conflict is paralleled and reinforced by mother/daughter tension between Kathy, Billy's fiancée, and her mother Minnie, a flamboyant former flame of Jacob's. Much of the play's comedy is provided by Minnie and her silent undertaker boyfriend, Harold, while contrast between the old and the new is given vivid aural presence through the sharp contrast between the Newfoundland accents of the older generation and the Torontonian speech of the younger. *Of the fields, lately* (1973, rpr. 1991) opened at Tarragon on 29 Sept. 1973. Two years after the events depicted in *Leaving home*, Ben returns from Regina, Saskatchewan, to attend an aunt's funeral.

Father and son are as far apart as ever, but in the course of the play Ben discovers that Jacob has suffered a heart attack and decides he will find work in Toronto so that his father will not have to return to his potentially dangerous job. However, coming to understand that his father's work is necessary to Jacob's sense of self, Ben changes his mind and once again leaves home. The play is a 'memory play', framed by direct address to the audience and placing some events in the past. Its core is to be found in three scenes between father and son, marvellously detailed but oblique—among the most effective uses of subtext to be found in Canadian dramatic literature. *Salt-water moon* (1985, rpr. 1988), which opened at Tarragon on 2 Oct. 1984, is a long one-act two-hander, a 'prequel' set in Coley's Point, Newfoundland, in 1926. Jacob has returned from a year in Toronto to discover that his former sweetheart, Mary, is engaged to Jerome McKenzie, a school teacher Jacob despises. Jacob finds Mary in the yard of the house where she works as a domestic, looking at the stars through a telescope; in the course of the evening he woos her back. While the essence of the play is this lyrical courtship, we get an insight into social conditions of place and time and see the reality behind Jacob's 'mythic' Newfoundland. A fourth Mercer play, *1949* (1989), premiered at Toronto's St Lawrence Centre on 20 Oct. 1988. With a cast of twelve, it is set on the eve of Newfoundland's entering Confederation, and incorporates a number of the characters seen or mentioned in the previous Mercer plays.

Mercy among the children (2000, rpr. 2001) is a novel by David Adams RICHARDS about the Hendersons, all victims, living in dire poverty near the Miramichi River in New Brunswick from the 1960s to the 1980s. Roy, the grandfather, went to prison for a crime he did not commit. His son, twelve-year-old Sydney, shovelling snow off the slanting church roof, gave a push to a nasty chum, who fell fifty feet and lay motionless below; Sydney vowed that if the boy was not dead 'he would never raise his hand or his voice to another soul'. The boy, Connie Devlin, got up laughing—and plagued Sydney for the rest of his life. Sydney acquired a wheelbarrow of books for twenty dollars, taught himself to read, became influenced by some great authors, including the Stoic philosopher Marcus Aurelius, and remained faithful to his vow. He also became a hated outcast. The bitter story of the Henderson family, stuck at the bottom rung of society (and enduring a predominance of winters and snowstorms), is narrated by

Sydney's son Lyle, who greatly resented his father's willed defencelessness in the face of untold wrongs inflicted on him by people, the church, and government: 'all the misery forced upon us was caused because he elected to be passive.' But Lyle also admired him, saw greatness in him: 'I envied him. He had made his life in spite of poverty, scorn, and intolerance.' Nevertheless, his father's example did not prevent Lyle from indulging in anger and seeking revenge, or submitting to a downward spiral in his own life. Other characters include Lyle's long-suffering mother Elly, who adored his father; his sister Autumn, an albino, who became a writer; his pure and loving little brother Percy; and, contributing to the Hendersons' chronic despair, the vicious Matthew Pit, his sister Cynthia, and the rich and devious landowner Leo McVicer, who dominated and exploited everyone in the community. The book presents a gallery of failures, and while Sydney's steadfast, though masochistic, virtue eventually becomes an example to others, it can also be seen as destructive. But the intensity and sincerity of Richards' depiction of his characters, both saintly and misbegotten, and the events that affected them, his unremitting exploration of a claustrophobic world of ill will besetting goodness and innocence, and the wry, ironic resolutions that conclude it invite strong reader involvement—and admiration. For this novel Richards was co-winner (with Michael ONDAATJE) of the GILLER PRIZE.

Merril, Judith (1923–97). Born in New York City, she acquired an international following among science-fiction enthusiasts for her stories, novels, reviews, and anthologies before she settled in Toronto in 1968, becoming a Canadian citizen in 1976. Her personal library of more than 5000 SF books and periodicals formed the basis of the Spaced Out Library, established at Rochdale College in 1969; the following year it became part of the Toronto Public Library system. Now the world's largest public collection of such literature, it is known as the Merril Collection of Science Fiction, Speculation, and Fantasy. From the first, Merril's fiction combined 'a sense of wonder' with 'a sense of gender'. Her influential anthologies cut across literary genres and championed the works of new and experimental writers. After coming to Canada she published *Survival ship and other stories* (1973), *The best of Judith Merril* (1976), and *Daughters of earth and other stories* (1985), and compiled the anthology *Tesseracts 1* (1988) devoted to new Canadian SF. A social activist, Merril drew public attention to the SF field, to the work of new writers, to the need for professional standards, and to a proper appreciation of the genre. *Better to have loved: the life of Judith Merril* (2002) is by Judith Merril and Emily Pohl-Weary.

Metcalf, John (b. 1938). Born in Carlisle, England, he came to Canada in 1962, having received an Honours B.A. (1960) and a certificate in education (1961) from the University of Bristol. He taught at high schools in Montreal and Cold Lake, Alberta, before accepting in 1969 a position at Loyola College, Montreal. Since 1971 he has devoted his time to writing, supplementing his income with part-time teaching, editing, and as writer-in-residence at a number of Canadian universities—and being very productive as a writer of short stories, novels, and essays, and as an editor of anthologies. Metcalf's first short-story collection, *The lady who sold furniture* (1970), contains—besides the title story, a novella—five stories set in England. Employing a fairly traditional technique and vivid observations, Metcalf injects a note of uneasiness into these stories, which sometimes explodes in a macabre or gruesome scene. *The teeth of my father* (1975) is a more uneven collection, though the control of tone and mood remains, and there are touches of humour. In the moving 'Beryl', two characters come together, but ultimately are unable to relieve each other's loneliness—a popular Metcalf theme. *Adult entertainment* (1986) shows a master stylist confidently at work in his favoured form. Its three short stories and two novellas are characterized by an episodic structure that achieves its effect through juxtaposition of images and scenes rather than narrative exposition; by dialogue that is nuanced and suggestive of unarticulated thought and feeling; by a cherishing of the particular and a concomitant fondness for lists; by a careful control of mood and pacing; by a comedic sense that is here more poignantly ironic than sharply satiric; and by a sensitivity to the artifice involved in any attempt at the real. Sometimes this artifice is brought to the fore, as in 'The Eastmill reception centre', where the narrator interrupts his story in order to comment on the inadequacy of its ending, proposes several alternative effects, dismisses the last and best of these on the grounds that he 'can't be bothered', then brings off a version of the ending he has just dismissed. Such metafictive effects are not unique in Metcalf's writings and demonstrate that he is by no means bound by the

modernist tradition he extols. In 1982 Metcalf published *Selected stories*, as well as his first book of essays, *Kicking against the pricks*. Three earlier novellas were republished under the title *Shooting the stars* (1993), with an introduction by Michael Darling that is a guide to the 'deflationary structures' that characterize Metcalf's work. *Standing stones: the best stories of John Metcalf* (2004), a long collection of eight stories, has an introduction by Clark BLAISE.

In Metcalf's first novel, *Going down slow* (1972), set in Montreal, he ridicules both the self-important staff of a high school and a society that would reward efficiency at the expense of intelligence and humanity. David Appleby is a recent English immigrant who battles the system in a series of fast-moving skirmishes, in contrast to his mistress Susan, who stays outside it, and his roommate Jim, who rises through the educational establishment. *Girl in gingham* (1978)—reprinted as *Private parts: a memoir* (1980)—contains two novellas with these titles. 'Girl in gingham' features a setting and dialogue that are nearly flawless, in addition to excellent satire. Peter Thornton, an appraiser of antiques who is slowly rebuilding his life after a traumatic divorce, is paired (after several computer-date mismatches) with his ideal woman, Anna, a rare-books librarian with a similar regard for the past. The title 'Private parts' alludes both to sex, which is treated lightly and entertainingly, and to the narrator's preservation of his inner self in a life-denying, puritanical milieu. About the coming-of-age of a precocious youth, it concludes with a sad irony: adulthood brings not liberation but disillusionment and boredom. The novel *General Ludd* (1980) combines vehement wit, understated humour, a black comedic vision, and occasional absurdity. Its hero, James Wells, poet-in-residence at St Xavier University—which, like society at large, has little appreciation for true poetry—becomes a modern-day Luddite and attempts to forestall the future by destroying the highly sophisticated Communication Arts Centre, the false idol of campus technocrats. The novel has passion and emotional range and offers a brilliant satire of a fast-food society oblivious to traditional values, art, and culture. Metcalf must have enjoyed writing the novella *Forde abroad* (2003), narrated by Robert Forde, a novelist, who is invited by the Literary and Cultural Association of Slovenia to attend a conference at a lake resort in the Alps called Splad. His wife Sheila is furious because she assumes he will meet Karla there, a young woman in the German Democratic

Republic who writes to him, professing admiration for his novels. Sheila calls her 'your Commie pen pal'. Forde expects to be given in Splad the translation of his third novel *Winter Creatures*. He flies to Europe and we are treated to an amusing account: his attempts to adjust to a foreign location where everything is strange, including his contacts with others—Karla does turn up, but their times together are harmless—and the modernist theorizing of the academics in their lectures (including two on L.M. Montgomery and Mazo de la Roche), which provoke the expletive 'Christ!'. Leaving, on the way to the airport, Forde's taxi driver stops so that he can watch two huge cranes perform an ungainly, comical mating ritual. 'The cranes trumpeted at the sky, first one then the fierce reply, reverberating blasts of noise bouncing off the stonework of the bridge filling the air with the clamour of jubilation. // Forde felt … // Forde exulted with them.'

Since 1983 Metcalf has laboured mightily as editor, anthologist, and cultural critic, publishing and promoting the work of other Canadians, particularly in the short-story form. He has produced nearly thirty anthologies over the course of his career and 'readied' many books for press for The PORCUPINE'S QUILL. His anthologies often include critical or authorial comment on the formal aspects of the writing, a practice extended in *How stories mean* (1993), a gathering of reflections by writers on questions of technique. Metcalf's effort to create a receptive climate for this work has led him into what he calls a guerilla campaign against academic critics who evaluate books from an extra-literary perspective. Metcalf edited with Claire Wilkinson *Writers talking* (2003), which includes interviews with and stories by eight writers (including Michael WINTER, Steven HEIGHTON, and Lisa MOORE) the editors thought were little known and deserved more attention. In *Freedom from culture* (1987), *What is a Canadian literature?* (1988), and *Volleys* (1990)—an exchange with academicians Sam Solecki and W.J. KEITH— he attacked the twin shibboleths of literary nationalism and government patronage of the arts. To further encourage spirited and accessible literary debate, Metcalf compiled two books of 'contentious essays and squibs': *The bumper book* (1986) and *Carry on bumping* (1988). His iconoclastic (penetrating, and sometimes cruel) evaluations of leading Canadian writers—and his anger over the neglect of what he considers to be true Canadian masterworks, and the submission of Canadian readers to the 'prizes and puffery' accorded to many well-known writers whose distinction he refuses to recognize—appeared under the title 'False Idols' in *Quill & Quire*, July 2000.

Metcalf has written two extensive autobiographies that are not only illuminating commentaries on the Canadian literary scene from the (more or less) 1960s to the present, but an informal, rambling account of his life; and they reveal the enormous range of his reading. *An aesthetic underground: a literary memoir* (2003), which begins (briefly) with his childhood and education, moves quickly to his arrival in Canada and his eventual contact—as mentor or publisher or friend—with a galaxy of Canadian writers. There are also descriptions of the numerous books he wrote or edited (sometimes with quotations), many sharp critiques (e.g., of the OBERON PRESS, *The ENGLISH PATIENT*), and accounts of the Porcupine's Quill and CANADIAN NOTES AND QUERIES, with which he became closely associated. There is more of the same in *Shut up he explained: a literary memoir: Vol. II* (2007)— 100 pages longer—which departs from the first volume in being greatly enlarged by a final 142-page chapter called 'The Century List', or the best forty Canadian short-story collections published in the twentieth century. It begins with Metcalf's longish discourse on the short story, which is followed by his list and then a few pages of appreciation for each author. Both books are illustrated with many photographs. The title *Shut up he explained* (clarified at the end of his first chapter called 'Titles') is drawn from Ring Lardner's parody of *The young visiters* (1919, rpr. 1949 and many times later) by Daisy Ashford (written when she was nine) in his story 'The young immigrants' (1920), in which Ring says to his four-year-old son Bill, 'Shut up he explained.' Metcalf was made a Member of the Order of Canada in 2004.

Michaels, Anne (b. 1958). Born in Toronto of Jewish parents, her father a Russian immigrant, she was educated in the city's schools and at the University of Toronto (B.A., 1980). Since 1988 she has taught a course in creative writing there. Michaels has published two important collections of poems, *The weight of oranges* (1986) and *Miner's pond* (1991)—appearing in one volume in 1997. Most of her lyrics—several of them complex, multi-layered sequences—can be categorized as love poems, elegies, or dramatic monologues, often about artists and historical figures. The love poems tend to be shorter, more purely lyrical, and to focus on what Michaels calls 'the passionate world' in which a relationship moves 'past the last familiar outpost', almost beyond space and time into a privacy available only to the lovers. In the longer poems, love and ecstasy are often celebrated as something lost, and her characteristic tone—despite the powerful verbal music and sensuous, natural, often visceral imagery—is a plangent one. Several of the most memorable poems—'Lake of two rivers', 'Words for the body', 'Miner's pond', 'Modersohn-Becker', and 'What the light teaches'—are retrospective meditations on something that has already happened and that is irretrievably lost, even though the words attempt to restore it. The longer poems show a tense interplay between a lyric intensity and an understated narrative drive. Their form, as well as some of the imagery—especially the concern with light—reflect Michaels' interest in music and painting. Though most of Michaels' poems are written in the first person, they are almost never directly autobiographical or confessional. In the more personal poems the 'I' maintains a taut balance between the subjective self and a more objective persona. In the historical dramatic monologues the speakers include Isak Dinesen, the German painter Paula Modersohn-Becker, the Russian poet Marina Tsvetaeva, and Marie Curie. The language of these poems—though characterized by a deceptively simple diction and syntax, and verse forms built on enjambment—communicates alternately with disarmingly simple sentences: 'No matter where you are/or who you're near,/we come up for air together'; and stanzas taut and highly metaphoric: 'There are nights in the forest of words/ when I panic, every step into thicker darkness,/ the only way out to write myself into a clearing,/which is silence.' Without being overtly about history, Michaels' poems are often suffused by a historical sense, an awareness of the ineluctable presence of the past in our lives. This is accompanied, however, by a concomitant awareness of how difficult it is to give adequate expression to the past, whether private or public, in words. In Michaels' small collection of mostly difficult poems, *Skin divers* (1999), the past is present in 'There is no city that does not dream'. It prevails in 'The second search', about Marie Curie's dealing with her husband's death ('The longer we lived together, the more / I loved you'); in 'Ice house', based on the journal of the widow, a sculptor, of the Antarctic explorer Robert Falcon Scott, who perished after reaching the South Pole in 1912 ('I took your face in my hands and your fine/ arms and long legs, your small waist,/and loved you into stone'); and in 'The hooded hawk', dedicated to A.W. (Adele WISEMAN), whose mother made dolls whose 'refugee' parts

represented history: 'History is the love that enters us/through death; its discipline/is grief.'

The concern with time, memory, and history is also evident in *Fugitive pieces* (1996, rpr. 2006), Michaels' remarkably strong first novel. It is made up of two closely related first-person narratives, the first by Jakob Beer, who is rescued by an archaeologist from the Nazi genocide of the Polish Jews, the second by Ben, a young Canadian professor, whose parents survived the death camps. Each narrative reveals an individual trying to understand a tragic, almost incomprehensible past in order to free himself to live in the present. Though the novel focuses on a handful of characters, it leaves one with the impression of a work that is much more inclusive and larger in scope—partly due to the shifts in setting from wartime Poland and postwar Greece to Toronto and back again to Greece; to Michaels' ability to sketch suggestively the lives of related minor characters; and to the fact that she situates the events not only against the background of the war—often registered in telling casual details—but also within the context of discussions of theology, geology, and art. *Fugitive pieces* has been translated into all the major European languages. In 1997 it won the Chapters/*Books in Canada* First Novel Award, the (Ontario) Trillium Award, the British Orange Prize for Fiction, given to women writers, and the Lannan Foundation Award for Fiction, USA. (Jeremy Podeswa's film *Fugitive Pieces* was released commercially in 2008.) *The winter vault* (2009, rpr. 2010) similarly offers layers of the present and the past (e.g., the dismantling of Abu Simbel for the Aswan Dam and the depredations preceding the St Lawrence Seaway) in a hermetic text beautifully written by a poet.

Micone, Marco (b. 1945). Born in Montelongo, Italy, he immigrated to Montreal with his family in 1958. His education includes an M.A. (1969) from McGill University with a thesis on the theatre of Marcel DUBÉ. While teaching Italian at Montreal's Vanier College, his first play, *Gens du silence*, was staged there in 1980 by Le Théâtre de l'Ouverture and published in 1982. The English translation by Maurizia Binda, *Voiceless people* (1984), about first-generation Italian immigrants, was premiered in Vancouver during Expo '86. The first French-language playwright to examine the immigrant experience in Québec, Micone achieved critical and popular success with repeated productions of *Gens du silence*, the more feminist *Addolorata* (1987)—translated by Binda with the same title (1994)—and *Déjà l'agonie* (1988), translated by Jill

MacDougall as *Beyond the ruins* (1995). All Micone's plays engage the polemics of Québec politics and the problematic place of immigrants in a nationalist country; they also recall the realism of Marcel Dubé's early works. *Addolorata*, which premiered in 1983 with the troupe La Manufacture at La Licorne theatre, Montreal, deals with a young woman who feels three-times marginalized: as an immigrant in Québec, as an Italian in Canada, and as a woman in a male-dominated society. *Voiceless people* and *Addolorata* were published in one volume in 1997 (rpr. 2005).

Millar, Margaret (1915–94). Born Margaret Sturm in Kitchener, Ontario, she studied at the Kitchener Collegiate Institute, and then at the University of Western Ontario. While still a student in Kitchener, she met Kenneth Millar (1915–83), an American-born fellow student. They were married in 1938 and the following year the couple taught English and History at KCI and then moved permanently to Santa Barbara, California, where they pursued parallel careers as writers of mystery fiction. (Kenneth Millar, who wrote as Ross Macdonald, created the private detective Lew Archer, who was renamed Harper for the film of that name starring Paul Newman.) Margaret Millar claimed she was a mystery fan years before she met her husband, avidly reading the detective magazines purchased by her two older brothers. She worked briefly as a screenwriter for Warner Brothers, but preferred to concentrate on her own mystery novels, which are prized for their psychological penetration of the hearts and minds of murderers. Her first novel was *The invisible worm* (1941), but she came to prominence with *Beast in view* (1955). Among her later novels are *Banshee* (1983) and *Spider webs* (1986). Margaret and Kenneth Millar were honoured independently by the Mystery Writers of America as Grand Masters.

Mills, John (b. 1930). Born in London, England, he came to Canada in 1953. While travelling widely in Canada and Europe, he held a striking variety of manual and technical positions. After he earned a B.A. from the University of British Columbia (1964) and an M.A. from Stanford University (1965), he began his career as a teacher of English at Simon Fraser University, Burnaby, British Columbia, where he is now Professor Emeritus. Mills is a sophisticated satirist of considerable forcefulness, and his novels are also assured parodies of literary conventions. *The land of is* (1972) is a blackly comic subversion of *The tempest*, transposed to contemporary

Vancouver; *The October men* (1973), set during the 1970 FLQ crisis, features a small-time confidence man whose associates, schemes, and fantasies imitate the stereotypes of pulp fiction. *Skevington's daughter* (1978), an inventive epistolary novel, is a caustic academic caricature, riddled with violence in action and rhetoric, which incidentally echoes late-Romantic travel writing. *Runner in the dark* (1992), with its subtext of literary allusion, is a somewhat archetypal thriller with a psychologically confounded hero, involuntary derring-do, and a spiritual climax set in a bleak New Mexican landscape. *Lizard in the grass* (1980) is a collection of Mills' amusing and unsentimental autobiographical pieces and some characteristically mordant and informed literary reviews. His interesting and poised autobiographical essays, several prompted by his Christian conversion, appeared in *Thank your mother for the rabbits* (1993). Both Mills' fiction and criticism often display a tone of articulate mockery that suggests uncompromising standards and complete individuality.

Miron, Gaston (1928–96). Born in Sainte-Agathe-des-Monts, Québec, he attended the Collège des Frères du Sacré-Coeur until 1946; the following year he went to Montreal, where he worked at various jobs. In 1953 he was one of the founders of Les Éditions de l'Hexagone, a publishing house devoted to the printing and distribution of poetry that influenced Québec's literary life for the next three decades. L'Hexagone was to become a convenient term not only for this business venture but also for the generation of poets it published. Miron's selflessness, and perhaps his ambivalence about his own writing, were illustrated by his concentration on political action. In the late 1950s he ran twice as an NDP candidate, but from 1962 devoted his energy to separatist movements. In Oct. 1970 he was jailed for ten days on account of his political opinions. Miron invested a considerable amount of energy in the everyday running of L'Hexagone, of which he was still the editor in the early 1980s; as a result, his own poetic output suffered. It was only in 1970, thanks to the initiative of the Presses de l'Université de Montréal, that *L'homme rapaillé* appeared, to great critical and public acclaim. In 1980 a long-awaited translation by Marc Plourde of one of its sections—with other poems not included in that volume—was published under the title *The agonized life*; it includes one of the three political essays in the original edition that detail his position on the disruption of the French language under the inevitable pressures of English, translated as 'A long road' ('Un long chemin'). The awards Miron received for *L'homme rapaillé* included the Prix Guillaume Apollinaire (1981), which traditionally goes to one of the great poets in the French language. Two images recur in Miron's work: one is of a woman—usually estranged, distant, and lost to the narrator; the other is of the land of Québec and its collective destiny. Both evoke unhappy ties, alienating and schizophrenic emotions; but they are also linked to a reconstruction process, a reconciliation of all forces. Humans are *rapaillé*: their life-giving faculties are collected, just as old bits of straw are picked up from the autumn fields of rural Québec. Though Miron's texts contend against the injustices of history and the plight of the Québec people, they include a message of invincible hope. The fact that his own writing destiny was inextricably linked to a specific historical situation made him one of the most visible and listened-to spokesmen for Québec's independence. But he also attracted more international attention, perhaps, than any Québécois poet. His poetry has been linked to that of Pablo Neruda and Aimé Césaire, who also expressed ideals of nationalism and social justice. A leader in Québec's cultural and political scene, Miron emphasized the role of the poet in expressing the reality of the 'nation' of Québec. See the bilingual edition, *L'homme rapaillé/Embers and earth: selected poems* (1984), translations by D.G. JONES and Marc Plourde, and the bilingual *Counterpanes* (1993), Dennis Egan's translation of Miron's *Courtepointes* (1975). Miron was awarded the Molson Prize in 1985.

Mistry, Rohinton (b. 1952). Born in Bombay, he completed his bachelor's degree at St Xavier's College, University of Bombay. He immigrated to Canada in 1975, worked for a time as a bank clerk, and also earned a B.A. (1982) from the University of Toronto. He lives in Brampton, Ontario, and is a full-time writer. Mistry's gift for writing fiction became evident when, as an undergraduate, he won the short-story contest conducted by Hart House at the University of Toronto in both 1983 and 1984. Since then he has published a collection of short stories, *Tales from Firozsha Baag* (1987, rpr. 2000, NCL)—about the occupants of the Bombay apartment building named in the title—and two novels. *Such a long journey* (1991, GGA, NCL), set in Bombay in 1971, is a beautifully written, richly textured narrative centred on the staunch Gustad

Noble, his family and friends, and relates the disappointments, reversals, betrayals, and deceit they cause or suffer—against the background of a corrupt government and political unrest. *A fine balance* (1995, rpr. 1997, NCL), which won the GILLER PRIZE, is set in India in the 1970s, but occasionally moves back in time to 1947. It is mainly about four people who share an apartment: a widow who is a seamstress, a student, and a man and his nephew who are tailors. Very few writers—Bapsi Sidhwa (b. 1938) is a notable exception—have so consistently and so rigorously dealt with the Parsi community as Mistry has. A Parsi himself, Mistry has focused on the aspirations, heroism, weaknesses, and marginality of the Parsi community with sympathy, humour, and love. Very much a realist, his strength lies in his capacity to create a strikingly referential surface and to draw his readers into the complex world he creates. In both his novels the political—particularly the period dominated by Indira Gandhi—and the personal intersect, and if at times the connection seems forced, it certainly leads to a completeness without which his characters would seem less engrossing. *A fine balance* also marks a growing point in that it reveals a desire to move beyond the Parsi community to extend the scope of his fiction. Mistry's work lacks the metafictional quality of Salman Rushdie or the artifice of Amitav Ghosh, yet it is no less important in the way it chooses to reflect, in the lives of a small community in India, the concerns that confront diasporic communities. Reading about the lives of the characters he so painstakingly creates is to recognize what it means to live on the cusp and to assert one's identity in the face of opposition that threatens to engulf it. Bombay—conveyed as a corrupt city filled with dangers—is also the setting for *Family matters* (2002), but the focus is on the family of Nariman Vakeel, a seventy-nine-year-old former professor and a widower suffering from Parkinson's disease. (A sad event in Nariman's past is revealed when we read about his love for Lucy, a Catholic, whom he was prevented from marrying because she was not a Parsi. Lucy, however, remains loyal to him by acting as a servant for a family in the Chateau Felicity where he lived with his wife and daughter.)

At the beginning of the novel he lives with Coomy and Jal, his stepdaughter and stepson, in the seven-room apartment in the Chateau Felicity he handed over to them; his daughter Roxana and her husband Yezad and their sons Murad and Jehangoo live in a two-room apartment (her dowry) called Pleasant Villa.

The long, engaging narrative—filled with natural-sounding dialogue—conveys the family's vicissitudes, beginning when Nariman goes out for a stroll and breaks his ankle. The bossy, selfish Coomy despairs of looking after him and foists him onto Roxana, who lives with her family in a small apartment. Yezad loses his job at the sporting-goods store when its friendly owner, Mr Kapur, dies (his widow lets him go cruelly), and there are two sudden accidental deaths. Yezad transforms himself as a religious zealot. The book ends with an Epilogue, by Jal.... and Murad's eighteenth birthday party is celebrated. He loved his grandfather, Nariman, and is still saddened by his death. 'I wonder what lies ahead for our family in this house, my grandfather's house, in this world that is more confusing than ever. I think of Daddy [Yezad], who makes me feel that my real father is gone, replaced by this non-stop-praying stranger.' He should well wonder, because the future does not bode well for him with such a father. But in the last few words his mother asks: 'Aren't you happy?' / 'Yes,' I say. 'Yes, I'm happy.' Filled with an easy unfolding of serious family matters, the novel leaves the reader with the feeling that family *matters*.

Mitchell, John (1880–1951). Born on the farm purchased by his grandfather in the Caledon Hills near Mono, Ontario, he moved in 1894 with his mother to Toronto, where he attended Harbord Collegiate; Victoria College, University of Toronto; and Osgoode Hall Law School. He practised law in Toronto for twenty-eight years, for the most part independently. Reticent, reclusive, and careless about the management of his personal affairs, Mitchell destroyed his professional standing in 1935 by confessing publicly to the misappropriation of trust funds. He was convicted, imprisoned for six months, and disbarred. Upon his release, he lived the rest of his life in obscurity. Under the pseudonym 'Patrick Slater' he wrote *The yellow briar; a story of the Irish in the Canadian countryside* (1933; rpr. 1970, with an account of his life by Dorothy Bishop), a fictional autobiography narrated by the Irish orphan 'Paddy Slater'. The book was initially accepted as genuine autobiography because it contained much authentic detail drawn from the experiences of Mitchell's grandparents. An engaging story of pioneering and early settlement in the Caledon region of southern Ontario and of life in Toronto, mainly in the 1840s, it captures and celebrates the seasonal and generational cycles with originality, tolerance, and garrulous good nature. It was an immediate success. Mitchell also wrote *Robert Harding* (1938), an unsuccessful novel about a man wrongly imprisoned for murder; *The water-drinker* (1938), a collection of sentimental verse; and a work of local history, *The settlement of York County* (posthumously published in 1952).

Mitchell, Ken (b. 1940). Born in Moose Jaw, Saskatchewan, he attended the University of Saskatchewan (B.A., 1965; M.A., 1967), and while still a student began publishing short fiction and writing radio plays for the regional and international networks of the Canadian Broadcasting Corporation. In 1967 he joined the English department of the University of Regina, teaching creative writing and Canadian literature, where be became a professor (1984–2005). In 1980–1 he was visiting professor of English, University of Nanjing, and has returned to China many times since. He is a Member of the Order of Canada (1999).

A populist writer, Mitchell is also an almost paradigmatic example of the regionalist artist; although his works are universal in appeal, it is difficult to conceive of them outside their prairie context, which is sometimes palpably physical and at other times little more than a mood or an attitude (as in his more recent works set outside the region, and even outside the country). In terms of characterization, this attitude appears in Mitchell's choice of protagonists—people who are, as he says, 'eccentric in the sense that they automatically resist being part of a consensus or any kind of conforming society.' Mitchell's love for, and enjoyment of, such people can be felt in his first novel, *Wandering Rafferty* (1972), in which the eponymous protagonist and his young sidekick endure a series of comic misadventures as they travel across the western provinces. Even the foolish young RCMP constable of the slapstick *The Meadowlark connection* (1975) is a bit of a nonconformist, albeit one who wants to belong. The stories collected in *Everybody gets something here* (1977) are essentially comic, though many have rather bleak subtexts. The protagonists, however, are always willing to flout authority. In *The con man* (1979) the rebel figure is a Métis who spends much of his time in jail because the people he meets keep insisting that he offer them something for nothing: he becomes the comic victim of a society that pretends to despise him but cannot do without him. *Stones of the Dalai Lama* (1993) is about Bob Harlow who, on a sabbatical trip to China, visits Tibet, and at a sacred region called Place of the Dead puts two mani stones, engraved funeral markers, in his pocket. Negative happenings in his life back home convince him that he is under a curse and he sets out to return the stones. *The heroic adventures of Donny Coyote* (2003, rpr. 2004) is a comical retelling of Cervantes' classic novel in which Donny Coyote, inspired by comic-book heroes, and his Métis companion Sandra Dollar set out in their Coyote Mobil truck from Moose Jaw, Saskatchewan, and head for the US and Las Vegas to perform noble deeds that somehow turn into misadventures.

Believing that theatre is 'the most powerful form of communication', Mitchell has especially enjoyed working on projects that involve various degrees of collaboration. *Cruel tears* (1977), a country-and-western 'opera' that transformed Othello into a tragicomic tale about truckers and their politics and jealousy over women, had songs by Humphrey and the Dumptrucks, who provided a kind of musical commentary on stage in an almost Brechtian manner. First performed in Saskatoon in 1975, it had a successful national tour the next year. *David the politician* (1979) recovers from Victorian silence the story of an early prairie politician and writer, Nicholas Flood Davin, and his feminist lover Kate Simpson-Hayes—both fitting Mitchell nonconformists; it was first produced in Regina in 1978. *The shipbuilder* (1979), written for actors and a percussion ensemble, is about a Finnish farmer who decides to build a ship by hand on his Saskatchewan farm in order to sail back to his homeland; unlike Mitchell's earlier plays, it is a stark tragedy of pride. It was first produced by the University of Regina in 1978. In *The medicine line* (1976), first produced in Moose Jaw in 1976, Mitchell created an epic outdoor drama about Major James Walsh of the North West Mounted Police and Chief Sitting Bull. *The great cultural revolution* (1980), first produced in Vancouver in 1979, sets a version of a kunchu-style Chinese opera inside a play about its staging in China in 1966; here he collaborated with the Chinese-Canadian composer David Liang. Mitchell has continued to explore the medium of drama, with musicals and revues, and especially in the startling and very popular one-man show based on the life of Norman Bethune, *Gone the burning sun* (1985, rpr. 1989), which premiered in Canada at the Guelph Spring Festival in 1984, and toured China in 1987 during Mitchell's second visit there. As Mitchell says in his Preface to *Rebels in time: three plays by Ken Mitchell* (1991), 'I have always been fascinated by rebels,' and the three revised plays in this anthology—*Davin*

the politician, Gone the burning sun, and *The great cultural revolution*—present heroic, rebellious, and tragic figures who insist on holding centre stage. *The plainsman* (1992) is about the Métis leader Gabriel Dumont, a hero of Mitchell's.

Mitchell has also published poetry. *Through the Nan Da Gate: a China journey* (1986) is a collection of mainly descriptive poems, with his own photographs, based on his first trip to China. *Witches & idiots* (1990) is in two sections, 'Coming of Age in Saskatchewan', poems about his childhood on the Prairies, and 'Pilgrimage', more poems about his travels in China and elsewhere.

Mitchell edited *Horizon: writings of the Canadian Prairie* (1977) and *Rhyming wranglers: cowboy poets of the Canadian West* (2007). *Ken Mitchell country* (1984), edited by Robert Currie, is a selection from his drama, poetry, short stories, and novels.

Mitchell, W.O. (1914–98). Born and raised in Weyburn, Saskatchewan, William Ormond Mitchell lost his father in 1921. He was raised thereafter in a largely female environment, though his boyhood was disrupted when he was diagnosed in 1926 as having bovine tuberculosis in his wrist. On medical advice his mother took him to the warmer climate of St Petersburg, Florida (and later California), where he attended high school. Throughout the 1930s he mixed formal education with travel and odd jobs. His pursuit of a medical degree at the University of Manitoba was interrupted by a further flare-up of the disease, whereupon he travelled through North America and Europe and worked at various jobs in Seattle and Calgary. In the early forties he completed his undergraduate studies and education degree at the University of Alberta, married Merna Hirtle, and began teaching in 'composite schools' in rural Alberta. At the same time he was experimenting in fiction, playwrighting, and journalism, stimulated by his creative-writing training at the University of Alberta and his Seattle theatre experience with the Penthouse Players. In the mid-forties, having been published in magazines like *Maclean's* and *The Atlantic Monthly* (his first three stories appeared in 1942), he determined to risk being a full-time writer and gave up teaching, moving his family to High River, Alta. A year after the successful publication of his first novel, WHO HAS SEEN THE WIND (1947, rpr. 2000), the Mitchells moved to Toronto, where he became fiction editor of *Maclean's* (1948–51). From 1950 to 1956 he wrote more than

300 weekly scripts for the popular Canadian Broadcasting Corporation radio series 'Jake and the Kid'—thirteen of which, originally written as short stories, were collected in *Jake and the Kid* (1961, rpr. 2000). From 1951, living mainly in Alberta, he enjoyed an immense popularity across the country over four decades as a popular lecturer, speaker, and performer. (See *An evening with W.O. Mitchell*, 1997.) He was made an Officer of the Order of Canada in 1973 and a Member of the Privy Council of Canada in 1992.

Though concerned with death, destructiveness, and negative values, Mitchell's work bubbles with energy and a persistent sense of joy: he is at heart a comic writer. His novels are remarkable for their exuberant talk, reflecting his fascination with oral tradition, inherited in part from Mark Twain and western American humour. Much influenced as well by the Romantic poets, particularly Wordsworth and Blake, Mitchell cherished innocence, spontaneity, and natural freedom, championing these virtues in the face of darkness, artificiality, and various forms of social restraint. *Who has seen the wind* was followed by *The kite* (1962, rpr. 1992), which is made memorable by the vibrant presence of Daddy Sherry, an irrepressible old maverick whose lifetime spans the 'white' history of the West and whose birthday provides the novel's focus. *The vanishing point* (1973, rpr. 1992), Mitchell's most ambitious and intriguing novel, is the story of Carlyle Sinclair's attempts as teacher and administrator on a Native reserve to bridge the cultural gap between himself and the Stonys, to break through his own puritanical inhibitions and recognize his love for a Native girl in a way that is neither paternalistic nor condescending. But the book's energy and power lie less with the agonies and earnestness of the middle-class protagonist than with the enterprising and clever Archie Nicotine and the self-serving evangelist, Healy Richards—characterizations that again reveal Mitchell's creative exuberance and his gift for dialect and comic situations. *How I spent my summer holidays* (1981, rpr. 2000) returns to the rich, sensory world of prairie boyhood, taking up where *Who has seen the wind* leaves off in dramatizing not the recognition of life, death, and the natural cycle, but the struggle a youth faces in discovering the presence of evil in a man he has romantically idolized.

Beginning in the 1980s Mitchell was at his most prolific, writing a series of novels that have near their centres the problems of aging, especially as they relate to the creative spirit

and the need to build bridges of communication. Since *Daisy Creek* (1984) has a university setting (Mitchell was writer-in-residence at many Canadian universities), as do *Ladybug, ladybug* ... (1988), which is in part about a retired Canadian professor's attempt to complete a biography of Mark Twain, and *For art's sake* (1992). *Roses are difficult here* (1990, rpr. 2000), first drafted in 1959, involves a return to the Alberta town of Shelby and to popular characters and character types from his earlier writing. *According to Jake and the Kid* (1989, rpr. 1994) is a second collection of 'Jake and the Kid' scripts.

Dramatic W.O. Mitchell includes five plays: two were previously published in small editions—*The devil's instrument* (1973) and *The black bonspiel of Wullie MacCrimmon* (1965), which was rewritten as a novella in 1993—while three were new: *The kite, For those in peril on the sea*, and what is perhaps Mitchell's most serious and affecting drama, *Back to Beulah*, which was effectively dramatized for CBC television by Eric Till. *The kite* (1992) is available separately. *The black bonspiel* and *The devil's instrument* were reissued as *The devil is a travelling man: two plays by W.O. Mitchell* (2009), edited by Ormond Mitchell and Barbara Mitchell, Mitchell's son and daughter-in-law, who also wrote *W.O.: the life of W.O. Mitchell; beginnings to Who Has Seen the Wind, 1914–1947* (1999) and *Mitchell: the life of W.O. Mitchell: the years of fame, 1948–1998* (2005). See *Magic lies: the art of W.O. Mitchell* (1997) edited by Sheila Latham and David Latham.

Montgomery, L.M. (1874–1942). Born at Clifton (now New London), Prince Edward Island, Lucy Maud Montgomery was raised by her maternal grandparents after her widowed father moved to Prince Albert, Saskatchewan. Educated at Prince of Wales College, Charlottetown, and at Dalhousie University, Halifax, Nova Scotia, she taught for some years; then, apart from working briefly for the *Halifax Daily Echo* (1901–2), she looked after her grandmother at Cavendish, P.E.I., from 1898 to 1911. Meanwhile, determined to become a writer, she wrote for American and Canadian children's magazines and gained international recognition with her first novel *ANNE OF GREEN GABLES* (1908, NCL; at least six other reprints are available). In 1911 she married the Rev. Ewan Macdonald, and while she pursued her writing career in her husband's charges at Leaskdale and Norval, Ontario, she performed her other roles as the minister's wife and as mother of a young family. The Macdonalds retired to Toronto in 1935. Their last years were plagued by her husband's deteriorating mental health and by Montgomery's severe depression over the Second World War. Both Montgomery and her husband died in Toronto and were buried in Cavendish. Several places associated with her are now museums: her birthplace at New London; her grandmother Macneill's homestead at Cavendish, where she wrote *Anne*; a house in Bala, Ontario, which is associated with her inspiration for *The blue castle*, her only Ontario novel; and two national historic sites, the 'Green Gables' farmhouse at Cavendish and the Presbyterian manse at Leaskdale.

Anne of Green Gables introduces the central situation in Montgomery's fiction: the imaginative adolescent girl's search for self-knowledge that results in liberation from adult authority and success in the male-female clash. An adoring public devoured not only this novel, but seven sequels about Anne's teaching career, her marriage to Gilbert Blythe, their family, and her responses to the changes wrought by the Great War and its aftermath, in *Anne of Avonlea* (1909, rpr. 1998), *Chronicles of Avonlea* (1912, rpr. 1987), *Anne of the Island* (1915, rpr. 1998), *Anne's house of dreams* (1917, rpr. 1983), *Rainbow Valley* (1919, rpr. 1987), *Rilla of Ingleside* (1921, rpr. 1987), *Anne of Windy Poplars* (1936, rpr. 1998), and *Anne of Ingleside* (1939, rpr. 1984). Anne, the spirited child, necessarily grows into a married matron who is highly conventional—to compensate, the later books develop sharp portraits of eccentric characters and rhapsodic descriptions of nature. The enduring quality of the Anne books is in their intense evocation of landscape and in their representation of female aspiration and power.

Following the success of *Anne of Green Gables*, Montgomery published several collections of stories, including her own favourite, *The story girl* (1911, rpr. 1987). In 1917, after a bitter lawsuit, she broke with her first American publisher, L.C. Page, and moved to a Canadian publisher. Page's unauthorized publication of her stories, *Further chronicles of Avonlea* (1920, rpr. 1987), embroiled her in another nine-year court battle that she finally won.

The Emily series is somewhat more autobiographical than the Anne books, and its themes are more deliberately feminist. Montgomery utilized her own reading of Charlotte Brontë's *Jane Eyre*, Elizabeth Barrett Browning's *Aurora Leigh*, and Olive Schreiner's *The story of an African farm* to write about Emily Byrd Starr's own reading and her discovery of her vocation. *Emily of New Moon* (1923, NCL; rpr. 1998) balances the child Emily's first-person journals against the author's third-person narrative. Misled by her male 'suitors', but sustained by her own Wordsworthian 'flashes' of creative insights, Emily's struggles as an adolescent and woman to understand her visions and find her voice as a writer are continued in *Emily climbs* (1925, NCL; rpr. 1998) and *Emily's quest* (1927, NCL; rpr. 1998). In deference to her publisher and her demanding readership, Montgomery eventually marries Emily to a suitor to end the trilogy, rather than focusing on her achievement and potential. Never comfortable with the frank realism of fiction after the Great War, Montgomery recognized that her talent lay in employing humour for the purpose of satirizing society.

Montgomery wrote two fictions aimed at a mature audience, which were well reviewed and sold well. The heroine Valancy of *The blue castle* (1926, rpr. 1988), the only novel without a P.E.I. setting, leaves her unhappy home in the Muskoka district of Ontario to care for a dying 'fallen woman' and child, and then to marry a local man who is suspected of being a shady character. He is revealed to be Valancy's favourite nature writer in disguise, as well as a millionaire's son. *A tangled web* (1931, rpr. 2009) depicts a manipulative, powerful old woman making sport of prospective heirs to a family heirloom. Montgomery then returned to two more adolescent heroines in *Pat of Silver Bush* (1933, rpr. 1988), *Mistress Pat* (1935, rpr. 1997), and *Jane of Lantern Hill* (1937, rpr. 1988). The latter work establishes a fascinating contrast between the city (Toronto) as a sterile wasteland of domineering adults and the P.E.I. countryside as an Edenic, organic community where self-realization is achieved. Posthumous collections of Montgomery's stories include Catherine McLay's edition of *The doctor's sweetheart and other stories* (1979, rpr. 1993) and Rea Wilmhurst's editions of stories (eight to date), beginning with *A kin to Anne: tales of other orphans* (1988). *The Alpine path: the story of my career* (1974, rpr. 2005) is a collection of 1917 magazine articles. See *Magic island: the fictions of L.M. Montgomery* (2008) by Elizabeth Waterston, who discusses the novels in terms of Montgomery's private life and her interests.

Early in the century Montgomery began a lifelong correspondence that—along with her journals, of which she left some ten volumes covering the years 1889 to 1942—provided her with much-needed intellectual and emotional outlets. Her letters were edited by Wilfrid Eggleston in *The Green Gables letters from L.M. Montgomery to Ephraim Weber 1905–1909* (1960, rpr. 1981); by Hildi Froese Tiessen and Paul

Tiessen in *After Green Gables: L.M. Montgomery's letters to Ephraim Weber 1916–1941*; and by Francis W.P. Bolger and Elizabeth R. Epperly in *My dear Mr M.: letters to G.B. MacMillan* (1980, rpr. 1992). The publication of selections from her journals brought to Montgomery a new and well-deserved reputation as a writer. Edited by Mary Rubio and Elizabeth Waterston, *The selected journals of L.M. Montgomery*—Volume I: *1889–1910* (1985, rpr. 2000), *Volume II: 1910–1921* (1987, rpr. 2003), *Volume III: 1921–1929* (1992, rpr. 2003), *Volume IV: 1929–1935* (1998, rpr. 2005), and *Volume V: 1935–1942* (2004, rpr. 2005)—cumulatively offer a vivid and powerful account of her early life and the tensions between her public image as minister's wife and successful author and her private life as wife, mother, and artist. *Volumes II, III, IV,* and *V* are a detailed record of the changes in Canadian society as Montgomery experienced them day by day.

As Elizabeth Epperly (in *The fragrance of sweet grass: L.M. Montgomery's heroines and the pursuit of romance*, 1992) has demonstrated, Montgomery's fictions are psychic biographies in which the self is idealized. She took over the Victorian fiction formulas of her youth and transformed them into romances of enduring appeal, which narrate the heroine's quest for empowerment; her tangles with parental authority figures; her rivalries with, and sexual attraction towards, males; and her triumph through marriage and the artist's vocation. At the same time, Montgomery's narrative strategies, as Mary Rubio has explained, rework the conventions of romance patterns in order to make 'serious social criticism' and to present women readers with an ironic recognition of how their culture oppresses them. Thus the continuing appeal of Montgomery's works lies in her ability to dramatize the psychology of adolescent girls, to be both empathetic and objective about them in her depiction of home and community that is an integral part of almost every story, her humour and irony, and in the *Journals'* portrait of a remarkably passionate and intelligent person.

All twenty volumes of fiction published in Montgomery's lifetime are in print, including many titles in translation, a testimony to their popularity around the world and to Anne's almost legendary status in Japan and Poland. There seems no end to the spinoffs. *Anne of Green Gables* was filmed in 1919 and 1934, and *Anne of Windy Poplars* in 1940. The musical version of *Anne* by Mavor MOORE, Donald Harron, and Norman Campbell has been performed annually at the Charlottetown Confederation Centre since 1965; stage versions of both *Anne of Green Gables* and *The blue castle* have been widely produced in Poland for several decades. The television movies *Anne of Green Gables* (1985), the sequel *Anne of Avonlea* (1987), and the ninety-one episodes of *The road to Avonlea* (1989–96) have been seen around the world and produced a generation of performers who enhanced live theatre in Canada. There is a charming realization of cooking and recipes by Kate Macdonald, Montgomery's granddaughter, in *The Anne of Green Gables cookbook* (1985), illustrated in colour and black and white by Barbara Di Lella. Elaine and Kelly Crawford published *Aunt Maud's recipe book* in 1996. One can browse the Internet sites for information on Montgomery's books and her literary clubs.

Biographies include F.W.P. Bolger, *The years before 'Anne'* (1974); Mollie Gillen, *The wheels of things: a biography of L.M. Montgomery* (1975); Mary Rubio and Elizabeth Waterston, *Writing a life: L.M. Montgomery* (1995); and, notably, Mary Henley Rubio, *Lucy Maud Montgomery: the gift of wings* (2008, rpr. 2010), the long-awaited definitive biography, in which the inconclusive discussion of the very unhappy last years of Montgomery's life indicates that she may or may not have committed suicide. See also Jane URQUHART's brief biography in Penguin Canada's series Extraordinary Canadians, *L.M. Montgomery* (2009).

Montreal Group, The. This influential group of students, with shared literary interests, at McGill University in the 1920s existed in four phases. The first was the founding by A.J.M. SMITH of the *Literary Supplement* (eighteen issues, 1924–5) to the *McGill Daily*, where he began his prolonged effort to introduce a modernist sensibility into Canadian writing. When the *Supplement* was abolished, probably because it was considered too 'highbrow', Smith and F.R. SCOTT—both graduate students—founded the *MCGILL FORTNIGHTLY REVIEW* (1925–7) as an independent journal, though it was supported by the student body. It attracted other young writers—among them A.M. KLEIN, Leo KENNEDY, John GLASSCO, Eugene FORSEY, and Leon EDEL, who was made managing editor. Here, too, Smith was the moving literary spirit, demanding high standards of taste and style, and precision of word and thought. A third phase, after the *Fortnightly* had run its course, was the *CANADIAN MERCURY*, subsidized and created by Louis Schwartz, who had been on the *Fortnightly* staff. Smith, Scott, Klein, Kennedy,

Montreal Group

Edel and others participated—Smith writing from Edinburgh, where he was working towards his Ph.D., and Edel from Paris. The final phase was the publication in 1936 of the seminal anthology of early Canadian modernism: *NEW PROVINCES: poems of several authors* (1936, rpr. 1976). See Leon Edel, *Memories of the Montreal Group* (Memorial University of Newfoundland, 1986).

Montreal Museum, The (Dec. 1822–Mar. 1834). This was the first periodical in British North America directed to female readers by a female editor and proprietor. While typical of its genre in its short publication span and its broad content—poetry, moralistic fiction, didactic and improving non-fiction, and supposedly true stories about historical figures—it was unique for its time and place in providing its readers with a monthly account of London fashions, and with material translated from French sources. The editor, Mary Graddon Gosselin, was the daughter of a Québec merchant who, in 1830, married Léon Gosselin, a Montreal lawyer, prominent reformer, and editor. The Montreal Museum was printed on the press of the newspaper *La Minerve*, of which Léon Gosselin was editor, and its termination may have been related to his departure from that position. The content was produced by writers of both sexes, most of them residents of the colony, although the poetry and fiction rarely had to do with anything distinctively Canadian. Women were more often the principal protagonists of stories than men, and were always depicted in a family context, as wives, mothers, daughters, or aunts, capable of independent action only within a limited sphere, where they were generally portrayed as strong, nurturing, sensible, and sensitive. A number of articles instructed women in their proper role as submissive wives; articles on the education of daughters emphasized the moral and practical, rather than frivolous accomplishments. In winding up the periodical, Mme Gosselin attributed its demise to a lack of subscribers. Its termination was publicly regretted.

Moodie, Susanna (1803–85). Born near Bungay, Suffolk, England, Susanna Strickland lived mostly at Reydon Hall, near Southwold, until her immigration to Canada in 1832. The last-born of six Strickland daughters, five of whom became writers, she was educated by her parents and, as her father's health began to fail, by her elder sisters, notably Elizabeth who, with Agnes, later gained fame and social status in England as authors of *Lives of the Queens of England* and other popular multi-volumed biographies of royalty and Anglican leaders. Like her sisters at isolated Reydon, Susanna began writing at an early age. She was especially attracted to heroic figures of history she judged to have been misunderstood. Her first narrative for young people, *Spartacus: a Roman story* (London, 1822), was followed by many stories for children and adolescents, and she continued writing for publication until 1830, when she met Lieut. John Wedderburn Dunbar Moodie. An Orkney gentleman and half-pay military officer, he had come to London from his Groote Valley farm to write an account of his ten years in South Africa. They married in London in April 1831, and later moved to Southwold, where their first child was born. They decided to immigrate to Canada in the spring of 1832. Arriving in Cobourg, Upper Canada (Ontario), in September, John Moodie chose not to take up their backwoods land grant near Susanna's brother, Samuel Strickland; rather, he bought a partially cleared farm near Lake Ontario and 'the Front'. 'Melsetter' (eight miles northwest of present-day Cobourg) is described in the first half (volume) of Susanna Moodie's *ROUGHING IT IN THE BUSH*. The problems of adjustment the Moodies faced there, compounded by a failed steamboat investment and the more encouraging prospects for a northern waterway (now the Trent-Severn system), prompted them to sell the farm and move in Feb. 1834 to their land grant, north of what is now Lakefield. Here they would be close to both Sam and Susanna's sister, Catharine Parr TRAILL. They remained on their 300-acre bush farm for nearly six years, which included the fearful days of the Rebellion of 1837 and the struggle to make ends meet on a farm distinguished more by cedar forest and rock deposits than by arable land. Only when Moodie was appointed sheriff of the newly established county of Hastings were Susanna and her five children finally able to leave the backwoods. They moved to the growing town of Belleville, where they lived until John Moodie's death in 1869.

Though she endured a great deal in her 'bush' experiences, Susanna Moodie never weakened in her literary aspirations. Initially few markets were available in Upper Canada. Only with the invitation of John Lovell to write for *The LITERARY GARLAND* (Montreal) did she at last find a sustained, paying outlet. During the life of that magazine (1838–51) she was its most prolific contributor, specializing in serialized fiction. As well, in 1847–8 Susanna and John Moodie jointly edited *The Victoria Magazine* in Belleville. The original sketches for *Roughing it in the bush* appeared in both *The Literary Garland* and *The Victoria Magazine* in 1847.

The high point of Susanna Moodie's literary career occurred during the 1850s when, through her husband's publisher Richard Bentley, her writing again found English publication. Her most enduring work is autobiographical in nature and includes her best-known book, *Roughing it in the bush: or, Life in Canada* (2 vols, London, 1852; rpr. 1989, 2009, NCL CEECT); its hastily put-together sequel, *Life in the clearings versus the bush* (London, 1853; rpr. 1989, 2010, NCL with an Afterword by Carol SHIELDS); and a fictionalized narrative, *Flora Lyndsay; or, Passages in an eventual life* (London, 1853). Together the three form a loose trilogy, Flora Lyndsay recounting the events leading up to the Moodies' move to Canada and concluding with their journey up the St Lawrence River. Marked by humour and an unusual frankness concerning pioneering experience, Susanna Moodie's extended account of her difficult adaptation from England to Canada has dramatic force as narrative and a perspicacity of observation rare in the literature of emigration and settlement. Between 1853 and 1868 she wrote three long-winded novels that drew heavily on Gothic and sentimental conventions and were published in both London by Bentley and New York, and a collection of three stories that had first appeared in *The Literary Garland*.

While the Belleville years appear to have been a generally stable and comfortable period for the Moodies, their finances were seldom secure and they were often the target of Tory lawyers who resented their reform (Baldwinite) politics and the advantages conferred upon them through John's appointment as sheriff by Sir George Arthur. Moreover, they suffered great personal losses in Belleville, first in a house fire in 1840 and then as a result of the drowning death of their five-year-old son John in 1844. Late in the 1850s, old political and personal grievances resurfaced in the form of a dubious charge against the aging sheriff for the 'farming' of his office. After exhausting much money and his legal recourses to appeal, John Moodie was at last forced to resign in 1863. After his death in 1869, Susanna outlived him by seventeen years, staying mostly with the families of her married children, though she often visited her sister Catharine Parr Traill in Lakefield.

She wrote little during these later years, turning increasingly to flower painting, a skill she had learned as a girl and had passed on to her daughter, Agnes (Moodie) Fitzgibbon (later Chamberlain), who illustrated *Canadian wildflowers* (Montreal, 1868), the text of which was written by Catharine Parr Traill. Moodie, however, made minor revisions to *Roughing it in the bush* for the first Canadian edition, brought out by Toronto publisher George Rose in 1871. During her last year she was bedridden, suffering in her final days from what her sister Catharine called brain fever. She died in Toronto in the home of her eldest daughter, Katie Vickers.

Much valuable information about Moodie's life and writing can be found in two collections of letters edited by Carl Ballstadt, Elizabeth Hopkins, and Michael Peterman: *Susanna Moodie: letters of a lifetime* (1985) and *Letters of love and duty: the correspondence of Susanna and John Moodie* (1993). See also Michael Peterman, *Susanna Moodie; or, passages from an eventful life* (1998) and Charlotte GRAY, *Sisters in the wilderness: the lives of Susanna Moodie and Catharine Parr Traill* (1999). Another joint biography, the large-format *Sisters in two worlds: a visual biography of Susanna Moodie and Catharine Parr Traill* (2007) by Michael Peterman (with an introduction by Charlotte Gray), is of exceptional interest because it is lavishly illustrated with modern colour photographs as well as archival photographs, paintings, letters, and family artifacts.

Moore, Brian (1921–99). Born and educated in Belfast, Northern Ireland, he served as a civilian employee of the British Ministry of War Transport during the Second World War in Algiers, Naples, and Marseilles, then for the United Nations commission for the resettlement of refugees (UNRRA) after the war, primarily in Warsaw. He immigrated to Canada in 1948, where he worked for the *Montreal Gazette* from 1948 to 1952 while writing his brilliant first novel *Judith Hearne* (1955) (US title *The lonely passion of Judith Hearne*, NCL), about a Belfast spinster whose feelings of loneliness and isolation are briefly and pathetically assuaged by an imaginary romance. A great critical success (and made into a 1987 film starring Maggie Smith), that novel was followed by *The feast of Lupercal* (1957) and *The luck of Ginger Coffey* (1960, GGA, NCL). Moore moved to the USA in 1959 but retained Canadian citizenship. References to Canada and the Canadian experience continued to appear in his fiction, as in *The great Victorian collection* (1975, GGA), which deals with a McGill University history professor, who, while visiting California, dreams about a 'Victorian collection' and awakens to find that his dream, to somewhat perverse effect, has come true.

Moore's other novels include *An answer from Limbo* (1962, rpr. 1982), *The emperor of ice-cream* (1965), *I am Mary Dunne* (1968), *Fergus* (1970), *Catholics* (1972), *The doctor's wife* (1976), *The Mangan inheritance* (1979), *The temptation of Eileen Hughes* (1981), *Cold heaven* (1983, rpr.1996), *The colour of blood* (1987, rpr. 1988), *Lies of silence* (1990, rpr. 2005), *No other life* (1993, rpr. 1994), *The statement* (1995, rpr. 1997), and *The magician's wife* (1997, rpr. 1998). Of Moore's many novels, *Black robe* (1985, rpr. 1997) seems his greatest departure. His only historical fiction, it portrays the mission of seventeenth-century French Jesuits to convert Native tribes in Canada and was made into a film (directed by Bruce Beresford, 1991).

In fact, all Moore's novels deal in some way with dilemmas of faith triggered by what he has called 'moments of crisis' that bring the accustomed into question. While his early Belfast-set novels assail a tyrannical version of Irish Catholicism that seems rooted in his own harshly clerical education there in the 1930s, his later books (beginning with *An answer from Limbo*) reveal the limitations of an opposite orientation, the attempt to find happiness through secular self-absorption. The books of this middle period betray a deep yearning for mystical and spiritual affirmation on the part of even his most rootless and worldly characters. Beginning with *The colour of blood*, Moore turned to the thriller genre as a way of exploring issues of conscience within the context of contemporary politics, from an uneasy complicity between Church and state, in the case of a French war criminal (*The statement*), to hostage-taking in Northern Ireland (*Lies of silence*). While not equally successful as literary productions, Moore's novels are on the whole remarkable for their transparency of style, and a leanness and dramatic economy of expression (perhaps honed by his occasional forays into scriptwriting) that manage to convey exceptional levels of nuance and psychological complexity. Moore is also notable for his success in depicting female characters and female sexuality, relating sexual autonomy for women to issues of identity and self-expression—and ultimately to their capacity for independent moral choice and moral responsibility (as in—apart from *Judith Hearne*—*The doctor's wife*, *Cold heaven*, *The temptation of Eileen Hughes*, and *I am Mary Dunne*).

See Denis Sampson, *Brian Moore: the chameleon novelist* (1998); and Colm Tóibín's long review of it in the *London Review of Books* (vol. 12, no. 15, 10 Aug. 2000), which is both an illuminating commentary on some of Moore's novels, particularly *Judith Hearne*, and a mini-biography.

Moore, Christopher (b. 1950). Born in Stoke-on-Trent, England, he was brought to Canada in 1954 by his parents, who settled in Nelson, B.C., and then Vancouver. He was educated at the University of British Columbia (B.A., 1971) and the University of Ottawa (M.A., 1977). As staff historian for Parks Canada (1972–5), he worked at Fortress of Louisbourg National Historic Park when a portion of the eighteenth-century town was being reconstructed. A significant book grew out of this experience: *Louisbourg portraits: life in an eighteenth-century garrison town* (1982, GGA; rpr. 1988), reprinted in 2000 with the subtitle *Five dramatic, true tales of people who lived in an eighteenth-century garrison town*—in which research on five unfamiliar figures associated with Louisbourg was transformed into vivid historical narratives. To *The illustrated history of Canada* (1987) edited by Craig Brown, Moore contributed the second chapter: 'Colonization and Conflict: New France and Its Rivals (1600–1760). *The Loyalists: revolution, exile, settlement* (1994) is an attractive, large-format history, with many illustrations, that focuses on individuals whose personal reminiscences were included in the Loyalist Claims. Moore's other books include *1867: how the Fathers made a deal* (1997, rpr. 1998), an illuminating 1990s examination of anomalies that were part of the process that led to Confederation—described by the author as 'a reading of some political history as if confederation mattered'; *Canada: our century* (1999), a rich photographic album that has texts by Mark Kingwell and Moore; and *The Law Society of Upper Canada and Ontario's lawyers 1797–1997* (1997). *McCarthy Tétrault: building Canada's premier law firm: 1855–2005* (2005) is the substantial history of a firm that was the result of the merger of four firms, including the well-known Toronto firm McCarthy & McCarthy, which was founded in 1855.

Moore has also written the texts of magnificently illustrated books for young people, beginning with *The story of Canada* (1992, rev. 1996), co-authored with Janet LUNN and illustrated by Alan Daniel. *The Big book of Canada: exploring the provinces and territories* (2002), illustrated by Bill Slavin, is indeed a big (and heavy) book in a large format, lavishly illustrated, that is both informative and entertaining in the way historical and modern information is provided. Combining Moore's informative texts with many archival and modern illustrations and photographs are *Adventurers: The Hudson's Bay Company—the epic story* (2000), produced for the HBC—though a short text (thirty-two pages) it is very revealing; and *Champlain* (2004), a remarkably informative and enjoyable treatment of the career of the Father of New France during three important decades of Canada's early history, with beautiful illustrations by Francis Back.

Moore, Lisa (b. 1964). Lisa Lynne Moore was born in Newfoundland, educated at the Nova Scotia College of Art and Design, and lives with her husband and two children in St John's. She has published two collections of stories and two novels. With her first book, *Degrees of separation* (1995), she revealed herself as a mistress of fragmented narratives that switch from subject to subject, scene to scene, mixing past and present and more than one viewpoint, to create not so much a story as the embodiment of a character, where she lives, and her complex experiences at one point in her life. The first sentence of the title story reads: 'The top half of Joan's house caught fire and burned while she slept downstairs.' Joan and her twelve-year-old son Wiley move in with the narrator, who goes on to tell us that she persuaded Joan to go with her, dressed as a man, 'to the only strip joint in town' (they do eventually go there) and that she had got 'into the habit of telling the woman who sells the coffee and muffins in the cafeteria of the building where I work the most intimate things about myself.' The woman wears a plastic name tag that says 'Cathy'. 'Once I said "Good morning, Cathy," and she said, "That's not my real name."' On the first page of the first story, 'Nipple of Paradise', we are told that the narrator's husband Cy 'had slept with Marie'. What follows are pre-natal classes (comical) and the birth (in some detail): 'My baby was too small to suck from the nipple so we had to feed her pumped breast milk from a bottle. I had to pump every night.' Marie comes over for supper and Cy takes her up to see the baby. The baby monitor is on: Cy says: 'Listen Marie, what happened, if Donna knew about it, it would really hurt her, I mean I really had a good time, but I think it was a sort of solitary thing.' After the birth, and after visiting hours, Cy phones his wife and reads to her from a book about Columbus, who is is revelling in

the myth that 'the garden of Paradise was on Earth. That the world was pear-shaped and the garden of Eden a protuberance on the top, like a woman's nipple.' When Columbus discovered fresh water off South America he thought it flowed 'from the nipple of paradise.' In *Open* (2002) people in St John's—though the location is almost invisible—receive a postmodern treatment in stories that are not narratives but riffs on random thoughts, incidents, friendships, memories (sometimes all interwoven in one paragraph), as well as on sex and uneasy marriages. The shapely, imaginative sentences often seem to invite admiration, but connection, coherence, and meaning are not prime considerations—the 'stories' and their seemingly irrelevant digressions are cumulations of *little* meanings, ambiguous and … open. In 'The way the light is' the narrator is making a five-minute film based on a poem by the Newfoundland poet John STEFFLER, and snatches of the screenplay are quoted among observations of, and conversations between, Mina, who is in the film, the narrator and her husband Jason, who shows Mina a video of his son's birth—graphically described by his wife. *Open* was a finalist for the 2002 GILLER PRIZE. The chapters in Moore's first novel, *Alligator* (2005) are headed by the names of ten characters, including teenaged Colleen, who at the beginning is viewing the archival shots made by her filmmaker aunt Madeleine (another repeated chapter title) of a man, called Loyola, who puts his head in an alligator's mouth—and the jaws close. 'He's still alive,' Madeleine says. 'He runs an alligator farm in Louisiana, an ecological reserve.' (Colleen eventually goes there to meet him.) She also tells Colleen: 'We had a little thing.' Other chapter titles: Beverly, Colleen's mother, an unhappy widow who is in despair when Colleen turns into an eco-terrorist, pouring sugar into Mr Duffy's bulldozers, and is arrested; young Frank, who attended his mother as she died of breast cancer, wants to have a hot-dog cart, and is victimized; and the unscrupulous Valentin, a survivor. 'The Russian vessel had been seized by the Canadian government in Harbour Grace with a crew of forty-three sailors on board. The shipping company responsible for the vessel and crew had folded without a trace and the men's wages were frozen or there were no wages and they had run out of supplies and had used up all their fuel after only a week in port.' Valentin succeeds as best he can, meeting the middle-aged actress Isobel (another chapter title), making love to her, telling her that he's decided to burn her house down so that he can benefit from the insurance money (giving a share to her—which he does). A cornucopia of visual details, abruptly changing scenes in the past or present, differing points of view as these people (and others) brush up against or oppose each other, the novel is a striking fusion of lives with, as background, St John's in an unfamiliar guise as a sophisticated and complex city. Moore has magically created a colourful, eventful reality of her own. In 2009 she published *February* (rpr. 2010), about the 1982 Ocean Ranger disaster, when that oil rig sank off Newfoundland, and how it affected the family of one of the eighty-four men who were killed.

Moore selected and introduced *The Penguin book of contemporary Canadian women's short stories* (2006).

Moore, Mavor (1919–2006). Born in Toronto to the Anglican clergyman Francis John Moore and the actress Dora (née Mavor) Moore, he grew up in Toronto, where he attended university, graduating with a B.A. (1941). Following service in Canadian army intelligence during the war, he and his mother founded the New Play Society in Toronto in 1946. He also worked for the Canadian Broadcasting Corporation during the 1940s and 1950s, becoming chief producer for CBC-TV (1950–4). From 1970 to 1984 he was Professor of Theatre at York University, Toronto, becoming Professor Emeritus. Throughout his career he was much involved in the theatre, acting as producer and director of the annual revue *Spring Thaw* between 1948–57 and 1961–5. He was the founding artistic director of the Charlottetown Festival (1964–8), general director of the St Lawrence Centre, Toronto (1965–9), founding chair of the Guild of Canadian Playwrights (1977), and chair of the CANADA COUNCIL (1979–83). From 1991 he was Research Professor of Fine Arts & Humanities at the University of Victoria on Vancouver Island.

Moore was the librettist for numerous musicals and operas, including *Sunshine Town* (produced in 1954), *The Ottawa Man* (produced in 1958), *Johnny Belinda* (produced in 1968), and *Fauntleroy* (produced in 1980). Perhaps his most important work in this genre was his libretto for the opera by Harry Somers, *Louis Riel* (1967), commissioned by the Canadian Opera Company for the centenary celebrations. A number of Moore's stage plays have been published in *Three one-act plays by Mavor Moore* (1973) and *Six plays* (1989). He was made an Officer of the Order of Canada in 1973, a Companion in 1988, and

in 1986 was awarded the Molson Prize for his outstanding achievement in the arts. See his memoirs, *Reinventing myself* (1994).

More joy in heaven (1973, NCL). From the publication of his first novel, *Strange fugitive* (1928), until that of *A time for Judas* (1983), one of the preoccupations of Morley CALLAGHAN's fiction has been the world of the criminal. Most concerned with this subject is *More joy in heaven*, the last and possibly the best novel by Callaghan from his most prolific period as a writer. It was clearly inspired by the life of the notorious bank robber Red Ryan, who was released from Kingston (Ont.) Penitentiary in the summer of 1935 after serving almost a dozen years of a life sentence. Ryan claimed that he had reformed, and his supporters included a priest, a senator, other citizens interested in prison reform, and even Prime Minister R.B. Bennett. The welcome that Ryan was given on his return to Toronto was equalled only by the bitterness that greeted the news, in May 1936, that he had been shot to death by police as he attempted to rob a liquor store in Sarnia, Ont. In the novel Red Ryan becomes the fictional Kip Caley, whose release from prison is also aided by a senator and a priest. Caley, however—unlike Ryan—has truly reformed. Having been turned into a celebrity by the press and the public, he begins to believe he has a mission to reform society, but is eventually overcome by its cynicism and violence. On one level *More joy in heaven* may be read as a novel of social comment; on another it is a religious parable, with the redeemed sinner being destroyed both by his illusions and by his fellow men.

Morency, Pierre (b. 1942). Born in Lauzon, Québec, he studied at the Collège de Lévis and Université Laval. In the 1970s he published four collections of poetry and, with Paul Hébert, a highly acclaimed French adaptation (1974) of J.T. McDonough's *Charbonneau and le Chef* (1968), a play about Maurice Duplessis's clash with the Archbishop of Montreal. In 1976 he co-founded *Estuaire*, the only Québécois magazine devoted exclusively to poetry. Morency then concentrated on his career as a broadcaster, producing programs and records on the birds of the St Lawrence and using to good effect his poetic gifts and his splendid speaking voice. A selection from some of his poetry collections of the sixties and seventies—*Poèmes de la froide merveille de vivre* (1967), *Poèmes de la vie déliée* (1968), *Au nord constamment de l'amour* (1970), *Lieu de naissance* (1973), *Torrentiel* (1978), and *Effets* *personnels* (1978)—was translated by Alexandre L. Amprimoz in *A season for birds: selected poems* (1990). Morency belongs to the generation of poets determined to end Québec's atavistic enslavement to the dualism of flesh and spirit. His poetry celebrates the world of things and people—the city, but above all the country, the Île d'Orléans, the North Shore of the St Lawrence River, and the wildlife of the region. He blatantly adopts a technical wildlife vocabulary in his poems to express his holistic vision of the human struggle against alienation and a reconciliation with the environment. His love of nature, and birds in particular, inspired prose pieces in which he invites readers to look more closely at the world around them: *L'oeil Américan: histoires naturelles du Nouveau Monde* (1989), translated by Linda Gaboriau as *The eye is an eagle: nature stories from the New World* (1992), is a long meditation on nature—on birds, trees, and insects—in twenty-four vivid, deeply felt 'stories'/ essays. Morency published in 1994 *Les paroles qui marchent dans la nuit*, which was translated by Lissa Cowan and René Brisebois as *Words that walk in the night, preceded by What Trom says: a story* (2001), a bilingual edition. The Trom section is made up of prose poems, in the first of which ('Portrait of a man alive') we read: that the poet notices his car. 'The license plate drew my attention. Along with three numbers, it had the letters TRM. A spontaneous leap of the imagination whispered to me the missing vowel.' The section called 'Glimmer on the mountain' is made up of untitled quatrains, e.g. 'I want you to meet a man who is gentle / he holds his tongue and keeps his word / he looks into your eyes touches without guilt / his serenity floats up the river love'. In 2000 Morency was awarded the prestigious Prix Athanase-David for the body of his work, and in 2002 he was made an Officer of the Order of Canada.

Morgan, Bernice (b. 1935). Born in St John's, Newfoundland, where she still lives, she undertook several jobs until 1986, when she resigned as communications director of the Newfoundland Teacher's Association to devote herself full time to writing (while being married with three children). Morgan's two novels tell a linked story about the families of Cape Random, an isolated, exposed point in the northeastern part of Newfoundland. She draws upon the history of her mother's family in Cape Island, a now-deserted outport, combining elements of Gothic romance with historically accurate and realistic details to form a sweeping

narrative. *Random passage* (1992) begins with the arrival of the Andrews family in 1824, and takes the form of a journal written chiefly by Lavinia Andrews in a shipping-records book. *Waiting for time* (1994) brings the narrative into the present with Lav Andrews, who is transferred from Ottawa to St John's to co-ordinate a report on the troubled cod fishery; it also recounts the story of Mary Bundle, one of the early settlers in Cape Random, that is inscribed in the margins of, and contests, the original journal that Lav finds. The interwoven stories layer fiction and history, evoking the tenuousness of life in the outports and the strength for survival that comes largely from the women. Morgan blends fast-paced narrative with haunting images of the people, land, and sea. *Cloud of bone* (2007) is a multiplotted novel made up of three narratives. The first, leading to the Battle of Britain in World War II—involving two young Newfoundlanders in the Royal Navy, Kyle Holloway and Gup—is in Kyle's memory, related in flashback. At the very end, describes a gripping scene that haunts him forever: Kyle throws a lifeline to a drowning German sailor and Gup tries to sever it with his knife. Kyle 'yanked the knife from between Gup's fingers' and it 'slipped smoothly into Gup's neck'; his body collapsed onto the deck and 'slithered like some huge fish below the rail and into the moon-drenched, oil-drenched sea.' The second story—a substantial and memorable one—is told in the words of Shanawdithit, who recounts her growing up among the Beothuk of Newfoundland and their gradual starvation and disappearance as Europeans encroached on their hunting grounds. (She died in St John's in 1829.) In the last section of the novel Judith Muir, an anthropologist, is in Rwanda with her husband when he is shot and killed. She returns to England to recover from her loss and, in the cottage of deceased Aunt Min, in a gas-mask box, she comes upon a skull that is numbered. Morgan holds the reader's interest as Judith follows clues that lead her to the Hunterian Collection of human and animal skeletal remains, where the number identifies the skull as being that of Shanawdithit. 'Apparently the doctor who attended her—a Dr. Carson—performed a post-mortem and decided that her skull exhibited certain peculiarities. He sent it to the Royal College of Physicians where it became part of the Odontological Society's collection, which was later acquired by us.' Judith keeps the skull, takes it to Newfoundland, meets the now elderly Kyle, who has become obsessed by the Beothuk maiden,

Morgan

Shanawdithit. She gives the skull to him. *Cloud of bone* is an ingenious, absorbing novel.

Moritz, A. F. (b. 1947). Born in Warren, Ohio, Albert Frank Moritz was educated at Marquette University, Milwaukee, Wisconsin (B.A., 1969; M.A., 1971) and the University of Toronto (Ph.D., 1975), where he is sessional lecturer in English literature and creative writing (1986–7, 1991–4, 1996–) at Victoria College, and was the Northrop FRYE Visiting Lecturer in Poetry in 1993–4. In 1990 he received a Guggenheim Foundation Fellowship Grant (poetry); and in 1991 he received a mid-career award in literature from the American Academy and Institute of Arts and Letters. As a poet Moritz is in the tradition of the Romantics. His poems are often philosophically dense meditations on visionary states embracing nature increasingly threatened by the mechanical world. His many books of poetry include *New poems* (1974), *Here* (1975); *Black orchid* (1981), *Between the root and the flower* (1982), *The visitation* (1983), *The tradition* (1986), *Song of fear* (1992), *The ruined cottage* (1993), *Phantoms in the ark* (1994), *Mahoning* (1994), and *Houseboat on the Styx* (1998). In the evocative and moving *Mahoning*—a long poem inspired by William Carlos Williams' *Paterson*—named after the river of his birthplace in Ohio, the poet seeks out the spirit of nature in a landscape blighted by the steel industry. In *Houseboat on the Styx* the speaker, Silenus, and his beloved, Diotima (Socrates's mentor in Plato's *Symposium*) are stuck in Hades in a marsh, which turns out to be a city, and the text encompasses remembered and imagined journeys, ancient and modern. It was inspired by an 1895 book with a similar title by John Hendrick Bangs, in which 'famous people drift along pleasantly on a houseboat in hell and make conversation that debunks history and received notions.' Michael Cameron, in his Introduction to *Black orchid*, wrote that 'Moritz's mental world has a haunted and haunting quality: the images are brilliant and correct as if seen in too harsh sunlight.' Moritz the intellectual poet is at his best in *Rest on the flight into Egypt* (1999, rpr. 2000), with poems that include 'The little walls before China', 'Landscape: on a line by Baudelaire', 'Kissinger at the funeral of Nixon', 'On a line by Catullus', and 'Ode to Apollo'; the title poem is a long meditation on thoughts inspired by the Bernard van Orley painting, seen in a reproduction on the cover. *The end of the age* and *Conflicting desire* were published in 2000. *Early poems* (2002)—which contains the poems in

Moriz's first five collections—has Forewords by Don MCKAY and John Hollander, who quotes words of praise for Moritz from two famous American literary figures, Harold Bloom ('Yes, I know his work. He is a true poet.') and Mark Strand ('Is that Al Moritz? He's wonderful.') *Night street repairs* (2004) was named after the poem 'Night street repairs in Mexico City'. Of this collection, Douglas BARBOUR has said: 'There is a dire pleasure in making one's way through these darkly labyrinthine poems to the possibly transcendent and hopeful hymns to sun, moon, and world that conclude *Night street repairs*....[Moritz] is certainly one of the contemporary masters of philosophical lyrical narrative.' *The sentinel* (2008), a collection of sixty-two poems (selected with the help of his editor Ken BABSTOCK), won the GRIFFIN POETRY PRIZE in 2009. The title poem begins: 'The one who watches while the others sleep / does not see. It is hoped, it is to be hoped / there is nothing to see. The camp has quieted / behind him and all is peace there....'

Moritz co-authored with his wife, Theresa Moritz, *Leacock: a biography* (1985), which was later revised as *Stephen Leacock: his remarkable life* (2001); *The pocket Canada: a guidebook* (1982); and *The Oxford illustrated literary guide to Canada* (1987). *Woman in dream* (2004) is Moritz's translation of *Mujer en sueño* by Ludwig ZELLER.

Morton, W.L. (1908–80). Born in Gladstone, Manitoba, William Lewis Morton was educated at the University of Manitoba and Oxford University as a Rhodes Scholar. He held various university teaching appointments in Manitoba until settling in the history department at the University of Manitoba in 1942, serving there until 1966 (from 1950 to 1964 as head). He then moved to Trent University, Peterborough, Ontario, as Master of Champlain College and Vanier Professor of History. After retiring from Trent in 1975, he returned to the University of Manitoba and continued to teach there until his death. He was made an Officer of the Order of Canada in 1969.

One of Morton's earliest books was *The Progressive Party in Canada* (1950, GGA; rev. 1967), which was partly a working-out of the Morton family past: the author's father had been elected to the Manitoba legislature as a Progressive and the study is deeply sympathetic to both regional grievances and the positive reforms of the movement. By this time, however, Morton had broken with his family's traditional political allegiances and become an active supporter of the

Conservative party; many of his later writings attempted to delineate a philosophy for Canadian Conservatism. Beginning in the mid-1950s Morton entered upon a decade of prodigious output, which saw him publish most of his major works and gradually change from a regional to a national historian. It included what many regard as his finest book, *Manitoba: a history* (1957, rev. 1967), a model provincial history. Stronger on the Red River period than the post-1870 one, it illustrated Morton's strong identification with the agrarian origins of the *province*, as well as his growing sense of Manitoba's cultural distinctiveness. (Morton later wrote a brilliant introduction to a related collection of documents: *Manitoba: the birth of a province*, 1965, for the Manitoba Record Society.) In 1957 he also published *One university a history of the university of Manitoba, 1877–1952*, which—while inevitably institutional in approach—captured the flavour of the disparate educational and cultural traditions in Manitoba that Morton always celebrated. Morton then turned to larger themes. An invitation to deliver a series of lectures in 1960 at the University of Wisconsin produced the bulk of *The Canadian identity* (1961, rev. 1972). In these lectures, and in his 1960 Canadian Historical Association presidential address, Morton sought to provide Canada with 'a self-definition of greater clarity and more ringing tone', emphasizing the nation's northern character, historical dependence, monarchical commitment, and special relationships with other states. These themes became the basis of his large-scale history *The kingdom of Canada* (1963), although they often became lost in a morass of encyclopedic and ill-digested detail. This work did not display Morton's abilities to the best advantage, nor did *The critical years: the union of British North America, 1857–1873* (1964), a volume in the Canadian Centenary Series, of which he was co-editor with Donald CREIGHTON. More than other studies of the Confederation period, *The critical years* focused on the aspirations of the outlying regions, stressing the cultural (rather than political) duality of Canada, a major preoccupation of Morton's later works. When he came to deal with regions outside Manitoba, however, Morton self-confessedly had difficulty in achieving the same *Verstehen* he displayed about his native province. His most insightful analysis and most stylish—often lyrical—prose is to be found in his writings on the early history of Manitoba. Although Morton was far more than merely a regional historian, it was as a regional historian that he

produced his most enduring and endearing work. Morton's shorter writings are accessible in A.B. McKillop, ed., *Contexts of Canada's past: selected essays of W.L. Morton* (1980).

Mosaic (1967–). Founded by the University of Manitoba in Canada's centenary year, it was originally intended to be a quarterly for the study of literature and ideas; its name suggests the cultural concept associated with Canada as a 'mosaic' of different ethnic groups rather than the American 'melting pot'. In 1980, however, the magazine changed direction to become 'A journal for the interdisciplinary study of literature', edited by Dr Evelyn Hinz, highlighting the theoretical, practical, and cultural relevance of literary works; one issue each year focuses on a topic of contemporary concern. The current editor is Dawne McCance.

Moses, Daniel David (b. 1952). A registered Delaware Native, he was born in Ohsweken, Ontario, on the Six Nations Reserve. He grew up on a farm there, attended elementary school on the reserve, and received his secondary education at Caledonia High School. He graduated with an Honours B.A. in General Fine Arts (1975) from York University, Toronto, and received an M.F.A. in Creative Writing (1977) from the University of British Columbia. Associate professor, Queen's National Scholar, at Queen's University (2003–), Kingston, Ontario, Moses co-edited *An anthology of Canadian Native literature in English* (3rd edn 2005).

His first collection of poetry, *Delicate bodies* (1980, rpr. 1993), was followed by *The white line* (1991), and *Sixteen Jesuses* (2000). He has also published six plays: *The dreaming beauty*, a one-act play in twelve scenes, published in *Impulse*, vol. 15, 3, 1989, was produced in a French version, *Belle fille de l'Aurore*, by Théâtre du Jour of Saskatoon and toured Canada in 1991; *Coyote City* (1990), produced by Native Earth Performing Arts, Toronto, in 1988; *Almighty Voice and his wife* (1992), produced in 1991 by the Great Canadian Theatre Company, Ottawa, and in 1992 by the Native Earth Performing Arts, Toronto; and *The Indian medicine shows* (1996), two linked one-act plays, produced by Theatre Passe Muraille, Toronto, in 1996. His *Big buck city*, produced by the Cahoots Theatre Project at the Tarragon Theatre, Toronto, in 1991, was published in one volume with *Coyote City* (1997). *Brébeuf's ghost*, workshopped at the University of Windsor's School of Drama in 1996, was published in 2000. Available in script format are *Kyotopolis*, workshopped by

Moses

the University of Toronto's Centre for Drama
(1993), and *City of shadows*, workshopped at
the School of Dramatic Art, University of
Windsor, in 1995. The pieces in the engaging
Pursued by a bear: talks, monologues, and tales
(2005) throw light on other Native writers and
on Moses' creativity and dramatic practice—
tracing the development of some of his
plays—and, in 'Queer for a day: writing the
status queer: reading beyond breeding', on
being gay.

Although Moses has one foot planted in a
world of tribal tradition and the other washed
by the eddies and currents of mainstream
Canada, he does not seem to be caught
between the two worlds in a cultural divide.
In his poetry he probes his world, trying to
find meaning from it, but there is no outrage;
the message is submerged in surreal images
characterized by unembittered wit and trickster wisdom. In his poetry his marvellously
lyric use of English seems to be inspired by
the King James version of the Bible, Gerard
Manley Hopkins, and e.e. cummings. Moses'
plays are boldly didactic, but the creative way
he uses his Native background as material for
his settings, characters, images, and humour is
remarkable. For example, his theme in *The
Indian medicine shows*, set in New Mexico in
the late nineteenth century, draws upon contemporary Native thought about homosexuality, which implies that gay people have a
dual nature, the male and the female inhabiting one body. According to Moses, the first of
the two plays, *The moon and dead Indians*, represents the destruction of the feminine; the
second, *Angel and the medicine show*, represents
its resurrection. Add to these themes fast-
paced action, the special lighting and sound
effects typical of theatre in the television age,
and the result is spectacular. Moses' plays are
profoundly imagined, the work of a circum-
spect and strong intelligence.

Mosionier, Beatrice Culleton. See
ABORIGINAL LITERATURE: 5.

Mouré, Erín (b. 1955), also known as Eirin
Mouré. Born in Calgary, she was educated at
the Universities of Calgary and British
Columbia. She has been living and working
in Montreal since 1984 as a freelance translator and communications specialist. Although
often conscious of how the Prairies reside in
her West, the cultural, political, and social
vibrancy of Montreal seems to have fired
much of Mouré's work. She shares with other
well-known women writers in that community, notably Nicole BROSSARD (Mouré, with

Robert Majzels, translated three poetry collections by Brossard) and Gail SCOTT, an
intensely urban-edged appreciation of life's
confusions, as well as a fascination with the
ways identity is shaped by the double play of
memory and experience. Broadly speaking,
one could say that the span of Mouré's poetry
tracks the progress of a woman's move from
west to east, from prairie grass to urban concrete, from heterosexual divorce to lesbian
love. Such a sweeping biographical formula-
tion ignores the intensely experiential quality
of Mouré's work, which has almost always
conveyed a high charge of immediacy,
demanding from the reader an uncompromising commitment to the page. Her first book
of poems, *Empire, York Street* (1979), was
nominated for a Governor General's Award. A
chapbook, *The whisky vigil* (1981), conveyed
the pain of divorce, but not without a characteristic co-mingling of rage and laughter.
Wanted alive (1983) marks a strengthening of
voice, an affirmation of the power of language, and an acknowledgement of the diur-
nal grind of work informed by Mouré's own
experience as a CN/VIA Rail employee.
Domestic fuel (1985) activates a passionate
awareness of the life of women, and a struggle
with the paradox of creating a world of collective challenge through private voice. *Furious* (1988, GGA) is a witty, fervent, and
intellectually intense appreciation of material
integration, and of memory, language, and
desire ('Your blue sweater bunched up in the
garden / & you in it, squatting over lettuce').
WSW (west south west) (1989) extends these
preoccupations through a clever series of
linked poems. A further poetic cycle, *Sheepish
beauty, civilian love* (1992), continues to map
the spaces where the personal and the political intersect. *Search procedures* (1996), Mouré's
most écomplex set of lyrics, contends that 'the
creation of experience is what the brain does',
a succinct manifesto of Mouré's own writing
principle. These collections were followed by
The green world: selected poems (1994), *A frame of
the book* (1999), and *Search procedures* (1999), a
difficult collection in which meaning is deliberately compromised.

Sheep's vigil by a fervent person (2001) is Eirin
Mouré's transelation—or, as she plays with this
word in a note, 'Trans-e-lations. Trans-eirin-
elations. Transcreations'—of the fifty poems in
a famous Portuguese work *O Guardador de
Rebanhos* by Fernando Pessoa (1888–1935).
The opening lines of the first poem are 'What,
me, guard sheep? / I made that up, this is
poetry. / It's my soul that's sheepish / Knows
wind and sun / Grabs onto every Season and

follows, looking.' The words of a solitary shepherd in the countryside of Portugal have been transmuted into the reflections of a female in Toronto, where Mouré wrote the book (staying in the house of Roo BORSON and Kim Maltman). Toronto and the twenty-first century are everywhere in these 'translations', make of them what you will. *Little theatres* (2005) is a strange potpourri of bilingual poems by Mouré (in Galician and English)— the effective 'Homages to water'—quotations about 'little theatres' and poems by the Galician poet (now living in Bucharest, Romania) Elisa Sampedrín; other poems by Mouré incorporate Galician lines, which the *Diccionario* at the end helps to interpret. The title *O cadoiro* (2007) means 'the place where falling is made'; the noun is a Galician word for waterfall, or cataract. 'Thus the fall,' she says in an endnote. 'This to me is the place of poetry, for whoever writes poetry must be prepared, ever, to fall down.' The lyrics in this collection (not all in English) were inspired by the medieval Galician *cantiga de amigo* (longing for an absent lover) and the Iberian songbooks written in Galacian-Portuguese. But their effect on Mouré's imagination has produced hermetic creations that only occasionally cast a shaft of light or meaning: '[B]y mine own eyes I saw her there / with terror and weighed grief and so lit / the pleasure that seeings craved / by eyes and yet what good is it to / see my lovely not at all.'

Mowat, Farley (b. 1921). Born in Belleville, Ontario, he grew up in Saskatoon, Saskatchewan, and was educated at the University of Toronto (B.A., 1949). After serving in the Hastings and Prince Edward Regiment during the Second World War, he spent two years in the Arctic before completing his degree in 1949 and becoming a freelance writer. With some forty books to his name, the author of many critically acclaimed and financially successful books, he was made an Officer of the Order of Canada in 1981.

Mowat's first book, *People of the deer* (1952, rev. 1975, rpr. 2005), caused much controversy by blaming government officials and missionaries for the plight of the caribou-hunting Ihalmiut Inuit, and was severely criticized for its obvious bias. Its sequel, *The desperate people* (1959; rev. 1975; rpr. 2006), is more moderate and much better researched, but lacks the impact of the first book, which sincerely and eloquently conveys the writer's sympathy for, and understanding of, a people whose culture and very lives were threatened by contact with European civilization.

Mowat's involvement with the North is a recurring theme in his books. *Coppermine journey* (1958) is an edited version of the narrative of Samuel Hearne; and the works known as the Top of the World Trilogy— *Ordeal by ice* (1960; rev. 1973; rpr. 1989), *The polar passion* (1967; rev. 1973; rpr. 1989), and *Tundra* (1973)—are edited journals of both famous and unknown explorers, with a linking commentary by Mowat. *Sibir: my discovery of Siberia* (1970, rev. edn 1990) is an account of the author's trips to the Soviet Union in the late 1960s, and *The snow walker* (1975, rpr. 2003) is a collection of stories about Canadian Inuit. *Canada North* (1967), a pictorial book with text by Mowat, was followed by *Canada North now: the great betrayal* (1976), an examination of living conditions in the Arctic during the 1970s. Mowat felt, in retrospect, that he did the Inuit a great disservice, after his first book about them encouraged assimilation: 'the government saw to it that no Eskimo died of malnutrition and the medical services were improved and nobody froze to death. But they turned the whole of the Canadian Arctic into a charity ward.' *Walking on the land* (2000), one quarter of which recycles material from *People of the deer* and *The desperate people*, is a recollection of his time spent with the Barrenground Inuit and reiterates, with many telling stories, the devastation of their culture after the depletion of the caribou herds.

Mowat's sympathy for the dispossessed is evident in the texts he wrote for two pictorial books about Newfoundland. In *This rock within the sea: a heritage lost* (1968), John de Visser's photographs are accompanied by Mowat's lament for a vanishing outport culture and his attack on Joseph Smallwood and the relocation program that wiped thousands of small communities off the map. In *The wake of the great sealers* (1973), David Blackwood's prints and drawings of the nineteenth- and early-twentieth-century seal hunt are complemented by a narrative in which Mowat draws on literature, folklore, and his own imagination to convey the heroism and tragedy of the sealing industry. Mowat's love affair with the people of Newfoundland, whom he described as 'the last primordial human beings left in our part of the world', was shattered after the events he describes in *A whale for the killing* (1972, rpr. 2005). His failed attempts to save the stranded whale and his account of the affair alienated him from the people he had been living among.

Mowat has been greatly criticized for his belief that one should never spoil a good story for lack of exaggeration. He has

Mowat

responded to a description of his work as 'subjective non-fiction' by saying that 'I try to tell the truth about the human condition without, on the one hand, letting the facts get in my way and, on the other hand, inventing situations which might suit my purpose.' Mowat's concern for endangered species has run the full gamut from Inuit to Newfoundland outports, to whales and wolves. In 1983, Disney made *Never cry wolf* (1963, rpr. 1992) into a heartfelt and convincing film conveying the book's message that wolves are not vicious but a necessary and useful element in the natural cycle.

Sailing has always been important to Mowat and he has written vividly about it in several books. *The grey seas under* (1959, rpr. 1981) is a history of the Foundation Company's salvage tug, and *The serpent's coil* (1961, rpr. 1989) is another sea narrative about a daring rescue accomplished during a hurricane. *Westviking: the ancient Norse in Greenland and North America* (1965, rpr. 1990) is a popular account of Viking exploration and settlement; the liberties Mowat took in this work, however, did not endear him to historians or archaeologists.

Mowat's broad definition of poetic license has been more enthusiastically received in his novels for young people: *Lost in the Barrens* (1956, GGA, rpr. 1987) was later made into a television film. Its sequel, *The curse of the Viking grave* (1974, rpr. 1987), and *The black joke* (1962, rev. 1987), about rum-running off the coast of Newfoundland, reflect the interests apparent in Mowat's books for adults. But his accounts of his own childhood in Saskatoon best display his abilities as a storyteller. Mutt, a canine of remarkable personality, is featured in *The dog who wouldn't be* (1957, rpr. 1993), along with Weep and Wol, who appear again in *Owls in the family* (1961, rev. 1989). The same wonderful light humour is evident in *The boat who wouldn't float* (1969, rpr. 1992).

Mowat turned again to his own youth for inspiration with *And no birds sang* (1979, rpr. 2003), about his experience of the Second World War, which covers essentially the same subject matter as *The regiment* (1955, rev. 1989). *The world of Farley Mowat* edited by Peter Davison (1980) was followed by *Sea of slaughter* (1984), which marked a return to discussions about the environment. His later books include *My discovery of America* (1985), *Virunga: the passion of Dian Fossey* (1987), *The new founde land: a personal voyage of discovery* (1989), *Rescue the earth* (1990), *My father's son: memoirs of war and peace* (1992, rpr. 1993), *Born naked* (1993, rpr. 1995), *Aftermath: travels in a post-war*

world (1995), *The farfarers: before the Norse* (1998), and *Walking on the land* (2000). *Bay of Spirits: a love story* (2006) is a memoir of Mowat's life in the 1950s when he met Claire Wheeler on the island of St Pierre (part of the Miquelon islands) and later married—this is one love story. The other is with Newfoundland: the book is also a wonderful account, by a great storyteller, of sailing along the southern coast of Newfoundland in his fishing schooner, the *Happy Adventure*. See also *A Farley Mowat reader* (1998), edited by Wendy Thomas, and James KING's biography, *The life of Farley Mowat* (2002). In 2008, at the age of eighty-seven, Mowat, published a beautifully written and interesting memoir called *Otherwise*.

Mulhallen, Karen (b. 1942). Born in Woodstock, Ontario, she was educated at Waterloo Lutheran University (B.A, 1963) and earned graduate degrees in the Department of English, University of Toronto (M.A., 1967, Ph.D., 1975). She taught English at what is now Ryerson University, Toronto, in 1966–70 and 1973–2000, when she became a full professor. She joined the University of Toronto as a professor in the Department of English in 2007. Her career has been manifold, encompassing, besides her teaching, most notably, her influential association with the magazine DESCANT, of which she was assistant editor for a year when it was founded in 1971 and became publisher and editor-in-chief, a role she has upheld admirably until the present, editing many special issues. She was associated with the CANADIAN FORUM as poetry review editor (1974–9) and arts features editor (1975–88). As a writer she has published many articles and reviews, and the prose work *In the era of acid rain* (1993), of which the author says 'This is a love story'. But it has also been described as a travel book, though one that has a fictional element when the author imaginatively alters the reality of people, places, and time. She is most devoted, however, to her work as a poet. Her collections include *Modern love: poems 1970–1989* (1990); *War surgery (1981–1995): a jazz catafalque* (1996); *The caverns of Ely* (1997), a long poem; *The grace of private passage* (2000); and *Sea light* (2003). In Mulhallen's impressionistic poems—focusing mainly on travel, landscape, and personal relationships—the world, in various ways, mirrors her psychic or emotional state, around which many of her poems are created.

Munro, Alice (b. 1931). Born Alice Laidlaw in Wingham, southwestern Ontario, Alice

Munro started writing in her early teens. After studying English for two years at the University of Western Ontario, she left to marry James Munro in 1951 and moved to Vancouver and then to Victoria, British Columbia, where her husband opened a bookstore. (Munro's is still a presence in the city.) While helping with the business and raising three daughters, Munro began her writing career with short stories published in magazines— 'Thanks for the ride' appeared in Issue 2 (1957) of *The TAMARACK REVIEW* and 'The peace of Utrecht' appeared in Issue 15 (1960)—and broadcast by the Canadian Broadcasting Corporation (CBC). Divorced in 1976, she returned to live in southwestern Ontario with her second husband, Gerald Fremlin; they divide their time between Clinton, Ont., and Comox, British Columbia.

Munro's first collection of stories, *Dance of the happy shades* (1968, GGA; rpr. 2005), was followed by *Lives of girls and women* (1971, rpr. 2009), Munro's only novel—but there is a story-like shape to the chapters. A second collection, *Something I've been meaning to tell you* (1974, rpr. 1996), was followed by *Who do you think you are?* (1978, GGA; rpr. 2006), a group of stories held together, like *Lives of girls and women*, by a single protagonist whose experiences are presented more or less chronologically. (The American and English editions are entitled *The beggar maid*.) Some of the stories in *The moons of Jupiter* (1982, rpr. 2006) were previously published in *The New Yorker*, where Munro has continued to appear. The book presents a variety of minutely observed characters dealing with familiar situations of everyday life. *The progress of love* (1986, GGA; rpr. 2006) explores relationships between the sexes and among families, with an increasing focus on the nature of storytelling. The stories in *Friend of my youth* (1990, rpr. 2007) focus almost exclusively on adult situations, in increasingly complex, multi-layered narratives. In *Open secrets* (1994, rpr. 2007) Munro pushes her fiction beyond realism, allowing for a variety of possible interpretations of 'truth'; the title is ironic, in that many of the stories do not fully reveal their secrets. Munro chose twenty-eight stories from the earlier books and arranged them in chronological order for her *Selected stories* (1996, rpr. 1998). This was followed by *The love of a good woman* (1998, rpr. 2007), another collection of stories that define important moments in women's lives. It was awarded the GILLER PRIZE.

By carefully focusing on the telling action or statement, Munro excels at revealing the surprising depth and complexity in the emotional lives of ordinary people. In the earlier books such revelations are often filtered through the consciousness of a girl who feels herself to be 'different' from those around her, usually because she is a secretly developing artist in an environment hostile to art. An imaginative girl's response to social pressures and the expectations of others, especially her mother, is the central subject of *Lives of girls and women*, as it is of many of the stories. The girl's steady desire to be like everyone else, to avoid mockery and humiliation, persists in many of Munro's adult women. Munro is par excellence the artist of social embarrassment and unease, capturing the obscure moments of shame that plague both child and adult. In the later stories her adult writer figures suffer from a sense of shame at being professional *voyeuses* who open secrets and lay things bare. Munro also depicts, with wry humour, the nuances of female response to what she sees as the pleasurable tyranny of sex. Del's mother in *Lives of girls and women* foresees a time when women will not assess their own worth only through their relationship with men; but in the life-story of Rose in *Who do you think you are?*, Munro shows how difficult it is for even the most competent women to break that 'connection'. Without a man, Rose feels undefined; an uncertain affair with a distant married man can validate her identity. Munro continues to explore this theme in several of the stories in *The moons of Jupiter*. The title story celebrates the father when a daughter must come to terms with his approaching death. (Munro's own father, shortly before his death, wrote a novel entitled *The MacGregors: a novel of an Ontario pioneer family*, 1979.) Although she creates accurate portraits of men, particularly in this volume, Munro only occasionally writes from a male point of view; her chief interest is in the lives of girls and women and in their influence on one another. The mother-daughter relationship is the central female connection; in the title story of *Friend of my youth*; the narrator accepts the fact that she will never fully understand or accurately describe her mother, never exorcize her guilt about their mutual past. In several of the later stories the narrator is herself a mother, painfully aware of the difficulty of communication across the generations. From her earliest stories, Munro has portrayed characters who have an interest in storytelling, whether as an art form or as an instinctive shaping of reality to make it understandable, bearable, or simply more dramatic. In the later work, especially in *Open secrets*, she experiments with an apparent realism that nevertheless moves to an area where seemingly contradictory interpretations are possible. Her narrators often seem puzzled by what they are telling; their non-linear accounts give the illusion of several stories being told at once, story lying behind or beside story. Letters, diaries, dreams, poems are devices to explore the mystery of communication, underscoring the notion that we can never know what 'really' happened, never fully understand other people or even ourselves. An exchange of letters begins the first story, 'Carried away' in *Open secrets*. It is 1817 and the letters are between two residents of Carstairs, Ontario, who don't know each other: Louisa, the librarian, is written to by Jack Agnew, overseas in the Great War, who had admired her in the library, and Louisa responds. Letters change the life of Joanna, the housekeeper for Mr McCauley and his granddaughter Sabitha, in the title story of *Hateship, friendship, courtship, loveship, marriage* (2002, rpr. 2008). Written by Edith, Sabitha's mischievous school friend, they involve Ken Boudreau, Sabitha's father who lives in Saskatchewan, and Johanna; exchanges between father and daughter are supplemented by Edith's sham letters that contrive a romance. Johanna leaves Mr McCauley, travels west to Boudreau, who is sick, and takes over his life. The essence of the story is not its surprise ending but the demonstrated power of storytelling, and the characters—their portrayal, their motives—and the inclusion of many details, such as Sabitha's game of the title, played by crossing out the duplication of letters in a boy's name and her own, counting the remainder, and ticking off the number to the refrain 'Hateship, Friendship….' 'The bear came over the mountain' in this collection inspired the film *Away From Her*, starring Julie Christie, Gordon Pinsent, and Olympia Dukakis; the collection with that title (2007) has a Foreword by the film's director, Sarah Polley. *Runaway* (2004, rpr. 2005) won the GILLER PRIZE. Other recent collections are *No love lost* (2003, NCL), selected and with an Afterword by Jane URQUHART, and *My best stories* (2006, rpr. 2009) with an Introduction by Margaret ATWOOD.

Munro has set some of her stories in British Columbia, Toronto, and elsewhere—one even as far afield as Albania—but it is with rural southwestern Ontario that she is most closely identified. She captures the look and atmosphere of small towns that resemble her birthplace, of the ramshackle dwellings at their outskirts and the rundown farms nearby. Reality is heightened with such clarity of remembered detail that it is, in Munro's words, 'not real but true'. She achieves her vivid re-creations of place and people by detailing all that the senses might register in a room, a street or on a person; she often lists objects, or qualifies a noun with a catalogue of adjectives that usually contains at least one surprising and satisfying oddity or paradox. It is characteristic of Munro's wit that a single word will strike home forcefully because it is both unexpected and yet completely right. Quasi-conversational repetition gives the appearance of artlessness to the prose, making the narrative seem spontaneous and immediate.

The view from Castle Rock (2006) is the result of Munro's researching the history of the Laidlaw side of her family, beginning with those who lived in the Ettrick Valley, about fifty miles south of Edinburgh. What she found began to shape itself into 'something like stories' and 'a curious re-creation of lives'. The Laidlaws who came to Canada left Scotland in 1818. (We also read about a literary ancestor who did not leave Scotland, James Hogg, whose mother was a Laidlaw. His collected works have so far appeared in twenty-three volumes, but he is best known as the author of *The private memoirs and confessions of a justified sinner*, first published in 1824.) When the narrative arrives at the time of her own parents, the reader takes pleasure in realizing that the complex feelings and acute observations she bestows on her fictional characters also enrich the portrayals here of her parents. Her father: 'He began to be talked about and thought about more as a trapper than as a young farmer…. He was edging away from the life of a farmer, just as he had edged away earlier from the idea of getting an education and becoming a professional man…. He was making money from his trapline. Some skins could bring him as much as a fortnight's work on a threshing gang.' The price of the furs fluctuated but in 1940, when he was married with a family, the prices were at their worst. Her mother was challenged. In the summer 1941 she went off with a trunkload of furs to a hotel in Muskoka. When Alice and her father drive up to collect her, they find the dining room and see two women sitting at a table near the kitchen having a late supper. One of the women turned, saw them, and came forward. 'The moment in which I did not realize this was my mother was not long, but there was a moment…. And even when I knew this was my mother, when she had put her arms round me and kissed me, spilling out an unaccustomed fragrance and showing none of her usual hurry and regrets, none of her usual dissatisfaction with my appearance, or my nature,

I felt that she was somehow still a stranger. She had crossed effortlessly, it seemed, into the world of the hotel, where my father and I stood out like tramps or scarecrows—it was as if she had always been living there.' She was full of her success in selling the furs. The final story in the book, 'What do you want to know for?', begins with the narrator and her husband driving through a country graveyard. She notices 'a large, unnatural mound blanketed with grass.' They looked around but found 'no clues as to who or what might be hidden inside.' A year after this the narrator learns the results of a mammogram: there was a lump deep in her left breast that 'neither my doctor nor I had been able to feel.' While waiting to see a city doctor about a biopsy, the challenge of finding the grass-covered crypt appealed to her strongly and the two themes—the investigative and the deeply personal—take over. The countryside and some of its people and history are revealed to them, and the grass-covered crypt is found, but its contents remain secret. In the end the narrator learns that a biopsy is not required: the lump is probably safe. 'Such frights will come and go. / Then there'll be one that won't. One that won't go.' In 2009 Munro published a new collection of ten stories, *Too much happiness*. She received the prestigious (and profitable) Lannan Literary Award (fiction) in 1995, and in May 2009 the Man Booker International Prize for Fiction ($100,000) for an entire body of work.

See *Lives of mothers and daughters: growing up with Alice Munro* (2001, rpr. 2008) by Sheila Munro, a delightful book that is both a biography and personal memoir, containing lots of enjoyable family snapshots; *Alice Munro: paradox and parallel* (1989) by W.R. Martin; and *Alice Munro: a double life* (1992) by Catherine Sheldrick Ross. See also two archival works published by the Canadian Archival Inventory, Literary Papers: *The Alice Munro papers: first accession* (1986) compiled by Jean M. Moore and Jean Tener, edited by Apollonia Steele; *Second accession* (1987) compiled by Jean M. Moore, edited by Apollonia Steele and Jean Tener.

Munsch, Robert (b. 1945). He was born in Pittsburg, Pennsylvania, as a middle child in a family of nine children. He earned a B.A. in history (Fordham University, 1969), an M.A. in anthropology (Boston University, 1971), and an M.Ed. in early childhood education (Tufts University, 1973), and devoted seven years of study towards becoming a Jesuit priest. Later, employed at the University of Guelph, Ontario, as a lecturer

(1975–80) and assistant professor (1980–4) in the Department of Family Studies, at the urging of a librarian he submitted for publication some of the stories he had made up and told to children. Now a full-time writer and oral performer living in Guelph, Ontario, Munsch has written over thirty books that have sold more than 20 million copies in North America. His storytelling performances are unique in that he often selects a child and makes up a story from details he elicits on the spot. Children like the respect he shows them in stories: they always cope successfully when events spin out of control. His stories usually contain repeated motifs, extraordinary vocal sound effects, surprising turns of event, humour that appeals to children, and something he calls an 'adult twist'. His first two books— *Mud puddle* (1979, rpr. 1996) and *The dark* (1979, rpr. 1997)—were followed by the immensely popular *The paper bag princess* (1980, rpr. 1994), a feminist fairy-tale retelling. His bestselling book, *Love you forever* (1986), which has sold more than 10 million copies and was on the *New York Times'* bestseller list of children's books, has also been controversial because of its darkness (like many of his stories) and its sadness. Other books include *Show and tell* (1991), *Get me another one* (1992), *Andrew's loose tooth* (1998), *Get out of bed!* (1998), and *Aaron's hair* (2000). The large-format *Much more Munsch!: a Robert Munsch collection* (2007)—illustrated by Michael Martchenko and Alan and Lea Daniel—includes five of his books and some new poems, and ends with questions and answers featuring author and artists. *Look at me!*, illustrated by Martchenko, is a 2008 publication. Munsch's titles have appeared as tapes, filmstrips, movies, and plays, and have been translated into a multitude of languages. He was made a Member of the Order of Canada in 1999.

Murray, John Clark (1836–1917). Born at Thread and Tannahill, near Paisley, Scotland, he was educated in religion and philosophy at Edinburgh, Scotland, and Heidelberg and Göttingen, Germany. In 1862 he came to Canada to teach at Queen's University, Kingston. Ten years later he moved to McGill University, Montreal, where he remained until his retirement. His *Outline of Sir William Hamilton's philosophy* (Boston, 1870) is a faithful presentation of the beliefs of his teacher at Edinburgh, but Murray had already begun to react against the 'common sense realism' of Hamilton. He emphasized the rational order and ultimate unity of reality in a manner closer to Hegel and the British idealists, and akin to that of his successor at Queen's, John WAT- SON. His theory is outlined in his two works on philosophical psychology: *Handbook of psychology* (London, 1885) and *Introduction to psychology* (1904), in which Murray denied the possibility of a mechanical explanation of the human mind, argued that the concept of per- sonality was central to psychology, and laid some of the foundations of his theory of value. His books were widely translated. His *Indus- trial kingdom of God*—probably written in 1887, but not published until 1981—advances pro- posals for economic reform that envisage chiefly a co-operative society and a system for the public determination of certain wages and prices. Murray read and commented on Marx and Henry George, but the main inspiration for this book was evidently the co-operative movement and his belief that Christianity provided the only basis for a just society of free human beings. Though he frequently quoted scripture in his social commentaries, he tried to develop his ethical theory from an analysis of the concept of person; he praised Christian- ity chiefly for having made the concept of person central to Western thought. Murray fought early, long, and hard for the education of women. His writings on this subject, and his defence of Canadian nationhood, are con- tained in letters, occasional newspaper and magazine articles, and handwritten notes. The basis of Murray's moral theory can be found in his *Introduction to ethics* (London, 1891) and *Handbook of Christian ethics* (Edinburgh, 1908), as well as in his social-gospel novel *He that received the five talents* (London, 1904), which undoubtedly helped to make popular the reformist views of Christianity that figured in other social-gospel novels.

Murrell, John (b. 1945). Born in Lubbock, Texas, he received a B.F.A. from Southwest- ern University, Texas (1966), after which he came to Canada and studied at the Univer- sity of Calgary (B.Ed., 1969). Murrell has been associated with a number of major Canadian theatres, including Alberta Theatre Projects, Calgary, where he was playwright- in-residence (1975–6); the Stratford Festival as an associate director (1977–8); Theatre Calgary as a dramaturge (1981–2); and the Banff Centre School of Fine Arts Playwrights Colony as Head (1986). From 1988 to 1992 he was the Head of The CANADA COUNCIL's Theatre Section. In 1999 he was appointed artistic director of the Theatre Arts Depart- ment of the Banff Centre for the Arts.

Among Murrell's early plays, Alberta Theatre Projects produced in 1975 *A great noise, a great light*, which is set in 1937 and deals with the politician William Aberhart, and marks the beginning of Murrell's recurring theatrical explorations of historical figures. Other early plays, which were produced, include *Hayden's head*, 1973; *Teaser*, 1975, with Kenneth Dyba; and *Arena*, 1975. Murrell received inter- national acclaim for *Memoir* (1978), which was produced at the Guelph Spring Festival (1977) in a production that starred the late Irish actor Siobhan McKenna as Sarah Bern- hardt. The play is starkly simple, a depiction of the reminiscences of the aging Bernhardt, who is attended by the play's only other character, her faithful secretary and servant Pitou, played in the original production by Gerard Parkes. The two actors reprised their roles in Dublin (1977) and London (1978). *Memoir* has been produced throughout Can- ada and was adapted for a CBC Radio pro- duction (1980). It has also been translated into a number of languages, and published in German (1979) and French (1979). An abridged French version, *Sarah et le crie de la langouste*, enjoyed a run of three years in Paris before being featured in the 1984 Edinburgh Festival. *Memoir* displays Murrell's gift for precise, elegant dialogue that reveals nuances of character, with an often understated, poi- gnant humour. These qualities are apparent in *Waiting for the parade* (1980), a study of five women living in Calgary during the Second World War. In *Farther west* (1986), May, a prostitute, moves 'farther west' in an attempt to escape the social and sexual constraints imposed by men who fall in love with her and demand that she settle into domesticity with them. Like many of Murrell's plays, *Farther west* deals with the character's fear of being constrained, which the playwright explores through spatial metaphors. When May finally reaches the Pacific Ocean she meets her death. In *New world* (1986) the three Rennie siblings gather at the edge of Canada, on the southwest coast of Vancouver Island, which serves as a metaphor for the edge of the world. On a single day the three speak of their yearnings, which amount finally to a longing for stability. *Democracy* (1992) depicts an exchange between Ralph Waldo Emerson and Walt Whitman, who is attending two young men, Pete and Jimmy. Set during a day spent by the characters at the side of a pond—evocative of Walden Pond—Whitman's idealism seems to flourish only in this natural idyll, removed from the violence and inhumanity of daily life.

Murrell admits to an admiration for artists whose work has nourished him. Two of his other plays, *October* and *The faraway nearby* (1995), both produced by Tarragon Theatre, Toronto (the former in 1988, the latter in 1995), depict artists. *October* offers an encounter between Eleonora Duse and Isadora Duncan, and *The faraway nearby* portrays the last year of the reclusive Georgia O'Keeffe and her friendship with the much younger artist, Juan Hamilton. Murrell was made an Officer of the Order of Canada in 2002.

Musgrave, Susan (b. 1951). Born in Santa Cruz, California, of Canadian parents who moved to Victoria, British Columbia, she is a great-granddaughter of Sir Anthony Musgrave, governor of the Crown colony of British Columbia, 1869–71. She attended Oak Bay High School until grade ten. Mentored by Robin SKELTON, whom she met as babysitter for his children, she had poems published in *The MALAHAT REVIEW* at sixteen. She travelled widely, living in California (1967–9), Ireland (1970–2), and her 'spiritual home', the Queen Charlotte Islands of B.C. (1972–4). She now lives in Sydney, B.C. Musgrave has led a flamboyant and notorious public personal life. Her three marriages were to a lawyer; to one of his clients, a drug dealer; and the third, nationally televised in a maximum-security prison, to a convicted bank robber, Stephen Reid, author of *Jackrabbit parole* (1988), whom she met through a correspondence writing course. Her husband, having been freed, has once again been imprisoned.

Musgrave's first poetry collection, *Songs of the sea-witch* (1970), published when she was eighteen, introduced many of her subsequent themes: roots, witches, fire, water, eroticism, and death. The landscape of the West Coast permeates her writing. Her poetic persona often searches for an identity against a mythological landscape of animated rocks and water. Her sensibilities incline towards both the contemporary and the aboriginal; her response to the modern urban world is either outrage or witty denunciation, though her often beautiful lyrics can slip into vagueness. *Entrance of the celebrant* (1972) celebrates the will of the imagination in brooding, mystical, ritualistic poems. *Grave-dirt and selected strawberries* (1973) includes a poetic sequence entitled 'Kiskatinaw songs', written in collaboration with Seán VIRGO during a period of homesickness in Cambridge, England. Originally published as a pamphlet, the poems were unsuccessful until they were republished under the pseudonym 'Moses

Bruce', an Amerindian. The 'strawberry poems' were inspired by a road sign. While most poets prefer a selected poems, Musgrave jokingly published *Selected strawberries* (1973), a book-length satire with gleanings from *The golden bough, Everything you always wanted to know about sex*, the journals of Anais Nin, *The Guinness book of records*, cookbooks, and self-help manuals. Beneath this satirical mythology, the strawberry emerges as a likeable main character. The collection, with minor revisions, was republished as *Selected strawberries and other poems* (1977), which includes *Entrance of the celebrant. The impstone* (1976) is a transitional book. More intimate, more approachable, more restrained and mature, it drew inspiration from the imp, the animal that helps a witch cast spells. In these fifty-three Gothic poems, the evocative and suggestive vocabulary of earth, stone, water, evil, witches, ghosts, moon, shadows, graves, dreams, night, and animals is utilized in a ritualistic manner to invoke an animistic landscape. Several of the poems deal with the problems of relationships. With mature poems like 'Fishing on a snowy evening', Musgrave moved from the sea-witch of youth to a more confident voice. In *Becky Swann's book* (1977)—reprinted in *A man to marry, a man to bury* (1979)—familiar images and simple details move quickly to a Dantesque moral vision in a Canadian setting, with scathing commentary on contemporary moral issues. The first poems invoke some of the most haunting love poems in Canadian letters, but they quickly move into a depressing world of loveless marriage, breakup, bizarre murder, degenerate ways among Native people, deformity, abortion, and dying. Musgrave counterbalances these with poems of genuine friendship (especially with the poet Marilyn BOWERING), caring, love, and acceptance in a carefully constructed sequence, 'Salmonberry Road', which explores friendship from delight to murderous fantasy to profound loss. *Tarts and muggers: poems new and selected* (1982)—mostly a selection from previous books—relies on shock values (rats on a face or dead-animal imagery) that produce a vision of an empty, hostile, loveless world. The best poem, 'Woodcutter, river God, and I', is a classic of mythological understatement. Musgrave's tenth collection, *Cocktails at the mausoleum* (1985), deals with the psyche, relationships, and her response to places where she has lived. A powerful awareness of being alone is countered with a tinge of hope in a deep need to love another person. She also includes a deeply felt Queen Charlotte Islands poem, 'Requiem for Talunkwun Island', a lament for the loss of the forest to loggers and a simple primordial life. *The embalmer's art* (1991) is a well-chosen selection from collections published between 1970 and 1991, with half-a-dozen new poems. *Forcing the narcissus* (1994) is filled with poems about brutality, death, violence, pain, and cruelty that are startling and even beautiful rather than depressing—and accepting, as these subjects are calmly examined. Pain and cruelty appear also in the love poems, referring to several loves, which can be ardent ('I take you into me, my heart / a wilder place than all the world beyond'—'The small night so alone out there') and, in 'Razor-wire, Millhaven Penitentiary', searing ('It slices through my heart / the way it surrounds you, / and something the colour of blood / spills out. In so much blackness / the heart leaps, jumps a beat / by the wall, goes over'). *Things that keep and do not change* (1999) is an outstanding Musgrave collection threaded with images of danger, fear, sex (even 'the sex of money'), and containing threatening dream poems as well as the light and humorous poem 'Do not make loon soup (valuable advice from the Eskimo cookbook)', in which, failing to write a poem about Canadian unity, she invites some poet friends for a party and Joe ROSENBLATT 'brought the entrée, a loon fresh / from Qualicum Beach'; after the cleaned bird was tossed into the stockpot and cooked, Lorna CROZIER found the title advice in the cookbook (but the poem on Canadian unity was written). *What the small day cannot hold: collected poems 1970–1985*, with an Introduction by Seán Virgo, was published in 2000. In 2009 Musgrave published *When the world was not our home: selected poems 1985–2000*.

Musgrave's interest in West Coast mythologies, Frazerian symbolism, militant feminism, and the mysterious is also evident in her first novel (called by her an apprentice work), *The charcoal burners* (1980), a modern horror story and a study in depravity, in which Matty, a sociologist married to an Amerindian living in East Oyster, B.C., is led by her lover, Christian Hawker, into the wilderness, where she meets a band of feminists from California who live off the land and practise a ritualistic religion based on ancient fertility rites and radical feminist ideology. Nearby live the charcoal burners, twentieth-century dropouts led by a Mansonesque madman known as the Chela. A powerful and original first novel, it has a serious structural flaw, with a naturalistic first half clumsily connected to a bizarre, almost surreal conclusion.

Musgrave's second novel, *The dancing chicken* (1987), which describes the degenerate life of a lawyer and his emotionally crippled family, was savagely reviewed and dismissed as clichéd and stilted, though it is a funny comedy of manners. *Cargo of orchids* (2000, rpr. 2001), which has an unnamed narrator who is on death row in the Heavenly Valley State Facility for Women, is weighed down by lurid details. Her past life—she became involved in a family-controlled drug cartel operating out of South America, fell in love with a son, became pregnant, was forcibly taken to Tranquilandia, an evil island off the coast of Colombia, and was made dependent on cocaine—is interwoven with the minutiae of her existence on death row, and her relationship with her fellow inmates: Rainey placed her Siamese twins on tracks to be run over by a train, and Frenchy killed her adolescent son. Disregard for human life, revenge, power, money, human vulnerability, and the horrors of capital punishment—all are given hyperbolic treatment.

Behind Musgrave's intelligence and often dark tone, there is charm and humour, which surface in her journalism. Two collections of her practical and entertaining newspaper and magazine articles, *Great Musgrave* (1989) and *Musgrave landing: musings on the writing life* (1994), present her always enjoyable, sometimes sarcastic thoughts on the often difficult life of a writer. Described in the first book are several love affairs and her wedding in prison. The title on the cover of Musgrave's latest memoir reads *You're in Canada now ...: a memoir of sorts* (2005), but the full title ends with 'motherfucker', quoting the words of a Mountie to an American dope smuggler in one of Musgrave's anecdotes. The book is a series of short pieces on a life full of waywardness, troubles, happiness, and love—including being institutionalized by her parents for nymphomania and leaving her first husband for a drug smuggler in Colombia—that evokes a vivid writer who has somehow managed to keep herself (and her two daughters) whole and continues to write informatively, sometimes memorably. Towards the end of the book she writes about her relationship with Stephen. 'Stephen and I were married in prison, in 1986, when he was serving the last months of a twenty-year sentence for bank robbery.... I visited him behind bars for two years before asking him to marry me. There was a small problem—I was already married at the time—but nothing our love couldn't rise above.... Our married life went into remission the day my husband failed to successfully rob the Royal Bank in the peaceful Cook Street Village, in Victoria, British Columbia on June 9th, 1999. Stephen remembers little of the car chase through Beacon Hill Park, or shooting at police officers who pursued him.'

Musgrave edited *Nerves out loud: critical moments in the lives of seven teen girls* (2001) and *Certain things about my mother: daughters speak* (2003).

Mysterious stranger, The. See Walter BATES.

N

NCL. See NEW CANADIAN LIBRARY.

Neatby, Hilda (1904–75). Born in Sutton, Surrey, England, and brought to a small Saskatchewan town two years later, she was educated at the University of Saskatchewan (B.A., 1924; M.A., 1927), at the Sorbonne, Paris, and at the University of Minnesota (Ph.D., 1934), supported by scholarships. Her doctoral thesis was published as *The administration of justice under the Quebec Act* (1937). Neatby was determined to invade the male preserve of historical scholarship, but it was not until 1945 that she secured a position as associate professor in the history department of the University of Saskatchewan, where she spent most of her academic career as a specialist in the history of Québec. Iconoclastic writings on education brought Neatby to the attention of Vincent Massey and appointment in 1949 to the Royal Commission on National Development in the Arts, Letters and Sciences. Her contributions were central to the Commission's report and Neatby became a speechwriter for Massey while he was governor general. In *So little for the mind* (1953) and *A temperate dispute* (1954), which aroused enormous debate, Neatby decried the emphasis placed in public education on physical facilities and administration at the expense of curriculum. She wrote for the Canadian Centenary Series *Quebec: the revolutionary age, 1760–1791*, which was published in 1966. The following year she was made a Companion of the Order of Canada. Frequently encountering male prejudice, and interested in promoting the place of women in intellectual life, Neatby was nevertheless typical of her generation in toeing the line to male consensus in her historical work. The subtitle of her last book, *Queen's University*

Vol. 1 1841–1914: and not to yield, published posthumously in 1978, was from a phrase in Tennyson's 'Ulysses', 'to strive, to seek, to find, and not to yield', and conveyed her own tenacity. A selection of her writings, *So much to do, so little time* (1983), was edited by Michael Hayden.

Nelligan, Émile (1879–1941). Born in Montreal, he was the son of David Nelligan, a postal inspector of Irish extraction, and Émilie-Amanda Hudon. He acquired his early education at Montreal's École Olier (1886–90) and Mont Saint-Louis (1890–3); his numerous absences set him back in his studies and forced him to repeat his third year. At the Collège de Montréal (1893–5) he twice repeated his course in elementary Latin and, after a six-month delay, registered at the Collège Sainte-Marie for two semesters (Mar. 1896–Feb. 1897). At seventeen he was two years behind his schoolmates and, against his parents' wishes, decided to abandon his studies. He wished only to be a poet; he was already writing verses and could envision for himself no other profession than that of an artist. In 1896 he answered a call for poems from *Le Samedi* and published his first poems, under the pseudonym 'Émile Kovar' (13 June– 19 Sept.), which plainly show the influence of Verlaine and Baudelaire. Nelligan introduced a '*frisson nouveau*' into a literary milieu dominated by the Romantic and patriotic epic. If he is sometimes Parnassian in his descriptions, he is so in the Symbolist manner, stressing the subjective impression ('Rythmes du soir', 'Rêve de Watteau'). Unlike his contemporaries, who produced philosophical and moralistic poetry, Nelligan showed a remarkable sensitivity to the power of words and the music of language. He adhered to Verlaine's precept, 'Music above all', and his revisions show a preoccupation with the evocative power inherent in sonority. Like his French masters, he expressed, in poems of melancholy ('Soir d'hiver') and nostalgia ('Le jardin de l'enfance'), an essential unfitness for life that was bound up in the demands of poetry itself. Poems published in *Le Monde illustré* (1897–8) appeared for the first time under his real name, which was sometimes modified to 'Émile Nellighan'. In 1898 Nelligan's poetic output fell off, possibly because of a journey he planned to make to England. His father, not content with his son's total preoccupation with poetry, would have found him a place in the merchant marine—a venture that never took place, however, since in October Nelligan was publishing poems in *La Patrie*. At the end of 1898 Nelligan joined the École littéraire de Montréal, which was increasingly becoming an important intellectual movement. By bringing together poets of diverse leanings, and refusing to address political and religious matters, the group declared its intention of giving special rules and autonomy to literature. During its heyday in 1899, when Nelligan was participating in the group's public readings, he achieved a great triumph after reciting his 'La romance du vin', an impassioned reply to detractors of poetry. But this, his most glorious moment as a poet, was his last public appearance. He was confined to the Saint-Benoît asylum, apparently for exhibiting signs of derangement. Nelligan had published only twenty-three poems, but in 1903, thanks to the devotion of his friend Louis Dantin (Eugène Seers), and with his mother's help, 107 poems were collected in *Émile Nelligan et son oeuvre*, which revealed his lyricism, his melancholy, and his nostalgia for childhood; it also contained 'Le vaisseau d'or' ('The ship of gold'), which has been perceived as a premonition of his madness. During more than forty years of confinement, Nelligan continued to write; but, having lost the capability to create a body of work, he contented himself with rewriting poems and fragments. The writer Dr Ernest Choquette, who visited him in 1909, remarked that 'he showed an undeviating obsession with literature'. After his father's death in Oct. 1925, Nelligan was transferred to the public ward of the Saint-Jean-de-Dieu hospital. But all that emerged from this period were notebooks containing the poet's revised versions of earlier poems and versions of Baudelaire and other poets. The increased number of visitors Nelligan received during the 1930s attests to the growing public interest in *Émile Nelligan et son oeuvre*, which came out in its third edition in 1932. The last thing he worked on was a version of 'La Benedictine', dated 5 Apr. 1941, seven months before his death in November. P.F. Widdows translated a few of Nelligan's poems under the title *Selected poems* (1960, rpr. 2004), and in 1983 Fred COGSWELL published *The complete poems of Émile Nelligan* in translation.

New, W.H. (b.1938). William Herbert New was born in Vancouver and educated at the University of British Columbia (B. Ed., 1961, M.A., 1963) and the University of Leeds (Ph.D., 1966). Professor of English at the University of British Columbia (1965–2003)—he held the McLean Chair in Canadian Studies from 1995 to 1997—and editor of *CANADIAN LITERATURE* (1977–95), he is now University Killam Professor Emeritus (2003–). New amazingly combined these roles with his activities as the editor or author of more than thirty publications, including books on Canadian literature and culture and eight books of poetry. He received the 2004 Governor General's International Award in Canadian Studies and in 2006 was appointed an Officer of the Order of Canada.

Two important literary reference books should perhaps be noted first. *A history of Canadian literature* (1989, 2nd edn 2003) is a solid work that, because of the enormous number of authors and works that had to be referred to in one volume, is a mere summary, but a wise and discriminating one that serves its purpose admirably. In some respects it strikes one as a contemporary, immensely abridged version of Carl KLINCK's *Literary history of Canada*, the second edition of which was published in three volumes in 1976. The New book concludes with a long, useful chronological table of publications, noting events in related periods. New's masterwork is *Encyclopedia of literature in Canada* (2002), of which he was editor, deciding on the wide range of (more than 1400) authors and subject entries and dealing with a huge number of contributors, for a work that is more than 1300 pages long and covers literature in English and French. What follows is a list of a few of the subject headings, some of them surprising. *Literary and publishing topics*: awards and literary prizes, archives, book history, book design, bookstores, comic-book literature, censorship, cowboy poetry, criticism and theory, editors and editing, Harlequin, life writing, literary history, long poem, music and literature, mystery and romance, newspapers, publishing industry, radio drama, reference guides, oral literature and history, reviewing. *Literary usages*: allegory, canon, imagery, irony, prosody. *Multicultural*: African-Canadian writing, Black history, cultural plurality, Mennonite writing, multicultural voices, Scottish and Gaelic literature. *Allusions in the literature to* Canadian Pacific Railway, Confederation, Halifax explosion, landscape, other countries (e.g., Africa, Australia, United States), Rebellions of 1837, Winnipeg General Strike, war. There are three indexes: of contributors, authors (including mentions of every name), and a supplementary index of names referred to in the entries. The author entries merely list book titles, for space reasons, with generalized comments about their content, but this is a phenomenal reference work and a substantial contribution to our culture.

New's large output of publications began with a biographical study, *Malcolm Lowry* (1971)—which was followed a few years later by another, *Margaret Laurence* (1977)—and *Articulating West: essays on purpose and form in modern Canadian literature* (1972), which contains essays on various Canadian authors or their books, including Frederick John NIVEN, E.J. PRATT, W.O. MITCHELL, Sinclair ROSS, Ethel WILSON, Hugh MACLENNAN, Mordecai RICHLER, Malcolm LOWRY, Margaret LAURENCE, Margaret AVISON, and Earle BIRNEY. He continued his Lowry studies with *Malcolm Lowry: a reference guide* (1978). In his Introduction to *Land sliding: imagining space, presence, and power in Canadian writing* (1997) New says: 'I am concerned in this book, then, not so much to explain what "land" is—to tabulate the dimensions of Canada, the statistics of ownership, the chronology of expansion—as to explain how various *configurations of land* function in literature (and so in Canadian culture at large) to question or confirm configurations of power.' *Borderlands: how we talk about Canada* (1998), in the Brenda and David McLean Canadian Studies Series, is made up of three provocative essays that explore the idea of the border as a metaphor (drawing on Canadians' interest in provincial borders, and the border with the US) as New discusses social issues, among them separatism, multiculturalism, national policies, language, and American influence. *Reading Mansfield and metaphors of form* (1999) is a penetrating critical study of the short stories of Katherine Mansfield, supported by research done in the Turnbull Library in New Zealand and the Newberry Library in Chicago. In *Grandchild of empire: about irony, mainly in the Commonwealth* (2003)—the 2002 Sedgewick lecture, Garnet

G. Sedgewick having been the founding head of the Department of English at the University of British Columbia—New glances at many topics, including family and family metaphors, social issues, language, and tone, in his readable overview of various kinds of irony. 'I see human affirmation as irony's oblique achievement.'

Among the many books New has edited are *Canadian writers in 1984: the 25th anniversary issue of Canadian Literature* (1984); and the textbook *Inside the poem: essays and poems in honour of Donald Stephens* (1992), which begins with poems by twenty-four well-known Canadian poets, followed by essays discussing the poems, and then twenty-eight new poems by more contemporary poets; the volume ends with a tribute to Donald STEPHENS by David WATMOUGH.

It is surprising that at least some of New's many collections of poetry are not better known outside of British Columbia. A resourceful poet, he writes for the most part clear, readable poems about his past, his environment time, memory, his travels, etc. The titles are *Science lessons* (1996) and in the same year *Raucous* (1999), *Stone/Rain* (2001), *Riverbook & ocean* (2002), *Night room* (2003), *Underwood log* (2004), *Touching Ecuador* (2006), and *Along a snake fence riding* (2007), a poem for eight voices. New's first collection, *Science lessons*, is a collection of mostly sonnet-length poems that seem to draw on his own growing up and the world around him at the time. *Stone/rain* is in three parts. 'Storyboards' was written after seeing the Northwest Coast Mask Exhibit at the Vancouver Art Gallery in 1998: 'Making the masks inscribes alter-/ natives, carves narratives/of being there://tree trans-/forming into teeth and painted/eye, turning wood to shadow/stories, spirit, played in breath.'; 'City limits' is a collective meditation on an unnamed city that is Vancouver; in the twenty-four short poems in 'Bicycle rack' bicycles are central as a traveller reflects on a city in China. In *Along a snake fence riding*, a long poem for eight voices, New meditates on time and memory: 'shouting a way out of nine months'/amniotic memory, we take whatever/time we have, to reach amnesia, saplings/fencing out—or in—the forest/we feed on: home, desire, the mountains whistling/*danger, come*'. Three collections of poems for children, illustrated by Vivian Bevis, are *Vanilla gorilla* (1998), *Llamas in the laundry* (2002), and *Dream helmet* (2005).

New Canadian Library. Officially launched on 17 Jan. 1958, MCCLELLAND & STEWART's

New Canadian Library

New Canadian Library is a quality paperback literary reprint series of outstanding or significant Canadian literary works. Malcolm ROSS, its general editor until 1978, conceived the idea in the early 1950s when he became frustrated by the lack of available texts to facilitate the teaching of Canadian literature in universities. While publisher and editor perceived post-secondary classes as the series' major market, they also hoped that some titles would appeal to secondary-school teachers and the public. An introduction, usually written by an academic, accompanied each of the more than 150 books issued under Ross's editorship. Mainly prose fiction, titles ranged from eighteenth-century works (Frances BROOKE's *The history of Emily Montague*) to such contemporary titles as Margaret LAURENCE's *The DIVINERS*. Financial concerns, related to book length, led to the abridgement of some works. This period also saw the emergence of two sub-series: NCL Originals, comprised of collections of poems or criticism, such as *Poets of the Confederation* and *Masks of fiction*, while the Canadian Writers Series, under the editorship of Dave GODFREY until the twelfth volume, consisted of brief monographs on Canadian writers. The NCL's success and the expansion of the study of Canadian literature encouraged other publishers to undertake similar reprint series, creating competition both in terms of sales and in the acquirement of titles. By the time of Ross's retirement in 1978, these circumstances had become troubling and provoked within M&S a lengthy period of reassessment. Titles added in the early 1980s were included at the publisher's sole discretion. After M&S's 1985 sale to Avie Bennett, plans for a revised NCL were initiated. David Staines was retained as general editor, an advisory board—Alice MUNRO, W.H. NEW, and Guy VANDERHAEGHE—was established, cover designs were in colour, many titles in the original series were allowed to go out of print, Introductions were abandoned in favour of Afterwords, and full texts replaced abridgements. The series was relaunched in 1988 and included four books by Margaret ATWOOD, two by Marie-Claire BLAIS, three by Morley CALLAGHAN, two by Mavis GALLANT, four by Frederick Philip GROVE, eight by Margaret LAURENCE, five by Stephen LEACOCK, four by L.M. MONTGOMERY, six by David Adams RICHARDS, nine by Mordecai RICHLER, seven by Gabrielle ROY, and six by Ethel WILSON, in addition to works by other writers. In 2007 a relaunched new edition of the NCL emerged, boasting all the books in trade paperback editions, their

Afterwords still maintaining prominence. This series, still under David Staines and his advisory board, now includes, for example, Robert KROETSCH and further translations from Québec literature. See *New Canadian Library: the Ross-McClelland years 1952–1978* (2007) by Janet B. Friskney.

New France, Writing in. 1. EXPLORATION LITERATURE forms the major part of writings related to New France, produced by missionaries, leaders of expeditions, or ghostwriters (partisans, compilers, printers). Most writers aimed to uphold the authority or defend the interests of an individual or group with business in New France, while also appealing to a public interested in new scientific information and exotic descriptions. Adopting one or more of numerous genres—chronicle, history, treatise, Utopia, satire, autobiography, official reports—this literature frequently projects a narrator's personality; it can also relate, as if it were the narrator's own experience, information acquired from various sources. Questions of veracity, plagiarism, or embellishment assail many of these books, which cannot always be understood as records of fact. Works discussed below are those available in English translation. The *JESUIT RELATIONS* are treated in a separate article.

Jacques Cartier (1491–1557) did not publish the accounts of his three journeys; in *Relations* (1986) Michel Bideaux defends their authenticity against the longstanding doubts of authorship reasonably raised by H.P. Biggar in his bilingual *The voyages of Jacques Cartier* (1924). The same title is given to an edition of the English translations in Biggar's book, with an introduction by Ramsay COOK, published in 1993; it includes documents relating to Cartier and the Sieur de Roberval. The first published work bearing Cartier's name, the *Bref récit ...* (Paris, 1515), is a third-person account of the second voyage (1535–6). It was followed by posthumous accounts of the first (1534) and third (1541–2) voyages. The latter is known only through fragments published in 1600 by Richard Hakluyt, while the account of the first voyage has an extremely complex publication history. The terse style of these works has led to the suggestion that they were derived from a ship's log, but the range of interest is fully that of a travel book, containing many memorable incidents and descriptions. Among these are the first meeting with an Iroquoian fishing party in the Baie des Chaleurs, the first sight of Stadac006 (Quebec City), the naming of Mont Royal, and the discovery of the much-needed cure for scurvy. Certain aphorisms, such as 'the land God gave to Cain', have become legendary, while data concerning vegetation, the Iroquoian language, and European adaptation are still prime information.

Marc Lescarbot (c. 1570–1642) was a Parisian lawyer and a writer before he was a traveller. His declared reason for going to Canada (at the invitation of Jean de Biencourt de Poutrincourt, who was one of his clients) was disgust with corrupt European society, particularly its courts (he had just lost a case). This was a conventional sentiment, but Lescarbot's originality lies in being the first writer in French to envision the New World as a desirable escape from the Old. Sailing for Acadia in 1606, he at once composed a poem, 'Adieu à la France', announcing a personal search for a lost Edenic paradise. In Port Royal he wrote commemorations of notable men and occasions. 'La défaite des sauvages armouchiquois' describes Native warfare in epic style. In his 'Le théâtre de Neptune', which was given the first theatrical performance in North America (1606), volleys of cannon and musket shot, trumpet fanfares, and the tomfoolery of sailors were ingeniously combined with verse speeches to mark the lieutenant-governor's return from an expedition. The written text, a mere 243 lines, has Neptune, six Tritons, four *sauvages*, and one cheery companion offering fulsome tribute to Poutrincourt. Native words and local objects are combined with classical poetic conventions. The play was obviously meant for fun, but the mock-pompous style contains a serious declaration of colonial ambitions for France. On his way to and from Acadia, Lescarbot also wrote twelve poems—later collected in *Les muses de la Nouvelle France* (Paris, 1609), which included 'Le théâtre de Neptune'—expressing enthusiasm for exploration. His clear, declamatory verse has no obvious continuity in Canada. In Lescarbot's *Histoire de la Nouvelle-France* (three Paris editions: 1609, 1611–12, and 1617–18) he brought together in a repetitious monument all discovery materials available to date, and included his 'Muses de la Nouvelle France'. Books I to III reproduce accounts by French explorers in the Americas (including Cartier and Roberval), with some editing and collation. Book IV recounts the abortive expedition of 1604 and the 1606–7 expedition in which Lescarbot took part; this book is marked by his indignation at failures. Book V recounts Champlain's voyages from 1608 to 1613, and those of the two Biencourts (father and son, 1610–15). Book VI contains 'the

Manner, Customs, and fashions of Life of the Western Indians of New France, and a comparison of them with those of the people of the old world....' The three editions of the *Histoire* testify to its popularity. Writing in a cultivated style, Lescarbot combined elements of ethnography and documentation with classical allusions and moral comment tending towards the myth of the '*bon sauvage*' and the regenerative power of the new land (Frenchmen become visibly more virtuous away from home). *The history of New France* (Toronto, 3 vols, 1907, 1911, 1914), translated for the Champlain Society and edited by W.L. Grant, follows Lescarbot's third edition; it contains 'Les muses de la Nouvelle France' without translation. An English translation by Pierre Erondelle of Books IV and VI of the first edition of the *Histoire* was published under the title *Nova Francia* (1609) and is available both in a modern edition (London, 1925) and in reprint (Amsterdam, 1977). A contemporary translation of *The theatre of Neptune* by Eugene BENSON and Renate Benson can be found in *Canada's lost plays*, vol. 4 (1982), edited by Anton Wagner.

Samuel de Champlain (c. 1570–1635) is celebrated as the explorer and navigator whose tireless efforts shaped the earliest successful colony in Canada. His prose is that of a man of action: terse, organized, sometimes peremptory. His life and works present some major mysteries. Was he a Protestant apostate? How did he appropriate the particle 'de' to his name? What was his status before 1608? What part did he have in writing 'his' first and last works? Did he make all the journeys described in them? His many biographers (listed in the DICTIONARY OF CANADIAN BIOGRAPHY, Vol. 1) reach no precise consensus. The available facts about Champlain's activities and writing may be summed up as follows. His earliest voyages were probably made on Spanish ships to the West Indies, and he had some hand in compiling travel literature about these. His first voyages to the St Lawrence (1603) and Acadia (1604 and 1606) gave him an opportunity; perhaps a motive, to display his knowledge. As the lieutenant of de Monts, Champlain returned to the St Lawrence in 1608 and established a trading post at Québec called the *Habitation*. In the years that followed he laid the foundations of New France, leading expeditions up the main inland water routes, crossing the Atlantic frequently, and writing and publishing his three volumes of *Voyages*. The first work undisputably by Champlain is *Des sauvages* (Paris, 1603), which offers a wealth of information on topography and commercial potential and succinct descriptions of rival Amerindian nations in the St Lawrence area. The first *Voyages...* (Paris, 1613) is regarded by some as Champlain's best work, mainly because of its highly factual character, covering the voyages from 1604 to 1612 (and using partly corrected material from *Des sauvages*). For the general reader what stands out most is the narration of striking episodes (such as the starving Natives crossing the ice floes in Feb. 1609) where the setting in the new country comes alive in action. Champlain's comments are usually curt: 'There are six months of winter in this country' (Ste-Croix, 1605) is typical of how he sums up a season of disasters. In the second volume of *Voyages...* (Paris, 1619) the canvas is richer, and the reader is better able to imagine the life of the little society at Québec. Here too are fuller descriptions of the Hurons, whom Champlain had at last seen in their own country (around Georgian Bay). They are no longer lost in vague generalities about '*sauvages*' (though some of these persist), nor reduced to physical measurements (though these are plentiful), and we get a lively impression of life in a longhouse with its fleas, spoilt children, and thick smoke. Champlain's account of his disputes with the fur-trading company, on the other hand, is a careful statement of legal positions without the drama and the personal clashes that must have accompanied them. The last volume of *Voyages...* (Paris, 1632), purporting to cover the period 1603 to 1631, presents the greatest complications. It contains a rewritten version of the voyages from 1603 (the rewriting is almost certainly not by Champlain, or not completed by him; the Jesuit Fathers in France and Champlain's young wife have both been suggested as possible ghostwriters); the new voyages to 1629; business surrounding the Treaty of St Germain-en-Laye; and a retrospective account of French exploration since 1504. It looks like a hasty job of rewriting Champlain's own accounts and runs into inconsistencies, particularly in trying to suppress all references to Recollect missionaries. Above all, a mellifluous moralizing tone seems quite unlike the brusque style of the two earlier *Voyages*. Whenever the 1632 *Voyages* sound patronizing or didactic we suspect a foreign hand, but Champlain himself can be recognized in places: the perfect navigator, he says, must be a decent God-fearing man and emulate Flemish cleanliness. H.P. Biggar's bilingual edition in the Champlain Society series, *The works of Samuel de Champlain* (6 vols, 1922–36), is authoritative. Among the selections

published in English, the most recent is the translation by Michael Macklem—*Voyages to New France* (1970), with an introduction by Marcel TRUDEL—which lends Champlain's accounts of the years 1615 to 1618 a liveliness that is not always present in the original. *Champlain's dream: the visionary adventurer who made a new world in Canada* (2008, rpr. 2009) by the Pulitzer Prize–winning American scholar David Hackett Fischer, is an unusually revealing biography of Champlain as the founder of New France and an explorer, his dream having to do with bringing about a way of life where the French and the Native people could live together amicably, in a way that is mutually beneficial. The substantial nature of this work can be summed up by its length: 834 pages that include 520 pages of biography, 100 pages of appendices, 109 pages of endnotes, and 40 pages of bibliography.

Gabriel Sagard (*fl.* 1614–38) was a simple though highly literate *Frère convers* in the Recollect branch of the Franciscan Order. He seems to have joined the Recollects about 1610, at the dawn of their existence as a strictly reformed branch, and he defected before 1638 when they were fully established. *Le grand voyage du pays des Hurons...* (Paris, 1632) is virtually a straightforward account of Sagard's own voyage to New France. He embarked at Dieppe in 1623 (his printer gives the wrong year) and describes all the stages of the journey to Ossossane in Huronia. His narrative gradually gives way to the need to describe things by categories, such as flora and fauna, burial customs, sexual behaviour, and family life. The book was written in a hurry; the Recollects needed publicity to make their presence and achievements in Canada known, since they had just been excluded from their mission. This may account for the frank spontaneity that most readers find in Sagard's narrative. His accounts of life in the longhouse are often unflattering, but nonetheless sympathetic, to the Hurons, of whom he gives the most integrated picture. His emphasis on their internal harmony is important in literary history because it gives observer support to the myth of the 'noble savage': Sagard was read and imitated down to the time of Voltaire. *Le grand voyage* was translated for the Champlain Society by H.H. Langton as *The long journey to the country of Hurons* (1939).

The most flagrant mixture of fact and fiction is in three volumes of voyages by Louis-Armand de Lom d'Arce, baron de Lahontan (1666–1716). Lahontan's military career in Canada gave him first-hand knowledge, while his quarrel with his senior officer in

Newfoundland drove him into exile and motivated his witty criticisms of the colonial administration. These constitute the main literary interest of *Nouveaux voyages*... (The Hague, 1703), of which there are several English translations: *New voyages*... (London, 1703; London, 1735; Chicago, 1905) and *Voyages* (1932), translated by Stephen LEACOCK.

Pierre-François-Xavier de Charlevoix (1682–1761) is one of the great Jesuit historians, known for his works on Japan and Paraguay. His two visits to Canada in 1705–9 and 1720–3 were backed up by his thorough use of Jesuit library resources, and he was actively concerned with the search for the Western Sea. His *Histoire et description générale de la Nouvelle France... avec le Journal... d'un voyage...* (Paris, 1744) was a longstanding authority and a model of literary style. Some passing remarks about the *Canadiens*, and the transfer to them of a name that had previously designated an Indian nation, suggest the emergence of a new people. There are separate English translations of the *Journal* (London, 1761; Chicago, 1923; and others), and of the *Histoire* as the *History and description...* (New York, 1866–72; rev. 1900).

Other writers dealing directly with the discovery of the new or not so new continent have attracted less attention in literary discussion. Pierre-Esprit Radisson (*c.* 1640–1710) mingles fiction with vivid fact, clearly in the hope of attracting financial support for his expeditions. His work is known only through an English version of 1669: *Voyages of Peter Esprit Radisson* (Boston, 1885, and New York, 1943), and *The explorations of Pierre Esprit Radisson* (1961) edited by Arthur T. Adams. Of many other accounts of New France—having perhaps less literary than documentary and historical interest—two will be mentioned here. Nicolas Jérémie (1669–1732), who served in Hudson Bay from 1694 to 1714, wrote 'Relation du Détroit et de la Baie d'Hudson', which was published in *Recueil d'arrests et autres pièces pour l'établissement de la Compagnie de l'Occident* (Amsterdam, 1720), the fourth edition of which was published in English: *Twenty years of York Factory, 1694–1714: Jérémie's account of Hudson Strait and Bay* (1926), translated by Robert Douglas and J.N. Wallace. In the realm of early western exploration the writings of Pierre Gaultier de Varennes et de La Vérendrye (1685–1749) and his sons are important. These were translated and edited by L.J. Burpee for the Champlain Society in *Journals and letters of Pierre Gaultier de Varennes de La Vérendrye and his sons with correspondence between the governors of Canada and the French court, touching the search for the western sea* (1927).

The *Journal du voyage de M. Saint-Luc de la Corne... 1761* (Montreal, 1778; Québec, 1863) relates the ill-fated journey of the *Auguste*, carrying émigrés to France after the Conquest. La Corne Saint-Luc (1711–84), born in Canada and one of the few survivors of the shipwreck, wrote of his hardships in a fine measured style. The shipwreck is exploration literature in reverse, best known through the fictionalized version in a chapter of Philippe AUBERT DE GASPÉ'S *CANADIANS OF OLD (Les anciens canadiens)*.

2. LETTERS. Letters attributed to the Jesuit missionary Antoine Silvy (1689–1711) were published in *Relation par lettres de l'Amérique septentrionale, années 1709 et 1710* (1904) and were included in translation in *Documents relating to the early history of Hudson Bay* (1916) edited by J.B. Tyrrell. Among other collections of letters, only a selection of those by MARIE DE L'INCARNATION have been translated—by Joyce MARSHALL in *Word from New France* (1967).

Newlove, John (1938–2003). Born in Regina, and raised in farming communities in eastern Saskatchewan where his mother was a school teacher, Newlove travelled extensively in Canada, lived for three years in Vancouver, where he worked at the University of British Columbia bookstore, was an editor for MCCLELLAND & STEWART in Toronto, a teacher, and a writer-in-residence at various institutions. Latterly he lived in Ottawa, where he worked as a freelance editor.

Newlove's books of poetry include *Grave sirs* (1961), *Elephants, mothers & others* (1963), *Moving in alone* (1965, rpr. 1977), *Black night window* (1968), *The cave* (1970), *Lies* (1972, GGA), *The fat man: selected poems, 1962–1972* (1977), *The green plain* (1981), *The night the dog smiled* (1986), *Apology for absence: selected poems 1962–1992* (1993), and *The Tasmanian devil & other poems* (1999). Two impulses dominate Newlove's poetry, the lyrical and the historical. As a lyric poet, Newlove is anything but precious and self-absorbed. While his work includes delicate musings on such traditional themes as love, beauty, and loss, moving away from cliché and towards ever-finer discriminations of thought and feeling, Newlove the singer also has a playful side, where he assumes the stance of stand-up comic, employing self-deflation, hyperbole, fantasy, and—especially in the treatment of domestic or mundane subjects—a deliberate rhetorical excess and archaic diction. Not only do words such as *song, music, melody,* and *measure* recur frequently in his poems, but also his best lyrics are characterized by a subtle modulation of image, idea, and sound; or, to use his own phrase, by a form of 'running verse' whose headlong movement recalls Charles Olson's description of the good poem: 'A high-energy construct' where 'one perception must lead immediately and directly to a further perception.' In 'No song', Newlove proposes to seek out a newer, more jagged music, appropriate for an age that has become increasingly violent and discordant. Like the crow perched on a branch, he must decline 'the privilege of music/or melody', instead 'fingering the absolute/wood beneath.' That wood represents the spiritual or psychological truth embodied in private and collective experience, which the poet must record. Thus Newlove assumes his second role, that of archivist of human consciousness, concerned to preserve history, to discover both the pride and the shame of his people, the nature of their origins and inheritance. In a number of fine poems—such as 'Ride off any horizon', 'Crazy Riel', and 'The pride'—he attempts to understand the contemporary relevance of Canada's Aboriginal heritage and its terrible burden of racial violence and social and economic oppression. The stories, 'whatever is strong enough/to be remembered', are everywhere, the poet says. In such historical meditations, the concrete rendering of fact and the temperamental scoring of emotion bring an almost perfect fusion of the lyrical and the documentary modes. *A long continual argument: the selected poems of John Newlove* (2007), edited by Robert McTavish, with an Afterword by Jeff Derksen, is an important and substantial selection covering forty years of Newlove's writing.

Newman, Peter C. (b. 1929). Born in Vienna, Peter Charles Newman came to Toronto in 1940 and was educated at Upper Canada College, and the University of Toronto (B.A., 1950; M. Com., 1954) before becoming an assistant editor at *The Financial Post* in 1951. His career has included executive positions in mass journalism, particularly as editor-in-chief of *The Toronto Star* (1969–71) and as editor of *Maclean's* (1971–82). His main interests, however, have always lain in distinct areas of political and financial journalism. His first book, *Flame of power: intimate profiles of Canada's greatest businessmen* (1959), is the embryo of the type of minutely detailed, anecdotal personality study he later combined with analyses of events. *Renegade in power: the Diefenbaker years* (1963, rpr. 1973) and *The distemper of our times* (1968; 2nd edn 1978), about the Pearson government, are stately

testaments to Newman's belief that the fate of nations is often the inevitable consequence of individual traits of personality acting in collusion; both books are wonderfully readable works of popular criminology. *Home country: people, places and power politics* (1973), a collection of magazine pieces, seemed to signal the end of Newman's life as a political analyst and the beginning of his career as the primary folklorist and explainer of Canada's proprietary class. *The Canadian establishment, vol. 1: The great business dynasties* (1975, rpr. 1999) and *vol. 2: The acquisitors* (1981, rpr. 1990) tell of the transition in Canadian entrepreneurship from owners to professional managers, and the not-unrelated partial shift in economic power from central Canada to the western provinces. Publication of the two volumes was separated by *Bronfman dynasty: the Rothschilds of the new world* (1978), the story of the rise to wealth and influence of the Montreal distilling family, so characteristic—in everything, perhaps, but scope—of Ontario and Québec financial life as it had been traditionally carried out. *The establishment man: a study of personal power* (1982) is a biography of Conrad Black, the prominent Canadian capitalist and the subject of some attention in *The acquisitors*; it was followed much later by *Titans: how the new establishment seized power* (1998).

Other books include three volumes on the Hudson's Bay Company: *Company of adventurers* (1985, rpr. 2005), *Caesars of the wilderness* (1987), and *Merchant princes* (1991). *True North, not strong and free* (1983), *Sometimes a great nation: will Canada belong to the 21st century?* (1988), *Canada 1892: portrait of a promised land* (1992), *The Canadian revolution: from deference to defiance, 1985–1995* (1995), and *Defining moments: dispatches from an unfinished revolution* (1997) signal a return to history/political analysis. More recent books are *Titans: how the new Canadian establishment seized power* (1998), and *The secret Mulroney tapes: unguarded confessions of a prime minister* (2005). Newman's memoir, *Here be dragons: telling tales of people, passion and power* (2004), is understandably voluminous (more than 700 pages), filled with anecdotes about the subjects he's researched and the prominent figures he's known and written about, and by no means neglecting his private life, including his second marriage to Christina MᴄCALL, about whom he writes admiringly. In 2008 Newman published *Izzy: the passionate life and turbulent times of Izzy Asper, Canada's media mogul.*

The recipient of a number of honorary doctorates, Newman was promoted to Companion of the Order of Canada in 1980.

New provinces: poems of several authors (1936, rpr. 1976). This landmark anthology, illustrating the advances of the early Canadian modernists in terms of technique, subject, and poetic perspective, contains eleven poems by Robert FINCH, ten by Leo KENNEDY, two by A.M. KLEIN, eight by E.J. PRATT, ten by F.R. SCOTT, and twelve by A.J.M. SMITH. In 1931 the Montreal poets began to collect their own work and in 1934 invited the Toronto poets, Pratt and Finch, to join them in a proposed anthology. Although collaboration began optimistically under Smith's instruction to 'avoid being merely Georgian', there was some debate between Smith and Scott over the selection. Smith wanted the volume to offer an up-to-the-minute statement on the contributors' work, while Scott wanted it to offer a more historical statement on the development of the contributors' poetry, in hopes of calling forth other, unknown modernist poets-in-the-making. There was also intense disagreement over Smith's proposed preface, which attacked the poetic achievements of the older Canadian poets. Without the placating, cajoling, and sometimes arbitrary insistence of Scott, New provinces would have foundered over this. When the anthology was finally published by MACMILLAN, Smith's lengthy Preface had been replaced by Scott's short one. A 1976 reprint contains an introduction by Michael Gnarowski that provides a history of the anthology's evolution, with particular reference to the incident of Smith's 'Rejected Preface' (which is included), laying the blame for its rejection at the feet of Pratt and Finch, who objected to his stringent attack on earlier Canadian poetry. The correspondence concerning New provinces reveals Scott's own reservations about it, which invited and strengthened the attack by Pratt and Finch. Smith's 'Rejected Preface' should be seen as an extension of his earlier article, 'Wanted: Canadian criticism', in The CANADIAN FORUM (Apr. 1928), to which Scott had taken exception in the next issue (June 1928).

Nichol, bp (1944–88). Barrie Phillip Nichol was born in Vancouver, and grew up there, and in Winnipeg and Port Arthur (now part of Thunder Bay), Ontario, returning to Vancouver in 1960. He entered the education faculty of the University of British Columbia in 1962 and received an elementary basic certificate in 1963. While there he audited creative-writing classes attended by younger members of the TISH group. After a difficult year in Port Coquitlam, B.C., where he taught a grade four class, he moved to Toronto and began

work as a book searcher at the University of Toronto and entered therapy with the lay analyst Lea Hindley-Smith. His inclusion in 1965 in a therapy-learning group taught by Hindley-Smith led Nichol in 1967 to join in the establishing of the lay-therapy foundation Therafields, and to work as a therapist and an administrator of this therapeutic community until 1983.

Although Nichol had been writing since 1961, he first attracted public notice in the mid-1960s with his hand-drawn or 'concrete' poems. He valued particularly the personal aesthetic ground that concrete poetry gave him amid that period's various controversies about poetic theory. With its informal postal network that reached from Switzerland to Brazil, concrete poetry also gave him almost immediately an international audience and reputation. The large range of Nichol's writing began to become apparent only with the publication of the relatively conventional free verse of *Journeying and the returns* (1967) and *Monotones* (1971)—which developed into Nichol's best-known work, *The martyrology*, published as *The martyrology: Books 1 and 2* (1972, rpr. 1997); *Books 3 and 4* (1976, rpr. 2000); *Book 5* (1982); *Book 6* (1987), *Book 7* and the posthumously published *Gifts* (1990), and *Book 9 Ad sanctos* (1993). Between 1967 and his death Nichol produced a prodigious number of books and pamphlets in a variety of genres. These included the prose text *Two novels* (1969); the essay collection *Craft dinner* (1978); the novels *Journal* (1977) and *Still* (1983); the poetry collections *Love: a book of remembrances* (1974), *Extreme positions* (1981), *Continental trance* (1982); the visual books *Still water* (1970), *ABC: the Aleph Beth book* (1971), and *Unit of four* (1974); the prose poems *Selected organs* (1988), the 'pataphysical' collections *Zygal* (1980), *Art facts* (1990), and *Truth: a book of fictions* (1993); a memoir, *Selected organs: parts of an autobiography* (1988); and the children's books *Moosequakes and other disasters* (1981), *ONCE: a lullaby* (1983), *The man who loved his knees* (1983), and *To the end of the block* (1984). *Still water*—together with the booklets *The true eventual story of Billy the Kid* (1970), *Beach head* (1970), and Nichol's collection of concrete poetry, *The cosmic chef* (1970)—won a Governor General's Award for poetry. All of Nichol's work was stamped by his desire to create texts that were visually engaging in themselves as well as in content, and to use indirect structural and textual devices to carry meaning. In *The martyrology* different ways of speaking testify to a journey through different ways of being. Language is both the poet's instructor and, through its various permutations, the dominant 'image' of the poem. The books of *The martyrology* document a poet's quest for insight into himself and his writing through scrupulous attention to the messages hidden in the morphology of his own speech. This attention to syntax and morphology characterizes both Nichol's concrete poetry and his prose fiction. His concrete poems were typically written as sequences, and involve the sequential development of syllabic relationships (*Still water*) or of alphabetic shapes (*Unit of four* and *Aleph unit*, 1973). His prose fiction employs Gertrude Stein's technique of using evolving yet repetitive syntax to develop language both as a correlative for intense emotional states, as in *Journal*, and as a medium to divine meaning, as in *The true eventual story of Billy the Kid*. See *Selected writing: as elected* (1980) edited by Jack David, *An H in the heart: bp Nichol, a reader* (1994), selected by George BOWERING and Michael ONDAATJE.

In the 1960s Nichol worked hard writing typewriter concrete 'poems', some of which found their way into *Konfessions of a Japanese fan dancer* (1967; rpr. 1969 in London, Eng.; rpr. 1973 by Weed Flower Press [run by Nelson Ball] in Canada)—which has reappeared in 2004, edited with an introduction and notes by Ball. Cycle #5 reads:

> sailboat
> boat sail
> sailboat sale
> sale boat sail

Nelson Ball writes: 'Nichol's typewriter concrete, although not extensive in itself, is at the core of his development as a writer. Through it he discovered aspects of language frequently ignored by other writers.' Four issues of OPEN LETTER are devoted to Nichol: *bpNichol + 10* (Tenth Series, Number 4, Fall 1998): *bpNichol + 20* (Thirteenth Series, Number 5, Spring 2008); *bpNichol + 21* (Thirteenth Series, Number 8, Spring 2009); and *The Martyrology: Survivors' Retrospective* (Fourteenth Series, Number 1, Fall 2009).

Nichol first began performing as a sound poet in the mid-1960s. His early work in this medium was documented, together with early reflective poems, in Ondaatje's film *Sons of Captain Poetry* (1970); in 'Borders', a small phonodisc included with *Journeying and the returns* in 1967; and in the long-playing record 'Motherlove' (1968). In 1970 Nichol began what proved to be an extended collaboration with fellow poets Rafael Barreto-Rivera, Paul Dutton, and Steve McCAFFERY, forming the sound-poetry group The FOUR HORSEMEN.

Together with McCaffery in 1973 he began the intermittent 'TRG' (Toronto Research Group) project of theoretical and 'pataphysical' writing—a project that McCaffery brought to a close in 1992 with the publication of *Rational geomancy: the kids of the book machine. The collected research reports of the Toronto Research Group 1973–1982*.

Nichol was also one of the most energetic and effective editors of the 1970s and '80s. He founded Ganglia Press in 1965 and the grOnk series of pamphlets in 1969. He joined COACH HOUSE PRESS in 1974 as an unpaid volunteer editor, and personally acquired and edited approximately one-quarter of the titles the press published between then and his death. In the early 1980s he helped found and fund the small writers' co-operative Underwhich Editions.

See Stephen SCOBIE, *bp Nichol: what history teaches* (1984); *Tracing the paths: reading/writing The Martyrology* (1988) edited by Roy Miki; *Zygal: a book of mysteries and translations* (2000); *Meanwhile: the critical writings of bp Nichol* (2002) edited by Roy Miki; *bp Nichol comics* (2002) edited by Carl Peters; and *Konfessions of an Elizabethan fan dancer* (2004) edited by Nelson Ball.

Nichols, Ruth (b. 1948). Born in Toronto and influenced by her mother's interest in literature, she was educated at the University of British Columbia (B.A., 1969, in religious studies) and McMaster University, Hamilton, Ont. (M.A., 1972, religion; Ph.D., 1977, theology). She began writing as a teenager and published her first novel at the age of twenty-one. She has written five novels for young people: *A walk out of the world* (1960), *Ceremony of innocence* (1969), *The marrow of the world* (1972), *Song of the pearl* (1976), and *The left-handed spirit* (1978). She gained recognition as a remarkable writer of fantasies with her first, third, and fourth books. The central figures in these novels are young girls searching for a place or true home where they can be redeemed from the constrictions of a divided self. Like many fantasy writers, Nichols is steeped in the tradition of Tolkien, Lewis, Spenser, and the King James Bible; her interest in the Renaissance and the history of religion are reflected throughout her work. The search for a spiritual home leads Judith, in *A walk*, and Linda, in *The marrow*, into fantasy landscapes. Restless, troubled, near despair over the condition of their 'real' lives, they find self-awareness and redemption in the world of fantasy. In *Song of the pearl* Nichols' use of metaphoric landscapes reaches a new level of power. Filled with hatred and melancholy, Margaret drifts calmly into death—which is her entrance into the realm of fantasy and a kind of heaven that is, ironically, both earth and the world of memory. Painfully she discovers that she has lived before—as Zawumatec, an Iroquois slave, and as Elizabeth, in Renaissance England—and learns that the uncle who raped her when she was Margaret, aged fifteen, was led to his fall by her own lust. After grappling with feelings she has denied or repressed, she gains another chance at life on earth. In this novel Nichols, putting the Tolkien-Lewis matrix behind her, succeeds in creating a powerful vision of the pilgrimage of the soul. Nichols' writing for young people is full of mystery, intrigue, and skilful plotting. She has also extended her interests and skills into historical fiction for adults. *The burning of the rose* (1990) and *What dangers deep* (1992) take us into Tudor and Elizabethan England. The latter novel is a fascinating study of Sir Philip Sidney's role as spy in the Polish capital Krakow in 1574 while he was attending the wedding of his godfather, the English ambassador. Told as Sidney's first-person account, the novel is clever and revealing, both as a character study of Sidney and as a portrait of some aspects of Elizabethan England that always fascinate: court drama, spying, power, and the search for truth.

Nicol, Eric (1919–2011). One of Canada's most prolific and versatile humorists, he was born in Kingston, Ontario, but his family moved to Vancouver when he was six. He served in the RCAF for three years during the Second World War and spent some time as a comedy writer for the BBC and as a student at the University of British Columbia (B.A., 1941; M.A., 1948); he also attended the Sorbonne (1949–50). Nicol has written for radio, television, and the stage, but it was his syndicated column in the Vancouver *Province* and his many books of humour (three of them winning the Leacock Medal for Humour) that brought him the most widespread attention. These include: *Sense and nonsense by E.P. Nicol (Jabez)* (1947), *The Roving I* (1950), *Twice over lightly* (1953), *Shall we join the ladies?* (1955), *Girdle me a globe* (1957), *In darkest domestica* (1959), *An uninhibited history of Canada* (1959), *Space age, go home!* (1964), *Don't move! Renovate your house and make social contacts* (1971), *Letters to my son* (1974), *There's a lot of it going around* (1975), *Canadadide: a patriotic satire* (1983), *Back talk: a book for bad back sufferers* (1992), and *Skiing is believing* (1996). His work has been anthol-ogized in *A herd of yaks: the best of Eric Nicol* (1962) and *Still a Nicol*

(1972). He has written a history of his city, *Vancouver* (1970, rev. 1978), and a book on his own profession, *One man's media, and how to write for them* (1973). Without having the highly individual view of the world that makes for a great humorist on the order of LEACOCK, Thurber or Twain, Nicol has a distinctive voice—fast-talking, wisecracking—and the consistency and durability of his work, rare in the field, is a tribute to his professional skill. Even the conventional pieces, in which he pictures himself struggling with social embarrassments and domestic misfortunes, stand up to rereading. His main strength is verbal inventiveness, shown in outrageous puns and verbal zig-zags that take the reader by surprise: for example, the title essay of *Shall we join the ladies?* refers not to after-dinner rituals but to sex-change operations.

As a playwright Nicol has had mixed success. *Like father, like fun* (1975, prod. 1966), about the attempt of a crass businessman to contrive his son's sexual initiation, was a hit in Vancouver, but (rewritten as *A minor adjustment*) flopped on Broadway, becoming a classic instance of the dangers of transplanting a play from one community to another. Nicol characteristically got a ruefully funny book out of the experience, *A scar is born* (1968). The scars also show on the central character of *The fourth monkey* (1975, prod. 1968), a frustrated playwright. Both plays combine frequently witty dialogue with structural weakness and arbitrary characterization. Nicol has also used drama as a vehicle for ideas, as in his contribution to *The centennial play* (prod. 1967) and *The Citizens of Calais* (1975, prod. 1974) where, through the comic squabbling of characters putting on a play, Nicol reflects on the cynicism and petty-mindedness that threaten Canada, and enters a plea for tolerance and common sense. *Pillar of sand* (1975, prod. 1972) pits the unreason of early Christian mysticism—for which we may read the unreason of Nicol's own time—against the rationality of a Roman soldier. Comedy and serious comment blend uneasily here; the mix works better in Nicol's childrens' plays, *The clam made a face* (1972, prod. 1967) and *Beware the quickly who* (1973, prod.1967), which celebrate the creative, playful side of life against the spoilsports who threaten it.

A substantial achievement is *Dickens of the Mounted: the astonishing long-lost letters of Inspector F. Dickens NWMP 1874–86* (1989), in which he presents himself as editor of the recently discovered letters of Frank Dickens, son of the great novelist, from his time as an officer of the North West Mounted Police. 'Dickens' writes in a modified version of Nicol's own wisecracking, pun-laden style, and shows a thoroughly modern anger at the government's treatment of Native peoples, combined with a wry affection for the parts of Canada that lie outside Ottawa. While he has a curious knack for bumping into famous people—like Gabriel Dumont, Louis Riel, and Harry Flashman—he is also ruefully aware of his own role as the unsatisfactory son of a great man. The result is an engaging blend of history, political commentary, fiction, and mischief. As an elderly man Nicol had fun writing the surprisingly substantial *The Casanova sexicon: a manual for liberated men* (2001), 'Dedicated to all my old girl friends—and why haven't you answered my letters?' Nicol's sixth collaboration with the cartoonist Peter Whalley is *Canadian politics unplugged* (2003). As an eighty-five-year-old, he wrote *Old is in: a guide for aging boomers* (2004). Nicol is a Member of the Order of Canada (2000). See his *Anything for a laugh: memoirs* (1998).

Niven, Frederick (1878–1944). Born to Scottish parents in Valparaiso, Chile, Frederick John Niven was taken to Glasgow at age five and educated in Hutcheson's Grammar School and the Glasgow School of Art. In his late teens he was sent to visit friends in the Okanagan Valley, British Columbia, as a treatment for a lung ailment. He spent what he described as 'a year or two' travelling in Canada and taking odd jobs, an experience that drew him into journalism on his return to Scotland. He began his career as a novelist with the publication of *The lost cabin mine* (1908), one of many adventure stories he set in the Canadian West, and established himself as a minor but promising novelist in Britain. His writing was stimulated by his Canadian travel, and more than half of his early publications—some of them adventure romances written 'to keep the wolf from the wife', to use Niven's phrase—include New World settings. He spent several months in 1912 and 1913 travelling as a freelance writer in Canada, to which, in 1920, he and his wife immigrated, living near Nelson, British Columbia, and in Vancouver until Niven's death. In B.C. Niven wrote seventeen novels, ending with *The flying years* (1935), *Mine inheritance* (1940), *Brothers-in-arms* (1942), and *The transplanted* (1944). These later books include his chief contribution to Canadian literature: a trilogy spanning the settlement of the West and incorporating his most serious themes. *Mine inheritance* is a historical romance of the struggle to establish the Selkirk Settlement amid the fur-trade wars on the Red River. Wholly sympathetic to the colonizers, it dramatizes their need to adapt mentally and spiritually, as well as physically, in order to overcome the isolation of the new land. *The flying years* is a panoramic narrative extending from the 1850s to the 1920s. Its protagonist, though not strongly characterized, becomes a representative immigrant, subject to the trials of adaptation through all stages of settlement, and of his life. He makes the Prairies his home without altogether relinquishing Scotland as that 'country of the mind' from which the Highland Clearances had driven him. *The transplanted*, which depicts the development of a settlement in the lumbering, mining, and ranching area of central British Columbia, completes the pattern by concentrating its thematic emphasis on the need for community to combat the destructive isolation that comes from seeking the freedom of the natural environment. Niven's significance in Canadian literature lies in his bringing to bear on western experience a developed writing talent influenced by British literary and cultural traditions. He became an immigrant as distinct from a colonial writer—recreating the West from a Canadian perspective.

Northern Review (1945–56). The result of a merger between two Montreal literary magazines, PREVIEW and FIRST STATEMENT, it was edited by John SUTHERLAND (managing editor), F.R. SCOTT, A.M. KLEIN, Irving LAYTON, Patrick ANDERSON, A.J.M. SMITH, Audrey Aikman, R.G. Simpson, and Neufville Shaw; regional editors were P.K. PAGE, Dorothy LIVESAY, James Wreford, and Ralph GUSTAFSON. The first issue appeared in Dec. 1945–Jan. 1946. The amalgamation was made uneasy by differences in literary philosophy among its editors. More significant, however, was the fact that the more nationalistic *First Statement* poets viewed Sutherland as editor-in-chief, whereas the *Preview* poets, used to Anderson's democratic editorial policies, saw Sutherland simply as a fellow editor in charge of production. The tension came to a head with Sutherland's aggressively critical review of Robert FINCH's Governor General's Award–winning book, *Poems*, in the issue of Aug.–Sept. 1947. Scott, Klein, Anderson, Smith, Shaw, Page, Livesay, and Gustafson all resigned in protest at not having approved the review. A year later, in the issue of Sept.–Oct. 1948, Layton's name disappeared from the masthead; the magazine subsequently became more conservative. Sutherland continued to publish *Northern Review* with the help of Aikman and Simpson and, in the issue of April–May 1951, announced the incorporation of *The Canadian Review of Music and Art*, through the generosity of Lorne PIERCE. Simpson retired from the editorial board with the Oct.–Nov. 1951 issue and his eventual replacement, A.E. Farebrother, withdrew when the magazine moved to Toronto in the spring of 1955 and changed from a bi-monthly to a quarterly. *Northern Review* had the largest circulation of any literary journal in the country (though it was not really large) and maintained a high quality of poetry, short stories, essays, and book reviews. Mavis GALLANT, Norman LEVINE, Brian MOORE, George WOODCOCK, Robert WEAVER, and Marshall McLUHAN are only a few of the contributors who appeared in its pages. It ceased publication with Sutherland's death in Sept. 1956, after forty issues.

Nova-Scotia Magazine and Comprehensive Review of Literature, Politics, and News, The. Published in Halifax between July 1789 and Mar. 1792, it was the first literary journal in Canada. It was issued monthly, printed by John Howe (father of Joseph HOWE), and edited by the Rev. William Cochran, first president of King's College, Windsor, Nova Scotia. Thirty-three numbers appeared; the first eighteen averaged over eighty pages, the last fifteen over sixty pages. The bulk of each issue was made up of material Cochran found in British and American books and magazines: passages by such well-known authors as Edward Gibbon, Richard Cumberland, Hester Piozzi, William Cowper, Dr Benjamin Rush, Joseph Priestly, and Benjamin Franklin, as well as little-known journalists. Prose fiction and poetry were prominently featured, and there were brief notices of new books; in addition there were detailed reports on the political scene in both Nova Scotia and Great Britain and a 'Chronicle' of current events, domestic and foreign. Of the few local contributions, all of which appeared anonymously the best-known pieces are 'A plan of a liberal education' by W. (possibly Cochran himself) and the poems of 'Pollio'. *The Nova-Scotia Magazine* was valuable for opening windows on the great world of science and literature that lay beyond Nova Scotia, and for attempting to draw Nova Scotian minds into that world.

Novascotian, The. See Joseph HOWE.

Nowlan, Alden (1933–83). Born in Windsor, Nova Scotia, he began working at fifteen in lumber mills and on farms. He completed his formal education at eighteen and left Nova Scotia for New Brunswick, where he became editor of the *Hartland Observer* and night-news editor of the *Saint John Telegraph-Journal*. Beginning to publish poetry and short stories in the mid-1950s, he was honoured with a Guggenheim Fellowship, a Governor General's Award (for *Bread, wine and salt*, 1967), and a Doctor of Letters from the University of New Brunswick. From 1969 he was writer-in-residence at the University of New Brunswick.

After the publication of Nowlan's first collection of verse, *The rose and the Puritan* (1958), his poetry was consistent in style and theme. The bulk of his poems are short anecdotal lyrics, conversational in tone and frequently directed towards some moral perception. He wrote chiefly about small-town New Brunswick, the constricted lives of its inhabitants, and the complexity of his own role as its compassionately observing poet—indicated by the title of his selected poems, *Playing the Jesus game* (1970); like Christ, Nowlan found that he must not only pity and forgive his fellow humans, but share personally their limitations and tragedies. Nowlan's emphasis on the essential innocence and helplessness of his variously benighted characters—escapist, credulous, treacherous, adulterous, murderous, insane—gives to many of his poems a suggestion of sentimentality that the poet must work to dispel through realistic imagery and colloquial dialogue. Nowlan's other collections of poetry are *A darkness in the earth* (1959), *Under the ice* (1960), *Wind in a rocky country* (1961), *The things which are* (1962), *The mysterious naked man* (1969), *Between tears and laughter* (1971), *I'm a stranger here myself* (1974), *Smoked glass* (1977), and *I might not tell everybody this* (1982).

Nowlan's first novel, *The wanton trooper*—about the difficult childhood of Kevin O'Brien—was written in 1960 but not published until 1988; it was reissued in 2009 in a reader's guide edition, with an Afterword by David Adams RICHARDS. The protagonist appeared again in Nowlan's autobiographical novel, *Various persons named Kevin O'Brien* (1973), recounts his childhood struggle against poverty in an ambitious, though not entirely successful, juxtaposition of adult and child viewpoints. The collection of short stories, *Miracle at Indian River* (1968)—technically less interesting than the novel—offers close-up views of the economically oppressed characters who populate much of his poetry. In the 1970s Nowlan collaborated with Walter Learning to write three stage plays: *Frankenstein* (1976), *The incredible murder of Cardinal Tosca* (1978), and *The dollar woman* (1981). Nowlan also wrote a travel book, *Campobello, the outer island* (1975), and collected twenty-seven of his magazine articles in *Double exposure* (1978). The following titles were published posthumously: *Alden Nowlan, early poems* (1983); *Will ye let the mummers in?* (stories, 1984); *An exchange of gifts: poems new and selected* (1985) edited by Robert GIBBS; *The wanton troopers* (novel, 1988); *The best of Alden Nowlan* (1993) edited by Allison Mitcham; *Alden Nowlan: selected poems* (1995) edited by Patrick LANE and Lorna CROZIER;

and *White madness* (1996), a selection by Gibbs of some of Nowlan's more personal columns from the *Telegraph-Journal. Nine Micmac legends*, children's stories, was published in 1983.

See Michael Oliver, *Alden Nowlan and his works* (1990), *The Alden Nowlan papers* (1992) edited by Jean M. Muir, and *Alden Nowlan: essays on his works* (2006) edited by Gregory M. Cook. See also Patrick Toner, *If I could turn and meet myself: the life of Alden Nowlan* (2000); and *Alden Nowlan: essays on his works* (2006) edited by Gregory M. Cook.

O

Oberon Press. One of the leading literary publishers in Canada, Oberon is a family company run by Michael Macklem and his son Nicholas, and was founded in 1966. It has a backlist of some 640 titles—all designed in house and many set in hot metal. It specializes in fiction and poetry, though it also publishes history, biography, and criticism. Its bestselling title is *Where to eat in Canada* by Anne Hardy, Michael's wife, and has been published annually since 1971. Among the writers of fiction on its list are Marie-Claire BLAIS, George BOWERING, Margaret GIBSON, Hugh HOOD, Isabel HUGGAN, W.P. KINSELLA, John METCALF, David Adams RICHARDS, Leon ROOKE, Audrey THOMAS, and W.D. VALGARDSON. Among the poets are Elizabeth BREWSTER, R.G. EVERSON, David HELWIG, Gwendolyn MacEWEN, Tom MARSHALL, bp NICHOL, Raymond SOUSTER, and Bronwen WALLACE.

Ocean to ocean (London, 1873 rpr. 1967). This enduring travel classic, subtitled *Sandford Fleming's expedition through Canada in 1872*, was written by George Monro Grant (1835–1902), who was president of Queen's University, Kingston, from 1877 until his death. He acted as secretary to Sandford Fleming, chief engineer of the Canadian Pacific Railway, when Fleming made an exploratory journey to the Pacific Ocean in search of a route. Grant's book ('simply a Diary written as we journeyed') is a record of the expedition's progress by train, steamer, canoe, wagon, and horseback from Halifax to Victoria between 1 July and 11 Oct. 1872. It presents memorable

descriptions of the landscape, the weather in different regions, various modes of travel, and personalities met en route; carefully records local place names and idioms; presents and analyzes the Native and Métis cultures; and constantly assesses the land's suitability for settlement. The members of the expedition themselves become vivid characters in a narrative that mingles humorous incidents with accounts of the unavoidable hardships of travel. Grant's delight in what he encounters is infectious, and his personal enthusiasms (including several rhapsodic comments about the merits of pemmican) make the book appealing.

Two volumes of the actual diary are among the Grant papers in Library and Archives Canada, and their records of the expedition often differ from the published version. It is apparent that Grant revised and expanded rough notes and structured his materials with some care for the purpose of defending both the proposed transcontinental railroad—which would firmly unite Canada, make possible the settlement of the West, and keep the Americans at bay—and the expansionist aspirations of English-speaking Canada. The Prairie West is seen as a potential garden, with the railroad as the means of bringing in settlers to make it bloom. Though treated with sympathy by Grant, the Métis and Native cultures stand in the way of necessary 'progress' and will need to be absorbed or controlled, paternalistically, by the new order. The new West, as Grant envisions it, will be in effect a colony of Ontario, a hinterland feeding the manufacturing metropolis of the East. Although *Ocean to ocean* did not save the Macdonald government from defeat in 1873, it was a defence of the prime minister's policies perhaps not coincidentally, a second edition (Toronto, 1879) appeared soon after Macdonald's return to power. There is a facsimile reprint (1967) of the second edition, with an introduction by L.H. Thomas.

Odell, Jonathan (1737–1818). Born in Newark, New Jersey, he was educated at the College of New Jersey (now Princeton University), graduating in 1759 with an M.A. in medicine. After serving as a surgeon in the British army in the West Indies, he went to London in 1763 to prepare himself for the Church of England ministry and was ordained in 1767; he was parish priest at St Mary's Church, Burlington, N.J., until Dec. 1776. His loyalist political sympathies led to his being forced to flee behind British lines to New York, where he was regimental chaplain, secretary to the chief British administrator, and a key intermediary in the espionage activities of Benedict Arnold and John André. Odell was the most skilled and trenchant of the loyalist satirists. His satiric activity reached its peak in 1779–80 with the publication of four major verse satires: 'The word of Congress' (1779), 'The congratulation, a poem' (1779), 'The feu de joie, a poem' (1779), and *The American times* (1780), all written in heroic couplets. The first three were published in a New York newspaper *The American times* was issued as a pamphlet in both London and New York. Perhaps the finest of the loyalist satires, it consists mainly of a series of biting satiric portraits of the chief participants in the rebel cause, culminating in an attack on personified Democracy. After the evacuation of New York in 1783 Odell lived in England for a year before being appointed secretary to the newly formed Province of New Brunswick. He arrived there in Nov. 1784 and served as provincial secretary, an influential political post, until 1812, at which time the position was passed on to his son. Odell's poetic activity declined after he moved to New Brunswick. There is an interesting series of verses dealing with the ethics of Thomas Carleton's absentee governing of New Brunswick (Carleton left in 1803 never to return, although he remained governor until 1817) and a small group of satiric poems inspired by the War of 1812. The most ambitious of these, 'The agonizing dilemma' (1812), is an extended travesty of the American general's report on his defeat at Queenston Heights. Odell's satires were collected by Winthrop Sargent in *The loyal verses of Joseph Stansbury and Doctor Jonathan Odell* (Albany, 1860).

'O God! O Montreal!' (1874)—the refrain from 'A psalm of Montreal' by the English writer (and sometime painter) Samuel Butler (1835–1902). This poem was circulated privately in England (to Matthew Arnold, among others) and was published in *The Spectator* on 18 May 1878. Butler composed it in 1875 while he was in Canada for several months overseeing a foundering business in which he had investments. His view of Montreal as provincial was strengthened when, on a visit to the Museum of Natural History, he found a copy of the Discobolus relegated to a storeroom, among stuffed animals. The curator in the poem says, 'The Discobolus is put there because he is vulgar,/He has neither vest nor pants with which to cover his limbs.' There is a connection with Butler's painting 'Mr. Heatherley's holiday', which hangs in the Tate Gallery. It shows Mr Heatherley, whose art school Butler attended, repairing a human skeleton amid pots and vases, the Discobolus, and other statuary.

O'Grady, Standish (1776 or 1777–1846). Born Standish O'Grady Bennett in County Limerick, he attended Trinity College, Dublin; there is at present no evidence that he graduated, in spite of the B.A. attached to his name on the title page of his poem. At the age of sixty, in 1836, he immigrated to Canada, settling on a farm on the south bank of the St Lawrence River near Sorel, where he failed at farming. He died destitute in Toronto. His one printed work, a long narrative poem in rhymed couplets, was self-published, dated 1841, and entitled *The emigrant: a poem in four cantos* (printed in Montreal by John Lovell). Despite the subtitle, the work has only one canto—2,160 lines on 117 pages—followed by 61 pages of notes that are frequently long anecdotal diversions with incidental verse incorporated. As a would-be man of letters O'Grady provides early evidence of how the lack of a congenial cultural climate limited pioneer literary effort. As a Protestant and a non-francophone, he was doubly displaced. Inexperienced at farming, he lived at Sorel among farmers who were experienced, French-speaking, and Catholic. His literary environment was equally unpromising. He dedicated his poem to 'Nobody', as no patron had offered himself 'on this vast portion of the globe to which myself and my Muse are perfect strangers'. O'Grady's use of heroic couplets, mostly competent, allows him to express his disillusionment in epigrams, hyperbole, and some whimsy; but his dependence on conventional and remote rhetoric reveals his distance from the immediate Canadian context. His reticence about things Canadian, and the frequent references to things Irish, testify to his continuing and limiting sense of displacement. Though his retrospection about life in Ireland was also gloomy, O'Grady warned Irish, Scots, and Britons to 'best engage your husbandry at home' rather than in a wintry country 'where nature seems one universal blank.' Along with winter's discomforts, he expressed dislike for French-Canadian law, education, and religious practice. Nonetheless he felt sure that eventually 'this expanded and noble continent will no doubt furnish fit matter for the Muse.' The identification of the poet as Standish O'Grady Bennett and other revisionist information at the beginning of this entry was established by Brian Trehearne in the long introduction to his 1989 scholarly edition of *The emigrant*, which he describes as having been written in the tradition 'of the eighteenth-century travel narrative, with its bewildering conventions of random observation, continual digression and narrative freedom.' It is 'typical of its period in Canada in its choice of a neoclassical form, style and structure as a vehicle for the poet's experiences and reflections in a new and difficult creative environment.'

O'Hagan, Howard (1902–82). He has been called 'the writer Canadian Literature forgot'. Born in Lethbridge, Alberta, he received a degree in law from McGill University in 1928 and while in Montreal began a long friendship with Stephen LEACOCK and A.J.M. SMITH. After practising law without having been called to the bar, he became a tour guide in Jasper National Park. He then travelled to Australia, where he began to write short stories; he returned to Montreal, where Leacock helped him get a job with the Canadian Pacific Railway, recruiting farm labourers from England; he later worked in New York and Jasper, Alberta, as a publicist for the Canadian National Railways, and in Buenos Aires for the Argentine Central Railway. While living in San Francisco he began the series of notes about Mounties, trappers, Natives, guides, mountain men, and railway workers that were used for his first novel *Tay John* (1939, NCL), which he completed on an island in Howe Sound, on the coast of British Columbia. During the 1950s O'Hagan was an occasional journalist for Victoria newspapers and also took odd jobs on the waterfront, in Gyproc mills, and on survey crews. Between 1963 and 1974 he and his wife lived in Sicily, until he decided to settle in Victoria, B.C., where he lived in poor health and semi-retirement while continuing to write. Even though he suffered from the lack of a supportive community, he became known as the mountain man of Canadian letters, and one of the best prose stylists of western Canada. He had a strong influence on Rudy WIEBE, Robert HARLOW, Jack HODGINS, Don GUTTERIDGE, and Michael ONDAATJE. *Tay John*—a remarkable novel that was possibly influenced by O'Hagan's reading of Joseph Conrad—is about a Métis, welcomed as the Messiah, who will lead his people across the Rocky Mountains to be reunited with the people of the B.C. coast. Born in his mother's grave, Tay John disappears into the earth with the body of a pregnant woman—O'Hagan touches on mythology and magic in this novel. A blend of fact, fiction, and historical re-creation, *Tay John* was reviewed favourably when it was published in England, but received little publicity because of the war. It was reprinted in the 1960s but remained relatively unknown until 1974, when it was reissued in the NEW CANADIAN LIBRARY; this edition now has an Afterword by Ondaatje. During the 1950s O'Hagan wrote wilderness articles for adventure magazines, some of which were collected in *Wilderness men* (1958). Although he referred to them as potboilers, they included incisive stories about such wilderness figures as Grey Owl (Archie BELANEY), Albert Johnson, the 'mad trapper of Rat River', and 'Almighty Voice'. O'Hagan also wrote excellent short stories, the best of which were collected in *The woman who got on at Jasper station* (1963, rpr. 1978). This and *Wilderness men* appeared together in *Trees are lonely company* (1993). Another novel, *The school-marm tree* (1977), was followed by a memorial volume edited by Gary GEDDES, *Coyote's song* (1983), a collection of essays that includes O'Hagan's word-portrait of Leacock. *Silence made visible: Howard O'Hagan and Tay John* (1992), edited by Margery Fee, includes an essay by W.J. KEITH, a memoir, and O'Hagan's spoofs of arts-club meetings.

Oliva, Peter (b. 1964). Born in Eugene, Oregon, he was educated at the University of Calgary (B.A., 1987; M.A., 1991). He is a presence in the literary community of Calgary, the former owner of the bookshop Pages on Kensington, which was well known for the many readings held there (he sold it in the summer of 2000); and a novelist who is attracted to complex subjects, which he addresses with technical adroitness and a vision of them that is compelling. *Drowning in darkness* (1993, rpr. 1999), set in a coal-mining community of southern Alberta's Crowsnest Pass, is about Italian miners who live in the district, called 'Dagoland', of a nearby town. But dominating the story is the mine itself, where 'methane swirls next to the coal face like a warm current in black sea…. It seduces a miner to sleep, to dream, to abandon life'— and after a mine blast he can drown. Celi, trapped in the mine, dreams—and remembers his fellow miner Pep; and Sera (Serafina), a strong-willed woman from Calabria (we read about her life there and its superstitions) who married him, then left him and disappeared. Oliva has taught English in both Italy and Japan. In *The city of Yes* (1999, rpr. 2001) a young Canadian man arrives in Japan in Nov. 1993 to teach English, and there unfolds a complicated but engrossing text that includes the narrator's bonding with Endo, a fellow teacher and close neighbour; illuminating accounts of Japanese culture (and culture clashes); mythological stories; the narrator's attraction to a Japanese woman; and constant discussions of language—of words and their meanings in Japanese and English. Interwoven in these narratives is the story—introduced to the narrator by Endo—of the real-life Canadian sailor Ranald MacDonald, who capsized his boat off Japan in 1848 because he wanted to go there, even though all foreigners were threatened with execution; he was imprisoned for a year. Past and present are therefore combined, and the book—like *Drowning in darkness*—tells a complex story that is lucid and often poetic in its illuminations. In an endnote Oliva says that the title 'comes from the old name for Hokkaido—Yesso—and from the beginning of a poem written by Yevgeny Yevtushenko: "I am like a train/rushing for many years now/between the city of Yes/and the city of No."' *The city of Yes* won the third Rogers Writers' Trust Prize in 2000.

Ollivier, Émile (1940–2002). Born in Port-au-Prince, Haiti, he lived in Montreal from 1965 and taught at the Université de Montréal until he retired, becoming Professor Emeritus. He published six novels in French that frequently treat migration, exile, and alienation. *Mère Solitude* (Paris, 1989)—translated by David Lobdell as *Mother Solitude* (1989)—portrays the search for past and future (in a fictional Caribbean city), contrasted with the social present. The success of this novel lies in the characters' retracing the history of Haiti, and the collective consciousness of Haitian people. The translation of *Passages* (1994) by Leonard Sugden—with the same title in English, 2003—tells two stories: that of Amédée Hosange, who leaves a Caribbean village with a group of destitute people in a frail boat in search of a new life; and of Normand Malavy, a Haitian living in Québec, who is in Miami for his health and meets Hosange, whose boat has shipwrecked. The power of memory, the sadness of exile, and the indomitable human spirit give life to this moving novel.

Ondaatje, Michael (b. 1943). Born in Ceylon (now Sri Lanka), he joined his mother in England in 1954 and moved to Canada in 1962. After studying at Bishop's University (Lennoxville, Qué, 1962–4), the University of Toronto (B.A., 1965), and Queen's University, Kingston, Ontario (M.A., 1967), he taught at the University of Western Ontario (1967–70) before joining the Department of English at Glendon College, York University, Toronto, in 1971. He is an Officer of the Order of Canada (1988).

Ondaatje has published seven collections of poetry—*The dainty monsters* (1967), *The man with seven toes* (1969), *Rat jelly* (1973), *There's a trick with a knife I'm learning to do: poems 1963–1978* (1979, GGA), *Secular love* (1984), *The cinnamon peeler* (1992), and *Handwriting* (1998, rpr. 2000)—and two chapbooks, *Elimination dance* (1980, rpr. 1991) and *Tin roof* (1982); a collage of poetry and prose, *The collected works of Billy the Kid* (1970, GGA); an autobiographical work, *Running in the family* (1982, rpr. 2001, NCL), combining prose and verse; and five novels: *Coming through Slaughter* (1976, rpr. 1998), *In the skin of a lion* (1987, rpr. 1996), *The* ENGLISH PATIENT (1992, GGA; rpr. 2006), *Anil's ghost* (2000, rpr. 2001), and DIVISADERO (2007, GGA; rpr. 2008). Three of these works—*Billy the Kid*, *The man with seven toes*, and *Coming through Slaughter*—have been performed as plays, while *The English patient*, a co-winner of the Booker Prize, was made into a film that won nine Academy Awards, including best picture. It is worth noting that *In the skin of a lion* finished in a tie with works by Nadine Gordimer and Toni Morrison for the Ritz-Hemingway prize; because the judges could not decide among the three, the prize was not awarded.

With the exception of *In the skin of a lion*, Ondaatje is not an obviously Canadian writer where subject matter, vision, and the verbal texture of a work are concerned. His style, owing almost nothing to an indigenous Canadian tradition, shows the influence of Wallace Stevens and of contemporary cinema artists, especially Louis Malle, Alfred Hitchcock, and Sergio Leone. His vision has been steadily directed at compelling the reader—by means of unusual settings and unexpected thematic, narrative, and stylistic shifts—to see reality as surreal, inchoate, and dynamic. Ondaatje's extraordinary settings, characters, and narratives function as a metaphoric or symbolic shorthand leading the reader to perceive reality anew. The central tension in his work, between self and reality, or between two aspects of self, results in a fascination with borders—between rationality and unconsciousness (in the poems 'Dragon', 'White dwarfs', 'Letters and other worlds'), peace and violence ('The time around scars', *The man with seven toes*), or reality and art ('Light', 'Spider blues', *Coming through Slaughter*). With his lyric poetry, Ondaatje has written a body of work as impressive as any among the poets of his generation. *Rat jelly* collects the best of the early poems, many of which are self-reflexive meditations on creativity: 'Letters and other worlds', 'King Kong meets Wallace Stevens', 'Spider blues', 'The gate in his head', 'Burning hills', and 'White dwarfs', all written between 1967 and 1973. These lyrics—for the most part in the first person—are his most self-reflexive poems; whatever their surface or narrative concerns, they are ultimately about poetry, and constitute Ondaatje's most explicit and complex exploration of the relationship between life and art. Ondaatje's most ambitious work in verse, and also his most personal, is *Secular love*, a book-length sequence made up of four chronologically arranged sections telling the story of the break-up of a marriage, the poet's own near-breakdown, and finally, after what one section calls 'Rock Bottom', his recovery and return through the love of another woman. The book should be read as a poetic journal rather than as a collection of discrete lyrics. Some of the poems, like the lovingly nuanced and mutedly elegiac 'To a sad daughter', can be read by themselves, yet the volume is so closely organized—with so much of the overall emotional and artistic effect depending on repetitions and echoes of sound, image, situation, and emotion—that the poems often seem more like the chapters of a narrative than parts of a collection. *Handwriting* is a short collection of poems written between 1993 and 1998 in Sri Lanka, their main subject, and Canada. Ancient Sri Lanka informs most of these delicate yet intense poems about such subjects as rock paintings

and burials against thievery, or destruction, of treasures like books and Buddhas: '750 AD the statue of a Samadhi Buddha/was carefully hidden, escaping war,/the treasure-hunters, fifty-year feuds./He was discovered by monks in 1968/sitting upright/buried in Anuradhapura earth,/eyes half closed, hands/in the gesture of meditation' ('Buried'). In the prose-poem 'Death at Kataragama' the speaker meditates on his approaching death and thinks of many things, 'Not goals considered all our lives but, in the final minutes, sudden choice…. that book I wanted to make and shape tight as a stone'—which can stand as a metaphor for *Handwriting*. As a fundraising project for World Literacy of Canada *The story* (2004) reprints one of the poems in the book—each line of which is repeated in Ondaatje's delicate handwriting (in red)—in a deluxe clothbound edition, illustrated with paintings by David Bolduc.

Billy the Kid uses a temporally discontinuous narrative with multiple viewpoints, and includes lyrics, photographs, prose passages, interviews, a play, and deliberately blank pages. The events are consistently ambiguous; and the central characters, Billy and Pat Garrett—drawn from history, legend, and fiction, and given a touch of autobiography—are both paradoxes. In Ondaatje's slightly romanticized narrative, Billy, certainly a killer, is described by Sallie Chisum as 'the pink of politeness/and as courteous a little gentleman/as I ever met'; while Pat Garrett, the sheriff, is a 'sane assassin' whose compulsive sanity and order bear traces of insanity.

Coming through Slaughter fictionalizes the life of Charles 'Buddy' Bolden (1876–1931), a legendary jazz cornetist who, like Billy the Kid, lived 'away from recorded history'. Ondaatje admires Bolden because for him art and life became almost indistinguishable. Bolden's sensibility is so compulsively responsive to the shifts and nuances of the lived moment that his self disappears into his art and, during the novel's climactic parade through Storyville, he loses his sanity. When he died in a state hospital twenty-four years later, his body was brought through the hamlet of Slaughter to New Orleans, where he was buried. The book's most disturbing suggestion is that in certain kinds of creativity, and in certain artists, 'making and destroying' are of necessity almost co-extensive: the tensions within them can be resolved only by being transmuted into art or madness. A visit to Sri Lanka to recapture the family past gave rise to *Running in the family*, a work that is ostensibly autobiographical, described in an authorial note as 'not a history but a portrait or "gesture"'. The various self-contained but interrelated sketches, stories, poems, and photographs offer a compassionate fictionalized portrait of Ondaatje's family's past in Sri Lanka. By the book's end the family exists for the reader somewhere between reality and legend, and we recognize that Ondaatje has quietly erased the boundary between autobiography and fiction. In the skin of a lion offers a similar and equally challenging blurring. Ondaatje's multi-textured and intricately structured semi-historical novel about Toronto between 1918 and 1938, though ostensibly focused on a young man named Patrick Lewis, presents a cross-section of Toronto life, interweaving scenes dealing with immigrant workers building the Bloor Street viaduct, and digging a two-mile tunnel to bring water into the Victoria Park Filtration Plant (called the 'Palace of Purification'), with the widely publicized search for the missing business tycoon, Ambrose Small. Based on Ondaatje's research in Toronto's archives, the book nevertheless subsumes the historical facts and names into a complex and challenging fictional vision of individuals in a rapidly changing society. This novel marks a turn in Ondaatje's fiction towards social and political concerns: though it is by no means a novel of ideas, it reveals a degree of social engagement only hinted at in his earlier work. Two of the characters, the thief Caravaggio and Patrick's daughter Hana, appear again in The English patient. The continuities between it and In the skin of a lion are immediately obvious: a prose style that is often memorably metaphoric and lyrical; the mixing of fact and fiction; the discontinuous narrative; the structuring of the story around a central mystery; and the reappearance of characters from the earlier novel in its successor. The English patient is set in a Tuscan villa during the last days of the Second World War, and involves four people brought together by chance: a young Canadian nurse, a Canadian soldier, an Indian soldier in the British army who is a bomb-disposal expert, and the mysterious English patient of the title, injured and burned in a plane crash. And though parts of the novel are set in England, Egypt, the Sahara, as well as Italy, it is ultimately less about geography and history than about the complex personal relationships of the main characters. The early interest in the relationship between legend and 'truth' or reality develops, in In the skin of a lion and The English patient, into a questioning of history and ideologies: the former novel focuses on history's lacunae and deliberate omissions, while the latter implicitly and ambiguously engages issues of nationalism and post-colonialism. Anil's ghost—lyrical, fragmented, and filled with literary artifice, like The English patient—is a brilliant and rich novel in which violent images of strife-torn Sri Lanka are a background for the work, in isolation, of Sri Lankan Anil Tissera, thirty-three, a forensic pathologist educated abroad and sent back to her homeland under the sponsorship of the Centre for Human Rights in Geneva; of Sarath Diyasena, an archaeologist, who discovers three skeletons, one identified by Anil as modern, in her eyes it is clearly a murder victim (it is eventually identified—Anil's ghost); and of his younger brother Gamini, a doctor made desperate by the crises surrounding him. Their past and present lives, and their association—and the eventual identification of the skeleton—are portrayed in the context of many other characters, and of the horrific background. Anil's ghost shared the GILLER PRIZE with MERCY AMONG THE CHILDREN by David Adams RICHARDS, and received France's Prix Médicis and a Governor General's Award. Ondaatje's next book, Divisadero is a long, often poetic novel set in both California and France, whose readers were divided. Some were puzzled by it and others went along with it and adored it: it won Ondaatje's fifth Governor General's Award. Ondaatje, who became friends with the distinguished film editor Walter Murch when he edited the film of The English patient, produced a wonderfully informative book on filmmaking in the form of conversations they had with a each other—with that word as the title: The conversations: Walter Murch and the art of editing film (2002, rpr. 2004). One of the revelations of the book is how editing affects storytelling in film, as self-imposed editing shapes Ondaatje's fragmented fiction. In the Introduction he says: 'I have made two documentary films, and my fictional works tend to follow this structural process: shooting or writing everything for a number of months or years, then shaping the content into a new form, till it is almost a newly discovered story. I move things around till they become sharp and clear, till they are in the right location. And it is at this stage that I discover the work's true voice and structure.' Divisadero reflects not only his interest in film but the slow, laborious structuring of a multitude of fragments, including echoes in the later text of early acts and events: beautifully written set pieces, historical and geographical research, detailed descriptions of various activities, such as fixing a leak in a water tower, and card games (leading to a discourse on such gambling movies as *The Cincinnati Kid*). The description of DIVISADERO is intended to provide an entry to the discontinuous and sometimes opaque text, illuminating it.

Sam Solecki's *Ragas of longing: the poetry of Michael Ondaatje* (2003) is a masterly work, with a long Introduction by the author in which he says he intends to 'examine the relationship between the life and the poetry; offer a chronological overview of his body of poetic work; comment on influence, development, and continuity; and give close readings to those poems that seem to require them.' All these goals he fulfils brilliantly. See also Ed Jewinski's biography, *Michael Ondaatje: express yourself beautifully* (1994).

Open Letter (1965–). This journal of experimental writing and criticism was founded in Victoria, British Columbia, by Frank DAVEY as a research project into 'open' form. The first series (each 'series' has contained nine issues) was titled 'The Open Letter' and offered selections from the current writing, reading, and correspondence of its contributing editors (George BOWERING, Daphne MARLATT, Fred WAH, David Dawson, and latterly Ted Whittaker). In typewritten format, this series served as a transitional publication between TISH, in which most of the editors participated, and the much larger and professionally printed issues that Davey later produced in eastern Canada. Numbers 5 and 6 of the first series were edited by Ted Whittaker.

The main period of *Open Letter* began when Davey moved to Toronto in 1970 and became associated with bp NICHOL, Victor COLEMAN, and the COACH HOUSE PRESS. Beginning in 1971 the second series featured Nichol, Coleman, Bowering, Wah, and Steve MCCAFFERY as contributing editors and limited its contents to experimental criticism, literary theory, and reviews. Coach House Press acted as publisher from 1971 to 1977. In the fourth (1978–81) and fifth (1982–4) series the magazine ceased publishing reviews and devoted itself to special issues on such topics as performance art, 'pataphysics', poetry and painting, prosody, or on single authors. After the death of bp Nichol in 1988, the editorial board was reorganized to include Davey, Barbara Godard, Terry Goldie, Smaro Kamboureli, McCaffery, Lola Lemire Tostevin, and Wah. (In 2009 they are called 'contributing editors') In its various editorial initiatives *Open Letter* has endorsed textual and phenomenological criticism, supported interchange between the Canadian and international avant-gardes,

proposed a linguistic foundation for both writing and criticism, championed western-Canadian writing, and argued against the centralization of the Canadian literary tradition that it saw implicit in both the Canadian nationalist movement of the 1970s and the 'thematic' criticism of Northrop FRYE, D.G. JONES, and Margaret ATWOOD. After its 1988 reorganization, many of its issues examined questions of feminism and the writing of younger members of racial-minority communities. Published three times a year in Strathroy, Ontario (102 Oak Street), *Open Letter* is still edited by Frank Davey; its subtitle is *A Canadian Journal of Writing and Theory*. It is worth noting that four issues are devoted to bp Nichol: Fall 1998, Spring 2008, Spring 2009, and Fall 2009.

Oppel, Kenneth (b. 1967). Born in Port Alberni, British Columbia, he was educated at the University of Toronto (B.A., 1989) and has been a freelance writer since the year he graduated, having published his first children's book, *Colin's fantastic video adventure*, with the encouragement of Roald Dahl, when he was fifteen. Oppel has written numerous books for younger readers, such as *A bad case of ghosts* (1993), *A strange case of magic* (1993), *A crazy case of robots* (1994), *An incredible case of dinosaurs* (1994), *A weird case of super-goo* (1996), and *Emma's emu* (1995). His more challenging books for older readers include *The live-forever machine* (1990), *Dead water zone* (1992), and the Silverwing saga—*Silverwing* (1997, rpr. 2002), *Sunwing* (1999, rpr. 2001, 2003), and *Firewing* (2002, rpr. 2004)—which has sold more than a million copies worldwide. *Silverwing*, which has sold more than 250,000 copies, is a long, riveting tale about talking bats, notably young Shade, who becomes lost on the event-filled migration south until he finally regains his family and friends in Hibernaculum. It is an adventure fantasy circumscribed by a night-time world and by the bats' being guided in total darkness by a sonar system based on an ultrasonic cry, brought to life by appealing characters, and enriched by their plausible 'society', 'culture', and habits: 'Breaking sharply, [Shade] scooped the beetle up with his tail membrane, flicked it into his left wing, and volleyed it straight into his open mouth. He veered up and away, and cracked the hard shell with his teeth, savoring the delicious beetle meat as it squirted down his throat. After a few good chomps, he swallowed it whole. Very tasty.' In October 2000 Oppel read from *Silverwing* in the Skydome, Toronto, with J.K. Rowling of Harry Potter fame and

Tim WYNNE-JONES at the International Festival of Authors. In the award-winning *Airborn* (2004, GGA, rpr. 2008)—it has received twelve honours—Matt Cruse, a cabin boy on the huge luxury airship *Aurora*, rescues the unconscious pilot of a crippled hot-air balloon. Before he dies the pilot tells Matt about the fantastic creatures he has seen flying through the clouds. In due course Matt is swept into unimaginable adventures. In *Skybreaker* (2005) a slightly older Matt is on a training ship and, at an enormous height, 16,000 feet, a lost and legendary airship, the huge Hyperion, is sighted. As it is known to be 'a floating treasure trove', much happens after that. In *Starclimber* (2008) Matt has a chance to become one of the world's first astralnauts on the space ship Starclimber. *Darkwing* (2007) takes place in the Paleocene epoch, some 65 million years ago when there was a sudden diversification of mammals, including the bat. As Oppel says, 'The Paleocene was a fascinating period of earth's history, full of drama and change, and it seemed an ideal setting for this story of the very first bats—the only mammal capable of powered flight.' The title *Half brother* (2010) refers to a chimp.

Oppel has written a thriller for adults, *The devil's cure* (2000), concerning cancer researcher Dr Laura Donaldson; David Haines, a death-row inmate with cancer whose immune system is killing his cancer cells and who breaks out of prison, determined to deprive the world of his body's secret; and Kevin Sheldrake, the FBI agent who had sent him to prison and is hunting him down in spite of other law-enforcement officers who want him dead—while, for obvious reasons, Laura wants him alive.

Ormsby, Eric (b.1941). Eric Linn Ormsby was born in Atlanta, Georgia, and raised in Florida. He received a B.A. from the University of Pennsylvania, majoring in oriental studies (Arabic and Turkish), and Princeton University (M.A., Ph.D.), where he specialized in Islamic theology and philosophy. He also pursued Islamic studies at the University of Tubingen, Germany, and in 1978 received a Master of Library Science degree from Rutgers University in New Jersey. From 1993 to 1996 he was associate professor in McGill University's Institute of Islamic Studies and from 1996 to 2005 full professor and director of the Institute. He now lives with his wife in London, England (he has two sons), where he is professor and chief librarian at the Institute of Ismaili Studies. He writes review articles for the *New York Sun*.

A distinguished poet whose work appears internationally in journals, he has published five poetry collections: *Bavarian shrine and other poems* (1990), *Coastlines* (1992), *For a modest God: new and selected poems* (1997), *Araby* (2001), *Daybreak at the straits* (2004), and *Time's covenant: selected poems* (2006). It is pertinent to reflect only on *Time's covenant*—in which the earliest poem was written in 1958 and the most recent in 2006—because it contains generous selections from Ormsby's first four books plus new poems. It therefore displays impressively his strengths as a poet: the clarity of his poems, the disciplined richness of his language, the infusion of wide knowledge, his ability to endow the most ordinary things with beauty ('The colours of disused railyards in winter;/the unnamed shades of iron at four o'clock;/the sun's curiosity along abraded stones;/corrosion that mimes the speckled lichen of woods' from 'Railyard in winter' in *Bavarian shrine*); and in 'Moths at nightfall' from the same book: 'The moths alarmed us./They were big and dark and they clung/Against the screen at night/Like starving children.' The delicate rendering of family devotion is another attribute: 'As my mother ages and becomes/Ever more fragile and precarious,/Her hands dwindle under her rings/And the freckled skin at her throat/Gathers in tender pleats like some startled fabric.' ('My mother in old age'). Ormsby can impress the reader with both sight and sound, as in 'Nova Scotia' in *Coastlines*, written 'south of Halifax, near Peggy's Cove':'... the hulls/Of summer pleasure boats aligned/And tarpaulined, and maybe there will be/A single lantern with its oily light/Reflected in the ocean of November./There in your seclusion from the wind/All night in dreams of home you'll listen for/The cold companionship of distant waves,/Hear squalls beating and the seethe of foam.' In *Araby*, which reflects Ormsby's knowledge of the Middle East, and his humour, there are many poems about Jaham (which means clouds), who is addressed by Allah in 'Allah answers Jaham in the days of dust': 'Consider the camel. *My*/design entirely. Consider how/her nubile nostrils can/asperge the sand: *I* came up/with that. Her popular hump/that wobbles as she strides/is *Mine* as well ....' Writing about the last section of the book, entitled 'Time's covenant', with a two-line epigraph containing that phrase from T.S. Eliot's 'Little gidding', Ormsby says that these poems 'represent a sample from a long collection which I've been working on for a number of years. Covenant itself is a fictional recreation of a nineteenth-century Utopian community in Tennessee, based on a similar settlement where my grandmother and her sisters and brother grew up ....': 'On Founder's Day I drove to Covenant/where my great-grandfather pitched his tent/one hundred and nineteen years ago today.'

Facsimiles of time: essays on poetry and translation (2001) is not only enjoyable to read but valuable for the insights of a man of great erudition. The very first essay, 'Poetry as isotope: the hidden life of words', is immediately interesting to anyone acquainted with Ormsby the poet, so sensitively attuned to words: 'We feel their power, the power of an energy as ancient as humanity itself, and which we are merely privileged to borrow for a time. This is what I mean by the words of my subtitle: the hidden life of words is that life they possessed in the past and will possess in the future, independent of us or of any generation of speakers.' The essays (many of which are book reviews) include two on the American poet Hart Crane (very interesting), followed by others on Keats, William Butler Yeats, and three Canadian poets: David SOLWAY, Pat LOWTHER, and ROO BORSON. Essays on translation have to do with Franz Kafka, Jorge Luis Borges, et al. This fine book ends with a brief memoir, mostly about Ormsby's grandmother, 'The place of Shakespeare in a house of pain'.

Ormsby's scholarly works are *Theodicy in Islamic thought: the dispute over al-Ghazali's 'best of all possible worlds'* (1984), *Handlist of Arabic manuscripts* (1987), *Moses Maimonides and his time* (1987), and *Ghazali* (2007), on al-Ghazali (1058–1111), considered the greatest theologian in Islam.

Ostenso, Martha (1900–63). Born near Bergen, Norway, she came to North America with her parents at the age of two and lived in various towns in Minnesota and North Dakota. Her family moved to Brandon, Manitoba—where Ostenso attended Brandon Collegiate and became interested in writing and painting—and then to Winnipeg, where she attended Kelvin Technical High School and the University of Manitoba. She taught school briefly about 100 miles northwest of Winnipeg—an experience that was to provide the background for her novel *Wild geese* (1925, NCL)—and worked as a reporter on the Winnipeg Free Press. She later joined Douglas DURKIN in New York and attended his course on 'The technique of the novel' at Columbia University, possibly in 1921–2. (It is now thought that the novels published under Ostenso's name were actually co-authored by Durkin, although *Wild geese* is considered to be primarily by Ostenso.) For two-and-a-half years she was a social worker in New York. Ostenso then went with Durkin to Gull Lake, Minnesota, in 1931; they married in 1945 and moved to Seattle in 1963. Ostenso published over a dozen volumes of fiction. *Wild geese* (originally called *The passionate flight*, the title of its English edition), which won a $13,500 prize for a best first novel, is set in Manitoba in the period between the arrival of the geese in the spring and their departure in the autumn. Lind Archer comes to teach at Oeland, and boards with the Gares. Caleb Gare controls his family as a means to the smooth and successful operation of the family farm. Described as 'a spiritual counterpart of the land, as harsh, as demanding, as tyrannical as the very soil from which he drew his existence', he exerts his power in part by emotional blackmail of his wife, Amelia, knowing that she has had, by her lover, a son, Mark Jordan, now an adult but still unaware of who either of his real parents are. When Mark comes to Oeland to manage the homestead of an ailing neighbour of the Gares, he and Lind meet and fall in love. A major figure in the novel is the Gares' daughter, Judith, beautiful as 'some fabled animal'; she is also described as 'vivid and terrible', and her strength and sexuality—which caused a sensation when the book was published—are contrasted with Lind's delicacy and capacity for fine feeling. A counter-example to the isolation experienced by the Gares, individually and as a family, is provided by the Bjarnasson family, in which four generations live in harmony. *Wild geese* represents a major development towards Canadian realism. See Stan Atherton, *Martha Ostenso and her works* (1990).

Other Canadians: an anthology of the new poetry in Canada. See John SUTHERLAND.

Ouellet, Fernand (b. 1926). He was born in Lac-Bouchette, Québec, and educated at Université Laval (B.A., 1948; L.ès L., 1950; D.ès L., 1965). He was professor of history at Laval (1961–5); Carleton University, Ottawa (1965–75); Université d'Ottawa (1975–85); and in 1986 he moved to York University, Toronto, where he has been Professor Emeritus since 1995. He was made an Officer of the Order of Canada in 1979. No other historian achieved more, after the Second World War, to alter the understanding of the first century of British rule in Canada than Ouellet. Through his writing, previous preoccupations were overturned or altered by fresh approaches and new research. Foremost among his concerns was the majority—Québec farmers and rural dwellers—but the activities of other groups such as merchants, politicians, and churchmen, whether francophone or anglophone, were not neglected. Since little had been written about ordinary people (most of it condescending), Ouellet plumbed hitherto neglected contemporary primary sources to provide a portrait of people on their own terms. Ouellet's *Histoire économique et sociale du Québec: 1760–1850: structures et conjoncture* (1966) and his *Le Bas-Canada: 1791–1840: changements structuraux et crise* (1976, GGA; 2nd edn 1980) were not only comprehensive, but also countered the emphasis that the Montreal school of history placed on the negative effects of the British conquest. The translation/adaptation of both books by Patricia Claxton resulted in *Economic and social history of Quebec, 1750–1850* (1980), and *Lower Canada 1791–1840: social change and nationalism* (1980) in the Canadian Centenary Series. In Ouellet's view, the principal forces altering Québec were changes in the nature of the fur trade, population increase, and the advent of the timber trade at the beginning of the nineteenth century. The rise of nationalism and the formation of political parties in the decade after 1800 allowed him to provide explanations of the intricate interplay of ethnicity and social class before the Rebellions of 1837–8. In concert with Ouellet, Marcel TRUDEL, and Jean Hamelin, the Laval school of history forged a perspective at odds with that expounded by their Montreal counterparts.

Ouellette, Fernand (b. 1930). Born in Montreal, he obtained a Licence en sciences sociales at the Université de Montréal (1952). For more than thirty years (1960–91) he directed and produced cultural programs for Radio-Canada. In 1959 he joined Jean-Guy Pilon and other young poets to found the influential literary journal *Liberté*, of which he has served as editor and to which he continues to contribute. Poet, essayist, and novelist, Ouellette has won three Governor General's Awards: the first (which he declined) for a book of essays, *Les actes retrouvé* (1970); the second for his third novel *Lucie; ou Un midi en novembre* (1985); and the third for poetry, *Les heures* (1987), one of his many poetry collections. Ouellette's themes are life, death, artistic

creation, love, sensuality, spiritual quest, and solitude. His images are those of light, sun and flame, night, the female body and the erotic experience, and nature perceived in material and symbolic landscapes. His poetry is highly condensed, its syntax reduced to the most basic structures with few modifiers. Ouellette makes frequent use, in both form and content, of seeming contradictions in theme, image, or structure to produce a metamorphosis and new syntheses through unresolved tensions. Because of the quality, vision, and courageous affirmation of human freedom found consistently throughout his work, Ouellette must be seen as one of Québec's leading writers, who has had a significant impact on the direction of poetry in Québec since the 1960s. EXILE EDITIONS published a bilingual volume of Ouellette's poetry, *Wells of light: selected poems by Fernand Ouellette (1955–1987)* (1989, rpr. 2003); the English translations of poems in seven Ouellette collections are by Ray Ellenwood and Barry CALLAGHAN: 'Did the world tumble/as summer brushed all breathing things?/Dire, desperate,/all too often surge uproots form,/the dead swarm under meadows,/shadows nudging daisies./Dazzled,/the great tree infolds.' ('Meadows'.)

Ouellette-Michalska, Madeleine (b. 1930). She was born in Saint-Alexandre de Kamouraska, Québec. As a child she was self-taught, receiving formal education only after enrolling at the Université de Montréal, where she received her B.A. (1965) and her Licence ès lettres (1968). She earned her M.A. (1978) from the Université du Québec à montréal and her doctorate in French studies (1987) from the Université de Sherbrooke. She is a short-story writer, a poet, and an award-winning novelist and essayist. *La femme de sable* (1979), a slim collection of short stories inspired by her stay as a teacher in Algeria, was translated by Luise Von Flotow under the title *The sandwoman* (1990). Her first book of poetry, *Entre le soufflé et l'aine* (1981), was translated by Wilson Baldridge under the title *Between breath and loins* (1990). Her writing as a whole is infused with desire, as reflected in a strongly sensual, corporeal language.

Outposts. This British literary magazine, founded by Howard Sergeant in 1944 to promote the work of younger writers (notably Muriel Spark), was the first foreign poetry journal to devote an entire issue solely to the work of Canadian poets. *Outposts* 10,

Summer 1948, was edited by Earle BIRNEY (then editor of *Canadian Poetry Magazine*), whom Sergeant had met during the Second World War. By 1948, *Outposts* had become a vehicle for the British Poetry Association, a London-based group dedicated to opening the horizons of national poetry to an international audience. *Outposts* 10 contained poems by Patrick ANDERSON, Louis DUDEK, Birney, E.J. PRATT, Malcolm LOWRY, P.K. PAGE, Robert FINCH, A.M. KLEIN, Dorothy LIVESAY, James REANEY, Roy DANIELLS, Miriam WADDINGTON, R.A.D. FORD, and Ralph GUSTAFSON. Space limitations prevented the inclusion of work by Margaret AVISON, Anne WILKINSON, and Raymond SOUSTER. Of the poems included, one of the most important, from a historical perspective, was Klein's satirical 'Quebec liquor commission', which appeared as 'Quebec liquor commission store' in his *The rocking chair and other poems* (1948). Also of interest is Livesay's sonnet, 'London rain'. The issue was introduced by Birney with a brief essay, 'Contemporary Canadian poetry', in which he charted the rise of Modernism in Canadian poetry, from the MONTREAL GROUP to the late 1940s, and noted the intense activity of such journals as FIRST STATEMENT, *Here and Now*, PREVIEW, CONTEMPORARY VERSE, and the then-new FIDDLEHEAD—anticipating the overwhelming importance that small magazines would play in the shaping of the Canadian literary identity.

Outram, Richard (1930–2005) Born in Oshawa, Ontario, he was educated at Victoria College, University of Toronto (B.A., 1953). He worked on technical crews for CBC-TV from 1956 to 1995, when he retired. With his beloved wife, the artist Barbara Howard, he founded Gauntlet Press in 1960. Outram's early book-length volumes—including *Exultate, jubilate* (1966), *Turns and other poems* (1976), and *The promise of light* (1979)—contain poems written in a loosely metaphysical mode, teasing out paradoxes and polarities with a meticulous playing with language, conceits, and mythological references. His poetry centres on the theme of the discrepancy between human aspirations and spirituality and the gross reality of the world. *Selected poems 1960–1980* (1984) indicated in some of its poems a new direction in Outram's poetry. While retaining a delight in metaphysical paradox, it shifted towards a more open form without losing its hold on structure. In the same way his language also opened into a more conversational and informal diction without letting go of formal elements. This newer style can be seen in *Hiram and Jenny* (1988), a series of poems about the lives and times of the two title characters in a small town in the Maritimes. *Mogul recollected* (1993) focuses on a shipwreck off the coast of New Brunswick, and in particular on an elephant drowned in that disaster—a subject approached with both seriousness and humour. Outram's own Gauntlet Press also published his *Around and about the Toronto islands* (1993), *Tradecraft* (1994), and *Eros descending* (1995). *Benedict abroad* (1998), published in the St Thomas Poetry Series, won the City of Toronto Book Award in 1999. His final book is a substantial collection, *Dove legend and other poems* (2001), a surprising mixture combining poems of high rhetoric and verbal brilliance, some empty of feeling, with restrained, elegant poems that are more appealing. It is dedicated to Barbara: 'She rests, beyond compare, beyond repose./ Between the armatures of darkness she has seen/light summoning the rose.' See *Richard Outram: essays on his works* (2007) edited by Ingrid Ruthig.

Oxley, James MacDonald (1855–1907). Born into a relatively wealthy Halifax family, Oxley was educated at Halifax Academy, Dalhousie University, and Harvard. He was admitted to the Nova Scotia Bar in 1878 and practised law in Halifax for five years before becoming a legal adviser to the federal Department of Marine and Fisheries. In 1891 he moved to Montreal to join the staff of the Sun Life Assurance Company. He spent the final years of his life in Toronto. Oxley wrote thirty-one books for boys, published between 1889 and 1905—unabashed adventure tales exploiting northern and seafaring settings already made popular by G.A. Henty, R.M. BALLANTYNE, and Frederick Marryat. In general, as many of their titles indicate, his stories turn on themes of initiation and the experience of a personable boy-hero whose physical courage is tested in an exotic setting. He usually set them in a remote historical period, though he occasionally used his native Nova Scotia as a backdrop. Among his titles are: *Bert Lloyd's boyhood* (London, 1889), *Up among the ice floes* (London, 1890), *The wreckers of Sable Island* (London, 1891), *Archie of Athabaska* (Boston, 1893; published in London, 1894, as *Archie Mackenzie, the young Nor'wester*), *The good ship Gryphon, or On the right track* (Boston, 1893), *Fife and drum at Louisbourg* (London, 1899), and *L'Hasa at last* (1900).

P

Pacey, Desmond (1917–75). Born in Dunedin, New Zealand, William Cyril Desmond Pacey lived in England from 1924 to 1931, when he came with his family to rural Ontario. He studied English and Philosophy at the University of Toronto (B.A., 1938) and also attended Cambridge University (Ph.D., 1941). He was professor of English at Brandon College, University of Manitoba, from 1941 to 1944, and then moved to the University of New Brunswick, where he remained, serving as head of the Department of English (1944–69), dean of graduate studies (1960–70), vice-president academic (1970–5) and University Professor until his death. Writing criticism that, like his teaching, was lucid, moderate, and modest in its claims, Pacey helped to establish Canadian literature as a legitimate field of study in both universities and schools. His many publications began with his *Frederick Philip Grove* (1945), an interest that continued with a selection of GROVE's stories, *Tales from the margin* (1971); an anthology of critical essays on Grove in the Critical Views of Canadian Writers series (1970); and his edition of *The letters of Frederick Philip Grove* (1976). His *Creative writing in Canada: a short history of English Canadian literature* (1952; rev. and enlarged, 1961) was the only handbook of its kind for many years. His *Ten Canadian poets: a group of biographical and critical essays* (1958) allowed him to treat more fully the work of SANGSTER, ROBERTS, CARMAN, LAMPMAN, D.C. SCOTT, PRATT, SMITH, F.R. SCOTT, KLEIN, and BIRNEY. Pacey was an editor of both editions of the *Literary history of Canada* (1965 and 1976). His *Essays in Canadian criticism: 1938–1968* (1969) and *Ethel Wilson* (1968), in the Twayne series, contain some of his best critical writing. He edited *A book of Canadian stories* (1947; 4th edn 1967) and *The selected poems of Sir Charles G.D. Roberts* (1956), as well as the school anthology *Our literary heritage* (1966). Two scholarly editions he was preparing at the time of his death were published posthumously: *The collected poems of Charles G.D. Roberts* (1985), completed by Graham Adams, and *The collected letters of Charles G.D. Roberts* (1989), completed by Laurel Boone. Pacey also published two collections of stories, *The picnic and other stories* (1958) and *Waken, lords and ladies gay: selected stories* (1974), edited by Frank M. Tierney.

Paci, F.G. (b. 1948). Born in Pesaro, Italy, he immigrated to Canada with his parents in 1952 and grew up in Sault Ste Marie, Ontario. His education includes a B.A. (1970), and B.Ed. (1975) from the University of Toronto, where he was encouraged by Margaret LAURENCE, who was writer-in-residence; and an M.A. (1980) from Carleton University. Paci—an outstanding Italian-Canadian novelist writing in English—lives in Toronto and teaches in Etobicoke. His first novel, *The Italians* (1978), is a realistic representation of a large and diverse Italian immigrant family in Sault Ste Marie, and became a bestseller. His best novel is *Black Madonna* (1982), the story of a young Canadian woman who totally rejects her Italian background and abandons her old-fashioned Italian mother to go off to university. Feminist ideas are also examined in *The father* (1984), where a strong mother takes over the family business. Following the conventions of realism, Paci's novels explore the struggle of Italian immigrant families in northern Ontario and the children of these families in Toronto. He has argued that his work is not so much about ethnic duality as about the essential self and the ultimate search for truth. Existentialist philosophical ideas are explored in a series of related novels beginning with *Black blood* (1991), followed by *Under the bridge* (1992), *Sex and character* (1993)—which recreates a scene with Margaret Laurence—and *The rooming-house* (1996). The setting of *Italian shoes* (2002) is Italy, when Mark Trecoci searches for his family roots in Venice, Florence, and Rome. *Losers* (2002) is an interesting, entirely believable novel about teenagers in high school. In *Hard edge* (2005) Mark Trecoci is a writer and painter and we are told on the first page that he and his girlfriend Lisa James, a serious painter, are 'into art, love, and knowledge.' The readable story—set in Ontario, New York, and Paris—also involves seduction and betrayal. See *F.G. Paci: essays on his works* (2003) edited by Joseph Pivato.

Packard, Frank (1877–1942). Born of American parents in Montreal, Frank Lucius Packard, who wrote more than thirty novels, was one of the first Canadian authors to reach a wide audience outside Canada. He trained as an engineer, attending McGill University (B.Sc., 1897) and L'Institut

Montefiore, Liège. While working as a civil engineer in the USA, he published his first short story in *Munsey's Magazine* in 1906, and in 1911 a collection of his magazine fiction, *On the iron at Big Cloud*, was brought out by Thomas Crowell of New York. Having married in 1910, Packard settled in Lachine, Québec, and wrote his first novel, *Greater love hath no man* (1913). His next novel, *The miracle man* (1914), which originally appeared in *Munsey's*, was a great success. Adapted for the stage by George M. Cohan, it played at the Astor Theatre, New York, and was made into a popular silent film. In 1917 Packard published another bestseller, *The adventures of Jimmy Dale*—the first of five Jimmy Dale novels—which set a pattern for his crime fiction. Thereafter he produced about a novel a year, all originally published in New York by Doran but reprinted in both Toronto and London. Packard used several formulas to gain mass-market appeal for his novels. He drew on his experience with railroads for *The wire devils* (1918), a crime novel with a surprise ending, and for many of the stories in *On the iron at Big Cloud*, reprinted, with additions, in *Running special* (1925). The same characters people the stories in *The night operator* (1919), tales stressing the technical competence and toughness of the railwaymen in the foothills of the American Rockies; despite melodramatic incidents, they present a believable social spectrum and suggest a heroic struggle to conquer a continent. For his highly successful series of Jimmy Dale crime novels, Packard haunted the streets of New York and joined police raids; but for all their authentic atmosphere, they have conventional plots that rely heavily on impenetrable disguise, miraculous escapes, and vital information overheard. Their chief character is a millionaire clubman and champion of honour and fair play who inhabits the underworld under various disguises and foils crime through his expertise in safe-cracking and lock-picking. By 1942 the series had sold an estimated 3 million copies and been made into a silent serial and a CBC Radio series (1942–5). Another group of Packard's novels, labelled 'romances' by his publisher, are also crime novels, but with more claim to serious consideration: they stress psychological themes of repentance, self-sacrifice, and redemptive love. In *Greater love hath no man* (1913), Varge shields his beloved foster mother by confessing to a murder he did not commit. Characteristically, Packard imbibed the atmosphere for this novel by visiting the St Vincent de Paul Penitentiary in Montreal, but he transferred the setting to an unnamed American location. *The miracle man* and *The sin that was his* (1917) describe the experiences of wrong-doers who are gradually converted by a religious power they set out to mock. Packard visited the South Seas in 1912, and in the 1920s he began to use them as a setting for novels with exotic titles like *Two stolen idols* (1927) and *The gold skull murders* (1931). Invention and careful attention to local colour, hardening into formula, are the main features of his enormous output.

Page, P.K. (b. 1916–2010). Patricia Kathleen Page was born at Swanage in the south of England. Her family came to Canada in 1919 and settled in Red Deer, Alberta. She was educated at St Hilda's School, Calgary, and, in later years, studied art under Frank Schaeffer in Brazil and Charles Seliger in New York. She also attended the Art Students' League and Pratt Graphics in New York. During the late 1930s she worked as a shop assistant and a radio actress in Saint John, New Brunswick; she then moved to Montreal, working as a filing clerk and a historical researcher. There, in the early 1940s, she associated with the writers who, for a time, made that bilingual city the most important centre of English-language poetry in Canada. Page published her first poems in Alan Crawley's CONTEMPORARY VERSE before she joined the MONTREAL GROUP—including F.R. SCOTT, with whom she had a close friendship—that had founded *PREVIEW*. It soon became apparent that among the younger poets of the group, she was the most accomplished. Her first collection, *As ten as twenty* (1946), showed a strong awareness of English poetic trends in the 1930s; and while Page did not make the extreme political commitments of those who at this time entered the Communist Party, it was evident that she had taken sides against the Anglo-Canadian establishment that then seemed to rule in Montreal. She also shared the psychoanalytic preoccupations of contemporary English poets, and some of the best of her early verse deals with various forms of neurosis. In terms of lyrical vision, the best poem in this first volume is undoubtedly the haunting 'Stories of snow', in which legend and dream and child memories are mingled—to quote A.J.M. SMITH—in 'a crystal clairvoyance'. In 1946 Page started to work as a scriptwriter for the National Film Board, and remained there until 1950, when she married William Arthur Irwin, at that time commissioner of the NFB. In this period she completed a poetry collection, *The metal and* *the flower* (1954, GGA). In their sharply visual presentations of concrete situations, and perhaps influenced by the space created in poetry by W.H. Auden for social commentary, the poems reflect the social concerns of a postwar world. They consider not ordinary political commitments but the plights of lonely people, or those whom circumstances have condemned to appear contemptible; some are miniature imaginary biographies that come as near as any writer can to the meeting of satire and compassion. In 1944, under the *nom-de-plume* of 'Judith Cape', she published a novel—or perhaps a romance— called *The sun and the moon*. Page has never explained her pseudonym, but Margaret ATWOOD noticed 'the visions of cloak-and-dagger and Holofernes' severed head raised by the last and first names respectively', and such associations are appropriate to a novel that deals with a young girl in touch with mysterious forces that almost destroy her artist husband. It was republished under Page's name in *The sun and moon and other fictions* (1973), which includes other stories from the 1940s that are less strained in credibility and at the same time more tightly organized. The best of them, as Atwood has said, are characterized by 'the bizarre perspectives and the disconcerting insights' that distinguish Page's best poems. Some, like 'The green bird' and 'George', project a wild yet pathetic sense of comedy. Others, such as 'The glass box', resemble early poems, like 'The landlady' and 'The stenographers', in their power to convey the sadness of lonely people trying to snatch a little meaning from their lives in the unfriendly city.

From 1953 to 1964—when W.A. Irwin acted as Canadian high commissioner in Australia and ambassador in Brazil and Mexico— Page lived away from Canada and wrote comparatively little poetry, concentrating on paintings and intricate drawings she made under the name P.K. Irwin—works that show how her two arts reflect each other, for they evoke poetic as well as aesthetic images. *Brazilian journal* (1987) is a rich, memorable account of her time in that country, embellished by her paintings, some in colour. The unity of her arts is stressed in the new poems she included in *Cry Ararat!* (1967) and *Poems selected and new* (1974), both of which consist largely of works chosen from her first books. The reproductions of Page's paintings and drawings in *Cry Ararat!*, although in black and white, and thereby missing the colour that is Page's distinctive signature as an artist, do give a sense of the dynamic movement and exquisitely detailed precision of her landscapes. The connections and correspondences between writing and painting are clear in 'Bark drawing', which shows her affinity with Australian Native art, and evokes with marvellous economy her double talents: 'an alphabet the eye/ lifts from the air/as if by ear/two senses/ threaded through/a knuckle bone.'

The newer poems demonstrate a movement towards verbal economy that one can link with Page's later philosophic inclination towards the mystical tradition of Sufism. In *Evening dance of the grey flies* (1981) there is an ever-increasing purification of the line. In the early poems the line was long and flowing, with the kind of full eloquence that belonged to the 1940s. In the newer poems there is still a fluidity, but it is more controlled, sparser, yet ever-moving. Similarly the pattern of thought is modified, and filled with a metaphysical intent that shifts its direction from the inward images of the earlier poems to the images of natural sublimity that pose a way of liberation from the alienated, imprisoned self. Increasingly Page's poems carry a kind of Delphic utterance, almost a possession by the vision; though the poems are perhaps more sharply and intensely visual than ever in their sensuous evocation of shape and colour and space, their imagery takes us magically beyond any ordinary seeing into a realm of imagining in which the normal world is shaken like a vast kaleidoscope, and revealed in unexpected and luminous relationships. The centrepiece is a remarkable futurist story, 'Unless the eye catch fire …', which ostensibly deals with the death of earth as a habitation of man, and the end of time as man dies; but on another level it projects a visionary perception, suggesting that one does not have to wait for the end of time to apprehend eternity. *The glass air: selected poems* (1985) ranges retrospectively over Page's body of work and includes drawings and two eloquent essays on the genesis of her art(s): 'Questions and images' and 'Traveller, conjuror, journeyman', which develop Page's idea that 'in all essential particulars writing and painting are interchangeable. They are alternate routes to silence.' This was reissued as *The glass air: poems selected and new* (1991), which contained a number of new poems—such as 'A little fantasy' and 'I-Sphinx'—that demonstrate Page's gift for creating dramatic voices in her poetry. *Hologram: a book of glosas* (1994) is a selection of fourteen elegant and intricate poems that resuscitate the late fourteenth-century Spanish poetic form, the *glosa*—which begins with a short stanza or *cabeza* of four consecutive lines taken from another poet, followed by four ten-line stanzas, each of which ends with a line from the *cabeza*. As Page explains in her preface, the poems allowed her to pay homage to those poets whose work she 'fell in love with' in her formative years. There is an elegiac quality to the poems as the poet looks back over a lifetime of experience, yet they build to a celebratory affirmation of the mystery of being human: 'We are the sea's, and as such we are at its beck. / We are the water within the wave and the water's form./And little will man—or woman, come to that—/know what he shall dream when drawn by the sea's wrack/or what he shall hope for once it is clear that he'll never go back.' Most important among Page's later publications is the impressive two-volume *The hidden room: collected poems* (1997). *Alphabetical* (1998) is an elegant chapbook that is intricate in its interlocking poems—one poem plays with a word in the preceding poem—on each letter of the alphabet.

Beginning when Page was in her middle eighties, her publications were prolific. *A kind of fiction* (2001) is a collection of eighteen stories, the earliest of which first appeared in *Preview* more than sixty years ago; others appeared in *The TAMARACK REVIEW, The MALAHAT REVIEW,* and *DESCANT,* etc. One enjoys in Page's fiction the astute observations, wit, and wide range of interests—a fairy tale, 'The sky tree', is included—that are apparent in all her writing. This was followed in 2007 by another collection of stories, *Up on the roof. Planet earth: poems selected and new* (2002) is a collection of ninety-four poems selected by Eric ORMSBY. He begins his Foreword by saying: 'It has become customary in Canada to describe P.K. Page as "distinguished", but that epithet betrays her. P.K. Page is simply too vivacious, too cunning, too elusive to be monumentalized. She is in fact the supreme escape artist of our literature. Try to confine her in a villanelle and she scampers off into free verse. Peg her as a prose poet and she springs forth with a glosa. Categorize her as a poet who writes fiction, but then note that you find very little "poet's prose" in her stories.' It is surprising that *Hand luggage: a memoir in verse* (2006) is not generally recognized because the apparently easy rendition of the known and little-known facts of Page's life are given to us in a compelling poetic narrative that one can hardly stop reading before it ends: 'Is it luck, is it destiny? How to account/for the fact, knowing nobody, I could connect,/a kid from the sticks,/with Abe Klein and Frank Scott,/Arthur Smith, Patrick Anderson, *Preview,* the lot?/A miracle.' When her great love takes over her life, 'someone in me was born and someone died.' She loses her lover, moves to Ottawa, and there is a happy marriage. The primary place of *Hand luggage* among Canadian memoirs should not be ignored. *The filled pen: selected non-fiction* (2007) was edited by Zailig Pollock. In a brief Foreword, Page the poet says that 'in actual word count I have written much more prose.' It is a short but memorable collection that includes 'A writer's life', and personal appreciations of two poets: George JOHNSTON, 'Notes on re-reading George Johnston', and A.M. KLEIN, 'The sense of angels: reflections on A.M Klein'. Page first saw Klein at a meeting of the *Preview* group during the war in the 1940s, when Abe wore a dark suit. She remembers it was summer. 'Summer dresses and open shirts. So Abe would not have been in the dark suit, which is how I see him in memory's eye.' Then there is a wonderful Page aphorism: 'Memory, so faithless to fact, so eager to please and quick to invent.' In 2008 *The essential P.K. Page* was published, edited by Arlene Lampert and Théa Gray—a collection of forty-nine poems that really do represent, in an attractive book, the poet at her best. The following year saw the publication of *Coal and roses: twenty-one glosas,* drawing on poems by internationally famous authors plus Canadians Dionne BRAND, Don McKAY, and Gwendolyn MacEWEN. With short biographies and photographs of the twenty-one poets represented, it is elegantly designed and produced (with a pretty cover) by Page's publisher since 2001, PORCUPINE'S QUILL. It was nominated for the 2010 GRIFFIN POETRY PRIZE.

Page has written the texts of six picture books for children: *A flask of sea water* (1989), *The goat that flew* (1993), *A grain of sand* (2003), *Jake the baker makes a cake* (2008), *The old woman and the hen* (2009), and *Three children's fables* (2009), plus *A Brazilian alphabet for the younger reader* (2005). Her poetry has been set to music by composers as various as Murray Adaskin, Bernard Naylor, Ruth Watson Henderson, Harry Somers, and Gavin Bryers. She was made a Companion of the Order of Canada in 1998 and has received honorary degrees from eight universities. See *P.K. Page: essays on her works* (2001) edited by Linda ROGERS and Barbara Colebrook Peace.

Page, Rhoda Anne (1826–63). Probably the bestknown Canadian poet for a brief period in the late 1840s, Page was brought to Canada from her native England at the age of six, when her family immigrated to a farm near Cobourg, Canada West (Ontario). Beginning in 1846, using the initials R.A.P., she published her poetry regularly in *The Cobourg*

Star, from which other newspapers copied it, and in other periodicals; her writing was therefore widely circulated through the Canadas. A pamphlet collection, *Wild notes from the backwoods*, was published in Cobourg in 1850. In 1856 she married William Faulkner, moved to the Rice Lake area, and had eight children. E.H. DEWART included five of her poems, using her married name, in his anthology *Selections from Canadian poets* (1864). Although a melancholy preoccupation with death runs through much of her work, Page was essentially a poet of nature. The Canadian backwoods, as she described them, was a tranquil world that owed its beauty and life to a genteel God. Her 'Rice Lake by moonlight: a winter scene', was the most widely reprinted Canadian poem of its day. One of the multitude of female lyric poets who peopled the literary world of the early nineteenth century, Page wrote verse that flows smoothly and effortlessly, with great charm, and the part of Ontario she described is recognizable today.

Panneton, Philippe (1895–1960). Better known under his pseudonym 'Ringuet' (his mother's family name), he was born in Trois-Rivières, Québec. He studied medicine at Université Laval, first in Quebec City, then in Montreal, and obtained his degree in 1920. He then left for Paris, spending three years on postgraduate studies in otorhinolaryngology. He returned to Canada in 1923 to practise medicine in Montreal, and in 1935 he became a professor in the faculty of medicine at the Université de Montréal. In 1956 he was appointed ambassador to Portugal, where he died. Panneton was very proud of being a physician: 'I am first a doctor and then a writer. Literature interests me like a sport. It is a distraction in my leisure time' (*La Revue populaire*, juillet 1939, p. 6). Nevertheless he diligently pursued this 'distraction', publishing numerous books, including three novels and a collection of short stories. Panneton achieved his greatest success as a writer with the publication of *Trente arpents* (1938), a classic of French-Canadian literature that was translated by Felix and Dorothea Walter as THIRTY ACRES (1940, GGA, NCL). It is the tragic story of Euchariste Moisan who, though devoted to his land, loses it and is sent by one son to his other son in the USA, where he is completely isolated by language. The title story of *L'héritage et autres contes* (1946), which is reminiscent of *Thirty acres* and was Panneton's favourite, was translated by Morna Scott Stoddart and appeared as 'The heritage' in *Canadian short stories* (1960, rpr. 2008) edited by Robert WEAVER.

Panych, Morris (b. 1952). Born in Calgary, he studied creative writing at the University of British Columbia (B.F.A., 1977) and acting at the E.15 Acting School in London, England. He lives in Vancouver. Working initially as an actor (he has performed in more than fifty plays), he is also a director, and has written some twenty-five works for the stage; his plays have been produced in over a dozen languages.

Panych first achieved prominence as a playwright in 1982 at Tamahnous Theatre, Vancouver—of which he was artistic director from 1984 to 1986—with *Last call: a postnuclear cabaret* (1983). This two-man musical, which he performed with Ken MacDonald (a frequent future collaborator), features the final two survivors of a nuclear holocaust, and plays with metatheatrical devices, such as a double ending to foreground the process of performance. Later plays continue to exploit the last stages of life as a convenient context for comic exaggeration. *Seven stories* (1990) moves into the surreal, isolating a solitary figure (The Man) on a ledge to contemplate suicide, while bizarre characters pop out of windows to play out their seven stories behind, across, and through him. Satiric references to philosophy, literature, politics, and art make highly comic the audience's attempts to fix meaning. *The ends of the earth* (1993, GGA) continues Panych's delight in comic philosophizing. In *Vigil* (1996, renamed *Auntie & me*) Panych once more finds black comedy in imminent death, as an old aunt refuses to die as scheduled, despite the harassing harangues of her impatient nephew. It played in London's West End and toured in the US and Canada; and under the title *Vigil*, in the fall of 2009, it was produced at the DR2 Theatre in New York. Another popular work that has toured, *The overcoat* (with Wendy Gorling, 1997), is wordless, a combination of movement, mime, and drama expressing two short stories by the Russian dramatist Nikolai Gogol. *Other schools of thought* (1994) is a collection of three short plays, all commissioned and first produced by Green Thumb Theatre for Young People, Vancouver. *Life science* and *Cost of living* are monologues, with accompanying slide projections in the first and a video in the second; and *2B WT UR* has three young people and two adults in the cast; all three plays portray young people discussing or reflecting on themselves and their future. In the expertly constructed two-character play *Lawrence and Holloman* (1998), the title characters meet and have surreal, Beckett-like conversations at various times and in various settings in the course of which the successful, confident Lawrence gradually declines into one-leggedness and blindness, and Holloman, the nobody, gains mastery, and the two are joined in a surprising end. It was first produced in Apr. 1998 by the Tarragon Theatre, Toronto, where three of Panych's subsequent plays were also produced: *Earshot* (2001), *Girl in the goldfish bowl* (2003, GGA), and *Benevolence* (2008). *Earshot* is a one-man play, a monologue by Doyle, who is driven almost crazy by sounds. For example, he hates public transit: 'I don't mean the inane conversations; that goes without saying. It's the incidental noise that clatters so unbearably in my ears. The jangling of cheap jewelry, the rattling of old men, the crackling of chewing gum. Humanity. What an excruciating burble.' In the award-winning *Girl in the goldfish bowl*, ten-year-old Iris has the first line: 'These are the last few days of my childhood.' With the appearances and exits of her mother Sylvia, Miss Rose and Owen, who live in the house, and Mr Lawrence, who comes to stay, Iris— whose fish, called Amahl, has died—has the most, and the most intelligent and knowing, things to say. 'OWEN: No one likes a ten-year-old with an opinion. IRIS: Especially a more interesting one.' The comings and goings of the characters and their dialogue—non-understanding, often fragmented, as in this exchange between Owen and Lawrence: 'Where are you going?/What?/Wait here./Where?/Just–/Just–?/–the two of us./Right. Got it. Just—who? Us?/No. Us.'—create a complex play, with many resonances, that may be most effective when seen rather than read, though it is still amusing and thought provoking to read. *The dishwashers* (2005) of the title work in the basement of a fancy restaurant and Moss, the old-timer, and Emmett, the 'new guy', are dominated by their boss, Dressler, who always has a lot to say. 'You don't need to tell me how people succeed. Running around like fucking jackrabbits, in their fast cars; shouting into phones. They're upstairs right now, eating off my plates. I'd like to kill them all, to be honest.' It's a clever funny-and-sad play. In *What lies before us* (2007) the experienced Scottish Ambrose and the young Englishman Keating are assistant surveyors for the Canadian Pacific Railway in the Rocky Mountains in 1885; the Chinese Mr Wing, who knows no English, appears off and on. Ambrose and Keating take part in a long, amusing dialogue that leads nowhere— and in the end Keating dies; and Ambrose, cared for by Wing, dies: 'Who are we to be remembered? Eh, Wing? Who are we?' Wing ends the play, speaking in Chinese (translated). *Benevolence* is an interesting, conversationally

brilliant play about what happens when Oswald Eichersen gives a street person, Terence Lomy, a hundred-dollar bill. In 2009 Panych published *Still laughing*, a collection of his adaptations of three comedy classics: *The government inspector, Hotel Peccadillo*, and *The amorous adventures of Anatol*.

In the 2008 season of the Stratford Festival, Herman Melville's *Moby-dick*, adapted and directed by Panych, was effectively produced in the Studio Theatre and praised. Panych directed his new family play, *The trespassers*, when it was produced in Stratford's Studio Theatre in (Aug.-Oct.) 2009.

Parizeau, Alice (1930–90). Born Alicja Poznanska in Luniec, Poland, she grew up in Cracow. She participated in the Polish resistance movement, and was sentenced to a German work camp. After the war, in 1945, she went to Paris, where she studied literature, political science, and obtained a master's degree in law (1953). She then immigrated to Canada and began a career as a journalist in Montreal. In 1956 she married Jacques Parizeau (premier of Québec, 1994–5), by whom she had a son and daughter. In 1970 she joined the criminology faculty of the Université de Montréal. Alice Parizeau published twelve novels. *Les lilas fleurissent à Varsovie* (1981)—translated by A.D. Martin-Sperry as *The lilacs are blooming in Warsaw* (1985)—was the first of three novels that make up her ambitious *cycle polonais*. Her subject was no less than the history of the Polish people, from the German occupation during the Second World War through Sovietization to the 1980's Solidarity movement. Told through the experiences of one family, in which the characters' individual happiness often conflicts with collective aspirations to political autonomy, this saga confirmed Parizeau as a master of short scenes, and of character and detail. As Alice Poznanska-Parizeau she was made an Officer of the Order of Canada in 1987.

Parker, Sir Gilbert (1862–1932). He was born in Camden Township East, Canada West (Ontario). After graduating from Trinity College, University of Toronto, he taught elocution there; he was later ordained a deacon in the Anglican Church. A short period as a parish assistant in Trenton, Ont., concluded with his departure in 1885 for Australia, where he rapidly rose as a journalist, becoming assistant editor of the Sydney *Morning Herald*. Before his departure for England in 1889 he travelled extensively in the South Pacific, penning romantic accounts of the spots he visited. In

England his skills as a writer of popular fiction, his position as a Member of Parliament (1900–18), and his 'good' marriage advanced him steadily. A knighthood (1902), a baronetcy (1915), and membership in the Privy Council (1916) testify that bright colonial sons like Parker (along with Bonar Law and Max Aitken) could aspire to the inner circles of the imperial motherland. During the Great War, Parker directed the British government's vast propaganda effort to move American public opinion in a pro-British direction, a project that was ultimately successful. Parker's last years were spent in California with the family of his brother. Parker's *Works* (1912–23) comprise twenty-three volumes, most of them historical novels of romance and adventure.

His contribution to Canadian letters rests on his fictional treatment of three subject areas: the romantic Northwest, picturesque Québec, and heroic New France. *Pierre and his people* (London, 1892), a collection of adventure tales about the colourful Métis, Amerindians, Mounties, and imperial adventurers in a Northwest he had never visited, put Parker on the map of literary London and was reprinted many times. Parker's Québec—the subject of *When Valmond came to Pontiac* (London, 1895), *The pomp of the Lavilettes* (Boston, 1896), *The lane that had no turning* (London, 1899), and *The money master* (1915), among other novels—is a quaint, agrarian society filled with simple rustics whose lives become momentarily ruffled by scheming villains, hot-headed lovers, and restless adventurers. New France offered an arena for heroic action in *The trail of the sword* (New York, 1894), *The seats of the mighty* (London, 1896), and *The power and the glory* (1925). *The seats of the mighty*—reprinted in 1982 edited by John Coldwell Adams—stemmed from the same source as *The GOLDEN DOG* by William KIRBY. Set at the time of the Conquest, it concerns the adventures in love and war of a British army spy, Robert Moray, and was based partly on the *Memoirs* of Robert Stobo (1727–70). Moray finally wins Alixe and defeats his rivals; the British take Québec; and English daring, drive, and hardihood are wedded to French charm, beauty, and emotional richness. No other novel quite sums up with such vigour and aplomb the imperialist view of Québec's role in Canada. See John C. Adams, *Seated with the mighty: a biography of Sir Gilbert Parker* (1979).

Parr, Joy (b. 1949). Born in Toronto, she was educated at McGill University, Montreal (B.A., 1971), and Yale University (M.Phil.,

1973; Ph.D., 1977). She taught at Queen's University, Kingston, Ontario, at Yale, and at the University of British Columbia, before joining the department of history at Queen's (1982–92), becoming professor there in 1988, and then Farley Professor of History at Simon Fraser University, Burnaby, British Columbia (1992–2003). She is now Canada Research Chair in Technology, Culture, and Risk, University of Western Ontario (2003–).

Indicative of the fresh approaches to Canadian historical scholarship in the late twentieth century are the subjects Parr has drawn attention to: the way in which children, women, gender, and consumerism figured in the past. *Labouring children: British immigrant apprentices to Canada, 1869–1924* (1980, rev. 1993) was the first thoroughly documented examination of the subject of dumping the unwanted offspring of industrial Britain on its North American colony. An informative and dispassionate analysis reveals the critical stages in which immigration had occurred and the means taken to govern it. With children rather than politicians as her focus, Parr concluded that while there had been injustices, sometimes so severe as to bring premature death, the movement of young people had transpired with increasing attention to their needs. The book was decentring: children, rather than economics or politics, became the criterion on which historical judgement was based. Parr conceived a seminal study that was published as *The gender of breadwinners: women, men, and change in two industrial towns, 1880–1950* (1990, rpr. 1998). Mastering industrial processes in textiles and furniture making, social structures, and economic change in the United Kingdom and Canada, she was able to show for the first time the gendered consequences of technological transfer and immigration as they were experienced in Paris and Hanover, Ontario. New directions were also indicated in *A diversity of women: Ontario, 1945–1980* (1995) and *Domestic goods: the material, the moral, and the economic in the postwar years* (1999). Parr edited with Nancy Janovicek *Histories of Canadian children and youth* (2003).

parti pris (1963–8). Founded by Pierre Maheu, André MAJOR, and Paul Chamberland, et al., it was a highly influential political and cultural review published in Montreal. Its founders reacted against the generation of intellectuals that preceded them, and specially those around the review *Cité libre*, reproaching them for denouncing the political corruption of the Duplessis régime and particular cases of injustice without attacking the fundamental injustices rooted in the economic and social structure of Québec society. This initial ideology, mainly centred on the idea of decolonization, later developed into a certain radicalization. The leaders of the review defined the situation from a Marxist perspective: the struggle for political independence appeared only as the first step towards social revolution. An internal conflict over whether René Lévesque's Mouvement souveraineté-association (1968, later the Parti Québécois) should be supported tactically or a new radical party founded, and the editors' view that the main aims of *parti pris* (independence, secularism, and socialism) had been widely disseminated, led them to cease publication. The magazine, and the publishing house Les Éditions parti pris (founded in 1961)—which was active for some three decades—played an important role in the literary and artistic development of Québec.

Pearson, Kit (b. 1947). Kit (Kathleen Margaret) Pearson was born in Edmonton, Alberta. She worked as a children's librarian in the public libraries of St Catharines and North York, Ontario, and Burnaby, British Columbia. After receiving her M.A. in children's literature from Simmons College, Boston, she settled in Vancouver. Pearson's novels for young people include *The daring game* (1986), an exploration of boarding-school life in 1960s Vancouver; *A handful of time* (1987), which blends fantasy and social history with the dynamics and secrets of family life; a historical trilogy—*The sky is falling* (1989), *Looking at the moon* (1991), and *The lights go on again* (1993), published in one volume as *The guests of war trilogy* (1998); and *Awake and dreaming* (1996, GGA), a ghost fantasy. These books are straightforward, clear, and tightly written with a gentle pace and, most often, episodic plots. A recurring theme is that of children being uprooted, leaving their homes, and forming their own societies as separate tribes apart from the intervention of parents and other adults. Another pattern is the exploration of personal integrity and courage as child characters become involved in moral choice and dilemmas. The novels have strong, memorable characters, usually eleven- or twelve-year-old girls in the pre-pubescent stage of personal strength, confidence, and imagination. All are rooted in the history and landscape of different parts of Canada. *A perfect gentle knight* (2007) draws the reader immediately into the lives of the six Bell children—particularly eleven-year-old Corrie (Cordelia) and her older brother Sebastian—who are dealing with the grief they feel over the death of their mother. They are more or less looking after themselves because their father is distant and uninvolved. One way they manage is to play at being Knights of the Round Table—Corrie is Sir Gawain and her older brother is Sir Lancelot. Like all Pearson's novels, this account of growing up is wonderfully readable; it skilfully and gently intertwines the conflicts of youth, the importance of imagination, and the significance of fantasy. The title is a line in Chaucer's *Canterbury Tales*. *The singing basket* (1990) is a picture book that retells a French-Canadian folktale of deceit and trickery as a woodcutter husband outwits his wife in a clever, lively manner. The text is a rewriting of the story that accompanied Ann Blades' fine watercolour paintings for an earlier edition of the tale. *Whispers of war: the War of 1812 diary of Susanna Merritt* (2002) is an engaging and persuasive work of fiction, though the events described and some of the characters are based on historical events and real people. Susanna Merritt is a fictional character.

Péloquin, Claude (b. 1942). Born and raised in Montreal, he began to write at thirteen and gave his first poetry reading shortly after his seventeenth birthday. He co-founded in 1964 a group called 'L'horloge du nouvel-age', whose presentations combining electronic music, slides, films, dance, and poetry gave birth to the era of collective creations and multi-dimensional shows in Québec. But this activity did not hinder Péloquin's commitment to writing: he has published numerous collections of avant-garde poetry and prose-poems. A selection has been translated by Lucie Ranger, titled *Pellucid waters* (1998). Péloquin has been called by some critics a 'death-obsessed poet', and by others 'an eternalist', descriptions that often tend to draw attention away from his essential concern: to transcend rational limits, to imitate the scientists' open-mindedness to new laws, based on new empirical evidence, and to decipher the 'incommensurable' within us. Péloquin's passion for rejecting conventional typography reveals his need to express himself beyond the confines of the written word through visual forms. By the mid-1980s, in keeping with his acute awareness of death, he came to embrace a somewhat more Christian approach, as can be seen in *Une plongée dans mon essentiel* (1985), which has been termed an autobiographical manifesto; it reproduces the 'open' character of the work published in the late 1970s and was prefaced by Roger LEMELIN, who had been critical in 1969 of Péloquin's anti-conformist texts. It was translated as *A dive into my essence* (1990) by Michel Albert and Jennifer Sullivan.

Penner, Henry. See ABORIGINAL LITERATURE: 5.

Percy, H.R. (1920–96). Born in Burham, Kent, England, he served in the Royal Navy from 1936 to 1952 and in the Royal Canadian Navy until 1971. He edited the *Canadian Author and Bookman* from 1962 to 1965 and in this period wrote a column for the *Ottawa Journal*. He was founding chair of the Writers' Federation of Nova Scotia. Percy's collection of stories, *The timeless island* (1960), largely features bittersweet romances and sentimental idylls in formally controlled language. In his novel *Flotsam* (1968) David Bronson's memories of social and nautical experiences are developed in an alternately lyric and realistic narrative. The memories of a dying painter, Emile Logan, structure Percy's second novel, *Painted ladies* (1983, rpr. 1984), which considers art and life with a characteristic poetic intensity of expression. *A model lover* (1986) collected most of his short stories. His evocative and sometimes puckish narratives are particularly distinguished by their metaphoric richness: three of his most accomplished, psychologically focused, and highly contained stories are 'An inglorious affair', 'Falling for Mavis', and 'A model lover'. The novel *Tranter's tree* (1987), a historical romance written in a whimsical, self-conscious style, with eccentric characterization, is an archly comic and sentimental Maritime tall tale about continuity and the spirits of place.

Peterson, Len (1917–2008). Leonard Byron Peterson was born in Regina of Norwegian stock. He received a B.Sc. (1938) from Northwestern University, Illinois. He established his reputation as a radio dramatist in the forties, collaborating with Andrew Allan and Esse Ljungh; during his long career he produced more than 1200 scripts. The 1930s left an indelible stamp on his work. A recurring theme in his plays is the destruction of the individual or the small community by impersonal states or societies. Variations on this theme are present in *Burlap bags* (1972, rpr. 1973), which presents a vertiginous vision of the world's absurdity and human insensitivity; *Almighty voice* (1974), a one-act children's play produced for Young People's Theatre, Toronto, in 1975, about the government's hunt for a Cree who stole a cow to feed his starving

people; *They're all afraid* (1981), which concerns a young man's alienation in a society governed by neurotic anxieties; and *The trouble with giants* (1973), a radio play that touchingly evokes the erosion of a unique Lithuanian culture by the acquisitive ruthlessness of both Germany and Russia. His best stage piece is *The great hunger* (1967), first produced by the Arts Theatre, Toronto, in Nov. 1960. Set in the Arctic, and about retribution for a killing, its theme is the importance of communal myths by which men—white or Inuit—live or perish. In attempting to explore the complexity of the self, Peterson frequently resorted to psychodrama in which fragments of the psyche assume distinct identities. *Women in the attic* (1971)—about a newspaperman who, while covering the funeral of a celebrated lady of pleasure, enters the reality of her life as it is revealed in her diary—and *Burlap bags* both use this expressionistic device in combination with moments of theatrical realism. Among the several one-act plays Peterson wrote for Young People's Theatre is *Billy Bishop and the Red Baron* (1975), about the Great War flying aces, Billy Bishop and Baron von Richthofen.

Philip, M. NourbeSe (b. 1947). Born Marlene Irma Philip in Tobago, and raised in Trinidad from the age of eight, she adopted 'NourbeSe', a Benin name from Nigeria. She earned a B.Sc. in economics at the University of the West Indies (1968), then immigrated to Canada, where she completed an M.A. in political science (1970) and an LL.B. (1973) at the University of Western Ontario. She practised law in Toronto from 1973 to 1982, working in the areas of immigration and family law, primarily as a partner in the firm Jemmott and Philip, the first black women's law partnership in Canada. During this period she also wrote the poetry that appears in two collections, *Thorns* (1980) and *Salmon courage* (1983). Since she turned to writing full time in 1982, Philip's publications include *Harriet's daughter* (1988), a novel for young people; *She tries her tongue, her silence softly breaks* (1989), a poetry cycle; *Looking for Livingstone: an odyssey of silence* (1991), an epic narrative in poetry and prose; and three collections of essays, *Frontiers: essays and writings on racism and culture* (1992), *Showing grit: showboating north of the 44th parallel* (1993), and *A genealogy of resistance and other essays* (1997). She is a charter member of Vision 21, a coalition of writers and artists opposing racism in the arts in Canada.

The poems in Philip's early collections deal powerfully with the experience of colonialism in the Caribbean, and particularly imperial attempts to smother a living, resonant culture under the spurious cover of transplanted hegemonic rituals and symbols—such as the English Queen's state visit, which is cleverly repudiated in the poem 'Oliver Twist'. In *She tries her tongue*, Philip portrays the English language itself, along with its literary conventions, as an instrument of colonization, a 'father tongue' that is inescapable yet patriarchically abusive in its systematic erasure of the native tongues of those under its sway— unlike the subversive tongue of the mother, which can blow into infant mouths an oppositional counter-speech with which to resist imperial fathers. Her most ambitious text, *Looking for Livingstone*, records a woman traveller's epic journey across time (18 billion years) and space (much of Africa) as she visits a series of mythic tribes, all of whose names are anagrams of the word SILENCE, who teach her the power of self-imposed and self-exploratory silence, the true 'dark continent' out of which full-voiced counter-discursive identity can ultimately emerge. Philip's powerfully written essays about issues of race, gender, and class speak particularly of the marginalization of writers of colour in Canada, a 'bordering' that must be countered, in her view, by reconstructing those borders as 'frontiers'. Referring to herself as 'Afrosporic', Philip sees herself, along with all other 'New World Africans', as exiled because severed from a nurturing linguistic and historical African past. Her children's story *Harriet's daughter* dramatizes the need for active reconstruction of black histories for African-Canadian children.

Coups and Calypsos (2001) is a three-character play that takes place in Tobago in 1990, when there was an uprising in Trinidad led by the Jamat al Muslimeen, a group of Muslim Trinidadians. Elvira Jackson is an African Caribbean woman from Trinidad who is a doctor in London and has been refused plane passage to fly back to England. At the airport she accidentally meets her former husband, Rohan Sankar, also from Trinidad, who has an Indian background and is a schoolteacher on holiday. He invites Elvira to share the small house he's occupying. The play is a series of conversations about all kinds of things—including ethnicity—between two intelligent people, with Rohan constantly and discreetly revealing his affection for Elvira, who is for the most part standoffish, sometimes testy, wedded to her career and her British passport. They are interrupted several times by Mrs Samuels, a good-hearted, talkative neighbour, and excellent cook,

whose dialect is a bit of a stumbling block: 'Dis life is a funny business. Butler [a politician] struggle and bring changes to stop white people exploiting we and today is we own Black people who putting de squeeze on we. Massa does come in all colour—oh yes. And bullet don't know no colour and gun don't care who shooting it—it doing what it have to do and dat is kill.' Radio reports of the state of affairs in Port of Spain and calypso music punctuate the lively discourse of Rohan and Elvira. We are told that the play received two (unidentified) productions in Toronto and London, England, in 1999.

Phillips, Edward O. (b. 1931). He was born in the Westmount district of Montreal (where he still lives), and was educated at McGill University (B.A., 1953) and graduated in law (1956) from the Université de Montréal. He also has an M.A. in teaching (1957) from Harvard, an M.A. in English literature (1962) from Boston University, and a diploma from the Montreal Museum of Fine Arts School of Art and Design (he has had several one-man exhibitions of his paintings). He taught English in Boston and Montreal (1957–65), but is now a full-time writer.

No one was more surprised than Phillips himself when he won an Arthur Ellis Award from the Crime Writers of Canada for *Buried on Sunday* (1986, rpr. 1999) because he saw himself not as a crime writer, but as the author of comic novels of manners (he is both). The novel is set in Québec cottage country north of Montreal, and features the gay and witty Westmount lawyer Geoffry Chadwick, who was introduced getting away with murder in *Sunday's child* (1981, rpr. 1998). It is replete with black humour and pokes wicked fun at Anglo pretensions, while being a cracking good mystery yarn. Geoffry Chadwick was brought back in *Sunday best* (1990, rpr. 2000), *Working on Sunday* (1998), and *A voyage on Sunday* (2004), which involves his friend Elinor Richardson (see below). Phillips' non-criminal novels include *Where there's a will* (1984), a hilarious tour de force; *Hope springs eternal* (1988); the witty and entertaining *The landlady's niece* (1992), in which Elinor Richardson, an engaging heroine for the 1990s, inherits a dilapidated apartment house in Montreal in this comedy of Westmount manners; *The mice will play* (1996, rpr. 1997); *No early birds* (2001)—the title refers to what some thought should be added to the ad for a garage sale when a large Westmount house had been sold; and *Queen's Court* (2007), an engaging novel, pleasing elderly people particularly, that describes the unusual transition of the recently widowed Louise Bingham when she moves from Victoria to Montreal, where she was born.

Pickthall, Marjorie (1883–1922). Born in Gunnersby, Middlesex, England, she immigrated with her family to Toronto in 1889. Educated at St Mildred's Girls School and the Bishop Strachan School for Girls, she was encouraged by her indulgent parents in writing, reading, and music (she studied the violin until she was nearly twenty), though she always had delicate health. Her literary career began with the publication of her story, 'Two ears', in the Toronto *Globe* in 1898; but her mother's death in 1910 so devastated her that it took the efforts of many prominent friends to encourage her to write again. She worked for a time in the library of Victoria College, University of Toronto, and in Dec. 1912 sailed for England to live with relatives and complete her recovery. During the war she trained as an ambulance driver, worked as a farm labourer, and assisted in the library of the South Kensington Meteorological Office. By 1920 she was, as she said, 'Canada sick', and sailed for home. After a brief visit with her father and friends in Toronto, she went to Vancouver, to indulge a long-cherished wish to see the West first-hand. She settled in a small cottage on Vancouver Island and resumed writing. Surgery to correct her continuing ill health was carried out in Vancouver in April 1922; but the initial rapid recovery was ended by an embolism. She was buried beside her mother in St James' Cemetery, Toronto.

Pickthall's literary reputation rests ultimately on the two major collections of poetry published during her lifetime: *The drift of pinions* (1913) and *The lamp of poor souls* (1916, rpr. 1972), which includes the poems published in the earlier volume. *The complete poems of Marjorie Pickthall* (1925), compiled by her father, includes 'fugitive and hitherto unpublished poems'. A 1936 edition, now regarded as definitive, includes the posthumously published *Little songs* (1925) and *The naiad and five other poems* (1931). *The selected poems of Marjorie Pickthall*, edited and with a sympathetic Introduction by Lorne PIERCE, appeared in 1957. The penchant for locations remote in place and time, the use of incantatory rhythms, a persistent sense of *ennui*, the evocation of an insular world of muted lights and a hushed atmosphere, and the recurrence of words such as 'silver', 'rose', and 'gold', suggest a perception of a world of ideal beauty and a literary

practice that originated at least as far back as the Pre-Raphaelite Brotherhood. To these mannerisms Pickthall added her own Anglo-Catholicism. The result is a poetry that evokes a dreamlike world that, although removed from the world of ordinary experience, only halfway approaches a more perfect existence in God. The frequently anthologized 'Père Lalement', 'The bridegroom of Cana', and 'Resurgam' show Pickthall's success in using cadence, delicate colouring, and apt word choice to create sustained moods. At their best the poems achieve a vision of beauty in earthly things that suggests a higher spiritual life; at their least inspired they are little more than versifications of poetic mannerisms. Like others of her generation, Pickthall wrote verse-drama. *The woodcarver's wife*, begun in England in 1919 and finished in Victoria in 1920, was first presented by the Community Players of Montreal at the New Empire Theatre. It appeared in published form in *The woodcarver's wife and other poems* (1922). Despite its convincing handling of incident and its contemporary issues (an artistic figure who can cope with aesthetics but not with life; a confined yet aspiring wife; and a chivalrous rescuer with fleshly appetites), this four-character one-act play, set in pre-Conquest days, is an academic exercise in which the characters mechanically mouth lines of verse to one another.

Pickthall also completed more than 200 short stories, two adult novels, and three juvenile novels. The short stories—many of which were written during the war years in England and submitted to various publications there, and suggest Pickthall's debt to Joseph Conrad, whose work she greatly admired—frequently imply deliberate manipulation of often violent incidents, or convey a facile conception of character. A representative selection of twenty-four stories was published posthumously in London under the inapt and misleading title *Angel's shoes* (1923). Of Pickthall's adult fiction, *Little hearts* (1915), set in the eighteenth-century Devonshire countryside, and *The bridge; a story of the Great Lakes* (1922), employ melodramatic incident. (*The bridge*, begun during the war years in England, and completed and revised on Vancouver Island, was published serially in *Everybody's*, New York, and the London *Sphere* in 1921.) Like most of her short stories, these novels failed to integrate fully descriptive detail, character, and incident. Pickthall was undoubtedly the most gifted of a group of minor writers who owed their inspiration, and a good deal of their literary practice, to the fading romanticism of an earlier day.

Pierce, Lorne (1890–1961). Born in Delta, Ontario, he was educated at Queen's University, Victoria University (University of Toronto), the Union Theological Seminary of New York, New York University, and Wesleyan Theological College, Montreal. He became a minister of the Methodist Church and later of the United Church of Canada. In 1920 he was named literary adviser to the RYERSON PRESS, and from 1922 to 1960 was its editor. As editor, and an ardent Canadian nationalist, Pierce consistently used his authority to encourage Canadian writers by both publication and advice. Among the poets he introduced were E.J. PRATT, Raymond KNISTER, Earle BIRNEY, A.J.M. SMITH, Dorothy LIVESAY, Louis DUDEK, and P.K. PAGE; and he was the first editor to accept a novel (*Settlers of the marsh*, 1925) by Frederick Philip GROVE. His desire to stimulate Canadian writing, however, led him to rely heavily on copy editors to redeem manuscripts of questionable promise. His sentiments and interests were expressed early in his editorial career when he instigated three series of short books on Canadian subjects: Makers of Canadian Literature (from 1925), the Ryerson Canadian History Readers (from 1926)—to celebrate past achievements—and the Ryerson Poetry Chapbooks (from 1925) to stimulate future efforts. In order to familiarize school children with Canadian literature, Pierce edited the *Ryerson* (later *Canada*) *books of prose and verse*, which began to appear in 1927. For adult readers he edited, with A.D. Watson, *Our Canadian literature: representative prose and verse* (1922). Its poetry section, edited with Bliss CARMAN, later became *Our Canadian literature: representative verse, English and French* (1922), and was revised in 1954 by V.B. Rhodenizer as *Canadian poetry in English*. Among Pierce's other books are *Marjorie Pickthall: a book of remembrance* (1925); *An outline of Canadian literature (French and English)* (1927); and *William Kirby, the portrait of a Tory loyalist* (1929). *Three Fredericton poets* (1933) reflected his close friendship with Sir Charles G.D. ROBERTS and Bliss Carman (who made him his literary executor). In numerous pamphlets Pierce urged upon Canadians the possibility of national greatness, to be achieved through awareness of spiritual foundations and the cultivation of *bonne entente* between English- and French-speaking Canadians. His many publications aside, Pierce has a claim to remembrance as a literary entrepreneur who unstintingly devoted his time and money to the promotion of Canadian literature and art. To this end he donated to the Royal Society of Canada the Lorne Pierce medal for distinguished service to Canadian literature; took a leading part in founding several organizations, including the Canadian Writers' Foundation; and built up an important collection of Canadian books, manuscripts, and correspondence that is now deposited at Queen's University. His career is described appreciatively by C.H. Dickinson, the Book Steward of the Ryerson Press from 1937 to 1964, in *Lorne Pierce: a profile* (1965).

Playwrights Guild of Canada. It grew out of the formation in 1971 of the Playwrights Circle, which was named Playwrights Co-op in 1972 and was incorporated as Playwrights Canada in 1979. This body merged in 1984 with the Guild of Canadian Playwrights to form the Playwrights Union of Canada, now named the Playwrights Guild. Among its many activities, the PGC negotiates standard contracts with the Professional Association of Canadian Theatres, distributes more than 3000 unpublished plays in a publish-on-demand photocopy format, distributes Canadian plays of more than forty publishers, and publishes a tri-annual *Directory of Canadian Plays & Playwrights*. Playwrights Canada Press, created in 1984, was incorporated as a for-profit publishing company in 2002. With its office in Toronto, PGC has a membership of 500 professionally produced playwrights. Foundation for the Recognition of Excellence in Drama (F.R.E.D.) is a charitable organization under the umbrella of PGC.

Pollock, Sharon (b. 1936). Mary Sharon Chalmers was born in Fredericton, the daughter of esteemed physician and longtime New Brunswick MLA Everett Chalmers. She was educated in the Eastern Townships of Québec and briefly at the University of New Brunswick, leaving in 1954 to marry Ross Pollock, a Toronto insurance broker. Separating in the early 1960s, she returned with her children to Fredericton, where she worked in various capacities, including acting, at the Playhouse Theatre (later Theatre New Brunswick). In 1966 she moved to Calgary with actor Michael Ball. That year Pollock won the Dominion Drama Festival best-actress award for her performance in Ann Jellicoe's *The knack*. Her play *Walsh* (1973, rev. 1974, 1983)— which premiered at Theatre Calgary in Nov. 1973, with a new production in July 1974 at the Stratford Festival's Third Stage—first drew Pollock to national attention as a playwright. She has also been active, artistically and administratively, in other aspects of theatre: as director, actor, dramaturge, artistic director, and theatre founder. In reaction to the restraints of subsidized theatre, in 1992 Pollock, in partnership with her son K.C. Campbell, established an independent company at the Garry Theatre, a former movie house in the neglected Inglewood district of Calgary. She has directed in many Canadian theatres, such as the Manitoba Theatre Centre, Neptune Theatre, Magnus Theatre, and Alberta Theatre Projects—including productions of her own plays: *One tiger to a hill* (1981) at the National Arts Centre in 1981; *Doc*, under the title *Family trappings*, at Theatre New Brunswick in 1986; and the premiere of *Saucy Jack* (1994) at the Garry Theatre in Nov. 1993.

Pollock's plays of the 1970s, drawn both from the past and from contemporary life, are marked by a strong commitment to political and social issues. The historical chronicle *Walsh*, structured in the episodic manner of the epic theatre, explores the treatment of Sitting Bull and his people when they fled from the USA to the Canadian Northwest after their defeat of General Custer at Little Big Horn. Major Walsh of the North West Mounted Police is caught between personal integrity and the political expediencies of the Macdonald government of the 1870s. Pollock returned to history with *The Komagata Maru incident* (1978), premiered at the Vancouver Playhouse in Jan. 1976, which is a stern indictment in presentational style of Canadian racism based on a historical event in 1914 when a shipload of Sikh immigrants in Vancouver harbour was denied permission to land. *One tiger to a hill*—which premiered at the Citadel Theatre, Edmonton, in Feb. 1980—was inspired by the New Westminster prison hostage-taking of 1975, in which an officer was shot, and attacks public apathy about prison reform. In a notable shift of emphasis in the plays of the next decade, Pollock subsumes the polemics of public controversy in the personal conflicts of family life, wherein conventional value systems are challenged by the rebellious behaviour of her protagonists. *Blood relations* (1981), a study of the famous New England spinster Lizzie Borden, acquitted by the courts for the axe murder of her parents in 1892, was first produced at Theatre 3, Edmonton, in Mar. 1980. Structurally it is Pollock's most sophisticated drama to date, taking the form of a play-within-a-play: ten years after the acquittal, Lizzie's actress friend (probably the historical Nance O'Neill) acts out the crucial scenes at the time of the murders, responding to stage directions from Lizzie herself. The play

explores not only the ambiguities of evidence, but also the social repressions of a middle-class spinster in the late nineteenth century. A more conventionally naturalistic work followed: *Generations* (1981)—first written for radio and premiered on stage at Alberta Theatre Projects, Calgary, in Oct. 1980—also evokes family tensions, but its conflicts inhere in contemporary prairie farm life. *One tiger to a hill*, *Blood relations*, and *Generations* were published in *Blood relations and other plays* (1981, GGA; 2nd edn 2002). *Whiskey six cadenza* (1987), premiered at Theatre Calgary in Feb. 1983, is a vivid recollection of prohibition days in a southern-Alberta mining community. Here the issues of an oppressive law and exploitative working conditions are expressed in the twisted relationship of parents and children. These climax in a destructive emotional triangle consisting of a flamboyant gospeller of free will who is also the local bootlegger, his adoptive daughter, and the rebellious son of a local temperance zealot. The play is published in *NeWest plays by women* (1987), edited by Diane Bessai and Don Kerr.

Pollock's next two plays, *Doc* (1986, GGA, rpr. 2003), which premiered at Theatre Calgary in Apr. 1984, and *Getting it straight*, show Pollock forging dramatic structures to accommodate an increasing interest in the subjectivity of female character. The theme of the former, partly autobiographical, is the conflict between a compulsively dedicated physician and his alcoholic wife, with particular emphasis on the impact of their discord on a growing daughter. The play rejects linear time, directly engaging the audience in the two present-time characters' associational memory patterns. In the monodrama *Getting it straight*, Pollock explores the subjective virtually to its dramatic limits in the fragmented mind of Eme, an escaped mental patient who broods brokenly on the horrors of male aggression—in particular as manifest in the events of Hiroshima and Nagasaki. It was published in *Heroines* (1992), edited by Joyce Doolittle. Pollock returned to historical subjects with *Fair liberty's call* (1995)—which premiered at the Stratford Festival in July 1993—and *Saucy Jack*. The former examines the moral and spiritual ravages of revolution in a Loyalist Boston family. Now living in the wilderness of early New Brunswick, the Roberts are further torn between principle and expediency in a life of hardship that is incongruously combined with the perpetuation of class privilege in the new community. In *Saucy Jack*, Pollock once more expresses her fascination with famous unsolved crimes, offering a variation on speculations concerning the identity of Jack the Ripper in which an actress is hired by an intimate friend of the heir-presumptive to the British throne to enact the roles of the viciously slaughtered East End prostitutes. While narratively the motive is to locate and cover up possible guilt in high places, the dramatist's main purpose is to give voice to the anonymous underclass victims. Pollock is also the author of a number of children's plays, and has written for radio and television. Her plays have been produced not only in Canada, but in Britain, the USA, Japan, and Australia. Pollock's plays *Moving pictures*, *End dream*, and *Angel's trumpet*—all first produced at Theatre Junction, Calgary, in 1999, 2000, and 2001 respectively—are collected in *Sharon Pollock: Three plays* (2003), with an introductory essay by Sherrill Grace. *Moving pictures* is about the Canadian actress Nell Shipman, who starred in silent films—the most famous of which was *Back to God's Country*—and formed her own production company. *End dream* was inspired by an event in Vancouver in 1924 when a young Scottish nanny was found dead in her employer's basement and a Chinese houseboy was charged with murder. *Angel's trumpet* focuses on the turbulent relationship of Scott Fitzgerald and his wife Zelda when her mental health was declining. See *Sharon Pollock: essays on her works* (2000) edited by Anna E. Nothof.

Porcupine's Quill, The. This small publisher, which began life as the production side of PRESS PORCÉPIC, was founded in 1974 by Tim and Elke Inkster, who in 2008 were both made Members of the Order of Canada. (The quill came from Porcépic, 'porcupine' in JOUAL.) It operates out of their combined home and printing/binding shop in Erin Village, Ontario, northwest of Toronto, with the assistance of the CANADA COUNCIL and the Ontario Arts Council. Its list includes works by new, experimental writers as well as works by many established authors, such as Caroline ADDERSON, Margaret AVISON, Matt COHEN, Don COLES, Elizabeth HAY, Steven HEIGHTON, George JOHNSTON, John METCALF, John NEWLOVE, Richard OUTRAM, P.K. PAGE, James REANEY, Robyn SARAH, Leo SIMPSON, Russell SMITH, Jane URQUHART, Paul Glennon, Andrew PYPER, and Mary Swan. It has reissued, in the Sherbrooke Street reprint series, books by Clark BLAISE, Hugh HOOD, Irving LAYTON, Norman LEVINE, Leon ROOKE, and Ray SMITH. In addition, its books have become known for being unusually attractive in design and production (sewn paperback bindings are standard) and often feature the work of wood engravers such as Gerard Brender à Brandis, George A. Walker, Wesley Bates, and Jim Westergard. The Heidelberg KORD is operated by Inkster himself. John Metcalf was for many years the senior editor. Porcupine's Quill books are distributed by the UNIVERSITY OF TORONTO PRESS. See *The Porcupine Quill's Reader* (1996) edited by John Metcalf and Tim Inkster.

Porter, Anna. Born Anna Szigethy in Budapest, Hungary, she was educated in New Zealand at the University of Canterbury, Christchurch (B.A., 1964; M.A., 1965). She worked in publishing in England in the late 1960s, and in Canada beginning in 1970, becoming vice-president and editor-in-chief of MCCLELLAND & STEWART, positions she held until 1979. She married Julian Porter in 1971. In 1982 she became publisher, CEO, and director of Key Porter Books, and continued to be a leading figure in Canadian publishing as the firm evolved its strong imprint. She was made an Officer of the Order of Canada in 1991. Porter has also been active as a writer— as the author of two entertaining Marsha Hillier crime novels, both having international publishing as their background, *Hidden agenda* (1985) and *The bookfair murders* (1997, rpr. 1998); and of the thriller *Mortal sins* (1987), set in Toronto and Hungary. *The storyteller: memory, secrets, magic and lies: a memoir of Hungary* (2000), is a fine memoir made up of stories told to her by her extraordinary grandfather, Vilmos Rácz, and recounting her difficult youth in Hungary and, in 1956, the move to New Zealand, and then to England and Canada.

In 2008 Anna Porter received the $15,000 Nereus Writers' Trust Non-Fiction Prize for *Kasztner's train: the true story of an unknown hero of the Holocaust* (2007). In April 1944, when the Nazi SS began the deportation of nearly 500,000 Hungarian Jews to Auschwitz, Rezső Kasztner (1908–57), a Hungarian journalist and politician, met Adoph Eichmann in Budapest and arranged for 1684 Hungarian Jews to reach Switzerland on 'Kasztner trains'; in 1944–5 he rescued some 15,000 others. Kasztner settled in Israel, became associated with David Ben-Gurion's faction of the Labour Party, and in 1952 was attacked in a leaflet by a right-wing journalist, who was prosecuted for libel. The case that followed went against Kasztner; it was then reversed on appeal. But in March 1957 Kasztner was shot and killed by right-wingers. Anna Porter's book on the subject—the result of heavy research and many interviews—is extensive (over 500 pages, including appendices) and very readable. As she says in her Introduction: 'This is a work of popular history. I have done my best to be accurate but have allowed myself the leeway to reconstruct scenes and dialogue based on the diaries, notes, taped interviews, courtroom testimonies, pretrial interrogations, and memoirs—both written and oral—of the participants in Hungarian, English, German, and Hebrew.'

Poulin, Jacques (b. 1937). Born in Saint-Gédéon, in the Beauce region of Québec, he was educated at Université Laval, where he took a bilingual Arts degree that enabled him to earn his living for a number of years as a commercial translator. As a novelist Poulin writes with ease, grace, and humour, seeming to share none of the usual preoccupations of Québécois novelists of his generation—the Church, the land (escaping from it or rediscovering it), Québec's political affairs. His first three novels were translated by Sheila FISCHMAN as *The Jimmy trilogy* (1979), which collected *My horse for a kingdom, Jimmy*, and *The heart of the blue whale*. A monument explodes in *Mon cheval pour un royaume* (1967), but this first novel is less interested in terrorism than in language and communication, love and sweetness, and strolls in old Quebec City. One of the chief influences in his first three novels is J.D. Salinger: the debt is obvious, but the novels—particularly *Jimmy* (1969), which was followed by *Le coeur de la baleine bleue* (1970)—are more an *hommage* than an imitation. The setting for these novels is largely the old part of Quebec City, which Poulin makes contemporary and North American, filled with light and childish delight. But one of the pervading themes is destruction—of an older order, of old buildings, old styles of life. New life springs from the old, however, and one is struck particularly by the humanity of the attitudes and characters in the novels of this very important, unjustly neglected, and appealing writer. *Les grandes marées* (1978), translated by Fischman as *Spring tides* (1986), shows the influence of Kurt Vonnegut Jr and Richard Brautigan. Here a translator of comic strips is sent to a deserted island in the St Lawrence, where he plays tennis with a ball-machine, does battle with dictionaries (though they are his friends), and discovers—or creates—a young 'dream' girl, Marie, before being destroyed by various agents of society who invade his island. For a writer, how is it possible to live without—or

with—the world? The narrative is now expanded, now interrupted, by quotations, questionnaires, flash cards, advertising clichés, bilingual announcements, recipes, instructions, equations, drawings, and comic strips. This novel—dream, narrative, fable, essay—is an exploration of the possibilities and the limits of narration. *Volkswagen blues* (1984)—translated by Fischman with the same title (1988), which was reissued as *Mr Blue* (1993)—is an extensive voyage of exploration in time and space, from the north-east to the south-west of America, from the cross planted by Jacques Cartier at Gaspé in 1534 to the Californian counterculture of the disciples of Allen Ginsberg and Lawrence Ferlinghetti. Everywhere the travellers—a writer with the *nom de plume* of 'Jack Waterman' and a young Métis woman mechanic—encounter traces (names) and records of the French exploration of the Mississippi and the Rockies. The ostensible reason for the trip is to find Theo, brother of Jack, in San Francisco—who turns out to be totally changed, aged, embittered, and stricken by a creeping paralysis. *My sister's blue eyes* (2007)—Fischman's translation of *Yeux bleus de Mistassini* (2002)—is narrated by twenty-five-year-old Jimmy, who is wandering through Vieux-Québec and comes across a bookshop, in the window of which is a blue book that interests him (he is devoted to the colour blue)—it is *The history of reading* by Alberto MANGUEL. He enters the shop and, questioned by the owner—an old man who turns out to be Jack Waterman—admits that he's interested in the Manguel book. Jack hands it to him and they have a conversation. Jimmy is offered a job in the shop and he accepts. His sister Mistassini, whom he calls Mist, turns up and also works for Jack, who likes her. (She and Jimmy have a romantic bond that he seems to understand is taboo because it is incestuous.) What follows is a series of quotidian events that have little point, and no dramatic impact, but they inform the portrayals of people and two places—unassertive people, their indistinct relationships—and the world of books and writing: authors Salinger, Hemingway, Brautigan, et al. are often referred to, writing is talked about, and the bookshop itself is a presence, along with Vieux-Québec—until Jack arranges for Jimmy to spend time in Paris in the apartment of friends (he should increase his experience if he wants to be a writer). The reader enjoys being there with Jimmy. He soon leaves the crowded apartment and acquires a Volkswagen minibus and sleeps in it. One chapter, a charmer, is called 'The Closerie des Lilas' and takes place in that famous restaurant because Jack asked Jimmy to draw the attention of a well-known Parisian, who frequents the Closerie, to Jack's latest novel. With Jimmy away, Mist helps out in the bookstore and writes him two letters 'without an end'—because Jack has Alzheimer's (he calls it 'Eisenhower's disease') and it's getting worse. Jimmy returns. Mist will look after the bookstore and Jimmy will write '… I wouldn't be really unhappy because I would always be able to put the things that made me sad into a story and attribute them to a character.' *My sister's blue eyes* has many echoes of Poulin's previous novels: Quebec City, to begin with; the names Jimmy and Jack Waterman; the colour blue (*Mr Blue*); a homeless cat; references to authors, mentioned above; and the occasional inexplicable use of the noun *zouave*, which must have a special meaning for Poulin.

Pour la patrie (Montreal, 1895). This separatist novel by Jules-Paul Tardivel (1851–1905), set in a hypothetical future, is the most enduring popular expression of Québec's nineteenth-century religious nationalism. Demand for his work among nationalist groups led to its reissue in the 1930s; and it was no doubt the revival of separatism that prompted a reprint in 1974 and the English translation, *For my country: an 1895 religious and separatist vision of Québec in the mid-twentieth century* (1975), by Sheila FISCHMAN. The federal government of 1945–6 is secretly dominated by a masonic lodge of devil worshippers that aims to destroy the French-Canadian society of Québec, the world's last stronghold of true religious (i.e., Catholic) life and values. The government proposes to change the Canadian constitution in a way that *seems* to perfect its federal character, but will in reality destroy Québec's autonomy and crush French Canada. A French-Canadian MP sees the danger, but is unable to convince a majority in Parliament. Only by the strength of his piety, his submission to divine will and acceptance of personal sacrifice, does he win the miraculous intervention from heaven that defeats the Satanists and brings about the ultimate independence of Québec. Tardivel was a Quebec City ultramontane journalist, accustomed to writing polemics, which may account for the novel's unsophisticated style, its superficial characterization, and its acceptance of Catholic faith at its simplest. He was the chief publicist in late nineteenth-century Québec for what he called 'thorough-going Catholicism', and it was to promote that cause, rather than to portray human character or drama, that he wrote

the novel. He defended the Church's important role in education and social service and held that in a Catholic society like Québec all public life must be informed by the spirit of religion and the Church's teachings. In *Pour la patrie* he argued that this would be possible only if Québec separated from Canada, freeing itself from non-Catholic influences. Called the father of Québec separatism, Tardivel had an important influence on twentieth-century French-Canadian nationalism.

Powe, Bruce (B.W.) (b. 1955). Bruce William Powe, son of the novelist Bruce Allen Powe, was born in Toronto and educated at York University, Toronto (B.A., 1977), and the University of Toronto (M.A., 1981). In this period he became deaf in one ear from being in a rock band, smoked dope, dropped acid, and tried to make sense of the hyperactive postwar baby boom. Since 1989 he has been professor of English and humanities at York University, Toronto. Powe's early writings explore the thesis that Canadians live in a condition of 'pluralistic' post-literacy, and thus lack any single identity: Canada is 'in process' as a communication state, and Canadians have lost their ability to think in an electronic and technological world—he is therefore the heir to Marshall MCLUHAN as a mass-age theorist. His first book was a modest series of essays on a community in transition, *Queen Street West* (1980). *The solitary outlaw* (1983, 3rd edn 1996) is an exploration of the lives and thoughts of Pierre Elliott Trudeau, Wyndham Lewis, Glenn Gould, McLuhan, and Elias Canetti—and concludes with his perception that literate men and women are now outlaws and exiles, with the task of maintaining language and making certain 'that human beings remain complex'. In *A climate charged: essays on Canadian writers* (1984, rpr. 1985, 1987) he is uneasy about the ever-increasing role of Canadian universities and the Toronto cultural establishment in shaping the idea of a national literature. Powe the iconoclast critiques several major Canadian authors—finding Margaret ATWOOD limited in her appeal, Irving LAYTON overrated, and Northrop FRYE limited by his impersonal approach to literature; he is affectionate towards his mentor, McLuhan, and fond of Robertson DAVIES, with reservations. He moved from his study of intellectual figures to reflections on the fate of Canada in the global world of corporatism and mechanized mass culture in the pamphlet *A tremendous Canada of light* (1993)—a long essay (originally intended to form an addendum to a larger book, which became his novel

Outage) on the elusive national identity of Canada. This was rewritten and extended in *A Canada of light* (1997), a sequence of brief meditations that put into often lyrical and aphoristic passages matters that plague the individual—overcome by 'the corporate mind and virtual models', leading to a loss 'of a frame of reference, a way of looking at colliding models of reality', and to Powe's visionary goal of 'a Canada of light' in which 'Canada's hidden destiny is to follow a path that diverges from egotism and violence, and to build a place where people could say, "All the forces and contradictions, the qualities and contrasts of our souls exist here side by side."' The third version, *Towards a Canada of light* (2006)—a fully revised, expanded, and updated edition—'was reconsidered, and redirected, in 2005, after September 11, 2001, after wars, and the morass for American soldiers and politicians in Iraq. One of those wars involves a considerable deployment of Canadian troops in Afghanistan.' *Outage: a journey into Electric City* (1995), a 'novel of ideas', is almost unclassifiable. It is part critical essay, part fiction, part memoir, part therapeutic release from a broken marriage. The main character, Bruce, wanders through Toronto in a series of vignettes in a world that involves too much TV, too many faxes, too many cellular phones, and too many radio, TV, and computer personalities. The jittery staccato style of the book tries to duplicate 'sound bytes' as Bruce, yearning for authentic communication in the fake world of electronic communication, moves towards a symbolic conclusion in Venice, birthplace of artistic perception and Renaissance humanism. The text of *Mystic Trudeau: the fire and the rose* (2007) combines long reflective passages addressed to 'Pierre' (set in sans serif type); accounts of friendly, informal lunch conversations with Trudeau in Montreal, in which he had little to say about any significant topic Powe hesitantly raised—the first lunch was in 1985, the last in 1998. In addition are Powe's meditations on a wide range of subjects the Trudeau myth inspired: for example, when Powe's neighbour expostulates about him and calls multiculturalism a disaster—'I don't know what a Canadian is now.... Trudeau did that.'—Powe examines the whole idea of identity, with quotes from McLuhan, Pascal, Frye, and Aquinas. Interwoven anecdotes, quotations, reflections; the 'fire' that drove Trudeau's ascendancy, popularity, and political message; the rose he wore in his lapel ('Perhaps you knew that the rose stands for the mystery of identity.'); and Powe's assumptions about Trudeau's spiritual life—these components of an interesting and imaginative tribute to Trudeau reveal no mystic qualities in the man, *pace* the title. Powe wrote him in July 2000 about having lunch and received a polite three-sentence reply, ending with: 'Let us wait until autumn.' He died on 28 Sept.

The unsaid passing (2005) is a substantial collection of poems, almost 200 pages long, written between 1995 and 2004. One is first struck by the many simple, loving poems about his daughter and son, twins. 'My ex came, took them/for a week..../My house never seemed so quiet,/or bare./The trace of harmony faded,/and I was left,/two parts of me/missing....' Also appealing are evocative poems inspired by some famous names: 'Beatrice, Dante', 'Song from Emily Dickinson', 'Isabelle Rimbaud' (written in the voice of the poet's sister), 'Song for Clara Schumann', 'Songs of Catherine Blake' ('Though I'm left to tell our patron,/*Mr. Blake's gone again to Paradise.*/He will be back shortly.')

Prairie Fire (1978–). The oldest and most important general-interest literary magazine in Manitoba was founded by Katherine Bitney, Elizabeth Carriere, and Andris Taskans as a Winnipeg newsletter named *Writers News Manitoba*, with the intention of establishing a provincial writers' organization. By the time the Manitoba Writers' Guild was founded in 1981, the newsletter had become a literary magazine, which changed its name to *Prairie Fire* in 1983. It became a quarterly in 1984 (published with the assistance of the CANADA COUNCIL, the Manitoba Arts Council, and the City of Winnipeg). Under editor Andris Taskans, *Prairie Fire: a Canadian Magazine of New Writing* has published writers from all of Canada (including Margaret ATWOOD, David BERGEN, Anne CARSON, Don Domanski, Sylvia Legris, Don MCKAY, P.K. PAGE, and Miriam TOEWS) while concentrating on writing from the Prairie provinces, especially Manitoba. Issues have featured David Arnason (29.1), Aboriginal writers (22.3), and surveys of Winnipeg poetry (28.1), non-fiction (29.1), and fiction (30.1). Other issues have featured work by the winners of the McNally Robinson Book of the Year Award and the John Hirsch Award for Most Promising Manitoba Writer., as well as the Anne SZUMIGALSKI Memorial Lecture. The magazine has sturdy and striking covers, usually in full colour.

Pratt, E.J. (1882–1964). One of the major figures in Canadian poetry, Edwin John Pratt was born in Western Bay, Newfoundland; but his father, a Methodist minister, moved the family at approximately four-year intervals among the fishing, sealing, and whaling outports of the British colony. After graduating from St John's Methodist College, Pratt served as a preacher and teacher in several remote island communities, and then attended Victoria College, University of Toronto, and majored in philosophy. Supporting his studies by doing missionary work in the West in the summers, and later serving as an assistant minister just outside Toronto, he earned his B.A. (1911), M.A. (1912) with a thesis on demonology, his B.D. (1913), and Ph.D. (1917) in theology, publishing his thesis *Studies in Pauline eschatology, and its background* (1917). In 1918 Pratt married Viola Whitney, who became a staunch United Church worker and a writer for young people. Their daughter, Mildred Claire, wrote a study of the Pratt family, *The silent ancestors: the forebears of E.J. Pratt* (1971).

In 1920 Pelham Edgar invited Pratt, who was then working as a demonstrator in the Department of Psychology, to join Victoria College's Department of English, thus re-initiating a teaching career that lasted until 1953. As a professor, Pratt published a number of articles, reviews, and introductions (including those to four Shakespeare plays), and edited Thomas Hardy's *Under the greenwood tree* (1937). Notes and commentaries by, and CBC interviews with, Pratt are available in *E.J. Pratt: on his life and poetry* (1983), and his selected prose, including texts of academic lectures, in *Pursuits amateur and academic: the selected prose of E.J. Pratt* (1995), both edited by Susan Gingell.

Pratt's first collection of poems, *Newfoundland verse* (1923), is frequently archaic in diction, and reflects a pietistic and sometimes preciously lyrical sensibility of late-Romantic derivation, characteristics that may account for Pratt's reprinting less than half these poems in the 1958 edition of his *Collected poems*. The most genuine feeling is expressed in humorous and sympathetic portraits of Newfoundland characters, and in the creation of an elegiac mood in poems concerning sea tragedies or Great War losses. The sea, which on the one hand provides 'the bread of life' and on the other represents 'the waters of death' ('Newfoundland'), is a central element as setting, subject, and creator of mood. The book contains the conclusion to the blank-verse narrative *Rachel: a sea-story of Newfoundland in verse* (1917), picking up the story of Rachel after she has already been widowed by the sea, and relating her decline into madness and death when the sea also claims her only

son. A better early indicator of Pratt's narrative skill is 'The ice-floes', a swift-paced account of a sealing disaster.

The witches' brew (1925) is a fanciful concoction of learning and nonsense, satire and celebration. Highly allusive in mythic structure and motif, it is written in the octosyllabic line that became the standard for Pratt's comedic poems. His zest for compiling humorous catalogues, his penchant for epic scale, and his interests in evolution and atavism clearly emerge for the first time. The three sea-witches' experiment to discover the effect of alcohol on fish may have been Pratt's high-spirited response to Prohibition; but the poem is really stolen by Tom, the Sea-Cat from Zanzibar, who serves as bouncer for the underwater bacchanal until Satan, scenting a way to expand his dominion into the heretofore amoral ocean, extends the experiment to Tom. Giving free rein to the primitive tendencies released by the brew, this evolutionary freak indulges in an orgy of destruction and is last seen headed for the Irish Sea, a destination no doubt chosen for Ireland's association with strong drink and pugnacious character.

In *Titans: two poems* (1926) Pratt achieves a fluid, engaging, and swiftly paced style by varying rhyme scheme, syllabic quantity, and stress patterns, and by frequently using enjambed lines. 'The cachalot' has as its epic hero a sperm whale whose dimensions are exaggerated in mock-heroic style. After a vividly described victory over a kraken, the cachalot engages in a mutually destructive battle with whalers. 'The great feud: a dream of a Pliocene Armageddon' examines the growth of racial hatred and wartime behaviour in its pictures of civil war between land and sea creatures that in the evolutionary process have only just been distinguished as species. An anachronistic *Tyrannosaurus rex* on the trailing edge of that process, and a female anthropoidal ape on the leading edge, indicate the poem's blend of the fantastic and the allegorical. The tiny-brained embattled dinosaur represents unreasoning violence that ends in self-destruction, but the ape uses her emergent intellectual powers to propagandize her forces. The poem's commentary on humanity's animal instincts is capped by the implication that the militaristic ape and her brood are the sole survivors of the volcanic eruption that ends the war.

The iron door: an ode (1927), written to commemorate Pratt's mother's death, gives voice to several positions on death and the afterlife. It ends with an affirmation of faith that is nonetheless ambivalent because the narrator is left dazzled to the point of blindness outside the door between the realms of life and death when the door opens to admit the dead. The theme of *The Roosevelt and the Antinoe* (1930) is the collective self-sacrificing heroism of sailors pitting themselves against the destructive powers of nature, and facing massive odds to rescue the crew of a ship sinking in a mid-Atlantic storm. Pratt here returns to the five-beat line that became standard for his extended treatments of serious subjects. This narrative was republished, with Pratt's notes and other poems, in *Verses of the sea* (1930); this verse-and-notes format was also used in *Ten selected poems* (1947) and in the anthology *Heroic tales in verse* (1941), a book Pratt edited and prefaced.

The nature pieces in *Many moods* (1932) seem to be a thematic throwback, though some reflect a precise image-making power, and the often-humorous vignettes of human character appear slight after the charting of new thematic territory in, and the stylistic vigour of, the narratives. Meditations on aging and death are numerous, but the emergence of a socially conscious voice strikes a new note. Pratt seeks antidotes to human misery in sacrifice or celebration. In a cosmic equivalent to 'The witches' brew' and a reflection of Pratt's expansive public personality, 'The depression ends' stages a banquet for all the world's unfortunates.

Irony is the structural principle on which *The Titanic* (1935) is built. The iceberg that embodies nature's Janus-faces of beauty and destructive power remains 'the master of the longitudes' when humans' hubris, in thinking they have built an unsinkable ship, combined with an ironic conjunction of circumstances, results in a collision of the forces of people and nature. Sombre intimations of war and failures of communication are the focus of *The fable of the goats and other poems* (1932, GGA), which indirectly treats humans' bellicose behaviour in a number of animal allegories, the best of which are 'Silences' and 'The prize cat'. Pratt chose to omit the title poem from his *Collected poems* (1958), perhaps because the pacifist conclusion to the territorial disputes between warring tribes of goats proved so futile a model for human behaviour.

Of all the volumes published during the war years, *Brébeuf and his brethren* (1940, GGA) is least overtly connected to the war. Pratt's research-oriented methodology is made clear in the precise diction and detailed, documentary-style recounting of events and observation in this, his first attempt to write a national epic; but in his ethnocentrism

Pratt presents the Jesuit priests as an enclave of civilization beleaguered by savages. *Dunkirk* (1941) and many of the poems of *Still life and other verse* (1943) are more immediately topical, picturing both the heroism and atavism of which people are capable, though the propagandistic cast of many of these poems should be recognized, for heroism seems the exclusive property of the Allies, and atavism characteristic solely of the Axis forces. *They are returning* (1945) is an occasional piece that strains to give the feats of Canadian veterans classical epic stature; but *Behind the log* (1947) successfully captures the drama of individuals' wartime experiences by chronicling the hounding of an Atlantic convoy by U-boats.

Pratt's concerns with communication and bringing alive Canadian history culminate in *Towards the last spike: a verse panorama of the struggle to build the first Canadian transcontinental from the time of the proposed terms of union with British Columbia [1870] to the hammering of the last spike in the Eagle Pass [1885]* (1952, GGA). Presenting an anglo/central-Canadian perspective, the poem interweaves the political battles between Sir John A. Macdonald and Edward Blake with the labourers' physical battles against mountains, mud, and the Laurentian Shield. In a metaphorical method typical of his style, Pratt characterizes the Shield as a prehistoric lizard rudely aroused from its sleep by the railroad builders' dynamite.

The collected poems of E.J. Pratt (1958) reprinted all but two poems in *Collected poems* (1944), while adding five earlier poems and a handful of previously unpublished ones. The 1958 edition, edited with an introduction by Northrop FRYE, serves as a map of the movement of Canadian poetry from its colonial phase to its becoming an identifiably independent national literature. A two-volume scholarly edition *E.J. Pratt: complete poems* (1989), edited by Sandra DJWA and Gordon Moyles, includes appendices of miscellaneous poems, previously unpublished verse drama and poetry, and a descriptive bibliography by Lila Laakso. See also *Selected poems: E. J. Pratt* (2000) edited by Djwa, W.J. KEITH, and Zailig Pollock.

Pratt's reputation as a major Canadian poet rests largely on his often powerfully evocative narrative poems, many of which show him as a mythologizer of the Canadian male experience; but a number of shorter philosophical works also command recognition. 'From stone to steel' asserts the necessity for redemptive suffering arising from the failure of humanity's spiritual evolution to keep pace without physical evolution and cultural achievements; 'Come away, death' is a complexly allusive account of the way the once-articulate and ceremonial human response to death was rendered inarticulate by the primitive violence of a sophisticated bomb; and 'The truant' dramatically presents a confrontation in a thoroughly patriarchal cosmos between the fiercely independent 'little genus homo' and a totalitarian mechanistic power, 'the great Panjandrum'. Pratt's choices of forms and metrics were conservative for his time; but his diction was experimental, reflecting in its specificity and its frequent technicality both his belief in the poetic power of the accurate and concrete that led him into assiduous research processes, and his view that one of the poet's tasks is to bridge the gap between the two branches of human pursuit: the scientific and artistic. See *Pursuits amateur and academic: the selected prose of E.J. Pratt* (1995) edited by Susan Gingell. See also David G. Pitt's biography, *E.J. Pratt: the truant years 1882–1927* (1984) and *E.J. Pratt: the master years 1927–1964* (1987).

Préfontaine, Yves (b. 1937). Born in Montreal, he studied anthropology and sociology in Montreal and Paris. He was a founder of Éditions de l'Hexagone in 1953. From 1978 he was a senior Québec civil servant. His very personal poetry is composed of long, luxuriant lines that occasionally betray a surrealist imagination. Among his many poetry collections, only *Le désert maintenant* (1987) has been translated—by Judith Cowan as *This desert now* (1993). As in previous collections, it explores issues of language and political engagement and focuses on the land as a site of change. Its lyrical and prose poems express a lingering hope for social renewal among the apathetic Québécois. The speaker locates the roots of a fertile language, which could give shape to Québec's experience, in the primitive, vital earth. The flowing rhythm of the long lines and internal rhymes underscore the potential for beauty and self-expression, even when the speaker's passionate call for awareness dissolves into bitter anger. Yves Préfontaine, from the Introduction: 'We started to read aloud, each in turn, from Judith Cowan's translation and my original. Then the miracle occurred: two citizens of this land breaking down word by word ... all the angry pride, the incomprehension, and the dull and stupid soliloquies that have been the distinguishing characteristics of our peoples' history for the last two

centuries.... As time passes it becomes more and more urgent to choose between the light and the darkness. And at this moment in my life I have chosen the light.'

Press Porcépic. It was founded by Dave GODFREY with Tim Inkster in 1972 in an old house in Erin, Ontario, not far from Toronto. Godfrey had left the House of ANANSI to form New Press with two partners; and then, out of a small but exceptional magazine *Porcépic* ('porcupine' in JOUAL), created his third company, Press Porcépic. (In 1974 Inkster took one 'quill' from the creature that served as the company logo and renamed his company the PORCUPINE'S QUILL.)

Godfrey had seen the potential of the new small offset-printing technology that made book production fast and economical. Within five years Porcépic was publishing up to seventeen titles a year, with an emphasis on young and experimental writers; but it also published Dorothy LIVESAY's poetry as well and her *Right wand left hand: a true life of the thirties*, as well as poetry collections by Eli MANDEL, Joe ROSENBLATT, P.K. PAGE, and Marilyn BOWERING. Among the fiction published by Porcépic was Godfrey's *The new ancestors* (1970, GGA) and *Dark must yield* (1978), a collection of fifteen stories; Kristjana GUNNARS' *The axe's edge* (183); and the English translation of Louky BERSIANIK's *L'Euguélionne*.

Press Porcépic opened editorial offices in Victoria, British Columbia, when Godfrey moved there in 1976. In 1980 Porcépic formed a division called Softwoods to become the first in Canada to publish computer titles and computer-assisted learning software. By 1985 the company had twenty-five employees, annual software sales over $1 million, and had developed a database for the Greater Victoria Public Library. Considered a world leader in the field of artificial intelligence, the company changed its name in 1987 to Porcépic Books, which in 1991 became part of Beach Holme Publishing, Victoria, whose books are distributed by the Dundurn Group, Toronto.

Preview (1942–5). This Montreal-based periodical, originally intended as a literary letter in which contributors would 'preview' or try out their work, was first published in Mar. 1942. Its editorial board was made up of F.R. SCOTT, Margaret Day, Bruce Ruddick, Neufville Shaw, and Patrick ANDERSON, who was its driving spirit and most influential editor. P.K. PAGE joined the board in Issue 2 (Apr. 1942) and A.M. KLEIN in Issue 19 (Mar. 1944), his work having appeared since Issue 5 (July 1942) and Day and Shaw having already resigned as editors. Planned as a monthly, but appearing irregularly over 23 issues until early 1945, *Preview* averaged 9 to 13 mimeographed pages and had a circulation of approximately 125. It featured poetry, short stories, frequently leftist essays, and became known for the wit, technical sophistication, and cosmopolitan interests of its talented and socially concerned editors. In Dec. 1945 it merged with FIRST STATEMENT to form NORTHERN REVIEW. The legendary rivalry between *Preview* and *First Statement* has been exaggerated.

Prewett, Frank (1893–1962). He was born on his maternal grandfather's pioneer farm at Kenilworth, near Mount Forest, Ontario, and raised in Toronto. He attended University College, University of Toronto, before enlisting in 1915 in the Third Contingent of the Canadian Expeditionary Force in a unit sponsored by the T. Eaton Company of Toronto, the Eaton Machine Gun Battery. On his arrival in England he was promoted to lieutenant in the Royal Artillery and was severely wounded and shell shocked in 1918. During his convalescence at a Scottish hospital, Lennels, and under the care of anthropologist/psychologist W.H.R. Rivers, Prewett met Siegfried Sassoon, who was impressed by the fact that Prewett wrote poetry and claimed (untruly) to have Native blood. Under the tutelage and guidance of Sassoon, who appears to have been seeking a surrogate for Wilfred Owen, who had returned to action in France, Prewett was introduced to the British literati of the period. Given his own room at Lady Ottoline Morrell's country house, Garsington, Prewett became friendly with D.H. Lawrence, T.S. Eliot, Ezra Pound, Aldous Huxley, Robert Graves, Edmund Blunden, E.M. Forster, Virginia Woolf, and the artists Dorothy Brett and Mark Gertler. Woolf, Sassoon, Morrell and others had a nickname for Prewett: 'Toronto'. Virginia Woolf herself handset Prewett's first publication, a collection of twenty-two poems that appeared as Hogarth Pamphlet Number 17, *Poems* (1920), which included some of Prewett's 'trench verses', notably 'Voices of women', 'The Somme Valley, 1917', and 'The card game', interspersed with many bucolic Georgian lyrics about pastoral landscapes and pleasant nature—a reaction to the savagery of war that had left him neurasthenic. Following on the success of the pamphlet, Edward Marsh chose eight of Prewett's poems for inclusion in *Georgian poetry 1920–1922*—the only

Canadian included in both the anthology and the movement. For his role in Georgianism, Prewett stands as the 'missing link' in Canadian verse between the CONFEDERATION POETS and the early Modernism of the MONTREAL GROUP. Prewett was ordered home from England in 1920 by the Canadian army after suffering from a suspected case of consumption. He hoped to establish a literary career in Canada, but found the cultural environment dry and stilted. To ease his neurasthenia, he studied organ with composer Healey Willan and escorted Siegfried Sassoon around Toronto during a tour that Sassoon records in *Siegfried's journey* (1945). By 1921 Prewett had returned to England to complete his undergraduate studies at Christ Church, Oxford (the University of Toronto never having conferred his B.A., breaking the promise that servicemen would be granted their degrees upon enlistment). *Poems* was followed by *The rural scene* (1922), in which Prewett continued in the tightly crafted lyrical style of the Georgian poetic. To the nature poems he added a number of love lyrics. By 1926 Prewett had fallen out with the Garsington circle and Georgianism was no longer fashionable. He attempted an experimental farm near Oxford with economist A.A. Carr Saunders and ecologist Charles Elton, failed at that, and took a teaching position at the Agricultural Economics Institute, Oxford, where he remained until the 1930s. In the early thirties he became a broadcaster on the BBC, devised the milk-marketing system for England, edited *The Farmer's Weekly* for Lord Beaverbrook, and wrote an unsuccessful novel about a nineteenth-century peasants' rebellion in England, *The Chazzey tragedy* (1933). (Even his own brother-in-law, the Toronto journalist Gordon Sinclair, gave the book a poor review.) During the Second World War, Prewett was dismissed from the army for frail nerves (he was guarding an ammunition depot), joined the Royal Air Force, and became Food Services and Supplies Adviser to Mountbatten in the South East Asian Command in Ceylon. Prewett's later life combined poverty and obscurity. His three 1954 BBC radio broadcasts, 'Farm life in Ontario fifty years ago', recalled his early days on his grandfather's farm at Kenilworth. He died in Scotland and was buried in Inverness. Robert Graves assembled *The collected poems of Frank Prewett* (1964), but the range of Prewett's talents was not revealed until the discovery by Bruce Meyer of Prewett's unpublished poems in the archives of the University of Texas, and the resulting publication of *The selected poems of Frank Prewett* (1987, rpr. 2000) edited by

Meyer and Barry CALLAGHAN. See Bruce Meyer, *Frank Prewett* (1991), in the series Profiles in Canadian Literature.

Priest, Robert (b. 1951). Born at Walton-on-Thames, England, he was brought to Toronto at the age of four. After briefly studying mathematics at the University of Waterloo, Priest devoted himself to writing poetry, plays for children, and songs, composing, and performing. Seven collections of his lively, amusing, and inventive poems have been published, beginning with *The visible man* (1979) and including *Scream blue living: new and selected poems* (1992) and *Time release poems* (1997), a tiny (to be kept in a shirt pocket) collection of one-sentence aphorisms. *Resurrection in the cartoon* (1997) consists of blackly humorous prose poems, ironic political poems, and mystical and transcendent meditations. *Blue pyramids: new and selected poems* (2002) is a long collection (slightly more than 200 pages) that of course includes Priest's best (witty) and poorest (sentimental) poems, though one can imagine how effective they would all be when read aloud by the author, i.e., heard in the voice of a great performer. 'Blue pyramids', the title poem, has as its subtitle 'A proposal for the ending of unemployment in Toronto', a lame fantasy about the unemployed building the 'blue pyramids of peace' on Yonge Street. The lighthearted vein of Priest's poems is maintained in poems that convey his spirituality, such as 'Christ is the kind of guy' ('… you just can't help hurting'), 'Getting close to God', and 'Testament of a new faith'. These poems are included in the 2008 collection *Reading the Bible backwards*, bearing the title and first line of the first poem ('… Christ Jesus pops his nails/And comes down/To give the karma back to the people/Bearing the cross downhill….' *How to swallow a pig* (2004) is a collection of Priest's brief, whimsical, imaginative prose narratives—he calls them prose poems—written over thirty years.

An accomplished children's entertainer, Priest has published eight books for youngsters (he has three offspring), including *Knights of the endless day* (1993), which began as a children's play that was performed in 1992 at Young People's Theatre, Toronto; *A terrible case of the stars* (1994); and *The secret invasion of bananas* (2001). He has performed as a rock musician, accompanied by his band Great Big Face, and has recorded LPs, CDs, and videos. COACH HOUSE PRESS released his audio tape *Rottweiler pacifist* (1990), which offers a selection of poems and songs. For Alannah Myles he wrote the lyrics of the award-winning hit 'Song Instead of a Kiss' (1992). His CD *The Great Big Face* (1997) features 'poems, songs, sayings, chants, and iterations'. One reviewer called the work of this unique rock poet 'a truly invigorating combination of rants, raves, and reveries'.

Proulx, Monique (b. 1952). Born in Quebec City, she now lives in Montreal and has written for radio, television, and film. Three of her books—two of them award-winning novels—have been translated by Matt COHEN. *Le sexe des étoiles* (1987), translated as *Sex of the stars* (1996), is an ingenious romp of a novel that tackles, with grace and humour, the loaded question of gender identity in the late twentieth century. At its heart is Marie-Pierre Deslauriers, previously Pierre-Henri, a world-famous scientist who was a Nobel Prize candidate shortly before he underwent the first of a series of operations to turn himself into the woman he always knew he was. All the other major characters are obsessed with Marie-Pierre: her (or his?) daughter Camille, who is in love with the stars and the best-looking boy in her class; Gaby, a researcher Marie-Pierre lives with; and Dominique Larue, an impotent writer who has produced nothing for twelve years and is convinced that Marie-Pierre can cure both ailments. If having a man's body does not necessarily make one a man, as Marie-Pierre claims, what does it mean to be a man or a woman? Does sexual difference lie in the body, in the brain cells, or in the depths of the soul? Through a series of improbable coincidences, the novel takes a long, steady look at the strange and often contradictory beliefs we cherish about masculinity and feminity. In *Homme invisible à la fenêtre* (1993), translated by Cohen as *Invisible man at the window* (1994), which is more ambitious and more complex, Proulx creates a character loosely based on a real person, the handicapped Montreal painter Yves Bussières, to whom the novel is dedicated. Since the 'Big Bang', the car accident that left him unable to move his lower limbs, Max has become obsessed with painting the infinite variety of the human body. The book is structured as a series of word portraits of the lost souls Max attracts: the actress Maggie, so beautiful she hates and envies her own smiling image on the movie screen; Julius Einhorne, a dubious—and obese—art collector in love with a very young girl; Julienne, Max's possessive mother; Lady, his lost love; and the nihilistic painter Gerald Mortimer, whose selfless devotion to Max is not accounted for until the novel's harrowing final pages. Using irony and self-mockery to keep his grief at bay, but full of clear-eyed, sometimes cruel, compassion for his fellow human beings, Max defines survival as forgetting what you once were rather than accepting what you have become. In the short opening chapter of *The heart is an involuntary muscle* (2003)—the translation by David Homel and Fred A. Reed of *Coeur est un muscle involontaire* (2002)—Florence, the narrator, describes her father's death, after which she is told by 'a man in white' in the hospital that her father's dying words were … the words of the title. Florence is the sole employee of Zeno Mahone, with whom she has a fraught relationship (they had 'tried to be lovers'). Mahone Inc. is some kind of agency for artists and writers. Florence hates writers and 'couldn't stand the heavy-handed arrogance of books. In a 300-page book, there are always 250 pages too many.' (As they finish this 359-page novel some readers might agree.) But Zeno has a favourite writer, Pierre Laliberté, 'whose books he carried with him wherever he went and leafed through respectfully, as if they were sacred texts.' When Florence discovers that her father's final words came from the mysterious Laliberté, the plot turns into a kind of mystery as she proceeds to uncover his true identity; a thread is interwoven relating to writers and writing; and there is romance as Florence gradually discards her self-absorption and gives herself to another (to Zeno). In English the novel is overwritten, weighed down by too many metaphors, but its force carries one along to the end.

Les aurores Montréalis (1996), translated as *Aurora Montrealis* (1997), is a series of stories and sketches about Montreal. The emphasis is on contrasts within the city—between English and French, rich and poor, beauty and ugliness—and on varying points of view: those of children, immigrants, lovers, vagrants, cleaning women, even a man who is writing a screenplay about a transsexual. This collection has been hailed by critics as one of the recent works of Québécois fiction that best sum up the 'soul' of Montreal—a world within a world in contemporary Québec culture, deeply, viscerally French, yet increasingly open to other cultures and voices.

Provincial: or Halifax Monthly Magazine, The. Published in Halifax between Jan. 1852 and Dec. 1853, it was the most prominent mid-century literary journal in Maritime Canada. A monthly edited by Mary Jane KATZMANN, each of its twenty-four issues ran to forty or more pages. Katzmann strove to make it a vehicle for local intellectual and literary development, giving the bulk of each issue to sentimental and moralistic poems, and fiction, by local writers, though there was a reasonably wide range of topics in the general articles. Three series on the early history of Nova Scotia were published, as well as occasional biographies of noted Nova Scotians, such as Samuel Cunard and Herbert Huntington. She also frequently reviewed books by local authors. At the same time, through reviews and articles on the literary and intellectual scene in Britain and the United States, Katzmann projected a sense of cultural interchange in the North Atlantic English-speaking communities.

Purdy, Al (1918–2000). Alfred Wellington Purdy (who, before settling on 'Al Purdy', signed his poems 'Alfred W. Purdy' and 'A.W. Purdy') was born in Wooler, Ontario, of what he described as 'degenerate Loyalist stock'. He spent most of his childhood in nearby Trenton and was educated at Albert College, Belleville. During the 1930s Purdy hitched rides on freight trains to Vancouver, where he worked for several years in a mattress factory and similar establishments. In the Second World War he served in the Royal Canadian Air Force, mostly at the remote base of Woodcock on the Skeena River in northern British Columbia. Having no university training (though his wide reading eventually turned him into a remarkably erudite man), he worked at casual and manual jobs while struggling to find time to write, and he sometimes lived in poverty well into his forties. The interaction, in his writing, of literary ambitions and working-class experience produced an anecdotal and powerfully direct poetry (visible, for example, in the title poem of *Piling blood*, 1984). He wrote poems restlessly and copiously in a career that spanned almost sixty years. The publication in 1944 of his first book, *The enchanted echo*, showed the young Purdy limited by formal preoccupations, his poetry conservatively traditional and largely derivative (in part, of the Canadian romanticism of ROBERTS and CARMAN). When he published his much superior fourth volume of poems in 1959, his choice of title, *The crafte so long to lerne* (the phrase is borrowed from Chaucer), wryly celebrated his sense that he had needed to serve a long apprenticeship. By steeping himself in the poetry of writers such as D.H. Lawrence and William Carlos Williams on the one hand, and W.H. Auden and Dylan Thomas on the other—as well as being influenced by

Purdy

the Canadian poets PRATT, BIRNEY, LAYTON, and ACORN—he had learned how to sound a distinctive contemporary note. Purdy fully achieved his own voice with the publication of *Poems for all the Annettes* (1962) and *The Cariboo horses* (1965, GGA). The latter book in particular shows him writing at the top of his form and attracted a broad readership. In these and the books that followed, he developed a long-lined and colloquially free poetry that allowed him to be intellectually direct without sacrificing powerful statement and evocative poetic imagery; they made him perhaps the foremost influence on the generation of Canadian poets who came after him. Drawing freely on the miscellaneous and extensive knowledge accumulated by his generalizing and autodidactic mind, Purdy created a poetry that is densely allusive, but never obscure.

He travelled widely in Canada and abroad, gaining experiences that recognizably shaped both the content and the mood of a great deal of his poetry. Some of his strongest poems, such as 'Shoeshine boys on the Avenida Juarez' (in *Wild grape wine*, 1968), emerge directly out of these journeys, and his most unified book of poetry, *North of summer: poems from Baffin Island* (1967), is virtually a travel book in verse. Nevertheless, the heart of Purdy's world remained the place that is named in so many of his poems, the symbolic omphalos of his imaginative world: Roblin Lake, deep in Loyalist country near Ameliasburgh, Ontario. A powerful sense of his local area informs most of the poems in *Wild grape wine*, such as 'Roblin's Mills (II)' and 'Wilderness Gothic', which have become classics in their own time. *In search of Owen Roblin* (1974) assembles a number of Purdy's poems of local history into a memorial cycle, one that powerfully evokes Canada as an old country already resonant with its own echoes. His attraction to the past also made the elegy one of his most effective forms, whether it was a commemoration of a member of his own family ('Elegy for a grandfather'—which he first published in *Emu, remember*, 1956, and revised several times over the next thirty years), of a public figure ('For Robert Kennedy', in *Sex & death*, 1973), of his home territory ('The country north of Belleville', in *The Cariboo horses*), or of a whole race ('Lament for the Dorsets' in *Wild grape wine*—one of his most affecting poems). A powerful and consistent persona is evident in the body of Purdy's poems: while the speaker may be capable of jokiness and broad comedy (see 'Birdwatching at the equator' in *The stone bird*, 1981; or 'Concerning Ms Atwood' in *Naked with summer in your mouth*,

1994), he was, perhaps as a result of his pervasive self-irony, also able to combine deeply felt emotion in a way that allowed him to explore what might otherwise seem outworn sentimentality ('Winter at Roblin Lake') and patriotism (as in the title poem of *A handful of earth*, 1977), or to register direct and intense responses to the beauty of nature ('Late rising at Roblin Lake' in *The Cariboo horses*). If in some of his late work—he published six books of new poems in the eighties and nineties—he also struck a loftier or more serious tone than in the work of his middle period, these later poems come across as shaped by a mature and hard-earned sense of perspective gained by a lifetime of poetic engagement with the world.

Over the years Purdy, who was made an Officer of the Order of Canada in 1982, published a number of books of selected poems (frequently revising earlier poems for their new appearance). *Being alive: poems 1958–78* (1978) shows his immense range and includes most of his best poems to that point. The shape of his entire career is visible in the 262 poems found in *The collected poems of Al Purdy* (1986, GGA) edited by Russell Brown—though its more than 350 pages comprise less that half Purdy's published work and about a quarter of the more than a thousand poems he estimated having written. Reading through this volume, one is impressed by the steady strengthening of quality as well as by his enormous productivity: it is a notable monument to a life dedicated to the making and reading of poems. Sam Solecki edited *Rooms for rent in the outer planets: selected poems 1962–1994* (1996). The title poem of *To Paris never again: new poems* (1997) alludes to an early experience of Paris, taking in all its associations and tramping through its sights, then returning 'back to Canada—and after a long time/finally beginning to understand/the man in my head was me'. *Beyond remembering: the collected poems of Al Purdy*, edited by Purdy and Solecki, was published in 2000. *The more easily kept illusions: the poetry of Al Purdy* (2006), selected with an Introduction by Robert Budde, with an Afterword by Russell Morton Brown is in the Laurier poetry series. On the east side of Queen's Park North, Toronto, is a handsome statue of Purdy—in rolled up shirtsleeves, sitting on a rock with a book in his right hand, his head turned to the left facing south—by sculptors Edwin and Veronica Dam de Nogales of Highgate, Ontario. It was unveiled in May 2008.

From the mid-1960s Purdy was able to earn a full-time living as a freelance writer and at related tasks, such as lecturing, poetry reading, and taking positions as writer-in-residence at various universities. He worked in virtually every literary form, writing radio and television plays and one novel, *A splinter in the heart* (1990, rpr. 2000), about the 1918 explosion of the British Chemical plant in Trenton, Ontario. A representative gathering of his critical essays, book reviews (written chiefly for *Canadian Literature*), travel pieces, and anecdotal portraits of people and places may be found in *Starting from Ameliasburgh: the collected prose of Al Purdy* (1995) edited by Sam Solecki. Although the childhood memoir published as *Morning and it's summer* (1983) is reprinted and supplemented with other prose recollections (some previously published) in *Reaching for the Beaufort Sea: an autobiography* (1993), a stronger sense of Purdy the man comes across in his four volumes of published letters: *The Bukowski/Purdy letters 1964–1974* (1983) edited by Seamus Cooney; *The Purdy-Woodcock letters: selected correspondence 1964–1984* (1988) edited by George Galt; and, especially, *Margaret Laurence—Al Purdy: a friendship in letters* (1993) edited by John Lennox. See also *Yours, Al: the collected letters of Al Purdy* (2004) edited by Sam Solecki. See also *Al Purdy: essays on his works* (2002) edited by Linda ROGERS and *The Al Purdy A-frame anthology* (2009) edited by Paul Vermeersch, with an introduction by Dennis LEE, a celebration of the Purdy house in Ameliasburgh, containing pieces by Purdy himself and many other well-known writers.

Pyper, Andrew (b.1968). Andrew Derek Pyper was born in Stratford, Ontario, and educated at McGill University (B.A., 1991, M.A., 1992) and in the Law Faculty of the University of Toronto (LL.B., 1995). He passed his Ontario Bar admission exams in 1996, but never practised law. We are told that when Pyper was bored in law classes he *wrote*, sketching descriptions, scenes, dialogue, and characters, focusing on young people, that later found their way into stories. Indeed, the thirteen stories in *Kiss me* (1996, rpr. 1999) are made up of well-written fragments of varying lengths. The father of the girl in 'Dime bag girl' gave her a car, 'a Plymouth Duster', and she liked taking the young narrator, who loves her, for drives in it; they smoke drugs and talk, until one day she says to him '... you're never going to see me again' and drives off. He finishes high school in a haze. There are no names. 'I'm right at the end and I didn't even tell you her name. Maybe I can't remember it now, not exactly.' The title of the story 'Call Roxanne' is what the young narrator sees, with phone number, in a washroom when his father is taking him to a hospital (we don't hear about that). The story is mostly reminiscences about the vicious attack on Carlotta Matson in the schoolyard when he was thirteen, and when he was told by the principal that his father had had a heart attack and took him to the hospital to see him. When he himself is taken to the hospital (why, we don't know), he feels in his pocket and finds a slip of paper. 'On it is Roxanne's number.' On the first page of the title story 'Kiss me', the narrator says: "*I am repulsive. That's a hell of a thing to say to yourself every day. I know it from seeing my face reflected in others*', the way the edges of their mouths drop and then tremble back up to an awkward mask of indifference.' It happened when he lit 'our third floor balcony barbecue with lighter fluid', which splashed over his face setting it on fire. His girlfriend Leah (herself a star university gymnast until a bad accident left her with scars and a limp) visited him every day in hospital, sometimes twice. When he returned home they stopped sleeping together because 'I took her invitations as charity, a gesture meant to bring me back into life.' When she looks at him steadily without aversion, he drops his eyes; he repels her declaration of love; she leaves him.

Before publication, Pyper's first novel, *Lost girls* (1999, rpr. 2003), earned for him two six-figure advances from international publishers; when published it was much praised both for its literary qualities—the nature of his prose, the complicated plotline involving secondary characters (who never contribute anything very revealing about the girls' disappearance)—and its attractiveness as a thriller, though it is not one. It begins with a Prologue, written in the third person, that is a tight, suspenseful narrative about two young people, a girl and a boy (cousins), that ends with a tragic canoe accident. It is unequalled by any other passage in the book, which becomes the first-person narrative of Bartholomew (called Barth) Christian Crane. This thirty-three-year-old lawyer in the firm of Lyle, Gederov, & Associate (called in Toronto Lie, Get 'Em Off & Associate), addicted to cocaine, has been assigned to defend Thomas Tripp in the Northern Ontario town of Murdoch, who has been accused of murdering two of his fourteen-year-old high-school students, Ashley and Krystal. The novel is overwritten, unnecessarily lengthened by gratuitous descriptions that dissipate the thrust of the plot. The similes are always off-key ('I'm uncomfortably aware of my buttocks squishing and slipping against each other like mating seals', 'a flood of circulation in my ears like poured sand', 'a face like a historical map'). A mythic figure in the town, the Lady of the Lake—a Polish immigrant who had two daughters taken away from her, drowned in Fireweed Lake, and appeared to Barth in his dreams—offers a ghostly element. Thom Tripp told the girls about her (they were fascinated) and took them in his car to the lake, where they themselves drowned, though the bodies were never recovered. The ending of *Lost girls* is anti-climactic, and most unsatisfactory for Barth. In Chapter Forty-Four, six chapters before the end, he recalls the event described in the Prologue, which presumably explains his celibate condition. *Lost girls* won the Crime Writers of Canada Arthur Ellis Award for Best First Novel.

The trade mission (2002) is a literary contrivance, with elements of a suspenseful thriller that lack the conviction, clarity, and disciplined intensity this genre requires. The novel begins with a wonderful set piece when two young boys, Marcus Wallace and Jonathan Bates, are caught in a snowstorm in the woods until they collapse in each other's arms. Will they be saved? How are they saved? (We do not hear about this until late in the novel.) Wallace and Bates, twenty-four years old, have invented a website called Hypothesys, a 'morality machine'—giving 'helpful advice', it teaches morality—and have strangely become millionaires. They embark on an official Canadian trade mission to Brazil, and while sailing as tourists on the Rio Negro with three others—including the narrator and translator Elizabeth Crossman—all five are kidnapped by guerrillas (we don't know why until towards the end of the novel); three of them submit to torture, the horrible details of which are provided. Escape (there are only three members by now) is followed by helpless wandering in the jungle (well described) until they reach a village of Yanomami Indians. When they eventually leave their village, Wallace follows them into the jungle; Bates dies; and the only survivor, Crossman, tells us that she returned home safely and had a child (Wallace is the father). The main part of the novel—their entrapment in the Brazilian jungle—is overloaded with endless conversations and disagreements that vitiate the narrative. Wallace and Bates (the slight but repeated suggestions of their being linked by a homoerotic bond lead nowhere) and the other characters—even Crossman the narrator (we are many pages into the novel before we realize that she is not a man but a woman)—remain distant and unconvincing. It is sad that much good writing went into a novel that is ambitious, implausible, and somehow misconceived. The damaging effects of fire are at the centre of *The wildfire season* (2005), which soon brings to mind the story 'Kiss me'. Miles McEwan—in love with Alex, they plan to marry—has been accepted by the Faculty of Medicine, University of Toronto, but heads west for the summer 'to work the wildfire season' in British Columbia. In the first week of August there is a conflagration. 'A blowup. The most feared event in fighting fires in the bush…. What begins as a series of spot fires sends hot, lighter air up, and the cooler, heavy air seeps in to take its place, creating a kind of burning tornado. The spot fires … join together. Invisible gases rise into the air hotter than the white heart of a flame. The ground itself is ignited.' The flames are advancing with speed and Miles sees Tim—his young co-worker, called 'the kid'—devoured by flames. He himself 'feels the first swipe of fire across the side of his face…. They keep him away from mirrors. Anything that can cast a reflection is hidden by the nurses.' Alex stays with Miles but he is devastated by his disfigurement and by his memory of the kid's death, for which he feels responsible. He and Alex live briefly in her apartment and make love once (she becomes pregnant), but Miles leaves her without writing a note. Six years later Alex searches for him in a car, accompanied by her five-year-old daughter, Rachel, and eventually finds him in Ross Lake, the Yukon, where he is the fire chief. The bulk of the novel that follows displays Pyper's skill in portraying uneasy relationships and emotions that change; his knowledge of bears when a bear with her two cubs enters the picture and is hunted, only to become the hunter; and his unusual ability to describe fire vividly when a final conflagration threatens Rachel. With all its suspense, and some violence, *The wildfire season* is, in the end, an unusual love story. In 2008 Pyper published his most engrossing novel, *The killing circle,* a successful thriller involving widower and wannabe novelist Patrick Rush and his eight-year-old son Sam; a 'writing circle' Patrick joins, in which Angela tells (and Patrick records) part of her story—which we read—about the Sandman, 'a terrible man who does terrible things'; a series of murders in Toronto—and the kidnapping of Sam.

Q

Quarrington, Paul (1953–2010). Born in Toronto, he attended the University of Toronto for one year in 1972. His early career was as a musician; he played bass with the rock band Joe Hall and the Continental Drift (and most recently the Porkbelly Futures) and co-produced and recorded an album, *Quarrington/Worthy* (1978), which featured a number-one hit single. While dealing with the travails of lung cancer, Quarrington wrote about his passionate devotion to making music, his writing, and facing death in a posthumously published memoir called *Cigar box banjo: notes on music and life* (2010).

Quarrington's novels are distinguished by their masterful handling of eccentric characterization and comic situations. His protagonists, fallen male figures drifting in the present, but haunted by their past, must undergo trials and suffering in order to redeem their lives. His uneven first book, *The service* (1978), introduces this recurring theme in its farcical treatment of a hapless man's struggle to understand his life. The mythic quest for meaning and redemption is also evident in *Home game* (1983, rpr. 1996), which revolves around a baseball game played between circus performers and religious fundamentalists, and in *Logan in overtime* (1990), about a down-and-out former National Hockey League goaltender in an industrial hockey league who finds himself playing in the longest overtime game in the history of hockey. In *The life of hope* (1985, rpr. 1996) the narrator leaves his problems in the city and flees to Hope, Ontario, where he researches the Utopian sect that founded the town in the nineteenth century.

Much of Quarrington's writing employs a variety of postmodernist narrative techniques that self-consciously foreground the act of writing and subvert traditional assumptions about narrative coherence and unity. He dispenses with disruptive intrusions in his finest works, *King Leary* (1987, rpr. 1994) and *Whale music* (1989, GGA, rpr. 1997). Both novels feature first-person interior monologues and flashbacks, an ideal narrative medium for Quarrington's linguistic dexterity and perfectly suited to his continued interest in the mind's intermingling of past and present. In *King Leary*, an aging hockey legend, Percival Leary, recalls his life and confronts the consequences of his previous actions. It won the 2008 edition of *Canada Reads*, CBC Radio's annual 'battle' of five books. *Whale music* both examines and parodies the world of rock music through the muddled brain of its drug-dependent narrator, Des Howell. Like Leary, Howell comes to understand how his earlier lack of compassion colours his present; his musical composition for whales is a redemptive act of reconciliation with his dead brother. Quarrington satirizes the false glamour of the movie industry and its blurring of appearance and reality in *Civilization: and its part in my downfall* (1994, rpr. 1995). Focused on the early days of Hollywood's first 'flickers', the book is narrated in the form of a memoir written by Thom Moss, former riding ace and cowboy-film star. *The spirit cabinet* (1999, rpr. 2000) is centred on two gay German professional magicians who become superstars in Las Vegas (bringing to mind the real-life Las Vegas entertainers Siegfried and Roy): Rudolfo, who is satisfied to perform mere tricks, in the belief that magic is a fake, and Jurgen, who is captivated by the possibility of real magic. But between them they put on a great show. Including bizarre performers and characters, among them an albino leopard, the novel is filled with weird and unexpected turnings while opening windows on the profession of magicians. *Galveston* (2004, rpr. 2005) is mainly about three 'weather chasers', people obsessed with storms, whose lives we read about in successive flashbacks: Caldwell (no first name), whose marriage has been destroyed by his winning $16 million dollars in a lottery, and Beverly (no last name), whose daughter Margaret has died. Both are fixated on Galveston, Texas, which was devastated by a hurricane in September 1900. Jimmy Newton photographs storms and has a large following as Mr Weatherman on Miami radio. Longing to experience a hurricane, they arrive, with others, on Dampier Cay, a small island in the Caribbean (discovered by William Dampier) that is not on any map. Hurricane Claire eventually hits the island. '"Category five," ' recited Newton. '"Catastrophe. Winds greater than 155 miles per hour. Storm surge greater than eighteen feet. Complete building failures with small utility buildings blown over or away."... That's us, baby.' The horrific results are fatal. The title of *The ravine* (2008) alludes to an event that took place in a Don Mills (Ontario) ravine, when the narrator Phil and his brother Jay, eleven- and ten-year-old Cubs, take part with other boys in some tomfoolery. But the novel is mainly about the adult Phil's life, in which everything seems to have gone wrong. In October 2009 the WRITER'S TRUST OF

Quarrington

CANADA named Quarrington the winner of the Matt COHEN Award ($20,000).

Quarrington has also written plays, including *The invention of poetry* (1990; performed by Canadian Stage, Toronto, and the Citadel Theatre, Edmonton, in 1989) and *Checkout time* (performed by the Fringe Festival, Toronto, in 1997). His works of non-fiction include three books about fishing, his avocation: *Fishing with my old guy* (1995), a humorous reflection on the sport of angling when four men, including the author, go to northern Québec in search of the largest speckled trout; *From the far side of the river: chest-deep in little fish and big ideas* (2003) is a follow-up to this book; and *Fishing for brookies, browns & bows: the old guy's complete guide* to *catching trout* (2001) by Gord Deval has 'an intelligent commentary' by Quarrington. In addition there are *Hometown heroes: on the road with Canada's national hockey team* (1988); and *The boy on the back of the turtle: seeking God, quince marmalade and the fabled albatross on Darwin's islands* (1997), based on Quarrington's visit to the Galapagos Islands with his father and daughter. This is less a travel book about the Islands and their fauna than a light-hearted account of the trip—in which all three Quarringtons are prominent—that interweaves historical background information, the author's personal/informational digressions, including anecdotes about Darwin, people met along the way, and considerations of Darwinism and God.

R

Raddall, Thomas (1903–94). Thomas Head Raddall was born in the married quarters of the British Army School of Musketry at Hythe, England, where his father was an instructor. The latter's posting to Halifax in 1913 made his son a Nova Scotian and resulted in Raddall's steadfast, intimate, and rewarding bond with that province. His engrossing and candid autobiography, *In my time* (1976), tells how Raddall, too poor to attend university, served as a wireless operator on coastal stations, at sea, and on Sable Island from 1919 to 1922; he then qualified as a bookkeeper, took a job with a lumber company on the Mersey River, and soon began to write, having developed an interest in the history of his province—in Mi'kmaqs, pre-Loyalist settlers, Loyalists, privateering, and the economic diseases that befell Canada's Atlantic littoral following the age of sail. These years—which introduced him also to hunting and fishing, logging, rum-running, business machinations, and backwoods politics—were the fullest of Raddall's life. Having published short stories in *Blackwood's Magazine* and elsewhere, Raddall chose in 1938 to become a professional writer. During the Second World War he was an officer in the West Nova Scotia Regiment, worked as a journalist and as a scriptwriter for radio, and published two collections of short stories and two novels.

Raddall's *The pied piper of Dipper Creek and other stories* (1939, GGA), with an introduction by John Buchan, was followed by *Tambour and other stories* (1945); *The wedding gift and other stories* (1947); *A muster of arms and other stories* (1954); and *At the tide's turn and other stories* (1959), a selection from the earlier books. All these collections demonstrate his knowledge of the texture of Nova Scotia life, past and present, and his facility for straightforward, entertaining storytelling.

Raddall's first historical novel, *His Majesty's Yankees* (1942, rpr. 1997), which deals with the conflicting political, economic, and emotional ties of Nova Scotians during the American Revolution, shows—in its sound use of J.B. Brebner's *The neutral Yankees of Nova Scotia* and Simeon Perkins' diaries—his enterprising, meticulous research. Its robust style also animates *Roger Sudden* (1944, rpr. 1996), a story of the Seven Years' War and the capture of Louisbourg, and *Pride's Fancy* (1946), a rousing tale of a privateer in West Indies waters during the fight for Haitian independence. *The governor's lady* (1960, rpr. 1992) offers a masterful re-creation of the personality and character of Fannie Wentworth, wife of the lieutenant-governor (1792–1808) of Nova Scotia. In *Hangman's beach* (1966, rpr. 1992) the focus is twofold: Raddall evokes the 1803–12 period of the Napoleonic Wars in Halifax, with particular emphasis on French prisoners held on Melville Island; and, through his portrayal of the Peter McLeod family, delineates the boom in Nova Scotia commerce during those years.

Though best known for his historical fiction, Raddall also wrote three novels set in the twentieth century—one of which, *The nymph and the lamp* (1950, rpr. 1994), is his masterpiece. With its superbly conveyed settings (Halifax, Sable Island, and the Annapolis Valley), its astutely interwoven themes, sexual tension, and powerful characterization of the protagonist, Isabel Jardine, it is a work of enduring merit that cannot be dismissed as a romance. *Tidefall* (1953) and *Wings of the night* (1956) are mediocre by comparison: the former has to do with a seafaring villain who makes and loses a fortune, the latter with forest life and economic troubles in Nova Scotia.

Raddall also wrote two books of history: the authoritative chronicle *Halifax, warden of the north* (1948, GGA; rev. 1965; rpr. 1993); the discerning and spirited popular history *The path of destiny: Canada from the British Conquest to home rule, 1763–1850* (1957, GGA); and *Footsteps on old floors: six tales of true mystery* (1968, rpr. 1988), containing essays on obscure but compelling 'mysteries' of Nova Scotia history, notably that of the derelict vessel *Mary Celeste* and her missing crew.

Raddall was made an Officer of the Order of Canada in 1970. See Alan R. Young, *Thomas Raddall and his works* (1990), and Alan R. Young, ed., *Time and place: the life and works of Thomas H. Raddall* (1991).

Radisson, Pierre-Esprit. See Writing in NEW FRANCE: 1.

Radu, Kenneth (b. 1945). Born in Windsor, Ontario, of Romanian heritage, he was educated at Victoria College, University of Toronto (B.A., 1970); at the University of Waterloo, Ontario (M.A., 1973); and was a doctoral student at Dalhousie University, Halifax (1973–5). He has taught in the English department of John Abbott College, Québec, since 1975. Radu has published three collection of poetry: *Letters to a distant father* (1987), *Treading water* (1992), and *Romanian suite* (1996); five novels: *Distant relations* (1989), *Home fires* (1992), *Strange and familiar places* (1999), *Flesh and blood* (2001), *The purest of human pleasures* (2005); and three collections of short stories: *The cost of living* (1987), *A private performance* (1990), and *Snow over Judaea* (1994). One is struck in Radu's writing by his engagement with a wide variety of characters—historical and modern, happy misfits, ordinary family members with psychological twists, struggling nonentities. The poems in *Letter to a distant father* include a sequence called 'Royal women', six poems on Marie Antoinette, Elizabeth of Austria, and

others; the title poem is the long final poem: 'Your language is not mine/so my hands grip a present/tense you won't understand.... / Will you understand these words/composed in the country of exile?/How will this passage/pass through translation?' The poems in *Romanian suite* were composed as a result of the visit of Radu's son Joshua to Romania and include meditations on famous figures (Prince Vlad and Dracula) and on two distinguished Romanian pianists, Dinu Lipatti, who died at thirty-three in 1950, and Radu Lupu ('His first name my last ...').

In Radu's first two novels a semi-stream-of-conscious mode is sometimes employed to accommodate the abundance of narrative ideas relating to both past and present. *Distant relations*, without chapters, tells the life story of Vera, in her last days at seventy-four, as she recalls her marriage to a country brute in the west; her children, whom she dislikes—except for her youngest, Louis, who became successful and has been living with his gay partner in Europe; and her lover, Amsterdam, a black doctor—all in the context of a family reunion that is about to take place, aggressively arranged by daughter Mary. *Home fires* is a much longer Montreal novel that portrays the present and past lives of several dysfunctional people: Brian, fairly happily married, who advertises for sex partners; Mariette, who answers his ad; Nick, a family man who has a sex shop and other enterprises related to sex—and gets his thrills by committing arson (known only by Wanda, his wife); the handsome Jacques, who works for him; and the destitute and alcoholic Roger, who is taken in by Mariette. *Strange and familiar places*, shorter and more controlled, is about Paul, a minister; his wife Evelyn, who likes to have 'sweet sex' with available men, here the janitor Armand, his young son Louis, and Charlie Buegler, a parishioner; and their daughter Cecily. The strongest thread in the novel is the strained but civilized and agreeable family life of Paul and Evelyn (though Paul knows about his wife's affairs) and the trip they and Cecily take to the Middle East; a sinister undercurrent of child kidnappings is not fully developed. Many of Radu's short stories, which always maintain narrative interest, are coloured by an attraction to plots with facile characterizations, and to the bizarre in both. In *Flesh and blood* Rose and Jacob—a loveless couple more or less forced to marry because Jacob was supposed to have a wife and Rose had no other offers—with their young children Nicky and Eva, are forced to leave the climate-scourged Saskatchewan in the 1930s and settle in southwestern Ontario, near

Radu

Windsor, in part of the house owned by Mr Washington, a handsome black man around forty, known as Bobby. What follows is an intricate and emotionally involving narrative describing Rose and Bobby's falling in love, their passionate affair conducted in the absence of Jacob, who is always looking for farming work and not often finding it. 'She had had so little in her life until now, so little to look back on with satisfaction. Bobby had given her the light of the sun and the softness of rain, had opened her heart and body until, looking up, she was white cloud and blue sky and the woman in the garden who grew food and flowers because life and energy flowed through her finger tips.' Rose, creating meals with homegrown vegetables, with little money to buy food, is tormented by anxiety, particularly when she becomes pregnant, though she is glad to be bearing Bobby's child. Sarah is born and she has to withstand Jacob's unexpressed fury. He finds a job, and more money enables Rose to produce delicious meals. There is another pregnancy (Rita is born) and Jacob erupts. He finds a job in Windsor and plans to move there with the family. Bobby has all this time pled with Rose to leave with him and start a new life, leaving Nicky and Eva (her flesh and blood) with Jacob. Rose cannot do this and there is a final separation, when Rose and Jacob and the children move to Windsor. We read about them ten years later, when Rose has two more sons. The remarkable quality of the novel has to do with Radu's sensitively combining an erotically charged relationship, and Rose's sensuous enjoyment of it, coupled with her stressful living conditions, while interweaving the backgrounds of Rose, Bobby, and Jacob. The denouement is not satisfactory for the two main characters—who, however, commit themselves to a new way of life. *The purest of human pleasures*—the title, from Francis Bacon, refers to gardens—opens (after a Prologue) in a lakeside community near Montreal: 'Loretta Ferroux congratulated herself on doing a good job of digging the compost and sheep manure into the new garden bed....The roots of the new astilbe, hosta, the arching fronds and delicate white flowers of Solomon's seal, Jacob's ladders, ferns, lungworts, and bleeding hearts (the white, not the maroon or red, for she agreed with Morris Bunter, her gardener, that *Dicentra spectabilis alba* would provide a lovely contrast in the shadows) had all arrived by post from her favourite nursery.' On this first page we are introduced to Loretta, a wealthy divorcee; Morris, her gardener; nineteen-year-old Kate Bunter, his daughter, who sometimes gives

him gardening assistance and is a university student involved in a sexual-harassment case against one of her professors, the artist Donald Ingoldsby; he lives next door to Loretta and is having an affair with her daughter Annick, much to her disgust. We deduce that there will be a prevalence of garden lore in the book, impressively displaying Radu's intimate knowledge of the subject, particularly of flowers and plants (especially poisonous plants), leading to an excess of gardening similes and metaphors. We soon learn that Annick is furious with her mother for not releasing money from the trust fund of a million dollars plus interest she will inherit at the age of thirty. Now twenty-four, Annick—who wants money to help Ingoldsby buy and remodel a house in Vermont—rushes outside and hurls her mother's blue-and-gold Lalique vase filled with daffodils and tulips against the fountain; it smashes in front of Kate, who is working in the garden. Among other characters, Morris and Kate (and their fretful father-daughter relationship) become central, particularly after Morris discovers Loretta lying dead in her garden, a hatchet in her head; old Mrs Grant is murdered later. But the murders and the discovery of their perpetrators are not central. The characters and their relationships, and Morris's gardens, attract the author more—until the Epilogue, which describes an act of devastation that is surprising, and in some ways unaccountable. Beautiful writing is the novel's strength, so that any weakness in the intricate plot does not take away from the reader's enjoyment. The ominous Prologue—an irritating device—makes little sense when first read; it becomes clearer after the novel is finished, though there are frustrating loose ends.

Radu's grandparents came to Saskatchewan from Romania in the early twentieth century. In *The devil is clever: a memoir of my Romanian mother* (2004, rpr. 2005) he portrays, as a gifted storyteller, the early life of his mother Annie Corches, born in 1913 in the town of Dysart. Her own mother (with five children) died the next year and her father died in 1920. Sent from home to home, often subjected to ill treatment, Annie survived with great strength the difficult early years of her life by finding comfort in her Romanian heritage, which suffuses the book (along with many Romanian recipes).

Rand, Silas T. See ABORIGINAL LEGENDS AND TALES: BIBLIOGRAPHY.

Rapoport, Janis (b. 1946). Born and raised in Toronto, she received a B.A. (1967) from the

University of Toronto. From 1968 to 1970 she lived in London, England, where she worked as an editor and researcher. She was an associate editor of the TAMARACK REVIEW from 1970 to 1982 and editor of *Ethos* from 1983 to 1987. She has been writer-in-residence at several Ontario libraries and participates regularly in readings, literary workshops, and conferences. Rapaport's books of poetry include *Within the whirling moment* (1967), *Foothills* (1973), *Jeremy's dream* (1974), *Winter flowers* (1979), *Upon her fluent route* (1991), and *After paradise* (1996). A lyric poet, her descriptive verse is layered verbally and punctuated with startling, visual images. Often she strikes an intellectual pose, which can result in a poetry of cool detachment. Soon after the appearance of her first slim volume, which favoured the brief, clipped line, Rapoport began to experiment with a longer, prose-like line, which became typical of her writing. In her first full-length collection, *Winter flowers*, she explored such common themes as love, human relationships, family, and children. Her later work reveals a lusher style and an interest in romanticism, introducing earth mothers, goddesses, and witches whose magical powers characterize a particularly female-centred world. Her writing asserts the value of the imagination, fantasy, faith, and change over the dullness of reason and order. Rapaport has also written *Dreamgirls* (1979), a two-act play featuring six female characters.

Reaney, James (1926–2008). 1. POETRY AND FICTION. Born in South Easthope near Stratford, Ontario, James Crerar (his mother's maiden name) Reaney won a scholarship to University College, University of Toronto, where he studied English literature (B.A, 1948; M.A., 1949). While an undergraduate he published two stories, 'The bully' and 'The box social', that are not only classic Canadian short stories but are the first examples of a modern tradition in fiction called SOUTHERN ONTARIO GOTHIC (having its origin in the novels of John RICHARDSON and some of the stories Susanna MOODIE tells) that make use of Gothic elements of the macabre. In the four-page 'The box social', for example, a young man bids for a prettily wrapped shoe box, from a girl he made pregnant, that contains 'the crabbed corpse of a stillborn child wreathed in bloody newspaper.' Margaret ATWOOD has remarked that 'without "The bully", my fiction would have followed other paths.' *The box social and other stories* (1996) presents eleven stories, written for the most part in the 1940s and 1950s. Reaney taught

English at the University of Manitoba from 1949 to 1956, when he returned to Toronto to complete a doctorate, which was awarded in 1958; his thesis, supervised by Northrop FRYE, was 'The influence of Spenser on Yeats'. In 1951 he married Colleen Thibaudeau, also a poet. In 1960 he began his long career as a professor of English at the University of Western Ontario. In that year he also started the magazine ALPHABET, on 'the iconography of the imagination', which lasted ten years. His first three collections of poetry all won Governor General's Awards: *The red heart* (1949), written when Reaney was twenty-three; *A suit of nettles* (1958, 2nd edn 1975); and *Twelve letters to a small town* (1962)—which was followed by *The dance of death at London, Ontario* (1963, drawings by Jack Chambers). *Poems* (1972)—which includes the four previous collections—*Selected shorter poems* (1975), and *Selected longer poems* (1976) were edited by Germaine Warkentin, with extensive introductions that are among the best Reaney criticism. These books were followed by *Imprecations: the art of swearing* (1984) and *Performance poems* (1990).

The red heart, a collection of forty-two lyrics, is an intensely private, even precious book. Already the playfulness and the somewhat childlike character of Reaney's poetic temperament—though not his technical mastery—are evident. Its central figure is a youthful artist coming to poetic terms with a provincial environment, the Perth County of Reaney's childhood. The poems are infused with a sentimental nostalgia as the poet, in the role of orphan, tries to create an imaginary play-box world of childhood as an antidote to a hostile cultural world. *A suit of nettles* is an extraordinary leap forward. Perhaps under the tutelage of Frye, Reaney draws on traditional literary structures to inform his poem, imitating Spenser's *The shepheardes calender*. A series of twelve pastoral eclogues, *A suit of nettles* focuses on a southern Ontario town, seen from the perspective of the barnyard geese in their twelve-month cycle from birth to ritual slaughter at Christmas. An opening invocation to the Muse of Satire 'to beat fertility into a sterile land' makes Reaney's satiric purpose clear: the geese provide a repertoire of human types—lover, teacher, philosopher, poet, critic—imitating an archetypal human community struggling against victimization by time and death and the negativism in humans that denies creativity. Made up of allegorical puzzles, dialogue poems, beast fables, and graphic poems—the sequence gives full play to the quirky, sardonic wit of

Reaney

Reaney, for whom poetry is game and mischief. In *Twelve letters to a small town*, a suite of lyrics, Reaney erects a model of Stratford, remembered from the late 1930s and early 1940s, and tries to recover the physical and spiritual environment that created him in the persona of a lively, imaginative boy, gifted with a capacity to see wonder and mystery in the simple and homely. Reminiscent of *Under Milk Wood* by Dylan Thomas, *Twelve letters* is an act of imagination by which the poet recreates his rural roots in their ideal mythological form. *The dance of death* and 'Two chapters from an emblem book', published in *Poems*, derive from Reaney's enduring fascination with iconography. As Germaine Warkentin has written, 'Reaney began to think … one could develop a virtual iconography of the imagination, an alphabet of images which would disclose the relationship between "the verbal universe which hovers over the seedbed of the so-called real and natural world" and the seedbed itself' ('Introduction', *Poems*). 'The emblem book', a combination of diagrams and verbal puns, tries to identify a whole unsorted alphabet of special diagrams in the triangles, circles, and crosses that recur in art. While this interest in hieroglyph and pictograph is engaged mostly at the level of game, it is rooted in Reaney's ambition to recover a traditional interest in graphic symbols as vehicles in articulating otherwise inapprehensible metaphysical insights. In *Imprecations: the art of swearing*, Reaney rediscovers cursing, describing it as a 'lost skill'. From childhood memories of swearing to actual cursing, he reminds the reader of the delight in finding appropriate objects for one's invective, from the giant grocery chain that has destroyed the local grocer to the minister of education who has damned the world to the bad teaching of poetry. *Performance poems* collects poems and prose poems written for performance since 1960, grouping them into a calendar cycle from January to December. In his preface, Reaney suggests the poems can be read silently, aloud, or scored for many voices, and can be illustrated by 'mime, dance, musique concrete, manipulation of props and body movement'. He also includes unfinished poems, challenging the reader to fill them out with local references. With delightful exuberance, he breaks down the barriers between theatre and poetry, reminding his readers of poetry's visceral roots in nursery rhymes and street games. In his hands, poetry becomes an environment, an entire world, and reading and performing his poetry becomes a medium by which his readers discover the latent but rarely tapped energy of their own creative imaginations. In *Souwesto home* (2005), published three years before Reaney died, his singular voice and vision depict and celebrate aspects of the small southwestern Ontario (Souwesto) town that was central in his imagination and in much of his writing: where 'The Old Huron Road curved only once,/Defeated by the Little Lakes/With their hemlock swamps/ Bottomless/Where they bent him south & then north/And caught, therefore, in their crooked snare/Painters & poets, storytellers, eccentrics/Who were born & lived & died there ('Little lake district [where I was born] poems'). 'Maps' ends with the lines:'Inside my school—the whole world/In a round globe, or flat maps;/Outside our school—a part of the world/Too big to be taught.' The poems stray to worldly subjects, with a surprising evolution: 'Department store Jesus', 'Moses', 'The birth of a pome', 'Descartes' ('He could not talk!/But he took a piece of chalk/And on a wall/Did he scrawl/For the cook & the farmer to see:/"Yes, I eat; therefore I be!"' The book is decorated with small line drawings ('clip art') by the author. Reaney will always have his devoted readers who, like Warkentin, find his poems among the most richly satisfying written in Canada.

Playing sophisticated games by switching voice, Reaney achieves a kind of 'magic realism', often through the distorted perspective and sense of disproportion of his child narrators. Reaney is also the author of two novels for young people: *The boy with an R in his hand: a tale of the type-riot at William Lyon Mackenzie's printing office in 1826* (1965, rev. edn 1980), about York (Toronto) in the 1820s, and *Take the big picture* (1986) about the large Delahay family: two girls and four boys, three of them triplets. Reaney was made an Officer of the Order of Canada in 1976.

2. DRAMA. James Reaney turned to writing drama after he had become established as a poet. The libretto for the chamber opera *Night-blooming Cereus* by John Beckwith was completed in 1953 (though the opera was not produced until 1960), and was published in *The killdeer and other plays* (1962), which also included *The sun and the moon* and *One-man masque*. This was followed by *Colours in the dark* (1969), *Listen to the wind* (1972), and *Masks of childhood* (1972), which contains three plays: *The Easter egg*, *Three desks*, and a revised version of *The killdeer*. Reaney has also written several children's plays, some of which have been published in *Apple butter and other plays for children* (1973), which includes

Geography match, Names and nicknames, and *Ignoramus.*

Reaney's early plays brought great imagination to English-Canadian drama. Some of them, written mainly or partly in verse, treat themes also found in his poetry: the contrasting worlds of innocence and experience, the underlying evil forces in everyone, love's power to redeem, the process of growth from childhood to adolescence to maturity. Reaney prefers a non-linear, kaleidoscopic drama to one based on the assumptions of the realistic theatre. Indeed, the complexity and profusion of events in his plays often bewilder and dissatisfy audiences accustomed to realistic drama. Rich in symbolism and patterns of imagery, the plays often present a fanciful, surrealistic world; and since little attempt is made to develop plot or character, their lack of emotional depth sometimes hinders audience involvement. The themes of the libretto for the chamber opera *Night-blooming Cereus* are loneliness and reconciliation. It was performed at Hart House Theatre, Toronto, in 1960, along with *One-man masque* (with Reaney himself as the performer)—a short poetic fantasy on birth, death, and other stages of human life. *The sun and the moon,* which includes elements of farce (as do most of Reaney's plays), shows the evil influences lurking in a small Ontario community and uses melodrama (a convention he is fond of) to bring these influences to the surface and to heighten the comic and redemptive dimensions of the play. The title of one collection of Reaney's plays, *Masks of childhood,* suggests the central place of the child's world in Reaney's work—as a symbol of unspoiled innocence, a mask to hide a deeper world of evil, and a shield for those who cannot enter the adult world of risk and responsibility. *The killdeer,* in its 1972 version, emphasizes the hold of a violent or inhibiting past on the lives of children from different families; only their mutual love and forgiveness enable them to break free. (In 1991 *The killdeer* was revised again for performance at the University of Western Ontario.) *Three desks* is a macabre and farcical treatment of the childishness and hostility that can affect the life of an academic community, in this case a small liberal-arts college on the Prairies. *The Easter egg* is a symbolic exploration of Christian redemption and resurrection. *Colours in the dark*—first produced at Stratford, Ont., in 1967 under the direction of John Hirsch—shows Reaney's surer command of the free dramatic form towards which all his plays tend. Of its forty-two scenes, which give impressions of growing up

in southwestern Ontario, Reaney said: 'This one has a new play before you every two minutes.' *Listen to the wind* adds a sombre note to the optimism of some of the earlier plays: a sick boy fails to reunite his parents, though he goes to bed believing he has succeeded. The play-within-a-play technique contrasts the worlds of imagination and reality.

Reaney's ability to confront more realistic situations, while developing new forms of dramatic structure, is evident in the Donnelly trilogy: *Sticks and stones: the Donnellys, part one* (1974), *The St Nicholas hotel, Wm Donnelly, Prop: the Donnellys, part two* (1976), and *Handcuffs: the Donnellys, part three* (1977)—about the famous Irish immigrant family that was massacred in Lucan, Ontario, in 1880. All three were published together as *The Donnellys* (1983) with scholarly apparatus by James Noonan. Combining history, poetry, music, dance, marionettes, magic lanterns, liturgy, mime, and myth, the plays were written after some eight years of research on the Donnellys and their times. Reaney is clearly sympathetic to the Donnellys and rejects their reputation as 'the Black Donnellys'; he presents them as superior and heroic, even Christ-like figures, who die for their own dignity and their right to be different. The trilogy was developed in workshops with director Keith Turnbull and the NDWT Company, which presented it at Toronto's Tarragon Theatre between 1973 and 1975. In the fall of 1975 *The Donnellys* was taken on a cross-Canada tour—to nineteen communities from Vancouver to Halifax—climaxed by a final presentation of all three plays in one day at the Bathurst St Theatre in Toronto on 14 Dec. 1975. Reaney wrote a personal account of the tour, the actors' experiences, and the plays' reception, in *14 barrels from sea to sea* (1977), which also contains reviews from all the cities in which they were performed.

While *The Donnellys* is the landmark achievement of Reaney's drama to date, he has continued to write plays based on local history, at times giving them universal significance. *Baldoon* (1976), co-authored with Marty GERVAIS, concerns events in a small community near Wallaceburg, Ontario, in the 1830s, involving poltergeists, witchcraft, and a witch hunter, often evoked by the use of puppets and marionettes. Liberation entails the defeat of Dr McTavish's dour Presbyterianism by the exorcist Dr Troyer's joyous Shaker brand of Christianity. Some later plays were commissioned for special groups or occasions. *The dismissal; or Twisted beards and tangled whiskers* (1978) was commissioned by Reaney's alma mater, University College, to mark the sesquicentennial of the University of Toronto in 1977. The play is above all entertainment and includes musical routines, vaudeville, and an actress playing the bearded 'President Fury' of the university in 1994–5. In *Wacousta* (1979) Reaney made a play from the melodramatic early-Canadian novel *WACOUSTA* by John Richardson. The published version of the play contains detailed descriptions of its development in workshops in London and Timmins, Ontario, before it toured Ontario in 1978. Reaney followed this with another elaborate work, *The Canadian brothers* (published in the anthology *Major Plays of the Canadian Theatre*, 1984, edited by Richard Perkyns, and performed by students at the University of Calgary in 1983), based on *The Canadian brothers; or, The prophecy fulfilled* (1840), Richardson's sequel to *Wacousta*. *King Whistle!* (1980, in the journal *BRICK*, no. 8), written for the centenary of the Central Secondary School in Stratford, Ont., was first performed at the Avon Theatre, Stratford, in Nov. 1979. The local subject matter lacks the wide appeal of some of Reaney's other plays, as does his next play *Antler River* (unpublished), commissioned by the Urban League of London, Ont. (where Reaney lives), to celebrate the city's 125th anniversary in 1980. *Stereoscope*, along with his *One-man masque* and *The perfect essay*, was performed at the University of Western Ontario in 1992 during month-long celebrations paying tribute to Reaney on his retirement from teaching there. *Gyroscope* (1983), performed at the Tarragon Theatre as part of the 1981 Toronto Theatre Festival, represents a return to personal vision and experience. It contains satire on sex, marriage, small-town life, and academia, and explores with humour the struggle for balance and understanding in a creative husband-wife relationship.

Much of Reaney's recent work has been librettos for Canadian composers. The first of these was the libretto for *The shivaree: opera in two acts* (1978), with music by John Beckwith, which Comus Music Theatre premiered at the St Lawrence Centre, Toronto, and on CBC Radio, in 1982. The title refers to the custom—still practised in parts of southwestern Ontario—of serenading a newly wedded couple on homemade percussion instruments. In 1982 Reaney was commissioned to write a play to celebrate the city of Waterloo, Ont. The result was *I, the parade: the story of professor C.F. Thiele* (director of the Waterloo Musical Society Band for thirty-five years). Two successive years saw the production of two operas

for which Reaney wrote the librettos: *Crazy to kill* (1988), a 'detective opera' with music by John Beckwith, heard at the Guelph Spring Festival in 1989; and *Serinette* (1990), a chamber opera with music by the late Harry Somers, produced as part of the Music at the Sharon Festival in 1990 to mark the tenth anniversary of that festival. Both operas were popular successes. Reaney scored another popular success with his adaptation for the stage of Lewis Carroll's *Alice through the looking-glass* (1994)—with music by Keith Thomas—which was performed at the Avon Theatre of the Stratford Festival in 1994, and repeated there in 1996. *Scripts: librettos for operas and other musical works* (2004) was edited with an introduction by John Beckwith, who says that he wrote music for all but one of 'scripts' in this valuable and attractive compilation published by the COACH HOUSE PRESS. It opens with a surprise, 'The Great Lakes suite' from *The red heart*—when it was published in 1949 Beckwith asked if he could set these five poems to music; also included are *Night-blooming Cereus*, *Twelve letters to a small town*, *The shivaree*, *Crazy to kill*, *Serinette*, and *Taptoo!*, an opera based on events surrounding the founding of the town of York (Toronto) and covering the years 1780 to 1810.

Rebel angels, The (1981, rpr. 2008). The first volume in the Cornish trilogy by Robertson DAVIES, it moves the novel towards 'anatomy' (one of the four categories of prose fiction Northrop FRYE defines in his 'Theory of genres', the Fourth Essay in his *Anatomy of criticism*) in its exploration of the nature of a university. Some of the characters thus appear not as fully rounded people but as mental attitudes, and ideas and theories are emphasized. The short form of the anatomy—the dialogue or colloquy—is present in the guest nights at Ploughwright College, and the exuberance of the anatomist appears in the piling up of erudite lore in catalogues, like the list of medieval terms for faeces of animals. By means of a web of allusions to Paracelsus, alchemy, medieval filth therapy, and Gypsies, Davies presents the university as an institution rooted in the Middle Ages—dedicated to the pursuit of learning and wisdom both secular and divine, but also prone to petty and gross betrayals of its professed standards. The story is narrated alternately by Maria Magdalena Theotoky, a gifted graduate student, and Simon Darcourt, a middle-aged Anglican priest and professor of New Testament Greek. Maria is preparing to write a doctoral thesis on a Rabelais manuscript. She works in the rooms of her supervisor Clement Hollier (whose field is the thinking of medieval people and with whom she imagines herself in love), takes various graduate courses, and furthers Hollier's research. At Hollier's urging she visits Ozias Froats to see whether his research into human excrement has revealed why medieval filth therapy worked. She also introduces Hollier to her mother, a Gypsy and a restorer of stringed instruments by the medieval method of burying their wooden cases in horse manure.

In his sections Darcourt describes various academic occasions—funerals and a wedding that take place in the chapel of the College of St John and the Holy Ghost, sherry parties given by a professor, college guest nights at Ploughwright College—because he is engaged in creating a record of collegiate life. He is also one of three academics who are sorting out the estate of their old friend and collector Francis Cornish. He thus has a chance to observe academic knowledgeability and cupidity in action. Several characters lust after (and one steals) the Rabelais manuscript that Maria has been promised and that Francis Cornish owned, and several lust after Maria herself. A high point is the Christmas dinner to which Maria's mother Mamusia invites Clement Hollier and Simon Darcourt. One of Davies' unforgettable set pieces, this encompasses a marvellous Gypsy *crèche*, a gargantuan feast, astute fortune telling, Gypsy music, and a misdirected love-philtre. The story winds through this and other highly coloured events towards the grotesque murder of a professor, a suicide, and Maria's Gypsy wedding, and comes to rest with the final guest night of the academic year at Ploughwright College.

The novel is something of a *roman à clef*. Ploughwright is clearly based on Massey College, and the College of St John and the Holy Ghost on neighbouring Trinity, both in the University of Toronto. Several characters have antecedents that have been identified. *The rebel angels* has been translated into ten languages.

Redbird, Duke (b. 1939). Born in Southampton, Ontario, the sixth and last child of Jack and Kathleen Richardson, he is a North American status Native. In 1978 he received an M.A. in interdisciplinary studies at York University, Toronto. In the sixties and seventies he was in the forefront of Native political organizations and was a prominent public speaker on Native issues, providing First Nations people in Canada with a new, young, and aggressive leadership. He was president of

the Ontario Métis and Non-status Indian Association and director of their Land Claims Research, as well as vice-president of the Native Council of Canada, and was the subject of a biography *Red on white* (1971) by Marty Dunn. His early poems—such as 'The beaver', 'A red nation', 'I am the redman'—are fuelled with the resentment of an angry young man disgusted with the white exploitation of Canada's Native people. In contrast, the poems in his collection *Loveshine and red wine* (1981) are about love of nature, of home and family, and are gentle and quietly domestic. In *I am a Canadian* (1978) he celebrates the people and the provinces of Canada in a stirring sixty-line prose poem. In 1989 he composed 'The Canadian Museum of Civilization' for 'Soirée Asticou', the pre-opening event of the new museum. His M.A. thesis, *We are Métis: a Métis view of the development of a Native Canadian people*, was published in 1980. Redbird has contributed significantly to film and television.

Redhill, Michael (b. 1966). Born in Baltimore, Maryland, he was raised in Toronto and educated at York University and the University of Toronto. A poet, playwright, and novelist, he was on the editorial board of COACH HOUSE PRESS from 1993 to 1996 and is the publisher and one of the editors of BRICK.

As a writer Redhill first achieved success in the 1990s as a poet, displaying a sure command of language and form and of the various themes he chose to write about, in *Impromptu feats of balance* (1990), *Lake Nora Arms* (1993), *Asphodel* (1997), and *Light-crossing* (2001). 'Nightfall' in *Lake Nora Arms* reads: 'The boat drives past the island cottage locked / in its privacy. Night falls on the lake, / You and I, drowsed with dusk, slowly talk / the darkness down and watch a gliding drake / dislodge the clouds around our boat and crack / the sky below us. In this clear weather / the stars seem to brighten for our sake—they appear like berries on the lake / glowing near the boat, close enough to gather.' The first part of *Asphodel* is called 'Coming to earth (Alzheimer Elegy)': 'That voyager can't come back, lifts / further away from the simplicities of beginning and / points its face into the darkness, welcomes it / in all the tongues of home.' In Part II 'Self Portrait' was inspired by *Window Façade,* a box by Joseph Cornell (see Redhill's novel *Martin Sloane* below). Part III, 'Going Under', was suggested by the sixth book of the *Aeneid*, in which the Sybil accompanies Aeneas to Hell and leads him to his father, Anchises; one of Redhill's poems

Redhill

(headed 18) echoes the 'Alzheimer elegy'—the father 'won't speak, / inclines his head, still suffers even here / from the forgetting that killed him in life.'

As a novelist Redhill made an impressive start with *Martin Sloane* (2001, rpr. 2001). The young American Jolene Iolas, an undergraduate at Bard College, New York, meets fifty-six-year-old Martin Sloane from Toronto, a well-known Irish-Canadian artist, when he is invited to the college to present an exhibition of his work. He arranges found objects in glass-fronted boxes in such a way that Jolene was captivated when she first saw an example of his work. (The Sloane career was inspired by that of Joseph Cornell, 1903–72, who created assemblages—positioning in his boxes surprising arrangements of beautiful and precious objects.) Jolene falls in love with Martin, as he does with her. She becomes a teacher at Bard and their happy affair lasts for several years—he comes down from Toronto to see her; she has a shed built in her backyard for him to work in. Jo invites her closest college friend, Molly, to visit them and the day the three spend together has tense undercurrents that result in Molly's going into Martin's shed to talk to him. The evening ends amicably, however. Jo and Martin sleep together, and when she wakes up he has gone, without a word. She never sees him again. The rest of the novel is an amalgam of Jo's devastation at her loss and slow recovery; the apparent disappearance of Molly from her life; Jo's search for Martin, beginning with a trip to Toronto, where she becomes a teacher and settles. (She embarks on a successful love affair with Daniel.) The narrative is interwoven with passages about Martin's early life in Dublin, his being hospitalized with TB, and the family's move to Galway in their effort to cure him. Suddenly, when Jo is thirty-five, Molly asks her to join her in Dublin. They reunite quite happily and join in a search for Martin that ends up in Galway. Jo enters a house lived in by Lenore, a crazy old lady, and meets her sister Mrs Bryson, also crazy, whom Martin married many years before. (Mrs Bryson never says where he lives.) But Jo also meets ninety-year-old Colin, the father, and talks to him about Martin. The reader is left with a poetic rendition of past and present, identity and nostalgia, that somehow satisfies without suggesting a convincing resolution. The hopeful marriage of Jolene and Daniel might be imagined as a happy ending. *Martin Sloane* won the *Books in Canada* First Novel Award (2001) and the Commonwealth Writers Prize (2002).

The ambitious novel *Consolation* (2006) is very much a Toronto book: the city appears as a resonant background character in two complementary narratives, set in 1997 and 1855–7 respectively. In the Victorian period the Englishman Jem Hallam arrives in Toronto and sets himself up as an apothecary, but fails; various events lead him to link up with, and learn photography from, the elderly photographer Samuel Ennis, and a young woman he calls Mrs Rowe: the three of them collaborate on a business. Hallam decides to photograph every aspect of the city, and his plates become valuable. He takes them to England, but on his return his boat is shipwrecked in Toronto harbour. The modern period centres on David Hollis (we are told in a prologue that he has thrown himself off the Hanlan's Point ferry)—a forensic archaeologist determined to protect the past, who is dying of Lou Gehrig's disease—and his wife Marianne and daughter Bridget (who are tediously given to inciting divisive arguments for no apparent reason apart from ill temper), and Bridget's fiancé John Lewis. (Sister Alison hardly appears.) David Hollis wrote a monograph saying he had evidence that a set of photographic plates in a strongbox, depicting Toronto in the 1850s, could be found in the remains of a boat that sank in Toronto harbour. This was respected by his peers until he refused to produce the diary that he said contained his evidence. His grieving widow takes a room on the thirty-second floor of a hotel overlooking a construction site (the Air Canada Centre?) on reclaimed land that may be in the very location where Hallam's boat sank. Indeed, traces of the boat are uncovered and for Marianne David's reputation is redeemed. Both narratives are filled with references to Toronto's streets and buildings, although we are not told that Campbell House, on its 'postage stamp of grass' at Queen Street and University Avenue, occupies Canada Life property and was moved from Duke and Frederick Streets in 1974. The novel is dedicated to the late architectural historian William Dendy—whose choice of old photographs and related commentary in his *Lost Toronto* inspired Redhill—and Jane Jacobs. *Consolation* won the 2007 ($11,000) City of Toronto Book Award.

The ten stories in *Fidelity* (2003) give evidence of Redhill's story-telling skill and ingenuity in constructing plots; weak characterizations and the lack of the author's emotional commitment to the stories will no doubt change if Redhill continues to write short stories. The first story, 'Mount Morris', is about the annual reunion of Tom, now a travelling photographer, and his ex-wife Lillian, when she cooks him dinner and they sleep together—but not this time. Tom says 'I have someone in my life now. I wanted to say something earlier.' The conversational exchanges between Tom and Lillian throughout the story are skilled. 'Split' is mainly a story about playing blackjack in a casino (we are impressed by Redhill's grasp of gambling protocol) and conversing with Arlene and her husband Jonas. Only on the last page do we discover that the narrator is Tom of the first story; when the game is over he drives home to Linda with his winnings. 'The victim, who cannot be named' opens with Margot weeping in front of the TV. Her husband sees that the screen is showing their daughter, a junior in high school, having sex with two even younger boys. The husband unaccountably thinks it's a matter of rape. 'We have to show this to the police,' he says. Margot: 'Rape victims don't smile, Peter.' The youngsters photographed themselves, putting the camera on automatic. The traumatic aftermath is gripping, though the story has two implausible episodes. There is no title story; the appropriateness of *Fidelity* as the title is not immediately apparent.

Redhill's published plays are *Building Jerusalem* (2000) and *Goodness* (2005). After several work-in-progress productions, *Building Jerusalem* was produced at the Factory Theatre, Toronto, in January 2000. It takes place on New Year's Eve 1899 in the home of Goldwyn SMITH, the Grange (now part of the Art Gallery of Ontario), and involves—besides a fictional character, twenty-one-year-old Alice—four historical figures: Adelaide Hoodless, who developed the study of 'domestic science' and was associated with the founding of the YWCA and the Victorian Order of Nurses in Canada; Silas Rand, a Protestant missionary in Nova Scotia and New Brunswick who translated the Bible into Mi'kmaq; Karl Pearson, an English scientist—a brilliant Darwinist, physicist, and mathematician; and Augusta Stowe-Gullen, the first woman in Canada to graduate from a Canadian medical school and the daughter of Emily Stowe, Canada's first woman doctor. Imaginatively contrived, it won the Dora Award for Best New Play in 2000 and the Chalmers Award in 2001. The central character of Redhill's *Goodness*—a postmodern play that is surely more enjoyable to see performed than it is to read—is Redhill himself (recently divorced), who at the beginning is immersed in a notebook writing a play. (His ex-wife Julia 'tears the notebook from Michael's hands.') He goes to Poland to research the loss of his Jewish relatives in the Holocaust. In London he is led to Althea, an elderly woman who tells him a story about being a prison guard for a man, with Alzheimer's, who is accused of fostering genocide and is about to be put on trial. Reality and deception, evil and goodness, and the role of memory are all ingredients in the plot. Apart from Michael and Althea, '... the rest of the characters act as a kind of chorus, who sing (African songs?)'. *Goodness* premiered at Tarragon Theatre, Toronto, in 2005, and was then produced in Edinburgh and New York.

Refus global (1948, rpr. 2008). If any single event marked the beginning of modern Québec, it was the appearance of this manifesto, which was published privately in 400 copies as a collection of loose typewritten mimeographed pages in a portfolio designed by Jean-Paul Riopelle. The title essay was written by the painter Paul-Émile Borduas (1905–60); it also carried the signatures of fifteen members of his circle (seven of them women). The manifesto's attack on the role of the clergy and capitalist powers in maintaining Québec's submission to the Church, and its description of the fear of authority, in which the majority of the population lived, provoked a *succès de scandale* in Duplessis's tightly controlled society, and brought about Borduas's dismissal from his teaching job and his subsequent exile to New York and later to Paris, where he died. Mainly because of its description of Québec as 'a colony trapped since 1760 within the slippery walls of fear, the usual refuge of the vanquished', *Refus global* has been viewed as the first step in the modern nationalist movement in Québec. The manifesto, however, goes on to describe a major crisis in Western values, whose emptiness is concealed behind a veil of abstract knowledge: the only hope is in a collective refusal to submit to the utilitarian conventions of society, and in the discovery of the liberating possibilities of art. No single label seems to fit *Refus global*. The fact that it has variously been called anarchist, surrealist, nationalist, Marxist, and Freudian may explain its lasting impact. Probably its most important influence on Québec culture derived from its clear message that art cannot isolate itself from society, and that to liberate his or her voice the artist must become allied with social revolution. An English translation can be found in *Paul Émile Borduas: Écrits / Writing 1942–1958* (1978), published by the Press of the Nova Scotia College of Art and Design. It was reissued in 2008 by EXILE EDITIONS, translated by Ray Ellenwood, as *Refus global / Total refusal*. See also Dennis Reid, *A concise history of Canadian painting* (2nd edn 1988), and Ray Ellenwood, *Égregore: the Montreal automatiste movement* (1993).

Reibetanz, John (b. 1944). Born in New York City, he was educated at Brooklyn College (B.A., 1965) and Princeton University (Ph.D., 1968). After living in Canada with his parents on several occasions, he settled in Toronto in 1968 and is professor of English at Victoria College, University of Toronto. His first poetry collection, *Ashbourn* (1986)—which grew out of his stay in Suffolk in the 1960s and his later research into local records and his transcription of oral accounts—brings to life a small community's characters and events in vivid poems. This was followed by *Morning watch* (1995), *Midland swimmer* (1996), *Near Finisterre* (1996), and *Mining for the sun* (2000). They include nature poems, memories of childhood, and poems about painters/paintings (Constable, Rembrandt, Mantegna, Hopper, Wyeth). A pleasing element of surprise is offered in the sequence of poems called 'Gibraltar Point', about York's (Toronto's) Governor John Graves Simcoe and his wife Elizabeth (*Morning watch*); in 'Verdigris', about a sculpture, 'Pulled / from a shipwreck near Marathon / a boy once bronze ... Greek boy, your green figure rises from the sea / like a dark sun, like life itself' (*Midland swimmer*); in 'Praise at Lindisfarne' about the writing of the Lindisfarne Gospels by Eadrith; and the title poem of *Near Finisterre*, which refers to 'the end of the earth' on the west coast of Spain to which the body of St James (Santiago) was transported from Jerusalem in a stone boat; and in translations of twenty-one short, energetic poems by Bertolt Brecht ('Buckow elegies' in *Morning watch*) that are liberated from any sign of studied diction or academic sensibility: 'Up far over the lake flies a bomber. / Up from rowboats look / Children, women, a greybeard. / From far / They look like little starlings, beaks wide open / Ready to be fed.' ('This summer's sky'). Reibetanz's most recent collections are *Mining for sun* (2000), in which a tribute to the American poet Elizabeth Bishop, 'Touching in detail: a gloss for Elizabeth Bishop' is memorable, along with 'Turner's eye', a wonderful evocation of Willliam Turner's sea paintings, which begins 'A perfect storm. // The sea thrashes its tail, agony / rides the bucking train / of its flailed, hanging flesh and exposed bone; / plummets, crashes, recoils ...' *Near relations* (2005) is remembered partly for the long prose poem 'Motherland', about his dying mother. In *Transformations* (2006) the beautiful Canoe Lake (in Algonquin Park, Ontario) is celebrated, in a poem of that name, along with the painter Tom Thomson, who was drowned in the lake in 1917. All these collections are unusual, in recent Canadian poetry publications, in offering the pleasure of reading a true poet's complex, but lucid.and satisfying evocations of wide-ranging subjects.

Renaud, Jacques (b. 1943). Born and brought up in the Montreal working-class district of Rosemont, he attended a public secondary school. After failing his grade eleven examinations, he began a series of manual jobs, then became a clerk in the municipal film library. He worked in advertising, as a journalist, as a researcher for a Radio-Canada TV program, and as a translator. Soon after it was founded in 1963, Renaud became associated with the *indépendantiste*/Marxist magazine PARTI PRIS. After a trip to India in 1970 he became attracted to yoga and Eastern mysticism. In the late 1980s he was active in the Equality Party, an extremist Anglo-rights party, only to leave it after a short time, though in 1993 he published a book that was critical of Québec's language legislation. Renaud's best-known novel—the first creative prose work in Québec to use JOUAL for dialogue and narration—is the powerful and shocking *Le cassé* (1964), written when the author was just twenty-one and living in the squalid area of Montreal's Centre-Ville. The best prose work of the *parti pris* group of writers, it was translated by Gérald Robitaille as *Flat broke and beat* (1968); a second translation, *Broke city* (1984), was done by David Homel. The French title, a *joual* word based on the English slang expression 'broke', also conjures up images of a central figure who is beaten, crippled, and disoriented. The hero, Tit-Jean, probably the most totally alienated character in Québec literature—the novel has been called '*le chant ultime de la dépossession*'—conceives and perpetrates the brutal murder of a 'goofball' pedlar, whom he wrongfully takes to be a secret lover of his mistress. The murder assumes an escapist and ritualistic character, giving temporary feelings of liberation to the frustrated hero. Despite some weak characterizations and occasional maladroit interjections by the narrator, *Le cassé* contains striking lower-depths poetry and skilful cinematic techniques. A second edition (1977) adds four short stories and the author's two-part 'Journal du cassé', the first part of which consists of short texts that discuss *Le cassé* directly or indirectly; the second part includes excerpts from reviews of the first edition of *Le cassé* that document the furore caused by its inclusion in a CEGEP course in the Sorel region in 1971. Renaud's other publications include novels, and collections of short stories and poems.

Ricci, Nino (b. 1959). Born in Leamington, Ontario, to parents from Molise, Italy, he obtained a B.A. in English at York University, Toronto, and an M.A. in creative writing at Concordia University, Montreal; he also completed a year of study in Italian literature at the University of Florence. He has taught English at a secondary school in Nigeria, through CUSO, and creative writing and Canadian literature at Concordia University. His first novel of a projected trilogy, *Lives of the saints* (1990, GGA), received international attention and was on the bestseller list in Canada for well over a year. This was followed by *In a glass house* (1993, rpr. 1994). Both novels deal with the protagonist's relationship with members of his Italian family, using first-person narration, a poetic and lucid prose style, and making ethnicity intrinsic to the representation of contemporary realities. Many of the topics that are developed (social estrangement, intergenerational conflict, the opposition of world views, the search for identity) typify some of the concerns of other writers in Canada involved in the depiction of ethnicity, especially in the area of Italian-Canadian fiction. In *Lives of the saints* there is a constant juxtaposing of different levels of experience, rendered through myth, superstition, folklore, and modernity. In *In a glass house* the acutely introspective Victor (Vittorio) Innocente, the protagonist-narrator, can neither be part of his social environment nor construct a stable interior world. Both novels examine the convulsions of cultural transformation, complex and conflicted family relations, and the existential dimensions of daily life; they present an ambiguous, contradictory view of Canadian society from an Italian perspective. In *Where she has gone* (1997), the third volume in the trilogy, Victor's feelings for his half-sister Rita obsess him until she leaves Toronto to travel with John, a much older man, and Victor leaves for Italy and the Apennine village where he was born, and where he is confronted with details of his mother's past, and with Rita and John, who visit him there. *Testament* (2002, rpr. 2003) describes aspects of the public ministry of Jesus Christ, ending with his crucifixion. There are four narrators (as there are four Gospels): Yihuda of Qiryat (Judas); Miryam of Migdal (Mary Magdalene);

Miryam (Mary), his mother; and Simon of Gergesa. There are many dissonances in the life story from the one we are acquainted with. Judas, a revolutionary opposed to Roman rule, is a follower but is alienated from Jesus because he sees him as doomed; he does not betray him. Jesus spends twelve years of his youth in Alexandria, learns Greek, and thinks 'more in the manner of a Greek than a Jew, finding recourse for his arguments in logic' rather than in parables: '... he had a way of leading us towards a thing as if we were ones who'd found it ourselves, taking us this way and that until finally we turned a corner and the answer sat in front of us as plain as stone.' The mother of Jesus was raped by a Roman soldier and forced to marry an old man, giving birth in his humble dwelling—Jesus says that he is a bastard. In the fourth section, the Syrian (non-Jewish) shepherd Simon, one of three Simons among the followers, describes Jesus's journey to Jerusalem for Passover and every episode from his arrest to his crucifixion—all details of which are related in chilling detail. Simon says: 'It won't be long, of course, before everyone has forgotten the man ....' This remark exemplifies the tone and vision of the book, the first three narrations being pedestrian descriptions of everyday life, with Yeshua (Jesus) appearing, off and on, only as a compelling figure of pure goodness, and for some a doorway leading to light. Ricci's reduction of the elevated language of the New Testament to a naturalistic, untranscendent narrative—and his deep research, which included travelling to Israel and Jordan and consulting the Jesus Seminar among other scholarly sources ('I have made every effort to work within the bounds of historical plausibility, based on what is known to us of the time and place in which Jesus lived.')—resulted in an ingenious, modernist recapitulation of biblical history that, in spite of the momentous content, is strangely inert. Because Jesus is not portrayed as divine, it will disappoint the true believer (for whom it was not written). Ricci has said: 'I find it much more interesting to think of him as having been a real person who tries to change things in a human way with only human powers.' *Testament* shared the (Ontario) Trillium Book Award with Austin CLARKE. In 2008 Ricci published another long, ambitious novel that has given much pleasure (particularly for its humour), *The origin of species* (rpr. 2009), in which Alex—living in Montreal in the 1980s, an unhappy graduate student over thirty, with a failed marriage behind him, working on a dissertation linking Darwin's theory of evolution with the history of human narrative—is affected by several people with their own demons, and draws on the memory of a visit to the Galapagos Islands, where various truths were revealed to him that changed his life. It won a GOVERNOR GENERAL'S AWARD. For the Penguin series Extraordinary Canadians, Ricci wrote *Pierre Elliot Trudeau* (2008).

Richards, David Adams (b. 1950). He grew up in Newcastle, New Brunswick, attended St Thomas University, Fredericton, which he left to pursue a career as a writer, and now lives in Toronto with his wife and children. He won the Norma Epstein $1000 prize for undergraduate creative writing with a portion of his first novel, *The coming of winter* (1974, rpr. 1992), which tells of a Miramichi Valley youth's tragicomic ineptitude and uninspired slide into marriage, counterbalanced by his love of the outdoors, and of the woods and rivers (so important to the author himself). Richards' ear for local speech patterns and his eye for the details of individual lifestyles have earned him a reputation for striking realism. *Blood ties* (1976, NCL) is a probing psychological examination of the lives of a larger number of characters from the same region. 'Ramsey Taylor', one of six stories in *Dancers at night* (1978), is about a grizzled guide, the American who hired him, and his young son. The deft characterization of the three, the building of the clear narrative, and its suspense—there is a canoe accident—are so effective that one regrets the absence of these qualities in Richards' long novels. The novel *Lives of short duration* (1981, NCL) continues in the Miramichi setting and shows an increased concern with the theme of cultural and economic deprivation, and an intensified sense of human compassion. An ambitious novel, it gives voice to a whole community and its history through the perceptions of three generations. *Road to the stilt house* (1985) has a more stark and compressed treatment in both subject and language. Carrying the theme of deprivation even further, it takes as its central figure a character and his family—seen by the community as mentally retarded—and discovers in this context some of the causes of social violence. *Nights below Station Street* (1988, GGA, rpr. 1997) began a trilogy of novels about an interrelated group of characters that was completed with *Evening snow will bring such peace* (1990, rpr. 2003) and *For those who hunt the wounded down* (1993, rpr. 2003)—which was made into a powerful film by Credo Films of Winnipeg, for which Richards wrote the script. Many of Richards' characters have a comic dimension that is often missed by those reviewers who feel uncomfortable in the world of his characters, but the humour is quite apparent in *Nights below Station Street*. We are intended to laugh at Adele when her nervous impatience completely derails her logical train of thought. At the centre of the novel is Joe, her father, a sort of moral hero who struggles to conquer his alcoholism. His hard-won sobriety, coupled with his fine woodsmanship, empower him to save the life of a friend at the novel's end. Such 'small heroics' are at the moral centre of Richards' universe. Joe does not understand his own accomplishment, but the characters in Richards' novels never comprehend, or are able to articulate, the whole meaning of their actions. *Hope in the desperate hour* (1996, rpr. 2001) expands the cast of Richards' characters into the academic world, which he came to know in Fredericton, both as a student and as writer-in-residence. The lives of two professors are entangled with those of a failed and dying hockey player, his family, and the Natives on a nearby reserve. All are struck in varying postures of failing or failed ambition and betrayal. The orchestration of this complex plot involves the heaviest reliance on an omniscient narrator that we have seen so far in Richards' work—resulting in a new clarity, though it is acquired at some cost to the novel's subtlety and dramatic intensity. *The bay of love and sorrows* (1998, rpr. 2002)—Richards likes portentous titles—set along a New Brunswick bay in the summer of 1974, presents an array of memorable characters—including Michael Skid, son of a judge, the farmhand Tommie Donnerel, and the charismatic, scheming Everette Hutch—who are carried into a dark world that includes a murder. It is possible to see Richards' themes as participating in a timeless tragi-comic world view that, when sown upon the exotic soil of New Brunswick, yields a unique wisdom. At the centre of MERCY AMONG THE CHILDREN (2000, rpr. 2001) is Sydney Henderson who, sworn to an enlightened pacifism, is punished by many trials, including the scorn of his neighbours and being framed for a murder, with tragic results for his family. The story is narrated by his despairing twenty-five-year-old son, Lyle, who has an understandably aggressive attitude to the wrongs inflicted on his father and sees his own desire for retaliation fulfilled. For this novel Richards was co-winner (with Michael ONDAATJE) of the GILLER PRIZE. *River of the brokenhearted* (2003, rpr. 2004)—the river is of course the Miramichi—opens with the marriage in the 1920s of Janie McLeary, an Irish Catholic, to George

King, an older Englishman and a Protestant (the union scandalized the locals), who run the first movie theatre in the town, and one of the first in New Brunswick. Their son Miles is born, Janie's husband dies; she is pregnant and her daughter Georgina is born. In spite of opposition, she runs the theatre herself. 'Of course by ten years of age Miles knew that the problem with his life was that his mother had fought with everyone. She had fought all her life. Yet those she fought with were not above inciting kids to exact revenge on him. But he couldn't tell her this. It would hurt her too deeply.' The self-seeking, deceptive villain of the novel, Joey Elias—who has his own little movie-house, the Biograph—is determined to take over Janie's Regent and resorts to sinister machinations (including the murder of Janie's father). In responding to one of these, Janie swims to the other side of the river to seek financial help. To her great surprise she meets Lord Beaverbrook, who saves her business. She earns the right to show all first-run sound pictures and becomes wealthy. (The indomitable Janie is based on Richards' grandmother—his family ran Newcastle's Uptown Theatre from 1911 to 1980.) The novel also depicts the results of the age-old feud of the McLeary and Drunken families. When Janie, out of pity, employs Rebecca Drunken (who becomes the mistress of Joey Elias) to look after her children, unpleasant complications ensue. Miles turns into a central character—although an alcoholic and often despairing, he is capable of uttering aperçus. He marries Elizabeth Whispers (one of nine children) and their offspring are Wendell, the narrator, and daughter Ginger, who is irrepressible, like her grandmother. 'Once I woke in the back seat ... to see my father slumped in the passenger seat, my mother sleeping next to me in the back, and Ginger herself, sitting on three books (one being Mother's Bible), navigating the turns of a solitary secondary road somewhere in the lost province of Nova Scotia.' Underlying the novel are the themes of evil and goodness, offence and atonement. Some critics, for whom the characters came to life, have praised it extravagantly. But this ingeniously contrived family saga—with envy, skulduggery, misjudgements, and the destructiveness of ne'er-do-wells prevailing, and the characters pretty much negative stereotypes, except for Janie and Miles—is flawed by its lack of discipline: it goes on too long; and there are paragraphs that do not make much sense. The forest that lies between the Miramichi and Chaleur Bay is the setting of *The friends of Meager Fortune* (2006), which

focuses on the logging industry and the mill of Byron and Mary Jameson. Byron is killed in an accident and is succeeded by his young son Will—whose abilities as a woodsman are celebrated; but he too is killed while clearing a log jam during a run. Mary takes over the mill with her brother until her second son Owen—sensitive, bookish—returns from the Second World War (with the Victoria Cross) and decides to go against his inclination to attend university and run the mill. (He walks with a cane because of a war wound, which he refused to have treated.) Owen is forced to take his team of men in winter up on dangerous Good Friday Mountain, site of one of the last great timber cuts in the province, where they set up camp. The 'camp keeper' is Meager Fortune, whom Owen met in the war; though small, in his twenties, and considered simple-minded and teased, he is an effective worker and turns out to be heroic. Much of Richards' narrative describes the men's activities as loggers, chilling the reader with descriptions of the fierce winter weather: 'Owen was up long before dawn. The first thing he had to do this morning was dig himself out of the camp, because the door was never free of the nightly drifts. The air was arctic and split his lip, so he tasted his blood a second before it froze.' The logging passages contrast with life in the town when Owen leaves his men to do their work and returns. He is seen to be friendly with Camellia, married to Reggie Glidden (whose life he had saved in the war). Then the gossip and rumours of more and more unpleasant people—suspicious, deceptive, ignorant—lead to a damaging series of events. 'The gossip had gone through a metamorphosis, from stage to stage, until it flowered into something—unrelenting, from the top of the town to the bottom.' Reggie disappears. Did Owen murder him? Is Camellia pregnant with Owen's lovechild? There is a trial and Owen is imprisoned (but he escapes). And there is a devastating climax after Easter with the spring run on Good Friday Mountain: '... the best drivers plunge the wood into the streams and brooks and run them down across Arron Brook, where the danger was....' Several men lose their lives. Meager Fortune says, tears streaming down his face, 'They was all my friends.' In the midst of this Owen dies too, at twenty-six, from a gangrenous leg that he never had treated. The identity of the narrator is not revealed until towards the end: it is Camellia's son by Reggie. The novel is an often powerful, richly detailed creation that is occasionally marred by inferior diction (such as 'gotten' for 'got', 'laying' for 'lying') and indecipherable sentences. The leading character of *The lost highway* (2007) is the ill-favoured Alex Chapman, an orphan raised by his tyrannical great uncle Jim Chapman. He enters a seminary, intending to become a priest; when that comes to nothing he spends nine years in a university, eventually working on a Ph.D. thesis, without ever displaying authentic academic knowledge or the slightest intellectual acuity, though he teaches a course in ethics. 'Alex thought of all the past ridicule he had suffered as a boy, after his mother died. And for what? For what reason was so much ridicule heaped on him? The horrible death of his mother. The taunting of kids on the bus. The failure of Minnie. The ultimate failure with his doctorate—and his consequential ouster at the university, a place where he had placed all his pride and certitude. All had floundered.' He indulges in fantasies and random, confused thoughts about ideas, ethics, etc.; and justifies committing one irrational, dishonest act after another, including deception and theft, leading to his being the accessory to a murder. (His absent uncle's unknowing possession of a winning lotto ticket worth $13 million incites the plot's devastating final complications.) The suspense in the last quarter of the book, describing the murder and the efforts of police officer Markus Paul (a Métis) to learn details of the victim's disappearance, certainly holds one's interest. But the novel is overwritten, interweaving too many digressions—for example, about Alex's parentage and school associations—and subject to such unappealing literary transgressions as repetition and grammatical errors ('For the first time Alex saw this relationship between he and his uncle as a kind of harsh and stupid love.'). A compressed version of the narrative would have aided the plot and added considerably to this reader's enjoyment. The novel, however, has been widely praised.

Richards—who was made a Member of the Order of Canada in 2010—has published six books of non-fiction. In *A lad from Brantford: and other essays* (1994) he is an armchair philosopher preoccupied with anti-Americanism, anti-intellectualism, and anti-materialism. *Hockey dreams: memories of a man who couldn't play* (1996), built around Richards' childhood passion for the sport and his adult disillusionment over the fate of Canada's national game, is notable for its poignant sketches of his fellow hockey hopefuls battling it out on the frozen Miramichi, and for Richards' sense of humour. His love of fishing gave rise to *Lines on the water: a fisherman's life on the Miramichi* (1998, GGA). For Penguin Canada's series of brief biographies, Extraordinary Canadians, Richards wrote *Lord Beaverbrook* (2008), which treats the great career of his fellow New Brunswickian with what one sees as a delicate suppression of its negative aspects. In April 2007 Richards delivered the second annual Antonine Maillet-Northrop Frye Lecture, *Playing the inside out* (2008). Raised as a Catholic, he published in 2009 *God is: my search for faith in a secular world. The Christmas tree: tales for the holidays* (2006), a small illustrated book for very young people, offers two charming stories related to Christmas: 'Carmichael's dog' and 'The Christmas tree'. See *David Adams Richards: essays on his works* (2005) edited by Tony Tremblay.

Richardson, John (1796–1852). The garrisons of Upper Canada shaped the early years of one of Canada's earliest novelists. Born in Queenston, Upper Canada (Ontario), John Richardson grew up in Amherstburgh (Fort Malden) on the Detroit River. His father was a British medical officer and his mother the offspring of John Askin, a leading fur trader and (probably) a Native, a member of the Ottawa tribe. In 1812 Richardson served as a gentleman-volunteer; he and his brother were allowed to raise the British colours over the captured Fort Detroit. Captured during Tecumseh's last stand at Moraviantown in 1813, Richardson was a prisoner of war in Ohio and Kentucky for a year. Tecumseh remained a lifelong hero to him, and his narratives are filled with the violence and savagery that he witnessed in forest warfare. His commission in the British army came too late for him to fight in the Napoleonic wars, so he spent 1816–18 in the garrisons of the West Indies. There he endured yellow fever and witnessed the brutalities of both the slaveholders and the army in which he served. Settling in London in 1818, then adventuring in Paris, he followed the rackety existence of a half-pay officer/adventurer on the make. In 1825 in Paris he married Jane Marsh, who died a few years later (in 1832 he wed Maria Caroline Drayson, who died in 1846).

In London again in 1826, Richardson began a productive but ill-paid career as a writer and journalist. While producing poetry, novels, memoirs, pamphlets, reports, and polemics, he also served for awhile in the army and then in other occupations. As a self-educated colonial, probably of mixed white-Native ancestry, he was touchy on a number of points. Arrogant, high-spirited, obtuse, he made quarrelsomeness (and duelling) a feature of his life. David Beasley, author of a remarkable (given the scarcity of written records) reconstruction of Richardson's life, *The Canadian Don Quixote* (1977), observes that a character in Richardson's novel *Ecarté* is a stand-in for his creator. That character's real-life counterpart ('endowed with a susceptibility which rendered him unable to endure even the shadow of slight or insult') suffered duelling injuries during the time in which the novel is set. In 1826 Richardson published an anonymous account of his 1812 war experiences in the *New Monthly Magazine*, London. His first imaginative use of his North American frontier experience came with the long poem *Tecumseh; or, The warrior of the West in four cantos with notes* (London, 1828; rpr. 1992 ed. by Douglas Daymond and Leslie Monkman). Lurid, written in a mock-epic verse form that undermines its claims to seriousness, it failed, and drove Richardson to exploit his Parisian experience in *Ecarté; or, The salons of Paris* (London, 1829; rpr. 2004) and *Frascati's; or Scenes in Paris* (an anonymous sequel now attributed to him; London, 1830). In the same year he published the satirical risqué poem *Kensington Gardens* (London, 1830). Also in 1830, inspired by James Fenimore Cooper's *The last of the Mohicans*, he began writing his best-known work, which used the wilderness of *Tecumseh* much more effectively. *WACOUSTA; or, The prophecy: a tale of the Canadas* (3 vols, Edinburgh, 1832; NCL, CEECT, rpr. 1998) takes place during the 1763 siege of Detroit during Pontiac's uprising. Its complex Gothic plot depicts Sir Reginald Morton's monstrous revenge upon his unscrupulous rival in love, Colonel De Haldimar. Forest and garrison alike are rife with inhumanity; the narrative is also marked by surprise, disguise, bizarre coincidence, and high rhetoric. Praised by reviewers, it attained a limited popularity in Britain and the United States (not in Canada), where it was fashioned into a melodrama. In 1835 Richardson went to Spain as a major in a mercenary force, the British Legion, fighting for the royalist side in the Carlist civil conflict of 1834–7—he wrote two influential books based on this experience—and in 1838 he returned to Canada, to Montreal, as special correspondent for *The Times* of London to cover Lord Durham's efforts to re-establish Upper and Lower Canada's political structures after the 1837 rebellions. Richardson's support of Durham led to differences with his editors, who fired him. *The Canadian brothers; or, The prophecy fulfilled* (Montreal, 1840; rpr. 1992 CEECT), a sequel to *Wacousta*, makes use of the author's 1812 experience as a prisoner of war in Kentucky. He then settled in Brockville (Ontario) and began the weekly *New Era; or The Canadian Chronicle* (1841–42).

There he serialized his memoir of the War of 1812, a vivid, highly partisan account of individuals and events interspersed with long stretches of documentary reprints, published as *War of 1812* (1902)

The failure of the Brockville venture sent Richardson to nearby Kingston and a new journal, *The Canadian Loyalist and Spirit of 1812* (1843–4). In 1845 his political connections landed him a superintendency of the Welland Canal police, where the insubordination of his men led to the disbandment of the force early the next year. His beloved wife died, and he shifted to Montreal until 1849, when he tried his luck in New York. During his last, desolate years in Canada, Richardson wrote pamphlets, collected in *Eight Years in Canada; embracing a review of the administrations of Lords Durham and Sydenham, Sir Charles Bagot, and Lord Metcalfe, and including numerous interesting letters from Lord Durham, Mr. Chas. Buller and other well-known public characters* (Montreal, 1847) and *The Guards in Canada; or The point of honour; being a sequel to … 'Eight years in Canada'* (Montreal, 1848). Both books combine reminiscence with political and personal polemic. Richardson's final, fatal gamble for success took place in New York. There he worked as a hack for Dewitt and Davenport, a publishing firm (devoted to pornography and anti-Catholicism) founded in 1848 by two young men. They published Richardson's *The monk knight of St. John; a tale of the Crusades* (New York, 1850; rpr. 2001), featuring the Middle Ages as background for a tale of adultery, slaughter, rape, and cannibalism. *Hardscrabble; or, The fall of Chicago. A tale of Indian warfare* (New York, 1850) and *Wau-nan-gee; or, The massacre at Chicago* (New York, [1852]) were volumes of a projected trilogy. Richardson severed his last ties with Canada with the publication of *Matilda Montgomerie; or The prophecy fulfilled* (New York, 1851), in which he attempted to Americanize his *Canadian brothers* by expunging its anti-American passages and retitling it with the name of his American villainess. *Matilda Montgomerie* and reissues of *Ecarté* and *Wacousta* were all successful American publications, though Richardson sold their rights and made little money from them. He published anonymously *Lola Montes; or, A reply to the 'Private history and memoirs' of that celebrated lady* (New York, 1851), a defence of the notorious Irish dancer and adventuress who had arrived in New York. *Westbrook, the outlaw; or, The avenging wolf* (New York, 1853; rpr. 2004), based on a historical figure who ravaged southwestern Ontario during 1812, appeared serially in the

Sunday Mercury and was published posthumously in book form; it sank without a trace until recovered and republished in 1973, and reprinted in 2004. Richardson died of a malnutrition-related illness, too poor to continue feeding his Newfoundland dog.

Restored texts of *Wacousta* and *The Canadian brothers*, edited by D.R. Cronk (1987) and D.G. Stephens (1992) respectively, have been published by the CENTRE FOR EDITING EARLY CANADIAN TEXTS. David Beasley edited *Major John Richardson's short stories* (1985).

Richler, Mordecai (1931–2001). Born in Montreal at the beginning of the Depression, Richler has depicted in his writing (particularly in the autobiographical sketches collected in *The street* (1969, rpr. 2001), his experience of growing up in the working-class Jewish neighbourhood around St Urbain Street and of attending Baron Byng, the predominantly Jewish public high school nearby. In 1948 Richler entered Sir George Williams College (now part of Concordia University), working part-time as a reporter for the *Montreal Herald*. Never comfortable in an academic milieu, he dropped out in 1950. The following year he went to Europe, joining in Paris the newest generation of North American expatriate writers, which included Allen Ginsberg, Terry Southern, and Mavis GALLANT, publishing a short story there, and beginning work on his first novel. Returning to Canada in 1952, he worked briefly at the CBC before moving to England in 1954. A professional writer since that time, Richler has worked as a journalist as well as a novelist. He has also written film scripts. (His credits include *Life at the top*, 1965, and *Fun with Dick and Jane*, 1977, as well adaptations of two of his own novels: *The apprenticeship of Duddy Kravitz*, 1974, and *Joshua then and now*, 1985.) Having spent his first eighteen years as a writer abroad, Richler remarked, 'I'm a Canadian and a Jew and I write about being both. I worry about being away so long from the roots of my discontent.' For many years he divided his time between residences in London and Québec province. In an early interview Richler said that he wrote from a compulsion to 'say what I feel about values and about people living in a time when … there is no agreement on values'. In his novels, as in his essays, he is a moralist who is nevertheless capable of shocking his readers with his choice and treatment of topics. His first novel, *The acrobats* (1954, rpr. 2002), published in England and poorly received in Canada, shows him beginning his career under the influence of Hemingway, Sartre, and Malraux. Though its cynical world-weariness seems more a product of the moment than of Richler's own vision, the novel embodies a set of interconnected concerns that recur in his later fiction: the Spanish Civil War as a testing ground of the engaged intellectual, the place of Jews in post-Holocaust society, a preoccupation with personal responsibility, and a sense that his own generation arrived at the wrong time to take heroic action. As well, this first novel exemplifies the characteristic quality that Richler would later describe as his 'persistent attempt to make a case for the ostensibly unsympathetic man'. Though clumsy in its use of the modernist technique of fragmented narrative, *The acrobats* was successful in its day. It was reissued (as *Wicked we love*) in an American paperback edition and translated into Danish, Norse, and German; but it didn't have a Canadian edition and Richler refused to let it be brought back into print. It was, however, reissued posthumously in 2002 in the NEW CANADIAN LIBRARY.

His greatest strength is his debunking of the myths of his culture. In Richler's fine second novel, *Son of a smaller hero* (1955, rpr. 2002, NCL), Melech Adler—family head, father of ten, and stern defender of Jewish tradition—hates the *goyim*. His eldest grandson Noah, who is attached to him (who has had an affair with a married French-Canadian woman), wants to leave the ghetto to gain 'some knowledge of himself independent of others.' It depicts a young man's need both to escape the limitations of the Montreal Jewish ghetto—it was attacked by some Montreal Jews as anti-Semitic—and to leave North American society. Once he himself was abroad, however, Richler was no more inclined to spare his new community than his old. His next novel, *A choice of enemies* (1957, NCL), satirizes as poseurs the expatriate film-makers in London who saw themselves as refugees from the political persecution of the American McCarthy era. It was not until his fourth novel, *The APPRENTICESHIP OF DUDDY KRAVITZ* (1959, rpr. 2001, 2005), that Richler fully exhibited the narrative skills and command of voice that made him one of the foremost writers of his generation. Featuring his most morally complex character, a bumptious young hustler obsessed with acquiring land as his way out of the ghetto, the novel presents Duddy Kravitz as unreliable, a moral coward who nonetheless has moments of genuine feeling and even nobility, and with whom the reader is invited to (and can) sympathize. One of Duddy's classmates was Jake Hersh, later the hero of Richler's *St Urbain's horseman*. Just as a youthful Jake can be glimpsed at several points in the 1959 novel, so a middle-aged Duddy later reappears in *St Urbain's horseman*. Duddy is not much changed, but, with Jake at the moral centre of the novel, he becomes a less sympathetic and more poignant figure. Together the two protagonists suggest the range of human possibility, almost two sides of the same personality—an idea implicit in the deathbed letter written to Duddy by his uncle Benjy, in which he tells him that he is 'two people' and urges him not to choose the 'brute inside you' but to be instead 'a gentleman. A *Mensch*.'

During the 1960s Richler published two surreal fables, *The incomparable Atuk* (1963, rpr. 1989) and *Cocksure* (1968, rpr. 2002, NCL), which marked him as one of the most caustic satirists of the era. Savage attacks on contemporary mores and mass society, these novels send up the poses and stereotypes of their decade. In *The incomparable Atuk* (American title: *Stick your neck out*), Richler ridiculed facile cultural nationalism by dramatizing the foolishness of an attempt to 'Canadianize' American pop culture. *Cocksure* extends his attack on the North American entertainment industry with its scabrous tale of a narcissistic Hollywood director aspiring to God-like powers, literally creating film stars tailored to the public's desires while cannibalizing his associates for their 'spare parts'. Its use of a more ribald humour than most readers then expected from serious Canadian fiction made it an object of controversy when it received (along with the collection of essays, *Hunting tigers under glass*, 1968) a Governor General's Award. However disturbing it may be, *Cocksure* is a deeply conservative work, a portrait of a 'square' protagonist who clings to old values, though bewildered by their inversion all around him. One of the novel's obvious influences is Evelyn Waugh, for whom Richler expressed admiration, but *Cocksure* really belongs to the more bitterly vitriolic tradition of Jonathan Swift.

St Urbain's horseman (1971, GGA, NCL, rpr, 2007) is a more humane novel, though it retains much of the comic tone and sharply satiric edge of his previous fiction. In this Kafkaesque story of Jake Hersch, a Montreal filmwriter who finds himself on trial for sexual indecencies he did not commit, Richler investigates the construction of both Canadian and Jewish identity, making the book an extended reconsideration of his previous topics of exile and home. The sense of loss that pervaded his earlier fiction broadens in this work into a depiction of an existence made almost meaningless by the horrors of recent history, the lack of roots for expatriates like Jake and his friends, and the 'competing mythologies' that result in the anomie of the contemporary era. Against these forces, Jake creates a compensatory myth by synthesizing diverse elements from popular culture, his Jewish inheritance, and the raw material of his cousin Joey's life in order to create something he can believe in: a superhuman figure of authority and heroism, 'St Urbain's Horseman'—a Jewish avenger (based on the myth of the Golem) who will right wrongs and punish evil-doers. In the novel's resolution, however, Jake finds he must also undertake the difficult but necessary task of confronting the limitations and even dangers of this myth-making, and must learn how to internalize his mythologies. Joshua Shapiro, the protagonist of *Joshua then and now* (1980, rpr. 2001, NCL), resembles Jake in his vulnerable humanity and in being another of Richler's misunderstood men. Where Jake was unjustly put on trial for sexual perversion, Joshua is mistakenly identified as a secret homosexual and transvestite. Where Jake wishes he could set right the wrongs of the past (his persistent fantasy is the pursuit of Joseph Mengele, then the most wanted of Nazi war criminals), Joshua avoids his present crisis by turning back to a past that haunts him because he feels he has earlier failed to show adequate moral commitment. Like Jake, Joshua must confront questions of personal responsibility and the taking of appropriate action, questions that for him are embodied in the Spanish Civil War rather than in anti-Semitism and Nazi genocide. He must eventually learn not only that the past can never be redeemed, but that to attempt to correct it may lead to a dangerous abandonment of the present. As with *St Urbain's horseman*, the novel ends with husband and wife clinging to one another, their affection and their bonds the best source of refuge and stability in a difficult world.

Solomon Gursky was here (1989, rpr. 2005), Richler's most ambitious work, is a complicated and sprawling novel that takes over (and sends up) the form of the multi-generational family saga. (For the second edition Richler provided a genealogical diagram to help readers with the complexities of the family line.) In this novel Richler comes to terms with the Canadian tradition he has often mocked: he writes into Canadian history and national mythology a previously overlooked Jewish dimension. Loosely based on real figures from

Richler

Canadian history (such as the early fur trader Ezekiel Solomons and, in particular, the Bronfman family), the development of the Gursky family (who, in the present, struggle over control of the giant liquor company that has emerged out of their Prohibition-era bootlegging) is shown to have been crucial to the formation of the Canadian nation and to Canada's national identity. Richler presents all of this in a long and episodic narrative that allows him to explore—and to burlesque—the myth of the Canadian North and to recast Northern and Native motifs that have become well established in Canadian writing and culture: shamanism; the Franklin expedition and the failed search for the Northwest Passage; and the Trickster figure. (Richler based his use of Raven as Trickster on the Haida myth recreated in Bill Reid's and Robert BRINGHURST's *Raven steals the light*.) In the figure of L.B. Berger, Richler also introduces a devastating caricature of A.M. KLEIN, a poet who has sometimes been treated as an icon in the Jewish cultural community, but a figure who has troubled Richler because, as he later wrote in *Saturday Night*, Klein 'was hired to fill the humiliating office of Sam [Bronfman]'s poet laureate. Degrading himself and his sullen craft ...' (July/August 1992). The novel is narrated by Moses Berger, L.B.'s son, who is preoccupied with understanding the truth about his father's employer, Bernard Gursky, and the nature of the mysterious and mythic figure who calls himself Sir Hyman Kaplansky. *Barney's version* (1997, rpr. 1998) is the memoir of Barney Panofsky, written to correct the 'scurrilous charges' in the autobiography of the writer Terry McIver, another Montrealer he got to know and dislike in Paris in the 1950s. Moving backward and forward in time, leaving no detail of his outrageous behaviour (laced with drink) and his current signs of aging undescribed, and no politically incorrect opinion or his love of jokes unexpressed, Barney unfolds his life, focusing on his three marriages, the first two disastrous and the third to his 'heart's desire', the beautiful Miriam, a paragon to whom he was happily married for thirty years and who bore him three children (though careless Barney let this marriage slip away from him). Behind all this is an event, from which he was exonerated, that haunted him from mid-life on (did he or did he not murder his friend Boogie?). Barney's text—sprawling, like that of *Solomon Gursky*—encompasses Montreal and Paris in the fifties to Montreal in 1995, leaving no critical stone unturned. But in all the mayhem of relationships and crises, love

(of one woman, of their children), and regret (for uncontrolled behaviour, for thoughtless cruelty), are paramount, and Barney is left with the reader's sympathy and liking. Towards the end of his memoir, he writes: 'Arguably the days when my memory functions perfectly are heavier to bear than those when it fails me.' The heaviness, as well as the lightness and humour, of his memories are indelibly recorded by Richler. *Barney's version* won the GILLER PRIZE.

Throughout his career Richler continued to write journalism. (He wrote a weekly column in the Toronto *National Post*.) Two early collections of his journalistic pieces appeared as *Hunting tigers under glass* (1968) and *Shovelling trouble* (1972). An American selection from these books was published as *Notes on an endangered species* (1974). *Home sweet home: my Canadian album* (1984) draws together pieces on Canada written over twenty-five years. In the 1990s Richler increasingly assumed the role of public intellectual by becoming the most prominent defender of the rights of Québec's anglophones. His opening sally was in what became a highly visible and protracted controversy over a 1991 article published in *The New Yorker*, which depicted the folly of Québec's language laws prohibiting or limiting the use of English on signs. It provoked hostile responses and vicious personal attacks in the Québec francophone press. Enjoying his role as gadfly, Richler expanded his polemics into a book-length diatribe, *Oh Canada! Oh Quebec! Requiem for a divided country* (1992), in which he further disturbed Québécois nationalists by also pointing to French-Québec's history of anti-Semitism. He continued his mordant critique of separatist politics and policies in his subsequent journalism. In 1994 Richler published his second full-length work of non-fiction, *This year in Jerusalem*. Partly memoir (about his early Montreal experiences with the Zionist movement's efforts to establish an independent country when he was growing up in Montreal and about his later journey to Israel to see the country that eventually emerged), partly travel book, and partly a meditation on the politics of Jewish identity in the modern world, it concludes with Richler—who began his career as an expatriate—confirming Canada as his spiritual homeland. There followed *Belling the cat: selected essays and reports* (1998), reprinted in 1999 with the subtitle *Essays, reports, and opinions*, a collection of his always interesting journalism. The entertaining *On snooker: the game and the characters who play it* (2001, rpr. 2002)—whose jacket shows the Queen Mother, wearing a hat and three strands of pearls, playing snooker—is filled with anecdotes not only about snooker and its players but about Richler himself and his favourite sports. The posthumous *Dispatches from a sporting life* (2002)—with an affectionate introduction by his son Noah—contains sports pieces Richler began writing for *Maclean's* magazine in the early 1960s and others he wrote until the 1990s; his sporting life was as a trenchant observer. Richler had considerable success as the author of three children's books, which feature a little boy who says everything twice: *Jacob Two-Two meets the hooded fang* (1975, rpr. 2009)—which has been made into a stage play and film, *Jacob Two-Two and the dinosaur* (1982, rpr. 2009), and *Jacob Two-Two's first spy case* (1995, rpr. 2009). Richler was appointed a Companion of the Order of Canada in 2000.

See *Mordecai Richler was here: selected writings* (2006), a lavish book—large, long, well illustrated, and with an Introduction by Adam Gopnik—and the biographies *The last honest man* (2004) by Michael Posner, *Mordecai Richler: leaving St Urbain* (2008) by Reinhold Kramer, and *Mordecai Richler* (2009) by M.G. VASSANJI in Penguin Canada's Extraordinary Canadians Series.

Riel trilogy. John COULTER's trilogy of plays about Louis Riel consists of *Riel* (1962), an epic of Elizabethan proportions; *The crime of Louis Riel* (1976), a free adaptation of the same play for less-experienced companies; and *The trial of Louis Riel* (1968), a documentary drama of Riel's trial.

Riel was first performed on 17 Feb. 1950 by the New Play Society, Toronto, at the Royal Ontario Museum Theatre, with Mavor MOORE in the title role. But not until 13 Jan. 1975 (at the height of the separatist movement in Québec) was it given the major Canadian stage production it deserved, when it was performed at the National Arts Centre, Ottawa, directed by Jean Gascon, with Albert Millaire as Louis Riel. It takes place in 1869–70 and 1885–6 in the Northwest Territories (in present-day Winnipeg, Manitoba, and Batoche, near Prince Albert, Saskatchewan). Part I is concerned with Riel's claim that the land belongs to his Métis people. In the ensuing uprising of 1869, incited both by the British attempt to take over their land and by Riel's decision to have the Ontario Orangeman Thomas Scott executed, Riel and his Métis followers are defeated—Riel escapes to Montana, where he marries and raises a family. Part II takes place in 1885 when the Métis

send a delegation to Riel begging him to return and lead another uprising against the British. He does so and is again defeated. He is imprisoned, put on trial, and condemned to death. The play ends with his hanging. There are echoes of the New Testament in the dialogue, with allusions to Riel as a Christ figure. Coulter imbues the 'voices' Riel hears with overtones of Joan of Arc, thus inviting comparisons between the two revolutionaries. In Part II Coulter hints at mental instability as Riel imagines himself to be an infallible religious leader, divinely inspired to lead his people to victory. The trial scene gives Coulter the opportunity to show his considerable gifts for depicting victims of injustice; as an Ulsterman, Coulter knew political unrest at first hand. The actual testimony of Riel (who insisted on defending himself) pales in contrast to that written by Coulter, which is more dramatic, though based on the substance of Riel's actual speech. Riel's subsequent hanging, accompanied by liturgical chanting, is strongly suggestive of the crucifixion and its aftermath. The play is a combination of epic, myth, legend, pageant, documentary, and montage. As epic it dramatizes the deeds of a historical hero in a series of events expressed in elevated language; as myth it is an allegory of a Christ-like prophet who symbolizes the larger and deeper beliefs of a nation; as legend it is the story of a Canadian hero who has assumed larger-than-life proportions; as pageant it is a procession of stylized events leading to a rich climax; as documentary it is a substantially accurate account of events and personalities; as a montage it is a composite picture of many elements produced through a rapid succession of scenes.

The crime of Louis Riel (1976) is a shortened version of *Riel* written for small-cast nonprofessional groups. Commissioned by the CANADA COUNCIL, it consists of a continuous flow of scenes set in motion by the 'Actor', who plays the part of the Crown Prosecutor. Functioning much like the stage manager in Thornton Wilder's *Our Town*, the 'Actor' also serves the same role as a Greek chorus. The audience is invited to join the jury to determine whether Riel will live or be hanged. *The trial of Louis Riel* was commissioned by the Chamber of Commerce, Regina, Saskatchewan, in 1967 to mark Canada's Centennial and to be an annual tourist event. It is a one-act documentary of the actual court scene in which Coulter takes Riel's own words and weaves them into a lively debate featuring twenty-eight characters. The play is performed in a replica of the original courthouse, where the audience, ushered in, as in a real courtroom, is scrutinized by the Constable as the Court assembles. Among the spectators are ladies of social prominence, colourfully dressed in period costume, and officers of the North West Mounted Police in scarlet uniforms. Once the counsel, witnesses, and jurymen arrive to take their seats the play begins with the usual formalities of a trial. Louis Riel, shackled with ball and chain, is placed in the dock, and the trial progresses as on the actual day. The play is not only moving, but direct and shocking in its re-creation of an infamous trial.

While the *Riel* trilogy brought John Coulter to the attention of the Canadian public, it also prompted some historians to research and re-evaluate the role of Louis Riel in Canadian history. Many of the tensions plaguing Canadian society are mirrored in Riel himself, who has become a symbol for both Native-rights groups and French Canadians.

Ringuet. Pseudonym of Philippe PANNETON.

Ringwood, Gwen Pharis (1910–84). Born in Anatone, Washington, she was educated at the Universities of Montana, Alberta, and North Carolina. Most of her adult life was spent in Alberta and, from 1953, in Williams Lake, British Columbia. Apart from a novel, *Younger brother* (1959), and occasional short stories, Ringwood's creative energies were devoted to drama. The author of more than sixty plays—dramas, musicals, children's plays, radio plays—she was a major force in the development of Canadian drama, particularly in the West. Many of her plays remain unpublished, but twenty-five of them appeared in *The collected plays of Gwen Ringwood* (1982), edited by Enid Delgatty Rutland, which is still in print; some typescripts are available in the theatre section of the Metropolitan Toronto Library and the Special Collections Division of the University of Calgary Library.

In 1937 Ringwood won a Rockefeller fellowship to the University of North Carolina, where she became part of the Carolina Playmakers group. Some of her best work belongs to this period. STILL STANDS THE HOUSE (1938) succeeds on two levels: as a powerful evocation of the severity of prairie life during the 1930s, and as an incisive psychological portrait of a spinster's resistance to change. *Dark harvest* (1945) shows an equally sensitive response to prairie environment and character, but is marred by stilted dialogue and a contrived ending. An earlier one-act version of the same play, *Pasque flower* (1939), benefits from a tighter structure, verse dialogue, and effective symbolism. The comic vein in Ringwood's work is revealed in a group of plays performed at the Banff School of Fine Arts in the early 1940s: *The courting of Marie Jenvrin* (1941), a flimsy piece; *The jack and the joker* (1944); and *The rainmaker* (1946). The gentle satire of small-town Alberta folly in the later two plays works well, especially in *The rainmaker*. They were both commissioned by the Alberta Folklore and Local History Project, as was *Stampede*, performed at the University of Alberta in 1946, which, in a laboured manner, eulogizes the Alberta cowboy. Comic invention returned with *A fine coloured Easter egg; or the drowning of Wasyl Nemitchuk* (1946) and *Widger's way* (1976), both adroitly controlled comedies that rely for their effect on character idiosyncrasies and improbable—yet, within their convention, credible—plots. (*Widger's way*, along with a later play, *The golden goose*, 1979, are still in print in separate editions.) *Wasyl Nemitchuk* also contains a serious element—seldom totally absent from Ringwood's comedies—in its reminder of the economic and social consequences of Alberta's oil discovery.

The first of Ringwood's plays about Canada's Native people, *Lament for Harmonica* (1975), is a melodramatic protest against exploitation, especially sexual exploitation, of Amerindians by white Canadians. *The stranger* has a similar theme, a slightly implausible plot, and flashes of poetry. Plot is also the weak point of *The deep has many voices*, but its expressionistic structure, imaginative use of visual and sound effects, and rich language mark this story of a young woman's search for her identity as a mature work. All the plays mentioned above are in *The collected plays*. Expressing many themes and utilizing many techniques, Ringwood was a constant explorer of dramatic structures and convention. But her main achievement was her skill in capturing a sense of place: the environment of western Canada and its people.

Ritchie, Charles (1906–95). Charles Stewart Almon Ritchie, the elder of the two sons of William Ritchie, K.C., and Lilian Stewart, was born in Halifax, Nova Scotia. (The younger son, Roland, later became Supreme Court Justice.) The boys' education was a moveable feast, including private tutors and schools in Nova Scotia, preparatory school in England, and Trinity College School, Port Hope, Ontario. Charles Ritchie earned his B.A. and

M.A. from Oxford University, and an M.A. from Harvard; he also attended the École libre des sciences politiques in Paris. Ritchie's public career began in 1934, when he joined Canada's fledgling Department of External Affairs. In 1939 he was posted to London—where, despite the war, as a clever and charming bachelor he had an active social life and his entry into the realms of both high culture and high society began. After the war (he married his cousin Sylvia Smellie in 1948) he was a member of the group of worldly wise Canadian civil servants whose efforts built one of the most highly respected foreign services in the modern world. Over his forty-year career as a diplomat, Ritchie was Canada's Ambassador to West Germany and the United States, High Commissioner in London, permanent representative to the United Nations and the North Atlantic Treaty Organization, and a special adviser to the Privy Council. He was made a Companion of the Order of Canada in 1969.

Ritchie began writing diaries in his adolescence, but did not offer them for publication until after his retirement in 1973. During his career he used them as a personal escape from the tedium of diplomatic life. However, in 1960 the British novelist Elizabeth Bowen encouraged him to publish them and by 1968 he was considering this as a retirement project. (Ritchie's love affair with Bowen, whom he met in 1941, inspired her novel The heat of the day, which is dedicated to him.) In his Foreword to The siren years: a Canadian diplomat abroad, 1937–1945 (1974, GGA; rpr. 2001) Ritchie says that a diary, though not an artistic creation, should have 'a breath of immediacy'—which his diaries certainly have. 'Life is not transmuted into art. Anyone who wishes to see how that miracle can be achieved should read the work of genius set in the London of those years, The Heat of the Day by Elizabeth Bowen.' His own account of those years, and the occasional bits of diplomatic and political gossip, had popular appeal; but it was the diary's wit and grace, its literary distinction, that established Ritchie's reputation as a writer. This was followed by An appetite for life: the education of a young diarist, 1924–1927 (1977, rpr. 1986), Diplomatic passport: more undiplomatic diaries, 1944–1962 (1981), and Storm signals: more undiplomatic diaries 1962–1971 (1983, rpr. 1987). Undiplomatic diaries: 1937–1971 (2008)—with an interesting introduction by Allan Gotlieb, who knew and admired Ritchie—includes in one volume The siren years, Diplomatic passport, and Storm

signals. Although he spent his working life cushioned by the security of the public service, Ritchie was a frustrated novelist, so that the diaries, on occasion, read like excerpts from novels. His last published work, My grandfather's house: scenes of childhood and youth (1987, rpr. 2002), richly combines autobiography and family memoir. Love's civil war: Elizabeth Bowen and Charles Ritchie: letters and diaries 1941–1973 (2008, rpr. 2009) was edited by the notable British biographer Victoria Glendinning with Judith Robertson, the daughter of the distinguished Canadian civil servant Norman Robertson, who hired young Ritchie for the Department of External Affairs. Ritchie's contribution to the book is made up of extracts from his diaries relating to Bowen (his letters to her were destroyed); Bowen's is made up of her wonderful letters to Ritchie, which have the grace, wit, and meticulous observations of her novels, and resound with her deep love for him.

Ritter, Erika (b. 1948). Born in Regina, Saskatchewan, she received a B.A. (1968) in English literature from McGill University and an M.A. (1970) from the University of Toronto's Graduate Centre for the Study of Drama. For three years she taught English and drama courses at Loyola College, Montreal, and then returned to Toronto to write—for radio, television, and the stage. She broadcasts often for CBC Radio 2 as a guest host. Ritter's first play was A visitor from Charleston (1975), produced by Loyola College in 1974, whose lead character, Eva, is addicted to the movie Gone with the wind. Her plan to see it for the forty-ninth time is postponed by the arrival of an earnest young salesman promoting Fantasia cosmetics. Thematically transparent and overwritten, the play has little of the liveliness and wit found in The splits (1978)—in which Ritter's specialty as a playwright comes to the fore: a skill in creating and mixing bright, snappy dialogue and zany, energetic, complex characters engaged in a battle of wit and wills. Megan, a writer of situation comedies for television, is as confused about her relationship to her work as she is about her relationships to men. Her estranged husband Joe—who is also a writer and reappears in her life at a most inopportune moment—serves as a model of artistic integrity. The supposition of the play is that his influence in this area will outlast their relationship. Ritter's skills as a playwright came to the fore in her hit comedy Automatic pilot

(1980), whose title refers to the emotional life of the central character, Charlie, a neurotic stand-up comic whose self-deprecating routine is based almost completely on auto-biographical material: her husband left her for another man, and two successive lovers have failed her. Funniest when she is making jokes about her own anxieties and disappointments, we watch her transform intimate personal details into comic material. Although Charlie might be considered a sad character locked into her own limitations, it becomes apparent that her humour—which expresses a form of self-protection, and vulnerability—is also a strength. Her resourcefulness, exuberance, and creativity transform and transcend complaint, even as only part of her act. *Automatic pilot* is a wonderful play, Ritter's best, because of the depth and poignancy of the characterization of Charlie, and because of the ingenuity and wit of the script. After its highly successful alternate-theatre run in Toronto, it was remounted in a more elaborate commercial production at Toronto's Bayview Playhouse in the summer of 1980, and has been produced by regional theatres across the country. Ritter's historical drama, *Winter 1671* (1979), focusing on the tragic love story of one of Louis XIV's *filles du roi* sent to New France, met a poor reception when it premiered at Toronto's St Lawrence Centre. A weighty period piece, it deals with unfamiliar terrain unsuited to Ritter's particular talents. In *The passing scene* (produced at the Tarragon Theatre, Toronto, in 1982), the central relationship between an investigative reporter and a lifestyle journalist extends beyond the issue of personal integrity and is given a broad public dimension. Partly because its central issues—kinds of journalism, the truth in any story—are of more interest to writers than to a general audience, the play was not consistently engaging. *Murder at McQueen* (produced by Tarragon, 1986) is the last full-length play Ritter has had staged to date. Members of the chic McQueen Club, four successful professional single women, share the struggle to achieve some kind of substantial centre for their lives. Finding themselves out of the conventional marriage plot, they have yet to feel comfortable with a different life-script. Although hampered by the confusions of its shifting focus and the defeated tone of the text, this play is a cleverly written post-feminist comedy of manners.

Ritter's first novel, *The hidden life of humans* (1997), is about the dysfunctional life of Dana, a writer whose ex-husband, whom she loves, is dying of AIDS, and who has short-term lovers, whom she also loves for a time. She is saddled with Murphy, a dog, with whom she bonds and who himself narrates the goings-on from his point of view every few chapters. Though often down, Dana is never out, and seems to transcend everything with her witty comments and wry sense of humour, like Charlie in *Automatic pilot*. Ritter has also published *Urban scrawl: the world as seen through the bemused eyes of Erika Ritter* (1984) and *Ritter in residence* (1987), amusing essays on city life. *The great big book of guys: alphabetical encounters with men* (2004) continues in this personal vein, the engaging brief memoirs beginning with Amigos, Bad Boys, Codgers, Dads, and ending with Younger Men and Zealots. In 2009 Ritter published *The dog by the cradle, the serpent beneath: some paradoxes of human-animal relationships*.

Roberts, Sir Charles G.D. (1860–1943). Charles George Douglas Roberts, a brother of Theodore Goodridge ROBERTS and a cousin of Bliss CARMAN, was born in Douglas, New Brunswick, and spent his childhood beside the Tantramar marshes near Sackville, N.B. His first teacher was his clergyman father, later eulogized in the poem Westcock hill, and another teacher was (Sir) George R. Parkin, who introduced him to the Pre-Raphaelite poets; Roberts was also educated at the University of New Brunswick. At the age of twenty he published a notable collection of poems, *Orion*, and in 1883 he became editor of the Toronto periodical *The WEEK*, but soon resigned after disagreeing with the views of its founder, Goldwin SMITH, on Canada's annexation to the United States. From 1885 to 1895 Roberts taught English literature at King's College, Windsor, Nova Scotia, and in 1896 he published his first collection of animal stories, *Earth's enigmas*. From 1897 to 1925 he supported himself by writing prose, living chiefly in New York from 1897 to 1907 and then on the Continent and finally in London, England, from 1907 to 1925. During the Great War he was a private in the British forces and was later commissioned and attached to the Canadian War Records Office in London. He returned to Canada in 1925 and spent the rest of his life in Toronto. He was knighted in 1935.

Roberts was called the father of Canadian literature because the international acclaim for his early poetry inspired his generation, among them Bliss Carman and Archibald LAMPMAN, into creativity. Also the inventor of the modern animal story, a distinction he shares with Ernest Thompson SETON, Roberts was the first writer to mythologize successfully, in both poetry and prose, the Maritime environment: its strong sense of the past, particularly the French and English struggle for Acadia; its New England heritage; its farming and fishing communities beside the Tantramar marshes of the Upper Bay of Fundy; and life in the remote forests of central New Brunswick. Rarely surpassed by other writers in recreating the outdoors, he was continually fascinated by the interpenetration of civilization and the wilderness. But it is nature without the human presence that evokes in Roberts two powerfully contrasting attitudes. In his poems he sees in nature a divine, even benevolent, spirit, finds permanence and consolation in the seasonal cycles, and emphasizes the kinship of all living things. In his animal stories, however, violence and destruction are the operative principles, and survival depends not merely on chance but on 'woodcraft'—Roberts' word for the individual creature's resourcefulness.

Roberts' best-known poetry was published between 1880 and 1898 (he published his last collection in 1941). While *Orion, and other poems* (Philadelphia, 1880) shows his assimilation of classical subjects and of Tennyson and Arnold, *In divers tones* (Boston, Montreal, 1886) and *Songs of the common day* (London, Toronto, 1893) reveal the mature artist's elegiac voice, his precise yet colloquial diction, and his scrupulous realism. In 'The tantramar revisited' the speaker refuses to inspect at close range a once-familiar landscape because in his memory it has transcended time and change. 'Canada', which was a popular patriotic piece in the 1890s, exhorts the young nation to draw its sustenance from its heroic French and British origins. The sonnet sequence of *Songs of the common day*, which describes the seasonal pattern of rural life in a detached, restrained style, contains Roberts' most satisfying poems, including 'The sower', 'The potato harvest', and 'The pea-fields'. With his departure from King's College and the separation from his wife and family in 1895–7 came a change in poetic subjects: his bohemian lifestyle, his sojourn in large cities, and his relationships with other women are recorded in the cityscapes, the love poems, and the philosophical pieces of *New York nocturnes and other poems* (Boston, 1898).

Roberts published his first animal story, 'Do seek their meat from God', in *Harper's* (Dec. 1892). This and three other stories appeared in *Earth's enigmas: a book of animal and nature life* (Boston, 1896). Unlike traditional animal stories, which were frequently parables illustrating human behaviour, Roberts' stories were based on direct observation and dispensed with sentimentality and didacticism—they freed him to deal with conduct outside the framework of Victorian morality. In the 'Introductory' to *The kindred of the wild* (1902), Roberts defined his animal story as 'a psychological romance constructed on a framework of natural science', one that 'helps us to return to nature, without requiring that we ... return to barbarism.' (*The kindred of the wild* was reissued in 2001 with one change: 'The king of the Mamozekel' was replaced by 'The gauntlet of fire'. There is a substantial Introduction by Seán VIRGO and the Afterword is Roberts' 'Introductory' to the original edition.) Alec Lucas, in his chapter 'Nature Writers and the Animal Story' in the *Literary history of Canada* identified three kinds of animal stories: the biography, which examines conduct or personality; the action story, which emphasizes plot and usually contains humans; and the sketch, which illustrates an elemental force governing the natural world. Accused by President Theodore Roosevelt in *Everybody's Magazine* (June 1907) of being a 'nature-fakir', Roberts argued that animals are not governed by instinct alone but by 'something directly akin to reason', an approach to animal psychology that was at odds with Darwinian determinism. Even though most of Roberts' animals are victims of the conflicting forces for survival in nature, they often evince a heroic spirit in their defeat. Occasionally, as in the full-length animal biography *Red fox* (1905), these creatures are observed by an adolescent boy much like the youthful Roberts, and here the intelligent fox eludes his animal and human enemies and finds freedom. The highly popular animal collections, Roberts' most important contribution to prose, also include *The watchers of the trails* (1904), and *The haunters of the silences* (1907), among many other titles. *The vagrants of the barren and other stories* (1992), edited by Martin Ware, is a modern collection.

Always sympathetic to French Canada, Roberts translated Philippe AUBERT DE GASPÉ's *Les anciens Canadiens* (Quebec, 1863) as *The CANADIANS OF OLD; an historical romance* (New York, 1890). Roberts also wrote eleven romances for adults, many of them set in eighteenth-century Nova Scotia, in which an escape or a rescue culminates in a marriage between French and English. An early example is *The forge in the forest: being the narrative of the Acadian Ranger, Jean de Mer* (1896, rpr. 2003). The international bestseller

Roberts

Barbara Ladd (1902) is the story of a New England girl on the eve of, and during, the American Revolution. After 1900 Roberts shifted to romances of contemporary New Brunswick, and produced two remarkable novels. *The heart of the ancient wood* (1900) tells of a young girl's kinship with the forest creatures around her; especially the she-bear Kroof, who—like Ben, the old bear in William Faulkner's novella *The bear*—is a symbol of the wilderness world that is endangered by the presence of humans. *The heart that knows* (1906, rpr. 2002), a realistic tale that is slightly marred by Roberts' deference to the expectations of his audience, deals with the cruel treatment given to an unmarried mother, and contains sympathetic portraits of Roberts' parents in the minister and his wife.

Available modern editions of Roberts' poetry are *The selected poems* (1974, rpr. 1980) edited by Desmond PACEY; *The collected poems of Sir Charles G.D. Roberts: a critical edition* (1985) edited by Pacey and Graham Adams; and *Orion, and other poems* (1999) edited by Ross Kilpatrick. Roberts' nature writing is well represented in *Lure of the wild* (1980) edited by John Coldwell Adams, and *The vagrants of the barren and other stories* (1992) edited by Martin Ware. *The collected letters of Charles G.D. Roberts*, edited by Laurel Boone, was published in 1989. See John Coldwell Adams, *Sir Charles God damn: the life of Sir Charles G.D. Roberts* (1986).

Roberts, Paul William (b. 1955). Born in Wales, and educated at Exeter College, Oxford, where he taught until 1977, when he spent three years in India, he thereafter settled in Toronto, where he has worked in television and as a journalist. He has written for *Vanity Fair*, *The New Yorker*, *The Atlantic Monthly*, *The Times Literary Supplement*, *The Washington Post*, and *The New York Times*. Roberts is the author of many books that have been praised for their literary distinction. The witty, picaresque, semi-autobiographical novel, *The palace of fears* (1994), involves Oxford University, high finance, filmmaking, and love. *Homeland* (2006) is narrated in 2050 by the 100-year-old self-loathing former public servant David Derklin Leverett. (His career in the American government goes back to the Carter era.) The US has become US-Global, a super-government above all other governments. He says in his Preface: 'Most of the great East Coast capitals never recovered from a deluge that came with the arctic meltdown, although human ingenuity knows no limits. Like the multitrillion-dollar transformation of the

former New York City into Big Aqua, the world's first underwater theme park, one of whose main attractions is a simulation of the attack on and collapse of the World Trade Towers. All under the sea.' The president and other government leaders 'are no longer identified for reasons of national security, and elections occur only to vote for the party, not an actual candidate. Indeed, no one knows where the President lives now. Or what he looks like. Or his name.' *Homeland* is an ingenious, frightening dystopian novel. The following travel books combine ironic views of unfamiliar locales with speculation about present-day remnants of traditions of hidden wisdom: *A river in the desert: modern travels in ancient Egypt* (1993, rpr. 1994), *Empire of the soul: some journeys in India* (1994, rpr. 2006), *Journey of the Magi: in search of the birth of Jesus* (1995, rpr. 1997; American title, *The birth of Jesus: the real journey of the Magi*), and *The demonic comedy: some detours in the Baghdad of Saddam Hussein* (1997). *Smokescreen: one man against the underworld* (2001), co-authored with Norman Snider, is about the extraordinary life of C. Calvin (Cal) Broeker, who worked in the 1990s as a Crown agent for the Royal Canadian Mounted Police and a paid agent for the United States Secret Service, infiltrating the Italian Mafia, the Hell's Angels and other biker gangs, the Russian Mafiya, Bulgarian government racketeers, and Native smuggling rings operating out of reservations/reserves on the US-Canadian border. It reads like a thriller—indeed, there is much dialogue. *A war against truth: an intimate account of the invasion of Iraq* (2004) is the result of Roberts' spending much time in Iraq, writing for the Toronto *Globe and Mail* and *Harper's* magazine. Preparing an article for the *Globe* at the end of March 2003, he writes in his notebook: 'The ruin of history. Even the air is red with blood, choking on sewage, cordite, burning oil, and my own fear. / The bombs are getting *closer* ... thumping of anti-aircraft batteries all around (this is bad location, likely target) ...' This preamble ends: 'Never in history was a war so well documented yet so poorly covered by the media.... I write in a state of raging anger, and shame, about what I saw and about what I am still seeing halfway through the year 2004.' Roberts' impassioned narrative, again with much dialogue, is a vivid, salutary counterweight to the present-day acceptance and optimistic appraisals of the condition of Iraq.

Roberts, Theodore Goodridge (1877–1953). He was born in the rectory of St Anne's

Parish, Fredericton, New Brunswick. Charles G.D. ROBERTS was his elder brother and Bliss CARMAN his cousin. At seventeen he left the University of New Brunswick without a degree and in 1897 acquired a position as sub-editor of *The Independent*, a New York weekly, which had published his first poem in 1888 when it was under the editorship of Carman. He was sent as a special correspondent to cover the Spanish-American war in 1898, an experience that inspired his novel *Hemming the adventurer* (1904). While there he caught 'Cuban fever' and returned to Fredericton to recover. During the next three years Roberts was editor of *The Newfoundland Magazine* and collected a wealth of information about out-port life and history that was to form the basis of his Newfoundland novels and his tales of the Beothuks. In this period he made a jour-ney to the Caribbean and South America on a full-rigged barkentine, an experience that he put to good use in *The wasp* (1914), and in numerous other tales and poems set in the South Seas. He returned to the Caribbean with Frances Seymour Allan on their honey-moon in 1903, and the couple remained in Barbados for two years while Theodore wrote. The first of four children—the painter Goodridge Roberts—was born there. In the next quarter-century the Roberts family trav-elled extensively—living in England, France, and various parts of Canada—while Theo-dore published thirty-four novels and over 100 pieces in periodicals, chiefly in *The Cana-dian Magazine*, *The Youth's Companion*, and *The Independent*. During the Great War he served in the 12th Battalion, at one point as A.D.C. to Max Aitken (Lord Beaverbrook), writing official accounts of the war, one of which was published as *Thirty Canadian V.C.'s* (1918). In 1930 he was awarded an honorary D.Litt. by the University of New Brunswick and in 1934 he was named a fellow of the Royal Society of Canada. In the same year he pub-lished a volume of poetry, *The leather bottle* (1934). He eventually settled in Digby, Nova Scotia.

Roberts' thirty-five novels, published between 1908 and 1922, were historical romances, backwoods mysteries and adven-tures, wartime adventures, South Seas adven-tures, tales of Newfoundland and Labrador, such as his best-known novel, *The harbor mas-ter* (1913, rpr. 1968), set on the Labrador coast, and Native stories, such as *The red feathers* (1907, rpr. 1976), an imaginative treatment of Native myth. Virtually all these fictions are best viewed as juveniles. All are rousing tales of adventure and romance that uphold the

basic virtues of courage, honesty, fair play, and self-reliance, with a strong flavour of English gentlemanliness, but a minimum of moral cant. Roberts' serious artistic accomplishment lies in his poetry. Some of his earliest pieces appeared in a family connection—with poems by his older brothers William Carman and Charles G.D., his sister Elizabeth Roberts MacDonald, and Bliss Carman—entitled *Northland lyrics* (Boston, 1899). In 1926 the RYERSON PRESS published more of Theo-dore's poems in *The lost shipmate*—a chap-book of 150 copies—many of which were included in *The leather bottle* (1934). Had this volume appeared forty years earlier, it might have won for Theodore a reputation equal to that of his brother Charles or of Bliss Carman. Poems such as 'The sandbar' and 'Magic' are unmatched in Canadian poetry for a facility and clarity of image suggestive of high-realist painting. See *That far river: selected poems* (1998) edited by Martin Ware.

Robin, Régine (b. 1939). Born Ryvka Ajz-ersztejn in Paris, of Polish-Jewish parents—whose Judaism, at least until the period of de-Stalinization, was subordinate to their dream of an egalitarian Communist society—Robin completed a doctorate in history at the Université de Paris (X Nanterre) before emi-grating and settling in 1977 in Montreal, where she taught at the Université du Qué-bec à Montréal. A member of the Royal Society of Canada, recipient of a Governor General's Award, and winner of the presti-gious Prix Jacques Rousseau (1994), she is not well known to the general public. Historian, essayist, novelist, Robin is one of Canada's most important thinkers, partly because of her interdisciplinarity and her questioning the very nature of memory and the historical process, but also because of her profound and innovative reflection on personal and collec-tive identity in a world characterized by shift-ing populations and ongoing confrontations in a multiplicity of cultures. Steering a diffi-cult path between the Scylla of the American 'melting pot' and the Charybdis of the Cana-dian multicultural mosaic, she explores in all her writings the question of (her) personal identity and its relation to society. Only one of her texts has been translated: *La Québécoite* (1983)—*The wanderer* (1997), translated by Phyllis Aronoff—is a novel about a novel yet to be written. The ambiguous title, a possible play on the word *cot/coite* (silent or non-plussed), refers to the main character, unable to feel quite Québécoise as she walks the streets of Montreal, ill at ease with a language that, while resembling her native French, in fact conceals a very different reality.

Robinson, Eden. See ABORIGINAL LITERATURE: 4, 5.

Robinson, Peter (b. 1950). Born in Yorkshire, England, he completed his B.A. in English literature at the University of Leeds before immigrating to Canada in 1974. He holds an M.A. (1975) from the University of Windsor, Ontario, where he studied with Joyce Carol Oates; and a Ph.D. (1983), on the sense of place in contemporary British poetry, from York University, Toronto. He is the author of a series of nineteen police procedurals featuring Detective Chief Inspector Alan Banks and set in Eastvale, a fictional Yorkshire dale. These include *Gallows view* (1987, rpr. 1988), *A dedicated man* (1988, rpr. 1989), *The hanging valley* (1989, rpr. 1990), *A necessary end* (1989, rpr. 1990), *Past reason hated* (1991; Arthur Ellis Award, rpr. 1992), *Wednesday's child* (1992, rpr. 1993), *Final account* (1994), *Innocent graves* (1996, Arthur Ellis Award), *Dead right* (1997, US title *Blood at the root*), *In a dry season* (1999), *Cold is the grave* (2000, Arthur Ellis Award), *Aftermath* (2001, rpr. 2002), *The summer that never was* (2003, rpr. 2008), *Playing with fire* (2004), *Strange affair* (2005), *Piece of my heart* (2006, rpr. 2010), *Friend of the devil* (2007), and *All the colours of darkness* (2008). The Banks series is most successful in its presentation of the character of Banks himself, a man sensitive about his working-class origins and limited education who has (somewhat ironically) moved his family from London to Yorkshire in search of a quieter life. With his methodical ways and infinite patience in pursuing his inquiries, Banks belongs to a particular British detective-fiction tradition that features cool, ruminative, and occasionally prickly investigators (ranging from Conan Doyle's Holmes through Ruth Rendell's Wexford and Colin Dexter's Morse). It is Banks' contemplative nature, in fact, that contributes to the success of the series in terms of its perceptive social and cultural commentary. As a newcomer to a rapidly disappearing ancient and venerable way of life in Yorkshire, Banks is well positioned to observe and lament its invasion by a double juggernaut consisting of egregious yuppie-style tastes migrating upward from the south of England, and of American popular culture with its proclivity toward self-absorption, instant pleasures, and gratuitous violence. *In a dry season* was inspired by Robinson's visit to Yorkshire in 1995 when a reservoir near the town of Oatley dried up, revealing a village that had been drowned. *Dead right* is the only Canadian title in *100 favourite mysteries of the century* published by the Independent Mystery Booksellers Association. (In 2009 Robinson published *The price of love and other stories* in which the 102-page novella 'Like a virgin'—one of only two stories about Banks—goes back twenty years when he was working in London. The Banks of this early period was much less admirable and appealing than the later Yorkshire Banks.) Robinson has also written two non-series crime novels: *Caedmon's song* (1990, rpr. 1991), a psychological thriller about a serial killer preying on university students in northern England, and *No cure for love* (1995, rpr. 1996), a police procedural that focuses on Detective Arvo Hughes of the Los Angeles Police Department's Threat Management Unit. They are less successful than his series fiction in evoking the sense of place that characterizes his writing at its best.

Robinson, Spider (b. 1948). Born in New York City, and educated at the State University of New York (Stonybrook), he settled in 1973 at Phinney's Cove on the Bay of Fundy, Nova Scotia; moved to Halifax; then moved again to Vancouver. He lives on Bowen Island, B.C. A voluminous science-fiction writer, and for some seven years a columnist in the Toronto *Globe and Mail*, he is praised for his novels and stories and prized for his wit and talent as a speaker at SF conventions. Robinson is best known for the Star books: *Stardance* (1978; co-written with his (late) dancer wife Jeanne Robinson), which describes a dance in zero gravity in space, and its lively successors *Starseed* (1991) and *Starmind* (1994). Puns predominate in the Callahan stories in nine collections, from *Callahan's Crosstime Saloon* (1977) to *Callahan's key* (2000) and *Callahan's con* (2003). Robinson was influenced by the bright, technological optimism of Robert A. Heinlein, but also by this SF master's conception of the 'Crazy Years' of social anarchy—consequently there is a dark, pessimistic aspect to Robinson's depiction of the uses of science and technology in such novels as *Telempath* (1976), *Mindkiller: a novel of the near future* (1982), and *Night of power* (1985). As a writer of short fiction, his range and resources are also shown to advantage in *Melancholy elephants* (1984), his sole Canadian publication, all others being published in the United States and widely translated. Robinson collected pieces he wrote for the *Globe and Mail* between 1996 and 2004 for *The crazy years* (2004), the title of course inspired by

Heinlein, who also influenced indirectly Robinson's crime mystery-cum-SF-novel, *Very bad deaths* (2004). It is narrated by Russell Walker (an amiable Spider Robinson figure), aged fifty-five, a columnist for the *Globe and Mail* who is devastated by the death of his wife. The action takes place in 2003, but there are frequent flashbacks to the 1960s. A former college roommate comes back into Russell's life, Zandor 'Smelly' Zudenigo—who is a genius at math and a telepath: he can read minds—and has just come upon a serial killer who has an obsessive desire to inflict pain and is about to commit a grisly murder. Smelly can't go to the police with this, so he persuades Russell to try to hunt the killer down, which he does, with the help of a sympathetic policewoman, Hilda Mandiç. The last quarter of the book, devoted to their confrontation, is exciting. One of the vivid, horrifying episodes in the novel has to do with Russell as the victim of pneumothorax, when the lung collapses and you can hardly breathe. Robinson had this at the age of fourteen; the condition was corrected by one of the most painful of all operations.

Rogers, Linda (b. 1944). Born in Port Alice, British Columbia, she was educated at the University of British Columbia (B.A., 1966; M.A., 1970), and has been active as a teacher and book reviewer, and in the Federation of B.C. Writers and The LEAGUE OF CANADIAN POETS, of which she was president in 1990 and 1991 respectively. Since the 1970s she has published more than ten collections of poetry. Among them are *Woman at Mile Zero* (1990), *Letters from the doll hospital* (1992), *Hard candy* (1994), *Love in the rain forest: new and selected poems* (1995), and *Heaven cake* (1997). *The saning* (1999) has graphic decorations and some typographical play. Rogers' poems about children (and outrage against wrongs inflicted on them), family, sex, love, lust, music, feminism—and others inspired by such real-life subjects as Jaqueline du Pré playing the cello ('Something brilliant for one hand'), a photograph by Man Ray ('Wrinkled coloratura'), Sylvia Plath and Marilyn Monroe ('Famous women')—can begin with a simple image then veer off in surprising directions, some of them surreal: her imagination knows no bounds. *The bursting test* (2002) is a large collection (seventy-seven poems) of prose-like verse ('"It's a miracle," they said of the child / who survived eight days and nights / in the crashed car without water'—'Walking over the floating'). In 2008 she was made Victoria's Poet Laureate, a three-year appointment.

Rogers' fiction includes *The half life of radium* (1994), a novella about Morgenstern who lives with her younger live-in lover Eliot, and The Lady Upstairs; and indulges in an argumentative correspondence with her mother. *Say my name: the memoirs of Charlie Louie* (2000) is a fictional account of the short life—told in his own words—of a young Native boy Rogers met and grew fond of in the seventies when she was living in the Cowichan Valley with her family. Sadly, he took his own life. The next two novels are redolent of family and of Victoria, where Rogers lives. *Friday water* (2003) is about Ariel, a former dancer, her daughter Rumer and sister Veronica, who goes to Cuba to look for Ariel's filmmaker husband Barin, who it turns out has been imprisoned. He doesn't know that Ariel has been operated on for breast cancer and has lost a breast. Veronica's long description of her trip to Cuba—and to Holguin, where they only have water on Friday—is an interesting central passage in the novel. But the whole book, covering little more than twenty-four hours, is readable. *The Empress letters* (2007) is an epistolary novel—the letters are written in 1927 on the *Empress of Asia*, en route from Victoria to Shanghai, by Poppy to her daughter Precious. She writes about many things, her past—about her Victoria home, a mansion called Casanora, which has a tunnel to the sea once used for opium smuggling; her second marriage to Olivier, a homosexual, who has nevertheless returned to her to live in the house with his lover Tony, who accompanies Poppy on the *Empress*. Emily Carr appears, along with the Dunsmuirs, a well-known Victoria family. Written over ten days of the voyage, the letters are packed with incident, mystery, and intrigue.

Rogers edited *P.K. Page: essays on her works* (2001), *Bill Bissett: essays on his works* (2002), *Al Purdy: essays on his works* (2002), *George Fetherling and his work* (2005), and *Joe Rosenblatt: essays on his works* (2006). She has written several books for children, and the young-adult novels *Frankie Zapper and the disappearing teacher* (1994) and *Molly Brown is not a clown* (1996). See *Linda Rogers: essays on her works* (2005) edited by Harold Rhenisch.

Rohmer, Richard (b. 1924). Born in Hamilton, Ontario, he attended high school in Fort Erie, Ontario. After serving in the Royal Canadian Air Force as a fighter pilot in the Second World War—participating in the D-Day invasion of Normandy—he attended the University of Western Ontario (B.A., 1948) and Osgoode Hall, Toronto, to become a Toronto lawyer and businessman. A major-general in the Militia (Air Command), he is an Officer of the Order of Canada and lives in Collingwood, Ontario. Rohmer is the undisputed Canadian king of the pot-boiler. His forte is the disaster novel and the polit-ical thriller, several of which deal with annexationist attempts by the USA to take over Canada, such as *Ultimatum* (1973), in which Canada's right to its own natural resources is called into question by an energy crisis; *Exxoneration* (1974), in which Canada thwarts an American invasion; *Exodus/UK* (1975), in which Britain has collapsed and the flood of Anglo-Celtic immigrants to Canada leads Québec to separate; *Separation* (1976), in which Québec has plans to secede, but Ottawa copes—and its sequel, *Separation II* (1981); and *Balls!* (1979), involving Cana-da's being blackmailed under threat of inva-sion by the USA. He has also written some 'Cold Warrior' novels preaching against the 'Red Menace', comprising *Periscope red* (1980), *Retaliation* (1982), *Triad* (1982), and *Red Arctic* (1989); science-fiction-like *Starma-geddon* (1986); and a war novel, *Rommel and Patton: armistice in Normandy* (1986), pub-lished in the USA as *The hour of the Fox*. While all these novels are devoid of literary values, they have an urgency and vitality that overcome their inherent implausibility and improbability, and they grip the reader. Rohmer is a nationalist, and his novels, even at their pulp-fiction level, touch a nerve that resonates. Among his novels there is one shining nugget, *John A.'s crusade* (1995), a his-torical espionage novel centred on Russia's sale of Alaska to the USA, of which the hero is Canada's first prime minister: it is one of the best Canadian political thrillers. *Death by deficit: a 2001 novel* (1995) is a portrait of a post-separation Canada on the verge of eco-nomic collapse. *Caged eagle* (2002) opens with a message from Garth Peters, written in a penitentiary, which includes the following: 'What got me started this writing goes this way. Some of my fellow inmates ... asked me to tell them about my escapades during the Second World War. As a fighter pilot in the UK and Europe I had a few, believe me. I told them about how, after the war, I became one of Canada's most famous and successful businessmen ...' *Ultimatum 2* (2007) is given by the American president to Russia when he insists that the Russians clean up high-level nuclear waste. A second ultimatum is given by the US, Russia, and the United Kingdom to Canada, which is seen as an international nuclear waste disposal site. The

Canadian prime minister says no and the Americans threaten to invade.

Non-fiction works by Rohmer include *The green North: mid-Canada* (1970); *The Arctic imperative: an overview of the energy crisis* (1973); *E.P. Taylor; the biography of Edward Plunket Tay-lor* (1978); *Patton's gap: an account of the Battle of Normandy 1944* (1981); *How to write a be$t $eller* (1984); *Massacre 747* (1984); and *Golden phoe-nix: the biography of Peter Munk* (1997). *Raleigh on the rocks: the Canada shipwreck of HMS Raleigh* (2003) is the well-researched story of a British cruiser that was commissioned in 1921 and ran aground at Forteau Bay, Labra-dor, the next year (it was blown up in 1926).

Generally speaking: the memoirs of Major-General Richard Rohmer (2004) focuses, after the first 36 pages on his early life, until page 185 on his military career in the Second World War when he flew 135 missions in the Royal Canadian Air Force, flying over the beaches of Normandy on D-Day. The rest of the book describes a very full life in which he had associations of one kind or another with a host of famous people, including the Queen, Prince Charles, Princess Diana, Prince Bernhard of The Netherlands, President Reagan—the book is a feast of name-dropping. See *A Richard Rohmer omnibus* (2003).

Rooke, Leon (b. 1934). He was born in Roa-noke Rapids, North Carolina, and lived in Victoria, British Columbia, between 1969 and 1988, when he moved to Ontario, where his wife, Constance Rooke (1942–2008), was appointed head of the English Department at the University of Guelph. He was educated at Mars Hill College, N.C. (1953–5), and at the University of North Carolina at Chapel Hill (1955–7, 1961), where he did both under-graduate and graduate work. He served in the US army in Alaska (1958–60), and edited the newspaper *Anvil* in Durham, N.C. (1967–9). He has taught English and creative writing at North Carolina, at Southwest Minnesota State University in Marshall, Minnesota, and at a number of universities in Canada. He was made a Member of the Order of Canada in 2007 and lives in Eden Mills, Ont., and Toronto.

The author, by his own estimate, of 300 stories, Rooke's collections include *Last one home sleeps in the yellow bed* (1968), *The love parlour* (1977), *The broad back of the angel* (1977), *Cry evil* (1980), *Death suite* (1981), *The birth control king of the Upper Volta* (1982), *Sing me no love songs I'll say you no prayers: selected stories* (1984), *A bolt of white cloth* (1984), *How I saved the province* (1989), *The happiness of others*

(1991), *Who do you love?* (1992), and *Oh! Twenty-seven stories* (1997). Two excellent selections from these books appeared in this millennium: *Painting the dog: the best stories of Leon Rooke* (2001) and *Hitting the charts: selected stories* (2006), with a Foreword by John MET-CALF. Rooke has also written eight novels: *Vault* (1973), *Fat woman* (1980), *The magician in love* (1981), *Shakespeare's dog* (1983, GGA; rpr. 1984), *A good baby* (1989), *Who goes there* (1999), *The fall of gravity* (2000), *The beautiful wife* (2005), and the novella *Balduchi's who's who* (2005). In continually testing the limits of fiction, Rooke deliberately weakens traditional elements of the realistic story. Often there is little unity of action: the narrator, as in 'Brush fire', prefers frequent digression to the tale he originally set out to tell. The development of character is often minimal, with the result that many of Rooke's stories have the quality of parable or fable—skeletal dramas enacted by generic figures. Although in some stories setting can be given in such detail that it becomes the dominant element—notably in stories that chiefly evoke a mood, such as 'For love of Eleanor'—in many it is completely absent. In *The magician in love* the lack of setting creates a temporal and spatial indeterminacy essential to the universality (attaining a level of fantasy) that Rooke seeks for the magician's experiences. Other stories offer little motivation for the action: characters act out of boredom, random impulse, or some unspecified, sometimes mysterious force, as in 'When swimmers on the beach have all gone home'. Occasionally the plot is dramatic yet visibly incomplete, as if Rooke wished to posit the incompleteness of our knowledge of some events. Most of Rooke's stories are first-person narrations by characters who, caring little to explain themselves, become known to us in a fragmentary way. Other stories are related by diary entries, biographical entries, in separate interlocking narratives, or from aloof third-person perspectives. Of particular note is the wide range of voices in Rooke's work—adolescent, American southern, West Indian, black American, even canine in his novel *Shakespeare's dog*, a tour de force written in pseudo-Elizabethan English. Because Rooke allows these voices to speak for themselves, without authorial mediation, they carry an intensity that more than compensates for the often fragmentary representation of action. The female narrator of Rooke's novel *Fat woman* is the most extravagant personality among his narrators and the most vivid of his characterizations. This work, *The magician in love*, and most of the story collections focus on the difficulty of male-female relations. Characters appear isolated within themselves, essentially unknown by their mates; they connect only out of secret and bizarre desires. The stories in *Cry evil* and *Death suite* move from the desultoriness of relationships to the despair and latent violence that underlie them; appearing as routine elements in human life are murder, sadism, and pornography. *Who goes there* is a prescient, picaresque novel about an aged right-wing senator and his abuse of interns (conceived before the Lewinsky scandal) and an array of other villains, and victims. Their activities are described with panache, but underpinning the novel are revelations of moral ambiguity that are thoughtful and even serious, though the narrative never strays from its light-hearted tone. *The fall of gravity* is an exuberant 'road novel': a year before the novel opens, Joyel Daggle has left husband Raoul and her tart-tongued eleven-year-old daughter, wending her way through various states and British Columbia for a year in a Plymouth that doesn't belong to her, and husband and daughter go after her because they want her back. Both trips, and the eccentrics met on the way, are described in a Rookeian narrative that is quirky, funny, not plot-driven, and yet transcends, in various scenes, the force of gravity behind the human bond with 'this sordid world'.

Muffins (1995) is a humorous, outrageous short story (accompanied by a 7" vinyl record of Rooke reading it) about a teenaged girl's relationship with her parents during and after a muffin-baking session in the kitchen. In 2009 he published *The last shot*, a collection of stories that includes a novella, 'Gator wrestling'. Rooke has also written several plays, including *Krokodile* (1973), *Sword/Play* (1974), *Ms America* (1984), *The good baby* (1986, rev. 1990), *Shakespeare's dog* (1989), and *The coming* (1991)—all of which have been produced. *Hot poppies* (2005) is a collection of poems, many of them prose poems, in which Rooke treats lightly, with surreal overtones, a great many subjects, including popular culture (summoning the names of Britney Spears, Mahalia Jackson, Martha Stewart, Lady Di) and American politics ('Cheney/Bush Rottweiler team', 'How we elect our president').

Roquebrune, Robert Laroque de (1889–1978). He was born at L'Assomption manor house into an aristocratic family that was deeply attached to the past. When he was four years old his parents moved to Montreal, where he was educated. He was one of the founders of the art magazine *Le Nigog*. In 1919 he began working for the Canadian Public Archives in Paris and became director in 1946. Throughout his life he was a contributor to many periodicals in France and Canada. He died in Cowansville, Québec. Roquebrune published four novels and a collection of short stories between 1923 and 1960, and two volumes of historical essays in the 1960s, but the only work to appear in English was his masterpiece, *Testament de mon enfance* (1951), translated by Felix Walter as *Testament of my childhood* (1964). In this first volume of his memoirs he recalls the comfortable and genteel existence led by his family in l'Assomption. The book is full of humorous sketches of adventurous ancestors and colourful people.

Roscoe, Patrick (b. 1962). Born of Canadian parents on the Spanish island of Formentera, he was raised in Canada and Tanzania, and left home at sixteen. He travelled widely throughout Canada, the United States, and Mexico, but feels most at home in Spain, dividing his time between Seville and Sidi Ifni, Morocco. As a writer, Roscoe has a natural exuberance that brought him, in his early twenties and later, numerous awards for his fiction. His story collections, *Beneath the western slopes* (1987, rpr. 1990) and *Love is starving for itself* (1994), are set in Mexico, and earned Roscoe a comparison with Gabriel García Márquez for his lyrical portrayals of fantasy, mystery, and fragility in a mythical Mexican village. He took a different direction with the nineteen autobiographical pieces in *Birthmarks* (1990)— powerful, often surreal accounts of how childhood experiences mark the forming identity of a young male prostitute growing up in Africa and British Columbia. Roscoe's novel *God's peculiar care* (1991) was even more unusual than his stories: it claims to complete the unfinished manuscript of Hollywood actress Frances Farmer, who was committed to an insane asylum in the 1940s. *Lost oasis* (1995) describes an emotionally bankrupt family and their travels; a poetic recitation of childhood grief, the book describes two decades of emotional history. *The truth about love* (2001) is described on the front cover as fiction; this is true, though it is not a novel but really a collection of stories, the first three of which—in Part One, entitled 'The Simple Rules of Life'—are linked. The first story is 'The last Casanova of Regina' about Louie, brought up by his elder sister Fan—who has two sisters, Lil and Annie and another brother, Michael—when their parents both died in 1911. Fan was always protective of Louie, even when he turned into a ladies' man. 'Louie was

always rushing off to another assignation, his lips were permanently swollen from too many kisses. Lipstick flowered on his collar in and out of season.' Fan defended his flirtations. '(What else could she do? She was almost his mother, after all.)' The story opens when he unaccountably marries in the 1930s. '"He chose the wrong floozy," decided Fan.' Annie calls her 'a bargain-basement bride.' Her name was Constance. 'What kind of a name was that? / "There's Constance Bennett," remembered Annie. A movie star name ... . False as a fair-weather friend.' Lil says, 'She won't last' And she didn't. Michael and his wife, and two sisters and their husbands, move to Brale, British Columbia; Fan (who has become a widow) and Louie stay in Regina. Roscoe's wonderful evocation of the everyday lives and banal utterances of these characters in this and another two stories—'Frozen blood' and 'Buried secrets', about Fan's cousin Etta and the mysterious Riley—stand in contrast to some pieces that are only two or three pages long, and to stories that are opaque, such as 'The murdered child', 'Touching darkness', and the enigmatic, rambling 'The laboratory of love' (fifty-eight pages). The title story, 'The truth about love', about the deeply felt, and mutual, love affair of two homosexuals, one of whom is the narrator; his lover is a serial killer. 'At first, it's true. I did feel jealous of your victims, of your special relationship with them. How their last earthly vision is of you. That interlocking of your eyes with theirs as they leave the world. How you carve out the shape of their unique destiny with your knife. Such shocking intimacy. But now I know you will always leave them to return to me. They hold your attention only briefly; our exchange lasts far longer than any death scream, any fading pulse.' (This powerful sociopathic episode is unique in the book.) A mundane explanation of 'the truth about love' may be that it has many aspects, illustrated here in story after story by an accomplished writer who is sometimes wilfully abstruse.

Rose-Belford's Canadian Monthly and National Review (1878–82). Hunter, Rose and Company, Toronto, which had printed *The Canadian Monthly and National Review* since its inception in 1872, in Jan. 1878 took control as publishers. Since Dec. 1876 they had also printed *Belford's Monthly Magazine: A Magazine of Literature and Art*, which combined serialized reprints of popular British and American stories with original contributions from many of the same Canadian writers appearing in *The Canadian Monthly*. In the spring of 1878 Hunter, Rose merged with Belford Brothers to form the Rose-Belford Publishing Company, and in June the two magazines were combined. The Belfords left the new company within the year, but the names of the publisher and the magazine remained unchanged until the magazine's demise in 1882. In its first year *Rose-Belford's* was edited by George STEWART, who continued the traditional serialized novels and social and literary comment. He introduced more American writers, as well as illustrated travel articles. After Stewart's departure Graeme Mercer ADAM, who had edited *The Canadian Monthly*, became editor. The magazine grew larger, although the illustrations disappeared and a greater emphasis was placed on original material by Canadian authors, such as Ethelwyn WETHERALD, William KIRBY, Sara Jeannette DUNCAN, Charles G.D. ROBERTS, and Frederick George SCOTT. Morality, ethics, and religious issues came to the fore, along with the fiction, poetry, and reviews. The publishers blamed 'our inchoate state as a nation' for the decision to cease publication in 1882: a greater patriotism would be required to support a magazine like *Rose-Belford's*, since the public preferred other types of literature.

Rosen, Sheldon (b.1943). Born in New York City, he grew up in Rochester and received his B.A. in psychology from the University of Rochester (1965). He then took an M.A. in telecommunications and spent several years producing radio and television commercials. He moved to Toronto in 1970. His first plays include a one-act absurdist comedy, *Love mouse* (1972), *Meyer's room* (1972), a surrealist one-act play, and *The wonderful world of William Bends (who is not quite himself today)* (1972), a dark comedy featuring a humanitarian who wants to spend his life as a mohair rug, and psychiatrists who are as crazy as their patients. Meanwhile Rosen was writing a number of shows for CBC television, which he continued to do after moving to Vancouver in 1973. There he became affiliated with the writer's-workshop program of the New Play Centre, which produced a number of his one-act plays, including *The box* (1975), and *Like father, like son* (produced in 1975)—later reworked as *The grand hysteric* and published with another one-act play, *Frugal repast*, in 1978. In *The box*, which begins with an extended movement sequence, two roommates fantasize about an unopened gift; in *Frugal repast* Picasso's harlequin figures come to life; and in *The grand hysteric* a seriously disturbed young man has a

traumatic session with his psychiatrist. Rosen's most successful play to date is *Ned and Jack* (1978), commissioned by the New Play Centre. Set in New York in 1922, it is about a late-night encounter between the popular American dramatist Edward Sheldon and his close friend John Barrymore, who—still in costume and full of the success of his opening night as Hamlet—climbs the fire-escape to Ned's penthouse apartment. Both artists are at a turning point in their lives: Jack is triumphant as an actor, while Ned has just learned that his paralysing illness is irreversible—he will be bedridden for the rest of his life. A sensitive and compassionate play, *Ned and Jack* combines humour, intense emotion, and careful character delineation. It was well received when it opened at the New Play Centre in 1977; after considerable rewriting it ran in two successive seasons at the Stratford Festival in 1978 and 1979. In 1980 its off-Broadway production was called one of the ten best plays of the year by Clive Barnes; but an 1981 Broadway production closed on opening night. *Souvenirs* (1985) was produced first off-Broadway in 1984 by the New York Theatre Workshop and subsequently by Factory Theatre Lab, Toronto, and Theatre Calgary. Set on an island off Australia, it is the account of a photographer's adventures during a political insurrection. *The duck sisters*, produced in 1990 by Toronto's Theatre Plus, returns to the comedic themes of Rosen's earlier writing. It is the story of two middle-aged sisters who wear duck masks as a way to advertise an out-of-the-way antique store. Even though this is their last day in business, the sisters are exuberant because a flying saucer is coming to take them away. The play was subsequently produced at the Half-Moon Theatre in Dallas, Texas. Rosen's imagistic adaptation of Ibsen's *An enemy of the people* was produced in 1994 by the National Theatre School, Montreal, of which Rosen was co-ordinator of the playwriting programs.

Rosenblatt, Joe (b. 1933). Born in Toronto, he attended Central Technical School, which he left in grade ten. During a decade of labouring jobs, the last seven years of which he spent as a freight handler with the Canadian Pacific Railway, he became increasingly interested in socialism, poetry, and drawing. With the help of a CANADA COUNCIL grant in 1963, he was able to leave the CPR and begin a career of writing, teaching, and editing. He now lives at Qualicum Beach on Vancouver Island, British Columbia. Since his first small-press publication, *The voyage of the mood* (1960), he has accumulated a witty and eccentric body of poetry and drawings. In *The LSD Leacock* (1963) he expressed in both serious and comic terms the idea that has permeated most of his writing: the essential unity of organic forms. He declared himself here a visionary who can see beyond civilization to the interconnectedness of human, reptile, and insect life. Rosenblatt's style reiterated the paradox expressed in the book's title: conventional and visionary vocabularies collide, scientific terms are invested with unexpected poetic resonance. After the much less adventurous *The winter of the lunar moth* (1968), and the collection of drawings *Greenbaum* (1970), Rosenblatt returned to the language of *The LSD Leacock* in *Bumblebee dithyramb* (1972), in which the poems vigorously celebrate humanity's sharing of the fecund energy of the animal and vegetable worlds, again marrying the vocabularies of mysticism and contemporary science. In *Dream craters* (1974) and *Virgins and vampires* (1975) Rosenblatt used more conventional forms of short poetry to explore other areas of his visionary bestiary. Frogs, cats, vampires, lizards, birds, toads, and goldfish here reflect, to one another, on their common piscine heritage. *Top soil* (1976, GGA) gathered poems from most of Rosenblatt's earlier books. His other books in this period included *The sleeping lady* (1979), a sonnet sequence exploring the 'salamander' joys of sexual love. In the 1980s Rosenblatt began writing sardonic long poems focused on ethical and political issues. *Brides of the stream* (1984) examined ecological and conservation questions; *Beds and consenting dreamers* (1994) reconsidered the history of Marxist government. His writings have been collected in *Poetry Hotel: selected poems 1963–1985* (1985), *The Joe Rosenblatt reader* (1995), and *The voluptuous gardener: the collected art and writing of Joe Rosenblatt 1973–1996* (1996). *Parrot fever* (2002) is a long poem inspired by his rage when Tuco, a West African parrot owned by his friend, the writer Brian Brett and his wife—with whom he was staying on Salt Spring Island, B.C.—'whose piercing shriek caused me to spill my drink in the early hours of the morning':'His primal jungle ululation, a seismic weapon / jarred my hand splattering my precious liquor / which slowly trickled across the weeping table.' The book is a visual feast, with stunning collages in colour by Michel Christensen on every black page and the poem's stanzas appearing in various colours— the poem and collages together producing a surrealistic extravaganza. Rosenblatt has also

published two volumes of memoirs, *Escape from the glue factory: a memoir of a paranormal Toronto childhood* (1985) and *The kissing goldfish of Siam* (1989), part memoir, part analysis, and part manifesto. *The lunatic muse: essays and reflections* (2008)—from which the anecdote above about Brian Brett's parrot was taken— includes discussions of troubled poets (MacEWEN, John Clare, Christopher Smart, Sylvia Plath) and a tribute to Rosenblatt's mentor, Milton ACORN. *Dog* (2008), by Rosenblatt and Catherine Owen, is a collection of sonnets about (what else?) dogs, with photographs by Karen Moe. See *Joe Rosenblatt: essays on his works* (2006) edited by Linda ROGERS.

Ross, Malcolm (1911–2002). Born in Fredericton, New Brunswick, he was educated at the University of New Brunswick (B.A., 1933), the University of Toronto (M.A., 1934), and Cornell University (Ph.D., 1941). He taught at the University of Manitoba (1945–50); Queen's University, Kingston (1950–60), when he was editor of *Queen's Quarterly* (1953–6); Trinity College, University of Toronto (1962–8); and Dalhousie University, Halifax (1968–82), where he became Professor Emeritus. He received many honorary degrees and was appointed an Officer of the Order of Canada. His books include several scholarly works and, on Canadian subjects, *Our sense of identity* (1954) and *The arts in Canada* (1958). But Ross is best known for being the first General Editor (1958–78) of the NEW CANADIAN LIBRARY, inaugurating this landmark series—which became the cornerstone for the study and dissemination of Canadian literature of the past and present— in order to provide texts for the study of Canadian literature in universities. See also CONFEDERATION POETS.

Ross, Sinclair (1908–96). Born on a homestead near Prince Albert, Saskatchewan, one of three siblings, James Sinclair Ross (familiarly known as Jim) grew up on prairie farms where his mother worked as a housekeeper after the breakdown of her marriage. Leaving high school after grade eleven, Ross worked as a bank clerk for the Union Bank of Canada (later the Royal Bank) in a succession of small towns in Saskatchewan before being transferred to Winnipeg in 1933 and then to Montreal in 1946. Apart from four years in the Canadian army (1942–6), when he was stationed in England, he remained with the bank until his retirement in 1968. He then lived for some years in Greece and Spain, returning to Canada in 1980 and settling in Vancouver, where he suffered declining health related to advancing Parkinson's disease. Sinclair Ross was appointed a Member of the Order of Canada in 1992.

Ross produced a substantial body of work that is more integrated than is usually acknowledged. His four novels—*As for me and my house* (1941, NCL), *The well* (1958, rpr. 2001), *Whir of gold* (1970, rpr. 2001), and *Sawbones memorial* (1974, rpr. 2001)—and eighteen short stories published between 1934 and 1972, feature both rural and urban settings and themes, but quite consistently focus on alienated, imaginative, and often artistic characters, many of them young boys or men, who experience social pressures and strictures as oppressive, and struggle to nurture a sensibility seemingly at odds with outside demands, particularly for conformity to gender expectations. His short stories were collected in *The lamp at noon and other stories* (1968, NCL), and *The race and other stories* (2nd edn 1993), edited and introduced by Lorraine McMullen. His early stories—such as 'No other way' (1934), 'The lamp at noon' (1938), and 'The painted door' (1942)—resonate with realistic detail reflecting the isolation, bone-wearying labour, helplessness in the face of the elements, and psychological strain, especially between husbands and wives, that Ross saw as characterizing life on the Prairies during hard times.

Reflecting these themes as well, AS FOR ME AND MY HOUSE attracted little critical attention until its release in a NEW CANADIAN LIBRARY edition in 1957 (it is still in the series), but has since become Canada's most critically discussed novel—an amazingly complex, elusive narrative that brings all of its own assertions into question before it closes. The story of Philip Bentley, a small-town minister during the Depression who is also (apparently) a frustrated artist, is told through the diary of his pinched and equally thwarted wife. While the story does deal with the artist's struggle to survive and express himself in a narrow, claustrophobic, critical, and hypocritical environment, it simultaneously—because of the rich ambiguities that surround Mrs Bentley's telling of the tale, and her agenda in doing so—suggests the provisionality of all truths, even those social and environmental constructions that at first seem so unassailably self-evident in this novel. (See *Sinclair Ross's 'As for me and my house': five decades of criticism* [1991] edited by David Stouck.) Ross's middle two novels, arising out of his own urban experience and his fascination with 'outlaws' and misfits,

were less well received. *The well*, set in Saskatchewan, is the story of a young fugitive from Montreal who is morally strengthened by spending a summer on a prairie farm. As his memories of his street gang recede and he manages to resist pressure to commit a second crime, it is clear that farm work, especially with horses, offers him a framework for spiritual renewal. *Whir of gold*, set in Montreal, portrays the near downfall of a down-and-out aspiring clarinetist from Saskatchewan, who is susceptible to the corrupting influence of a fellow roomer. His final rejection of criminal life is due less to the love of a generous woman than to the strength of his dream of becoming a musician—a dream connected to his memories of his farm family and the spirited horse he loved as a boy. Though often dismissed as melodramatic and sentimental, both novels explore Ross's most persistent themes, and invite revisionary critical thinking, particularly in the light of the now-public knowledge of Ross's homosexuality and the ways in which these novels draw together a particular constellation of elements (young men, artistic leanings, work with horses, and the ambiguities that surround prairie life and farm work for such young people) whose exploration is likely to shed new light on the rest of Ross's work. His fourth novel, *Sawbones memorial*, is in many ways a return to the territory of *As for me and my house*. Set in 'Upward', Sask., in 1948, the narrative reflects a single evening, during a retirement party for the town doctor that coincides with the opening of a long-awaited hospital named in his honour. Comprised of unlinked snippets—dialogue, speeches, interior monologues, and songs—it is, like its antecedent, a profoundly disquieting story, wherein the doctor's public capitulation to Upward's norms and conventions has conferred on him a level of social power and prestige that is undercut by the evidence of secrecy, deviation, dishonesty, and sheer rebellion that are made evident through the unmediated 'bits and pieces' that make up this text, and that seem to indicate the existence of contestatory elements just below the surface of any seemingly orderly—but essentially repressive—social entity. This novel also testifies to Ross's abiding interest in narrative experiment and his debt to European writers, such as Proust and Claude Mauriac, on whose *Diner en ville* Ross's novel was modelled.

See *Sinclair Ross* (2nd edn 1991) by Lorraine McMullen; Keath FRASER's *As for me and my body: a memoir of Sinclair Ross* (1997), which argues for a reconsideration of Ross's work in the light of his homosexuality and personal sexual history. *As for Sinclair Ross* (2005) by David Stouck is a substantial, authoritative biography. Stouck knew Ross in his late years (calling him Jim) and learned that he was actually bisexual, having had sexual relations with women; on pages 282–3 there is an interesting exchange, in Vancouver in 1992, between Mavis GALLANT and 'Jimmy' Ross about writing stories. See also *Sinclair Ross and his works* (1990) edited by Morton Ross and *Sinclair Ross: an annotated bibliography* (1981) edited by David Latham.

Ross, W.W.E. (1894–1966). Born in Peterborough, Ontario, William Wrightson Eustace Ross studied geophysics at the University of Toronto. He returned from England after the Great War to begin a long career as a geophysicist at the Dominion Magnetic Observatory, Agincourt, Ont. He contributed his first imagist poems in 1928 to *The Dial* and *Poetry* (Chicago). He published many of these in *Laconics* (1930) and in the less-interesting *Sonnets* (1932). However, despite an admiring review by Marianne Moore (*Poetry* 35, 1931), he was not recognized as Canada's first imagist poet until a retrospective collection, *Experiment 1923–29* (1956), appeared, edited by Raymond SOUSTER, who also co-edited with John Robert COLOMBO *Shapes and sounds* (1968), a selection of Ross's poems with a memoir by Barry CALLAGHAN. In Ross's spare, vertically narrow poems, the inquiring spirit of the New World seeks release from old sentiments, customs, and poetic conventions. Spurning the cliché of the 'old graveyards of Europe', Ross seeks 'something of the sharper tang of Canada' in the surface reflections and dark shadows of pine-surrounded lakes, where reality is recognized as profound and mysterious. The modern poet of the New World seeks illumination by objectifying the ordinary sensations of sight and sound. His explorations of the land of lake and loon thereby serve as metaphors for illumination and rejuvenation. Barry Callaghan edited, with an introductory memoir, and his EXILE EDITIONS published *Irrealities, sonnets, & laconics* (2003), a collection of Ross's poems, the 'irrealities' being his surrealist poems.

Ross's correspondence with A.J.M. SMITH, edited by Michael E. Darling in *Essays on Canadian writing* 16 (1979–80), reveals his virtuosity with forty-two parodies of American, British, and Canadian poets, including a self-parody. See also Bruce Whiteman's edition,

A literary friendship: the correspondence of Ralph Gustafson and W.W.E. Ross (1984).

Roughing it in the bush; or, Forest life in Canada (2 vols, London, 1852, NCL, CEECT). This series of autobiographical sketches by Susanna MOODIE describes her experiences, and those of her husband and their growing family, during their first seven years in Upper Canada (Ontario). The first volume (1832–4) deals with their arrival in Canada and settlement on a partially cleared farm in Hamilton Township, near Port Hope; the second (1834–9) dramatizes their struggle to wrest a living from the uncleared, largely unarable farm north of Lakefield that was part of Lt John Moodie's military land grant. Loosely chronological, the chapters are organized into subjects appropriate to the then-popular form of the sketch: studies of unusual or eccentric characters ('John Monaghan', 'Brian the still-hunter'), descriptions of local customs ('The logging bee', 'The borrowing system'), anecdotal accounts of special places or events ('Quebec' and 'The Outbreak' [of the 1837 Rebellion]), and accounts of outings or adventures ('The walk to Dummer', 'A trip to Stony Lake') are designed to provide entertainment and variety and to celebrate the genteel values, patriotism, and spirit of progressiveness that for Moodie were inherent in her English middle-class roots. She also included a good deal of her own poetry, much of which she had written in the backwoods, and added several more documentary chapters by her husband ('The land jobber', 'The village hotel', and 'Canadian sketches', the latter added to the second English edition in late 1852) and by her brother Samuel Strickland.

The importance and prominence of this work among nineteenth-century 'Canadian' books follows from Susanna Moodie's intense emotional engagement in her experiences. She sought to increase narrative interest by placing herself near the centre of all she described, much as if she were the heroine of her own autobiographical novel. In the process she offered a surprisingly candid record of her fascination with what she had encountered during what she called 'this great epoch of our lives'. Writing of her adventures nearly a decade later, and well aware of the extent to which her sister Catharine Parr TRAILL's optimism had characterized *The BACKWOODS OF CANADA*, she wished to mark not only the various kinds of alienation and discomfort she had experienced as a pioneer but also her engagement in and commitment to the future of the rising colony. The book's richness of representation owes much to her comedic ability in describing and puzzling over the curious individuals she met in the backwoods, and to her trenchant, no-nonsense examination of pioneering experience, an outlook that gives the book a strong cast of documentary authority. Its influence can be measured in part by the extent to which contemporary writers—for instance, Margaret ATWOOD in the poems that make up The JOURNALS OF SUSANNA MOODIE (1970) and Carol SHIELDS in her novel Small ceremonies (1976)—have been fascinated by the complexity of Moodie's voice and vision. While ostensibly written to warn members of her class not to subject themselves to conditions of wilderness and radical deculturation, Moodie's sketches suggest, finally, not so much an aversion to her experiences as a fascination with and deep involvement in them that no amount of genteel condemnation can effectively diminish. This tension is rooted in Moodie's English background and romantic temperament; it also finds force in the fact that even as Moodie lamented much of what happened to her, she recognized the psychological and emotional importance of those events in the lives of her husband and herself and sought to measure how she had been tested and how much she had grown.

Many of the sketches were composed specifically for Canadian readers and were first published in The LITERARY GARLAND and in The Victoria Magazine in 1847. Much of the book's negative cast about Canada (see the lengthy articulations of her nostalgia and the introduction of language appropriate to a highly genteel readership) was added later for the book's English audience. A sequel, Life in the clearings versus the bush (London, 1853; 1989, NCL; rpr. 2010), presents a more consistently positive view of the worth of settling in 'this great and rising country'.

Roughing it in the bush went through several editions in England and the United States in the nineteenth century. The influential NEW CANADIAN LIBRARY edition of 1962 edited by Carl KLINCK introduced Canadian students to Moodie, but the volume suffered because of its omissions. The current NCL version provides the whole text (of Richard Bentley's edition of Dec. 1852). However, students interested in a close study of Moodie's intentions, the book's evolution and textual history, and the historical sources of the events and people Moodie describes, should consult the CENTRE FOR EDITING EARLY CANADIAN TEXTS edition of 1988 edited by Carl Ballstadt.

Roy, André (b. 1944). Born in Montreal, he edited the Prose du jour series for Éditions du Jour and the Écrire series for Éditions de l'Aurore; was editor-in-chief of the literary magazines Spirale and Hobo-Québec, of which he was a founder; and has written much film criticism, publishing two collections of his reviews. But Roy is best known as a Modernist poet, with well over twenty collections to his credit, notably his Passions cycle, written in a filmic form: Les passions du Samedi (1979), Petit supplément aux passions (1980), and Monsieur Désir (1981). All are represented in The passions of Mister Desire (selected poems) (1986), translated by Daniel Sloate, which concludes with The beds of America (Les lits d'Amérique, 1983). Dealing frankly with homosexuality in a compressed style, a sensitive and well-read narrator describes the amorous gestures and fantasies of male love in all their everyday immediacy.

Roy, Gabrielle (1909–83). Born in Saint-Boniface, Manitoba, she was educated there and at the Winnipeg Normal School. After teaching for some years in rural Manitoba, she travelled to England and France, where she studied drama and began to write. When war forced her return to Canada, she continued to write stories and articles in Montreal, meanwhile observing the people of the Saint-Henri district, who were to provide the material for Bonheur d'occasion (1945), her immensely successful first novel. She was elected to the Royal Society of Canada in 1947 and in the same year married Dr Marcel Carbotte. Made a Companion of the Order of Canada in 1967, she was also awarded the Molson Prize (1978) for the entire body of her work. She lived in Quebec City until she died.

Gabrielle Roy's prairie background and passion for the Canadian Arctic gave her writing a breadth and an absence of regional pettiness not common among French-Canadian writers. Fully bilingual, she hesitated at first about whether to write in English or in her native French. She was a fine craftsman with a style that is at once simple, strong, and delicately poetic. Her characters are usually rather humble people, whom she handled without falsity or over-emotion so that they become symbols of humanity's quest for a joy that is often ephemeral, of persistent courage and striving for an understanding with one's fellows that is seldom more than fleeting and often too late. Roy was highly adept at portraying strong women characters like the mothers in Bonheur d'occasion and La petite *poule d'eau*. Awarded the Prix Fémina, *Bonheur d'occasion* was the first Canadian work to win a major French literary prize. The first English version was translated by Hannah Josephson as *The TIN FLUTE* (1947, GGA). A new translation (1980) by Alan Brown was published in a deluxe boxed edition with two drawings of the author by Harold Town; this text was reprinted in the NEW CANADIAN LIBRARY. The central figure of Roy's other Montreal novel, *Alexandre Chenevert* (1955)—translated by Harry Binsse as *The cashier* (1955, NCL)—is a middle-aged, emotionally inhibited bank teller who is tormented by his inability to express love in his own life and by his uselessness in face of the miseries of which he is informed daily by radio and newspapers. He dies a slow death from cancer, but learns finally that love exists, even for him, and that his life has not been as valueless as he believed.

Three Manitoba books—all linked short stories rather than novels—make imaginative use of material from Roy's own past. *La petite poule d'eau* (1950)—translated by Binsse as *Where nests the water hen* (1950, NCL)—is a poetic account of life in a remote settlement in northern Manitoba; in 1971 it was published in a deluxe edition with twenty-four original woodcuts by Jean-Paul Lemieux. The lively and varied stories in *Rue Deschambault* (1955)—translated by Binsse as *Street of riches* (1957, GGA, NCL)—cover a girl's growth from childhood to adolescence in Saint-Boniface among people of every nation, pioneers of the West. *La route d'Altamont* (1966)—translated by Joyce MARSHALL as *The road past Altamont* (1966, NCL)—provides more intense insight into the same period in this girl's life, focusing on the girl, her mother, and grandmother in four connected stories that describe a circle of time in which the generations succeed and pass one another, meeting in rare flashes of understanding, and in which journeys always lead back to their beginnings.

In *La montagne secrète* (1961)—translated by Binsse as *The hidden mountain* (1962)—a young painter's Arctic journey and the mountain that he finds, loses, and finds again, frame a parable of the artist's lifelong quest for his subject and his efforts to express it. The four stories of *La rivière sans repos* (1970) use the Arctic background more explicitly to depict the Inuit in a state of transition, drawn without choice into the white man's world and still uneasy with his gifts: his medicine that uselessly prolongs life, a wheelchair, the telephone. In the long title story—which was published separately in a translation by Joyce Marshall as *Windflower* (1970, NCL)—a child is born of a brief brutal meeting between an American soldier and a young Inuit girl. In her efforts to bring up and keep her son, the mother shifts between white and Inuit ways, not quite at home with either, and loses the boy finally to the white man and his wars. *Cet été qui chantait* (1972)—translated by Marshall as *Enchanted summer* (1976)—is a collection of nineteen stories and sketches, many very brief, each adding a dab of light or intensity to the picture of a summer in Charlevoix County in Québec. In two later works Roy dipped again into her Manitoba past to provide new pictures and new insights. *Un jardin au bout du monde* (1975)—translated by Alan Brown as *Garden in the wind* (1977, NCL)—recaptures prairie solitude and multiculturalism in four sensitive and evocative stories. *Ces enfants de ma vie* (1977, GGA)—translated by Brown as *Children of my heart* (1979, rpr. 2000 in a film tie-in)—returned once more to Roy's days as a teacher in a series of narrative sketches, each centring on a single child in a lonely prairie hamlet or a Winnipeg slum.

Fragiles lumières de la terre (1978)—translated by Brown as *The fragile lights of earth* (1982)—is a selection of Roy's non-fiction from 1942 to 1970: early journalistic pieces describing prairie immigrant communities (Doukhobors, Sudeten Germans, and Ukrainians, among others), and some later writing in which she expressed her debt, both literary and personal, to her prairie past. It is invaluable to students of her work. Roy also wrote three books for children: *Ma vache Bossy* (1976), translated by Brown as *My cow Bossy* (1986); *Courte-Queue* (1979), translated by Brown as *Cliptail* (1980); and *L'espagnole et la pékinoise*, published posthumously (1986) and translated by Patricia Claxton as *The tortoise shell and the pekinese* (1989). Other posthumous publications were *La détresse et l'echantement* (1984), translated by Patricia Claxton as *Enchantment and sorrow* (1987), an autobiography of Roy's life until 1939 that was incomplete on her death; and *Ma chère petite soeur, lettres à Bernadette 1943–1970* (1988), translated by Claxton as *Letters to Bernadette* (1990). Claxton also translated the 1996 French edition of the illuminating *Gabrielle Roy: a life* (1999) by François Ricard, who was a friend during the last decade of Roy's life. This full-scale biography is more stringent and on occasion more precise than *Enchantment and sorrow*; it is also affectionate, and warmly appreciative of Roy as writer and human being. See *Intimate strangers: the letters of Margaret Laurence and Gabrielle Roy* (2004) edited by Paul G. Socken, and *In translation: the Gabrielle Roy–Joyce Marshall correspondence* (2006) edited by Jane Everett.

Rule, Jane (1931–2007). Born in Plainfield, New Jersey, Jane Vance Rule spent her childhood in various parts of the American mid-west and California. She received a B.A. in English (1952) from Mills College, California, and spent the following year studying seventeenth-century literature at University College, London. From 1954 to 1956 she taught English and biology at Concord Academy, Massachusetts, where she met Helen Sonthoff, with whom she has lived since 1956. In that year she moved to Vancouver and worked at the University of British Columbia—as assistant director of International House (1958–9) and periodically as lecturer in English or creative writing—until 1976, when she moved to Galiano Island, British Columbia, where she made her home until she died in 2007, the year she was appointed a Member of the Order of Canada.

Rule is perhaps best known for her unapologetic and clear-eyed writing on lesbian themes. Her first two novels focus on contrasting types of relations between women. In *Desert of the heart* (1964, rpr. 1991), set in Reno, Nevada, where the seemingly sterile but startlingly beautiful desert provides a powerful contrasting image to the Vanity Fair commercialism of the casino, two women overcome their fears and prejudices and start living together; the novel is structured on their alternating points of view. Donna Deitch's film of this novel appeared as *Desert hearts* in 1986. *This is not for you* (1970, rpr. 2005), which takes the form of a long, self-justifying letter that is not meant to be mailed, portrays a woman so trapped by her conventional attitudes and desire to conform to social norms that she withholds her love for another woman. It would be a mistake, however, to categorize Rule as being interested in lesbian subjects that appeal to a specialized minority. She writes novels of social realism that naturally include both homosexuals and heterosexuals, but in her later novels the central focus is not on any one sort of character. She matches fictional form to the structure of society as she experiences it—not as a hierarchy but as a democratic 'concert' of characters, all of whose voices are given equal attention. In her third novel, *Against the season* (1971), the small-town setting draws characters into a group where, despite violence, pain, and a guilt imposed by the dead as well as the living, affection and love triumph. In *The young in one another's arms* (1977, rev. 2005) residents of a Vancouver boarding house slated for demolition form a voluntary 'family' and work together to establish a restaurant on Galiano Island. *Contract with the world* (1980) is Rule's most successful experiment in making the form of the novel reflect its egalitarian philosophy. Though the events concerning the life and work of six Vancouver artists are told almost entirely in chronological sequence, they are described from a different point of view in each chapter: the reader's view of each character is subtly changed by the perceptions of the others. This multiple voice also presents a variety of aesthetic theories and comments on the relations of art and the artist to society. In these three novels voluntary communities offer protection against stultifying isolation and such hostile outside forces as police harassment, mindless commercial exploitation, and philistinism. Tempering their serious concerns are a gentle sense of humour and a sharp ear for contemporary speech, with literary associations.

Rule's last two novels (she declared her retirement from writing in 1990, caused in part by severe arthritis) include in their study of communities a clear-eyed and sensitive focus on aging. In *Memory board* (1987), a retired doctor in her sixties is reconciled with the twin brother from whom she has been estranged for decades, to some extent because of her lesbianism. Her lover suffers from loss of memory, while the brother must reconstruct his memories of the past in order to come to terms with a new phase of his life. The new sharing of their lives is set in counterpoint to the more conventional families of his children and grandchildren. *After the fire* (1989) tells of five women, each of whom—from widowhood, divorce, or personal choice—learns to live alone, among a community of islanders who recognize the need for mutual support and for shared rituals to mark deaths and disasters.

Rule has been a prolific writer of short stories, published in three collections: *Themes for diverse instruments* (1975), *Outlander* (1981), and *Inland passage and other stories* (1985). The title story of the first is a stylistic tour de force, outlining the branches of a family tree in patterns evocative of an orchestral piece. Several stories in each volume concern children, whose characters Rule creates convincingly and without sentimentality; this is especially apparent in a related group of family stories in *Inland passage*. The stories in *Outlander* all deal with some form of lesbian experience, whether of survivors, as in the title piece, or of the deeply damaged, as in the vivid, painful story 'In the attic of the house'; the volume ends with a selection of Rule's polemical columns from the newspaper *Body politic*, many of which are also included in the collection of essays *A hot-eyed moderate* (1985, rpr. 1993).

Rule's work consistently presents love between women as one of the many natural and acceptable forms of human expression; the question of why this viewpoint was seldom projected in the past—even by homosexual writers—is addressed in her commissioned book *Lesbian images* (1975), whose introductory essay surveys attitudes to female sexuality over the centuries and condemns the prejudices fostered by churchmen and psychologists. Its chapters on individual writers such as Radclyffe Hall, Colette, Violette Leduc, May Sarton, and Vita Sackville-West are pioneering studies of the sometimes tortured, often veiled, forms in which these women created images of their love for other women.

Jane Rule's account of her own life appears in the Gale autobiography series Contemporary Authors 18 (1994) and she appears in the film about her life and work entitled *Fiction and Other Truths* (1994). See Marilyn R. Schuster, *Passionate communities: reading lesbian resistance in Jane Rule's fiction* (1999).

Russell, Ted (1904–77). Born and reared in Coley's Point, Conception Bay, Newfoundland, Edward Russell completed his high-school education at Bishop Field College in St John's, and later qualified to become a teacher at Memorial University College. He taught in a number of Newfoundland communities between 1920 and 1935, starting his career in remote Pass Island in Hermitage Bay, which was possibly the model for the imaginary outport of Pigeon Inlet in his Uncle Mose stories. In 1935 Russell joined the magistracy and eight years later became director of co-operation with the Newfoundland government. Part of his responsibilities in this position was to write co-operative tracts and make radio broadcasts. From 1949 to 1951 he was a member of J.R. Smallwood's administration. Subsequently he worked as an insurance salesman, broadcaster, writer, and teacher. When, late in life, he returned to teaching, he gave up what he called the 'hobby' of writing.

Russell is best known for his Uncle Mose stories, which he wrote and narrated himself on the Canadian Broadcasting Corporation in St John's, beginning in 1954. Five selections

from these stories were published: *The chronicles of Uncle Mose* (1975), *Tales from Pigeon Inlet* (1977), and three titled *The best of Ted Russell* (1982–8), all edited by his daughter, Elizabeth Russell Miller. In these sketches of outport life, Russell created a gallery of intriguing local characters and summoned up a way of life that was fast changing. He was not opposed to change; he had no affection for what he once called the 'ignorance and isolation' of Newfoundland's past. But neither did he wish to rush towards some vulgar prosperity. He wanted a renovated, modern Newfoundland, with the best retained from the old values. His stories, at their best, are gentle, whimsical, and shrewd evocations of the lives of ordinary people. Russell also wrote radio plays, including *The holdin' ground/Ground swell* (1990) edited by Elizabeth Russell Miller, further expressions of his love for the people in the Newfoundland outports. See Miller's *The life and times of Ted Russell* (1981).

Rybczynski, Witold (b. 1943). Born in Edinburgh, of Polish parentage, he was educated in Jesuit schools in England and Montreal, and at McGill University (B.Arch., 1966; M. Arch, 1972). He practised as an architect from 1970 to 1982 and was a professor of architecture at McGill from 1974 to 1993. Since 1994 he has been Meyerson Professor of Urbanism at the University of Pennsylvania. Drawing upon his knowledge and practise of architecture, and enlarging the range of his study and thinking to become a cultural and social historian, Rybczynski has achieved another career as a writer of books that enter the realm of literature for the clarity, wit, and ease with which he illuminates a wide range of subjects. *Paper heroes: a review of appropriate technology* (1980) was followed by *Taming the tiger: the struggle to control technology* (1983), which is in two sections— 'The shock of the machine' and 'The environment of technology'—and demonstrates the real connection between technology and humans, reminding the reader that 'mass production is precisely how nature reproduces itself' and that people and machines exist 'not in two different worlds, but at two ends of the same continuum ... . the struggle to control technology has all along been a struggle to control ourselves.' Rybczynski's masterpiece, *Home: a short history of an idea* (1986, rpr. 1987), discusses, in historical terms, a subject that evokes many emotions. For example, it was in Holland, where the idea of family life was most central, that the concept of 'home' appeared a hundred years earlier than elsewhere, not only as a house, but also as 'everything that was in it and around it, as well as the people, and the sense of satisfaction and contentment that all these conveyed'. Also examined are past and present ideas of such things as furniture (particularly chairs), efficiency, ventilation, mechanization, decoration, style, domesticity, and comfort, which 'incorporates many transparent layers of meaning—privacy, ease, convenience— some of which are buried deeper than others.' *The most beautiful house in the world* (1989, rpr. 1990)—the title refers to 'the one that you build for yourself'—grew out of the author's plan to build a boatbuilding workshop in Québec near the Vermont border; this changed to a long shed, then a barn; and when that was built—by Ryczynski, his wife, and a friend—the barn was turned into a house, which was made to look like a home by the addition of a small portico. The accounts of these stages of development are complemented by the author's characteristic informal reflections on subjects that connect in his mind with his building experience, from the Chinese reverence for the natural landscape, feng shui (wind and water), to famous homes and their builders (Palladio, Sir Walter Scott, Robert Louis Stevenson, Samuel Clemens, William Randolph Hearst, and Frank Lloyd Wright). The first pages of *Waiting for the weekend* (1991), a study of leisure, describe the author's enjoyment of Vivaldi's *The Four Seasons* and lead from the influence of the changing seasons on everyday life to 'the rhythmic cadence of the week' as experienced in his youth, to 'the sovereignty of the weekend'—which is then examined in a multitude of aspects, considering that 'Most North Americans enjoy about 130 days off each year.' In his Introduction to *Looking around: a journey through architecture* (1992, rpr. 1993) Rybczynski says that he has no interest in reviewing buildings (stating his reasons), but likes writing about buildings 'in a different way—as places rather than objects, and as part of a larger social and cultural context rather than as diverting works of art.' It is in this context that he examines architecture loosely under the section headings 'Homes and Houses', 'Special Places', and 'The Art of Building'—demolishing many preconceptions along the way.'If European cities seemed like beautiful architectural museums, our cities were more like unfinished building sites where each generation was free to try its hand.' This statement, in the Preface to *City life: urban expectations in a new world* (1995, rpr. 1996), underlies Rybczynski's discussion of

the planning and characteristics of Montreal and many American cities, with references to those aspects of London, Paris, and Rome. The last chapter, 'The Best of Both Worlds', accounts for his move from rural Hemmingford to a city, Philadelphia—but to a garden suburb, Chestnut Hill. *One good turn: a natural history of the screwdriver and the screw* (2000, rpr. 2002) is a delightful and fascinating history that, surprisingly, begins with Archimedes. Rybczynski also wrote *A place for art: the architecture of the National Gallery of Canada* (1993) and *A clearing in the distance: Frederick Law Olmsted and America in the 19th century* (1999, rpr. 2000), a study of the famous landscape architect—most notably of Central Park, New York. *The look of architecture* (2001), a lecture in the annual series sponsored by the New York Public Library and Oxford University Press, discusses style and fashion in architecture and examines the work of a number of modern architects with these characteristics of a distinctive manner. Before even reading *The perfect house: a journey with the renaissance master Andrea Palladio* (2002), it can be recognized that this illuminating and delightful book is the consummate union of subject and writer. The long subtitle of Rybczynski's next book pretty well tells you what it is about: *Last harvest: how a cornfield became New Daleville: real estate development in America from George Washington to the builders of the twenty-first century, and why we live in houses anyway* (2007): the charming, intimate account of the creation of a new residential subdivision in rural Pennsylvania, an hour or so west of Philadelphia.

Ryerson Press, The. In 1828, when Canadian Methodists severed their formal ties with the American Methodist Episcopal Church, they determined at the same meeting to secure a press and to begin a journal and book room. Soon after its foundation in Toronto in 1829, the Methodist Book Room began to issue denominational materials, and by 1835 general trade books. In 1919 the name 'Ryerson Press' was adopted in honour of the first editor, the Methodist minister and educator Egerton Ryerson (1803–82). After 1829, for half a century, the publication of general books was undertaken haphazardly. A coherent publishing policy emerged only with the election of William Briggs in 1879 as Book Steward; his astute business sense enabled him to amass, through agencies for British and American firms, sufficient revenue to build a Canadian list. W.H. Withrow, longtime editor of Sunday school publications, was the first editor who actively sought out writers. Since the chief market for his books was in Sunday school libraries, he depended largely on fellow clerics for wholesome narratives, such as John Carroll's *My boy life* (1882) and Egerton Ryerson Young's *By canoe and dog-train among the Cree and Saulteaux Indians* (1890). Edward S. Caswell, who joined the Press as a reader in 1881 and eventually headed the book department, made contact with a wider literary circle. His initiative fostered such books as Catharine Parr TRAILL's *Pearls and pebbles* (1894), *The poems of Wilfred Campbell* (1905), and *The collected poems of Isabella Valancy Crawford* (1905), along with Canadian editions of several of Charles G.D. ROBERTS' collections of poetry. After Caswell's departure in 1909, Briggs depended more and more on agency titles, virtually allowing his Canadian publishing program to lapse by the time of his retirement in 1918. Lorne PIERCE, who was appointed in 1920 as literary adviser and in 1922 as editor, was determined to restore the Press to its former position as the foremost publisher of Canadian writers. He overcame opposition within his own organization partly by building up a very profitable line of school texts. His great achievement, especially during his first decade, and again after the Second World War under the sympathetic regime of C.H. Dickinson as book steward, was to start many promising authors—such as Frederick Philip GROVE, Earle BIRNEY, Dorothy LIVESAY, and Louis DUDEK—on careers that led them eventually to other publishers. In 1970, mainly through losses incurred in connection with the purchase of an expensive but unsatisfactory colour press, The Ryerson Press was sold to the American firm McGraw-Hill.

Ryga, George (1932–87). Born in Deep Creek, in the Athabasca region of northern Alberta, he was raised in a Ukrainian farming community there. His formal education consisted of seven years in a one-room schoolhouse and a brief period at the University of Texas in 1949, after which he worked as a farm labourer, in construction, and at a radio station in Edmonton. In 1962 he decided he could make his living as a writer, and in the following year he and his wife Norma, with their children, moved to Summerland, British Columbia, where they resided until his death. His writings included the plays and novels for which he is best remembered, along with essays, short stories, poetry, and film scripts.

Ryga's dramatic technique often blends realism, poetry, dance and song, and juxtaposes past and present, though the surrealistic devices in his plays are not always successful. Invariably he sided with the oppressed and the exploited, and spoke out against injustices in Canadian society. Three of his early plays, included in *The ecstasy of Rita Joe and other plays* (1971, rpr. 1991), edited by Brian Parker, contain heroes who are rebelling against their society or who are trapped in almost unbearable social situations. The one-act play *Indian* (1967) vividly portrays a Canadian Native labourer harassed by a heartless employer and an impersonal government official. *The ECSTASY OF RITA JOE* (1970), in which the heroine is unable to live by the old ways of her people or adapt to the white man's ways in the city, offers a much fuller and grimmer presentation of the Canadian Aboriginal's plight. Commissioned by the Vancouver Playhouse for Canada's centennial year, and starring Frances Hyland in the title role and Chief Dan George as her father, *Rita Joe* was the first play in English presented in the theatre of the National Arts Centre, Ottawa, in 1969; like many other of Ryga's plays, it has since been performed internationally, often in Europe. A less-enduring play, though very popular when first produced at the Vancouver Playhouse in 1969, is *Grass and wild strawberries* (1971), which dramatizes the conflicts between the hippie culture of the 1960s and middle-class society; but it is often a disharmonious mixture of film projection, dance, song, dialogue, and recorded vocal and musical sound. *Captives of the faceless drummer* (1971), commissioned by the Vancouver Playhouse for production in Feb. 1971, centres on the kidnapping of a Canadian diplomat by a group of young revolutionaries—there are many parallels with the October Crisis of 1970. When the board of directors of the Playhouse reversed its decision to produce the play, there was a bitter controversy during which the artistic director, David Gardner, was dismissed. It was subsequently produced in Vancouver, Toronto, and Lennoxville, Québec. *Sunrise on Sarah* (1973) is the somewhat confusing story of a troubled woman and her search for liberation from the ghosts that haunt her—her parents and the men in her past. *Paracelsus*, staged at the Vancouver Playhouse in 1986, has more dramatic power, though the production was not well received. It is a wide-ranging historical drama about the pioneering sixteenth-century Swiss physician and alchemist, whose relation to the present is heightened by scenes in a contemporary hospital. It was published in *Two plays* (1982), along with Ryga's adaptation of Aeschylus's *Prometheus bound*, with an introduction by Mavor MOORE. *Ploughmen of the glacier* (1977) and *Seven hours to sundown* (1977) show Ryga's continuing preoccupation with the quality of life in Canada. *Ploughmen* examines realistically 'the myth of the men who made the West' through an old prospector, Volcanic Brown, who represents the adventurous, exploitative spirit of the gold seekers, and a retired newspaperman, the somewhat dissolute but human Lowery. *Seven hours to sundown* is based on a confrontation in Ryga's own town between officials wanting to demolish a heritage building and a citizens' group (of which Ryga was a member) wishing to preserve it for use as a cultural centre. Though some of the characters lack sufficient motivation and the ending is inconclusive, it is a strong statement of Ryga's concern and involvement in social, political, and cultural issues. Some of these issues are touched upon again in a one-act play, *Laddie boy*, published in *Transactions I: short plays* (1978), edited by Edward Peck. Set in a Halifax jail, it gives, in Ryga's best realistic style, a cameo picture of the gulf between rich and poor in Canada. *A letter to my son* (1982) is the story of Ukrainian immigrant Ivan Lepa's struggles to adjust to life in Canada. *Portrait of Angelica* (1984), published in *A letter to my son*, and produced at the Banff School of Fine Arts in the summer of 1973, presents a picture of the people in a Mexican town seen through the eyes of a Canadian tourist, Danny Baker. Reminiscent of Dylan Thomas's *Under Milk Wood*, it is Ryga's most mellow play. Other plays by Ryga that were performed but are as yet unpublished are *Nothing but a man* (in 1967), *Just an ordinary person* (in 1968), *The last of the gladiators* (in 1976, an adaptation of his novel *Night desk*), *Jeremiah's place* (1978), a children's play, and *One more for the road* (in 1985). *The other plays* (2004) is a collection of sixteen plays (excluding *Rita Joe*) edited by James Hoffman. Ryga published four novels: *Hungry hills* (1963, rpr. 1977), *Ballad of a stonepicker* (1966, rpr. 1976), *Night desk* (1976), and *In the shadow of the vulture* (1985). *Hungry hills* is the story of an unloved youth, Snit Mandolin, who links up with another outcast, Johnny Swift, and they make their way as best they can, honestly and dishonestly. *George Ryga's HUNGRY HILLS* is a 2009 film adapted by screenwriter Gary Fisher and directed by Rob King. *Ballad of a stonepicker* depicts the

struggles, physical and psychological, of a sensitive man who has sacrificed much of his life by staying with his parents on the family farm so that his younger brother can pursue studies leading to a Rhodes scholarship. *Night desk* takes the form of a rambling monologue by a vibrant, self-centred, riotous, though humane ex-wrestler and fight promoter, Romeo Kuchmir, and brings him to life as a memorable personality. *In the shadow of the vulture* is the story of indentured Mexican workers doing slave labour for Americans in subhuman conditions in a border town. The hero of this heavily symbolic action tale is Sandy Wade, a veteran of the Vietnam war who leads the Mexicans' escape to freedom from their fascist chicken-farmer owner. While in none of these novels was Ryga able to present more than one character in depth, all four are evocative and share an intensity of narration; all are both authentic and suspenseful.

Beyond the crimson morning: reflections from a journey through contemporary China (1979) is a partly fictionalized, impressionistic account of Ryga's visit to China. Two posthumous volumes brought together many of Ryga's unpublished writings. *The Athabasca Ryga* (1990) is a collection of three essays, seven short stories, two short plays, and selections from a novel *The bridge*—which was mostly written before the Rygas moved from Alberta to British Columbia—and a lengthy introduction on Ryga's early life and work by the editor, E. David Gregory. *Summerland* (1992), a much larger collection edited by Ann Kujundzic, includes essays and letters, screen plays and radio plays, short stories, and his final work, a five-page poem entitled appropriately 'Resurrection'. All were written during Ryga's life in Summerland, and are arranged in the book by decade.

Ryga always insisted on the rights of common people, and decried their violation by governments, bureaucracies, and oppressors of whatever origin. Even when he was shunned by the powerful and by the theatrical establishment, he continued to address these issues in eloquent speeches, in briefs to the Canadian government, in his essays, short stories, and novels, and in plays for local theatre groups that shared his concerns. Always direct and confrontational, Ryga had a large following, both of readers and of people who came to his Okanagan home for advice and encouragement. See the authorized biography, *The ecstasy of resistance: a biography of George Ryga* (1995) by James Hoffman.

S

Sagouine, La (1971, Eng. edn 1979). This series of sixteen monologues by Antonine MAILLET—translated with the same title by Luis de Céspedes in 1979—is composed of the reminiscences, grievances, anecdotes, opinions, and homilies of a seventy-two-year-old charwoman, a former prostitute, who is the wife of an Acadian fisherman. A garrulous, indomitable old woman, La Sagouine (freely translated as 'the Slattern') narrates a personal history that forms a mosaic in which generations, social classes, temperaments, and ideologies all find their authentic and rightful place. Expressed in a roughened, coarsened version of old domestic French, the monologues bring her world to life, from her youth to her observations on death, in tones that are sometimes pathetic—she is after all old and ailing—and sometimes laceratingly vengeful. But these qualities are offset by her irreverent humour. La Sagouine is the Acadian sister of Gratien GÉLINAS's Fridolin, both of whom speak in monologues for want of knowing how to converse or behave. First created for radio in Moncton, New Brunswick, a selection of the monologues—brilliantly acted by Viola Léger—has been widely and successfully performed in both French and English since its presentation at the Centre d'essai des auteurs dramatiques in Montreal in Oct. 1972. On stage La Sagouine's colourful language, and the tone and timbre of her voice, are more compelling than her ruddy complexion, grim countenance, and props—mop, pail, clogs, and apron. Faithfully rendering the contradictions in La Sagouine's fascinating character, Léger skilfully endowed her simplicity with complexity.

Saint-Denys-Garneau, Hector de (1912–43). Born in Montreal, he spent his early childhood at the family's manor in Sainte-Catherine-de-Fossambault, and from 1923 lived in Montreal's middle-class Westmount district under the shadow of the Depression. His studies at Collège Saint-Marie were interrupted by an illness that left him with a 'cardiac lesion'. With friends such as André Laurendeau, Robert Élie, Paul Beaulieu, and Jean LE MOYNE he founded a small journal, *La relève*. In 1937 Saint-Denys-Garneau underwent a spiritual crisis that filled him with self-doubt and loneliness. Reported to have once been joyous, even dynamic, he gradually withdrew from contact with others and in 1941 moved to Sainte-Catherine-de-Fossambault, where he died. (While his name has been variously given, the most recent practice is to present it as in this entry.)

Considered to be the founder of modern 'liberated' poetry in Québec, Saint-Denys-Garneau published only one book of poems during his lifetime, *Regards et jeux dans l'espace* (1937), a highly symbolic title for a book that holds a promise of conquering space through poetic vision. Later poems were published posthumously by Robert Élie under the title 'Les solitudes'—a title he thought appropriate—as part of *Poésies complètes—Regards et jeux dans l'espace, Les solitudes* (1949). Some poems were translated by F.R. SCOTT in *Saint-Denys Garneau and Anne Hébert: translations/traductions* (1962, rev. 1978); John GLASSCO translated the *Complete poems of Hector de Saint-Denys Garneau* (1962). Saint-Denys-Garneau's diary of 1935–9, entitled *Journal* (1954), edited by Élie and Le Moyne—an English translation by Glassco was published in 1962—discusses many facets of life, art, and literature; gradually, however especially towards the end, it turns to painful self-analysis.

Influenced perhaps by his experience as a painter and by the Platonic tinge of his philosophical and religious thinking, Saint-Denys-Garneau searched in his poetry for a transforming poetic vision, inaccessible to the materialists who dominated society. This vision, however, was threatened from within and without and led to progressive alienation. The poetry conveys not only the anguish of Saint-Denys-Garneau's personal experience but also his striving for a non-traditional form of expression, its themes and symbols often suggesting isolation from others, even from God, and distrust of himself. Whether his alienation and despair were caused by the moralizing attitudes to sex of Saint-Denys-Garneau's educators; the social, economic, and cultural dispossession experienced by young Québécois intellectuals in the thirties; the pressure of capitalistic English Canada upon Québécois nationhood; or a painful Oedipus complex—Saint-Denys-Garneau the poet has been viewed by his successors as a vanquished hero whose violence was directed towards himself rather than towards the injustices of the world.

St Pierre, Paul (b. 1923). Born in Chicago, he was a columnist for the *Vancouver Sun* from 1947 to 1968 and 1972 to 1979, and was Liberal MP for Coast Chilcotin from 1968 to 1972. He lives in Fort Langley, British Columbia, but has also maintained a residence in Sinaloa, Mexico. St Pierre is beloved as a writer for his tales of the Chilcotin ranching country and its people, both white and Native, 'who have marched to the beat of a different drummer' and are portrayed with affection and humour. (They grew out of his successful CBC-TV series 'Cariboo Country'.) Throughout the classic novel *Breaking Smith's quarter horse* (1966, rpr. 1984), Smith wants Ol Antoine to break his quarter horse, but this never happens; instead we are told about eccentric and agreeable rogues. For example, Gabriel Jimmyboy, who committed a murder, gave himself up, and stood trial in the courthouse at Williams Lake, when things turned to farce: Smith attacks the detested Walter Charlie in the courtroom and is given sixty days; as a witness for the defence Ol Antoine delivers a speech in Chilcotin (with a translator), without ever mentioning Gabriel Jimmyboy, but making a good impression. Samuels, the defence lawyer, in his summing-up, says no expense was too great for the government of Canada to collect its evidence, while it could afford only forty-three cents a day to pay teachers of an Indian child, as Gabriel once was, in a residential school—he also says there were no eyewitnesses. The jury finds the accused not guilty because he was too drunk to know what he was doing. On the last page, when Smith gets out of jail, he simply 'climbed aboard that quarter horse and bucked him out in the usual way. He turned out to be just another horse.' In the first story of *Smith and other events: stories of the Chilcotin* (1983, rpr. 1985) Smith and the other ranchers are told that Ol Antoine has died and they find that the Namko Cattlemen's Association has a surplus of over $1200, enough money to buy him a 'wooden overcoat'. For a handsome coffin Smith gives this sum to the undertaker in Williams Lake, who was saving it for a deceased local rich man. When everything is ready for the funeral and wake, Smith tells Norah, his wife, that in fact Ol Antoine is still alive and will soon arrive to attend his own funeral; it stands to reason that Smith could not lose face with the undertaker by returning the coffin, so he filled it with rocks. St Pierre's other Chilcotin books are *Chilcotin holiday* (1970, rev. 1984)—'a man on a Chilcotin holiday takes only a horse, a rifle, and a shaker of salt' (St Pierre travelled by car)—and

Chilcotin and beyond (1989), both made up of *Sun* columns; and *Boss of the Namko drive* (1965, rpr. 1986), written for young people: the drive is ready to move 200 miles to Williams Lake when Frenchie breaks his leg and his fifteen-year-old son takes over, becoming Boss of the drive and completing a three-week trip. *Sister Balonika* (1973, rpr. 1986) is an effective play for television—first produced by CBC-TV, Vancouver, in 1969—about three nuns in a Yukon school, and the children, among them Telegraph Jim (a girl) and the disabled Sitkum Memaloose. Sister Balonika (the children's name for Sister Veronica) responds to them sympathetically, and to the adult Forty Horse Johnson, but is unwittingly connected with a tragedy at the play's end. *In the navel of the moon* (1993) is both a mystery novel and a comedy, set in a small town in Mexico, wherein Mac, a retired Canadian newspaperman, is assigned by bureaucrats in Ottawa to look into drug smuggling; but he is more interested in observing the Mexicans he lives among, whose activities are described with St Pierre's dry wit and keen eye for the absurd—though a mystery does unfold. *Tell me a good lie: tales from the Chilcotin country* (2001) is a collection of fifty-two stories, the title being a Chilcotin greeting. In *Old enough to know better* (2002) the outspoken St Pierre has collected his opinions on all kinds of subjects that he wanted to get off his chest for his descendants and others. 'Here are set out the truths that eluded me when I was a kid under seventy and the questions I should haves been asking.' In 2000 St Pierre won the $5000 BC Lifetime Achievement Award.

St Ursula's Convent (Kingston, 1824; rpr. 1991). The first novel published in British North America by a native-born author, *St Ursula's Convent; or, The nun of Canada* was begun by Fredericton's Julia Catherine Beckwith (see HART) when she was only seventeen and was visiting relatives in Nova Scotia. Family stories and childhood journeys to Québec probably influenced the content of the novel, but the writer's emphasis on coincidence, sentimentality, and melodrama also reflect her preoccupation with the conventions of popular romance. Focusing on the personal history of Mother St Catherine before and after she entered the Ursuline convent at Quebec, the novel eventually sees this gentlewoman reunited with her long-lost husband and children. Collateral figures add to the complexity of the plot, which introduces shipwrecks, exchanged babies, potential incest, and a nefarious priest into the drawing-room society of seigneurial Québec and eighteenth-century Europe. Always highly moral in tone despite its melodramatic elements, the novel predictably marries off most of its titled lovers. Published by Hugh C. Thomson of Kingston, Upper Canada, for 9s. 4d., the two-volume work received support from 147 subscribers in England, the United States, Nova Scotia, New Brunswick, and the Canadas. It was sold by booksellers in the Maritimes as well as in the Canadas and was reviewed in 1824 in *The Scribbler, The Canadian Magazine and Literary Repository*, and *The Canadian Review and Literary and Historical Journal*. Considered an immature work even in its own time, the novel survives today because of its historical importance. A scholarly edition, edited by Douglas LOCHHEAD, was published in 1991 by The CENTRE FOR EDITING EARLY CANADIAN TEXTS.

Sakamoto, Kerri (b. 1959). Born to a Japanese-Canadian family in Toronto, she was educated at the University of Toronto (B.A., 1982) and New York University (M.A., 1992). She has written two acclaimed novels. *The electrical field* (1998, rpr. 1998), set in the mid-1970s in Ontario, has as it background the internment of Japanese Canadians in 1942 in British Columbia; Sakamoto was born seventeen years later, but her parents were interned. (This infamous subject is also treated by Joy KOGAWA in *Obasan*.) It is narrated by Asaka Saito, who lived in the internment camp—her mother died shortly after their release—and who now lives with her younger brother Stum and her senile father in a house in Ontario that is separated from the town by a stretch of huge electric pylons—the electrical field of the title. A complex, divided personality, Asaka is alienated from herself, resorting to being simply a dutiful daughter and sister. She reminisces often about her beloved older brother Eiji, who died of pneumonia in the camp. Members of the Nakamura and Yano families, her neighbours, were also affected by being interned. Masashi Yano spends time distributing circulars calling for compensation for their internment. (A Redress Settlement was granted in 1988.) Asaka befriends the teenaged Sachi Nakamura and admires, and converses with, the beautiful Chisako Yano, the Japanese-born wife of her much older husband and the mother of two children—her boss, Mr Spears, is her lover. We learn early in the novel that Chisako and Mr. Spears had been killed. It is revealed only towards the end that Yano killed them, his children, and himself. Though overlong, with

the accretion of countless extraneous descriptions, *The electrical field* is a beautifully written treatment of human relationships in a Japanese-Canadian community and of the traumas effected by an injurious event some three decades before: it stays in the mind. (See 'Monsters and monstrosity: Kerri Sakamoto, *The electrical field*' in *Contemporary Canadian Women's Fiction* [2003] by Coral Ann Howells.) Sakamoto's second novel, *One hundred million hearts* (2003, rpr. 2004) is about Miyo Mori, a young Canadian-born Japanese woman (a *nisei*) living in Toronto with her father Masao, who raised her. 'He saw me for what I was and still he took care of me, fed me, helped to dress me because I was clumsy, not used to my body. I had to learn how to coddle its weak parts, to compensate for my left with my right.' Miyo, who is lame, has an accident leaving the subway car in a crowd and collapses. A young stranger—David—tends to her, puts his arms around her gently, takes her home in a taxi, sees her again—and they become lovers and live together. Maseo dies and Setsuko reappears in Miyo's life for the first time since she was eight. It turns out that Setsuko is her stepmother—she and Maseo were secretly married in Japan and had a daughter, Hana. Setsuko and Miyo travel to Tokyo to meet Hana and the lives of the half-sisters become intertwined. Miyo learns that her father was sent from Canada to attend university in Japan and in 1943 volunteered as a kamikaze pilot (one who, in an aircraft loaded with explosives, crashed on its target in the hope of receiving eternal glory). She also learns how he survived. The novel is another sensitive revelation of relationships and character, and in this case of life in Japan in the present and the past. The title comes from the Japanese government's wartime slogan: 'One hundred million hearts beating as one human bullet to defeat the enemy.'

Sale, Medora (b. 1943). Born in Windsor, Ontario, she was awarded a Ph.D. in medieval studies (1974) from the University of Toronto (under her birth name, Caroline Medora Roe) and taught at Branksome Hall, Toronto, before turning to writing full time. Her six detective novels featuring Toronto police Inspector John Sanders and Harriet Jeffries, an architectural photographer, include *Murder on the run* (1985), winner of an Arthur Ellis Award, *Murder in focus* (1989), *Murder in a good cause* (1990), *Sleep of the innocent* (1991), *Pursued by shadows* (1992), and *Short cut to Santa Fe* (1994). Like Robert Barnard and Reginald

Hill, whom she cites as favourite crime-fiction authors, Sale is a traditionalist whose emphasis is on complicated plotting and the solution of tangled crimes that are often interestingly and complexly connected to upper-class Toronto interests and milieux. *Murder on the run*, for example, investigates the slaying of female joggers in Toronto's parks and ravines and involves staff at one of the city's exclusive private girls' schools, while *Murder in a good cause* deals with philanthropy and poisoned herbal tea in Toronto's affluent Rosedale neighbourhood. While clever and reasonably entertaining, the series on the whole is somewhat unfocused in terms of continuity and emotional texture. The relationship between Sanders and Jeffries often seems flat and desultory, and they are at times too peripherally connected to the investigations in particular novels to permit the books to be experienced as a successful investigator-centred series.

Salutin, Rick (b. 1942). Born in Toronto, he received a B.A. in Near Eastern and Jewish Studies from Brandeis University, Massachusetts; an M.A. in religion from Columbia University, New York; and worked on a Ph.D. in philosophy at the New School for Social Research in New York. He once considered becoming a rabbi; but, unable to find what he was looking for in religion, he was attracted by the trade-union movement on his return to Toronto in 1970, taking part in the Artistic Woodwork strike there in the early 1970s. He has written on a variety of issues for magazines, receiving National Newspaper Awards for comment and criticism in 1982 and 1984, and for some time has written a Friday column of engaging left-wing commentary for the Toronto *Globe and Mail*. His interest in the labour movement and social issues is evident in *The organizer: Kent Rowley: a Canadian union life* (1980), a biography of a Canadian union leader.

Salutin's first published play, *1837: the farmers' revolt* (1976), was created in collaboration with the dynamic group of actors at Theatre Passe Muraille, Toronto, and its innovative director Paul Thompson, in 1972 and 1973. His sympathy is clearly with the rebels in the abortive 1837–8 uprising led by William Lyon MACKENZIE. Salutin answered many questions raised by the drama in a lengthy introduction to another edition of the play entitled *1837: William Lyon Mackenzie and the Canadian revolution: a history/a play* (1975, rpr. 1997). The Passe Muraille production has toured many parts of Canada as well as Scotland, and was produced on CBC television in 1975. For the 150th anniversary of the 1837 rebellion, Salutin wrote a ten-part radio play for CBC 'Morningside' entitled *The reluctant patriot* (unpublished) about Samuel Chandler, a wagonmaker who spirited the fugitive Mackenzie across the border into the United States after the rebellion was suppressed. *The false Messiah: a Messianic farce* (1981)—its title suggests its serio-comic nature—was produced at Theatre Passe Muraille in 1975. About a seventeenth-century Jew in a Constantinople prison who claims to be the Messiah, it shows effectively the need for hope even in the form of illusion. Salutin's most popular and successful play is *Les Canadiens* (1977), which premiered at Montreal's Centaur Theatre in 1977. It was written with an 'assist' from goaltender Ken Dryden, who also wrote a preface to the published version. Salutin used the Montreal hockey team as a metaphor for the failures and triumphs of French Canadians from the defeat of 1759 on the Plains of Abraham to the Parti Québécois victory on 15 Nov. 1976. It has been performed across Canada.

Salutin turned next to the Canadian cultural scene to portray one of its most influential figures in *Nathan Cohen: a review* (1981), based on the life and work of the drama critic (q.v.) who died in 1971. Produced at Theatre Passe Muraille in 1981, it starred the eminent Canadian actor Douglas Campbell. Although the play is well researched, it lacks character exploration and unity, a weakness that is evident in *Joey* (unpublished)—presented at Toronto Workshop Productions in 1982—based on the life of Joseph Smallwood, former premier of Newfoundland, and written in collaboration with the Rising Tide Theatre company of St John's. It was warmly received in both Toronto and Newfoundland, as well as at the National Arts Centre, Ottawa. Salutin's next two plays examined Canada's security system. *S: portrait of a spy* (1985), written with Ian Adams, on whose novel of the same name it was based, explored the character of a 'mole' who became director of counter-espionage for the Royal Canadian Mounted Police before being discovered, and raised important questions about the efficiency of Canada's security service. The play premiered at the Great Canadian Theatre Company in Ottawa, directed by Patrick McDonald. In *Grierson and Gouzenko* (unpublished), a ninety-minute docudrama produced on CBC television in 1986, Salutin condemned Canada's treatment of John Grierson, founder of the National Film Board, who was forced to leave the country after allegations of espionage by Igor Gouzenko, the Russian agent turned informer.

Somewhat disillusioned by the theatre in Canada, Salutin turned his creativity into writing novels. The first was *A man of little faith* (1988) about a director of religious education at a temple in Toronto. With humour and warmth, it explores his journey of self-discovery in a mid-twentieth-century Jewish community, such as the one from which Salutin came. Very different was his next novel, *The age of improv: a political novel of the future* (1995, rpr. 1996). More a satire and a novel of ideas, it takes place about the year 2005 when Canada's present political parties have collapsed and a disillusioned actor, Matthew Deans, becomes prime minister by using his skill at improvisation. It adroitly brings together both Salutin's experience in theatre, and his experience as a political and social analyst. The first sentence of *The womanizer: a man of his time* (2002, rpr. 2003) is 'Let's consider the little Casanova at age eight'—in 1950, referring to Max, no last name given, whose lifetime fixation on women and sex are central to the novel. Many years later the Big Event 'happens under the dining room table at her house, a floor below her parents' bed.' In retrospect, it was like 'you're up north, camped on a lonely lake, you awaken at midnight and step outside the tent to pee and the stars are so close and bright you actually duck to get out of their way.' Max, a freelance economist, in middle age 'starts to replay his life as a womanizer, like counting sheep.' Part II, called 'The Huck Finn of Sex', details the respective 'versions' of Jenny, Francie, Cyndi, Amy, Deb, Marguerite, Elyse, and Olivia. (Part III is 'Max's Version'.) Though amusingly and discreetly conveyed, it is not this aspect that is most interesting but the bulk of the novel that displays Max the thinker commenting—often searchingly and wittily, always with strong narrative interest—on everything under the sun, including Toronto and Canada (bringing to mind Salutin the columnist), London, and happenings of more than local interest, such as 'when [John Kenneth] Galbraith and Milton Friedman are in town. The two of them are touring as a tag team, like G. Gordon Liddy, the Watergate burglar, and Timothy Leary, the acid guru.' Max says that Galbraith 'is the representative today of the intellectual current that represents the best of our era, the voice that speaks out for the public.....' His Canadian connection is 'like a cherry on top.' Towards the end of the book Max apparently finds his true love, Anita. 'It already feels like something has changed for the better, and they did *nothing*. // Change remains the best trick, better than money, better than sex.....' She is pregnant and bears Max a son. 'The arrival looks around, alert and inquisitive. Around and round he gazes, the most arresting moment of his life is already almost over.... Max holds the baby boy, who already has a name.... How do you give someone you don't know a name they have to carry all their life? He rains tears down on the wrinkly, alert face. *Owen.*' *The womanizer*—whose subtitle, *A man of his time*, perhaps suits the novel better—smoothly introduces many concerns of Max's time, in addition to his many liaisons.

Salutin has voiced his concerns in more concrete terms in articles and columns, many of them in *This Magazine*, which became the basis of two books. The first is *Marginal notes: challenges to the mainstream* (1984), which includes pieces he had written from 1970 to 1983. Claiming marginality as a strength, it confirms his position as the most incisive left-leaning commentator in Canada. His next collection, bringing together pieces written between 1984 and 1991, is *Living in a dark age* (1991), the title reflecting the more pessimistic view he took in the years immediately before and after the Free Trade Agreement between Canada and the United States. Reflections on the 1988 federal election campaign may be found in *Waiting for democracy: a citizen's journal* (1989), a book-length memoir of Salutin's travels interviewing Canadians during the weeks leading up to election day that ends with surprisingly positive comments on the results. Even more positive is his introduction to *Spadina Avenue* (1985) by Rosemary Donegan—based on a photographic history she curated at A Space Gallery in Toronto in 1984—in which Salutin comments on growing up in this Toronto area, on his father's and two uncles' work as salesmen there, and on the working people who gave him the stimulus to spend his career advocating a better life for them.

James Noonan wrote an overview of Salutin's life and work in the Profiles in Canadian Literature series, vol. 8 (1991).

Salverson, Laura Goodman (1890–1970). Laura Goodman was born in Winnipeg of Icelandic immigrant parents. Her education there and in the United States was frequently interrupted by illness and her parents' hopeful wandering throughout North America, and she was ten years old before she began to learn English. Married in 1913 to George Salverson, a railwayman, she continued to lead a transient life in Canada, supplementing her income by writing short stories for periodicals. Salverson was one of the first Canadian novelists to fictionalize the drama of immigration in the West. In her three novels that concentrate on the Scandinavian immigrant experience, she drew upon her family's failures in order to inveigh against the falsity of the Canadian dream. Her first novel, *When sparrows fall* (1925), deals with Norwegian immigrants in an American city (a thinly disguised Duluth). Dedicated to Nellie McCLUNG, it emphasizes the feminist struggle as well as the dilemma of immigrants pressured into choosing between their ancestral traditions and the American melting pot. In *The Viking heart* (1923; rev. 1947; NCL 1975), considered to be her best work because of its breadth of history and almost documentary authenticity, Salverson traces the immigration of 1400 Icelanders in 1876 to the area of Gimli, Manitoba. After chronicling their subsequent difficulties and the development of their settlement up to 1919, she concludes with the immigrants' disillusionment over Canada's participation in the Great War. A confirmed pacifist, Salverson presents Canada as a nation whose great potential had been betrayed and neglected by its leaders. In *The dark weaver* (1937, GGA), which reinforces this pacifist theme, a composite group of Nordic immigrants settles in the West and prospers until the war culls their second generation and reimposes Old-World chaos upon them. The title refers to the apparent indifference of a God who weaves His plots oblivious to the tragedies and prayers of the people involved. Salverson's autobiography, *Confessions of an immigrant's daughter* (1939, GGA; rpr. 1981), covers her life to 1923 and describes with compassion and a sense of social injustice the struggles of immigrants in a New World that fell far short of their hopes and expectations. Salverson argued for the preservation of the Icelandic cultural identity in what she felt was a cultural vacuum in Canada.

Sandwell, B.K. (1876–1954). Bernard Keble Sandwell was born at Ipswich, England. He was brought to Canada as a child and educated at Upper Canada College and the University of Toronto (B.A., 1897). In Montreal he was drama critic at the *Herald* (1905–11), editor of the *Financial Times* (1911–18), taught economics at McGill University (1919–23), and headed the English department at Queen's University, Kingston (1923–5). Editing *Saturday Night* from 1932 to 1951, he gave a long-running performance few journalists

anywhere have equalled. By the time he became editor of *Saturday Night*, at the age of fifty-six, he was able to discuss both the new Morley CALLAGHAN novel and the federal debt with equal confidence. He not only put out a thick weekly paper and made it the articulate voice of liberal Canada, but he also wrote many of its best pieces—in one issue he might contribute three or four anonymous editorials, a major book review under his own name, and a charming theatre review under a pen name, 'Lucy Van Gogh'. He carried this off with style and integrity, becoming what Robertson DAVIES (who worked briefly for Sandwell in the 1940s) called 'unquestionably the most influential journalist in Canada'. Civil liberties were Sandwell's favourite cause, and in the 1940s he was one of a tiny minority of Canadians who vehemently criticized the expulsion of the Japanese and Japanese-Canadians from the coastal areas of British Columbia. His essays were collected in *The privacity agent and other modest proposals* (1928) and in the posthumously published *The diversions of Duchesstown and other essays* (1955). The Sandwell lines most often quoted today are those with which he greeted the appointment in 1952 of Vincent Massey as the first Canadian-born Governor General: 'Let the Old World, where rank's yet vital,/Part those who have and have not title./Toronto has no social classes—/Only the Masseys and the masses.'

Sangster, Charles (1822–93). Born at the Navy Yard, Kingston, Upper Canada (Ontario), Sangster left school to make cartridges at Fort Henry during the Rebellion of 1837 and remained there as a clerk until 1849, when he turned to a modest career in journalism: first as editor of the *Amherstburg Courier*, then as a proofreader and bookkeeper for Kingston's *British Whig*; and finally as a reporter for Kingston's *Daily News*. He moved to Ottawa in 1868 to join the new federal post-office department, where he remained until he retired in 1886.

Demonstrating his wish, as a poet, to be 'Canadian in his choice of subjects', Sangster secured his reputation as the 'poet-laureate of colonial Canada' with three books of poetry: *The St Lawrence and the Saguenay and other poems* (Kingston, 1856), *Hesperus and other poems and lyrics* (Montreal, 1860), and *Our Norland*, an undated fourteen-page chapbook issued by Copp Clark, Toronto. One of his best poems, the patriotic 'Brock', was commissioned for the 1859 inauguration of the monument to General Brock at Queenston Heights. It is a secular celebration of the collective self-sacrifices that passed beyond the bounds of time as all Canadians inherited the heroic tradition: 'The hero deed can not expire,/The dead still play their part.' Sangster's most ambitious work, 'The St Lawrence and the Saguenay', presents a voyage from Kingston down the St Lawrence and up the Saguenay—a journey away from civilization towards nature and the divine creator. Modelling his tour on Byron's *Childe Harold's pilgrimage* and Wordsworth's *The River Duddon*, and drawing on his own steamer tour recorded in 'Etchings by the way', his series of travel letters for the Kingston *British Whig* (1853), Sangster was stirred by the picturesque scenery to muse upon its rich history (Wolfe and Montcalm and the Plains of Abraham) and rich legend (the Native maiden of the Thousand Islands who paddles nightly to care for her fugitive father). As the voyage nears the poet's source of inspiration (symbolized by the river's divine origin), he questions whether art can compete with the splendour of God's work, humbly musing that the expressive calm of silence in the northern wilderness is a 'Godlike eloquence'. But at Trinity Rock he envisions the Dream of Love achieved through the trinity of man, maiden, and God, which in turn empowers the poet to achieve the Dream of Art through the trinity of art, nature, and love. As love excites us to perceive the earth as heavenly, God inspires us to share that vision with others. See *The St. Lawrence and the Saguenay* (1990) edited by D.M.R. Bentley.

Frank M. Tierney edited three collections Sangster projected, but did not live to publish: *Norland echoes and other poems and lyrics* (1976), *The angel guest and other poems* (1978), and the revised *Hesperus and other poems and lyrics* (1979). Many weak, overly conventional poems in these books show why the young Archibald LAMPMAN took no notice of Sangster when they worked in the same postal department.

Sarah, Robyn (b. 1949). Born in New York City to Canadian parents, she trained as a classical musician at the Conservatoire de musique du Québec. Sarah has made Montreal—where she studied philosophy at McGill University, receiving her B.A. and M.A.—her home. Her first publication was the chapbook *Shadowplay* (1978). Until 1984 Sarah's poetry was known mostly in small-press, anthology, and magazine publications, though her reputation as a poet with an exquisite ear and sensibility was already established. *Anyone skating on that middle ground* (1984) was Sarah's first book-length publication and in it she demonstrated the mature, accomplished style that also characterizes the poems in *Becoming light* (1987). *The touchstone: poems new & selected* (1992) focuses on the achieved work from her previous two collections to produce a volume of consistently high quality. This was followed by *Questions about the stars* (1998), which includes a long collage poem, 'A brief history of time: digest and subtext', that incorporates chapter headings and 'found' material from Stephen Hawking's book. Margaret AVISON has been quoted as saying that in Sarah's poems 'an elegant play is going on even in the most acutely painful moment of clarity, a play of pure energy.' Sarah is a formalist who moves effortlessly along a broad range of available forms, as at home with the sestina as she is with the prose poem. This flexibility pays off for the reader in the variety and depth of voices and moods the work as a whole expresses. *A day's grace: poems 1997–2002* (2003), an enjoyable and beautiful collection, begins with a prose poem, 'Only a child, alone', which begins 'At the bottom of the slatted iron fire escape there was a place where we used to play', and moves from places to spaces, 'small, enclosed spaces, glimpsed from bus windows, from other people's balconies, through dusty screen doors: spaces that breathe a promise which has no words... . One glimpses these spaces in passing but does not enter them. Only a child, alone, may play there.' One trivial event after another during a day: 'a dead / bird on the stoop, a gift / from the cat', 'a friend's letter, / homesick on the other side / of the world', seeing 'a woman weeping / in a parked car' // 'Random grains in the day's sieve....' ('Cipher'); and on another day a plaster face, broken in two, being 'handed out a window / carefully, / one by one, / to two / waiting upon the lawn / with upstretched arms' ('The face')—are beyond explanation. But 'A grace resides in mysteries like these.' The imagery— 'Something has jarred loose in the mind. / An old grief, like a marble rolling around / in an empty drawer' ('Rattled')—and family matters, such as a bereavement—'The words gather in density / like banks of cloud on the horizon / blocking the sunset light, / and still / they spin like mist, / they wind like wool.' ('A silence')—and birth in the poignant poem 'To N, *in absentia*', which begins 'I do not know how you went out of my life / or when exactly... . But I remember as if yesterday the day / you came out of my body into this world... . .' The clarity of imagination and musical language of Robyn Sarah draws the reader gladly into the sensibility and life of a real poet. His latest collection, *Pause for breath*, was published in 2009.

A nice gazebo (1992) gathers stories whose restraint and depth are reminiscent of the subtle fictions of Alice MUNRO (Sarah's main concern is with the lives of girls and women), Mavis GALLANT, and Elisabeth HARVOR. The eight stories in *Promise of shelter* (1997), though no story has that title, suggest variations on the theme of shelter (the title of one story), refuge, and home. Much of Sarah's writing appears to be autobiographical—the stories perhaps less so than the poetry, though it is only in them that any allusions are drawn from Sarah's Jewish background. Her focus in all her writing is on apparently insignificant surfaces, the details of things that amount, finally, to a life. The quotidian, at times overwhelming in the earlier poems, takes on a kind of visionary sanctity in the later work. *Little eurekas: a decade's thoughts on poetry* (2007) is an unusual compilation of essays and reviews by a poet who is also a critic and an excellent writer of prose. The essays in the first section, beginning with 'How I fell for poetry', discuss teaching, publishing, and editing poetry. Section II, 'Appreciations', includes 'How poems work', and appreciations of a single poem by each of five poets, including Margaret Avison, and the English poet Philip Larkin; Don COLES, Richard SOMMER, and especially George JOHNSTON are other poets treated appreciatively in this section. There are interesting short book reviews, followed by 'Collaborations', in which Sarah exchanges thoughts and ideas with Steven HEIGHTON, Dennis LEE, and Robert BRINGHURST, and has a conversation (in the form of an email correspondence) about writing poetry with Eric ORMSBY. Robyn Sarah selected the poems in *The essential Don Coles* (2009), concluding it with an interesting summary of Coles's life and career.

Sarah Binks (1947, NCL). Long before this book was published, its author, Paul Hiebert (1892–1987)—then professor of chemistry at the University of Manitoba—had entertained public and private gatherings in Winnipeg with readings from the works and life of the 'Sweet Songstress of Saskatchewan'. A gentle combination of parody and burlesque (Hiebert insisted that the book is not satirical), *Sarah Binks* invites our laughter at the foibles and excesses of literary biography and criticism, and at the brilliantly bad naive poetry of his heroine: many of Sarah's poetic effusions are masterpieces of deliberately contrived incompetence, the product of a sensibility both unknowingly academic and earthy. The account of Sarah's upbringing, her family and friends, her development as a poet, her eventual success, and her untimely death, is appropriately 'scholarly' in its plodding quest for facts and its ample quotations from the poet's works. Yet Hiebert treats Sarah with humorous affection, much as Stephen LEACOCK did the inhabitants of Mariposa, and many of the poems reveal a nostalgic understanding of life in the rural Canadian West before the Depression: 'Then all in fun they feed the pigs, / And plough the soil in reckless glee, / And play the quaint old-fashioned game / Of mortgagor and mortgagee' ('The farmer and the farmer's wife'); 'I sing the song of the simple chore, / Of quitting the downy bed at four, / And chipping ice from the stable door— / Of the simple chore I sing' ('The song of the chore'). Hiebert dedicated *Sarah Binks* to those 'of the West' who have seen its beauty and endured its hardships.

Additional Binksiana may be found in Hiebert's *Willows revisited* (1967) and *For the birds* (1980). Sarah is not a central figure in these books, but her shade may be said to haunt *Willows revisited*. *Sarah Binks* is in the NEW CANADIAN LIBRARY and has been dramatized.

Saul, John Ralston (b. 1947). Born in Ottawa, he studied politics, economics, and history at McGill University (B.A., 1969) and earned a doctorate at King's College, University of London (Ph.D., 1972), with a thesis on the modernization of France under Charles de Gaulle, emphasizing civil-military relations and the role of the armaments industry. From 1972 to 1975 he ran Chapel Land, a subsidiary of an English investment house in Paris; from 1976 to 1978 he was assistant to Maurice Strong, chairman of Petro-Canada; from 1978 to 1982 he was chairman of Filmfive Inc. and Secretary of the Canada-China Trade Council. He has received fourteen honorary degrees and was made a Companion of the Order of Canada in 1999. From 1999 to 2006 he lived in Ottawa as Canada's viceregal consort while his wife, Adrienne Clarkson, was Governor General. He and his wife now live in Toronto. He is the series editor of Penguin's Extraordinary Canadians.

Over some thirty years Saul has created an *oeuvre* of taut, telling fiction and trenchant social criticism. His books have been published in English in Toronto, London, and New York; in Paris in French; and in other languages, including Italian, Spanish, and German. While his early work was entirely fiction, in recent years he has published books of commentary and philosophy, establishing himself as an iconoclast and polymath. His novels—which have the intrigue of Graham Greene and the social relevance of Dickens and Balzac—have an enduring existential quality. In *The birds of prey* (1977, rpr. 1997) he builds on the true story of the mysterious crash of a military aircraft and the death of the French Chief of Staff to expose the Machiavellian workings of the military and political hierarchy. He has denied that the book was a *roman à clef*, but its verisimilitude unnerved the French establishment and it sold 2 million copies. His next three novels are a thematic trilogy addressing the struggle of the individual against authority. *Baraka; or The lives, fortunes and sacred honor of Anthony Smith* (1983, rpr. 1997) describes the involvement of an international oil company in a multi-million-dollar arms deal, illuminating business in the late twentieth century. *The next best thing* (1986, rpr. 1997) follows the obsession of an art smuggler in Burma. *The paradise eater* (1988, rpr. 1997) is a black comedy that deals with arms, murder, and politics in Bangkok. These novels have in common not just exotic venues and quixotic characters, but corruption, power, and morality.

Saul's growing influence in Canada and abroad flows from his social philosophy, which shows a spirited distaste for convention and an eagerness to challenge orthodoxy; this has been expressed in both books and the popular press. His signature work is *Voltaire's bastards: the dictatorship of reason in the West* (1992, rpr. 2005), a provocative treatise that questions the failure of reason to create a rational world and takes aim at the modern power elite, Voltaire's misguided descendants. *The doubter's companion: a dictionary of aggressive common sense* (1994, rpr. 2005) is a companion volume of pointed skepticism that is less a classical dictionary than witty and biting alphabetized commentaries on Saul's affections and aversions. *The unconscious civilization* (1995, rpr. 2005, GGA), another critique of reason and of the rise of technocratic elitism, challenges corporatism and laments the erosion of democracy. Saul argues that the individual and democracy matter less in Western society than is widely thought: legitimacy now lies in negotiation between relevant groups based on expertise, interest, and the ability to exercise power. The book grew out of the CBC Massey Lectures, which Saul delivered in 1995. A successor to this trilogy is *On equilibrium* (2001), a substantial book

(328 pages plus notes) about balancing six qualities—common sense, ethics, imagination, intuition, memory, and reason—as positive forces in our lives. *Reflections of a Siamese twin: Canada at the end of the twentieth century* (1997, rpr. 2005)—a long, and often illuminating, sequence of ruminations on the Canadian past and present, drawn from Saul's immersion in the country's history and literature—is an attempt to make sense of Canada today. The title refers to the discordant bond between English and French Canada. In discussing various mythologies that obtain in Canadian issues, he rejects negative myths and promotes Canada's complexity, its 'central characteristic'. The then-current condition of the country had to do with the fact that our leaders, subsumed by neo-conservative ideology, no longer cared about the common good, having become servants of corporations and their foreign affiliations. *The collapse of globalism: and the reinvention of the world* was published in 2005. Emerging in the 1970s, the idea of globalization propounded the supreme importance of global markets, rather than nation-states, and of economics in determining the course of human events. The beneficial effects of the growth of international markets would include the disappearance of poverty and the conversion of dictatorhips into democracies. In 2005 the results included 'some remarkable successes, some disturbing failures and a collection of what might best be called running sores.' In 2005, when this was written, the worldwide financial collapse and economic disarray had yet to happen. In 2008 Saul published *A fair country: telling truths about Canada*: 'To insist on describing ourselves as something we are not is to embrace existential illiteracy. We are not a civilization of British or French or European inspiration. We never have been. Our society is not an expression of *peace, order and good government*. It never was…. We are a people of Aboriginal inspiration organized around a concept of peace, fairness and good government.' Saul shared in *The LaFontaine-Baldwin lectures, volume one: a dialogue on democracy in Canada* (2002), made up of his conversations with Alain Dubuc and George Erasmus. *Joseph Howe & the battle for freedom of speech* (2006) is the inaugural Joseph Howe Lecture delivered at the University of King's College School of Journalism on 20 Mar. 2004. In Oct. 2009 Saul was elected president of the International PEN organization, the first Canadian to hold this position.

Saunders, Marshall (1861–1947). Born in the Annapolis Valley of Nova Scotia, the daughter of an eminent Baptist minister, and educated in Halifax and for one year in Edinburgh and Orléans, France, Margaret Marshall Saunders returned to teach and write in Halifax. Holiday travels to Europe produced the shipboard atmosphere of the romantic novel *My Spanish sailor: a love story* (London, 1889), for which 'Beauty and the Beast' supplied the plot. In her late twenties she attended Dalhousie University for a year; the next year, in Ottawa, she heard the story of a gentle, homely dog; it would become the germ of *BEAUTIFUL JOE: an autobiography* (Philadelphia, 1894, rpr. 1994), which became a phenomenal bestseller. She then went on to write almost thirty formulaic novels; four more sentimental romances for adults; *The girl from Vermont: the story of a vacation school teacher* (1919), a sombre attack on children's problems, such as abuse, enforced labour, and lack of schooling and playgrounds; and many stories for children and young people, mostly about animals and birds. From 1916 she lived in Toronto and died there.

Savard, Félix-Antoine (1896–1982). Born in Quebec City, he spent most of his youth and early manhood in Chicoutimi. He became a priest in 1922 and taught at the Chicoutimi Seminary until 1927. After serving as curate in several locations within the diocese, he established Saint-Phillipe-de-Clermont parish (Charlevoix) in 1931 and remained there until 1945, while also launching a literary career. During this period, in collaboration with Luc Lacourcière, Savard began to assemble folksongs and folktales, an initiative that led to the formation of Université Laval's folkloric archives (1944). In 1943 he began to lecture in the faculty of arts at Laval, where in 1950 he was honoured with the title of Monsignor and appointed dean of the faculty, a position he held until 1957. He received many distinctions, in both France and Canada, including a Governor General's Award for *Le barachois* (1959), a mixture of prose and verse that is a tribute to the Acadian people, whom he came to know and love during his investigation of their folklore. The only one of his many books that has been published in English is a classic of French-Canadian literature, *Menaud, maître-draveur* (1937), which was translated twice: by Alan SULLIVAN as *Boss of the river* (1947) and by Richard Howard as *Master of the river* (1976). It is a lumber-camp story set in the Charlevoix region in northeastern Québec, about a veteran of the log drive who—incensed by the foreign (Anglo-Canadian)

businessmen exploiting Québec's resources—is fired by words he reads in Louis HÉMON's *MARIA CHAPDELAINE*: 'Around us have come strangers we scorn as foreigners. They have taken all the money. Yet in the land of Québec nothing will change.' Misfortune comes to Menaud in the harshest fashion when his son drowns while trying to free a log jam. His efforts to rally the people to oppose the foreigners meet with no success. When, distraught, he goes into the forest during a snowstorm in search of the 'stranger' who has threatened to cut off the local people from access to the territory, he is barely saved from freezing to death. After that he sinks into madness. The novel ends with the words of a farmer: 'This is no ordinary madness! It is a warning!' *Menaud* is the last in a long line of traditional novels on French-Canadian nationalism, though in its conflicts and its portrayal of madness it is far removed from the rural idylls of the past. Savard was made an Officer of the Order of Canada in 1968.

Savoie, Jacques (b. 1951). Born in Edmundston, New Brunswick, he studied creative writing and cinema at Bathurst College, N.B., and at the University of Aix-en-Provence. A scriptwriter for cinema and television in Montreal, he is also a novelist and writer of children's books. Only two of Savoie's novels have been published in English. *The revolving doors* (1989) is Sheila FISCHMAN's translation of *Les portes tournantes* (1984), which was made into a movie by Francis Mankiewicz. It begins: 'My name is Antoine. I'm ten years old and I'm a musician.' He lives with the painter Blaudelle and is recording his 'memoirs' because Blaudelle doesn't know how to write. These are interspersed with letters of Antoine's grandmother, and the result is a text that 'revolves' around three generations—with writing, music, and painting as a subtext—and that has as a central image the revolving doors of the Grand Théâtre in Quebec City. *The blue circus* (1997) is Fischman's translation of *Le cirque bleu* (1995), which exploits a theme familiar to the author: the reunited family. This story of a tender, complex love—where music and poetry, realism and the fantastic, are mixed—confirms Savoie's great technical abilities, but also reveals a certain difficulty in maintaining to the end the interest aroused by the novel's beginning: about the arrival (from Chicago) in Montreal of Hugo, a circus performer, in search of his half-sister Marthe, whom he soon finds. At their first meeting he tells her about his girlfriend Sally and how she died during a performance at the hands of a knife-thrower, her uncle.

Sawyer, Robert J. (b. 1960). Born in Ottawa, he was educated at Toronto's Ryerson Polytechnic University (B.A., 1982). In setting out to become a professional writer of science fiction, Sawyer masterfully bonded together concerns about technology and an interest in compelling storylines to publish short stories and many novels—and to win more than forty national and international awards. He is the only Canadian to win all three of the world's top awards for best science-fiction novel of the year: the Hugo, the Nebula, and the John W. Campbell Memorial Award. In August 2007 he was named 'the most popular foreign author of the year' at the Chengdu International Science Fiction and Fantasy Festival in China. He is the editor of Robert J. Sawyer Books.

In *Golden fleece* (1990) the element of detection plays a critical role aboard a starship guided by a homicidal computer. The Quintaglio trilogy chronicles life on a planet populated by sentient dinosaurs and consists of three closely written, highly detailed novels: *Far-seer* (1992), *Fossil hunter* (1993, rpr. 2005), and *Foreigner* (1994, rpr. 2005), whose main characters are Galileo-like, Darwin-like, and Freud-like respectively. Dinosaurs and their fate figure in *End of an era* (1994), a time-travel novel set in Canada during the Cretaceous period. Toronto in the year 2011 is the setting of *The terminal experiment* (1995), a thoughtful consideration of the consequences of the discovery of proof of the existence of the human soul. It won the Nebula Award. Subsequent novels include *Starplex* (1996), a far-future novel that explores the origin and fate of the universe; *Frameshift* (1997), an SF thriller; and *Illegal alien* (1997), a courtroom drama with an extraterrestrial defendant. *Factoring humanity* (1998) begins in 2007 when an unintelligible message is detected coming from outer space; it is followed by ten years of signals until they stop. Heather Davis, a professor at the University of Toronto, discovers a revolutionary new technology and deciphers the messages. *Flash-forward* (1999) is posited on a universal event: virtually everyone in the world blacks out for two minutes and has a vision of what he or she will be experiencing for two minutes in the year 2030. The immediate results of this, and the overview of humans coping with fore-knowledge, make for a gripping narrative. *Flashforward* led to a TV series. *Calculating God* (2000) is an enjoyable light novel that begins when an alien ship lands outside the Royal Ontario Museum in Toronto and a

scientist—Hollus of the Forhilnor race—steps out, asking to speak to a paleontologist, and meets Dr thomas Jericho, with whom he has many discussions about the nature of God. The Neanderthal Parallax trilogy—*Hominids* (2002), which won the Hugo Award, *Humans* (2003), and *Hybrids* (2003)—was followed by *Mindscan* (2005), winner of the Hugo and Nebula Awards as well as the Campbell Memorial Award. *Rollback* (2007), which begins in 2048, is an enjoyable novel even for non-SF readers. Dr Sarah Halifax—who decoded the first radio transmission received from aliens—received another message thirty-eight years later, when she's eighty-seven. Can she decipher it? The rollback of the title is a very costly experimental rejuvenation procedure and a wealthy industrialist offers it to Sarah, who insists that Donald, her husband of sixty years, also receive it. It takes with Don but not with Sarah—and an interesting novel ensues. It is redolent of ethical and moral considerations when futuristic science and modern technologies affect human relationships. Sawyer himself has called the novel 'a scientific romance'. *Wake* (2009) centres on young Caitlin Decter, born blind, who receives a retinal implant that gives her not only ordinary sight but that of the data streams that make up the World Wide Web. Webmind grows out of this and leads to the entertainingly complex second novel in Sawyer's WWW trilogy, *Watch* (2010)—the third novel is to be called *Wonder*. His short-story collections are *Iterations and other stories* (2002, rpr. 2008), *Relativity: essays and* stories (2004), and *Identity theft and other stories* (2008).

Scheier, Libby (1946–2000). She was born in New York and educated at Sarah Lawrence College (B.A.) and the State University of New York (M.A.). She lived in France, where she studied at the Sorbonne, California, and Israel before coming to Canada in 1975. Scheier taught a creative-writing course at York University from 1988 to 1995 and founded the Toronto Writing Workshop in 1994. A gifted poet, she published four collections: *The larger life* (1983), *Second nature* (1986), *Sky: a poem in four pieces* (1990), and *Kaddish for my father: new and selected poems 1970–1999* (1999). Foreshadowing recurrent themes in her later work, her first book, *The larger life*, contains the polemical 'Why poems should not be fictions' ('…because Ms Magazine puts Margaret Thatcher and Indira Gandhi / on the cover…') and the surrealistic 'Fetal Suite' ('I dreamed it came out slowly, / easily, soft and wet / I caught its head with my hands / it was made of clay'). *Sky* is made up of four sequences—Sky, Ocean, Earth, and Fire—that employ memory ('memory is a strange thing a strange sting its little / brain flames hotting up this and that corner of skull / till cells flare into snapshots'). A larger collection, *Second nature*, contains 'A poem about rape', which is calm and detached because after seven years since she was raped the poet's 'anger / has waned and cannot feed a poem'. 'Cotton Bowl, New Year's Day', begins, 'I have finally understood why I don't understand / North America. /It has to do with football', and a section called 'Manhood' contains the prose poem 'Husband's lament' ('I didn't want constant and earnest intellectual agreement.... I wanted agreement of the body. A place to soothe my bones. You are not the wife I wanted.') Poems from all three collections are included in *Kaddish for my father*, which is particularly memorable for the title sequence that makes up almost half the book. Scheier had a conflicted relationship with her father ('My father's death inhabits me like a gourd, / a stone-cold vegetable / petrified'), but the prose passages and poems about painful recollections, caring in old age, 'making peace', and grieving express emotions that are intense, controlled, and direct: 'you win, Dad, / or is it me? / the God in the moon won't take sides / but looks on us and sees us all / to be looked at and seen is / after all / a great gift'. Scheier's one work of fiction, *Saints and a runner: stories and a novella* (1993), is surprising, often amusing and touching, as the linked stories replay some of the ideas and concerns in her poetry. At their centre is Arla, a single mother with a son (like Sheier herself), and the collection opens with 'Letters to my family'—to her mother, her father ('Dear Dad: What do men want? What if it's not what I want? It's not what I want. Please advise'), her lover, Sam, and her brother ('Dear Mark: What are brothers for? Please write'). 'The saint who frequented prostitutes' is named Francis ('which made a lot of sense') and is the narrator's lover. 'Donna and Carmina' is about attempts at lesbian love, and 'The runner', a novella, is about a mysterious unnamed girl, 'the redhaired runner beat up by the cops', who seems to dominate Arla's life when they enter a relationship based on caring for each other's child. A passionate writer of poetry and prose, Scheier expressed a wide range of emotions grounded in a tough, disenchanted view of everyday reality redeemed by a light touch and mordant humour.

Schermbrucker, Bill (b. 1938). Born in Eldoret, Kenya, of white parents of South African roots, Schermbrucker has been a teacher of English and creative writing at Capilano College, North Vancouver, since 1968, and was an editor of the *Capilano Review* from 1977 to 1982. Much of his writing has dealt with his youth in Africa. *Chameleon and other stories* (1983) depicts, with exotic colour and detail, life in Kenya during the time of the Mau Mau uprising that eventually led to independence from Britain in 1963. *Mimosa* (1988) is a fictional memoir of his mother. *Motor therapy* (1993), a light and pleasant collection of stories describing trips in cars in Africa and North America, has all the exuberance of Jack Kerouac's *On the road*.

Schoemperlen, Diane (b. 1954). Born in Thunder Bay, Ontario, she graduated in 1976 from Lakehead University, Thunder Bay, and immediately attended a six-week writing workshop at the Banff School ('mostly because Alice Munro was going to be there'). She stayed for several years in Alberta, and now lives in Kingston, Ontario. She has published six collections of short fiction: *Double exposures* (1984); *Frogs and other stories* (1986); *Hockey night in Canada* (1987); *The man of my dreams* (1990), which includes the anthologized story 'Red plaid shirt'; *Hockey night in Canada and other stories* (1991); *Forms of devotion* (1998, GGA), and *Red plaid shirt: stories new & selected* (2002). This most recent collection includes not only 'Red plaid shirt' but 'The man of my dreams'. 'Red plaid shirt' is divided into eight sections, each one featuring an item of clothing and its colour—it is worn in honour of a new lover, who eventually evaporates—ending with a list of words suggested by the colour: RED: *crimson cochineal cinnabar sanguine, scarlet* etc. 'The man of my dreams' happily transgresses the cautionary advice to writers: 'Stay away from dreams'—there are thirty-six of them, many of them ending with mythological beliefs: '*To dream of eating oranges is signally bad, foretelling pervasive discontentment and the sickness of friends or relatives.*' Containing stories written from 1976 to 1996, this collection ends with 'Five small rooms (a murder mystery)', in which each room and the colour it is painted is described, giving force to the opening words: 'I have learned not to underestimate the power of rooms ... .' Referred to occasionally is an unidentified 'you', and the last words are: 'It is time to make it clear that I did not kill him. But yes, oh yes, I wanted to.' Schoemperlen cites as influences Alice MUNRO, Carol SHIELDS, and Margaret ATWOOD, whose dry sense of humour she shares. Several of her stories are characterized by formal experimentalism that puts a premium on the role of the reader to fill in parentheses ('Life sentences'), to make subtle connections ('Waiting'), and to view digression in the story as the sort of natural impulse it is in real life ('A simple story'). A typical setting is the small town, where 'freedom means flirting with your best friend's husband or lover or both' ('This town'). The pitfalls of romantic relationships are common to Schoemperlen's characters, whose intimate reflections create a potent psychological realism. Also characterizing what John METCALF calls 'a recognizable Diane Schoemperlen story' is domestic realism: an attention to the furniture, food, and habits of Canadian families in the late 1960s and 1970s—especially those of younger women who struggle towards finding a sense of self. *Forms of devotion: stories and pictures* is an imaginative departure from her other collections. The title story is made up of ten brief meditations on virtues of the faithful: Faith, Memory, Knowledge, Innocence, etc. 'Innocent objects' describes Helen's activities away from her house, punctuated by one-sentence italicized parentheses noting a thief's actions as he goes through the house, touching and taking objects that are described in charming, informative footnotes. 'The spacious chambers of her heart', a story about Evangeline Clark, is punctuated by descriptions (and illustrations) of the four chambers of the heart. The 'pictures' of the collection's subtitle are wood engravings and line drawings from the seventeenth to the nineteenth centuries, aptly chosen by the author and adding to the pleasure of the book.

In the language of love: a novel in 100 chapters (1994, rpr. 2000) is organized around the 100 stimulus words of the Standard Word Association Test—Dark, Music, Sickness, Man, Deep, etc.—and they head the 100 short, story-like chapters that relate the familiar and surprising realities of Joanna's life from childhood to adulthood and of her search for love, which she receives from lover, husband, and son. Schoemperlen's first novel, it was published in the USA, Sweden, and Germany. *Our Lady of the Lost and Found* (2001, rpr. 2005) is about belief, faith, the spiritual life. One morning in April the narrator finds a woman standing in her living room. 'She was wearing a navy blue trench coat and white running shoes. She had a white shawl draped over her hair like a hood... .—Fear not, she said.—It's me, Mary, she said. Mother of God.' She stays for a week and is a delightful guest; the two become friends, exchange stories about their lives, and

the narrator (Schoemperlen?) interjects amazing stories about Mary's role in history—Marian Apparitions are described enthusiastically. Though somewhat convoluted, *Our Lady* is infused with feeling and very readable, but it remains an imaginative construct rather than a persuasive novel. In 2008 Schoemperlen published *At a loss for words* (rpr. 2009), which is a long sequence of fragments (some three to a page, some two or three pages long). It begins with the sentence 'I am a writer who cannot write.' The writer's block was instigated by the return, after thirty years, of a former lover at a book-signing. The ending: 'I am no longer at a loss for words.'

In 2004 Schoemperlen published *Names of the dead: an elegy for the victims of September 11.* In her Preface she says: 'For four months I worked only on the names.' She was consulting published lists—which impressed her with 'the power of naming'—that changed every day. 'Faced with such large losses of life, we find that the *numbers* of the dead tend to remain as abstractions in the mind but the *names* ... the names are real. They take your breath away with their power. They can only be read with your heart in your mouth.' Many of the names, arranged alphabetically, are complemented by brief personal details that Scheomperlen discovered in her research. She frequently interrupts the list with what she calls 'fragments'—some factual, referring briefly to the day's events, some 'short narrative scenes of events that had happened in the lives of the victims.' This sad list of names—presented in a handsome, large-format book—is a worthy memorial to the victims of the horrific tragedy. As a writer in mid-career, Schoemperlen received in 2008 the WRITERS' TRUST Marian Engel Award ($15,000).

Schroeder, Andreas (b. 1946). Born in Hoheneggelsen, Germany, he was brought by his family to Canada in 1951. He studied creative writing under Michael BULLOCK and J. Michael YATES at the University of British Columbia (B.A., 1969; M.A., 1972). Schroeder has been founder and editor of *The Journal of Contemporary Literature in Translation* (1968–80); a columnist for the Vancouver *Province* (1968–73); and lecturer on creative writing at the University of Victoria (1974–5), the University of British Columbia (1985–7), and Simon Fraser University (1989–90), where, since 1993, he has been professor of creative non-fiction. He lives with his wife in Roberts Creek, B.C. Much of Schroeder's writing in the 1970s, his most productive period, was influenced by European surrealism. His first two works were poetry collections, *The ozone minotaur* (1969) and *File of uncertainties* (1971), which focused on the violent unpredictability of twentieth-century life. He then published a collection of concrete poetry, *UNIverse* (1971), and his strongest work, a collection of short stories, *The late man* (1972). He has also written a novella, *Toccata in 'D'* (1984), and a novel, *Dustship glory* (1986). In 2008 Schroeder published *Renovating heaven: a novel in triptych*, an entirely delightful work that is obviously autobiographical, about growing up with Mennonite parents and two sisters, all of whom emigrated from Germany in the 1950s. The first part (really a story), 'Eating my father's island', is narrated by young Peter and turns on his father's winning, in a contest, an island off the British Columbia coast. When the family are driven from their farm in the Fraser Valley to view it from a distance, it looks like a pile of rocks. Much transpires in this rich, entertaining story, including a severe loss on the farm. When poverty threatens, the father, Reinhard Neibuhr, sells his island and a wonderful meal is enjoyed from the proceeds (thus the title). The second story bears the title of the book—the renovation is of the house (more like a shack) Reinhard bought when the family were forced to moved from their farm to Vancouver. In the third story, 'Toccata in "D"', Peter travels to Germany in 1971 to try to put himself in touch with his parents' life there, and their meeting, during the war.

Renovating heaven should become Schroeder's best-known book, which at present may be *Shaking it rough: a prison memoir* (1976, rpr. 1983), a journal of the eight-month term he spent in British Columbia prisons on a minor narcotics conviction. His other non-fiction titles include *The Mennonites: a pictorial history of their lives in Canada* (1990), which he wrote as a 'defunct Mennonite', and *Carved from wood: Mission, B.C. 1891–1992* (1991), a history of the place where he once lived. His entertaining stories about 'the world's most outrageous' swindles and rip-offs broadcast on CBC Radio's 'Basic Black' led to the publication of three popular collections: *Scams, scandals, and skulduggery* (1996), *Cheats, charlatans, and chicanery* (1997), and *Fakes, frauds, and flimflammery* (1999).

Schoolcraft, Henry Rowe. See ABORIGINAL LEGENDS AND TALES: BIBLIOGRAPHY.

Scobie, Stephen (b. 1943). Born in Carnousie, Scotland, he took an M.A. at the University of St Andrews before immigrating to Canada in 1965. After completing a doctorate in English at the University of British Columbia in 1969, he taught for ten years at the University of Alberta, then returned to the West Coast to teach at the University of Victoria as professor of english; since 2005 he has been Professor Emeritus. He has been very active in both the promotion of Canadian literature abroad and the examination of North American popular culture, as in his prose work *Alias Bob Dylan* (1991).

Scobie has published numerous short stories and more than a dozen books of poetry, including *The birken tree* (1973), *McAlmon's Chinese opera* (1980, GGA), *A grand memory for forgetting* (1981), *Expecting rain* (1984), *The ballad of Isabel Gunn* (1987), *Dunino* (1989), *Remains* (1990), *Gospel* (1994), and *The spaces in between: selected poems 1965–2001* (2003). *Taking the gate: a journey through Scotland* (1996) includes poetry. *Ghosts: a glossary of the intertext* (1990) is a series of short prose ruminations.

The breadth of Scobie's poetic gifts was already apparent in *A grand memory*, which includes catchy verses that recall the songs of Leonard COHEN, some resonant and carefully modulated lyrics, such as 'The seventh wave' and 'I like to think of you asleep', and a number of intricate and finely tuned historical meditations, such as 'Darien' and the extended sequence 'Elegy'; such poems indicate clearly that Scobie ranges freely from free verse to formalism, from sound and performance poetry to tightly woven art-for-art's-sake compositions. Although he rationalizes his own lack of political engagement with the question, 'Who has the right/to tell us torture?', he nevertheless feels compelled constantly to dredge up the past, lament *temps perdus*, and 'pay/the duty of attention to the dead.' Paying attention to the dead is what Scobie does best, in his lyrics and in his long poems. *McAlmon's Chinese Opera*, which is a subtle and moving tribute to an era and to Robert McAlmon (portrayed in John GLASSCO's *MEMOIRS OF MONTPARNASSE*), the American writer who didn't make it in the Paris of the twenties and ended up selling trusses in Arizona. This poem has a certainty of voice and a dramatic force that derive from the blending of narrative fragments and imagistic detail. (A truly great writer, Robert Louis Stevenson, also a Scot, inspired Scobie's book-length poem *At the world's end* [2009].) In the narrative poem *The ballad of Isabel Gunn*, which has been transformed into an opera, he lovingly reconstructs the story of a young Orkney woman who disguised herself as a man in order to accompany her lover to

Scobie

Canada, where she worked for the Hudson's Bay Company until the birth of her first child ended her gender-bending adventure. A similar impulse towards historical reconstruction is at work in *Gospel*, Scobie's first-person poetic rendering of the life of Christ, which plays with and exploits the slippage between poetic language—lower-case 'word'—and the biblical reference to Christ as the Word made flesh.

While Scobie may be seen enthusiastically announcing the death of the Author, defending the postmodernist, feminist, and deconstructionist critical barricades in Canada, and giving lively performances of his sound-poems, Scobie the poet-scribe stands well back in the shadows, observing the unfolding not only of critical theory, but also of contemporary history. From this vantage point, and with an ingrained, perhaps even Scottish, ambivalence, he composes his subtly contrived, intensely measured, and very accessible poetic fictions.

As a critic Scobie has written a full-length study, *Leonard Cohen* (1978); a critical monograph, *Sheila Watson and her works* (1984); and a provocative collection of critical essays, *Signature event Cantext* (1989).

Scofield, Gregory. See ABORIGINAL LITERATURE: 4, 5.

Scott, Chris (b. 1945). Born in Hull, Yorkshire, England, he was educated at the University of Hull (B.A., 1966), Manchester University (M.A., 1967), and then at the University of Pennsylvania. After a period of teaching at York University, Toronto, he moved to a small town north of Kingston. Scott unleashed his formidable literary learning in *Bartleby* (1971), an anti-novel, in which the reader is guided by a Shandean narrator through a series of intricate, clever literary parodies. Much of the novel turns on literary puns and references. *To catch a spy* (1978) takes the delicate convolutions of the Le Carré thriller a step further—towards a world in which the doubleness of agents is both assumed and unprovable. The plot is a fictional response to the Burgess-MacLean-Philby spy scandals of the Cold War years that moves towards a meditation on the necessity of living with borrowed faiths and contingent truths in the face of an inscrutable divinity. A historical novel, *Antichthon* (1982; UK title, *The heretic*, 1985), continues where the spy novel left off, exploring the universal suspicion in the Renaissance world of casuistry and the Inquisition in which Giordano Bruno

is burnt as a heretic. Like the previous novel, it centres on a 'fictional' death, whose reality is called into question, making truth itself the subtlest corrosive in a corrupt world. Scott's concept of the suppleness of truth underlies the serious vitality he has brought to two otherwise hackneyed genres—the espionage novel and the historical novel. *Hitler's bomb* (1985) returns to the twentieth century, which becomes increasingly more horrifying. A canny handling of spy-trade tools produces an unnerving and exciting twist of mind and motive. *Jack* (1988) is a confession. In this mode the Ripper, Thomas Neill Cream, M.D. (McGill, 1876), uttered his claim, 'I am Jack ...' as the trap-door opened below him for the crimes of poisoning young women. The first-person narrative becomes an objectifying tool that serves to mask the Ripper's identity while the body parts of crime after crime are described. Blood flows rather freely between the elusive ego boundaries of the narrator/murderer. Scott writes about a hugely disappointing organization, his world, with an inexhaustible delight in his craft, and an intellect that feeds equally on sadness and fun, comfort and terror. The razzle-dazzle of the boisterous *Bartleby* has moved into the harder material world of late-twentieth-century monsters, which, as Scott shows us, we are just beginning to imagine.

Scott, Duncan Campbell (1862–1947). The son of a Methodist minister, he was born in Ottawa. He attended school in Smith's Falls, Ontario, and college in Stanstead, Québec. In 1879 his father asked Prime Minister Sir John A. Macdonald to assist him in getting his son a position in the civil service. Shortly thereafter Scott became a clerk, at $1.50 a day, in the Indian Branch (later the Department of Indian Affairs). The poet Scott's career as a civil servant brought him into contact with Canada's Native peoples, particularly during an extensive 1905 trip to the James Bay area as one of the commissioners to the tribes in that region, where he was called 'Da-ha-wen-non-tye', meaning 'flying or floating voice, us-ward', a reference to the poetry he wrote that sympathized with their plight.

Scott's earliest poems, heavily influenced by the Romantics and Victorians, demonstrate a growing facility with language and verse forms but in content reflect nothing Canadian. *The magic house and other poems* (Ottawa, 1893) contains the meditative 'In the country churchyard', a poem honouring the poet's late father and all those who struggle and toil. The belief in the dignity of labour, a crucial element of high Victorianism, is also evident in the title poem of Scott's second book, *Labor and the angel* (Boston, 1898). Though the poems in both books could as easily have been written in London as in Ottawa, *Labor and the angel* reveals Scott's first attempts to deal with subject matter that is indigenous to the land of his birth. 'The Onondaga madonna' offers a portrait of a young Native mother whose race is dying and whose child will never know the thrill of battle. While the subject of the poem is drawn from Scott's first-hand knowledge of Canada's Native peoples, the poet is unable to divest himself of the weight of European sensibilities to which he is heir: the language is Romantic, and the poem's central metaphor, the madonna, is imposed upon the protagonist. Scott's decision to write the poem in the form of a Petrarchan sonnet further distances form from content. *New world lyrics and ballads* (1905), in which Scott struggles to bring form and content together, contains his best-known and most frequently anthologized poem, 'The forsaken', chronicling the sacrifices made by a Chippewa woman as she struggles to save her young son from starvation; when she becomes old, she is left by her son to die in the wilderness. The poem's language is drawn from, rather than imposed upon, its subject. The Chippewa woman's baby is wrapped in the lacings of the *tikanagan*, a Chippewa word, whereas the child in 'The Onondaga madonna' had slept in his mother's 'shawl', a European word. Scott is attempting to find a language, as well as a rhythm, that is appropriate to the life he is documenting—though he is unwilling to relinquish his Christian perspective of the world for the Amerindians' radically different view of experience. In 'The forsaken' the abandonment of the old woman is consistent with her tribe's custom (its purpose being to free the tribe of the burden of caring for the elderly), but Scott interprets the custom in the light of Christian values: the woman is forsaken. The poem contains a number of communion and resurrection metaphors and ends with the pantheistic image of the woman's being shrouded with snow before being drawn up to God's breast—the Christian imagery drawn from Scott's, and not his heroine's, culture. In 'On the way to the mission' (also in *New world lyrics*) the Christian perspective is less forced. A Native is ambushed and killed by three white men who plan to steal what they believe to be a pile of furs on his toboggan. In fact he is not transporting furs but is taking his wife's corpse to the mission for burial. The white men

discover her body, with a crucifix 'under her waxen fingers', when they attempt to gather their spoils. As the Natives here are Christian, the pantheistic conclusion of the poem is appropriate: the Native and his wife are the recipients of God's beneficence as the moon goes 'on to her setting', and covers 'them with shade'. The encroachment of European civilization on the Aboriginal way of life is Scott's most frequent theme. In 'The half-breed girl' (*Via Borealis*, 1906), the agony of being caught between the world of 'the trap and the paddle' and the world of 'loch and shieling' leads the young heroine to desperation.

Although his reputation rests largely on his Amerindian poems, Scott wrote poetry on other subjects. 'The piper of Arll' (*Labor and the angel*), as well as 'The sea by the wood', and its companion piece 'The wood by the sea' (*New world lyrics and ballads*), are among the most-often-anthologized of his non-Native poems. A balance of Native and non-Native poems may be found in *The poems of Duncan Campbell Scott* (1926). *The green cloister: later poems* (1935) and *The circle of affection and other pieces in prose and verse* (1947) contain poems written during Scott's extensive travels in Europe. Yet even in his later years Scott published poems about the history and suffering of the Native Peoples—in 'Powassan's drum', one of the new poems included in *The poems of Duncan Campbell Scott*, and in 'At Gull Lake, 1810' in *The green cloister*, which argues that human dignity can survive the oppression and savagery by which it is so often threatened. Three selections of Scott's poetry have been published since his death: *Selected poems of Duncan Campbell Scott* (1951), with a memoir by E.K. BROWN; *Duncan Campbell Scott: selected poetry* (1974), edited by Glenn Clever; and *Powassan's drum: selected poems of Duncan Campbell Scott* (1985), edited by Raymond SOUSTER and Douglas LOCHHEAD.

Scott was the author of two collections of short stories: *In the village of Viger* (Boston, 1896, NCL) and *The witching of Elspie: a book of stories* (1923). (*The circle of affection* also contains stories.) *In the village of Viger*, set in nineteenth-century Québec, details the lives of both the villagers and those whose lives are intertwined with them. Although the characters are more appropriate to romance than to realism (a shoemaker, a pedlar, an aristocrat fallen on hard times), there is a degree of realism in these stories that is uncommon in the short fiction of the 1890s: encroaching upon the idyllic village are the forces of industrialization and urbanization. In examining a closed society being penetrated by forces that threaten to disrupt its unity, Scott is being consistent with the themes he explores in his poetry about Natives. Glenn Clever has gathered a representative number of Scott's short stories in *Selected stories of Duncan Campbell Scott* (1972, rpr. 1987). It contains 'Charcoal', written some time between 1898 and 1904, based on the case of an Alberta Native who murdered both his wife's lover and a Mounted Policeman, and wounded a farm instructor. (The Native was tried and executed.) Although in a letter to John Masefield, Scott said that the story was 'almost a transcript of the evidence at [Charcoal's] trial, plus facts the Indian agent gave me', it is a blend of fact and romance. See *Uncollected stories of Duncan Campbell Scott* (2001) edited by Tracy Ware.

An important dimension of Duncan Campbell Scott's literary career concerns his relationship with his friend and fellow poet Archibald LAMPMAN. Lampman, Scott, and Wilfred CAMPBELL collaborated on 'AT THE MERMAID INN', a column that ran in the Toronto *Globe* in 1892 and 1893. Scott sought patronage for Lampman and, after Lampman's premature death, became his literary executor. He edited *The poems of Archibald Lampman* (1900, rpr. 1974), the immediate purpose of which was to raise money for Lampman's impoverished widow and children. (Scott even shared the funeral expenses when Mrs Lampman died in 1910.) He subsequently edited Lampman's *Lyrics of earth: sonnets and ballads* (1925); joined E.K. Brown in editing *At the Long Sault and other new poems* (1943, rpr. 1974); and edited *Selected poems of Archibald Lampman* (1947). Although Scott took editorial liberties with the manuscripts, he was almost single-handedly responsible for bringing Lampman's work to the attention of twentieth-century readers.

See *Addresses, essays, and reviews* (2000), Volumes 1 and 2, edited by Leslie Ritchie.

Scott, F.R. (1899–1985). The son of Frederick George SCOTT, Francis (Frank) Reginald Scott was born in the Rectory of St Matthew's Church, Quebec City. He was educated at Bishop's College, Lennoxville, Québec, and at Oxford University, where he held a Rhodes scholarship, receiving a B.A. (1922) and a B.Litt. (1923) for a thesis on 'The annexation of Savoy and Nice by Napoleon III, 1860'. On his return to Canada he taught briefly at Lower Canada College and in 1924 entered the law faculty at McGill University, graduating with a B.C.L. in 1926. In 1927 he was called to the bar and in 1928 returned to McGill to teach; he was dean of law from

1961 to 1964 and retired from McGill in 1968. In 1952 he was technical-aid representative for the United Nations in Burma and from 1963 to 1971 a member of the Royal Commission on Bilingualism and Biculturalism. Scott—who has contributed equally to Canadian law, literature, and politics in both official languages—received a Molson Prize for outstanding achievements in the arts, the humanities, and the social sciences in 1967, the year in which he was made a Companion of the Order of Canada. His dedication to interpreting Québec poetry culminated with a Canada Council Translation Prize for *Poems of French Canada* (1977), and his work as a social philosopher and his life as a poet won him two Governor General's Awards, for *Essays on the constitution: aspects of Canadian law and politics* (1977) and *The collected poems of F.R. Scott* (1981) respectively.

In his career as an inspiring law teacher and social philosopher, Scott was most concerned with the nature of the constitutional and political 'forms' that must be developed to meet the needs of an emerging Canadian society. His interest in social philosophy was sparked by the Depression: he became active in left-wing political movements, and with Frank Underhill was an organizer of the League for Social Reconstruction (1932). President of the League in 1935–7 and national chairman of the Co-operative Commonwealth Federation from 1942 to 1950, he was co-author with David Lewis of *Make this your Canada: a review of CCF history and policy* (1943). *A new endeavour: selected political essays, letters, and addresses* (1986) was edited by Michiel Horn. An authority on constitutional law and civil rights—who has been described by Walter Tarnopolsky as an 'architect of modern Canadian thought on human rights and fundamental freedoms'—Scott argued several major civil-rights cases before the Supreme Court, including Switzman v. Elbing (1957) and Roncarelli v. Duplessis (1958). In addition, Scott is one of the most important catalysts of modern Canadian poetry, partly because of the influence of his own poetry and partly through his personality and his association with several literary groups and 'little magazines'. As a satirist in the late twenties and early thirties, he helped battle an outworn Canadian Romanticism in order to introduce the 'new poetry'; and in landscape poems such as 'Old song', 'Lakeshore', and 'Laurentian Shield' he established a northern evolutionary view of Canadian nature that later influenced such poets as Al PURDY and Margaret ATWOOD. While achieving distinction as a poet, political activist, and leading authority on constitutional law, Scott also became a figure of extraordinary importance as a commentator on both Canadian society and Canadian literature. All these activities found expression in his poetry, and all stemmed from the nationalistic concerns of Canadian intellectuals in the 1920s.

At McGill Scott met A.J.M. SMITH, who introduced him to the new poets, mostly English, who were developing a 'modern' poetry. In 1925 he collaborated with Smith and Leon EDEL in founding *The McGILL FORTNIGHTLY REVIEW*, an iconoclastic journal of modernist literature and opinion. Scott's attacks on the orthodox were to range widely, but his first broadside was launched against the old poetry and its traditional forms. In 1927, in the *McGill Fortnightly*, he published a first draft of 'The Canadian authors meet', a jaunty indictment of the Canadian literary establishment, inspired by visiting a meeting of the CANADIAN AUTHORS' ASSOCIATION. When the *McGill Fortnightly* ceased publication in 1927, Scott became one of the editors of its successor, *The CANADIAN MERCURY* (1928–9). His association with influential literary journals and anthologies continued over succeeding decades. In 1936, with Smith, he co-edited, and wrote a short Preface for, the first anthology of modern Canadian poetry, *NEW PROVINCES: poems of several authors* (1936: rpr. 1976), which included his own verse. In 1942 he was a moving spirit in the founding of *PREVIEW*—edited by a small group that included Patrick ANDERSON, P.K. PAGE, and A.M. KLEIN. In 1945 Scott played a leading role in its merger with a rival publication, *FIRST STATEMENT*, which became *NORTHERN REVIEW* (1945–56).

Scott's career as a poet exemplifies the transition from a Victorian Romanticism to the modern. But, as with most moderns, there was to be a strong infusion of Romanticism in his own poetry, primarily in his use of nature as symbol, but also in his belief that poetry can change society. His poems show a progressive development: from the imagism of late-1920s' poems like 'Old song', through the proletarian realism of the thirties, into a new, almost metaphysical richness of thought and form in the mid-forties and fifties. His first collection of poems, delayed by the Depression, was *Overture* (1945), followed by *Events and signals* (1954); *The eye of the needle* (1957), a collection of satires; *Signature* (1964); and *Selected poems* (1966). Scott's subject is often man in the generic sense, silhouetted against a natural horizon, and his characteristic metaphors

develop from the exploration of man's relationships to nature and society: they involve time and infinity, world and universe, love and spirit—terms that emerge as twentieth-century humanist substitutes for the Christian vocabulary. A typical Scott poem moves from specific image (the great Asian moth of 'A grain of rice', for example), or from the natural landscape ('Hidden in wonder and snow, or sudden with summer,/This land stares at the sun in a huge silence'), to a consideration of the significance of the image in the larger pattern of human life. The human journey, in turn, is seen as a moment in time, a part of the larger cosmic flux in which matter, striving to realize itself, is thrown up briefly in waves. Scott perceives that humans, as physical beings, come and go; yet he maintains that there is continuity in the human spirit and in the shared human experience. His poetry reflects not only the wide diversity of such experience, ranging in style from the reportorial and satiric 'Summer camp' to the fine lyric 'Departure', but a strikingly flexible speaking voice that can move from the playful ('Did you ever see such asses/As the educated masses?') to the tenderly reflective, as in 'Windfall'. Scott has remarked that satire is 'inverted positive statement', and certainly the obverse of Scott the lyrical idealist is Scott the satirist. But even from the satirical inversions of poems such as 'W.L.M.K.' and 'The Canadian authors meet', we can infer both the political and poetic ideals for which Scott stands. As a socialist poet, Scott was most concerned with the kind of social order or 'writing' that humans choose to shape their world. His fear, expressed in 'Laurentian shield' (1945), was that the language of a developing Canada—'prewords,/Cabin syllables,/Nouns of settlement'—might be reduced to the syntax of rapacious technology, 'The long sentence of its exploitation'. In 'Fort Providence' he comments ironically on the toll of the 'firetrap mental gaol'—the religious residential school that oppresses First Nations people.

Scott's later books of poetry include *Trouvailles: poems from prose* (1967), *The dance is one* (1973), and *Collected poems* (1981). He also collaborated with A.J.M. Smith in editing *The blasted pine: an anthology of satire, invective and disrespectful verse: chiefly by Canadian writers* (1957, rev. 1967). An early translator of poetry, he published *St-Denys Garneau and Anne Hébert* in 1962. *Dialogue sur traduction* (1970) is an exchange of letters between Anne HÉBERT and Scott. Northrop FRYE commented in a preface: 'One can hardly learn more in less compass about the kind of craftsmanship that goes into the making of poetry than is given in these few pages.' This was followed by Scott's *Poems of French Canada* (1977).

See *The politics of the imagination: a life of F.R. Scott* (1987, rpr. 1989) by Sandra DJWA, a cultural biography that unifies the thought underlying Scott's poetry, politics, and his work as a legal activist in the context of a developing Canada.

Scott, Frederick George (1861–1944). Born in Montreal, he received a B.A. from Bishop's College, Lennoxville, Québec, in 1881 and an M.A. in 1884. After studying theology at King's College, London, in 1882 and being refused ordination in the Anglican Church of Canada for his Anglo-Catholic beliefs, he was ordained at Coggeshall, Essex, in 1886. He served first at Drummondville, Québec, and then in Quebec City, where he became rector of St Matthew's Church (in whose rectory his son F.R. SCOTT was born in 1899). In 1906 he was appointed a canon of the cathedral and in 1925 archdeacon. During the Great War he was chaplain to the Canadian First Division, where his courage at the front was legendary; his book *The Great War as I saw it* (1922, rpr. 2005) is a vivid war memoir. Scott was created CMG in 1916 and was awarded the DSO in 1918. After the war he was chaplain of the army and navy veterans and was renowned for his radical social views during the Winnipeg and Besco strikes. F.G. Scott was popularly known as the 'poet of the Laurentians'—a lesser member of the group now known as the CONFEDERATION POETS—and was recognized in his time for his nature lyrics and for his hymns of Empire, which stressed both the new nationality and Canada's roles in the Boer and Great Wars. Scott's first book, *Justin and other poems*, privately printed in 1885, contains poems on religion, death, and evolution informed by Victorian pessimism—in which Justin is made to ask, 'Why men should be, why pain and sin and death,/And where were hid the lineaments of God?'; this collection was included in *The soul's quest and other poems* (Toronto, 1885; London, 1888). In 'A mood', dated Mar. 1882, Scott writes of his intense fear of death, speaking of a demon that had haunted him since childhood with 'death and dreams of death'. Several of the early narrative poems, and his later didactic novel *Elton Hazelwood* (1891), describe typically Victorian crises of faith and the recognition of 'life and death as they are'. Hazelwood links his spiritual crisis with that described in John Stuart Mill's *Autobiography*. Scott's lyrics were collected in numerous other books, from *My lattice and other poems* (Toronto, 1894) and *The unnamed lake and other poems* (Toronto, 1897) to *Selected poems* (1933) and *Collected hearts* (1941). His best-known poem, 'The unnamed lake', was an important precursor of 'Old song' by F.R. Scott, and his social radicalism undoubtedly influenced his son. Scott's poetry, with its Christian and evolutionary concerns, is nostalgically Victorian, striking an authentic and original note only in his poems of the Northland.

Scott, Gail (b. 1945?). Born in Ottawa, she grew up in a bilingual community in eastern Ontario. She was educated in English and modern languages at Queen's University (B.A., 1966) and in 1966–7 studied French literature at the Université de Grenoble. From 1967 to 1980 she worked as a journalist in Montreal, covering key political and cultural events in Québec for an English-Canadian audience. Scott was a founding editor of the alternative political publication *The Last Post* (1970), the feminist magazine *Des luttes et des rires des femmes* (late 1970s), and the French-language cultural magazine *Spirale* (1979–83); she also co-founded and worked as Québec editor for the bilingual journal *Tessera* (1984–9). From 1980 to 1991 she taught journalism at Concordia University and since 1991 has devoted her time to writing and translating.

Scott's first book, *Spare parts* (1981), is a collection of stories that parody journalistic style: non-sequiturs disturb the logic of cause and effect, the extraordinary clashes with the matter-of-fact, and strings of simple sentences generate emotional charges that trouble the even surface of newspaper writing. Scott's essays, collected in *Spaces like stairs* (1989), also reject the neutrality and objectivity of her former *métier*. The issue of who is writing for whom, she asserts, shapes what can and cannot be said in a given text. Scott's is a feminist project of opening spaces for women to speak, one that recognizes the variegations in the category 'women'. Her own specificity as an anglophone writing in English in Québec who finds sustenance in French-language culture is a case in point. Traces in her writing of French rhythms and syntax are signs of the influence a minority culture (French) can have on a majority culture (English). *Spare parts: plus two* (2002) is an expanded edition, with two new pieces: 'The virgin denotes; or the unreliability of adverbs to do with time' and 'Bottoms up', two essays on narrative. Scott's novels *Heroine* (1987) and *Main brides* (1993) raise questions about the novel genre, particularly its presentation of female character and her inscription in history. *Heroine* is narrated in the present tense by a woman sitting in a bathtub whose thoughts float from her struggle to write, to an old love affair set against the leftist and independence movements of 1970s Québec, to her interest in the woman in the next room. *Main brides* is a kind of 'installation' that allows a slippage between the woman narrator sitting in a bar on Boulevard St Laurent and the women who come within her field of vision. In both novels innovation begins at the level of the sentence, with strategies of statement-making that resist fixing the subject within the field of relations. Narrative is a fleeting, incomplete structure available only indirectly through a recurring image, a glance, an encounter, or a superficial detail. The privileged centre of consciousness is abandoned in favour of making visible those subjects at the limits of the narrator's consciousness. *My Paris* (1999) is mainly composed by a diarist of numbered sections (to 120) that in telegraphic (sometimes one-word) sentences combine a multitude of riffs on Paris and on lives lived. Scott here acknowledges the influence of Walter Benjamin (1892–1940) and his 'revolutionary method of recovering history through montage of "found" textual objects and anecdotes'—as well as that of Gertrude Stein. See *Gail Scott: essays on her works* (2002) edited by Lianne Moyes.

Scott, Peter Dale (b. 1929), The son of F.R. SCOTT and the painter Marian Dale Scott, he was born in Montreal and educated at McGill University; University College, Oxford; and the Institute d'Études Politiques, Paris. Scott was a foreign service officer for the Canadian Embassy in Warsaw, Poland (1959–61), a professor in the Speech Department at the University of California, Berkeley (1961–6), and a professor in the English Department there (1966–95). His poetry is deeply informed by his childhood in Montreal, his time abroad and in the United States, and his close connections to his family and friends. His first book, *Poems* (1952), was followed by *Prepositions of jet travel* (1981) and *Heart's field* (1986). But Scott established his reputation as a major poet with *Coming to Jakarta: a poem about terror* (1988). This remarkable work—with its distinctive three-line stanzas reminiscent of Ezra Pound, its spare clarity, and its seamless integration of the political and the personal—redefines the possibilities of the long poem for the twentieth century. It addresses the little-known massacre of more than a million Indonesians in 1965, and its frequent references convey Scott's familiarity with a vast array of sources, from

CIA classified documents to works by politicians and anthropologists, newspaper articles, and essays. The poem's haunting drama draws the reader slowly, carefully, and above all responsibly into a world of political terror and uncertainty: the reader does not make this journey simply to witness what Scott records, but rather, like Scott, to grapple with the urgent question of personal responsibility for world events that often seem remote from everyday concerns. *Coming to Jakarta*, like Scott's other works, is also intensely personal, its force stemming from Scott's adept integration of the personal with the political in a manner that illustrates how the two are interdependent. The poetic exploration of personal issues is further deepened in the long poem *Listening to the candle: a poem on impulse* (1992), which moves between different events as it records personal stories of love and loss, in the three-stanza form familiar from *Coming to Jakarta*. The poet's voice itself is marked by an unusual rigour, honesty, and integrity. A trilogy was formed by these two books and the publication of *Minding the dark* (2000). Two collections of Scott's work draw together poems that are not thematically organized—*Rumors of no law: poems from Berkeley 1968–1977* (1981) and *Murmur of the stars: selected shorter poems* (1994)—which communicate the range of Scott's poetic vision: again the poems combine a gentle, compassionate perspective with keen and incisive analysis. Succeeding volumes of Peter Scott's poetry include *Minding the darkness: a poem for the year 2000* (2000) and *Mosaic Orpheus* (2009).

Scott is also well known for numerous works of prose, or what he calls 'parapolitics', their titles indicating his interest in the covert actions and conspiracies that also inform his poetry. These works include *The war conspiracy* (1972), *The assassinations: Dallas and beyond* (1976, in collaboration with Paul L. Hoch and Russell Stetler), *Crime and cover-up: the CIA, the Mafia, and the Dallas-Watergate connection* (1977), *The Iran-Contra connection: secret teams and covert operations in the Reagan era* (1987, with Jonathan Marshall and Jane Hunter); *Cocaine politics: drugs, armies, and the CIA in Central America* (1991, with Jonathan Marshall); and *Deep politics and the death of JFK* (1993), *Deep politics II: the new revelations in government files, 1994–1995* (1994, rpr. 1997), *Drugs, oil, and war: the United States in Afghanistan, Colombia, and Indochina* (2003), *The road to 9/11, and the deep politics of war* (2008).

Second Scroll, The (1951, scholarly edition 2000). A.M. KLEIN's novel, or philosophical parable, was written after he made a trip to Israel in the summer of 1949—an exciting one for a Zionist—when the country was one year old; he also visited, more briefly, the Jewish ghettos in Casablanca, and Rome—all of which are locations in the book. Using his 'Notebook of a journey', Klein composed a symbolic, allusive fulfillment of his trip in the form of a narrative of five 'books' (Genesis to Deuteronomy). The narrator, on a mission to identify the new poets of Israel, is determined to meet his uncle, Melech Davidson. The representative of universal Jewry and also a Messiah figure, Uncle Melech is never met; he is murdered by 'assailants, who were many against one', his body covered with gasoline. Historically, the first scroll contained the first five books of the Bible, the Pentateuch. Melech's life story—encapsulating contemporary Jewish history (and details of Klein's own life history)—becomes the second scroll, written in what Klein called 'the aftermath of a great death, European Jewry's, and in the presence of a great resurrection'. There are five 'glosses', or interpretative variations on spiritual aspects, including a poem, 'Autobiographical' (Gloss Aleph), first published in 1943 in the CANADIAN FORUM; another poem, 'Elegy' (Gloss Beth); 'On first seeing the ceiling of the Sistine Chapel' (Gloss Gimel), a long, dazzling explication in the form of a letter from Melech; a verse-drama, 'The three judgements' (Gloss Dalid); and prayers (Gloss Hai).

Segal, Y.Y. (1896–1954). Yakov Yitzhak (Jacob Isaac) Segal, a major Yiddish-Canadian poet, was born in Koretz, a small village in Ukraine. He immigrated to Canada in 1911 and settled in Montreal, where he worked first in a pants factory, later as a teacher in secular Yiddish schools, and finally as a journalist and editor for the Yiddish-language daily *Der Kanader Odler* (*The Canadian Eagle*). For a time (1923–8) he lived in New York, where he came under the influence of a group of modern Yiddish poets, *Die Junge* (The Young Ones). After his return to Montreal, where he lived until his death, he became a close friend of A.M. KLEIN.

Segal had his first Canadian poem published in *Der Kanader Odler* in 1915, and thereafter he published a great many poetry collections—until *Letzte Lieder* (*Last poems*), which was published posthumously in Montreal in 1995. His first collection, *Vun mein Velt* (*Out of my world*; Montreal, 1918) brought him immediate recognition, not only in Canada but in New York and Poland, the two world

centres of Yiddish literature before the Second World War. Although Segal was a secular Jew, he was learned in the Torah and steeped in Chassidic tradition and folklore. His lyric poetry combines religious and folk tradition, modernist American literary practice, and Canadian landscape and atmosphere. His warm, intimate style unites Jewish lament, prayer, and celebration with a modern consciousness in a highly original way. Some of Segal's poems have been translated into English in *A treasury of Yiddish poetry* (1969) edited by Irving Howe and E. Greenberg; *The first five years: a selection from the Tamarack Review* (1962) edited by Robert WEAVER; and in a renowned picture book of poems for children, *The wind has wings: poems from Canada* (1969, rev. 1984) compiled by Mary Alice Downie and Barbara Robertson and illustrated by Elizabeth Cleaver.

Sellar, Robert (1841–1919). Born in Glasgow, the son of an estate factor, he was brought to Upper Canada as a boy. In 1863 he moved from a job on the Toronto *Globe* to become first editor of *The Gleaner*, a Reform paper in Huntingdon, Québec—in that 'eastern wedge of the province between Ontario and Yankeedom'. Sellar's early editorials rejected Annexationism, deplored lavish government spending, and urged temperance; his 'In defence of the Quebec minority', reprinted in 1894, attacked Roman Catholic encroachment into school and political systems. His editorial wrath at the 'clerical conspiracy' culminated in *The tragedy of Quebec: the expulsion of the Protestant farmers* (1907; republished, with an introduction by Robert Hill, in 1974). Independent, self-published, never part of any literary establishment, Sellar nevertheless became widely known, not only for his partisan regional journalism, but also for his complex use of local materials in both historical fiction and essays.

Gleaner tales (Huntingdon, 1885) draws on interviews with Scots and Loyalist families to create vivid anecdotes of feuds, fires, and harvests; the same material is given non-fictional treatment in *History of the county of Huntingdon and of the seigniories of Beauharnois and Châteauguay* (Huntingdon, 1888), comparable as regional history to the work of James MacPherson Le Moine. *Gleaner tales: second series* (Huntingdon, 1895) adds 'Archange and Marie', a pathetic tale of Acadian exiles in Châteauguay, and 'The summer of sorrow, 1847', about Irish survivors of the cholera epidemic. Sellar's novels illustrate three types of historical fiction: the heroic romance, the group-focused survival story, and the anti-romance of laborious achievement. In *Hemlock: a tale of the War of 1812* (Montreal, 1890), a young British officer is captured by invading Americans, and a Scots settler's daughter bravely travels to the isolated mission at Oka, Québec, to call into action the Native warrior Hemlock. He frees the captive, who then leads a force through the Châteauguay Valley and up the St Lawrence to successful battle at Crysler's Farm. *Morven: a legend of Glengarry* (1910), written in an archaic rhythm suggesting Gaelic, follows a group of Highlanders, cleared from their shielings in the 1770s, who are transported to virtual slavery in Virginia, rescued by the folk-hero Morven, and led with the help of friendly Natives through the wild Adirondacks towards the bush country north of Cornwall. *True makers of Canada: Gordon Sellar—a Scotsman of Upper Canada* (1915), covering the period 1825 to 1838, catches the naive vigour of genuine immigrant journals and is written from the perspective of a Scottish lad, Gordon Sellar; hard times in Scotland lead to Gordon's arduous voyage to York County.

Selvadurai, Shyam (b. 1965). Born in Colombo, Sri Lanka, he came to Canada after the Colombo riots in 1983 and was educated at York University, Toronto (B.F.A.). He lives in Toronto. Of Selvadurai's three novels, two are set in Colombo, at a time when Tamil/Sinhalese enmities—and issues of culture, religion, and caste—provide many charged moments. *Funny boy: a novel in six stories* (1994, rpr. 1997) describes the growth to self-knowledge in the 1970s of Arjie Chelvaratnam, a Tamil boy, who at the age of seven prefers to play with girls; his young Aunt Rhada's benighted attraction to a young Sinhalese man; his mother's ill-fated love affair, in his father's absence, with a friend from her youth who had returned from Australia; his father's attempt to help the young son of a close friend from the past, who may or may not have been attached to the dangerous Tamil Tigers; and Arjie's transference in his teens to the strict and often tormenting Queen Victoria School because, in his father's words, it 'will force you to become a man'—where Arjie realizes he is gay and has a love affair with a fellow student, a Sinhala boy (Arjie's parents had insisted that he learn Sinhalese). The final story, entitled 'Riot journal: an epilogue', ends with emigration. Richly detailed about Sri Lankan family life, and delicately nuanced in describing human relations, *Funny boy* is a memorable, simply told story of

a few years in the life of a young Sri Lankan, and of his family. It won the Smith Books/*Books in Canada* First Novel Award. *Cinnamon Gardens* (1998)—the title refers to a suburb of Colombo that had once been a cinnamon estate and houses 'the best of Ceylonese society'—is set in the 1920s, and the Gardens are where the Kandiah family live: Louisa, a Christian Tamil who left her husband in Malaya, and her three daughters, of whom Annalukshmi (Anna) is a key figure in the novel and teaches at the school of Miss Lawton, to whom she becomes close, as she does to Miss Lawton's adopted daughter Nancy. A family connection, the powerful, ruthless, and hypocritical Mudaliyar Navaratnam, owner of one of the finest houses in the Gardens, and his younger son, Balendran (Bala), are other important characters. Married and with a son, Bala, while being educated in London fell in love and lived with Richard Howland. Howland's arrival in Colombo twenty years later, and the brief renewal of their love affair, provides one of the threads in this family novel of many complications, all smoothly and lucidly described. *Swimming in the Monsoon Sea* (2005) is also set in Colombo, in 1980 in the season of monsoons, but it is described as a young-adult's novel—though there is no reason why the plot, and the vivid, accomplished writing, would not interest adults. It is about Amrith, a fourteen-year-old orphan, living with his godmother (his mother's best friend), Aunty Bundle (her real name was Beatrice 'but she was such a happy baby her parents called her Bundle-of-Joy and then just Bundle') and her husband Uncle Lucky (real name Lukshman Manuel-Pillai). They have two daughters, both close to Amrith. His everyday life in a well-to-do family, with Sri Lankan mores gracefullly injected, is supplemented by his receiving an award in his boys' school for his portrayal of Juliet in scenes from *Romeo and Juliet*, learning to type in the office of Uncle Lucky (at his insistence), his ambition to play Desdemona in the next school play, the last scene of *Othello*, and, most crucially, the arrival of his mother's brother and cousin Neresh from Canada. The two cousins take to each other, but Amrith falls in love with Neresh, bringing about his sexual awakening, and ending—as Neresh leaves for Canada—a memorable coming-of-age story. It was a runner-up for the GGA (Juvenile). Selvadurai edited *Story-Wallah: short fiction from South Asian writers* (2005), an engaging anthology that includes, among other writers, Michael ONDAATJE, Salman Rushdie, Jhumpa Lahiri, and Anita Desai.

Service, Robert W. (1874–1958). Robert William Service was born in Preston, England, and grew up in Scotland, first in Ayrshire with his grandfather and aunts and later in Glasgow with his parents. After leaving school in 1888 he worked for the Commercial Bank of Scotland between 1889 and 1896 when, having cultivated a keen taste for a life (and literature) of adventurous, romantic experience, he left Scotland for Canada. He worked on a farm and, later, on a ranch near Duncan, Vancouver Island. In 1897–8 he wandered through the southwestern USA and Mexico, but by 1899 was again working on the Vancouver Island ranch, where he stayed until 1903, when he resumed his banking career with the Bank of Commerce, Victoria. In the summer of 1904 the bank transferred him to Kamloops; in the autumn of 1904 to Whitehorse; and in 1908 to Dawson, Yukon Territory, the setting for his best-known verse. By 1909 Service had published *Songs of a sourdough* (1907), *The spell of the Yukon* (1907), *Ballads of a cheechako* (1909), and *Rhymes of a rolling stone* (1912), which established his reputation as a writer of humorous, melodramatic ballads—such as 'The shooting of Dan McGrew' and 'The cremation of Sam McGee'—and brought him enough money to give up banking in order to write his first novel. In 1912 Service left Canada, visiting the Balkans as correspondent and eventually settling in Paris. He spent 1914–16 as a war correspondent and stretcher-bearer, and was later a reporter for the Canadian government. He settled finally in Monte Carlo, where he died, although he spent the Second World War in Los Angeles.

Service published many more collections of verse. *Collected poems* (1940) contains most of the early verse and *More collected verse* (1955) contains poems published between 1949 and 1953. *Later collected verse* (1960) appeared posthumously. The best of his verse offers vivid, colourful, and often lurid tales of the Canadian North, told by either the observing or participating 'I'. The heroes of the early work are frequently wanderers, vagabonds, or outsiders, caught between regret for what they have left behind and desire to find a new home in the cold and heartless North. In the verse of his middle period, Service seeks to wring meaning out of the carnage of the Great War, and also balances his experience with death with a close attention to details of life in postwar Europe. In his later verse he repeats frequently and rather tediously his literary commitment to the tales and the idioms of ordinary people. Service also published six works of popular fiction between 1911 and 1927. Anne Watts edited *The best of Robert Service* (1995). See also James A. MacKay, *Vagabond of verse: Robert Service: a biography* (1995).

Seton, Ernest Thompson (1860–1946). Born Ernest Thompson in South Shields, England, he later adopted the name Seton, which he claimed reflected his descent from the Scottish Lord Seton, Earl of Winton. In 1866 the Thompson family immigrated to Canada, settling near Lindsay, Ontario; after 1870 they moved to Toronto, where Seton received his early education. His boyhood experiences near Lindsay and in Toronto's Don Valley, then wilderness areas, formed the basis for many of his writings. Although his talents were diverse, all his work was rooted in the single commitment, formed when he was a boy, to be a naturalist—a term that for him had a visionary as well as scientific meaning. After graduating from the Toronto Grammar School (now Jarvis Collegiate), Seton enrolled at the Ontario College of Art. He graduated in 1879, having earned a Gold Medal and a scholarship to study at the Royal Academy in England. In 1881 he returned to Ontario, and in the following year joined his brother on a homestead near Carberry, Manitoba. His program of self-education as a naturalist then became increasingly rigorous as he made meticulous records of the behaviour of animals and birds and published *The birds of Manitoba* (Smithsonian Institution, 1891). In the meantime he travelled frequently to New York, where he was in demand as an illustrator, having been commissioned to do 1000 illustrations of birds and animals for the twelve-volume *Century dictionary*. Encouraged by his success as an artist, he studied in Paris for several years after 1890. In 1891 his painting *The Sleeping Wolf* won first prize in the annual competition held at the Paris Salon. His later submissions were more controversial. The painting *Triumph of the Wolves* (1892), depicting wolves devouring the body of a man, caused an uproar that contributed to his decision to return to Canada. In 1892 Seton was appointed official naturalist for Manitoba, a position that was largely honorary. In the same year he had made a brief visit to New Mexico and his experiences there became the basis for his most famous animal story, 'Lobo, the king of Currumpaw'. He then returned to Paris for another year, submitting another painting to the Salon competition and publishing *Studies in the art anatomy of animals* (New York, 1896). But the cool reception given in Paris to his pro-wilderness paintings led him to return in 1896 to the United States where, with the exception of various expeditions to Canada, he spent the rest of his life. Seton's work as a scientist never abated. In 1908 he published the two-volume *The life histories of northern animals: an account of the mammals of Manitoba*; and, after he made a journey into the Far North, *The arctic prairies: a canoe-journey of 2,000 miles in search of the caribou* (1911). He continued to work as an illustrator, publishing *Pictures of wild animals* (1901) and *Bird portraits* (1901).

But it was Seton's animal stories that ensured his lasting fame. He contributed, along with Sir Charles G.D. ROBERTS, to the creation of a distinctive literary genre: the realistic animal story. His first collection—containing the story of Lobo, a grey wolf—was WILD ANIMALS I HAVE KNOWN (New York, 1898; 1977, NCL; rpr. 1991, 2009); it was an immediate success and was followed by numerous animal stories and collections—such as *The biography of a grizzly* (1900), *Lives of the hunted; containing a true account of the doings of five quadrupeds and three birds, and, in elucidation of the same, over 200 drawings* (1901), *Monarch, the big bear of Tallac* (1904), *Animal heroes* (1905)—until 1945. The best of Seton's stories derive their power from his ability to synthesize his knowledge of animal behaviour, and from his prophetic vision (the worst are maudlin). Romantic primitivism, with its glorification of a sublime wilderness, forms a necessary context for an understanding of that vision. At the same time, later criticism has remarked that the wilderness in Seton's tales is also Darwinian. In Margaret ATWOOD's *SURVIVAL*, Seton's stories appear as a central example of a tendency to identify with the hunted victim, which Atwood views as peculiarly Canadian. Seton's strange blend of Romantic and Victorian attitudes to nature resulted from his synthesis of British, American, and Canadian influences.

In the midst of his busy writing career, Seton found time to become deeply involved in the development of a youth organization called Woodcraft Indians. His childhood interest in 'playing Indian' formed the basis for his children's story TWO LITTLE SAVAGES; *being the adventures of two boys who lived as Indians and what they learned* (1906), a classic in the genre. He also wrote numerous other books about woodcraft. In 1910 Seton joined Lord Baden-Powell and Daniel Beard in establishing the Boy Scouts of America. His writings formed the basis for the *Boy Scouts of America Official Manual* (1910). For many years

he held the post of Chief Scout and enjoyed immense popularity. At the same time he began a prolonged disagreement with the administration of the association, levelling charges of militarism; they, in turn, accused Seton of pacifism. Finally, in 1915, the association expelled him on the pretext that he was not an American citizen. Until the end of his life Seton remained so bitter about this episode that he was urged by his publisher to leave all mention of it out of his autobiography. Nevertheless, the incident did nothing to stop the flow of books about woodcraft.

There had been constant criticism of Seton's animal stories from scientists who charged him with anthropomorphism. Books like *The natural history of the Ten Commandments* (1907), in which Seton attempted to demonstrate the biological source of biblical morality, added fuel to these charges. The so-called nature-fakir controversy, however—the epithet was used by President Theodore Roosevelt in 1907 to dismiss the animal stories of Seton and Roberts—merely acted as a catalyst, leading Seton to redouble his scientific activity. Between 1925 and 1927 he published four volumes in a series entitled Lives of Game Animals that won him the John Burroughs and the Elliott Gold Medals, then the highest awards given for naturalist work. The last sixteen years of Seton's life were spent near Santa Fe, New Mexico, where he settled in 1930. In 1931 he took out American citizenship. With his much younger second wife, Julia Buttree, who had been his assistant, he set up Seton Village, a study centre for naturalists. He continued to publish books until 1945.

See *Selected stories of Ernest Thompson Seton* (1977) edited by Patricia Morley, and Betty Keller, *Black wolf: the life of Ernest Thompson Seton* (1984).

Sherman, Francis Joseph (1871–1926). Born in Fredericton, New Brunswick, he attended the Collegiate School and entered the University of New Brunswick at the age of fifteen, but was forced to abandon his studies for financial reasons and joined the Merchants' Bank of Halifax. Advancing quickly through the ranks while serving in Woodstock, N.B., Fredericton, Montreal, and Havana, Sherman had established the bank's influence throughout Cuba and the Caribbean by 1901, when the Merchants' Bank changed its name to the Royal Bank of Canada. He returned to the head office in Montreal in 1912 as assistant general manager. In 1919 he retired because of ill health caused by his military service in the Great War. He died in Atlantic City, USA, and is buried in Fredericton. Although encouraged in his writing of poetry by the literary ambience of Fredericton in the post-Confederation period, Sherman was never as public or as prolific a writer as his friends Bliss CARMAN, Charles G.D. ROBERTS, and Theodore Goodridge ROBERTS. His collections include *Matins* (Boston, 1896), a series of romantic poems praised by both Rudyard Kipling and Carman; *In memorabilia mortis* (Cambridge, Mass., 1896), a tightly crafted sonnet series commemorating the 'eminent Victorian' William Morris, who was a poet, among many other occupations, and whose poetry was much admired by Sherman and was an influence on his style; and *The deserted city* (Boston, 1899), nineteen lyrical and finely disciplined sonnets on faith and love, described by Roberts as the work of a 'master sonneteer'. Lorne PIERCE edited *The complete poems of Francis Sherman* (1935), with a foreword by Sir Charles G.D. Roberts. Pierce and Roberts both acknowledged the sure craftsmanship, fastidious attention to language, and control of the sonnet form that continue to earn Sherman admiration among a sympathetic circle of poetry readers. *An Acadian Easter: the collected poems of Francis Sherman* was published in 1999.

Sherman, Jason (b.1962). Born in Montreal, Sherman (the seventh of eight sons) graduated from the Creative Writing Program of York University, Toronto, in 1985. That year he founded *What Publishing*, which produced *What Magazine*, which he edited from 1985 to 1990. While Sherman is best known for his swift attainment of acclaim as a dramatist, his venture with *What* marks his alternative career as a journalist whose reviews, essays, and interviews have appeared not only in the magazine he edited but in the Toronto *Globe and Mail* and elsewhere. He has been playwright-in-residence at Tarragon Theatre, Toronto, since 1992.

The league of Nathans (1996), produced in a co-production by Orange Dog Theatre and Theatre Passe Muraille, Toronto, tells of a reunion as adults of three boyhood friends and introduces themes that pervade Sherman's work, including the complex problem of how an individual, in the context of histories that are both personal and social, behaves ethically. Sherman, a Canadian and a Jew, raises this issue against the context of the politically fraught creation of the state of Israel. In having the three boyhood friends

bear the same given name, Sherman suggests that seemingly different, contradictory perspectives on being Jewish are nevertheless related. This history weighs on the response each of the Nathans has to the creation of the state and to the violence that Israel has levelled against Palestinians.

This complexity, of the political and personal, features strongly in *Three in the back, two in the head* (1994, GGA), which deals with the search of Paul Jackson for answers about the murder of his father, Donald, who was working on a defence system that would create a shield against incoming missiles. The son's search for the truth about his father's death is impelled by both his personal sense of grief and his sense of his father's place in the nation's history. The father's work, like his death, is shrouded in secrecy; its true implications are suppressed for political reasons. Faced with the suppression of truth, the problem facing Paul is knowing who in the government will tell him the truth about his father, his work and his death. Sherman returned to the impact of history on individual lives and the difficulty of being an ethical citizen in *The retreat* (1996). At a writers' retreat in the mountains (like those at Banff) two film producers, David Fine and Jeff Bloom, meet with a writer, Rachel Benjamin. Sherman again raises the troubling question: in a web of histories, how can individuals be certain that they are making ethically correct choices? Sherman's *Reading Hebron* (1997) was produced by Factory Theatre in 1996 and *None is too many* was produced in 1997 by Winnipeg's Jewish Theatre and the Manitoba Theatre Centre. *It's all true*—which was produced twice in Toronto in 1999, first at the Tarragon Theatre and ten months later, somewhat revised and sharpened, at Buddies in Bad Times—is about the 1937 musical by Marc Blitzstein, *The cradle will rock*, that depicts decadent capitalism, social injustice, and labour unity; it was directed by Orson Welles. The government padlocked the theatre on opening night and the actors were forced to perform while sitting in their seats at a different theatre. The complexities of the situation—which includes censorship and the illusion of theatre—and of the characters were skilfully handled to create a production that was described as magical. See *Jason Sherman: the plays* (2000) and *Jason Sherman: six plays* (2001)—the plays are *The retreat*; *Three in the back, two in the head*; *The league of Nathans*; *Reading Hebron*; *It's all true*; and *Patience*.

The title *An acre of time: the play* (2001)—inspired by the book of the same title by Phil Jenkins—refers to an acre of land near the

Ottawa River. Its discovery by a surveyor, Julia Wright, leads to a poignant fantasy about its historical past and the people who passed through it. It was first produced at the Tarrragon Theatre, Toronto, in March 2001. *Remnants [a fable]* (2003), about anti-Semitism in Canada, is a modern retelling of the biblical story of Joseph and his brothers, taking place between 1925 and 1946, the setting shifting from Egypt and Poland to Canada. Young Joseph goes to Canada, becomes educated and Canadianized, and changes his last name to Taylor. He eventually becomes an adviser to Prime Minister Mackenzie King, who entrusts him with the task of rejecting a boatload of Jewish refugees, among whom are his brothers. Unfortunately characterization in this play is given a weak secondary place to the dramatic plot. It was commissioned by the Canadian Stage Company and premiered at Tarragon Theatre, Toronto, in September 2003. *Adapt or die: plays new and used* (2006) is made of four modern play adaptations based on works by three great Russian writers: *The brothers Karamazov* from the Dostoevsky novel (first produced by the Stratford Festival, Ontario, in May 2005); *The bear*, based on the farce by Anton Chekhov (first produced by Soulpepper Theatre, Toronto, in September 2002); *Enemies*, an adaptation of the play by Maxim Gorky (first produced by Ryerson University, Toronto, in February 2006); and *After the orchard*, inspired by Chekhov's *The cherry orchard* (first produced by the National Arts Centre, Ottawa, in September 2005). Sherman edited *Modern Jewish plays* (2006), containing plays by six Canadian playwrights: Arthur Milner (*Masada*), Motti Lerner (*The Murder of Isaac*, translated), Jonathan Garfinkel (*The trials of John Demjanjuk: a holocaust cabaret*), Simon Block (*Hand in hand*), Joshua Sobol (*Shooting Magda [the Palestinian girl]*, translated), and Sherman (*Reading Hebron*).

Shields, Carol (1935–2003). Carol Warner was born in Oak Park, Illinois. In 1957 she received her B.A. from Hanover College, Indiana, and in the same year married a Canadian, Donald Hugh Shields (whom she had met the year before when she was on an exchange program with Exeter University, England); they had five children. Carol Shields became a Canadian citizen in 1971 and in 1975 received an M.A. in English from the University of Ottawa; a revision of her thesis was published as *Susanna Moodie: voice and vision* (1972, rpr. 1977). She has taught English at the Universities of Ottawa, British

Columbia, and Manitoba (Don Shields was appointed professor of civil engineering in the University of Manitoba), where she became professor of English. In 1996 she was appointed Chancellor of the University of Winnipeg. She was made a Companion of the Order of Canada in 2002. In 2000 she and her husband moved to Victoria, B.C., where she died. Shields's unusual array of attributes was widely mourned. These included, of course, her literary gift, but also her gift for friendship, her love of family and domesticity, and her indelible curiosity about life and human behaviour, which found memorable expression in her writing.

Shields published three volumes of poetry: *Others* (1972), *Intersect* (1974), and *Coming to Canada* (1992, rev. 1995), which contains eleven poems from each of the previous collections, a section of new poems, and an introduction by Christopher Levenson. The poems are simple, domestic, generous in spirit, though often technically undistinguished. Our satisfaction typically comes in the moments of insight, but as if these moments somehow existed apart from the language and final shape of the whole. Shields is best known as a writer of novels and stories. *Small ceremonies* (1976, rpr. 1995) was followed by *The box garden* (1977, rpr. 1990), *Happenstance* (1980 and 1982, rpr. 1997), and *A fairly conventional woman* (1982). These novels are characterized by gentle satire and careful, pleasingly accurate domestic observation. Very much concerned with the threads that connect domestic and artistic or intellectual life, Shields represents in her fiction both her experience as a wife and mother and her literary ventures: the heroine of *Small ceremonies*, for example, writes fiction and has produced a book about Susanna MOODIE (as Shields did). Disillusioned in early middle age, Shields' protagonists are nevertheless survivors and celebrants. They find consolation in the texture of daily life, the rush of love, and the intersection of their ordinary worlds with something really extraordinary—such as the party of deaf-mutes who dine out together so marvellously at the end of *Small ceremonies*. This sudden, lyrical blossoming in Shields' fiction is like a signature attesting to the writer's love for her own gift of observation. *Happenstance*, however, suggests that some part of perception (even when it is specifically of love) always remains stillborn: 'He loved her. But feared that something in his greeting might fall short. Some connection between perception and the moment itself would fail, would always fail.' The plot of *The box garden*—the least successful of these novels—relies on far-fetched coincidence, and *A fairly conventional woman* is flawed by sentimentality and spates of unconvincing dialogue. For *Happenstance* Shields used a male protagonist for the first time. *Small ceremonies*, in this period the best and most consistently believable of her novels, illustrates most clearly her special gifts of observation. The story collection *Various miracles* (1985, rpr. 1996) features Shields' sharp-eyed observations, and odd incidents rather than plotted stories. 'Mrs Turner cutting the grass' is about an elderly woman in shorts and halter pushing a lawnmower in front of her Winnipeg house—a repellent sight to her neighbours. What if they knew of her youth in New York where she gave birth to a black baby she left in a carriage in Brooklyn Heights? Or that she likes to travel and with her two sisters went to Japan, where they caught the attention of 'the Professor', a poet, who later wrote a cruel and funny poem about the three philistines that was always the most popular poem at his readings. Like Chekhov, Shields writes about ordinary people who outwardly lead unremarkable lives. In one of the stories in *The orange fish* (1989, rpr. 1990) Hazel is trying to mourn her late husband, a man who had a habit of sleeping with her best friends. On an impulse she answers a newspaper ad and gets a job, her first. To the astonishment of friends and family, she is a success.

The heroine of *The republic of love* (1992, rpr. 1994) is Fay McLeod, a folklore scholar, aged thirty-five, who is ending yet another affair. Tom Avery is a radio disc jockey, thrice divorced, and forty. These two search for love, and find it, in this good-humoured urban fantasy. *Swann: a mystery* (1987, rpr. 1996) unfolds as a mild satire on the world of scholarship. We meet a professor, Sarah, who is a successful feminist writer; Morton, a biographer of famous poets; Rose, a librarian in a small Ontario town; Frederic, an octogenarian journalist and publisher—each one is described in a separate chapter. All four come together at a Toronto symposium in honour of a dead Canadian poet, Mary Swann. Her poems have attracted much interest because she was murdered by her husband, who dismembered her body before shooting himself. Each of the characters wants to be seen as the authority on Mary Swann. But the symposium—described in the last chapter in the form of a film script—ends in a shambles: Swann's notebooks, copies of her book, a rare photograph, and notes for a speech have vanished. These disappearances, Swann herself and her violent death, remain mysterious. We

are led on a fine chase and learn very little. But Shields' characters entertain us while the hunt is on. The film *Swann*, directed by Anna Benson Gyles, was released in 1997.

Shields came to her full power in *The Stone diaries* (1993, rpr. 2008), which won both a Governor General's Award and the Pulitzer Prize. It is set at first in a company mining town in Manitoba early in the twentieth century, and opens as Mercy Stone Goodwill, a stonemason's wife, is startled and bewildered by birth pangs. The novel is mainly about Daisy, the daughter she bears, and follows her through childhood, marriage, widowhood, a second marriage, motherhood, and old age in Florida. When she returns to Canada from her father's home in Indiana in search of her roots, she finds a husband, a home, and a garden. It is the last that becomes her passion. What an eye Shields has for detail! And how well she describes lonely eccentric men: Mercy's husband, the quarryman; Barker Flett, the shy botanist Daisy marries; and Barker's curmudgeon father. They are ordinary; they are unforgettable. *Larry's party* (1997, rpr. 1998) is about another ordinary person, Larry Weller of Winnipeg, from 1977 to 1997. His relationships—with parents, two wives, his son, his friends, a lover—and the events of his life, notably his developing a career as a successful designer of garden mazes after being inspired by the Hampton Court maze, seen on his honeymoon, are embroidered with Shields' wonderful and witty eye for detail (as in *The Stone diaries*) pertaining to things and people. Fifteen chapters that are really linked short stories examine Larry's life: 'Larry's love', 'Larry's folks', 'Larry's work' ... ending with 'Larry's party', at which both of his ex-wives are present, along with his lover—it anticipates one more change in his life. *Larry's party* won the prestigious Orange Prize for Fiction. A musical based on the novel, produced by Canadian Stage, Toronto—book and lyrics by Richard Ouzounian, music by Marek Norman—opened in Jan. 2001. *Unless* (2002, rpr. 2003), Shields' last novel, begins with the sentence: 'It happens that I am going through a period of great unhappiness and loss just now.' The narrator, Reta Winters—a feminist, happily married to Dr Tom Winters for twenty-six years, with three daughters, living on a farm in an old house in Orangetown, an hour's drive north of Toronto—is referring to the loss of her nineteen-year-old daughter Norah, who for an unfathomable reason has left university and sits cross-legged at the corner of Bloor Street and Bathurst, in front of Honest Ed's, with a hand-lettered cardboard sign saying GOODNESS hanging from her neck. (It might occur to some readers that the opening sentence could also refer to Shields' having been diagnosed with breast cancer around the time she began to write the novel.) Norah does not speak when members of her family visit her. The novel, however, is mainly about Reta as she describes the commonplace events of her daily life, which Shields' artistry and keen observation turn into a succession of clear-eyed, sometimes poignant or comical set-pieces. Reta is a translator from the French —specializing in the works of a great French writer, Danielle Westerman—and has published a light novel called *My thyme is up* (writers and the satirical treatment of a publisher's editor are among the topics searchingly dealt with in this discursive novel), which had a moderate success, won an award, and occasioned a promotional trip to New York, Washington, and Baltimore, wittily described. *Unless* is a compelling and probing account of a short period in one woman's life. The final chapter, called 'Not Yet', focuses indirectly on Norah, the horrific event that traumatized her, the collapse of her health, her father's finding the hospital she is in—until Reta writes in the last paragraph: 'Day by day Norah is recovering at home. Awakening atom by atom, and shyly planning her way on a conjectural map. It is bliss to see ... .'

Shields ended the millennium, or began the new millennium, with a highly praised collection of stories, *Dressing up for the carnival* (2000, rpr. 2001). Her three story collections are represented in *The collected stories* (2004, rpr. 2005), which opens with 'Segue', Shields' last story, the first-person narrative of sixty-seven-year-old Jane Sexton who discusses her husband, the well-known Chicago novelist Max Sexton (the story opens with their shopping) and her interests—she is a poet who describes writing sonnets, tries to write one sonnet every fourteen days, and is the retiring chair of the Sonnet Society—in a day-long discursive memoir (thus the title) that is filled with Shields' characteristic warm, acute observations and ends at night when Jane begins to fall asleep, thinking: '...if it weren't for my particular circumstances I would be happy.'

Shields collaborated with the novelist Blanche Howard in writing *A celibate season* (1991, rpr. 1998), an epistolary novel about the unavoidable ten-month separation of a married couple. She is also a published playwright. *Departures and arrivals* (1990), which takes place in an airport, was first performed in Manitoba in 1984; and she collaborated with

her daughter, Catherine Shields, in writing *Fashion, power, guilt* (1995). Her most successful play is *Thirteen hands* (1993), which premiered at Winnipeg's Prairie Theatre Exchange in 1993, and in 1997 was co-produced by the National Arts Centre, Ottawa, and the Canadian Stage Company, Toronto. It presents four actors who play a group of women, most of whom have been weekly bridge partners for forty-three years. These housewives and mothers form an important bond of friendship on the Tuesday evenings when they do not have to be at home and have 'a dozen eyes and thirteen hands'. They are types we recognize with pleasure, and some of their stories are moving. *Thirteen hands and other plays* (2002) includes three other plays: *Departures and Arrivals, Anniversary*, and *Fashion, Power, Guilt, and the Charity of Families*.

For the Penguin / Weidenfeld & Nicolson Lives series, Shields wrote *Jane Austen* (2001), a brief (152 pages) but satisfying, sensitive study of Austen's life and works: 'Jane Austen is a dramatic rather than descriptive writer, concerned with morality and using speech as her medium. Readers know how rarely she stops to describe a gown or a meal or a piece of furniture, and how those of her characters who are given to such descriptions are exposed, gently or severely, as being inferior.' *A memoir of friendship: the letters between Carol Shields & Blanche Howard* (2007), edited by Blanche Howard and Allison Howard, is a substantial (549 pages) collection of letters written from 1975 to 2003, with a Foreword by Anne Giardini, Carol Shields' daughter. *The staircase letters: an extraordinary friendship at the end of life* (2007), by Arthur Motyer with Elma Gerwin & Carol Shields, records the thoughts of two dying women who were friends—Gerwin (afflicted with colon, lung, then brain cancer) and Shields (afflicted with breast cancer)—through email letters, in which Motyer took part as Gerwin's friend and former professor at Mount Allison University. He links the letters with sensitive commentaries on death and dying.

See Adriana Trozzi, *Carol Shields' magic wand: turning the ordinary into the extraordinary* (2001, published in Rome), *Carol Shields: narrative hunger, and the possibilities of fiction* (2003) edited by Edward Eden and Dee Goertz; *Carol Shields: the arts of a writing life* (2003) edited by Neil Kalman Besner, *Carol Shields and the extra-ordinary* (2007) edited by Marta Dvořák and Manina Jones, and Eleanor WACHTEL's *Random illuminations: conversations with Carol Shields* (2007).

Shiels, Andrew (1793–1879). Born in rural Roxburghshire, Scotland, and largely self-educated, he immigrated to Nova Scotia in 1818 and worked as a blacksmith in Halifax. In 1828 he established himself on a farm in Dartmouth and became a leading citizen in the area, serving as a justice of the peace and in 1857 being appointed a magistrate. Perhaps the most prolific poet in nineteenth-century Nova Scotia, he wrote and published verse for over fifty years under the pseudonym 'Albyn'—frequently in local newspapers, but also in eleven books and pamphlets of verse, including *The witch of the Westcot* (Halifax, 1831), *The water lily* (Halifax, 1852), *Letter to Eliza* (Halifax, 1876), *John Walker's courtship* (Halifax, 1877), and *Dupes and demagogues* (Halifax, 1879). Although he tried his hand at a wide variety of verse forms, he was at his best writing songs and light lyrics (in the manner of Burns) and verse tales, in which he often turned to history and legend for his subjects: he was particularly interested in the history and folk stories of Nova Scotia. For Shiels, one of the main functions of verse was to dramatize and amplify human experience so that what appeared commonplace took on special meaning. He strove to express the mysterious, vital, magical spirit that lay at the heart of the world, and was able to make his readers feel the force of his love of life.

Sime, Jessie Georgina (1868–1958). She was born in Scotland, and at the age of eleven moved with her parents to London, England, where, through her parents, both writers, Sime became acquainted with such notable Victorian writers as Thomas Carlyle and William Morris. Immigrating to Montreal in 1907, she soon became involved in the city's literary and intellectual community. Sime was an early modernist and realist, in her fiction and non-fiction directing attention to the social, economic, and emotional difficulties of working-class women and the urban poor. Her fiction includes *Sister woman* (1919, rpr. 1992), stories mainly about working-class immigrants to Canada, and *Our little life: a novel of today* (1921, rpr. 1994): set in Montreal, it is a significant early attempt at urban realism in Canadian fiction. Sime may have returned to England about 1950.

Simon, Lorne. See ABORIGINAL LITERATURE: 4.

Simons, Beverley (b. 1938). Born in Flin Flon, Manitoba, Simons grew up in Edmonton, and was preparing for a career as a concert pianist when she won a creative-writing scholarship to the Banff School of Fine Arts for her one-act verse drama, *Twisted roots* (1956). After two years at McGill University, where she formed an experimental theatre group, she completed her B.A. in English and theatre at the University of British Columbia in 1959. Following two more years of working and studying in Europe, she settled in Vancouver and produced several stage, television, and film scripts while raising a young family. In 1968 and 1986 she visited the Orient, studying theatre. In 1972 she received a CANADA COUNCIL Senior Arts Award. Criticism over the award, and continual difficulties in getting her plays produced, led her to abandon playwriting in the mid-seventies. While most of her plays have been published and are often studied in drama courses, they are now rarely performed. *Crabdance* (1969, rpr. 1972), which had several productions in the sixties and seventies, has been aptly compared to *Waiting for Godot*: in both plays a few characters, in a setting that is 'suggestive rather than detailed', perform the rituals and word games that denote a meaningless existence and the failure of communication. While Beckett's Vladimir and Estragon wait, Sadie Golden prepares for an inevitable end. The emptiness of her life is gradually revealed as she struggles to assert her significance in a series of ritualistic relationships with three visiting salesmen. But, tragically her efforts to use the buyer-seller, mother-son, wife-husband, mistress-lover roles for self-discovery become confused circular patterns of exploitation and victimization that can be resolved only by her death. In *Green lawn rest home* (1973), a one-act play, Simons again reveals how fragile and pointless one's sense of identity can be as three elderly residents of a nursing home experience the loss of their senses, passions, and memories in a series of empty social rituals that do nothing to calm their fear of the death they cannot mention. *Preparing* (1975) is a quartet of short plays— *Preparing, Prologue, Triangle,* and *The crusader*— that offer different models of the preparation for death. They employ experimental forms ranging from the naturalistic one-woman monologue of the title play, through the formalistic patterning of *Triangle*, to the stylized rituals of Japanese theatre in *The crusader*. Simons' experimentation with form, however, is most radical in *Leela means to play* (1976). Relying heavily on the symbolic devices of oriental theatre, it destroys conventional time and space with an episodic exploration of 'man's evolution through relationships, the interaction of people'. In Simons' plays there is a progression from the personal rituals shaping *Crabdance* to the formal rituals that define *Leela means to play*, and this gradual solidification of form becomes an effective metaphor for her view of life as a preparation for death, the final meaningless ritual.

Simpson, Leo (b. 1934). Leo James Pascal Simpson was born in Limerick, Ireland, and was educated in that country. He lived in England and Spain before coming to Canada in 1961. After working as publicity director and editor at MACMILLAN OF CANADA, he moved to Queensborough Township north of Belleville, Ontario, in 1966 and then settled in Madoc in 1972. He and his wife Jacqueline spent years completely and faithfully restoring the Susanna MOODIE house in Belleville, moving into the house in 1987.

Simpson is a rarity among Canadian writers, a comic novelist of ideas. His protagonists continually find themselves in absurd plights when they struggle to purge the evil influences of contemporary technology and business, and of small-town conformity. Addison Arkwright, the hero of Simpson's ambitious first novel, *Arkwright* (1971), describes himself as 'holding my ripped humanity together comically'. A violent iconoclast, he is obsessed with exposing his multi-millionaire uncle's scheme to exploit a bogus religion founded on the exaltation of failure, and is torn by contrary and ineffectual impulses throughout most of the novel. He finally attains an idyllic refuge in Crete, though he imagines that he will be forever engaged in seeking personal 'reformation'. Two of Simpson's other novels, *The Peacock papers* (1973) and *Kowalski's last chance* (1980), are set in Bradfarrow, modelled on Belleville. Jeffrey Anchyr, the intellectual upper-class protagonist of *The Peacock papers*, and Joe Kowalski, a low-brow policeman, have in common their sense of contact with a fantasy realm scorned by their obtuse fellow citizens. Anchyr believes himself to be guided by the nineteenth-century British novelist Thomas Love Peacock in a campaign to resist the conversion of the Bradfarrow Public Library into a computerized data centre, a scheme undertaken by a character based on Marshall MCLUHAN. In part a loving imitation of the real Peacock's fiction, the novel upholds Peacock's preaching of traditional humanism and attacks the false faith of communications technology. The events of the book take a tragi-comic turn when Anchyr, troubled by 'much confused dying' in the modern world, proves a martyr to his sensitivity. Joe Kowalski,

equally sensitive in his own sphere to human injustice, is persecuted by his chief for taking pity on an alleged bank robber who declares himself to be a leprechaun. Unlike *The Peacock papers*, *Kowalski's last chance* focuses on social rather than intellectual satire, but in both novels Simpson concocts an ingenious blend of fantasy, farce, and intellectual insight. *The lady and the travelling salesman: stories by Leo Simpson* (1976), edited by Henry Imbleau, collects stories written over the previous decade and a half. Many involve the sudden reversal of stereotyped roles, as in the title story, in which an arms salesman is assaulted by a militant do-gooder, or 'The savages', in which teenagers on the rampage are massacred by an earnest computer expert. Both the themes and manner of Simpson's previous work can be found, in as lively and challenging a form as ever, in *Sailor man* (1996). Part of this novel is set in Belleville, but most of it takes place within an Ottawa commercial and residential complex that in its comprehensive range of money-making services, from a hospital maternity wing to a nursing home, is an emblem of the greed of contemporary hucksterism and a distortion of the role of a traditional community. Drawing on the stock roles of *commedia dell'arte* for his own symbolic purposes, Simpson relies on a witty narrator and farcical confrontation scenes to create a darkly comic vision of contemporary alienation: technology no longer seems to be an evil in itself so much as an easy target for commercial manipulation. Like all Simpson's fiction, *Sailor man* is playfully inventive, but also fundamentally serious in its skeptical view of contemporary life.

Skelton, Robin (1925–97). He was born at Easington, England, emigrating after his education at Christ's College, Cambridge, and the University of Leeds (B.A., 1950, M.A., 1951). In 1963 he joined the Department of English at the University of Victoria, British Columbia, establishing a network between that university and British writers that would enrich the Creative Writing Department, which he founded in 1967, staying on as head until 1976. A renaissance man, who perhaps preferred to be mainly regarded as a poet, Skelton was also scholar, editor, biographer, critic, mentor, literary angel, visual artist, and translator.

Despite the chiaroscuro of Skelton's poems—which, starting with *Patmos and other poems* (1955), extend to several baker's dozens of volumes, including *Selected shorter poems 1947–1977* (1981) and *One leaf shaking: collected later poems 1977–1990* (1996, rpr. 2000), *Facing* the light (2004), and *In this poem I am: selected poetry of Robin Skelton* (2007)—edited with an introduction by Harold Rhenisch, 'A portrait of the poet as a book'—he was, in his own words, always 'marching syntax toward a ceremony of love'. This march is measured by his understanding and devotion to form, to writing as a monastic discipline. Unlike most contemporary poets, he believed that the shape of the poem is a conscious component in the act of writing—implying discipline, while not denying sensuality, passion, or intimacy. There is always a perceptible restraint: Skelton the shaman transcends Skelton the man. The poet, dressed in black with a snow-white beard like that of some Celtic Father Christmas, wearing exotic jewelry, is the persona presented in the many volumes of verse that mark his career as a writer and consummate performer. The thrilling voice that made his readings memorable can almost be heard in every poem as it explores and re-explores the exile's no man's land of memory and desire. Skelton's intellectual devotion to poetry resulted in an extraordinary posthumous publication, *Shapes of our singing: a comprehensive guide to verse forms and metres from around the world* (2002), featuring more than 300 verse forms illustrated by an original poem.

Skelton's short fiction—like his children's poems and stories, *I am me* (1994) and *Long, long ago* (1995)—illuminates the dark corners inhabited by an often melancholic poet who also had lighter moments. A lover of language, he took delight in its comic arrangements, as a child does. His fiction titles—including *The parrot who could* (1987), *Hanky panky* (1990), and *Higgledy piggledy* (1992)—suggest the playfulness of his stories.

A respected scholar of Anglo-Irish literature, Skelton was also the author of three books on J.M. Synge, co-authored a book on W.B. Yeats, and edited the work of English and North American poets for various anthologies. With the late John Peter he was a founding editor of *The MALAHAT REVIEW*, which quickly acquired an international reputation. The Thursday-night salons at the house of Robin and Sylvia Skelton were for many years a catalyst in the dialogue among Victoria's artistic communities—which the Skeltons, he as poet and visual artist and she as artist/calligrapher, were much involved in. The Skeltons were also members of the Limners, a loose association of artists and friends, including the painters Myfanwy Spencer Pavelic and Herbert Siebner, which was seminal to the artistic development of Victoria. Robin Skelton's writings about the visual arts

include *Painters talking* (1957), *Herbert Siebner* (1979), and *House of dreams* (1983).

A practising healer, Skelton drew upon the tradition of witchcraft in his obsession for finding the language for making spells to heal a troubled world, and shapes to cut out and paste in collages of found wisdom that reveal the lost-and-found aspects of truth—an English tradition he endeavoured to impress on the New World in as many ways as he could think of. Some of his books on the occult are *Spellcraft* (1978), *Talismanic magic* (1985), and *The practice of witchcraft* (1995).

Skelton's *Memoirs of a literary blockhead* (1988) tell much of his story, but does not mention the high esteem in which he was held. A compulsive writer, he produced an enormous body of published work. Some would argue that he published too much, thus obscuring his best writing. But there is no argument about his enormous contribution to literature. Issue 160 of *The MALAHAT REVIEW* (September 2007) is 'A celebration of Robin Skelton'.

Škvorecký, Josef (b. 1924). Born in Náchod, Bohemia, then Czechoslovakia, he entered the faculty of medicine at Charles University, Prague, but soon transferred to philosophy, graduating in 1949 and receiving his Ph.D. in 1951. Over the next two decades he was a teacher in a girls' school, a translator of contemporary American fiction (including Faulkner's *A fable*), an editor on the Prague magazine *World Literature*, and a scriptwriter working with, among others, Miloš Forman and Jiří Menzel (*Closely watched trains*). From the early 1950s he was a central figure in the postwar Czechoslovak cultural renaissance, much of whose impetus came from the underground circle of writers and artists in Prague. In 1968, after the Soviet invasion of Czechoslovakia, Škvorecký immigrated to Canada with his wife, the writer-actress Zdena Salivarová, lecturing on English literature at the University of Toronto, where he became a professor in 1971. In that year he and his wife founded Sixty-Eight Publishers, and during the next twenty years it published more than 200 books banned in their homeland. He retired from the University of Toronto in 1990—he is Professor Emeritus—and in the same year President Václav Havel awarded the Škvoreckýs the Order of the White Lion, Czechoslovakia's highest award for foreigners (they are Canadian citizens). Škvorecký was made a Member of the Order of Canada in 1992 and has received numerous honorary doctorates.

He has written and edited more than fifty books, including novels, mysteries, and critical works on literature, music, and film. The majority of his novels and short stories have been translated into English—variously by Rosemary Kavan, Peter Kussi, Jeanne Němcová, Káca Poláčková-Henley, and Paul Wilson—with the best-known novels being *The cowards, The bass saxophone, Miss Silver's past, The miracle game,* and *The engineer of human souls.*

The publication in Prague of his first novel *Zbabělci* (1958)—later translated as *The cowards* (1970, rpr. 1995)—resulted in the banning of the book, Škvorecký's loss of his editorial post, and an extensive purge of the intellectual community. In the next ten years Škvorecký published novels, novellas, and short-story collections. Works from this period available in English translation are *The mournful demeanor of Lieutenant Boruvka* (1974, rpr. 1987), a collection of mystery stories (followed later by *The end of Lieutenant Boruvka,* 1989, and *The return of Lieutenant Boruvka,* 1990); *The bass saxophone* (1980, rev. 2001) and *Emoke,* two novellas published in one volume in 1977; and *Miss Silver's past* (1975, rpr. 1995), a mystery novel dealing with literature and censorship in a totalitarian society. In Canada during the 1970s he published in Czech two of his most ambitious and longest novels: *Mirákl* (1972)—*The miracle game* (1990, rpr. 2002)—and *Příběh inženýra lidských duší* (1977)—*The engineer of human souls* (1984, GGA; rpr. 1993).

The highest praise of Škvorecký's work has come from Graham Greene, for whom *The bass saxophone* and *Emoke* are 'in the same rank as James Joyce's *The dead* and the very best of Henry James's shorter novels'. The first deals with a young Czechoslovak who plays a bass saxophone for a German band during the Second World War; the second is a poignant love story about a relatively cynical young man's attempt to seduce Emoke, a woman who doesn't seem to believe that love is possible in Communist Czechoslovakia. Yet Škvorecký's most substantial work seems to be in the longer novels, *The cowards, The miracle game,* and *The engineer of human souls,* which form part of a cycle dealing with the life and times of Daniel Smiricky, a thinly disguised portrait of the author. Also in the series are *The republic of whores* (1993, rpr. 1995) and the interrelated stories of *Prima sezona,* which has been translated as *The swell season* (1982). The series spans forty years in Danny's life, beginning in wartime Czechoslovakia (*The cowards*) and ending in Canada of the 1970s (*Engineer of human souls*). Smiricky fulfils the role of an Everyman who, as an East European, has experienced some of the tragic events of the past half-century. The stories (with various translators and narrated by Danny Smiricky) in *When Eve was naked: a journey through life* (2000) are autobiographical: its four sections cover the main stages of Škvorecký's life. The title story is about Danny, aged eight, who falls in love with Eve, aged about six. When a teacher takes Eve, with Danny and some of his friends, swimming, the boys undress to their swim trunks, while Eve came out of a tent 'naked and red in the face.' She and the teacher 'ran off to the sea. I could see the teacher's turquoise two-piece bathing suit and the girl's white naked behind, above which bounced two bows in long braids.' Danny Smiricky is also the narrator of *Ordinary lives,* published in 2008. As Danny, who graduated in 1943, attends two class reunions—one in 1963, one in 1993, for which he returns to Czechoslovakia from Toronto—we are transfixed by his memories, particularly of the political turmoil affecting his life and the lives of his classmates during the war years and later. There are two interesting, informative appendixes, 'Danny's Classmates' and 'Notes', which lists references to characters in Škvorecký's novels and stories, to the works themselves, and to political events etc. *Ordinary lives* is a good introduction to the Danny Smiricky novels.

The concern with Czechs and history is taken in a new direction in *Dvorak in love* (1986, rpr. 1992). While focusing on the Czech composer's life and work, especially his visit to the United States in the 1890s, the novel also deals with nearly fifty years of Czech and Slovak history and the lives of other Czechs and Slovaks who immigrated to the United States. Škvorecký's research for the novel led directly to *The bride of Texas* (1995, rpr. 1996), which is also set in the United States, but thirty years earlier during the Civil War. Like *Dvorak in love,* the novel is polyphonic and the characters and events (especially Sherman's march through the South) are described from various perspectives. Two other important narratives involve the Czech Toupelik family, especially their daughter Lida—the 'bride' of the title—and Lorraine Henderson Tracy, a writer with feminist tendencies. With *The bride of Texas,* Škvorecký's novels as a group offer a 150-year fictional social history of the Czech people.

If one of Škvorecký's dominant themes is people's fate in history, his other is the central function played by art (Smiricky is a writer), which is a metaphor for freedom and free activity—a means of resisting the ideological demands of a state that insists on writing and rewriting reality and history to suit its needs. The writers and jazz musicians of Škvorecký's fiction, whether they know it or not, are what Solzhenitsyn calls a 'second government'—people who use art to celebrate the dignity and worth of human life, the necessity of certain basic human freedoms, and so on. While Škvorecký's themes are serious and weighty, there is an unsettling interweaving of the tragic and the comic in his fiction. This is evident in his crime novel *Two murders in my double life* (1999), written in English, in which the narrator, a Czech-born teacher of detective fiction at a Toronto college, combines a serious, sad account of accusations against his wife, related to the secret police in Czechoslovakia, with a rather playful treatment of a murder at the college and the detection that ensues. All Škvorecký's fiction is the work of a natural storyteller with a fundamentally ironic vision. *An inexplicable story or The narrative of Questus Firmus Siculus* (English translation, 2002) is a clever (and convincing scholarly) literary diversion for the author. Seven narrow scrolls of the Questus manuscript—from the first century A.D., written in Latin in the time of Augustus—were found by Mayan archeological students in Honduras in a cracked pottery urn. (How did they get there?) Questus is nineteen and would like to be an inventor, creating machines for the army. His father, a military figure is absent; his mother, a great beauty, is a favourite of the Emperor and of the poet Ovid, whose *The art of love* (*Ars amatoria*) has just been published—its sexual secrets may have included his mother. Ovid was exiled by Augustus Caesar (to the Black Sea, in modern-day Romania). Was this the reason? (We discover at the end that Ovid was Sextus's father.) Commentaries by the editor, mystery writer Patrick Oliver Enfield (P.O.E.—the writings of Edgar Allan Poe and Jules Verne influenced Švorecký's own writing), two illuminating letters from readers, and a mysterious short text by Questus throw light on the main narrative and give rise to further game playing by the author. In an Author's Note, Škvorekcý explains why he became interested in Ovid in exile and how he created a plot in the form of fragments of a narrative, with many scholarly footnotes, some of them long. For anyone with the slightest interest in ancient Rome, this is a well-contrived, enjoyable creation.

For an autobiographical perspective on Škvorecký's years in Czechoslovakia, especially the 1950s and 1960s, the essay 'I was born in Nachod' in *Talkin' Moscow blues: essays about literature, politics, movies, and jazz* (1988), edited by Sam Solecki, and *Headed for the blues: a memoir with ten stories* (1997, rpr. 1998), are particularly interesting.

Slater, Patrick. Pseudonym of John MITCHELL.

Slipperjack, Ruby. See ABORIGINAL LITERATURE: 5.

Smart, Elizabeth (1913–86). Born in Ottawa, she was the daughter of a lawyer who was a member of the Anglo-Canadian social establishment. She attended Hatfield Hall, a private school, and at eighteen travelled to England to study piano. When she returned to Canada in 1933, she briefly joined the staff of the *Ottawa Journal*, writing society notes. With the ambition to become a writer, she submitted poems to Lawrence Durrell's Paris magazine *Booster*, and at his suggestion began a literary correspondence with the English poet George Barker. While staying at a writers' colony in Big Sur, California, in the fall of 1940, she secured passage for Barker and his wife to the United States. A passionate love affair ensued. Barker became the father of her four children.

In 1941 Smart travelled alone to Pender Harbour, British Columbia, where she completed her first novel, BY GRAND CENTRAL STATION I SAT DOWN AND WEPT (1945, rpr. 1977), a prose poem—part incantation and part cry of pain—about passion and the loss of love. (It was reissued in England in 1966, with a Foreword by Brigid Brophy.) After giving birth in Pender Harbour to her first child, Smart took a job as a file clerk in the British Army Office in Washington, D.C., to be with Barker, who had been barred from entry into Canada on her mother's instigation. She was transferred to the Ministry of Defence in London in 1943, and supported herself and her children for the next two decades by writing copy for fashion magazines like *Vogue* and *Queen*, of which she became literary editor.

In 1977, following almost three decades of silence, Smart published a collection of poems, *A bonus*. After the poetic incantatory style of her novel, it is surprising in its casual conversational language and clipped rhythms. The book is largely about writing: the struggle to speak when silence is seductive; the battle against a sense of inadequacy; the release and elation that comes out of the pain of writing. The impulse to order and cultivate is explored in many poems about gardening. The poems are moving in their efforts to examine the problems of the writer who chooses to abandon the distractions of love for the necessary self-absorption of the artist. Smart's second novel, *The assumption of the rogues and rascals* (1978), like its predecessor, is essentially a poetic meditation without a plot structure. Set in postwar England, it explores the psychology of a woman of thirty-one, trapped in despair, who 'stops at its ardent, obstreperous source, every hopeful passion', and who cannot decide whether her hell is self-created or life's failure. The novel is structured by means of associations: snippets of conversation, dreams, memories (the fiction of Samuel Beckett provides a precedent). The rogues and rascals of the title—the misfits who at least have the courage to resist the forces of normalcy and mediocrity—are the outlawed. The novel ends with the dilemma of the writer—how and why to write—and offers an archetypal model: Philoctetes, isolated on his island with his body a running sore.

Smart lived in Canada from 1982 to 1984, and, encouraged by her friend Alice Van Wart, contemplated publishing her journals. In 1984 she published an interim collection of her writings, *In the meantime*, which contains the remarkably titled story 'Dig a grave and let us bury our mother', written in 1940 while Smart stayed briefly in Mexico with the surrealist painters Wolfgang Paalen and Alice Rahon. It is about a love affair between two women, recorded with an erotic intensity that would have been shocking in its day. The book also contains poems and a diary from which the book draws its title: 'In the meantime: diary of a blockage'. Shortly after Smart died, the first volume of her journals appeared: *Necessary secrets: the journals* (1986), edited by Van Wart. Recording Smart's life from 1933 to 1941, it makes clear that the diary form was—for Smart, as it was for Virginia Woolf—less a space for confession than for rigorous experimentation as she undertook her self-imposed apprenticeship in writing. Some of the lyrical passages about landscape and love from Smart's early entries would eventually appear in *By Grand Central Station*. After Smart's death, several new books appeared: *Autobiographies* (1987), edited by Christina Burridge, a miscellaneous collection of Smart's documents, letters, and journals dating from 1940 to 1982; *Juvenilia* (1987), edited by Van Wart, a collection of early stories written between the ages of eleven and nineteen, with family letters; and *Elizabeth's garden: Elizabeth Smart on the art of gardening* (1989), which collects some of the columns she wrote for the British magazine *Harper's Bazaar*, with excerpts from

her garden journals. Smart was a celebrated gardener; her garden in Suffolk was featured in an issue of *Harper's Queen* in 1975. *The collected poems*, with a Foreword by the British poet David Gascoyne, was published in 1992 and adds significantly to the material in *A bonus*. What Gascoyne called her 'wry', 'cheeky' truthfulness is evident in poems like 'All I know about why I write', but the most moving poem in the volume is the harrowing elegy to her daughter, Rose, who died at the age of thirty-five. *On the side of the angels* (1994), the second volume of Smart's journals dating from the 1940s to the 1980s, was also edited by Van Wart. Its often exquisite lyric prose and subject—the intense confrontation with the difficulties of trying to live as mother and writer, explored with such candour as to become universal—confirmed Smart's talent for the autobiographical mode. The aphorisms she crafted to render a compassionate account of life's frustrations, particularly for women, are often brilliant, and make her journals an important contribution to women's writing.

See Rosemary SULLIVAN's biography *By heart: Elizabeth Smart/a life* (1991); *Elizabeth Smart: a fugue essay on women and creativity* (2004) by Kim Echlin; and the play *Memories of you* (1989) by Wendy LILL, based on Smart's life.

Smith, A.J.M. (1902–80). Arthur James Marshall Smith was born in Westmount, Montreal, the only son of English immigrant parents. He attended Westmount High School, but in his second year was taken to England, where he lived from 1918 to 1920, studied for the Cambridge Local Examinations, 'and failed everything except English and history' (he later wrote). However, in London he frequented Harold Monroe's bookshop, then the citadel of Georgian poetry, and read much in the recent war poets and the imagists. On his return to Montreal in 1920 he completed his high-school studies, graduated in 1921, and in the same year was admitted to McGill University where, yielding to parental pressure, he studied for a bachelor of science; but during his undergraduate years he edited a singularly mature *Literary Supplement* to the *McGill Daily*, in which some of his early poems appeared. On graduating in 1925, he undertook a master's program in English and wrote a dissertation on Yeats and the symbolist movement. At this time he met F.R. SCOTT, newly returned from Oxford. Both were in full revolt against Montreal's lingering Victorianism and conservatism, and both felt their vocation to be poetry, although Scott was studying law. The two founded *The* McGILL FORTNIGHTLY REVIEW (1925–7), which, behind its solemn title, displayed an artistic and political maturity that exerted an influence beyond the collegiate boundaries, and in effect represented the innovative spirit of the 1920s in Canada. *The McGill Fortnightly* drew to it other young writers—among them A.M. KLEIN, Leo KENNEDY, and Leon EDEL—on whom, as well as on Scott, Smith had an enduring influence. Smith in turn came under the influence of a young biology professor at McGill, Lancelot Hogben (the future author of *Mathematics for the million* and a peripheral figure in London's Bloomsbury). Hogben, who wrote pseudonymous poems for *The McGill Fortnightly*, gave Smith the early poems of T.S. Eliot to read, and encouraged him in his revolt against philistinism and Montreal parochialism.

After receiving his M.A. in 1926, Smith taught briefly in a Montreal high school and then received a fellowship for study in Edinburgh, where he worked with H.J.C. Grierson, the pre-eminent authority on Donne, and began a doctoral dissertation on the metaphysical poets of the Church of England in the seventeenth century (Ph.D., 1931). Returning to Canada during the Depression, Smith was unable to find an academic post and taught in a series of small American colleges until he received an appointment at Michigan State College (later University). There he remained during the rest of his career and was, in later years, poet-in-residence. He became a naturalized American, but spent all his summers in his country place near Magog, Québec.

In 1936 Smith, Scott, Klein, and Kennedy—the 'MONTREAL GROUP', as they now began to be called—joined with E.J. PRATT and Robert FINCH of Toronto in producing *NEW PROVINCES: poems of several authors* (1936, rpr. 1976), a landmark in Canada's modern poetry. Smith wrote a lightly ironic and mocking Preface about the concern of Canada's poets with 'pine trees, the open road, God, snowshoes or Pan'. The Toronto contributors felt Smith's words would produce a controversy at the expense of the volume's contents, and the preface was shelved in favour of a brief anonymous foreword (by Scott). It pointed out that the poems, appearing in the mid-thirties during an economic Depression, in reality reflected innovations of the 1920s in 'freer diction and more elastic forms'. It added that 'the search for new content was less successful than had been the search for new techniques.' Smith published his 'rejected'

Preface thirty-five years later in *Towards a view of Canadian letters* (1973) and in the 1976 reprint of *New provinces*, showing that he had also expressed in it his own poetic stance: a disciplining of form and emotion by which intensity is attained; a sense of the poem as 'a thing in itself'; and the discarding of artificial forms (like mechanical rhyme) in favour of 'arbitrarily chosen verse patterns'. The poems in *New provinces* had an impact on Canadian verse far beyond any prefatorial pronouncements: in its implicit call for new findings and new attitudes in Canadian writing, it might be likened to the effect of the Wordsworth-Coleridge *Lyrical ballads* in 1798 on the Romantics. Smith included in this anthology at least five of his own poems that were destined for wide publication: the repeatedly anthologized 'The lonely land', 'The creek', 'News of the phoenix', 'Like an old proud king in a parable', and 'The two sides of the drum'. The effect of *New provinces* was that it established the Montreal Group as the Canadian avant-garde of its time.

During his twenties and thirties Smith wrote a great deal of poetry: some of it appeared in *The* CANADIAN FORUM; the *Dial*, then edited by Marianne Moore; *Poetry* (Chicago); and in England he was published in *New Verse*. He created a kind of reservoir of his poems—some 200—which, in the ensuing years, he polished and published in his five collections. The first did not appear in book form until he was forty-one: *News of the phoenix and other poems* (1943, GGA). *A sort of ecstasy: poems new and selected* (1954) reprinted one third of the *Phoenix* and added some twenty new poems. *Collected poems* (1962) contained 75 poems from the two previous collections and 25 not hitherto collected: 100 good poems, Smith argued, represented sufficient yield for any poet's lifetime. In reprinting this collection as *Poems new and collected* (1967), Smith retained 99 poems, but added another 22. In *The classic shade: selected poems* (1978) he used 60 poems from the previous collection and added some 20 occasional, satiric, and burlesque poems. In four of these collections Smith used a single epigraph from Santayana: 'Every animal has his festive and ceremonious moments, when he poses or plumes himself or thinks; sometimes he even sings and flies aloft in a sort of ecstasy.' This remained Smith's permanent view of his own poetry—that its function was decorative or ornamental—and caused critics to characterize his verse as 'lapidary'. Smith was master of a wide range of styles: he used pastiche, satire, burlesque, and bawdy. Yet his ribaldry could give way to simple lyricism and sensuality; he was on occasion meditative, and often colloquial. He was always authoritative, and always in quest of formal beauty, so that George WOODCOCK spoke of him as being 'among the most memorable lyric poets writing in the whole English-speaking world.' Northrop FRYE discerned the same lyrical qualities, but felt the poems betrayed a certain lack of energy. Smith defined his own tendency to the 'metaphysical' as expressing 'ideas that have entered so deeply into the blood as never to be questioned.' His poems possess an aristocratic coolness and a shrinking from common vulgarities; they also show a singular joy in life and an uneasy fear of death. The life-game of love is subsumed in his bawdy. The world's irrationalities and aggressivities are mocked and vigorously attacked, as in his poem 'News of the phoenix', or in his mordant verses on the atom bomb. See Anne COMPTON, *A.J.M. Smith: Canadian metaphysical* (1994). Smith's career as an important poet has been definitively recognized and documented by *The complete poems of A.J.M. Smith* (2007), edited by Brian Trehearne and published by Canadian Poetry Press, London, Ontario (edited by D.M.R. Bentley). Illuminated by a long, brilliant introduction by Trehearne, it is a substantial volume of 740 pages, containing not only previously published poems but unpublished, archival poems. The extensive notes are made up of editorial emendations, and interesting and helpful explanatory and textual notes, which throw light on Smith's mythological sources and historical references, etc.

Calling himself a 'compulsive anthologist', Smith edited many anthologies. The Canadian anthologies, which established a canon of Canadian poetry, included *The Book of Canadian poetry: a critical and historical anthology* (1943; 2nd edn 1948; 3rd edn 1957), a college anthology that became a kind of national textbook, and *The Oxford book of Canadian verse: in English and French* (1960), with its important introductory essay that refines his earlier selections and gains an even greater importance by including French-Canadian poetry. Smith's other Canadian anthologies include *Modern Canadian verse* (1967), again both in English and French; *The blasted pine*, with F.R. Scott (1957, rev. 1967), which bears the lengthy subtitle *An anthology of satire, invective and disrespectful verse chiefly by Canadian writers*; and *The colonial century: English-Canadian writing before Confederation* (1965, rpr. 1986).

Smith's critical essays—written in an easy, lucid, and sometimes poetic prose—reassert his doctrines of intensity gained through discipline; the negative effects of colonialism, which Smith equated with parochialism; and his reiterated belief that a poem is 'not the description of an experience, it is in itself an experience.' His essays were collected in *Towards a view of Canadian letters: selected critical essays 1928–1971* (1973) and in *On poetry and poets: selected essays of A.J.M. Smith* (1977) in the NEW CANADIAN LIBRARY of the time.

Smith was one of the most influential figures in Canadian poetry in the twentieth century. As a critic and anthologist he set, for the first time in Canada, high standards of poetic taste and discrimination; as a poet who combined classical Anglo-American forms with the modern temper, he infused an assured cosmopolitan strain into modern Canadian poetry—though towards the end of his life Smith felt, incorrectly, that the new generation's use of looser and less-demanding forms had shelved his own work. Whatever the vagaries of his reputation as both poet and critic, his total achievement marks Smith as a vigorous but also delicate reformer of Canadian taste through the power of his knowledge, wit, and craft.

Smith, Goldwin (1823–1910). Born in Reading, England, and educated at Eton and Oxford, he established an international reputation as a journalist and controversialist. He first achieved notice in England with his advocacy of university reform and his subsequent participation in the Royal Commission examining the academic reform of Oxford University. In 1858 he was appointed Regius professor of modern history at Oxford (the future King Edward VII was one of his pupils). Writing a constant stream of letters and articles for popular journals on the religious, political, economic, and imperial issues of the day, Smith spoke from the perspective of the Manchester school of laissez-faire economics and frequently adopted unpopular positions, especially with his support of the Northern cause during the American Civil War. He resigned his professorship in 1866 to care for his father, following whose death Smith accepted an offer to join the staff of newly founded Cornell University in Ithaca, New York. During his tenure (1868–71), he contributed much to the young university, including his personal library, while attempting to interpret England to America and vice versa. Closer contact with party politics, however, eroded Smith's admiration for American political institutions. In 1871 he moved to Toronto, living with relatives until his marriage in 1875 to Harriet Boulton, a widow, and took up residence in her home, The

Grange, now part of the Art Gallery of Ontario.

In Canada Smith lived in comfortable affluence, founded on both an inheritance from his father and his wife's money, and used his means for charitable works and to establish periodicals that commented on Canadian and international issues: *The Canadian Monthly and National Review* (1872–8), *The Evening Telegram* (1874), *The Bystander* (1880–90), *The WEEK* (1883–96), and *The Weekly Sun* (1896–1909). He wrote extensively on religious, literary, and historical subjects, concentrating on the twin issues of nationalism and imperialism. Hostile to all forms of political oppression, Smith expressed sympathy for the Canada First movement, decried the Boer War, and ridiculed the concept of Imperial federation. He generated great public hostility with his argument for commercial union with the United States, presented most cogently in *Canada and the Canadian question* (London, 1891), which declares that geography, history, and race demand a single North American, Anglo-Saxon nation, and that attempts to frustrate these forces would lead to economic suffering for Canada. Smith's views of Canada's future—based on his idiosyncratic brand of liberalism rather than on research—reveal his underestimation of the strength of the Canadian national spirit and the influence of French Canada. Though Smith undoubtedly enriched Canadian political discussion, his influence on events was minimal. His greatest contribution may have been through the periodicals he was involved with, which helped to disseminate the work of the poets and authors of the time. See Elizabeth Wallace, *Goldwin Smith: Victorian liberal* (1957).

Smith, Ray (b. 1941). Born in Inverness, Cape Breton Island, Nova Scotia, he received his B.A. (1963) from Dalhousie University, Halifax, and his M.A. (1985) from Concordia University, Montreal. After serving in the RCAF and working as a systems analyst, he began writing fiction in 1964. Since 1970 he has taught at Dawson College, Montreal. Smith has published seven books of fiction: *Cape Breton is the thought control centre of Canada* (1969, rpr. 2008), *Lord Nelson Tavern* (1974), *Century* (1986), *A night at the opera* (1992), *The man who loved Jane Austen* (1999), *The man who hated Emily Brontë* (2004), and *The flush of victory: Jack Bottomly among the virgins* (2007). *Cape Breton* is a collection of stories, of which the most interesting are 'Colours' and 'Galoshes' (apparently influenced by J.P. Donleavy's *The ginger man*). In *Lord Nelson*

Tavern—usually called a novel, but actually a collection of linked stories as in *Century*—Smith begins with a group of university students, habitués of a Halifax saloon, who weave in and out of one another's lives over the years, exchanging women, delivering monologues. The complex design is not anchored chronologically. Smith's remarkable control of voice, however, is evident throughout and is especially fine in a very funny seduction monologue delivered by a thirteen-year-old girl ('Sarah's summer holidays'). *A night at the opera*, a novel, is an unconvincing satire of German culture and manners. These books are clearly within the tradition of postmodernist fiction as defined by writers like Borges and William Gass. They are elaborately crafted, playful, self-referential. In Smith's words, 'the writer says what the story is about *in the whole story*'—so that the story can equally be 'about' its linguistic components or punctuation (including an especially artful semicolon) and 'about' relations between the sexes, a prominent theme in his work, on which Smith can be peculiarly disturbing. There is something brutal in the attitude to women displayed by the men; but this nastiness, while evidently recognized as such by Smith, is not purged or contained by his awareness. *The man who loved Jane Austen* is a departure. It is a straightforward narrative about Frank, a widower with two sons under ten, who lectures at a CEGEP in Montréal—he teaches Jane Austen, among other subjects. A thoroughly good man, he is subjected to the machinations of his late wife's unspeakable family, who want to wrest the boys away from him, and to a disaster in his teaching career that was probably caused by his in-laws. At the same time, this is a sympathetic novel about family, and about Montreal (and Québec). *The man who hated Emily Brontë* is an exuberant satire on life in a small junior college in Montreal in which all the characters but the protagonist, Will Franklyn, bounce smart repartee off each other. The man who hates Brontë is not Will but his officemate Harrison Morgan, who tells him: 'You'll have 120 mouth-breathers who are intellectually challenged by the instructions on a chocolate bar wrapper'. Will asks: 'Harrison, are all the teachers here—I mean in the English department—as, well, as eccentric as you?' 'Me? Eccentric? I'm not eccentric, I'm starkers. And so are all the rest of them.' He quotes W.S. Gilbert: 'Things are seldom what they seem,/Skim milk masquerades as cream.' Later on he says: 'I hate Emily Brontë and every other nineteenth-century romantic peddler of passion.' All chapter epigraphs are from *Wuthering Heights. The flush of victory* is narrated by Major Jack Bottomly, who is an intelligence officer—'Back when I first joined the shop, when it was still Royal Canadian Air Force Intelligence ... back before we were forced into a shotgun marriage with the Army and Navy and renamed [in 1968] the Canadian Armed Forces ... .' The events and misadventures that follow have to do with a trip to Vancouver and an apparent airplane sabotage, the discovery of an international conspiracy, travel in Europe, with American, Russian, and British figures turning up as stock characters, while Bottomly himself focuses on a retirement plan that is illegal and involves a Swiss bank account. This farcical novel, which takes nothing seriously, is redolent with the occasionally funny but rude lines of the unappealing Bottomly (and his unfunny toilet humour), whose secretary Lureen suddenly gives him a kiss: 'It may be true that only the brave deserve the fair but, I reflected as I cradled her bum in my mitts, with a little luck the merely cunning can get a handful now and then.' He eventually seduces her while she's asleep. In spite of the shenanigans and salty language, the novel doesn't amount to much—though it might be the first in a series of Bottomly fictions.

Smith, Russell (b. 1963). Born in Johannesburg, South Africa, he was educated in Halifax schools, at Queen's University, Kingston, Ontario (B.A., 1986; M.A., 1987), and at the Université de Poitiers and the Université de Paris III. As a journalist he has written for many periodicals and writes a weekly column on the arts, culture, and entertainment for the Toronto *Globe and Mail*. His novels *How insensitive* (1994) and *Noise* (1998) are sharply observed satires of small communities of people between twenty and thirty in Toronto, in the late eighties and early nineties, getting along as best they can and enjoying themselves, as they drift in and out of media and fashion jobs, relationships, and pads. At the end of *Noise* a man in a bar complains about Canadian fiction: '... it's still linear narrative. It's still the same old nineteenth-century tell the story, use a narrator, have characters with identities ... it's the same old bourgeois shit.' This is not true of *How insensitive*, in which there is little story and the characters do not have identities, they are merely voices. But a real society of the time is revealed and adroitly travestied in their conversations in John's house, where most of them live, in nightclubs of ever-increasing bizarreness, and in such situations as a popular TV interview

program where the central character, the writer Ted Owen, confused by the nonsensical nature of the program, finds himself uttering nonsense of his own in the few minutes allotted that is received with 'huge applause' and brings him five minutes of fame. In *Noise* James Willing—who writes restaurant reviews and other pieces for magazines with such titles as *Dental Week, Reams and Reams*, and *Glitter*—is asked to interview an elderly national literary icon, winner of the *Prairie Afternoon* Responsible Fiction Award, who has not published a book since 1974, spends part of the interview in a drunken sleep, and whose wife supplies the interview quotes. Willing bonds with Piers De Courcy, who is gay (he is unaware of this until the end of the novel), and with one woman after another. About Alison: 'He wondered why he didn't want to see her again and decided that he didn't know.' Noise from neighbours besets the house where De Courcy and others live, and to which James moves in desperation. Most of the stories in *Young men* (1999) are about Dominic, Lionel, and James. In one of the stories about Lionel he repeats to himself that he is 'a very well-known author', having been shortlisted for the Ontario Booksellers' Award, before he is subjected to a disastrous book-signing in Yarmouth, Nova Scotia, during a heavy snowstorm. 'Responsibility', a story about James, is a long and sensitive conversation between mother and son (it might well have taken place, with few changes, between most of the other two books' characters and a respective parent) in which James's mother gently wants him to settle down and he, less gently, upholds his present selfish way of life. She breaks into tears, saying: '*Nice people don't do things for themselves....* "I'm sorry Mom," he said. "*You're* nice."' At the end he realized 'that he wasn't nice'. In 'Young Women', the last section of *Young men*, Margaret, an actress / waitress in Chez Giovanni, survives a well-described chaotic evening at Giovanni's packed restaurant. Smith's next novel, *Muriella Pent* (2004), is a departure, named for a well-to-do but socially insecure widow who lives in Toronto in a large house in Stillwoode (Wychwood?) Park and is a member of the literature committee of the City Arts Board, called the Action Council. When the city offers money for an exchange program for a Developing Region ('what they used to call the Third World'), the middle-aged Marcus Royston is chosen—he was a successful poet some twenty years ago and is from the (fictional) island of St. Andrew's in the Caribbean. Muriella offers a self-contained basement apartment in her house for him to live in. A light-skinned black, Royston when he arrives turns out to be not at all the man they expected: he is well-educated, sophisticated, with intellectual interests that alienate him completely from issues some Torontonians want to raise with him—such as race, and turning libraries into 'community centres'—as he makes his thoughts known. He is also a drinker and romantically inclined—the first chapter is mainly a post-coital conversation between Royston and Muriella. But this is a satirical novel about several things, including arts committees, their members, their inane exchanges at meetings—and Toronto. Royston writes in a letter home: 'The house is in the middle of a very large and ugly city, but it is hidden in a park that's full of trees and other lovely houses, built just for rich people.' Among other important characters, Royston and Muriella are memorable. When Royston's plane is leaving Ontario he stared 'at the darkening floor of forest and wondered where he had been.... he didn't really know where he had been ....' Muriella, however, is transformed, full of self-confidence as she meets a Dr Winthrup at the airport. An entirely different Toronto atmosphere is portrayed in the highly praised *Girl crazy* (2010), in which thirty-two-year-old Justin, who teaches at a community college, becomes obsessed with Jenna, a beautiful twenty-year-old stripper, and is drawn into the drug-ridden subculture that is her world.

The princess and the whiskheads (2002), a fable for adults, tells of Princess Juliana, the ruler of the kingdom of Liralove. The beautiful towers of the city are called Architectrons but they have no function. Her admirer Lord Lucas wants to overhaul the kingdom's sewage system; and her friend Count Bostock tells her about a group called 'whiskheads' who take pride in going through a strange and dangerous operation: having a very fine wire inserted form one ear to the other through the brain, the ends 'woven into fine patterns like jewellery.' Juliana asks Bostock why he said she wouldn't want to know about them. 'Well ... because they are not pleasant. They are a rather angry sort. They have political meetings at which there is much shouting and jeering ... they are unhappy.' 'They are unhappy? About what?' He looked away. 'About me,' she said. 'Yes.' Juliana puts on borrowed clothes to disguise herself and goes out to investigate the whiskheads. She is taken to the Convolutionists' meeting hall inside an Architecton and while there is attracted to a tall blond boy called Jan (their meeting leads to some pleasing erotic scenes). For all its elaborate construction and detailed descriptions, however, *The princess* lacks conviction and verisimilitude; the moral of the fable is obscure or non-existent, and the story seems pointless in the end. As befits a fable, however, the book is beautifully designed, with handsome wood engravings by Wesley W. Bates. *Diana: a diary in the second person*—first published in 2003 by Gutter Press, Toronto, and then in 2008 by BIBLIOASIS—is described as a work of pornography in Smith's long, mildly defensive Introduction, in which he declares that 'there is nothing wrong with liking it.... Pornography is sometimes dismissed as merely practical, as something whose sole purpose is physical arousal. As if there were anything ignoble about such a useful and, to my mind, beautiful goal.'

Smith was derided by at least one reviewer for writing *Men's style: the thinking men's guide to dress* (2005), which grew out of columns he wrote for the Toronto *Globe and Mail*. Itself stylishly designed, with drawings by Edwin Fotheringham, it is also stylishly written—informed and informative, both sensible (it begins with a chapter called 'Why Bother?') and admirable in taste. He should be applauded for writing such a book when surely 90 per cent of Canadian males are oblivious of style—I pray that some of them read it.

Smucker, Barbara (1915–2003). Born in Newton, Kansas, and raised as a Mennonite, she immigrated to Kitchener, Ontario, with her husband, a professor, and worked there as a librarian from 1969 to 1982. She eventually made her home in Bluffton, Ohio. Her numerous books for young people have dealt with political or religious oppression, racial and class discrimination, and culture clashes. *Underground to Canada* (1977, rpr. 1978) treats the subject of American slavery; *Days of terror* (1979, rpr. 1991) chronicles the mass migration of Mennonites from Ukraine to North America; *Amish adventure* (1983, rpr. 1991) explores cultural differences between the empire-building Scots-Canadians and the Amish-Canadians who eschew modernization; and *White mist* (1985, rpr. 1987) uses time-fantasy to focus on Native-white relations in the context of environmental destruction. Smucker's carefully researched books, mostly historical fiction, give children insight into how adult power struggles have caused pain and social injustice. *Selina and the shoo-fly pie* (1998), about Mennonites in Upper Canada, is a picture book for children illustrated by Janet Wilson.

Smyth, Donna E. (b. 1943). Born in Kimberley, British Columbia, she was educated at the Universities of Victoria, Toronto, and London (Ph.D., 1972). She has taught English at the University of Victoria (1967–9), the University of Saskatchewan (1972–3), and, from 1973, taught at Acadia University, Wolfville, Nova Scotia. She lives on an old farm in Hants County. Her writing combines inquiry into philosophical questions, poetic response to the natural world, and sensitivity to the lives and thought of ordinary working people. Her novel *Quilt* (1982, rpr. 1994) is set in rural Nova Scotia; its main characters are a young battered wife whose husband kills himself in a rage, and an older widow who lives with the memory of having helped her invalid husband to die. Offsetting their dramatic stories are the subtle tensions in the life of a couple facing retirement and ill health. The vicissitudes of human life are counterpointed by the cycle of the natural world. Like the quilt the women are sewing, the novel is a patchwork of different styles, suggesting an image of community and underlying purpose in apparent chaos. Smyth used a similar patchwork technique in her scripts written for Nova Scotia's touring Mermaid Theatre. *Susanna Moodie* (1976) dramatizes the story of MOODIE's experience both as told in *ROUGHING IT IN THE BUSH* (1852) and as Margaret ATWOOD reinterpreted it in *The JOURNALS OF SUSANNA MOODIE* (1970). Atwood's poems are recited between dramatized episodes, each implicitly commenting on the other. Smyth also wrote *Running to paradise: a play about Elizabeth Bishop* (1999). Her novel *Subversive elements* (1986) weaves together a supposedly fictional story of two seemingly unlikely lovers, a former monk and a much older woman, with a factual account of the writer's real-life involvement in a successful grassroots movement to halt plans for uranium mining in Nova Scotia. Included in the text are newspaper clippings reporting the notorious libel case brought against Smyth by a prominent academic, following her opinion piece in a Halifax newspaper. The love of nature reflected in the narrator's vegetable gardening and goat farming is linked to love of the earth in general as well as to love between human beings. *Among the saints* (2003) is a collection of nine stories, well told with believable dialogue, that often incorporate an oddity matter-of-factly. In the first story, 'The temptation of Leafy', Leafy is an old woman and her closest friend is Sarah, a goose. 'Sarah watched Leafy lovingly, followed every inflection of thought and voice with a kind of intelligence

Leafy never doubted.' When things were going well 'Sarah seemed to know and rejoice with her. She'd sidle closer until, absent-mindedly, Leafy put out a hand to stroke the soft feathers. If a goose could purr like a cat, Sarah purred, Leafy swore she did, not out loud but with a body hum that vibrated through Leafy's fingers. Hum of goose contentment.' The title 'A fine and private place' refers to a grave. Ashley is an apprentice in an undertaking parlour so that she can enrol in a course. She is put in charge of Mrs McGregor, who insisted on being buried with her (real) pearls and her cellphone. It rings and Mrs McGregor's voice is heard, giving instructions! Much happens in this long story—which ends after the funeral service—including Ashley's witnessing a clash over the pearls between the deceased's unpleasant daughter, Carol Laskey, and gay son, Gordon (the siblings hate each other). Underneath the various exchanges that take place among the undertaker, Ashley, Mrs Laskey, and Gordon is a satirical critique of the undertaking profession. In the unfocussed title story it is not clear who the saints are, though the central character is Jude—but she's a woman (unlike Saint Jude, one of the Apostles), with a husband and children. She divides herself in three—Jude, Judy, and Judith—and is receiving professional treatment. As the story ends, the narrator (a therapist?) thinks 'Jude.// The patron saint of lost causes, last refuge of those without hope.'—sentiments that have no place in the story.

Loyalist runaway (1991), written for young people, is an adventure story set in Halifax and Boston during the American Revolution; it is based on the diaries of a Nova Scotia family.

Snow Drop, The (Apr. 1847–June 1853). *The Snow Drop; or Juvenile Magazine*, one of the first Canadian periodicals for children, was edited by two sisters (née Foster) who had moved to Montreal from Boston: Mrs Eliza Lanesford Cushing (b. 1794) and Mrs Harriet Vining Cheney (b. 1796). It was published in Montreal by the firm of Lovell and Gibson, which also published *The LITERARY GARLAND*. Setting out to instruct and amuse, the magazine was directed primarily to girls, each issue providing one or two stories along with articles on historical events, famous people, natural history, and faraway places; the slight Canadian content had to do mostly with the past or with the quainter aspects of Canadian life. Most of *The Snow Drop*'s identified authors were from old or New England, like the books and periodicals from which it published selections.

Snow Drop

Although its final numbers contained an increasing proportion of original contributions, it made little impact on the Canadian literary scene. Late in its six-year existence it had a short-lived competitor, *The Maple Leaf* (June 1852–Dec. 1854), which deliberately featured Canadian content, including work by Susanna MOODIE and her sister Catharine Parr TRAILL.

Solway, David (b. 1941). Born in Montreal, he was educated at McGill University (B.A., 1962; Q.M.A., 1966), Concordia University (M.A., 1988), and Lajos Kossuth University (Ph.D., 1998). From 1971 to 1997 he taught English and creative writing at John Abbott College, Montreal. His first book of poems, *In my own image* (1962), appeared when he was only twenty-one, and in its rebellious romanticism it suggests the influence of Leonard COHEN. After several experimental slim volumes—*The crystal theatre* (1971), *Paximalia* (1972), *The Egyptian airforce* (1973), and *Anacrusis* (1976)—Solway came to poetic maturity with *The road to Arginos* (1976). Here the influence of Cohen is still discernible, notably in the way the poetry rises from a fruitful tension between his Jewish background and interests and a Greek-island lifestyle that he found creatively stimulating and attractive. But Solway has since shed his 'pop-culture' influences and espoused a rigorous technical discipline that has resulted in poetry that manages to combine the lyric facility and intensity of W.B. Yeats and the classical fastidiousness of Robert Graves. His subsequent volumes include *Mephistopheles and the astronaut* (1979); *Selected poems* (1982); *The Mulberry men* (1982), children's verse; *Stones in winter* (1983); *Bedrock* (1993), which includes one poem by 'Andreas Karavis' (see below); and *Chess pieces* (1999); for the most part they continued and extended the Hebraic/Hellenic debate. But *Modern marriage* (1987), a tour de force, is a series of fifty conversational sonnets where a human marital dispute, in the tradition of George Meredith's *Modern love* (1862), is the convenient basis for a witty and profound inquiry into life's oppositions: art / nature, soul / blood, reality / illusion, poetry / prose, movement / stasis. Solway caused a stir—and some interest and amusement—when he published *Saracen Island: the poems of Andreas Karavis* (2000) and *An Andreas Karavis companion* (2000). In a subsequent article (*National Post*, 6 Jan. 2001) he confessed that Karavis, the so-called Greek poet he claimed to have translated, was an invention, representing 'the spirit of play, of imagination, of seductive risk … . I needed

Karavis in order to materialize on the plane of literary existence in this country.' Solway carried this 'spirit of play' one step further in documenting the aftermath of Karavis's liaison with Nesmine Rifat in *The pallikari of Nesmine Rifat* (2004)—*pallikari* means 'young man' in Turkish. (Rifat was born in Istanbul in 1965, according to Solway's short Preface); in Karavis's language it means brave man, hero, warrior. In Solway's Afterword he describes Rifat's poetry, his acquaintance with her, and says: '*Pallikari* furnishes an ongoing record of the author's changing reactions and emotions in the wake of a failed love affair ….' *The lover's progress: poems after William Hogarth* (2001)—with paintings and drawings (in black and white) by Marion Wagschal—was inspired by Hogarth's series of paintings and engravings, *The Rake's Progress*, executed in the 1730s. Set in the present century, Solway's poems are introduced by a longish pedantic Preface that attempts to connect the modern lover of his poems with Hogarth's rake—unconvincingly. (To an ordinary reader there seems to be no connection.) It is followed by a list, 'The lover's itinerary'—the lover was a traveller. 'Club Med' begins: 'Tomorrow I'll pack up and go to Paradise / and there, among pelicans and fishingboats, / watch the beautiful people at their trades' *Franklin's passage* (2003), published in the Hugh MacLennan Poetry Series, recaptures and memorializes John Franklin's disastrous attempt to sail through and map the Northwest Passage, and does this evocatively: 'I bequeath this revelation / to all who shall come after. / Ice is the Northwest Passage, // our navigable route / to the distant coast, / land of shadow and cold.' And: 'It is a thing in itself, the cold, / a creature rising from below the threshhold / of human consciousness …' In his Preface to *The properties of things: from the poems of Bartholomew the Englishman* (2007)—Bartholomew being an obscure thirteenth-century scholar whose only surviving work, *De proprietatibus rerum*, was translated a century or so later—Solway says, 'I have taken all kinds of liberties in trying to reconceive Bartholomew not as a theologian and peregrine cleric but as a poet preoccupied with the things a poet would be interested in: poetry itself, the nature of imagination, the annoyances and marvels of the natural and quotidian worlds, and the complexities of love … .': 'Darkness is a kind of holding back / for it binds the eyes / that it may not see the sun or any other light, / and so darkness is nothing else / than curbing and limitation' ('Darkness').

Solway has also written *Education lost: reflections on contemporary pedagogical practice* (1989) and *Lying about the wolf: essays in culture and education* (1997), two independent and persuasive indictments of modern pedagogical philosophy and method; *The anatomy of Arcadia* (1992), a diary-style meditation on the all-but-forgotten distinction between tourism and genuine travel; and *Random walks: essays in elective criticism* (1997). His prose is close-packed, exuberant, and intellectually challenging. The salutary essays in *Director's cut* (2003) are defended in Solway's Preface:'I sense that the time has arrived to take stock and engage passionately if our literature, and especially our poetry, is ever to be rescued from the swamp of second-rateness into which it has so complaisantly descended... . I am convinced that almost all of the poetry (and much of the fiction) being written in Canada these days—with only a couple [?] of redeeming exceptions that stand out like crop circles in a featureless plain—is turgid, spurious and pedestrian stuff, the lame result of two highly questionable developments.' These are creative-writing courses and the large amount of subsidization. He argues with George Elliott CLARKE ('The colour of literature'), praises Milton ACORN ('Acorn, Lemm and Ojibway'), has little patience with Anne CARSON ('The trouble with Annie'), and discusses Louis DUDEK ('A personal memoir'), Al PURDY ('Standard average Canadian'), Lorna CROZIER ('An open letter'), and Richard OUTRAM ('I would like to like the poetry of Richard Outram more than I do'—'Reading Richard Outram').The book ends with a long essay on Canadian poets and poetry,'The great disconnect'.This is a collection that should surely be better known and discussed. Solway was a liberal-leftist until 9/11—the horrific TV images of which he witnessed on the remote Greek island of Tilos. This forced him 'to remake my thinking', and the book that grew out of the catastrophe was *The big lie: on terror, antisemitism, and identity* (2007), an impassioned polemic in the form of two long essays: I. 'Platform'—the English title of Michel Houellebecq's Islam-bashing French novel that linked the domestic disorder of Western society and its weakness in the face of Islamic threats; II. 'On being a Jew'. Solway's new mindset has him seeing liberal intellectuals—all liberals, for that matter—and journalists as 'lovers of those who would annihilate us, human shields for the adversary, guarantors of the dysfunctional Muslim world', made up of people who 'can scarcely be considered, in the vocabulary of Western humanism, as "ethical subjects" but remain in the service of an exclusionary universal and as such are inaccessible to us.' He scorns the claim that there are 'moderate Muslims'. Though of course one respects the strong feelings that occasioned the essays, which have been assiduously researched and are well-informed, they are also self-indulgent, undisciplined, rambling, given to hyperbole and inaccuracies. It is not true that 'there is now little that may serve to distinguish our notable news organs from, let us say, the Palestinian daily *Al-Hayat al-Jadida* or the Arabic television channel Al Jazeera'; nor that the editorial policy of the *New York Times* 'opposes the validity of the Jewish state'. Anti-Semitism begins with unpleasant occurrences in Solway's childhood and youth in a small town in Québec and tars anyone who criticizes Israel's current policies—a sadly clouded and prejudiced view of determinedly impartial critical opinions. Part II, however, is a rich and eloquent outpouring. There are forty-four pages of Notes—some of them very long, many of them angry—but no index. Hitler's words in *Mein kampf* provided the title: 'In the big lie there is always a certain force of credibility....'
See *David Solway: essays on his works* (2001) edited by Carmine Starnino.

Sommer, Richard (b. 1934). Born, raised, and educated in Minnesota, he attended Harvard University before coming to Canada in 1962 to teach at Concordia University, Montreal, from which he retired. Sommer has published eight volumes of poetry, including *Blue sky notebook* (1973), *The other side of games* (1977), *Selected and new poems* (1984), *Fawn bones* (1986), and *The shadow sonnets* (1992). A constant theme of much of his poetry is one of placing himself inside reality to experience and then report any events impinging on the self, which, as he states in one of his sonnets, 'is all we really have.' Irony flickers through the poems: as he expresses the external world directly, he lets irony surround his responses to that reality. Much of Sommer's concern for the life of nature and the violent inroads made on it figures in his *Fawn bones*. His poetic voice has remained consistent, though he moved to a more open language, trying to merge directness and the colloquial with the inwardly musing sides of his nature. This is particularly true of *The shadow sonnets*, a collection of 100 poems recording a wide range of personal experiences, both painful and joyous. While he retains a firm hold on the intricacies of rhyme and rhythm, many of the sonnets jostle and pull at the constraints as he juggles with slant rhyme and expanded rhythms—a worrying at the form that creates an added tension to the poetry.

Sono Nis Press (1968–) was founded in Victoria, British Columbia, by J. Michael YATES as a literary press to publish poetry and avant-garde fiction in quality editions. The name of the press is nonsensical, taken from a character in Yates's *The man in the glass octopus* (1968), a collection of stories and the first book published by the press. (*Sono* in Italian means 'I am'; *nis* in Anglo-Saxon means 'is not'.) From 1968 to 1972 the press published nearly fifty poetry or short-fiction titles, high-quality hardcover books printed and bound by the Morriss Company of Victoria. In 1976 Yates sold the press to them. Richard Morriss had a long-standing relationship with writers and literary publishers in B.C. ('in any typeface you want, as long as it's Baskerville'), and, under the initial advisory editorship of Robin SKELTON, he extended the publishing program to a dozen diversified titles a year: local histories, artbooks, journals, biographies, literary criticism, and scholarly books, as well as poetry collections. Its authors included Susan MUSGRAVE, Andreas SCHROEDER, Seán VIRGO, Robert HARLOW, Robin SKELTON, Robert BRINGHURST, John Robert COLOMBO, George Amabile, George JONAS, and Yates himself. Sono Nis books were never remaindered. After Richard Morriss's death, his daughter Diane took over the company in 1994. In 2002 she and her husband, graphic designer Jim Brennan, moved Sono Nis from Victoria to Winlaw, B.C. In 2007 they celebrated 39 years of publishing, with 'more than 300 titles, 300 authors, and a fabulous string of Canadian poetry and history prize nominations and awards'.

Souster, Raymond (b. 1921). Born in Toronto, he has lived there nearly all his life and rooted most of his poetry in its landscape. He grew up in the western Humberside area of the city, becoming an outstanding softball pitcher in his late teens. He joined the Bank of Commerce as a teller in 1939 and enlisted as a tradesman in the Royal Canadian Air Force in 1941. He was posted to continental defence squadrons in Nova Scotia and Newfoundland before a posting to England brought him to Europe for the final day of the war. While in Nova Scotia, Souster was inspired by John SUTHERLAND's FIRST STATEMENT to publish his first little magazine, *Direction* (1943–6), mimeographed on borrowed RCAF paper. A large selection of his poetry was included in Ronald Hambleton's *Unit of five*

(1944). On demobilization he returned to what is now the Canadian Imperial Bank of Commerce, where he worked for forty-five years until his retirement, and proceeded to write poetry steadily. He was made an Officer of the Order of Canada in 1995. Souster's first book, *When we are young* (1946), published by John Sutherland's First Statement Press, was followed by his inclusion in Sutherland's anthology *Other Canadians: an anthology of the new poetry in Canada, 1940–1946* (1947) and by the RYERSON PRESS's publication of his *Go to sleep, world* (1947). He attempted his second little magazine, *Enterprise*, in 1948 and published a pseudonymous war novel, *The winter of time*, by 'Raymond Holmes', in 1949. His third volume of poetry, *City Hall street*, appeared in 1951. The poetry of this and the preceding volumes was romantic in diction, often overstated, and opposed nature and youthful love to the ugliness of war and factory.

In 1951 Souster became a close friend of Louis DUDEK, who had just returned to Montreal from New York, and who introduced him to the work of William Carlos Williams and the poets of Cid Corman's US magazine *Origin*. With Dudek's encouragement he launched his third magazine, CONTACT (1952–4), in which he was able to publish work by Corman and other *Origin* writers. In the spring of 1952 he joined with Dudek and Irving LAYTON to begin Contact Press (1952–67), the chief publisher of new poetry in Canada during the 1950s. Under the influence of Williams and Corman, Souster's style changed drastically; his line became the brief 'variable foot' of Williams, his diction became concrete and austere. In his publications of the fifties—*Shake hands with the hangman* (1953), *A dream that is dying* (1954), *For what time slays* (1955), *Walking death* (1955), *The selected poems* (1956), *Crêpe-hanger's carnival* (1958)—Souster continued his early theme of the opposition between the 'outside' forces of love, nature, and sport and the 'inside' ones of industry and commerce. Because this was also an opposition between small and large, Souster's new poetic of understatement and economy was ideally suited to it. Late in the decade Souster began his fourth mimeographed little magazine, *Combustion* (1957–60), which reflected his continuing interest in the poetry of Corman and other American writers.

The 1960s were a period of consolidation for Souster. He published three outstanding collections: *A local pride* (1962), *The colour of the times* (1964, GGA), and *As is* (1967); and began the lengthy process of publishing or re-publishing his entire body of work with *Lost & found: uncollected poems 1945–1965* (1968) and *So far, so good* (1969). He also published the less-important books *Place of meeting* (1962), *At Split Rock Falls* (1963), *Twelve new poems* (1964), and *Ten elephants on Yonge Street* (1965); edited for Contact Press the influential anthology of young poets *New wave Canada: the new explosion in Canadian poetry* (1966); and on the demise of CONTACT PRESS in 1967 began work on another novel loosely tied to his war experiences, *On target* (1972), privately published under the 'John Holmes' pseudonym. The re-publication of Souster's early work continued in the 1970s with *The years* (1971), *Selected poems* (1972), *Double-header* (1975), and *Rain-check* (1975). The poems in *Change-up* (1974), *Extra innings* (1977), and *Hanging in* (1979) took on a retrospective tone, particularly the series Pictures of a Long-Lost World, in which Souster directed his nostalgic vision towards recapturing specific moments of twentieth-century history. Other later volumes are *Jubilee of death: the raid on Dieppe, a poem* (1984), *Flight of the roller coaster: poems for children* (1985), *It takes all kinds* (1986), *The eyes of love* (1987), *Asking for more* (1988), *Running out the clock* (1991), *Riding the long black horse* (1993), *Old bank notes* (1993), *No sad songs wanted here* (1995), *Close to home* (1996). *Of time & Toronto* (2000) ends with a sequence called 'Pictures from a long-lost world', recapturing a famous moment in American history when the abolitionist John Brown raided Harper's Ferry (in October 1859): a canny rearrangement of a prose text, it does not rise to being a prose-poem. Between 1980 and 1992, and including poetry from 1940 to 1992, Souster published seven volumes of *Collected poems* (1980, 1981, 1982, 1983, 1984, 1989, and 1992). His poetry is notable for its skilled use of imagism, for its vivid affirmations of the value of the commonplace object, and for its depictions of Toronto streets, parks, and suburbs. Deliberately avoiding the formally elegant poem, Souster compiled a body of disarming lyrics in which the craft is concealed so that incidents and scenes may have all possible prominence.

In 2001 Souster lost the sight of his left eye, and not long after his right eye gave him trouble; he is now almost blind. Nevertheless, in 2002 a collection of his baseball poems, *Take me out to the ballgame*, was published, with an Introduction by W. P. KINSELLA; and in 2003 *Twenty-three new poems*, in which he encapsulates his memory of wartime stories so that they won't be 'lost forever'. In 2006 a trilogy was published: *Uptown downtown: new poems of the GTA*, with an Introduction by Robert FULFORD; *Wondrous wobbly world*, including Souster's 'found poems' based on extracts from a selection of letters Archibald LAMPMAN wrote to Edward William THOMSON (with a commentary by William Toye); and *Down to earth: new poems to catch up*, including many poems about warfare from 1893 to the Iraq war, with a Foreword by Eleanor Cook. Undertaking a strange challenge—researching the French Indo-China war of 1946–54 and the decisive battle of Dien Bien Phu of 1954 and turning many relevant texts into simulated 'found poetry', Souster produced—with the help of his neighbour Les Green—*What men will die for: a docu-poem in many voices of the first Vietnam (French Indo-China) war* (2007). It is an extraordinary work because it is perverse, and so long, some 400 pages with maps.

Southern Ontario Gothic. Graeme GIBSON's interviews in *Eleven Canadian novelists* (1973) marked the appearance in print of a passionate recognition by Ontario writers of the Southern Ontario Gothic. The fiction of Margaret ATWOOD, Matt COHEN, Marian ENGEL, Timothy FINDLEY, Alice MUNRO, and Scott SYMONS shares a sense of distinct regional, even mythological, place where horror, murder, and bodily violations are not uncommon. Rooted in the nineteenth-century romances of John RICHARDSON and the survival stories of Susanna MOODIE's pioneer experiences, the Gothic tradition extends forward to Raymond KNISTER's chronicles of the living dead in *White narcissus* (1929), Munro's *Selected Stories* (1996), and Atwood's *Alias Grace* (1996). James REANEY's plays— *Colours in the dark* (1969), *Baldoon* (1976), and *The Donnellys* (1974–7)—as well as his short stories 'The bully' and 'The box social' (reprinted in *The box social and other stories* in 1996), also assume Gothic elements of the macabre rooted in nightmarish families and uncanny action. Carol SHIELDS' novel *Swann* (1987) makes the murder and dismemberment of poet Mary Swann by her husband, an Ontario farmer, a secret at the heart of the narrative that must be investigated and resolved, in keeping with Gothic conventions. The best expressions of Southern Ontario Gothic celebrate life, while exhuming the deadening and deforming forces beneath genteel surfaces, manifest in the merciless forces of Perfectionism, Propriety, Presbyterianism, and Prudence. Traditionally the Gothic deals with confinement, illness, madness, demonism, secrets, live burial, and fear; usually an

Southern Ontario Gothic

imperilled heroine searches for the clues to her identity in a ruin or a confining architectural space like a dungeon. In the Southern Ontario tradition, however, the threat to the female protagonist can come from the wilderness, from cabin fever, or from uncommunicative husbands. Because the Gothic often deals with the supernatural, it challenges rationality. Irrational figures like the Wild Man, the Wild Woman, fool-saints, or wendigos provide the apparition of the supernatural within the Canadian bush. In other cases the Gothic concerns family secrets and social oppression—what might be called the irrationality of civilized institutions. This may take the form of religious difference, as in the case of 'demonic' Catholicism in *The Donnellys*. It may also take the form of finding dead or ill mothers, like the sickly Mrs Dempster in Robertson DAVIES' *FIFTH BUSINESS* (1970). Sometimes the female principle is threatening and requires elimination, such as the smart but spell-casting Zenia in Atwood's *The robber bride* (1993). In this sense the Gothic is about the impossibility of dealing with women and their bodies. It is sometimes located in desperate domestic circumstances that produce insanity or criminal action. Novels like Joan BARFOOT's *Dancing in the dark* (1982), Tom MARSHALL's *Changelings: a double fugue* (1991), Timothy Findley's *Headhunter* (1993), and Atwood's *The blind assassin* (2000) make madness in the home or in the streets an aspect of the bizarreness that underlies much of 'ordinary' Southern Ontario experience. What makes this locale so prone to Gothic tales is the failure of communication between family members or social groups. In the absence of communication, strange projections and psychological grotesqueries spring up and rapidly grow to unmanageable proportions. Malevolent fantasies are the source and sustenance of the Gothic tradition.

Spalding, Esta (b. 1966). Born in Boston to Philip Spalding and Linda SPALDING, she has a B.A. from the University of Chicago and an M.A. from Stanford University. Living now in Vancouver, she is both a screenwriter and poet. She adapted Barbara GOWDY's novel *Falling angels* into a 2003 feature film and that year co-wrote the script adaptation of Carol SHIELDS' *The republic of love*, which was filmed. Her 2007 movie-of-the-week for CTV, *In God's Country*, was a great success. But it is Esta Spalding's gifts as a poet—her sensitive command of diction, the striking imagery and beautiful touches of eroticism—that compel attention. Her collections are *Carrying place*

(1995), *Anchoress* (1997), *Lost August* (1999)—in which 'Aperture' won the Long Poem Prize of the *MALAHAT REVIEW,* and 'Bee verse' ('Let the bees come then. Let / there be another time & *enough.* / Let this empty cup brim / another cup.') won the League of Canadian Poets' National Poetry Contest—and *The wife's account* (2002). *Anchoress,* a remarkable long poem, opens with Peter Hull's invocation to his dead wife: 'Helen, I'm drowning. If I lie down in darkness will you come, if I lie down in rain will you rescue me, arrive with torches to dry my skin, tell me again the things that mattered? ... I want you inside me, a second, deeper skin, my anchoress.' He explores his own past as well as Helen's: 'Helen is with the dead. With my father, gone before I knew / him. I grew up staring at his photograph: Private Peter H–. / *Canadian Armed Forces.* He had a secret only I might / understand. Since I had his name .... You cannot outrun the dead. They are in the elements—/ even at my birth, Lake Ontario was dying. From the / Thousand Islands to the bilge harbours of Hamilton where I / grew up, it unspooled itself. Restless as a virus.' Helen's response to the Gulf War: 'she soaks in gasoline, pours it down her neck, / heavy canister, sloshing gas on her back, / ribbons of gasoline / splash on her jeans, her feet, the snow / on the ground catches it / in pools that rainbow around her, furious / birds overhead, and squirrels, feeding, / oblivious.' (In a note at the end Spalding tells us that 'On February 16, 1991, Gregory Levey burned himself to death to protest the Persian Gulf War.') Helen's sister is France: 'two sisters make love to the same man .... We make love again and again ... ' *The wife's account*—of a marriage over a year—is a favourite Spalding collection and takes in the pharaoh Ramses II and his wife Nefartari, Lady Diana, and Alicia from the Hitchcock film *Notorious,* but it is notably about love: 'You lie beside me / sand on the back of your arms / & legs your back / grains in your hair & behind your ears ... I made my life with this man / the one who walked up to me at a party / he was someone else's / but the shape his hands made in air when he spoke / was a place to put my grief // That man whose head touches my head in the sand / whose eyes open to the same clawed sky' ('Hinge'). 'Nothing love / could make me leave / you nothing / though my body has broken / beneath yours a thousand times / & after each we come up / for air forgetting / what we sought' ('Anniversary') *'What are we going to do / with this love?* Sun roses snow / on the branches. I lift my face from / the window glass. // We're tied to each other. Where you climb, I will // climb. This light, ungraspable, / all we have.' ('Train window'). The poem 'The wife's account' begins: 'Here's what happened: At lunch your mother gave me one / of those tapes. She has a whole library—have you seen them in her closet? Lose weight impotent no more grief divorce—I'm driving home on Marine Drive & I pop the tape in / The first thing it says *Do not operate a motor / vehicle while listening to this recording.*' The title character of *Mere* (2001), a non-fiction work by Esta and Linda Spalding, is the twelve-year-old daughter of Faye Holmes who lives on the sailboat Faye skippers on the Great Lakes—on Lake Ontario when she docks twice a year in Toronto to collect an envelope of cash. Also on board is Mark, a mysterious teenaged runaway and a pal of Mere's. In Toronto Mere connects, to her pleasure, with her father Merrill, estranged from Faye. Flashbacks tell of Mere's parents' unlawful involvement in an anti-Vietnam War protest in Chicago, in 1968, which explains the paranoia and fear that weigh on them both to the present day. A novel containing many interesting ingredients (including sailing), the narrative is disruptive, sometimes withholding information, or suddenly and briefly injecting surprising new information without following it up clearly. The boat is called *Persephone*. The combination of the myth of Demeter, mother of Persephone (by Zeus), and the daughter-mother pairing in both the authorship and the leading characters, does not add to one's enjoyment of the plot.

Esta Spalding is one of the editors of BRICK and co-edited—with Michael REDHILL, Michael ONDAATJE, and Linda Spalding—the anthology *Lost classics* (2000).

Spalding, Linda (b. 1943). Born Linda Dickinson in Topeka, Kansas, she received her B.A. (1965) at the University of Colorado; married Philip Spalding and had two daughters, Esta SPALDING and Kristin; they divorced. She pursued graduate studies at the University of Hawaii at Monoa from 1970 to 1972. In Hawaii she met Michael ONDAATJE and they became partners; they live in Toronto, where she is one of the editors of BRICK (along with Ondaatje and Esta). She has written two novels. In *Daughters of Captain Cook* (1988) the past is a mirror that reflects and refracts the present-day life of Jesse, the female protagonist. From the narrative frame, 'Album', Jesse describes family photographs that speak of lost events, a reality past. In reminiscing about her past and contemplating her marital

disappointments, Jesse wonders if her present circumstances are an inescapable fate, a legacy bequeathed to her by female ancestors, one she will pass down to her own daughter, Kit. Countering Jesse's family history is that of Paul, her husband. His is a history imbedded in ancient Hawaiian tradition and mythology and one that forces Jesse to struggle with conflicting points of view. A marked feature of *Daughters* is how Spalding acknowledges traditional Hawaiian beliefs as they are both reflected and denied by contemporary life. In *The paper wife* (1994, rpr. 1995) Colorado and Mexico provide the disparate cultural landscapes. The naivety of a 1960s Kennedy-era American idealism confronts political issues that raise moral dilemmas for the characters. Vietnam War conscription, an illegal adoption agency operating under the guise of a beneficent orphanage in Mexico, and the inextricable links between money and power and identity provide the novel's political underpinnings. Spalding's *The follow: a true story* (1998) has one characteristic of fiction in its plentiful dialogue, but it is non-fiction, the matter-of-fact account of Spalding's three visits to Borneo. The title refers to the silent watch of a tracker over an orangutan's movements, and also to Spalding's quest. She had been inspired by the study of endangered orangutans undertaken by the Canadian anthropologist Dr Biruté Galdikas, whom she heard lecture in 1995 in Los Angeles and with whom she later had a hectic dinner. The book recounts Spalding's sojourns in Borneo, her bonding with her guide Riska, her relations with many others, her growing knowledge of orangutans, and the anti-climax of her difficult journey up the Sekonyer River, when she and her two companions finally stood in front of Galdikas, but were ignored. (This expedition led to Riska's memoirs, which Spalding edited, writing a long Introduction: *Riska: memories of a Dayak girlhood* [1999] by Riska Orpa Sari.) *Who named the knife: a book of murder and memory* (2006) grew out of a trial that took place in 1982 over the 1978 murder in Hawaii of Larry Hasker, for which William Acker, twenty-eight, and his wife Maryann, eighteen—a notably amoral married couple—were prosecuted. (Also in 1978 they were implicated in the murder of Cesario Arauzo in California.) They had a Smith and Wesson gun and a knife (never used) called 'Justice'. When William is tried he said that Maryann fired the shots, but he was still imprisoned as an accessory. (Years later he admitted that he lied.). For Maryann's trial Spalding was called as an alternate witness. Towards its end, owing to an unexpected happening, she was five minutes late arriving at the courtroom and was dismissed. This always haunted her, as she thought that her doubts about Maryann's guilt might have kept her out of prison. Eighteen years later, while living in Toronto, she discovers the diary she kept during the trial. Phone calls eventually put her in touch with Maryann in prison—she visited her three times, there was much correspondence—and they became close (Maryann was eventually released.) All this and more is related in a fascinating text that incorporates Maryann's early life, along with William's (the victims of the murders receive virtually no attention). Interweaving this narrative with details of her own early life and marriage as a young woman, and later divorce, Spalding attempts to draw a connection between the two. *Mere* (2001), a non-fiction work that Linda wrote with her daughter, is described in the entry on Esta Spalding.

Linda Spalding is an editor of BRICK and co-edited (with Ondaatje) *The Brick reader* (1999) and (with Michael REDHILL, Esta Spalding, and Ondaastje) the anthology *Lost classics* (2000).

Sparshott, Francis (b. 1926). Francis Edward Sparshott was born in Chatham, England, and educated at Oxford University. He came to the University of Toronto in 1950 as a lecturer in philosophy and in 1955 joined the staff of Victoria College. He was professor of philosophy from 1964 until he retired in 1991, and was appointed University Professor in 1982. Philosopher by profession and poet by inclination, Sparshott remarked that, while poetry and philosophy are two distinct things, there is common ground, for the purpose of both is to 'discover connections that are not evident'. Sparshott's philosophical concerns pervade his poetry; he is skilled at perceiving hidden relations between ideas. This is nowhere more evident than in his *The cave of Trophonius and other poems* (1983), which he describes as a 'trip of the shaman through the universe'; it won the first prize for poetry in the 1981 CBC literary competition. His first two poetry collections, *A divided voice* (1965) and *A cardboard garage* (1969), focus on poems of introspection that speak to themes of unfulfilled love, unattainable pleasures, and the sense of waste in human loneliness and isolation. Formally graceful, the poems are by turns romantic, humorous, passionate, and profound. *The naming of the beasts* and *The rainy hills* (haiku), both published in 1979, tend to feature observations and descriptions of commonplace events. All the poems in these collections have an elegant clarity of language and often give

voice to a capricious irreverence, refined colloquialisms, scholarly allusions, and witty asides. Sparshott's later books of poetry include *The hanging gardens of Etobicoke* (1983, rpr. 1994), *Storms and screens* (1986), *Sculling to Byzantium* (1989), *Views from the zucchini gazebo* (1994, rpr. 1997), *Home from the air* (1997), and *The city dwellers and other poems* (2000). His themes continue to display a wonderment at the banality of life's tiny moments. Increasingly they reveal a painful resignation to the temporality of the human condition. For the most part, Sparshott's poetry is not joyous: decay as a theme creeps frequently into his work.

Sparshott's early philosophy books display the irreverence and witty asides of his early poetry, giving them a literary panache that is rare in philosophical writing. Sparshott made his reputation as a philosopher with *An enquiry into goodness and related concepts* (1958), a distinguished work that tackles the traditional concerns of ethics and explores the various meanings of 'goodness' and their relation to human satisfaction. But he is perhaps best known for his work on aesthetics. In *The structure of aesthetics* (1963) he examines the concept of a work of art, the meanings of artistic language, the legitimacy and purpose of artistic criticism, and the role of art as an expression of the human condition. It concludes with a warning against scholarly theses that suggest a single function or analysis of art. *The concept of criticism* (1967) argues for the interrelatedness of theories and functions, and urges the use of reasonable techniques, 'not just one method of criticism'. *Looking for philosophy* (1972) is a mixture of witty essays, interludes, and lively dialogues that investigate the discipline of philosophy and the philosopher's task. Sparshott accepts St Ambrose's dictum that salvation cannot be achieved by philosophy, but adds that this belief was easy for Ambrose, since he was no philosopher. This book aroused the ire of some critics, who believed that philosophers should not make jokes about philosophy. (Sparshott's humour also surfaces frequently in the footnotes accompanying his philosophical works.) *The theory of the arts* (1982), which he has described as his magnum opus, distinguishes between the classical definition of 'fine arts'—which regards art as productivity, 'a performance with respect to its design'—and the modern concept of art considered as pure creativity and expressed intuitions. Sparshott concludes that he has offered an aesthetic meta-theory—a theory about theories of art. Sparshott then turned his attention to dance as an art in *Off the ground: first steps to a philosophical consideration of the dance* (1988), a landmark work that offers historical review, hermeneutical exegesis, and ontological speculations—concluding that dance is a 'visible object of cognition' sustained by 'a system of virtual energies', representing a 'sense of achievement or wonder, a celebration of life'. But he warns the reader incessantly that these are suggestions among multiple interpretations. After his retirement he published three more major works of philosophy: *Taking life seriously: a study of the argument of the Nichomachean ethics* (1994), *A measured pace: toward a philosophical understanding of the arts of dance* (1995), and *The future of aesthetics* (1998). For all Sparshott's interest in dance, only one of his poems directly addresses the art: 'Arabesque' (*Storms and screens*). Perhaps each book of poetry is in its own right Sparshott's choreographed metaphor for life. The reader knows that he/she is living: as in dancing, the struggle for excellence is painful, and the performance is brief.

Spears, Heather (b. 1934). Born in Vancouver, she received a diploma from the Vancouver School of Art and a B.A. in English (1956) from the University of British Columbia. The same year an Emily CARR Scholarship enabled her to leave for art studies in London. Marrying Lenny Goldenberg, a potter from Montreal, she settled in 1962 with her growing family on the Danish island of Bornholm, moving to Copenhagen in the 1980s. She continues to live in Copenhagen, where she teaches drawing and runs a small gallery called Upper Canada, besides making regular trips to Canada to teach, exhibit, and give readings. As a writer Spears began with poetry, writing *Asylum pieces* (EMBLEM BOOKS, 1958) as an undergraduate after two summers working in mental hospitals. It has been followed by ten collections: *Drawings from the newborn: poems and drawings of infants in crisis* (1986); *How to read faces* (1988); *The word for sand* (1989, GGA); *Human acts* (1991); *Moonfall* (1991); *The Panum poems* (1996), which Spears wrote while making anatomical drawings at the Panum Institute, Copenhagen; *The taming* (1996); *Selected poems* (1997); and *Poems selected and new* (1999). The poems and drawings in *Required reading* (2001) document the trial—during which Spears was the courtroom artist—of two teenagers from Victoria, B.C., charged with the 1997 beating death of fourteen-year-old Reena Virk. The horrific event and the trial are brought to life vividly. Turning to fiction, Spears has written

a post-apocalypse trilogy—*Moonfall* (1991), *The children of Atwar* (1993), and *The taming* (1996)—in which twins inhabit the same body. *The flourish: murder in the family* (2004) is a stunning departure for which she draws on her research into the lives of her forebears in Victorian Scotland, particularly Charlotte Spears (her great-aunt), who was murdered in 1883, aged thirty-six. Spears says: 'The events in this story are true. The characters all lived'—though there is a fictional element in the family history, which is partly a murder mystery.

As writer and artist Spears has scrupulously trained herself both to see and to render what she sees—scenes, activities, persons, relationships—with great candour and objectivity, and including the emotional truth of what is seen. In most of her work no added information or explanation is supplied, and the reader is required to give very full attention—to participate in the seeing. The poems are, so to speak, craggy but exhilarating. This uncompromising approach works effectively in her first three novels as well: plunged into a strange world, the reader is brought close to the characters' perceptions and emotional life, while groping after the half-stated structures and connections that shape their surroundings. In her fourth novel, *The flourish*, Spears' storytelling skills animate the rich inner life of Charlotte and the Victorian world she lives in as well as 'the flourish' itself—its several meanings including the harsh weather giving way to the promise of spring, or a wholesome life giving way to violence. Spears also produced *Line by line* (2002), drawings of Canadian poets with a selection of their poems.

Stacey, C.P. (1906–89). Charles Perry Stacey was born in Toronto and educated at the University of Toronto (B.A., 1927), Oxford University (B.A., 1929), and Princeton University (A.M., 1931; Ph.D., 1933), where he taught from 1934 to 1940. Having served in reserve units, and being interested in military history, he was commissioned into the Canadian army in 1940 and joined the Historical Section of the General Staff, Army Headquarters, rising, with the rank of colonel, to be its director from 1945 to 1959, the year he was appointed professor of history at the University of Toronto. He was made an Officer of the Order of Canada in 1969. The author of more than a dozen books, Stacey was a pivotal historian in depoliticizing history and ensuring its freedom from censorship. He made the official history of the Canadian army in the Second World War more accessible to the intelligent general reader than its ponderous predecessors, but he did not foresee the battle he was forced to wage with Liberal governments to produce accounts free from censorship. Not only did Stacey succeed, but he also wrote three of the volumes: *The Canadian Army, 1939–1945* (1948, GGA), *Six years of war* (1955), and *The victory campaign* (1960). His *Quebec, 1759: the siege and the battle* (1959) became a classic on the subject. The monumental *Men, arms, and governments: the military policies of Canada 1939–1945* (1970) brought together a lifetime's work. After retirement in 1975 Stacey produced a controversial study of Mackenzie King's private world in *A very double life* (1976, rpr. 1985). The two-volume *Canada and the age of conflict: a history of Canadian external policies* (1977, 1981)—Vol. I, *1867–1921*, and Vol. II, *1921–1940: The Mackenzie King era*—includes an examination of foreign policy free from the partisan biases that had been prominent in twentieth-century historiography called his autobiography *A date with history: memoirs of a Canadian historian* (1983).

Stansbury, Joseph (1742?–1809). Born in London, England, he immigrated to Philadelphia, arriving there on 11 Oct. 1767. He opened a china shop and gradually became a prominent member of the British social set. He had the reputation of being intelligent, with an ability to write satirical and humorous political poems and songs. 'As a writer of satirical verse, free from hatred and bitterness, he was "without a rival among his brethren"' (M.C. Tyler, *The literary history of the American Revolution*, 1897). With talk of a revolution in the air, he opposed independence of the American colonies and became a British agent, acting as a go-between for Benedict Arnold and the British headquarters. He moved to New York City, where he continued to write satires directed against the Whigs. In 1783 Stansbury moved his family to the Loyalist settlement of Shelburne, Nova Scotia; but after two years of hardship and disappointment he returned to New York, where he died. His well-known poem 'To Cordelia' vividly records his feelings about pioneer life in Nova Scotia. Winthrop Sargent's *The loyal verses of Joseph Stansbury and Dr. Jonathan Odell* (Albany, 1860) is the best collection of his verse.

Stead, Robert J.C. (1880–1959). Robert James Campbell Stead was born in Middleville, Ontario, and grew up in Cartwright, Manitoba. He attended Winnipeg Business College, and from 1898 to 1909 published and edited a local weekly. Stead worked at other temporary occupations, including selling automobiles, and by 1912 was in Calgary, first on the editorial staff of *The Albertan*, then from 1913 directing publicity for the colonization department of the Canadian Pacific Railway. In 1919 he moved to Ottawa to be publicity director for the Department of Immigration and Colonization, and from 1936 until his retirement in 1946 he held this position for parks-and-resources aspects of the Department of Mines and Resources. He was active in the CANADIAN AUTHORS' ASSOCIATION from its inception, and became its president in 1923.

Stead was the only writer to span the development of prairie fiction from the popular genre of romances of pioneering to realistic novels scrutinizing the values of prairie society. Five volumes of his slight, patriotic verse, published between 1908 and 1918, are of interest mainly as evidence of Stead's devotion to the imperial vision of the Prairies. Except for *The copper disc* (1931), a mystery published in the Doubleday Crime Club series, Stead's novels have prairie or foothills settings. *The bail jumper* (1914); *The homesteaders* (1916, rpr. 1973); *The cow puncher* (1918), which sold 70,000 copies; *Dennison Grant* (1920); and *Neighbours* (1922)—all combine romantic plots and an authentic depiction of western life. They brought Stead immediate popularity rather than a lasting reputation—with the exception of *The homesteaders*, which went through five printings by 1922 and has since earned critical recognition as a central romance of pioneering. Tracing the lives of an ideal pioneer couple from their arrival in Manitoba in 1882 to the land boom before the Great War, it develops such traditional motifs and themes of its genre as harmony with the land, the marriage of eastern refinement and western vitality, and the dangers of falling from idealism into mammonism. It has been argued that Stead, the journalist and publicist, exploited a shrewd sense of the popular taste in fiction; yet even his romances show a sometimes obtrusive concern for social issues, and in his last two prairie novels he turned away from the formulas that had brought him popularity to develop his ideas and his craft. In *The smoking flax* (1925) sociological theories about rural life overpower a weak plot; but it prepared the themes and techniques that Stead developed in his next and best novel, *Grain* (1926, NCL). Set partly against a background of the Great War, it portrays, from an ironic perspective, the life of Gander Stake, a pacifist who loves the land for what it can offer, but whose growth as a human being is stunted by an almost erotic absorption in the romance of mechanization and by the culturally impoverished environment of a prairie farm—which he leaves for Winnipeg. The technical nature and function of Stead's realism are subjects of critical debate, but he is credited, along with Frederick Philip GROVE and Martha OSTENSO, with initiating the sober assessment of man's spiritual alienation from the land that distinguishes prairie realism from the earlier romances of pioneering. *Dry water: a novel of western Canada*—of which Stead wrote three versions, the first in 1932–5—was not published until 1983, with an Introduction and Notes by Prem Varma. Another homesteading novel, it is a story, told in thirty-three very short chapters, about Donald Strand, who as a boy in 1890 travels to the mid-west to live with his farmer uncle, and in his early twenties buys a farm for $1400, then marries and has children. Unlike *Grain*, it is less about farming than about human relationships: the interraction of Donald, his wife Clara, his cousin Jimmie, and Ellen, the woman Jimmie marries who is the love of Donald's life—and about their difficulties, and some crises, related in an even, undramatic manner, and with the stable, resigned farmer Donald Strand always central.

Steffler, John (b. 1947). He was born in Toronto and raised in a rural area north of the city, near Thornhill. He received a B.A. (1971) from the University of Toronto and an M.A. (1974) from the University of Guelph. From 1975 he was professor of English at Sir Wilfred Grenfell College, Memorial University of Newfoundland, in Corner Brook.

Steffler has published six volumes of poetry: *An explanation of yellow* (1980), *The Grey Islands: a journey* (1985, rpr. 2000), *The wreckage of play* (1988), *That night we were ravenous* (1998), *Helix: new and selected poems* (2002), and *Lookout* (2010). Atlantic-coast folklore reveals its influence in the storytelling nature of much of Steffler's poetry. His syntax is that of speech, and his translucent images show that the lessons taught by the imagists have been learned well. Family, love of nature, and an often anxious contemplation of the past are some of the recurring themes in his poems. *The Grey Islands*, in which the speaker writes of a journey to islands off the east coast of northern Newfoundland, consists of poems and prose. As the journey progresses, the poet reveals his fascination for 'Carm', the last man to remain

on the islands, a fisherman who lived an eccentric life full of deprivation and grief and was considered 'mental', but whose relationship to the island and to isolation the poet attempts to absorb. *Helix* contains poems from this book, from *Wreckage of play*, and from *That night we were ravenous*. The title poem is one of the new poems: taking off for Amsterdam in rain and mist, the poet 'looks straight down on the Jacques Cartier bridge, the docks/where thirty-five years ago I got on the *Yildun*/and sailed as a deck-hand to Holland—confused/to be suddenly at the railing of time's helix, seeing/my younger self from this unforeseeable ledge.' Steffler has been quoted as saying that *Lookout* is 'a kind of goodbye to the island'. His interest in multiple narratives reasserted itself in his best-known work, *The afterlife of George Cartwright* (1992), which is a novel based on the life of the eighteenth-century diarist and entrepreneur who ran a trading post in Labrador and wrote about his experiences in a journal published in 1792. Steffler managed both to convey sympathy for Cartwright and to condemn his exploitation of the Natives with whom he lived and worked. Part history, part fiction, the novel is remarkable for its successful manipulation of a complex chronology in which the narrative ricochets through three centuries. *George Cartwright* won the Smithbooks/*Books in Canada* First Novel Award and the Thomas RADDALL Atlantic Fiction Award. Steffler was Poet Laureate of Canada in 2006–8 and now lives in Perth, Ontario.

Stein, David Lewis (b. 1937). Born and raised in Toronto, he attended the University of Toronto, studying philosophy (B.A., 1960; Master of Science, Urban and Regional Planning, 1974) and became interested in journalism; he was features editor of the *Varsity*. After graduation he worked as a reporter for *Maclean's*, the New York *Herald Tribune* in its Paris bureau, and the *Star Weekly*, and in 1977 joined *Toronto Star* as an editorial writer and columnist, writing on urban affairs from 1984 until 2001, when he retired. He teaches in the urban studies department of Innis College, University of Toronto, where he was made adjunct professor in 2002.

Stein's journalism, often studying political activism and its social roots, stands behind two early non-fiction books, *Living the revolution: the Yippies in Chicago* (1969) and *Toronto for sale: the destruction of a city* (1972), as well as his play, *The hearing* (1978), which depicts the comic and tragic dimensions of municipal battles between real-estate developers and home-owners' associations. Fifteen years later he published *Going downtown: reflections on urban progress* (1993). Like his journalism, Stein's fiction takes the form of political protest and social commentary, with the influence of George Orwell always evident. In his fine first novel, *Scratch one dreamer* (1967), Joe Fried, a middle-class Jewish liberal individualist, returns home to Toronto and his dying uncle, once a labour leader of the 1940s. Maintaining a careful and frequently comic balance between the cynical and the sentimental, the novel is a detached yet passionate study of political activism in the 1960s and of the hero's growing acceptance of individual moral choices. *My sexual and other revolutions: the memoirs of Daniel Johnson as told to David Lewis Stein* (1972) is his most vitriolic work; yet the vehemence of Stein's social criticism—moving sometimes awkwardly among parody, satire, pornography, and blatant attack—makes the book less effective than his first novel. Given his reputation as an insightful and empathetic chronicler of life in Toronto, it is not surprising that Stein uses that city as both setting and character in two later novels: *The Golden Age Hotel* (1984) and *Taking power* (1992), the latter a topical work that explores the public and private lives of a large cast of characters during the tumultuous 1970s. Stein's collection *City boys* (1978) includes both published and unpublished short fiction.

Sterling, Shirley. See ABORIGINAL LITERATURE: 5.

Stevens, Peter (b. 1927). Born in Manchester, England, he graduated in English and education from the University of Nottingham (B.A., 1951). He came to Canada in 1957 and taught at both a private school and McMaster University while working on his M.A. (1968). He then taught at the University of Saskatchewan (1964–8) and was the first person to receive a doctorate there in Canadian literature (1968). Stevens' thesis topic, 'The growth of modernism in Canadian poetry between the wars', led eventually to the publication of *The McGill movement* (1969), and to his editing Raymond KNISTER's *The first day of spring and other stories* (1976). He has also written critical monographs on the poetry of Dorothy LIVESAY and Miriam WADDINGTON, whose modernist poetics profoundly influenced Stevens' sense of versification and vocalized personal presence in his poems. From 1969 to 1996 he taught English literature and creative writing

at the University of Windsor, Ontario, where he is now Professor Emeritus. Stevens began writing poetry after his arrival in Canada, and his first collection, *Nothing but spoons* (1969), focuses on domestic events and Canadian places and landscapes. Poems such as 'Saskatchewan' from that collection represent a diary of adjustment to the new country. These subjects are expanded in *A few myths* (1971), which accommodates both conventional and experimental forms. Stevens' fascination with narrative and with individuals who observe the world from the periphery are characteristics of the books from the middle of his career, such as *Breadcrusts and glass* (1972), *Family feelings* (1974), and the chapbook *A momentary stay* (1980). *And the dying sky like blood* (1974) is a collage of poems that examine the life of Dr Norman Bethune and draws from such sources as found poetry, narrative vignettes, and lines from jazz songs of the 1930s and 1940s—material of special interest to Stevens, who contributed to CBC's *Jazz Radio Canada* program and conducted a Saturday-morning jazz show on a local radio station in Windsor. *The Bogman Pavese tactics* (1977) is divided into four sections, of which the first is based on P.V. Glob's discoveries of human sacrifices in northern European bogs (the same source inspired some of the best work of Irish poet Seamus Heaney), while the third continues Stevens' fascination with character-based narratives and focuses on Italian poet Cesare Pavese. *A momentary stay* (1974), which examined the brevity and fragility of life in the context of an alienated and dispassionate world, and the chapbook *Coming back* (1981), were followed by *Revenge of the mistresses poems* (1981), which draws upon a collection of erotic photographs by fashion photographer Helmut Newton and gives voice to, and avenges, the 'used' women of the pictures. For *Out of the willow trees* (1986) Stevens returned to the material of his childhood and the important relationships in his life in a process of self-examination and re-evaluation. *Swimming in the afternoon: new and selected poems* (1992), edited by Bruce Meyer, takes its title from Kafka's off-hand diary remark about the beginning of the Great War and contains poems that confront the ways individuals are ambushed by the unexpected in life. Long attracted to the dark side of human nature and the Gothic underbelly of the contemporary psyche, Stevens' *Rip rap: Yorkshire Ripper poems* (1995) takes a documentary approach to the murders and the murderer. It establishes a link between the Yorkshire of the mass murderer and that of Stevens' own past, and examines the ways in which actions become sublimated in consciousness and the process by which reality is transformed into memory—a sublimation that is both horrific and entangling. This collection was followed by *Thinking into the dark* (1997) and *Attending to this world* (1998).

Stewart, George, Jr (1848–1906). Born in New York City, he came to Canada with his parents in 1851 and was educated in London, Canada West (Ontario), and in Saint John, New Brunswick. At sixteen he founded *The stamp collector's monthly gazette* (1865–7), the first periodical of its kind in Canada, and at nineteen STEWART'S LITERARY QUARTERLY MAGAZINE. From 1872 to 1878 he was city editor of the Saint John *Daily News* and literary and dramatic editor of *The Weekly Watchman*; he went to Toronto in 1878–9 as editor of *ROSE-BELFORD'S CANADIAN MONTHLY*, but resigned after losing his court battle to get royalties from *Rose-Belford's* for his *Canada under the administration of the Earl of Dufferin* (Toronto, 1878). He next edited the Quebec *Daily Chronicle* from 1879 to 1896. He then purchased and edited the *Quebec Daily Mercury*, and when it ceased publication in 1903 he returned to the *Chronicle*. For many years he freelanced for American and Canadian magazines and contributed to reference works. Stewart was an innovative editor whose career illustrates the hazards of professional literary journalism in nineteenth-century Canada. His *Literary Quarterly*, founded on the belief that good literature could 'elevate and refine' emotions and morals, ran out of Canadian contributors of fiction. He introduced illustrated articles into *Rose-Belford's Canadian Monthly* and expanded its fiction department to include American writers. He was a prolific reviewer of theatre productions in Saint John and Quebec City, and was one of the first Canadian journalists to deal with contemporary events in book form. *The story of the great fire in St John, New Brunswick* (Saint John, Toronto, Detroit, 1877) is still a reliable source book; *Canada under the administration of the Earl of Dufferin*, however, is less a history of the country than a eulogistic record of the Governor General's public duties, with long excerpts from his speeches, though Stewart narrates events like the public reaction to the Pacific Scandal (1873) in a simple and dramatic way. While he advocated higher critical standards that he had evolved under the influence of William Wordsworth and Matthew Arnold, his articles on Carlyle, Thoreau, Emerson, and Longfellow were appreciative rather than judgemental; these were collected in *Evenings in the library* (Toronto, 1878) and *Essays from reviews* (Quebec, 1st series, 1882; 2nd series, 1893). Attacking the apathy towards local writers, he pressed for a native publishing industry and for Canada's adherence to international copyright, and was a fervent interpreter of French Canada in many articles that ranged from the scholarly to the travel guide. Stewart was one of the first critics to argue that the literatures of Canada and America were distinct entities from British literature. His activities and writings brought him international recognition, including honorary membership in the Athenaeum Club of London; the distinction of becoming the first Canadian member (1879) of the International Literary Congress; and honorary degrees from Laval, McGill, and Bishop's Universities, and from King's College, Halifax. Despite his fame and success, however, Stewart died in straitened circumstances in Quebec City.

Stewart's Literary Quarterly Magazine, Devoted to Light and Entertaining Literature (Saint John, Apr. 1867–Oct. 1872). This was the only Canadian magazine of its day to rely entirely on original contributions. The editor and publisher to Jan. 1872 was its young founder George STEWART, Jr; it continued for three numbers until Oct. 1872 as *The New Brunswick Quarterly*, of which the joint editors and publishers were A.A. Stockton and G.W. Burbidge. To counter the spread of 'trashy weeklies and immoral monthlies' from the United States, Stewart believed that 'the time had come for literary development in Canada, and especially in New Brunswick. Our best writers ... were sending their work to the British and American magazines, and I was convinced that the country could and would afford a decent support to a monthly or quarterly magazine.' Financially the *Quarterly* was not successful, even though its printer, George James Chubb, took no profit from it. Although Stewart attracted little fiction, he published poetry by James Hannay, Charles SANGSTER, Alexander McLACHLAN, and Ewan McColl; biographical sketches; and articles on history, drama, and literature. As a critic, Stewart tried to evaluate Canadian writers by the same standards that he applied to the British and the Americans. It was now time, he maintained in a review of Charles MAIR's *Dreamland, and other poems* (Jan. 1869), to judge a work on its artistic merits rather than merely as a phenomenon of Canadian authorship and publishing. While the articles were frequently cosmopolitan and lively, however, *Quarterly* writers never quite shook off a self-conscious provincialism in dealing with Canadian writing; and a spirit of parochialism infected its successor. Nevertheless, *Stewart's Quarterly* showed that Canadian journalism had the potential for higher standards.

Still stands the house (1938). This one-act 'drama of the Canadian frontier' (as it is subtitled) is one of five plays Gwen Pharis RINGWOOD wrote while earning her M.A. in drama at the University of North Carolina. First produced by the Carolina Playmakers on 3 Mar. 1938, and first published in 1938 in the *Carolina Playbook*, vol. II, it is one of the most popular plays in the Canadian dramatic repertory. The cast consists of four characters, and the action, which takes place in the Warrens' prairie farmhouse during a blizzard, is stark and simple. A real-estate salesman offers Ruth a vision of a new future near a city. Opposed to her is Hester, her sister-in-law, whose allegiance is to a house and farm as sterile as her own life. Caught between them is Hester's brother Bruce Warren, who is married to Ruth. Bruce is lost in a blizzard, and Ruth is murdered by Hester, who lapses into madness. With its claustrophobic setting in the livingroom of the isolated farmhouse, presenting a powerful metaphor of Canadian life during the Depression and its winter blizzards, offering an image of a disorder in nature that is reflected in the disorder of the Warren household, the play is a folk tragedy. Its key symbols—a broken hyacinth, a lamp not filled, a mare about to foal—reinforce Ringwood's theme of disorder and madness.

Stone Angel, The (1964, NCL). This novel by Margaret LAURENCE, which established her international reputation, is the first of her books to have a Canadian setting, and the first volume of what is known as the Manawaka cycle. A draft was completed in 1962, when Laurence was living in Vancouver, and rewritten the next year in England. In 1964 it was published simultaneously in Toronto, London, and New York. Originally entitled *Hagar*, it is a character study of the narrator, ninety-year-old Hagar Shipley, who is fiercely battling the threat of banishment to an old-people's home and the ravages of terminal disease. Friction with her son and daughter-in-law, with whom she lives, and her desperate attempt to preserve some dignity, contribute to a powerfully realized study of old age. A meeting with a stranger leads her to acquire a measure of grace before she is put into hospital where, in her last days, she is able to offer a little of the love and humility she has previously, to her cost, always withheld. Hagar's narrative, with its wit and humorous self-awareness, alternates between present action and reminiscences of the past: her Manawaka childhood; her defiant marriage to the handsome but lackadaisical Bram Shipley; life on his dusty, ramshackle farm during the Depression with her two sons; and her partial responsibility for the death of her younger son. The interweaving of past and present is part of a larger pattern of contrasts, which are most marked in the duality of Hagar's character: she has tried to hold to the stony, puritanical pride of her Scots-Presbyterian ancestors while denying the life-loving, wild, spontaneous part of her nature that gives such vigour to her narrative. Like the stone angel marking her mother's tomb, she has been 'doubly blind' in all her human relations. Incorporating many biblical allusions, the novel offers a modern version of the archetypal quest for spiritual vision. Kari Skogland's film of *The stone angel,* starring Ellen Burstyn, was released in 2008.

Storm, Jennifer. See ABORIGINAL LITERATURE: 5.

Stringer, Arthur (1874–1950). Born in Chatham, Ontario, he studied at the University of Toronto (1892–4) and briefly at Oxford University, before beginning a career in journalism and freelance writing, first with the Montreal *Herald* (1897–8) and then in New York, where he established himself as a capable producer of popular fiction and a minor but flamboyant figure on the fashionable literary scene. His first marriage was to actress Jobyna Howland, known as the original 'Gibson Girl'. In 1903 he bought a farm at Cedar Springs on the north shore of Lake Erie, where he lived intermittently for the next eighteen years, a period that included a brief, costly attempt at grain farming in Alberta around 1914. In 1921 he sold his Ontario farm and moved permanently to an acreage in New Jersey.

Stringer was as versatile as he was prolific. In addition to writing fifteen volumes of undistinguished verse and non-fiction prose, and more than forty works of fiction, he wrote copiously for magazines and occasionally for the stage, and for the serial 'The perils of Pauline' for Hollywood. His popularity was based mainly on a series of crime adventure novels, beginning with *The wire tappers* (1906), and on a series of wilderness adventures of the North (a region unfamiliar to

Stringer), beginning with *Empty hands* (1924). He occasionally attempted psychological sophistication, as in *The wine of life* (1921), and has been hailed as an early realist; but generally he worked within the conventions of sentimental romance popular around the turn of the century. Though Stringer used Canadian settings in a few of his novels, and Canadian characters in others, the bulk of his work belongs to American literature. One of his most popular books was *Lonely O'Malley* (1905), a sentimentalization of his boyhood in Chatham and London; but he made an enduring contribution to Canadian literature with his prairie trilogy: *Prairie wife* (1915), *Prairie mother* (1920), and *Prairie child* (1921). Stringer's narrator, a New England socialite married to a dour Scots-Canadian wheat farmer, develops gradually from the optimism typical of pioneering romances, through disillusionment as her marriage deteriorates, to mature resolve as she begins an independent life on the Prairies. Stringer's use of the diary form (though the narrative ostensibly opens as a letter to a friend) anticipates Sinclair ROSS's *AS FOR ME AND MY HOUSE* and places Stringer's trilogy in the Canadian tradition of confessions of a refined sensibility confronting the crudeness of pioneer life. His last work was a biography of Rupert Brooke, *Red wine of youth* (1948).

Strube, Cordelia (b. 1960). Born in Montreal and now living in Toronto, she was educated at Dawson College, Montreal, in the Professional Theatre Program (1978–81). She became an actress in theatre, television, film, and on radio (1981–8), and has written ten radio plays for CBC Radio drama (1988–94) and two screenplays. But Strube is perhaps best known as an accomplished novelist—publishing a novel a year over four years: *Alex & Zee* (1994, rpr. 1998), *Milton's elements* (1995, rpr. 1997), *Teaching pigs to sing* (1996), and *Dr Kalbfleisch & the chicken restaurant* (1997). Novels about dysfunctional partners and families (and others), they come to life in an adroit combination of dialogue and inner monologues or third-person observations that veer off in every direction—focusing on overheard conversations, horrific newspaper items, bizarre moments in the lives of movie stars and in movies and TV programs, all of them metaphors for the skewed world the characters live in, justifying their alienation. Bickering marks the relationship of Alex and Zee (his real name is Theodore)—they need each other but can't live together, and he leaves her, moving in with his mother, but is obsessed by her, as

Alex is by Zee. And of Milton and Judith ('He wanted to love Judith. He just wasn't comfortable around her. It was like every word he said was wrong before he said it.'). After Milton hits Judith she leaves him, and he is joined in his house, one by one, by his mother whom he hates, a sister who is a prostitute, another sister (and her two sons) who has left her alcoholic husband, and a brother who is dying of AIDS. Rita in *Pigs* thinks 'maybe pointlessness is a fact of life. She personally wants to stop trying to see a point to anything because it only gives her headaches.' Her mother has Alzheimer's, her brother is schizoid, her father is impossible, and she is plagued by mice in her kitchen; but her life and love are centred on her son, six-year-old Max, who yearns for a father. This man—Nolan, a doctor—appears, but he is a wreck; and Max is sodomized by someone unknown (he appears to have no memory of this). In the fourth novel Raymond, manager of Dr Kalbfleisch's chicken restaurant, Chez Simon, discovers his biological mother, Gloria, a pathological liar, and learns that she lives with his identical twin, who proceeds to harass Mara, Raymond's ex-wife, and even makes love to her when he thinks he's Raymond. These novels have been described as comic—there is black comedy in some of the grotesqueries, and there are sentences that induce laughter. But they contain an unrelenting parade of characters who are anxiety-ridden, depressed, affectless, cruel, vulnerable, or mentally retarded, for whom happiness is unknown, and events that shock (Milton and Judith's three-year-old daughter Ariel pulls the TV down on herself and is crushed, Rita's operation for fibroids, the report of Max's rape, the remains of a baby found in Mara's backyard, Raymond's viewing the cremation of his adoptive mother's body), as the author portrays a bleak urban landscape populated by losers. This dark vision, however, is offset by the light tone of the narratives, and by the steady relaying of minutiae of everyday life, which strike the reader as witty and true. *The barking dog* (2000) has many of the characteristics of the previous novels. A story containing many grim details and including both dread and humour, it is about Greer Pentland, a real-estate agent (her job provides some comedy), who has had a mastectomy (the sufferings and treatment of a cancer patient are described); whose son is on trial for murdering an elderly couple while sleepwalking; and who is troubled by her ex-husband, a seriously ill elderly aunt, a sister in an abusive relationship, and the disturbed daughter of the couple her son is on trial for killing. In *Blind night*

Strube

(2004) McKenna, a hairdresser and the single mother of Logan, hasn't a good word to say for men. Her father abused her; her ex-boyfriend Payne (Logan's father), her brother, and her Greek boss Kristo are all hopeless. At the outset of the novel McKenna's house burns down and she and Logan have to live in a motel; the stress affects her eyesight. Building on these ingredients, Strube has McKenna dealing as best she can with various clients, and several crises that befall her. Her dying father 'was supposed to die, is lost, forever drooling, and I want to ask him why he won't let them shut down the respirator. But this would be too intimate for us.' She is horrified to discover that Logan, the centre of her life, suffered a trauma when Mr Beasley fondled her intimately. Payne has a trial by fire and his face is disfigured. McKenna cares for him and he bonds with Logan. 'I hug him a lot …. It started with restraining him because he'd wake up screaming, flailing, dreaming of flames and dressing changes. I'd hold him and tell him he wasn't dead, that we were all here, together in the house …. When he had pneumonia in both lungs, when the nurses stopped making eye contact with me, I figured out I wanted him to live. Because we're bound by our daughter's DNA. Because our world would be smaller without him. Because nobody's perfect, because nothing stays the same.' The focus of *Planet Reese* (2007) is a troubled man with an unpleasant wife. Reese Larkin is a former Greenpeace activist who has become a 'for-profit' marketer. His marriage to Roberta (their offspring are Clara and Derek) has foundered; he irritates her. '"Do you think it makes children happy," Roberta had asked, rhetorically, "to hear about species extinction and loss of wilderness … and corporate take-overs?"' She ejects him from the family. Later Reese persuades her to join him on a family cruise (for the sake of the children) and the novel opens on the plane, when he has to sit separately. Some confusion ensues when turbulence begins, the plane drops fifty feet, and Reese accidentally kills a fellow passenger. As for the cruise, Reese thought it went rather well, but Roberta didn't. Returning home, she insisted that the limo drop Reese off first, at his basement apartment. Her farewell words were 'We'll be in touch.'—'Whenever someone says they'll be in touch it means they'll never be seen again. What did he do wrong this time?' Reese's tribulations—quite apart from newspaper headlines brandishing the state of the world—multiply, with bickering parents, the marketing company he works for, his attempts to find a 'quality mattress' that

will enable him to sleep, and Roberta's having her reasons for obtaining total custody of the children. The book ends when Reese learns that Roberta (too) was abused by her father. She learns that her suspicions of Reese were unfounded, so that custody of the children can now be shared. After one of their visits, when Reese has to return the children to Roberta and is alone, 'he is developing a confidence in his solitude … despite knowing that there are far too many people for nature to digest, that we are all going down together, that as the planet sickens, so shall we. He has begun to suspect that he is privileged to be able to contemplate his life before it is over, to function without mediation, to be apparently going nowhere.'

Such, Peter (b. 1939). Born in London, England, he immigrated to Canada in 1953 and completed his secondary schooling in Toronto before obtaining a B.A. and an M.A. in English from the University of Toronto. He has taught in high schools, colleges, and universities in Ontario and became professor of humanities at York University, Toronto; he is now Professor Emeritus (1999–). He lives in Victoria, B.C. Such's first novel, *Fallout* (1969, rpr. 1977), grew out of his experience as a miner in the uranium mines near Elliot Lake while he was a student. Told in fragments, it is about the violent rape of the landscape in the search for ore—a rape that is mirrored in the violent lives of the Natives and white men caught up in the rush for precious metal—and argues that exploitation of the land demands its price in exploitation of the Native peoples. The novel's grimness is somewhat tempered by a lyrical love affair between one of the Natives and a young white woman. *Riverrun* (1973, rpr. 1982) is about the last days of the Beothuk people of Newfoundland, who were systematically wiped out by the white settlers, becoming extinct by 1829. Told convincingly from the point of view of the Beothuks as they make their last desperate stand for survival, having been driven from the sea's edge by the newcomers, it is a bitter epitaph for a people in tune with the riverrun, the annual migration of salmon and caribou, on which the Beothuks largely depended. *Dolphin's wake* (1979) is a thriller about an archaeologist and his wife who have spent many years in Greece. *Earthbaby* (2005) is dystopian SF set in 2039 after the planet has been devastated by global warming. Earthbaby is a deep-space habitat; some of its crew turn the novel into a psychological thriller.

Suknaski, Andrew (b. 1942). Born on a homestead near Wood Mountain, Saskatchewan, of a Polish mother and a Ukrainian father, Suknaski attended Simon Fraser University and the University of British Columbia, as well as the Kootenay School of Fine Arts and the Montreal Museum of Fine Arts School of Art and Design. A poet and visual artist, he has worked at various jobs across the Prairies and in 1976 listed his occupation as 'migrant worker'. Though he has lived all over western Canada, his true home and centre remains Wood Mountain.

English was not Suknaski's first language, and the vocabulary of his poems contains a rich strain of Polish and Ukrainian, as well as many attempts to render an approximate transliteration of ethnic speech and pronunciation. Much of his early poetry, published in pamphlets by his own Elfin Plot Press, is visual in nature: concrete poems based on East Asian characters and on collage. His full emergence as an important voice in western Canadian poetry came with the publication of *Wood Mountain poems* (1976). (A thirtieth anniversary edition, with an Introduction by Tim Lilburn, was published in 2006.) Subsequent collections include *The ghosts call you poor* (1978), *In the name of Narid* (1981), *Montage for an interstellar cry* (1982), and *Silk Trail* (1985). Later, poor health largely prevented him from writing. A volume of selected poems, *The land they gave away: new and selected poems* (1982), was edited with an introduction by Stephen SCOBIE. Suknaski's central subject has been the people and the heritage of Wood Mountain, and of the Prairies generally. He writes of the town's inhabitants, both present and past, of the various nationalities and generations of the settlers, and of the Native peoples whose land it first was. (The historical association of Wood Mountain with Sitting Bull is a recurrent topic.) Suknaski sees himself as a mythographer who honours his subjects, rather than as a historian who describes or analyzes them. Like many Prairie writers, he loves the tall tale, the beer-parlour story, and the accents of the voices that recount them. Because he tries to recreate on the printed page the vividness and variety of spoken narrative, his poems tend to be long and rambling, somewhat diffuse in form, their poetic effect depending upon the choice and juxtaposition of anecdotes. The later work shows an increasing concern for those ethnic groups that have historically been relegated to the margins of society, and for a large-scale sense of world mythology. His historically based anecdotal style, employing the rhythms of the speaking voice, became for a time a dominant influence in Prairie poetry, and in the late 1970s Suknaski himself—with his beard, pipe, and coil of sweetgrass—was a presiding shaman of the region's literature. Perhaps the best view of Suknaski and his work can be found in Harvey Spak's film *Wood Mountain poems* (National Film Board, 1978). His collection *There is no mountain* was published in 2007 but was unobtainable.

Sullivan, Rosemary (b. 1947). Born in Montreal, she attended McGill University (B.A., 1968), the University of Connecticut (M.A., 1969), and the University of Sussex, where she earned her Ph.D. in 1972 for a thesis that was published as *The garden master: the poetry of Theodore Roethke* (1975). After teaching for a year each at the Université de Dijon and the Université de Bordeaux, she taught at the University of Victoria, British Columbia, from 1974 to 1977, when she joined the English faculty at the University of Toronto, becoming a full professor of English in 1991. Sullivan has published three collections of poetry: *The space a name makes* (1986) contains evocative poems about family history, love, neighbourhood, and travel; *Blue panic* (1991) intensifies this exploration of the ordinary world and extends it to include a Chilean sequence. Both collections—embracing occasionally her many travels—portray life as lived in the context of a psychological hinterland subject to both tenderness and violence. They were followed by *The bone ladder: new & selected* poems (2000).

Sullivan's first two biographies of writers— *By heart: Elizabeth Smart, a life* (1991, rpr. 1992) and *Shadow maker: the life of Gwendolyn MacEwen* (1995, GGA)—are substantial and engrossing. While seeking to understand the creativity of SMART and MacEWEN, Sullivan illuminates the complexities of the interactions between life and art. In *Shadow maker* she reveals the process of writing a biography in ways that enhance our understanding not only of her subject, but of the form itself. In *The red shoes: Margaret Atwood/starting out* (1998) she takes ATWOOD's life and career into the 1970s with an informed understanding and valuation of Atwood's works. *Labyrinth of desire: women, passion, and romantic obsession* (2001, rpr. 2004) is made up of an enjoyable and illuminating series of reflection on her subject that range widely over literature (*Madame Bovary*, *The sorrows of young Werther*, *Wuthering Heights*, *Jane Eyre*, *Rebecca*, *Doctor Zhivago*, *By Grand Central Station I sat down and wept*, *Gone with the wind*), films (the three versions of *Love affair, Casablanca, Rebecca, The lover, Wide Sargasso Sea, Sleepless in Seattle*), personages (D.H. Lawrence and Frieda, Aristophanes, Simone de Beauvoir and Sartre, Charlotte Brontë, Jean Rhys, Virginia Woolf, Elizabeth SMART, Frida Kahlo and Diego Rivera, Madonna, Leonora Carrington)—engaging one's interest in references to all these subjects and in conversations with friends. The book begins with a romantic story, and ends with its conclusion (in which Varian Fry—see below—appears). In her Afterword, Sullivan writes that romantic love 'can turn into something more real and durable' than obsessive passion.

In a work of historical non-fiction, *Villa Air-Bel: World War II, escape, and a house in Marseille* (2006), Sullivan describes in fascinating detail events that followed an attempt to rescue anti-Nazi refugees from Germany and Austria by the Emergency Rescue Committee, an organization set up by some New York intellectuals and recent émigrés in June 1940. They sent Varian Fry—thirty-two years old, a Harvard classics scholar—to Marseille, with the result that he led a phenomenal rescue operation, helping 2000 or more to escape Vichy France (including, before the book begins, the famous writer Franz Werfel and his wife Alma—formerly Alma Mahler—and Hanna Arendt and her husband). Sullivan focuses on a run-down mansion in the outskirts of Marseille, the Villa Air-Bel, rented by an American heiress, Mary Jane Gold, between the fall of 1940 and the summer of 1941. Frye and his colleagues welcomed a stream of painters and writers who visited the mansion. Among those they helped to escape were Max Ernst, Marc Chagall and his wife, Jacques Lipchitz, and Marcel Duchamp. Numerous memoirs and biographies have related most of the details in Sullivan's book, but she has brought everything together in a memorable narrative. The seventeen essays in *Memory-making: selected essays* (2001) include three that draw on research for her biographies: 'Romantic obsession' (Elizabeth Smart), 'Memory-making and the stamina of the Poet' (Gwendolyn MacEwan), and 'Alias Margaret: the Radcliffe years (Margaret Atwood). There are also essays on P.K. PAGE, Al PURDY, an interview with Margaret LAURENCE, and 'Confessions of an anthologist'. It's a wonderful collection, full of interest. *Cuba: grace under pressure* (2003) is a large-format picture-book tribute to Cuba, with photographs by Malcolm David Batty (and an Introduction by Margaret Atwood), in which Sullivan's text

brings aspects of the country to life, particularly (for someone who has only a distant interest in Cuba) in her fifteen-minute interview with the legendary ballerina Alicia Alonso, in her eighties. Alonso was asked how she could continue to dance while blind. She replied by referring to Beethoven, who was deaf: 'I admire him not only as a composer but as a man because I know what it is to compose without hearing since I have had to dance without seeing.'

Sullivan has edited several important anthologies, including *Stories by Canadian women* (1984), *More stories by Canadian women* (1987), *Poetry by Canadian women* (1989), and *The Oxford book of stories by Canadian women in English* (1999). In 2008 she received the Trudeau Foundation Fellowship ($225,000).

Sullivan, Alan (1868–1947). Born in Montreal, he spent his childhood in his father's Anglican rectories in Chicago, Montreal, and Sault Ste Marie, Ontario, and attended Loretto School, the most Spartan of British public schools, in Scotland. After studying civil engineering for a year at the University of Toronto (1886–7), he began a rugged career in northern Ontario that included surveying and construction for the Canadian Pacific Railway, lumbering, industrial engineering, gold mining, and prospecting. In 1904 he settled in Toronto, began to raise his large family, and, finding the sedentary life confining, turned in his free time to the literary re-creation of his past experiences. His short-story collection, *The passing of Oul-i-but* (1913), marked the beginning of his full-time career as a writer at age forty-five. After a stint with the RAF during the First World War, Sullivan wrote *Aviation in Canada: 1917–18* (1919). In 1920 he moved to England, where he lived—making numerous extended trips to Canada—until his death. Sullivan wrote forty-three works of fiction, including some two dozen lightweight novels of romance, mystery, and adventure set mainly in England, three of which deal with the paranormal; novels whose heroes discover their identity when they leave the Old Country for Canada; two novels set in the Canadian Arctic; and three historical novels that combine accurate detail and real and fictional characters. The best known of these is *Three came to Ville Marie* (1941, GGA), which is set in seventeenth-century Montreal. Sullivan also produced poetry, radio scripts, and magazine fiction, and in his heyday was widely read and reviewed. Several of his novels were made into films, including *The great divide* (1935), about the building of the Canadian Pacific Railway, which received a glittering premiere in England as *The great barrier* (1937). Workmanlike if not supremely talented, Sullivan conveyed an ethos of mainly masculine hard work, perseverance, and loyalty, which helped define Canada to itself and others.

Summers, Merna (b. 1933). Born in Mannville, Alberta, now living in Edmonton, she was a reporter and freelance writer before turning to the writing of fiction. Summers has written three collections of short stories: *The skating party* (1974), *Calling home* (1982), and *North of the battle* (1988). Widely anthologized, her stories have won numerous literary awards. She writes with insight, clarity, and in a richly textured prose about the activities and occasions of ordinary people in small-town farming communities in rural Alberta. In *The skating party* the stories convey the dailyness of life in the fictional but credible town of Willow Bunch during the 1930s and 1940s, recalling an era when life was guided by old-fashioned mottoes, and social occasions united family and community. In *Calling home*, small-town values clash with city ones, and familiar ways of behaving contradict a more contemporary etiquette. Astrid in 'City wedding' makes a trip to the city to help plan her son's wedding, only to learn that her hopes for a family occasion are at odds with the bride's mother's fuss-and-feathers plans. As in Summers' first collection, memory is a significant underlying theme that reveals layer on layer of irony and meaning when characters probe their past to understand their present. *North of the battle* is made up of selected stories from Summers' first two books plus 'A time for rising', in which Glen, from Ontario, takes over the farm he inherits and finds neither a common language nor a common set of values by which to understand the mid-western locale; he is consumed by an impulse to cut down trees and pile up rocks—to change things. It is a story that marks the beginning of the end of life as it once was in rural Alberta.

Sunshine sketches of a little town (1912, NCL). This has remained the most popular of Stephen LEACOCK's books. Set in Mariposa, a typical small Ontario town closely based on Orillia, where Leacock had his summer home, it caused great offence to the townspeople. The 'sketches' are dominated by Josh Smith, a hotel keeper who becomes Mariposa's Member of Parliament. The Mariposans believe that Smith is a hero and benefactor, but he is in fact a ruthless

individualist who sees through, and plays upon, the townspeople's desire for importance and sophistication. There has been some debate over the tone of the book, with Robertson DAVIES, most notably, seeing it as particularly harsh and unforgiving. However, most readers would agree that the tone is gently ironic: there are no real villains, not even Josh Smith, whose machinations never actually do any harm; and Leacock shows genuine affection in his portrayal of the foolish but good-natured Mariposans, such as the barber-financier Jefferson Thorpe, the 'enchanted' lovers Peter Pupkin and Zena Pepperleigh, and the 'mugwump' minister Dean Drone. Underlying the book's genuine affection and sympathy is serious criticism of the Mariposans' foolish desire to become part of the big urban world of material success, and of their failure to realize that there is no place in such a world for the social continuity and genuine fellow-feeling that Mariposa, for all its limitations, fosters.

Survival: a thematic guide to Canadian literature (1972, rpr. 2006, with a new Introduction by the author). This widely read critical work by Margaret ATWOOD was written while the author was associated with the House of ANANSI. Conceived as a handbook on Canadian literature for the average reader, it was written at a time when Canadians were notoriously diffident about themselves and their culture, and when Canadian literature was not considered a legitimate area of study. Based on the premise that Canadian literature was a colonial literature, imbued with implied preoccupations, the book offered an inductive study of the collective literary imagination, and of the key patterns that at that time constituted the shape of Canadian literature. The book's thesis—that every culture has a central symbol that functions like a code of beliefs—followed the well-known theory proposed by Northrop FRYE, who suggested that 'in every culture there is a structure of ideas, images, beliefs ... which express the view of man's situation and destiny generally held at the time' (*The modern century*, 1967). According to Atwood, the central image of Canadian culture before 1972 was that of a collective victim struggling for survival—an image that was the legacy of both a hostile natural environment and a colonial history. As a consequence, the national psychology was fatalistic, the expression of a victim mentality. There was considerable polemical anger in Atwood's assertion that Canadians had a will to lose, and that Canadian culture was characterized by a failure of nerve (one chooses to be a victim to avoid the responsibility of self-definition). In a series of chapters exploring archetypal images in Canadian literature—nature as monster, animals as victims, Natives as persecuted, the artist as paralysed, woman as ice maiden or absent Venus—Atwood described Canadian writers as living in an unknown territory, as exiles in their own country. Written with intelligence, wit, and considerable audacity, *Survival* was partly a political manifesto that protested the neglect of Canadian culture in Canada. It fell on the ears of its Canadian audience like a call to order, at a time when the realization was dawning that a Canadian literature indeed existed. Perhaps more than any other work, it helped galvanize the flurry of energy that characterized Canadian writing in the 1970s. An interesting three-way discussion of *Survival*—by Philip MARCHAND, Noah Richler, and Lynn Coady—appears in the December 2007 issue of *Quill & Quire*.

Sutherland, Fraser (b. 1946). Born in Pictou, Nova Scotia, he was educated at the University of King's College, Halifax, and graduated in journalism from Carleton University in 1969. In 1965–70 he worked as a reporter and staff writer on the *Wall Street Journal*, New York, and the Toronto *Globe and Mail* where he has been a regular book-reviewer since 1984. He was the founding editor of the literary magazine *Northern Journey* (1971–6). The approach Sutherland takes to his poetry is suggested by the title of his first book, *Strange ironies* (1972). Other collections of poems include *Within the wound* (1976), *Madwomen* (1978), *Whitefaces* (1986), and his most ambitious work, *Jonestown: a poem* (1996), about a religious cult leader, that combines dramatic, narrative, and epic elements. The title poem, written in 1971, of *The Matuschka case: selected poems 1970–2005* (2006) is named for Sylvestre Matuschka, 'who could only get sexual satisfaction blowing up trains./This interesting Hungarian blew up several/before he was finally captured, costing the railroads/a lot of money and killing quite a few people along the way.' He is a hero, a 'very rare human being,/a man who truly knew what his pleasure was.' *Manual for emigrants* (2007) includes poems about exile and belonging. The author says in a note at the end: 'Since I've long regarded myself as an internal exile, it was natural to interest myself in *real* exiles…. Connecting with the other is a way of connecting with the otherness within myself, a way of recognizing and validating difference.'

In Part I, 'A Manual for Emigrants', the nine poems turn these sentiments on their head, with a straight-faced series of anti-immigrant, racist commands: 'No, keep to yourselves. You'll be happier that way.' ('Mates'); 'If you speak English we may let you stay for a while.' ('English'); 'We don't want your warlords, your rapes and death camps, your borders erased and redrawn, your revenge and your resentments. We don't want your wars.' ('War'); 'What do you do with the money? // You send it off to your bombsites, your barrios, your famine villages. You buy the airfare for more of you to come and take more money and send it back.' ('Money'); 'What's wrong about white? // Where do you get off with your skin?' ('White'); 'We keep our distance. That's how we get along…. Don't get in the way of our distance.' ('Enough').

Sutherland is also the author of a novel, *In the village of Alias* (1986), and of three non-fiction works: *The style of innocence* (1972), a study of Ernest Hemingway and Morley CALLAGHAN, *John Glassco: an essay and bibliography* (1984), and *The monthly epic: a history of Canadian magazines* (1989). Sutherland edited the *Collected poems and translations of Edward LACEY* (2000), the expatriate (born in Lindsay, Ontario), interesting gay poet.

Sutherland, John (1919–56). Born in Liverpool, Nova Scotia, he attended Queen's University, Kingston (1936–7), where he developed tuberculosis of the kidney after an athletic injury. He was confined to bed in the family home in Saint John, New Brunswick, until 1941, when, against doctor's orders, he enrolled at McGill University, Montreal, though he left several months later. In Sept. 1942, after his poems had been rejected by the Montreal magazine *PREVIEW*, he founded *FIRST STATEMENT*, with the help of Audrey Aikman (whom he married) and other McGill undergraduates. The next year Irving LAYTON and Louis DUDEK became members of the editorial board and joined Sutherland in pursuit of a Canadian realism that would express the local and particular in simple language. In 1943 Sutherland acquired a printing press and in 1945, under the imprint of First Statement Press, he made an impact with a series of important chapbooks, the first of which was Layton's *Here and now*. In late 1945 *First Statement* merged with *Preview* to form *NORTHERN REVIEW*, with Sutherland as managing editor. In response to A.J.M. SMITH's *The book of Canadian poetry: a critical and historical anthology* (1943), Sutherland edited *Other Canadians: an anthology of the new poetry in Canada, 1940–46* (1947), in the introduction to which he vigorously attacked Smith's literary views, notably his use of the categories 'native' and 'cosmopolitan', and emphasized the need for Canadian poetry that was North American in perspective and technique. His hostile criticism (in *Northern Review*, Aug.–Sept. 1947) of Robert FINCH's *Poems*, which had won a Governor General's Award, led to the departure of the *Preview* poets from *Northern Review*'s editorial board. A year later Layton resigned. (Dudek had previously left to pursue studies in New York.) Sutherland continued to edit the magazine almost single-handedly, supporting himself by odd jobs; but his literary interests took on a conservative slant, culminating in the article, 'The past decade in Canadian poetry' (Dec. 1950–Jan. 1951), in which he turned his back on many of his former literary ideals, including the importance of vitality and a kind of Nietzschean spiritual health in poetry. He continued to publish *Northern Review* until his death in Sept. 1956. Sutherland returned in his literary philosophy to the views of his early *First Statement* days, but the emphasis on spiritual health was now more religious than Nietzschean because of an earlier conversion to Roman Catholicism. *The poetry of E.J. Pratt: a new interpretation* (1956), Sutherland's study of his favourite poet, reflects his Roman Catholic beliefs to an extent that does not benefit his criticism of Pratt's poetry. A selection of Sutherland's writings, together with a memoir by the editor, Miriam WADDINGTON, was published in *John Sutherland: essays, controversies and poems* (NCL, 1972). Bruce Whiteman edited *The letters of John Sutherland, 1942–1956* (1992).

Sutherland, Ronald (b. 1933). Born in east-end Montreal, he was educated at McGill University (B.A., 1954; M.A., 1955) and Wayne State University (Ph.D., 1960). From 1959 he taught at the Université de Sherbrooke, heading the English department from 1962 to 1974 and founding its graduate program in comparative Canadian literature in 1963. He is the author of three books of criticism—*Frederick Philip Grove* (1969), *Second image* (1971), and *The new hero* (1977)—and three novels: *Snow lark* (1971), *Where do the MacDonalds bury their dead?* (1976), and *How Elvis saved Quebec* (2003). With the exception of his first book, Sutherland's criticism is principally concerned with themes common to novels by French- and English-speaking Canadian writers of the past century.

It is sustained by a theory fully expressed in 'The mainstream', a chapter in *The new hero*: Canadian literature, properly speaking, provides imaginative expression of the interaction between the French and English founding cultures of Canada. In *Second image* he groups Canadian fiction according to three interlocking themes: the land and the divine order; the breakup of the old order; and the search for vital truth. Sutherland convincingly demonstrates the affinities that link writers as diverse as GROVE, Ringuet (Philippe PANNETON), W.O. MITCHELL, Gabrielle ROY, Hubert AQUIN, Jean Simard, and others, showing how these authors, though writing in isolation from each other, have expressed a common sensibility informed by a shared attitude towards the land, religion, and the self. Sutherland's theory—rooted in a generous, sensitive vision of modern Canada from a specific Québec vantage point—is manifested in his fiction. *Snow lark*, the story of Suzanne MacDonald, offspring of a French-English marriage who grows up in Montreal's east end, dramatizes the two cultures as they act upon an individual's search for self-knowledge and happiness. Suzanne's reconciliation of the claims of mixed ancestry is emblematic of the emergence of modern Canada. While *Snow lark* is set in Montreal, *Where do the MacDonalds bury their dead?* traces its protagonists' search for self from Québec to Michigan, California, and Mexico. Ti-Mac, Suzanne's cousin, eventually returns home, a wiser person through his exposure to cultural diversity. The two novels are interrelated by characterization and theme, and by the world view that frames Sutherland's two principal books of criticism: the articulation of the Canadian identity lies in the recognition of its bilingual and bicultural nature. This theme is enjoyable variation in *How Elvis saved Quebec*, which begins with the arrival of Frank Collins—a Ph. D. anthropology candidate from Wayne State University—to study the people in the town of North Chadley in the Eastern Townships of Québec. Frank very quickly gets to know some of the residents: Wilton Wadleigh, the proprietor of the small inn he stayed in; the beautiful Lisette (Mrs Wadleigh, an excellent cook); and William Martin, a history professor at the Université de Brooke (a friend of Frank's department chairman) and his daughter. Back in his room he scratches his head over what he has learned, including the issue that 'in about three months' time there was going to be a referendum to decide whether Québec would remain a province in the Canadian

Confederation or become an independent nation.' The affairs of the people in North Chadley, Frank's progress with his thesis, and the result of the referendum give special pleasure to anyone who is acquainted with the charms of North Hatley, Québec, on Lake Massawippi, and with the Université de Sherbrooke not far away. *The Massawippi monster and other friends of mine* (2004) is described by the author in his Preface as a 'selection of my more humorous and whimsical vignettes' (having appeared in various newspapers), which convey 'a kind of autobiography.'

Swan, Susan (b. 1945). Born in Midland, Ontario, she studied English at McGill University, Montreal (B.A., 1967) and then began working as a journalist with the *Toronto Telegram*. She now divides her time between writing and teaching in the Department of humanities at Glendon College, York University, Toronto, where she is now professor of humanities (1991–). Swan's first three novels—*The biggest modern woman of the world* (1983), *The last of the golden girls* (1989), and *The wives of Bath* (1993, rpr. 1994)—display her powerful grasp of the subtleties of the social construction of gender, depicting also the sexuality of her female characters. Her first novel tells the story of Anna Swan (1846–88), a Nova Scotian giantess. While staying true to the basic facts of Anna's biography—she worked for many years for the American showman, P.T. Barnum—the novel invents and explores her inner life. Swan sets up three major themes—an exploration of the dichotomies of man/woman, 'normal'/giant, and American/Canadian—and draws explicit parallels between the subordinate or marginalized element of each pair. *The last of the golden girls* is the story of the sexual awakening of Jude and her two best friends, Bobby and Shelly. Their blossoming sexuality sparks a competition for men, which continues over ten years and poisons their friendships. A playful eroticism provides an optimistic counterpoint to a more pessimistic look at the subtleties of male control over female sexuality. *The wives of Bath* is an intriguing amalgam of genres that Swan has labelled sexual gothic. Set in the 1960s at an all-girls' school, Bath Ladies College, the novel chronicles the coming of age of Mouse Bradford, a lonely girl struggling with feelings of extreme alienation, caused in part by her misshapen body, and in part by her struggle to resist adopting any of the feminine roles she sees available. *What Casanova told me* (2004) is an enjoyable, complicated semi-epistolary novel (there are many

letters), with two narratives set, respectively, in 1797 and modern times, and in Toronto, Venice, Istanbul, Greece (Athens and Sounion), and Crete. Luce Adams, an archivist, has come into the possession of the journal of her ancestor Asked For Adams, extracts from which tell us of Asked For's friendship, and love affair, with Jacob (Jacopo) Casanova in the year before he died—she travels with him to Turkey. Other characters in the novel include Luce's mother, Dr Kitty Adams, who has died accidentally—an archeaologist and an authority on Minoan Crete, she appears in letters and Luce's memories—and Kitty's former (female) lover, Lee Pronski; she takes a protective interest in Luce, who resents her at first, but in time they become friends. Among all the complexities, one remembers with particular pleasure the many scenes in Venice, in the present and the past, and Casanova himself, who is presented not only as a good writer but as the interesting and appealing man he probably was: 'My vices never burdened anyone but me, and seduction was never characteristic of my behaviour because I never seduced anyone except unconsciously, always being seduced myself first.'

Swan has also published two collections of short stories: *Unfit for paradise* (1982) and *Stupid boys are good to relax with* (1996).

Symons, Scott (1933–2009). Born in Toronto into a highly respected Rosedale family of distinguished Loyalist ancestry, he was educated at Trinity College, University of Toronto; King's College, Cambridge; and the Sorbonne. In 1965, when he was married with a son, curator of the Canadiana collection at the Royal Ontario Museum, and assistant professor of fine arts at the University of Toronto, he left wife, home, and job to live in Montreal and write his first novel, *Place d'Armes*. Bisexual from schooldays, he was frequently at odds with parents, teachers, and institutions, and often seethed at what he believed to be the betrayal of his country by the 'Blandmen'—Liberal politicians and businessmen, satellites of Mackenzie King. *Place d'Armes: a personal narrative* (1967, rpr. 1978), which takes the form of a combat journal, contains five different typefaces and two narrators, both closely modelled on Symons himself. It is by turns lyrical, bathetic, inspiring, and banal. Chiefly about the discovery of the self through the body's encounter with another man, it also concerns the discovery of French-Canadian culture through a sensuous experience of architecture and artifacts. An energetic, if confusing, work, it attacks modern advertising and what Symons saw as the accelerating destruction of both English and French traditions in Canada. *Civic Square* (1969) is a huge, chaotic work that was boxed, not bound, because Symons would not reduce the 848 typewritten pages to conventional book length. Symons decorated each container with red felt-pen pictures of birds, flowers, and phalli as his personal present to DR, the imaginary Dear Reader to whom the book is addressed. *Civic Square* is not only a blistering attack on the 'Blandmen' but also a lyrical appreciation of the natural beauty of the Ontario countryside. It is repetitive, dislocated and, once again, full of high energy. Symons then went to Mexico with a young male lover. A series of flights, escapes, and hardships followed: *Place d'Armes* had been savagely reviewed; Symons' marriage was ending in divorce; his family would neither speak to him nor of him. He was awarded the Beta Sigma Phi Best First Canadian Novel Award for *Place d'Armes*, however, and Symons claimed that this prevented his suicide. He returned to Canada and lived for a time in northern British Columbia and Newfoundland. He wrote, on commission, a coffee-table book on Canadian furniture: *Heritage—a romantic look at early Canadian furniture* (1972), with photographs by John de Visser. Filled with passion, knowledge, and taste—Symons called it his 'furniture novel'—the book transformed the furniture and artifacts into characters who speak in a variety of authentic accents about Canada's past, and the Western tradition from which they sprang. There followed more travel in Europe and a move to Morocco, where Symons began work on *Helmet of flesh* (1986), a riotously rich episodic account of life, love, and travels in Morocco, with a long flashback to Osprey Cove, Newfoundland. The novel is in essence an attempt to find the spiritual meaning of life through the exploration of all the senses—a poetic, dreamlike vision of life under a tropical sun. In Symons' passion and hyperbole there are echoes of D.H. Lawrence; in his lyricism and intensity, of Malcolm LOWRY; in his elegance and opulence, of Henry James—probably his three major influences. Charles Taylor wrote a fine study of his life and writings in *Six journeys: a Canadian pattern* (1977). In 2005 the *Literary Review of Canada* named *Place d'Armes* one of the 100 most important books in Canadian history—partly, one supposes, for its depiction of gay desire.

Szumigalski, Anne (1922–99). Anne Davis was born in London, England, and educated privately in nearby Hampshire. During the war she worked with refugees from Belgium, and with the British Red Cross Civilian Relief as medical auxiliary, interpreter, and welfare officer. In 1946 she married Jan Szumigalski, a retired Polish army officer. After the birth of two children she lived in Wales, then immigrated to Saskatchewan, and lived in or near Saskatoon from 1951. Her husband worked as a surveyor and in the 1960s two more children were born. She then began a career as an arresting, complex, and experimental poet, translator, editor, and playwright who was deeply involved with the Saskatchewan and Saskatoon writing community.

Most of Szumigalski's work shows a preoccupation with matters of the spirit, and the visionary qualities of the imagination. Many of her poems have a childlike appreciation of place and a mystical relationship with the encounter of landscape. She cited as her greatest influences the King James Bible, *The book of common prayer*, William Blake, and contemporary visual artists, though critics have also cited the influence of gnostic mythology, botany and herbal lore, and the occult traditions. Many of her works employ prose poems linked to myth and fable— sources of her poetic power in poems that always surprise. Szumigalski's publications include *BOooOm* (1973; poems for elementary schools, with Terrence Heath); *Woman reading in bath* (1974)—the title poem is about a woman swimming in the sea with God; two collaborations with Terrence Heath, *Wild man's butte: long poem for voices* (1979) and *Journey/Journée* (1988); *A game of angels* (1980), which connects the poems of this world to the inspirational other world in comic or ironic ways; *Risks* (1983); *Litany of the baglad-ies: words for dance* (1983); *Doctrine of signatures* (1983); *Instar* (1985); and *Dogstones* (1986). *Rapture of the deep* (1991) deals with childhood memories, which develop from those of the Christ child and the Holy Family. *Voice* (1995, GGA) is a collaboration between Szumigalski and the painter Elysa St George: full-colour reproductions, poems, and shared imagination give 'voice' to each other and create the book itself. Szumigalski's most substantial collection is *On glassy wings: poems new and selected* (1997), which contains poems and prose poems from nine previous collections and thirteen new poems. *The word, the voice, the text: essays and memoirs* (1990) is an exploration of the writer's life as it looks at the sources of her imagination in childhood experience. Her play *Z: a meditation on oppression, desire, and freedom* (1995) draws upon her war experiences as she laments the Holocaust and celebrates the regenerative capacity of the human spirit to create art. In the posthumously published *When the earth leaps up* (2006), with a Preface by Hilary Clark and an Afterword by Mark Abley, Szumigalski's voice is resplendent.

T

Talonbooks. One of the most important Canadian small publishers, it arose from a small poetry magazine, *Talon*, founded by an editorial collective based at Magee High School in Vancouver in 1963. It moved in 1965 to the University of British Columbia, where it continued to publish as a literary magazine. By 1967 it had published so many young writers that Talon decided to become a book publisher for its authors. Talonbooks began as a combined imprint with Very Stone House, formed by Patrick LANE, Seymour MAYNE, and bill BISSETT, and Talon editors David Robinson, Gordon Fidler, and Jim Brown—a collectivity that did not last beyond the first year. By 1958 Talonbooks had ceased publication of its literary magazine and continued as a book publisher under the general direction of David Robinson, who resigned in 1984. He was succeeded by Karl Siegler, who had joined, and incorporated the company, in 1974; he remains Talon Books Ltd's publisher to date. The important drama list of Talonbooks, established by editor Peter Hay, includes both English- and French-Canadian and some American playwrights.

Starting out with poetry, including the first book (*Sticks & stones*) of Canada's first Parliamentary Poet Laureate, George BOWERING, Talonbooks diversified into drama, with Beverley SIMONS' *Crabdance*, George RYGA's *The ECSTASY OF RITA JOE*, and James REANEY's *Colours in the dark* in 1969; into fiction with Jane RULE's *Desert of the heart* and Audrey THOMAS's *Songs my mother taught me* in 1973; into Québec literature in translation with Robert GURIK's *The trial of Jean Baptiste M.* and Michel TREMBLAY's *Les BELLES-SOEURS* in 1975; and into non-fiction with the collected works of ethnographer Charles Hill-Tout, *The Salish people, Volumes I–IV* in 1979.

In the early 1980s Talonbooks experimented with publishing commercial titles, which were highly successful. It found, however, that these not only took too much time away from its literary work but also threatened the company's solid literary backlist by putting it at too great a risk. It therefore returned, in 1985, to its original exclusively literary mandate. Over the past decade Talonbooks has diversified its literary non-fiction list to include works on current global flashpoints in the Middle East and the Balkans, and on Canadian issues and politics.

At the end of December 2008 publisher Karl Siegler and production manager Christy Siegler sold a majority interest in Talonbooks to Kevin and Vicki Williams. While the Sieglers both retain their roles as publisher and production manager respectively, Kevin Williams is now president. Talonbooks is distributed in Canada by Publishers Group Canada and in the United States by Northwestern University Press.

Tamarack Review, The (1956–82). This literary quarterly devoted to stories, poems, essays, and reviews by new and established Canadian writers was conceived by Robert WEAVER at a time when John SUTHERLAND's NORTHERN REVIEW was about to cease publication. Weaver enlisted as co-editors Kildare DOBBS, Millar MacLure, Ivon Owen, William Toye, and Anne WILKINSON. The editorial board was later altered by the death of Wilkinson, by resignations (Weaver and Toye remained editors to the end), and by the addition of Patricia Owen, John Robert COLOMBO, and Janis RAPOPORT as co-editors. *Tamarack* was founded in Toronto when a new generation of now-prominent writers was just beginning to publish, and before the onset of Canadian nationalism, when Canadian literature was of slight general interest. Produced in a handsome format—with covers by graphic designers that included Theo Dimson, Allan Fleming, Fred Huffman,

Frank Newfeld, and Toye—it attempted to maintain a standard of literary excellence, without regional or ideological emphasis, and published early, and sometimes the first, work by Timothy FINDLEY and Jay MACPHERSON (both of whom appeared in the first issue), Dave GODFREY, Hugh HOOD, Alice MUNRO, Mordecai RICHLER, and others. Dependent on volunteer editorial services and precarious financial support (much of it provided by the CANADA COUNCIL and the Ontario Arts Council), *Tamarack* did not realize its aims consistently. But for twenty-five years it was the most respected literary magazine in English Canada.

Tardivel, Jules-Paul. See *POUR LA PATRIE*.

Taylor, Charles M. (b. 1931). Born in Montreal, he was educated at McGill University (B.A., 1952) and Oxford University (B.A., 1955; D.Phil., 1961; Fellow of All Souls' College, 1956–61). He began teaching at McGill in 1961, and was appointed professor of political science and professor of philosophy in 1973; Professor Emeritus, 1999. From 1976 to 1981 he was the Chichele Professor of Social and Political Theory at Oxford. He has lectured widely throughout the world, is a Fellow of the British Academy and the Royal Society of Canada, and received the prestigious Le Prix Léon Gérin in 1992 for his outstanding contribution to the civic and intellectual life of Québec. He was made a Companion of the Order of Canada in 1995. In 2007 he received the $1.5 million (US) Templeton Prize for those who 'advance progress toward research or discoveries about spiritual realities.' And in 2008 he was awarded Japan's Kyoto Prize ($460,000) honouring his development of a philosophy that 'actively pursues the harmonious co-existence of diverse cultures.'

Recognized throughout the world as one of today's outstanding moral and political philosophers, Taylor has written more than a dozen books and hundreds of articles that articulate the moral and political identity of the modern age in all its complexity and density; he has also written eloquently about his Roman Catholic faith. The best introductions to his work are *Sources of the self: the making of the modern identity* (1989) and his popular Massey Lectures, *The malaise of modernity* (1991, rpr. 2003). At the heart of Taylor's philosophy is the view that people come to discover and revise their identities in *dialogues* with others—dialogues that are *interpretative* in character. Almost all of Taylor's work

revolves around this central and brilliant insight. We discover who we are in dialogue by interpreting what Taylor calls 'sources' that are articulated most clearly by exemplary texts in philosophy and literature. In *Sources of the self* he shows that the many and seemingly contradictory faces of modern identity can be clarified, and perhaps even reconciled, by returning to works—the 'sources'—from Plato to Nietzsche that give us their clearest articulation. Moreover, since the language we use in dialogues, from childhood on, will itself partly constitute our identity, Taylor has devoted much of his time to the philosophy of language (see the two-volume *Philosophical papers*, 1985). Of particular concern to him, given the cultural and linguistic diversity of modern societies, is the nature of cross-cultural understanding in bilingual and polylingual circumstances (*Philosophical arguments*, 1995). His political philosophy is also based on his insights regarding dialogue and interpretation. Democracy is the form of government in which citizens rule themselves by entering into deliberative public dialogues on the identity and good of their political association. He applied this theory of democracy to the problems of Canadian identity and the Canada/Québec problem in *Multiculturalism and the 'politics of recognition'* (1992) and *Reconciling the solitudes: essays on Canadian federalism and nationalism* (1993). *A secular age* (2007) is a huge study (874 pages), difficult to read but with brilliant insights. Secularism takes us from 'a society in which it was virtually possible not to believe in God to one in which faith, even for the staunchest believer, is one human possibility among others'—a state that he calls 'exclusive humanism ... a humanism accepting no final goals beyond human flourishing, nor any allegiance to anything else beyond that flourishing.' His context seems to be limited to Europe, and parts of North America, including Québec. Much of this book grew out of the Gifford Lectures Taylor gave at the University of Edinburgh in 1999, which perhaps explains the exclusion of the present-day non-secular Middle East, Africa, and parts of the US.

See James Tully, ed., *Philosophy in an age of pluralism: the philosophy of Charles Taylor in question* (1994).

Taylor, Drew Hayden (b. 1962). The son of an Ojibwa mother and a white father he never knew, he grew up on the Curve Lake Reserve near Peterborough, Ontario, attending school on the reserve and in Lakefield, Ontario. He graduated from Seneca College, Toronto, where he studied radio and television broadcasting, and has become a prolific writer who explores Native issues in plays, stories, and two novels; he has also written TV scripts and worked on countless documentaries exploring the Native experience. Taylor was artistic director of Native Earth Performing Arts, Toronto (1994–7). His plays are both emotional and humorous. *Toronto at Dreamer's Rock* is a one-act fantasy that involves three Native teenagers from different time periods who meet at Dreamer's Rock, a tourist attraction that was once a sacred site. It was published, in 1990, in the same volume as another one-act play, *Education is our right*, a political satire that draws upon Dickens' *A Christmas carol*. Over sixteen years Taylor wrote his Blues quartet: *The bootlegger blues* (1991), *The baby blues* (1999), *The buz'gem blues* (2002), and *The Berlin blues* (2007). The first two plays are comedies, the second play described by the author as 'what some have called a Native version of a British sex farce'. *The Berlin blues*, which was first produced in March 2007 at Autry National Center/Wells Fargo Theatre in Los Angeles, centres on German developers who appear at the Otter Lake Reserve with an offer to create a Native theme park called 'OjibwayWorld' to attract European tourists. In Taylor's two-act play *Someday* (1993), which has had six productions, winning a lottery allows an impoverished mother, Anne Wabung, to search for Grace, her first-born daughter, who had been taken away from her ('scooped up') by social services and placed with a white family thirty-five years earlier; there is an eventual reunion. Its sequel, *Only drunks and children tell the truth* (1998)—performed at the Native Canadian Centre, Toronto, in 1996—continues the story five months later. Janice Wirth (Grace), now a successful Toronto entertainment lawyer who had been raised by adoptive parents, discovers her Ojibway birth family when, after the death of her birth mother, she goes home again to the Otter Lake reserve in Northern Ontario to reconcile herself with her Native heritage In *400 kilometres* (2005)—the distance between Otter Lake and London, Ontario—Janice/Grace is pregnant by a Native father-to-be and must choose her future. *The girl who loved her horses/The boy in the tree-house* (2000) are two plays about children becoming adults. *In a world created by a drunken God* (2006), which was nominated for a Governor General's Award, is a two-character play in which Jason Pierce, a half Native, is visited by Harry Deiter, who tells him they are half-brothers and that their father, who left Jason's Native mother when he was two months old, is in

need of a kidney transplant: Harry wants Jason to agree to a compatability test. The emotions that this situation arouses in both men make for a powerfully effective play. In *Fearless warriors* (1998, rev. 2008), a collection of twelve engaging stories, the title story is mainly about an accident on the highway when Andrew is driving his friend William—they call themselves 'fearless warriors'—and their girlfriends home: the car hits but does not kill a deer, and we witness each of the fearless warriors' incapability of using a tire iron to bring an end to the deer's suffering. Taylor's novel *The night wanderer: a Native Gothic novel* (2007) is for teens: sixteen-year-old Tiffany Hunter and her boyfriend are confronted by an Ojibway vampire. An adult novel, *Motorcycles & sweetgrass*, was published in 2010. He has also written humorous commentaries on Native issues in the *Globe and Mail*, the *Toronto Star*, and magazines that have been collected in *Funny, you don't look like one: observations from a blue-eyed Ojibway* (1998), which opens with his much-anthologized article 'Pretty like a White Boy'. Three other *Funny, you don't look like one* collections followed: *Further adventures of a blue-eyed Ojibway* (1999), *Furious observations of a blue-eyed Ojibway* (2002), and *Futile observations of a blue-eyed Ojibway* (2004).

See *Drew Hayden Taylor: essays on his works* (2007) edited by Robert Nunn.

Tecumseh. See ABORIGINAL LITERATURE: I.

Teleky, Richard (b. 1946). Born in Cleveland, Ohio, he attended Case-Western University (B.A., 1968) and immigrated to Canada in 1968, during the Vietnam War protest years, to study at the University of Toronto (M.A., 1969; Ph.D., 1973). After teaching for three years at York University, Toronto (1972–5), he worked as a senior editor and later managing editor of Oxford University Press Canada until 1991. While working for Oxford he co-edited, with Marie-Claire BLAIS, *The Oxford book of French-Canadian short stories* (1983), and produced collections by many of Canada's leading poets, including Margaret AVISON, Daryl HINE, Patrick LANE, and P.K. PAGE. He also edited books by Linda HUTCHEON, Robert KROETSCH, Janice KULYK KEEFER, Miriam WADDINGTON, and Adele WISEMAN in the series Studies in Canadian Literature. He is now a professor in the Division of Humanities of York University, where he directed the creative writing program for ten years. Teleky's books include *Goodnight, sweetheart and other stories* (1993), stories that portray loss and isolation in a wide range of voices; *Hungarian rhapsodies: essays on ethnicity, identity and culture* (1997), a blend of scholarship and personal essay about Central European and Hungarian immigrant culture in North America that examines issues such as ethnic representations in the arts, ethnic trauma, and nostalgia; and his first novel, *The Paris years of Rosie Kamin* (1998, rpr. 1999). About an American Jewish woman, the child of a Holocaust survivor, and her troubled life in a contemporary multicultural Paris, it is entirely unromantic, encompassing Rosie's love, loneliness, grief, and survival in a spare and meticulously observant text that also portrays, not without humour, an unfamiliar Parisian setting in vivid detail. It received an important American award, the Harold U. Ribalow Prize for the best novel of 1999, won the previous year by Anne MICHAELS. Teleky's short story 'Some of the old good feelings' was made into a film (1995), starring John Neville, for the Bravo television network.

In 2001 and 2006 respectively Teleky published two novels that for their vivid atmosphere and settings, their recognizable, interesting characters, their natural dialogue, the engrossing situations they become involved in, and the sophisticated narratives that drive them forward are in a class by themselves, arousing more involvement and empathy than most other Canadian novels of the period. In *Pack up the moon* (2001, rpr. 2002)—W.H. Auden's words provide the title: 'The stars are not wanted now: put out every one;/Pack up the moon and dismantle the sun...'—Canadian Karl Marton, now teaching in the US, returns to Toronto for his friend Jay's funeral. At a dinner party for college friends, Karl learns that his best friend, Charlotte Fleury, has been murdered (based on an actual murder). Set in 1992 and 1965—in Toronto, Oberlin, Ohio, where Karl teaches, Sarasota, and Paris (briefly)—it is mainly a novel about love and loyalty as Karl reminisces about Jay and Charlotte, her sister Bunny and her mother. The narrative is fleshed out with Teleky's assured rendering of the times, places, and people he is writing about (and the murder), with draft dodgers and chats about films included for good measure. '"Most love stories end up the same," Charlotte finally said, pulling Digs closer to her. "A big zero."/"But people keep going back for more," I said./"I don't." Lighting a Gitane, she rested her head against the wall and inhaled languidly. "It made more sense when people married for money./The dog put its chin on her thigh and looked up in vacant bliss."' Chapter 7 ('Sex Talk at Christmas, 1968') begins: 'Later

in October, when Jackie Kennedy married Aristotle Onassis on his Greek island, my family took little interest, while the Canadians I knew acted as if they'd been personally insulted.' *Winter in Hollywood* (2006) is about Irene Toth, who married Hal Dunne in the late 1940s (thus acquiring the name of a once-famous movie star). Hal died in 1998 after a happy marriage. The novel begins when seventy-five-year-old Irene—who has flown to Hollywood because her daughter Holly, a film producer, has been killed in a car accident—is opening Holly's condo. She meets Holly's friends and becomes attached to some of them: Tony Nakamura 'from down the hall', a gay florist who runs the Paramount Flower Shop, 'the last in-studio shop of its kind in Hollywood. He seemed proud of the fact'; the flamboyant Magda El Masri, a Hungarian, who sells babies; pregnant Juli, her niece, and others. Becoming involved in their lives, Irene prolongs her visit. Towards the end of the novel she visits Magda's apartment in the midst of an ugly scene having to do with a baby and Irene falls, smacking her head against a stucco wall, and has a concussion. The novel delicately portrays her physical decline as a patient in a hospital: 'This morning, after she woke to find a nurse straightening her sheets, she wondered if she was dead yet./Maybe I'm dead and I don't know it.'//'Irene Dunne,' the supervisor says [to her colleague Consuelo]. 'I think you should call her Irene. Won't that be nice?'/'I saw one of her movies on TV. She was a big star long ago.'/'Someone else said that,' the supervisor remarks. 'We get all types here.'

Teleky's *The hermit's kiss* (2006) is among the better Canadian poetry collections published in recent years. Many interests are accounted for in poems both long and short whose clear, disciplined diction, concision, and elegance are unusual in present-day poetry: *literature* ('Re-reading *Anna Karenina*'—one of the longer poems), 'George Herbert's glass of blessings', 'For Simone Weil'; *aging* ('Of course'—'No one wants old men,/not even each other./Bald spots, slack fat,/these aren't the worst/of it. Old dreams, yes,/now here we begin.'); *mythology and music* ('The return' about Pandora and Debussy and Ravel—dedicated to the flautist Nora Shulman); *friendship* ('The German breakfast'—dedicated to Teresa Stratas); and *Garbo* ('Following Garbo'—'Dead?' she once remarked,/'I've been dead for many years.') The title prose poem honours St Roch, a native of Montpellier, France, a popular saint as a protector from plague (a statue of whom is in St Clare's Roman Catholic Church, St Clair Avenue West, Toronto). Teleky is the editor of *The 'Exile' book of Canadian dog stories* (2009).

Théoret, France (b. 1942). Born in Montreal into a working-class family, she was educated at the Université de Montréal (B.A., 1968; M.A., 1977) and the Université de Sherbrooke (Ph.D., 1982). After teaching literature at the CEGEP level in Montreal from 1968 to 1987, she devoted herself full time to writing. The author of many books, Théoret defies traditional classification in her writings, which integrate modernity with feminism. She has written prose poetry, short stories, essays, pieces for the theatre, personal and travel journals, and 'novels'. Most are texts that blur the categories as she pursues her difficult (re-)search for language to alter the stultifying and inhibiting patriarchal codes of the past. Autobiography, fiction, and theory are intertwined in her discourse, which is characterized by the presence of a female figure/voice, however designated (the narrative pronoun may change within the text), seeking to establish her identity in a language, culture, and society from which, as a woman, she feels excluded. Few of her books are available in translation. *The tangible word, poetry and texts 1977–1983* (1991), translated by Barbara Godard, includes translations of *Bloody Mary* (1977), *Une voix pour Odile* (1978), *Vertiges* (1979), and *Nécessairement putain* (1980)—relatively brief, elliptical, and poetic texts, each illustrating differently the dialectic of revolt and alienation and seeking, with painful difficulty, the narrator's release through language, which may itself be a trap. *Une voix pour Odile*, which consists of twelve brief monologues, was the first of Théoret's writings to attract broad critical attention; the inflections of the voice(s) and the swift rhythm give unity to the different texts. *Bloody Mary* is the most violent and anarchical in expression; *Vertiges* is more introspective; *Nécessairement putain* centres on the figure of the prostitute, the woman most excluded from society, and develops the analogy of the prostitute and the woman writer. *The man who painted Stalin: stories and a novella* (1991) is a translation by Luise von Flotow of *L'homme qui peignait Staline* (1989). Closer to traditional form—although without dialogue or psychological description—is *Laurence* (1998), a translation by Gail SCOTT of a novel with the same title published in French in 1996. It follows the life of a courageous young woman of humble origins and meagre

finances who achieves a measure of emancipation and happiness through her own efforts. It is also a remarkable socio-economic portrait of Québec from the 1920s to the 1940s. *Girls closed in* (2005), a translation by von Flotow of *Huis clos entre jeunes filles* (2000), is a study of introspection, as a solitary young woman (the narrator), in a Catholic school for teachers in training, is attracted to Yolande, with whom she spends a few friendly times—until: 'I don't want to talk to you anymore, [Yolande] says. You're too superficial.... I'm twenty and you're sixteen. It doesn't work.' Muriel and Danielle are two other young woman she relates to. And there was handsome Lionel, sitting beside her on the bus; they exchange glances and she has a sudden desire: 'I wanted this man I didn't know to kiss me, to put his arms around me.' He does kiss her. 'I could still feel the kiss when I arrived at school.' As the books ends she remains solitary and self-involved. 'When the joy of learning is tied to learning introspection, this wakes you up to the dark side of things.... //I see myself from the inside, and the outside. The realm of the unconscious, which I have visited so many times, has never been totally clarified. It is unstable, shifting. I think there is always a part of oneself that is out of sight.' Théoret was made a Member of the Order of Canada in 2000.

Thériault, Yves (1915–83). The only son of Alcide Thériault, an Acadian of partly Montagnais ancestry, and Aurore Nadeau, he was born in Quebec City and from the age of seven was able, he claimed, to speak the Cree dialect taught to him by his father. He received his primary and secondary education in Montreal, but quit school at fifteen to work at a host of odd jobs. After working as a radio announcer and radio scriptwriter in several Québec cities, and as a tractor salesman, he published his first short story in *Le Jour* in 1941. A year or two later he became a public-relations officer and scriptwriter for the National Film Board. From 1945 to 1950, while working as a scriptwriter for Radio-Canada, Thériault published anonymously, or under pseudonyms, an enormous quantity of 'ten-cent novels' (thirty-two pages); at one point he was producing eleven a week. In 1952 he travelled around the world aboard an Italian freighter, and lived for several years in Italy. From 1965 to 1967 he was cultural director for the Department of Indian and Northern Affairs in Ottawa. A period of increasing personal difficulties, compounded by health problems, persuaded him to leave Ottawa, and in 1968 he purchased a small farm at Saint-Denis-sur-Richelieu, Québec. In June 1970 Thériault suffered a cerebral thrombosis that left him paralysed and unable to speak, write, or talk. After a prolonged convalescence he resumed his career, becoming co-director in 1977 of a film company with his companion Lorraine Boisvenue. He received a Molson Prize in 1970, was made an Officer of the Order of Canada in 1975, and lived at Rawdon, a village west of Joliette, Québec.

Thériault was the most prolific and versatile of contemporary Québec writers. Largely self-taught, he was animated by driving dynamism, bohemian restlessness, a passion for liberty that caused him to revolt against conformism and convention, and a vast experience of the seamier and more violent sides of life that are reflected in some forty books he published after *Contes pour un homme seul* (1944). These unusual, captivating, and brutal stories announced the themes that he would later develop: naturalism, primitivism, exoticism, eroticism, and sublimated sexuality struggling for expression. Basic human instincts and passions, in conflict with the forces of tradition and repression, are the occasion for biting criticism of our civilization and of French-Canadian society in particular. The quantity, quality, and variety of his prodigious output assured his popularity with the French-Canadian reading public. Only three of his books are available in English, but with the publication of *Agaguk* (1958)—translated in 1967 by Miriam Chapin, and since available as *Agaguk: shadow of the wolf* (1992)—Thériault achieved international recognition for this almost epic evocation of love and fatherhood among the Inuit of the Canadian North. Agaguk's evolution towards maturity is the mainspring of the action and of the various conflicts he has with the whites, his own tribe, his father, and the harsh realities of the vast and hostile tundra. The gradual civilizing of Agaguk is the work of Iriook, his wife, who twice saves her husband's life. The crux of the novel occurs when Iriook—opposing the merciless Inuit tradition—demands at gunpoint that Agaguk spare the life of the daughter she has borne him. She then convinces Agaguk to accept his daughter and the risks and responsibilities that this decision involves. *Ashini* (1960, GGA; translated by Gwendolyn Moore, 1972) is not so much a novel as a lyric poem to the glory of the Montagnais (despite Ashini's suicide). Native myths are evoked with great beauty. Thériault ranked this book, which is a plea for justice as well as a work of art, as one of his best. In 1968 Thériault published, among five other books, *N'Tsuk* (translated by Gwendolyn Moore, 1972), which has often been compared to *Ashini* because both books were written in highly poetic language, and the main characters in both are critical of modern society.

Thesen, Sharon (b. 1946). Born in Tisdale, Saskatchewan, she was raised in various parts of western Canada and educated in British Columbia. She received her B.A. (1970) and her M.A. (1974) in English literature from Simon Fraser University. From 1976 until 1992 she taught in the Department of English at Capilano College, North Vancouver. *Artemis hates romance* (1980), Thesen's first book of poetry, in its skilful use of the rhythms of speech, hints at the influence of Charles Olson, Robert Creeley, and the West Coast *TISH* poets. Pointed, lean, and occasionally angry, the *Artemis* poems scrutinize failed relationships and small-town life. Thesen contemplates the mundane partly by recasting it through philosophy and myth, which undergird her work. A brief stay in Montreal is one of the subjects of Thesen's chapbook *Radio New France Radio* (1981). All of the poems in this small book were republished in *Holding the pose* (1983), in which Thesen adapts the rhythms of country music, gospel, and jazz to examine loneliness, separation, torture, and ennui in poems that, even when they probe the darkness, never succumb to it. *Confabulations: poems for Malcolm Lowry* (1984), which Thesen has identified as a long poem, is dedicated to Michael ONDAATJE, whose influence on this volume is evident. In LOWRY's self-destructiveness, Thesen finds an Ondaatjean subject, and her verse echoes Ondaatje's in its point-blank language and slightly jagged, free-verse metre. With *The beginning of the long dash* (1987) Thesen reveals her broad reach as a poet. The ordinary is shadowed by the profound; the apparently innocent particulars of daily life reverberate with questions about the nature of being. *The pangs of Sunday* (1990), a selected volume, includes almost two dozen new poems, and is a showcase for Thesen's great skill. One detects the influence of the American poet Sharon Olds in the slightly longer lines of the new poems, in which narrative is carefully balanced with lyric. In *Aurora* (1995), one of her most accomplished works, Thesen experiments with form, using traditional stanzas (e.g., *terza rima*), free verse, and a poetic adaptation of stream-of-consciousness narrative to deepen the complexity of her response to the sensory world. Ideas are in abundance, and—as in all of Thesen's work—they live in the interstices between the lines. The title of the collection *A pair of scissors* (2000)—two lines of the epigraph by Pablo Neruda are 'Time cannot be cut/With your exhausted scissors'—is also that of a twenty-poem sequence in which striking images of daily life are interjected by two of Virginia Woolf's characters, Mrs Dalloway and the man she had loved, here called Mr Walsh.

Weeping willow (2005) is a slim volume of twelve poems that pays tribute to her friendship with the late Angela Bowering, wife of George BOWERING. The first section of *The good bacteria: poems* (2006) bears the book's title, which is explained in the first (untitled) poem: 'In the morning they ate again, and took their penicillin pills./The penicillin killed the good bacteria as well as the bad.//It killed all the bacteria, good and bad, like death and God.' Another section, 'The Fire', memorializes a terrible British Columbia forest fire Thesen witnessed: 'Go ahead fire ... //just go ahead, you/ and your nasty little freaky friend/the wind.' ... 'My woods are charred/bituminous//black bark bleeds/red resin plasma//between the standing/broiled branchless poles//new unwelcome views of the lake//and of shocked humps of hills/self-conscious and sad, evicted// from their leafy life ...'

Thesen edited *The new long poem anthology* (1992, 2nd edn 2001), a large and heavy (nearly 500 pages) collection that includes twenty-five poets, almost all of whom have entries in this *Companion*.

Thirty acres (1940, GGA, NCL). This is the translation by Felix and Dorothea Walter of a classic of French-Canadian literature by Philippe PANNETON (pseud. 'Ringuet'), *Trente arpents* (1938), which was warmly received by critics both in France, where it first appeared, and in Canada. It is the tragic story of the rise and fall of Euchariste Moisan, who is entirely devoted to his land. After years of success—he was the envy of his neighbours—the sale of a piece of his land and the failure of a law suit against one of his neighbours bring Euchariste humiliation and ruin. His son Étienne, who persuades Euchariste to cede his land to him and to visit his favourite son Ephrem in the USA, refuses to send his father the money for a return ticket to his village, and the old man will likely end his life as a nightwatchman in an American industrial town, unable to communicate with anyone but his son— not even with his own grandchildren and his son's wife, since he speaks no English and they speak no French. Set in a Trois-Rivières area between 1887 and 1932, the novel reveals a society on the verge of radical change, opposing progress to traditions, city life to rural life, younger to older generations, and life to death. Above all, it denounces the farmer's subservience to his land. The main character is the land itself, and that is what gives the novel its universality. Panneton, who took nine years to write *Trente arpents*, did not want the term 'regionalist' to be applied to his novel; he was anxious to achieve realism by avoiding the extremes of both naturalism and idealism, and refused to use literature as an excuse for reviving the past or putting it to the service of a political cause.

Thomas, Audrey (b. 1935). Audrey Grace Callahan was born in Binghamton, New York, and educated at Smith College, with a year at St Andrews University, Scotland. After teaching for a year in England, she married Ian Thomas in 1958; the couple immigrated to Canada in 1959. She received an M.A. in English (1963) from the University of British Columbia and did further work there, on Anglo-Saxon language and literature, towards a Ph.D. that was not awarded. The years 1964–6 were spent in Ghana, where her husband taught at the University of Science and Technology, Kumasi. Much of her fiction recalls her life in Africa; the foreignness of the land and its customs provide a metaphor for emotional alienation, the threat and challenge of the unknown, and exploration of the dark side of the self. After her return to Vancouver, Thomas published her first collection of stories, *Ten green bottles* (1967), in the same year that the youngest of her three daughters was born. The lead story, 'If one green bottle', is based on the author's confinement and eventual miscarriage in a Ghanaian hospital. The sense of futility and shame accompanying this six-month-long experience haunts the narrator of *Mrs Blood* (1970), a novel that expands the material of the story into a moving characterization of a woman so distressed by her condition that she sees herself as a nameless, fragmented being, speaking sometimes as the fearful, self-conscious, acted-upon 'Mrs Thing', sometimes as the guilt-ridden bundle of memories and poetic visions, 'Mrs Blood', wracked by physical and psychic forces she cannot control. In 1969 Thomas found the cabin on Galiano Island, B.C., in which, after separating from her husband in 1972, she made her home. The Gulf Island atmosphere is captured in the second of two related novellas, published in one volume: *Munchmeyer* and *Prospero on the island* (1971). This is the diary of Miranda who, in an island cabin, is writing *Munchmeyer*, a novel about a male writer who also keeps a diary. The two works can be read separately, but together they reveal subtle explorations of the nature of creativity, the interdependence of art and craft, and the emotional demands made on the artist. Such reminders of *The tempest* as Miranda's name, and the existence of a Caliban figure, provide a sometimes ironic framework for events on the 'magic' island.

Thomas's first novel, *Songs my mother taught me* (1973, rev. 1991) is set in the New York State of the author's childhood, and chronicles a girl's growing up, from Blakean 'innocence' in the emotionally violent world of her home and social life to 'experience', acquired through grotesque revelations of human misery in a mental hospital where she had a summer job. What appears at first to be a conventional first-person narrative is in fact a curiously constructed record of two voices, the speaker sometimes referring to herself as 'I', and sometimes as Isobel, a third person she observes from a distance, or addresses directly. *Blown figures* (1974) is Thomas's most experimental novel, where a collage method of narration and the use of space on the page reflect the schizophrenia of a woman haunted by guilt and the sense of loss from a miscarriage. She relives psychically a journey to Africa, gradually turning in her own mind into a doomed and destructive witch.

Ladies and escorts (1977) confirmed Audrey Thomas's reputation as a brilliant writer of short stories. The complex emotions and ideas explored never strain the capacities of the form, whether in stories depicting the subtle nuances of sexuality and the unfathomable depths of pain, violence, and sadness in human relations (as in 'Kill day at the government wharf' and 'Aquarius'), or in aesthetic enquiries into the mirror relationship of art to life (as in 'Rapunzel' and, powerfully, in 'Initram'). These stories show a gift for evoking place that is also one of the strengths of the epistolary novel *Latakia* (1979, rpr. 1989), which captures the atmosphere of Crete as well as of places visited on a sea voyage to Europe. The Syrian port of Latakia, where language difficulties trigger a fierce culture-shock, provides a metaphor for the love affair, now over, between two Canadian writers who, despite strong physical attraction, are separated by a gulf of non-comprehension, created in part by Michael's need to make Rachel his subordinate and by his resentment of her superiority as a writer. Similar doomed relationships appear in *Real mothers* (1981), which contains one of Thomas's best stories,

the delicate, haunting 'Natural history', which celebrates the love of a mother and daughter and draws together several levels of narrative into one moment of illumination. *Two in the bush and other stories* (1981) contains a selection from *Ten green bottles* and *Ladies and escorts*. The stories in *Goodbye Harold, good luck* (1986) and *The wild blue yonder* (1990) develop similarly subtle analyses of emotional life, often with a witty ironic touch that eases the pain of failed human relationships.

The mother-daughter relationship introduced in 'Natural history' is further developed in the novel *Intertidal life* (1984, rpr. 1991), where the narrator and her young daughter spend an island summer studying marine life exposed to view at low tide. This and the moon, 'shining always by reflected light', serve as metaphors for woman's place in a man's world. Gulf Island flora and fauna, stories of the Spanish explorers who navigated the coastal waters, and wry depictions of the various island communities are woven into the narrator's analysis of her failed marriage and her desperate need for love. In the novel *Graven images* (1993), two women travel to England in search of their roots (the great trees felled by the actual hurricane of 1987 offer a natural metaphor). The genealogy studied by the narrator is that of the Corbetts, Thomas's own family on her mother's side. The nuances of a grown daughter's uneasy relationship with her ninety-year-old mother are woven into a re-creation of the past and impressions of the present. *Coming down from Wa* (1995) is another version of the return to Africa, again in search of family history, but this time with a male protagonist. The Ghanaian scene is vividly evoked, as are the traveller's discomfort, sickness, frustration, exhilaration, and joy. The eventual disclosure of the family's dark secret is, however, far less successfully handled than the epiphanic encounter with ancestors in *Graven images*. A vigorous experimenter with narrative method and language, Thomas shows a special interest in the derivation of words, their ambiguities, and multiple connotations. She plays with literary allusions and puns (almost too flamboyantly at times) as she stretches language to catch the experience of people, mostly women, hovering on the verge of disintegration. Intertextual reference to both her own work and a multitude of literary sources serves to underscore the notion of the connectedness of experience. A notable departure for Thomas is *Isobel Gunn* (1999, rpr. 2000), a historical novel about a woman from the Orkney Islands, where she lived a harsh life, who in 1806 signs on as a man, John Fubbister, to work for the Hudson's Bay Company in Rupert's Land, which she did successfully. But things fall apart when she suddenly appears before the chief factor at Pembinah, Alexander Henry the younger, in great pain—this event was actually recorded in Henry's journal of Dec. 1807. Having been raped by a fellow worker, she is pregnant and bears a son, James, whom she is eventually forced to give away; with her gender disclosed she is made to work as a washerwoman and then is returned to the Orkneys by the chief factor at Fort Albany, who wants to raise the boy as his own. She has one friend, however, the kindly schoolteacher/minister Magnus Inkster, who tells her story—the book is as much about him as about Isobel and is also about various forms of love, beginning with Isobel's love for her son, whom she never sees again. Growing out of one brief recorded incident, this is a richly detailed imaginary reconstruction that has the ring of truth. Though it is not long (slightly over 200 pages), *Tattycoram* (2005) is a clever, enjoyable pastiche of a Victorian novel. The narrator Harriet (called Hattie) Coram is left by her birth mother at the Foundling Hospital in London—she is No. 19,176—and her last name is that of the founder, Thomas Coram. She was soon put in the care of a foster family, brothers Sam and Jonnie, blind Grandfather, and the only parents she ever knew. When she was five, her mother said to her: '"Hattie, we have never made a secret of the fact that you are on loan to us from the good people at the hospital. We have loved you as our own little daughter and watched you grow. But now the time is coming when we must give you back." Her voice broke and she sobbed into her apron.' Hattie got used to what she called the Foundling and was well treated. But a surprise awaited her. The secretary, Mr Brownlow, called her to his office. 'There was a gentleman with him, quite a young man, shortish, with a bright embroidered waistcoat under his coat./"Harriet," Mr Brownlow said, "do you know who this man is?"/"My father, sir?"/"No, no, child, this is Mr Dickens. He has come to engage you as a servant. He is a regular attendant at chapel on Sunday and takes a keen interest in all that goes on here. I think you could not ask for a better placement."' Hattie moves into Charles Dickens' house on Doughty Street. Both Dickens and his wife like Hattie and are kind to her; but Mrs Dickens' sister Georgina resents her and trains Charles Dickens' raven to call her Tatttycoram, because of all the tatting (lace-work) she does. In Thomas's

smooth-flowing narrative much goes on—more than can be related here. Hattie becomes a teacher; Dickens employs her to run the home for fallen women he has helped to found called Urania Cottage. Sam and Jonnie, her foster brothers, come back into her life and she marries Sam, happily, and bears him a daughter. She has a shock when she learns that Dickens has used her as a character—the bad-tempered maid of Mr and Mrs Beagles, called Tattycoram—in his novel of the 1850s, *Little Dorrit*. This last episode does not end satisfactorily for Hattie—she goes to London to talk to Dickens, but he rebuffs her and dies not long after. She 'could not judge him harshly and was sorry he was gone.' *The path of totality: new and selected* stories (2001), comprising twenty-two stories, is a generous selection of Thomas's short fiction. In her Introduction she says: 'I do love words, but I don't trust them, for although I have seen how words can elevate or charm or heal, I have also seen how they can wound or be misunderstood. If language is a bridge over the gap between one person and another, it is often a very shaky bridge, a swaying bridge of vines (with maybe crocodiles down below.)' Audrey Thomas was appointed an Officer of the Order of Canada in 2008.

Thomas, Clara McCandless (b. 1919). Born in Strathroy, Ontario, she was educated at the University of Western Ontario (B.A., 1941; M.A., 1944) and the University of Toronto (Ph.D., 1962). In 1969 she was appointed professor of English at York University, Toronto, and in 1984 became Professor Emeritus. Her first book, *Canadian novelists: 1925-1945* (1946, rpr. 1970), began as an M.A. thesis and was innovative in its compilation of biographical and bibliographical listings of 122 writers. Thomas has written three biographies: a book that grew out of her Ph.D. thesis, *Love and work enough: the life of Anna Jameson* (1967, rpr. 1978), a groundbreaking study of the accomplished early feminist writer, art historian, and visitor to Upper Canada in 1836-7; *Ryerson of Upper Canada* (1969), on the career and times of the famous clergyman and educator, Egerton Ryerson; *William Arthur Deacon: a Canadian literary life* (1982, with John Lennox), a detailed study of the life, letters, and work of the well-known literary journalist (q.v.). Thomas is probably best known for the depth and breadth of her work on Margaret LAURENCE, which includes many articles and chapters in books, and for *The Manawaka world of Margaret Laurence* (1975), the earliest and most influential book-length study of Laurence's writings.

Our nature—our voices (1973), Thomas's guide-book to Canadian literature, was translated into Japanese and published in Japan in 1981. Many of Thomas's writings have been collected in *All my sisters: essays on the work of Canadian women writers* (1994). See Thomas's interesting memoir, *Chapters in a lucky life* (1999), in which her friendship with Margaret Laurence figures prominently; it ends with an account of her final years.

Thompson, David. See EXPLORATION LITERATURE IN ENGLISH: 2.

Thompson John. (1938–76). Born in Timperley, Cheshire, England (not Manchester as he later stated), Thompson was all but orphaned at the age of two when his father died of a heart attack and his mother sent him to live with various relatives in Manchester. He grew up parentless as a full boarder in several schools, finally attaining a scholarship to the academically excellent Manchester Grammar School. After graduation he attended the University of Sheffield, where he took his B.A. in honours psychology in 1958. After service in the British army intelligence corps for two years, he went to the United States, where he studied comparative literature at Michigan State University and received a Ph.D.; his thesis, directed by mentor A.J.M. SMITH, was translations of poems by the French surrealist poet René Char. He moved to New Brunswick in 1966 to teach in the English department of Mount Allison University, living with his wife and daughter in a farmhouse near the Bay of Fundy shore, a locale that inspired his best poetry. His poems and translations, including sequences by Québec poets Roland Giguère and Paul-Marie LAPOINTE, began appearing in Canadian quarterlies, and his first poetry collection was *At the edge of the chopping there are no secrets* (1973). The publication of his second and last collection, *Stilt Jack* (1978), was preceded by conflicts with the university, divorce, psychiatric treatment, a long struggle with alcoholism, and finally his death, apparently by suicide, at thirty-eight.

Although reviewers praised Thompson's accurate evocation of landscape in *At the edge of the chopping*, it went unnoticed that as a sophisticated student of modern poetry—Lorca, Trakl, Yeats, Neruda, and Roethke are clear influences—he was working on a more ambitious level than many Canadian critics of the time could recognize. Like René Char, Thompson sought to reveal the core truths of nature, to name the unnameable secrets,

through a poetry of brief, intensely concentrated but carefully structured images. The poems in his first collection open with a series of precise metaphors: an apple tree is 'a cauldron of leaves,/the sun a deadly furnace' that in winter bears 'a head of burnt hair/crackling faintly' against the snow. The 'plot' moves from images of fertile decay to the frozen zero of winter, when both women and the air can get thin and cold. The icy purity of stars, knives, frozen trout, and the heart's isolation are at once feared, celebrated, penetrated, embraced, abhorred. In many lines Thompson's terror seems absolute; knowledge can leave us 'cold-broken, earthed'; but the final poems in the book are restorative, offering to a grateful eye the curative power of onions and roots and redemptive words. The indifferent reception given this astonishing book did nothing to brighten Thompson's difficult last years. He moved to Toronto for a sabbatical rest, only to hear that his house in the Tantramar Marsh had burned to the ground. *Stilt Jack* begins with the lines: 'Now you have burned your books: you'll go/with nothing but your blind, stupefied heart', and the bereft poet then enters a night-world that inverts the life-affirming natural sphere celebrated in his first collection. *Stilt Jack's* thirty-eight poems, their insistent negations and glittering cascade of images, tell of a man pushed to the limit: the title, after Yeats, can allude to a hooked fish, or to a man on stilts. Yet Thompson's charity and good sense flash out in the blackness; he reminds us that after all, 'I'm still here like the sky/and the stove'. The lines shine with his scrupulous care for language and a wry Yorkshire humour. Thompson considered his form carefully; he explains in a prefatory note that his model is the ancient Persian ghazal, which proceeds by orderly couplets, but is a 'poem of contrasts, dreams, astonishing leaps'. The publication of *I dream myself into being: collected poems* (1991), with an Introduction by James Polk, preceded that of *John Thompson: collected poems & translations* (1995), a definitive edition of all Thompson's poems, published and unpublished, including the translations, with textual notes, a bibliography, and a detailed biographical essay by the editor, Peter Sanger.

Thompson, John Sparrow (1795–1867). He was born in Waterford, Ireland, and as a young man went to London. In 1827 he immigrated to Halifax, marrying Charlotte Pottinger in 1829 and fathering seven children (one of whom, his namesake, was prime minister of Canada from 1892 to 1894). He was a schoolteacher who started a private school in Halifax; an editor of newspapers and literary magazines; and a civil servant. His government posts included that of Queen's Printer (1843-4, 1848-54). In the late 1820s and 1830s Thompson earned a limited reputation as a poet and essayist, appearing in *The Novascotian* and *The Halifax Monthly Magazine*. Thompson made his contribution to the literary life of Nova Scotia as an editor of newspapers and magazines and as a friend and critic of young poets; in the 1830s and 1840s he was a major catalyst in stimulating literary activity, a role he shared with his friend Joseph HOWE. As editor of *The Halifax Monthly Magazine* (1830-3), *The Acadian Telegraph* (1836-7), *The Novascotian* (1838, 1840-2), *The Pearl* (1839-40), and *The Mirror* (1848), he published all the best young Nova Scotia poets of the day: Joseph Howe, Sarah and Mary Eliza HERBERT, John McPHERSON, Angus Gidney, Samual Elder, Andrew SHIELS, and Mary Revett. He knew most of them personally, introduced them to one another, and was instrumental in getting them to think critically about their craft. Without him, literary activity would have been thinner and more diffuse.

Thompson, Judith (b. 1954). Born in Montreal, and raised in Connecticut, USA, and Kingston, Ontario, she graduated from Queen's University with a B.A. in English (1976) and in 1979 from the acting program of the National Theatre School. She is the mother of five children and lives in Toronto with her husband Duncan Campbell.

Thompson's first play, *The crackwalker* (1981), was produced by Theatre Passe Muraille, Toronto, in 1980 and has since been staged in major theatres worldwide. A dark, compassionate presentation of disadvantaged young people, the play explodes with unexpected violence, using language that penetrates to the viscera. As playwright-in-residence at Tarragon Theatre, Toronto, Thompson continued to create psychologically rich characters struggling to understand the secrets of their contradictory selves. *White biting dog* (1984, GGA) combines emotional intensity with a highly metaphoric theatricality, while *I am yours* (1987) reveals the subconscious desires of the characters in a more realist structure. *Lion in the streets* (1992, rpr. 1996) moves through fear and confrontation as a young girl stalks her murderer, to a state of grace imaginatively offered through forgiveness. The prowling presence of the dead girl, on the fringes of every scene, tends to unite the disparate scenes, but other devices

in language and structure open the play to multiple interpretations, foregrounding the constructed nature of the reality it depicts. *Sled* (1997) pursues the theme of innocence tainted or destroyed by evil, juxtaposing animal images from Native spirituality with those from Catholic sources. *Perfect pie* (2000) is about a farm wife in eastern Ontario and her childhood friend who has become a famous actress and visits her; it was produced (and directed by the playwright) at Tarragon in Feb. 2000. *Capture me* (2004) is a lively, gripping play about Jerry, a thirty- to fortyish kindergarten teacher, Aziz, an Arabic immigrant she's in love with, and Dodge, her ex-husband who is stalking her; it was produced at Tarragon in 2004. *Palace of the end* (2007) is an electrifying theatrical experience—one hour and forty minutes long—in the form of three monologues (*My Pyramids, Harrowdown Hill, Instruments of Learning*) drawn from the Iraqi war, delivered by Lynndie (based on Lynndie England, who was photographed in the Abu Ghraib prison); Dr David Kelly, who killed himself after he was revealed as the source of the BBC's report that claims about Iraq's weapons program had been doctored by the British government; and an Iraqi woman (Nehrjas Al Saffarh), who was tortured, along with her sons, under Saddam Hussein, and then died when her house was destroyed by American bombs in the Gulf War. *Palace of the end* had three very successful premieres: in North Hollywood, California (The NOHO Arts Centre) in June 2007; in Toronto (Berkeley Theatre, January 2008); and off-Broadway in New York (Epic Theatre Ensemble production, June 2008). In his *New Yorker* review (7 and 14 July 2008) of the New York production, Hilton Als said that Thompson's 'rhythmic language reaches its full flowering in the beautiful closing monologue.' *Palace of the end* won for Thompson in 2008 the ($20,000 US) Susan Smith Blackburn Prize, presented in Houston, Texas, and in 2009 the Amnesty International Freedom of Expression Award for the best play at the Edinburgh Fringe Festival that dealt with human rights.

Thompson's two-character play *Enoch Arden in the Hope Shelter* (2006), the text of which is short, is a strange (for Thompson) amalgam of words and music—playing on Tennyson's popular poem *Enoch Arden*, Richard Strauss's piano work of that title, and his haunting song 'Morgen'—that is unfolded by the psychotic Jabber, who has logorrhea and connects himself with Tennyson's poem, and Ciel, catatonic but musical—she can play Strauss's piece and sing his 'Morgen'. The play was performed at Theatre Centre, Toronto, in September 2005, with John Fitzgerald Jay as Jabber and Kristen Mueller as Ciel.

The collection *The other side of the dark: four plays* (1989, GGA, rpr. 1997) contains *The Crackwalker, Pink, Tornado,* and *I Am Yours. Judith Thompson: late 20th century plays 1980–2000* (2002) contains *The Crackwalker, White biting dog, I am yours, Lion in the street, Sled,* and *Perfect pie.* Thompson compiled and edited the anthology *She speaks: monologues for women* (2004). Ric Knowles edited *Judith Thompson* (2005), volume three in the series Critical Perspectives on Canadian Theatre in English, and *The masks of Judith Thompson* (2006).

In 2007 Thompson received the $50,000 Walter Carsen Prize for Excellence in the Performing Arts. She was made an Officer of the Order of Canada in 2005.

Thompson, Kent (b. 1936). Born in Waukegan, Illinois, he was educated at Hanover College (B.A., 1957), and, after serving in the US army from 1958 to 1961, at the University of Iowa (M.A., 1962) and the University of Wales (Ph.D., 1965). In 1966 he moved to the University of New Brunswick at Fredericton, where he was appointed professor of English and creative writing in 1974; he retired in 1994. He was editor of *The* FIDDLEHEAD from 1967 to 1971 and from 1974 to 1975. He lives in Annapolis Royal, Nova Scotia.

Thompson is the author of six novels: *The tenants were Corrie and Tennie* (1973), *Across from the floral park* (1974), *Shacking up* (1980), *Married love: a vulgar entertainment* (1988), *Playing in the dark* (1990), and *Hollywood secrets* (2000). His fiction often deals with the consequences of protagonists who find themselves in an unfamiliar situation with a sexually attractive stranger. For example, the fable-like *Across from the floral park* is told by a wealthy and idle narrator who discovers that a young and alluring tenant is mysteriously occupying a house he has purchased. She resists the narrator's attempts to evict her and seduces him into marriage. Although the narrator begins to learn about his new wife's past and to create a present for the two of them, in the novel's conclusion he finds himself locked out for no reason he can understand and he fatalistically begins life anew in a nearby hotel. Thompson's concern with the way obsession and fantasies control individuals' lives is extended in *Playing in the dark*, a story told in several voices about a violent, desperate love affair that runs its course without understanding, without hope. Like most of Thompson's

fiction, it focuses on people barely able to cope with their lives, locked into existences of limited possibility. The byline of *Hollywood secrets* reads Kent Thompson writing as Hugo Hepworthy. It is a *jeu d'esprit* whose opening lines are: 'It is a fine thing to watch your mother being strangled ....//Isn't that how a memoir should begin? With something shocking?'.

His mother is a film actress, the narrator is ten, and the shoot is in Quebec City in 'a foreign country where they speak a foreign language'. The studio insisted that his mother marry (the handsome man who plays) Tarzan, who they later discover likes boys. The story goes on from there, until Hugo meets Loretta and he helps her try to make money by being a burglar. She is sent to prison, where she learns to read and write. On the last page: 'My beard is white, long and scraggly. I look like a mad prophet. I am a prophet. I am. Listen to my words: You are going to die.'

Thompson's short stories have been collected in *Shotgun and other stories* (1979) and *A local hanging and other stories* (1984). (In the latter collection, some of the characters from *Shacking up* reappear.) Usually quiet in tone, his short fiction has an intensity that makes it effective. Thompson has been particularly noted for his interest in what he calls 'postcard' fiction, extremely brief stories such as those collected in *Leaping up sliding away* (1986).

Thompson has also published two books of poetry—*Hard explanations* (1968) and *A band of my ancestors* (1975), which is a sequence of twenty-four poems spoken by a Viking invading the New World—and *Biking to Blissville* (1993), a tour guide of New Brunswick, which was followed by *Getting out of town by book and bike* (2001), a series of charming personal essays on the role of the bicycle in both literature and life, illustrated with attractive archival bicycle drawings and photographs.

Thomson, E.W. (1849–1924). Edward William Thomson was born in Peel County, now part of Toronto. In 1864, while visiting an American relative, he briefly joined and fought with the Union army in the American Civil War and in 1866 enlisted in the Queen's Own Rifles to fight the Fenians. Discharged the next year, he studied civil engineering for five years and from 1872 to 1878 surveyed for eastern Ontario lumbering and railway concerns. In Dec. 1878 he became a political journalist for the Toronto *Globe*, where, except for a return to surveying in 1882 and 1883 during the Winnipeg land boom, he remained for twelve years, serving for a time as its Montreal correspondent. In 1891, disagreeing with the Liberal election platform on unrestricted reciprocity, he left the *Globe*, where he was by this time in charge of the editorial page. He became a revising editor for the Boston *Youth's Companion*—a weekly magazine that was at the height of its popularity, with the widest circulation of any American periodical—to which he had been contributing stories since winning first prize in a *Youth's Companion* short-story competition in 1886 with 'Petherick's peril'. He remained with that magazine as a revising and contributing editor until 1901, when he returned to Canada—first to Montreal, where he worked for the *Star*, and a year later to Ottawa, where he was Canadian correspondent for the Boston *Transcript*. In 1909 he was made a Fellow of the Royal Society of Literature (England) and in 1910 a Fellow of the Royal Society of Canada. He died in Boston at the home of his grandson. A fluent writer, a politically uncompromising and independent thinker, and an entertaining conversationalist, Thomson was a friend of Duncan Campbell SCOTT and Ethelwyn WETHERALD, and a close friend and admirer of Archibald LAMPMAN, whose *Lyrics of earth* (1895), after receiving several rejections, was finally published by Copeland and Day of Boston through the efforts of Thomson. (He also edited the selection and arrangement of the manuscript at Lampman's invitation.) While in Boston, Thomson remained in close touch with the Canadian literary scene, and during his tenure with the *Youth's Companion* many Canadian writers appeared in its pages. While he lived in Ottawa, he became a close friend and admirer of Henri Bourassa and Wilfrid Laurier.

Although most of Thomson's stories were published in the *Youth's Companion*, several of his best first appeared elsewhere: 'Privilege of the limits' in *Harper's Weekly* (25 July 1891); 'Old Man Savarin' and 'Great Godfrey's lament' in the New York magazine *Two tales* (Oct. 1892); and 'Miss Minnelly's management' in *The UNIVERSITY MAGAZINE* (Oct. 1910). In the 1890s he published three collections: *Old Man Savarin and other stories* (Toronto, 1895) and two collections that seem to have been designed for a juvenile audience: *Walter Gibbs, the young boss; and other stories* (Toronto, 1896) and *Between earth and sky, and other strange stories of deliverance* (Toronto, 1897); all three were published simultaneously in Canada and the United States. After his return to Canada in 1901 Thomson produced little fiction. In 1909 a collection of his poetry was published in Canada as *The*

many-mansioned house and other poems and in the United States, slightly altered, as *When Lincoln died and other poems* (as a boy, on a visit to Philadelphia, Thomson had an encounter with Lincoln). Thomson reissued *Old Man Savarin* as *Old Man Savarin stories: tales of Canada and Canadians* (1917, rpr. 1974) with changes in content: two stories from the 1895 collection were omitted, while two from *Between earth and sky* and three later stories were added. This collection was dedicated to Sir Arthur Quiller-Couch, who had included Thomson's poem 'Aspiration' in *The Oxford book of Victorian verse* (1912). Some of Thomson's stories are excessively sentimental; some are simply boys' stories; but the best are fine realistic stories of early Canadian life. Among the Irish, Scottish, and French-Canadian settlers and lumbermen he wrote about are some memorable characters portrayed with economy, gentle humour, liveliness of language, felicity of dialogue, and a skilful use of dialect. See the *Selected stories of E. W. Thomson* (1973, rpr. 1992) edited by Lorraine McMullen. See also *An annotated edition of the correspondence between Archibald Lampman and Edward William Thomson (1890–1898)* (1980), edited by Helen Lynn—and Raymond SOUSTER's 'found poems' based on a selection of them (with an introduction by William Toye), in Souster's *Wonderful wobbly world: poems for the new millennium* (2006).

Tin flute, The (1947, NCL). This is the translation of the first novel, *Bonheur d'occasion* (1945), by Gabrielle ROY. A poetic, compassionate, and authentic portrayal of a Montreal slum family whose fortunes rise ironically—unique in French-language fiction for its sweep, its masterful characterization, and its creative unity—it has been seen as a progenitor of the protest literature that would explode in Québec in the 1960s. It is set in Saint-Henri, and the action focuses on Florentine's search for security and love, and on the trials of the Lacasse family. As in other Québec novels of the period, the family is in a state of disintegration: at the end, pregnant Florentine marries Emmanuel, who, like Florentine's father and brother, goes off to war; one brother gets a job in a munitions factory, one dies of leukemia, and a sister decides to become a nun. The novel is deeply rooted in a historical period and sharply questions the value of a social system that 'solves' its crises through war. The first translation, by Hanna Josephson, won a Governor General's Award. A translation by Alan Brown is in the NEW CANADIAN LIBRARY.

Tippett, Maria (b. 1944). Born in Victoria, British Columbia, she began her training as a cultural historian at Simon Fraser University (Hons. B.A., 1972). (The university conferred on her the honorary degree of Doctor of Laws in 2006.) She wrote with her then-husband, the late Douglas Cole, *From desolation to splendour: changing perceptions of the British Columbia landscape* (1977). This was followed by her distinguished biography, *Emily Carr* (1979, GGA; rpr. 1982; rev. 1994, rpr. 2006), which threw a new light on the character and works of the well-known Canadian painter and writer (q.v.). In 1982 she received a Ph.D. from the University of London. Her *Art at the service of war: Canada, art, and the Great War* (1984) was followed by *Making culture: English-Canadian institutions and the arts before the Massey Commission* (1990). *By a lady: celebrating three centuries of Canadian women in the visual arts* (1992) is a significant and lavishly illustrated addition to the study of this branch of Canadian culture. *Between two cultures: a photographer among the Inuit* (1994), for which Tippett wrote the text, represents another direction of her research. *Stormy weather: F.H. Varley, a biography* (1998) is a carefully documented and informative account of Varley's life, with less attention paid to his work as a renowned landscape artist and portraitist. *Bill Reid: the making of an Indian* (2003)—about an artist of mixed heritage—is a carefully researched biography of the jeweler and carver in wood of Haida images who was associated with the revival of Northwest Coast Native art, that is in effect the unmasking of a man whose mother was only part Haida and whose white father was of German and Scottish descent. Bill Reid identified himself with the world of whites until relatively late in his life, when his superb artistic creations of Native (Haida) images—such as *The Spirit of Haida Gwaii*, a huge sculpture (over six tons) produced for the Canadian embassy in Washington—began to make him famous. At the end of her book Tippett says that Bill Reid 'was a linchpin ... between the Native and non-Native communities. At various points in his career he justified the museum world's salvage, restoration, and reclassification of Native artifacts as works of art.' *Portrait in light and shadow: the life of Yousuf Karsh* (2008, rpr. 2009) is a handsome biography—with many well-reproduced celebrity (and other) Karsh photographs—of the immigrant from an Armenian family who lived in Mardin, Turkey, and made a spectacular career for himself in Canada through talent and canniness and a great deal of self-promotion. The 'light and shadow' of the title, which dramatized his portraits, evokes more shadow than light in Tippett's biography, which is nevertheless enjoyable. Karsh—who died in 2002 at the age of ninety-three—and his second wife Estrillita moved to Boston in 1997. Tippett describes him at the end of his life sitting in his hospital bed with the Order of Canada pin attached to his pajamas. He was made an Officer in 1969 and a Companion in 1990.

Becoming myself: a memoir (1996) is an engaging and frank account of Tippett's life, until the publication of *Emily Carr*, that includes her not entirely happy time as an adopted child; a period in Europe, particularly Germany; and the first phase of her university education. She has also published a collection of stories, *Breaking the cycle and other stories from a Gulf Island* (1989). In 1995 Tippett was made a Senior Research Fellow of Churchill College, Cambridge University. She had married in 1991 the distinguished English historian Peter Clarke, who for several years was Master of Trinity Hall, Cambridge. They now divide their time between two houses: on Pender Island, BC., and in East Anglia, England.

Tish (1961–9). Founded in Vancouver in Sept. 1961, this mimeographed magazine began the writing careers of its poet-editors: Frank DAVEY, George BOWERING, Fred WAH, David Dawson, and James Reid. It was influenced by the work of both the San Francisco poet Robert Duncan and the CONTACT PRESS editors Louis DUDEK and Raymond SOUSTER. The '*Tish*-group', as the five editors soon became known, argued for a poetry of spoken idiom written in lines determined by oral rhythms. Nineteen consecutive monthly issues, marked by extensive discussion of poetic theory and numerous attempts at extended or series poems, notably Bowering's Margins series, were published by the original editors. Writers associated with *Tish* during this period included critic Warren Tallman, playwright Carol BOLT, and poets Daphne MARLATT (Buckle), David Cull, Red LANE, Robert Hogg, and Lionel KEARNS. Following five issues edited between Aug. 1963 and June 1964 by a group headed by David Dawson, the general editorship of *Tish* was assumed by Dan McLeod, who later founded the counterculture newspaper *The Georgia Straight*. Under McLeod, *Tish* directed itself mainly to the Vancouver writing community and lost the awareness of central and eastern Canada that had characterized the earlier period. The last four issues, published in 1968–9, were edited by Karen Tallman from offices shared with *The Georgia Straight* and were given over mostly to prose, particularly the diary and reflective essay. In 1969 *Tish* was unofficially replaced by *The Georgia Straight Writing Supplement.*

The founding of *Tish* marked the beginning of a distinct but inward-looking West Coast writing community that later published such journals as *Iron, The Pacific Nation, BLEW OINTMENT, Air, Island, Pulp, Talon,* and *Writing*—journals rarely seen elsewhere in Canada. Paradoxically, in a national context *Tish* was also the most dramatic evidence of the emergence across the country of a new generation of poets more open to the colloquial and popular than were their forebears—a generation that included not only the *Tish* editors but such writers as John NEWLOVE and Andrew SUKNASKI in Saskatchewan and Margaret ATWOOD and David McFADDEN in Ontario. The first nineteen issues of *Tish* were reprinted by TALONBOOKS as *Tish 1–19* (1975). Critical and historical materials concerning *Tish* were collected by C.H. GERVAIS in *The writing life* (1976), and by Douglas BARBOUR in *Beyond 'Tish'* (1991).

Tit-Coq (1950, tr. 1967). This famous play by Gratien GÉLINAS concerns the illegitimate young soldier Arthur Saint-Jean—called Tit-Coq (little rooster) for his fighting spirit—and his search for acceptance and love. Though there is some melodrama and much comedy in its three acts with thirteen scenes, the way Tit-Coq and his fiancée Marie-Ange are caught in the cultural and religious web of Québec in the 1940s is genuinely tragic. The play can also be read as a statement about the plight of French Canadians in a world dominated by Anglo-American culture and traditions. Tit-Coq, in his search for acceptance and identity in a hostile world, can be seen as a metaphor for Québec in an English-speaking continent. Much of its success in Québec can be attributed to Gélinas's use of the French spoken by working-class Québécois, who were shown in this play that their situation and language were worthy materials for the stage. Although the play may seem dated now and some of its characters stereotypes, it remains a moving presentation of Québec society before the Quiet Revolution. The first production of *Tit-Coq* opened at Montreal's Théâtre Monument National on 22 May 1948 and was directed by Gélinas and Fred Barry. An immediate success, it ran at that theatre until the summer recess, after which it transferred to the Théâtre du Gesù, where it played in both French and English until 1951

with basically the same cast—Gélinas played Tit-Coq in both versions—for more than 500 performances. In English it had a successful run at the Royal Alexandra Theatre, Toronto, and in Chicago. This encouraged Gélinas in 1951 to take the English version to New York, where it closed on Broadway after three performances. In 1953 it was made into a film, starring Gélinas and directed by him and René Delacroix; a subtitled English version was also made. In 1981 *Tit-Coq* had a very popular revival at the Théâtre Denise Pelletier by the Nouvelle Compagnie Théâtrale, Montreal; directed by Gélinas, this production had a dynamic young actor, Daniel Gadouas, in the title role. A televised production, starring Alain Gélinas, Gratien's son, was aired on Radio-Canada in 1984. In 1992 and 1993 it had highly popular productions at the Théâtre de la Bordée in Quebec City.

Tit-Coq was first published in French in 1950 and in English—in a too-literal translation by Kenneth Johnstone, in co-operation with the author—in 1967; this remains its only English translation.

Toews, Miriam (b. 1964). Of Mennonite descent, Miriam Toews (pronounced *taves*) was born and grew up in Steinbech, Manitoba, and earned a B.A. from the University of Manitoba and a Bachelor of Journalism degree from the University of King's College, Halifax. She lived in Montreal and London, England, before settling in Winnipeg, Manitoba, with her husband Neal Rempel and three (now grown) children. Her first novel, *Summer of my amazing luck* (1996, rev. 2006), focuses on single welfare mothers—two of them, Lucy and Lish, living in a house they call Half-a-Life (real name Have-a-Life). Both have children. Lucy, the narrator, says: 'Somewhere along the line I became pregnant. With Dill, my son who is now nine months old. His full name is Dillinger. I don't know who the father is.' Lish has four daughters 'two of them with the same guy and the other two, twins, with a carefree street performer who had fallen in love with Lish's hands'—he disappears. (Even so, Lish pines for him.) Life on the dole is not funny, but the everyday lives of the inhabitants of Half-a-Life, and of Serenity Place across the street, provide a vein of humour in Toews' hands. Humour also infuses *A boy of good breeding* (1998, rev. 2005), which is set in Canada's smallest town, called Algren in Manitoba. 'It was possible to walk anywhere in town in less than fifteen minutes'. The mayor, Hosea Funk (he was named after the book in the Bible) is determined to keep the population at 1500 because he has received a letter from the prime minister's office saying that the PM might visit Canada's smallest town on July 1, 1996. Hosea is constantly disturbed when the population fluctuates: Knute and her young daughter Summer Feelin' arrive from Winnipeg so that Knute can help her mother Dory look after her father Tom, who has had a heart attack; Leander Hamm dies; Bertha Plenty has triplets (the names of the three boys are Finbar, Callemachus, and Indigo—more of Toews' outlandish names), and the possibility of other additions and subtractions threaten. Hosea was born in 1943 because his mother, Euphemia Funk, allowed herself to be seduced by a handsome stranger when she attended a dance. 'Afterwards they sat together, and Euphemia said "well," and turned and smiled at him. And the stranger smiled back and squeezed her hand and said, "Thank you." Then he walked over to where his horse was tied up, just on the other side of the dance hall, and rode away.' On her death bed Euphemia told Hosea that his father was the prime minister of Canada. Did she make up this 'final ridiculous story'? Was this 'her parting gift to Hosea'? That he was a boy of good breeding? Max, the estranged husband of Knute—and the son of Combine Jo, who used to drive her late husband's combine up and down Main Street—comes back to see his daughter, Summer Feelin', whom he adores. A narrative of trivial happenings laced with humour among not-so-intelligent people, the novel unfolds seamlessly and the characters are alive. *A complicated kindness* (2004, GGA, rpr. 2008) is narrated by sixteen-year-old Nomi (Naomi) Nickel, who lives in East Village (Steinbech?), a community of Mennonites. Founded 500 years ago by Menno Simons, the Mennonite faith led to such modern-day proscriptions as 'the media, dancing, smoking, temperate climates, movies, drinking, rock'n roll, having sex for fun, swimming, make-up, jewelry, playing pool, going to cities, or staying up past nine o'clock. That was Menno all over. Thanks a lot, Menno.' Nomi, who indulges in some of these things, lives with her kindly, religious father Ray, a schoolteacher, because her mother Trudie (Gertrude) and elder sister Tash (Natasha) left the family, several weeks apart, without a word, rejecting completely the church and its teachings—they are both excommunicated. The reason for Trudie's leaving? 'The idea of my mom leaving town to spare my dad the pain of having to choose between the church and her, knowing it would kill him, was the story I liked best.'—a complicated kindness. Nomi's restless, episodic narrative—moving back and forth in time—includes memories of Tash and Trudie. Another character is The Mouth, her mother's brother Hans, the minister of the church. 'Everything in this town, the school, the church, the museum, the chicken plant, is connected to everything else, like the sewers of Paris. There's no separation of Church and State, just of reality and understanding, and The Mouth is behind the wheel of it all.' In the museum, replicating earlier Mennonite times for tourists, Nomi's boyfriend Travis 'has to go behind a rope in the authentic house barn pretending to be the husband of a fake pioneer girl in a long skirt and bonnet who rocks a Cabbage Patch doll in a cradle. He sits there reading the Bible with a candle. They're supposed to smile at each other periodically.' ('Please don't be happy with that girl, I said./He said okay, he wouldn't be.') Like J.D. Salinger with Holden Caulfield, Toews portrays a credibly articulate teenaged Nomi who conveys the vicissitudes of her own life, both its sad and humorous aspects, and of her father's, who eventually leaves her (because he knows she will never leave him), with a note about 'how to deal with the sale of the house, how to change the oil in the car, not to get a basement apartment if I could help it....' Deep feeling along with social diminution encapsulate Nomi's captivating scattershot observations that make up the narrative. *The flying Troutmans* (2008, rpr. 2009) begins when Hattie Troutman flies back from Paris at the behest of her eleven-year-old niece Thebes, whose mother Min is in hospital with a psychotic breakdown and she and her brother, the rebellious fifteen-year-old Logan, need someone to look after them. To oversimplify, Hattie gets the kids into the family van and heads for the United States, as far south as the Mexican border, in search of their father. Details of the road trip, many of them humorous—the people they meet, Hattie's memories of her difficult relationship with Min, the wayward behaviour of Thebes and Logan—make up much of the novel. It was awarded the Rogers WRITERS' TRUST Fiction Prize ($25,000).

Swing low: a life (2005), a tribute to Toews' father Mel, begins with a prologue:'"Nothing accomplished."/I don't know what my father meant when he said it. I had asked him, the day before he took his own life, what he was thinking about, and that was his reply. Two hopeless words, spoken in a whisper by a man who felt he had failed on every level. This book is my attempt to prove my father wrong.' From the age of seventeen Mel Toews suffered from bipolar disorder. His daughter brilliantly reconstructs his life for this book, presenting it in the form of a vivid, touching first-person narrative in her father's voice.

Torgov, Morley (b. 1928). He was born and raised in Sault Ste Marie, Ontario, where his family was part of the city's small Jewish community. A full-time lawyer with a practice in Toronto, he writes in his leisure time. Torgov has published a memoir and five novels, each of which explores Jewish themes with humour and irony that are gentler than in either Mordecai RICHLER or Philip Roth, with whom he is often compared. *A good place to come from* (1974) won the LEACOCK Medal for Humour and was adapted as a mini-series for television and for the stage in Canada and the United States. A series of vignettes, it describes Torgov's experience of growing up Jewish in the predominantly Gentile world of Sault Ste Marie. *The Abramsky variations* (1977), written in three parts and set in Toronto and France, concerns three generations of the Abramsky (later Brahms) family: father Louis, son Hershel, and grandson Bart (né Kevin). Each character struggles to reconcile Jewish identity with secular ambition and all are more strongly attracted to fantasizing about people they want to emulate than to facing reality. Torgov's second novel, *The outside chance of Maximilian Glick* (1982, rpr. 2002), which also won the Leacock Medal, was first written as a children's story. It takes a comic look at twelve-year-old Maximilian, so named because his parents thought it would look impressive on the door of a law office. It is the story of a boy raised in the tiny Jewish community of Steelton, northern Ontario. Maximilian seeks to escape the overwhelming love of his parents and grandparents, who envision him making a career as a surgeon, judge, or scientist. With the help of Rabbi Kalman Teitelman, who replaces Steelton's former rabbi and with whom Maximilian forms a relationship, he eventually releases himself from the stifling expectations of others. *St Farb's day* (1990) concerns Isadore Farb, an honest, respectable lawyer on Toronto's Bay Street. As Farb struggles with an ethical dilemma—he finds himself involved in a conflict of interest with several clients—he confronts larger moral issues linked to his Jewish identity. *The war to end all wars* (1998)—the title refers to the competition between owners of two clothing stores in a town in northern Michigan—begins in 1917 in the Austrian trenches. Elliot Pines (born Eliezar Pinsky) is a Russian soldier who flees after his squadron is destroyed by a German regiment, of which Karl Sternberg, who is decorated for bravery, is a member. We next see Elliot arriving, with the intention of opening a clothing store, in the fictional town of Oreville, where his competitor turns out to be Sternberg, working with his sister-in-law Hannah, who begins the War to End All Wars. The novel incorporates other characters, including the infuriated mother of the young woman Karl is having an affair with and a criminal oppressor of Elliot, and it has many surprises, two of them acts of violence; but it is a calm and polished narrative, laced with humour, that has survival and love as underlying themes. *Murder in A-Major* (2008) is Torgov's ingenious attempt to draw on his love of music and musicians to create a crime novel involving Robert and Clara Schumann, and Brahms, in the Germany of the 1850s, along with Düsseldorf's leading detective, Inspector Hermann Preiss. *Stickler and me* (2002) is an engaging book for young people—with characters and dialogue that are entirely believable—about part of a summer in 1962 that thirteen-year-old Ben Marshall spends with his crusty grandfather, Ira Lamport, called Ira the Stickler, aged seventy-five and a lawyer for nearly fifty years, who is on a difficult case regarding his wealthiest client, who has died. Ben cannot help but be involved and the narrative becomes entertaining and poignant.

Traill, Catharine Parr (1802–99). Born in Kent, England, Catharine Strickland spent her first thirty years in rural Suffolk. At Reydon Hall, on the outskirts of Southwold, Thomas and Elizabeth Strickland conscientiously educated their six daughters and two sons. Thomas's library provided much imaginative stimulus for his daughters, who were drawn to the romance of history and experimented in writing stories, plays, and poetry to pass the time. By the late 1820s all but one of them had become published writers. The eldest, Elizabeth and Agnes, later achieved fame and social prominence in England as co-authors of *Lives of the Queens of England* and other multivolumed royalist biographies; Jane Margaret specialized in moral tales and histories; Catharine, like her younger sister Susanna (MOODIE), began as a writer of children's stories. Three members of this remarkable family—Catharine, Susanna, and their younger brother Samuel (b. 1807)—immigrated to Canada (Samuel in 1825, his sisters in 1832) and there earned recognition as recorders and interpreters of pioneer life and settlement in early-nineteenth-century Upper Canada.

Catharine was the first Strickland offspring to appear in print, producing virtually a book a year between 1822 and 1831. One pre-emigration book deserves special mention. *The young emigrants; or, Pictures of life in Canada. Calculated to amuse and instruct the minds of youth* (1826) anticipates her own removal to Canada six years later and reflects her positive approach to the challenges involved in a dramatically new life. Based on information from family friends in Canada and travel books, it is structured as a series of letters and promotes the worth of an adventurer's spirit, British resoluteness, and a Crusoe-like acceptance of untoward fate, all in the context of stable domestic life and family solidarity. In May 1832 Catharine married Lt. Thomas Traill, a sensitive, sociable, and well-read widower who had attended Oxford. Following the plans for emigration already formulated by Catharine's sister Susanna and her husband John Moodie, they set out immediately for Scotland to arrange their finances, bid farewell to Traill's family, and book summer passage for Canada.

Thomas Traill adapted to life in the Canadian backwoods far less effectively than his younger, more capable wife. Though their arrival and settlement (near present-day Lakefield, Ontario) was buffered by the kindness and resourcefulness of Catharine's brother Samuel—their neighbour, and soon the area's most successful pioneer—Thomas Traill was never happy with clearing trees, farming, or his remoteness from congenial society. Nevertheless, out of the early—and generally positive—years of pioneering experience, Catharine Traill drew the materials for her most important book, one of the few she wrote exclusively for an adult audience: *The BACKWOODS OF CANADA: being letters from the wife of an emigrant officer, illustrative of the domestic economy of British America* (London, 1836; rpr. 2000; NCL, CEECT). Thomas Traill's attempts to sell the farm on Lake Katchwanook, begun in 1835, succeeded in 1839. The family moved to Peterborough, but mounting debts, illnesses, and more mouths to feed hampered their progress in the town, despite Catharine's attempt to run a school. When in 1846 the sudden death of a young Scottish friend left them liable for his debts, they accepted the timely offer of an English friend, the Rev. George Bridges, to live rent-free in his Rice Lake home, 'Wolf Tower'. For the next thirteen years

they lived in that area, particularly at 'Oaklands', where Thomas Traill, increasingly incapacitated by depressions, relied upon his wife not only to raise their seven surviving children but also to write for publication when time and opportunity allowed. To these most difficult years of the Traills' Canadian experience belong two of Catharine's children's books, *Canadian Crusoes. A tale of the Rice Lake plains* (London, 1852, CEECT) and *Lady Mary and her nurse; or, A peep into the Canadian forest* (London, 1856). The former—drawing upon the attractive landscape of the Rice Lake plains, what she knew of the history of its Native peoples, and the lost-child theme—dramatizes the exemplary survival of three adolescents of Scottish and French roots who, though lost in the backwoods for nearly two years, succeed in bringing their high-minded and civilized attitudes to bear on wilderness experience and bring into their midst a Native girl whom they rescue. The novel is at once a testimony to British resourcefulness and a hopeful allegory of Canadian survival and unity. *Lady Mary*—which, like *Crusoes*, was reprinted under variant titles in Britain and the United States to disguise its Canadian specificity—is a stylized dialogue between teacher and child that manifests Traill's fondness for nature and her skill at close observation. Her other book of this period, *The female emigrant's guide, and hints on Canadian housekeeping* (Toronto, 1854), returns to the spirit of *The backwoods of Canada*, providing supportive counsel and practical information for women faced with the prospect of emigration and settlement in remote British-American locales. Though repetitive, anecdotal, and uneven, this miscellany went through ten editions in the 1850s.

Some of Traill's best writing from the late 1830s to 1860, including a sequel to *The backwoods*, did not find its way into book form. Various sketches and stories about bush life that appeared in British and Canadian magazines have been collected under the title *Forest and other gleanings: the fugitive writings of Catharine Parr Traill* (1994), edited by Michael Peterman and Carl Ballstadt. Traill's strengths as a writer are her clarity, firm sense of identity, optimistic spirit, and above all her attention to natural detail. While her interest in flora and fauna is clearly shown in *The backwoods*, it was only after her husband's death in 1859, her subsequent removal to Lakefield, Ontario, and the maturation of her children that she had the opportunity to focus that attention. *Canadian wild flowers* (Montreal, 1868) combined her text and the paintings of Susanna

Moodie's daughter, Agnes Fitzgibbon. Agnes took the initiative in the project, learning lithography, organizing the material, finding a publisher, and arranging for the necessary subscribers. In the 1880s, while living in Ottawa with her second husband, Brown Chamberlain, Agnes also made possible her aunt's most significant work as a naturalist, *Studies of plant life in Canada; or, Gleanings from forest, lake and plain* (Ottawa, 1885), a fond and detailed study that earned Traill the praise of several professional botanists. In her last decade Traill produced two more books: *Pearls and pebbles; or, Notes of an old naturalist* (Toronto, London, 1894), which includes reminiscences of her childhood and a useful biographical sketch by her grand-niece, Mary Agnes Fitzgibbon, and *Cot and cradle stories* (Toronto, 1895), another children's collection. She died in Lakefield at the age of ninety-seven, still at work on book projects, her life having virtually spanned the entire nineteenth century.

See *I bless you in my heart: selected correspondence of Catharine Parr Traill* (1996), edited by Carl Ballstadt, Elizabeth Hopkins, and Michael Peterman. See also Charlotte GRAY, *Sisters in the wilderness: the lives of Susanna Moodie and Catharine Parr Traill* (1999) and the large-format *Sisters in two worlds: a visual biography of Susanna Moodie and Catharine Parr Traill* (2007) by Michael Peterman (with an Introduction by Charlotte Gray). It is of exceptional interest because it is lavishly illustrated with modern photographs in colour as well as archival photographs, paintings, letters, and family artifacts.

Tregebov, Rhea (b. 1953). Born Rhea Block in Saskatoon, she was raised in Winnipeg. She married Alan Tregebov in 1971, attended the University of Manitoba (B.A., 1974), and then did graduate work at Cornell and Boston Universities (M.A., 1978). Since 1978 she has lived in Toronto, and has been a freelance editor, poetry-workshop instructor, and business writer. A lyric poet, Tregebov has published six books of poetry: *Remembering history* (1982), *No one we know* (1987), *The proving grounds* (1991), and *Mapping the chaos* (1995). Her work explores the impact of history and memory on personal lives. Stylistically she prefers the long, punctuated line and often uses the striking details of daily life to evoke sensual images. In her first volume, Tregebov sees history as fixed and permanent, a view she reconsiders in the collections that follow. Increasingly she comes to recognize and celebrate the mutable 'chaos' of life in poems that treat such varied themes as the legacy of

the Holocaust, the destructiveness of nuclear power, her son's near-death from severe asthma, the death of loved ones, urban life, and gardening, a favourite subject. Always aware of the potential tragedy that looms beneath the surface of life, she seeks to integrate darkness and light in verse that finally rejects pessimism. *The strength of materials* (2001) is a collection of elegies. "Paris Elegy (Atget)' begins: '"How private and public spheres intersect" and/how it is observed, tacitly, that trees,/in twenty-five years, grow but buildings/do not;...' The opening quotation is from the catalogue for the exhibition of photographs by Eugène Atget at the Art Gallery of Ontario in March 2001. *(alive): selected and new poems* (2004) is an enjoyable volume that makes one appreciate Tregebov's ability to turn intense life/family experiences into poems that, while sometimes complex and indirect, hit home with the reader. Among the new poems is 'Scare': 'She had ten years on me,/the doctor. She wasn't looking/at me, she was watching the screen,/one hand expertly stroking/the dumb snout of the ultrasound/over and then over and again over/my right breast,/her fine face focused.// She wasn't looking at me/but all I wanted to look at/was her human face.' In 2009 Tregebov published her first novel, *The knife sharpener's bell,* about a ten-year-old girl who leaves Winnipeg with her family in the 1930s and returns to Stalinist Russia.

Tregebov edited *A long life of making: poems from the Pat Lowther Memorial Award winners* (2000), which includes poems by M. Travis LANE, Tregebov, Bronwen WALLACE, JILES, MOURÉ, SPEARS, MacEWEN, CROZIER, and Marilyn BOWERING. She also edited the charming *Gifts: poems for parents* (2002), a collection of thirty-four poems by Canadian poets (many of whom have entries in this *Companion*) that should be better known. Tregebov also edited *Arguing with the storm: stories by Yiddish women writers* (2007); the title comes from the poem 'My home', by the Yiddish poet Rachel (Rokhl) KORN. Tregebov has also written books for children: *The extraordinary ordinary everything room* (1991), *The big storm* (1992), *Sasha and the wiggly tooth* (1993), and *Sasha and the wind* (1996).

Tremblay, Michel (b. 1942). Born and raised on rue Fabre in the Plateau Mont-Royal section of Montreal (where most of his plays and novels are set), he studied graphic arts after high school and became a linotype operator, like his father and brother. His first play, *Le train,* written in 1959, won first prize in the 1964 'Jeunes auteurs' contest of Radio-Canada, and was produced on television. But Les BELLES-SOEURS (1968), written in 1965 and produced in 1968, is regarded as the true beginning of a career that rapidly brought fame to Tremblay, enabling him to devote himself entirely to his writing. (A translation by Bill Glassco and John Van Burek was published in 1974; rev. 1992; rpr. 2007) A full cycle of plays followed, describing other facets and characters of the same universe; it ended with Damnée Manon, sacrée Sandra (1977), translated by Van Burek in 1981 with the same title. Tremblay later wrote L'impromptu d'Outremont (1980; translated by Glassco and Van Burek as The impromptu of Outremont, 1981), which reflects the preoccupations of the more bourgeois neighbourhood he moved to in 1974 and, at the same time, sets the scene for major changes in Tremblay's writing: in tune with the new post-referendum dramaturgy of the 1980s, the time had come to tone down 'kitchen-sink realism' and nationalist symbolism. Two major plays exemplify this new trend: Albertine, en cinq temps (1984; translated as Albertine in five times in 1986 by Glassco and Van Burek), a fascinating and innovative depiction of Albertine between the ages of thirty and seventy, and Le vrai monde? (1987; translated in 1988 by Glassco and Van Burek as The real world?), a self-reflexive Pirandellian play about the playwright describing his own family life. La maison suspendue (1990, translated with the same title by Van Burek in 1991) and Marcel poursuivi par les chiens (1992; translated by Van Burek in 1992 as Marcel pursued by hounds) link characters on stage with those described in the novels about the Plateau Mont-Royal and in two autobiographical novels, Le coeur découvert (1986, translated by Sheila Fischman in 1989 as The heart laid bare) and Le coeur éclaté (1993), which draw on his love affair with a young actor.

The Plateau Mont-Royal setting must be seen as a true microcosm of alienated Québec: most characters are doomed, from birth to death, to a dead end. The most powerfully tragic play in this regard is À toi, pour toujours, ta Marie-Lou (1971)—translated by Glassco and Van Burek as Forever yours, Marie-Lou (1975, rev. 1999)—in which two sisters, Carmen and Manon, confront their parents, Leopold and Marie-Lou, who have been dead ten years. Manon sits in a rocking chair trying to resemble her mother, whose destiny she perpetuates in a masochistic acceptance of a frustrated and dull life, while Carmen, dressed as a cowgirl, has become a country-and-western singer in a cheap nightclub. Carmen reappears in Sainte Carmen de la Main (1976; translated by Glassco and Van Burek in 1981 as Sainte-Carmen of the Main), in which she is killed for having tried to liberate (or 'redeem') her transvestite and prostitute friends. Carmen is a central figure in Tremblay's plays, for she exemplifies the full meaning of transvestism (in the sense of le travestissement, which means not only cross-dressing but misrepresentation)—a major theme in his plays dealing mainly with show-business or homosexuality, such as La Duchesse de Langeais (1970; translated, with other plays, by Van Burek in 1976), Hosanna (1973; translated by Glassco and Van Burek in 1974), and Damnée Manon, sacrée Sandra. These plays present an interesting and basically realistic depiction of a marginal milieu, where the struggle for social recognition and true human love is often dramatic. However, one must also consider their characters as symbolic figures for a whole collectivity—Québec—in which borrowing someone else's identity always seems the only way to success and respectability. Hence Carmen's decision to drop the lyrics and tunes learned in Tennessee, and to sing her own songs describing the real problems of her friends, can lead only to her death. Hence also (but more positively) the final scene of Hosanna, in which the two male lovers—one of them, 'Hosanna', garbed as Elizabeth Taylor in Cleopatra—undress, shedding all pretences and make-believe to accept their true selves and affirm their identities. Other aspects of the metaphorical use of transvestism are shown in Damnée Manon, sacrée Sandra. Manon, Marie-Louise's daughter, is still rocking her life away in the kitchen chair, but her mysticism now verges on fetishism and madness. 'Sandra' is a male transvestite whose sole concern in life seems to be with sex. He is opposed to Manon as sharply as his white costume is opposed to her black dress, his 'avocado sea-green' lipstick to the burgundy colour of her rosary. But as Sandra describes the black 'god' from Martinique whom he loves, and Manon tells about her love for Christ, the true meaning of the play becomes clear: 'religion and sex stem from the same craving for an absolute', as the playwright explained to Martial Dassylva in La Presse (26 Feb. 1977).

Remembering Tremblay's repeated statement that there are no 'real men in Québec', most critics have noted that Tremblay's world is dominated by women—just as Québec society, and particularly its French and religious characteristics, owe much to the obstinacy of women. Bonjour, là, bonjour (1974)—translated by Glassco and Van Burek in 1975—seems to shed new light on this matter. It deals with the love between a brother and sister, Serge and Nicole, a social taboo seldom treated so openly; such a relationship meets social and family attitudes head on—but these are shown to be hypocritical, for the whole family is unknowingly entangled in incestuous desires. But very strikingly, the characters who stand out in this mostly feminine universe are two men, father and son; all the women are trying to seduce or possess Serge, who craves only the love of his deaf father. The play climaxes in Serge's long-contained cry: 'I love you, Papa!' Thus his love for his sister—and this might apply to some homosexual relationships depicted by Tremblay—seems a perverse manifestation of his quest for his father's love. More generally, this might allow us to see the portrayal of ineffectual men in other plays from the same perspective. The weak and sometimes despicable male characters in Les belles-soeurs, Forever yours, Marie-Lou, and En pièces détachées (1970)—translated by Allan Van Meer as Like death warmed over (1973)—are the hidden face of this obsessive quest, the importance of which is again shown in Les anciennes odeurs (first produced and published in 1981), in which the older lover is clearly identified as a father image by the younger one, who talks incessantly about his dying father. It was translated by John Stowe as Remember me (1984). Trois petits tours (1971) contains three short plays, which appear in English as Berthe, Johnny Mangano and his astonishing dogs, and Gloria Star, along with Surprise! Surprise!—translated by Van Burek in La Duchesse de Langeais and other plays (1976). Encore une fois, si vous permettez (1998), and the translation by Linda Gaboriau, For the pleasure of seeing her again (1998), employs two actors in a portrait of Tremblay's very supportive mother. Assorted candies for the theatre (2007)—Gaboriau's translation of Bonbons assortis au théâtre (2006)—is a stage adaptation of Tremblay's fourth book of autobiographical sketches, about his childhood in the Plateau Mont-Royal neighbourhood. Tremblay's plays have been performed widely in English Canada—many of them first at Toronto's Tarragon Theatre—and internationally. In Scotland, William Findlay and Martin Bowman translated Les belles-soeurs into Scottish dialect as The guid sisters (1988) and La maison suspendue as House among the trees: the production of these plays had an enormous success and gave a significant impulse to the cultural life of Scotland. Bowman and Findlay also translated Messe solennelle pour une pleine lune d'été as Solemn Mass for a full moon in summer (2000), also in a Scots dialect, which was first performed in 2000 at Edinburgh's Traverse Theatre and then at the Barbicon Centre, London. The form of the play, based on the Mass, is fourteen short scenes featuring troubled couples: a male gay couple, one of whom cares for the other who has AIDS; two middle-aged lesbians; a daughter who cares for her father with amputated arms; a mother whose son (with a wife and child) has become gay and been abandoned by his lover... It is not so much a play as a theatrical tone poem, with the actors exchanging dialogue in short scene after scene and ending up dancing a tango. The driving force (2003)—Gaboriau's translation of L'impéretif présent (2003)—encapsulating the disharmony that lies beneath family relationships, is in two acts, each one a monologue: of the son Clarke (fifty-five), a successful playwright, and of the father Alex (seventy-seven). First Alex is confined to an Alzheimer's ward and tended by his son, at the same time berating him for all his grievances; in the second act we find Clarke in the same helpless position, being attacked verbally by Alex. Each monologue quotes passages from the other speaker, giving a different perspective. At the end of both acts the speaker leaves, 'throws open the door and stares'. Well acted, this can make for a powerful theatrical experience.

In the field of fiction, Tremblay published as early as 1966 Contes pour buveurs attardés, translated by Michael BULLOCK as Stories for late-night drinkers (1977); this was followed by La cité dans l'oeuf (1969), a fantasy, translated by Bullock as The city in the egg (1999). None of these seemed a major work, whereas the six Plateau Mont-Royal chronicles—La grosse femme d'à-coté est enceinte (1978), Thérèse et Pierrette à l'école des saints-anges (1980), La Duchesse et le roturier (1982), Des nouvelles d'Édouard (1989), Le premier quartier de la lune (1989), and Un objet de beauté (1997)—have been generally hailed by readers and critics as important. Unlike his plays, which were often written out of anger, these novels are imbued with love, tenderness, and a generosity of spirit; they made Tremblay a major novelist of the 1980s. Sheila FISCHMAN translated them as The fat woman next door is pregnant (1981), Thérèse and Pierrette and the little hanging angels (1984), The duchess and the commoner (1999), News from Édouard (2000), The first quarter of the moon (1994), and A thing of beauty (1998)—an ironic novel about Marcel, a twenty-three-year-old 'child in a man's body', whose mother is called Albertine, and whose working-class family is dysfunctional. In

News from Édouard the title character, a shoe salesman by day but the Duchess of Langeais in a transvestite show by night, sails for Paris, where he is disillusioned—telling all this to his sister-in-law, the 'fat woman'. *Some night my prince will come* (2004), a translation by Fischman of *La nuit des princes charmants* (1995), can only be thought of as autobiographical, beginning with a night at the opera, *La Bohème*, continuing with a happy and unhappy search for love, and ending with the narrator 'stretched out on the living-room sofa, my ear practically glued to the speaker, and I'd closed my eyes.' He was listening to the third act of *La Bohème*. Two novels that have a large cast of lively characters are *Le cahier noir* (2003) and *Le cahier rouge* (2004), which were translated by Fischman and published as *The black notebook* (2006)—about Céline Poulin, a waitress on the night shift of a cheap restaurant called the Sélect (she is a midget)—and *The red notebook* (2008), which takes place in 1967, the year of Expo, and Céline is now a hostess in a bordello. In *The blue notebook* (2009) Céline returns to the Sélect and begins an affair with Gilbert.

Tremblay has also published several books of memoirs in which he discusses the works that most influenced his life and writing in the fields of cinema, theatre, and literature. These include (pertaining to cinema) *Les vues animées* (1990), translated by Fischman as *Bambi and me* (1998), and *Twelve opening acts* (2002)—Fischman's translation of *Douze coups de théâtre* (1992)—a collection of twelve stories that are related to the theatre and have to do with his own life. It opens with 'Babar the elephant', a theatrical performance he attended when he was six. Other chapters are stories connected with his seeing two famous plays by Marcel DUBÉ—in English 'Lilac time' and 'A simple soldier'. Some chapters have opera titles—'The Abduction from the Seraglio', 'The Threepenny Opera', and 'Tristan and Isolde'—in which Tremblay describes his brief (sexual) encounter with a formerly famous Montreal radio actor and his borrowing the actor's recording of *Tristan,* with Kirsten Flagstad, conducted by Furtwängler—ending with his mother's hearing the voice of her broadcasting idol in a phone call to her son. In *Birth of a bookworm* (2003)—Fischman's translation of *Un ange cornu avec des ailes de tôle* (1994)—each chapter heading refers to a book (or books) and author, but the chapters themselves are stories, not only about Tremblay's reading but also about his early life until the publication in 1966 of his first book,

Contes pour buveurs attardés. A valuable social history of Montreal and Québécois mores in the period, *Birth of a bookworm* is among Tremblay's best books.

Tremblay has received many honours, including the title Chevalier de l'Ordre des Arts et des Lettres de France in 1984, promoted to Officer in 1991; the Prix David in 1988 for his entire work; and many honorary doctorates from Canadian universities. See Renate Usmiani, *Michel Tremblay* (1981).

Trower, Peter (b. 1930). Born in St Leonards, England, he attended the Vancouver School of Art for two years and was a logger in the British Columbia forest for twenty-two years, an experience that has informed much of his writing as a poet and novelist; he is also a singer and songwriter, and lives in Gibson's, BC. Al PURDY, in his Introduction to *The slidingback hills* (below), said that 'British Columbia lives and breathes in nearly all [Trower's] writing'. On Trower's seventieth birthday in August 2000, his friends and some fellow poets, considering him unrecognized outside British Columbia, presented him with the first annual Peter Trower Alternative Poetry Award. His poetry collections include *The alders and others* (1976); *Ragged horizons* (1978); *Bush poems* (1978), with logging drawings by Bus Griffiths; *Goosequill snags* (1982); *The slidingback hills* (1986)—'The hills are sliding back/slipping into distance/more profound than miles/floating into remoteness/down time's wrong-way telescope.'; *Unmarked doorways* (1989); *Where roads lead* (1994); *Hitting the bricks: urban jazz poems* (1997); and *A ship called Destiny* (2000), love poems. *Chainsaws in the cathedral: collected woods poems: 1964-1998* (1999) has another Introduction by Purdy: 'Pete's words jump and push and leap and whisper and roar in your ears.' But in this gathering of logging poems, previously printed flush left, the energy, drama, passion, and roughness have been subdued by the centring of every line (as in the low-life poems of *Hitting the bricks*). *There are many ways: poems new and revised* (2002), with illustrations by Jack Wise, opens with the poem 'Upwind From Yesterday', the third stanza of which reads: 'Upwind from yesterday/the shape of things alters and twists,/the hurts diminish,/the misapprehensions pack their bags./We are left with the trembling gist.' *Haunted hills & hanging valleys: selected poems 1969-2004* (2004) opens with an admiring Foreword by Don MCKAY, in which he says that in much modernist writing 'art "purifies the tribe," lifting it out of the workplace into its own rarefied air. But strong work poets like Peter Trower exercise a pull in the other direction, reminding the angels of poesy of the workaday world that the tribe inhabits.' There are, however, many personal poems. One of the last in this collection is 'A Voice from the Edge' dedicated to Pat LOWTHER: 'I will never forget your voice/on that last day of your days/it ghosted over the phone like audible darkness/strained sapped utterly empty/bled of all hope all joy/the merest echo of you/the voice of someone who faced/the naked unfaceable.'

Trower's three novels have a logging background. In *Grogan's Café: a novel of the B.C. woods* (1993) nineteen-year-old Terry Belshaw tries his hand at logging in various 'gyppo' (independently owned) camps in the 1950s, and is a short-order cook for Davies Grogan (in his cafe, not accented) between jobs. This vivid account of the life of BC loggers—an experienced logger says to Terry: 'Trees are funny. They can split on you and do things you're not expecting. Sometimes it almost seems as though the bastards are fighting back.'—encompasses characters who are both good and bad, much rough language, and a romance with the wife of a friend that is prevented from becoming disastrous. Terry Belshaw also narrates *Dead man's ticket: a novel of the streets and the woods* (1996), a thriller that centres on the mysterious death in Vancouver of his best friend Frankie, reportedly 'found dead of a heroin overdose in an East End hotel room', and his urge to pursue the mystery, first by returning to Frankie's camp in his place, on a 'dead man's ticket'. Completing the novel trilogy, *The Judas Hills* (2000) continues Belshaw's logging adventures.

Trudel, Marcel (b. 1917). Born at St-Narcisse-de-Champlain, Québec, he was educated at Université Laval (B.A., 1938; L.ès L., 1941; D.ès L., 1945) and did research at Harvard University (1945–7). He was professor of history at Laval from 1947 to 1965, director of the Institute of Canadian Studies at Carleton University, Ottawa (1965–6), and head of the history department at the Université d'Ottawa (1966–8). He was made an Officer of the Order of Canada in 1971 and a Companion in 2008 and was awarded the Molson Prize in 1980. He was directeur adjoint of the first four volumes of the DICTIONAIRE BIOGRAPHIQUE DU CANADA. The author of more than two dozen titles—some of them in two volumes—and specializing in the history of New France, Trudel became an essential figure in transforming Québec's history from wishful romanticism to

rigorous intellectual pursuit, and in putting an end to the rhetorical indulgence that had turned Québec historical writing into religious and ideological manifesto. He emphasized extensive work on contemporary historical sources, turning some of his graduate seminars into an extended examination of just one historical text. The three volumes of his *Histoire de la Nouvelle-France—Les vaines tentatives, 1524–1603* (1963), *Le comptoir, 1604–1627* (1966, GGA), and *La seigneurie des Cent-Associés, 1627–1663* (1973)—were condensed and translated by Patricia Claxton for the Canadian Centenary Series to create *The beginnings of New France, 1524–1663* (1973), of which Chapter 18 was based on Trudel's *Le terrier du Saint-Laurent en 1663* (1972) and *La population du Canada en 1663* (1973). All these books explored vast unplumbed areas of Québec's past. Writing also on slavery in New France, on demographic and settlement history, on the beginnings of Montreal, among other subjects, Trudel revealed his skill in meticulous reconstruction. His autobiography *Mémoires d'une autre siècle* (1987) was translated by Jane Brierly as *Memoirs of a less travelled road: a historian's life* (2001, GGA)—a fascinating book.

Twigg, Alan (b. 1952). Born in West Vancouver, he has had a central influence in promoting the work of British Columbia writers, writing for the Vancouver *Province* as a book columnist (1979–88) and an editorial-page columnist (1995–8), and as the publisher/owner of the quarterly *BC BookWorld* (1988–), which features interviews, articles, photographs, etc. in a lively format and has been said to have the largest circulation of any Canadian periodical devoted to books. In honour of George WOODCOCK, Twigg organized a symposium and other events that took place in May 1994, the year before Woodcock died. He has also produced six television documentaries. He lives in Vancouver ('when he is not in Placentia, Belize').

Twigg has written fifteen books, and has been especially productive in the last few years. His books include *Hubert Evans: the first ninety-three years* (1985), a brief biography of EVANS, with chapters on his writings and an interview; *Vancouver and its writers: a guide to Vancouver's literary landmarks* (1986); *Strong voices: conversations with fifty Canadian authors* (1988); *Twigg's directory of 1,001 BC writers* (1992) and *Twigg's 200: a selection of significant BC literature* (1998), short notes on BC authors and their works; and *Cuba: a concise history for travellers* (2000), which fulfils the promise of the subtitle in an informative, readable, and not-too-long text; it was followed by *101 top historical sites of Cuba* (2004). *Understanding Belize: a historical guide* (2006) is another authoritative, interesting travel book. *First invaders: the literary origins of British Columbia* (2004) presents early writers who were also explorers, priests, traders, scientists, and their books relating to British Columbia. In his Foreword to *Aboriginality: the literary origins of British Columbia, Vol. 2* (2005) Twigg says that he is introducing 'more than 170 Aboriginal authors (including painters, carvers, illustrators and editors) who have produced three hundred books since 1900.' *Thompson's highway: British Columbia's fur trade, 1800–1850* (2006) discusses the lives of the famous explorers and fur traders Alexander Mackenzie, Simon Fraser, David Thompson, and others. In 2008 Twigg published *Full time: a soccer story*, which focuses particularly on what the game means to his team of players fifty and over (not all of them in good health), and climaxes with a trip to Spain and a game in which they didn't score a goal. 'We came, we saw, we were conquered, but our resiliency had brought rewards that were as good as any victory.' The wonderful colour photograph on the jacket is of Alan Twigg in midair with a soccer ball above his head. A friend of George and Ingeborg WOODCOCK, he published in 2009 *Tibetans in exile: the Dalai Lama and the Woodcocks*.

Intensive care: a memoir (2002)—made up of poems written for his family—grew out of the discovery (after a soccer game) that Twigg had a brain tumour. A five-hour operation fortunately resulted in his recovery: 'He walks. He talks./He gets get-well cards./ While flossing his teeth in the mirror/he sees a carnival attraction/–Miracle Boy at 49–/ and his detachment is mildly depressing.// He had hoped for an After/different from his Before' ('Wonderland').

Two little savages (1906). For many years considered a classic of children's literature, this story by Ernest Thompson SETON (translated into many languages, but because of its politically incorrect title has been out of print for over thirty years) grew out of his work with youth groups in the United States. By 1903 fifty 'tribes' had formed, calling themselves 'Seton's Indians' or 'Woodcraft Indians'. In that year Seton published, in *Ladies Home Journal*, a serialized story for boys, an expanded version of which later became *Two little savages: being the adventures of two boys who lived as Indians and what they learned*. Although written in the third person, the story is semi-autobiographical and records Seton's adventures in the summer of

1876, when he holidayed with the Blackwell family near Lindsay, Ontario. In the woods near the farm, Seton and the son of Blackwell 'played Indian' and developed games that were later incorporated in Boy Scout rituals still used in many parts of the world. An episodic adventure story, it provided Seton with a framework into which he could interpolate instructions on woodcraft (generously illustrated with his own detailed drawings), and in which an initiation rite tests a boy's knowledge of birds and trees and merges with an archetypal pattern. Yan (as the young Seton) confronts a sequence of trials, demonstrates his courage, and is finally pronounced a hero. Since the story ends with Yan's resolve to 'strive and struggle as a naturalist', the book could be viewed as an autobiographical *Bildungsroman*. Variations of many of the same episodes appear in Seton's autobiography, *Trail of an artist-naturalist* (1940).

Two solitudes (1945, GGA, NCL; rpr. 2003). This novel by Hugh MacLENNAN aroused more public interest than critical attention because of its theme of Canadian unity, which had been strained in the 1942 plebiscite on conscription, and its apposite title, drawn from Rilke. Although Rilke and MacLennan both had individuals in mind as the solitudes that touch and protect each other, the application to the dominant cultural groups in Canada has since become a cliché. The novel is structured in four parts: the first two treat the period 1917 to 1921 and the second two the years 1934 and 1939. Part I, set in the rural Québec parish of Saint-Marie-des-Érables, has two interests. One is the struggle between the proud, anti-clerical, progressive Athanase Tallard and the anglophobe parish priest, Father Beaubien, who opposes change. The second interest is the attempt of Yardley, a retired sea captain, to settle in the parish where, ironically, he is more acceptable than Tallard, whose political loyalties, affiliation with English-speaking capitalists, estrangement from his anglophobe son Marius, and second marriage to an Irish girl threaten the status quo. Part II ends in utter defeat for Tallard: a failed marriage, a broken family, financial ruin, the loss of his family home, and death, which is preceded by a return to the Church. MacLennan's treatment in the first half of Tallard, Yardley, and the younger generation is deft and sympathetic; the story moves with almost tragic inevitability. But as George WOODCOCK and others have noted, the second half of the book—centring on Paul Tallard, the son of

Athanase by his second marriage, and on Paul's courtship of Heather Methuen against the backdrop of the English community of Montreal and the business career of Huntley McQueen—is neither sympathetic nor dramatic. McQueen is treated satirically (he has overtones of Mackenzie King); and Paul's and Heather's marriage, intended to suggest a French-English détente, is unconvincing. Paul is more like a spokesman for the author's beliefs and hopes than a fully realized character. It is typical of MacLennan's early optimistic writing about national problems that the realities of the situation should be rendered more persuasively than their resolution. The novel, then, is not an unqualified success.

With its abrupt period divisions, its point of view that changes from the objective to the personal and didactic, leading characters who in the beginning are lively and realistic (Tallard *père*, Yardley) and then become mere symbols (Paul, Heather, and the other *Anglais*) or shadows (Marius), it lacks cohesiveness. If the sense that the components are ill-yoked does not suit the theme, however, it suits the title. For all its faults, *Two solitudes* is a sensitive and creditable attempt to portray the tensions and differences in Québec that culminated in the Quiet Revolution (a decade and a half before that event took place) and the possibility of reconciliation. It is a landmark in Canadian nationalistic fiction.

U

Uguay, Marie (1955–81). Born in Montreal, she studied at the Collège Marguerite Bourgeoys and at the Université du Québec à Montréal. In her short life—she died at twenty-six—she published only two collections of poems, *Signe et rumeur* (1976) and *L'outre-vie* (1979); they were followed by the posthumous collection *Autoportraits* (1982). English translations by Daniel Sloate of some of these poems, with a Foreword by Jacques Brault, were collected in *Selected poems (1975–1981)* (1990). Uguay's first collection immediately revealed a poetry that is personal, intimate, and concise, and that stood apart from the formalist tendencies of the 1970s; the poems attempt to reconcile art and life through exploration of the possibilities of aphorism and analogy. Uguay emerged in her second collection as one of the most outstanding voices of her generation, pursuing her search for a poetic language intimately connected with life, though she knew she had cancer. Illness gave a tragic depth to her introspection, but even in her late poems she did not abandon the idea of reconnecting with the world, beyond the cruel experience she was living through.

Uher, Lorna. See Lorna CROZIER.

University Magazine, The (1907–20). A Montreal quarterly edited by Andrew MACPHAIL, it succeeded the semi-annual *McGill University Magazine* (1901–6), edited by Charles Moyse, which had appeared ten times. The new periodical took over its subscription list of under 1000 and numbered its volumes consecutively, beginning with vol. VI. Although theoretically directed by an editorial committee drawn from McGill, the University of Toronto, and Dalhousie University, Halifax, *The University Magazine* was under Macphail's control from the beginning. Notable for paying its contributors—the average fee of $25 was more than many a weekly wage—the magazine was financially guaranteed by Macphail himself, although McGill University and the University of Toronto and various benefactors made occasional contributions. It drew upon the best contributors from English-speaking Canada, along with some from outside the country, and under Macphail's rigorous editorial direction set a standard of excellence, while attaining a circulation of nearly 6000, a level that no comparable Canadian quarterly has subsequently matched. Macphail himself contributed forty-three pieces of political comment and social criticism (for which he took no payment). Although welcoming purely literary contributions—for example, 'Addison as a literary critic' by E.K. Broadus (Feb. 1909)—the magazine, for Macphail, was a vehicle to advance what he described as 'correct thought', which had to do with a Canada that was rural, traditional, imperial in sentiment, and, aside from Québec, overwhelmingly British in ethnic composition. When his ideals had seemed to become things of the past—and for various other reasons, including failing eyesight and financial pressures—Macphail discontinued the magazine.

University of British Columbia Press. The third largest university press in Canada, UBC Press was founded in 1971 to replace the University of British Columbia's Publication Centre, which had been in operation since 1961. From 1971 to 1980, under its first director Anthony Blicq and editor Jane Fredeman, it published an average of ten books a year within four areas of concentration: western North America, English and French Canadian literary criticism, Asia and the Pacific Rim, and international law. Blicq was succeeded by James Anderson as the Press struggled unsuccessfully to establish a fresh mandate and editorial direction. In 1989 the University took the extraordinary step of replacing the entire senior management group. The next year Peter Milroy was appointed Director, and he made Jean Wilson senior editor; they in turn set about refocusing the publication program. Among the new policies adopted by Milroy and the Press's publication board was the exclusion of literary criticism from the subjects published, focusing on areas of strength such as Native Studies and western Canadian history. The Press continues to publish in these areas, and over the last two decades has gradually added publications in the social sciences, becoming a leading publisher of Canadian history, politics, law, environmental studies, military history, and Asian studies—regularly achieving national and international recognition. By 2009 the average annual output grew to sixty titles, including such notable works as the nine-volume *Canadian democratic audit*; the four-volume *The birds of British Columbia*; Tina Loo's *States of nature*; Cole Harris's *Making Native space* and *The reluctant land*; Alan Cairn's *Citizens plus*; John Helliwell's *Globalization and well-being* and Julia Cruickshank's *Do glaciers listen?*; and the outstanding series Law and Society and Nature, History, Society. To date the Press's list of textbooks, monographs, and collections in print contains some 900 titles.

University of Toronto Press Incorporated. Founded in 1901, the first university press to be established in Canada and the tenth to be established in North America, the University of Toronto Press Incorporated is today one of the largest university presses on the continent. It began as a small printing department of the University, producing examination papers and calendars. It now comprises, along with its publishing activities, a digital print operation, seven bookstores on three Toronto campuses, and distributes books for about seventy other publishers, most of them Canadian. It was incorporated in 1992 as an independent, not-for-profit corporation maintained outside the university budget. It issues about 150 new books annually and has a backlist of about 1500 titles. It also publishes some textbooks for Higher Education and some sixteen academic journals, most of them quarterlies. General policies are determined by a board appointed by the University, and publications are approved by an academic editorial board appointed by the provost of the university. Its net income, after all operating and capital expenses have been met, is devoted to the publication of scholarly research, reference works, and general books of culture and social significance. Its publications—which have won many international and national awards for their contributions to knowledge and for their design and production—are sold worldwide through a network of exclusive agents and representatives, and, in the United States, through its own office and warehouse in Buffalo.

Publishing in the humanities, social sciences, and now in business, the Press draws its authors from across Canada and from many other countries. Major multi-volume publications include the *Collected works of John Stuart Mill*, the *Collected works of Erasmus* (translated into English), the DICTIONARY OF CANADIAN BIOGRAPHY, the *Collected Works of Northrop Frye*, the *Letters of Bernard Shaw*, the *Records of early English drama,* and the David Milne Project. Although most of its works are intended for an academic readership, it also publishes general books of mainly Canadian interest, including the three-volume *History of the book in Canada* (2004–7), the *Encyclopaedia of music in Canada* (1982, 2nd edn 1992), the three-volume *Historical atlas of Canada* (1987–93), and *Canadian Who's Who*. Long-term bestsellers have included John Porter's *Vertical mosaic* (1965) and Marshall McLUHAN's *Gutenberg galaxy* (1962).

Urquhart, Jane (b. 1949). Born Jane Carter in Little Long Lac, Ontario, she moved with her family to Toronto at the age of five. She was educated at the University of Guelph, earning a B.A. in English in 1971 and in art history in 1976, the year she married the painter Tony Urquhart. Jane Urquhart's first publications were books of poetry: *I'm walking in the garden of his imaginary palace* (1982, with illustrations by her husband), *False shuffles* (1982), and *The little flowers of Madame de Montespan* (1984). (The first and third of these collections were combined in *Some other garden: poems* [2000].) Her delicately worded verse explores, among other things, illusion, memory, history, and transformation in different areas of human experience. Similar themes are found in her fiction, beginning with *The whirlpool* (1986, rpr. 1993), three stories of nineteenth-century Canadians whose lives are interconnected by different events and symbols, notably that of the whirlpool—to which Canadian history is also linked: a character reflects that the whirlpool is like 'history … moving nowhere and endlessly repeating itself'. (In a French translation it was the first Canadian book to win, in 1992, France's prestigious Prix de Meilleur Livre Étranger.) *Storm glass* (1978, rpr. 2000) is a collection of stories related to perception, memory, and transformation; it includes an unusual five-story sequence about wheelchairs. *Changing heaven* (1990, rpr. 1996) is a modern-day *Wuthering Heights*: Ann, a Canadian scholar, travels to England to research Emily Brontë, while two ghosts—the spirits of Brontë herself and of another nineteenth-century woman killed in a balloon crash—haunt the same territory. Always intrigued by nineteenth-century culture, Urquhart was influenced by some 'creative and passionate' contemporary criticism, including Gilbert and Gubar's *The madwoman in the attic* (1979) and Fanny Ratchford's *The Brontës' web of childhood* (1941). The passion that suffused Brontë's fiction is woven throughout this strange, evocative novel as Ann encounters a latter-day Heathcliff. In *Away* (1993) a new series of transatlantic and historical connections are found in her exploration of the Irish influence in Canada. Urquhart, herself of Irish extraction, grew up listening to a wealth of Celtic tales. In the novel, oral tales about the O'Malley family, passed down through four generations of women, encompass aspects of both Irish and Canadian history. Urquhart was co-winner of the (Ontario) Trillium Award for *Away*. The central character of *The underpainter* (1997, GGA; rpr. 1998) is Austin Fraser, born in 1894 in Rochester, New York, who in his eighties narrates the story of his life, in which painting is central—he becomes a well-known artist, mostly as a painter of landscapes. He spent boyhood summers in the town of Davenport on the Canadian side of Lake Ontario and returns to it throughout his life to see his friend George, who served in the Great War but lived to return to his passion for china and china painting. Other characters are Robert Henri, the New York painter and teacher who taught Fraser; a painter-friend, Rockwell Kent; Sara, his model and lover whom he visits and paints over fifteen summers at Silver Islet on the north shore of Lake Superior; and George's lover Augusta, who had been a nurse in the war. The novel is informed not only by Fraser's keen observations but by his coldness—he keeps himself at a distance from everyone he knows. Henri taught him to put his feelings into his painting, but when Fraser asks Kent what he thinks of his nude paintings of Sara, the answer is 'They're as cold as ice.' Though emotion is plentiful in the novel, it is merely inferred, from Sara's responses to Fraser; from Augusta's account of her life; and from the result of Fraser's accidentally meeting Vivian, with whom George had a brief marriage before the war, and his driving her from New York to Davenport so that she can meet him again—an event that has tragic consequences.

The stone carvers (2001), a more successful novel, is also more ambitious and more compelling. It is complex, beginning in Bavaria in the 1860s, when Father Archangel Gstir is instructed—by (mad) King Ludwig—to go to 'the wilds of Canada' (southern Ontario) to minister to the people there who have no priest. He meets Joseph Becker, another Bavarian, a miller and wood-carver. The village of Shoneval takes shape and a narrative unfolds, embracing not only the church Father Gstir eventually had built but Joseph's family and particularly his granddaughter Klara, trained as a woodcarver, and her brother Tilman, who as a boy tried to run away until his father, at his wife's bidding, attached him, in his sleep, to an iron harness and a chain. He manages to escape—and disappears. Klara falls in love with the young Irishman Eamon O'Sullivan, who goes off to war in 1914—and disappears. In 1934 Tilman turns up at Klara's house, swinging a wooden leg. He tells her about his past and shows her a beautiful wooden box he has carved. 'I've done marble carving too. My friend Giorgio apprenticed with a man who made tombstones and he got me a job there. He tried to get me into lettercarving too.' Giorgio 'got a job overseas … working on some Jesus huge Canadian war memorial that's going to be built at Vimy Ridge, where I lost my leg in France.' The last third of the novel is devoted to the completion of the Vimy Memorial, when Klara (disguised as a man) and Tilman go there, meet Giorgio, and are hired to assist in various ways. The designer of the Memorial, the sculptor Walter Allward, is a fictional character. Both Klara and Tilman find loving relationships and Klara connects with at least the *name* of Eamon on the monument—he died at Vimy. With Urquhart's detailed, admiring description of the Memorial's completion, and of some fictional people closely involved, the novel ends as a romantic tribute. A strong romantic element also pervades *A map of glass* (2005), a long, intricate novel with many characters, of whom the Woodmans are central. Irish-born Joseph Woodman is granted Timber Island at the eastern end of Lake Ontario: timber, and rafts taking it through the St Lawrence to Québec, become his life. His son is Branwell, and *his* son is Maurice, whose son Andrew opens the book as an old man with Alzheimer's walking, fatally, in the snow towards 'the island'. Young Jerome McNaughton—a photographer who 'wanted to mark the moment of metamorphosis, when something [e.g., the natural environment] changed from what it had been in the past.'—discovers Andrew's body embedded in ice. Sylvia Bradley, a woman in her fifties who lives in a world of her own, had had a secret affair with Andrew, the love of her life. 'What matters is the miracle that we ever met... the miracle of the life I never could have lived without the idea of him....' A year later Sylvia finds Jerome in Toronto and gives him Andrew's journals to read. His life is revealed—and, in conversation, their affair, and Jerome's own life. The conceptions of change (and Sylvia's resistance to it), memory, history, geography, maps, diagrams, landscape, possessions dominate the narrative, reducing the dramatic effectiveness of the actions and exchanges of the somewhat lifeless characters. Urquhart has written, for Penguin Canada's Extraordinary Canadians series, *L.M. Montgomery* (2009), a brief biography. She was appointed an Officer in the Order of Canada in 2004. See *Jane Urquhart: essays on her works* (2005) edited by Laura Ferri.

Not the idea, but the result of *The Penguin book of Canadian short stories* (2007), which Urquhart edited, was unwelcome for several reasons. It is a big, hefty book (hard to handle), overlong (683 large pages set in small type) containing sixty-nine stories by sixty-six writers, the number inflated by the many writers (including Ethel WILSON, who wrote distinguished short stories) represented by extracts from novels or memoirs, and by the writers who should *not* have been included—e.g., Adrienne Poy (Clarkson), Virgil Burnett, et al. For all her gifts, Urquhart—who refers to her 'uncertainty' in her Introduction—lacked the instinct for discovering and valuing great short stories that comes from years of reading them. The anthology has undergone much criticism, notably in *CNQ: CANADIAN NOTES & QUERIES* 74 and its 'Salon des refusés' (Mark Anthony JARMAN, Clark BLAISE, Ray SMITH, Douglas GLOVER, Diane SCHOEMPERLEN, Cynthia FLOOD, and Hugh HOOD are among the writers excluded).

V

Valgardson, W.D. (b. 1939). William Dempsey Valgardson was born in Winnipeg, but spent most of his childhood in Gimli, Manitoba. He received a B.A. (1961) from United College, a B.Ed. (1966) from the University of Manitoba, and an M.F.A. (1969) in creative writing from the University of Iowa. He served as chair of the English department of Cottey College in Nevada, Missouri, from 1970 to 1974, when he returned to Canada to join the creative-writing department of the University of Victoria, British Columbia, of which he was chairman from 1982 to 1987. Valgardson is the author of two novels, *Gentle sinners* (1980) and *The girl with the Botticelli face* (1992); two collections of poetry, *In the gutting shed* (1976) and *The carpenter of dreams* (1986); and four collections of short stories: *Bloodflowers* (1973), *God is not a fish inspector* (1975), *Red dust* (1978), and *What can't be changed shouldn't be mourned* (1990)—all of which draw on his knowledge of the Icelandic communities near Gimli. In the short stories Valgardson's spare and rigorously concrete style mirrors both the cold, brittle landscape in which the stories are set and the harsh fates that befall most of the central characters. Occasionally, however, they are marred by endings that strain for subtlety. *Gentle sinners* departs from the realism of the stories to give mythological complexity to the familiar theme of a country boy's struggle against the corruption of town life. In contrast, *The girl with the Botticelli face* is a rather disagreeable novel about a troubled, misogynistic, recently divorced man whose hatred of women, particularly his ex-wife, is at odds with his claimed belief in love and acceptance. Valgardson is also the author of books for children and young people: *Sarah and the people of the Sand River* (1996), *Garbage Creek and other stories* (1997), *The divorced kids club and other stories* (1999), and *Frances* (2000), a delightful story about Frances Sigurdsson who discovers in an old family trunk her Icelandic great-grandmother's diary. When translated, it reveals family secrets and, more importantly, puts her in touch with her heritage.

Van Camp, Richard. See ABORIGINAL LITERATURE: 4, 5.

Vanderhaeghe, Guy (b. 1951). Born and raised in Esterhazy, Saskatchewan, he majored in history at the University of Saskatchewan (B.A., 1971; M.A., 1975) and pursued further studies at the University of Regina (B.Ed., 1978). Since 1993 he has been visiting professor of English at the University of Saskatchewan. He has received honorary D. Litts from the University of Saskatchewan and York University, Toronto, and was appointed an Officer of the Order of Canada in 2003. He lives in Saskatoon.

Influenced by such prairie novelists as Margaret LAURENCE, Sinclair ROSS, and Robert KROETSCH, Vanderhaeghe began writing short stories in the late 1970s. The twelve stories in *Man descending* (1982, GGA; rpr. 2000)—ranging in setting from the drought and economic depression of the Prairies in the 1930s to Jubilee year in London—follow in a roughly chronological pattern, from childhood to old age, the pain and disillusionment of various male protagonists as they struggle to transcend their fear and loneliness. Suffused with compassion and subtle humour, Vanderhaeghe's compelling fiction belongs in the prairie tradition to which he is indebted. He collected a number of his earlier short fictions in *The trouble with heroes* (1983, rpr. 1986), a title that signals his preoccupation with heroes and notions of heroism in both the

classical and the contemporary worlds. What unites these complex forays through time and space is Vanderhaeghe's uniformly affirmative vision of the stubbornness of the human spirit; each story can be read as a brief testament to the determination of individuals to survive physically, emotionally, and spiritually even when circumstances prove bleak and unforgiving. Indeed, in these stories some truer heroism proves to lie in the survival of life, rather than just in the survival of death, in 'the stubborn refusal of men and women to submit to circumstances'. *Things as they are?* (1992, rpr. 1993) is made up of ten polished stories that reflect on what one character describes as 'the pitiless refusal to delude oneself' and to see clearly in order to struggle towards the 'acceptance of things as they are'.

In the 1980s Vanderhaeghe turned to writing novels. *My present age* (1984, rpr. 2000) centres on Ed, a 'man descending', who was already developed in the final two stories of the first collection. Abandoned by his wife Victoria, Ed, an existential anti-hero of the 1980s, embarks on a quixotic quest to find her, the quest becoming his journey back into his own past and his comic and painful confrontations with his own self-deceptions. In *Homesick* (1989, rpr. 1993) Vanderhaeghe returned to the deeply troubled and troubling setting of eastern Saskatchewan. At the novel's centre is the strong-willed Vera Monkman, a widow and the mother of a young boy. A complex and compelling story of her fitful reunion with her father, an aging widower, and of the prairie community in which she lives, *Homesick* probes the often exhausting emotional dynamics of individuals and communities whose sense of 'home' is marked by equal parts longing and claustrophobic terror. Vanderhaeghe's third novel, *The Englishman's boy* (1996, GGA; rpr. 1997), is composed of two casually linked and masterfully entwined stories: the cold-blooded massacre of an encampment of Assiniboine at Cypress Hills in 1873 (based on a historical incident) in which 'the Englishman's boy' was involved, and the wholly fictional recounting of a 1920s Hollywood mogul's obsessive drive to manipulate this event in support of his own morally degraded social vision. Serving this mogul is Harry Vincent, a relocated Saskatchewan native whose own moral passivity and stalled writing career render him the stereotypical Canadian foil to the American's powerful revisionist impulse. Hired to track down the elusive Shorty McAdoo, a cowboy extra and reputed 'Indian fighter' who may (or may not) know the 'true' story of the sadistic massacre, Vincent remains woefully unwilling or unable to scrutinize his own complicity as an increasingly sinister chain of events unfolds around him. Vanderhaeghe eschews his usual comic overtones in *The Englishman's boy* in order to foreground the intense though characteristically understated ironies permeating the lives and stories of his main characters. It is an accomplished work, displaying his ear for well-tuned dialogue, his sensitivity to language and sparse rhythms, and his apparently effortless evocation of character, and of sharply contrasting times and places. *The last crossing* (2002) is an epic novel, beginning in England, that takes a caravan of ill-assorted people in 1871 from Fort Benton, Montana, across the 'Medicine Line', the border between the United States and Canada. The central character is Charles Gaunt, a painter, who is sent by his father—with his brother Addison—to search for Charles's twin brother Simon, who has disappeared (having joined a missionary, the Rev. Obadiah Witherspoon, to convert the American Indians). Addington takes command of the mission, but his fecklessness works against it; he is mainly interested in hunting and adventure and eventually becomes deranged (he has syphilis). They are joined by Custis Straw, a veteran of the American Civil War who reads his Bible while drinking whiskey and longs for Lucy Stoveall. When both her parents died, young Lucy Dray was left with her thirteen-year-old sister Madge; her landlord gives them 'a month to get off the property.' What could she do but marry Abner Stoveall, who was older than her father, and submit to his ill treatment, while discovering that his eighty acres were actually owned by his younger brother Wisdom. 'It was hard to learn my husband was a liar, and worse, a lazy liar.' Fortunately he abandons Lucy. It is when Madge is raped and murdered that Lucy joins the Gaunt brothers, hoping to find the murderer, and becomes the cook for the expedition. There are four narrators—Charles Gaunt, Custis, Lucy, and Aloysius, a bartender friend of Custis—and periodically a third-person narrative. Jerry Potts, partly Scots and partly Blackfoot, joins them as a valuable guide. (A real, extraordinary person, he is the subject of a biography.) He is capable of scalping: 'A quick cut, a foot braced to the corpse, a sharp tug, and the hair ripped free. The blood froze dark to the blade of his skinning knife.' 'And what am I to call you now?' his wife Mary asks him. 'Jerry Potts or Bear Child? What do you wish to be, White or Kanai?// She knew his secret. He wanted to be both and could

not pardon her for reminding him of the impossibility of it.' Jerry Potts becomes 'the sensitive antennae of the caravan.' *The last crossing* is a rich novel, filled with believable characterizations—all four narrators have different voices—and its well-handled play of incidents, stories, romance, suspense, and events (some of them violent) holds the interest from beginning to end, which is satisfying. In retrospect the novel may seem stuffed with material the author found in his research that he could not persuade himself to omit, but never mind. It's all compelling—perhaps Vanderhaeghe's most admirable achievement as a novelist.

He has also published two plays that garnered critical and public attention: *I had a job I liked, once* (1992) and *Dancock's dance* (1996). In the former, which was first performed at Saskatoon's Persephone Theatre in 1991, a police station serves as the setting for a young man's confrontation with the law; his interrogation by a rule-conscious sergeant leads the officer to the painful discovery of the impossibility of passing judgement. In the latter, which was first performed at the Persephone in 1995, the setting is the Saskatchewan Hospital for the Insane during the great flu epidemic of 1918. The inmates, led by the shell-shocked Lieutenant John Dancock, take over the hospital's nursing and administrative duties and teach a rigid superintendent the relative impossibility of strict codes of conduct and the need for human and humane compassion.

Van der Mark, Christine (1917–69). Born in Calgary, she attended Normal School and taught for five years in rural Alberta schools. She then completed a B.A. and M.A. at the University of Alberta, studying creative writing under F.M. Salter. In 1946 she submitted her first novel, *In due season*, as her thesis, and it was published the next year (it was reprinted in 1966). It explores, from a distinctive female point of view, the human costs of pioneering. Its protagonist develops a farm in the northern Alberta bush and raises a family through the 1930s with no help from her amiably shiftless husband. In the process she becomes hard and unscrupulous, alienating her neighbours and losing her daughter to a Métis sweetheart. A vivid and convincing evocation of northern life, the novel won the Oxford-Crowell prize for Canadian fiction. During three years of writing and university teaching van der Mark married, and from 1953 to 1964 her husband's work led the family to Montreal, Pakistan, the USA, England, and the Sudan, before they settled in Ottawa. Despite her many travels she continued writing stories, articles, and in 1960 she began *Honey in the rock* (1966). It is less elemental and more social in its emphasis than *In due season*. Interweaving the romantic awakenings and frustrations of a tightly knit community of Brethren in Christ in southern Alberta in 1936–7, it has moments of dramatic intensity; but the plot dissipates its force in complications, and the setting lacks the compelling quality of her first novel.

van Herk, Aritha (b. 1954). Born in Wetaskiwin, Alberta, to Dutch immigrant parents, she studied at the University of Alberta (B.A., 1977; M.A., 1978). Her first published short story won a significant award in 1976 and her first novel, *Judith* (1978), won the $50,000 Seal Books First Novel Award. Since 1983 she has taught at the University of Calgary, where in 1991 she was appointed professor of Canadian literature and creative writing and is now University Professor. *Judith*, the story of a young woman's awakening into feminist consciousness as a secretary/mistress-turned-pig-farmer (a revisioned Circe), launched van Herk's career as a bawdy/body images-of-women novelist whose work merges mythic and historical women with contemporary feminist heroines. Judith struggles with an inheritance that would insist she remain 'Judy', as she comes to terms with her eroticized relationships with her father, her boss, her neighbours' son, and herself. The novel reduces formal experiment to a disturbing narrative slippage between the present and past selves of the protagonist, Judith/Judy, to illustrate her struggle with the stereotypes of Daddy's girl, boss's mistress, spinster farmer, and potential wife. Van Herk's second novel, *The tent peg* (1981), fuses the Biblical Jael with J.L., a young woman who disguises herself as a man in order to be hired as cook to a geological survey team working in the Far North. There, once her gender identity is known, the story seems less about her search for independence (it comes remarkably easily) and more about how her presence mythically transforms the lives of the men with whom she works. Van Herk's own experience in the North, as well as her love/hate affair with the masculine penchant for naming, mapping, and mining the land, receives its first fictional treatment in this novel. She returned to these matters in her most bawdy novel, *No fixed address: an amorous journey* (1986), a picaresque journey that reverses the usual gender dynamics of the genre with its sexually aggressive, multi-talented heroine Arachne Manteia, pantyless regional sales rep for Ladies' Comfort Limited, specializing in women's underwear. This job supplies the material reason for Arachne's travels, but the psychic reason is that Arachne loves motion for its illusion of escape from her constricted possibilities as a woman, and the opportunity it affords for mapless intercourse with the land and actual intercourse with as many different types of men as possible. Arachne eventually disappears off the map into the Far North, leaving only a trail of coloured panties behind her. Travel has occupied the life of the narrator (a courier) of *Restlessness* (1998), the first sentence of which is 'I am alone in a room with the man who has agreed to kill me.' The room is in the Palliser Hotel, Calgary, and the novel is made up of reminiscences, brief meditations, reflections on the places she has visited, and conversations with her hired assassin, Derrik Atman, an intelligent, sensitive, companionable man: they go out for a walk, have dinner, talking all the time. It is a mesmerizing novel that takes place over a few hours that are suffused with tension: from beginning to end the reader awaits the narrator's signal for an act that will cause the death she craves. *Places far from Ellesmere: a geografiction: explorations on site* (1990) is a fusion of autobiography, travel book, fiction, and criticism, the latter in the form of an extended essay on *Anna Karenina*. Taking herself and Anna (in Tolstoy's novel) to Ellesmere Island offers revisionist opportunities similar to those in her earlier work, but in more theorized and personalized forms. Novelist turned historian, van Herk published *Mavericks: an incorrigible history of Alberta* (2001), a hefty book in a large format that attests both to her abilities as a researcher and a writer (it is very readable) and to her devotion, both loving and critical, to her native province. The first chapter is entitled 'Aggravating, Awful, Awkward, Awesome Alberta'. *Audacious and adamant: the story of maverick Alberta* (2007) is a slim illustrated version of this book.

A blend of the theoretical, personal, fictional, and critical is the hallmark of van Herk's two collections of essays, *In visible ink: crypto-frictions* (1991) and *A frozen tongue* (1992), where the writer-as-critic engages in dialogue and debate with her multiple and conflicting predecessors/contemporaries, particularly writers from the Canadian West. These essays are stylistic and self-consciously gendered rivals to Robert KROETSCH's essays on similar themes. See *Aritha van Herk: essays on her works* (2001) edited by Christl Verduyn.

van Vogt, A. E. (1912–2000). Alfred Elton van Vogt was born to parents of Dutch ancestry in Winnipeg, and raised in Neville and

Swift Current, Saskatchewan, and then in Morden and Winnipeg, Manitoba. He wrote his earliest science-fiction and fantasy stories in the Winnipeg Public Library before moving to Ottawa, where he was employed by the Department of National Defence. He then lived for two years in Toronto. Van Vogt's first story, 'Black destroyer', appeared in the July 1939 issue of *Astounding Science Fiction*, along with stories by Robert A. Heinlein and Isaac Asimov, and this conjunction of talents marked the beginning of SF's so-called Golden Age. *Transgalactic* (2006), edited by Eric Flint and David Drake, contains the original stories that van Vogt wrote for that magazine, 'not the later versions which A.E. van Vogt reworked for various novelizations.' The stories appear under the collective titles *Clane of Linn*, *The Ezwal*, and *Mission to the stars*. With 'Black destroyer'—subsequently included in *The voyage of the Space Beagle* (1950)—van Vogt found his métier: incident-packed prose, concepts galore, superhuman conflict, heroic action to save civilization if not entire solar systems, and dream-like logic. He wrote some 600,000 words of fantastic fiction during the Canadian years, including much of his most imaginative prose. Between 1940 and 1942 he published in magazines the original versions of *The wagon shops of Isher* (1951), an epic of libertarianism, and *Slan* (1946, rev. 1951), a classic novel of the persecution of a mutant whose telepathic powers hold the key to the survival of individualism. *Slan hunter* (2007), unfinished when van Vogt died, was completed by Kevin J. Anderson.

In 1944 van Vogt immigrated to the United States and lived in Hollywood, California, where he was briefly associated with Dianetics and Scientology. He wrote more than fifty novels and collections of stories, including *The world of Null-A* (1948), *The war against the Rull* (1959), *The Silkie* (1969), and *The battle of forever* (1971). As he once explained, 'Science fiction, as I personally try to write it, glorifies man and his future.'

Vassanji, M. G. (b. 1950). Moyez G. Vassanji was born in Nairobi, Kenya, and grew up in Dar es Salaam, Tanzania. He moved to the United States, where he studied physics at the Massachusetts Institute of Technology (B.Sc., 1974) and at the University of Pennsylvania (Ph.D., 1978). He came to Canada in 1978 to work in the nuclear lab at Chalk River, Ontario, and in 1980 moved to Toronto (where he now lives with his family), lecturing in physics at the University of Toronto until 1989, when he became a full-time writer.

Vassanji began his literary career—for which he was made a Member of the Order of Canada in 2004—with the publication in 1989 of his novel *The gunny sack*. *No new land* (1991, rpr. 1997), set in Toronto, deals with the immigrant community in the suburb of Don Mills, and recalls the Indians from East Africa whose mistreatment in Uganda inspired a mass exodus. His novel *The book of secrets* (1994, rpr. 1997) won the first GILLER PRIZE. At the end of the first chapter of *No new land* the narrator claims that 'we are but creatures of our origins, and however stalwartly we march forward … the ghosts from our past stand not far behind and are not easily shaken off.' These ghosts were Vassanji's preoccupation in his early fiction as he attempted to reclaim the past and give expression to the experiences of his community that migrated from India to East Africa at the turn of the century. The need to portray the complexity of his Indian community in Africa gives to his writing a sense of urgency, commitment, and a strong referential surface. Vassanji combines realism in *The book of secrets*, but his fiction took a different direction in *Amriika* (1999, rpr. 2000)—'America' was pronounced thus by the narrator's grandmother in Dar es Salaam—which relates the life, from 1968 through the nineties, of Ramji, a Muslim immigrant student from Tanzania who first lives with an Episcopalian couple in New Jersey, and then begins his attempt to adjust to, and understand, America. The period includes student politics, protests against the Vietnam war, his marriage, an affair, Iranian exiles versus Muslim fundamentalists, other immigrants from Tanzania—and mystery and violence.

Vikram Lall, the narrator of *The in-between life of Vikram Lall* (2003, rpr. 2004), tells the story of his life when he is a middle-aged man living in Ontario. He was born in 1945 and grew up in Kenya, a British protectorate, where his Indian parents lived in Nakuru, running a grocery store. It is 1953, the Coronation year, and the revolutionary Mau Mau are running rampant, murdering entire English families. But eight-year-old Vikram, called Vic, is having a happy childhood, playing with his younger sister Deepa and friends Bill Blair and his sister Annie (whom Vic loves), and Njoroge, grandson of the gardener, a black Kikuyu (he loves Deepa)—their games echo their identities. There is a traumatic crisis when the Blair family is slaughtered by the Mau Mau. Vic, deeply affected, is unable to love as he grows up. 'There was a frozen core buried deep inside me that I could not dislodge or melt.' Colonial Kenya achieves independence, which is betrayed by tribal rivalries and corrupt politicians, including Jomo Kenyatta (a former Mau Mau)—who is released from prison and appointed president of Kenya, and with whom Lall becomes associated as a money launderer. Lall always felt 'in-between', even as a child, when his playmates were genuine and he was 'in the middle', and later when he tried to protect the lovers Deepa and Njoroge, and as a brown Asian with white English people and black Africans on either side. The Ontario frame of the story is slight: Deepa sends Joseph, Njoroge's son (by his wife Mary), to attend university in Toronto and tells Lall on the phone: 'You are his family there, Vic. ... Be his anchor when he needs you.' While *The in-between world of Vikram Lall* has its ups and downs as an ambitious narrative, it offers a compelling portrait of Kenya in the fifties and sixties, along with countless memorable moments, emotional and political. The novel won for Vassanji his second Giller Prize. *The assassin's song* (2007) begins on the birthday of Karsan Dargawalla, aged eleven, when he is taken for a stroll by Bapu-ji, his father, the 'lord and keeper' of the Sufi shrine Pirbaag—'as was his father before him, as were all our ancestors for many centuries.' (The shrine honours Nur Fazal, and several chapters dated 1260 tell *his* story.) Young Karsan is weighed down by 'a heaviness of the heart' when he realizes that it was intended that he would be his father's successor. As he grows up he longs to be 'ordinary', to experience the outside world; to his surprise he achieves this ambition in the 1970s when he wins a scholarship to Harvard University to study English literature. This, of course, changes his life. 'America of those days is a blurry experience now, its narratives interweaving, shifting perspectives. So much happened so fast.' He marries Marge Thompson, an Indian Canadian, earns his doctorate, becomes a professor at Simon Fraser University in Burnaby, British Columbia, and has a son (their happiness is short-lived). In February 2002 Karsan's father writes him a long, touching letter: 'My son, I have this one wish of you: that you return to Pirbaag once and let your father set his eyes on you again. Will you come? Let me know. But right now is not a good time to come; we are going through bestial times yet again [i.e., communal violence between Hindus and radical Muslims]; demons are on the roam feeding on blood and the screams of the innocent.... Your father, who longs for you.' Karsan replies that he will come in the summer, but six weeks later his brother Mansoor tells him in a

telegram that their father is dead. Karsan returns to India and enters a whole new world, with echoes from his youth. Books tell him about the Assassins, a controversial medieval Shia sect 'who disdained the outer forms of worship and the Muslim laws of Sharia for inner spiritual truths.' From mountain fortresses in western Persia they set out to murder or intimidate their enemies. (Karsan decides that Nur Fazal had been an Assassin.) There is a massacre at Pirbaag and the shrine is devastated. Karsan says finally: 'I am the caretaker of Pirbaag. I do advise people on their worldly affairs when called upon and supervise some projects in the town.... But here I stop, to begin anew. For the call has come for me, again, and as Bapu-ji would say, this time I must bow.' Much of *The assassin's song* is fictional. Nur Fazal and the shrine of Pirbaag, and the characters, are all fictional; but Vissanji's novel embraces, and persuades the reader about, a stretch of periods, unfamiliar customs, generational cultural conflicts, family dissensions and loyalties, in an engaging narrative whose ethnic complexities are masterfully surmounted.

A witty and poignant collection of short stories, *Uhuru Street*, set in Dar es Salaam, came out in 1992. The stories in *When she was queen* (2005) make use of memory, displacement, and immigration in various ways to produce absorbing, tight narratives. The title story begins with the sentence: 'My father lost my mother one evening in a final round of gambling at the poker table.' The narrator learns from his sisters that wealthy John Chacha bid his mansion against the wife of Rashid. 'If I have a palace, you have the Queen of Kisumu.' Rashid lost. When he protests, Chacha says: 'I could have lost, and you would have won my house.... I won your wife for a night, Rashid. Tonight I'll send a car for her.' The narrator wonders if Chacha was his real father. Years later, when his elderly mother is living in Don Mills and the Chachas live in Scarborough, he seeks out John Chacha and learns what happened that evening when his mother went to him. The story has a surprising ending that is both ingenious and satisfying. The first sentence of 'The sky to stop us' is 'His wife had left him.' She left a note: 'I want to think things over for myself.' Nazir is incredulous and irritated—he was 'right in the midst of a major deal, worth millions....' When striving to go from rags to riches, he told his wife: 'Where we're going there's only the sky to stop us.' As he thinks about the success he has achieved, the riches he has garnered, his emotional neglect of his wife and children becomes clear (but only to the reader). He phones his son Shaf in Montreal and asks him to tell him where his mother is. 'I can't, Dad. I promised.' The ending simply confirms the justice of Nazir's wife's abandonment. A long, surprising story is 'Elvis, Raja', about classmates Rusty (Rustam Mehta) from Bombay and Diamond from Nairobi, who meet years later when Diamond, who lives in Toronto, looks up Rusty who is a professor in a college three hours away from Chicago. 'I'm one of the pioneers in Elvis Studies in this country,' he says. 'It wasn't easy to get my course accepted, I can tell you that.' Diamond stays with the Mehtas and one evening they have a 'séance' with an ouija board and Elvis Raja is summoned and spells out satisfactory answers to Rusty's questions. Rusty shows Diamond his extravagant 'shrine' to Elvis. In addition to all this, Vassanji cleverly and smoothly incorporates many details of the Mehtas' and Diamond's family life.

In 2008 Vassanji published *Place within: rediscovering India,* an interesting collage made up of journal entries from several visits, family narratives, myths and legends, and beautifully written descriptions and observations. The next year he published *Mordecai Richler* (2009) in Penguin Canada's Extraordinary Canadians Series.

Véhicule Press. It began in the summer of 1973 as a small printing and literary publishing co-op in the back room of the Véhicule Art Gallery in Montreal, sustaining itself with printing jobs for the artistic community and LIP (Local Initiative Program) money. Simon Dardick joined the co-op in the fall of 1973. In 1979 Véhicule was accepted into the block-grant program of the CANADA COUNCIL. Dardick and his wife Nancy Marelli became publishers when the printing company was dissolved in 1981. Véhicule publishes Canadian poetry and fiction, and a series that documents Québec's social history. Among poetry books published (with the imprint Signal Editions, edited by Carmine Starnino) are *White stone: the Alice poems* by Stephanie BOLSTER, *Helix: new and selected poems* by John STEFFLER; *Heresies: the complete poems of Anne WILKINSON 1924–1961*; and *How we all swiftly,* comprising the first six books by Don COLES. The noted historian Marcel TRUDEL is also represented, in translation, by *Memoirs of a less-travelled road: a historian's life.*

Victims of tyranny, The (2 vols, Buffalo, 1847). This early Canadian novel by Charles E. Beardsley is a republican's version of the political and personal conflicts in the brief public career of a young Irish immigrant to York (Toronto), Upper Canada. The hero, Joseph Wilcox, is a thinly disguised representation of the actual Joseph Willcocks, a member of the legislative assembly and critic of government who was killed fighting with the Americans in the War of 1812. Wilcox is presented as a romantic paragon, a champion of truth and justice and tragic victim of the forces of self-serving oligarchy—the 'Family Compact', epitomized by the Rev. Whifler, the principal antagonist, and Mr Carleton (caricatures of the Rev. John Strachan and Provincial Secretary William Jarvis). These power-obsessed villains eventually provoke Wilcox's enlistment with the invading American forces and he is ultimately killed while championing republican ideas. The compression of events, covering more than a decade in the space of several months, heightens the drama of the novel. One of its more engaging characters, ironically, is Sam Johnson—to his unresourceful creator a resourceful and witty model American, clearly patterned on the stereotyped Sam Slick of Thomas Chandler HALIBURTON. Though characterization tends towards caricature, and dialogue towards diatribe, and though the novel's concluding section is too diffuse, *The victims of tyranny* is nonetheless an impassioned and provocative narrative of actual characters and events from early Canadian history. The author, about whom nothing is known, was apparently a member of the republican branch of an American family divided by the American Revolution. The Loyalist branches of the Beardsleys settled in New Brunswick and Upper Canada, where the men became prominent lawyers, and maintained contact with the American branches. The knowledge of the internal affairs of York and Upper Canada displayed in the novel suggests that Beardsley must have lived, for a while at least, in Toronto. He very likely had his novel published in Buffalo because he could not find a Toronto publisher.

Viets, Roger (1738–1811). Born in Simsbury, Connecticut, he prepared himself for Church of England orders at Yale College, graduating in 1758. After several years as a lay reader, he was ordained in London in 1763 and returned to Simsbury, where he was parish priest until he immigrated to Nova Scotia as a Loyalist refugee in late 1785. During the American Revolution, Viets had remained loyal to the monarchy and was jailed in 1777 on suspicion of aiding British fugitives. Upon immigrating to Nova Scotia he was assigned to the parish of Digby, a new Loyalist town, and served there as rector of Trinity Church until his death. He published six sermons between 1787 and 1800, and left a large collection in manuscript form. His theology was orthodox and not particularly challenging intellectually, but in their logical clarity and persuasive rhetoric his sermons reveal a strong, active, passionate mind as they project a vision of an ordered, cohesive society bound together by unanimity and mutual respect. The implication is that all the fundamental elements of human happiness lie within the reach of the Loyalist refugees. Viets' *Annapolis Royal, a poem* (Halifax, 1788), written in the same vein, is of historical interest as the first separate imprint of verse written and published in what is now Canada. The author's emphasis falls on harmony—in nature, in man, in the universe—and the image that emerges is therefore idyllic; but the poem explicitly integrates life in Loyalist Nova Scotia into the vision of emotional, moral, and spiritual contentment that was central to prevailing eighteenth-century views of human experience and social purpose. The poem is inspirational because it asserts that the recently dispossessed refugees are not isolated from the mainstream of human civilization. T.B. Vincent has edited a modern edition of this poem (1979).

Villemaire, Yolande (b. 1949). Born in Saint-Augustin, Comté des Deux-Montagnes, near Montreal, she holds a B.A. in dramatic art (1970) and an M.A. in literary studies (1974) from the Université du Québec à Montréal. Beginning in 1974 she taught literature at the Rosemont CEGEP. A prolific feminist writer—playwright, novelist, and poet—Villemaire is best known for her 1980 novel *La vie en prose* (not available in English), which caused a sensation because of its exuberance and formal experimentation. At once a novel, poem, and essay, it presents several female characters—members of a women's editorial collective—in a chronicle in which lives lived and written collide. Only four of Villemaire's books have been translated. The poems in *Quartz and micea* (1987), Judith Cowan's translation of *Quartz et mica* (1985), relate to the poet's stay in New York. In *Amazon angel* (1993), Gérald Leblanc's translation of *Ange amazone* (1982), Villemaire pursues the exploration of writing that began with *La vie en prose*. It is a colourful fantasy in which the Amazon angel travels through time, touching the lives of women and men in the past and the future. Two

novels, both translated by Leonard Sugden, trace the upheavals of the inner life and the movements from place to place of young Montreal artist Miliana Tremblay. She is in The Netherlands in *Midnight tides of Amsterdam* (2003—*La déferlante d'Amsterdam*, published in the same year)—having left her lover Dragan. She roams the streets, canals, and museums of Amsterdam, finds she's pregnant, makes friends with other artists, and visits, among other places, Delft: 'As soon as she gets off the train at the station.... Miliana is struck by a feeling of déjà vu. She meanders along the canal as far as the Oudekerk, allowing the muffled noon-time church bells to guide her along and make her heart beat thunderously ... she recognizes this house, this bridge, this door and the colour of the sky. Vermeer, of course! It's because of Vermeer.' Toward the end of the novel Dragan appears—a friend had phoned and told him Miliana was pregnant. The book ends when they make love. '...she rolls with her Centaur in this garden of happiness while the wind blows relentlessly upon Amsterdam.... She abandons herself once again and her cry is an unfurling of love, a billowing of shadow and of desire.' Dragan turns up on the first page of *Poets and centaurs* (2006)—the translation of *Poètes et centaures* (2003)—along with Miliana's baby Atalanti, whom Dragan adores and regularly looks after, for he and Miliana no longer live together. There is a trip to Mexico—she exhibits her paintings at a Symposium of Poets of the Latin World (and spends a night with the Mexican poet Carlos Esteban Flores). A man who calls himself Aladin, whom she knew in Europe, makes love to her in Montreal. (Villemaire's descriptions of sexual passion are vivid.) Dreams and memories of Miliana's travels, of her past and echoes of her present, unfold occasionally in italicized prose poems that are perhaps enabling her to come to terms not only with her past but with her roles as mother, artist, and lover.

Virgo, Séan (b. 1940). Born in Mtarfa, Malta, to an Anglo-Irish family, Virgo has experienced the picaresque lifestyle of Ireland's Travelling People (Gypsies). He has lived in England (B.A., University of Nottingham), Greece, Ireland, and finally, beginning in 1966, in various parts of Canada—always looking for a possible state of grace. (He now lives in rural Saskatchewan.) He has earned his living from writing, and from teaching at various Canadian universities. In 2008, the hundredth anniversary of the birth of Roderick HAIG-BROWN, the University of Victoria appointed

Virgo the Haig-Brown Writer in Residence (from 15 Sept. to 15 Dec.).

Virgo's collections of poetry—*Pieces for the old earth man* (1973); *Island* (1975), with Paul and Lutia Lauzon; *Kiskatinaw songs* (1977), with Susan MUSGRAVE; *Deathwatch on Skidegate Narrows* (1979); and *Selected poems* (1992)—resonate with the influences of Native culture and spirit religion from time spent in the Queen Charlotte Islands (Haida Gwaii) of British Columbia. In these books Virgo is the medium for a fusion of both Celtic and Aboriginal voices. His style—clean, cryptic, and allusive—is almost liturgical in its artful simplicity. In Virgo's fiction—*White lies and other fictions* (1979), *Through the eyes of a cat: Irish stories* (1983), *Selakhi* (1987), *Wormwood* (1989), *White lies ... plus two* (1990), *Waking in Eden* (1990), and the chapbook story *The scream of the butterfly* (1996), an account of a metaphysical experience on the west coast of Vancouver Island—the poetic dialectic of innocence and experience is his machinery for confabulation. *Selakhi* is a recreation of the life of the artist Paul Rimbaud. Central to every story is lost or potential salvation and apocalyptic intimations that forever threaten the human and natural order. *A traveller came by: stories about dying* (2000) is made up of eleven of Virgo's stories, five of them new. Even though it is about death and dying, the long, eloquent introduction has a cheerful component—it opens with a descriptions of the idyllic setting of Lesbos, where Virgo was finishing a novel, and describes new friends made there, one of whom is a doctor, 'a healer of the dying'. Virgo says he has 'continued to write about dying, and death. I don't know why—I'm in no way a morbid person, and the stories have always been about people, not victims, as far as I'm concerned, and quite often tinged by laughter.' They are good stories, the work of a fine writer. Each one begins with a prelude explaining how and why it came to be written. The title story—along with 'Keepsakes' and 'The scream of the butterfly'—is included in Virgo's *Begging questions* (2006), in which some of the stories are mannered, arch, possessing a degree of incomprehensibility that stands in the way of reading enjoyment. 'Delivered by hand' is a long letter addressed to Madame Doctor Deputy, between whom (and her brother), and the letter writer, there is a mysterious, perhaps sinister estrangement. When he attempts to visit her, she says: 'Are you mad? ... //Well, Madame Doctor, disgrace may be a disease, old age may be contemptible, but do they add up to madness?'... 'Our country is less than a century old; it is falling

apart in your hands. You are willing to let this happen....' The 'Idea', apparently a potent force, is referred to several times without explanation. The narrator says: '...we are all just Songbirds... I am a Blackbird... And we shared the land... with many others. With the Sparrows, the Robins, the Larks and the Canaries—and in the later years of the Idea, with the migrant Whitethroats....' The letter ends with: 'I was your uncle, your sponsor, your benefactor.//This curse upon both of you.' The title story is made up of disconnected episodes—personal memories of the narrator (who is a woman, though one assumes in the first few pages that it is a man). She has a Greek father and an English mother (who 'said she had Gypsy blood, maybe that's why she fell for a Greek. My father laughed and said all Greeks hate Gypsies, it couldn't be that.') When she asks her father why there were not other children in the family, his answer is different from her mother's. 'But who was lying to whom, she wondered.//And that is a begging question.' Other questions in the narrative are followed by the parenthesis (B.Q.). The next episode features one of the two people 'I'm most grateful to in the world.... Herant Gavilian. The sad Maestro. He seduced me when I was 14, after I met him in the Railway Café.'

'A Mother's dead face on a pillow is all Begging Questions rolled into One.'

'All at once I am blessed with ignorance. Is that not, B.Q., what Sanctuary must mean? How can you pity yourself when there's still so much you don't know?'

Virgo edited *The eye in the thicket* (2002), fifteen essays on natural history and the world of nature. The writers include Barry CALLAGHAN, Patrick LANE, Don McKAY, Susan MUSGRAVE, and Jan ZWICKY. The title is from a line in Zwicky's poem 'Recovery': 'The wren's bright eye in the thicket.'

Visser, Margaret (b. 1940). Margaret Lloyd was born in South Africa; came to Canada with her husband, Colin Visser, in 1964; and was educated at the University of Toronto (B.A., 1970; M.A., 1973; Ph.D., 1980). As a teacher of classics, she was course director at York University, Toronto (1976–9, 1982–8) and research fellow in the Department of Classics (1988–93). She lives in Toronto, Paris, and the south of France. As a writer, Visser is a socioanthropologist and a historian of culture. The first sentence of her first book—'The extent to which we take everyday objects for granted is the precise extent to which they govern and inform our lives'—could be the starting point for her books about everyday things that are familiar to us all, and that receive illumination and new meaning from her learned accounts of them. *Much depends on dinner* (1986, rpr. 1997, 2000)—the title is from Byron's *Don Juan*: 'Since Eve ate apples, much depends on dinner'—devotes a chapter to every ingredient in the following meal: corn with salt and butter; chicken with rice; lettuce with olive oil and lemon juice; ice cream. The result is a long and fascinating book. *The rituals of dinner: the origins, evolution, eccentricities, and meaning of table manners* (1991, rpr. 1992) is another substantial and highly readable study about 'how we eat, and why we eat as we do'. *The way we are* (1994, rpr. 1995) is made up of brief articles Visser wrote for the magazine *Saturday Night* on sixty ordinary subjects (including Santa Claus, spoonerisms, beards, tipping, vacations, parades, bells, taking a shower, tap-dancing, chewing gum). Visser's devotion to the traditions of the Roman Catholic Church informs *The geometry of love: space, time, mystery, and meaning in an ordinary church* (2000), the church being Rome's Sant' Agnese fuori le Mura, founded in 342 to honour the twelve-year-old Agnese, who was martyred in 305, and her placed of burial. This extraordinary study of one small church—covering, in many digressions, history, politics, theology, anthropology, art history and technology, iconography, hagiography, and folklore in exploring the meanings of the architectural details—reveals its 'language' against the background of the historical periods associated with its construction and enrichment. In 2008 Visser published *The gift of thanks: the roots, persistence, and paradoxical meanings of a social ritual.* Her typically erudite but very readable consideration of this subject has resulted in a large-format book that is long—458 pages including notes. In her Introduction she writes: 'The book takes seriously the plural form of the English word *thanks.* Through the variety of its contents it reflects the multi-faceted nature of gratefulness, starting with the simplest and apparently most trivial of its expressions, which is verbal thanking, and ending with gratitude at its highest level.'

In *Beyond fate* (2002), Visser's 2002 CBC Massey Lectures, she reflects on the meaning of fate, and the human tendency to believe in it and accept it. The titles of the five lectures are 'Drawing a line', 'Fate and the furies', 'Free fall', 'Transgression', and 'Beyond fate'.

Vizinczey, Stephen (b. 1933). Born in Káloz, Hungary, he had three youthful plays banned by Communist censors, but graduated with honours from Budapest's Academy of Theatre and Film Arts in the spring of the fateful year 1956. A few months later he was fighting in the revolution; not long after, with the revolutionaries defeated by the Soviets, he was on his way to the West. In retrospect, this early life presages his development as a romantic intellectual who injects contemporary ideas into works of wide popular appeal. By 1957 he was in Montreal, learning English while writing scripts for the National Film Board, and became a Canadian citizen. In 1961 he founded and edited a short-lived but much-admired magazine, *Exchange.* In the mid-1960s he wrote his first novel while working on CBC radio documentaries in Toronto. Discouraged by the tepid response of Canadian publishers, he created a one-book publishing company, Contemporary Canada Press, and brought out *In praise of older women: the amorous recollections of András Vajda* (1965, rpr. 2010), a crisply written account of a young man's sexual awakening, narrated by a Hungarian-born philosophy professor at the University of Saskatchewan. A celebrated bestseller in Canada, it eventually appeared in many translations, selling more than 5 million copies. In 2010 it was reprinted by Penguin Modern Classics—but not by Penguin Canada because Vizinczey could not come to terms with them. (*In praise of older women* was made into two feature films, in 1978 and 1997. In 2007 Vizinczey sued the producer of the 1978 film, Robert Lantos—who says in a DVD that it earned some $20 million—for his share of the film's gross, and received a settlement in six figures.) Shortly after his first novel was published Vizinczey moved to England—he lives in London with his wife Gloria—and began writing for, among other newspapers, *The Times* and the *Sunday Telegraph;* his essays have appeared in two impressive collections: *The rules of chaos* (1969) and *Truth and lies in literature* (1986). His long-awaited second novel, *An innocent millionaire* (1983), turned out to be a sweeping Balzacian view of modern American society, examining the Mafia, corporate polluters, and a corrupt justice system through the eyes of a young man who finds sunken treasure in the Caribbean. *The man with the magic touch* (1994) is a novel of social criticism influenced by magic realism. Vizinczey translated and introduced *Be faithful unto death* (1995), a Hungarian classic by Zsigmond Móricz, originally published in 1921.

Voaden, Herman (1903–91). Born in London, Ontario, he graduated from Queen's University, Kingston, in 1923 and then embarked on a long teaching career that included positions at Toronto's Central High School of Commerce (head of English, 1928–64), Queen's University, and the University of Toronto. In the 1920s Voaden was also active as a director and actor at Hart House Theatre, University of Toronto; the Detroit Repertory Theatre; and the Sarnia Little Theatre. In 1930–1 he studied drama at Yale University with George Pierce Baker, and later held several key administrative positions in Canadian arts organizations. He was made a Member of the Order of Canada in 1974. His career as a playwright began with the expressionist *Symphony: a drama of motion and light for a new theatre*, co-written with the painter Lowrie Warrener in 1930; it was published in the journal *Canadian Drama* in 1982. Rejecting what he saw as the mediocrity and stifling uniformity of contemporary theatre, he created in *Symphony* what he termed 'symphonic theatre', consisting of a striking coalescence of light, music, dance, and rhythmic speech. At Yale, Voaden wrote a realistic drama of the North called *Wilderness*—in *Canada's last plays: the developing mosaic*, vol.3 (1980) edited by Anton Wagner; a revised version, *Rocks*, first produced in 1932, again revealed Voaden's interest in dramatic innovation. The experimentation continued with *Earth song* (1976, prod. 1932), *Hill-land* (prod. 1934), and *Murder pattern* (1980, prod. 1936). *Murder pattern* (based on an actual Ontario murder case) is Voaden's best play, and combines a clear narrative line with drum-beats, chorus, and an expressionistic set and lighting. Adaptations and more original work followed. As a playwright Voaden remained isolated from predominant fashions and conventions; on the whole, his plays were too complex (and too expensive) for regular production. As an anthologist (he edited several anthologies) and as theatrical administrator and theorist, however, he had a vital and positive effect on the shape of twentieth-century Canadian theatre. *A vision of Canada: Herman Voaden's dramatic works 1928–1945* (1993), edited by Anton Wagner, contains a selection of Voaden's plays, together with a comprehensive and sympathetic introduction and several useful appendices.

Wachtel, Eleanor (b. 1947). She was born in Montreal and educated at McGill University (B.A., 1969, with a First Class Honours degree in English). She then joined a graduate program in journalism at Syracuse University (1969–70), which she disliked and did not complete. With her then-husband she lived in Kenya in 1973–4 and they moved in 1975 to Vancouver, where she began a freelance career. This included being an adjunct professor in women's studies at Simon Fraser University (1984–7); she was editor of the literary quarterly *Room of One's Own* (1976–1989); a contributing editor of *Books in Canada* (1976–89); and a theatre and film critic for CBC Radio, Vancouver (1979–1987). She now lives in Toronto. She is a Member of the Order of Canada and has received eight honorary degrees.

As a writer (who has contributed to numerous books) Wachtel wrote the Introduction to the 2008 edition of *Stones* by Timothy FINDLEY, the Foreword to *My life as a dame* (2008) by Christina McCALL, and important introductions to the collections of interviews mentioned below. Beginning in 1990, for CBC Radio, Wachtel has hosted 'Writers & Company', an apparently never-ending (one hopes) series of remarkable interviews with a galaxy of international writers, including many Canadians. The renown of her interviews—some of which stand as definitive revelations of the authors' distinction—is due to her literary knowledge, intellectual sensitivity, oral skills, and of course to her meticulous preparation for each interview. They have been published, so far, in the following collections (with partial lists of the authors interviewed): *Writers & Company* (1993)—Ozick, Banks, ONDAATJE, Oz, Byatt, MUNRO, Rushdie, Gordimer, ATWOOD, Lessing, Drabble); *More Writers & Company* (1996, rpr. 1997)—Sacks, Ishiguro, SHIELDS, Trevor, Said, Allende, Winterson, Walker, Doctorow, Erdrich, Harold Bloom, Fuentes, BROSSARD, Martin Amis, Kincaid, Berger; and *Original minds* (2003), which has a Foreword by Carol

Shields—Jonathan Miller, Goodall, Berto-lucci, Steiner, Tutu, Sontag, Steinem, Sacks, Jane Jacobs, Eco, Chomsky, and Bloom (for the second time). As an interviewer Wachtel is perhaps best described by Shields, who was often interviewed by her—they were friends: '...she enters into conversations, opens debates, sketches in background. She interprets and suggests, but never imposes. She projects curiosity, spontaneity, humour and goodwill. Her sense of respect, her tact, her utter lack of obsequiousness, even with the famous, and her uncanny ability to ask difficult questions—don't I know it!—have endeared her to readers and listeners.... Think of the moment when, instead of going on to another question, Eleanor pauses to consider the writer's last answer. "How so?" she asks and then the writer pauses too. The silence lingers. The listener wonders, what else is there to be said? And then comes the response: thoughtful, revealing. We sense the mind of the writer reaching into some zone of experience not before articulated. We admire the sweep of this mind, the way it connects ideas and feelings.' Wachtel's *Random illuminations: conversations with Carol Shields* (2007), containing interviews and some letters from Shields, is eloquent proof of the Shields/Wachtel bond.

Wacousta; or, The prophecy (3 vols, Edinburgh, 1832; NCL, CEECT). The complex plot of this Gothic forest romance by John RICHARDSON unfolds through surprise and flashback: each chapter opens with an astonishment that is followed by an explanation. Set in Fort Detroit during Pontiac's 1763 rollback of British power, the story is the culmination of a grievance that originated during the savaging of the Scottish Highlands following the defeat of the Jacobites in 1745. We learn at the novel's end that Sir Reginald Morton fell in love with the sequestered Clara Beverley while on occupation duty, only to lose her to the treachery of his friend, Charles De Haldimar. Through a frame-up, Morton also lost his commission. Two decades later, having fled to France and served as an officer in the famous battle on the Plains of Abraham in 1759, Morton has become the dreaded Wacousta, Pontiac's chief adviser during the siege of the fort commanded by De Haldimar. Wacousta's scheme of revenge, ultimately fatal, also ends in the deaths of De Haldimar, his younger son Charles, and his daughter Clara. With an epigraph from an eighteenth-century imitation of Elizabethan revenge tragedy, the novel depicts a noble spirit maddened by injustice,

whose scheme of vengeance exceeds in horror the original wrong. The violence and suspense that mark the narrative—the surefire formula of hushed expectancy broken by shock—coexist with tedious exposition and courtship scenes, and florid, crudely rhetorical dialogue: '"Almighty Providence," aspirated the sinking Clara... "can it be that the human heart can undergo such change?"' And '"Ha! ha! By heaven, such cold, pompous insolence amuses me," vociferated Wacousta.' Nevertheless *Wacousta's* intensity and energy, its moments of passion and high feeling, its depiction of nature as both comforting and monstrous, its sexually perverse undertones—and its development of the potential of Canadian space and time to include all this—have bestowed upon it a continuing critical interest. In addition, its garrison-versus-wilderness theme, and its ultimate moral equation of the two, have influenced much subsequent Canadian writing; its preoccupation with violence and terror and its inclusion of sexual perversity interest a contemporary public; and the sheer exuberance of its plotting appeals to a postmodern sensibility. Rather than sober speculation and representation, *Wacousta* resembles a nightmare: it embodies an aspect of the Canadian imagination in search of the fantastic and surreal. The current NEW CANADIAN LIBRARY edition is complete and unabridged. In 1987 the CENTRE FOR THE EDITING OF EARLY CANADIAN TEXTS published a scholarly edition, edited by D.R. Cronk. James REANEY's dramatization was staged in 1978. For *Wacousta: based on the novel by John Richardson* (2005) Helen Kirk produced a simplified, much shorter version of the novel in the interests of greater readability.

Waddington, Miriam (1917–2004). Miriam Dworkin was born into an intellectual Jewish family in Winnipeg, where she lived for fourteen years. She was educated at the University of Toronto (B.A., 1939), and studied social work in Toronto and Philadelphia. Married to Patrick Waddington (from whom she was later divorced), she had two sons. In 1945 she moved to Montreal, where she was active in social work and the literary life there, contributing to John SUTHERLAND's FIRST STATEMENT. In 1960 she moved back to Toronto, where she worked for the North York Family Service. She joined the English faculty at York University in 1964 and retired as a professor in 1983, becoming Professor Emeritus. She eventually moved to Vancouver.

Waddington's first collection of poems, *Green world* (1945), was published by First

Statement Press. In it and *The second silence* (1955), both of which celebrate childhood, greenness, and sun, her experiences are transmuted through traditions of fairy tale and of a pastoralism that suggests Blake, Wordsworth, and Archibald LAMPMAN. Her imagery is intense and visual. The more abstract social poems present a green world as an antidote to broken lives; in a world of lost vision she would have us move into suspended moments from the past, put on 'bandages of light'. Doors and windows offer thresholds to 'other selves' that we are invited to recover, and memory emerges in metaphors of water, presenting the need for descent and flow. In *The season's lovers* (1958), which uses set forms and a public voice to convey important truths, some messages snap aphoristically into place, while others trail off in irresolute language. The last, more metaphysical part works well with playful, intimate language. There is, however, a falling off from her earlier lyricism, which critics generally believe informs her best mode. *The glass trumpet* (1966) represents a great leap forward. Content to live with uncertainties and small topics, Waddington here presents life in touchingly simple words and finds a style that is whimsical and clever. The poems shove forward with gusto, becoming expressively staccato through a shift to very short, lightly punctuated lines, a departure she assigns in part to the influence of Gertrude Stein. She frees up sounds and meanings by breaking syllables across lines, and by using the line itself as a unit of meaning. *Say yes* (1969), affected by Apollinaire's experiments with the page, shows further formal departures: punctuation and capitalization virtually disappear, and the left margin begins to crumble; words disintegrate even more into new units and meanings; and the voice begins to imitate sounds for which we have no words. The modest claims and understatements in the love poems show Waddington's skill in finding symbolic weight in ordinary things. *Call them Canadians* (1968) includes humane poems (all untitled) in response to a set of photographs. *Dream telescope* (1972) lacks the charge of her best work, while *Driving home* (1972)—her 'Selected' poems, combined with forty-six pages of later material—contains only five or six outstanding new pieces. *The price of gold* (1976), *Mister Never* (1978), and *The visitants* (1981) contain excellent work and continue to articulate the centres of Waddington's poetry, though few poems reach the level of her writing in the 1960s. Several concerns that emerged in the 1970s—prophecy, feminism, and aging—occasionally turn into coyness or didacticism; but in these collections Waddington's lifelong outrage at injustice (which in her essays she attributes to her Jewish upbringing) takes on new life. In *Collected poems* (1986), which adds forty pages of 'Uncollected Poems' and includes the poems in *Call them Canadians*, Waddington, out of respect for history, chose to forgo 'both omissions and revisions' to her published material. The 'Afterword' is a brief but illuminating literary memoir. This was followed by the collection *The last landscape* (1992).

The short fiction in *Summer at Lonely Beach* (1982)—stories about initiation that are mainly anecdotal and meditative, with little dialogue—is close to poetry, making use of rapid summary and tenuous closures. Like many of Waddington's poems, the stories draw on her early childhood in southern Manitoba. Waddington has written valuable criticism in numerous reviews and essays, seeking to foster our appreciation of writing that addresses our cultural and political lives. Much of her prose has been gathered in *Apartment Seven: selected essays* (1989), in which she articulates her political idealism, her romantic aesthetics, and her abiding sense of what it is to be positioned as the outsider.

Wade, Bryan (b. 1950). Born in Sarnia, Ontario, he studied creative writing at the University of Victoria before taking an M.F.A. in motion pictures and television at the University of California in Los Angeles. He has written and directed for television and worked as a screenwriter. As a playwright he was especially prolific in the 1970s, writing surrealist fantasies typical of the period. The one-act play *Alias* (1974, prod. 1975) is characteristic: its cast includes the Lone Ranger (who is having an identity crisis), Tonto, and a mobile six-foot penis. Other one-act plays are *Lifeguard* (1973, prod. 1973) and *Electric gunfighters* (1976, prod. 1973). The dialogue of *Blitzkreig* (1974, prod. 1974), featuring Hitler and Eva Braun, alternates between lurid fantasies of sex and violence that seem merely self-indulgent and a banality that is quite chilling. The latter vein is more effectively explored in *Underground* (1975), a three-character play of sex and power games, conventional in its subject matter and technical formality, but full of enigmatic menace. These plays are collected in *Blitzkrieg and other plays by Bryan Wade: alias, lifeguard, underground, electric gunfighters* (1979). *This side of the Rockies* (1977, prod. 1977) is split between the surrealist style and a new realism; it also introduces a sense of the uncanny in the characters' relationship to nature that resurfaces occasionally in later plays despite their generally realistic manner. The one-act *Tanned* (1976, prod. 1976), set in British Columbia's cottage country, creates a languid, erotic atmosphere with frustration and violence beneath the surface; a three-act version was published in 1979. *Breakthrough* (1986, prod. 1978) concerns the relations between the painter Tom Thomson and a woman from England; it explores a number of promising themes but fails to relate them convincingly. There is a stronger sense of direction in *Polderland* (1984, prod. 1985): set in a Dutch farmhouse during the Second World War, it features a group of Canadian soldiers who have taken a German prisoner; some human contact develops among the characters, but in the end the imperatives of war take over. *The right one* (1989) is an engaging if surprisingly conventional romantic comedy about a disaster-plagued wedding in which the occasional touches of Wade's earlier non-realistic manner seem out of place. It is as though he had lost touch with the impulses of his earlier work but still felt an obligation to them.

The title of *Brave new play rites: 20 years of dramatic engagement from UBC's creative writing program* (2006), edited by Bryan Wade, is that of the annual public festival that produces the kind of one-act plays that are included in this anthology, which presents the work of twenty-five writers.

Wagamese, Richard. See ABORIGINAL LITERATURE: 4, 5.

Wah, Fred (b. 1939). Born in Swift Current, Saskatchewan, Wah grew up in the Kootenay region of British Columbia, in Trail and Nelson. Although he studied music at the University of British Columbia, his primary interest has been poetry. While in Vancouver in the sixties he was part of the TISH movement, helping to found the group's poetry newsletter. As a graduate student he went to the University of New Mexico to study with Black Mountain poet Robert Creeley and to the State University of New York in Buffalo to work with Creeley and Charles Olson, the founder and major theorist of the Black Mountain school. After completing his M.A. at Buffalo, Wah returned to the Kootenays, where he taught at Selkirk College and then became founding co-ordinator of the writing program at David Thompson University Centre during its brief existence. In 1989 he joined the English faculty of the University of Calgary.

Wah has published sixteen books of poetry. *Selected poems: Loki is buried at Smoky Creek* (1980), edited by George BOWERING, collects poems from his early books: *Lardean: selected first poems* (1965), *Mountain* (1967), *Tree* (1972), *Among* (1972), *Earth* (1974), and *Pictograms from the interior of B.C.* (1975)—along with newer poems, some of which reappear in *Breathin' my name with a sigh* (1981). One can see in *Loki* a style characteristic of most of Wah's writing: following the tenets of Black Mountain and the *Tish* group, it is spare, imagistic poetry largely concerned with nature and the events of daily life. In *Breathin' my name* Wah's playful connection of the sound of his name to the sounds of air being exhaled is partly grounded in the Black Mountain concern for breath; it also reveals his fascination with the interplay of language and pure sound. Wah's playfulness is also evident in *Owner's manual* (1981), in which the poems take the form of a set of instructions about how to live.

Waiting for Saskatchewan (1985, GGA) picks up poems from *Breathin' my name with a sigh* and *Grasp the sparrow's tail* (1982), and, adding new poetry, transforms the selections into a unified work in which Wah continues his exploration of the auditory aspects of his poetry, in the context of both Black Mountain ideas about breath and concepts connected to Asian practices of concentration. As well, believing that in order to understand who we are, we must be conscious not only of our physical existence but also of part of our heritage, Wah also begins, through an imagined exploration of his father's experience, what has become an ongoing exploration of his own inheritance. His mother was a Swedish-born Canadian while his father, born in Canada but raised in China, was a mixture of Chinese, Scots, and Irish, and Wah inherited not only his father's Chinese surname but also a sense of not belonging to a specific ethnic group. Wah's later collections—such as *Rooftops* (1987), *Limestone lakes utaniki* (1989), and *So far* (1991)—have made this exploration not one into ethnic identity so much as into the experience of being of mixed-heritage. Wah's message in these collections is not that of one forever displaced, but of the complexity of inheritance and of the consequent need to explore it without attempting to create a clear definition of its nature. As well, Wah shows that there is another dimension of belonging: one's physical reality. The present reality of the Kootenays, his family, his friends, and his own experience are shown to constitute identity as much as his complicated inheritance.

The linked books *Music at the heart of thinking* (1987) and *Alley alley home free* (1992) reveal Wah's continuing interest in sound. In both, Wah seeks to escape the way in which articulation limits meaning by introducing the principles of jazz improvisation into his writing. Although the attempt to escape the fixed nature of the word may be foredoomed, one can see in these books Wah's increasing control over the musicality of his language. In Wah's 2008 publication *Sentenced to light*, the positive strips of black-and-white film by Mexican photographer Eric Jervaise, the colour photographs, line drawings, and heavy paper (drawing attention, no doubt unintentionally, to the expensive production values TALONBOOKS assigned to this book) complement the esoteric 'poems' and 'transcreations' of Wah's perversely hermetic experimental texts.

Diamond Grill (1996, rpr. 2007), Wah's first work of prose, is a return to the world of his parents and his childhood and is his most ambitious book. This partly invented memoir (he calls it a 'biotext') moves towards the prose poem and blurs the line between fiction and fact. In its invocation of both the intensely localized and Canadian experience of a small-town Chinese diner in 1951, and in its investigation of the complicated international history that surrounds it, *Diamond Grill* attempts to deal with the nature of hybridity in a country in which identity has traditionally been defined in terms of belonging to well-defined ethnic groups.

Walker, David (1911–92). He was born in Dundee, Scotland, and attended the Royal Military College, Sandhurst (1929–30). He pursued a military career in the Black Watch (1931–47), serving in India (1932) and the Sudan (1936). His first connection with Canada occurred in 1938 when he was aide-de-camp to the Governor General, Lord Tweedsmuir. Walker was captured in France in 1940 and held prisoner-of-war until 1945, an experience on which he based his novel *The pillar* (1952, GGA). In 1945–6 he served as an instructor at Staff College, Camberly, England, before taking up his last official military post as comptroller to the Viceroy of India. In 1947 he retired, with the rank of major, to take up a new career as professional writer, ultimately settling in St Andrews, New Brunswick. From 1957 to 1961 he was a member of the Canada Council. Walker won a second Governor General's Award for *Digby* (1953).

A prolific writer of fast-paced adventure stories, Walker tried his hand at everything from international espionage (*Cab-intersec*, 1968; published in England as *Devil's plunge*), to children's stories (*Dragon Hill*, 1962). Set in Canada are *Mallabec* (1965), *Where the high winds blow* (1960), *Pirate Rock* (1969), and some of the short stories in *Storms of our journey and other stories* (1964). Two of his novels—*Geordie* (1950) and *Harry Black* (1956)—were made into films. Walker's other novels are *The storm and the silence* (1949), *Sandy was a soldier's boy* (1957), *Winter madness* (1964), *Come back, Geordie* (1966), *Big Ben* (1970), *The Lord's pink ocean* (1972), *Black Dougal* (1973), *Ash* (1976), and *Pot of gold* (1977). In 1984 David Walker published his memoirs, *Lean, wind, lean*. He was made a Member of the Order of Canada in 1987.

Walker, George F. (b. 1947). The youngest of four children of working-class parents, he was born and raised in Toronto's East End. In 1970 he responded to a call for scripts from Toronto's newly founded Factory Theatre Lab by writing *Prince of Naples* (1972), a two-character farce in which a young and ostensibly liberated student challenges the rational thinking of his older and more conventional mentor. Produced by the Factory in 1971, it marked the beginning of a long association that included Walker's being the theatre's playwright-in-residence from 1971 to 1976 and its artistic director in 1978–9. In 1977 he began a three-year association with Toronto Free Theatre, which produced a number of his plays. In 1981 he was playwright-in-residence at the New York Shakespeare Festival, which produced in 1982 the American premiere of his first critically acclaimed work, *Zastrozzi: the master of discipline* (1977, rpr. 1979). In addition to his ongoing association with the Factory Theatre, Walker's plays have premiered in Toronto at the Tarragon (*Science and madness*, 1983) and the Canadian Stage (*Better living*, 1986); at the Mark Taper Forum, Los Angeles (*Nothing sacred*, 1988); at Vassar College in a production by the New York Film and Stage Co. (*Escape from happiness*, 1991); and at the Green Thumb Theatre for Young People, Vancouver (*Tough!*, 1994). *Zastrozzi* had a successful production in the Studio Theatre of the Stratford Festival in (Aug.–Oct.) 2009. Wallace became a Member of the Order of Canada in 2005.

Walker's career has been unprecedented in English Canada. He has won two Governor General's Awards (for *Criminals in love* and *Nothing sacred*), among many other awards. He is also a director of his own productions, notably the remount of *Nothing sacred*—an adaptation of Turgenev's *Father and sons*—at the Winter Garden Theatre, Toronto. Walker has produced a body of work that includes over twenty stage plays and numerous radio and television scripts, making him the most published and produced playwright in English Canada. His plays have been mounted in hundreds of productions around the world, have been translated into several languages, and have developed a critical and popular respect that led to Walker's being named in 1993 one of the hundred most powerful people in American theatre, and to the publication of a critical anthology of his work, *Shared society: selected plays* (1994).

If Walker's plays have been a rich source of material for actors and directors, they have posed somewhat more of an enigma for critics, who have not always known quite what to make of the seemingly pastiched concoctions of cinematic forms and techniques, cartoon characters, serious political and philosophical issues, and bizarre, even grotesque, theatrical flourishes. Early critics, for example, mistook Walker for an absurdist or a surrealist because of the very early plays' evocation of patterns from those theatrical traditions. *Prince of Naples* (1972) and *Ambush at Tether's End* (1972), for example, use stock absurdist devices to reach decidedly non-absurdist conclusions. Critic Gregory Sinclair has described Walker's dramatic technique as 'scouring artistic graveyards for dead stereotypes and mouldy subgenres, stitching them all together and watching them career madly across the stage.' The Frankensteinean metaphor is, perhaps, apt for a playwright who delights in revivifying traditional theatrical conventions by inserting pop-cultural and B-movie references into them. At first Walker's unorthodox technique and periodic stylistic changes suggested a playwright who was himself careering madly across the theatrical landscape. However, as his craft has matured, a consistent theatrical technique has emerged, one that Richard Knowles has described as 'perversion', a persistent warping and reconfiguration of received forms into new, independent ones in order to disrupt dominant discourses. If there are any threads running through all Walker's plays, they can be located in his understanding of language, style, even structural forms as the building blocks out of which not only art but human subjectivity and culture are constructed, and through which power is constituted and wielded. By twisting, or perverting, these forms and processes, Walker's plays both foreground the forms' role in cultural constructions and suggest new ways of constituting such power.

Much has been written about Walker's use of cinematic forms, a stylistic preference that continues even in the more recent plays' use of 'gangster' and 'tough' movie plots and characters. Walker himself has remarked that 'I tend to like to frame the world, and use various genres to do that. "B" movies are a generic frame that gives me freedom to jump off in any direction that I want to or that the characters will take me.' Thus, for example, the cartoon exaggerations and comic grotesques that pervade his early plays shift to stereotypical characters and structural clichés of Hollywood B-movies in the plays anthologized in *Three plays by George F. Walker* (1978). But in all these plays Walker perverts the conventions and thus exposes their ideological blindness. A play such as *Beyond Mozambique* (1975), for example, uses the B-movie conventions to express what the B-movies themselves did not express: the desperation and ugliness of a decaying imperialist centre endlessly regurgitating its own cultural debris.

In the middle group of plays the comic structure becomes somewhat more conventional, but the emphasis on manipulating these conventional forms to raise questions about their attendant political and philosophical ideologies continues. *Gossip* (1981) and *Filthy rich* (1981), two 'detective movies', expose the bankrupt morality and decadent mores of the rich and famous that Walker locates at the centre of media-warped society. In *Gossip* the crime-drama convention of the revelation scene is exaggerated out of all proportion, and in *Filthy rich* the crime-drama conventions themselves break down when their basic requirement of clear and distinguishable good and evil proves to be naive. In *Theatre of the film noir* (1981) and *The art of war* (1984) Walker again draws on the formats of cinematic suspense to spin the webs of sexual and political intrigue that are his metaphors for contemporary confusion and decay. Using the characters and conventions of horror films in *Science and madness* (1982), he expands upon this technique, developing a Gothic collage whose portrayal of the classic struggle between good and evil revives the conflict of Zastrozzi, in which Zastrozzi, the arch-villain of Western Europe—derived from Shelley's play of the same name—confronts Verezzi, his idealistic opposite. *Zastrozzi* demonstrates the playwright's ability to merge philosophical issues with powerful characterizations, urbane dialogue, and intricate plot in a fast-paced series of visually striking scenes that are as intellectually sophisticated as they are theatrically exciting.

A group of plays often called the 'East End plays'—after the title of the 1988 anthology that collects three of them (*Criminals in love, Better living,* and *Beautiful city*), as well as for their evocation of the working-class neighbourhoods of Walker's own East End Toronto upbringing—are his most mature plays to date. Though in them Walker turns to the conventions of realist drama, he does not abandon the cartoonish characters or the interest in cultural forms and relations of power that characterized his earlier works. The first of the East End plays, *Criminals in love* (1984), introduces a set of characters that reappear over some later plays. They include several matriarchal figures who battle the forces of corruption in their neighbourhoods in order to carve out a safe place for their families to flourish. The heroes in these plays are typically 'ordinary folk' who have been pushed too far and are finally standing up for themselves, and the villains typically represent the organized forms of power, whether the Mafia, politicians, or the police, who have taken them for granted. The women in these families are almost all strong, and the men either weak or violently controlling. The development of more overt political, particularly class, issues—begun already in *Gossip* and *Filthy rich*—becomes predominant in these plays. Walker's plays are all highly metatheatrical, and the East End plays are no exception, with characters often resolving conflicts through ruses, disguises, and performances. In *Love and anger* (1990), for example, the characters win a victory over the corrupt newspaper boss, Conner, by fabricating evidence against him and by 'trying' him in a mock courtroom. Performance, itself a form of power, thus offers one resolution of the fascination all Walker's plays have with the various forms power can take, from the ruthless cruelty of Zastrozzi and Hackman (*The art of war*), to the homespun wisdom and dangerous stubbornness of Nora Quinn (*Better living* and *Escape from happiness,* 1992) and Gina Mae Sabatini (*Beautiful city*), to the creative and unorthodox performances of numerous characters, such as Petie Maxwell (*Love and anger*) and William (*Criminals in love*). What is perhaps not especially obvious, because of its subtlety in the East End plays, is Walker's unusual ability to hold up the quotidian and reveal the magical, the sublime, and the ridiculous, harnessing them all to the service of a theatricality that is at once politically, aesthetically, culturally, and philosophically astute. *East End plays: Part 2* (1999) contains

Beautiful city, Love and anger, and *Tough!.* Other recent collections of Walker's plays are *Somewhere else* (1999)—containing *Beyond Mozambique, Zastrozzi, Theatre of the film noir, Nothing sacred,* and *Suburban motel* (1999), a group of six plays all set in the same hotel room: *Problem child, Adult entertainment, Criminal genius, Featuring Loretta, The end of civilization* and *Risk everything.* Walker's most recent play, *Heaven* (2000), was produced in Toronto by Canadian Stage in Mar. 2000. 'It's all about pain,' Walker has said, and this rough, funny, confrontational play about culture, religion, and race addresses the statement of one character: 'They don't know your private battle against everything that isn't honest or real—to eradicate all the bullshit from the world.'

Wallace, Bronwen (1945–89). She was born in Kingston, Ontario, and educated at Queen's University (B.A., 1967; M.A., 1979). Her mother was of United Empire Loyalist stock, and her father's family lived on the same farm for over 200 years. A political activist, she worked in Windsor, Ontario, in the 1970s with auto-workers, and co-founded a women's bookstore; in Kingston in the 1980s she worked in a battered women's shelter. All these experiences appear in her poetry. In the late 1980s she was a teacher of creative writing and women's studies at Queen's. She also wrote a highly personal and feminist column for two years on the Monday op-ed page of the Kingston *Whig-Standard.* A late-starter, she published her first book at thirty-five. (In her memory, the WRITERS' DEVELOPMENT TRUST established an annual award for the best writer under thirty-five with achievements in fiction or poetry.) She had a vital and humane voice, free of rhetoric.

Wallace was heavily influenced by Al PURDY, whose example taught her to structure poems as narratives instead of lyrics. Her intention was to organize poems the way women get together to tell stories. Story, for Wallace, achieved its meaning through cumulative effect. Her poems are often two or three pages long, with exact details of ordinary lives shining from within. Her first collection, *Marrying in the family* (later published alone in 1994), was published in one volume with Mary DI MICHELE's *Bread & chocolate* (1980). She followed this with *Signs of the former tenant* (1983, rpr. 1992), *Common magic* (1985), and the dazzling collection *The stubborn particulars of grace* (1987). Magic and love are found in the most common things: a kitchen or living room; the places people live in, even the poet's hands, become 'wings'. *Common magic* also includes poems of marital strife and male anger; *Stubborn particulars* includes poems about working in a battered women's shelter, the importance of conversation over the dinner table, and planting daffodils as an act of faith in the future. Wallace's posthumous publications include short stories about nurturing female relationships, love and its obstacles, and finding the divine in the commonplace, in *People you'd trust your life to* (1990, rpr. 2001); *Keep that candle burning bright and other poems* (1991), a short collection of prose poems dedicated to 'Emmylou Harris, sparked by a song called "Burn That Candle"'; *Arguments with the world: essays* (1992), a collection of her newspaper columns, edited by Joanne Page; and the exchanges of Wallace and Erin MOURÉ in *Two women talking: correspondence 1985–1987* (1993). Wallace made two films: *All You Have To Do* (1982) about living with cancer, made seven years before she was diagnosed with the disease; and *That's Why I'm Talking* (1985), which celebrates four poet-friends, Robert PRIEST, Mary di Michele, Pier Giorgio DI CICCO, and Carolyn Smart.

Wallace, Frederick William (1886–1958). The son of a ship captain, Wallace was born in the seafaring dockland community of Govan, then on the outskirts of Glasgow, where he was educated in local schools. He was naturally drawn to the world of the sea, idealizing the courage, skill, and strength of such men as his father. To his immense frustration, however, he came of age just as the world he admired was coming to a close, as iron and steam replaced sail and wood. Instead of apprentice seaman, his first job was as a shipping clerk, initially in Glasgow, and then—following his family's move to Hudson, Québec, in 1904—in Montreal. Wallace continued to dream of life at sea from behind his desk, and began to write short stories based on events in his father's career. These were sufficiently popular with his friends that in 1908 he became a freelance writer, specializing in adventure stories for various magazines directed at men such as himself, office-bound and bored. But it was a vicarious existence, to which he could bring no experience of his own. The turning point in Wallace's life came in August 1911, when he was sent by *Canadian Century* magazine to cover a fishermen's regatta in Digby, Nova Scotia, where he was introduced to Grand Banks fishermen, who still made their living on the water and under sail. Insinuating himself aboard a working trip, he quickly gained the respect of the fishermen for his skill, knowledge, and

fortitude, and was accepted as a working member of the crew. Six more such trips with the fishermen of Digby were the grist from which he milled his publications: three novels, *Blue water* (1914), *The Viking blood* (1920), and *Captain Salvation* (1925); three collections of short stories, *The shack locker* (1916), *Salt seas and sailormen* (1922), and *Tea from China* (1926); as well as innumerable magazine and newspaper writings, both fiction and non-fiction. In 1914 Wallace was hired as the founding editor of the industrial journal *Canadian Fisherman*, a position he held almost continuously until shortly before his death. He then began to compile records relating to the deep-sea wooden sailing vessels built in the Maritime region, which led to the publication of his enjoyable *Wooden ships and iron men* (1924), *In the wake of the windships* (1926), and *The record of Canadian shipping* (1929). He also wrote an account of a voyage he made aboard one such vessel in 1920, *Under sail in the last of the clippers* (1936). Wallace's reputation as a writer rested for a long period on these historical compilations, which helped to establish an image of a nineteenth-century golden age of economic activity in the Maritime region. Recent scholarship, however, has superseded, and in large measure discredited, this work. His fiction was quickly dated by its stock characters and romantic plots—boy wins girl after much adventure—but it nevertheless retains historical interest for those exploring issues of gender and the development of urban middle-class masculinity, and for providing detailed and realistic accounts of the working life of the Banks fishermen on the eve of mechanization. Indeed, Wallace's writings were praised by fishermen, in marked contrast to the reception they gave to Frank Parker DAY's near-contemporary novel *Rockbound* (1928). Wallace returned to the description of the world of the Banks fishing schooner at length in his autobiography, *Roving fisherman* (1955), which, shorn of the romanticism of his fiction, offers a unique picture of men at work on the water. It might be considered his lasting contribution to Canadian literature and history.

Wallace, J.S. (Joe) (1890–1975). Toronto-born, raised in Truro and North Sydney, Nova Scotia, he attended St Francis Xavier University and worked in advertising, running as a candidate in provincial and federal elections before joining the Communist Party of Canada the year following its formation in 1921. He wrote for the labour press, attended the Conference for the Unemployed in Ottawa in 1933, and when the Party was outlawed was interned at Petawawa, Ontario, in 1941–2. Imprisonment inspired his early verse. Five collections of lyric and satiric poems appeared, beginning with *Night is ended* (1942) and ending with *A radiant sphere* (1964). The latter volume was issued in Moscow in three editions of 10,000 copies each—in Russian, English, and Chinese. With Wilson MacDONALD, he toured Russia and China in 1956–7. Both a committed Communist and a devout Roman Catholic, he died in a Catholic convalescent home in Vancouver. *Joe Wallace: poems* (1981) brings together 300 poems and verses that show his ability to write socially committed light verse ('The American way of life:/You can get away with murder/If you use a golden knife') and, on occasion, lyric poems of intensity, notably his elegy for Norman Bethune and his poem on tolerance, which begins 'All my brothers are beautiful.'

Walmsley, Tom (b. 1948). Born in Liverpool, England, he came to Canada in 1952 and was raised in Oshawa, Ontario, and Lorraine, Québec, dropping out of high school in grade ten. Life on the streets of Toronto and Vancouver followed—which included welfare fraud, robbery, and an addiction to heroin and alcohol—until he turned to writing. Surviving a period of ill health and becoming sober, he converted to Roman Catholicism and now lives in Toronto.

In Vancouver Walmsley joined up with some alienated intellectuals who, under Stephen Osborne, formed Pulp Press (later Arsenal Press), Walmsley's publisher. They dreamed up the idea of a Three-Day Novel contest, which Walmsley won with *Doctor Tin* (1979), which was followed in 1992 by *Shades: the whole story of Doctor Tin*: 'I had my hand on my gun when the doors opened and there he was, a service revolver in either hand..../ Doctor Tin, I said./Not for a lot of years, McGraw.' An aimless extravaganza featuring the private-eye McGraw, sex, a rock star named A.J. who is also a murderer, lots of action, and no quotation marks—plus a bizarre literary contrivance in the middle section called 'The Main Drag', in which each of roughly 100 pages contains two narratives divided by a line. *Kid stuff* (2003)—filled with smart dialogue (as usual, no quotation marks)—focuses on young people on the edge of adulthood who are driven to transgress the principles of the small town they live in, with devastating consequences.

Walmsley is perhaps most gifted as a playwright: *The working man* (1976), *The Jones boy*

(1978), *Something red* (1980), *White boys* (produced in 1982), *Getting wrecked* (produced in 1985), and *Mr Nice Guy* (produced in 1986), written with Dolly Reisman. The plays are by far the best part of his work. The only conventional facet of Walmsley's drama is its formal realism. Sex and violence pervade his stage: obscenities riddle his dialogue. But his plays are never simply exercises in sensationalism. Even *The working man*, for all its graphic violence, focuses on the psychological drama. Although the principal characters in *The Jones boy* are drug addicts, the play is not 'about' heroin but about the quest for self-knowledge and the meaning of courage and honour in a criminal subculture that offers only unreflective barbarism as an ideal. *Something red*, Walmsley's most ambitious play, moves through scenes of extreme physical and psychological brutality to climactic moments in which a character stands revealed to others and himself. The protagonist, Bobby, whose life has been an abject saga of flight and betrayal, is a memorable creation. Dishonourable and self-seeking in all his relationships, revolting in his sexual obsessions, he also bears traces of tragic grandeur. He is faithful only to his most wayward impulses—the 'monstrous forms of being', in Ionesco's words, that inhabit the human psyche; yet when he makes his last appearance, having committed an appalling sex murder, our responses are pity and fear. Revised versions of both the above plays, *Something red* and *The Jones boy*, were published in one volume in 2008. In *White boys* the playwright presents his familiar character types within the framework of farce. The full-length play works well at the level of a revue skit; but the idiom obstructs the necessary development of the theme, which is, once again, infantile impulse baffled by the demands of adult experience. *Getting wrecked* is a musical treatment of the theme of teenage abuse of alcohol, and *Mr Nice Guy* treats the theme of wife battering. The most serious limitation of Walmsley's theatre is its narrow focus. The characters and milieu offer only a remote relation to society at large. His work, although increasingly expert, tends to turn in on itself as the playwright delves ever deeper into extreme, anarchic states of being. But within their restricted compass, Walmsley's plays—*The Jones boy* and *Something red* in particular—generate a power that is rare in contemporary Canadian drama.

His published works include four books of poetry. *Rabies* (1975)—there is no poem called 'Rabies' in this uninteresting collection—and *Lexington hero* (1976) preceded *Honeymoon in*

Berlin (2004). With illustrations by Sandy McClelland, it is a little book of poems that fantasize Jake the narrator, Loretta, and Veronika discovered on the Internet—along with love, death, shit, and Berlin ('The city is my mind, I said./Berlin is my soul, she said.'), bringing to life brief moments that collectively have little apparent meaning. The poems in *What happened* (2007)—written entirely in lower case (except for God) and without punctuation (except for a final period)—are satisfying to read for their clarity and amusingly unassuming manner, even as the poet draws on some surprising (often sexual) life experiences: 'i woke up beside a/loaded shotgun i remembered/nothing until she came home told/me she'd held it to my head the/night before but changed her mind &/went to bed so//i put away the gun &/we ate dinner watched TV &/stayed together another year' (part ten of 'Little honey').

Warland, Betsy (b. 1946). Born in Fort Dodge, Iowa, she attended Luther College, Decorah, Iowa, taking courses in Art and Education (B.A.1970); she immigrated to Canada in 1973 and became a citizen in 1980. She is associated with the Writer's Studio at Simon Fraser University, Burnaby, B.C. Becoming a significant figure in feminist and lesbian writing, she helped conceive and co-ordinate in 1983 the landmark conference 'Women and Words/Les femmes et les mots' at the University of British Columbia, and she has edited extensively, helping to bring to publication the work of many feminist writers in such vehicles as *Telling it: women and language across cultures* (1990) and, as sole editor, *InVersions: writing by dykes, queers & lesbians* (1991).

Warland's poetry is intensely personal, and in *A gathering instinct* (1981) she records sequences of pain and loss in relationships. She highlights the difficulties of constructing a self in language, using a lower-case 'i' to identify her first-person voice. In the wake of the 'Women and Words' conference, the 1980s in Canada became a period of intense feminist experimentation with language, and Warland participated energetically in this collective investigation. In *open is broken* (1984) she explores etymological and homonymic webs of meaning, and breaks the bounds of conventional discourse. Increasing syntactical fracture characterizes her contribution to a feminist poetics, a process she continues in *serpent (w)rite: (a reader's gloss)* (1987) and *Proper deafinitions: collected theorograms* (1990). *The bat had blue eyes* (1993) examines memories of childhood sexual abuse and the mechanisms by which language paralyses and erases experiences whose articulation is taboo. For instance, in the phrase 'I clings', Warland syntactically relegates the first-person pronoun to the third-person, objectifying her own voice and thus illustrating its erasure. In *What holds us here* (1998)—in widely spaced lines, some of a few words—capture feelings of desire, love, and illumination. A similar typographic style is exercised in *Bloodroot: tracing the untelling of motherloss* (2000) and *Only this blue: a long poem with an essay* (2005), which grew out of her life-threatening experience of breast cancer and how this changed her daily life. All lines are set in lower case (on the right-hand page only), with space between lines and longer spaces equaling perhaps silence or perhaps breath. (Warland has said: 'Blank space on the page is not empty.') Colour is important: red suggests cutting, blue the sanguine observer. Warland has also written collaboratively with Daphne MARLATT in *Double negative* (1988) and *Two women in a birth* (1994).

Warr, Bertram (1917–43). Born in Toronto, Warr was educated there. After working in Muskoka and Halifax during the late 1930s, he decided to leave Canada to pursue his literary ambitions in England. He arrived in England after stowing away on a passenger liner, worked as a clerk for a London oyster company, and joined the Fire Service at the start of the Second World War. Though a pacifist, he was 'called up' and joined the Royal Air Force in 1941. He perished on a raid over Essen, Germany, in April 1943. Warr's poetry appeared in various British literary magazines and anthologies. Shortly before joining the RAF he published a small pamphlet, *Yet a little onwards* (1941), in the Resurgam Younger Poets Series. That collection of fourteen poems reflects Warr's early response to the war, particularly in 'War widow', and his socialist leanings in 'Working class' and 'To a passionate socialist'. Warr shared with his British contemporaries of this period a desire to blend both politics and realism in a controlled free-verse style that is metaphorically sensual. But unlike English poets of the Apocalyptic or Personalist movements (e.g., Henry Treece, Nicholas Moore, and G.S. Fraser), Warr maintained a conscious and open-eyed attitude, and an imagistic system of realism that locates his work closer to that of Dorothy LIVESAY and Earle BIRNEY. Warr's sense of uneasy pessimism, declared in the introduction to *Yet a little onwards*—'ours is an age of renunciation … of probing and reflection'—lends his work a contemplative aspect that goes beyond mere agitprop or manifesto poetry, hallmarks of other verse from the Second World War. His poetry was revived by Birney (who had discovered Warr's work in England during his own service) and Len Gasparini and published in *Acknowledgement to life: the collected poems of Bertram Warr* (1970). In his Preface, Birney asserts that had Warr survived the hostilities he would likely have become an important voice in Canadian poetry.

Wars, The (1977, GGA; rpr. 2005). This novel, his third, brought Timothy FINDLEY to prominence in Canadian literary circles, though he had published his first novel a full decade before. It expresses a general trend in Canadian fiction of the 1970s: the self-conscious exploration of history as text— what the critic Linda HUTCHEON has called 'historiographic metafiction'. For his tale of a nineteen-year-old Canadian soldier in the Great War, as told through the eyes of a researcher and various witnesses, Findley drew much of the documentary materials from letters written by his uncle (Thomas Irving Findley), who served with the artillery in France, and he supplemented them with readings in the published texts of the period—from the poetry of Wilfred Owen and Siegfried Sassoon to Erich Remarque's *All quiet on the Western Front* (1929). Far from decrying the indebtedness of Findley's novel to powerful fictional and poetic predecessors, reviewers tended to praise his use of such materials as a means of validation. Of the many features of *The wars* that have attracted critical inquiry, the spare, cinematic style is prominent. Findley's division of the novel into five sections, themselves subdivided into numbered sections and punctuated by transcripts of witnesses' memories, suggests a concern with history's construction and the very status of knowledge. Documented fact is radically destabilized: Robert, trapped in a barn at the end of the novel, cries out, 'We shall not be taken.' To the male-centred mindset that Findley would continue to critique in later novels such as *Not wanted on the voyage* (1984), 'we' can only be construed as Robert plus other human beings—he is part of a conspiracy against authority and is therefore punished by fire. In the literary nationalism that dominated the early 1970s there was an imperative to locate *The wars* either in cosmopolitan literary company or in a newly reconceptualized Canadian 'tradition'. For this reason the novel is a pivotal text for students of Canadian literary canonization in the years following the centennial celebrations of 1967. It won a Governor General's Award and became a film (directed by Robin Phillips, 1983); its popularity continues unabated, and it is regularly taught in literature courses.

Watmough, David (b. 1926). Born in Epping Forest, near London, England, Watmough spent most of his childhood in Cornwall, where he learned the idiosyncratic rhythm of his prose. Forced by the Depression to leave his boyhood home, he has forever after employed the voice of the exile in stories that describe the outsider looking homeward, back to the disintegrating family and now unfamiliar landscape. He was educated at Cooper's School, London, served in the Royal Navy during wartime, then attended King's College, University of London, (1945–9), where he studied theology, the subject of his first book, *A church renascent*. After a few years working as a journalist in New York and San Francisco, Watmough immigrated to Vancouver in 1960 (he became a Canadian citizen in 1969), where he worked as a print, radio, and television critic (living with his partner, the late Floyd St Clair, for over fifty years) and produced a cycle of plays, stories, and novels—all with an autobiographical impulse. Watmough's novels are *No more into the garden: chronicles of Davey Bryant* (1978), for which he was given the Best Novel of the Year Award by Giovanni's Room, a leading gay bookstore in Philadelphia; *Unruly skeletons* (1982); *The year of fears* (1987); *Thy mother's glass* (1992); *The time of the kingfishers* (1994); *Hunting with Diana* (1996); *The moor is dark beneath the moon* (2002), in which Davy Bryant returns to Cornwall; *Vancouver voices* (2005), about a gay priest who has been accused of child abuse; and *Geraldine* (2007), a tribute to a woman, now an elderly grandmother, who had once been professionally successful in the man's world of biochemistry. Watmough's collections of stories are *From a Cornish landscape* (1975), *Love and the waiting game* (1975), *The Connecticut countess* (1984), *Fury* (1984), and *Vibrations in time* (1986). *The shorter fiction of David Watmough: 1972–82* was published in 1982. Davey Bryant is the persona we encounter in most of Watmough's fiction. In fact, every story would appear to belong to a composite Davey, his life in transparent layers, as if by telling and reading variations on the story the writer and the reader will finally come to an understanding of what it means to be a man alienated from his own culture by the accident of his homosexuality and the progress of history. Irony is Watmough's way of dealing with inevitable cruelties—it distances him from a sentimental childhood, which is also the paradise he seeks in each new fiction and every human relationship. In 2008 Watmough published *Myself through others: memoirs* in which he chose to tell about aspects of his own life through his (sometimes slight) connections with other people, some of them famous—such as W.H. Auden and Stephen Spender, whom he did know over a period of time, and the movie star Jean Arthur and Tennessee Williams (dinner only with both). Canadian writers included are Jane RULE, Ethel WILSON, Margaret LAURENCE, Robin SKELTON, George WOODCOCK, and Carol SHIELDS. Unfortunately Watmough's short chapters on them (as on others), while admiring and affectionate, offer little but generalities about the writers—and in the case of Ethel Wilson, just a few unsatisfying lines.

Watmough has also written monodramas—solo performance pieces—in which he takes the role of writer/performer. These were published in *Ashes for Easter & other monodramas* (1972, rpr. 1976).

Watson, John (1847–1939). Born in Glasgow and educated at Glasgow University, he came to Queen's University, Kingston, Ontario, in 1872 to be a professor of logic, metaphysics, and ethics, replacing John Clark MURRAY, who had accepted a chair at McGill. Watson was the central figure in the Hegelian movement that dominated Canadian philosophy from the 1870s until after the First World War, and did much to shape religious, political, and cultural ideas in Canada in this period. His rational version of Christianity formed a significant part of the intellectual basis of the union that resulted in the formation of the United Church of Canada in 1925. Religion was central to Watson's work. His religious views were first expounded in *Christianity and idealism: the Christian life in relation to the Greek and Jewish ideals and to modern philosophy* (New York, 1896). Believing that all reality formed a rational unity within which the highest values could be realized, Watson sought a rational religion that could unite all people around demonstrable truths, and render intelligible both human history and the life of the individual. Though a decade separates *The philosophical basis of religion: a series of lectures* (1907) from *Christianity and idealism*, his fundamental position remained the same. Watson's books attracted international recognition and this

culminated in the invitation to give the Gifford Lectures in Scotland in 1910–12, which led to his monumental *Interpretation of religious experience* (2 vols, 1912). Much of Watson's reputation rests on his *Philosophy of Kant explained* (1908) and *Kant and his English critics: a comparison of critical and empirical philosophy* (Glasgow, 1881), both of which were frequently reprinted and continue to be read. His *Philosophy of Kant as contained in extracts from his own writings* (Glasgow, 1888) was widely used by undergraduates. His introductory texts, *Comte, Mill & Spencer, an outline of philosophy* (Glasgow, 1895), later adapted as *An outline of philosophy* (1908), helped shape the minds of two generations of Canadian students. These books also contain a good deal of original philosophy, as does Watson's *Hedonistic theories from Aristippus to Spencer* (Glasgow, 1895). The Great War gave rise to *The state in peace and war* (1919), a treatise devoted to the ideal of a world government based on the principles of tolerance and the integral development of national cultures, which Watson thought characteristic of the emerging British Commonwealth and of the established pluralist tradition in Canada. Watson's lucid prose style made his books accessible and helped to account for their wide readership. His influence generally stemmed from the generations of Presbyterian clergymen who were educated by him, and from the frequency with which his students attained senior posts in the civil service in Ottawa.

Watson, Sheila (1909–98). Born in New Westminster, British Columbia, she lived during her early years on the grounds of the Provincial Mental Hospital, in New Westminster, where her father, Dr Charles Edward Doherty, was superintendent until his death in 1922. She received a B.A. (1931) in Honours English from the University of British Columbia; earned her academic teaching certificate in 1932; and completed an M.A. (1933) at UBC. During the next few years Watson taught elementary school in a succession of British Columbia classrooms. In 1941 she married the poet Wilfred WATSON. In the postwar years Sheila Watson undertook another series of short-term teaching posts at Moulton College, Toronto (1946–8), a sessional lectureship at UBC (1948–50), and at a high school in Powell River, B.C. (1950–1) before spending two years in Calgary, during which she wrote her celebrated novel *The double hook* (1959, NCL). After short periods in Edmonton and France, she undertook doctoral studies at the University of Toronto in

1957, completing a dissertation on Wyndham Lewis, under the direction of Marshall McLU-HAN, in 1965. (See her *Wyndham Lewis and expressionism* [2004].) She was appointed to the faculty of the University of Alberta in 1961, and retired as full professor in 1975. *Four stories* (1979) was followed by *Five stories* (1984), which added a fifth story, 'And the four animals', to the original four. See *A father's kingdom: the complete short fiction of Sheila Watson* (2004, NCL). A second novel, *Deep Hollow Creek* (NCL)—written in the 1930s, but not published until 1992—has a semi-autobiographical basis in Watson's experiences as a teacher at Dog Creek in the interior of British Columbia in 1935-7, and can be read as an early writing of various aspects of *The double hook*, which is considered by many to be the first truly modern Canadian novel. Concerned to avoid both regionalism and realistic reportage, Watson created in this text a highly poetic and elliptical narrative written in biblical rhythms, in chapters that resemble stanzas, and in images that dwarf plot and action. The novel depicts the struggle of members of a small village to move from despair to hope, from apathy to action, in a world where pagan and Christian symbolisms have blurred, and silence proves more eloquent than language. The discontinuous and highly imagistic style of the work reiterates the distrust of discursive language that it embodies. Watson's stories, written in the same period as *The double hook*, reflect a similarly austere and precise use of language and image. Most focus on spiritual paralysis, and give mythological names to the characters to avoid the semblance of realism. The characters thus appear oppressed by myth, and struggle against its authority as personified in parent, priest, or nun.

Watson, Wilfred (1911–98). Born in Rochester, England, and educated at Maldon Grammar School, Maldon, Essex, he immigrated with his family in 1926 to Duncan, British Columbia. After a year at Duncan High School he began thirteen years of work in a tidewater sawmill, meanwhile reading, writing poetry, and exploring the coasts and mountains of Vancouver Island. In 1940 he enrolled in English at the University of British Columbia, graduating in 1943, whereupon he joined the Canadian navy for the remainder of the war. He received an M.A. from the University of Toronto in 1946 and a Ph.D. in 1951. After teaching English briefly at the University of British Columbia, he taught at the University of Alberta, first in Calgary

and later in Edmonton, where he served as a distinguished teacher and scholar until his retirement in 1976. With his wife Sheila WATSON he co-founded the little magazine *White Pelican* (1971–8).

As both experimental poet and dramatist, Watson explored contemporary media-conditioned sensibilities. His first collection of poems, *Friday's child* (1955, GGA) contained apparently conventional verse that nevertheless bore the seeds of the radical writing to follow. The poems of his second collection, *The sorrowful Canadians and other poems* (1972), are curiously analogous to his drama in their use of space, for which Watson uses the term *mise en page*. Unlike most concrete poetry, Watson's offers both context and content: the size or positioning of various typefaces modulates verbal intensity, so that the eye is bombarded by a typographical 'voice' speaking with the insistence of choral utterance in the plays. His number/grid poems—in which each stanza or grid provides for seventeen words juxtaposed typographically to the numbers one to nine—were published in *I begin with counting* (1978) and *Mass on cowback* (1982). The discipline of the grid method of ordering his poems is also reflected in the finely honed short verse-play *Woman taken in adultery* (published in Diane Bessai, ed., *Prairie performance*, 1980; produced 1987), which concisely illustrates Watson's facility for drawing satiric portraits within rapidly shifting time-space environments. A comprehensive gathering of the poetry is found in *Poems: collected/unpublished/new* (1986), with an introduction by Thomas Peacocke.

As the author of many experimental plays, Watson was influenced by the Theatre of the Absurd and by his interest in the theories of Marshall McLUHAN, with whom he collaborated in *From cliché to archetype* (1970). He also wrenches the language of biblical and literary tradition into contemporary contexts, and traditionally sacred questions are filtered through the distorting lens of modern-day secularity. Watson's full-length plays are gathered in *Plays at the Ironbridge; or The autobiography of Tom Horror* (1989), edited by Shirley Neuman with an Introduction by Gordon Peacock. His *The Baie-Comeau angel and other stories* (1993) contains the same mordant prisms of irony, fantasy, and humour through which Watson eyes the world in all his writing.

Wayman, Tom (b. 1945). Born in Hawkesbury, Ontario, he was raised in Prince Rupert and Vancouver, British Columbia. He attended the University of British Columbia, where he edited the student newspaper, *The Ubyssey*, and did graduate work at the University of California. He teaches at the University of Calgary, and has an estate, 'Appledore', in the Selkirk Mountains of southeastern British Columbia. The wide variety of jobs he has had in the United States and Canada is reflected in his poetry.

Wayman's first collection was *Waiting for Wayman* (1973). His many subsequent volumes include *For and against the rain: blues, yells, and chuckles* (1974), *Free time: industrial poems* (1977), *A planet mostly sea* (1979), *Living on the ground: Tom Wayman country* (1980), *The face of Jack Munro* (1985), and *The astonishing weight of the dead* (1993, rpr. 1994). There is one major volume of selected poems: *Did I miss anything?* (1993). Wayman's poetry is about what he describes as 'the central experience of every-day life—which is what people do for a living, their work.' He writes of the various jobs he has held; tells the stories of people he has worked with; and speculates on the social, political, and even metaphysical implications of the work experience. While his point of view is clearly pro-labour, Wayman seldom makes dogmatic political statements, though he can be aroused to passionate indignation (as in the powerful title poem of *The face of Jack Munro*). His analyses of the effects of people's jobs on their lives are clear, sensible, often humorous, and convincingly argued. Much of this poetry is necessarily narrative, conveyed in a straightforward, realist tone, with very little reliance on metaphor or self-consciously 'poetic' figures of speech. Often the poetic effect depends on the witty deployment of an ironic persona—the third-person 'Wayman' who acts as a self-deprecatory character and narrator. The rhythms are prosaic and some-times flat; while this effect works well in the ironic narrative mode, it is less successful in more conventionally 'lyric' poems. Wayman's major concern and achievement have been to rescue realism in poetry from its position, as he sees it, 'somewhere at the bottom of the heap', and to assert the worth, dignity, and complex-ity of daily work as a poetic subject.

The death of Wayman's father gave rise to *My father's cup* (2002). 'In Memory of A.W. Purdy': 'Sid Marty phoned/from his ranch up Willow Valley Road/in the Alberta foothills/ to let me know./ "All the fathers are dying," I responded/—my own father, exhausted to the core by a hospital's/intrusive and agonizing procedures/to restore one collapsed bodily system after another,/had convinced his doc-tors the previous May to grant/the peace of

the hospice ward/in which he could sleep his solitary way out of the world.' In the poem 'Two Poets I Admire Contact Me on the Same Day'—the poets are Sid MARTY and Peter Christensen—Wayman is moved to write 'The friendships of men/to me are remotely beautiful' and goes on to say 'Good words, good poems/possess the beauty/of a tree in winter: a formal perfection,/.... But friendship is that tree/leaving out in April, each curled green nub/fulfillment alike of summer/and of shade.' Later poems, how-ever—as in *High speed through shoaling water* (2007)—employ a more relaxed style focused on many other subjects, such as aging, teach-ing, the writing of poetry, and nature: 'Alder, birch, mountain ash detonate/on the hills or alongside the roads./ ... until the valley resounds/with an incessant green concussive roar.' ('Springbomb'.)

Entering the world of fiction in 2007, Way-man published two collections of stories. The twelve stories in *Boundary country* have a one-page preface entitled 'Welcome to Boundary Country', in which he refers to the 'places and moments' when 'we encounter a bound-ary'—such as 'the line between self and oth-ers, between individuals and their community.' The final story in *A vain thing: four novellas* (2007)—overlong stories that lack the narra-tive discipline and depth of novellas—is 'Love in the afterlife', the easiest story to read, and perhaps the most enjoyable for a Torontonian. It sets up a conflict between two cities and two lovers, Vancouverite Dennis and Toronto-nian Elizabeth. Dennis's collection of stories has been nominated for a Governor General's Award; Elizabeth is a freelance writer with many friends in the literary community of Toronto. Dennis's Vancouver friend Wayne tells him: 'Toronto is just a place you go after you've accomplished something elsewhere. It's the Afterlife for poor schmucks like you.' What happens when the married writer Mark Gould enters the picture and he and Elizabeth become lovers? Dennis has an epiphany when he sees her with her Toronto friends.

Wayman has also published two collections of critical essays on the subject of work: *Inside job: essays on the new work writing* (1983) and *A country not considered: Canada, culture, work* (1993). He edited *The dominion of love: an anthology of Canadian love poems* (2001), which includes poems by fifty Canadian poets, most of whom have entries in this *Companion*.

Weaver, Robert (1921–2008). Born in Niag-ara Falls, Ontario, from 1942 to 1945 he served first in the RCAF, and then in the Canadian army. After his discharge he enrolled at University College, University of Toronto, and took his degree in philosophy and English (B.A., 1948). In the same year he was hired by the Canadian Broadcasting Corporation as a program organizer in the Talks and Public Affairs Department, and in this role he was associated with a number of the most important cultural programs on Canadian radio. These included 'Critically Speaking', which he began shortly after joining the CBC; 'Stories with John Drainie', which ran from 1959 to 1965; and 'Anthology', which he launched in 1953 and produced until 1985. Weaver was also closely involved in the cultural flagship program 'CBC Wednesday Night', which began in 1948, and with its successors. He retired from the CBC in 1985. In 1979 he founded, and was organizer of, CBC Radio's Canadian Literary Awards. He was an Officer of the Order of Canada.

As a program organizer and producer for radio, Weaver played an important role as a kind of impresario in the Canadian literary world, encouraging writers, producing their works, and giving them employment as critics and commentators. At a time when publishers and magazine editors lost interest in short stories, Weaver produced them on his radio programs, and in the process virtually discovered Mordecai RICHLER, Alice MUNRO, and other writers. His editing activities soon extended beyond radio: when the cessation of NORTHERN REVIEW and CONTEMPORARY VERSE in the early 1950s left Canada without a literary magazine of any consequence, he and a group of Toronto writers and publishers established The TAMARACK REVIEW (1956–82), of which he was the inspiring force. Weaver's interest in the short story led him into the preparation of anthologies. These include the five Oxford volumes Canadian short stories: First series (1960, rpr. 2008), Second series (1968), Third series (1978), Fourth series (1985), and Fifth series (1991)—all of them reprinted several times; and Ten for Wednesday night (1961). Another of his anthologies, The first five years (1962), consists of writings selected from the early issues of Tamarack. Weaver also edited a collection of stories by Mavis GALLANT, The end of the world and other stories (1973, NCL); with William Toye The Oxford anthology of Canadian literature (1973, 2nd edn 1981); Small wonders: new stories by twelve distinguished Canadian writers (1982); The Anthology anthology: a selection from 30 years of CBC Radio's 'Anthology' (1984); and, with Margaret ATWOOD, The Oxford book of Canadian short stories in English (1986, 2nd edn 1995).

See *Robert Weaver: godfather of Canadian literature* (2007) by Elaine Kalman Naves.

Webb, Phyllis (b. 1927). Born in Victoria, British Columbia, and educated at the University of British Columbia (B.A., 1949), she ran as a CCF candidate for the provincial legislature at the age of twenty-two. In 1950 she travelled to Montreal, where she did a year of graduate studies at McGill University. Webb lived in England, Paris, San Francisco, and Toronto, then taught at UBC for four years. In Toronto she conceived the CBC Radio program 'Ideas' and was its executive producer from 1966 to 1969, after which she returned to the west coast to settle on Salt Spring Island. She was made an Officer of the Order of Canada in 1992.

Webb's early poetry—published with poems by Gael Turnbull and Eli MANDEL in *Trio* (1954), and separately in *Even your right eye* (1956)—is both formal and rhetorical, with considerable clarity of statement and elegance of diction. With the publication of *Naked poems* (1965), language and sentiment are pared to the bone in a series of interconnected minimalist poems, whose narrator claims to be 'only remotely/human' and determined to ensure that 'the area of attack/ is diminished'. In *Selected poems: 1954–65* (1971), Webb's work becomes steadily more expansive, taking greater risks with content and form while not forgetting the hard-won lessons of economy and control. Her subsequent collections include *Wilson's bowl* (1980), *Sunday water: thirteen anti ghazals* (1982), *The vision tree: selected poems* (1982, GGA), *Water and light: ghazals and anti ghazals* (1984), and *Hanging fire* (1990). Her poetry is unique for its musicality and intellectual play, achieving a wonderful synchronicity of sound and idea. Her readers are invited to participate in the choreography of a nimble and discriminating mind as it selects, examines, and shapes its poetic materials. From this privileged position the reader can, to use Webb's own phrase, respond to 'the dance of the intellect in the syllables'.

As well as being a poet's poet, Webb has written a number of important and finely spun essays on poetry and poetics. Her essays, reviews, and radio talks were first collected in *Talking* (1982); a second volume, *Nothing but brush strokes: selected prose*, appeared in 1995, and included a photo-collage of the visual art that became her chief focus. Of particular interest are her comments on the poetic line, and the process by which many of her poems have come into being. In 'Message machine'

Webb characterizes herself as an ambivalent minimalist with a hyper-sensitive inner ear, so preoccupied with picking up subtle messages and fine-tuning them that she sometimes appears out of touch with her earlier political self; and yet, she argues, the poems deal with 'Marxian class struggle, animals rights, violent revolution, if only by means of glancing blows. The dialectic goes deep in my nature.'

Week, The (1883–96). This 'Canadian Journal of Politics, Society, and Literature' was founded by Goldwin SMITH and published in Toronto for the purpose of 'stimulating our national sentiment, guarding our national morality, and strengthening our national growth'. It appeared between 6 Dec. 1883 and 20 Nov. 1896. (Charles G.D. ROBERTS was editor for the first three months.) *The Week* conveyed an accurate impression of the intellectual currents and cultural taste of its day. Leading writers and intellectuals contributed stories, poems, essays, commentary on current issues, and reviews of literature, drama, and music. Topics frequently debated included realism and naturalism in literature, the problem of reconciling religion with Darwinism, and the Canadian copyright situation. Awareness of international trends in fiction was indicated in the reviews, while the publication of villanelles, rondeaux, and triolets demonstrated Canadian interest in the revival of French fixed forms that was currently underway in English poetry. Frequent poetry contributors included Archibald LAMPMAN, Susie Frances HARRISON, Ethelwyn WETHERALD, and Frederick George SCOTT. The liveliest columnist and essayist was Sara Jeannette DUNCAN.

Weintraub, William (b. 1926). Born in Montreal and educated at McGill University (B.A., 1947), Weintraub began his career at the Montreal *Gazette* where he worked as a reporter for two years. He subsequently freelanced as a journalist and broadcaster and held a staff position at *Weekend Magazine* before launching a successful and prolific career as a script writer, film producer, and director, primarily with the National Film Board, writing scripts and commentaries for more than 100 documentary NFB films. In 1985 he was program producer of sixteen half-hour dramatic films (a co-production of the NFB and Atlantis films) based on short stories by, among other Canadian authors, Alice MUNRO, Brian MOORE, Margaret LAURENCE, Timothy FINDLEY, and Mordecai RICHLER. Weintraub took early retirement from the NFB in 1986 to devote himself to writing. He is the author of five critically acclaimed books: the satirical novels *Why rock the boat?* (1962) and *The underdogs* (1979), another novel *Crazy about Lili* (2005); a lively history of Montreal in one of its most exciting periods, *City unique: Montreal days and nights in the 1940s and '50s* (1996); and *Getting started: a memoir of the 1950s with letters from Mordecai Richler, Mavis Gallant, and Brian Moore* (2001). The memoir aspects of Weintraub's life in Montreal and Europe in the 1950s—combined with the letters of Richler, GALLANT, and Moore—make for a wonderful book.

His first two novels lampoon the almost lunatic qualities of life in Québec. *Why rock the boat?* parodies the workings of a fictional Montreal English-language newspaper, delighting critics everywhere but in Montreal, where the local papers were frosty in their reception. Published three years after the first electoral success of the Parti Québécois, *The underdogs* is set in the future, twenty years after the purported creation of the Republic of Québec. This time the main butt of Weintraub's biting humour is the nationalist policy of the separatists, in particular their restrictive linguistic and cultural legislation. Weintraub adapted both his novels to other dramatic forms. He wrote and directed the film version of *Why rock the boat?* (1974), which became one of the most widely viewed Canadian features in its time, and he turned *The underdogs* into a play (1998). Rejected as being unfair to francophones by Montreal's Centaur Theatre, which had initially rented space for the production in 1989, it was not performed until 1996, and then not in Montreal but in Cobourg, Ontario. The title *Crazy about Lili* refers to Richard Lippman's attraction to the striptease artist Lili L'Amour in a farcical novel that mocks all kinds of things in the Montreal (and Québec) of the 1940s.

Weinzweig, Helen (1915–2010). Helen Tenenbaum was born in Poland and came to Toronto with her family at the age of nine. Her formal education ended abruptly after high school when the Depression impelled her to go to work—successively as a stenographer, receptionist, and salesperson. She married the composer John Weinzweig in 1940 and had two sons. Helen Weinzweig, who read widely—especially the work of Conrad, Jerzy Kosinski, John Barth, Borges, and Ivy Compton Burnett—published her first novel, *Passing ceremony* (1973), when she was fifty-seven. Its 117 pages display the ellipses and compression of good poetry. About a weird wedding between a homosexual and a promiscuous woman, the story is recounted by the principals and wedding guests through bits of internal monologue. Everyone is bored with the ceremony and trapped in various isolations of ennui, hatred, sickness, fantasy, or self-disgust. Composed of reverie, memory, quick perceptions, and fantasy, this novel is a tour de force on an unattractive subject. Weinzweig's second novel, *Basic black with pearls* (1980, rpr. 1990), as technically assured as *Passing ceremony*, is a more unified work; also short (only 135 pages), it consists of the internal monologue of one person, Shirley Kazenbowski, née Silverberg, alias Lola Montez. Shirley is in pursuit of her lover, Coenraad, a secret agent, who has apparently given her a coded message for an assignation in Toronto. Written totally subjectively, the novel never discloses whether the adventure is madness or sanity. It is both comic and pathetic: high romance and sordid reality collide and collude in a slow waltz through a labyrinth that is also the familiar cityscape of Toronto. *A view from the roof* (1989) is a collection of thirteen of Weinzweig's short stories—including 'Causation', 'A view from the roof', 'What happened to Ravel's bolero?', and 'The man with memories'—that have many of the qualities of her longer fiction.

Wetherald, Agnes Ethelwyn (1857–1940). The daughter of English Quaker parents, she was born in Rockwood, Ontario, received her early education at home, and later studied at a Quaker school in New York State and at Pickering College in Ontario. She became a journalist and contributed to many Canadian and American periodicals; for a time she was the editor of the women's department of the Toronto *Globe*, using the pseudonym 'Bel Thistlewaite'. Although Wetherald's poems had begun appearing in the late 1870s, her first collection, *The house of the trees and other poems* (Boston), was not published until 1895. Five other collections followed between 1902 and the publication of her collected *Lyrics and sonnets* in 1931. Her early work was favourably received by reviewers on both sides of the Atlantic, and praised by influential contemporaries, including Archibald LAMPMAN. Major anthologies of the time, including Wilfred CAMPBELL's *Oxford book of Canadian verse* (1913) and John Garvin's *Canadian poets* (1916), gave her extensive representation. Her treatment of nature, the main subject of many of her poems, has been described as shallow and sentimental, and much of her other work is

judged to be conventional in style and thought. This criticism, however, is too dismissive: Wetherald's presentation of nature is often sensual and occasionally erotic; her technical skill, particularly in the sonnet form, is at times of a very high order. Some poems, in their gravity and restraint, recall the work of Emily Dickinson, a resemblance that Wetherald's as-yet unexamined Quaker background and New England connections (most of her books were published in Boston) would clarify.

Wetherald also wrote *An Algonquin maiden: a romance of the early days of Upper Canada* (Montreal, 1887) in collaboration with G. Mercer ADAM, a novel that—as Pauline JOHNSON once noted—failed to avoid the usual inaccuracies and sentimental stereotypes.

Wevill, David (b. 1935). Born in Yokohama, Japan, of Canadian parents, he left Japan shortly before the Second World War and was educated in Toronto, and at Trinity College School, Port Hope, Ontario, before taking his B.A. (1957) at Caius College, Cambridge University. During this period Wevill won England's Eric Gregory Award for Poetry, the only Canadian to do so. He was also the only Canadian to appear in A. Alvarez's landmark anthology, *The new poetry* (1965). In 1960 he became the third husband of Assia Lipsey. He and his wife made friends with Sylvia Plath and Ted Hughes, who in time became Assia's lover (they had a daughter). Six years after Plath committed suicide, Assia did the same, in 1969. Following a period in Burma, where he taught at the University of Mandalay, and a sojourn in Spain, Wevill moved to Austin, Texas, where he became professor of English at the University of Texas, Austin; he is now Professor Emeritus.

Wevill's poetry weaves an intricate mixture of cultural legend and autobiographical reflection in which he sets the understanding of his own life, its joys and various personal difficulties, against the suffering of other artists (Ezra Pound, Robert Schumann, Yasunari Kawabata) as if they are conduits to the solace he seems to crave. The early works, which portray an uncertain, often lonely individual; the middle works, which offer a modern man in search of a dependable though oblique personal mythology; and the later works, which present an understanding of a man's position within the experience of his own life—form an opus of self-exploration where the only answer is the Faulknerian edict of endurance and perseverance. His poems often depict the women in his life—his dying mother, his three daughters, and his lost lovers—and they become more than recurring characters or motifs, muse-like in their presence, both troubling and inspiring him. His poetry—especially in his most recent collections, *Other names for the heart: new and selected poems, 1964–1984* (1985), *Figure of eight: new poems and selected translations* (1987), and *Child eating snow* (1994)—show the marked influence of poets whose works he has translated, namely Lorca, Neruda, Machado, Paz, and the Hungarian Ferenc Juhász. Wevill has noted their influence, particularly in reference to his use of landscape, which he views not as 'nature, but as "something out there"'. Into this landscape Wevill often interjects a solitary, contemplative figure who is more at home in his own mind than in his physical environment, as in the early poem 'At Rideau Falls' from *Birth of a shark* (1964), or in the title poem from *A Christ of the ice-floes* (1966). Wevill's is a poetry of the searcher, a recurring theme that signals both his personal restlessness and the need to 'create complete poems, not just passing observations'. One of his most complete poems is the title piece in *Birth of a shark*, in which the world is seen from the obtuse perspective of a young shark that finds himself among a threatening hoard of swimmers. Wevill's next three collections—*Firebreak* (1971), *Where the arrow falls* (1974), and the prose poems in *Casual ties* (1983)—mark an experimental phase in his work where he appears to be looking for direction and foundation in both poetry and life. *Casual ties* concludes with a vision of a man, like Shakespeare's Prospero, casting his book into the sea. However, in *Other names for the heart*, a poetic rebirth at the urging of publisher Barry CALLAGHAN, Wevill rediscovers his poetic and personal roots in Japan in 'Snow country', a reflection on Japanese novelist Yasunari Kawabata's tragic story of a geisha and a wealthy businessman. The title poem—in which the persona sees human passion as a form of obsession that must be endured in the name of life and art—examines the isolated passions of Robert Schumann during that composer's final days. In 'Summer morning', which concludes *Child eating snow*, Wevill re-examines his personal life from the perspective of a survivor: 'You see the world / you saw fifty years ago but had / no words for. Having the words / now makes the light hold still a moment / and the moment resembles your life.' These collections were followed by *Solo with grazing deer* (2001) and *Asterisks* (2007), which was also published by Barry Callaghan's EXILE EDITIONS. It is a collection of forty-nine numbered short poems—little epiphanies: 'I am not carried away / by poetry. // If a poem were to / carry me off, I'd say // put me down, we've / come a long way together. // Now tell me / what it was all about. // Oh, nothing. Nothing.' The year 2010 saw the publication of *To build my shadow a fire: the poetry and translations of David Wevill*, edited by Michael McGriff.

White, Howard (b. 1945). Born in Abbotsford, British Columbia—and living now in Madeira Park, BC—he had a working-class background of driving trucks and bulldozing in logging country, which he often refers to in his writings. But in 1969–74 he published a community newspaper, *The Peninsula Voice*, and in 1974 he founded—and is now the president and publisher of—HARBOUR PUBLISHING, which has had an enormous influence in the region and beyond in publishing BC writers. He is also known for editing the series Raincoast Chronicles. The first issue of this magazine-format publication—featuring stories and articles about the history of the British Columbia coast—*Raincoast chronicles first five* (1975), sold over 40,000 copies, and the series continued to issue 20 (2004). White's own writings have appeared in numerous books, including *Writing in the rain: stories, essays & poems* (1990), which includes his popular story 'The bomb that mooed', about a cow 'whose greatest caper was the time it ate the dynamite'—the book won the Leacock Medal for Humour. White's poetry collections, *The men were then* (1983) and *The ghost in the gears* (1993), include poems about work in the mines and work camps of British Columbia, as well as such poems (in *The ghost*) as 'Poem ending with a line by Raymond Carver', in which an acquaintance 'tells me the oil industry is quaking/in their boots over a/bacterium/that inhabits the swift-flowing/corridors of the world's great/oil pipelines ... those bacteria [the poem ends]/are the heroes of this poem'; and 'Invisible minority': 'There are 1 million Canadian unemployed./ That's enough to stretch from Vancouver/to Calgary if placed head to foot/on their bellies along the Trans Canada Highway.' White received the Order of British Columbia in 1997, an honorary LL.D from the University of Victoria in 2003, and was made a Member of the Order of Canada in 2008.

White savannahs, The (1936, rpr. 1975). This was the first book-length work on English-Canadian literature written from a purely critical standpoint, that of the modernist movement of the years after the First World War. Its author, William Edwin Collin (1893–1984), an English-born academic trained in France, taught Romance languages at the University of Western Ontario from 1923 to 1959. To his study of eight English-speaking poets and one French prose-writer, he brought (i) the inwardness and subjectivity of late nineteenth-century French critical writing; (ii) the 'neoclassical' critical theories of T.E. Hulme; and (iii) the influence of myth criticism, which was then being felt by such poets as T.S. Eliot. Collin was attracted to the first English-Canadian writers able to assimilate and learn from the modernist movement whose writing directly challenged the genteel tradition then dominant in Canadian literature. He first explored these new green shoots of creativity, struggling to emerge beneath the frozen 'white savannahs' of Canadian culture, in several essays produced between 1931 and 1934 for *The Canadian Forum* and *The University of Toronto Quarterly*. In Archibald LAMPMAN and Marjorie PICKTHALL Collin saw a retreat from the search for cosmic order into a repressed fiction of 'nature'. An essay—somewhat unrelated to the others—on the French novelist Marie Le Franc, who lived for twenty years in Montreal and set some of her novels in Canada, hints at how Collin connected myth criticism with both a theory of style and a general view of civilization. But the core of the book was his attentive and enthusiastic reading of the MONTREAL GROUP—F.R. SCOTT, A.M. KLEIN, A.J.M. SMITH, Leo KENNEDY—and their contemporaries E.J. PRATT and Dorothy LIVESAY. For Collin most of these poets, like their 'metaphysical' forebears in the seventeenth century, redefined the word 'natural' in terms that would preserve the human in 'a real world of living and mechanical forces'. Though Collin recognized their common ground, his critical method richly elicited the independent virtues of each writer: the link between imagist and socialist in Livesay, the stern ethical centre in Scott, the fruitful confrontation of heritages in Klein, a certain austerity and reserve in Smith. His deepest rapport was with Kennedy, whom he saw—not very persuasively—as providing at last the redemptive pattern linking man with the natural order that Lampman could not envision. Though *The white savannahs*—which was reprinted in 1975 with an introduction by Germaine Warkentin—did not sell well in 1936, its influence on Canadian poetry and critical writing was considerable, both in its contribution to what A.J.M. Smith called 'a new climate of opinion among readers and publishers of poetry in Canada' and in the exemplary wit, enthusiasm, and elegance of its critical prose.

Whittaker, Herbert (1910–2006). Born in Montreal, he studied design at the École des Beaux-Arts. He began designing for Montreal amateur theatres in 1933 and reviewing film, ballet, and theatre for the Montreal *Gazette* in 1934, serving as the paper's lead critic from 1937 to 1949. In 1949 he joined the Toronto *Globe and Mail* as theatre and film critic. He became its theatre and ballet critic in 1952, and reviewed theatre until his retirement in 1975, when he was named the *Globe's* critic emeritus. He was an Officer of the Order of Canada. In his theatre criticism Whittaker was a strong supporter of Canadian actors, playwrights, and directors. Besides designing and directing several prize-winning productions for over twenty amateur companies in Montreal and Toronto from 1933 to 1982, Whittaker directed and designed for the Jupiter Theatre in Toronto in 1951; directed for the Crest Theatre in 1954 and 1956; and designed sets and costumes for the 1961–2 tour of the Canadian Players. He served as a governor of the Dominion Drama Festival from 1949 to 1968 and was a member of the Board of Trustees of the National Arts Centre from 1976 to 1982. Unlike Nathan COHEN, who kept aloof from the theatre community, Whittaker maintained an involvement in live theatre that made him aware of the economic and artistic difficulties of Canadian productions. His criticism (unlike Cohen's) generally accented positive aspects. He has said: 'Appreciation has always been more important than fault-finding in the theatre critic's lexicon. I think I make my points quite clear without a hammer.'

See Whittaker's *Setting the stage: Montreal theatre 1920–1949* (1999). His career is surveyed in John Rittenhouse's 'Herbert Whittaker: a theatre life', and in *Theatre history in Canada* (Spring 1982). A collection of his theatre criticism appears in *Whittaker's theatre: a critic looks at stages in Canada and thereabouts 1944–1975* (1985) edited by Ronald Bryden with Boyd Neil.

Who has seen the wind (1947, rpr. 2000), by W.O. MITCHELL, is one of Canada's most beloved novels. Structured in four parts and set in a Saskatchewan town, it dramatizes Brian O'Connal's growth from age four to twelve, and his youthful struggle to comprehend 'the ultimate meaning of the cycle of life' in the face of loss and death.

Prairie, family, and town all contribute to his awakening sense of perspective and social responsibility. By the novel's end young Brian, originally self-centred in his innocence, has matured to the point that he imagines his future as a 'dirt doctor', pledged to minister to the land and the difficult environmental conditions affecting the lives of the people he loves. But Brian's growth has an inverse quality, as Mitchell's allusions to Wordsworth suggest. In childhood Brian is closest to nature and the divine; he experiences intimations of immortality particular to a prairie boyhood. As he ages his social identity begins to take shape; 'the feeling' he often experienced occurs far less frequently. In Brian's growth the prairie is a vast romantic stage, its vitality symbolized by characters like the Bens and Saint Sammy. In contrast, the town seems ruled by the restrictions and cruelties of a life-denying puritanism. Brian's most effective teachers are associated with the prairie or the peripheries of town, where waspish elitism, racial prejudice, unfairness, and hypocrisy have less place. Though melodramatically schematized, the novel has a freshness of perspective, a cogency of theme, a vividness of voice and event, and a vitality of presentation that contribute to its continuing popularity and prominence—its status as a 'classic'—in Canadian letters. First published in Canada by MACMILLAN, and in the United States by Little, Brown, the shorter and edited American version was the basis for reprints for over thirty years. A coffee-table edition, with illustrations by William Kurelek, appeared in 1976. It was not until 1991, however, that McCLELLAND & STEWART published an edition that restored the text as Mitchell had intended it. A paperback edition (1993) and a fiftieth-anniversary commemorative edition (1997) followed. A 1977 film based on the novel was directed by Alan King.

Wiebe, Rudy (b. 1934). Born on the family farm at Speedwell, a small Mennonite community near Fairholme, Saskatchewan, of parents who came to Canada from the Soviet Union in 1930, Rudy Henry Wiebe began writing seriously as an undergraduate at the University of Alberta (B.A., 1956; M.A., 1960). He studied at the University of Tübingen, West Germany, in 1957-8 and then at the Mennonite Brethren Bible College (Th.B., 1961). In 1967 he joined the English Department of the University of Alberta, Edmonton, becoming a full professor in 1977, and since 1992 has been Professor Emeritus. He was made an Officer of the Order of Canada in 2000.

Wiebe has written nine novels: *Peace shall destroy many* (1962, rpr. 2001), *First and vital candle* (1966, rpr. 2006), *The blue mountains of China* (1970, NCL), *The temptations of Big Bear* (1973, rpr. 1999, GGA, NCL), *The scorched-wood people* (1977, rpr. 2004), *The mad trapper* (1980), *My lovely enemy* (1983), *A discovery of strangers* (1994, rpr. 1995, GGA), and *Sweeter than all the world* (2001, rpr. 2002). He has also produced collections of short stories: *Where is the voice coming from?* (1974) and *Alberta/a celebration* (1979), which contains photographs by Tom Radford and commentary by Harry Savage—selections from these books were reprinted in *The angel of the tar sands and other stories* (1982); a play, *Far as the eye can see* (1977); and two picture books for children, *Chinook Christmas* (1992), illustrated by David More, and *Hidden buffalo* (2003), illustrated by Michael Lonechild. The two aspects of Wiebe's life that are most important to his art are that he is a Westerner and that he was born, and continues to be, a Mennonite, having spoken Russian Mennonite Low German at home, High German in church, and English when he entered grade one. His fiction, though experimental in style and form (his major novels are among our most successful experimental works), is resolutely committed to a radical and an ecumenical Christian vision. *Peace shall destroy many, First and vital candle*, and *The blue mountains of China* are essentially about people's struggle to live a moral and spiritual life in a world where such terms and assumptions are increasingly considered archaic and even obsolete. The first dramatizes—in a realistic style and within a relatively conventional four-part seasonal structure—the conflicts that arise during the Second World War in a Mennonite community in Wapiti, Sask. Most of the action is seen through the eyes of the protagonist, Thom Wiens, an earnest and inquiring young man who is torn between the old ways (represented by the dogmatic and bullying Deacon Block) and the new (embodied in, and articulated by, the reforming Joseph Duecke). The novel's central question—how does one live a truly Christian life in a fundamentally non-Christian world?—is raised again in *First and vital candle*, which depicts the life of Abe Ross, who has lost his faith. An ambitious, closely organized work, containing many powerful scenes of Native and Inuit life, the novel is finally too portentous and didactic. In *The blue mountains of China* Wiebe turned to the historical and epic mode characteristic of his major novels. It offers both a criticism of the materialism and one-dimensionality

(Marcuse's term) of modern life, and an affirmative alternative. At the centre of this episodic novel, covering almost a century of Mennonite history—including the heroic 1920s emigration from Soviet Russia to Canada and later to Paraguay—is a vision of various forms of Christian action and commitment: from the passive but firm belief of Frieda Friessen to the active witnessing of the cross-carrying John Reimer, who is walking through western Canada in search of the scattered Mennonite communities that still cling to the original revelation. The culmination of Wiebe's fictional writings about the Mennonites is surely the sweeping *Sweeter than all the world*, which is set both in the historical European past—the Netherlands, Danzig, London (and Russia) and in the twentieth century, when it tells of Adam Wiebe, who was born in Saskatchewan in 1935. Wiebe has said that he was prompted to write it when he discovered that his family name went all the way back 'to the 1500s in Harlingen, Friesland—now the Netherlands—and the historical Wybe Adams [to whom the novel is dedicated], a brilliant water engineer who, during the Thirty Years War that devastated Europe between 1618 and 1648, invented the cable car to move masses of earth to build and strengthen the walls of the city of Danzig.' *Sweeter than all the world* is one of Wiebe's signal literary accomplishments.

Wiebe has written extensively about Canada's Native peoples, in part because they resemble the Mennonites in their concern for a community embodying spiritual values, and because they exist on the periphery of, and in opposition to, modern society. Wiebe's commitment to this body of western experience—which is traditionally ignored, or misinterpreted, in Canadian history and fiction—is reflected in minor works, such as some of the stories in *Alberta/a celebration* and *Where is the voice coming from?* and in the adventure novel *The mad trapper*, as well as in *The temptations of Big Bear*, *The scorched-wood people*, and *A discovery of strangers*. By means of a complex polyphonic, multiple-viewpoint narrative structure, incorporating much documentary material, Wiebe tries in *The temptations of Big Bear* to present the Native point of view, especially Big Bear's struggle to understand the changes taking place in the West in the last decades of the nineteenth century. This often brilliant, often difficult novel covers twelve years—from Big Bear's refusal to sign a treaty in 1876, through his inadvertent involvement in the killings at Frog Lake in 1884, to

his imprisonment and death. (See also Wiebe's biography *Big Bear* [2008] in Penguin's Extraordinary Canadians Series.) A massive attempt at fictive translation, it attempts to give one culture (ours) an imaginative sense of another (the Cree's). To emphasize the conflict between the two cultures Wiebe uses opposed sets of images: the whites, described predominantly in images drawn from civilization, are all angles and straight lines; the Natives are represented in images drawn from nature, with the result that Big Bear is a curve, a wave of life, a bird, a tree, and finally, in the novel's resonant closing image, a rock. More significantly, however, he is associated with the wind, with spirit, and—like most of Wiebe's fictional heroes—with speech and vision. Big Bear—in this novel, and in the tragic nature of his life—anticipates another visionary and revolutionary, Louis Riel, the central, heroic figure in *The scorched-wood people*. (Riel appears on the periphery of *The temptatiaons of Big Bear*, is mentioned in *Peace shall destroy many*, and his grave is visited by Abe Ross in *First and vital candle*.) Like Big Bear, Riel articulates and embodies a vision of western community. Wiebe's complex portrait of him (both in form and content), and of the Métis, is historical revisionism with a vengeance: Wiebe refuses to accept the traditional interpretations of the man and his era offered by some noted historians. Instead of presenting Riel as mad (and the Métis as a marginal group impeding progress), Wiebe describes him in Christological terms as a visionary and a millenarian, the prophet of a vision of community that stands in direct opposition to the expansionist capitalist 'vision' of the prime minister, Sir John A. Macdonald. Wiebe has argued that the border between fiction and history has been called into doubt in our era. In *The scorched-wood people* he holds our interest by filling in the lacunae of history, providing details that no one person could have known by means of an omniscient posthumous narrator, Pierre Falcon, the poet of the Métis, who had seen Riel. *My lovely enemy* uses the story of a love affair between a professor of history at the University of Alberta and a graduate student as the basis for an exploration of Wiebe's traditional concerns: man's relationship to God, the relevance of Christianity, and the nature and scope of human and divine love. The challenging narrative technique, combining realism and fantasy, is the perfect medium for Wiebe's central theme that love, erotic or spiritual, transcends time. However, this ambitious novel, which includes a rewriting of Dostoevsky's 'Grand Inquisitor' episode, has a major weakness: the author's slightly sentimental attitude towards his three central characters. *The mad trapper* is a novel that fleshes out Wiebe's essay and short story, 'The naming of Albert Johnson', about Johnson, the 'mad trapper' who shot a Mountie and became the object of a lengthy and widely publicized chase through the North. (The essay can be found in *Figures in a ground: Canadian essays on modern literature collected in honour of Sheila Watson* [1978] edited by Diane Bessai and David Jackel; the story can be read in Robert WEAVER's *Canadian short stories: third series*, 1978.) Wiebe's least ambitious work, it is in essence a well-told adventure story.

Focusing on the 1820–21 expedition of John Franklin (1786–1847) to the Arctic coast of what is today Canada, *Playing dead: a contemplation concerning the Arctic* (1989, rev. 2003) is a series of interrelated essays in which Wiebe weaves his impressions of the North, Inuit narratives, and discussions of various explorers from Franklin to Vilhjalmur Stefansson. Like the novel it anticipates, the book is notable both for its sensitive and informed treatment of Native and Inuit ways of life, as well as for its refusal to simplify or sentimentalize them. In retrospect the book seems like a set of preparatory sketches for *A discovery of strangers*, which recasts the sections dealing with Franklin's first expedition in the form of a historical novel that shows the English explorers and their misconceived expedition from several viewpoints, including that of the Tetsot'ine or Yellowstone Natives who helped them survive. Thoroughly researched and often drawing on period materials, the novel interweaves excerpts from journals kept by Robert Hood and John Richardson, Native narratives, myths, and songs, and the story of the expedition, which provides it with a unifying narrative drive. At the heart of the novel are Franklin's obsession with the journey and the love affair between Robert Hood and Greenstocking, a historical figure named in Franklin's narrative and perhaps Wiebe's most fully realized female portrait. This relationship serves, ironically, to emphasize the irreconcilable disparity between Europeans and Natives when, at the novel's end, Greenstocking refuses to acknowledge to the English that her child is Hood's.

Wiebe's novels and stories stress that the 'signs' of God's presence are, and will always be, visible and available: people need only be receptive to the various incarnations taking place around them. The writings are filled with homely figures who, shadowed by biblical originals, function as Christ-like scapegoats,

reminding others of a fully Christian life. No other Canadian writer, French or English, has made as concerted an attempt to give the peoples of the First Nations a voice in fiction. Critical debate about Wiebe's novels, however, has often focused less on his themes than on his style, which some readers have found ponderous in rhythm and tortuous in syntax. For his admirers, Wiebe's style became smoother in later writings; his so-called difficult style is the necessary expression of the fiction's complex attitude to life and its ambitious attempt to render non-European modes of thought, being, and expression.

Two other publications reveal Wiebe in a different light. *Stolen life: the journey of a Cree woman* (1998), of which Yvonne Johnson is co-author, had its beginning when Johnson—imprisoned in 1991 in the Kingston Federal Prison for Women for her involvement in a murder—wrote Wiebe (whose *The temptations of Big Bear* she had read) a long letter in which she told him that 'my grandfather's grandfather was the Cree chief Big Bear.' They met in the prison four times between 1991 and 1995, when Johnson was transferred to the minimum-security Okimaw Ohci Healing Lodge for Native Women in Saskatchewan. With Wiebe as a mentor, she filled seventeen prison notebooks of reminiscences with ever-increasing skill and self-insight. The book is mainly Wiebe's presentation of an engrossing and vivid account, in Johnson's own words, of one Native's troubled life that is illuminated by his linking texts. *River of stone: fiction and memories* (1995), a collection of Wiebe's short fiction (including 'The naming of Albert Johnson'), is supplemented by personal narratives.

The many books he has written and the growing refinement of his literary skills, along with a vibrant memory of his childhood in Speedwell—his schooling, books, nature as he experienced it—resulted in what one hopes is the first volume of Wiebe's memoirs, the engaging and vivid *Of this earth: a Mennonite boyhood in the boreal forest* (2006). The influence of the 'seemingly endless land' he lived in, and the 'visitation of wind', is summed up as follows: 'Bracing myself into that breathing wind, I would grow to feel it: a land too far to see, fathomless to the looking eye—but, perhaps, touchable by words. Words strung out with the utmost care, like the thin, high steel of the railroad bridge at Lethbridge stretching itself across the immense canyon of the Oldman River, words forged and bolted together into the living architecture of story.' This wonderful evocation of the source of perhaps all of Wiebe's writing won the 2007 Charles Taylor Prize for Literary Non-Fiction.

See *Rudy Wiebe and his works* (1986) by Susan Whaley, *The Rudy Wiebe papers: first accession* (1986) edited by Apollonia Steele, and *Rudy Wiebe: a tribute* (2002) edited by Hilde Froese Tiessen.

Wild animals I have known (New York, 1898; 1977, NCL; rpr. 1991, 2009). The first and most famous of many collections of animal stories by Ernest Thompson SETON, it includes the perenially popular 'Lobo, the King of Currumpaw' and seven other stories. Since publication it has never been out of print and exists in numerous translations. Along with Charles G.D. ROBERTS' *The kindred of the wild* (1902), it marked the beginning of a new genre: the realistic animal story. Seton's innovation was to make an animal, rather than a human, the central character. His goal was to make a moral point about humanity's relation to animals and to the wilderness they inhabit, emphasizing the need to live in harmony with nature. His work as a naturalist supplied the raw material for his stories. He insisted that his animal biographies were all fact, but admitted that they were often composite portraits, based on his observations of many animals of a species. The story of the wolf Lobo was first published in *Scribner's Magazine* (Nov. 1894). Based on a real episode that took place in 1892 when Seton visited New Mexico, it describes the killing of Blanca, the capture of her mate Lobo, and his mysterious death during captivity. Seton's fellow scientists, arguing that a wolf cannot die of a broken heart, challenged his assertion that his stories were factual. Repeated charges of anthropomorphism—the 'nature-fakir' controversy—acted as a catalyst to increase Seton's productivity in scientific publications; but they did not keep him from writing numerous collections of stories following his popular formula.

Wilkinson, Anne (1910–61). Born in Toronto, Anne Gibbons spent her early years there and in London, Ontario; she was educated privately by tutors, and at progressive schools in the USA and France. She married F.R. Wilkinson, a surgeon, in 1932 (they were divorced twenty-two years later) and brought up a family of two sons and a daughter in Toronto.

Anne Wilkinson's reputation as a writer was founded on two books of poetry, *Counterpoint to sleep* (1951) and *The hangman ties the holly* (1955), but she was equally accomplished

in prose. In *Lions in the way* (1956) she traced the story of her distinguished family, the Oslers, who originally settled in the backwoods of Ontario, in Tecumseth Township. Her great-grandmother, Ellen Osler, raised nine children, four of whom developed outstandingly successful careers: Featherston and Britton Bath Osler as eminent lawyers; Sir William Bath Osler as Regius Professor of Medicine at Oxford; and her grandfather Sir Edmund Osler as a financier and Member of Parliament. The figure who emerges most clearly, however, is Ellen, to whose courage and strong personality these men owed their success. The book provides a lively social history of Upper Canada. An epilogue brings the tale up to Wilkinson's own childhood, when she spent long periods in her grandfather's Toronto mansion, Craigleigh. This luxurious house is also described in the beautifully written autobiographical piece, 'Four corners of my world', originally published in *The TAMARACK REVIEW* 20 (Summer 1961), of which she was a founding editor and generous patron. A.J.M. SMITH included this memoir in *The collected poems of Anne Wilkinson* (1968), where poems and fragments from periodicals and manuscripts are added to the two volumes of poetry published in her lifetime. Smith's edition was re-issued, with a new introduction by Joan Coldwell, as *The poetry of Anne Wilkinson and a prose memoir* (1990). 'Four corners of my world' is a much-abridged version of the full-length autobiography that Wilkinson submitted for publication late in her life but that remained unpublished until it was included in *The tightrope walker: autobiographical writings of Anne Wilkinson* (1992) edited by Joan Coldwell. This volume also contains the journals Wilkinson wrote between 1947 and 1956, the years of her productivity as a poet as well as of the disintegration of her marriage. The journals create an intimate portrait of a woman balancing the demands of motherhood and poetry; they also provide a valuable record of social and literary history, relating to both Toronto and Canada. The autobiography and the journals testify to Wilkinson's love for, and close bond with, her mother, Mary Osler Gibbons Boyd.

The 'four corners' of Wilkinson's world are seen as archetypes: the Gothic family home in London; the classical Craigleigh; the romantic summer home on Lake Simcoe; and the mysteriously evocative oceanside house in Santa Barbara, California, where her mother spent winters. A similar shaping of material into a quaternity characterizes Wilkinson's poetry, where this method of seeing unity in multiplicity, especially in imagery of the four elements, emphasizes her own sense of identity and her oneness with nature. Her poetry is both highly sensuous and wittily intellectual; even in the most passionate of her love poems she plays with puns and with references to her eclectic reading. Her subjects range from the landscapes of her family's 'summer acres', where she insists on the spirituality of the senses, to philosophical enquiries based on Kafka, Empedocles, and medieval texts. A.J.M. Smith's prefatory essay to *The collected poems* gives a fine analysis of these aspects of her work, as also of her poems of love and death, pointing to the celebration of metamorphosis in her poetry—a motif found, too, in her story for children, *Swann and Daphne* (1960). Delightfully illustrated by Leo Rampen, it tells of two mysterious children: instead of hair the boy has feathers and the girl has leaves. In an ironic comment on the relation of the sexes, the girl sacrifices her own plans and turns into a birch tree in order to free the boy for a life of adventure with the wild swans.

A fairly recent publication elucidates and honours Wilkinson's poetry: *Heresies: the complete poems of Anne Wilkinson 1924–1961* (2003), edited, with an Introduction and textual notes, by Dean Irvine. Including forty-six previously uncollected poems, this is a distinguished scholarly achievement, containing a perceptive account of the biographical background and throwing light on the composition of Wilkinson's poems.

Williams, David (b. 1945). Born in Souris, Manitoba, he grew up in a number of Saskatchewan towns, most importantly in Lac Vert. His parents and paternal grandfather, strong fundamentalists, tried to block his entry into journalism at the University of Western Ontario, and succeeded in sending him to Briercrest Bible Institute (near Moose Jaw), from which he graduated with a pastor's diploma in 1965. He nevertheless attended the University of Saskatchewan (B.A. Hons., 1968) and the University of Massachusetts (M.A., 1970; Ph.D., 1973). Since 1983 he has taught English literature at St Paul's College, University of Manitoba, where he became a full professor, teaching Canadian literature and Milton. Brilliantly evoking prairie landscapes and social conflict, Williams' three novels—the Lacjardin trilogy—show the influence of Milton's and Melville's searching for myths that would make sense of suffering. *The burning wood* (1975), built on his haunting memory of sitting in his grandfather's Stony Lake Bible Camp and

hearing the drums of the Chagoness Indian Reserve, follows Williams' alter-ego, Joshua Cardiff, as he runs away from Bible Camp with his Cree friend Thomas. Joshua's sense of personal damnation, and of a Christian society that has betrayed its ideals, results in his wish to 'go Indian', but the hilarious attempt to resurrect the buffalo hunt—with stolen Clydesdales and reluctant cattle—ends in tragedy. *The river hosemen* (1981) even more convulsively mixes Cree culture with prairie fundamentalism by calling up personal and collective pasts in an effective use of Faulkner's interior monologues. Having lost parents, women, and God in the Depression, the four horsemen paddle up the South Saskatchewan River from Lacjardin to Saskatoon. The river's monstrous underworld of corpses and inexplicable drownings matches the dissolving world on shore, where not only dust, but also the Regina Riots and Edward VIII's abdication oppress. As funny as it is apocalyptic, the novel expands in a series of layered parodies: of the gospels and revivalism in the faith healer Jack Cann; of the Cree trickster Wisahkecahk in Many Birds and Billy O'Jibway; of the shaman in Fine Day; and of a Huck Finn figure in the profane Ukrainian boy, Nick. Jack Cann, believing that he must die as God, and Many Birds, believing that his ex-lover Agnes ought to feel his sexual prowess one more time, bring the novel to its explosive conclusion, while more humane possibilities are imagined in Fine Day's hesitant remembering of the spirit world and Nick's location of his abused mother. Struck by the parallels between his own family history and the Brynhild cycle, Williams next fictionalized his maternal grandfather in *Eye of the father* (1985) as the scapegrace Magnus Vangdal, whose flight from his father's house in Hardangerfjorden (Norway) lands him in Lacjardin. His alias, Magnus Sigurdson, proves prophetic as he goes through fire to rescue Hilda and later abandons her. Finally a lost soul in a new country, Magnus becomes one of the Old Ones from whom he fled. Hilda, however, refuses a Wagnerian immolation. Under the rune that signifies necessity or constraint, she and her descendants struggle to accept Magnus's legacy without repeating his life.

Williams has also published *Confessional fictions: a portrait of the artist in the Canadian novel* (1991), *Imagined nations: reflections on media in Canadian fiction* (2003), and *Media, memory, and the First World War* (2009).

Wilson, Budge (b. 1927). Born Budge Marjorie Archibald in Halifax, Nova Scotia, she was educated at Dalhousie University

(B.A., 1949, Dip. Ed., 1953) and the University of Toronto (1949–51), and married Alan Wilson in 1953; they have two daughters and two grandsons. After living in Ontario for thirty-three years, the Wilsons returned to Halifax, and Budge Wilson—a teacher, fitness instructor, photographer, and illustrator—began to write seriously for children and young people. Her early books are *The best/worst Christmas present ever* (1991), *Mr John Bertrand Nijinsky and Charlie* (1986), *A house far from home* (1986), *Mystery lights at Blue Harbour* (1987). In *Thirteen never changes* (1989) Lorinda inherits her grandmother's diaries and reads the diary when she was *her* age, thirteen. Budge Wilson said in an interview: 'The grandmother died when she was sixty; I wrote the book when I was sixty.... World War II was on. The British Guest Children had arrived and were about to make an enormous impact on all our lives.' Wilson has published more than thirty books—many of which have won awards—with twenty-seven foreign editions in fourteen languages. *The leaving* (1990, rpr. 1993; American edn 1992)—a collection of nine beautifully written, vivid stories about the family relationships of girls in Nova Scotia—won the Canadian Young Adult Book Award and earned many other citations, such as 'Best Book', 'Notable Book', 'Noteworthy Book', *Horn Book* 'Fanfare Book'. It is of particular interest because it includes a story, 'Lysandra's poem', that is taught in high schools and is extremely popular with grade nine students. Wilson also achieved great success with her 2008 publication, *Before Green Gables*, a prequel to ANNE OF GREEN GABLES, in which she describes Anne's life before she went to Green Gables, capturing her voice and personality delightfully. Budge Wilson was made a Member of the Order of Canada in 2004.

Wilson, Ethel (1888–1980). Born Ethel Davis Bryant at Port Elizabeth, South Africa, where her father was a Methodist missionary, she was taken to England in 1890 on the death of her mother and had a happy life with her father and relatives. In 1898, after her father died, she was sent to Canada and lived with her domineering Methodist grandmother in Vancouver in circumstances—'it was impossible to be young'—drawn upon later for *The innocent traveller* (1949, NCL). Like Frankie Burnaby in *Hetty Dorval* (1947, NCL), she attended boarding schools, first in Vancouver and then in England. After receiving a teacher's certificate from the Vancouver Normal School in 1907, she taught at various local schools until 1920. In 1921 she married Dr Wallace Wilson, then

at the beginning of a distinguished medical career (he was president of the Canadian Medical Association in 1946–7).

Wilson's writing career—for which she was appointed an Officer of the Order of Canada in 1970–began late. She started to publish short stories in the *New Statesman and Nation* in the late 1930s, and her first novel did not appear until 1947. In *Hetty Dorval* (influenced by Willa Cather's *My mortal enemy*) the story of the 'experienced' Hetty Dorval is told through the 'innocent' Frankie Burnaby, a girl growing up in the British Columbia hinterland. The plot is a trifle forced, but Wilson demonstrates an ability to combine stylistic clarity and technical sophistication with the authorial poise, humour, and good sense that characterize all her fiction. Her next novel, *The innocent traveller*, employs elements from her own family history in tracing the life of Topaz Edgeworth from precocious three-year-old in the English Midlands to still irrepressible centenarian in Vancouver. Besides offering a wholly credible portrait of a character rarely encountered in fiction—the unconventional, unfrustrated middle-class spinster who lives a passive, unremarkable yet full and happy life—the novel offers a convincing presentation of social developments in England and Canada over a long period (the 1840s to the 1940s). Wilson's later fiction reveals an increasing interest in portraying various kinds of women at times of personal crisis, and in exploring spiritual and religious values. *The equations of love* (1952, NCL) is made up of two novellas. 'Tuesday and Wednesday' follows the life of an ordinary couple for two days, on the second of which the husband dies; 'Lilly's story' traces an unmarried mother's determination to bring up her child independently and decently. Both involve people who never penetrate below the surface of life, but they are portrayed with understanding and sympathy. *Swamp angel* (1954, NCL), perhaps Wilson's finest artistic success, divides its attention between a woman escaping a disastrous marriage to start a new life on a remote lake in northern British Columbia, and a retired circus-performer whose memories of her past threaten to spoil her present. It is a touching, sensitively written, wise novel that delicately raises profound questions about human responsibility and the meaning of life. Wilson's final novel, *Love and salt water* (1956, NCL), is darker in tone. Most of the characters are wounded, physically or emotionally, by the Second World War. The central figure, Ellen Cuppy, had a painful childhood (she discovered her mother dead; her father soon remarried), and her initiation into the adult world is deftly presented in all its clumsiness and uncertainty. Here, as elsewhere in Wilson's novels, the focus is not so much on what happens as on personal responses to what happens. Human relationships, especially love, are invariably Wilson's main subject; and in this novel the pain and danger implicit in emotional commitments, symbolized by the salt water of the title, are given particular emphasis.

Unfortunately Wilson published little after 1961. Her later years, after her husband died in 1966, were spent in seclusion and often ill-health until her death. The novels she wrote are about everyday topics—love, the failure to love, hope and despair, all-too-human fear and courageous determination. Her characters are not immediately memorable, but Wilson shows that they are more remarkable than they seem. She approaches them with compassion balanced by firmness; she is not afraid to discuss her characters with her readers in Victorian fashion, but her attitudes belong solidly to her own time. George WOODCOCK caught the curious tensions in her work by describing Wilson as an Edwardian sensibility who acquired a contemporary ironic intelligence. She wrote with wit and grace but did not ignore human triviality or evil. Her novels demonstrate that it is possible to combine serenity, good humour, and intelligence in twentieth-century fiction without seeming incongruous. The majority of Wilson's short stories, many of them predating the novels, were collected and published in *Mrs Golightly and other stories* (1961, NCL). They range in tone from the warm comedy of 'Mrs Golightly and the First Convention' to the bleak presentation of gratuitous violence in 'Fog' and 'Hurry, hurry'; from garrulous monologue in 'I just love dogs' to sophisticated experiments with narrative viewpoint in 'A drink with Adolphus'. The last story in the collection, 'The window', is an effective moral parable that draws together many strands from her work as a whole. While there is much variety in her short stories, the collection is unified by Wilson's mature perception and unostentatious artistic control. David Stouck collected other writings in *Ethel Wilson: stories, essays, letters* (1987). He also wrote *Ethel Wilson: a critical biography* (2003), which not only portrays her life with much detail but identifies her literary accomplishment and her pronounced literary association with British Columbia. See also Mary McAlpine's biography, *The other side of silence* (1988).

Winter, Michael (b. 1965). Michael Hardy Winter was born in Jarrow, England, Three years later his father moved the family to Newfoundland, where they settled in Corner Brook. After high school Winter attended Memorial University, where he graduated in economic geography (B.A., 1986). He has published two collections of short stories and four novels. He and his partner Christine Pountney have a young son and spend summers in Conception Bay, Newfoundland, where Winter bought an old house, and the rest of the time in Toronto.

Winter's two short-story collections and three novels collectively offer a resonant portrayal not only of the landscape and weather of Newfoundland but the particularities of Corner Brook and St John's, and the speech and concerns of people who live there. All but one of his books have to do with Gabriel English, Winter's alter ego, educated as an economic geographer (like Winter), wanting to become a writer, and sharing other aspects of Winter's past. One notices first about his books that the titles are never attractive or seem appropriate. The title story of *Creaking in their skins* (1994) begins with the narrator's meeting Lynn on a cold night, 'four below'; he has a wife, Paula, and two children, Jenny and Peter, and leaves Paula because of a mole under her chin that he first saw when she became fat. A year later he moves into a house that Lynn lives in. One cold winter night he's walking home. 'It was after midnight and all the houses and trees were encased in a film of ice. The telephone wires creaking in their skins.' In these early stories the language is graceless: 'There are trees out on the islands that are two thousand years old. The roots go way down. There was a fire out there and they couldn't put it out.' In 'Introduced' the narrator is living with Dina Tumova, a Bulgarian, but before he met her in St John's he had met her parents in Bulgaria, and her ex-husband Ivailo. But the story is mainly about what happens when he (the narrator) and Dina prepare a canoe to go fishing on Indian Lake and Dina sees the bloated carcass of a moose on the beach. They attempt to sink it and finally do. Dina: 'I can't stop thinking about it under there. It's stuck under a meter of water in a bog, with stones tied to it. Imagine finding that. Imagine your sister swimming into that.' / 'It'll rot. The fish'll have it gone. It's better that it's under water.' The stories in *One last good look* (1999, rpr. 2001) describe various events in Gabriel English's early life as he grows up, and—in 'The ground that owns you'—his relationship with his brother Junior, called June, and his father and *his* dog Elsie, with memories of the past mingling with an accidental disaster of the present when Gabe and June are out grouse shooting and Gabe accidentally shoots Elsie (we don't read about this). June phones his father and tells him. 'Who shot her? Oh, you ... fools.' But when the boys map out the scene–'You can follow the path of the shot, how the pattern caught the dog before it reached the grouse.'– their father simply says: 'You better put her in the back [of the car]' 'The pallbearer's gloves' is a touching story of Gabriel's elder brother Bruce's dying, and death, from cancer at forty-two. He is joined by June, who arrives with his girlfriend Carol. 'Junior: Bruce thinks he's going to get better./What else can he think./He can be realistic./You can't be realistic. Death isn't realistic.' After the funeral the pallbearers wear gloves (why?) and lay them on the casket (why?) as it sinks into the ground. Winter introduces his novel *This all happened* (2000, rpr. 2001), saying that Gabriel English is a writer and is supposed to be writing a historical novel about the American artist Rockwell Kent, who spent eighteen months in Brigus, Newfoundland, until he had to leave because he was suspected of being a German spy after he sang German songs and declared his admiration for German culture. Gabriel turns against the novel he is writing and doesn't finish it. 'Instead, he writes a collection of daily vignettes over a full calendar year. These small windows onto moments follow the evolving passion and anguish Gabriel feels for Lydia Murphy. The vignettes also document the desperate relationships that blossom and fail around him .... *This all happened* is a literary tableau of Newfoundland life, for better or for worse, seen from within.' *The big why* (2004) is perhaps the novel Gabriel wished he could write. It is indeed about Rockwell Kent (1882–1971) in Brigus in 1914, and his friend Brigus-born Bob Bartlett (1875–1946), a renowned ice navigator and explorer who sailed on the arctic and polar expeditions of Robert Peary and Vilhjalmur Stefanson. (Bartlett: 'The question, Rockwell, is did you get to be who you are. And if not, then why. That, my friend, is the big why.') Without much of a plot but with lots of happenings, it is well written; everyday life, and the conversations and relationships of characters, unfold in a natural and readable way. Rockwell Kent—who is joined by his wife Kathleen and their children—is portrayed not all that favourably: he commits infidelities and Kathleen is the first of three wives. But his art remains paramount: 'Painting is a solitary and isolating work .... If a farmer saw me up in his fields, painting his cows and his hills, he no longer waved to me. He seemed annoyed at my presence, as though by giving me leave to use his property to stand and paint on, he was guilty of fraternizing with a strange and corrupting influence.' At the age of eighty-six he is surprised to receive an invitation from the premier of Newfoundland (now a province of Canada), Joey Smallwood, to 'be this Government's guest on a visit back to Newfoundland, including Brigus.' ... 'And so the next summer I returned, with my third wife, Sally. I have lived with Sally for longer than I did my first two wives put together.' *The architects are here* (2007, rpr. 2008) begins with the narrator saying 'This is a story about my friend David Twombly and about the nature of our friendship. David is gone now ....' Many pages are read before one learns that the narrator is Gabriel English. The story of the lives of David and Gabriel and others over forty years is permeated by one crisis or disaster after another, beginning when they were children growing up in Corner Brook and 'one entire side' of the igloo they had built 'was sheered off and the loud orange blade of a snow-plough ran past us'; David in his teens and his older brother Zac are in a motor-boat in a rainstorm, the lake swells, 'a rogue wave swamped them' (well described) and Zac drowns; the adult Gabriel's Toronto apartment is destroyed by a gas explosion; a heavy mirror falls on David's head and leaves him with a gash; on their way back to Newfoundland they accidentally acquire a dog, their beloved Bucephalus, and when she has been tied to the 'trailer hitch' David starts up the car and drives off at full speed, dragging the dog and killing it; David survives a shipwreck. The complex personal events are no less arresting. At university David and Gabe meet a fellow student, Nell Tarkington (we are told she is the great-granddaughter of the bestselling American novelist Booth Tarkington), who is attracted to one of her professors—Arthur Twombly, David's father—has an affair with him, becomes pregnant, and bears Anthony, who is adopted by the Hurleys in Corner Brook. Gabriel and Nell fall in love and become a couple, until she confesses to Gabe that she has had a sporadic affair with David. They separate, and Nell flies to Santa Fe, where she reunites with Arthur's friend Richard Text, who is gay, whom she had previously married. Eighteen years later much happens. In Toronto David's wife Sok Hoon has left him, taking their son Owen with her to

Montreal. David's father has been nearly killed in a car accident (?)—he was hit by a van with a moose bar—and is in hospital seriously incapacitated. David persuades Gabe to accompany him back to Corner Brook—every stop-over is described in detail—which they eventually reach. The denouement involves not only Gabriel but pregnant Nell, her son Anthony, Arthur Twombly, and David. The overlong narrative—wedding the series of disasters referred to above—is made up of many rambling conversations and minute-by-minute descriptions, with the occasional intrusion of a paragraph that makes one ask: What does it mean? Why is it here? Though Gabe describes David often, his descriptions do not bring him to life; and none of the main characters seem to be connected with what they do in the story. An overall feeling of unreality pervades this complex novel; but Winter's verbal dexterity—his fluent but undisciplined use of language—cannot be denied. This particular reader (who did not enjoy *The architects are here*) is clearly at odds with the many reviewers who praised it in the four pages of quotations that open the paperback edition (and with 'the seventy-one people who helped make this book'). As for the title, 'The architects are here' is an exclamation frequently made by David Twombly—it is a guard's utterance prior to Julius Caesar's assassination, which (Gabriel tells us) David fastened on when, as a student, he read Suetonius, the Roman biographer of the Caesars—suggesting the onset of bad times.

Wiseman, Adele (1928–92). Born in Winnipeg, Manitoba, to Jewish parents who emigrated from Ukraine, she received a B.A. in English and psychology (1949) from the University of Manitoba and then, to support her early intention to be a writer, took a variety of jobs as executive secretary, teacher, and social worker in Canada and abroad. She and her husband, Dmitry Stone, made their home in Toronto; they had one daughter, Tamara.

Wiseman's imagination was shaped by her Eastern European Jewish heritage. Her first novel, *The sacrifice* (1956, GGA, NCL), was followed by *Crackpot* (1974, NCL). In both novels Wiseman interprets modern Jewish experience as reflected in the lives of people who immigrated to the Canadian Prairies between the two world wars. *The sacrifice* uses the biblical story of the patriarch's willingness to sacrifice his son as the metaphorical base for the tragic story of a new Abraham—who settles with Sarah and their son Isaac in the Jewish community of an unnamed Winnipeg—who repeatedly suffers the blows of a hostile fate and, though he is dedicated to the search for moral and spiritual perfection, is eventually driven to murder. Like the heroes of Greek tragedy, Abraham is over-proud; only at the end does he recognize the need to love, to accept weakness in himself and others, and to acknowledge the mysterious co-existence of creativity and destruction. The novel depicts the hardships of immigrant experience, with sharp criticism of exploitation in the garment trade, ruthless business practices, and social snobbery. *Crackpot* is also set in a Jewish ghetto, now recognizably the north end of Winnipeg during the Depression. Unlike the former novel, which used a traditional pattern and an omniscient narrator, it experiments with unconventional sentence structures and language appropriate to the uneducated perceptions of Hoda, a fat prostitute who never loses her childlike trust and clear-sightedness. Through this seemingly unprepossessing character, Wiseman celebrates life in all its richness and complexity and, at the moment when Hoda must choose to commit incest, demonstrates the paradoxical knotting of good and evil within one action. *Crackpot* is full of laughter as well as pathos and is given poetic richness by an intricate symbolism, especially to do with light, based on the Kabbalah. Like its predecessor, this novel contains much social criticism, particularly of the educational and welfare systems, but the method is more satirical and, in the tradition of Jewish humour, much of the laughter is self-directed. Rachel WYATT's dramatized version of *Crackpot* was staged in Calgary and Victoria in 1996.

Wiseman wrote the short text that accompanies Joe ROSENTHAL's drawings in *Old markets, new worlds* (1964), stressing the importance of the old-style markets to an immigrant community. This piece is reprinted in *Memoirs of a book-molesting childhood* (1987), a collection of personal and often witty essays, of which the final one reflects on her parents' death. Much of their life story is told episodically in *Old woman at play* (1978), an illustrated book whose main concern is the formation of an aesthetic theory drawn from her mother's craft of doll-making. Wiseman spent many years on two plays of social criticism: *Testimonial dinner* (1978), a study of three generations of a Canadian Jewish family, was published privately; a portion of *The lovebound*, set on a Jewish refugee ship in 1939, appears in *Journal of Canadian Fiction* 31/32 (1981), which also contains Wiseman's story 'The country of the hungry bird' and Roslyn Belkin's interview with Wiseman, 'The consciousness of a

Jewish artist'. A final short story about physically handicapped youth was published in *The MALAHAT REVIEW* (Spring 1992). *We who can fly: poems, essays and memories in honour of Adele Wiseman* (1997) was edited by Elizabeth Greene. Wiseman wrote the texts for two children's picture books: *Kenji and the cricket* (1988), beautifully illustrated by Shizuye Takashima, and *Puccini and the prowlers* (1992), illustrated by Kim La Fave (Pucci is a pup).

See *Adele Wiseman: essays on her works* (2001) edited by Ruth Panofsky. See also *Selected letters of Margaret Laurence and Adele Wiseman* (1997) edited by John Lennox and Ruth Panofsky.

Wiseman, Christopher (b. 1936). Born, raised, and educated in England, teaching there and in Scotland, he settled in Canada in 1969 after completing graduate studies in creative writing at the University of Iowa, joining the English faculty of the University of Calgary (from which he retired in 1997; he is now Professor Emeritus), where he founded the creative-writing department in 1973. His first two books of poetry published in Canada were *Waiting for the barbarians* (1971) and *The barbarian file* (1974). The persona of the titles is a questioning and at times gullible man striving to be decent in an increasingly uncivilized world. He speaks in a satirical voice that comments, sometimes sardonically, sometimes with honest doubt or inquisitive ignorance, on the foibles, immoralities, mischiefs, and betrayals of contemporary society. The direct honesty of approach is part of the poet's continuing quest for sensible and serious values that are often undermined by loss and insensitivity. The poems are included in the prize-winning *Postcards home: poems new and selected* (1988). Other collections are *The upper hand* (1981), *An ocean of whispers* (1982), *Missing persons* (1989), *Remembering Mr Fox* (1994), and *Crossing the salt flats* (1999)—in which the salt flats of the title poem are a metaphor for memory. The substantial *In John Updike's room: new and selected poems* (2005) contains poems from all the preceding volumes. 'In the Banff Springs Hotel' (from *Postcards home*) is a wonderful tribute to that memorable building and its original guests: 'Their ghosts/Sit with rugs on their knees/Looking down the valley. The red/Of the map brought them all this way//To take the healing waters, or feel/The real sublime before they died ...//To dream of building this out here,/So far from anything, and then/Transform it into magnificence....' The title poem was inspired by one the late John Updike wrote when he stayed at the Marine Hotel, North Berwick, Scotland, in May 1998. Wiseman stayed there too, and was given the same room. Updike's dark thoughts were occasioned by seeing on TV the film *High Society* with Grace Kelly (and Crosby and Sinatra)—there is a photograph of the young Grace on the paperback cover—and Wiseman is led to meditate on Updike's mood in this town 'where I spent my summers before/Grace sang ...' In 2008 Wiseman published *36 Cornelian Avenue*, poems about his wartime childhood at Wheatcroft, Yorkshire, when he was seven: 'The thing we dreaded most/was the bike painted bright red,/strong official leather bag/behind the saddle, a man/in uniform riding it,/bringing official telegrams.' ('What we sometimes saw'.)

Wood, Joanna E. (1867–1927). Born in Lesmahagow, Scotland, Joanna (also known as Nelly) Ellen Wood—the youngest of eleven children—was taken by her parents, Robert and Agnes, and their five surviving offspring to join the eldest son William in Irving, New York. They later moved to Queenston, Ontario. In 1874 Robert bought a farm called The Heights overlooking the Niagara River at Queenston. He sold it in 1893 to his son William, who later put it in the hands of Joanna. During her writing career Joanna did much travelling in Britain and Europe, and lived for periods in the USA, particularly New York and Boston. Research for her last-known novel *Farden Ha'* (London, 1902)—set in a coalmining village—was carried out on a journey to Scotland. She died of a stroke in the Detroit home of her sister Jessie Maxwell. She is buried in Fairview Cemetery, Niagara Falls, Ontario.

Wood wrote eight sentimental novels whose central theme is love. Her characters are often two-dimensional, her plots melodramatic, her language ornate and artificial. However, her work is transitional, at its best containing passages of penetrating social analysis and statement, with a clear indebtedness to the school of realism, particularly to Thomas Hardy, which was noted by contemporary critics. She shows remarkable insight into the Canadian small town, whose cultural character, folkways, and speech she depicts with a skill that goes well beyond much of the local-colour fiction of her day. Her most successful novel in this respect is *The untempered wind* (New York, 1894; Toronto, 1898; rpr. 1994, edited by Klay Dyer), in which an unmarried woman, betrayed in love, raises her child in a moralistic and censorious Ontario town with the fictional name of Jamestown (Queenston?): the strict moral codes, hypocrisy, and parochialism of the small town are clearly delineated. The first novelist to express what E.K. BROWN would later define as the central impediments to creativity in Canada—puritanism, colonialism, and the frontier spirit—Wood stands at the beginning of a tradition of fiction that examines the Canadian small town critically. In *Judith Moore; or, Fashioning a pipe* (Toronto, 1898) and *A daughter of witches* (1900) a more humorous tone emerges as she captures the colour and vitality of rural life through the speech of her minor characters. Wood is also significant as a member of the important post-Confederation group of writers who sought a native literature in local settings and characters. While not blind to the limitations of the small town, she does subscribe to a myth of Canada, shared by many of her generation, as an unspoiled place of innocence and potential, a refuge from the corruption and pressures of Europe and the United States. This myth is expressed in powerful, mystical terms in *Judith Moore*. Wood enjoyed a favourable reputation in literary circles in the late 1890s, largely based on *The untempered wind*. *Current literature* (vol. XVI, 1894, p. 378) called this novel 'the strongest and best American novel of the year.' Canadian critics were slower to respond, but the *Canadian Magazine* (vol. X, 1898, p. 460) assessed Wood as one of the three leading Canadian novelists of the day, in the ranks of Gilbert PARKER and Charles G.D. ROBERTS. Her novels were reviewed in Britain, where she was discussed as a writer who had an individual style, the particular strengths of which were a quiet humour and strong character portraits.

Wood, Ted (b. 1931). Born Edward John Wood in Shoreham, Sussex, England, he lived in London until the outbreak of the Second World War and served in RAF Coastal Command. In 1954 he immigrated to Canada, where he was a policeman in Toronto for three years. In 1957 he joined MacLaren Advertising, Toronto, as a copywriter, eventually becoming a creative director. While employment in law enforcement and advertising provided food and shelter for his growing family, Wood found time to write and sell short stories to Canadian and American magazines and to write television plays; he also collaborated on the musical comedy *Mister Scrooge*, which was produced in Toronto and on CBC television. In 1974 he published a collection of Chekhovian short stories,

Somebody else's summer, but he is best known as a crime novelist. His *Dead in the water* (1984)—which won the Scribner's Crime Novel Award, and publication in both the USA and Canada—features a small-town policeman, Reid Bennett, and his dog Sam—the entire law enforcement needs of Murphy's Harbour, a fictional resort community in the Kawartha region of Ontario. Bennett's and Sam's popularity was enough to extend the series through *The killing cold* (1984; UK title, *Murder on ice*) to its current tenth title, *A clean kill* (1995), and to have the books also published in England and in many translations. A second series (published under the name Jack Barnao), featuring a peripatetic Toronto-based bodyguard, John Locke, has thus far extended to three titles: *Hammerlocke* (1986), *Lockstep* (1987), and *Timelocke* (1991).

Woodcock, George (1912–95). Born in Winnipeg to British parents, he was raised and educated in England. In the late 1930s, while mixing in the London literary world that included Dylan Thomas, Roy Campbell, Herbert Read, and George Orwell, Woodcock emerged as a poet and radical pamphleteer, part of a socially committed literary underground whose pacifism only intensified as a world war approached. During the war he performed non-military duties as a conscientious objector, edited the anarchist publication *War Commentary* (later *Freedom*), and founded the radical literary magazine *Now*, which he edited until 1947. In retrospect the pamphlets he wrote in this period fathered his later more lasting works, such as *Anarchism: a history of libertarian ideas and movements* (1962, rpr. 2004) and *Gandhi* (1971), though the young Woodcock gave little indication of the important and prolific literary figure he would later become. His early work ran from collections of verse, such as *The white island* (1940) and *The centre cannot hold* (1943), to *The incomparable Aphra: a life of Mrs Aphra Behn* (1948, rpr. in 1989 as *Asphra Behn: the English Sappho*) and *The writer and politics: essays* (1948). They all reflect the fluent writing style and the precise mixture of literary and political curiosity that seemed peculiar to him alone. Within the general view that society is best served by individuals who are not organized under the yoke of government, Woodcock found room for himself as an independent journalist, historian, and literary commentator equally unconstrained by the academy or by slavish devotion to only one or two disciplines. As an anarchist, his antecedents were the notable libertarian thinkers of the nineteenth century whose biographer he became in such books as *William Godwin: a biographical study* (1946, rpr. 1989) and *Pierre-Joseph Proudhon: a biography* (1956, rpr. 1987). In the same vein is *The anarchist prince: a biographical study of Peter Kropotkin* (1950), written in collaboration with Ivan Avakumovic, as was *The Doukhobors* (1968). Woodcock's literary ancestors, however, would stretch from Defoe and William Cobbett to any of the late-Victorian generalists to whom nothing humanly interesting could be totally foreign. In 1949 Woodcock returned to Canada, settling in British Columbia, eventually in Vancouver, where he founded and edited, under the auspices of the University of British Columbia, the literary magazine CANADIAN LITERATURE from 1959 until 1977, when he had edited seventy-three issues. In spite of this responsibility he carried on his profession as a writer with even greater vigour. All his Canadian writings, even the most personal, tended to be informed by his interest in the role of the arts in a free society and the way many past eras and more primitive cultures point up weaknesses in our own. While one should be wary of seeing his career as compartmentalized, it is possible to break down his work into several convenient, if maddeningly overlapping, categories.

As a prolific travel writer Woodcock produced personal narratives rather than guidebooks, through such stylized works as *To the city of the dead: an account of travels in Mexico* (1957) and *Incas and other men: travels in the Andes* (1959), filled with observations on the history, geography, economy, and culture of the regions being examined. Other travel books are *Faces of India: a travel narrative* (1964), *Asia, gods and cities: Aden to Tokyo* (1966), *Kerala: a portrait of the Malabar coast* (1967), and *South Sea journey* (1976). It is no coincidence that all the above deal with areas once part of either the Spanish or the British empires, for in Woodcock colonialism is often seen as government writ large, and the lowly native as a metaphor for the individual within the dreaded state. These ideas are still more apparent in related works of history, such as *The Greeks in India* (1966), *The British in the Far East* (1969), *Into Tibet: the early British explorers* (1971), and *Who killed the British Empire?* (1974).

Woodcock's travel books, all of them examples of a type more common in Britain than in North America—informal and objective in approach, wide-ranging in subject-matter—were thus the fountainhead for other of his works, including his many publications on Canada. After *Ravens and prophets: an account of journeys in British Columbia, Alberta and southern Alaska* (1952, rpr. 1993), in which he saw the region as deliciously untamed yet foreign, Woodcock gradually became a Canadian nationalist whose nationalism was rooted in the cause of regionalism and decentralization. Such is the viewpoint conveyed to foreign audiences in *Canada and the Canadians* (1970; rev. 1973) and *The Canadians* (1979), and expressed more stridently for domestic consumption in *Confederation betrayed!* (1981), whose format harks back to his numerous early pamphlets. The underlying concern with local cultural history surfaced fully in such biographical studies as *Amor De Cosmos, journalist and reformer* (1975) and *Gabriel Dumont: the Métis chief and his lost world* (1975, rpr. 2003). The subtitle of the latter is significant, for, as in *Peoples of the coast: the Indians of the Pacific Northwest* (1977), Woodcock often laments or tries to evoke a lost world—one in which anarchism was people's natural state. Also in this vein are *The walls of India* (1985) and *Caves in the desert: travels in China* (1988).

In his literary criticism, too, one can see Woodcock constantly refining certain tenets that came early to him. In its search for the perfect marriage of imaginative and political activity (somewhat akin to Tolstoy's idealized balance of the intellectual and the physical), *The paradox of Oscar Wilde* (1950, rpr. 1989 as *Oscar Wilde: the double image*) is virtually a blueprint for later bio-critical studies, such as *The crystal spirit: a study of George Orwell* (1966, GGA; rpr. 2005); *Dawn and the darkest hour: a study of Aldous Huxley* (1972); and *Herbert Read: the stream and the source* (1972, rpr. 2008). These books also showed his preference for the radical and Woodcock's inclination towards sociological over textual criticism (which he did not disregard), as did *Odysseus ever returning: essays on Canadian writers and writing* (1970, NCL), *The world of Canadian writing: critiques and recollections* (1980), and *Northern spring: the flowering of Canadian literature* (1987). All are important collections, showing to best advantage the style and disposition that are also obvious in two monographs, *Hugh MacLennan* (1969) and *Mordecai Richler* (1971), which present Woodcock as a questioner and leveller rather than as an explainer and champion, which he tended to be when discussing younger regionalist authors. Woodcock also wrote introductions (*Introducing...*) to single works by ATWOOD, LAURENCE, MacLENNAN, RICHLER, and ROSS.

As regards influences, Woodcock was both a transmitter and a receiver—the latter particularly in his verse. In poetry collections

Woodcock

from *Imagine the South* (1947) to *Selected poems* (1967), he was essentially a British poet from between the wars in outlook and style. In his newer verse—collected in *Notes on visitations: poems, 1936–1975* (1975) and *The kestrel and other poems* (1978)—Auden had been supplanted as an influence by Margaret Atwood, and the writer had been virtually redefined and rejuvenated. His most finely crafted collection of poetry was likewise his last: *The cherry tree on Cherry Street* (1994).

Among Woodcock's many other books—each expressing strains in his previous writings—are *Civil disobedience* (1966), *Henry Walter Bates: naturalist of the Amazon* (1969), *Thomas Merton, monk and poet: a critical study* (1978), and *Two plays* (1978). He also edited several anthologies drawn from CANADIAN LITERATURE. *The rejection of politics and other essays on Canada, Canadians, anarchism and the world* (1972) suggests the spread of his journalism, while *A George Woodcock reader* (1980), edited by Douglas (George) FETHERLING, gives a broader hint of its scope. In his last few years Woodcock turned to history with renewed vigour, and with as much concern for historiographical ideas as for mere historical information. Three such works were *A social history of Canada* (1988, rpr. 1989); the unjustly overlooked distillation of his ideas, *The marvellous century: archaic man and the awakening of reason* (1988, rpr. 2005); and *The century that made Canada 1814–1914* (1989). *Taking it to the letter* (1982) is a selection of Woodcock's correspondence with other Canadian writers. *Letter to the past* (1982) is the first volume of his autobiography, covering the years before his return to Canada. He completed the story of his life in *Beyond the blue mountains* (1987) and *Walking through the valley* (1994).

A voluminous writer—thirty of his titles remained in print in 2006—Woodcock was a vital force in Canadian writing, and a constant link between the Canadian tradition and those of other English-language cultures. See Fetherling's *The gentle anarchist: a life of George Woodcock* (1998). Alan TWIGG, a friend of both George Woodcock and his wife Ingeborg, published in 2009 *Tibetans in exile: the Dalai Lama and the Woodcocks*.

Wright, Eric (b. 1929). Born in South London, England, he immigrated to Canada at the age of twenty-one, completed his B.A. (1957) at the University of Manitoba and his M.A. (1963) at the University of Toronto, then taught English at Ryerson Polytechnic University, Toronto (1958–89). He is best known for his series of eleven police procedurals featuring Metropolitan Toronto Police Inspector Charlie Salter, beginning with *The night the gods smiled* (1983), which won an Arthur Ellis Award, a City of Toronto Book Award, and Britain's John Creasy Memorial Award for a best first crime novel, followed by *Smoke detector* (1984), *Death in the old country* (1985), which also won an Arthur Ellis Award, *A single death* (1986), *A body surrounded by water* (1987), *A question of murder* (1988), *A sensitive case* (1990), *Final cut* (1991), *A fine Italian hand* (1992), *Death by degrees* (1993), and *The last hand* (2001). While officially assigned to Special Duties rather than Homicide, Salter tends to stumble across or inherit stubborn investigations, and the chief interest in the series lies less in the solving of recalcitrant murders (which tend to be ordinary and fairly easily unravelled in any case) than in the character, peregrinations, and observations of Salter himself, a husband and father whose life revolves around his twenty-year marriage. But it is the life of Toronto itself, as Salter observes its landmarks and moves through its neighbourhoods, that most distinguishes the series, along with Salter's wry comments about class and power in a society that imagines itself to be classless. The novels are noteworthy, too, for Wright's lucid and agreeably laconic style. See *A Charlie Salter omnibus* (2003). Wright has also written several non-Salter books. *Moodie's tale* (1994) is a satirical account of post-secondary education in Ontario in general and academic posturing in particular, as told through the precocious rise of British immigrant William Moodie through the ranks at the 'W.C. Van Horne Institute' in Toronto—an ascent that is followed by an equally precipitous descent into a second career as a backwoods fishing guide, a job that proves the need for remarkably similar survival skills. *Buried in stone* (1996, rpr. 1997) features Mel Pickett, a retired Toronto detective who first appeared in *A sensitive case* and finds himself investigating a murder at 'Larch River', a small town on the edge of the Canadian Shield. Lucy Trimble is the detective in *Death of a Sunday writer* (1996, rpr. 2000) and *Death on the rocks* (1999). They were followed by *The kidnapping of Rosie Dawn* (2000), which features Joe Barley, part-time English professor and part-time private detective, as does *The Hemingway caper* (2003), in which Barley becomes involved with some missing Hemingway Papers. How much Wright's early-life experiences contributed to his fiction is revealed indirectly in Eric Wright's remarkable memoir, *Always give a penny to a* *blind man* (1999, rpr. 2001). He was born into a large, poor family in a tenement in London, S.E.—he was one of ten children—and grew out of his Dickensian childhood to immigrate to Canada (to Churchill, Manitoba). University followed. His memoir is filled with stories—without being fictional, they reveal his gift for fiction. *Finding home* (2007) is another wonderful novel (with autobiographical underpinnings) in which Will Prentice—a Canadian for thirty years, though English-born—whose wife has asked him for a divorce, returns to England for his mother's funeral and decides to drive through England to recapture memories. He is joined by Fred, a young relative, who is a Cambridge graduate and is interested in Canadian studies. Fred becomes the driver through the English countryside while Will talks to him about Canada, the resulting dialogue giving rise to a portrait of both Britain and Canada. Wright edited with Howard ENGEL the anthology *Criminal shorts: mysteries by Canadian crime writers* (1992).

Wright, L.R. (1939–2001). Laurali Rose (Bunny) Appleby was born in Saskatoon, Saskatchewan, received an M.A. from Simon Fraser University, Burnaby, British Columbia, and worked for the Fraser Valley Record, the *Calgary Albertan*, and the *Calgary Herald* (1968–77), before retiring from newspaper work. Although she wrote four mainstream novels under her married name—*Neighbours* (1979), *The favorite* (1982), *Among friends* (1984), and *Love in the temperate zone* (1988)—Wright was best known for her crime-fiction series featuring Staff Sergeant Karl Alberg of the Sechelt detachment of the Royal Canadian Mounted Police. Located on the 'Sunshine Coast', a peninsula just north of Vancouver, accessible only by ferry, the Alberg series includes *The suspect* (1977, rpr. 1986), which was the first Canadian novel to win an Edgar Award from the Mystery Writers of America in the best-novel category; *Sleep while I sing* (1986, rpr. 1998); *A chill rain in January* (1990, rpr. 1998), which won an Arthur Ellis Award; *Fall from grace* (1991, rpr. 1997); *Prized possessions* (1994, rpr. 1997); *A touch of panic* (1995); *Mother love* (1996), which also won an Arthur Ellis Award; *Strangers among us* (1997); and *Acts of murder* (1997, rpr. 1998). Wright's interest in this series was less in the actual detection of crime or criminals (the criminal is often known or easily suspected from the outset) than in the question of criminal or psychological motivation. Often compared to Ruth Rendell, P.D. James,

and Patricia Highsmith, Wright created atmosphere and suspense superbly as crimes appear to unfold with a certain chilling inevitability within the boundaries of an otherwise normal, indeed pristine and picturesque, islanded community. The series is animated by the continually developing relationship between the divorced Alberg, who is forty-four at the start of the series, and Cassandra Mitchell, the town's librarian, who is several years younger: in *Strangers among us* they are poised to marry and in *Acts of murder* they marry. Wright's novels attest to the unexpected (often bizarre) levels of emotional complexity that may characterize even apparently ordinary human lives. Her interleaved narratives—in which several parallel stories typically impact smoothly upon one another within the framework of the novel—testify to the ways (in Wright's view) in which individuals, however independent they may imagine themselves to be, ultimately share the fate of the community at large. *Kidnap* (2000, rpr. 2001), 'An Edwina Henderson Mystery', introduces Sergeant 'Eddie' Henderson (though she appears in *Acts of murder*), who investigates the kidnapping of five-year-old Samantha. It is an outstanding crime novel that is also an engrossing study of character—that of both Eddie and the kidnapper, whose mind it explores.

Menace (2001, rpr. 2002), published posthumously, takes place in Gibsons, a few miles south of Sechelt, and Eddie Henderson has been made the new chief of the Gibsons RCMP detachment. The villain, whose thoughts we are introduced to at the beginning of the novel, is not identified until the end.

Wright, Richard B. (b. 1937). Born in Midland, Ontario, Richard Bruce Wright attended Ryerson Polytechnic Institute, Toronto, receiving a degree in Radio and TV Arts (1959). He then worked briefly in journalism before embarking on a decade of work for two Toronto publishers, Macmillan and Oxford University Press. He left publishing in 1970, received a B.A. degree in 1972 from Trent University, and in 1976–9 and 1985–2001 he taught English at Ridley College, St Catharines, Ontario, retiring in 2001. He is a Member of the Order of Canada (2007).

Wright's first work of fiction, *Andrew Tolliver* (1965), was a children's book. His first novel for adults, *The weekend man* (1970, rpr. 2001), was widely praised, and like his subsequent fiction was published in the United States and England as well as Canada; it has also been translated into French, Italian,

Japanese, Spanish, and Swedish. Wes Wakeham is the first example of a type found throughout Wright's fiction: a man of gentle instincts out of sympathy with the common ambitions of his society and embittered by separation from a rich and domineering wife. Having drifted from one inconsequential job to another, Wakeham is an outsider by temperament and conviction; he defines a weekend man as 'a person who has abandoned the present in favour of the past or the future', and has an air of amused detachment in common with the hero of Walker Percy's *The moviegoer*, a novel Wright says influenced his work. Fred Landon, the protagonist of *In the middle of a life* (1973, rpr. 2001), approaches life with middle-aged wariness and resignation rather than with youthful cynicism. His efforts to find harmony with his family and to establish a new romantic bond are related in a style that reflects the wistful melancholy of his character. This novel won the Faber fiction award in England. Wright abandoned sober realism for exuberant comedy in *Farthing's fortunes* (1976). Presented as the artless tape-recorded memoirs of an ancient wandering Canadian, the novel incorporates graphic vignettes of the social history of half a century, including Toronto's low and high life in the 1890s, the Yukon gold rush, the Battle of the Somme, and the Depression. The book cleverly manipulates storytelling conventions and deliberately evokes well-worn stereotypes—the good-hearted whore, the loud-mouthed American entrepreneur, the love-starved poet—in imitation of the picaresque novel. In *Final things* (1980, rpr. 2004) Wright returned to the novel of character with a memorable portrait of a burnt-out sportswriter who is consumed by thoughts of revenge when his teenage son is brutally murdered. As a study of a decent middle-aged man tortured by feelings of failure, the novel has much in common with *In the middle of a life*; but it attains a shattering emotional intensity beyond the range of the earlier book as the protagonist closes in on his son's killer. An astute observer of social realities, Wright explores in *The teacher's daughter* (1982, rpr. 2004) the relationship of a lonely teacher and a young ex-convict. *Tourists* (1984, rpr. 2002) has as its middle-aged protagonist a private-school teacher who, with his perpetually unfaithful wife, becomes immersed in a series of increasingly violent encounters with an American couple while on holiday in Mexico. The novel is a dark comedy that draws on the irritations founded on trans-border 'cultural stereotypes': the narrator thinks of the

appropriately named Ted Hacker as 'just another vulgar, loud-mouthed know-it-all American', while Hacker regards him, with some justice, as 'a stuffy, uptight little Canadian shit'. In Richard Wright's portrait gallery of lonely, wistful people, no character is more appealing than Kay Ormsby, the idealistic, literary former teacher who is a central figure in *Sunset Manor* (1990, rpr. 2002). As the title suggests, a retirement home (or 'facility', as its formidable administrator calls it) is at the heart of the novel, and old age, seen in an unsentimental, often unsparingly comic way, is its underlying subject. All the characters are, as Wright says of an imaginary novelist in another book, 'psychologically cornered by the prospect of finitude'. Only Miss Ormsby, though urged by her cheerful young doctor to 'forget all this nonsense about death', realizes that 'only by thinking of death can one come to value and enjoy life.' *The age of longing* (1995, rpr. 2001) returns to Wright's familiar territory of middle-age, and to some of the settings of Wright's own life in a Georgian Bay town (pictured in the mid-1930s, shortly before Wright was born) and the publishing business. At the same time, the novel has a more unvaried gravity than most of its predecessors, a tone that is imparted to the novel by its intelligent but melancholy narrator, an editor who returns to his hometown to cope with his mother's death and his own heart attack. The class divisions of Huron Falls, mirrored in Howard Wheeler's own puritanical mother and fun-loving father, are searchingly explored. Two characters who never meet embody much of the book's pathos in their doomed attempts to convert talent and early promise into lasting success: Buddy Wheeler seeks the prize most valued by Huron Falls—success in the National Hockey League—but returns home defeated 'like thousands of young men in small towns everywhere'; Charles Pettinger is an embittered, isolated novelist who, after a fictional debut much like Wright's own, and many years of silence, produces a failed magnum opus. Particularly in his latest novels, Wright shows his characters stumbling as they seek through various expedients to 'forget for a while the muddle and death that await us all'. There is much art as well as sad truth in his images of Ontario life.

Clara Callan (2001, rpr. 2009, GGA)—winner not only of the Governor General's Award but the GILLER PRIZE and the (Ontario) Trillium Award—must be Wright's most popular novel. It features Clara, who teaches in an elementary school in the village of Whitfield, Ontario, and her sister Nora, who has moved to New York, where she has achieved success in the leading role of a popular daily soap opera, 'The House on Chestnut Street'. Their lives are revealed in Clara's journal entries and in her many letters to Nora (which often repeat details we have learned from the journal) and in Nora's to her—between 1934 and 1938. A third well-rounded, truly lifelike letter-writing character is Evelyn Dowling, who creates the scripts for Nora's soap opera, becomes a friend of Nora's (though Evelyn is a lesbian) and later of Clara's. Clara's quiet life—living alone in her father's house, stoking the furnace in winter, visiting Toronto—is not uneventful: she is raped, becomes pregnant, responds to Nora's desire to help by going to New York (where Evelyn arranges an abortion); she later meets a man in Toronto who becomes her ardent lover (he is not only married with four children but turns out to have other lovers) and she becomes pregnant again, bears the child, a daughter, and keeps her. Nora has a lover, Lewis Mills, an esteemed writer who is much beyond her intellectually; they, with Clara, travel to Rome, Florence, and Venice together. Nora and Lewis break up and Nora gives in to Les Cunningham, the handsome announcer on her radio program (he also is married, with children, and is an Irish Catholic). Much more is incorporated in this long, layered novel, which works in, rather mechanically, various period details and happenings (the New York Automat, the Quintuplets, Orson Welles's Mercury Theatre radio play about a Martian invasion) and political events (the abdication, fascist Italy, the domination of Hitler). The predictable events of the novel, the clichés and sometimes stilted language of the letters do not seem inappropriate because the sisters were not all that well educated (though Clara was a great reader—e.g., Keats's letters—while Nora read *Gone With the Wind*) and did not affect the book's popularity—thanks, perhaps, to Wright's ability to draw the reader into the sisters' lives with compelling narrative skill. *Adultery* (2004, rpr. 2005) opens with a long, gripping chapter that begins with the protagonist Daniel Fielding—the fifty-five-year-old editor in a Toronto publishing firm—being interrogated by police officers in England. He and his editorial colleague Denise, in her twenties, after attending the Frankfurt Book Fair, began an affair and she accompanied him to London and then to a town called Glynmouth in Devon (which Fielding had visited with his wife Claire). There is a walk on the beach when Fielding sees a strange man coming towards them, and passing them, 'with his

greying hair pulled into a ponytail, and the surly, vacant face that had reminded Fielding of a clenched fist.' It began to rain and they climbed up the stairs on the cliff and reached the car in the car-park. They had a drink from the pint of Ballantine's in their possession. '"Let's have a quickie, Daniel," she said.... When he thought about it now, the entire episode seemed preposterous: fucking in a car in a rainstorm on Saturday afternoon; they must have been in some kind of sexual delirium.' She leaves the car to have a pee; Daniel falls asleep, waking up to find that she has vanished. He fantasizes that the man with the ponytail had watched them in the car and abducted her. He phoned the police: thus the interrogation. The next morning a police officer phones him in his hotel to say that Denise Crowder's body had been found, and that the murderer, not long out of prison— the man with the ponytail—had been turned in by his brother-in-law. Interwoven into all this are scenes with Fielding's wife Claire and his daughter Heather. The conversations when he phones Claire to tell her he's in a bad situation, and the second time when he tells her the body had been found involve the reader masterfully in the characters' extreme despair. Another terrible phone conversation, with Denise's horrified mother Lucille Crowder, ends the chapter. The rest of the novel includes difficult family and other situations—Denise's brother Ray is antagonistic—and ends with the funeral. At the reception afterwards Lucille converses with Fielding at length, saying she likes him, but drunken Ray knocks him down with a punch in the face. When he drives home, Claire exclaims over his bruised face. 'Closing his eyes, Fielding leaned his head against her stomach, and felt her fingers on his face. It was enough. For now it was enough.' While his experience has been shattering, he strikes the reader as weak and ineffectual. The narrator of *October* (2007, rpr. 2008) is James Hillyer, a widower and retired English professor, who is visiting his daughter in England because she has told him she has an aggressive cancer. (Their conversations about this, over a few days, are delicately underlain with grief, fear, bravery, tact.) In London, about to leave England, James is taken aback to see, in front of the Dorchester Hotel, and to meet again, Gabriel Fontaine, an old man in a wheelchair, whom he had known sixty years before as a boy of fourteen, for one summer in 1944 at Percé, Québec. The willful young Gabriel from a wealthy American family—stricken by polio and in a wheelchair—was sixteen and staying with his mother in the St Lawrence Hotel. Now, in 2004–looked after by an attentive young man called Adam—Gabriel is delighted to be reunited with James and invites him for dinner at his hotel, the Dorchester. In the course of the evening he tells James he is going to Zurich to die. 'Don't worry, it's all legal. They're very enlightened about these things, the Europeans.' 'You're going to commit suicide, then?' 'In a manner of speaking, yes. But it will all be done professionally in the presence of a doctor.... Good God, man, surely you can tell looking at me that I've got only a few months left and every day is a fucking torment. I've got pancreatic cancer. I can't wait to get it over with.' He pleads with James to accompany him and Adam to Zurich, to be with him when he dies. The chapters alternate between Percé and England, then Zurich. The boys had an uneven relationship—they were both attracted to Odette, a young chambermaid in the hotel (it is Gabriel who conquers her sexually)—though they often spend time together as James pushes Gabriel around in his wheelchair. Seamlessly including James Hellyer's reminiscences about his family and teaching life, the narrative is a wonderful portrayal of the end of childhood, and human relationships, that also treats, from more than one perspective, mortality—though it is not in the least depressing.

Wright, Ronald (b. 1948). Born in England, he studied at Cambridge University, where he received a B.A. and M.A. in archaeology. He immigrated to Canada in 1970 and began, but gave up after two years, doctoral studies at the University of Calgary (which gave him an honorary doctorate in 1996), supported himself as a truck driver, failed at farming, and began a series of long trips to South America. After living in Port Hope, Ontario, Wright and his wife moved to Saltspring Island, British Columbia.

He writes mainly non-fiction, on both national and international subjects, but he also writes fiction. His first book, *Cut stones and crossroads: a journey in the two worlds of Peru* (1984, rpr. 2001), deftly evokes the complex world of contemporary Andean Peru, leading the reader on a bracing overland journey to the major sites of the Incas, and offering an acutely perceptive cultural commentary on the world of their descendants—Wright acquired a working knowledge of the Quechua language. *On Fiji Islands* (1986), the least erudite of Wright's non-fiction books, is an exploration of Fijian society leavened by the

low comedy of serendipitous, on-the-road encounters. *Time among the Maya: travels in Belize, Guatemala, and Mexico* (1989, rev. 2005) offers a *tour d'horizon* of early and contemporary Mayan culture. Like Wright's book on Peru, this one takes the form of a literary travel narrative, yet delves deeply into ethnology and pre-Columbian history. These intellectual concerns are again pursued in *Stolen continents: the New World through Indian eyes since 1492* (1992, rpr. 2003), published to coincide with the quincentenary of Columbus's first voyage to America. A chronicle of the post-Columbian period from the point of view of five Native-American peoples (the Aztecs, Mayas, Incas, Cherokees, and Iroquois), it gives a dramatic account of the European invasions experienced by these five nations, their centuries-long resistance to annihilation, and their reaffirmation of themselves in recent decades. *Home and away* (1993, rpr. 1994) is a collection of Wright's journalism. His travel writing is distinguished by its wit, learning, and supple prose. Unlike many literary sojourners from the industrialized world, Wright exhibits a deep sympathy for less materially advanced cultures and accepts them on their own terms. His mocking eye is reserved for hypocrisy and self-delusion wherever he finds them.

A short history of progress (2004), is a brilliant series of five CBC Massey Lectures, the first of which is titled 'Gaugin's questions', alluding to the famous painter while he was living in Tahiti: 'Where do we come from? What are we? Where are we going?' The lectures meditate on the fact that the present-day problems of human civilization conform to a pattern of progress and disaster that goes back thousands of years. The text of the book, which was published worldwide in more than a dozen languages, was amplified by illustrations in the handsome *The illustrated short history of progress* (2006, rpr. 2007). In 2008 Wright published *What is America? A short history of the New World Order*. A litany of the negative aspects of America, past and present, and its power, that are marshalled in a provocative and readable text, it is well documented, with 100 pages of Notes and a 20-page Bibliography, and is filled with quotable sentences: 'The argument at the heart of this book—that the New World made the modern world and now threatens to undo it—came to me from the final chapter of my last one, *A Short History of Progress*, which outlined the long record of collisions between Nature and human nature.' '... through military might, big business, popular culture, covert operations and above all through social example and the shining promise of modernity, the United States has Americanized the world.' 'America, which helped set the Europeans on their new path half a century ago, must now examine its own record—the facts, not the myths—and free itself from the potent yet potentially fatal mix of forces that created its nation, its empire, and the modern world.'

The title of Wright's first novel, *A scientific romance* (1997, rpr. 1998), is a Victorian term for speculative fiction, like H.G. Wells's *The time machine*. The narrator, David Lambert, an expert on Wells, comes into the possession of a letter Wells wrote in 1946, 'TO BE OPENED ON DECEMBER 21st, 1999', in which he says that the time machine of his novel would appear at a certain location. David goes there and is shocked to find himself looking at it. He boards it and flies 500 years into the future, when Britain has become a semi-tropical landscape without people, when industrial civilization is but a faint archaeological memory. The novel is a brilliant dystopian satire that hands down a wry judgement on contemporary avarice and on late industrial society's ravaging of the natural world, but in which David's memories of his past, and a lost love, also play a part. Wright's second novel, *Henderson's spear* (2001), is made up of two elements: a very long letter Olivia Wyvern writes in 1990—from a women's prison in Arue, Tahiti—to a daughter she gave up at birth, describing her heritage. Alternate chapters by a family connection, Francis Barkley Henderson, are his journals, what he calls 'Occasional Papers', written in the late nineteenth century. (They incorporate passages from the journal of the real-life Frank Henderson, who was a cousin of the author's father.) Most of them describe his sailing around the world in 1879–82, on a corvette called *Bacchante*, with Queen Victoria's teenaged grandsons, Prince Edward (Eddy) and his younger brother Prince George, who are in the charge of their tutor Dalton, a clergyman. The writers Olivia and Frank are appealing but shallow characterizations; this reader was most taken by Wright's confident rendering of world travels by sea, and colonial affairs in both Africa and the South Pacific, including French Polynesia (Tahiti, Society Islands, Marquesas Islands, etc.) and independent Fiji, and the culture of South Sea islands. Brief satirical thrusts (re: imperialism, missionaries) were also enjoyed. Of secondary interest in the voyages of the *Bacchante* are the princes. George loved the sea and loved being on shipboard; Eddy was always ill-at-ease and

unhappy. 'The former's eyes were acquiring their father's well-known sparkle in female company, roving after the many pretty figures to be seen in Sydney.... Eddy was also delighted to be once again among feminine influences, but not, I believe, for the same reasons.' (Eddy is revealed to be a homosexual. Some ten years later, as the Duke of Clarence, he died; his brother became George V.) Olivia's father had not returned from the Korean War and was last seen in Tahiti. Inspired by Herbert Melville's *Typee: a peep at Polynesian life* (1846), Olivia was determined to find evidence of his life or death in Polynesia. In Papeete, Tahiti, she joined some Greenpeacers on a fifty-two-foot schooner. They saw a woman 'floating face down, her yellow hair fanned and pulsing in the swell like fronds of seaweed.' The body was heaved onto the boat, and it was this event that led to Olivia's imprisonment. The climactic revelation about her father, and the intricate Henderson/Wyvner connection, cannot be gone into here, nor can Henderson's acquiring a wooden African spear. This is a complex novel, but it is accomplished and has many narrative attractions.

Writers' Trust of Canada, The. Founded in 1976 by Margaret ATWOOD, Pierre BERTON, Graeme GIBSON, Margaret LAURENCE, and David Young, it is a registered charitable organization, incorporated under federal charter, whose primary goal is the advancement of Canadian literature and the support, including financial support, of Canadian writers. Its specific objectives are to increase recognition of the contribution writers make to the cultural richness of Canada; use the knowledge and insights of established writers to inspire gifted young students; recognize and reward excellence in the craft of writing and the creation of literature; provide financial aid to Canadian writers; and accept and administer funds obtained through wills, bequests, endowments, and donations. Among the awards it administers are the Rogers Writers' Trust Fiction Prize, the Writers' Trust Non-Fiction Prize, the Writers' Trust of Canada/McClelland & Stewart Journey Prize, and the Shaughnessy Cohen Prize for Political Writing. It also administers the Woodcock Fund, endowed initially by George WOODCOCK and his wife Ingeborg in 1989, which offers emergency grants to senior writers in financial distress, and the RBC Bronwen WALLACE Award for Emerging Writers of $5000 annually to help young poets or short-fiction writers at the beginning of their career. The

Writers' Trust of Canada

Trust supports the annual Thomas RADDALL Atlantic Fiction Award of $10,000 and sponsors the annual Margaret Laurence Memorial Lecture (by a distinguished Canadian writer on the subject of writing). It owns and operates the Berton House Writers' Retreat in Dawson City, Yukon, which was inspired by Pierre Berton and began in 1996.

Writers' Union of Canada, The. It is a professional association of writers founded in 1973 and a participant in the late-twentieth-century renaissance of Canadian writing and publishing. In 1971, the exclusion of writers from an Ontario Royal Commission on the State of Canadian Publishing led Toronto writers Farley MOWAT, Graeme GIBSON, and several colleagues to advocate a new organization for professional writers. Margaret LAURENCE, then English-Canada's most prominent novelist, served as interim Chair, and the Writers' Union was founded on 3 Nov. 1973 at a meeting in Ottawa. The word 'union' was chosen to convey militancy and to stress the need for Canadian writers to write.

From the start, the union was directed at writers' professional concerns. Its goals were 'to unite writers for the advancement of their common interests; to foster writing in Canada; to maintain relations with publishers; to exchange information among members; to safeguard the freedom to write and publish; and to advance good relations with other writers and their organizations in Canada and all parts of the world.' Membership is open to fiction and non-fiction writers and poets (Canadian citizens or landed immigrants) who have published at least one trade book The initial cost of membership was $43; it has risen to over $1500. The Union has campaigned successfully for the implementation of the Public Lending Right in Canada (implemented in 1986), pushed for improvements in granting policies at the CANADA COUNCIL and other public agencies; promoted copyright reform and the collective licensing of photocopying rights; conducted royalty audits and negotiated with publishers for better contract standards; and lobbied for effective federal and provincial Status of the Artist legislation. The Union and its members helped organize agencies such as the WRITERS' TRUST, the Book and Periodical Council, Access Copyright, and PEN English Canada.

The Union played a vital role in raising the profile of Canadian writers and in bringing professional writers together, notably at its three-day Annual General Meetings, where in the early years a large proportion of the membership gathered to debate writers' issues. Among the national debates, for which the Union has provided a platform, was the subject of 'appropriation of voice' and the role of racial minority voices in Canadian culture. Services for members, administered by a small staff in Toronto and Vancouver, have included contract advice, the funding of reading tours, manuscript evaluation for beginning writers, a grievance committee for disputes with publishers and agents, and professional development workshops across the country.

Prominent writers who have led the Union and contributed to its influence and public stature include Marian ENGEL, Timothy FINDLEY, June CALLWOOD, Matt COHEN, Margaret ATWOOD, Pierre BERTON, Susan Crean, Paul QUARRINGTON, and Audrey THOMAS. Margaret Atwood has written:'One of the most important achievements of the Union is to have fostered a spirit of professionalism and respect among writers. This organization, founded by writers for writers, has enabled them to meet and know one another and to take collective responsibility for decisions which affect the ways in which they are seen and treated.'

CHRISTOPHER MOORE

Wyatt, Rachel (b. 1929). Born in Bradford, England, she was educated in Yorkshire and studied nursing in London before immigrating to Canada with her husband and children in 1957. She began writing radio drama in the early 1970s; more than seventy-five of her deftly constructed radio plays have been produced by the CBC, thirty by the BBC. As an instructor in, then director of, the Writing Program at the Banff Centre for the Arts in Alberta from 1986 to 1999, Wyatt was active in the Canadian literary scene. For eight years she managed a series of radio-drama workshops at Arctic College, Iqaluit, Baffin Island. In the early 1990s she moved with her family to Victoria, British Columbia. In 2002 she was appointed a Member of the Order of Canada.

Wyatt has published six novels: *The strong box* (1970), *The Rosedale hoax* (1977), *Foreign bodies* (1982), *Time in the air* (1985), *Mona Lisa smiled a little* (1999), and *Time's reach* (2003). The early books in particular suggest British comedies-of-manners in the vein of Evelyn Waugh or Nancy Mitford, but the merriment is tempered by the melancholy of the characters, often expatriates who seem dislocated, lost in the surreal cityscapes of North America. Thus *The strong box* follows a British journalist, pining for pubs and greensward, through the carnival world of Toronto broadcasting. *Foreign bodies,* perhaps her best novel, revisits the classic Canadian theme of genteel British immigrants making do, as Yorkshire academics on an exchange program, in a Toronto of vile weather, folkways, and high prices, while also finding their lives wrenched askew by an equally displaced Pakistani. In *Mona Lisa,* Almeida Kerwell, at fifty-six, leaves her husband to try life on her own, and this period is explored through the people she meets, until she retires and is invited to take a trip to China with her husband, when they are reconciled, only to come home to a family tragedy. The chapters in this episodic novel are like short stories; indeed, three of them appeared (slightly altered) in *The day Marlene Dietrich died* (1995), a collection of stories about middle-edged retirees who are shadowed by memories of the sex goddess of the 1930s and 1940s, as well as by a sense of roads not taken, opportunities missed. *Time's reach* is a novel about intense family relationships, focusing on an English family: the elderly Robert Parkes, his wife Frieda, their daughter Maggie visiting from Canada as the book opens, and David, their son. Robert becomes obsessed with the idea that he does not want to be considered an ordinary man. 'I would like you to know, he began to say to [Maggie] under his breath, what I did in the war.' A thread runs through the narrative having to do with brief references to Robert's involvement in wartime happenings in Europe when he worked as a wool merchant; without context and meaningless, they are irritating, though they are clearly pointing to a climactic resolution. There are also strange, unexplained phone calls. 'She [seventy-three-year-old Frieda] had always, well maybe not always, but for a long time, known there was something in his past that preyed on him.' After Robert dies, uttering the name Dora (infuriating Frieda, who turns against her dead husband), Bertie, Maggie's enterprising young daughter, organizes a family trip to Europe to investigate Robert's wartime past. In certain family ways it was disastrous, but some anti-climactic revelations of Robert's war years are finally revealed, along with the meaning of Dora. Much more takes place in the novel and Wyatt's handling of its intricacies is evidence of her skill.

Wyatt has published two short-story collections. The title story of *The last we heard of Leonard* (2002) is the strangely uneventful account of, 'two years ago', of Leonard's connection with Jenny, Fran, Alice, and the narrator, when 'he came round to the apartment to show us some of his work, the way he often

did.' He is an artist. The story is mainly about the girls, but after they comment unfavourably on his drawings he leaves Toronto to work for an advertising agency in Chicago. In 'The view from here', Emma is on a bus, having left the drunken Donald, exchanges comments with the driver, Roger Staines, and two passengers—neither of them interesting. In the long title story, however, of *The magicians's beautiful assistant* (2005), much happens. Paul—a successful political lobbyist—is married to Grazia, his second wife, and chooses her clothes for his various political gatherings, which she wears, looking gorgeous. At one party for donors she rebels, and appears wearing jeans and a wrinkled sweater and serves cheap sparkling wine instead of champagne. 'She throws the contents of her glass into his face. He grabbed her arm and slapped her.// She didn't scream or cry out but simply pushed him so that he flopped onto an armchair like a seal.' All the guests leave. The story switches to Barbara, a thirty-six-year-old lawyer who has trained herself as a magician, The Amazing Sandro, and entertains at parties with twenty-year-old Jack. He imagines being asked 'And what do you do, sir? I'm the Magician's Beautiful Assistant.' They part when he decides to let his dad pay his fees at UBC; lawyer Barbara takes on a case that involves her former lover. While there are real relationships in this story, they are shallow; and the two parts, which relate only slightly, and the story itself, is downgraded by an unpersuasive element of contrivance. The final story in this collection 'Scenes from her life' begins with the sentence: 'Lorraine lay in the open coffin stripped of all knowledge, free from facts.... Tomorrow others would come to view the woman who hadn't been easy to like.' The unpleasant scenes are with her sister Jane and her brother Sam. Michel was attracted to her. 'He'd only wanted to get this brilliant woman into bed, to "own" her, at least for that weekend. But she had taken him on. She had embraced him. And her embrace was like that of a giant octopus. She grasped him. She understood him. She improved him.' 'We'll stay friends, she'd said when he moved out.' As a result of the brief 'scenes' the reader is craftily provided with the sketch of a strong-willed woman who affects other people ambivalently, and becomes a poignant figure in memory when it is revealed that she was murdered by a thief.

Wyatt's two stage plays presented at Tarragon Theatre, Toronto, *Geometry* (1983) and *Chairs and tables* (1984), are nominally comedies, but a painful unease lurks beneath the witty verbal surfaces and marital chess games of Canada's upper-middle classes. Her 1995 stage adaptation of Adele WISEMAN's novel *Crackpot* for Theatre Calgary, about an earthy Winnipeg prostitute, may be seen as a distinctively uncharacteristic departure. Wyatt's substantial body of work displays confident technique, irony, craftsmanship, and a keen sense of the dislocation that can undermine characters who may seem, at first, very much at home.

Wyatt has also written a biography of the first woman elected to the Canadian House of Commons: *Agnes Macphail: champion of the underdog* (2000).

Wylie, Betty Jane (b. 1931). Born Betty Jane McKenty in Winnipeg, she was educated at the University of Manitoba (B.A., 1951; M.A., 1952). In 1952 she married William T. Wylie and had two daughters and two sons. While raising her family she pursued a career as a writer—as a journalist and an author of more than thirty books (five of which were in print in 2006). These include self-help, advice, and inspirational books, cookbooks, plays, poetry, and children's books. Wylie's writing, informal and chatty, is braced with good sense and careful research. Among her most popular books are *Beginnings: a book for widows* (4th edn, 1997), *All in the family: a survival guide for family living and loving* (1988), *The book of Matthew: the story of a learning-disabled child* (1984), *Betty Jane's diary: lessons children taught me* (1993), *Reading between the lines: the diaries of women* (1995), *Life's losses: living through grief, bereavement and sudden changes* (1996), and *Letters to Icelanders: exploring the northern soul* (1999). *The book of Matthew*—about her youngest son, who was born with brain damage—is an intimate chronicle of the first twenty-three years of his life (which included such setbacks as the death of his father when he was twelve and the onset of epilepsy), and of Wylie's experiences in nurturing the development of the mind and skills of the appealing young man Matthew became, who found enjoyment in life and family, and could say at the end of the book, 'I'm okay as I am.' *Letters to Icelanders* was inspired by Wylie's Icelandic heritage on her mother's side, and is made up of letters to her grandparents, one daughter, her grandchildren, and others. Icelandic history, lore, and recipes are combined with the life of the so-called western Icelanders, who settled on Lake Winnipeg and created the town of Gimli, the birthplace of her mother. *The write track: how to succeed as a freelance writer in Canada* (2003) is a revised and expanded second edition of a work that was found very useful. It begins with two full pages listing, in double column, all Wylie's 'published and produced works' (including radio plays, musicals, recordings, TV programs, and journalism). She was made a Member of the Order of Canada in 2003.

Wynand, Derk (b. 1944). Born in Bad Suderode, Germany, he came to Canada with his family in 1952 and was educated at the University of British Columbia (B.A., 1966; M.A., 1969). In 1969 he joined the Creative Writing Department of the University of Victoria, from which he retired as a full professor in 2004. He had a long association with *The MALAHAT REVIEW* as assistant editor (1973–5) and editor (1992–8).

Wynand's poetry and fiction are strongly influenced by the Surrealists, fabulists, and absurdists, including the Austrian H.C. Artmann (whom Wynand has translated), Karl Krolow, Franz Kafka, and Friederike Mayröcker. Because Wynand's writings originate from such esoteric sources, his work has not received much critical attention in Canada. However, his sparse and laconic poems, stories, and translations have appeared in more than 300 periodicals in the USA, Canada, and Europe and have been broadcast on various CBC radio programs. His chapbooks *Locus* (1971) and *Pointwise* (1979) are filled with metaphors about the double standards of contemporary living. His style is precise, but his disturbing imagery often relies on symbolist or fabulist devices to create jarring images of alienation. *Locus* is vaguely surreal and *Pointwise* is at once bleak and wittily ironic about nebulous human relationships. In *Snowscapes* (1974) Wynand counterpoints prose poems and poetic styles about snow, in which he finds searching metaphors for the dilemma of modern humanity. Human experience becomes a white void. Love, children, poetry, and the barest acts of survival are only muffled communications that leave no trace. *Airborne* (1994) is a chapbook written as a 3000-word sentence about loneliness, using the metaphor of a solo pilot; *Door slowly closing* (1995) is another chapbook. Other poetry titles include *Second person* (1983), *Heat waves* (1988), and *Closer to home* (1997)—which, as the titles suggests, leaves experimentation in favour of lyric, vivid takes on the familiar, the domestic. *One cook, once dreaming* (1980) is an admirable series of vignettes in stripped-down prose about an anonymous cook and his wife some place in Central Europe. Dreams, scenes, fantasies, and role reversals accumulate to form a single powerful metaphor about the search for a meaningful relationship. The poems in *Dead man's float* (2002) are in three sections: 'Creature Comforts', 'Tropical Snowman', and 'Night Window', which include imaginative poems about creatures—'Heron', 'Pigeons', 'Mexican Dogs'.

Wynne-Jones, Tim (b. 1948). He was born in Bromborough, Cheshire, England, and brought to Canada at the age of three. He graduated from the University of Waterloo (B.A.), Waterloo, Ont., and York University (M.F.A.), Toronto. He lives with his family in Perth, Ont. His fiction, whether for adults or children, engages and entertains, provides exotic atmosphere and characterization, and can include fantasy, the gothic, and the comic. The prize-winning *Odd's end* (1980), a thriller about a psychotic intruder that was adapted for a British-French film in 1995, was followed by *The knot* (1982), a murder mystery set in Toronto. His best-known adult work is *Fastyngange* (1988), the name of a ruined castle near Glastonbury, England, which captivates Alexis from Toronto. Parts of the novel are narrated by an oubliette (a small dungeon)—'"I am a hole," I said. "An oubliette. Such a pretty word from the French, to forget, to be forgotten."'—which eventually follows Alexis back to Toronto. *The uninvited* (2009) is about nineteen-year-old Mimi Shapiro, who has just finished her first year in drama studies at New York University, and drives north into Ontario to spend the summer in the ramshackle house owned by her estranged father (who abandoned her mother when she was four). A half-brother is living in the house—and the story goes on from there, with the appearance of Cramer, another half-brother and the beginning of dark currents of suspense.

Among Wynne-Jones's many popular books for children and young adults—all attractively literary in the sense of featuring well-turned language, humour, puns, and natural, playful dialogue—are the picture-book trilogy, *Zoom at sea* (1983), *Zoom away* (1985), *Zoom upstream* (1992), illustrated by Eric Beddows; and *The boat in the tree* (2007) illustrated by John Shelley, about several kinds of boats including the rowboat in the tree. *Ned Mouse breaks away* (2003), for older children because it has more text, was illustrated with cartoonish black-and-white drawings by Dušan Petričić. Wynne-Jones has also published three collections of stories: *Some of the kinder planets* (1993, GGA),

The book of changes (1994), and *Lord of the fries* (1999), in which the title story is about a curmudgeonly short-order cook. *On Tumbledown Hill* (1998), illustrated by Dušan Petričić, is about a painter threatened by monsters in which the text diminishes and is taken over by the illustrations. Among his novels for young people, *The maestro* (1995, GGA) is about an abusive father and his son who leaves him. In *Stephen Fair* (1998) the father and Stephen's older brother have left, and Stephen's nightmares at the beginning of the story (related to ones his brother had) eventually help to sort out his family life. *The boy in the burning house* (2000) is a plot-driven thriller involving Father Fisher, who is being blackmailed; and his stepdaughter Ruth Rose, who plays detective and is helped by fourteen-year-old Jim Hawkins, whose father, Fisher's childhood friend, has mysteriously disappeared.

The first volume of another trilogy, for children ten and up, *Rex Zero and the end of the world* (2006), is set in Ottawa in 1962, a rather chaotic time. Rex Norton-Norton (Norton minus Norton equals Zero), whose family has moved from Vancouver; and his new adolescent friends become involved in adventures and mysteries. It was followed by *Rex Zero, king of nothing* (2007) and *Rex Zero: the great pretender* (2009). The teenaged Rex—outspoken, intelligent, uncertain, affectionate—is a memorable characterization. All three are entertaining novels. Wynne-Jones's ability to draw young readers immediately into a good story, and never lose their interest, is also evident in *The thief in the house of memory* (2004). Declan Steeple, who is sixteen, lives with his father and sister in a modern house on the family estate, on which stands the empty Big House, from which his mother disappeared six years ago. When Dec and his sister discover the dead body of a local man who has broken into the old house, memories of his mother and mysteries about the past and the present overwhelm him, until secrets are revealed, there are revelations about his mother, and he begins to grow up.

Among Wynne-Jones's picture books are versions for children of two classics: *The hunchback of Notre Dame* (1996), illustrated by Bill Slavin, and *Dracula* (1997), illustrated by Laszlo Gall. Wynne-Jones edited *Boys' own: an anthology of Canadian fiction for young readers* (2001), which includes stories by Monica HUGHES, Sarah ELLIS, Brian DOYLE, Wynne-Jones himself, Lesley CHOYCE, Joan CLARK, and W.D. VALGARDSON.

Y

Yates, J. Michael (b. 1938). Born in Fulton, Missouri, he was educated at the University of Kansas City (B.A., 1960; M.A., 1961), then studied comparative literature at the University of Michigan. He taught comparative literature at Ohio University and the University of Alaska from 1963 to 1966. In 1967 he moved to Vancouver, where he served until 1971 as an influential and highly regarded professor of creative writing at the University of British Columbia. While at UBC, Yates founded SONO NIS PRESS. He was a key figure in the early 1970s in the development of a distinctive style of fiction and poetry that he called 'West Coast surrealism'. Widely read in European and Latin American literatures, he writes in a 'non-realist' or abstract style; his subject is consciousness itself, not the description of the external details of everyday life. Much of his work centres on 'the polarities between absolute wilderness and absolute technology'. Dismantling accepted views of reality and discourse, his poetry is innovative, moody, intellectual, metaphysical, and occasionally puzzling. Critics have called him self-indulgent, referring not only to his work but to his lavish self-published collections, which often reprint existing volumes. His early collections—*Spiral of mirrors* (1967), *Hunt in an unmapped interior* (1967), and selections from *The Great Bear Lake meditations*—were reprinted in *Nothing speaks for the blue moraines: new and selected poetry* (1973). *Canticle for electronic music* (1967), which made Yates's reputation as a poet, is an intriguing, enigmatic volume in which the mind is seen as a vast library consumed by the fire of consciousness, which cannot be located; our knowledge is left behind as scorched paper. The poems are twenty-four canticles, each with eight stanzas, three lines long. *The Great Bear Lake meditations* (1970)—in which a kind of nightmarish surrealism is grafted onto the experience of the North, with death seen as the ultimate desire—is a remarkable sequence of prose-poems. Yates meditates on madness, travelling north to escape from civilization, fear, isolation, and death. 'Great Bear' becomes a place, a legend, the edge of the mind, a totem power rising from darkness, as the poetic voice, on the verge of suicide, searches for the elusive nothing of the self. Jumping to collections of the 1980s, which are still in print, *Fugue Brancusi* (1983) is a challenging philosophical exploration using fugal arrangements of statement, variation, and coda, with repetitions of certain words and phrases, and suggestions that a poem can be as pure as music, or as abstract as sculpture. *INSEL: the Queen Charlotte Islands meditations* (1983) explores the idea of an island of the self surrounded by a sea so dark it cannot properly be expressed even by poetry. This was the result of a trip to the Queen Charlotte islands, off B.C.'s northwest coast, and is one of Yates's most profound works. Sensitive to the conflicting concerns of loggers, the environmentalists, and the plight of the Haida, Yates meditates in free verse on life and death, consciousness, and eternity. A selection from seven volumes of Yates's poetry up to 1986 appears in two volumes: *The completely collapsible portable man: selected shorter lyrics* (1984) and *Schedules of silence: the collected longer poems, 1960–1986* (1986).

Yates's short fiction, 1960–1987, has been collected in two volumes, *Torque* and *Torpor*, both published in 1988. He calls his Borges-inspired stories 'fictions' to emphasize their parabolic or allegoric nature. Often plotless, and with characters unnamed, they are set in technological worlds where cameras, radios, telephones, and libraries are seen as threats to individuality.

On the way to work as a Vancouver CBC-radio public-relations employee in 1978, Yates was injured in a car accident that resulted in memory loss. He stopped writing, taking a job as a prison guard, and for twelve years worked in three different prisons. His 'unrepentant memoir', *Line screw: my twelve riotous years working behind bars in some of Canada's toughest jails* (1993), is a fast-paced, upbeat debunking of prison myths; he sees guards and convicts as allies, at the mercy of a bureaucracy that is both obsessive and badly managed.

Yee, Paul (b. 1956). Born in Spalding, Saskatchewan, orphaned when very young, and raised by an aunt in Vancouver's Chinatown, he received a B.A. (1978) and an M.A. (1983) from the University of British Columbia and, trained as an archivist, worked in the Archives of Vancouver (1979–88) and Ontario (1988–91). Now living in Toronto, he is multicultural coordinator for the Archives of Ontario. His first books were for young people. *Roses sing on new snow: a delicious tale* (1991), a folktale about an artist, and *Tales from Gold Mountain: stories of the Chinese in the New World* (1989), a collection of original tales, use many of the conventions of European folktales but adapt them to the pioneer Chinese-Canadian setting and to the demands of Yee's persistent themes: the inability of an Old World culture to survive on New World soil; the wrong-headedness of attempts at such transplantation; and the power of food and art to assuage the sense of cultural and geographical displacement immigrants feel. These 'New World folk tales', as Yee calls these stories, were supplemented by *Dead man's gold and other stories* (2002), illustrated by Harvey Chan, a collection of ten ghost stories, a popular narrative form in China. Yee writes: 'I wanted to dramatize the history of the Chinese in North America and create a New World mythology where immigrant stories can be told and retold.' *The curses of third uncle* (1986) and *Breakaway* (1994) are both historical novels. Distilled into clean, concrete prose and naturally paced dialogue are the dramas of young adults struggling with identity and assimilation—struggles that are partly worked out through the paradoxical achievement of individualism through community. *Ghost train* (1996, GGA) is set, like Yee's other fiction, in pioneer British Columbia and records the historical segregation, dislocation, and loneliness of Chinese immigrants in Canada. The protagonist is a painter whose art performs the dual function Yee, as historian and storyteller, envisions for his own art: it provides a conduit into the past from which it records the sufferings and triumphs of a pioneer Chinese-Canadian community; it thereby works as an instrument of spiritual consolation and liberation. *The bone collector's son* (2003, rpr. 2004) is a ghost story set in Vancouver in 1907. Bing-wing Chan's father, Ba, a bone collector, digs up the bones of deceased Chinese so that they can be sent to China and buried permanently. *What happened this summer* (2006) is about the conflict between Chinese-Canadian teenagers' attraction to urban youth culture and their parents' traditional values. *Learning to fly* (2008) is a lively seventeen-year-old Chinese Canadian's first-person account of his everyday life, including school.

Yee has written four picture books. *The boy in the attic* (1998), illustrated by Gu Xiong, is about Kai-Ming Wong, who leaves China with his family to settle in a North American city, in an old house with an attic, where he meets and bonds with Benjamin, who turns out to be a ghost. *The jade necklace* (2002), illustrated by Grace Lin, begins when Yenyee's fisherman father gives her a jade pendant. 'This small gift comes from me and your friend, the sea.'—and he drowns in a storm at sea. A *song for Ba* (2004), beautifully illustrated by Jan Peng Wang, is about Wei Lim's father Ba, who sings in the Chinese opera in the Chinatown of a large city on the Pacific Ocean. *Bamboo* (2005), illustrated by Shaoli Wang, is about a farmer (named Bamboo) who falls in love with Ming and marries her. They plant a grove of bamboo trees to celebrate their marriage. Shaoli Wang also illustrated in black and white *Shu-Li and Tamara* (2007), for older children. Shu-Li works in her parents' shop, the Yum Yum Chinese Deli, and there is a lot in the book about making cookies and other treats (with some recipes at the end).

Saltwater City: an illustrated history of the Chinese in Vancouver, 1886–1986 (1988, rpr. 1997) is a handsome large-format publication with many black-and-white illustrations. It grew out of an exhibition of the same name held at the Vancouver Chinese Cultural Centre in 1986. Saltwater City was the name early Chinese immigrants gave to Vancouver to distinguish it from the older city of New Westminster on the freshwater Fraser River. A second edition of the book was published in 2006, with a seventh chapter added called 'Massive Change', referring to the diversity of the Chinese community today, with large numbers of immigrants from Hong Kong, Taiwan, the People's Republic of China, Vietnam, and other places. Yee also wrote *Struggle and hope: the story of Chinese in Canada* (1995) and *Chinatown: an illustrated history of the Chinese communities of Victoria, Vancouver, Calgary, Winnipeg, Toronto, Ottawa, Montreal and Halifax* (2005).

Z

Zeller, Ludwig (b. 1927). Born in Río Loa, Chile, and educated at the University of Chile, he worked in Santiago for the ministry of education (1953–68), exhibiting and publishing collages and surrealist texts. With his wife, the artist Susana Wald, he settled in Toronto in 1971, where he attracted a following as artist and poet and issued texts in English, French, and Spanish under the Oasis imprint. In 1979 the Hamilton Art Gallery held a major retrospective of the couple's work titled 'By Four Hands'. Since 1994 Wald and Zeller have maintained a second residence in Oaxaca, Mexico, where their art and poetry have found enthusiastic acceptance. *In the country of the antipodes: poems 1964–1979* (1979), edited and largely translated by A.F. MORITZ and Susana Wald, collects more than sixty of Zeller's poems from ten publications and includes a concise bibliography of his verbal and visual work. In his introduction Moritz finds four characteristics of the poetry: it questions, it presents man as pilgrim, it displays distrust of rationality, and it offers an 'examination of reality'. Moritz and the poet's daughter Beatriz Zeller were the translators for *The ghost's tattoos* (1989), which contains a long sequence entitled 'Exercises for the third hand', one long poem, 'Visible-invisible', and a selection of twenty-seven poems headed 'The ghost's tattoos'. Moritz and Theresa Moritz translated the poems in *Body of insomnia* (1996) and the novel *Rio Loa: station of dreams* (1998). Intensely surreal, Zeller's work consists of dream imagery replete with audacious references and rhetorical flourishes that are entirely out of keeping with the hitherto realistic mode and anecdotal idiom of English-Canadian poetry. The year 2007 saw the publication of *The eye on fire*, translated by Moritz, a suite of twenty-seven interconnected poems that maintain Zeller's surrealistic vision in the face of aging.

Zend, Robert (1929–85). Born in Budapest, he graduated from Péter Pázmány University in 1953 and worked for the Budapest press as cartoonist and columnist. Following the revolution in 1956, he left Hungary and settled in Toronto. In 1969 he received an M.A. in Italian Studies from the University of Toronto. He held staff and then contract positions with the Canadian Broadcasting Corporation, first as shipper, film librarian, and film editor, then as radio producer, writing and producing more than 100 programs for CBC Radio's 'Ideas'. Zend wrote prose and poetry in both Hungarian and English; after 1964 he favoured English. His earliest substantial collections of poems are *From zero to one* (1973) and *Beyond labels* (1982), both in English versions undertaken with John Robert COLOMBO. Zend's poems display a ready wit and a willingness to take flights of fancy. Imaginative, almost surreal fugues are characteristic of the longer poems: in *From zero to one* an automatic record player begins to play records for its own enjoyment; the ghost of a

dead wife continues to haunt the family home; office workers take refuge in a secret room that seems to exist in another dimension; and a message from outer space proves to be either nonsense or higher sense. The poems in *Beyond labels* are similar, except that here the poet shows more formal ingenuity and invention, especially with his 'Ditto poems' and 'Drop poems', which are reminiscent of concrete poetry. This book also includes the poet's address to Amnesty International, which examines the destructive compulsion some people feel to label other people. Zend explored the visual elements in poetry in the post-concrete experiments that make up *OAB* (vol. 1, 1983; vol. 2, 1985), a curious yet characteristic composition that is difficult to describe because its effects are predominately graphic. He explored the verbal elements in public readings, having formed with Robert PRIEST and Robert Sward the poetry-performance group known as The Three Roberts.

Since Zend's death five books have appeared, their publication arranged by the poet's wife Janine Zend: three in Hungarian and two in English. *Daymares: selected fictions on dreams and time* (1991), with a Foreword by Colombo and an Afterword by Northrop FRYE, collects Zend's shorter prose and some free-ranging poems that display a decision to be lighthearted in dealing with the darker aspects of life. *Nicolette: a novel novel* (1993) is written in short 'takes', ranging over two continents, with vivacity and charm that are more French than Hungarian or English. Frye wrote: 'Zend was a notably free spirit who was among us for a while and who, now that he has gone, is irreplaceable. All we can do is read and admire what he has left us.'

Zieroth, Dale/David (b. 1946). Born in Neepawa, Manitoba, a farming community north of Winnipeg, where his German grandfather settled, he attended local schools and moved to Toronto in the mid-sixties, where his strongly felt, plain-spoken poems of prairie life began appearing in such anthologies as ANANSI's *Mindscapes* and *Storm warning*, edited by Al PURDY. Zieroth's first collection with Anansi, *Clearing: poems from a journey* (1973), contains his most widely anthologized work, poems drawing on prairie memories (e.g., 'Father', 'Hunters of the deer'), set forth in a soberly reflective, unadorned style. A move to Invermere, British Columbia, where he worked as a park ranger, inspired *Mid-river* (1981), which uses Banff-Kootenay landscapes for meditations on the vulnerability and redemptive strengths of the natural world. After a move to Vancouver came *When the stones fly up* (1985), poems that reach back in time to the poet's Manitoba roots, and back yet further to European ancestors preparing their voyage to the New World. *The weight of my raggedy skin* (1991) wryly focuses on fatherhood, family, and scenes from domestic life as lived in North Vancouver, where much of Zieroth's energies have gone into his teaching at Douglas College and his longtime editorship of *Event*, a West Coast magazine concentrating on new talent in Canadian poetry and prose. Published under the name David Zieroth are *How I joined humanity at last* (1998), *Crows do not have retirement* (2001), and *The village of sliding time* (2006). In the second book there are two poems about crows: the title poem has an epigraph from Ted Hughes ('... the infinite depth/of crowiness in the crow's flight.') and begins 'Crows do not have retirement/homes to go to when finally/their wings break down.' The poem 'Men'—which is also about women, children, family— begins: 'At a gathering of men who consider/ the penis a marvel of liquid/engineering, I wander off/to the kitchen and the women/and who talk about the coven and the oven/and what/comes out....' The title section of *The village of sliding time*—an evocative long poem in three sections that is a memoir, treating mainly Zieroth's early life in Neepawa— begins: 'An early morning/knock on my apartment door/it is myself, a younger/teen- aged boy/come to take me back//and guide me through/what I had thought gone'. In 2009 he published *The fly in autumn: poems* (GGA). Zieroth has also recalled his early years in an effective prose memoir, *The education of Mr Whippoorwill: a country boyhood* (2002)

Zwicky, Jan (b. 1955). Born in Calgary, Alberta, she was educated at the University of Calgary (B.A., 1976) and the University of Toronto (M.A., 1977; Ph.D., 1981). A musician (she is a freelance violinist), she also teaches philosophy and the humanities and has taught at several universities, including the University of Waterloo, Ont. (1981, 1984, 1985, 1989), Princeton University (1982), and the University of New Brunswick (1994, 1995); since 1996 she has taught at the University of Victoria, B.C. Her poetry has been collected in *Where have we been* (1983), *Wittgenstein elegies* (1986), *The new room* (1989), and *Songs for relinquishing the earth* (1996, GGA; rpr. 1998). *Wittgenstein elegies* is made up of five sequences based on the philosophy and life of the Viennese philosopher (1889–1951),

who taught at Cambridge University—from philosopher 'Philosophers' stone', inspired by the only work by him published in his lifetime, to 'Rosro, County Galway', named after the cottage in Ireland he rented in 1948. The poems (sometimes including italicized 'found' poetry from his book) are lucid, approachable interpretations or echoes of Wittgenstein, using imagery about everyday things, personal matters, colour. *The new room*, which includes a long eight-part poem, 'Leaving Home', and seven elegies to the poet's father ('Death is not/a stumbling in the dark;/a friend; an enemy; a season,/silence, shadow, refuge, cloud. It is not/ash. The body is ash.'). *Songs for relinquishing the earth*, which won a Governor General's Award, was first published by Zwicky in 1996 as a handmade book, 'each copy individually sewn for its reader in response to a request.' The constant demand led to its publication by BRICK BOOKS. It is a fine collection of poems that is informed by Zwicky's background in music and philosophy, both of which also resonate in lyrical poems about other things.'Kant and Bruckner: twelve variations' begins with an interesting prose preface connecting the philosopher and the composer; the first variation (about Kant) begins: 'What did they want of me?/What's worth saying?/A terrible thing always losing your socks./God is everywhere, everywhere.' And 'The geology of Norway', about Wittgenstein's visit to that country, includes the lines, 'The sound of wind in leaves,/that was what puzzled me. It took me years/to understand that it was music.' Two poems are about works by Beethoven that inspired lyrical, personal meditations. Other of the best poems—'Border station', 'Recovery', 'Shade', 'Lancey Meadows'—are simply and effectively about what the titles suggest. *Robinson's crossing* (2004), though slender, is a rich collection that includes three long poems—the title poem, 'Nostalgia', and 'Black spruce', a prose poem—and poems inspired by music and musicians, such as 'Bee music' ('Deaf as tiny/Beethovens, you bend/ the goldenrod/beneath your weight.'), the prose poem 'Mozart and Haydn' ('It's as though Mozart can relieve us of being human for a while, but Haydn knows being human is all we've got.'), 'String practice', 'Three mysterious songs' ('Lost Music', 'Music's Breath', 'Forgotten Music'), 'Glenn Gould: Bach's *Italian Concerto*, BVW 971' ('the friend/I had once who hoped he might die/listening to this music'). And much else besides. *Thirty-seven small songs & thirteen silences* (2005) is a physically attractive collection of short poems in which every page is a delight. The second stanza of 'Small Song: Mozart' reads: 'What are you, music–/that in entering/undoes us? And undoing,/makes us whole.' One of 'Six variations on silence': 'The jade river in its skin of wind/below. sudden coolness/of cloud shadow, even at mid-day.'

In her Foreword to *Wisdom & metaphor* (2003)—a philosophical meditation on the nature of metaphor—Zwicky describes the unusual arrangement of the texts: 'The series of aphorisms that make up the left-hand text is organizationally dominant, and the entries in the parallel right-hand text [quotations from many writers, often Ludwig Wittgenstein, Simone Weil, Charles Simic, Herakleitos] are, for the most part, attempts to illustrate, extend, or comment on the left's claims and arguments.' The book is extraordinary not only for its content but for its handsomeness

and its very large page size—just under eleven inches from top to bottom; one right-hand page has nothing on it but a one-line quotation from Herakleitos and his name—the rest is white space. In a way the large format relieves the esoteric nature of the texts, inviting one to ponder.

Jan Zwicky with Brad Cran edited *Why I sing the blues: lyrics & poems* (2001). As Zwicky says in her interesting Foreword, '... what an astonishing *poetic* form the blues was. I wondered if it might be possible for poets to write in that form, even if they'd never tuned a guitar or tightened a drumskin in their lives.' The anthology includes poems by many writers who have entries in this *Companion*, including P.K. PAGE and her surprising 'Empty house blues' ('My house is empty but I don' want no one here/My bed is empty and the friggin' fridge is bare'). The book was accompanied by a '13 Song CD'.